FINANCIAL ASSET

Financial Asset Pricing Theory

CLAUS MUNK

OXFORD
UNIVERSITY PRESS

Great Clarendon Street, Oxford, OX2 6DP,
United Kingdom

Oxford University Press is a department of the University of Oxford. It furthers the University's objective of excellence in research, scholarship, and education by publishing worldwide. Oxford is a registered trade mark of Oxford University Press in the UK and in certain other countries

First published 2013
First published in paperback 2015

Published in the United States of America by Oxford University Press
198 Madison Avenue, New York, NY 10016, United States of America

British Library Cataloguing in Publication Data
Data available

Library of Congress Cataloging in Publication Data
Data available

ISBN 978–0–19–958549–6 (Hbk.)
ISBN 978–0–19–871645–7 (Pbk.)

Preface

The book is intended to serve as a textbook for a course in Asset Pricing Theory or Advanced Financial Economics, either in a Ph.D. programme or in an advanced Master of Science programme. It will also be a useful reference book for researchers and finance professionals.

The overall purpose of the book is that, after reading through and understanding the book, the reader will

- have a comprehensive overview of the classic and the current research in theoretical asset pricing,
- be able to read and understand state-of-the-art research papers in the field,
- be able to evaluate and discuss such papers, and
- be able to apply the concepts and results of the book to their own research projects or to real-life asset valuation problems.

A large part of the material is covered by other asset pricing textbooks. The books by Ingersoll (1987), Huang and Litzenberger (1988), Merton (1992), and (earlier editions of) Duffie (2001) laid the foundation for my knowledge of asset pricing theory as a graduate student. Later I have learned a lot from reading the books by LeRoy and Werner (2001), Lengwiler (2004), Cochrane (2005), and Altug and Labadie (2008). The key distinctive features of my book are the following:

- A balanced presentation offering both formal mathematical modelling and economic intuition and understanding. Most major results are formulated as theorems which, in most cases, are accompanied by mathematical proofs and discussions clarifying the economic meaning and intuition. Readers from the mathematical finance or mathematical economics communities will surely miss some precision in various statements and details in some of the proofs, but I do not want the reader to focus on mathematical quibbles nor to pay too much attention to unlikely special cases that need special care—at least not until the main concepts, methods, ideas, and results are well understood.
- Asset pricing is developed around the single, unifying concept of a state-price deflator. All other valuation techniques and modelling approaches (e.g. factor models, term structure models, risk-neutral valuation, option pricing models) are seen in connection with state-price deflators.
- The book is divided into chapters according to economic concepts and theories, not according to the type of model used. This contrasts with most

other advanced asset pricing textbooks that first contain some chapters presenting concepts and results in a simple one-period setting, then the following chapters present basically the same concepts and results in a multiperiod, discrete-time setting, and finally other chapters do the same in the continuous-time setting. In my view, such an organization of the material makes it hard for the reader to take the intuition and simplicity from the one-period and discrete-time settings to the mathematically more demanding continuous-time setting. Also, the usual division into a discrete-time part and a continuous-time part tempts lecturers and readers not to cover both frameworks, which has the unfortunate implication that those who have studied only the discrete-time part (often empirically oriented readers) are not able to communicate with those who have only studied the continuous-time part (often theoretically oriented readers). Good future researchers should be able to handle and understand both discrete-time and continuous-time asset pricing studies.

- The book covers recent developments in asset pricing research that are not covered by competing books. For example, the book offers an accessible presentation of recursive preferences and shows how asset prices are affected by replacing the usual assumption of time-additive utility by recursive utility. In particular, the book goes through the long-run risk model introduced by Bansal and Yaron (2004) which has been very successful in explaining many apparently puzzling empirical asset pricing findings and, consequently, is becoming a benchmark asset pricing model.
- The existing advanced books on asset pricing do not give much attention to how modern asset pricing models can be applied for valuing a stream of dividends coming from a stock or an investment project. The books typically represent the contents of a given asset pricing model by an equation linking the expected return on an asset over a certain period to one or more covariances or 'betas' between the asset return and some 'pricing factors'. While this is useful for empirical studies, where time series of returns and factors are inputs, the formulation is not directly useful for valuing a stream of dividends—although this should be a fundamental application of asset pricing models. In contrast, this book also explains how the models are used for pricing.
- Each chapter ends with a number of problems. While the key points are, of course, explained in the text, many of the problems are based on research papers and offer additional insights—and show the reader that he/she can handle actual research problems.

The book does not attempt to cover all topics in asset pricing theory. Some important topics that are only briefly touched upon or not discussed at all are asset pricing in an international setting, liquidity and trading imperfections, heterogeneous information and beliefs, ambiguity about model and parameters, production-based asset pricing, and behaviourial asset pricing. If used as the primary readings in a course, the book can be supplemented by selected surveys or research papers on some of these topics.

I have strived to provide references both to all the major original contributions presented in the book and to relevant further readings. However, the literature is so large and so rapidly expanding that I am sure that I have overlooked a number of papers that would have deserved mentioning. I offer my apologies to authors who miss references to their work, but I can assure them that the omissions are not intentional from my side.

I appreciate comments and corrections from Simon Lysbjerg Hansen and students exposed to earlier versions of these notes in courses at the University of Southern Denmark, Aarhus University, the Danish Doctoral School of Finance, and the Graduate School of Finance in Finland. I also appreciate the secretarial assistance and financial support from the University of Southern Denmark and Aarhus University where I was employed while major parts of this book were written. I am very grateful to Oxford University Press and the people I have been in touch with there for their willingness to publish the book and their remarkable patience and professional assistance. I am indebted to my former teachers and supervisors Peter Ove Christensen and Kristian Risgaard Miltersen who led me into a career in finance research. I also thank all the people I have worked with on research projects over the years and from whom I have learned so much. Finally, I am deeply grateful to my wife Lene for her continuing love and support.

Claus Munk

1 July 2012

Contents

List of Figures

List of Tables

1

Introduction and Overview

1.1 WHAT IS MODERN ASSET PRICING?

This book presents general methods and specific models for the pricing of financial assets. These models are important for understanding the pricing mechanisms in seemingly complex financial markets. Asset pricing models are also important tools for individuals and corporations in analysing and solving a number of financial concerns and decisions such as

- asset allocation: how individual and institutional investors combine various financial assets into portfolios;
- the measurement and management of financial risks, for example in banks and other financial institutions;
- capital budgeting decisions in firms: how firm managers should select and time investments in real assets such as factories and machines;
- capital structure decisions in firms: how firm managers should select the mix of equity and debt financing;
- the identification and possible resolution of potential conflicts of interest between the stakeholders of a firm, for example shareholders vs. creditors and shareholders vs. managers.

Central banks and governments often try to control or at least influence financial markets, for example by setting interest rates or limiting stock market volatility. For that purpose, they also need a deep understanding of the asset pricing mechanisms and the link between financial markets and macroeconomics.

Undoubtedly, the Capital Asset Pricing Model (CAPM) developed by Sharpe (1964), Lintner (1965), and Mossin (1966) is the most widely known asset pricing model. The key message of the model is that the expected excess return on a risky financial asset is given by the product of the market-beta of the asset and the expected excess return on the market portfolio. In symbols, the relation can be written as

$$\mathrm{E}[R_i] - R^f = \beta_i \left(\mathrm{E}[R_M] - R^f \right). \tag{1.1}$$

Here the 'excess return' of an asset or a portfolio is the return R_i less the risk-free return R^f, and the 'market-beta' of an asset is the covariance between the return on this asset and the return on the market portfolio, divided by the variance of the return on the market portfolio, that is $\beta_i = \mathrm{Cov}[R_i, R_M]/\mathrm{Var}[R_M]$. Only the risk correlated with the market gives a risk premium in terms of a higher expected return (assuming the market-beta is positive). The remaining risk can be diversified away and is therefore not priced in equilibrium. In principle, the market portfolio includes all assets, not only traded financial assets but also non-traded assets like the human capital (the value of future labour income) of all individuals. However, the market portfolio is typically approximated by a broad stock index, although this approximation is not necessarily very precise.

The CAPM has been very successful as a pedagogical tool for presenting and quantifying the tradeoff between risk and (expected) return, and it has also been widely used in practical applications. It captures some important characteristics of the pricing in financial markets in a rather simple way. However, the CAPM is insufficient in many aspects and it is based on a number of unrealistic assumptions. Here is a partial list of problems with the CAPM:

1. The original CAPM is formulated and derived in a one-period world where assets and investors are only modelled over one common period. In applications, it is implicitly assumed that the CAPM repeats itself period by period which intuitively demands some sort of independence between the pricing mechanisms in different periods, which again requires the unrealistic assumption that the demand and supply of agents living for several periods are the same in all periods.
2. The CAPM is not designed to capture variations in asset prices over time and cannot do so.
3. Typical derivations of the CAPM assume that all asset returns over the fixed period are normally distributed. For assets with limited liability you cannot lose more than you have invested so the rate of return cannot be lower than -100%, which is inconsistent with the normal distribution that associates a positive probability to any return between $-\infty$ and $+\infty$. Empirical studies show that for many assets the normal distribution is not even a good approximation of the return distribution.
4. The true market portfolio contains many unobservable assets, so how can you find the expected return and variance on the market portfolio and its covariances with all individual assets?
5. The CAPM is really quite unsuccessful in explaining empirical asset returns. Differences in market-betas cannot explain observed differences in average returns of stocks.

6. The CAPM is not a full asset pricing model in the sense that it does not say anything about what the return on the risk-free asset or the expected return on the market portfolio should be. And it does not offer any insight into the links between financial markets and macroeconomic variables like consumption, production, and inflation.

The overall purpose of this book is to develop a deeper understanding of asset pricing than the CAPM can offer. We will follow the traditional scientific approach of setting up mathematical models with explicit assumptions from which we try to derive relevant conclusions using the logic and tools of mathematics. Assumptions and results will be accompanied by economic interpretations and intuition. Both general, rather abstract, models and specific, more concrete, models are studied. Assumptions are varied in order to gauge the impact on the conclusions. While this book has a clear theoretical focus, the evolution of theoretical asset pricing models is naturally guided by empirical observations and statistical tests on actual data. This book will therefore refer to empirical findings where relevant, but does not include new empirical tests and does not discuss how such tests should be performed.

The modern approach to asset pricing is based on the following intuition. When an investor purchases a given asset, she obtains the right to receive the future payments of the asset. For many assets the size of these future payments is uncertain at the time of purchase since they may depend on the overall state of the economy and/or the state of the issuer of the asset at the payment dates. Risk-averse investors will value a payment of a given size more highly if they receive it in a 'bad' state than in a 'good' state. This is captured by the term 'state price' introduced by Arrow (1953). A state price for a given state at a given future point in time indicates how much investors are willing to sacrifice today in return for an extra payment in that future state. Rational investors will value a given payment in a given state the same no matter which asset the payment comes from. Therefore state prices are valid for all assets. The value of any specific asset is determined by the general state prices in the market and the state-contingent future payments of the asset. Modern asset pricing theory is based on models of the possible states and the associated state prices.

The well-being of individuals will depend on their consumption of goods throughout their lives. By trading financial assets they can move consumption opportunities from one point in time to another and from one state of the world to another. The preferences for consumption of individuals determine their demand for various assets and thereby the equilibrium prices of these assets. Hence, the state price for any given state must be closely related to the individuals' (marginal) utility of consumption in that state. Most modern asset pricing theories and models are based on this link between asset prices and consumption.

1.2 ELEMENTS OF ASSET PRICING MODELS

1.2.1 Assets

For potential investors the important characteristics of a financial asset or any other investment opportunity are its current price and its future payments which the investor will be entitled to if she buys the asset. Stocks deliver dividends to owners. The dividends are uncertain because they will depend on the well-being of the company, which again may depend on the state of the general economy. Bonds deliver coupon payments and repayments of the outstanding debt, usually according to some predetermined schedule. For bonds issued by some governments, you might consider these payments to be certain, that is risk-free. On the other hand, if the government bond promises certain dollar payments, you will not know how many consumption goods you will be able to buy for these dollar payments, that is the payments are risky in real terms. As the sovereign debt crisis that started in late 2009 has made painfully clear, bonds issued by some countries are uncertain even in nominal terms. The payments of bonds issued by corporations are also uncertain because of the risk of default of the issuer. The future payments of derivatives such as forwards, futures, options, and swaps depend on the evolution of some underlying random variable and therefore are also uncertain.

Let us simply refer to the payments of any asset as 'dividends'. More precisely, a dividend means the payment of a given asset at a given point in time. The uncertain dividend of an asset at a given point in time is naturally modelled by a random variable. If an asset provides the owner with payments at several points in time, we need a collection of random variables to represent all the dividends, namely one random variable per payment date. Such a collection of random variables is called a stochastic process. A stochastic process is therefore the natural way to represent the uncertain flow of dividends of an asset over time. We will refer to the stochastic process representing the dividends of an asset as the dividend process of the asset.

1.2.2 Investors

In reality, only a small part of the trading in financial markets is executed directly by individuals. The majority of trades are executed by corporations and financial institutions such as pension funds, insurance companies, banks, broker firms, etc. However, these institutional investors trade on behalf of individuals, either customers or shareholders. Productive firms issue stocks and corporate bonds to finance investments in production technology they hope will generate high earnings and, consequently, high returns to their owners in future years. In the end, the decisions taken at the company level are also driven by the desires of individuals to shift consumption opportunities across time and states. In our basic models we will assume that all investors are individuals and ignore the many good reasons for the existence of various intermediaries. For example, we will assume that assets are traded without transaction costs. We will also ignore taxes and the role of the government and central banks in the financial markets. Some authors use the term 'agent' or 'investor' instead of 'individual', possibly in order to indicate that some investment decisions are taken by other decision-making units than individual human beings.

How should we represent an individual in an asset pricing model? We will assume that individuals basically care about their consumption of goods and services throughout their life. The consumption of a given individual at a future point in time is typically uncertain, and we will therefore represent it by a random variable. Note that using a random variable to represent consumption at a given date simply means that the individual will allow her consumption to depend on the state of the economy at that date. For example, she will probably choose to consume more if she receives a high income that day compared to the case where she receives a low income. The consumption of an individual at all future dates is represented by a stochastic process: the consumption process of the individual. Again, this is nothing but a collection of random variables, one for each relevant point in time.

Although real-life economies offer a large variety of consumption goods and services, we assume in our basic models that there is only one good available for consumption and that each individual only cares about her own consumption and not the consumption of other individuals. The single consumption good is assumed to be perishable, that is it cannot be stored or resold but has to be consumed immediately. In more advanced models discussed in later chapters we will relax these assumptions and allow for multiple consumption goods, for example we will introduce a durable good (like a house). We will also discuss models in which the well-being of an individual depends on what other individuals consume, which is often referred to as the 'keeping up with the Joneses' property. Both extensions turn out to be useful in bringing our theoretical models closer to real-life financial data, but it is preferable to understand the simpler models first. Of course, the well-being of an individual will also be affected by the number of hours she works, the physical and mental challenges offered by her position, etc., but such issues will also be ignored in basic models.

We will assume that each individual is endowed with some current wealth and some future income stream from labour, gifts, inheritance, etc. For most individuals the future income will be uncertain. The income of an individual at a given future point in time is thus represented by a random variable, and the income at all future dates is represented by a stochastic process: the income process. We will assume that the income process is exogenously given and, hence, ignore labour supply decisions.

If the individual cannot make investments at all (not even save current wealth), it will be impossible for her to currently consume more than her current wealth and impossible to consume more at a future point in time than her income at that date. Financial markets allow the individual to shift consumption opportunities from one point in time to another, for example from working life to retirement. Financial markets also allow the individual to shift consumption from one state of the world to another, for example from a state in which income is extremely high to a state in which income is extremely low. The prices of financial assets define the prices of shifting consumption through time and states of the world. The individuals' desire to shift consumption through time and states will determine the demand and supply and, hence, the equilibrium prices of the financial assets. To study asset pricing we therefore have to model how individuals choose between different, uncertain consumption processes. The preferences for consumption of an individual are typically modelled by a utility function. Since this is a text on asset pricing, we are not primarily interested in deriving the optimal consumption stream and the associated optimal strategy for trading financial assets. However, since asset prices are set by the decisions of individuals, we will have to discuss some aspects of optimal consumption and trading.

1.2.3 Equilibrium

For any given asset, that is any given dividend process, our aim is to characterize the set of 'reasonable' prices which, in some cases, will only consist of a single, unique, reasonable price. A price is considered reasonable if the price is an equilibrium price. An equilibrium is characterized by two conditions: (1) supply equals demand for any asset, that is markets clear, (2) any investor is satisfied with her current position in the assets given her preferences, wealth, and income and given the asset prices. Associated with any equilibrium is a set of prices for all assets and, for each investor, a trading strategy and implied consumption strategy.

1.2.4 The Time Span of the Model

As discussed above, the important ingredients of all basic asset pricing models are the dividends of the assets available for trade and the consumption preferences, current wealth, and future incomes of the individuals who can trade the assets. We will discuss asset pricing in three types of models:

1. **One-period model**: all action takes place at two points in time, the beginning of the period (time 0) and the end of the period (time 1). Assets

pay dividends only at the end of the period and are traded only at the beginning of the period. The aim of the model is to characterize the prices of the assets at the beginning of the period. Individuals have some initial beginning-of-period wealth and (maybe) some end-of-period income. They can consume at both points in time.

2. **Discrete-time model**: all action takes place at a finite number of points in time. Let us denote the set of these time points by $\mathcal{T} = \{0, 1, 2, \ldots, T\}$. Individuals can trade at any of these time points, except at T, and consume at any time $t \in \mathcal{T}$. Assets can pay dividends at any time in $\mathcal{T}$, except time 0. Assuming that the price of a given asset at a given point in time is ex-dividend, that is the value of future dividends excluding any dividend at that point in time, prices are generally non-trivial at all but the last point in time. We aim to characterize these prices.
3. **Continuous-time model**: individuals can consume at any point in time in an interval $\mathcal{T} = [0, T]$. Assets pay dividends in the interval $(0, T]$ and can be traded in $[0, T)$. Ex-dividend asset prices are non-trivial in $[0, T)$. Again, our goal is to characterize these prices.

In a one-period setting there is uncertainty about the state of the world at the end of the period. The dividends of financial assets and the incomes of the individuals at the end of the period will generally be unknown at the beginning of the period and are thus modelled as random variables. Any quantity that depends on either the dividends or income will also be random variables. For example, this will be the case for the end-of-period value of portfolios and the end-of-period consumption of individuals.

Both the discrete-time model and the continuous-time model are multi-period models and can potentially capture the dynamics of asset prices. In both cases, T denotes some terminal date in the sense that we will not model what happens after time T. We assume that $T < \infty$, but under some technical conditions the analysis extends to $T = \infty$.

Financial markets are by nature dynamic and should therefore be studied in a multiperiod setting. One-period models should serve only as a pedagogical first step in the derivation of the more appropriate multiperiod models. Indeed, many of the important conclusions derived in one-period models carry over to multiperiod models. Other conclusions do not. And some issues cannot be meaningfully studied in a one-period framework.

It is not easy to decide whether to use a discrete-time or a continuous-time framework to study multiperiod asset pricing. Both model types have their virtues and drawbacks. Both model types are applied in theoretical research and real-life applications. We will therefore consider both modelling frameworks. The basic asset pricing results in the early chapters will be derived in both settings. Some more specific asset pricing models discussed in later chapters will only be presented in one of these frameworks. Some authors prefer to use a discrete-time model, others prefer a continuous-time model. It is comforting that, for most purposes, both models will result in identical or very similar conclusions.

At first, you might think that the discrete-time framework is more realistic. However, in real-life economies individuals can in fact consume and adjust portfolios at virtually any point in time. Individuals are certainly not restricted to consuming and trading at a finite set of pre-specified points in time. Of course no individual will trade financial assets continuously due to the existence of explicit and implicit costs of such transactions. But even if we take such costs into account, the frequency and exact timing of actions can be chosen by each individual. If we were really concerned about transaction costs, it would be better to include those in a continuous-time modelling framework.

Many people will find discrete-time models easier to understand than continuous-time models. If you want to compare theoretical results with actual data it will usually be an advantage if the model is formulated with a period length closely linked to the data frequency. On the other hand, once you have learned how to deal with continuous-time stochastic processes, many results are clearer and more elegantly derived in continuous-time models than in discrete-time models. The analytical virtues of continuous-time models are basically due to the well-developed theory of stochastic calculus for continuous-time stochastic processes, but also due to the fact that integrals are easier to deal with than discrete sums, differential equations are easier to deal with than difference equations, and so on.

1.3 DEFINING RETURNS

Stylized empirical facts about the returns of major asset classes will be reported below, but before doing so we had better explain how to define returns and how to average them. A return refers to the gains from holding an asset (or a portfolio of assets) over a given time period. We need to distinguish between nominal returns and real returns. A nominal return is a measure of the monetary gains, whereas a real return is a measure of the gains in terms of purchasing power.

Let us be more precise. The nominal price of an asset is the number of units of a certain currency, say dollars, that a unit of the asset can be exchanged for. Likewise, a nominal dividend is simply the dividend measured in dollars. If, for any t, we let $\tilde{P}_t$ denote the nominal price at time t of an asset and let $\tilde{D}_t$ denote the nominal dividend received in the period up to time t, then the *gross nominal rate of return* on the asset between time t and time $t+1$ is $\tilde{R}_{i,t+1} = \left(\tilde{P}_{i,t+1} + \tilde{D}_{i,t+1}\right)/\tilde{P}_{it}$. The *net nominal rate of return* is $\tilde{r}_{i,t+1} = \left(\tilde{P}_{i,t+1} + \tilde{D}_{i,t+1} - \tilde{P}_{it}\right)/\tilde{P}_{it} = \tilde{R}_{i,t+1} - 1$. For brevity, we will sometimes drop the words 'rate of' when referring to returns.

The real value of an asset reflects how much consumption the asset can be exchanged for. For simplicity, we can think of the economy as having a single consumption good with a unit price at time t of $\tilde{F}_t$. The gross inflation rate between time t and $t+1$ is then $\Phi_{t+1} = F_{t+1}/F_t$ and the net inflation rate is $\varphi_{t+1} = \Phi_{t+1} - 1 = (F_{t+1} - F_t)/F_t$. More broadly, we can think of F_t as the value of the Consumer Price Index at time t which tracks the price of a certain basket of goods.

An asset with a nominal price of $\tilde{P}_t$ has a real price of $P_t = \tilde{P}_t/\tilde{F}_t$ since this is the number of units of the consumption good that the asset can be exchanged for. Similarly, a nominal dividend of $\tilde{D}_{t+1}$ has a real value of $D_{t+1} = \tilde{D}_{t+1}/\tilde{F}_{t+1}$ (throughout the book, a 'tilde' above a symbol indicates a nominal value, whereas the same symbol without a tilde indicates the corresponding real value). The *gross real rate of return* between time t and time $t+1$ is then

$$R_{i,t+1} = \frac{P_{i,t+1} + D_{i,t+1}}{P_{it}} = \frac{\tilde{P}_{i,t+1}/\tilde{F}_{t+1} + \tilde{D}_{i,t+1}/\tilde{F}_{t+1}}{\tilde{P}_{it}/\tilde{F}_t}$$

$$= \frac{\tilde{P}_{i,t+1} + \tilde{D}_{i,t+1}}{\tilde{P}_{it}} \frac{\tilde{F}_t}{\tilde{F}_{t+1}} = \tilde{R}_{i,t+1} \frac{\tilde{F}_t}{\tilde{F}_{t+1}} = \frac{\tilde{R}_{t+1}}{\Phi_{t+1}}.$$

The *net real rate of return* is

$$r_{i,t+1} = R_{i,t+1} - 1 = \frac{1 + \tilde{r}_{i,t+1}}{1 + \varphi_{t+1}} - 1 = \frac{\tilde{r}_{i,t+1} - \varphi_{t+1}}{1 + \varphi_{t+1}} \approx \tilde{r}_{i,t+1} - \varphi_{t+1}.$$

The above equations show how to obtain real returns from nominal returns and inflation. Given a time series of nominal returns and inflation, it is easy to compute the corresponding time series of real returns.

Sometimes we will work with a *log-return*, which is also referred to as a *net continuously compounded rate of return*. For example, the real log-return is defined as $\ln R_{t+1} = \ln((P_{t+1} + D_{t+1})/P_t)$. We will sometimes follow the standard notation in the asset pricing literature and let small letters denote the log of the corresponding capital letters so that, in particular, $r_{t+1} = \ln R_{t+1}$. Therefore, when you see a symbol like r_{t+1} you will have to deduce from the context whether it denotes the periodic ('uncompounded') or the continuously compounded net rate of return. Note that in the bond and money markets other compounding frequencies, and thus other return definitions, are also used, see Section 11.2.

Since the end-of-period dividend and price are generally unknown at the beginning of the period, any of the returns defined above will be a random variable as seen from time t (and earlier). If, given the information at time t, the return (with any of the above definitions) is going to be the same no matter what will happen over the period until time $t+1$, the return is said to be risk-free. We will write the risk-free gross rate of return between t and $t+1$ as R^f_t

and the risk-free net rate of return (with a certain compounding frequency) as r_t^f.

Computing a return on an asset over a period in which the asset delivers multiple dividends (at different points in time) seems challenging at first since you should discount appropriately to adjust for the value of time. A given dollar dividend is worth more when paid early in the period than when paid late. As dividends are generally risky, it is not clear what discount rate to apply. In fact, this is one of the key questions we study throughout this book. Such discussions can be avoided by assuming that as soon as a dividend is received, it is reinvested in the same asset by purchasing additional (fractions of) units of the asset. Suppose you purchase one unit of the asset at time t and you reinvest all dividends as you go along, then you will end up with some number $A_{t,s}$ of units of the asset at time s, with $A_{t,s} \geq 1$ when all dividends are non-negative. The gross rate of return on the asset between time t and time s is then computed as $R_{t,s} = A_{t,s}P_s/P_t$ and the net rate of return is $r_{t,s} = R_{t,s} - 1$. We will go into more detail in Chapter 3.

Given a time series of (net rate of) returns, real or nominal, $r_1, r_2, \ldots, r_T$ over T time periods of equal length, we are often interested in the average return as this can be a good estimate of the return that we can expect from the asset in the future. You can compute the *arithmetic average* (net rate of) return as

$$\bar{r}_{\text{arith}} = \frac{1}{T}\sum_{t=1}^{T} r_t.$$

This may be a good measure of the return you can expect over any single period. On the other hand, it is not necessarily a good measure for the return you can expect to get over multiple periods. This is due to the fact that returns are compounded. If you invested 1 unit of account (that is 1 dollar if dividends and prices are measured in dollars) at the starting date of the time series and kept reinvesting dividends by purchasing additional units of the asset, then you will end up with

$$(1 + r_1)(1 + r_2) \ldots (1 + r_T)$$

after the last period. The *geometric average* (net rate of) return is computed as

$$\bar{r}_{\text{geo}} = [(1 + r_1)(1 + r_2) \ldots (1 + r_T)]^{1/T} - 1.$$

The geometric average is lower than the arithmetic average. The difference will be larger for a very variable series of returns.

As a simple example, assume that the percentage return of an asset is 100% in year 1 and -50% in year 2. Then the arithmetic average return is $(100\% - 50\%)/2 = 25\%$ and the geometric average return is $[(1 + 1)(1 - 0.5)]^{1/2} - 1 = 1 - 1 = 0$, that is 0%. An investment of 1 in the beginning of the first year has grown to 2 at the end of year 1 and then dropped to $2 \times 0.5 = 1$ at the end of year 2. The zero return over the two periods is better reflected by the geometric average than the arithmetic average.

1.4 EFFICIENT MARKETS AND IMPLICATIONS FOR PRICES AND RETURNS

The return over a given period is determined by the dividend(s) over the period and the price change. Since the price of an asset should equal the sum of the expected future dividends, discounted appropriately, any price change must be due to changes in expected future dividends or the appropriate discount rates or a combination thereof. The discount rate can be separated into a risk-free rate and a risk premium. The classic view was to assume constant discount rates so that returns were driven by revisions of expected future dividends. But over the last couple of decades, understanding the level and the variations of discount rates has taken most of the attention in the asset pricing literature and is also at the centre of this book.

A key question in the 1970s was whether financial markets were informationally efficient or not, that is whether the price of a given stock reflected all the available information about its fundamentals (future dividends). Informational efficiency means that prices move because of news. It rules out the idea that risk-adjusted profits can be systematically made on trading strategies using only the information available to the market participants and, in particular, strategies based on historical price patterns. Competition in the financial markets should lead to informational efficiency, and empirical studies generally confirm that financial markets are informationally efficient. Informational efficiency was originally believed to imply that the price of any asset should follow a random walk and thus be completely unpredictable, see, for example, Samuelson (1965) and Fama (1970). This is an incorrect conclusion. Returns in efficient markets can be predictable if there are variations in expected returns over time as noted, for example, by Fama and French (1988). As shown in later chapters, many reasonable models lead to time variations in risk premia and risk-free rates and can thus explain return predictability without introducing informational asymmetries or inefficiencies.

Every now and then a trading strategy is discovered that involves only liquidly traded assets and offers an apparently abnormal high return. But the conclusion that most economists draw today is that such an anomaly is due to an inadequate adjustment for risk or trading frictions, not that the market is informationally inefficient. Some economists still believe that various anomalies are due to behavioural biases in the sense that investors are unable to process the available information correctly or systematically make decisions that are incompatible with rational behaviour and typical assumptions about preferences. This book does not discuss the behavioural finance views on asset pricing. The reader is referred to Hirshleifer (2001) and Barberis and Thaler (2003) for an introduction to behaviourial finance and to Constantinides (2002), Ross (2005), and Cochrane (2011) for a critique of that approach.

1.5 SOME STYLIZED EMPIRICAL FACTS ABOUT ASSET RETURNS

This book is on the theory of financial asset pricing, but theoretic developments are naturally guided by empirical observations. One purpose of having a theory or a model is to help us understand what we see in reality. Hence, theories and models designed with that intention should be able to match at least some of the key findings of empirical studies. Of course, some asset pricing models are developed for other purposes, for example to make a certain argument in as simple a setting as possible without trying to price all assets in accordance with the data.

Throughout most of the book we will focus on stocks and default-free (government) bonds, and in this section we summarize some general empirical findings about these asset classes. Derivatives are covered in the final chapter. We do not discuss other major asset classes such as corporate bonds, foreign exchange, and commodity-linked financial assets. For more on empirical asset pricing the reader is referred to the textbook presentations of Campbell, Lo, and MacKinlay (1997), Cuthbertson and Nitzsche (2004), Cochrane (2005), and Singleton (2006).

1.5.1 Stock Returns

Stocks have high average returns. Based on quarterly US asset returns, Campbell (2003) reports that the (geometric) average annualized real return on the stock market was 7.2% over the period 1891–1998, 8.1% in 1947–1998, and 6.9% in 1970–1998. These average returns are high compared to the average annualized real return on a 3-month Treasury bill (US government bond), which was 2.0%, 0.9%, and 1.5% over the same periods. Both the high average stock returns and the big difference between average stock returns and average bond returns are found consistently across countries. Table 1.1 is a slightly edited version of Table 4-2 in the book *Triumph of the Optimists* by Dimson, Marsh, and Staunton (2002) which provides an abundance of information about the performance of financial markets in 16 countries over the entire 20th century. Over that period, the (arithmetic) average real US stock return was

Table 1.1. Means and standard deviations (StdDev) of annual real asset returns in different countries over the period 1900–2000.

Country	Stocks		Bonds		Bills	
	Mean	StdDev	Mean	StdDev	Mean	StdDev
Australia	9.0	17.7	1.9	13.0	0.6	5.6
Belgium	4.8	22.8	0.3	12.1	0.0	8.2
Canada	7.7	16.8	2.4	10.6	1.8	5.1
Denmark	6.2	20.1	3.3	12.5	3.0	6.4
France	6.3	23.1	0.1	14.4	−2.6	11.4
Germany	8.8	32.3	0.3	15.9	0.1	10.6
Ireland	7.0	22.2	2.4	13.3	1.4	6.0
Italy	6.8	29.4	−0.8	14.4	−2.9	12.0
Japan	9.3	30.3	1.3	20.9	−0.3	14.5
The Netherlands	7.7	21.0	1.5	9.4	0.8	5.2
South Africa	9.1	22.8	1.9	10.6	1.0	6.4
Spain	5.8	22.0	1.9	12.0	0.6	6.1
Sweden	9.9	22.8	3.1	12.7	2.2	6.8
Switzerland	6.9	20.4	3.1	8.0	1.2	6.2
United Kingdom	7.6	20.0	2.3	14.5	1.2	6.6
United States	8.7	20.2	2.1	10.0	1.0	4.7

Notes: Numbers are in percentage terms. Means are arithmetic averages. Bonds mean long-term (approximately 20-year) government bonds, while bills mean short-term (approximately 1-month) government bonds. The bond and bill statistics for Germany exclude the year 1922–23, where hyperinflation resulted in a loss of 100% for German bond investors. For Swiss stocks the data series begins in 1911
Source: Table 4-2 in Dimson, Marsh, and Staunton (2002)

8.7%. The table shows that in any of the listed countries the average return on stocks was much higher than the average return on long-term bonds, which again is higher than the average short-term interest rate. As we will see in later chapters, standard asset pricing models have a hard time explaining why average stock returns should be so much higher than average bond returns and risk-free interest rates.

Stock returns are very volatile. Panel (a) of Fig. 1.1 shows the return on the S&P 500 US stock index in each year over the period 1928–2010. Obviously, stock returns vary a lot from year to year. The standard deviation or volatility of the annualized US real stock returns is reported as 15.6% in the study of Campbell (2003) and 20.2% in Dimson, Marsh, and Staunton (2002), compare Table 1.1. The table also shows similar levels of stock market volatility in other countries. For individual stocks, the volatility is often much higher. For example, Goyal and Santa-Clara (2003) report that the average volatility on individual stocks is four times the volatility of an equally-weighted stock market index, which also demonstrates that shocks to individual stocks can be diversified away to a large degree by forming portfolios. Stock volatilities vary over time and tend to cluster so that there are periods with low volatility and periods with high volatility, a phenomenon first noted by Mandelbrot (1963). In technical terms, stock volatility exhibits positive autocorrelation over several days. Stock volatility tends to be negatively correlated with the return so that volatility is high in periods of low returns and vice versa, as originally observed by Black (1976b). The volatility is far from perfectly correlated with the price so it has a separate stochastic component that is not linked to the stochastic price. Finally, the level of the stock market volatility tends to peak in periods with high political or macroeconomic uncertainty, as documented by Bloom (2009) among others.

Stock returns are not normally distributed. Daily returns on stock market indices tend to be negatively skewed: returns that are, say, Δr below the mean are observed more frequently than returns of Δr above the mean, at least for small-to-medium values of Δr. In contrast, daily returns on individual stocks are roughly symmetric (zero skewness) or slightly positively skewed. See Albuquerque (2012) for a recent empirical documentation and an attempt to reconcile the differences between individual stocks and indices. Stock return distributions have heavy tails or excess kurtosis: very low and very high returns are observed more frequently than would be the case if returns followed a normal distribution. This is true for both individual stocks and indices. However, increasing the length of the period over which returns are computed results in the distribution becoming less heavy-tailed and less skewed and thus closer to a normal distribution. So the shape of the return distribution varies with the period length. Such results are reported by Campbell, Lo, and MacKinlay (1997, Sec. 1.4) among others.

Stock dividends have different statistical properties than stock returns. According to Campbell (2003) the annual growth rate of real stock market dividends has a standard deviation of 6%, which is much lower than the return standard deviation of 15.6% (at much shorter horizons dividend volatility is considerably higher because of seasonality in dividend payments). The high return volatility reflects large variations in stock prices, that is large variations in expected discounted future dividends. The low volatility of dividends suggests that the discount rates involved in the valuation must vary substantially over time. A discount rate for a future dividend consists of a risk-free rate plus a risk premium, and, since risk-free rates are quite stable, the risk premium apparently varies a lot over time. The correlation between quarterly real dividend growth and real stock returns is only 0.03, but the correlation increases with the measurement period up to a correlation of 0.47 at a 4-year horizon.

The ratio between current dividends and prices varies substantially over time. Figure 1.2 shows the variations in the price-dividend ratio and its reciprocal, the dividend yield, on the US stock market between 1927 and 2010. Extensive research has investigated whether future dividend growth can be predicted by the current price-dividend ratio (or the dividend yield). The evidence is

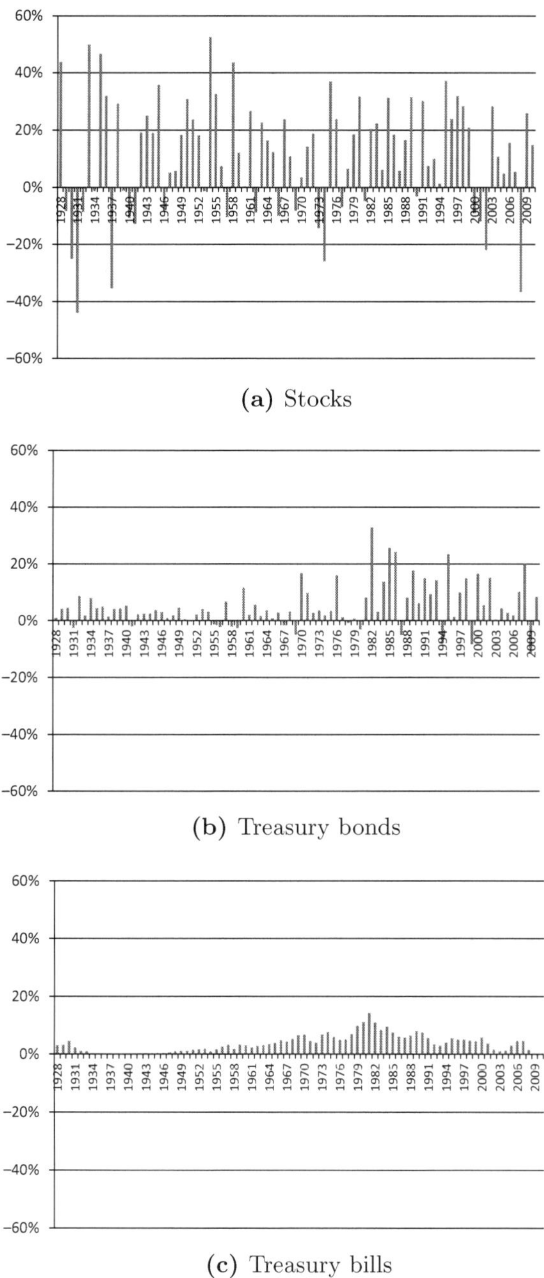

Fig. 1.1. Annual returns on the stock market index, Treasury bonds, and Treasury bills in the US over the period 1928–2010.

Notes: Stock returns are the returns on the S&P 500 market index. The Treasury bill rate is a 3-month rate and the Treasury bond is the constant maturity 10-year bond. The Treasury bond return includes coupon and price appreciation. The data are taken from the homepage of Professor Aswath Damodaran at the Stern School of Business at New York University, see http://pages.stern.nyu.edu/~adamodar

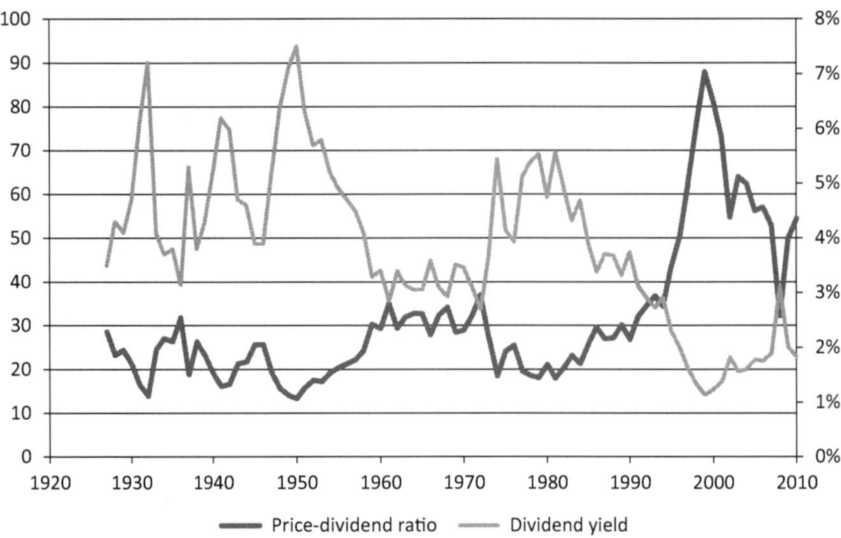

Fig. 1.2. The relation between prices and dividends on the US stock market over the period 1927–2010.

Notes: Stock returns are the returns on the S&P 500 market index. The black graph (left-hand vertical axis) shows for each year the price-dividend ratio, that is the ratio of the end-of-year value of the S&P 500 index to the dividends paid out during that year. The grey graph (right-hand vertical axis) shows the dividend yield, which is just the reciprocal of the price-dividend ratio. The data are taken from the homepage of Professor Aswath Damodaran at the Stern School of Business at New York University, see http://pages.stern.nyu.edu/~adamodar

mixed as the conclusion depends on the country and time period used in the study, compare Campbell and Shiller (1988), Campbell and Ammer (1993), Ang and Bekaert (2007), Cochrane (2008), Chen (2009), van Binsbergen and Koijen (2010), Engsted and Pedersen (2010), and Rangvid, Schmeling, and Schrimpf (2011).

Average stock returns are not constant, but seem to vary counter-cyclically. For example, average 1-year returns are higher in recessions than in expansions. The counter-cyclical pattern is also seen in price-dividend ratios, average excess stock returns, and the ratio of average excess stock returns and the standard deviation of the stock return (the so-called Sharpe ratio). See, for example, Fama and French (1989) and Lettau and Ludvigson (2010).

Returns over different periods are not statistically independent. The returns on stock portfolios exhibit positive autocorrelation at fairly short horizons (daily, weekly, and monthly) and most strongly so at very short horizons (daily). For example, a positive [negative] return over the previous month tends to be followed by a positive [negative] return over the next month. This pattern is referred to as *short-term momentum*. Over longer horizons (one to five years), the autocorrelation tends to be negative. This is referred to as *long-term reversal* or *mean reversion*. Past returns positively predict returns in the near future and negatively predict returns some years into the future. These effects seem more predominant for individual stocks than for broad indices. Examples of estimates and discussions thereof can be found in Fama and French (1988), Campbell, Lo, and MacKinlay (1997, Sec. 2.8), and Cochrane (2005, Sec. 20.1). Further evidence of momentum is provided by Moskowitz, Ooi, and Pedersen (2012), who show that the return over the past 12 months strongly and positively predicts the return over the next month and that this holds for many different asset classes. The momentum effect is also present in relative returns: an asset that has outperformed similar assets in the recent past tends to outperform the same assets in the near future as documented by Jegadeesh and Titman (1993), Rouwenhorst (1998), and Asness, Moskowitz, and Pedersen (2012) among others.

Stock returns appear to be predicted by other variables than past returns such as:

- the price/dividend ratio or, equivalently, the dividend yield (see, for example, Campbell and Shiller 1988; Boudoukh, Michaely, Richardson, and Roberts 2007),
- the price/earnings ratio (Campbell and Shiller 1988),
- the book-to-market ratio (Kothari and Shanken 1997),
- the short-term interest rate (Ang and Bekaert 2007),
- the consumption-wealth ratio (Lettau and Ludvigson 2001a),
- the housing collateral ratio (Lustig and van Nieuwerburgh 2005),
- the ratio of stock prices to GDP (Rangvid 2006),
- the ratio of aggregate labour income to aggregate consumption (Santos and Veronesi 2006),
- the output gap, that is the difference between actual GDP and the potential GDP (Cooper and Priestley 2009).

However, there are various statistical challenges in measuring predictability, and there is still a lot of debate among academics about whether predictability is there or not, see for example Ang and Bekaert (2007), Boudoukh, Richardson, and Whitelaw (2008), Campbell and Thompson (2008), Cochrane (2008), Goyal and Welch (2008), and Lettau and Van Nieuwerburgh (2008). Koijen and Van Nieuwerburgh (2011) survey the recent research on return and dividend predictability. As explained in Section 1.4, predictability of stock returns does not imply that markets are informationally inefficient. Trading strategies trying to exploit return predictability provide fairly low returns after adjusting for transaction costs and for market risk according to the CAPM, and any apparently abnormal return can be due to an insufficient adjustment for systematic risks.

There are systematic differences in average returns of different stocks. According to the standard CAPM, differences in expected returns across stocks should be entirely due to differences in their market-beta, see Eq. (1.1). This is contradicted by empirical facts. Stocks of companies with low market capitalization (small stocks) offer higher average returns than stocks in companies with high market capitalization (large stocks), even after controlling for differences in market-betas. This is the so-called *size effect* or size premium originally identified by Banz (1981). The size effect seems to have weakened substantially in recent decades, compare Schwert (2003).

Average stock returns also depend on the book-to-market ratio of the company, that is the ratio of the book value of the stocks of the company to the market value of these stocks. Stocks in companies with high book-to-market ratios are called *value stocks*. Stocks in companies with low book-to-market ratios are called *growth stocks*; if the market value of equity is high relative to the book value, it is probably because the company has substantial and valuable options to grow over time and boost future earnings and dividends. Rosenberg, Reid, and Lanstein (1985) and Fama and French (1992) showed that value stocks provide a higher average return than growth stocks, even after controlling for differences in market-betas. This is the so-called *value premium*. For a discussion of other apparent anomalies, see Schwert (2003).

1.5.2 Bond Returns and Interest Rates

Next, we describe some empirical characteristics of nominal bonds issued by the US government or, more precisely, the United States Department of the Treasury. Depending on their time to maturity when issued, these bonds are referred to as Treasury bills (maturity up to one year), Treasury notes (from two to ten years), or Treasury bonds (exceeding 10 years, typically 30 years). The bonds are nominal in the sense that they promise certain dollar payments at certain dates. Since they are backed by the US government and thus the US taxpayers, they are traditionally considered to be free of default risk. However, the purchasing power of the future promised dollar payments is uncertain because of inflation risk. The US Treasury also offers the so-called TIPS (Treasury Inflation-Protected Securities) which are bonds with a face value adjusted by the change in the Consumer Price Index, but in the following we focus on the nominal bonds.

Returns on long-term government bonds are lower on average and less volatile than returns on stocks. Short-term government bonds have even lower average returns and lower volatility. Note that if you take the standard deviation as a measure of risk, the historical estimates confirm the conventional wisdom that higher average returns come with higher risk. These assertions are backed by Table 1.1 and Fig. 1.1. The standard deviation of the ex-post real return on 3-month US Treasury bills was only 1.7% over the period 1947–98 (Campbell 2003) and much of this is due to short-run inflation risk. Therefore, the standard deviation of the ex-ante real interest rate is considerably smaller.

Short-term interest rates exhibit considerable persistence. The autocorrelation in 3-month real interest rates on US Treasury bills was 0.5 over the period 1945–2000. Interest rates tend to mean revert, in particular short-term interest rates. The volatility of short-term interest tends to increase with the level of interest rates, see for example Chan *et al.* (1992). Interest rate volatility has stochastic components that are not linked to the current interest rate level or yield curve, so-called unspanned stochastic volatility, as documented by Collin-Dufresne and Goldstein (2002) among others.

The yield curve at a given point in time is the graph of the yields of different bonds as a function of their time to maturity. The yield curve is typically upward-sloping, but in some short periods short-term yields have exceeded long-term yields. These observations can be made from Fig. 1.3 which shows the 3-month, 5-year, and 20-year yields on US government bonds over the period 1951–2008. Before economic expansions the yield curve tends to be steeply upward-sloping, whereas it is often downward-sloping before recessions, compare Chen (1991) and Estrella and Hardouvelis (1991). In other words, the slope of the yield curve forecasts economic growth.

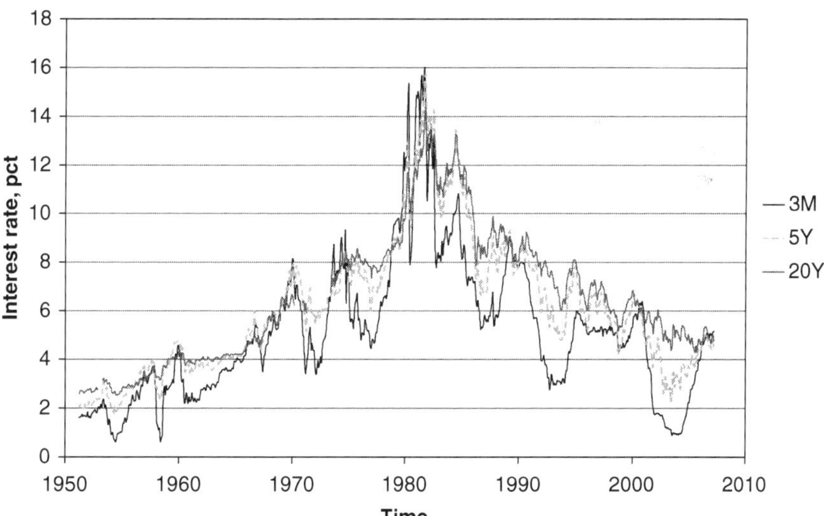

Fig. 1.3. Short-, medium-, and long-term yields on US government bonds over the period 1951–2008.

Notes: Data are taken from the homepage of the Federal Reserve, http://www.federalreserve.gov/releases/h15/data.htm

When the yield curve is upward-sloping, it is typically concave, that is relatively steep for short maturities and almost flat for long maturities. Campbell (2000) reports that the average historical yield difference (spread) to the 1-month yield is 33 basis points (0.33 percentage points) for the 3-month yield, 77 basis points for the one-year yield, and 96 basis points for the two-year yield, whereas there is only little difference between the average 2-year and 10-year yields. In periods where the yield curve is downward-sloping, it is typically convex, that is steeply decreasing for short maturities and almost flat for long maturities.

The excess returns on US Treasury bonds relative to very short-term interest rates are predictable by changes in the yield spreads over time. Campbell and Shiller (1991) and Campbell, Lo, and MacKinlay (1997, Ch. 10) find that a high yield spread between a long-term and a short-term interest rate forecasts an increase in short-term interest rates in the long run and a decrease in the yields on long-term bonds in the near future. Other studies indicate that a combination of forward rates can predict bond returns, see for example Fama and Bliss (1987), Stambaugh (1988), and Cochrane and Piazzesi (2005).

1.5.3 Asset Cross-Correlations

Price changes (and thus returns) of stocks and long-term bonds tend to be positively correlated as shown by Shiller and Beltratti (1992) and Campbell and Ammer (1993) among others. This makes sense if we think of the price of an asset as being the sum of the expected future dividends discounted by an appropriately risk-adjusted discount rate. If the discount rates of the stock and the long-term bonds move together then, assuming expected dividends do not change, the prices should move together. However, the risk-free discount rate of the long-term bond and the risk-adjusted discount rate of the stock do not have to move in lockstep as the equity risk premium might vary with the risk-free interest rates. More recent studies show that the stock–bond correlation varies over time and is even negative in some periods, see for example Ilmanen (2003), Cappiello, Engle, and Sheppard (2006), and Andersson, Krylova, and Vähämaa (2008). In periods of financial market turbulence some investors tend to shift from stocks to bonds (the so-called flight-to-quality) causing opposing changes in the price of the two asset classes. Negative stock–bond correlation is often seen around stock market crashes.

Ibbotson Associates Inc. publishes an annual book with a lot of statistics on the US financial markets. The cross-correlations of annual nominal and real returns on different asset classes in the US are shown in Table 1.2. Note the fairly high correlation between the real returns on the two stock classes and between the real returns on the three bond classes, whereas the correlations between any bond class and any stock class is modest.

Table 1.2. Cross-correlations of annual returns between bills (short-term government bonds), long-term government bonds, long-term corporate bonds, stocks in companies with large capitalization, stocks in companies with small capitalization, and the inflation rate derived from the Consumer Price Index (CPI).

	Treas. bills	Treas. bonds	Corp. bonds	Large stocks	Small stocks	CPI inflation
Nominal returns						
bills	1.00	0.24	0.22	-0.03	-0.10	0.41
gov. bonds	0.24	1.00	0.91	0.16	0.00	-0.14
corp. bonds	0.22	0.91	1.00	0.24	0.09	-0.15
large stocks	-0.03	0.16	0.24	1.00	0.79	-0.03
small stocks	-0.10	0.00	0.09	0.79	1.00	0.08
inflation	0.41	-0.14	-0.15	-0.03	0.08	1.00
Real returns						
bills	1.00	0.58	0.59	0.12	-0.06	—
gov. bonds	0.58	1.00	0.95	0.24	0.04	—
corp. bonds	0.59	0.95	1.00	0.30	0.12	—
large stocks	0.12	0.24	0.30	1.00	0.79	—
small stocks	-0.06	0.04	0.12	0.79	1.00	—

Notes: The upper panel shows correlations for nominal returns, the lower panel correlations for real returns. Data from the United States in the period 1926–2000

Source: Ibbotson Associates (2000)

1.6 THE ORGANIZATION OF THIS BOOK

The remainder of this book is organized as follows. Chapter 2 discusses how to represent uncertainty and information flow in asset pricing models. It also introduces stochastic processes and some key results on how to deal with stochastic processes which we will frequently apply in later chapters.

Chapter 3 shows how we can model financial assets and their dividends as well as how we can represent portfolios and trading strategies. It also defines the important concepts of arbitrage, redundant assets, and market completeness.

Chapter 4 defines the key concept of a state-price deflator both in one-period models, in discrete-time multiperiod models, and in continuous-time models. A state-price deflator is one way to represent the general pricing mechanism of a financial market. We can price any asset given the state-price deflator and the dividend process of that asset. Conditions for the existence and uniqueness of a state-price deflator are derived as well as a number of useful properties of state-price deflators. We will also briefly discuss alternative ways of representing the general market pricing mechanism, for example through a set of risk-neutral probabilities.

The state-price deflator and therefore asset prices are ultimately determined by the supply and demand of investors. Chapter 5 studies how we can represent the preferences of investors. We discuss when preferences can be represented by expected utility, how we can measure the risk aversion of an individual, and we introduce some frequently used utility functions. In Chapter 6 we investigate how individual investors will make decisions on consumption and investments. We set up the utility maximization problem for the individual and characterize the solution for different relevant specifications of preferences. The solution gives an important link between state-price deflators (and, thus, the prices of financial assets) and the optimal decisions at the individual level.

Chapter 7 deals with the market equilibrium. We will discuss when market equilibria are Pareto-efficient and when we can think of the economy as having only one representative individual instead of many individuals.

Chapter 8 further explores the link between individual consumption choice and asset prices. The very general Consumption-based Capital Asset Pricing Model (CCAPM) is derived. A simple version of the CCAPM is confronted with data and leaves several stylized facts unexplained. A number of recent extensions that are more successful are discussed in Chapter 9.

Chapter 10 studies the so-called factor models of asset pricing where one or multiple factors govern the state-price deflators and thus asset prices and returns. Some empirically successful factor models are described. It is also shown how pricing factors can be identified theoretically as a special case of the general CCAPM.

While Chapters 8–10 mostly focus on explaining the expected excess return of risky assets, most prominently stocks, Chapter 11 explores the implications of general asset pricing theory for bond prices and the term structure of interest rates. It also critically reviews some traditional hypotheses on the term structure of interest rates.

Chapter 12 shows how the information in a state-price deflator can be equivalently represented by the price of one specific asset and an appropriately risk-adjusted probability measure. This turns out to be a powerful tool when dealing with derivative securities, which is the topic of Chapter 13.

Each chapter ends with a number of exercises which either illustrate the concepts and conclusions of the chapter or provide additional related results.

1.7 PREREQUISITES

We will study asset pricing with the well-established scientific approach: make precise definitions of concepts, clear statements of assumptions, and formal derivations of results. This requires extensive use of mathematics, but not very complicated mathematics. Concepts, assumptions, and results will all be accompanied by financial interpretations. Examples will be used for illustrations. A useful general mathematical reference 'manual' is Sydsaeter, Strom, and Berck (2000). The main mathematical disciplines we will apply are linear algebra, optimization, and probability theory. Linear algebra and optimization are covered by many good textbooks on mathematics for economics such as the companion books by Sydsaeter and Hammond (2005) and Sydsaeter *et al.* (2005) as well as many more general textbooks on mathematics.

Appendix A reviews the main concepts and definitions in probability theory. Appendix B summarizes some important results on the lognormal distribution which are useful in many specific models.

We will frequently use vectors and matrices to represent a lot of information in a compact manner. For example, we will typically use a vector to represent the prices of a number of assets and use a matrix to represent the dividends of different assets in different states of the world. Therefore some basic knowledge of how to handle vectors and matrices (so-called linear algebra) is needed. Appendix C provides an incomplete and relatively unstructured list of basic properties of vectors and matrices. We will use boldface symbols like $\boldsymbol{x}$ to denote vectors and vectors are generally assumed to be column vectors. Matrices will be indicated by double underlining like $\underline{\underline{A}}$. We will use the symbol $^{\top}$ to denote the transpose of a vector or a matrix.

2

Uncertainty, Information, and Stochastic Processes

2.1 INTRODUCTION

Uncertainty is a key component of any asset pricing theory. The future dividends of most financial assets are unknown. Other variables that may affect the valuation of the future dividends, such as future labour income and consumption, are also unknown. When building and studying asset pricing theories and models, we have to be able to handle such uncertainties, know how to associate probabilities to them, and know how these probabilities may change over time. This chapter provides the tools from probability theory that are being used in the asset pricing models covered in the remaining part of the book.

Some of the basic concepts from probability theory—including random variables, distribution functions, density functions, expectations, variances, and correlations—are briefly explained in Appendix A. Section 2.2 reviews the concept of a probability space that underlies any standard mathematical representation of uncertainty.

Modern asset pricing models are formulated in multiperiod settings and models should capture the fact that we learn more and more as time passes. For example, dividends that were once uncertain eventually become known and actually paid out to investors. Information grows over time. When investors take decisions, they will use all the relevant information they have. Section 2.3 discusses how to represent the flow of information mathematically.

The dividend of an asset at a given point in time is well represented by a random variable. In multiperiod settings, assets may pay dividends at several dates, so to capture the entire dividend stream of an asset we need a collection of random variables, one for each relevant point in time. Such a collection of random variables is called a stochastic process. Section 2.4 introduces some terminology used in relation to stochastic processes. Section 2.5 gives an overview of important discrete-time stochastic processes where the basic uncertainty is generated by a time series of normally distributed shocks to the quantities we intend to model. Continuous-time stochastic processes involve certain so-called stochastic integrals and are therefore more difficult to understand and handle without adequate training. Section 2.6 offers a relatively short what-you-need-to-know presentation of stochastic integration and continuous-time stochastic processes. Finally, Section 2.7 discusses how we can handle multiple stochastic processes simultaneously, which we have to do in most asset pricing models.

2.2 PROBABILITY SPACE

Any model with uncertainty refers to a probability space $(\Omega, \mathcal{F}, \mathbb{P})$, where

- Ω is the state space of possible outcomes. An element $\omega \in \Omega$ represents a possible realization of all uncertain objects of the model. An event is a subset of Ω.
- $\mathcal{F}$ is a sigma-algebra in Ω, that is a collection of subsets of Ω with the properties
  (i) $\Omega \in \mathcal{F}$,
  (ii) for any set F in $\mathcal{F}$, the complement $F^c \equiv \Omega \setminus F$ is also in $\mathcal{F}$,
  (iii) if $F_1, F_2, \dots \in \mathcal{F}$, then the union $\cup_{n=1}^{\infty} F_n$ is in $\mathcal{F}$.

  $\mathcal{F}$ is the collection of all events that can be assigned a probability.
- $\mathbb{P}$ is a probability measure, that is a function $\mathbb{P} : \mathcal{F} \to [0, 1]$ with $\mathbb{P}(\Omega) = 1$ and the property that $\mathbb{P}(\cup_{m=1}^{\infty} A_m) = \sum_{m=1}^{\infty} \mathbb{P}(A_m)$ for any sequence $A_1, A_2, \dots$ of disjoint events.

An uncertain object can be formally modelled as a random variable on the probability space. A random variable X on the probability space $(\Omega, \mathcal{F}, \mathbb{P})$ is a real-valued function on Ω which is $\mathcal{F}$-measurable in the sense that for any interval $I \subseteq \mathbb{R}$, the set $\{\omega \in \Omega \mid X(\omega) \in I\}$ belongs to $\mathcal{F}$, that is we can assign a probability to the event that the random variable takes on a value in I.

What is the relevant state space for an asset pricing model? A state $\omega \in \Omega$ represents a possible realization of all relevant uncertain objects over the entire time span of the model. In one-period models dividends, incomes, and so on, are realized at time 1. A state defines realized values of all the dividends and incomes at time 1. In multiperiod models a state defines dividends, incomes, and so on, at all points in the time considered in the model, that is all $t \in \mathcal{T}$, where either $\mathcal{T} = \{0, 1, 2, \dots, T\}$ or $\mathcal{T} = [0, T]$. The state space must include all the possible combinations of realizations of the uncertain objects that may affect the pricing of the assets. These uncertain objects include all the possible combinations of realizations of (a) all the future dividends of all assets, (b) all the future incomes of all individuals, and (c) any other initially unknown variables that may affect prices, for example variables that contain information about the future development in dividends or income. The state space Ω therefore has to be 'large'. If you want to allow for continuous random variables, for example dividends that are normally distributed, you will need an infinite state space. If you restrict all dividends, incomes, and so on, to be discrete random variables, that is variables with a finite number of possible realizations, you can do this with a finite state space.

For some purposes we will have to distinguish between an infinite state space and a finite state space. When we consider a finite state space we will take it to be $\Omega = \{1, 2, \ldots, S\}$ so that there are S possible states of which exactly one will be realized. An event is then simply a subset of Ω and $\mathcal{F}$ is the collection of all subsets of Ω. The probability measure $\mathbb{P}$ is defined by the state probabilities $p_\omega \equiv \mathbb{P}(\omega)$, $\omega = 1, 2, \ldots, S$, which we take to be strictly positive with $p_1 + \cdots + p_S = 1$, of course. With a finite state space we can represent random variables with S-dimensional vectors and apply results and techniques from linear algebra. In any case we take the state probabilities as given and assume they are known to all individuals.

2.3 INFORMATION

In a one-period model all uncertainty is resolved at time $t = 1$. At time 0 we only know that the true state is an element in Ω. At time 1 we know exactly which state has been realized. In a multiperiod model the uncertainty is gradually resolved. Investors will gradually know more and more about the true state. For example, the dividends of assets at a given point in time are typically unknown before that time, but known afterwards. The consumption and investment decisions taken by individuals at a given point in time will depend on the available information at that time and therefore asset prices will also depend on the information known. We will therefore have to consider how to formally represent the flow of information through time.

To illustrate how we can represent the information at different points in time, consider an example of a two-period, three-date economy with six possible outcomes simply labelled 1 through 6. In Fig. 2.1 each outcome is represented by a dashed horizontal line. The probability of each outcome is written next to each line. At time 0, we assume that investors are unable to rule out any of the six outcomes—if a state could be ruled out from the start, it should not have been included in the model. This is indicated by the ellipse around the six dots/lines representing the possible outcomes. At time 1, investors have learned either (i) that the true outcome is 1 or 2, (ii) that the true outcome is 3, 4, or 5, or (iii) that the true outcome is 6. At time 2, all uncertainty has been resolved so that investors know exactly which outcome is realized.

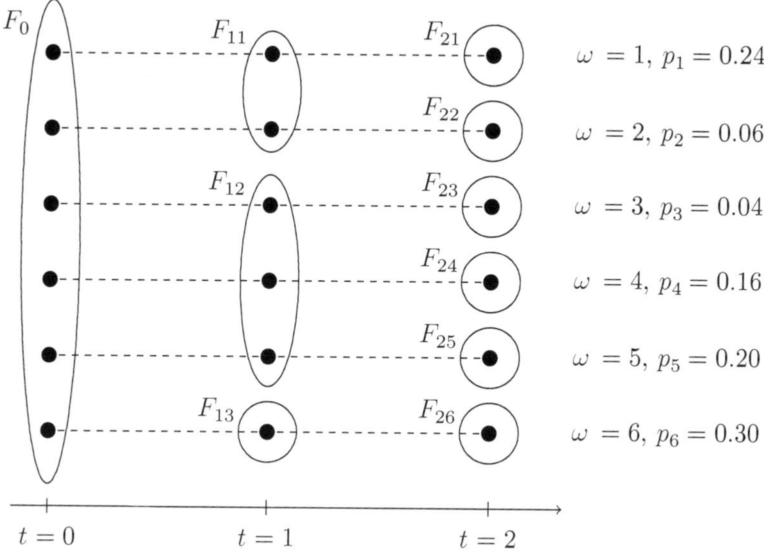

Fig. 2.1. An example of a two-period economy.

We can represent the information available at any given point in time t by a *partition* $\mathbb{F}_t$ of Ω, which means that $\mathbb{F}_t$ is a collection of subsets $F_{t1}, F_{t2}, \dots$ of Ω so that

(i) the union of these subsets equal the entire set Ω: $\cup_k F_{tk} = \Omega$,

(ii) the subsets are disjoint: $F_{tk} \cap F_{tl} = \emptyset$ for all $k \neq l$.

In our example, the partition $\mathbb{F}_0$ representing time 0 information (or rather lack of information) is the trivial partition consisting only of $F_0 = \Omega$, that is

$$\mathbb{F}_0 = \{\Omega\}.$$

The partition $\mathbb{F}_1$ representing time 1 information consists of F_{11}, F_{12}, and F_{13}, that is

$$\mathbb{F}_1 = \big\{\{1,2\}, \{3,4,5\}, \{6\}\big\}.$$

The partition $\mathbb{F}_2$ that represents time 2 information (full information) is

$$\mathbb{F}_2 = \big\{\{1\}, \{2\}, \{3\}, \{4\}, \{5\}, \{6\}\big\}.$$

In a general multiperiod model with a finite state space Ω, the information flow can be summarized by a sequence $(\mathbb{F}_t)_{t \in \mathcal{T}}$ of partitions. Since investors learn more and more, the partitions should be increasingly fine, which more formally means that when $t < t'$, every set $F \in \mathbb{F}_{t'}$ is a subset of some set in $\mathbb{F}_t$.

An alternative way of representing the information flow is in terms of an *information filtration*, that is a sequence $(\mathcal{F}_t)_{t\in\mathcal{T}}$ of sigma-algebras on Ω. Given a partition $\mathbf{F}_t$ of Ω, we can construct a sigma-algebra $\mathcal{F}_t$ as the set of all unions of (countably many) sets in $\mathbf{F}_t$, including the 'empty union', that is the empty set $\emptyset$. Where $\mathbf{F}_t$ contains only the disjoint 'decidable' events at time t, $\mathcal{F}_t$ contains all 'decidable' events at time t. For our simple two-period example above, we get

$$\mathcal{F}_0 = \{\emptyset, \Omega\},$$

$$\mathcal{F}_1 = \{\emptyset, \{1,2\}, \{3,4,5\}, \{6\}, \{1,2,3,4,5\}, \{1,2,6\}, \{3,4,5,6\}, \Omega\},$$

while $\mathcal{F}_2$ becomes the collection of *all* possible subsets of Ω. In a general multiperiod model we write $(\mathcal{F}_t)_{t\in\mathcal{T}}$ for the information filtration. We will always assume that the time 0 information is trivial, corresponding to $\mathcal{F}_0 = \{\emptyset, \Omega\}$. We also assume that all uncertainty is resolved at or before the final date so that $\mathcal{F}_T = \mathcal{F}$, the set of all subsets of Ω that can be assigned a probability, which is generally all the subsets you can think of. The fact that we learn more and more about the true state as time goes by implies that we must have $\mathcal{F}_t \subset \mathcal{F}_{t'}$ whenever $t < t'$, that is every set in $\mathcal{F}_t$ is also in $\mathcal{F}_{t'}$.

Above we constructed an information filtration from a sequence of partitions. We can also go from a filtration to a sequence of partitions. In each $\mathcal{F}_t$, simply remove all sets that are unions of other sets in $\mathcal{F}_t$. Therefore there is a one-to-one relationship between information filtration and a sequence of partitions.

In models with an infinite state space, the information filtration representation is preferable. We will therefore generally write the formal model of uncertainty and information as a *filtered probability space* $(\Omega, \mathcal{F}, \mathbb{P}, (\mathcal{F}_t)_{t\in\mathcal{T}})$, where $(\Omega, \mathcal{F}, \mathbb{P})$ is a probability space and $(\mathcal{F}_t)_{t\in\mathcal{T}}$ is an information filtration.

Whenever the state space is finite we can alternatively represent the uncertainty and information flow by a multinomial tree. For example, we can depict the uncertainty and information flow in Fig. 2.1 by the multinomial tree in Fig. 2.2. Each node at a given point in time corresponds to an element in the partition representing the information. For example, the node labelled F_{11} at time 1 represents the element $\{1,2\}$ of the partition $\mathbf{F}_1$. We can think of F_{11}, F_{12}, and F_{13} as the three possible 'scenarios' at time 1. At time 0, there is only one possible scenario. At time 2, when all uncertainty is resolved, there are as many scenarios as states. The arrival of new information in a given period can be thought of as the transition from one scenario at the beginning of the period to a scenario at the end of the period. In our example, there are three possible transitions in the first period. If the economy is in scenario F_{11} at time 1 (that is the true state is 1 or 2), there are two possible transitions over the next period, either to F_{21} (state 1) or to F_{22} (state 2). If the economy is in scenario F_{12} at time 1 (the true state is known to be 3, 4, or 5), there are three possible transitions over the next period, to F_{23} (state 3), to F_{24} (state 4), or to

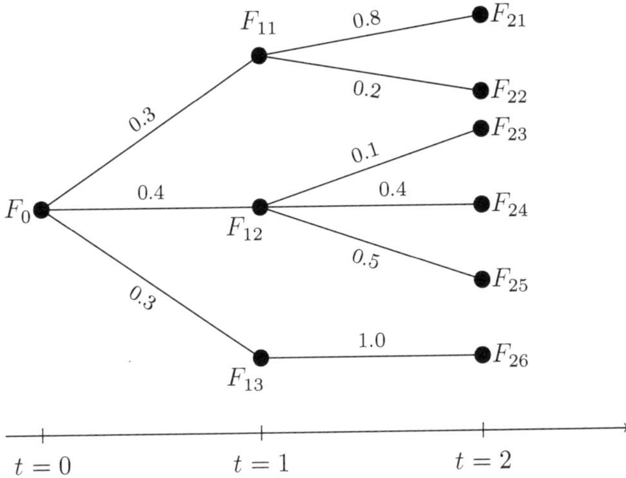

Fig. 2.2. The multinomial tree version of the two-period economy in Fig. 2.1.

F_{25} (state 5). If the economy is in scenario F_{13} at time 1, the true state is already known to be state 6, and there is only one possible transition over the next period, corresponding to no new information arriving. Each state corresponds to a path through the tree.

The transitions are illustrated by the lines in Fig. 2.2. The numbers along the lines are conditional probabilities of the transitions happening. Over the first period there is really no information to condition on. The transition from F_0 to F_{11} will happen with a probability of 0.3, which is simply the sum of the probabilities of the two outcomes in F_{11}, namely the probability of 0.24 for state 1 and the probability of 0.06 for state 2. This holds similarly for the other transitions over the first period. The probabilities assigned to the transitions over the second period are true conditional probabilities. Conditional on the economy being in scenario F_{11} at time 1, it will move to F_{21} with a probability of $0.24/(0.24 + 0.06) = 0.8$ since that is the probability of state 1 given that the state is either 1 or 2 as represented by scenario F_{11}. This holds similarly for the other transitions over the second period. Of course, given the conditional probabilities in the multinomial tree, we can also recover the state probabilities. For example, the state $\omega = 5$ corresponds to a transition from F_0 to F_{12} over the first period, followed by a transition from F_{12} to F_{25} over the second period. The probability of this sequence of transitions is given by the product of the probabilities of each of the transitions, that is $0.4 \times 0.5 = 0.2$, which equals the probability of state $\omega = 5$.

In our asset pricing models we will often deal with expectations of random variables, for example the expectation of the dividend of an asset at a future point in time. In the computation of such an expectation we should take the information currently available into account. Hence we need to consider conditional expectations. Recall that the information at a given point in time t is represented by a sigma-algebra $\mathcal{F}_t$ (or, equivalently, a partition $\mathbf{F}_t$). One can generally write the expectation of a random variable X given the sigma-algebra $\mathcal{F}_t$ as $\mathrm{E}[X|\mathcal{F}_t]$. For our purposes the sigma-algebra $\mathcal{F}_t$ will always represent the information at time t and we will write $\mathrm{E}_t[X]$ instead of $\mathrm{E}[X|\mathcal{F}_t]$. Since we assume that the information at time 0 is trivial, conditioning on time 0 information is the same as not conditioning on any information, hence $\mathrm{E}_0[X] = \mathrm{E}[X]$. Since we assume that all uncertainty is resolved at time T, we have $\mathrm{E}_T[X] = X$. We will frequently use the following result:

Theorem 2.1 (The Law of Iterated Expectations). *If $\mathcal{F}$ and $\mathcal{G}$ are two sigma-algebras with $\mathcal{F} \subseteq \mathcal{G}$ and X is a random variable, then* $\mathrm{E}\left[\mathrm{E}[X|\mathcal{G}] \mid \mathcal{F}\right] = \mathrm{E}[X|\mathcal{F}]$. *In particular, if $(\mathcal{F}_t)_{t\in\mathcal{T}}$ is an information filtration and $t' > t$, we have*

$$\mathrm{E}_t\left[\mathrm{E}_{t'}[X]\right] = \mathrm{E}_t[X].$$

Loosely speaking, the theorem says that what you expect today of some variable that will be realized in two days is equal to what you expect today that you will expect tomorrow about the same variable. The Law of Iterated Expectations is also known as the *Tower Rule* or *Tower Property* of conditional expectations.

We can define conditional variances, covariances, and correlations from the conditional expectation exactly as one defines (unconditional) variances, covariances, and correlations from (unconditional) expectations:

$$\mathrm{Var}_t[X] = \mathrm{E}_t\left[(X - \mathrm{E}_t[X])^2\right] = \mathrm{E}_t[X^2] - (\mathrm{E}_t[X])^2,$$

$$\mathrm{Cov}_t[X, Y] = \mathrm{E}_t\left[(X - \mathrm{E}_t[X])(Y - \mathrm{E}_t[Y])\right] = \mathrm{E}_t[XY] - \mathrm{E}_t[X]\,\mathrm{E}_t[Y],$$

$$\mathrm{Corr}_t[X, Y] = \frac{\mathrm{Cov}_t[X, Y]}{\sqrt{\mathrm{Var}_t[X]\,\mathrm{Var}_t[Y]}}.$$

Again the conditioning on time t information is indicated by a t subscript.

In the two-period model of Figs. 2.1 and 2.2, suppose we have an asset paying state-dependent dividends at time 1 and 2 as depicted in Figs. 2.3 and 2.4. Then the expected time 2 dividend computed at time 0 is

$$\begin{aligned}\mathrm{E}[D_2] = \mathrm{E}_0[D_2] &= 0.24 \times 0 + 0.06 \times 20 + 0.04 \times 10 + 0.16 \times 5 \\ &\quad + 0.2 \times 20 + 0.3 \times 20 = 12.4.\end{aligned}$$

What is the expected time 2 dividend computed at time 1? It will depend on the information available at time 1. If the information corresponds to the event $F_{11} = \{1, 2\}$, the expected dividend is

$$\mathrm{E}_1[D_2] = 0.8 \times 0 + 0.2 \times 20 = 4.$$

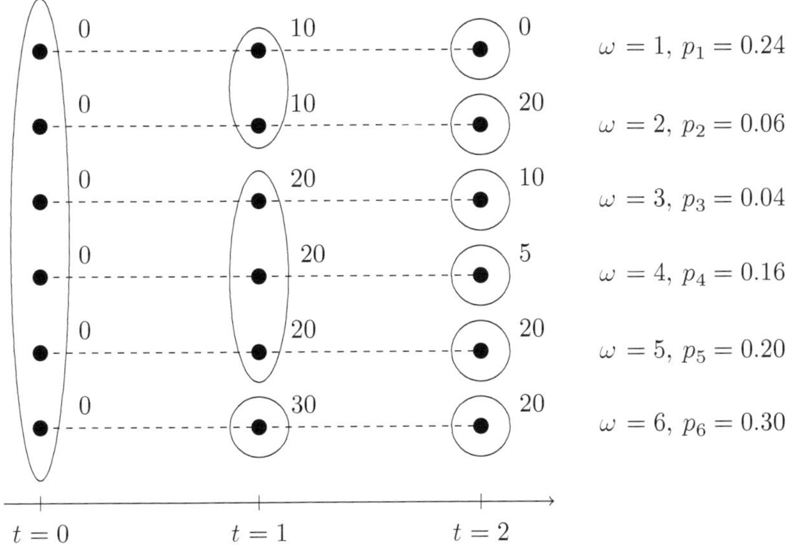

Fig. 2.3. The dividends of an asset in the two-period economy.

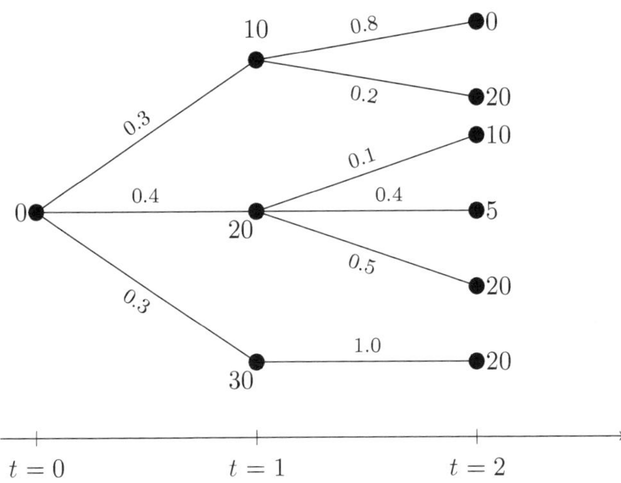

Fig. 2.4. The multinomial tree version of the dividend process in Fig. 2.3.

If the information corresponds to the event $F_{12} = \{3, 4, 5\}$, the expected dividend is

$$E_1[D_2] = 0.1 \times 10 + 0.4 \times 5 + 0.5 \times 20 = 13.$$

If the information corresponds to the event $F_{13} = \{6\}$, the expected dividend is

$$E_1[D_2] = 1.0 \times 20 = 20.$$

The time 1 expectation of the time 2 dividend is therefore a random variable which is measurable with respect to the information at time 1. Note that the time 0 expectation of that random variable is

$$\mathrm{E}\left[\mathrm{E}_1[D_2]\right] = 0.3 \times 4 + 0.4 \times 13 + 0.3 \times 20 = 12.4 = \mathrm{E}[D_2],$$

consistent with the Law of Iterated Expectations.

Obviously, the state space must contain all possible realizations of exogenous quantities such as dividends and income. But it must also contain all the possible revisions of probabilities of future events. Consider a simple two-period example with a single risky asset that only pays a dividend D_2 at time $t = 2$ and nothing at time $t = 1$. The dividend can be either 50, 150, or 250. At time $t = 0$, an individual associates a probability of $5/18$ both to a dividend of 50 and a dividend of 150 and a probability of $4/9$ to a dividend of 250. At time $t = 1$, the individual may receive the information signal A that leads him to revise the probabilities to $1/2$ both for a dividend of 50 and a dividend of 150 (and thus zero probability for a dividend of 250). Alternatively, he may receive the information signal B that leads him to revise the probabilities to $1/3$ for each of the three possible dividends. Or he may receive the information signal C that tells him that the future dividend will be 250 for sure. Seen from time 0, the three signals are equally likely. This setting is illustrated by the tree in Fig. 2.5, which happens to have the same structure as the tree considered above. Note that these conditional probabilities are consistent with the stated unconditional probabilities of the final dividend. For example, the probability of a dividend of 50 is $1/3 \times 1/2 + 1/3 \times 1/3 = 5/18$. Although there are only three possible outcomes of the final dividend, we need six states to capture the

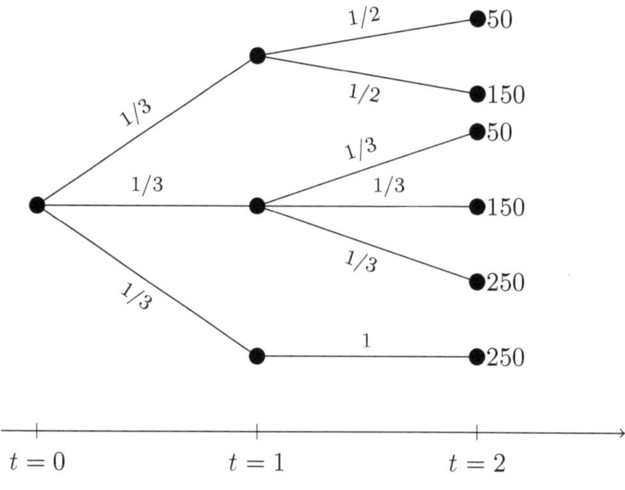

Fig. 2.5. A multinomial tree with revised probabilities of terminal outcomes.

flow of information about the final dividend. The time 1 information about the time 2 dividend will certainly affect the demand for, and thus the price of, the asset at time 1.

2.4 STOCHASTIC PROCESSES: DEFINITION AND TERMINOLOGY

In one-period models all uncertain objects can be represented by a random variable. For example, the dividend (at time 1) of a given asset is a random variable. In multiperiod models we have to keep track of dividends, asset prices, consumption, portfolios, (labour) income, and so on, throughout the time set $\mathcal{T}$, where either $\mathcal{T} = \{0, 1, 2, \dots, T\}$ or $\mathcal{T} = [0, T]$. For example, the dividend of a given asset, say asset i, at a particular future date $t \in \mathcal{T}$ can be represented by a random variable D_{it}. Recall that, formally, a random variable is a function from the state space Ω into $\mathbb{R}$, the set of real numbers. To represent the dividends of an asset throughout all dates, we need a collection of random variables, one for each date. Such a collection is called a *stochastic process* (we will often just write 'process' instead of 'stochastic process'). The dividend of asset i is thus represented by a stochastic process $D_i = (D_{it})_{t \in \mathcal{T}}$, where each D_{it} is a random variable. We can form multidimensional stochastic processes by stacking one-dimensional stochastic processes. For example, we can represent the dividends of I assets by an I-dimensional stochastic process $\boldsymbol{D} = (\boldsymbol{D}_t)_{t \in \mathcal{T}}$, where each $\boldsymbol{D}_t = (D_{1t}, \dots, D_{It})^{\top}$ is an I-dimensional random variable.

In general, for any $t \in \mathcal{T}$, the dividend at time t will be known at time t, but not before. The random variable D_{it} is then said to be $\mathcal{F}_t$-measurable, where $\mathcal{F}_t$ is the sigma-algebra representing the information at time t. If this information is equivalently represented by a partition $\mathbb{F}_t = \{F_{t1}, F_{t2}, \dots\}$, measurability means that D_{it} is constant on each of the elements F_{tj} of the partition. Note that this is indeed the case in our example in Fig. 2.3. If D_{it} is $\mathcal{F}_t$-measurable for any $t \in \mathcal{T}$, the stochastic process $D_i = (D_{it})_{t \in \mathcal{T}}$ is said to be *adapted* to the information filtration $(\mathcal{F}_t)_{t \in \mathcal{T}}$. Since the dividends of assets and the income of individuals are assumed to be part of the exogenous uncertainty, it is natural to assume that dividend processes and income processes are adapted to the information filtration. In fact, most concrete models write down stochastic processes for all the exogenous variables and define the information filtration as the smallest filtration to which these exogenous processes are adapted.

An individual can choose how much to consume and which portfolio to invest in at any point in time, subject of course to a budget constraint and other feasibility constraints. The consumption and portfolio chosen at a given future date are likely to depend on the income the individual has received up to that point and her information about her future income and the future dividends of assets. The consumption rate at a given future date is therefore a random variable, and the consumption rates at all dates constitute a stochastic process, the consumption process. Similarly, the portfolios chosen at different dates form a stochastic process: the portfolio process or the so-called trading strategy. Representing consumption and investments by stochastic processes does not mean that we treat them as being exogenously given and purely determined by chance, but simply that the individual will condition her consumption and portfolio decisions on the information received. Since we assume that the underlying model of uncertainty includes all the uncertainty relevant for the decisions of the individuals, it is natural to require that consumption and portfolio processes are adapted to the information filtration.

Now consider prices. In a multiperiod model we need to keep track of prices at all points in time. The price of a given asset at a given point in time depends on the supply and demand for that asset from all individuals, which again depends on the information individuals have at that time. Hence, we can also represent prices by adapted stochastic processes. To sum up, all the stochastic processes relevant for our purposes will be adapted to the information filtration representing the resolution of all the relevant uncertainty.

Next, we introduce some further terminology often used in connection with stochastic processes. A stochastic process $X = (X_t)_{t\in\mathcal{T}}$ is said to be a *martingale* if, for all $t, t' \in \mathcal{T}$ with $t < t'$,

$$\mathrm{E}_t[X_{t'}] = X_t,$$

which means that no change in the value is expected. Since the conditional expectation depends on the probability measure $\mathbb{P}$ and the information filtration $(\mathcal{F}_t)_{t\in\mathcal{T}}$, we should really call the process X a $(\mathbb{P}, (\mathcal{F}_t)_{t\in\mathcal{T}})$-martingale if the above condition is satisfied. Throughout the book we will only consider a single information filtration in any given model, and until Chapter 12 we will only consider a single probability measure. The appropriate probability measure and information filtration are therefore clear from the context.

A *sample path* of a stochastic process X is the collection of realized values $(X_t(\omega))_{t\in\mathcal{T}}$ for a given outcome $\omega \in \Omega$. The *value space* of a stochastic process is the smallest set $\mathcal{S}$ with the property that $\mathbb{P}(\{X_t \in \mathcal{S}\}) = 1$ for all $t \in \mathcal{T}$. If the value space has countably many elements, the stochastic process is called a discrete-value process. Otherwise, it is called a continuous-value process. Of course, if the state space Ω is finite, all processes will be discrete-value processes. If you want to model continuous-value processes, you need an infinite state space.

For the modelling of most time-varying economic objects it seems reasonable to use continuous-value processes. Admittedly, stock prices are quoted on exchanges as multiples of some smallest possible unit (often 0.01 currency units), and interest rates are rounded off to some number of decimals. But the set of possible values of such objects is approximated very well by an interval in $\mathbb{R}$ (maybe $\mathbb{R}_+$ or $\mathbb{R}$ itself). Also, the mathematics involved in the analysis of continuous-value processes is simpler and more elegant than the mathematics for discrete-value processes. However, there are economic objects that can only take on a very limited set of values. For these objects discrete-value processes should be used. An example is the credit rating assigned by credit rating agencies (such as Moody's and Standard and Poor's) to debt issues of corporations and governments.

As time goes by, we can observe the evolution in the object which the stochastic process describes. At any given time t', the previous values $(X_t)_{t\in[0,t')}$ will be known (at least in the models we consider). These values constitute the *history* of the process up to time t'. The future values are still stochastic.

As time passes, we will typically revise our expectations of the future values of the process. More precisely, we will revise the probability distribution we attribute to the value of the process at any future point in time, compare the discussion in the previous section. Suppose we stand at time t and consider the value of a process X at a future time $t' > t$. The distribution of the value of $X_{t'}$ is characterized by probabilities $\mathbb{P}(X_{t'} \in A)$ for subsets A of the value space $\mathcal{S}$. If, for all $t, t' \in \mathcal{T}$ with $t < t'$ and all $A \subseteq \mathcal{S}$, we have that

$$\mathbb{P}\left(X_{t'} \in A \mid (X_s)_{s\leq t}\right) = \mathbb{P}\left(X_{t'} \in A \mid X_t\right),$$

then X is called a *Markov process*. Broadly speaking, this condition says that, given the present, the future is independent of the past. The history contains no information about the future value that cannot be extracted from the current value.

2.5 SOME DISCRETE-TIME STOCHASTIC PROCESSES

In most discrete-time financial models the basic uncertainty is described by a sequence $\varepsilon_1, \varepsilon_2, \dots, \varepsilon_T$ of random variables, one for each point in time. Think of ε_t as an exogenous shock to the financial market at time t. We assume that the shocks at different points in time are mutually independent, that each shock has a mean of zero and a variance of one. The shock at any given point in time t can be multivariate, in which case we will write it as a vector $\boldsymbol{\varepsilon}_t$. In that case the elements of the vector are assumed to be mutually independent. We assume that the shocks at all points in time have the same dimension. The distribution of the exogenous shocks has to be specified in the model. Typically, the shocks are assumed to be normally distributed (infinite state space), but models with a binomial or multinominal structure (finite state space) also exist.

The filtered probability space $(\Omega, \mathcal{F}, \mathbb{P}, (\mathcal{F}_t)_{t\in\mathcal{T}})$ is defined implicitly from the assumptions on the exogenous shocks. For example, assume that the exogenous shocks $\varepsilon_1, \dots, \varepsilon_T$ are $N(0,1)$ distributed. The state space is then the set of all possible realizations of all the T shocks, which is equivalent to $\mathbb{R}^T$. The sigma-algebra $\mathcal{F}$ is the set of events that can be assigned a probability, which is the set of (Borel-)subsets of $\mathbb{R}^T$. The probability measure $\mathbb{P}$ is defined via the normality assumption as

$$\mathbb{P}(\varepsilon_t < h) = N(h) \equiv \int_{-\infty}^{h} \frac{1}{\sqrt{2\pi}} e^{-a^2/2}\, da, \quad t = 1, \dots, T,$$

where $N(\cdot)$ is the cumulative distribution function for an $N(0,1)$ variable. Probabilities of other events will follow from the above. The information at time t is represented by the smallest sigma-algebra with respect to which the random variables $\varepsilon_1, \dots, \varepsilon_t$ are measurable.

Stochastic processes for dividends, income, and so on, can be defined relative to the assumed exogenous shocks. It is easy to obtain non-zero means, non-unit variances, and dependencies across time. A discrete-time stochastic process $X = (X_t)_{t\in\mathcal{T}}$ is typically specified by the initial value X_0 (a constant in $\mathbb{R}$) and the increments over each period, that is $\Delta X_{t+1} \equiv X_{t+1} - X_t$ for each $t = 0, 1, \dots, T-1$. The increments ΔX_{t+1} are defined in terms of the exogenous shocks $\varepsilon_1, \dots, \varepsilon_{t+1}$, which implies that the process X is adapted.

Let us look at some discrete-time stochastic processes frequently used in asset pricing models. In all the examples we assume that the exogenous shocks $\varepsilon_1, \dots, \varepsilon_T$ are independent, one-dimensional $N(0,1)$ distributed random variables.

Random walk: $\Delta X_{t+1} = \sigma\varepsilon_{t+1}$ or, equivalently, $X_{t+1} = X_0 + \sigma(\varepsilon_1 + \varepsilon_2 + \dots + \varepsilon_{t+1})$. Here σ is a positive constant. A random walk is a Markov process since only the current value X_t and not the previous values $X_{t-1}, X_{t-2}, \dots$ affect X_{t+1}. Since the expected change over any single period is zero, the expected change over any time interval will be zero, so a random walk is a martingale. Conditionally on X_t, X_{t+1} is normally distributed with mean X_t and variance σ^2. X_{t+1} is unconditionally (that is seen from time 0) normally distributed with mean X_0 and variance $(t+1)\sigma^2$.

Random walk with drift: $\Delta X_{t+1} = \mu + \sigma\varepsilon_{t+1}$, where μ is a constant (the drift rate) and σ is a positive constant. Also a random walk with drift is a Markov process. The expected change over any single period is μ so, unless $\mu = 0$ and we are back to the random walk without drift, the process $X = (X_t)_{t\in\mathcal{T}}$ is not a martingale. Conditionally on X_t, X_{t+1} is normally distributed with mean $\mu + X_t$ and variance σ^2. X_{t+1} is unconditionally normally distributed with mean $X_0 + (t+1)\mu$ and variance $(t+1)\sigma^2$.

Autoregressive process: A process $X = (X_t)_{t\in\mathcal{T}}$ with

$$\Delta X_{t+1} = (1-\rho)(\mu - X_t) + \sigma\varepsilon_{t+1},$$

where $\rho \in (-1, 1)$, is said to be an autoregressive process of order 1 or simply an AR(1) process. It is a Markov process since only the current value X_t affects the distribution of the future value. The expected change over the period is positive if $X_t < \mu$ and negative if $X_t > \mu$. In any case, the value X_{t+1} is expected to be closer to μ than X_t is. The process is pulled towards μ, and therefore the process is said to be mean-reverting. This is useful for modelling the dynamics of variables that tend to vary with the business cycle around some long-term average. Note, however, extreme shocks may cause the process to be pushed further away from μ.

Observe that

$$X_{t+1} = X_t + (1-\rho)(\mu - X_t) + \sigma\varepsilon_{t+1} = \rho X_t + (1-\rho)\mu + \sigma\varepsilon_{t+1}.$$

Hence, conditional on X_t, X_{t+1} is normally distributed with mean $\rho X_t + (1-\rho)\mu$ and variance σ^2. Also note that the covariance between the subsequent values X_t and X_{t+1} is

$$\mathrm{Cov}[X_t, X_{t+1}] = \rho\,\mathrm{Cov}[X_t, X_t] = \rho\,\mathrm{Var}[X_t]$$

so that $\rho = \mathrm{Cov}[X_t, X_{t+1}]/\,\mathrm{Var}[X_t]$ is the so-called autocorrelation parameter.

Solving backwards, we find

$$\begin{aligned}
X_{t+1} &= \rho X_t + (1-\rho)\mu + \sigma\varepsilon_{t+1} \\
&= \rho\left(\rho X_{t-1} + (1-\rho)\mu + \sigma\varepsilon_t\right) + (1-\rho)\mu + \sigma\varepsilon_{t+1} \\
&= \rho^2 X_{t-1} + (1+\rho)(1-\rho)\mu + \sigma\varepsilon_{t+1} + \rho\sigma\varepsilon_t \\
&= \dots \\
&= \rho^{k+1} X_{t-k} + \left(1 + \rho + \dots + \rho^k\right)(1-\rho)\mu + \sigma\varepsilon_{t+1} + \rho\sigma\varepsilon_t + \dots \\
&\quad + \rho^k\sigma\varepsilon_{t-k+1} \\
&= \rho^{k+1} X_{t-k} + \left(1 - \rho^{k+1}\right)\mu + \sigma\sum_{j=0}^{k}\rho^j\varepsilon_{t+1-j}.
\end{aligned}$$

In particular,

$$X_{t+1} = \rho^{t+1}X_0 + \left(1 - \rho^{t+1}\right)\mu + \sigma\sum_{j=0}^{t}\rho^j\varepsilon_{t+1-j},$$

and, consequently, X_{t+1} is unconditionally normally distributed with mean $\rho^{t+1}X_0 + (1-\rho^{t+1})\mu$ and variance $\sigma^2\sum_{j=0}^{t}\rho^{2j}$.

More generally, a process $X = (X_t)_{t\in\mathcal{T}}$ with

$$X_{t+1} = \mu + \rho_1(X_t - \mu) + \rho_2(X_{t-1} - \mu) + \dots + \rho_\ell(X_{t-\ell+1} - \mu) + \sigma\varepsilon_{t+1}$$

is said to be an autoregressive process of order ℓ or simply an AR(ℓ) process. If the order is higher than 1, the process is not a Markov process.

(G)ARCH process: ARCH is short for Autoregressive Conditional Heteroskedasticity. An ARCH(ℓ) process $X = (X_t)_{t\in\mathcal{T}}$ is defined by

$$X_{t+1} = \mu + \sigma_{t+1}\varepsilon_{t+1},$$

where

$$\sigma_{t+1}^2 = \delta + \sum_{i=1}^{\ell} \alpha_i \varepsilon_{t+1-i}^2.$$

The conditional variance depends on squares of the previous ℓ shock terms. ARCH processes were introduced by Engle (1982).

GARCH is short for Generalized Autoregressive Conditional Heteroskedasticity. A GARCH(ℓ, m) process $X = (X_t)_{t\in\mathcal{T}}$ is defined by

$$X_{t+1} = \mu + \sigma_{t+1}\varepsilon_{t+1},$$

where

$$\sigma_{t+1}^2 = \delta + \sum_{i=1}^{\ell} \alpha_i \varepsilon_{t+1-i}^2 + \sum_{j=1}^{m} \beta_j \sigma_{t+1-j}^2.$$

GARCH processes were suggested by Bollerslev (1986). ARCH and GARCH processes are often used for detailed modelling of stock market volatility. Various extensions exist.

More generally we can define an adapted process $X = (X_t)_{t\in\mathcal{T}}$ by the initial value X_0 and the equation

$$\Delta X_{t+1} = \mu(X_t, \dots, X_0) + \sigma(X_t, \dots, X_0)\varepsilon_{t+1}, \quad t = 0, 1, \dots, T-1,$$

where μ and σ are real-valued functions. If $\varepsilon_{t+1} \sim N(0,1)$, the conditional distribution of X_{t+1} given X_t is a normal distribution with mean $X_t + \mu(X_t, \dots, X_0)$ and variance $\sigma(X_t, \dots, X_0)^2$. However, the unconditional distribution of X_{t+1} depends on the precise functions μ and σ and is generally not a normal distribution.

We can write the stochastic processes introduced above in a different way that will ease the transition to continuous-time processes. Let $z = (z_t)_{t\in\mathcal{T}}$ denote a unit random walk starting at zero, that is a process with the properties

(i) $z_0 = 0$,

(ii) $\Delta z_{t+1} \equiv z_{t+1} - z_t \sim N(0,1)$ for all $t = 0, 1, \dots, T-1$,

(iii) $\Delta z_1, \Delta z_2, \dots \Delta z_T$ are independent.

Then we can define a random walk with drift as a process X with

$$\Delta X_{t+1} = \mu + \sigma\,\Delta z_{t+1},$$

an AR(1) process is defined by

$$\Delta X_{t+1} = (1-\rho)(\mu - X_t) + \sigma\,\Delta z_{t+1},$$

and a general adapted process is defined by

$$\Delta X_{t+1} = \mu(X_t,\dots,X_0) + \sigma(X_t,\dots,X_0)\Delta z_{t+1}.$$

We will see very similar equations in continuous time.

2.6 CONTINUOUS-TIME STOCHASTIC PROCESSES

2.6.1 Brownian Motions

In the continuous-time asset pricing models we will consider in this book, the basic uncertainty in the economy is represented by the evolution of a so-called *standard Brownian motion*. This is a (one-dimensional) stochastic process $z = (z_t)_{t\in[0,T]}$ satisfying the following conditions:

(i) $z_0 = 0$,

(ii) for all $t, t' \geq 0$ with $t < t'$, the random variable $z_{t'} - z_t$ is $N(0, t'-t)$ distributed [normally distributed increments],

(iii) for all $0 \leq t_0 < t_1 < \cdots < t_n$, the random variables $z_{t_1} - z_{t_0}, \dots, z_{t_n} - z_{t_{n-1}}$ are mutually independent [independent increments],

(iv) z has continuous sample paths.

The first three conditions are equivalent to the discrete-time case studied above. We can informally think of $dz_t \approx z_{t+dt} - z_t \sim N(0, dt)$ as an exogenous shock to the economy at time t. The state space Ω is in this case the (infinite) set of all paths of the standard Brownian motion z. The information filtration $(\mathcal{F}_t)_{t\in[0,T]}$ is generated by the standard Brownian motion z in the sense that, for each t, $\mathcal{F}_t$ is the smallest sigma-algebra on which the random variable z_t is measurable. The probability measure $\mathbb{P}$ is fixed by the normality assumption.

Any continuous-time stochastic process $X = (X_t)_{t\in[0,T]}$ in the financial models in this book will be defined in terms of the standard Brownian motion by an initial constant value X_0 and an equation of the form

$$dX_t = \mu_t\,dt + \sigma_t\,dz_t.$$

Here μ_t and σ_t are known at time t (measurable with respect to $\mathcal{F}_t$) but may depend on X_s and z_s for $s \leq t$. We can informally think of dX_t as the increment

$X_{t+dt} - X_t$ over the 'instant' (of length dt) following time t. Since dz_t has mean zero and variance dt, we can informally compute the conditional mean and variance of dX_t as

$$\mathrm{E}_t[dX_t] = \mu_t\, dt, \qquad \mathrm{Var}_t[dX_t] = \sigma_t^2\, dt.$$

Therefore we can interpret μ_t and σ_t^2 as the conditional mean and conditional variance of the change in the value of the process per time unit. The properties of the process X will depend on the specification of μ_t and σ_t. We will be more formal and give examples below.

The standard Brownian motion is basically the continuous-time version of a random walk with initial value 0. The standard Brownian motion is a Markov process because the increment from today to any future point in time is independent of the history of the process. The standard Brownian motion is also a martingale since the expected change in the value of the process is zero.

The name Brownian motion is in honour of the Scottish botanist Robert Brown who in 1828 observed the apparently random movements of pollen submerged in water. The standard Brownian motion is also known as a *Wiener process* in honour of the American mathematician Norbert Wiener. In the 1920s, he was the first to show the existence of a stochastic process with these properties, and he developed a mathematically rigorous analysis of the process. As early as 1900, standard Brownian motion was used in a model for stock price movements by the French researcher Louis Bachelier in his derivation of what appears to be the first option pricing formula.

The defining characteristics of a standard Brownian motion look very nice, but they have some drastic consequences. It can be shown that the sample paths of a standard Brownian motion are nowhere differentiable, which means that the sample paths bend at all points in time and are therefore strictly speaking impossible to illustrate. However, one can get an idea of the sample paths by simulating the values of the process at different times. If $\varepsilon_1, \dots, \varepsilon_n$ are independent draws from a standard $N(0, 1)$ distribution, we can simulate the value of the standard Brownian motion at time $0 \equiv t_0 < t_1 < t_2 < \dots < t_n$ as follows:

$$z_{t_i} = z_{t_{i-1}} + \varepsilon_i \sqrt{t_i - t_{i-1}}, \quad i = 1, \dots, n.$$

With more time points, and hence shorter intervals, we get a more realistic impression of the sample paths of the process. Figure 2.6 shows a simulated sample path for a standard Brownian motion over the interval $[0, 1]$ based on a partition of the interval into 200 subintervals of equal length.[1] Note that since

[1] Most spreadsheets and programming tools have a built-in procedure that generates uniformly distributed numbers over the interval $[0, 1]$. Such uniformly distributed random numbers can be transformed into standard normally distributed numbers in several ways. One example: given uniformly distributed numbers U_1 and U_2, the numbers ε_1 and ε_2 defined by

$$\varepsilon_1 = \sqrt{-2 \ln U_1} \sin(2\pi U_2), \qquad \varepsilon_2 = \sqrt{-2 \ln U_1} \cos(2\pi U_2)$$

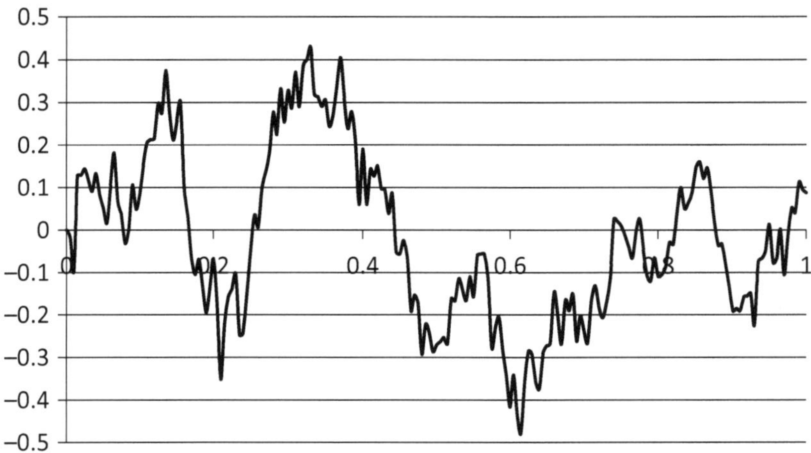

Fig. 2.6. A simulated sample path of a standard Brownian motion based on 200 subintervals.

a normally distributed random variable can take on infinitely many values, a standard Brownian motion has infinitely many sample paths that each have a zero probability of occurring. The figure shows just one possible sample path. Note that the picture resembles typical stock price charts.

Another property of a standard Brownian motion is that the expected length of the sample path over any future time interval (no matter how short) is infinite. In addition, the expected number of times a standard Brownian motion takes on any given value in any given time interval is also infinite. Intuitively, these properties are due to the fact that the size of the increment of a standard Brownian motion over an interval of length Δt is proportional to $\sqrt{\Delta t}$, in the sense that the standard deviation of the increment equals $\sqrt{\Delta t}$. When Δt is close to zero, $\sqrt{\Delta t}$ is significantly larger than Δt, so the changes are large relative to the length of the time interval over which the changes are measured.

The expected change in an object described by a standard Brownian motion equals zero, and the variance of the change over a given time interval equals the length of the interval. This can easily be generalized. As before let $z = (z_t)_{t \geq 0}$ be a one-dimensional standard Brownian motion and define a new stochastic process $X = (X_t)_{t \geq 0}$ by

$$X_t = X_0 + \mu t + \sigma z_t, \quad t \geq 0,$$

where X_0, μ, and σ are constants. Here X_0 is the initial value of the process X. It follows from the properties of the standard Brownian motion that, seen from

will be independent standard normally distributed random numbers. This is the so-called Box-Muller transformation. See for example Press *et al.* (2007).

time 0, the value X_t is normally distributed with mean $X_0 + \mu t$ and variance $\sigma^2 t$, that is $X_t \sim N(X_0 + \mu t, \sigma^2 t)$.

The change in the value of the process between two arbitrary points in time t and t', where $t < t'$, is given by

$$X_{t'} - X_t = \mu(t' - t) + \sigma(z_{t'} - z_t).$$

The change over an infinitesimally short interval $[t, t + \Delta t]$ with $\Delta t \to 0$ is often written as

$$dX_t = \mu\, dt + \sigma\, dz_t, \tag{2.1}$$

where dz_t can be loosely interpreted as a $N(0, dt)$-distributed random variable. To give this a precise mathematical meaning, it must be interpreted as a limit of the expression

$$X_{t+\Delta t} - X_t = \mu \Delta t + \sigma(z_{t+\Delta t} - z_t)$$

for $\Delta t \to 0$. This process X is called a *generalized Brownian motion* or a generalized Wiener process. It is basically the continuous-time version of a random walk with drift. The parameter μ reflects the expected change in the process per unit of time and is called the drift rate or simply the *drift* of the process. The parameter σ reflects the uncertainty about the future values of the process. More precisely, σ^2 reflects the variance of the change in the process per unit of time and is often called the *variance rate* of the process. σ is a measure for the standard deviation of the change per unit of time and is referred to as the *volatility* of the process.

A generalized Brownian motion inherits many of the characteristic properties of a standard Brownian motion. For example, a generalized Brownian motion is also a Markov process, and the sample paths of a generalized Brownian motion are also continuous and nowhere differentiable. However, a generalized Brownian motion is not a martingale unless $\mu = 0$. The sample paths can be simulated by choosing time points $0 \equiv t_0 < t_1 < \cdots < t_n$ and iteratively computing

$$X_{t_i} = X_{t_{i-1}} + \mu(t_i - t_{i-1}) + \varepsilon_i \sigma \sqrt{t_i - t_{i-1}}, \quad i = 1, \ldots, n,$$

where $\varepsilon_1, \ldots, \varepsilon_n$ are independent draws from a standard normal distribution. Figure 2.7 shows simulated sample paths for two different values of σ but the same μ. The paths are drawn using the same sequence of random numbers ε_i so that they are directly comparable. The straight line represents the deterministic trend of the process, which corresponds to imposing the condition $\sigma = 0$ and hence ignoring the uncertainty. The parameter μ determines the trend, and the parameter σ determines the size of the fluctuations around the trend.

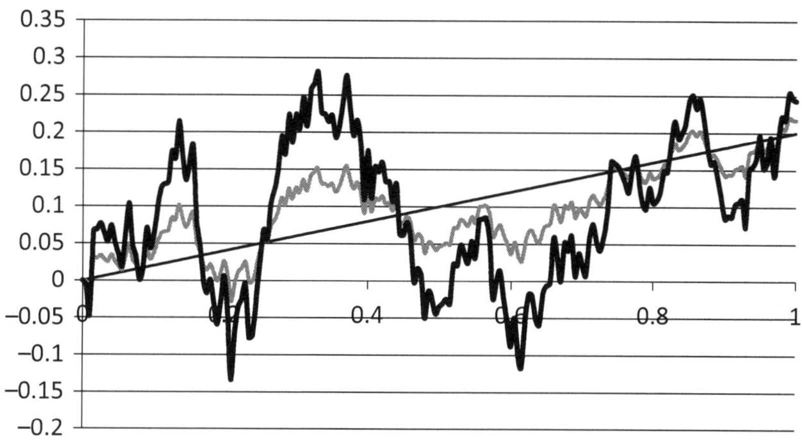

Fig. 2.7. Simulation of a generalized Brownian motion with $\mu = 0.2$ and initial value $X_0 = 0$.

Notes: The thin straight line shows the trend corresponding to $\sigma = 0$. The grey line is for $\sigma = 0.2$ and the thick black line for $\sigma = 0.5$. The simulations are based on 200 subintervals using the same sequence of random numbers for both σ-values

If the parameters μ and σ are allowed to be time-varying in a deterministic way, the process X is said to be a *time-inhomogeneous* generalized Brownian motion. In differential terms such a process can be written as

$$dX_t = \mu(t)\, dt + \sigma(t)\, dz_t. \tag{2.2}$$

Over a very short interval $[t, t + \Delta t]$, the expected change is approximately $\mu(t)\Delta t$, and the variance of the change is approximately $\sigma(t)^2 \Delta t$. More precisely, the increment over any interval $[t, t']$ is given by

$$X_{t'} - X_t = \int_t^{t'} \mu(u)\, du + \int_t^{t'} \sigma(u)\, dz_u.$$

The last integral is a so-called stochastic integral, which we will define (although not rigorously) and describe in a later section. There we will also state a theorem, which implies that, seen from time t, the integral $\int_t^{t'} \sigma(u)\, dz_u$ is a normally distributed random variable with mean zero and variance $\int_t^{t'} \sigma(u)^2\, du$.

2.6.2 Diffusion Processes

For both standard Brownian motions and generalized Brownian motions, the future value is normally distributed and can therefore take on any real value, that is the value space is equal to $\mathbb{R}$. Many economic variables can only have values in a certain subset of $\mathbb{R}$. For example, prices of financial assets with limited liability are non-negative. The evolution in such variables cannot be well represented by the stochastic processes studied so far. In many situations we will instead use so-called diffusion processes.

A (one-dimensional) *diffusion process* is a stochastic process $X = (X_t)_{t\geq 0}$ for which the change over an infinitesimally short time interval $[t, t + dt]$ can be written as

$$dX_t = \mu(X_t, t)\, dt + \sigma(X_t, t)\, dz_t, \tag{2.3}$$

where z is a standard Brownian motion, but where the drift μ and the volatility σ are now functions of time and the current value of the process.[2] This expression generalizes Eq. (2.1), where μ and σ were assumed to be constants, and Eq. (2.2), where μ and σ were functions of time only. An equation like (2.3), where the stochastic process enters both sides of the equality, is called a *stochastic differential equation*. Hence, a diffusion process is a solution to a stochastic differential equation.

If both functions μ and σ are independent of time, the diffusion is said to be *time-homogeneous*, otherwise it is said to be *time-inhomogeneous*. For a time-homogeneous diffusion process, the distribution of the future value will only depend on the current value of the process and how far into the future we are looking—not on the particular point in time we are standing at. For example, the distribution of $X_{t+\delta}$ given $X_t = x$ will only depend on x and δ, but not on t. This is not the case for a time-inhomogeneous diffusion for which the distribution will also depend on t.

In the expression (2.3) one may think of dz_t as being $N(0, dt)$-distributed so that the mean and variance of the change over an infinitesimally short interval $[t, t + dt]$ are given by

$$\mathrm{E}_t[dX_t] = \mu(X_t, t)\, dt, \qquad \mathrm{Var}_t[dX_t] = \sigma(X_t, t)^2\, dt.$$

To be more precise, the change in a diffusion process over any interval $[t, t']$ is

$$X_{t'} - X_t = \int_t^{t'} \mu(X_u, u)\, du + \int_t^{t'} \sigma(X_u, u)\, dz_u. \tag{2.4}$$

Here the integrand of the first integral $\int_t^{t'} \mu(X_u, u)\, du$ depends on the values X_u for $u \in [t, t']$, which are generally unknown at time t. It is therefore natural to define the integral $\int_t^{t'} \mu(X_u, u)\, du$ as the random variable which in state $\omega \in \Omega$ has the value $\int_t^{t'} \mu(X_u(\omega), u)\, du$, which is now just the integration of a real-valued function of time. The other integral $\int_t^{t'} \sigma(X_u, u)\, dz_u$ is a so-called stochastic integral, which we will discuss in Section 2.6.5.

[2] For the process X to be mathematically meaningful, the functions $\mu(x, t)$ and $\sigma(x, t)$ must satisfy certain conditions. See for example Øksendal (2003, Ch. 7) and Duffie (2001, App. E).

We will often use the informal and intuitive differential notation of Eq. (2.3) instead of the mathematically more rigorous form of Eq. (2.4). The drift rate $\mu(X_t, t)$ and the variance rate $\sigma(X_t, t)^2$ are really the limits

$$\mu(X_t, t) = \lim_{\Delta t \to 0} \frac{\mathrm{E}_t\left[X_{t+\Delta t} - X_t\right]}{\Delta t},$$

$$\sigma(X_t, t)^2 = \lim_{\Delta t \to 0} \frac{\mathrm{Var}_t\left[X_{t+\Delta t} - X_t\right]}{\Delta t}.$$

Note that the diffusion process is completely determined by the functions μ and σ, that is by the first- and second-order local moments.

A diffusion process is a Markov process as can be seen from Eq. (2.3) since both the drift and the volatility only depend on the current value of the process and not on previous values. A diffusion process is not a martingale, unless the drift $\mu(X_t, t)$ is zero for all X_t and t. A diffusion process will have continuous, but nowhere differentiable, sample paths. The value space for a diffusion process and the distribution of future values will depend on the functions μ and σ. In Section 2.6.7 we present an example of a diffusion process often used in financial modelling, the so-called geometric Brownian motion. Other diffusion processes will be used in later chapters.

2.6.3 Itô Processes

It is possible to define even more general continuous-path processes than those in the class of diffusion processes. A (one-dimensional) stochastic process X_t is said to be an *Itô process* if the local increments are of the form

$$dX_t = \mu_t \, dt + \sigma_t \, dz_t, \tag{2.5}$$

where the drift μ and the volatility σ themselves are stochastic processes. A diffusion process is the special case where the values of the drift μ_t and the volatility σ_t are given as functions of t and X_t. For a general Itô process, the drift and volatility may also depend on past values of the X process and also on past and current values of other adapted processes. It follows that Itô processes are generally not Markov processes. They are generally not martingales either, unless μ_t is identically equal to zero (and σ_t satisfies some technical conditions). The processes μ and σ must satisfy certain regularity conditions for the X process to be well defined. We will refer the reader to Øksendal (2003, Ch. 4) for these conditions. The expression (2.5) gives an intuitive understanding of the evolution of an Itô process, but it is mathematically more rigorous to state the evolution in the integral form

$$X_{t'} - X_t = \int_t^{t'} \mu_u \, du + \int_t^{t'} \sigma_u \, dz_u. \tag{2.6}$$

Again the first integral can be defined 'state-by-state', and the second integral is a stochastic integral.

2.6.4 Jump Processes

Above we have focused on processes having sample paths that are continuous functions of time so that one can depict the evolution of the process by a continuous curve. Stochastic processes having sample paths with discontinuities (jumps) also exist. The jumps of such processes are often modelled by Poisson processes or related processes. It is well known that large, sudden movements in financial variables occur from time to time, for example in connection with stock market crashes. There may be many explanations of such large movements, for example a large unexpected change in the productivity in a particular industry or the economy in general, perhaps due to a technological breakthrough. Another source of sudden, large movements is a change in the political or economic environment, such as unforeseen interventions by the government or central bank. Stock market crashes are sometimes explained by the bursting of a bubble (which does not necessarily conflict with the usual assumption of rational investors). Whether such sudden, large movements can be explained by a sequence of small continuous movements in the same direction or jumps have to be included in the models is an empirical question, which is still open. While jump processes may be relevant for many purposes, they are also more difficult to deal with than processes with continuous sample paths so that it will probably be best to study models without jumps first. This book will only address continuous-path processes. An overview of some financial models with jump processes is given by Cont and Tankov (2004).

2.6.5 Stochastic Integrals

In Eqs. (2.4) and (2.6) and similar expressions, a term of the form $\int_t^{t'} \sigma_u \, dz_u$ appears. An integral of this type is called a stochastic integral or an Itô integral. For given $t < t'$, the stochastic integral $\int_t^{t'} \sigma_u \, dz_u$ is a random variable. Assuming that σ_u is known at time u, the value of the integral becomes known at time t'. The process σ is called the integrand. The stochastic integral can be defined for very general integrands. The simplest integrand is a constant. For a constant σ, we define the stochastic integral $\int_t^{t'} \sigma \, dz_u$ simply as

$$\int_t^{t'} \sigma \, dz_u = \sigma (z_{t'} - z_t).$$

We can easily generalize that to a piecewise constant integrand. Assume that there are points in time $t \equiv t_0 < t_1 < \cdots < t_n \equiv t'$ so that σ_u is constant on each subinterval $[t_i, t_{i+1})$. The stochastic integral is then defined by

$$\int_t^{t'} \sigma_u \, dz_u = \sum_{i=0}^{n-1} \sigma_{t_i} \left(z_{t_{i+1}} - z_{t_i} \right).$$

It can be shown that if the integrand process σ is not piecewise constant, there will exist a sequence of piecewise constant processes $\sigma^{(1)}, \sigma^{(2)}, \ldots$, which converges to σ. For each of the processes $\sigma^{(m)}$, the integral $\int_t^{t'} \sigma_u^{(m)} \, dz_u$ is defined as above. The integral $\int_t^{t'} \sigma_u \, dz_u$ is then defined as a limit of the integrals of the approximating processes:

$$\int_t^{t'} \sigma_u \, dz_u = \lim_{m \to \infty} \int_t^{t'} \sigma_u^{(m)} \, dz_u.$$

We will not discuss exactly how this limit is to be understood nor which integrand processes we can allow. Again the interested reader is referred to Øksendal (2003). The distribution of the integral $\int_t^{t'} \sigma_u \, dz_u$ will, of course, depend on the integrand process and can generally not be completely characterized, but the following theorem gives the mean and the variance of the integral:

Theorem 2.2 *Let z be a standard Brownian motion, and let σ be a stochastic process satisfying some regularity conditions. Then the stochastic integral $\int_t^{t'} \sigma_u \, dz_u$ has the following properties:*

$$\mathrm{E}_t \left[\int_t^{t'} \sigma_u \, dz_u \right] = 0,$$

$$\mathrm{Var}_t \left[\int_t^{t'} \sigma_u \, dz_u \right] = \int_t^{t'} \mathrm{E}_t[\sigma_u^2] \, du. \tag{2.7}$$

The result (2.7) is often referred to as the Itô isometry.

Proof. Suppose that σ is piecewise constant and divide the interval $[t, t']$ into subintervals defined by the time points $t \equiv t_0 < t_1 < \cdots < t_n \equiv t'$ so that σ is constant on each subinterval $[t_i, t_{i+1})$ with a value σ_{t_i} which is known at time t_i. Then

$$\mathrm{E}_t \left[\int_t^{t'} \sigma_u \, dz_u \right] = \sum_{i=0}^{n-1} \mathrm{E}_t \left[\sigma_{t_i} \left(z_{t_{i+1}} - z_{t_i} \right) \right] = \sum_{i=0}^{n-1} \mathrm{E}_t \left[\sigma_{t_i} \mathrm{E}_{t_i} \left[\left(z_{t_{i+1}} - z_{t_i} \right) \right] \right] = 0,$$

using the Law of Iterated Expectations. For the variance we have

$$\begin{aligned}\mathrm{Var}_t\left[\int_t^{t'} \sigma_u\, dz_u\right] &= \mathrm{E}_t\left[\left(\int_t^{t'} \sigma_u\, dz_u\right)^2\right] - \left(\mathrm{E}_t\left[\int_t^{t'} \sigma_u\, dz_u\right]\right)^2 \\ &= \mathrm{E}_t\left[\left(\int_t^{t'} \sigma_u\, dz_u\right)^2\right]\end{aligned}$$

and

$$\begin{aligned}&\mathrm{E}_t\left[\left(\int_t^{t'} \sigma_u\, dz_u\right)^2\right] \\ &\quad= \mathrm{E}_t\left[\sum_{i=0}^{n-1}\sum_{j=0}^{n-1} \sigma_{t_i}\sigma_{t_j}(z_{t_{i+1}} - z_{t_i})(z_{t_{j+1}} - z_{t_j})\right] \\ &\quad= \sum_{i=0}^{n-1}\sum_{j=0}^{n-1} \mathrm{E}_t\left[\sigma_{t_i}\sigma_{t_j}(z_{t_{i+1}} - z_{t_i})(z_{t_{j+1}} - z_{t_j})\right] \\ &\quad= \sum_{i=0}^{n-1} \mathrm{E}_t\left[\sigma_{t_i}^2(z_{t_{i+1}} - z_{t_i})^2\right] + 2\sum_{i=0}^{n-1}\sum_{j=i+1}^{n-1} \mathrm{E}_t\left[\sigma_{t_i}\sigma_{t_j}(z_{t_{i+1}} - z_{t_i})(z_{t_{j+1}} - z_{t_j})\right] \\ &\quad= \sum_{i=0}^{n-1} \mathrm{E}_t\Big[\sigma_{t_i}^2 \underbrace{\mathrm{E}_{t_i}\left[(z_{t_{i+1}} - z_{t_i})^2\right]}_{=t_{i+1}-t_i}\Big] \\ &\qquad + 2\sum_{i=0}^{n-1}\sum_{j=i+1}^{n-1} \mathrm{E}_t\Big[\sigma_{t_i}\sigma_{t_j}(z_{t_{i+1}} - z_{t_i})\underbrace{\mathrm{E}_{t_j}\left[(z_{t_{j+1}} - z_{t_j})\right]}_{=0}\Big] \\ &\quad= \sum_{i=0}^{n-1} \mathrm{E}_t\left[\sigma_{t_i}^2\right](t_{i+1} - t_i) = \int_t^{t'} \mathrm{E}_t[\sigma_u^2]\, du,\end{aligned}$$

where we have used the Law of Iterated Expectations to get the fourth equality. If σ is not piecewise constant, we can approximate it by a piecewise constant process and take appropriate limits. □

If the integrand is a deterministic function of time, $\sigma(u)$, the integral will be normally distributed so that the following result holds:

Theorem 2.3 *If z is a standard Brownian motion, and $\sigma(u)$ is a deterministic function of time, the random variable $\int_t^{t'} \sigma(u)\, dz_u$ is normally distributed with mean zero and variance $\int_t^{t'} \sigma(u)^2\, du$.*

Proof. Dividing the interval $[t, t']$ into subintervals defined by the time points $t \equiv t_0 < t_1 < \cdots < t_n \equiv t'$, we can approximate the integral by a sum:

$$\int_t^{t'} \sigma(u)\, dz_u \approx \sum_{i=0}^{n-1} \sigma(t_i)\left(z_{t_{i+1}} - z_{t_i}\right).$$

The increment of the Brownian motion over any subinterval is normally distributed with mean zero and a variance equal to the length of the subinterval. Furthermore, the different terms in the sum are mutually independent. It is well known that a sum of normally distributed random variables is itself normally distributed. Moreover, the mean of the sum is equal to the sum of the means, which in the present case yields zero. Due to the independence of the terms in the sum, the variance of the sum is also equal to the sum of the variances, that is

$$\begin{aligned} \mathrm{Var}_t\left[\sum_{i=0}^{n-1} \sigma(t_i)\left(z_{t_{i+1}} - z_{t_i}\right)\right] &= \sum_{i=0}^{n-1} \sigma(t_i)^2\, \mathrm{Var}_t\left[z_{t_{i+1}} - z_{t_i}\right] \\ &= \sum_{i=0}^{n-1} \sigma(t_i)^2 (t_{i+1} - t_i), \end{aligned}$$

which is an approximation of the integral $\int_t^{t'} \sigma(u)^2\, du$. The result now follows from an appropriate limit where the subintervals shrink to zero length. □

Note that the process $y = (y_t)_{t \geq 0}$ defined by $y_t = \int_0^t \sigma_u\, dz_u$ is a martingale since

$$\begin{aligned} \mathrm{E}_t[y_{t'}] &= \mathrm{E}_t\left[\int_0^{t'} \sigma_u\, dz_u\right] = \mathrm{E}_t\left[\int_0^t \sigma_u\, dz_u + \int_t^{t'} \sigma_u\, dz_u\right] \\ &= \mathrm{E}_t\left[\int_0^t \sigma_u\, dz_u\right] + \mathrm{E}_t\left[\int_t^{t'} \sigma_u\, dz_u\right] = \int_0^t \sigma_u\, dz_u = y_t \end{aligned}$$

so that the expected future value is equal to the current value. More generally $y_t = y_0 + \int_0^t \sigma_u\, dz_u$ for some constant y_0, is a martingale. The converse is also true in the sense that any martingale can be expressed as a stochastic integral. This is the so-called *martingale representation theorem*:

Theorem 2.4 (Martingale representation). *Suppose the process $M = (M_t)$ is a martingale with respect to a probability measure under which $z = (z_t)$ is a* *standard Brownian motion. Then a unique adapted process $\theta = (\theta_t)$ exists such that*

$$M_t = M_0 + \int_0^t \theta_u \, dz_u$$

for all t.

For a mathematically more precise statement of the result and a proof, see Øksendal (2003, Thm. 4.3.4).

Now the stochastic integral with respect to the standard Brownian motion has been defined, we can also define stochastic integrals with respect to other stochastic processes. For example, if X_t is a diffusion given by $dX_t = \mu(X_t, t)\, dt + \sigma(X_t, t)\, dz_t$ and $\alpha = (\alpha_t)_{t\in[0,T]}$ is a sufficiently 'nice' stochastic process, we can define

$$\int_0^t \alpha_u \, dX_u = \int_0^t \alpha_u \mu(X_u, u)\, du + \int_0^t \alpha_u \sigma(X_u, u)\, dz_u.$$

2.6.6 Itô's Lemma

In continuous-time models a stochastic process for the dynamics of some basic quantity is often taken as a given, while other quantities of interest can be shown to be functions of that basic variable. To determine the dynamics of these other variables, we shall apply Itô's Lemma, which is basically the chain rule for stochastic processes. We will state the result for a function of a general Itô process, although we will frequently apply the result for the special case of a function of a diffusion process.

Theorem 2.5 (Itô's Lemma, one-dimensional). *Let $X = (X_t)_{t\geq 0}$ be a real-valued Itô process with dynamics*

$$dX_t = \mu_t \, dt + \sigma_t \, dz_t,$$

where μ and σ are real-valued processes, and z is a one-dimensional standard Brownian motion. Let $g(X, t)$ be a real-valued function which is two times continuously differentiable in X and continuously differentiable in t. Then the process $y = (y_t)_{t\geq 0}$ defined by

$$y_t = g(X_t, t)$$

is an Itô process with dynamics

$$dy_t = \left(\frac{\partial g}{\partial t}(X_t, t) + \frac{\partial g}{\partial X}(X_t, t)\mu_t + \frac{1}{2}\frac{\partial^2 g}{\partial X^2}(X_t, t)\sigma_t^2 \right) dt + \frac{\partial g}{\partial X}(X_t, t)\sigma_t \, dz_t.$$

The proof of Itô's Lemma is based on a Taylor expansion of $g(X_t, t)$ combined with appropriate limits, but a formal proof is beyond the scope of this presentation. Once again, we refer to Øksendal (2003) and similar textbooks. The result can also be written in the following way that may be easier to remember:

$$dy_t = \frac{\partial g}{\partial t}(X_t, t)\, dt + \frac{\partial g}{\partial X}(X_t, t)\, dX_t + \frac{1}{2}\frac{\partial^2 g}{\partial X^2}(X_t, t)(dX_t)^2. \qquad (2.8)$$

Here, in the computation of $(dX_t)^2$, one must apply the rules $(dt)^2 = dt \times dz_t = 0$ and $(dz_t)^2 = dt$ so that

$$(dX_t)^2 = (\mu_t\, dt + \sigma_t\, dz_t)^2 = \mu_t^2 (dt)^2 + 2\mu_t\sigma_t\, dt \times dz_t + \sigma_t^2 (dz_t)^2 = \sigma_t^2\, dt,$$

which equals the instantaneous variance $\mathrm{Var}_t[dX_t]$. The intuition behind these rules is as follows: when dt is close to zero, $(dt)^2$ is far less than dt and can therefore be ignored. Since $dz_t \sim N(0, dt)$, we get $\mathrm{E}[dt \times dz_t] = dt \times \mathrm{E}[dz_t] = 0$ as well as $\mathrm{Var}[dt \times dz_t] = (dt)^2\, \mathrm{Var}[dz_t] = (dt)^3$, which is also very small compared to dt and is therefore ignorable. Finally, we have $\mathrm{E}[(dz_t)^2] = \mathrm{Var}[dz_t] - (\mathrm{E}[dz_t])^2 = dt$, and it can be shown that[3] $\mathrm{Var}[(dz_t)^2] = 2(dt)^2$. For dt close to zero, the variance is therefore much less than the mean, so $(dz_t)^2$ can be approximated by its mean dt.

In standard mathematics, the differential of a function $y = g(X, t)$ where X and t are real variables is defined as $dy = \frac{\partial g}{\partial X}\, dX + \frac{\partial g}{\partial t}\, dt$. When X is a stochastic process, Eq. (2.8) shows that we have to add a second-order term.

2.6.7 The Geometric Brownian Motion

The geometric Brownian motion is an important example of a diffusion process. A stochastic process $X = (X_t)_{t \geq 0}$ is said to be a *geometric Brownian motion* if it is a solution to the stochastic differential equation

$$dX_t = \mu X_t\, dt + \sigma X_t\, dz_t, \qquad (2.9)$$

where μ and σ are constants. The initial value for the process is assumed to be positive, $X_0 > 0$. A geometric Brownian motion is the particular diffusion process that is obtained from Eq. (2.3) by inserting $\mu(X_t, t) = \mu X_t$ and $\sigma(X_t, t) = \sigma X_t$.

The expression (2.9) can be rewritten as

$$\frac{dX_t}{X_t} = \mu\, dt + \sigma\, dz_t,$$

[3] This is based on the computation $\mathrm{Var}[(z_{t+\Delta t} - z_t)^2] = \mathrm{E}[(z_{t+\Delta t} - z_t)^4] - \left(\mathrm{E}[(z_{t+\Delta t} - z_t)^2]\right)^2 = 3(\Delta t)^2 - (\Delta t)^2 = 2(\Delta t)^2$ and a passage to the limit.

which is the relative (percentage) change in the value of the process over the next infinitesimally short time interval $[t, t + dt]$. If X_t is the price of a traded asset, then dX_t/X_t is the rate of return on the asset over the next instant, assuming no dividends are paid in that period. The constant μ is the expected rate of return per period, and σ is the standard deviation of the rate of return per period. In this context μ is often called the drift (rather than μX_t) and σ the volatility (rather than σX_t). Strictly speaking, one must distinguish between the *relative* drift and volatility (μ and σ, respectively) and the *absolute* drift and volatility (μX_t and σX_t, respectively), but when referring to a volatility it will often be clear from the context whether it is the relative or the absolute volatility. An asset with a constant expected rate of return and a constant relative volatility has a price that follows a geometric Brownian motion. For example, such an assumption is used for the stock price in the famous Black–Scholes–Merton model for stock option pricing, see Chapter 13. In the framework of consumption-based capital asset pricing models it is often assumed that the aggregate consumption in the economy follows a geometric Brownian motion, see Chapter 8.

Next, we will find an explicit expression for X_t. We can then also determine the distribution of the future value of the process. We apply Itô's Lemma with the function $g(x, t) = \ln x$ and define the process $y_t = g(X_t, t) = \ln X_t$. Since

$$\frac{\partial g}{\partial t}(X_t, t) = 0, \qquad \frac{\partial g}{\partial x}(X_t, t) = \frac{1}{X_t}, \qquad \frac{\partial^2 g}{\partial x^2}(X_t, t) = -\frac{1}{X_t^2},$$

we get from Theorem 2.5 that

$$dy_t = \left(0 + \frac{1}{X_t}\mu X_t - \frac{1}{2}\frac{1}{X_t^2}\sigma^2 X_t^2\right) dt + \frac{1}{X_t}\sigma X_t\, dz_t = \left(\mu - \frac{1}{2}\sigma^2\right) dt + \sigma\, dz_t.$$

Hence, the process $y = (y_t)$ is a generalized Brownian motion. Consequently, we have

$$y_{t'} - y_t = \left(\mu - \frac{1}{2}\sigma^2\right)(t' - t) + \sigma(z_{t'} - z_t),$$

which implies that

$$\ln X_{t'} = \ln X_t + \left(\mu - \frac{1}{2}\sigma^2\right)(t' - t) + \sigma(z_{t'} - z_t).$$

Taking exponentials on both sides, we get

$$X_{t'} = X_t \exp\left\{\left(\mu - \frac{1}{2}\sigma^2\right)(t' - t) + \sigma(z_{t'} - z_t)\right\}. \tag{2.10}$$

This is true for all $t' > t \geq 0$. In particular,

$$X_t = X_0 \exp\left\{\left(\mu - \frac{1}{2}\sigma^2\right) t + \sigma z_t\right\}.$$

This is the solution to the stochastic differential equation (2.9). Since exponentials are always positive, we see that X_t can only have positive values. The values of the standard Brownian motion z_t are unbounded, so the exponent can take any real value. Hence, the value space of a geometric Brownian motion is $\mathcal{S} = (0, \infty)$.

Suppose now that we stand at time t and have observed the current value X_t of a geometric Brownian motion. Which probability distribution is then appropriate for the uncertain future value, say at time t'? Since $z_{t'} - z_t \sim N(0, t' - t)$, we see from Eq. (2.10) that the future value $X_{t'}$ (conditional on X_t) is lognormally distributed. The probability density function for $X_{t'}$ (given X_t) is defined for $x > 0$ by

$$f(x) = \frac{1}{x\sqrt{2\pi\sigma^2(t'-t)}} \exp\left\{-\frac{1}{2\sigma^2(t'-t)}\left(\ln\left(\frac{x}{X_t}\right) - \left(\mu - \frac{1}{2}\sigma^2\right)(t'-t)\right)^2\right\},$$

and the mean and variance are

$$\mathrm{E}_t[X_{t'}] = X_t e^{\mu(t'-t)},$$

$$\mathrm{Var}_t[X_{t'}] = X_t^2 e^{2\mu(t'-t)}\left[e^{\sigma^2(t'-t)} - 1\right],$$

compare the results on the lognormal distribution stated in Appendix B.

Paths can be simulated by recursively computing either

$$X_{t_i} = X_{t_{i-1}} + \mu X_{t_{i-1}}(t_i - t_{i-1}) + \sigma X_{t_{i-1}} \varepsilon_i \sqrt{t_i - t_{i-1}}$$

or, more accurately,

$$X_{t_i} = X_{t_{i-1}} \exp\left\{\left(\mu - \frac{1}{2}\sigma^2\right)(l_i - t_{i-1}) + \sigma\varepsilon_i\sqrt{t_i - t_{i-1}}\right\}.$$

Figure 2.8 shows a single simulated sample path for $\sigma = 0.2$ and a sample path for $\sigma = 0.5$. Both sample paths are generated using $\mu = 0.2$ and $X_0 = 1$ as well as the same sequence of random numbers.

We will consider other specific diffusions in later chapters when we need them. For example, we shall use the Ornstein–Uhlenbeck process defined by

$$dX_t = \kappa\,(\theta - X_t)\,dt + \sigma\,dz_t,$$

which is the continuous-time equivalent of the discrete-time AR(1) process, and the square root process defined by

$$dX_t = \kappa\,(\theta - X_t)\,dt + \sigma\sqrt{X_t}\,dz_t.$$

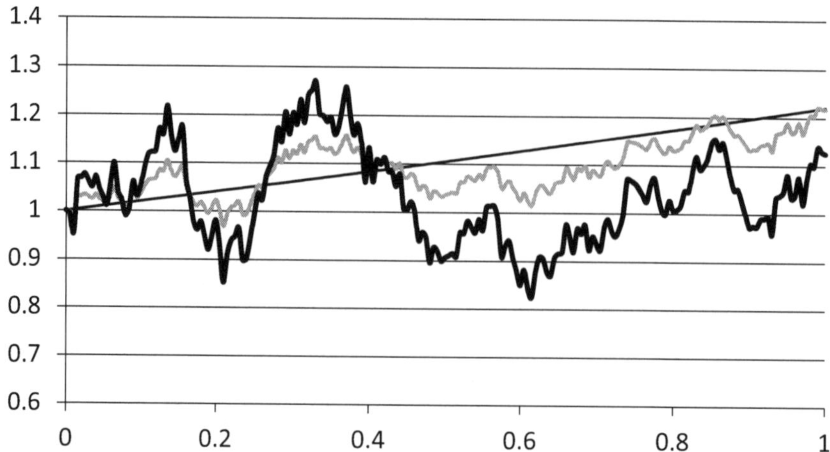

Fig. 2.8. Simulation of a geometric Brownian motion with initial value $X_0 = 1$ and relative drift rate $\mu = 0.2$.

Notes: The thin smoother line shows the trend corresponding to $\sigma = 0$; it may appear to be linear, but is in fact exponentially increasing. The grey curve is for a relative volatility of $\sigma = 0.2$, whereas the thick black line is for $\sigma = 0.5$. The simulations are based on 200 subintervals of equal length, and the same sequence of random numbers has been used for both σ-values

Such processes are used, among other things, to model the dynamics of interest rates.

2.7 MULTIDIMENSIONAL STOCHASTIC PROCESSES

So far we have only considered one-dimensional processes, that is processes with a value space equal to $\mathbb{R}$ or a subset of $\mathbb{R}$. In most asset pricing models we need to keep track of several processes, such as dividend and price processes for different assets, and we will often be interested in covariances and correlations between different processes.

If the exogenous shocks in the model are one-dimensional, then increments over the smallest time interval considered in the model will be perfectly correlated. In a discrete-time model where the exogenous shocks $\varepsilon_1, \ldots, \varepsilon_T$ are one-dimensional, changes in any two processes between two subsequent points in time, say t and $t+1$, will be perfectly correlated. For example, suppose X and Y are two general processes defined by

$$\Delta X_{t+1} = \mu_{Xt} + \sigma_{Xt}\varepsilon_{t+1}, \qquad \Delta Y_{t+1} = \mu_{Yt} + \sigma_{Yt}\varepsilon_{t+1}$$

where ε_{t+1} has a mean of zero and a variance of one. Here $\mu_{Xt}, \mu_{Yt}, \sigma_{Xt}$, and σ_{Yt} are known at time t and reflect the conditional means and standard deviations of the increments to the processes over the next period. By using the properties of covariances and variances we get

$$\mathrm{Cov}_t[\Delta X_{t+1}, \Delta Y_{t+1}] = \sigma_{Xt}\sigma_{Yt}\,\mathrm{Var}_t[\varepsilon_{t+1}] = \sigma_{Xt}\sigma_{Yt},$$
$$\mathrm{Var}_t[\Delta X_{t+1}] = \sigma_{Xt}^2, \quad \mathrm{Var}_t[\Delta Y_{t+1}] = \sigma_{Yt}^2,$$

and, consequently, the correlation is

$$\mathrm{Corr}_t[\Delta X_{t+1}, \Delta Y_{t+1}] = \frac{\mathrm{Cov}_t[\Delta X_{t+1}, \Delta Y_{t+1}]}{\sqrt{\mathrm{Var}_t[\Delta X_{t+1}]\,\mathrm{Var}_t[\Delta Y_{t+1}]}} = \begin{cases} +1, & \text{if } \sigma_{Xt}\sigma_{Yt} > 0, \\ 0, & \text{if } \sigma_{Xt}\sigma_{Yt} = 0, \\ -1, & \text{if } \sigma_{Xt}\sigma_{Yt} < 0. \end{cases}$$

If σ_{Xt} and σ_{Yt} are both non-zero, the increments to X_t and Y_t over the next period will be either perfectly positively correlated or perfectly negatively correlated. In general, increments in two processes over more than one subperiod are not perfectly correlated even with a one-dimensional shock.

In a continuous-time model where the exogenous shock process $z = (z_t)_{t\in[0,T]}$ is one-dimensional, the instantaneous increments of any two processes will be perfectly correlated. For example, if we consider the two Itô processes X and Y defined by

$$dX_t = \mu_{Xt}\,dt + \sigma_{Xt}\,dz_t, \qquad dY_t = \mu_{Yt}\,dt + \sigma_{Yt}\,dz_t,$$

then $\mathrm{Cov}_t[dX_t, dY_t] = \sigma_{Xt}\sigma_{Yt}\,dt$ so that the instantaneous correlation becomes

$$\begin{aligned}\mathrm{Corr}_t[dX_t, dY_t] &= \frac{\mathrm{Cov}_t[dX_t, dY_t]}{\sqrt{\mathrm{Var}_t[dX_t]\,\mathrm{Var}_t[dY_t]}} = \frac{\sigma_{Xt}\sigma_{Yt}\,dt}{\sqrt{\sigma_{Xt}^2\,dt\;\sigma_{Yt}^2\,dt}} \\ &= \begin{cases} +1, & \text{if } \sigma_{Xt}\sigma_{Yt} > 0, \\ 0, & \text{if } \sigma_{Xt}\sigma_{Yt} = 0, \\ -1, & \text{if } \sigma_{Xt}\sigma_{Yt} < 0. \end{cases}\end{aligned}$$

The conclusion is thus the same as in the discrete-time setting. Increments over any non-infinitesimal time interval are generally not perfectly correlated, that is for any $h > 0$ a correlation like $\mathrm{Corr}_t[X_{t+h} - X_t, Y_{t+h} - Y_t]$ is typically different from ± 1, but close for small h.

To obtain non-perfectly correlated changes over the shortest time period considered in the model, we need an exogenous shock of a dimension higher than one, that is a vector of shocks. It is without loss of generality to assume that the different components of this shock vector are mutually independent because non-perfect correlations between the relevant processes can be generated by varying the sensitivities of those processes towards the different exogenous shocks. We will first consider the case of two processes and later generalize further.

2.7.1 Two-Dimensional Processes

In the discrete-time example above, we can avoid the perfect correlation between ΔX_{t+1} and ΔY_{t+1} by introducing a second shock. Suppose that

$$\Delta X_{t+1} = \mu_{Xt} + \sigma_{X1t}\varepsilon_{1,t+1} + \sigma_{X2t}\varepsilon_{2,t+1}$$

and

$$\Delta Y_{t+1} = \mu_{Yt} + \sigma_{Y1t}\varepsilon_{1,t+1} + \sigma_{Y2t}\varepsilon_{2,t+1},$$

where $\varepsilon_{1,t+1}$ and $\varepsilon_{2,t+1}$ are independent and have zero mean and unit variance. Now the covariance is given by

$$\mathrm{Cov}_t[\Delta X_{t+1}, \Delta Y_{t+1}] = \sigma_{X1t}\sigma_{Y1t} + \sigma_{X2t}\sigma_{Y2t},$$

and the variances are

$$\mathrm{Var}_t[\Delta X_{t+1}] = \sigma_{X1t}^2 + \sigma_{X2t}^2, \quad \mathrm{Var}_t[\Delta Y_{t+1}] = \sigma_{Y1t}^2 + \sigma_{Y2t}^2.$$

The correlation is thus

$$\mathrm{Corr}_t[\Delta X_{t+1}, \Delta Y_{t+1}] = \frac{\sigma_{X1t}\sigma_{Y1t} + \sigma_{X2t}\sigma_{Y2t}}{\sqrt{(\sigma_{X1t}^2 + \sigma_{X2t}^2)(\sigma_{Y1t}^2 + \sigma_{Y2t}^2)}}.$$

Since

$$\sigma_{X1t}^2\sigma_{Y2t}^2 + \sigma_{X2t}^2\sigma_{Y1t}^2 - 2\sigma_{X1t}\sigma_{Y1t}\sigma_{X2t}\sigma_{Y2t} = (\sigma_{X1t}\sigma_{Y2t} - \sigma_{X2t}\sigma_{Y1t})^2 \geq 0,$$

it follows that

$$(\sigma_{X1t}\sigma_{Y1t} + \sigma_{X2t}\sigma_{Y2t})^2 \leq (\sigma_{X1t}^2 + \sigma_{X2t}^2)(\sigma_{Y1t}^2 + \sigma_{Y2t}^2),$$

and therefore the squared correlation is generally smaller than one. The correlation will equal -1 or $+1$ only if $\sigma_{X1t} = \sigma_{Y1t} = 0$ or $\sigma_{X2t} = \sigma_{Y2t} = 0$ so that we are effectively back to the single shock case.

Similarly, in the continuous-time setting we add a second standard Brownian motion so that

$$dX_t = \mu_{Xt}\,dt + \sigma_{X1t}\,dz_{1t} + \sigma_{X2t}\,dz_{2t}, \quad dY_t = \mu_{Yt}\,dt + \sigma_{Y1t}\,dz_{1t} + \sigma_{Y2t}\,dz_{2t},$$

where $z_1 = (z_{1t})$ and $z_2 = (z_{2t})$ are independent standard Brownian motions. This generates an instantaneous covariance of

$$\mathrm{Cov}_t[dX_t, dY_t] = (\sigma_{X1t}\sigma_{Y1t} + \sigma_{X2t}\sigma_{Y2t})\,dt,$$

instantaneous variances of

$$\mathrm{Var}_t[dX_t] = \left(\sigma_{X1t}^2 + \sigma_{X2t}^2\right) dt, \quad \mathrm{Var}_t[dY_t] = \left(\sigma_{Y1t}^2 + \sigma_{Y2t}^2\right) dt,$$

and thus an instantaneous correlation of

$$\mathrm{Corr}_t[dX_t, dY_t] = \frac{\sigma_{X1t}\sigma_{Y1t} + \sigma_{X2t}\sigma_{Y2t}}{\sqrt{\left(\sigma_{X1t}^2 + \sigma_{X2t}^2\right)\left(\sigma_{Y1t}^2 + \sigma_{Y2t}^2\right)}},$$

which again can be anywhere in the interval $[-1, +1]$.

In order to define a two-dimensional process (X, Y), we need to specify the first- and second-order local moments. Obviously, μ_X and μ_Y fully characterize the first-order local moments. The shock coefficients σ_{X1t}, σ_{X2t}, σ_{Y1t}, and σ_{Y2t} determine the second-order local moments, which are the two instantaneous variances and the instantaneous correlation. But many combinations of the four shock coefficients will give rise to the same variances and the same correlation. Hence, we have one degree of freedom in fixing the shock coefficients. For example, we can put $\sigma_{X2t} \equiv 0$, which has the nice implication that it will simplify various expressions and interpretations. Then the dynamics of X and Y are

$$dX_t = \mu_{Xt}\, dt + \sigma_{Xt}\, dz_{1t}, \qquad dY_t = \mu_{Yt}\, dt + \sigma_{Yt}\left(\rho_t\, dz_{1t} + \sqrt{1-\rho_t^2}\, dz_{2t}\right).$$

The instantaneous variances are now $\mathrm{Var}_t[dX_t] = \sigma_{Xt}^2\, dt$ and

$$\begin{aligned}
\mathrm{Var}_t[dY_t] &= \mathrm{Var}_t\left[\sigma_{Yt}\left(\rho_t\, dz_{1t} + \sqrt{1-\rho_t^2}\, dz_{2t}\right)\right] \\
&= \sigma_{Yt}^2\, \mathrm{Var}_t\left[\rho_t\, dz_{1t} + \sqrt{1-\rho_t^2}\, dz_{2t}\right] \\
&= \sigma_{Yt}^2\left(\rho_t^2\, dt + (1-\rho_t^2)\, dt\right) \\
&= \sigma_{Yt}^2\, dt.
\end{aligned}$$

The instantaneous covariance is

$$\mathrm{Cov}_t[dX_t, dY_t] = \sigma_{Xt}\sigma_{Yt}\, \mathrm{Cov}_t\left[dz_{1t}, \rho_t\, dz_{1t} + \sqrt{1-\rho_t^2}\, dz_{2t}\right] = \rho_t\sigma_{Xt}\sigma_{Yt}\, dt.$$

If σ_{Xt} and σ_{Yt} are both positive or both negative, then ρ_t will be the instantaneous correlation between the two processes X and Y. If σ_{Xt} and σ_{Yt} have opposite signs, the correlation will be $-\rho_t$.

In many continuous-time financial models, one stochastic process is defined in terms of a function of two other stochastic processes. In such a case the following two-dimensional version of Itô's Lemma is useful.

Theorem 2.6 (Itô's Lemma, two-dimensional). *Suppose $X = (X_t)$ and $Y = (Y_t)$ are two stochastic processes with dynamics*

$$dX_t = \mu_{Xt}\,dt + \sigma_{X1t}\,dz_{1t} + \sigma_{X2t}\,dz_{2t}, \quad dY_t = \mu_{Yt}\,dt + \sigma_{Y1t}\,dz_{1t} + \sigma_{Y2t}\,dz_{2t}, \tag{2.11}$$

where $z_1 = (z_{1t})$ and $z_2 = (z_{2t})$ are independent standard Brownian motions. Let $g(X, Y, t)$ be a real-valued function for which all the derivatives $\frac{\partial g}{\partial t}$, $\frac{\partial g}{\partial X}$, $\frac{\partial g}{\partial Y}$, $\frac{\partial^2 g}{\partial X^2}$, $\frac{\partial^2 g}{\partial Y^2}$, and $\frac{\partial^2 g}{\partial X \partial Y}$ exist and are continuous. Then the process $W = (W_t)$ defined by $W_t = g(X_t, Y_t, t)$ is an Itô process with

$$\begin{aligned} dW_t = \Bigg(& \frac{\partial g}{\partial t} + \frac{\partial g}{\partial X}\mu_{Xt} + \frac{\partial g}{\partial Y}\mu_{Yt} + \frac{1}{2}\frac{\partial^2 g}{\partial X^2}\left(\sigma_{X1t}^2 + \sigma_{X2t}^2\right) \\ & + \frac{1}{2}\frac{\partial^2 g}{\partial Y^2}\left(\sigma_{Y1t}^2 + \sigma_{Y2t}^2\right) + \frac{\partial^2 g}{\partial X \partial Y}\left(\sigma_{X1t}\sigma_{Y1t} + \sigma_{X2t}\sigma_{Y2t}\right)\Bigg) dt \\ & + \left(\frac{\partial g}{\partial X}\sigma_{X1t} + \frac{\partial g}{\partial Y}\sigma_{Y1t}\right) dz_{1t} + \left(\frac{\partial g}{\partial X}\sigma_{X2t} + \frac{\partial g}{\partial Y}\sigma_{Y2t}\right) dz_{2t}, \end{aligned}$$

where the dependence of all the partial derivatives on (X_t, Y_t, t) has been notationally suppressed.

Alternatively, the result can be written more compactly as

$$\begin{aligned} dW_t = & \frac{\partial g}{\partial t}\,dt + \frac{\partial g}{\partial X}\,dX_t + \frac{\partial g}{\partial Y}\,dY_t + \frac{1}{2}\frac{\partial^2 g}{\partial X^2}(dX_t)^2 + \frac{1}{2}\frac{\partial^2 g}{\partial Y^2}(dY_t)^2 \\ & + \frac{\partial^2 g}{\partial X \partial Y}(dX_t)(dY_t), \end{aligned}$$

where it is understood that $(dt)^2 = dt \times dz_{1t} = dt \times dz_{2t} = dz_{1t} \times dz_{2t} = 0$. This implies that

$$(dX_t)^2 = \mathrm{Var}_t[dX_t], \quad (dY_t)^2 = \mathrm{Var}_t[dY_t], \quad (dX_t)(dY_t) = \mathrm{Cov}_t[dX_t, dY_t].$$

Most of our applications of the two-dimensional Itô's Lemma will be covered by the following two examples. See Exercise 2.7 for a different application.

Example 2.1 Suppose that the dynamics of X and Y are given by Eq. (2.11) and $W_t = X_t Y_t$. In order to find the dynamics of W, we apply the above version of Itô's Lemma with the function $g(X, Y) = XY$. The relevant partial derivatives are

$$\frac{\partial g}{\partial t} = 0, \quad \frac{\partial g}{\partial X} = Y, \quad \frac{\partial g}{\partial Y} = X, \quad \frac{\partial^2 g}{\partial X^2} = 0, \quad \frac{\partial^2 g}{\partial Y^2} = 0, \quad \frac{\partial^2 g}{\partial X \partial Y} = 1.$$

Hence,

$$dW_t = Y_t\, dX_t + X_t\, dY_t + (dX_t)(dY_t).$$

In particular, if the dynamics of X and Y are written in the form

$$\begin{aligned} dX_t &= X_t\left[m_{Xt}\, dt + v_{X1t}\, dz_{1t} + v_{X2t}\, dz_{2t}\right], \\ dY_t &= Y_t\left[m_{Yt}\, dt + v_{Y1t}\, dz_{1t} + v_{Y2t}\, dz_{2t}\right], \end{aligned} \tag{2.12}$$

we get

$$\begin{aligned} dW_t = W_t\Big[& (m_{Xt} + m_{Yt} + v_{X1t}v_{Y1t} + v_{X2t}v_{Y2t})\, dt \\ & + (v_{X1t} + v_{Y1t})\, dz_{1t} + (v_{X2t} + v_{Y2t})\, dz_{2t}\Big]. \end{aligned}$$

For the special case in which both X and Y are geometric Brownian motions so that m_x, m_Y, v_{X1}, v_{X2}, v_{Y1}, and v_{Y2} are all constants, it follows that $W_t = X_tY_t$ is also a geometric Brownian motion. □

Example 2.2 Define $W_t = X_t/Y_t$. In this case we need to apply Itô's Lemma with the function $g(X, Y) = X/Y$ which has derivatives

$$\frac{\partial g}{\partial t} = 0, \quad \frac{\partial g}{\partial X} = \frac{1}{Y}, \quad \frac{\partial g}{\partial Y} = -\frac{X}{Y^2}, \quad \frac{\partial^2 g}{\partial X^2} = 0,$$
$$\frac{\partial^2 g}{\partial Y^2} = 2\frac{X}{Y^3}, \quad \frac{\partial^2 g}{\partial X \partial Y} = -\frac{1}{Y^2}.$$

Then

$$\begin{aligned} dW_t &= \frac{1}{Y_t}\, dX_t - \frac{X_t}{Y_t^2}\, dY_t + \frac{X_t}{Y_t^3}(dY_t)^2 - \frac{1}{Y_t^2}(dX_t)(dY_t) \\ &= W_t\left[\frac{dX_t}{X_t} - \frac{dY_t}{Y_t} + \left(\frac{dY_t}{Y_t}\right)^2 - \frac{dX_t}{X_t}\frac{dY_t}{Y_t}\right]. \end{aligned}$$

In particular, if the dynamics of X and Y are given by (2.12), the dynamics of $W_t = X_t/Y_t$ becomes

$$\begin{aligned} dW_t = W_t\Big[& \left(m_{Xt} - m_{Yt} + (v_{Y1t}^2 + v_{Y2t}^2) - (v_{X1t}v_{Y1t} + v_{X2t}v_{Y2t})\right) dt \\ & + (v_{X1t} - v_{Y1t})\, dz_{1t} + (v_{X2t} - v_{Y2t})\, dz_{2t}\Big]. \end{aligned}$$

Note that for the special case in which both X and Y are geometric Brownian motions, $W = X/Y$ is also a geometric Brownian motion. □

We can apply the two-dimensional version of Itô's Lemma to prove the following useful result relating expected discounted values and the relative drift rate. Note that if $X = (X_t)$ is a stochastic process with dynamics of the form $dX_t = X_t[m_t\, dt + \sigma\, dz_t]$, then m is referred to as the relative drift rate of X.

Theorem 2.7 *Under suitable regularity conditions, the relative drift rate of an Itô process $X = (X_t)$ is given by the stochastic process $m = (m_t)$ if and only if $X_t = \mathrm{E}_t[X_T \exp\{-\int_t^T m_s\, ds\}]$.*

Proof. Suppose first that the relative drift rate is given by m so that $dX_t = X_t[m_t\, dt + v_t\, dz_t]$. Let us use Itô's Lemma to identify the dynamics of the process $W_t = X_t \exp\{-\int_0^t m_s\, ds\}$ or $W_t = X_t Y_t$, where $Y_t = \exp\{-\int_0^t m_s\, ds\}$. Note that $dY_t = -Y_t m_t\, dt$ so that Y is a locally deterministic stochastic process. From Example 2.1, the dynamics of W becomes

$$dW_t = W_t\left[(m_t - m_t + 0)\, dt + v_t\, dz_t\right] = W_t v_t\, dz_t.$$

Since W has zero drift, it is a martingale. Therefore, $W_t = \mathrm{E}_t[W_T]$, which means that $X_t \exp\{-\int_0^t m_s\, ds\} = \mathrm{E}_t[X_T \exp\{-\int_0^T m_s\, ds\}]$. It now follows easily that $X_t = \mathrm{E}_t[X_T \exp\{-\int_t^T m_s\, ds\}]$ as was to be shown.

On the other hand, suppose $X_t = \mathrm{E}_t[X_T \exp\{-\int_t^T m_s\, ds\}]$ for all t. Then

$$\begin{aligned}
\frac{1}{\Delta t}\mathrm{E}_t[X_{t+\Delta t} - X_t] &= \frac{1}{\Delta t}\mathrm{E}_t\left[\left(\mathrm{E}_{t+\Delta t}\left[X_T e^{-\int_{t+\Delta t}^T m_s\, ds}\right]\right) - \left(\mathrm{E}_t\left[X_T e^{-\int_t^T m_s\, ds}\right]\right)\right] \\
&= \frac{1}{\Delta t}\mathrm{E}_t\left[X_T e^{-\int_{t+\Delta t}^T m_s\, ds} - X_T e^{-\int_t^T m_s\, ds}\right] \\
&= \mathrm{E}_t\left[X_T e^{-\int_t^T m_s\, ds}\frac{e^{\int_t^{t+\Delta t} m_s\, ds} - 1}{\Delta t}\right],
\end{aligned}$$

where we have applied the Law of Iterated Expectations (Theorem 2.1) to obtain the second equality. For small Δt, we have $\int_t^{t+\Delta t} m_s\, ds \approx m_t \Delta t$ so that

$$\frac{e^{\int_t^{t+\Delta t} m_s\, ds} - 1}{\Delta t} \approx \frac{e^{m_t \Delta t} - 1}{\Delta t} \approx m_t$$

since $e^x \approx 1 + x$ for $x \approx 0$. It now follows that

$$\frac{1}{\Delta t}\mathrm{E}_t[X_{t+\Delta t} - X_t] \to m_t\, \mathrm{E}_t\left[X_T e^{-\int_t^T m_s\, ds}\right] = m_t X_t$$

for $\Delta t \to 0$, which means that the relative drift rate equals m_t as was to be shown. □

Similarly, a stochastic process $X = (X_t)$ has an absolute drift rate of $m = (m_t)$ if and only if $X_t = -\mathrm{E}_t\left[\int_t^T m_s\, ds\right]$. That m is the absolute drift rate of X means that the dynamics of X is of the form $dX_t = m_t\, dt + \sigma_t\, dz_t$.

2.7.2 K-Dimensional Processes

The simultaneous modelling of the dynamics of a lot of economic quantities requires the use of a lot of shocks to those quantities. For that purpose we will work with vectors of shocks. In particular for continuous-time modelling, we will represent shocks to the economy by a vector standard Brownian motion. We define this below and state Itô's Lemma for processes of a general dimension.

A *K-dimensional standard Brownian motion* $\boldsymbol{z} = (z_1, \dots, z_K)^\top$ is a stochastic process for which the individual components z_i are mutually independent one-dimensional standard Brownian motions. If we let $\mathbf{0} = (0, \dots, 0)^\top$ denote the zero vector in $\mathbb{R}^K$ and let $\underline{\underline{I}}$ denote the identity matrix of dimension $K \times K$ (the matrix with ones in the diagonal and zeros in all other entries), then we can write the defining properties of a K-dimensional Brownian motion $\boldsymbol{z}$ as follows:

(i) $\boldsymbol{z}_0 = \mathbf{0}$,

(ii) for all $t, t' \geq 0$ with $t < t'$, the random variable $\boldsymbol{z}_{t'} - \boldsymbol{z}_t$ is $N(\mathbf{0}, (t' - t)\underline{\underline{I}})$ distributed (normally distributed increments),

(iii) for all $0 \leq t_0 < t_1 < \cdots < t_n$, the random variables $\boldsymbol{z}_{t_1} - \boldsymbol{z}_{t_0}, \dots, \boldsymbol{z}_{t_n} - \boldsymbol{z}_{t_{n-1}}$ are mutually independent (independent increments),

(iv) $\boldsymbol{z}$ has continuous sample paths in $\mathbb{R}^K$.

Here, $N(\boldsymbol{a}, \underline{\underline{b}})$ denotes a K-dimensional normal distribution with mean vector $\boldsymbol{a}$ and variance-covariance matrix $\underline{\underline{b}}$. Just as in the one-dimensional case, we can also define multidimensional generalized Brownian motions which are simply vectors of independent one-dimensional generalized Brownian motions.

A *K-dimensional diffusion process* $\boldsymbol{X} = (X_1, \dots, X_K)^\top$ is a process with increments of the form

$$d\boldsymbol{X}_t = \boldsymbol{\mu}(\boldsymbol{X}_t, t)\, dt + \underline{\underline{\sigma}}(\boldsymbol{X}_t, t)\, d\boldsymbol{z}_t, \tag{2.13}$$

where $\boldsymbol{\mu}$ is a function from $\mathbb{R}^K \times \mathbb{R}_+$ into $\mathbb{R}^K$, and $\underline{\underline{\sigma}}$ is a function from $\mathbb{R}^K \times \mathbb{R}_+$ into the space of $K \times K$-matrices. As before, $\boldsymbol{z}$ is a K-dimensional standard Brownian motion. The evolution of the multidimensional diffusion can also be written componentwise as

$$\begin{aligned} dX_{it} &= \mu_i(\boldsymbol{X}_t, t)\, dt + \boldsymbol{\sigma}_i(\boldsymbol{X}_t, t)^\top\, d\boldsymbol{z}_t \\ &= \mu_i(\boldsymbol{X}_t, t)\, dt + \sum_{k=1}^{K} \sigma_{ik}(\boldsymbol{X}_t, t)\, dz_{kt}, \quad i = 1, \dots, K, \end{aligned}$$

where $\boldsymbol{\sigma}_i(\boldsymbol{X}_t, t)^\top$ is the i'th row of the matrix $\underline{\underline{\sigma}}(\boldsymbol{X}_t, t)$, and $\sigma_{ik}(\boldsymbol{X}_t, t)$ is the (i, k)'th entry (that is the entry in row i, column k). Since $dz_{1t}, \dots, dz_{Kt}$ are mutually independent and all $N(0, dt)$ distributed, the expected change in the i'th component process over an infinitesimal period is

$$\mathrm{E}_t[dX_{it}] = \mu_i(X_t, t)\,dt, \quad i = 1, \dots, K,$$

so that μ_i can be interpreted as the drift of the i'th component. Furthermore, the covariance between changes in the i'th and the j'th component processes over an infinitesimal period becomes

$$\begin{aligned}
\mathrm{Cov}_t[dX_{it}, dX_{jt}] &= \mathrm{Cov}_t\left[\sum_{k=1}^{K} \sigma_{ik}(X_t, t)\,dz_{kt}, \sum_{l=1}^{K} \sigma_{jl}(X_t, t)\,dz_{lt}\right] \\
&= \sum_{k=1}^{K}\sum_{l=1}^{K} \sigma_{ik}(X_t, t)\sigma_{jl}(X_t, t)\,\mathrm{Cov}_t[dz_{kt}, dz_{lt}] \\
&= \sum_{k=1}^{K} \sigma_{ik}(X_t, t)\sigma_{jk}(X_t, t)\,dt \\
&= \boldsymbol{\sigma}_i(X_t, t)^{\top}\boldsymbol{\sigma}_j(X_t, t)\,dt, \quad i, j = 1, \dots, K,
\end{aligned}$$

where we have applied the usual rules for covariances as well as the independence of the components of z. In particular, the variance of the change in the i'th component process of an infinitesimal period is given by

$$\mathrm{Var}_t[dX_{it}] = \mathrm{Cov}_t[dX_{it}, dX_{it}] = \sum_{k=1}^{K} \sigma_{ik}(X_t, t)^2\,dt = \|\boldsymbol{\sigma}_i(X_t, t)\|^2\,dt,$$

$$i = 1, \dots, K.$$

The volatility of the i'th component is given by $\|\boldsymbol{\sigma}_i(X_t, t)\|$, the length of the vector $\boldsymbol{\sigma}_i(X_t, t)$. The variance-covariance matrix of changes of X_t over the next instant is $\underline{\underline{\Sigma}}(X_t, t)\,dt = \underline{\underline{\sigma}}(X_t, t)\underline{\underline{\sigma}}(X_t, t)^{\top}\,dt$. The correlation between instantaneous increments in two component processes is

$$\mathrm{Corr}_t[dX_{it}, dX_{jt}] = \frac{\boldsymbol{\sigma}_i(X_t, t)^{\top}\boldsymbol{\sigma}_j(X_t, t)\,dt}{\sqrt{\|\boldsymbol{\sigma}_i(X_t, t)\|^2\,dt\,\|\boldsymbol{\sigma}_j(X_t, t)\|^2\,dt}} = \frac{\boldsymbol{\sigma}_i(X_t, t)^{\top}\boldsymbol{\sigma}_j(X_t, t)}{\|\boldsymbol{\sigma}_i(X_t, t)\|\,\|\boldsymbol{\sigma}_j(X_t, t)\|},$$

which can be any number in $[-1, 1]$ depending on the elements of $\boldsymbol{\sigma}_i$ and $\boldsymbol{\sigma}_j$.

Similarly, we can define a *K-dimensional Itô process* $\boldsymbol{x} = (X_1, \dots, X_K)^{\top}$ to be a process with increments of the form

$$dX_t = \boldsymbol{\mu}_t\,dt + \underline{\underline{\sigma}}_t\,dz_t, \tag{2.14}$$

where $\boldsymbol{\mu} = (\boldsymbol{\mu}_t)$ is a K-dimensional stochastic process and $\underline{\underline{\sigma}} = (\underline{\underline{\sigma}}_t)$ is a stochastic process with values in the space of $K \times K$-matrices.

In fact, the values of $\underline{\underline{\sigma}}(X_t, t)$ in Eq. (2.13) and $\underline{\underline{\sigma}}_t$ in Eq. (2.14) do not have to be square matrices. For example, if $z = (z_t)$ is an M-dimensional standard Brownian motion, $\boldsymbol{\mu} = (\boldsymbol{\mu}_t)$ is a K-dimensional process, and $\underline{\underline{\sigma}}_t$ is a stochastic process with values in the space of $K \times M$ matrices, then a K-dimensional Itô process X can be defined by

$$dX_t = \boldsymbol{\mu}_t \, dt + \underline{\underline{\sigma}}_t \, dz_t. \tag{2.15}$$

The instantaneous $K \times K$ variance-covariance matrix $\underline{\underline{\Sigma}}_t \equiv \underline{\underline{\sigma}}_t \underline{\underline{\sigma}}_t^{\top}$ is symmetric and positive semidefinite (because $\boldsymbol{\pi}^{\top} \underline{\underline{\Sigma}}_t \boldsymbol{\pi} \, dt = \mathrm{Var}_t[\boldsymbol{\pi}^{\top} d\boldsymbol{X}_t]$ and any variance is non-negative); see Appendix C for matrix concepts and results. Therefore, $\underline{\underline{\Sigma}}_t$ can be Cholesky decomposed as $\underline{\underline{\Sigma}}_t = \hat{\underline{\underline{\sigma}}}_t \hat{\underline{\underline{\sigma}}}_t^{\top}$ for some lower-triangular $K \times K$-matrix $\hat{\underline{\underline{\sigma}}}_t$ with non-negative diagonal entries. The Itô process X defined by

$$dX_t = \boldsymbol{\mu}_t \, dt + \hat{\underline{\underline{\sigma}}}_t \, d\hat{z}_t, \tag{2.16}$$

where $\hat{z} = (\hat{z}_t)$ is a K-dimensional standard Brownian motion, will thus have the same local mean and the same local variance-covariance matrix as the process defined by Eq. (2.15). Since the probabilistic properties of a K-dimensional Itô process are completely specified by the local mean and the local variance-covariance $\underline{\underline{\Sigma}}$, the definitions (2.15) and (2.16) are equivalent. Therefore, when formulating the dynamics of a multidimensional Itô process, it is without loss of generality to assume that the sensitivity matrix is a square matrix. However, if we have already attached a certain meaning or interpretation to the exogenous shock process z, we cannot just transform the shocks but should proceed applying the formulation (2.15).

Because $\hat{\underline{\underline{\sigma}}}_t$ is lower-triangular, we may write the dynamics (2.16) componentwise as

$$\begin{aligned}
dX_{1t} &= \mu_{1t} \, dt + \hat{\sigma}_{11t} \, d\hat{z}_{1t} \\
dX_{2t} &= \mu_{2t} \, dt + \hat{\sigma}_{21t} \, d\hat{z}_{1t} + \hat{\sigma}_{22t} \, d\hat{z}_{2t} \\
&\vdots \\
dX_{Kt} &= \mu_{Kt} \, dt + \hat{\sigma}_{K1t} \, d\hat{z}_{1t} + \hat{\sigma}_{K2t} \, d\hat{z}_{2t} + \cdots + \hat{\sigma}_{KKt} \, d\hat{z}_{Kt}.
\end{aligned} \tag{2.17}$$

We can think of starting the modelling of the dynamics of X with X_1. The shocks to X_1 are represented by the standard Brownian motion z_1 and its coefficient $\hat{\sigma}_{11}$ is the volatility of X_1. Then we extend the model to include X_2. Unless the infinitesimal changes to X_1 and X_2 are always perfectly correlated we need to introduce another standard Brownian motion, z_2. The coefficient $\hat{\sigma}_{21}$ is fixed to match the covariance between changes to X_1 and X_2, and then $\hat{\sigma}_{22}$ can be chosen so that $\sqrt{\hat{\sigma}_{21}^2 + \hat{\sigma}_{22}^2}$ equals the volatility of X_2. The model may be extended to include additional processes in the same manner.

Some authors prefer to write the dynamics in an alternative way with a single standard Brownian motion $\hat{z}_i$ for each component X_i such as

$$\begin{aligned} dX_{1t} &= \mu_1(\mathbf{X}_t, t)\, dt + V_1(\mathbf{X}_t, t)\, d\hat{z}_{1t} \\ dX_{2t} &= \mu_2(\mathbf{X}_t, t)\, dt + V_2(\mathbf{X}_t, t)\, d\hat{z}_{2t} \\ &\vdots \\ dX_{Kt} &= \mu_K(\mathbf{X}_t, t)\, dt + V_K(\mathbf{X}_t, t)\, d\hat{z}_{Kt}. \end{aligned} \tag{2.18}$$

Clearly, the coefficient $V_i(\mathbf{X}_t, t)$ is then the volatility of X_i. To capture an instantaneous non-zero correlation between the different components, the standard Brownian motions $\hat{z}_1, \dots, \hat{z}_K$ have to be mutually correlated. Let ρ_{ij} be the correlation between $\hat{z}_i$ and $\hat{z}_j$. If (2.18) is meant to represent the same dynamics as (2.17), we must have

$$V_i = \sqrt{\hat{\sigma}_{i1}^2 + \dots + \hat{\sigma}_{ii}^2}, \quad i = 1, \dots, K,$$

$$\rho_{ii} = 1; \quad \rho_{ij} = \frac{\sum_{k=1}^{i} \hat{\sigma}_{ik}\hat{\sigma}_{jk}}{V_i V_j}, \; \rho_{ji} = \rho_{ij}, \quad i < j.$$

As in the one-dimensional case, the above differential expressions are strictly speaking just convenient notation for more precise integral expressions. For example, the equation

$$dX_{it} = \mu_{it}\, dt + \boldsymbol{\sigma}_{it}^{\top}\, d\mathbf{z}_t$$

for the dynamics of the process $X_i = (X_{it})$ means that

$$X_{it'} = X_{it} + \int_t^{t'} \mu_{iu}\, du + \int_t^{t'} \boldsymbol{\sigma}_{iu}^{\top}\, d\mathbf{z}_u$$

for any $t' > t$. The challenge is again to define and derive relevant properties of the latter integral. Concerning the definition, we refer to the short explanation in the one-dimensional case, see Section 2.6.5. For a sufficiently nice $\boldsymbol{\sigma}_i$-process, the conditional mean and variance of the stochastic integral $\int_t^{t'} \boldsymbol{\sigma}_{iu}^{\top}\, d\mathbf{z}_u$ are given as in Theorem 2.2. In general, we cannot say anything about the probability distribution of the stochastic integral and, therefore, about the probability distribution of the future value $X_{it'}$. When $\boldsymbol{\sigma}_i$ is deterministic, the stochastic integral will be normally distributed in accordance with Theorem 2.3.

In the multidimensional setting, the conditional covariance between two stochastic integrals is sometimes of interest. If $\boldsymbol{\sigma}_i$ and $\boldsymbol{\sigma}_j$ are sufficiently nice stochastic processes, it can be shown that

$$\mathrm{Cov}_t\left[\int_t^{t'} \boldsymbol{\sigma}_{iu}^\top \, dz_u, \int_t^{t'} \boldsymbol{\sigma}_{ju}^\top \, dz_u\right] = \mathrm{E}_t\left[\left(\int_t^{t'} \boldsymbol{\sigma}_{iu}^\top \, dz_u\right)\left(\int_t^{t'} \boldsymbol{\sigma}_{ju}^\top \, dz_u\right)\right]$$
$$= \int_t^{t'} \mathrm{E}_t\left[\boldsymbol{\sigma}_{iu}^\top \boldsymbol{\sigma}_{ju}\right] du,$$

which simplifies to the variance rule (or so-called Itô isometry) when $\boldsymbol{\sigma}_i = \boldsymbol{\sigma}_j$. Of course, when $\boldsymbol{\sigma}_i$ and $\boldsymbol{\sigma}_j$ are deterministic functions, we then have

$$\mathrm{Cov}_t\left[\int_t^{t'} \boldsymbol{\sigma}_i(u)^\top \, dz_u, \int_t^{t'} \boldsymbol{\sigma}_j(u)^\top \, dz_u\right] = \int_t^{t'} \boldsymbol{\sigma}_i(u)^\top \boldsymbol{\sigma}_j(u) \, du.$$

Next, we state a multidimensional version of Itô's Lemma, which applies to the case in which a one-dimensional process is defined as a function of time and a multidimensional process.

Theorem 2.8 (Itô's Lemma, multidimensional). *Let $\boldsymbol{X} = (\boldsymbol{X}_t)_{t \geq 0}$ be an Itô process in $\mathbb{R}^K$ with dynamics $d\boldsymbol{X}_t = \boldsymbol{\mu}_t \, dt + \underline{\underline{\sigma}}_t \, dz_t$ or, equivalently,*

$$dX_{it} = \mu_{it} \, dt + \boldsymbol{\sigma}_{it}^\top \, dz_t = \mu_{it} \, dt + \sum_{m=1}^{M} \sigma_{imt} \, dz_{mt}, \quad i = 1, \ldots, K,$$

where $z = (z_1, \ldots, z_M)^\top$ is an M-dimensional standard Brownian motion, and μ_i and σ_{im} are well-behaved stochastic processes.

Let $g(\boldsymbol{X}, t)$ be a real-valued function for which all the derivatives $\frac{\partial g}{\partial t}$, $\frac{\partial g}{\partial X_i}$, and $\frac{\partial^2 g}{\partial X_i \partial X_j}$ exist and are continuous. Then the process $y = (y_t)_{t \geq 0}$ defined by $y_t = g(\boldsymbol{X}_t, t)$ is also an Itô process with dynamics

$$dy_t = \left(\frac{\partial g}{\partial t}(\boldsymbol{X}_t, t) + \sum_{i=1}^{K} \frac{\partial g}{\partial X_i}(\boldsymbol{X}_t, t)\mu_{it} + \frac{1}{2}\sum_{i=1}^{K}\sum_{j=1}^{K} \frac{\partial^2 g}{\partial X_i \partial X_j}(\boldsymbol{X}_t, t)\gamma_{ijt}\right) dt$$
$$+ \sum_{i=1}^{K} \frac{\partial g}{\partial X_i}(\boldsymbol{X}_t, t)\sigma_{i1t} \, dz_{1t} + \cdots + \sum_{i=1}^{K} \frac{\partial g}{\partial X_i}(\boldsymbol{X}_t, t)\sigma_{iMt} \, dz_{Mt},$$

where $\gamma_{ijt} = \boldsymbol{\sigma}_{it}^\top \boldsymbol{\sigma}_{jt} = \sigma_{i1t}\sigma_{j1t} + \cdots + \sigma_{iMt}\sigma_{jMt}$ is the covariance between the processes X_i and X_j.

The result can also be written as

$$dy_t = \frac{\partial g}{\partial t}(\boldsymbol{X}_t, t) \, dt + \sum_{i=1}^{K} \frac{\partial g}{\partial X_i}(\boldsymbol{X}_t, t) \, dX_{it} + \frac{1}{2}\sum_{i=1}^{K}\sum_{j=1}^{K} \frac{\partial^2 g}{\partial X_i \partial X_j}(\boldsymbol{X}_t, t)(dX_{it})(dX_{jt}),$$

where in the computation of $(dX_{it})(dX_{jt})$ one must use the rules $(dt)^2 = dt \times dz_{it} = 0$ for all i, $dz_{it} \times dz_{jt} = 0$ for $i \neq j$, and $(dz_{it})^2 = dt$ for all i. This implies that

$$(dX_{it})(dX_{jt}) = \mathrm{Cov}_t[dX_{it}, dX_{jt}].$$

Alternatively, the result can be expressed using vector and matrix notation:

$$\begin{aligned} dy_t = &\left(\frac{\partial g}{\partial t}(X_t, t) + \left(\frac{\partial g}{\partial \boldsymbol{X}}(X_t, t)\right)^{\top} \boldsymbol{\mu}_t + \frac{1}{2}\,\mathrm{tr}\left(\left[\frac{\partial^2 g}{\partial \boldsymbol{X}^2}(X_t, t)\right] \underline{\underline{\sigma}}_t \underline{\underline{\sigma}}_t^{\top}\right)\right) dt \\ &+ \left(\frac{\partial g}{\partial \boldsymbol{X}}(X_t, t)\right)^{\top} \underline{\underline{\sigma}}_t \, dz_t, \end{aligned} \tag{2.19}$$

where

$$\frac{\partial g}{\partial \boldsymbol{X}} = \begin{pmatrix} \frac{\partial g}{\partial X_1} \\ \vdots \\ \frac{\partial g}{\partial X_K} \end{pmatrix}, \quad \frac{\partial^2 g}{\partial \boldsymbol{X}^2} = \begin{pmatrix} \frac{\partial^2 g}{\partial X_1^2} & \frac{\partial^2 g}{\partial X_1 \partial X_2} & \cdots & \frac{\partial^2 g}{\partial X_1 \partial X_K} \\ \frac{\partial^2 g}{\partial X_2 \partial X_1} & \frac{\partial^2 g}{\partial X_2^2} & \cdots & \frac{\partial^2 g}{\partial X_2 \partial X_K} \\ \vdots & \vdots & \ddots & \vdots \\ \frac{\partial^2 g}{\partial X_K \partial X_1} & \frac{\partial^2 g}{\partial X_K \partial X_2} & \cdots & \frac{\partial^2 g}{\partial X_K^2} \end{pmatrix},$$

and tr denotes the trace of a quadratic matrix, that is the sum of the diagonal elements.

As a special case, we get the following extension of Theorem 2.6:

Theorem 2.9 *Suppose that $X = (X_t)$ and $Y = (Y_t)$ are two stochastic processes with dynamics*

$$dX_t = \mu_{Xt}\, dt + \boldsymbol{\sigma}_{Xt}^{\top}\, dz_t, \qquad dY_t = \mu_{Yt}\, dt + \boldsymbol{\sigma}_{Yt}^{\top}\, dz_t,$$

where $z = (z_t)$ is an M-dimensional standard Brownian motion, and $\boldsymbol{\sigma}_{Xt}$ and $\boldsymbol{\sigma}_{Yt}$ are M-dimensional vectors. Let $g(X, Y, t)$ be a real-valued function for which all the derivatives $\frac{\partial g}{\partial t}$, $\frac{\partial g}{\partial X}$, $\frac{\partial g}{\partial Y}$, $\frac{\partial^2 g}{\partial X^2}$, $\frac{\partial^2 g}{\partial Y^2}$, and $\frac{\partial^2 g}{\partial X \partial Y}$ exist and are continuous. Then the process $W = (W_t)$ defined by $W_t = g(X_t, Y_t, t)$ is an Itô process with

$$\begin{aligned} dW_t = &\left(\frac{\partial g}{\partial t} + \frac{\partial g}{\partial X}\mu_{Xt} + \frac{\partial g}{\partial Y}\mu_{Yt} + \frac{1}{2}\frac{\partial^2 g}{\partial X^2}\|\boldsymbol{\sigma}_{Xt}\|^2 + \frac{1}{2}\frac{\partial^2 g}{\partial Y^2}\|\boldsymbol{\sigma}_{Yt}\|^2 \right. \\ &\left. + \frac{\partial^2 g}{\partial X \partial Y}\boldsymbol{\sigma}_{Xt}^{\top}\boldsymbol{\sigma}_{Yt}\right) dt + \left(\frac{\partial g}{\partial X}\boldsymbol{\sigma}_{Xt} + \frac{\partial g}{\partial Y}\boldsymbol{\sigma}_{Yt}\right)^{\top} dz_t, \end{aligned}$$

where the dependence of all the partial derivatives on (X_t, Y_t, t) has been notationally suppressed.

The following example generalizes Examples 2.1 and 2.2.

Example 2.3 Suppose X and Y are two Itô processes with dynamics of the form

$$dX_t = X_t \left[\mu_{Xt}\, dt + \boldsymbol{\sigma}_{Xt}^{\top}\, d\boldsymbol{z}_t\right], \quad dY_t = Y_t \left[\mu_{Yt}\, dt + \boldsymbol{\sigma}_{Yt}^{\top}\, d\boldsymbol{z}_t\right].$$

With $W_t = X_t Y_t$, Theorem 2.9 implies that

$$\begin{aligned} dW_t &= Y_t\, dX_t + X_t\, dY_t + (dX_t)(dY_t) \\ &= W_t \left[\left(\mu_{Xt} + \mu_{Yt} + \boldsymbol{\sigma}_{Xt}^{\top}\boldsymbol{\sigma}_{Yt}\right) dt + \left(\boldsymbol{\sigma}_{Xt} + \boldsymbol{\sigma}_{Yt}\right)^{\top} d\boldsymbol{z}_t\right]. \end{aligned}$$

For $W_t = X_t / Y_t$, we obtain

$$\begin{aligned} dW_t &= W_t \left[\frac{dX_t}{X_t} - \frac{dY_t}{Y_t} + \left(\frac{dY_t}{Y_t}\right)^2 - \frac{dX_t}{X_t}\frac{dY_t}{Y_t}\right] \\ &= W_t \left[\left(\mu_{Xt} - \mu_{Yt} + \|\boldsymbol{\sigma}_{Yt}\|^2 - \boldsymbol{\sigma}_{Xt}^{\top}\boldsymbol{\sigma}_{Yt}\right) dt + \left(\boldsymbol{\sigma}_{Xt} - \boldsymbol{\sigma}_{Yt}\right)^{\top} d\boldsymbol{z}_t\right]. \end{aligned}$$ □

2.8 CONCLUDING REMARKS

This chapter has provided an overview of the concepts and results in probability theory and stochastic calculus that are needed to develop modern asset pricing models. In the following chapters we will frequently apply these concepts and results, often without providing all the intermediate steps in the relevant computations. The reader is recommended to check all such computations in full detail.

2.9 EXERCISES

Exercise 2.1 In the two-period economy illustrated in Figs. 2.1 and 2.2 consider an asset paying a dividend at time 2 given by

$$D_2 = \begin{cases} 0, & \text{for } \omega = 3, \\ 5, & \text{for } \omega \in \{1, 2, 4\}, \\ 10, & \text{for } \omega \in \{5, 6\}. \end{cases}$$

(a) What is the expectation at time 0 of D_2? What is the expectation at time 1 of D_2? Verify that the Law of Iterated Expectations holds for these expectations.

(b) What is the variance at time 0 of D_2? What is the variance at time 1 of D_2? Confirm that $\text{Var}[D_2] = \text{E}\left[\text{Var}_1\left[D_2\right]\right] + \text{Var}\left[\text{E}_1\left[D_2\right]\right]$.

Exercise 2.2 Let $X = (X_t)$ and $Y = (Y_t)$ be the price processes of two assets with no intermediate dividends and assume that

$$dX_t = X_t \left[0.05\, dt + 0.1\, dz_{1t} + 0.2\, dz_{2t}\right],$$
$$dY_t = Y_t \left[0.07\, dt + 0.3\, dz_{1t} - 0.1\, dz_{2t}\right].$$

(a) What is the expected rate of return of each of the two assets?

(b) What is the return variance and volatility of each of the two assets?

(c) What is the covariance and the correlation between the returns on the two assets?

Exercise 2.3 Suppose $X = (X_t)$ is a geometric Brownian motion, $dX_t = \mu X_t\, dt + \sigma X_t\, dz_t$. What is the dynamics of the process $y = (y_t)$ defined by $y_t = (X_t)^n$? What can you say about the distribution of future values of the y process?

Exercise 2.4 Suppose that the continuous-time stochastic process $X = (X_t)$ is defined as

$$X_t = \frac{1}{2} \int_0^t \lambda_s^2\, ds + \int_0^t \lambda_s\, dz_s,$$

where $z = (z_t)$ is a one-dimensional standard Brownian motion and $\lambda = (\lambda_t)$ is some 'nice' stochastic process.

(a) Argue that $dX_t = \frac{1}{2}\lambda_t^2\, dt + \lambda_t\, dz_t$.

(b) Suppose that the continuous-time stochastic process $\xi = (\xi_t)$ is defined as $\xi_t = \exp\{-X_t\}$. Show that $d\xi_t = -\lambda_t \xi_t\, dz_t$.

Exercise 2.5 (Adapted from Björk (2009)) Define the process $y = (y_t)$ by $y_t = z_t^4$, where $z = (z_t)$ is a standard Brownian motion. Find the dynamics of y. Show that

$$y_t = 6 \int_0^t z_s^2\, ds + 4 \int_0^t z_s^3\, dz_s.$$

Show that $\mathrm{E}[y_t] \equiv \mathrm{E}[z_t^4] = 3t^2$.

Exercise 2.6 (Adapted from Björk (2009)) Define the process $y = (y_t)$ by $y_t = e^{az_t}$, where a is a constant and $z = (z_t)$ is a standard Brownian motion. Find the dynamics of y. Show that

$$y_t = 1 + \frac{1}{2} a^2 \int_0^t y_s\, ds + a \int_0^t y_s\, dz_s.$$

Define $m(t) = \mathrm{E}[y_t]$. Show that m satisfies the ordinary differential equation

$$m'(t) = \frac{1}{2} a^2 m(t), \quad m(0) = 1.$$

Show that $m(t) = e^{a^2 t/2}$ and conclude that

$$\mathrm{E}\left[e^{az_t}\right] = e^{a^2 t/2}.$$

Exercise 2.7 The dynamics of the continuous-time stochastic processes $X = (X_t)$ and $Y = (Y_t)$ are given by

$$dX_t = X_t\,[\mu_X\,dt + \sigma_X\,dz_{1t}]\,,$$

$$dY_t = \mu_Y\,dt + \rho\sigma_Y\,dz_{1t} + \sqrt{1-\rho^2}\sigma_Y\,dz_{2t},$$

where z_1 and z_2 are independent standard Brownian motions, and $\mu_X, \sigma_X, \mu_Y, \rho, \sigma_Y$ are constants with $\sigma_X, \sigma_Y \geq 0$ and $\rho \in [-1, 1]$.

(a) State the conditional expectation and variance of the increments of the two processes, that is state $\mathrm{E}_t[dX_t]$, $\mathrm{Var}_t[dX_t]$, $\mathrm{E}_t[dY_t]$, and $\mathrm{Var}_t[dY_t]$. State the conditional covariance and correlation between the increments of the two processes, that is $\mathrm{Cov}_t[dX_t, dY_t]$ and $\mathrm{Corr}_t[dX_t, dY_t]$.

Define a process $W = (W_t)$ by $W_t = X_t e^{Y_t}$.

(b) Determine the dynamics of W, that is find dW_t. Describe what type of process W is.

3

Portfolios, Arbitrage, and Market Completeness

3.1 INTRODUCTION

Assets are characterized by their dividends and their prices. Using the language of stochastic processes developed in Chapter 2, we explain in Section 3.2 how to represent assets in our mathematical models of the financial markets and how to compute asset returns over shorter and longer periods.

Most investors hold a portfolio of several assets and change the decomposition of the portfolio over time. Section 3.3 shows how the dividend, the value, and the return of a portfolio are related to that of the individual assets in the portfolio.

Section 3.4 formalizes the key concept of an arbitrage, which is basically an investment strategy that offers something for nothing. Arbitrage cannot exist in equilibrium, so when looking for equilibrium asset prices we can focus on no-arbitrage prices.

Section 3.5 introduces the term redundant asset and discusses the pricing of such assets.

Finally, Section 3.6 explains the concept of market completeness, which turns out to be important for many results in subsequent chapters.

3.2 ASSETS

An asset is characterized by its dividends and its price. We will refer to an asset as a *basic asset* if the dividends of the asset are always non-negative and if, any point in time before the terminal date, there is a positive probability of a positive dividend at the terminal date of the model. We let I denote the number of basic assets that are available for trade throughout the time span of the model. We can safely assume (since equilibrium prices will be arbitrage-free; see precise definition below) that the prices of the basic assets are always positive. We assume without loss of generality that assets pay no dividends at time 0. We use the convention that the price of an asset at a given point in time is exclusive of any dividend payment at that time, that is prices are ex-dividend. At the last point in time considered in the model, all assets must then have a zero price.

3.2.1 The One-Period Framework

In a one-period model any asset i is characterized by its time 0 price P_i and its time 1 dividend D_i, which is a random variable. If the realized state is $\omega \in \Omega$, asset i will give a dividend of $D_i(\omega)$. We can gather the prices of the basic assets in the I-dimensional vector $\boldsymbol{P} = (P_1, \dots, P_I)^\top$ and the dividends of the basic assets in the I-dimensional random variable $\boldsymbol{D} = (D_1, \dots, D_I)^\top$. We assume that all variances of dividends and that all pairwise covariances of dividends are finite.

We defined returns in Section 1.3. In a one-period framework the net rate of return on asset i is $r_i = (D_i - P_i)/P_i$, the gross rate of return is $R_i = D_i/P_i = 1 + r_i$, and the log-return or continuously compounded rate of return is defined $\ln R_i = \ln(D_i/P_i)$. We will write the risk-free gross rate of return as R^f. We can stack the returns on the different assets into vectors. For example, the gross rate of return vector is $\boldsymbol{R} = (R_1, \dots, R_I)^\top$. Defining the $I \times I$ matrix

$$\operatorname{diag}(\boldsymbol{P}) = \begin{pmatrix} P_1 & 0 & \dots & 0 \\ 0 & P_2 & \dots & 0 \\ \vdots & \vdots & \ddots & \vdots \\ 0 & 0 & \dots & P_I \end{pmatrix}, \tag{3.1}$$

we can write the link between the dividend vector and the gross rate of return vector as

$$\boldsymbol{R} = \left[\operatorname{diag}(\boldsymbol{P})\right]^{-1} \boldsymbol{D} \quad \Leftrightarrow \quad \boldsymbol{D} = \operatorname{diag}(\boldsymbol{P})\boldsymbol{R}. \tag{3.2}$$

Given our assumptions about dividends, all the gross rate of returns will have finite variances, and all the pairwise covariances of gross rate of returns will also be finite.

Note that if we know the expected dividend of asset i, $\mathrm{E}[D_i]$, then finding the expected return $\mathrm{E}[R_i]$ is equivalent to finding the price P_i. In one-period models we can therefore study equilibrium expected returns instead of equilibrium prices, and many asset pricing models are typically formulated in terms of expected returns. This is for example the case for the classic CAPM.

The so-called *Sharpe ratio* on an asset is defined as the expected excess return on the asset divided by standard deviation of the return on the asset. Here the excess return of an asset means the return on the asset minus the risk-free return. In symbols, the Sharpe ratio for asset i is $(\mathrm{E}[R_i] - R^f)/\sigma[R_i]$.

3.2.2 The Discrete-Time Framework

In a discrete-time model with $\mathcal{T} = \{0, 1, 2, \dots, T\}$, we allow for dividends at all dates except time 0 so that the dividends of an asset are represented by an adapted, non-negative stochastic process $D_i = (D_{it})_{t\in\mathcal{T}}$ with initial value $D_{i0} = 0$. The random variable D_{it} represents the dividend payment of asset i at time t. We are interested in prices at all dates $t \in \mathcal{T}$. Let $P_i = (P_{it})_{t\in\mathcal{T}}$ denote the price process of asset i. By our assumptions, $P_{iT} = 0$ in all states. We assume that, for any basic asset, there will be a positive (conditional) probability that the terminal dividend is positive no matter what the information at time $T-1$ is. We collect the prices and dividend processes of the I basic assets in I-dimensional processes $\boldsymbol{P} = (\boldsymbol{P}_t)_{t\in\mathcal{T}}$ and $\boldsymbol{D} = (\boldsymbol{D}_t)_{t\in\mathcal{T}}$ with $\boldsymbol{P}_t = (P_{1t}, \dots, P_{It})^\top$ and similarly for $\boldsymbol{D}_t$.

The gross rate of return on asset i between two adjacent points in time, say t and time $t+1$, is $R_{i,t+1} = (P_{i,t+1} + D_{i,t+1})/P_{it}$, the net rate of return is $r_{i,t+1} = R_{i,t+1} - 1$, and the log-return is $\ln R_{i,t+1}$. Note that now the relation between the expected gross rate of return $\mathrm{E}_t[R_{i,t+1}]$ and the beginning-of-period price P_{it} involves both the expected dividend $\mathrm{E}_t[D_{i,t+1}]$ and the expected future price $\mathrm{E}_t[P_{i,t+1}]$. Therefore we cannot easily switch between statements about expected returns and statements about prices. We will consider both formulations of asset pricing models and the link between them in later chapters.

We can also define returns over longer holding periods. Now, we could define the gross rate of return on asset i between time t and time $t+n$ as $R_{i,t,t+n} = (P_{i,t+n} + D_{i,t+1} + \dots + D_{i,t+n})/P_{it}$ but, unless the intermediate dividends $D_{i,t+1}, \dots, D_{i,t+n-1}$ are all zero, we will add values at different dates without any discounting which should be avoided. More appropriately, we can compute the return assuming that intermediate dividends are reinvested in the asset. Suppose we buy one unit of asset i at time t. For the dividend of $D_{i,t+1}$ received at time $t+1$, we can buy $D_{i,t+1}/P_{i,t+1}$ extra units of the asset so that the total holdings are $A_{t+1} \equiv 1 + D_{i,t+1}/P_{i,t+1}$ units. The total dividend received at time $t+2$ is then $(1 + D_{i,t+1}/P_{i,t+1})D_{i,t+2}$, which will buy you $(1 + D_{i,t+1}/P_{i,t+1})D_{i,t+2}/P_{i,t+2}$ additional units of the asset, bringing the total up to

$$A_{t+2} \equiv 1 + \frac{D_{i,t+1}}{P_{i,t+1}} + \left(1 + \frac{D_{i,t+1}}{P_{i,t+1}}\right)\frac{D_{i,t+2}}{P_{i,t+2}} = \left(1 + \frac{D_{i,t+1}}{P_{i,t+1}}\right)\left(1 + \frac{D_{i,t+2}}{P_{i,t+2}}\right)$$

units. Continuing like this, we end up with

$$A_{t+n} \equiv \prod_{m=1}^{n}\left(1 + \frac{D_{i,t+m}}{P_{i,t+m}}\right) = \left(1 + \frac{D_{i,t+1}}{P_{i,t+1}}\right)\dots\left(1 + \frac{D_{i,t+n}}{P_{i,t+n}}\right)$$

units at time $t+n$. The gross rate of return on asset i between time t and time $t+n$ is therefore

$$R_{i,t,t+n} = \frac{A_{t+n} P_{i,t+n}}{P_{it}} = \frac{P_{i,t+n}}{P_{it}} \prod_{m=1}^{n} \left(1 + \frac{D_{i,t+m}}{P_{i,t+m}}\right). \tag{3.3}$$

Again, we can define the corresponding net rate of return or log-return.

In the discrete-time framework, an asset is said to be risk-free if the dividend at any time $t = 1, \dots, T$ is already known at time $t-1$, no matter what information is available at time $t-1$. The risk-free gross rate of return between time t and $t+1$ is denoted by R^f_t so that the subscript indicates the point in time at which the return will be known to investors, not the point in time at which the return can be cashed in. Before time t, the risk-free return R^f_t for the period beginning at t is not necessarily known. Risk-free rates fluctuate over time so they are only risk-free in the short run. If you roll-over in one period risk-free investments from time t to $t+n$, the total gross rate of return will be

$$R^f_{t,t+n} = \prod_{m=0}^{n-1} R^f_{t+m} = R^f_t R^f_{t+1} \dots R^f_{t+n-1}.$$

Note that this return is risky seen at, or before, time t. In contrast, an asset that provides a risk-free return from time t to time $t+n$ is a default-free, zero-coupon bond maturing at time $t+n$. If it has a face value of 1 and its time t price is denoted by B^{t+n}_t, you will get a gross rate of return of $1/B^{t+n}_t$.

3.2.3 The Continuous-Time Framework

In a continuous-time model over the time span $\mathcal{T} = [0, T]$, the price of an asset i is represented by an adapted stochastic process $P_i = (P_{it})_{t\in[0,T]}$. In practice, no assets pay dividends continuously. However, for computational purposes it is sometimes useful to approximate a stream of frequent dividend payments by a continuous-time dividend process. On the other hand, a reasonable model should also allow for assets paying lump-sum dividends. We could capture both through a process $\mathcal{D}_i = (\mathcal{D}_{it})_{t\in[0,T]}$ where $\mathcal{D}_{it}$ is the (undiscounted) sum of all dividends of asset i up to and including time t. The total dividend received in a small interval $[t, t+dt]$ would then be $d\mathcal{D}_{it} = \mathcal{D}_{i,t+dt} - \mathcal{D}_{it}$ and the dividend yield would be $d\mathcal{D}_{it}/P_{it}$. A lump-sum dividend at time t would correspond to a jump in $\mathcal{D}_{it}$. For notational simplicity, we assume that the basic assets of the economy will pay a lump-sum dividend only at time T. The terminal dividend of asset i is modelled by a random variable D_{iT}, assumed non-negative with a positive probability of a positive value. Up to time T, dividends are paid out continuously. In general, the dividend yield can then be captured by a specification like $d\mathcal{D}_{it}/P_{it} = \delta_{it}\,dt + \nu_{it}\,dz_{it}$ for some one- or multidimensional standard Brownian motion z_i, but for simplicity we assume that there is no uncertainty about the dividend yield over the next instant, that is $\nu_{it} = 0$. To sum up, the dividends of asset i are represented by a dividend yield process $\delta_i = (\delta_{it})_{t\in[0,T]}$ and a terminal lump-sum dividend D_{iT}.

Next consider returns. If we buy one unit of asset i at time t and keep reinvesting the continuous dividends by purchasing extra (fractions of) units of the assets, how many units will we end up with at time $t' > t$? First divide the interval $[t, t']$ into N bits of length Δt so that dividends are cashed in and additional units bought at times $t + \Delta t, t + 2\Delta t, ..., t + N\Delta t \equiv t'$. We can then proceed as in the discrete-time case discussed above. Let $A_{t+n\Delta t}$ denote the number of units of the asset we will have immediately after time $t + n\Delta t$. We start with $A_t = 1$ unit. At time $t + \Delta t$ we receive a dividend of $\delta_{it}P_{i,t+\Delta t}\Delta t$ which we spend on buying $\delta_{it}\Delta t$ extra assets, bringing our holdings up to $A_{t+\Delta t} = 1 + \delta_{it}\Delta t$. At time $t + 2\Delta t$ we receive a total dividend of $A_{t+\Delta t}\delta_{i,t+\Delta t}P_{i,t+2\Delta t}\Delta t$ which will buy us $A_{t+\Delta t}\delta_{i,t+\Delta t}\Delta t$ extra units. Our total is now $A_{t+2\Delta t} = A_{t+\Delta t} + A_{t+\Delta t}\delta_{i,t+\Delta t}\Delta t$. Continuing like this we will find that, at any time $s = t + n\Delta t$ for some integer $n < N$, our total holdings immediately after time $s + \Delta t$ are given by $A_{s+\Delta t} = A_s + A_s\delta_{is}\Delta t$ so that

$$\frac{A_{s+\Delta t} - A_s}{\Delta t} = \delta_{is}A_s.$$

If we go to the continuous-time limit and let $\Delta t \to 0$, the left-hand side will approach the derivative A'_s, and we see that A_s must satisfy the differential equation $A'_s = \delta_{is}A_s$ as well as the initial condition $A_t = 1$. The solution is

$$A_s = \exp\left\{\int_t^s \delta_{iu}\,du\right\}.$$

So investing one unit in asset i at time t and continuously reinvesting the dividends, we will end up with $A_{t'} = \exp\{\int_t^{t'} \delta_{iu}\,du\}$ units of the asset at time t'. The gross rate of return on asset i over the interval $[t, t']$ is therefore $R_{i,t,t'} = \exp\{\int_t^{t'} \delta_{iu}\,du\}P_{it'}/P_{it}$.

The net rate of return per time period is

$$\begin{aligned}
r_{i,t,t'} &= \frac{1}{t'-t}\left(R_{i,t,t'} - 1\right) = \frac{1}{t'-t}\left(e^{\int_t^{t'} \delta_{iu}\,du}\frac{P_{it'}}{P_{it}} - 1\right) \\
&= \frac{1}{t'-t}\left(e^{\int_t^{t'} \delta_{iu}\,du}\frac{P_{it'} - P_{it}}{P_{it}} + e^{\int_t^{t'} \delta_{iu}\,du} - 1\right) \\
&= e^{\int_t^{t'} \delta_{iu}\,du}\frac{1}{t'-t}\frac{P_{it'} - P_{it}}{P_{it}} + \frac{1}{t'-t}\left(e^{\int_t^{t'} \delta_{iu}\,du} - 1\right).
\end{aligned}$$

Now let us take the limit as $t' \to t$. In the first term, $\int_t^{t'} \delta_{iu}\,du \to 0$ as the integration interval disappears. Hence, $e^{\int_t^{t'} \delta_{iu}\,du} \to 1$. The limit of the term $\frac{1}{t'-t}\frac{P_{it'}-P_{it}}{P_{it}}$ is exactly what we mean by $\frac{1}{dt}\frac{dP_{it}}{P_{it}}$. To find the limit of the term $\frac{1}{t'-t}\left(e^{\int_t^{t'} \delta_{iu}\,du} - 1\right)$, recall that

$$e^x = \sum_{n=0}^{\infty} \frac{1}{n!}x^n = 1 + x + \frac{1}{2}x^2 + \dots,$$

and for t' close to t we have $\int_t^{t'} \delta_{iu}\,du \approx \delta_{it}(t'-t)$. Therefore,

$$\begin{aligned}
\frac{1}{t'-t}\left(e^{\int_t^{t'} \delta_{iu}\,du} - 1\right) &\approx \frac{1}{t'-t}\left(e^{\delta_{it}(t'-t)} - 1\right) \\
&= \frac{1}{t'-t}\left(\delta_{it}(t'-t) + \frac{1}{2}\delta_{it}^2(t'-t)^2 + \dots\right) \\
&= \delta_{it} + \frac{1}{2}\delta_{it}^2(t'-t) + \dots.
\end{aligned}$$

Taking the limit as $t' \to t$, we get δ_{it} (all the approximations are exact in the limit). In sum,

$$r_{it} = \lim_{t'\to t} r_{i,t,t'} = \frac{1}{dt}\frac{dP_{it}}{P_{it}} + \delta_{it}.$$

The first term on the right-hand side is the instantaneous percentage capital gain (still unknown at time t), the second term is the dividend yield (assumed to be known at time t).

We will typically write the dynamics of the price of an asset i as

$$dP_{it} = P_{it}\left[\mu_{it}\,dt + \boldsymbol{\sigma}_{it}^{\top}\,dz_t\right], \tag{3.4}$$

where $z = (z_t)$ is a standard Brownian motion of dimension d representing shocks to the prices. Furthermore, μ_{it} is the expected capital gain so that the total expected net rate of return per time period is $\mu_{it} + \delta_{it}$, and $\boldsymbol{\sigma}_{it}$ is the vector of sensitivities of the price with respect to the exogenous shocks. The volatility is the standard deviation of instantaneous relative price changes, which is $\|\boldsymbol{\sigma}_{it}\| = \left(\sum_{j=1}^{d} \sigma_{ijt}^2\right)^{1/2}$. Using Itô's Lemma exactly as in Section 2.6.7, one finds that

$$P_{it'} = P_{it}\exp\left\{\int_t^{t'}\left(\mu_{iu} - \frac{1}{2}\|\boldsymbol{\sigma}_{iu}\|^2\right)du + \int_t^{t'} \boldsymbol{\sigma}_{iu}^{\top}\,dz_u\right\}. \tag{3.5}$$

Therefore, the gross rate of return on asset i between t and t' is

$$
\begin{aligned}
R_{i,t,t'} &= \exp\left\{\int_t^{t'} \delta_{iu}\, du\right\} \frac{P_{it'}}{P_{it}} \\
&= \exp\left\{\int_t^{t'} \left(\delta_{iu} + \mu_{iu} - \frac{1}{2}\|\boldsymbol{\sigma}_{iu}\|^2\right) du + \int_t^{t'} \boldsymbol{\sigma}_{iu}^\top\, d\boldsymbol{z}_u\right\}.
\end{aligned}
$$

For a short period, that is with $t' = t + \Delta t$ for Δt small, we have

$$
R_{i,t,t+\Delta t} \approx \exp\left\{\left(\delta_{it} + \mu_{it} - \frac{1}{2}\|\boldsymbol{\sigma}_{it}\|^2\right) \Delta t + \boldsymbol{\sigma}_{it}^\top \Delta \boldsymbol{z}_t\right\}, \tag{3.6}
$$

where $\Delta \boldsymbol{z}_t = \boldsymbol{z}_{t+\Delta t} - \boldsymbol{z}_t$ is d-dimensional and normally distributed with mean vector $\mathbf{0}$ and variance-covariance matrix $\underline{\underline{I}} \times \Delta t$ (here $\underline{\underline{I}}$ is the $d \times d$ identity matrix). The gross rate of return is thus approximately lognormally distributed with mean

$$
\begin{aligned}
\mathrm{E}_t\left[R_{i,t,t+\Delta t}\right] &\approx \exp\left\{\left(\delta_{it} + \mu_{it} - \frac{1}{2}\|\boldsymbol{\sigma}_{it}\|^2\right) \Delta t\right\} \mathrm{E}_t\left[\exp\left\{\boldsymbol{\sigma}_{it}^\top \Delta \boldsymbol{z}_t\right\}\right] \\
&= e^{(\delta_{it} + \mu_{it})\Delta t},
\end{aligned}
$$

compare Appendix B.

The log-return is

$$
\ln R_{i,t,t'} = \int_t^{t'} \left(\delta_{iu} + \mu_{iu} - \frac{1}{2}\|\boldsymbol{\sigma}_{iu}\|^2\right) du + \int_t^{t'} \boldsymbol{\sigma}_{iu}^\top\, d\boldsymbol{z}_u
$$

with mean and variance given by

$$
\begin{aligned}
\mathrm{E}_t[\ln R_{i,t,t'}] &= \int_t^{t'} \mathrm{E}_t\left[\delta_{iu} + \mu_{iu} - \frac{1}{2}\|\boldsymbol{\sigma}_{iu}\|^2\right] du \approx \left(\delta_{it} + \mu_{it} - \frac{1}{2}\|\boldsymbol{\sigma}_{it}\|^2\right) \Delta t, \\
\mathrm{Var}_t[\ln R_{i,t,t'}] &= \int_t^{t'} \mathrm{E}_t\left[\|\boldsymbol{\sigma}_{iu}\|^2\right] du \approx \|\boldsymbol{\sigma}_{it}\|^2 \Delta t,
\end{aligned}
$$

according to Theorem 2.2, where the approximations are useful for a short time period $t' - t = \Delta t$. The expected log-return is (approximately) $\left(\delta_{it} + \mu_{it} - \frac{1}{2}\|\boldsymbol{\sigma}_{it}\|^2\right) \Delta t$, whereas the log of the expected gross rate of return is (approximately) $(\delta_{it} + \mu_{it})\Delta t$. The difference is due to the concavity of the log-function so that Jensen's Inequality implies that $\mathrm{E}[\ln X] \leq \ln \mathrm{E}[X]$ with equality only for the case of a deterministic X.

We can write the dynamics of all I prices compactly as

$$
d\boldsymbol{P}_t = \mathrm{diag}(\boldsymbol{P}_t)\left[\boldsymbol{\mu}_t\, dt + \underline{\underline{\sigma}}_t\, d\boldsymbol{z}_t\right], \tag{3.7}
$$

where $\text{diag}(\boldsymbol{P}_t)$ is defined in (3.1), $\boldsymbol{\mu}_t$ is the vector $(\mu_{1t}, \ldots, \mu_{It})^\top$, and $\underline{\underline{\sigma}}_t$ is the $I \times d$ matrix whose i'th row is $\boldsymbol{\sigma}_{it}^\top$.

A risk-free asset is an asset where the rate of return over the next instant is always known. We can think of this as an asset with a constant price and a continuous dividend yield process $r^f = (r_t^f)_{t\in[0,T]}$ *or* as an asset with a zero continuous dividend yield and a price process accumulating the interest rate payments, $P_t^f = \exp\left\{\int_0^t r_s^f \, ds\right\}$.

3.3 PORTFOLIOS AND TRADING STRATEGIES

Individuals can trade assets at all time points of the model except for the last date. The combination of holdings of different assets at a given point in time is called a *portfolio*. We assume that there are no restrictions on the portfolios that investors may form and that there are no trading costs.

3.3.1 The One-Period Framework

In a one-period model an individual chooses a portfolio $\boldsymbol{\theta} = (\theta_1, \ldots, \theta_I)^\top$ at time 0 with θ_i being the number of units held of asset i. It is not possible to rebalance the portfolio, and the individual simply cashes in the dividends at time 1. Let $D^{\boldsymbol{\theta}}$ be the random variable that represents the dividend of the portfolio $\boldsymbol{\theta}$. If state ω is realized, the total dividend from a portfolio $\boldsymbol{\theta}$ is

$$D^{\boldsymbol{\theta}}(\omega) = \sum_{i=1}^{I} \theta_i D_i(\omega) = \boldsymbol{\theta} \cdot \boldsymbol{D}(\omega),$$

that is $D^{\boldsymbol{\theta}} = \boldsymbol{\theta} \cdot \boldsymbol{D} = \boldsymbol{\theta}^\top \boldsymbol{D}$.

Denote the price or value of a portfolio $\boldsymbol{\theta}$ by $P^{\boldsymbol{\theta}}$. We will throughout this book make the following assumption about prices:

Assumption 3.1 *Prices satisfy* the Law of One Price, *that is prices are linear so that the price of any portfolio* $\boldsymbol{\theta}$ *is given by*

$$P^{\boldsymbol{\theta}} = \sum_{i=1}^{I} \theta_i P_i = \boldsymbol{\theta} \cdot \boldsymbol{P} = \boldsymbol{\theta}^\top \boldsymbol{P}. \tag{3.8}$$

Since we ignore transaction costs, any candidate for an equilibrium pricing system will certainly have this property. In Section 3.4 we will discuss the link between the Law of One Price and the absence of arbitrage.

The fraction of the total portfolio value invested in asset i is then $\pi_i = \theta_i P_i / P^\theta$. The vector $\boldsymbol{\pi} = (\pi_1, \dots, \pi_I)^\top$ is called the *portfolio weight* vector. If we let $\mathbf{1} = (1, \dots, 1)^\top$, we have $\boldsymbol{\pi} \cdot \mathbf{1} = \sum_{i=1}^I \pi_i = 1$. Note that $\operatorname{diag}(\boldsymbol{P})\,\mathbf{1} = \boldsymbol{P}$ and thus $P^\theta = \boldsymbol{P}^\top \boldsymbol{\theta} = \left(\operatorname{diag}(\boldsymbol{P})\,\mathbf{1}\right)^\top \boldsymbol{\theta} = \mathbf{1}^\top \operatorname{diag}(\boldsymbol{P})\boldsymbol{\theta}$ so that

$$\boldsymbol{\pi} = \frac{\operatorname{diag}(\boldsymbol{P})\boldsymbol{\theta}}{\boldsymbol{P}^\top \boldsymbol{\theta}} = \frac{\operatorname{diag}(\boldsymbol{P})\boldsymbol{\theta}}{\mathbf{1}^\top \operatorname{diag}(\boldsymbol{P})\boldsymbol{\theta}}. \tag{3.9}$$

Given $\boldsymbol{\theta}$ and the price vector $\boldsymbol{P}$, we can derive $\boldsymbol{\pi}$. Conversely, given $\boldsymbol{\pi}$, the total portfolio value P^θ, and the price vector $\boldsymbol{P}$, we can derive $\boldsymbol{\theta}$. We therefore have two equivalent ways of representing a portfolio.

The gross rate of return on a portfolio $\boldsymbol{\theta}$ is the random variable

$$R^\theta = \frac{D^\theta}{P^\theta} = \frac{\sum_{i=1}^I \theta_i D_i}{P^\theta} = \frac{\sum_{i=1}^I \theta_i P_i R_i}{P^\theta} = \sum_{i=1}^I \frac{\theta_i P_i}{P^\theta} R_i = \sum_{i=1}^I \pi_i R_i = \boldsymbol{\pi} \cdot \boldsymbol{R}, \tag{3.10}$$

where π_i is the portfolio weight of asset i. We observe that the gross rate of return on a portfolio is just a weighted average of the gross rates of return on the assets in the portfolio. Similarly for the net rate of return since $\sum_{i=1}^I \pi_i = 1$ and thus

$$r^\theta = R^\theta - 1 = \left(\sum_{i=1}^I \pi_i R_i\right) - 1 = \sum_{i=1}^I \pi_i (R_i - 1) = \sum_{i=1}^I \pi_i r_i = \boldsymbol{\pi} \cdot \boldsymbol{r},$$

where $\boldsymbol{r} = (r_1, \dots, r_I)^\top$ is the vector of net rates of return on the basic assets.

3.3.2 The Discrete-Time Framework

In a multiperiod model individuals are allowed to rebalance their portfolio at any date considered in the model. A *trading strategy* is an I-dimensional adapted stochastic process $\boldsymbol{\theta} = (\boldsymbol{\theta}_t)_{t \in \mathcal{T}}$ where $\boldsymbol{\theta}_t = (\theta_{1t}, \dots, \theta_{It})^\top$ denotes the portfolio held at time t or rather immediately after trading at time t. Here θ_{it} is the number of units of asset i held at time t.

A trading strategy $\boldsymbol{\theta}$ generates a dividend process D^θ. Immediately before time t the portfolio is given by $\boldsymbol{\theta}_{t-1}$ so the investor will receive dividends $\boldsymbol{\theta}_{t-1} \cdot \boldsymbol{D}_t$ at time t and then rebalance the portfolio to $\boldsymbol{\theta}_t$ immediately after time t. The net gain or dividend at time t is therefore equal to

$$\begin{aligned} D_t^\theta &= \boldsymbol{\theta}_{t-1} \cdot \boldsymbol{D}_t - (\boldsymbol{\theta}_t - \boldsymbol{\theta}_{t-1}) \cdot \boldsymbol{P}_t \\ &= \boldsymbol{\theta}_{t-1} \cdot (\boldsymbol{P}_t + \boldsymbol{D}_t) - \boldsymbol{\theta}_t \cdot \boldsymbol{P}_t, \quad t = 1, 2, \dots, T-1. \end{aligned} \tag{3.11}$$

We can think of this as a budget constraint saying that the sum of the withdrawn dividend and our additional investment $(\boldsymbol{\theta}_t - \boldsymbol{\theta}_{t-1}) \cdot \boldsymbol{P}_t$ has to equal the dividends we receive from the current portfolio. The terminal dividend is

$$D_T^{\theta} = \boldsymbol{\theta}_{T-1} \cdot \boldsymbol{D}_T.$$

Given the Law of One Price, the initial price of the trading strategy is $P^{\theta} = \boldsymbol{\theta}_0 \cdot \boldsymbol{P}_0$. We can let $D_0^{\theta} = 0$ so that the dividend process D^{θ} is defined at all $t \in \mathcal{T}$.

For $t = 1, \dots, T$ define

$$V_t^{\theta} = \boldsymbol{\theta}_{t-1} \cdot (\boldsymbol{P}_t + \boldsymbol{D}_t)$$

which is the time t value of the portfolio chosen at the previous trading date. This is the value of the portfolio just after dividends are received at time t and before the portfolio is rebalanced. Define $V_0^{\theta} = \boldsymbol{\theta}_0 \cdot \boldsymbol{P}_0$. We call $V^{\theta} = (V_t^{\theta})_{t \in \mathcal{T}}$ the *value process* of the trading strategy $\boldsymbol{\theta}$. According to Eq. (3.11), we have $V_t^{\theta} = D_t^{\theta} + \boldsymbol{\theta}_t \cdot \boldsymbol{P}_t$ for $t = 1, \dots, T$ and, in particular, $V_T^{\theta} = D_T^{\theta}$. The change in the value of the trading strategy between two adjacent dates is

$$\begin{aligned} V_{t+1}^{\theta} - V_t^{\theta} &= \boldsymbol{\theta}_t \cdot (\boldsymbol{P}_{t+1} + \boldsymbol{D}_{t+1}) - \boldsymbol{\theta}_{t-1} \cdot (\boldsymbol{P}_t + \boldsymbol{D}_t) \\ &= \boldsymbol{\theta}_t \cdot (\boldsymbol{P}_{t+1} + \boldsymbol{D}_{t+1}) - D_t^{\theta} - \boldsymbol{\theta}_t \cdot \boldsymbol{P}_t \\ &= \boldsymbol{\theta}_t \cdot (\boldsymbol{P}_{t+1} - \boldsymbol{P}_t + \boldsymbol{D}_{t+1}) - D_t^{\theta}. \end{aligned} \tag{3.12}$$

The first term on the right-hand side of the last expression is the net return on the portfolio $\boldsymbol{\theta}_t$ from time t to $t+1$, the latter term is the net dividend we have withdrawn at time t.

The trading strategy is said to be *self-financing* if all the intermediate dividends are zero, that is if $D_t^{\theta} = 0$ for $t = 1, \dots, T-1$. Using Eq. (3.11) this means that

$$(\boldsymbol{\theta}_t - \boldsymbol{\theta}_{t-1}) \cdot \boldsymbol{P}_t = \boldsymbol{\theta}_{t-1} \cdot \boldsymbol{D}_t, \quad t = 1, \dots, T-1.$$

The left-hand side is the extra investment due to the rebalancing at time t, the right-hand side is the dividend received at time t. A self-financing trading strategy requires an initial investment of $P^{\theta} = \boldsymbol{\theta}_0 \cdot \boldsymbol{P}_0$ and generates a terminal dividend of $D_T^{\theta} = \boldsymbol{\theta}_{T-1} \cdot \boldsymbol{D}_T$. At the intermediate dates no money is invested or withdrawn so increasing the investment in some assets must be fully financed by dividends or by selling other assets. If $\boldsymbol{\theta}$ is self-financing, we have $V_t^{\theta} = P_t^{\theta} \equiv \boldsymbol{\theta}_t \cdot \boldsymbol{P}_t$, the time t price of the portfolio $\boldsymbol{\theta}_t$, for $t = 0, 1, \dots, T-1$. Moreover, the change in the value of the trading strategy is just the net return as can be seen from Eq. (3.12).

For any trading strategy $\boldsymbol{\theta}$ we can, at any point in time, compute a portfolio weight vector $\boldsymbol{\pi}_t$ corresponding to the vector $\boldsymbol{\theta}_t$ of units of the individual assets, exactly as in the one-period setting, see Eq. (3.9). The return on a self-financing trading strategy over any period of time can be computed as for single assets, see Eq. (3.3).

3.3.3 The Continuous-Time Framework

Also in the continuous-time framework with $\mathcal{T} = [0, T]$, a trading strategy is an I-dimensional adapted stochastic process $\boldsymbol{\theta} = (\boldsymbol{\theta}_t)_{t \in \mathcal{T}}$ where $\boldsymbol{\theta}_t = (\theta_{1t}, \dots, \theta_{It})^{\top}$ denotes the portfolio held at time t or rather immediately after trading at time t.

Consistent with the discrete-time framework we define the value of the trading strategy $\boldsymbol{\theta}$ at any given time t as the price of the portfolio just chosen at that time plus any lump-sum dividends received at that time. Since we only allow for lump-sum dividends at the terminal date, we define

$$V_t^{\boldsymbol{\theta}} = \boldsymbol{\theta}_t \cdot \boldsymbol{P}_t, \quad t < T$$

and $V_T^{\boldsymbol{\theta}} = \boldsymbol{\theta}_T \cdot \boldsymbol{D}_T \equiv D_T^{\boldsymbol{\theta}}$, the terminal lump-sum dividend. The time 0 value is the cost of initiating the trading strategy. We assume that between time 0 and time T no lump-sum dividends can be withdrawn from the investment, but funds can be withdrawn at a continuous rate as represented by the process $\alpha^{\boldsymbol{\theta}} = (\alpha_t^{\boldsymbol{\theta}})$. Intermediate lump-sum withdrawals could be allowed at the expense of additional notational complexity. For later use note that an application of Itô's Lemma, Theorem 2.8, implies that the increment to the value process is given by

$$dV_t^{\boldsymbol{\theta}} = \boldsymbol{\theta}_t \cdot d\boldsymbol{P}_t + d\boldsymbol{\theta}_t \cdot \boldsymbol{P}_t + d\boldsymbol{\theta}_t \cdot d\boldsymbol{P}_t. \tag{3.13}$$

Assume for a moment that we do not change our portfolio over a small time interval $[t, t + \Delta t]$. The total funds withdrawn over this interval are $\alpha_t^{\boldsymbol{\theta}} \Delta t$. Let $\Delta\boldsymbol{\theta}_{t+\Delta t} = \boldsymbol{\theta}_{t+\Delta t} - \boldsymbol{\theta}_t$ and $\Delta \boldsymbol{P}_{t+\Delta t} = \boldsymbol{P}_{t+\Delta t} - \boldsymbol{P}_t$. The total dividends received from the portfolio $\boldsymbol{\theta}_t$ over the interval are $\sum_{i=1}^{I} \theta_{it}\delta_{it}P_{it}\Delta t$, which we can rewrite as $\boldsymbol{\theta}_t^{\top} \operatorname{diag}(\boldsymbol{P}_t)\boldsymbol{\delta}_t\Delta t$ where $\operatorname{diag}(\boldsymbol{P}_t)$ is the matrix defined in Eq. (3.1). Then the budget constraint over this interval is

$$\alpha_t^{\boldsymbol{\theta}} \Delta t + \Delta\boldsymbol{\theta}_{t+\Delta t} \cdot \boldsymbol{P}_{t+\Delta t} = \boldsymbol{\theta}_t^{\top} \operatorname{diag}(\boldsymbol{P}_t)\boldsymbol{\delta}_t\Delta t.$$

The left-hand side is the sum of the funds we withdraw and the net extra investment. The right-hand side is the funds we receive in dividends. Let us add and subtract $\Delta\boldsymbol{\theta}_{t+\Delta t} \cdot \boldsymbol{P}_t$ in the above equation. Rearranging we obtain

$$\alpha_t^{\boldsymbol{\theta}} \Delta t + \Delta\boldsymbol{\theta}_{t+\Delta t} \cdot \Delta\boldsymbol{P}_{t+\Delta t} + \Delta\boldsymbol{\theta}_{t+\Delta t} \cdot \boldsymbol{P}_t = \boldsymbol{\theta}_t^{\top} \operatorname{diag}(\boldsymbol{P}_t)\boldsymbol{\delta}_t\Delta t.$$

The equivalent equation for an infinitesimal interval $[t, t + dt]$ is

$$\alpha_t^{\boldsymbol{\theta}}\, dt + d\boldsymbol{\theta}_t \cdot d\boldsymbol{P}_t + d\boldsymbol{\theta}_t \cdot \boldsymbol{P}_t = \boldsymbol{\theta}_t^{\top} \operatorname{diag}(\boldsymbol{P}_t)\boldsymbol{\delta}_t\, dt.$$

Using this, we can rewrite the value dynamics in Eq. (3.13) as

$$dV_t^{\theta} = \theta_t \cdot dP_t + \theta_t^{\top} \operatorname{diag}(P_t)\delta_t \, dt - \alpha_t^{\theta} \, dt.$$

Substituting in Eq. (3.7), this implies that

$$dV_t^{\theta} = \theta_t^{\top} \operatorname{diag}(P_t) \left[(\mu_t + \delta_t) \, dt + \underline{\underline{\sigma}}_t \, dz_t \right] - \alpha_t^{\theta} \, dt.$$

As discussed earlier we can define a portfolio weight vector

$$\pi_t = \frac{\operatorname{diag}(P_t)\theta_t}{P_t^{\top}\theta_t} = \frac{\operatorname{diag}(P_t)\theta_t}{V_t^{\theta}}.$$

The value dynamics can therefore be rewritten as

$$dV_t^{\theta} = V_t^{\theta}\pi_t^{\top} \left[(\mu_t + \delta_t) \, dt + \underline{\underline{\sigma}}_t \, dz_t \right] - \alpha_t^{\theta} \, dt. \tag{3.14}$$

A trading strategy is called *self-financing* if no funds are withdrawn, that is $\alpha_t^{\theta} \equiv 0$. In that case the value dynamics is simply

$$dV_t^{\theta} = \theta_t^{\top} \operatorname{diag}(P_t) \left[(\mu_t + \delta_t) \, dt + \underline{\underline{\sigma}}_t \, dz_t \right] = V_t^{\theta}\pi_t^{\top} \left[(\mu_t + \delta_t) \, dt + \underline{\underline{\sigma}}_t \, dz_t \right].$$

This really means that for any $t \in (0, T)$,

$$\begin{aligned} V_t^{\theta} &= \theta_0 \cdot P_0 + \int_0^t \theta_s^{\top} \operatorname{diag}(P_s) \left[(\mu_s + \delta_s) \, ds + \underline{\underline{\sigma}}_s \, dz_s \right] \\ &= \theta_0 \cdot P_0 + \int_0^t \theta_s^{\top} \operatorname{diag}(P_s) (\mu_s + \delta_s) \, ds + \int_0^t \theta_s^{\top} \operatorname{diag}(P_s) \underline{\underline{\sigma}}_s \, dz_s. \end{aligned}$$

The return on a self-financing trading strategy over any period of time can be computed as for single assets.

3.4 ARBITRAGE

We have already made an assumption about prices, namely that prices obey the Law of One Price or, in other words, prices are linear. We will generally make the stronger assumption that prices are set so that there is no *arbitrage*. An arbitrage is basically a risk-free profit or 'money for nothing'.

3.4.1 The One-Period Framework

In the one-period framework we define an arbitrage as follows:

Definition 3.1 *In a one-period setting, an arbitrage is a portfolio $\boldsymbol{\theta}$ satisfying one of the following two conditions:*

(i) $P^{\boldsymbol{\theta}} < 0$ *and* $D^{\boldsymbol{\theta}} \geq 0$,
(ii) $P^{\boldsymbol{\theta}} \leq 0$ *and* $D^{\boldsymbol{\theta}} \geq 0$ *with* $\mathbb{P}\left(D^{\boldsymbol{\theta}} > 0\right) > 0$.

Recall that $D^{\boldsymbol{\theta}}$ is the random variable representing the dividend of the portfolio $\boldsymbol{\theta}$. The inequality $D^{\boldsymbol{\theta}} \geq 0$ means that the dividend will be non-negative no matter which state is realized, that is $D^{\boldsymbol{\theta}}(\omega) \geq 0$ for all $\omega \in \Omega$. In a finite-state economy this can be replaced by the condition $\boldsymbol{D}^{\boldsymbol{\theta}} \geq 0$ on the dividend vector, which means that all elements of the vector are non-negative. The condition $\mathbb{P}\left(D^{\boldsymbol{\theta}} > 0\right) > 0$ can then be replaced by the condition $\boldsymbol{D}^{\boldsymbol{\theta}}_{\omega} > 0$ for some state ω.

An arbitrage offers something for nothing. It offers a non-negative dividend no matter which state is realized and its price is non-positive so that you do not have to pay anything. Either you get something today (case (i)) or you get something at the end in some state (case (ii)). This is clearly attractive to any greedy individual, that is any individual preferring more to less. Therefore, a market with arbitrage cannot be a market in equilibrium. Since we are interested in equilibrium pricing systems, we need only worry about pricing systems that do not admit arbitrage.

Arbitrage is linked to the Law of One Price in the following way:

Theorem 3.1 *If prices in a financial market do not allow for arbitrage, then the Law of One Price holds.*

Proof. Given any portfolio $\boldsymbol{\theta}$, we need to show that $P^{\boldsymbol{\theta}} = \boldsymbol{\theta}^{\top}\boldsymbol{P}$. Suppose that $P^{\boldsymbol{\theta}} < \boldsymbol{\theta} \cdot \boldsymbol{P}$. Then an arbitrage can be formed by purchasing the portfolio $\boldsymbol{\theta}$ for the price of $P^{\boldsymbol{\theta}}$ and, for each $i = 1, \ldots, I$, selling θ_i units of asset i at a unit price of P_i. The end-of-period net dividend from this position will be zero no matter which state is realized. The total initial price of the position is $P^{\boldsymbol{\theta}} - \boldsymbol{\theta} \cdot \boldsymbol{P}$, which is negative. Hence, in the absence of arbitrage, we cannot have that $P^{\boldsymbol{\theta}} < \boldsymbol{\theta} \cdot \boldsymbol{P}$. The inequality $P^{\boldsymbol{\theta}} > \boldsymbol{\theta} \cdot \boldsymbol{P}$ can be ruled out by a similar argument. □

On the other hand, the Law of One Price does not rule out arbitrage. For example, suppose that there are two possible states. Asset 1 gives a dividend of 0 in state 1 and a dividend of 1 in state 2 and costs 0.9. Asset 2 gives a dividend of 1 in state 1 and a dividend of 2 in state 2 and costs 1.6. Suppose the Law of One Price holds so that the price of any portfolio $(\theta_1, \theta_2)^{\top}$ is $0.9\theta_1 + 1.6\theta_2$. Consider the portfolio $(-2, 1)^{\top}$, that is a short position in two units of asset 1 and a long position of one unit of asset 2. The dividend of this portfolio will be 1 in state 1 and 0 in state 2 and the price is $0.9 \times (-2) + 1.6 \times 1 = -0.2$. This portfolio is clearly an arbitrage.

3.4.2 The Discrete-Time and Continuous-Time Frameworks

In both the discrete-time and the continuous-time frameworks we define an arbitrage like this:

Definition 3.2 *In a multiperiod economy, an arbitrage is a self-financing trading strategy $\boldsymbol{\theta}$ satisfying one of the following two conditions:*

(i) $V_0^{\boldsymbol{\theta}} < 0$ and $V_T^{\boldsymbol{\theta}} \geq 0$ with probability one,

(ii) $V_0^{\boldsymbol{\theta}} \leq 0$, $V_T^{\boldsymbol{\theta}} \geq 0$ with probability one, and $V_T^{\boldsymbol{\theta}} > 0$ with strictly positive probability.

As we have seen above, $V_T^{\boldsymbol{\theta}} = D_T^{\boldsymbol{\theta}}$ and $V_0^{\boldsymbol{\theta}} = P^{\boldsymbol{\theta}}$ for self-financing trading strategies. A self-financing trading strategy is an arbitrage if it generates non-negative initial and terminal dividends with one of them being strictly positive with a strictly positive probability. Due to our assumptions on the dividends of the individual assets, the absence of arbitrage will imply that the prices of individual assets are strictly positive.

Ruling out arbitrages defined in (i) and (ii) will also rule out shorter term risk-free gains. Suppose for example that we can construct a trading strategy with a non-positive initial value (that is a non-positive price), always non-negative values, and a strictly positive value at some time $t < T$. Then this strictly positive value can be invested in any asset until time T generating a strictly positive terminal value with a strictly positive probability. The focus on self-financing trading strategies is therefore no restriction. Note that the definition of an arbitrage implies that a self-financing trading strategy with a terminal dividend of zero (in any state) must have a value process identically equal to zero.

3.4.3 Continuous-Time Doubling Strategies

In a continuous-time setting it is theoretically possible to construct some strategies that generate something for nothing. These are the so-called *doubling strategies*, which were apparently first mentioned in a finance setting by Harrison and Kreps (1979). Think of a series of coin tosses numbered $n = 1, 2, \ldots$. The n'th coin toss takes place at time $1 - 1/n \in [0, 1)$. In the n'th toss, you get $\alpha 2^{n-1}$ if heads comes up, and loses $\alpha 2^{n-1}$ otherwise, where α is some positive number. You stop betting the first time heads comes up. Suppose heads comes up the first time in toss number $k + 1$. Then in the first k tosses you have lost a total of $\alpha(1 + 2 + \cdots + 2^{k-1}) = \alpha(2^k - 1)$. Since you win $\alpha 2^k$ in toss number $k + 1$, your total profit will be $\alpha 2^k - \alpha(2^k - 1) = \alpha$. Since the probability that heads comes up eventually is equal to one, you will gain α with probability one. The gain is obtained before time 1 and can be made as large as possible by increasing α.

Similar strategies, with appropriate discounting of future dividends, can be constructed in continuous-time models of financial markets—at least if a risk-free asset is traded—but these strategies are clearly impossible to implement in real life. As shown by Dybvig and Huang (1988), doubling strategies can be ruled out by requiring that trading strategies have values that are bounded from below, that is that some constant K exists such that $V_t^{\theta} \geq -K$ for all t. A trading strategy satisfying such a condition is said to be credit-constrained. A lower bound is reasonable since nobody can borrow an infinite amount of money. If you have a limited borrowing potential, the doubling strategy described above cannot be implemented. If you have no future income at all, $K = 0$ seems reasonable. An alternative way of eliminating doubling strategies is to impose the condition that the value process of the trading strategy has finite variance, compare Duffie (2001). For a doubling strategy the variance of the value process is, in fact, infinite.

It seems evident that any greedy investor would implement a doubling strategy, if possible, since the investor will make a positive net return with a probability of one in finite time. However, Omberg (1989) shows that a doubling strategy may in fact generate an expected utility of minus infinity for risk-averse investors. In some events of zero probability, a doubling strategy may result in outcomes associated with a utility of minus infinity. When multiplying zero and minus infinity in order to compute the expected utility, the result is indeterminate. Omberg computes the actual expected utility of the doubling strategy by taking an appropriate limit and finds that this is minus infinity for commonly used utility functions that are unbounded from below. Although this questions the above definition of an arbitrage, we will stick to that definition which is also the standard of the literature.

In the rest of this book we will—often implicitly—assume that some conditions are imposed so that doubling strategies are not implementable or nobody wants to implement them.

3.5 REDUNDANT ASSETS

An asset is said to be *redundant* if its dividends can be replicated by a trading strategy in other assets. For example, in the one-period framework asset i is redundant if a portfolio $\boldsymbol{\theta} = (\theta_1, \dots, \theta_I)^{\top}$ exists with $\theta_i = 0$ and

$$D_i = D^{\boldsymbol{\theta}} \equiv \theta_1 D_1 + \cdots + \theta_{i-1} D_{i-1} + \theta_{i+1} D_{i+1} + \cdots + \theta_I D_I.$$

Recall that the dividends are random variables so the above equation really means that

$$D_i(\omega) = \theta_1 D_1(\omega) + \dots + \theta_{i-1} D_{i-1}(\omega) + \theta_{i+1} D_{i+1}(\omega) + \dots + \theta_I D_I(\omega),$$
$$\forall \omega \in \Omega.$$

Such a portfolio is called a *replicating portfolio* for asset i. In other words, when the dividends of all the assets are linearly dependent, then at least one of the assets is redundant.

If an asset i is redundant, its price follows immediately from the Law of One Price:

$$P_i = \theta_1 P_1 + \dots + \theta_{i-1} P_{i-1} + \theta_{i+1} P_{i+1} + \dots + \theta_I P_I.$$

We can thus focus on pricing the non-redundant assets, then the prices of all the other assets, the redundant assets, follow.

Note that the number of non-redundant assets cannot exceed the number of states. If there are more assets than states, there will be some redundant asset.

Example 3.1 Consider a one-period economy with three possible end-of-period states and four traded assets. The dividends are given in Table 3.1. With four assets and three states at least one asset is redundant. The dividend vector of asset 4 can be written as a non-trivial linear combination of the dividend vectors of assets 1, 2, and 3 since

$$\begin{pmatrix} 1 \\ 1 \\ 1 \end{pmatrix} - \begin{pmatrix} 0 \\ 1 \\ 2 \end{pmatrix} + 2 \begin{pmatrix} 4 \\ 0 \\ 1 \end{pmatrix} = \begin{pmatrix} 9 \\ 0 \\ 1 \end{pmatrix}.$$

A portfolio of one unit of asset 1, minus one unit of asset 2, and two units of asset 3 perfectly replicates the dividend of asset 4, which is therefore redundant. In terms of random variables, we have the relation

$$D_1 - D_2 + 2D_3 = D_4$$

among the dividends of the four assets. On the other hand, asset 1 is redundant since it can be perfectly replicated by a portfolio of one unit of asset 2, minus two units of asset 3, and one unit of asset 4. Similarly, asset 2 is redundant and asset 3 is redundant. Hence, either of the four assets can be removed without affecting the set of dividend vectors that can be generated by forming portfolios. Note that once one of the assets has been removed, neither of the three remaining assets will be redundant anymore. Whether an asset is redundant or not depends on the set of other assets available for trade. This implies that we must remove redundant assets one by one: first we remove one redundant asset, then we look for another asset which is still redundant—if we find one, we can remove that, and so on. □

In the multiperiod model an asset is said to be redundant if its dividend process can be generated by a trading strategy in the other assets. In the discrete-

Table 3.1. The state-contingent dividends of the assets considered in Example 3.1.

	State-contingent dividend		
	State 1	State 2	State 3
Asset 1	1	1	1
Asset 2	0	1	2
Asset 3	4	0	1
Asset 4	9	0	1

time framework, asset i is redundant if there exists a trading strategy $\boldsymbol{\theta}$ with $\boldsymbol{\theta}_{it} = 0$ for all t and all ω so that

$$D_{it} = D_t^{\theta} \equiv \boldsymbol{\theta}_{t-1} \cdot (\boldsymbol{D}_t + \boldsymbol{P}_t) - \boldsymbol{\theta}_t \cdot \boldsymbol{P}_t, \quad t = 1, \dots, T.$$

Such a $\boldsymbol{\theta}$ is called a *replicating trading strategy* for asset i.

Just as in the one-period setting, redundant assets are uniquely priced by no-arbitrage.

Theorem 3.2 *If $\boldsymbol{\theta}$ is a replicating trading strategy for asset i, the unique arbitrage-free price of asset i at any time t is*

$$P_{it} = \boldsymbol{\theta}_t \cdot \boldsymbol{P}_t.$$

Proof. The trading strategy $\hat{\boldsymbol{\theta}}$ defined by $\hat{\boldsymbol{\theta}}_t = \boldsymbol{\theta}_t - \boldsymbol{e}_i$, where $\boldsymbol{e}_i = (0, \dots, 0, 1, 0, \dots, 0)^{\top}$, is self-financing and $V_T^{\hat{\theta}} = 0$. No-arbitrage implies that $V_t^{\hat{\theta}} = 0$. The result now follows since $V_t^{\hat{\theta}} = \hat{\boldsymbol{\theta}}_t \cdot \boldsymbol{P}_t = \boldsymbol{\theta}_t \cdot \boldsymbol{P}_t - P_{it}$. □

The above definition of redundancy can be generalized to a continuous-time setting, where the theorem is also valid.

The theorem is useful for the pricing of derivatives and applied, for example, in the Cox, Ross, and Rubinstein (1979) binomial model (see Exercise 3.1 at the end of this chapter) and the Black and Scholes (1973) continuous-time model for the pricing of stock options. There is more on derivatives pricing in Chapter 13.

3.6 MARKET COMPLETENESS

By forming portfolios and trading strategies investors can generate other dividends than those offered by the individual basic assets. Any dividend that can be generated by trading the basic assets is said to be a *marketed dividend* or to be *spanned by traded assets*. If all the dividends you can think of are marketed, the financial market is said to be *complete*. Otherwise the financial market is said to be incomplete. We will see in later chapters that some important results will depend on whether the financial market is complete or incomplete. Below we provide formal definitions and characterize complete markets.

3.6.1 The One-Period Framework

In the one-period framework dividends are random variables. A random variable is said to be a marketed dividend if it is identical to the dividend of some portfolio of the traded assets. The dividend of a portfolio $\boldsymbol{\theta}$ is the random variable $D^{\boldsymbol{\theta}} = \boldsymbol{\theta} \cdot \boldsymbol{D}$. The set of marketed dividends is thus

$$\mathcal{M} = \left\{ x \,|\, x = \boldsymbol{\theta} \cdot \boldsymbol{D} \text{ for some portfolio } \boldsymbol{\theta} \right\}.$$

Note that $\mathcal{M}$ is a subset of the set $\mathcal{L}$ of all random variables on the probability space $(\Omega, \mathcal{F}, \mathbb{P})$ with finite variance. Intuitively, $\mathcal{L}$ consists of all the dividends investors could potentially be interested in.

Definition 3.3 *The financial market is said to be complete if* $\mathcal{M} = \mathcal{L}$.

If some of the basic assets are redundant, they will not help us in generating dividends. Suppose that there are $k \leq I$ non-redundant assets. The k-dimensional random variable of dividends of these assets is denoted by $\hat{\boldsymbol{D}}$ and a portfolio of these assets is denoted by a k-dimensional vector $\hat{\boldsymbol{\theta}}$. We can obtain exactly the same dividends by using only the non-redundant assets as by using all dividends so

$$\mathcal{M} = \left\{ x \,|\, x = \hat{\boldsymbol{\theta}} \cdot \hat{\boldsymbol{D}} \text{ for some portfolio } \hat{\boldsymbol{\theta}} \right\}.$$

With k non-redundant assets, the set of marketed dividends will be a k-dimensional linear subspace in $\mathcal{L}$. You have k choice variables, namely how much to invest in each of the k non-redundant assets. The dimension of $\mathcal{L}$ equals the number of possible states. For each state ω you have to make sure that the dividend of the portfolio will equal the desired dividend $x(\omega)$. Whether the market is complete or not is therefore determined by the relation between the number of states and the number of non-redundant assets. If the state space is infinite, the market is clearly incomplete.

With a finite state space $\Omega = \{1, 2, \ldots, S\}$, there can be at most S non-redundant assets, that is $k \leq S$. If $k < S$, the market will be incomplete. If $k = S$, the market will be complete. Here is the mathematical explanation: with a finite state space, dividends can be represented by S-dimensional vectors and the dividends of all the I basic assets by the $I \times S$ dividend matrix $\underline{\underline{D}}$. A marketed dividend is then an S-dimensional vector $\boldsymbol{x}$ for which a portfolio $\boldsymbol{\theta}$ can be found such that

$$\underline{\underline{D}}^{\mathsf{T}}\boldsymbol{\theta} = \boldsymbol{x}.$$

Removing redundant assets we eliminate rows in the dividend matrix $\underline{\underline{D}}$. As long as one of the assets is redundant, the rows of $\underline{\underline{D}}$ will be linearly dependent. The maximum number of linearly independent rows of a matrix is called the *rank* of the matrix. It can be shown that this is also the maximum number of linearly independent columns of the matrix. With k non-redundant assets, the rank of $\underline{\underline{D}}$ is equal to k. Removing the rows corresponding to those assets from $\underline{\underline{D}}$ we obtain a matrix $\hat{\underline{\underline{D}}}$ of dimension $k \times S$, where $k \leq S$ since we cannot have more than S linearly independent S-dimensional vectors. Then the set of marketed dividend vectors is

$$\mathcal{M} = \left\{ \hat{\underline{\underline{D}}}^{\mathsf{T}}\hat{\boldsymbol{\theta}} \mid \hat{\boldsymbol{\theta}} \in \mathbb{R}^k \right\}$$

since we can attain the same dividend vectors by forming portfolios of only the non-redundant assets as by forming portfolios of all the assets.

In the finite-state economy, the market is complete if $\mathcal{M} = \mathbb{R}^S$, that is any state-contingent dividend can be generated by forming portfolios of the traded assets. The market is complete if and only if for any $\boldsymbol{x} \in \mathbb{R}^S$, we can find $\boldsymbol{\theta} \in \mathbb{R}^I$ such that

$$\underline{\underline{D}}^{\mathsf{T}}\boldsymbol{\theta} = \boldsymbol{x}.$$

Market completeness is thus a question of when we can solve S equations in I unknowns. From linear algebra we have the following result:

Theorem 3.3 *With a finite state space, $\Omega = \{1, 2, \ldots, S\}$, the market is complete if and only if the rank of the $I \times S$ dividend matrix $\underline{\underline{D}}$ is equal to S.*

Clearly, a necessary (but not sufficient) condition for a complete market is that $I \geq S$, that is that there are at least as many assets as states. If the market is complete, the 'pruned' dividend matrix $\hat{\underline{\underline{D}}}$ will be a non-singular $S \times S$ matrix.

Example 3.2 Consider an economy with only two states. First suppose that a single asset is traded and that this asset provides a dividend of 2 in state 1 and a dividend of 1 in state 2. This corresponds to the black arrow in Fig. 3.1. An investor who can only trade in this asset can obtain all the dividend vectors corresponding to the grey line through the origin. Since he cannot obtain dividend vectors off the line, the market is incomplete. A second asset with a dividend vector that is already on the grey line would be redundant and not expand the set of marketed dividends. When adding such an asset to the market, the market would still be incomplete. In contrast, if we add a second asset with a dividend vector that is not on the grey line, we would have two linearly independent and thus non-redundant assets, and the market will then

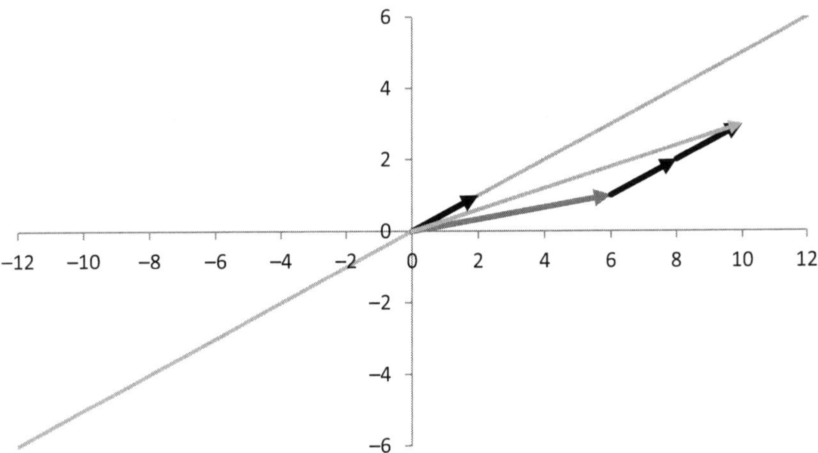

Fig. 3.1. Dividends in a two-state economy.

Notes: The black arrow from the origin corresponds to the asset with dividend vector $(2, 1)^{\top}$. The thick dark-grey arrow from the origin corresponds to the asset with dividend vector $(6, 1)^{\top}$. The light-grey arrow from the origin shows that the dividend vector $(10, 3)^{\top}$ can be obtained by a portfolio of two units of the asset with dividend vector $(2, 1)^{\top}$ and one unit of the asset with dividend vector $(6, 1)^{\top}$

be complete. Any dividend vector in $\mathbb{R}^2$ can be obtained by some combination of the two non-redundant assets. For example, as illustrated in the figure, if the dividend vector of the second asset is $(6, 1)^{\top}$, we can obtain the dividend vector $(10, 3)^{\top}$ by forming a portfolio of two units of the first asset with dividend $(2, 1)^{\top}$ and one unit of the second asset with dividend $(6, 1)^{\top}$. □

Example 3.3 The market considered in Example 3.1 is complete since there are as many non-redundant assets as there are states. Any potential dividend vector can be formed by some portfolio of three of the traded assets. For example, if we let $\underline{\underline{D}}$ be the dividend matrix of the first three assets, we can generate any dividend vector $\boldsymbol{x}$ by solving $\underline{\underline{D}}^{\top}\boldsymbol{\theta} = \boldsymbol{x}$ for the portfolio $\boldsymbol{\theta}$ of the first three assets, that is $\boldsymbol{\theta} = \left(\underline{\underline{D}}^{\top}\right)^{-1} \boldsymbol{x}$. In the present case, we have

$$\underline{\underline{D}} = \begin{pmatrix} 1 & 1 & 1 \\ 0 & 1 & 2 \\ 4 & 0 & 1 \end{pmatrix}, \; \underline{\underline{D}}^{\top} = \begin{pmatrix} 1 & 0 & 4 \\ 1 & 1 & 0 \\ 1 & 2 & 1 \end{pmatrix}, \; (\underline{\underline{D}}^{\top})^{-1} = \begin{pmatrix} 0.2 & 1.6 & -0.8 \\ -0.2 & -0.6 & 0.8 \\ 0.2 & -0.4 & 0.2 \end{pmatrix}.$$

For example, the portfolio providing a dividend vector of $(5, -10, 5)^{\top}$ is given by

$$\boldsymbol{\theta} = \begin{pmatrix} 0.2 & 1.6 & -0.8 \\ -0.2 & -0.6 & 0.8 \\ 0.2 & -0.4 & 0.2 \end{pmatrix} \begin{pmatrix} 5 \\ -10 \\ 5 \end{pmatrix} = \begin{pmatrix} -19 \\ 9 \\ 6 \end{pmatrix}.$$

□

3.6.2 Multiperiod Framework

In a multiperiod setting the market is said to be complete if any imaginable state-dependent terminal payoff can be obtained by a self-financing trading strategy in the basic assets. The terminal payoff is represented by a random variable on the probability space $(\Omega, \mathcal{F}, \mathbb{P})$ since $\mathcal{F}_T = \mathcal{F}$. Hence, the market is complete if for any random variable X there is a trading strategy $\boldsymbol{\theta}$ such that $D_T^{\boldsymbol{\theta}} = X$ in all states. Let $\mathcal{M}$ represent the set of marketed terminal dividends, that is the set of random variables $D^{\boldsymbol{\theta}}$ for all self-financing trading strategies $\boldsymbol{\theta}$. Then market completeness is still defined by Definition 3.3.

If you think of a payment before the terminal date T, this can be transformed into a terminal payment by investing it in a given asset until time T. Hence the definition covers all relevant dates, and the market will thus be complete if any adapted stochastic process can be generated by some trading strategy in the given assets.

How many assets do we need in order to have a complete market? In the one-period model, Theorem 3.3 tells us that with S possible states we need S sufficiently different assets for the market to be complete. To generalize this result to the multiperiod setting we must be careful. Consider once again the two-period model illustrated in Figs 2.1 and 2.2 in Chapter 2. Here there are six possible outcomes, that is Ω has six elements. Hence, one might think that we need access to trade in at least six sufficiently different assets in order for the market to be complete. This is not correct. We can do with fewer assets. This is based on two observations: (i) the uncertainty is not revealed completely at once, but little by little, and (ii) we can trade dynamically in the assets. In the example there are three possible transitions of the economy from time 0 to time 1. From our one-period analysis we know that three sufficiently different assets are enough to 'span' this uncertainty. From time 1 to time 2 there are either two, three, or one possible transition of the economy, depending on which state the economy is in at time 1. At most, we need three sufficiently different assets to span the uncertainty over this period. In total, we can generate any dividend process if we just have access to three sufficiently different assets in both periods.

If we think of the multinomial tree version of a more general, finite-state discrete-time market, we can for each node in the tree define the *spanning number* as the number of branches of the subtree leaving that node. The market is then complete if, for any node in the tree, the number of linearly independent traded assets over the following period is equal to the spanning number.

Loosely speaking, 'linearly independent' assets are 'sufficiently different'. In the one-period setting, this means that the matrix of the dividends of the assets in a given period is of full rank. In the discrete-time multiperiod model the value of a given asset at the end of each period is the sum of the price and the dividend in that period. The relevant matrix is therefore the matrix of possible values of price plus dividend at the end of the period. This matrix tells us how the assets will react to the exogenous shocks over that sub-period. If we have at least as many assets that respond sufficiently differently to the shocks as we have possible realizations of these shocks, we can completely hedge the shocks. Note that these observations imply that, in general, you cannot decide whether a market is complete or not just by looking at the possible dividends of the traded assets, you have to take into account the dynamics of the equilibrium asset prices.

Next, think about a continuous-time model in which the uncertainty is generated by a d-dimensional standard Brownian motion. Then the state space is infinite, but nevertheless the market can be complete! Here is the precise result:

Theorem 3.4 *A continuous-time financial market with uncertainty generated by a d-dimensional standard Brownian motion is complete if, at all points in time, investors can trade in an instantaneously risk-free asset and d risky assets having a price sensitivity matrix* $\underline{\underline{\sigma}}_t$ *of rank d.*

The formal proof of this result is pretty complicated and will not be given here. We refer the interested reader to Harrison and Pliska (1981, 1983) and Duffie and Huang (1985). However, the result is quite intuitive given the following observations:

(i) For continuous changes over an instant, only means and variances matter.

(ii) We can approximate the d-dimensional shock dz_t by a random variable that takes on $d+1$ possible values and has the same mean and variance as dz_t.

For example, a one-dimensional shock dz_t has mean zero and variance dt. This is also true for a random variable ε which equals $\sqrt{dt}$ with a probability of 1/2 and equals $-\sqrt{dt}$ with a probability of 1/2.

The order one and two moments of a two-dimensional standard Brownian motion $z = (z_1, z_2)$ are $\mathrm{E}[dz_{it}] = 0$, $\mathrm{Var}[dz_{it}] = dt$, $\mathrm{Cov}[dz_{1t}, dz_{2t}] = 0$. These moments are shared by a random variable $(\varepsilon_1, \varepsilon_2)$ with just three states:

$$\begin{aligned} \varepsilon_1 &= \frac{\sqrt{3\,dt}}{\sqrt{2}} \text{ and } \varepsilon_2 = \frac{\sqrt{dt}}{\sqrt{2}} && \text{with prob. } 1/3 \\ \varepsilon_1 &= 0 \text{ and } \varepsilon_2 = -\sqrt{2\,dt} && \text{with prob. } 1/3 \\ \varepsilon_1 &= -\frac{\sqrt{3\,dt}}{\sqrt{2}} \text{ and } \varepsilon_2 = \frac{\sqrt{dt}}{\sqrt{2}} && \text{with prob. } 1/3 \end{aligned}$$

(iii) With continuous trading, we can adjust our exposure to the exogenous shocks at every instant.

Over each instant we can thus think of the model with uncertainty generated by a d-dimensional standard Brownian motion as a discrete-time model with $d+1$ states. Therefore it only takes $d+1$ sufficiently different assets to complete the market. For example, if all market prices are affected by a single shock, a one-dimensional Brownian motion, the market will be complete if you can always find two assets with different sensitivities towards that shock. One of the assets could be a risk-free asset. Note however that when counting the number of shocks you should include shocks to variables that contain information about future asset prices.

Example 3.4 Suppose that assets pay no intermediate dividends and that the price dynamics of an arbitrary asset, asset i, is given by

$$dP_{it} = P_{it}\left[\mu_i\, dt + \sigma_i\, dz_t\right],$$

where $z = (z_t)$ is a one-dimensional standard Brownian motion and μ_i, σ_i are constants. Suppose that assets i and j have different sensitivities towards the shock so that $\sigma_i \neq \sigma_j$. From (3.14), it follows that a self-financing trading strategy with a weight of π_t on asset i and $1-\pi_t$ on asset j will generate a value process V_t with dynamics

$$dV_t = V_t\left[\left(\pi_t(\mu_i - \mu_j) + \mu_j\right)\, dt + \left(\pi_t(\sigma_i - \sigma_j) + \sigma_j\right)\, dz_t\right].$$

We can obtain any desired sensitivity towards the shock. If you want to have a portfolio return sensitivity of ν_t, you can achieve that with a portfolio weight of $\pi_t = (\nu_t - \sigma_j)/(\sigma_i - \sigma_j)$. Now suppose that each μ_i is a function of some variable x_t and that the dynamics of x_t is affected by another shock represented by a standard Brownian motion $\hat{z} = (\hat{z}_t)$ independent of z:

$$dx_t = m(x_t)\, dt + v(x_t)\left(\rho\, dz_t + \sqrt{1-\rho^2}\, d\hat{z}_t\right).$$

Then the full uncertainty of the model is generated by a two-dimensional shock $(z, \hat{z})$. Since the instantaneous price changes are affected only by z, the market is now incomplete. You cannot hedge against the shock process $\hat{z}$. □

Note that the condition for market completeness stated in Theorem 3.4 depends on the dynamics of asset prices, just as in the discrete-time setting as explained above. Anderson and Raimondo (2008) provide conditions on the dividends of the basic assets under which an equilibrium exists in which the price dynamics is such that the market is indeed complete.

For a moment think about a continuous-time model in which there can be a jump in the value of one of the key variables. Suppose that when a jump occurs, the variable can jump to K different values. The change over an instant in such a variable cannot be represented only by the expectation and the variance of the jump. To obtain any desired exposure to the jump risk, you need K assets which react sufficiently different to the jump. Typical models with jump risk assume that the size of the jump is normally or lognormally distributed. In both cases there are infinitely many possible realizations of the jump size and, consequently, a market with finitely many assets will be incomplete.

3.6.3 Discussion

As we shall see in later sections, some fundamental results require that the market is complete. It is therefore important to assess the realism of this property. Market completeness means that every relevant risk is traded. Individuals can insure against all risks that are relevant for asset prices through trading in financial assets. Clearly, individuals would like to have that opportunity so if the market is incomplete there will be an incentive to create new non-redundant assets that will help complete the market. In fact, at least part of the many new assets that have been introduced in the financial markets over the last decades do help complete the market, for example assets with dividends depending on the stock market volatility, the weather at a given location, or the number of natural catastrophes.

On the other hand, some risks are difficult to market. For example, due to the obvious information asymmetry, it is unlikely that individual labour income risk can be fully insured in the financial market. Maybe you would like to obtain full income insurance, but who should provide that? You probably know a lot more about your potential income than anybody else, and you can influence your own income while most other individuals cannot affect your income. Hence, we should not expect that real-life financial markets are complete in the strict sense.

If the market is incomplete, it is not possible to adjust your exposure to one or several shocks included in the model. But maybe investors do not care about those shocks. Then the model is said to be effectively complete. Before solving for prices and optimal decisions of the individuals, it is generally impossible to decide whether an incomplete market is really effectively complete. We will return to this discussion and some formal results on it in Chapter 7.

3.7 CONCLUDING REMARKS

This chapter has explained how to represent assets and portfolios of assets in both one-period, discrete-time, and continuous-time models. The key concepts of arbitrage and complete markets were introduced. In later chapters we will explore what conclusions we can draw about prices by assuming the absence of arbitrage and sometimes also market completeness.

3.8 EXERCISES

Exercise 3.1 Consider a one-period model with only two possible end-of-period states. Three assets are traded in an arbitrage-free market. Asset 1 is a risk-free asset with a price of 1 and an end-of-period dividend of R^f, the risk-free gross rate of return. Asset 2 has a price of S and offers a dividend of uS in state 1 and dS in state 2.

(a) Show that if the inequality $d < R^f < u$ does not hold, there will be an arbitrage.

Asset 3 is a call-option on asset 2 with an exercise price of K. The dividend of asset 3 is therefore $C_u \equiv \max(uS - K, 0)$ in state 1 and $C_d \equiv \max(dS - K, 0)$ in state 2.

(b) Show that a portfolio consisting of θ_1 units of asset 1 and θ_2 units of asset 2, where

$$\theta_1 = (R^f)^{-1}\frac{uC_d - dC_u}{u-d}, \qquad \theta_2 = \frac{C_u - C_d}{(u-d)S}$$

will generate the same dividend as the option.

(c) Show that the no-arbitrage price of the option is given by

$$C = (R^f)^{-1}\left(qC_u + (1-q)C_d\right),$$

where $q = (R^f - d)/(u - d)$.

Exercise 3.2 Imagine a one-period economy with two possible end-of-period states that are equally likely. Two assets are traded. Asset 1 has an initial price of 1 and pays off 1 in state 1 and 2 in state 2. Asset 2 has an initial price of 3 and gives a payoff of 2 in state 1 and a payoff k in state 2, where k is some constant.

(a) Argue that if $k = 4$, the Law of One Price does not hold. Is the Law of One Price violated for other values of k?

(b) For what values of k is the market complete?

(c) For what values of k is the market free of arbitrage?

(d) Assume $k = 8$. Is it possible to obtain a risk-free dividend? If so, what is the risk-free rate?

Exercise 3.3 Verify Eq. (3.5).

Exercise 3.4 In a one-period two-state economy the risk-free interest rate over the period is 25%. An asset that pays out 100 in state 1 and 200 in state 2 trades at a price of 110.

(a) What is the no-arbitrage price of a second risky asset that pays out 200 in state 1 and 100 in state 2?

(b) If this second risky asset trades at a higher price than what you computed in (a), how can you obtain a risk-free profit?

4

State Prices

4.1 INTRODUCTION

If you want to price a set of assets, you could take them one by one and evaluate the dividends of each asset separately. However, to make sure that you evaluate all assets in a consistent way (avoiding arbitrage for example), it is a better strategy first to figure out what your general pricing rule should be and then you can subsequently apply that rule to any given dividend stream. The general pricing rule can be represented by a state-price deflator, which is the topic of this chapter. Basically, a state-price deflator contains information about the value of additional payments in different states and at different points in time. Combining that with the state- and time-dependent dividends of any asset, you can compute a value or price of that asset.

Section 4.2 defines the state-price deflator in each of our general frameworks (one-period, discrete-time, and continuous-time) and derives some immediate consequences for prices and expected returns. Further important properties of state-price deflators are obtained in Section 4.3. Section 4.4 contains examples of concrete distributional assumptions on the state-price deflator and the dividends that will simplify the computation of the present value of the dividends and in some cases even lead to closed-form solutions. Section 4.5 explains the difference between real and nominal state-price deflators. Finally, Section 4.6 gives a preview of some alternative ways of representing the information in a state-price deflator. These alternatives are preferable for some purposes and will be studied in more detail in later chapters.

The concept of state prices was introduced and studied by Arrow (1951, 1953, 1971), Debreu (1954), Negishi (1960), and Ross (1978).

4.2 DEFINITIONS AND IMMEDIATE CONSEQUENCES

This section gives a formal definition of a *state-price deflator*. Some authors use the name stochastic discount factor, event-price deflator, or pricing kernel instead of state-price deflator.

4.2.1 The One-Period Framework

Here is how we define a state-price deflator in a one-period framework.

Definition 4.1 *A state-price deflator is a random variable ζ satisfying*

(i) ζ has finite variance,

(ii) $\zeta > 0$, that is $\zeta(\omega) > 0$ for all states $\omega \in \Omega$,

(iii) the prices of the I basic assets are given by

$$P_i = \mathrm{E}[\zeta D_i], \quad i = 1, 2, \dots, I, \tag{4.1}$$

or, more compactly, $\boldsymbol{P} = \mathrm{E}[\zeta \boldsymbol{D}]$.

The finite variance assumptions on both the state-price deflator and the dividends ensure that the expectation $\mathrm{E}[\zeta D_i]$ is finite.

The definition has some interesting immediate implications for prices and returns which we summarize in the following theorem.

Theorem 4.1 *Suppose ζ is a state-price deflator. Then the following is true:*

(a) For any portfolio $\boldsymbol{\theta}$, the price satisfies $P^{\boldsymbol{\theta}} = \mathrm{E}\left[\zeta D^{\boldsymbol{\theta}}\right]$, where $D^{\boldsymbol{\theta}}$ is the dividend of the portfolio.

(b) For any asset i, the gross return $R_i = D_i/P_i$ satisfies

$$1 = \mathrm{E}[\zeta R_i]. \tag{4.2}$$

If a risk-free asset is traded, then its gross return is given by

$$R^f = \frac{1}{\mathrm{E}[\zeta]}. \tag{4.3}$$

(c) The price of any asset i can be stated as

$$P_i = \mathrm{E}[\zeta]\,\mathrm{E}[D_i] + \mathrm{Cov}[D_i, \zeta], \tag{4.4}$$

or, if a risk-free asset is traded, as

$$P_i = \frac{\mathrm{E}[D_i] + R^f\,\mathrm{Cov}[D_i, \zeta]}{R^f}. \tag{4.5}$$

(d) The gross return R_i on any asset i satisfies

$$\mathrm{E}[R_i] = \frac{1}{\mathrm{E}[\zeta]} - \frac{\mathrm{Cov}[R_i, \zeta]}{\mathrm{E}[\zeta]}. \tag{4.6}$$

If a risk-free asset is traded, then

$$\mathrm{E}[R_i] - R^f = -\frac{\mathrm{Cov}[R_i, \zeta]}{\mathrm{E}[\zeta]}, \tag{4.7}$$

and the Sharpe ratio of asset i is

$$\frac{\mathrm{E}[R_i] - R^f}{\sigma[R_i]} = -\operatorname{Corr}[R_i, \zeta]\frac{\sigma[\zeta]}{\mathrm{E}[\zeta]}. \tag{4.8}$$

In particular, the maximal Sharpe ratio is the ratio $\sigma[\zeta]/\mathrm{E}[\zeta]$.

Proof. (a): Straightforward from Eq. (4.1) and the Law of One Price (3.8):

$$P^{\theta} = \sum_{i=1}^{I} \theta_i P_i = \sum_{i=1}^{I} \theta_i \mathrm{E}[\zeta D_i] = \mathrm{E}\left[\zeta\left(\sum_{i=1}^{I} \theta_i D_i\right)\right] = \mathrm{E}\left[\zeta D^{\theta}\right].$$

(b): Divide through by P_i in Eq. (4.1). On the right-hand side we can divide by P_i inside the expectation since P_i is not stochastic. Inside the expectation we then have the gross rates of return, $R_i = D_i/P_i$, which leads to Eq. (4.2). If the return is risk-free, we can move it outside the expectation so that $1 = R^f\,\mathrm{E}[\zeta]$ and therefore Eq. (4.3) holds.

(c): Eq. (4.4) follows directly from Eq. (4.1) and the covariance relation $\operatorname{Cov}[x,y] = \mathrm{E}[xy] - \mathrm{E}[x]\,\mathrm{E}[y]$. The expression (4.5) follows by applying Eq. (4.3).

(d): By definition of the covariance, Eq. (4.2) implies that $1 = \mathrm{E}[\zeta]\,\mathrm{E}[R_i] + \operatorname{Cov}[R_i, \zeta]$ from which Eq. (4.6) results. With a risk-free asset, we can replace $1/\mathrm{E}[\zeta]$ by R^f so that Eq. (4.10) follows. Rewriting the covariance as the product of the correlation and the standard deviations, we obtain Eq. (4.8). Since the correlation is between -1 and 1, the maximal Sharpe ratio is as stated. □

Note that a dividend of a given size is valued more highly in a state for which the state-price deflator is high than in a state where the deflator is low. Equation (4.5) shows that, if a risk-free asset is traded, the value of a future dividend is given by the expected dividend adjusted by a covariance term, discounted at the risk-free rate. If the dividend is positively [negatively] covarying with the state-price deflator, the expected dividend is adjusted upwards [downwards]. Defining the dividend-beta of asset i with respect to the state-price deflator as

$$\beta[D_i, \zeta] = \frac{\operatorname{Cov}[D_i, \zeta]}{\operatorname{Var}[\zeta]}$$

and $\eta = -\operatorname{Var}[\zeta]/\mathrm{E}[\zeta] < 0$, we can rewrite the above pricing equation as

$$P_i = \frac{\mathrm{E}[D_i] - \beta[D_i, \zeta]\eta}{R^f}.$$

Some basic finance textbooks suggest that a future uncertain dividend can be valued by taking the expected dividend and discounting it by a discount rate reflecting the risk of the dividend. For asset i, this discount rate $\hat{R}_i$ is implicitly defined by

$$P_i = \frac{\mathrm{E}[D_i]}{\hat{R}_i}, \tag{4.9}$$

and combining this with the above equations, we must have

$$\hat{R}_i = \frac{R^f \,\mathrm{E}[D_i]}{\mathrm{E}[D_i] - \beta[D_i, \zeta]\eta} = R^f \frac{1}{1 - \frac{\beta[D_i,\zeta]\eta}{\mathrm{E}[D_i]}}.$$

The risk-adjusted discount rate does not depend on the scale of the dividend in the sense that the risk-adjusted discount rate for a dividend of kD_i for any constant k is the same as for a dividend of D_i. Note that the risk-adjusted discount rate will be smaller than R^f if $\beta[D_i, \zeta]\eta / \mathrm{E}[D_i] < 0$ which, since $\eta < 0$, is the case if $\beta[D_i, \zeta]$ and $\mathrm{E}[D_i]$ are of the same sign. And if $0 > \mathrm{E}[D_i]/\beta[D_i, \zeta] > \eta$, the risk-adjusted gross discount rate will be negative! While this possibility is rarely recognized in textbooks, it is not really surprising. Some assets or investments will have a negative expected future dividend but still a positive value today. This could be the case for insurance contracts that typically have $\mathrm{E}[D_i] < 0$ and may have $\beta[D_i, \zeta] > 0$. The lesson here is to be careful if you want to value assets by discounting expected dividends by risk-adjusted discount rates.

We can also rewrite the expected return relations in terms of a 'beta'. Defining the return-beta as

$$\beta[R_i, \zeta] = \frac{\mathrm{Cov}[R_i, \zeta]}{\mathrm{Var}[\zeta]},$$

Equation (4.7) implies that

$$\mathrm{E}[R_i] - R^f = \frac{\mathrm{Cov}[R_i, \zeta]}{\mathrm{Var}[\zeta]}\left(-\frac{\mathrm{Var}[\zeta]}{\mathrm{E}[\zeta]}\right) = \beta[R_i, \zeta]\eta, \tag{4.10}$$

which is in the same style as the traditional CAPM. An asset with a positive [negative] return-beta with respect to the state-price deflator will have an expected return smaller [larger] than the risk-free return.

The expressions involving expected returns and return-betas are not directly useful if you want to value a future dividend. For that purpose the equations with expected dividends and dividend-betas are superior. On the other hand the return-expressions are appropriate for empirical studies, where you have a historical record of observations of returns and, for example, of a potential state-price deflator.

Example 4.1 Let ζ be a state-price deflator and consider a dividend given by

$$D_i = a + b\zeta + \varepsilon,$$

where a, b are constants, and where ε is a random variable with mean zero and $\mathrm{Cov}[\varepsilon, \zeta] = 0$. What is the price of this dividend? We can use the original pricing condition to get

$$P_i = \mathrm{E}[D_i\zeta] = \mathrm{E}\left[(a + b\zeta + \varepsilon)\,\zeta\right] = a\,\mathrm{E}[\zeta] + b\,\mathrm{E}[\zeta^2],$$

using $\mathrm{E}[\varepsilon\zeta] = \mathrm{Cov}[\varepsilon, \zeta] + \mathrm{E}[\varepsilon]\,\mathrm{E}[\zeta] = 0 + 0 = 0$. Alternatively, we can compute

$$\mathrm{E}[D_i] = a + b\,\mathrm{E}[\zeta], \qquad \mathrm{Cov}[D_i, \zeta] = b\,\mathrm{Var}[\zeta],$$

and use (4.4) to get

$$P_i = \mathrm{E}[\zeta]\,(a + b\,\mathrm{E}[\zeta]) + b\,\mathrm{Var}[\zeta] = a\,\mathrm{E}[\zeta] + b\,\mathrm{E}[\zeta^2],$$

applying the identity $\mathrm{Var}[\zeta] = \mathrm{E}[\zeta^2] - (\mathrm{E}[\zeta])^2$. □

After these quite general findings, some specialized results are listed in the following.

4.2.1.1 *Exponential State-Price Deflators*

In many cases of interest, the next-period state-price deflator is given as an exponential function of some specified random variables, and it is then useful to work with $\ln\zeta$. The first-order Taylor approximation of $\ln x$ for $x \approx \bar{x}$ is

$$\ln x \approx \ln\bar{x} + \frac{1}{\bar{x}}(x - \bar{x}),$$

so

$$\ln\zeta \approx \ln\mathrm{E}\left[\zeta\right] + \frac{1}{\mathrm{E}\left[\zeta\right]}\left(\zeta - \mathrm{E}\left[\zeta\right]\right),$$

and therefore

$$\zeta \approx \mathrm{E}\left[\zeta\right]\left(1 + \ln\zeta - \ln\mathrm{E}\left[\zeta\right]\right).$$

Substituting that into (4.7) we obtain

$$\mathrm{E}[R_i] - R^f \approx -\,\mathrm{Cov}\left[R_i, \ln\zeta\right]. \qquad (4.11)$$

4.2.1.2 *Lognormal State-Price Deflator and Return*

In many specific models the state-price deflator ζ is assumed to have a lognormal distribution. It follows from Appendix B that

$$\mathrm{E}[\zeta] = \mathrm{E}\left[e^{\ln\zeta}\right] = e^{\mathrm{E}[\ln\zeta] + \frac{1}{2}\mathrm{Var}[\ln\zeta]}.$$

In particular, if a risk-free asset exists, the continuously compounded risk-free rate of return is

$$r^f = \ln R^f = -\ln \mathrm{E}[\zeta] = -\mathrm{E}[\ln \zeta] - \frac{1}{2}\mathrm{Var}[\ln \zeta]. \tag{4.12}$$

For a risky asset that has a gross rate of return R_i with the property that R_i and the state-price deflator ζ are jointly lognormally distributed, the product ζR_i will also be lognormally distributed. Hence, we find

$$1 = \mathrm{E}\left[\zeta R_i\right] = \mathrm{E}\left[e^{\ln \zeta + \ln R_i}\right] = \exp\left\{\mathrm{E}[\ln \zeta + \ln R_i] + \frac{1}{2}\mathrm{Var}\left[\ln \zeta + \ln R_i\right]\right\},$$

and thus

$$\begin{aligned} 0 &= \mathrm{E}[\ln \zeta + \ln R_i] + \frac{1}{2}\mathrm{Var}\left[\ln \zeta + \ln R_i\right] \\ &= \mathrm{E}[\ln \zeta] + \frac{1}{2}\mathrm{Var}\left[\ln \zeta\right] + \mathrm{E}[\ln R_i] + \frac{1}{2}\mathrm{Var}\left[\ln R_i\right] + \mathrm{Cov}\left[\ln \zeta, \ln R_i\right]. \end{aligned}$$

If we let $r_i = \ln R_i$ denote the continuously compounded rate of return on asset i and apply Eq. (4.12), we obtain

$$\mathrm{E}[r_i] - r^f = -\mathrm{Cov}[\ln \zeta, r_i] - \frac{1}{2}\mathrm{Var}[r_i]. \tag{4.13}$$

Hence, a log-version of the Sharpe ratio is

$$\frac{\mathrm{E}[r_i] - r^f + \frac{1}{2}\mathrm{Var}[r_i]}{\sigma[r_i]} = -\mathrm{Corr}[\ln \zeta, r_i]\sigma[\ln \zeta]. \tag{4.14}$$

4.2.1.3 *Excess Returns*

Some empirical tests of asset pricing models focus on excess returns, where returns on all assets are measured relative to the return on a fixed benchmark asset or portfolio. Let $\bar{R}$ be the return on the benchmark. The excess return on asset i is then $R_i^e \equiv R_i - \bar{R}$. Since the above equations hold for both asset i and the benchmark, we get that

$$\mathrm{E}[\zeta R_i^e] = 0$$

and

$$\mathrm{E}[R_i^e] = -\frac{\mathrm{Cov}[R_i^e, \zeta]}{\mathrm{E}[\zeta]} = \beta[R_i^e, \zeta]\eta,$$

where $\beta[R_i^e, \zeta] = \beta[R_i, \zeta] - \beta[\bar{R}, \zeta]$.

4.2.1.4 State-Price Vectors with a Finite State Space

If the state space is finite, $\Omega = \{1, 2, \ldots, S\}$, we can alternatively represent a general pricing rule by a *state-price vector*. This is an S-dimensional vector $\boldsymbol{\psi} = (\psi_1, \ldots, \psi_S)^\top$ with the properties

(i) $\boldsymbol{\psi} > 0$, that is $\psi_\omega > 0$ for all $\omega = 1, 2, \ldots, S$,

(ii) the prices of the I basic assets are given by

$$P_i = \boldsymbol{\psi} \cdot \boldsymbol{D}_i = \sum_{\omega=1}^{S} \psi_\omega D_{i\omega}, \quad i = 1, 2, \ldots, I, \tag{4.15}$$

or, more compactly, $\boldsymbol{P} = \underline{\underline{D}}\boldsymbol{\psi}$ where $\underline{\underline{D}}$ is the dividend matrix of all the basic assets.

Suppose we can construct an Arrow–Debreu asset for state ω, that is a portfolio paying 1 in state ω and nothing in all other states. From Eq. (4.15) the price of this portfolio will be equal to ψ_ω, the 'state price for state ω'. The price of a risk-free dividend of 1 is $P^f \equiv \boldsymbol{\psi} \cdot \mathbf{1} = \sum_{\omega=1}^{S} \psi_\omega$ so that the gross risk-free rate of return is

$$R^f = \frac{1}{\sum_{\omega=1}^{S} \psi_\omega} = \frac{1}{\boldsymbol{\psi} \cdot \mathbf{1}}.$$

There is a one-to-one correspondence between state-price vectors and state-price deflators. With a finite state space, a state-price deflator is equivalent to a vector $\boldsymbol{\zeta} = (\zeta_1, \zeta_2, \ldots, \zeta_S)^\top$, and we can rewrite Eq. (4.1) as

$$P_i = \sum_{\omega=1}^{S} p_\omega \zeta_\omega D_{i\omega}, \quad i = 1, 2, \ldots, I.$$

We can then define a state-price vector $\boldsymbol{\psi}$ by

$$\psi_\omega = \zeta_\omega p_\omega. \tag{4.16}$$

Conversely, given a state-price vector this equation defines a state-price deflator. Note that we can think of the state-price deflator for a given state as the state price per unit of probability. Other things equal, the value of getting a certain dividend in a state is higher the more likely it is that that state is realized. The state-price deflator reflects the value of a dividend in different states after controlling for differences in the probabilities of the states. With infinitely many states we cannot meaningfully define state-price vectors, but we can still define state-price deflators in terms of random variables.

Example 4.2 Consider the same market as in Example 3.1. Suppose there is a state-price vector $\boldsymbol{\psi} = (0.3, 0.2, 0.3)^\top$. Then we can compute the prices of the four assets as $\boldsymbol{P} = \underline{\underline{D}}\boldsymbol{\psi}$, that is

$$\begin{pmatrix} P_1 \\ P_2 \\ P_3 \\ P_4 \end{pmatrix} = \begin{pmatrix} 1 & 1 & 1 \\ 0 & 1 & 2 \\ 4 & 0 & 1 \\ 9 & 0 & 1 \end{pmatrix} \begin{pmatrix} 0.3 \\ 0.2 \\ 0.3 \end{pmatrix} = \begin{pmatrix} 0.8 \\ 0.8 \\ 1.5 \\ 3 \end{pmatrix}.$$

In particular, the gross risk-free rate of return is $1/(0.3 + 0.2 + 0.3) = 1.25$ corresponding to a 25% risk-free net rate of return.

If the state probabilities are 0.5, 0.25, and 0.25, respectively, the state-price deflator corresponding to the state-price vector is given by

$$\zeta_1 = \frac{0.3}{0.5} = 0.6, \quad \zeta_2 = \frac{0.2}{0.25} = 0.8, \quad \zeta_3 = \frac{0.3}{0.25} = 1.2.$$

□

4.2.2 The Discrete-Time Framework

We extend the definition of a state-price deflator to the discrete-time setting with $\mathcal{T} = \{0, 1, 2, \dots, T\}$ as follows:

Definition 4.2 *In the discrete-time multiperiod framework a state-price deflator is an adapted stochastic process $\zeta = (\zeta_t)_{t \in \mathcal{T}}$ such that*

(i) $\zeta_0 = 1$,

(ii) $\zeta_t > 0$ *for all* $t = 1, 2, \dots, T$,

(iii) for any $t \in \mathcal{T}$, ζ_t *has finite variance,*

(iv) for any basic asset $i = 1, \dots, I$ *the price satisfies*

$$P_{it} = \mathrm{E}_t \left[\sum_{s=t+1}^{T} D_{is} \frac{\zeta_s}{\zeta_t} \right], \quad \text{all } t \in \mathcal{T}. \tag{4.17}$$

The condition (i) is just a normalization. If some process ζ satisfied the other three conditions, then these conditions would also be satisfied by the process $k\zeta$ for any strictly positive constant k. By fixing the initial value, we avoid this indeterminacy. Condition (ii) requires the state-price deflator to be strictly positive at all points in time and in all states of the world. No matter what happens, we should always associate a positive value to any positive future payment. The condition (iii) is purely technical and will ensure that some relevant expectations exist. Condition (iv) gives the price at time t in terms of all the future dividends and the state-price deflator. This condition will also hold for all trading strategies.

We can restate the pricing condition Eq. (4.17) in two alternative ways:

Theorem 4.2 *The pricing condition Eq. (4.17) is equivalent to the following two conditions:*

(a) *For any asset* $i = 1, \dots, T$ *the price satisfies the recursive relation*

$$P_{it} = \mathrm{E}_t\left[\sum_{s=t+1}^{t'} D_{is}\frac{\zeta_s}{\zeta_t} + P_{it'}\frac{\zeta_{t'}}{\zeta_t}\right], \qquad \text{all } t, t' \in \mathcal{T} \text{ with } t < t'. \tag{4.18}$$

(b) *For any assets* $i = 1, \dots, T$ *the state-price deflated gains process* $G_i^\zeta = (G_{it}^\zeta)_{t\in\mathcal{T}}$ *defined by*

$$G_{it}^\zeta = \sum_{s=1}^{t} D_{is}\zeta_s + P_{it}\zeta_t$$

is a martingale.

Proof. (a) If we let $t' = T$ in (4.18), we directly obtain (4.17) because $P_{iT} = 0$. Conversely, from (4.17) we have

$$P_{it'} = \mathrm{E}_{t'}\left[\sum_{s=t'+1}^{T} D_{is}\frac{\zeta_s}{\zeta_{t'}}\right].$$

We can now rewrite the price P_{it} as follows:

$$\begin{aligned}
P_{it} &= \mathrm{E}_t\left[\sum_{s=t+1}^{T} D_{is}\frac{\zeta_s}{\zeta_t}\right] \\
&= \mathrm{E}_t\left[\sum_{s=t+1}^{t'} D_{is}\frac{\zeta_s}{\zeta_t} + \sum_{s=t'+1}^{T} D_{is}\frac{\zeta_s}{\zeta_t}\right] \\
&= \mathrm{E}_t\left[\sum_{s=t+1}^{t'} D_{is}\frac{\zeta_s}{\zeta_t} + \frac{\zeta_{t'}}{\zeta_t}\sum_{s=t'+1}^{T} D_{is}\frac{\zeta_s}{\zeta_{t'}}\right] \\
&= \mathrm{E}_t\left[\mathrm{E}_{t'}\left[\sum_{s=t+1}^{t'} D_{is}\frac{\zeta_s}{\zeta_t} + \frac{\zeta_{t'}}{\zeta_t}\sum_{s=t'+1}^{T} D_{is}\frac{\zeta_s}{\zeta_{t'}}\right]\right] \\
&= \mathrm{E}_t\left[\sum_{s=t+1}^{t'} D_{is}\frac{\zeta_s}{\zeta_t} + \frac{\zeta_{t'}}{\zeta_t}\mathrm{E}_{t'}\left[\sum_{s=t'+1}^{T} D_{is}\frac{\zeta_s}{\zeta_{t'}}\right]\right] \\
&= \mathrm{E}_t\left[\sum_{s=t+1}^{t'} D_{is}\frac{\zeta_s}{\zeta_t} + P_{it'}\frac{\zeta_{t'}}{\zeta_t}\right].
\end{aligned}$$

Here the fourth equality follows from the Law of Iterated Expectations, Theorem 2.1.

(b) We need to show that, for $t < t'$, $G^{\zeta}_{it} = \mathrm{E}_t[G^{\zeta}_{it'}]$, that is

$$\sum_{s=1}^{t} D_{is}\zeta_s + P_{it}\zeta_t = \mathrm{E}_t\left[\sum_{s=1}^{t'} D_{is}\zeta_s + P_{it'}\zeta_{t'}\right].$$

Subtracting the left-hand side sum and dividing by ζ_t yield (4.18). Conversely, Eq. (4.18) implies that G^{ζ}_i is a martingale. □

A particularly simple version of Eq. (4.18) occurs for $t' = t + 1$:

$$P_{it} = \mathrm{E}_t\left[\frac{\zeta_{t+1}}{\zeta_t}\left(P_{i,t+1} + D_{i,t+1}\right)\right]. \tag{4.19}$$

This equation shows that the ratio ζ_{t+1}/ζ_t acts as a one-period state-price deflator between time t and $t+1$ in the sense of the definition in the one-period framework, except that the price at the end of the period (which is zero in the one-period case) is added to the dividend. Of course, given the state-price deflator process $\zeta = (\zeta_t)$, we know the state-price deflators ζ_{t+1}/ζ_t for each of the sub-periods (note that these will depend on the realized value ζ_t which is part of the information available at time t). Conversely, a sequence of 'one-period state-price deflators' ζ_{s+1}/ζ_s and the normalization $\zeta_0 = 1$ define the entire state-price deflator process since

$$\zeta_t = \zeta_0 \frac{\zeta_1}{\zeta_0}\frac{\zeta_2}{\zeta_1}\cdots\frac{\zeta_t}{\zeta_{t-1}}.$$

This link between state-price deflators in the discrete-time and in the one-period settings has direct implications for risk-free rates and expected returns over each sub-period in the multiperiod framework. Recall from Section 3.3 that R^f_t denotes the gross risk-free return over the period between t and $t+1$ and that $R_{i,t+1}$ denotes the gross return on a risky asset i over the same time interval.

Theorem 4.3 *Suppose that $\zeta = (\zeta_t)$ is a state-price deflator in the discrete-time setting and let $t \in \mathcal{T}$ with $t < T$. Assume that a risk-free asset exists over the period from t to $t+1$. Then the following holds:*

(a) For any risky asset i

$$1 = \mathrm{E}_t\left[\frac{\zeta_{t+1}}{\zeta_t} R_{i,t+1}\right]. \tag{4.20}$$

(b) The risk-free gross return is

$$R^f_t = \left(\mathrm{E}_t\left[\frac{\zeta_{t+1}}{\zeta_t}\right]\right)^{-1}. \tag{4.21}$$

(c) For any risky asset i, the excess expected return from t to t + 1 is

$$\mathrm{E}_t[R_{i,t+1}] - R^f_t = -\frac{\mathrm{Cov}_t\left[R_{i,t+1}, \frac{\zeta_{t+1}}{\zeta_t}\right]}{\mathrm{E}_t\left[\frac{\zeta_{t+1}}{\zeta_t}\right]}, \tag{4.22}$$

and the Sharpe ratio is

$$\frac{\mathrm{E}_t[R_{i,t+1}] - R^f_t}{\sigma_t[R_{i,t+1}]} = -\,\mathrm{Corr}_t\left[R_{i,t+1}, \frac{\zeta_{t+1}}{\zeta_t}\right] \frac{\sigma_t\left[\frac{\zeta_{t+1}}{\zeta_t}\right]}{\mathrm{E}_t\left[\frac{\zeta_{t+1}}{\zeta_t}\right]}.$$

In particular, the maximal Sharpe ratio is $\sigma_t\left[\frac{\zeta_{t+1}}{\zeta_t}\right] / \mathrm{E}_t\left[\frac{\zeta_{t+1}}{\zeta_t}\right]$.

The proof is similar to the one-period case and is left for the reader. If a risk-free asset does not exist, the expression (4.22) has to be restated as

$$\mathrm{E}_t[R_{i,t+1}] - \frac{1}{\mathrm{E}_t\left[\frac{\zeta_{t+1}}{\zeta_t}\right]} = -\frac{\mathrm{Cov}_t\left[R_{i,t+1}, \frac{\zeta_{t+1}}{\zeta_t}\right]}{\mathrm{E}_t\left[\frac{\zeta_{t+1}}{\zeta_t}\right]}. \tag{4.23}$$

The 'beta-version' of Eq. (4.22) is

$$\mathrm{E}_t[R_{i,t+1}] - R^f_t = \beta_t\left[R_{i,t+1}, \frac{\zeta_{t+1}}{\zeta_t}\right]\eta_t,$$

where

$$\beta_t\left[R_{i,t+1}, \frac{\zeta_{t+1}}{\zeta_t}\right] = \frac{\mathrm{Cov}_t\left[R_{i,t+1}, \frac{\zeta_{t+1}}{\zeta_t}\right]}{\mathrm{Var}_t\left[\frac{\zeta_{t+1}}{\zeta_t}\right]}, \qquad \eta_t = -\frac{\mathrm{Var}_t\left[\frac{\zeta_{t+1}}{\zeta_t}\right]}{\mathrm{E}_t\left[\frac{\zeta_{t+1}}{\zeta_t}\right]}.$$

The same relation holds for net rates of return. Just substitute $R_{i,t+1} = 1 + r_{i,t+1}$ and $R^f_t = 1 + r^f_t$ on the left-hand side and observe that the ones cancel. On the right-hand side, use that $\mathrm{Cov}_t[R_{i,t+1}, x] = \mathrm{Cov}_t[1 + r_{i,t+1}, x] = \mathrm{Cov}_t[r_{i,t+1}, x]$ for any random variable x. Therefore we can work with gross or net rate of returns as we like in such expressions.

The above theorem implies that the variations over time in the conditional mean and the conditional standard deviation of the next-period state-price deflator determine the variations in the risk-free rate and the Sharpe ratios (the latter may also vary because of a time-varying correlation). Since real-life risk-free rates and Sharpe ratios vary, our models of the state-price deflator should allow for variations in the conditional one-period mean and standard deviation.

In many cases of interest, the next-period state-price deflator is given as an exponential function of some specified random variables, and it is then useful to work with $\ln(\zeta_{t+1}/\zeta_t)$. We can follow the procedure leading to Eq. (4.11) and use the first-order Taylor approximation

$$\ln \frac{\zeta_{t+1}}{\zeta_t} \approx \ln \mathrm{E}_t\left[\frac{\zeta_{t+1}}{\zeta_t}\right] + \frac{1}{\mathrm{E}_t\left[\frac{\zeta_{t+1}}{\zeta_t}\right]}\left(\frac{\zeta_{t+1}}{\zeta_t} - \mathrm{E}_t\left[\frac{\zeta_{t+1}}{\zeta_t}\right]\right),$$

which implies that

$$\frac{\zeta_{t+1}}{\zeta_t} \approx \mathrm{E}_t\left[\frac{\zeta_{t+1}}{\zeta_t}\right]\left(1 + \ln\frac{\zeta_{t+1}}{\zeta_t} - \ln \mathrm{E}_t\left[\frac{\zeta_{t+1}}{\zeta_t}\right]\right).$$

Substituting that into Eq. (4.22) we obtain

$$\mathrm{E}_t[R_{i,t+1}] - R^f_t \approx -\operatorname{Cov}_t\left[R_{i,t+1}, \ln\frac{\zeta_{t+1}}{\zeta_t}\right]. \tag{4.24}$$

In a situation where the next-period state-price deflator ζ_{t+1}/ζ_t and the next-period gross rate of return $R_{i,t+1} = e^{r_{i,t+1}}$ on a risky asset are jointly lognormally distributed conditional on time t information, it follows from our one-period analysis that the expected excess continuously compounded rate of return is

$$\mathrm{E}_t[r_{i,t+1}] - r^f_t = -\operatorname{Cov}_t\left[\ln\left(\frac{\zeta_{t+1}}{\zeta_t}\right), r_{i,t+1}\right] - \frac{1}{2}\operatorname{Var}_t[r_{i,t+1}],$$

where

$$r^f_t = \ln R^f_t = -\ln \mathrm{E}_t\left[\left(\frac{\zeta_{t+1}}{\zeta_t}\right)\right] = -\mathrm{E}_t\left[\ln\left(\frac{\zeta_{t+1}}{\zeta_t}\right)\right] - \frac{1}{2}\operatorname{Var}_t\left[\ln\left(\frac{\zeta_{t+1}}{\zeta_t}\right)\right]$$

is the continuously compounded risk-free rate of return over the next period. In line with Eq. (4.14) the log-version of the conditional Sharpe ratio is

$$\frac{\mathrm{E}_t[r_{i,t+1}] - r^f_t + \frac{1}{2}\operatorname{Var}_t[r_{i,t+1}]}{\sigma_t[r_{i,t+1}]} = -\operatorname{Corr}_t\left[\ln\frac{\zeta_{t+1}}{\zeta_t}, r_{i,t+1}\right]\sigma_t\left[\ln\frac{\zeta_{t+1}}{\zeta_t}\right]. \tag{4.25}$$

For the valuation of a future dividend stream we have to apply Eq. (4.17). Applying the covariance definition once again, we can rewrite the price as

$$P_{it} = \sum_{s=t+1}^{T}\left(\mathrm{E}_t[D_{is}]\,\mathrm{E}_t\left[\frac{\zeta_s}{\zeta_t}\right] + \operatorname{Cov}_t\left[D_{is}, \frac{\zeta_s}{\zeta_t}\right]\right).$$

By definition of a state-price deflator, a zero-coupon bond maturing at time s with a face value of 1 will have a time t price of

$$B^s_t = \mathrm{E}_t\left[\frac{\zeta_s}{\zeta_t}\right].$$

Define the corresponding (annualized) yield $\hat{y}_t^s$ by

$$B_t^s = \frac{1}{(1+\hat{y}_t^s)^{s-t}} \quad \Leftrightarrow \quad \hat{y}_t^s = \left(B_t^s\right)^{-1/(s-t)} - 1.$$

Note that this is a risk-free rate of return between time t and time s. Now we can rewrite the above price expression as

$$\begin{aligned} P_{it} &= \sum_{s=t+1}^{T} B_t^s \left(\mathrm{E}_t[D_{is}] + \frac{\mathrm{Cov}_t\left[D_{is}, \frac{\zeta_s}{\zeta_t}\right]}{B_t^s} \right) \\ &= \sum_{s=t+1}^{T} \frac{\mathrm{E}_t[D_{is}] + \frac{\mathrm{Cov}_t\left[D_{is}, \frac{\zeta_s}{\zeta_t}\right]}{\mathrm{E}_t\left[\frac{\zeta_s}{\zeta_t}\right]}}{\left(1+\hat{y}_t^s\right)^{s-t}}. \end{aligned} \tag{4.26}$$

Each dividend is valued by discounting an appropriately risk-adjusted expected dividend by the risk-free return over the period. This generalizes the result of the one-period framework.

4.2.3 The Continuous-Time Framework

The state-price deflator in a continuous-time setting is defined similarly to the discrete-time framework:

Definition 4.3 *A state-price deflator in the continuous-time framework is an adapted stochastic process $\zeta = (\zeta_t)$ with*

(i) $\zeta_0 = 1$,

(ii) $\zeta_t > 0$ *for all* $t \in [0, T]$,

(iii) for each t, ζ_t *has finite variance,*

(iv) for any basic asset $i = 1, \ldots, I$ *and any* $t \in [0, T)$, *the price satisfies*

$$P_{it} = \mathrm{E}_t\left[\int_t^T \delta_{is} P_{is} \frac{\zeta_s}{\zeta_t}\, ds + D_{iT}\frac{\zeta_T}{\zeta_t}\right]. \tag{4.27}$$

Under technical conditions, Eq. (4.27) will also hold for all reasonable trading strategies. As in the discrete-time case the pricing equation (4.27) implies that for any $t < t' < T$

$$P_{it} = \mathrm{E}_t\left[\int_t^{t'} \delta_{is} P_{is} \frac{\zeta_s}{\zeta_t}\, ds + P_{it'}\frac{\zeta_{t'}}{\zeta_t}\right].$$

Again, the condition (iv) can be reformulated as follows: for all basic assets $i = 1, \ldots, I$ the state-price deflated gains process $G_i^\zeta = (G_{it}^\zeta)_{t \in \mathcal{T}}$ defined by

$$G^{\zeta}_{it} = \begin{cases} \int_0^t \delta_{is} P_{is} \zeta_s \, ds + P_{it}\zeta_t & \text{for } t < T, \\ \int_0^T \delta_{is} P_{is} \zeta_s \, ds + D_{iT}\zeta_T & \text{for } t = T \end{cases} \tag{4.28}$$

is a martingale.

If we invest in one unit of asset i at time t and keep reinvesting the continuously paid dividends in the asset, we will end up at time T with $\exp\{\int_t^T \delta_{iu} \, du\}$ units of the asset, compare the argument in Section 3.2.3. Therefore, we have the following relation:

$$P_{it} = \mathrm{E}_t \left[e^{\int_t^T \delta_{iu} \, du} D_{iT} \frac{\zeta_T}{\zeta_t} \right]. \tag{4.29}$$

As in the discrete-time case we can derive information about the short-term risk-free rate of return and the expected returns on the risky assets from the first and second local moment of the state-price deflator. Recall from Chapter 2 that in continuous-time models driven by Brownian motions, a stochastic process is fully determined by its local mean (drift) and standard deviation (from the sensitivity towards the shocks). This leads to a one-to-one relation between state-price deflators on one hand and risk-free rates and excess returns on the other hand. Before we can formalize this relation, we need to define the concept of a *market price of risk*:

Definition 4.4 *In a continuous-time setting in which the fundamental uncertainty is represented by a standard Brownian motion $z = (z_t)$ and a locally risk-free asset is traded at all times, a market price of risk is a process $\boldsymbol{\lambda} = (\boldsymbol{\lambda}_t)$ satisfying*

$$\mu_{it} + \delta_{it} - r^f_t = \boldsymbol{\sigma}^{\top}_{it} \boldsymbol{\lambda}_t \tag{4.30}$$

for all risky assets $i = 1, \dots, I$.

If the price of some asset, say asset i, is only sensitive to the j'th exogenous shock, then Equation (4.30) reduces to

$$\mu_{it} + \delta_{it} - r^f_t = \sigma_{ijt} \lambda_{jt},$$

implying that

$$\lambda_{jt} = \frac{\mu_{it} + \delta_{it} - r^f_t}{\sigma_{ijt}}.$$

Therefore, λ_{jt} is the compensation in terms of excess expected return per unit of risk stemming from the j'th exogenous shock. This explains the term 'market price of risk'.

If $\boldsymbol{\lambda}$ is a market price of risk, it follows immediately from Eq. (4.30) that the expected relative price appreciation of any risky asset i is

$$\mu_{it} = r_t^f + \sigma_{it}^\top \lambda_t - \delta_{it}$$

and that the total expected rate of return is

$$\mu_{it} + \delta_{it} = r_t^f + \sigma_{it}^\top \lambda_t.$$

The general price dynamics in Eq. (3.4) can then be restated as

$$dP_{it} = P_{it}\left[\left(r_t^f + \sigma_{it}^\top \lambda_t - \delta_{it}\right) dt + \sigma_{it}^\top \, dz_t\right]. \tag{4.31}$$

We define the *instantaneous Sharpe ratio* of asset i at time t to be the ratio of the excess expected rate of return $\mu_{it} + \delta_{it} - r_t^f$ to the volatility $\|\sigma_{it}\|$. According to Eq. (4.30), the instantaneous Sharpe ratio can be expressed as

$$\frac{\mu_{it} + \delta_{it} - r_t^f}{\|\sigma_{it}\|} = \frac{\sigma_{it}^\top \lambda_t}{\|\sigma_{it}\|}.$$

For any two vectors a and b, the Cauchy–Schwartz inequality $|a^\top b| \le \|a\| \, \|b\|$ holds. Therefore,

$$\frac{|\mu_{it} + \delta_{it} - r_t^f|}{\|\sigma_{it}\|} \le \frac{\|\sigma_{it}\| \, \|\lambda_t\|}{\|\sigma_{it}\|} = \|\lambda_t\|$$

so that $\|\lambda_t\|$ is the maximal instantaneous Sharpe ratio.

Now we can state the following important result characterizing state-price deflators:

Theorem 4.4 *Consider a continuous-time model in which the fundamental uncertainty is represented by a standard Brownian motion $z = (z_t)$ and a locally risk-free asset is traded at all times. Then, under technical conditions, a process $\zeta = (\zeta_t)$ is a state-price deflator if and only if*

$$d\zeta_t = -\zeta_t\left[r_t^f \, dt + \lambda_t^\top \, dz_t\right], \quad \zeta_0 = 1, \tag{4.32}$$

where r^f is the continuously compounded risk-free rate process and λ is a market price of risk.

The finite variance condition on the state-price deflator can be ensured by imposing an appropriate condition on λ. Note that Eq. (4.32) implies that

$$\zeta_s = \zeta_t \exp\left\{-\int_t^s r_u^f \, du - \frac{1}{2}\int_t^s \|\lambda_u\|^2 \, du - \int_t^s \lambda_u^\top \, dz_u\right\} \tag{4.33}$$

for any $s > t$. This can be confirmed by an application of Itô's Lemma on $\ln \zeta_t$ following the steps in Section 2.6.7.

Proof. Write the dynamics of the state-price deflator as

$$d\zeta_t = -\zeta_t\left[m_t \, dt + v_t^\top \, dz_t\right] \tag{4.34}$$

for some relative drift m and some 'sensitivity' vector ν (this is without loss of generality because of the martingale representation theorem and the fact that ζ_t is positive). We have to show that $m_t = r^f_t$ and that $\nu = (\nu_t)$ is a market price of risk. We give both an informal proof based on a discrete-time approximation and a limiting argument as well as a more formal proof based on Itô's Lemma.

Informal proof: consider a discrete-time approximation with period length Δt. In such a model, the risk-free one-period gross rate of return satisfies

$$\frac{1}{R^f_t} = \mathrm{E}_t\left[\frac{\zeta_{t+\Delta t}}{\zeta_t}\right],$$

according to Eq. (4.21). In terms of the annualized continuously compounded one-period risk-free rate r^f_t, the left-hand side is given by $\exp\{-r^f_t \Delta t\}$. Subtracting one on both sides of the equation and changing signs, we get

$$1 - e^{-r^f_t \Delta t} = -\,\mathrm{E}_t\left[\frac{\zeta_{t+\Delta t} - \zeta_t}{\zeta_t}\right].$$

Dividing by Δt and letting $\Delta t \to 0$ we get

$$r^f_t = -\lim_{\Delta t \to 0} \frac{1}{\Delta t}\,\mathrm{E}_t\left[\frac{\zeta_{t+\Delta t} - \zeta_t}{\zeta_t}\right] = -\frac{1}{dt}\,\mathrm{E}_t\left[\frac{d\zeta_t}{\zeta_t}\right].$$

The left-hand side is the continuously compounded short-term risk-free interest rate. The right-hand side is minus the relative drift of the state-price deflator which, using Eq. (4.34), equals m_t. Hence, $m_t = r^f_t$ as was to be shown.

To obtain an expression for the current expected return on a risky asset, we start with the equivalent of Eq. (4.20) in the approximating discrete-time model, that is

$$\mathrm{E}_t\left[\frac{\zeta_{t+\Delta}}{\zeta_t} R_{i,t+\Delta t}\right] = 1,$$

which implies that

$$\mathrm{E}_t\left[R_{i,t+\Delta t}\right] \mathrm{E}_t\left[\frac{\zeta_{t+\Delta}}{\zeta_t}\right] - 1 = -\,\mathrm{Cov}_t\left[R_{i,t+\Delta t}, \frac{\zeta_{t+\Delta}}{\zeta_t}\right]. \qquad (4.35)$$

First note that, for small Δt, we have $\mathrm{E}_t\left[\frac{\zeta_{t+\Delta t}}{\zeta_t}\right] \approx e^{-r^f_t \Delta t}$. Next, recall from Eq. (3.6) that we can approximate the gross rate of return as

$$R_{i,t+\Delta t} = e^{\int_t^{t+\Delta t} \delta_{iu}\,du} \frac{P_{i,t+\Delta t}}{P_{it}} \approx \exp\left\{\left(\delta_{it} + \mu_{it} - \frac{1}{2}\|\boldsymbol{\sigma}_{it}\|^2\right)\Delta t + \boldsymbol{\sigma}_{it}^{\top}\Delta z_t\right\}$$

so that $\mathrm{E}_t\left[R_{i,t+\Delta t}\right] \approx e^{(\delta_{it}+\mu_{it})\Delta t}$. Moreover,

$$\begin{aligned}\mathrm{Cov}_t\left[R_{i,t+\Delta t}, \frac{\zeta_{t+\Delta}}{\zeta_t}\right] &= e^{\int_t^{t+\Delta t}\delta_{iu}\,du}\,\mathrm{Cov}_t\left[\frac{P_{i,t+\Delta t}}{P_{it}}, \frac{\zeta_{t+\Delta t}}{\zeta_t}\right] \\ &= e^{\int_t^{t+\Delta t}\delta_{iu}\,du}\,\mathrm{Cov}_t\left[\frac{P_{i,t+\Delta t}-P_{it}}{P_{it}}, \frac{\zeta_{t+\Delta t}-\zeta_t}{\zeta_t}\right].\end{aligned}$$

Substituting these expressions into Eq. (4.35), we obtain

$$e^{(\delta_{it}+\mu_{it}-r^f_t)\Delta t} - 1 \approx e^{\int_t^{t+\Delta t}\delta_{iu}\,du}\,\mathrm{Cov}_t\left[\frac{P_{i,t+\Delta t}-P_{it}}{P_{it}}, \frac{\zeta_{t+\Delta t}-\zeta_t}{\zeta_t}\right].$$

Now apply the approximation $e^x \approx 1 + x$ on the left-hand side, divide by Δt, and let $\Delta t \to 0$. Then we arrive at

$$\begin{aligned}\mu_{it} + \delta_{it} - r^f_t &= -\lim_{\Delta t\to 0} e^{\int_t^{t+\Delta t}\delta_{iu}\,du}\frac{1}{\Delta t}\,\mathrm{Cov}_t\left[\frac{P_{i,t+\Delta t}-P_{it}}{P_{it}}, \frac{\zeta_{t+\Delta t}-\zeta_t}{\zeta_t}\right] \\ &= -\frac{1}{dt}\,\mathrm{Cov}_t\left[\frac{dP_{it}}{P_{it}}, \frac{d\zeta_t}{\zeta_t}\right]. \qquad (4.36)\end{aligned}$$

The left-hand side is the expected excess rate of return over the next instant. The right-hand side is the current rate of covariance between the return on the asset and the relative change of the state-price deflator. Using Eq. (4.34), the right-hand side is $\boldsymbol{\sigma}_t^{\top}\boldsymbol{\nu}_t$, and Eq. (4.36) then implies that $\boldsymbol{\nu} = (\boldsymbol{\nu}_t)$ indeed is a market price of risk as claimed.

Formal proof: first, focus on the risk-free asset. By the pricing condition in the definition of a state-price deflator, the process G^{ζ}_f defined by $G^{\zeta}_{ft} = \zeta_t \exp\{\int_0^t r^f_u\,du\}$ has to be a martingale, that is it must have a zero drift. By Itô's Lemma,

$$dG^{\zeta}_{ft} = G^{\zeta}_{ft}\left[(-m_t + r^f_t)\,dt - \boldsymbol{\nu}_t^{\top}\,d\boldsymbol{z}_t\right]$$

so we conclude that $m_t = r^f_t$. The relative drift of a state-price deflator is equal to the negative of the continuously compounded short-term risk-free interest rate.

Next, for any risky asset i the process G^{ζ}_i defined by Eq. (4.28) must be a martingale. From Itô's Lemma and the dynamics of P_i and ζ given in Eqs. (3.4) and (4.34), we get

$$\begin{aligned}dG^{\zeta}_{it} &= \delta_{it}P_{it}\zeta_t\,dt + \zeta_t\,dP_{it} + P_{it}d\zeta_t + (d\zeta_t)(dP_{it}) \\ &= P_{it}\zeta_t\left[\left(\mu_{it} + \delta_{it} - m_t - \boldsymbol{\sigma}_{it}^{\top}\boldsymbol{\nu}_t\right)\,dt + (\boldsymbol{\nu}_t + \boldsymbol{\sigma}_{it})^{\top}\,d\boldsymbol{z}_t\right].\end{aligned}$$

With a risk-free asset, we know that $m_t = r^f_t$. Setting the drift equal to zero, we conclude that the equation

$$\mu_{it} + \delta_{it} - r_t^f = \boldsymbol{\sigma}_{it}^{\top} \boldsymbol{\nu}_t$$

holds. This implies that $\boldsymbol{\nu}$ is a market price of risk. □

If we know or specify the dynamics of the state-price deflator and the dividend stream from an asset, we can in principle price the asset using Eq. (4.27). However, only in special cases is it possible to compute the price in closed form. Examples are given in Section 4.4. In other cases one can use Monte Carlo simulation to approximate the relevant expectation.

4.3 PROPERTIES OF STATE-PRICE DEFLATORS

After defining state-price deflators, two questions arise naturally: Under what conditions does a state-price deflator exist? Under what conditions will it be unique? We will answer these questions in the two following subsections.

4.3.1 Existence

Here is the answer to the existence question:

Theorem 4.5 *A state-price deflator exists if and only if prices admit no arbitrage.*

Since we have already concluded that we should only consider no-arbitrage prices, the theorem implies that we can safely assume the existence of a state-price deflator. As shown in the following proof, it is easy to show that the existence of a state-price deflator implies the absence of arbitrage. The proof given here of the converse implication is purely mathematical. In Chapter 6 we provide an economically more insightful proof by constructing a state-price deflator from the solution to the utility maximization problem of any individual. That solution will only exist in the absence of arbitrage.

Proof. Let us start with a one-period framework and assume that a state-price deflator ζ exists. Then the price of any random dividend D is $P = \mathrm{E}[\zeta D]$. If D is non-negative in all states, it is clear that ζD will be non-negative in all states and, consequently, the expectation of ζD will be non-negative. This rules out arbitrage of type (i), compare Definition 3.1. If, furthermore, the set of states $A = \{\omega \in \Omega : D(\omega) > 0\}$ has strictly positive probability, it is clear that ζD will be strictly positive on a set of strictly positive probability and otherwise non-negative, so the expectation of ζD must be strictly positive. This rules out type (ii) arbitrage.

The same argument applies to the discrete-time framework. In the continuous-time setting the argument should be slightly adjusted in order to incorporate the lower bound on the value process that will rule out doubling strategies. It is not terribly difficult, but involves local martingales and supermartingales which we will not discuss here. The interested reader is referred to Duffie (2001, p. 105).

Now assume that prices do not admit arbitrage. For simplicity, take a one-period framework with a finite state space $\Omega = \{1, 2, \ldots, S\}$ and assume that none of the I basic assets are redundant (the proof can easily be extended to the case with redundant assets). Define the sets A and B as

$$A = \{\kappa \boldsymbol{P} \mid \kappa > 0\}, \quad B = \{\underline{\underline{D}}\boldsymbol{\psi} \mid \boldsymbol{\psi} \in \mathbb{R}^S_{++}\},$$

where R^S_{++} is the set of S-dimensional real vectors with strictly positive components. As before, $\boldsymbol{P}$ is the I-dimensional vector of prices of the basic assets, and $\underline{\underline{D}}$ is the $I \times S$ matrix of dividends. Both A and B are convex subsets[1] of $\mathbb{R}^I$. A is convex since $\alpha\kappa_1\boldsymbol{P} + (1-\alpha)\kappa_2\boldsymbol{P} = (\alpha\kappa_1 + (1-\alpha)\kappa_2)\boldsymbol{P} \in A$ for any $\alpha \in [0,1]$ and any $\kappa_1, \kappa_2 > 0$. Likewise, B is convex because, given $\boldsymbol{\psi}_1, \boldsymbol{\psi}_2 \in \mathbb{R}^S_{++}$ and $\alpha \in [0,1]$, then $\alpha\underline{\underline{D}}\boldsymbol{\psi}_1 + (1-\alpha)\underline{\underline{D}}\boldsymbol{\psi}_2 = \underline{\underline{D}}\left(\alpha\boldsymbol{\psi}_1 + (1-\alpha)\boldsymbol{\psi}_2\right)$ which belongs to B.

Suppose now that no state-price vector exists. Then we would have $A \cap B = \emptyset$. By the Separating Hyperplane Theorem,[2] a non-zero vector $\boldsymbol{\theta} \in \mathbb{R}^I$ exists so that

$$\kappa\boldsymbol{\theta}^\top\boldsymbol{P} \leq \boldsymbol{\theta}^\top\underline{\underline{D}}\boldsymbol{\psi} = (\underline{\underline{D}}^\top\boldsymbol{\theta})^\top\boldsymbol{\psi}, \qquad \text{for all } \kappa > 0,\ \boldsymbol{\psi} \in \mathbb{R}^S_{++}.$$

This implies that $\boldsymbol{\theta}^\top\boldsymbol{P} \leq 0$ and $\underline{\underline{D}}^\top\boldsymbol{\theta} \geq 0$. Since we have assumed that none of the basic assets are redundant, the dividend matrix $\underline{\underline{D}}$ has full rank so there is no $\boldsymbol{\theta}$ for which $\underline{\underline{D}}^\top\boldsymbol{\theta} = 0$. Hence, $\boldsymbol{\theta}$ must satisfy $\boldsymbol{\theta}^\top\boldsymbol{P} \leq 0$ and $\underline{\underline{D}}^\top\boldsymbol{\theta} > 0$, and therefore $\boldsymbol{\theta}$ is an arbitrage. This contradicts our assumption. Hence, a state-price vector must exist. □

Just assuming that prices obeyed the Law of One Price—instead of the stronger no-arbitrage assumption—would lead to the existence of a vector $\boldsymbol{\psi}$ satisfying $\boldsymbol{\psi} \cdot \boldsymbol{D}_i = P_i$ for all i, but we could not conclude that $\boldsymbol{\psi}$ would be strictly positive. For that we need the stronger no-arbitrage condition and then $\boldsymbol{\psi}$ is indeed a state-price vector. Dividing by state probabilities, $\zeta_\omega = \psi_\omega/p_\omega$, we obtain a state-price deflator.

Example 4.3 Consider again the market in Example 3.1 and ignore asset 4, which is redundant. Suppose the market prices of the three remaining assets are 1.1, 2.2, and 0.6, respectively. Can you find a state-price vector $\boldsymbol{\psi}$? The only candidate is the solution to the equation system $\underline{\underline{D}}\boldsymbol{\psi} = \boldsymbol{P}$, that is

[1] A set $X \subseteq \mathbb{R}^n$ is convex if, for all $x_1, x_2 \in X$ and all $\alpha \in [0,1]$, we have $\alpha x_1 + (1-\alpha)x_2 \in X$.

[2] The version of the Separating Hyperplane Theorem applied here is the following: suppose that A and B are non-empty, disjoint, convex subsets of $\mathbb{R}^n$ for some integer $n \geq 1$. Then there is a non-zero vector $\boldsymbol{\theta} \in \mathbb{R}^n$ and a scalar ξ so that $\boldsymbol{\theta}^\top\boldsymbol{a} \leq \xi \leq \boldsymbol{\theta}^\top\boldsymbol{b}$ for all $\boldsymbol{a} \in A$ and all $\boldsymbol{b} \in B$. Hence, A and B are separated by the hyperplane $H = \{x \in \mathbb{R}^n | a^\top x = \xi\}$. See, for example, Sydsaeter *et al.* (2005, Them. 13.6.3).

$$\boldsymbol{\psi} = \left(\underline{\underline{D}}\right)^{-1} \boldsymbol{P} = \begin{pmatrix} 1 & 1 & 1 \\ 0 & 1 & 2 \\ 4 & 0 & 1 \end{pmatrix}^{-1} \begin{pmatrix} 1.1 \\ 2.2 \\ 0.6 \end{pmatrix} = \begin{pmatrix} -0.1 \\ 0.2 \\ 1 \end{pmatrix},$$

which is not strictly positive. Hence there is no state-price vector for this market. Then there must be an arbitrage, but where? The computation above reveals that the three assets are priced such that the implicit value of an Arrow–Debreu asset for state 1 is negative. The portfolio of the three assets that replicates this Arrow–Debreu asset is given by

$$\boldsymbol{\theta} = \left(\underline{\underline{D}}^{\top}\right)^{-1} \boldsymbol{e}_1 = \begin{pmatrix} 0.2 & 1.6 & -0.8 \\ -0.2 & -0.6 & 0.8 \\ 0.2 & -0.4 & 0.2 \end{pmatrix} \begin{pmatrix} 1 \\ 0 \\ 0 \end{pmatrix} = \begin{pmatrix} 0.2 \\ -0.2 \\ 0.2 \end{pmatrix},$$

which indeed has a price of $0.2 \times 1.1 - 0.2 \times 2.2 + 0.2 \times 0.6 = -0.1$. You get 0.1 today for a portfolio that pays you 1 if state 1 is realized and 0 in other states. This is clearly an arbitrage. □

4.3.2 Uniqueness

Here is a general result on the uniqueness of state-price deflators:

Theorem 4.6 *Assume prices admit no arbitrage. Then there is a unique state-price deflator if and only if the market is complete. If the market is incomplete, several state-price deflators exist.*

We first give a detailed proof for a one-period economy with a finite state space $\Omega = \{1, 2, \ldots, S\}$. Recall that there is a one-to-one relation between state-price deflators and state-price vectors in that setting.

Proof. (One period, finite state space.) A state-price vector is a strictly positive solution $\boldsymbol{\psi}$ to the equation system $\underline{\underline{D}}\boldsymbol{\psi} = \boldsymbol{P}$ or, equivalently, $\hat{\underline{\underline{D}}}\boldsymbol{\psi} = \hat{\boldsymbol{P}}$, where $\hat{\underline{\underline{D}}}$ is the dividend matrix and $\hat{\boldsymbol{P}}$ the price vector of the non-redundant assets. A redundant asset has a dividend vector which is a linear combination of the dividend vectors of other assets and, because of the no-arbitrage assumption, the price of the redundant asset will equal the same linear combination of the prices of the other assets. In technical terms, $\operatorname{rank}(\underline{\underline{D}}) = \operatorname{rank}(\underline{\underline{D}}_P)$, see Appendix C.

First, assume the market is complete so that any dividend vector in $\mathbb{R}^S$ is marketed. By the absence of arbitrage, we know that at least one state-price vector exists. Suppose we have two state-price vectors $\boldsymbol{\psi}$ and $\hat{\boldsymbol{\psi}}$. Then for any dividend vector $\boldsymbol{D}$, the price is given by $P = \boldsymbol{D} \cdot \boldsymbol{\psi} = \boldsymbol{D} \cdot \hat{\boldsymbol{\psi}}$. For any state ω, the Arrow–Debreu asset paying out 1 in state ω and 0 in all other states is marketed. Let $\boldsymbol{e}_\omega$ denote that dividend vector. Then the price of that asset is equal both to $\boldsymbol{e}_\omega \cdot \boldsymbol{\psi} = \psi_\omega$ and to $\boldsymbol{e}_\omega \cdot \hat{\boldsymbol{\psi}} = \hat{\psi}_\omega$. Therefore, $\psi_\omega = \hat{\psi}_\omega$. Since this argument works for any ω, we conclude that $\boldsymbol{\psi} = \hat{\boldsymbol{\psi}}$. Hence, the state-price deflator is unique.

Next, assume that the state-price vector $\boldsymbol{\psi}$ is unique. Suppose the market is incomplete so that the number of non-redundant assets, k, is smaller than the number of states, S. Then the pruned $k \times S$ dividend matrix $\hat{\underline{\underline{D}}}$ has the property that for $\hat{\underline{\underline{D}}}\boldsymbol{\varepsilon} = \mathbf{0}$ for some $\boldsymbol{\varepsilon}$ in $\mathbb{R}^S$. Note that this is true for any scaling $k\boldsymbol{\varepsilon}$ of $\boldsymbol{\varepsilon}$. In particular, we can find an $\boldsymbol{\varepsilon} \in \mathbb{R}^S$ satisfying $\hat{\underline{\underline{D}}}\boldsymbol{\varepsilon} = \mathbf{0}$ and $\varepsilon_\omega > -\psi_\omega$ for all $\omega = 1, 2, \ldots, S$. Now define $\hat{\boldsymbol{\psi}} = \boldsymbol{\psi} + \boldsymbol{\varepsilon}$. Since $\hat{\boldsymbol{\psi}}$ is strictly positive and

$$\hat{\underline{\underline{D}}}\hat{\boldsymbol{\psi}} = \hat{\underline{\underline{D}}}(\boldsymbol{\psi} + \boldsymbol{\varepsilon}) = \hat{\underline{\underline{D}}}\boldsymbol{\psi} + \hat{\underline{\underline{D}}}\boldsymbol{\varepsilon} = \hat{\underline{\underline{D}}}\boldsymbol{\psi} = \hat{\boldsymbol{P}},$$

then $\hat{\boldsymbol{\psi}}$ is also a state-price vector, different from $\boldsymbol{\psi}$. This contradicts the uniqueness of $\boldsymbol{\psi}$. Therefore, the market must be complete. □

In a one-period setting with an infinite state space, the market is incomplete. According to the theorem, there will then be more than one state-price deflator. With finitely many assets and an infinite state space, we can find a non-zero random variable ε so that $\mathrm{E}[\varepsilon D_i] = 0$ for all i. Note that this is also true for any scaling $k\varepsilon$, where $k \in \mathbb{R}$. If ζ is a state-price deflator, it now follows that

$$\mathrm{E}[(\zeta + \varepsilon)D_i] = \mathrm{E}[\zeta D_i] + \mathrm{E}[\varepsilon D_i] = \mathrm{E}[\zeta D_i] = P_i.$$

After appropriate scaling, we can make sure that $\zeta + \varepsilon$ is strictly positive, and then it will be a state-price deflator different from ζ. Thus, more than one state-price deflator exists.

The arguments given above for a one-period economy can be adapted to a discrete-time economy. In a continuous-time economy, the line of proof is somewhat different.

Proof. (Continuous time.) Assume that a locally risk-free asset is always traded and let r^f_t denote the continuously compounded risk-free rate. Theorem 4.4 implies that the number of state-price deflators is then equal to the number of market prices of risk, that is the number of stochastic processes $\boldsymbol{\lambda} = (\boldsymbol{\lambda}_t)$ satisfying for each t the equation system

$$\boldsymbol{\mu}_t + \boldsymbol{\delta}_t - r^f_t \mathbf{1} = \underline{\underline{\sigma}}_t \boldsymbol{\lambda}_t.$$

Again we can eliminate entries corresponding to redundant assets so that the equation system reads

$$\hat{\boldsymbol{\mu}}_t + \hat{\boldsymbol{\delta}}_t - r^f_t \mathbf{1} = \hat{\underline{\underline{\sigma}}}_t \boldsymbol{\lambda}_t. \tag{4.37}$$

Recall that the uncertainty is generated by a d-dimensional standard Brownian motion $z = (z_t)$. Let $k \leq d$ denote the number of non-redundant assets, then $\hat{\underline{\underline{\sigma}}}_t$ is the $k \times d$ matrix of price sensitivities. If the market is complete, then

$k = d$ according to Theorem 3.4, we see that there is a unique solution $\boldsymbol{\lambda}_t$ to (4.37). If the market is incomplete so that $k < d$, then there will be more than one solution. The claim in Theorem 4.6 now follows. □

In a continuous-time model with k non-redundant assets, it follows from the considerations in Section 2.7.2 that we can assume, without loss of generality, that the price dynamics of the non-redundant assets are of the form

$$d\hat{\boldsymbol{P}}_t = \operatorname{diag}(\hat{\boldsymbol{P}}_t)\left[\hat{\boldsymbol{\mu}}_t\,dt + \underline{\underline{\hat{\sigma}}}_t\,d\hat{\boldsymbol{z}}_t\right],$$

where $\hat{\boldsymbol{z}} = (\hat{\boldsymbol{z}}_t)$ is a k-dimensional standard Brownian motion and $\underline{\underline{\hat{\sigma}}}_t$ is a (lower-triangular) non-singular $k \times k$ matrix. If the market is complete so that $k = d$, we have a unique market price of risk defined by $\boldsymbol{\lambda}_t = \hat{\boldsymbol{\lambda}}_t$, where

$$\hat{\boldsymbol{\lambda}}_t = \left(\underline{\underline{\hat{\sigma}}}_t\right)^{-1}\left(\hat{\boldsymbol{\mu}}_t + \hat{\boldsymbol{\delta}}_t - r^f_t\boldsymbol{1}\right). \tag{4.38}$$

If the market is incomplete so that $k < d$, it must be because $\hat{\boldsymbol{\mu}}_t$ or $\underline{\underline{\hat{\sigma}}}_t$ or both depend on a $(d-k)$-dimensional standard Brownian motion $\tilde{\boldsymbol{z}} = (\tilde{\boldsymbol{z}}_t)$ independent of $\hat{\boldsymbol{z}}$. If we let $\underline{\underline{0}}$ denote a $k \times (d-k)$ matrix of zeros, we can rewrite the price dynamics as

$$\begin{aligned} d\hat{\boldsymbol{P}}_t &= \operatorname{diag}(\hat{\boldsymbol{P}}_t)\left[\hat{\boldsymbol{\mu}}_t\,dt + \underline{\underline{\hat{\sigma}}}_t\,d\hat{\boldsymbol{z}}_t + \underline{\underline{0}}\,d\tilde{\boldsymbol{z}}_t\right] \\ &= \operatorname{diag}(\hat{\boldsymbol{P}}_t)\left[\hat{\boldsymbol{\mu}}_t\,dt + \left(\underline{\underline{\hat{\sigma}}}_t, \underline{\underline{0}}\right)\,d\boldsymbol{z}_t\right], \end{aligned}$$

where $\boldsymbol{z}$ is the d-dimensional standard Brownian motion obtained by stacking up $\hat{\boldsymbol{z}}$ and $\tilde{\boldsymbol{z}}$. A market price of risk $\boldsymbol{\lambda}$ must then satisfy

$$\hat{\boldsymbol{\mu}}_t + \hat{\boldsymbol{\delta}}_t - r^f_t\boldsymbol{1} = \left(\underline{\underline{\hat{\sigma}}}_t, \underline{\underline{0}}\right)\boldsymbol{\lambda}_t,$$

which is true for any $\boldsymbol{\lambda}$ with $\boldsymbol{\lambda}_t = (\hat{\boldsymbol{\lambda}}_t, \tilde{\boldsymbol{\lambda}}_t)$, where $\hat{\boldsymbol{\lambda}}_t$ is given by Eq. (4.38) and $\tilde{\boldsymbol{\lambda}}_t$ is *any* well-behaved vector of dimension $d-k$. Clearly, this confirms that we have several market prices of risk, and thus several state-price deflators, in an incomplete market.

The arguments above already indicate that when there is more than one state-price deflator, there will in fact be infinitely many. This is also a consequence of the following theorem. Before we state the precise result, we need some terminology. A convex combination of some objects (such as vectors, random variables, stochastic process, etc.) $x_1, x_2, \dots, x_L$ is given by

$$x = \sum_{l=1}^{L} \alpha_l x_l,$$

where $\alpha_1, \dots, \alpha_L$ are positive constants summing up to one.

Theorem 4.7 *If $\zeta_1, \dots, \zeta_L$ are state-price deflators, and $\alpha_1, \dots, \alpha_L > 0$ satisfy $\sum_{l=1}^{L} \alpha_l = 1$, then the convex combination*

$$\zeta = \sum_{l=1}^{L} \alpha_l \zeta_l$$

is also a state-price deflator.

The theorem holds both in the one-period, the discrete-time, and the continuous-time framework. In particular, it tells you that once you have two different state-price deflators, you can generate infinitely many state-price deflators. The proof of the theorem is left as Exercise 4.3.

4.3.3 Spanned Deflators

In the one-period framework with a finite state space, a state-price vector $\boldsymbol{\psi}$ is a strictly positive solution to the equation system $\underline{\underline{\hat{D}}}\boldsymbol{\psi} = \hat{\boldsymbol{P}}$. In the case of a complete market, the matrix $\underline{\underline{\hat{D}}}$ is non-singular so that the unique solution is

$$\boldsymbol{\psi}^* = \underline{\underline{\hat{D}}}^{-1} \hat{\boldsymbol{P}}.$$

Whether the market is complete or not, the S-dimensional vector

$$\boldsymbol{\psi}^* = \underline{\underline{\hat{D}}}^{\top} \left(\underline{\underline{\hat{D}}}\, \underline{\underline{\hat{D}}}^{\top} \right)^{-1} \hat{\boldsymbol{P}}$$

is a solution since

$$\underline{\underline{\hat{D}}}\boldsymbol{\psi}^* = \underline{\underline{\hat{D}}}\, \underline{\underline{\hat{D}}}^{\top} \left(\underline{\underline{\hat{D}}}\, \underline{\underline{\hat{D}}}^{\top} \right)^{-1} \hat{\boldsymbol{P}} = \hat{\boldsymbol{P}}.$$

Hence, *if* $\boldsymbol{\psi}^*$ is strictly positive, it will be a state-price vector. Note that $\boldsymbol{\psi}^*$ is in fact exactly equal to the dividend generated by the portfolio $\hat{\boldsymbol{\theta}}^* = \left(\underline{\underline{\hat{D}}}\, \underline{\underline{\hat{D}}}^{\top} \right)^{-1} \hat{\boldsymbol{P}}$. Hence, it is spanned by the traded assets.

In the special case of a complete and arbitrage-free market the elements of $\boldsymbol{\psi}^*$ will be strictly positive. Why? Since the market is complete, we can construct an Arrow–Debreu asset for any state. The dividend vector of the Arrow–Debreu asset for state ω is $\boldsymbol{e}_\omega = (0, \dots, 0, 1, 0, \dots, 0)^{\top}$, where the 1 is the ω'th element of the vector. The price of this portfolio is $\boldsymbol{\psi}^* \cdot \boldsymbol{e}_\omega = \psi^*_\omega$. To avoid arbitrage, ψ^*_ω must be strictly positive. This argument works for all $\omega = 1, \dots, S$. Hence, $\boldsymbol{\psi}^*$ is a state-price vector if the market is complete.

Now let us turn to state-price deflators. Due to the one-to-one correspondence between state-price vectors and state-price deflators we expect to find similar results. Define the S-dimensional vector $\boldsymbol{\zeta}^*$ by

$$\boldsymbol{\zeta}^* = \underline{\underline{\hat{D}}}^{\top}\left(\mathrm{E}\left[\hat{\boldsymbol{D}}\hat{\boldsymbol{D}}^{\top}\right]\right)^{-1}\hat{\boldsymbol{P}}.$$

To see the meaning of this, let us for simplicity assume that none of the basic assets are redundant so that $\boldsymbol{\zeta}^* = \underline{\underline{D}}^{\top}\left(\mathrm{E}\left[\boldsymbol{D}\boldsymbol{D}^{\top}\right]\right)^{-1}\boldsymbol{P}$. Recall that $\boldsymbol{D}$ is the I-dimensional random variable for which the i'th component is given by the random dividend of asset i. Hence, $\boldsymbol{D}\boldsymbol{D}^{\top}$ is an $I \times I$ matrix of random variables with the (i,j)'th entry given by $D_i D_j$, that is the product of the random dividend of asset i and the random dividend of asset j. The expectation of a matrix of random variables is equal to the matrix of expectations of the individual random variables. So $\mathrm{E}\left[\boldsymbol{D}\boldsymbol{D}^{\top}\right]$ is also an $I \times I$ matrix and so is the inverse $\left(\mathrm{E}\left[\boldsymbol{D}\boldsymbol{D}^{\top}\right]\right)^{-1}$. For the general case we see from the definition that $\boldsymbol{\zeta}^*$ is spanned by the traded assets: it is the dividend vector generated by the portfolio

$$\hat{\boldsymbol{\theta}}^* = \left(\mathrm{E}\left[\hat{\boldsymbol{D}}\hat{\boldsymbol{D}}^{\top}\right]\right)^{-1}\hat{\boldsymbol{P}}$$

of the non-redundant assets. We can think of the vector $\boldsymbol{\zeta}^*$ as a random variable ζ^* given by

$$\zeta^* = \hat{\boldsymbol{D}}^{\top}\hat{\boldsymbol{\theta}}^* = \hat{\boldsymbol{D}}^{\top}\left(\mathrm{E}\left[\hat{\boldsymbol{D}}\hat{\boldsymbol{D}}^{\top}\right]\right)^{-1}\hat{\boldsymbol{P}}. \tag{4.39}$$

We can see that

$$\mathrm{E}\left[\hat{\boldsymbol{D}}\zeta^*\right] = \mathrm{E}\left[\hat{\boldsymbol{D}}\hat{\boldsymbol{D}}^{\top}\left(\mathrm{E}\left[\hat{\boldsymbol{D}}\hat{\boldsymbol{D}}^{\top}\right]\right)^{-1}\hat{\boldsymbol{P}}\right] = \mathrm{E}\left[\hat{\boldsymbol{D}}\hat{\boldsymbol{D}}^{\top}\right]\left(\mathrm{E}\left[\hat{\boldsymbol{D}}\hat{\boldsymbol{D}}^{\top}\right]\right)^{-1}\hat{\boldsymbol{P}} = \hat{\boldsymbol{P}}.$$

It follows that, *if* ζ^* is strictly positive, then it is a state-price deflator. In a complete market, ζ^* will be a state-price deflator and it will be unique.

Recall that there is a one-to-one relation between state-price vectors and state-price deflators. In general ζ^* is not the state-price deflator associated with ψ^*. However, this will be so if the market is complete. To see this, let $\mathrm{diag}(\boldsymbol{p})$ denote the diagonal $S \times S$ matrix with the state probabilities along the diagonal and zeros away from the diagonal. In general, $\mathrm{E}\left[\hat{\boldsymbol{D}}\hat{\boldsymbol{D}}^{\top}\right] = \underline{\underline{\hat{D}}}\,\mathrm{diag}(\boldsymbol{p})\underline{\underline{\hat{D}}}^{\top}$ and the state-price vector associated with a given state-price deflator $\boldsymbol{\zeta}$ is $\mathrm{diag}(\boldsymbol{p})\boldsymbol{\zeta}$, compare Eq. (4.16). With a complete market, $\underline{\underline{\hat{D}}}$ is a non-singular $S \times S$ matrix so

$$\begin{aligned}\boldsymbol{\zeta}^* &= \underline{\underline{\hat{D}}}^{\top}\left(\mathrm{E}\left[\hat{\boldsymbol{D}}\hat{\boldsymbol{D}}^{\top}\right]\right)^{-1}\hat{\boldsymbol{P}} = \underline{\underline{\hat{D}}}^{\top}\left[\underline{\underline{\hat{D}}}\,\mathrm{diag}(\boldsymbol{p})\underline{\underline{\hat{D}}}^{\top}\right]^{-1}\hat{\boldsymbol{P}} \\ &= \underline{\underline{\hat{D}}}^{\top}\left(\underline{\underline{\hat{D}}}^{\top}\right)^{-1}[\mathrm{diag}(\boldsymbol{p})]^{-1}\underline{\underline{\hat{D}}}^{-1}\hat{\boldsymbol{P}} = [\mathrm{diag}(\boldsymbol{p})]^{-1}\underline{\underline{\hat{D}}}^{-1}\hat{\boldsymbol{P}},\end{aligned}$$

and the state-price vector associated with $\boldsymbol{\zeta}^*$ is

$$\mathrm{diag}(\boldsymbol{p})\boldsymbol{\zeta}^* = \underline{\underline{\hat{D}}}^{-1}\hat{\boldsymbol{P}} = \boldsymbol{\psi}^*.$$

Note that $\boldsymbol{\psi}^*$ and ζ^* are defined in terms of the prices of the basic assets. Observing the prices and state-contingent dividends of the basic assets, we can extract the state-price vector or deflator. While this might be useful for empirical studies based on observed prices, it does not tell you how to compute the prices of the basic assets from their state-contingent dividends. We need to add more structure to link the state-price vector and deflator to other variables, for example the consumption and portfolio decisions of the individuals in the economy. This is what concrete asset pricing models have to do.

Example 4.4 Consider again the complete market first studied in Example 3.1. We ignore asset 4, which is in any case redundant. Let $\underline{\underline{D}}$ be the dividend matrix and $\boldsymbol{P}$ the price vector of the first three assets. If we assume that $\boldsymbol{P} = (0.8, 0.8, 1.5)^{\top}$, we can compute the unique state-price vector $\boldsymbol{\psi}^*$ as

$$\boldsymbol{\psi}^* = \underline{\underline{D}}^{-1}\boldsymbol{P} = \begin{pmatrix} 1 & 1 & 1 \\ 0 & 1 & 2 \\ 4 & 0 & 1 \end{pmatrix}^{-1} \begin{pmatrix} 0.8 \\ 0.8 \\ 1.5 \end{pmatrix} = \begin{pmatrix} 0.3 \\ 0.2 \\ 0.3 \end{pmatrix},$$

which is consistent with the results of Example 4.2. The portfolio generating this dividend vector is $\boldsymbol{\theta}^* = (0.14, 0.06, 0.04)^{\top}$.

Since the market is complete, the unique state-price deflator ζ^* is the one associated with $\boldsymbol{\psi}^*$. From Example 4.2, we have $\zeta_1^* = 0.6$, $\zeta_2^* = 0.8$, $\zeta_3^* = 1.2$. The portfolio generating this dividend is $\boldsymbol{\theta}^* = (0.44, 0.36, 0.04)^{\top}$.

Suppose now that only assets 1 and 2 were traded with the same prices as above, $P_1 = P_2 = 0.8$. Then

$$\underline{\underline{D}} = \begin{pmatrix} 1 & 1 & 1 \\ 0 & 1 & 2 \end{pmatrix}, \quad \underline{\underline{D}}\,\underline{\underline{D}}^{\top} = \begin{pmatrix} 3 & 3 \\ 3 & 5 \end{pmatrix}, \quad \left(\underline{\underline{D}}\,\underline{\underline{D}}^{\top}\right)^{-1} = \begin{pmatrix} \frac{5}{6} & -\frac{1}{2} \\ -\frac{1}{2} & \frac{1}{2} \end{pmatrix}$$

and we get

$$\boldsymbol{\psi}^* = \underline{\underline{D}}^{\top}\left(\underline{\underline{D}}\,\underline{\underline{D}}^{\top}\right)^{-1}\boldsymbol{P} = \begin{pmatrix} \frac{4}{15} \\ \frac{4}{15} \\ \frac{4}{15}, \end{pmatrix},$$

which is strictly positive and therefore a state-price vector. It is the dividend of the portfolio that only consists of $4/15 \approx 0.2667$ units of asset 1. But we can find many other state-price vectors. We have to look for strictly positive solutions $(\psi_1, \psi_2, \psi_3)^{\top}$ of the two equations

$$\psi_1 + \psi_2 + \psi_3 = 0.8, \quad \psi_2 + 2\psi_3 = 0.8.$$

Subtracting one equation from the other we see that we need to have $\psi_1 = \psi_3$. Any vector of the form $\boldsymbol{\psi} = (a, 0.8 - 2a, a)^{\top}$ with $0 < a < 0.4$ will be a valid state-price vector (this includes, of course, the state-price vector in the three-asset market). All these vectors will generate the same price on any marketed dividend, but different prices on non-marketed dividends. For example, the value of the dividend of asset 3, which we now assume is not traded, will be $\boldsymbol{\psi} \cdot (4, 0, 1)^\top = 5a$, which can be anywhere in the interval $(0, 2)$.

Let us compute ζ^* in the two-asset market. The computations needed for $\mathrm{E}[\boldsymbol{D}\boldsymbol{D}^\top]$ are given in Table 4.1. We get

$$\mathrm{E}[\boldsymbol{D}\boldsymbol{D}^\top] = \begin{pmatrix} 1 & 0.75 \\ 0.75 & 1.25 \end{pmatrix}, \quad \left(\mathrm{E}[\boldsymbol{D}\boldsymbol{D}^\top]\right)^{-1} = \begin{pmatrix} 1.8182 & -1.0909 \\ -1.0909 & 1.4545 \end{pmatrix},$$

$$\boldsymbol{\theta}^* = \left(\mathrm{E}[\boldsymbol{D}\boldsymbol{D}^\top]\right)^{-1} \boldsymbol{P} = \begin{pmatrix} 0.5818 \\ 0.2909 \end{pmatrix}, \quad \boldsymbol{\zeta}^* = \underline{\underline{D}}^\top \boldsymbol{\theta}^* = \begin{pmatrix} 0.5818 \\ 0.8727 \\ 1.1636 \end{pmatrix}.$$

Since $\boldsymbol{\zeta}^* > 0$, it is a valid state-price deflator. Note that this is *not* the state-price deflator associated with the state-price vector $\boldsymbol{\psi}^*$ computed above. We have infinitely many state-price deflators for this market. Given any state-price vector $\boldsymbol{\psi} = (a, 0.8 - 2a, a)^\top$ for $0 < a < 0.4$, the associated state-price deflator is given by $\zeta_\omega = \psi_\omega / p_\omega$, that is

$$\boldsymbol{\zeta} = \begin{pmatrix} a/0.5 \\ (0.8 - 2a)/0.25 \\ a/0.25 \end{pmatrix} = \begin{pmatrix} 2a \\ 3.2 - 8a \\ 4a \end{pmatrix}.$$

Letting $b = 2a$, any state-price deflator is of the form $\boldsymbol{\zeta} = (b, 3.2 - 4b, 2b)$ for $0 < b < 0.8$. □

In the multiperiod discrete-time framework all the above observations and conclusions hold in each period.

Now consider the continuous-time framework and assume again that an instantaneously risk-free asset is traded. Whether the market is complete or not, we can write one solution to Eq. (4.37) as

$$\boldsymbol{\lambda}_t^* = \underline{\underline{\hat{\sigma}}}_t^\top \left(\underline{\underline{\hat{\sigma}}}_t \underline{\underline{\hat{\sigma}}}_t^\top \right)^{-1} \left(\hat{\boldsymbol{\mu}}_t + \hat{\boldsymbol{\delta}}_t - r_t^f \mathbf{1} \right). \tag{4.40}$$

Table 4.1. Computation of expectations for $\boldsymbol{\zeta}^*$ in Example 4.4.

Probabilities	State 1	State 2	State 3	Expectation
	0.5	0.25	0.25	
D_1^2	1	1	1	1
$D_1 D_2$	0	1	2	0.75
D_2^2	0	1	4	1.25

If the market is complete, this simplifies to

$$\boldsymbol{\lambda}_t^* = \underline{\underline{\hat{\sigma}}}_t^{-1} \left(\hat{\boldsymbol{\mu}}_t + \hat{\boldsymbol{\delta}}_t - r_t^f \mathbf{1} \right).$$

Let ζ^* be the state-price deflator associated with $\boldsymbol{\lambda}^*$, that is

$$\zeta_t^* = \exp\left\{ -\int_0^t r_s^f \, ds - \frac{1}{2} \int_0^t \|\boldsymbol{\lambda}_s^*\|^2 \, ds - \int_0^t (\boldsymbol{\lambda}_s^*)^\top \, d\boldsymbol{z}_s \right\}. \tag{4.41}$$

The ζ^* is closely related to the value process of a specific trading strategy, which can be seen as an analogue of the spanned state-price deflator discussed in the one-period framework. More precisely, it is the self-financing trading strategy given by the fractions of wealth $\boldsymbol{\pi}_t^* = \left(\underline{\underline{\hat{\sigma}}}_t \underline{\underline{\hat{\sigma}}}_t^\top \right)^{-1} \left(\hat{\boldsymbol{\mu}}_t + \hat{\boldsymbol{\delta}}_t - r_t^f \mathbf{1} \right)$ in the non-redundant risky assets and the fraction $1 - (\boldsymbol{\pi}_t^*)^\top \mathbf{1}$ in the instantaneously risk-free asset. It follows from Eq. (3.14) that the dynamics of the value V_t^* of this trading strategy is given by

$$\begin{aligned} dV_t^* &= V_t^* \left[\left(r_t^f + (\boldsymbol{\pi}_t^*)^\top \left(\hat{\boldsymbol{\mu}}_t + \hat{\boldsymbol{\delta}}_t - r_t^f \mathbf{1} \right) \right) dt + (\boldsymbol{\pi}_t^*)^\top \underline{\underline{\hat{\sigma}}}_t \, d\boldsymbol{z}_t \right] \\ &= V_t^* \left[\left(r_t^f + \|\boldsymbol{\lambda}_t^*\|^2 \right) dt + (\boldsymbol{\lambda}_t^*)^\top \, d\boldsymbol{z}_t \right]. \end{aligned} \tag{4.42}$$

It can be shown that $\boldsymbol{\pi}_t^*$ is the trading strategy with the highest expected continuously compounded growth rate, that is the trading strategy maximizing $\mathrm{E}[\ln \left(V_T^{\boldsymbol{\pi}} / V_0^{\boldsymbol{\pi}} \right)]$, and it is therefore referred to as the *growth-optimal trading strategy*. Consequently, $\boldsymbol{\lambda}_t^*$ defined in Eq. (4.40) is the relative sensitivity vector of the value of the growth-optimal trading strategy. One can show that $\zeta_t^* = V_0^*/V_t^*$ (see Exercise 4.12) so we have a state-price deflator defined in terms of the value of a trading strategy.

4.3.4 The Candidate Deflator ζ^* and the Hansen–Jagannathan Bound

The candidate deflator $\boldsymbol{\zeta}^*$ from the one-period framework is interesting for empirical studies so it is worthwhile studying it more closely. Let us compute the return associated with the dividend ζ^*. This return turns out to play an important role in the characterization of the mean-variance efficient portfolios given in Chapter 10. For notational simplicity suppose that no assets are redundant so that

$$\zeta^* = \boldsymbol{D}^\top \left(\mathrm{E}\left[\boldsymbol{D}\boldsymbol{D}^\top \right] \right)^{-1} \boldsymbol{P}, \quad \boldsymbol{\theta}^* = \left(\mathrm{E}\left[\boldsymbol{D}\boldsymbol{D}^\top \right] \right)^{-1} \boldsymbol{P}.$$

Let us first rewrite ζ^* and $\boldsymbol{\theta}^*$ in terms of the gross rates of return of the assets instead of prices and dividends. Using Eq. (3.2), we get

$$\begin{aligned}\left(\mathrm{E}\left[\boldsymbol{D}\boldsymbol{D}^{\top}\right]\right)^{-1} &= \left(\mathrm{E}\left[\operatorname{diag}(\boldsymbol{P})\boldsymbol{R}\boldsymbol{R}^{\top}\operatorname{diag}(\boldsymbol{P})\right]\right)^{-1} \\ &= \left(\operatorname{diag}(\boldsymbol{P})\,\mathrm{E}\left[\boldsymbol{R}\boldsymbol{R}^{\top}\right]\operatorname{diag}(\boldsymbol{P})\right)^{-1} \\ &= [\operatorname{diag}(\boldsymbol{P})]^{-1}\left(\mathrm{E}\left[\boldsymbol{R}\boldsymbol{R}^{\top}\right]\right)^{-1}[\operatorname{diag}(\boldsymbol{P})]^{-1}, \end{aligned} \tag{4.43}$$

using the facts that prices are non-random and that $(AB)^{-1} = B^{-1}A^{-1}$ for non-singular matrices A and B. Consequently, applying the fact that $[\operatorname{diag}(\boldsymbol{P})]^{-1}\boldsymbol{P} = \mathbf{1}$, we obtain

$$\boldsymbol{\theta}^* = \left(\mathrm{E}\left[\boldsymbol{D}\boldsymbol{D}^{\top}\right]\right)^{-1}\boldsymbol{P} = [\operatorname{diag}(\boldsymbol{P})]^{-1}\left(\mathrm{E}\left[\boldsymbol{R}\boldsymbol{R}^{\top}\right]\right)^{-1}\mathbf{1}$$

and

$$\begin{aligned}\zeta^* &= \boldsymbol{D}^{\top}\left(\mathrm{E}\left[\boldsymbol{D}\boldsymbol{D}^{\top}\right]\right)^{-1}\boldsymbol{P} \\ &= \boldsymbol{D}^{\top}[\operatorname{diag}(\boldsymbol{P})]^{-1}\left(\mathrm{E}\left[\boldsymbol{R}\boldsymbol{R}^{\top}\right]\right)^{-1}\mathbf{1} \\ &= \left([\operatorname{diag}(\boldsymbol{P})]^{-1}\boldsymbol{D}\right)^{\top}\left(\mathrm{E}\left[\boldsymbol{R}\boldsymbol{R}^{\top}\right]\right)^{-1}\mathbf{1} \\ &= \boldsymbol{R}^{\top}\left(\mathrm{E}\left[\boldsymbol{R}\boldsymbol{R}^{\top}\right]\right)^{-1}\mathbf{1} \\ &= \mathbf{1}^{\top}\left(\mathrm{E}\left[\boldsymbol{R}\boldsymbol{R}^{\top}\right]\right)^{-1}\boldsymbol{R}, \end{aligned}$$

where we have used Eq. (3.2) and various rules from matrix algebra that can be found in Appendix C. The portfolio weight vector is obtained by substituting $\boldsymbol{\theta}^*$ into Eq. (3.9). Since

$$\operatorname{diag}(\boldsymbol{P})\boldsymbol{\theta}^* = \operatorname{diag}(\boldsymbol{P})[\operatorname{diag}(\boldsymbol{P})]^{-1}\left(\mathrm{E}\left[\boldsymbol{R}\boldsymbol{R}^{\top}\right]\right)^{-1}\mathbf{1} = \left(\mathrm{E}\left[\boldsymbol{R}\boldsymbol{R}^{\top}\right]\right)^{-1}\mathbf{1},$$

we get

$$\boldsymbol{\pi}^* = \frac{\left(\mathrm{E}\left[\boldsymbol{R}\boldsymbol{R}^{\top}\right]\right)^{-1}\mathbf{1}}{\mathbf{1}^{\top}\left(\mathrm{E}\left[\boldsymbol{R}\boldsymbol{R}^{\top}\right]\right)^{-1}\mathbf{1}}. \tag{4.44}$$

The gross rate of return on this portfolio is

$$R^* = (\boldsymbol{\pi}^*)^{\top}\boldsymbol{R} = \frac{\mathbf{1}^{\top}\left(\mathrm{E}\left[\boldsymbol{R}\boldsymbol{R}^{\top}\right]\right)^{-1}\boldsymbol{R}}{\mathbf{1}^{\top}\left(\mathrm{E}\left[\boldsymbol{R}\boldsymbol{R}^{\top}\right]\right)^{-1}\mathbf{1}}. \tag{4.45}$$

This is the gross rate of return corresponding to the dividend ζ^*.

We can also compute R^* directly as ζ^* divided by the price of ζ^* (well-defined since it is a dividend), that is $R^* = \zeta^*/P(\zeta^*)$. Since $\zeta^* = \mathbf{1}^{\top}\left(\mathrm{E}\left[\boldsymbol{R}\boldsymbol{R}^{\top}\right]\right)^{-1}\boldsymbol{R}$, the price of ζ^* is

$$P(\zeta^*) = \mathrm{E}[\zeta^*\zeta^*] = \mathrm{E}\left[P^\top \left(\mathrm{E}\left[DD^\top\right]\right)^{-1} DD^\top \left(\mathrm{E}\left[DD^\top\right]\right)^{-1} P\right]$$
$$= P^\top \left(\mathrm{E}\left[DD^\top\right]\right)^{-1} P = \mathbf{1}^\top \left(\mathrm{E}\left[RR^\top\right]\right)^{-1} \mathbf{1}.$$

Dividing ζ^* by $P(\zeta^*)$ we get (4.45).

In Exercise 4.4 you are asked to show the properties collected in the following lemma:

Lemma 4.1 *R^* has the following properties:*

$$\mathrm{E}[R^*] = \frac{\mathbf{1}^\top \left(\mathrm{E}\left[RR^\top\right]\right)^{-1} \mathrm{E}[R]}{\mathbf{1}^\top \left(\mathrm{E}\left[RR^\top\right]\right)^{-1} \mathbf{1}}$$
$$\mathrm{E}[(R^*)^2] = \frac{1}{\mathbf{1}^\top \left(\mathrm{E}\left[RR^\top\right]\right)^{-1} \mathbf{1}} = \frac{1}{P(\zeta^*)},$$
$$\mathrm{E}[R^* R^i] = \mathrm{E}[(R^*)^2], \quad i = 1, \dots, N.$$

In particular,

$$\frac{\mathrm{E}[R^*]}{\mathrm{E}[(R^*)^2]} = \mathbf{1}^\top \left(\mathrm{E}[RR^\top]\right)^{-1} \mathrm{E}[R]. \tag{4.46}$$

Any random variable ζ that satisfies $P_i = \mathrm{E}[\zeta D_i]$ for all assets i can be decomposed as

$$\zeta = \mathrm{E}[\zeta] + (P - \mathrm{E}[\zeta]\,\mathrm{E}[D])^\top \underline{\underline{\Sigma}}_D^{-1} (D - \mathrm{E}[D]) + \varepsilon,$$

where $\underline{\underline{\Sigma}}_D = \mathrm{Var}[D]$ and ε is a random variable with $\mathrm{E}[D\varepsilon] = \mathbf{0}$ and $\mathrm{E}[\varepsilon] = 0$. In particular $\mathrm{Cov}[D, \varepsilon] = \mathbf{0}$. So taking variances we get

$$\mathrm{Var}[\zeta] = (P - \mathrm{E}[\zeta]\,\mathrm{E}[D])^\top \underline{\underline{\Sigma}}_D^{-1} \mathrm{Var}[D - \mathrm{E}[D]]\, \underline{\underline{\Sigma}}_D^{-1} (P - \mathrm{E}[\zeta]\,\mathrm{E}[D]) + \mathrm{Var}[\varepsilon]$$
$$\geq (P - \mathrm{E}[\zeta]\,\mathrm{E}[D])^\top \underline{\underline{\Sigma}}_D^{-1} (P - \mathrm{E}[\zeta]\,\mathrm{E}[D])$$
$$= (\mathbf{1} - \mathrm{E}[\zeta]\,\mathrm{E}[R])^\top \underline{\underline{\Sigma}}^{-1} (\mathbf{1} - \mathrm{E}[\zeta]\,\mathrm{E}[R]),$$

where $\underline{\underline{\Sigma}} = \mathrm{Var}[R]$. The possible combinations of expectation and standard deviation of state-price deflators form a hyperbolic region in $(\mathrm{E}[\zeta], \sigma[\zeta])$-space. This result is due to Hansen and Jagannathan (1991), and the right-hand side of the above inequality (or the boundary of the hyperbolic region) is called the Hansen–Jagannathan bound. In Exercise 4.5 you are asked to show that ζ^* satisfies

$$\zeta^* = \mathrm{E}[\zeta^*] + \left(P - \mathrm{E}[\zeta^*]\,\mathrm{E}[D]\right)^\top \underline{\underline{\Sigma}}_D^{-1} (D - \mathrm{E}[D]). \tag{4.47}$$

Note that no ε is added on the right-hand side. It follows that ζ^* satisfies the Hansen–Jagannathan bound with an equality.

4.4 MULTIPERIOD VALUATION MODELS

This section studies some cases in which the computation of the present value of a dividend (stream) is relatively simple and leads to nice solutions. These cases are based on concrete distributional assumptions on both the state-price deflator and the dividends to be priced.

4.4.1 Lognormal Dividend and State-Price Deflator

Consider a single terminal dividend of D_T. Suppose that $D_T = \mathrm{E}_t[D_T]e^X$ for a normally distributed random variable X. To ensure $\mathrm{E}_t[e^X] = 1$, we need $X \sim N(-\frac{1}{2}\sigma_X^2, \sigma_X^2)$, compare Theorem B.2 in Appendix B. Also assume that $\zeta_T = \zeta_t e^Y$, where X and Y are jointly normally distributed with correlation ρ and $Y \sim N(\mu_Y, \sigma_Y^2)$. Then the present value of the dividend is

$$P_t = \mathrm{E}_t\left[D_T\frac{\zeta_T}{\zeta_t}\right] = \mathrm{E}_t\left[\mathrm{E}_t[D_T]e^X e^Y\right] = \mathrm{E}_t[D_T]\,\mathrm{E}_t\left[e^{X+Y}\right].$$

Since $X + Y \sim N(-\frac{1}{2}\sigma_X^2 + \mu_Y, \sigma_X^2 + \sigma_Y^2 + 2\rho\sigma_X\sigma_Y)$, we get

$$\begin{aligned}\mathrm{E}_t\left[e^{X+Y}\right] &= \exp\left\{-\frac{1}{2}\sigma_X^2 + \mu_Y + \frac{1}{2}\left(\sigma_X^2 + \sigma_Y^2 + 2\rho\sigma_X\sigma_Y\right)\right\} \\ &= \exp\left\{\mu_Y + \frac{1}{2}\sigma_Y^2 + \rho\sigma_X\sigma_Y\right\}\end{aligned}$$

and thus

$$P_t = \mathrm{E}_t[D_T]\exp\left\{\mu_Y + \frac{1}{2}\sigma_Y^2 + \rho\sigma_X\sigma_Y\right\}.$$

The exponential term on the right-hand side of this equation is the appropriately risk-adjusted discount factor for the given dividend. The risk adjustment depends on how risky the dividend is (captured by σ_X) and how correlated the dividend is with the state-price deflator (captured by ρ).

In a continuous-time setting the distributional assumption on $Y = \ln(\zeta_T/\zeta_t)$ is satisfied if the market price of risk vector is a constant $\boldsymbol{\lambda}$ and the short-term risk-free rate is a constant r^f since then

$$\begin{aligned}Y &= -\left(r^f + \frac{1}{2}\|\boldsymbol{\lambda}\|^2\right)(T-t) - \int_t^T \boldsymbol{\lambda}^{\top}\,dz_u \\ &\sim N\left(-\left(r^f + \frac{1}{2}\|\boldsymbol{\lambda}\|^2\right)(T-t), \|\boldsymbol{\lambda}\|^2(T-t)\right),\end{aligned}$$

in which case we can rewrite the present value as

$$P_t = \mathrm{E}_t[D_T] \exp\left\{-r^f(T-t) + \rho\sigma_X\sigma_Y\right\}.$$

If we substitute in σ_Y and write $\sigma_X^2 = \sigma_d^2(T-t)$, where σ_d^2 is the annualized variance of the dividend, we get a present value of

$$\begin{aligned} P_t &= \mathrm{E}_t[D_T] \exp\left\{-r^f(T-t) + \rho\sigma_d\|\boldsymbol{\lambda}\|(T-t)\right\} \\ &= \mathrm{E}_t[D_T] \exp\left\{-(r^f - \rho\sigma_d\|\boldsymbol{\lambda}\|)(T-t)\right\}. \end{aligned}$$

The expected dividend is discounted with a risk-adjusted percentage interest rate, which equals the risk-free rate minus $\rho\sigma_d\|\boldsymbol{\lambda}\|$.

Note that if $\rho > 0$, the dividend is positively correlated with the state-price deflator so that the dividend tends to be high exactly when investors value extra payments the most. Therefore, the price will be relatively high. Equivalently, the expected dividend should be discounted at a low rate.

4.4.2 Discrete-Time Valuation

Consider a discrete-time multiperiod framework in which the state-price deflator $\zeta = (\zeta_t)$ satisfies

$$\mathrm{E}_t\left[\frac{\zeta_{t+1}}{\zeta_t}\right] = \mu_\zeta, \quad \mathrm{Var}_t\left[\frac{\zeta_{t+1}}{\zeta_t}\right] = \sigma_\zeta^2$$

for each $t = 0, 1, 2, \dots, T-1$. In particular, $\mathrm{E}_t\left[(\zeta_{t+1}/\zeta_t)^2\right] = \sigma_\zeta^2 + \mu_\zeta^2$. Consider an uncertain stream of dividends $D = (D_t)$ for which the dividend growth rate is given by

$$\frac{D_{t+1}}{D_t} = a + b\frac{\zeta_{t+1}}{\zeta_t} + \varepsilon_{t+1}, \quad t = 0, 1, \dots, T-1,$$

where $\varepsilon_1, \dots, \varepsilon_T$ are independent with $\mathrm{E}_t[\varepsilon_{t+1}] = 0$ and $\mathrm{E}_t[\varepsilon_{t+1}\zeta_{t+1}] = 0$ for all t.

First note that

$$\begin{aligned} \mathrm{E}_t\left[\frac{D_{t+1}}{D_t}\frac{\zeta_{t+1}}{\zeta_t}\right] &= \mathrm{E}_t\left[\left(a + b\frac{\zeta_{t+1}}{\zeta_t} + \varepsilon_{t+1}\right)\frac{\zeta_{t+1}}{\zeta_t}\right] \\ &= a\,\mathrm{E}_t\left[\frac{\zeta_{t+1}}{\zeta_t}\right] + b\,\mathrm{E}_t\left[\left(\frac{\zeta_{t+1}}{\zeta_t}\right)^2\right] \\ &= a\mu_\zeta + b\left(\sigma_\zeta^2 + \mu_\zeta^2\right) \equiv A \end{aligned}$$

for every $t = 0, 1, \dots, T-1$. Together with the Law of Iterated Expectations this implies that for each $s > t$

$$\begin{aligned}
\mathrm{E}_t\left[\frac{D_s}{D_t}\frac{\zeta_s}{\zeta_t}\right] &= \mathrm{E}_t\left[\frac{D_{s-1}}{D_t}\frac{\zeta_{s-1}}{\zeta_t}\frac{D_s}{D_{s-1}}\frac{\zeta_s}{\zeta_{s-1}}\right] = \mathrm{E}_t\left[\frac{D_{s-1}}{D_t}\frac{\zeta_{s-1}}{\zeta_t}\,\mathrm{E}_{s-1}\left[\frac{D_s}{D_{s-1}}\frac{\zeta_s}{\zeta_{s-1}}\right]\right] \\
&= A\,\mathrm{E}_t\left[\frac{D_{s-1}}{D_t}\frac{\zeta_{s-1}}{\zeta_t}\right] = \dots = A^{s-t}.
\end{aligned}$$

The price-dividend ratio of the asset is therefore

$$\begin{aligned}
\frac{P_t}{D_t} &= \mathrm{E}_t\left[\sum_{s=t+1}^{T}\frac{D_s}{D_t}\frac{\zeta_s}{\zeta_t}\right] = \sum_{s=t+1}^{T}\mathrm{E}_t\left[\frac{D_s}{D_t}\frac{\zeta_s}{\zeta_t}\right] \\
&= \sum_{s=t+1}^{T} A^{s-t} = A + A^2 + \dots + A^{T-t} \\
&= \frac{A}{1-A}\left(1 - A^{T-t}\right).
\end{aligned}$$

The price is thus

$$P_t = D_t\frac{A}{1-A}\left(1 - A^{T-t}\right).$$

If $|A| < 1$ and you let $T \to \infty$, that is assume dividends continue forever, you get

$$P_t = D_t\frac{A}{1-A}.$$

In particular, the price-dividend ratio is a constant. As described in Section 1.5 the price-dividend ratio of the entire stock market (and for typical individual stocks) varies over time. To obtain that, we would have to allow for time-variation in the conditional moments of the state-price deflator or for a different relation between dividend growth and the state-price deflator than assumed above.

The pricing formula derived above has some similarity to the Gordon Growth Formula which was developed by Gordon (1962) and is apparently still frequently applied by many financial analysts. Gordon's model assumes that expected dividends grow forever at a constant rate of g and that the appropriate risk-adjusted percentage discount rate is a constant $\bar{r} > g$. Then the present value of all future dividends is

$$P_t = \sum_{s=t+1}^{\infty} D_t(1+g)^{s-t}(1+\bar{r})^{-(s-t)} = D_t\sum_{u=1}^{\infty}\left(\frac{1+g}{1+\bar{r}}\right)^u = D_t\frac{1+g}{\bar{r}-g}$$

so that the price-dividend ratio is constant. However, it is not clear how to find the appropriate risk-adjusted discount rate. The above derivations avoid that and produce a result which is just as simple as the Gordon Growth Formula.

Other examples leading to a simple closed-form expression for the price of a dividend stream are addressed in Exercises 4.9 and 4.10.

4.4.3 Continuous-Time Valuation

Let us consider how to compute the time t value P_t of a single lump-sum dividend payment D_T at time T. From the definition of the state-price deflator and Eq. (4.33), we know that

$$P_t = \mathrm{E}_t\left[\frac{\zeta_T}{\zeta_t} D_T\right] = \mathrm{E}_t\left[D_T \exp\left\{-\int_t^T r_s^f\,ds - \frac{1}{2}\int_t^T \|\boldsymbol{\lambda}_s\|^2\,ds - \int_t^T \boldsymbol{\lambda}_s^{\top}\,d\boldsymbol{z}_s\right\}\right].$$

Suppose now that an m-dimensional diffusion process $\boldsymbol{x} = (\boldsymbol{x}_t)_{t\in[0,T]}$ exists with dynamics of the form

$$d\boldsymbol{x}_t = \boldsymbol{\mu}_x(\boldsymbol{x}_t)\,dt + \underline{\underline{\sigma}}_x(\boldsymbol{x}_t)\,d\boldsymbol{z}_t \tag{4.48}$$

and the property that

$$r_s^f = r^f(\boldsymbol{x}_s), \quad \boldsymbol{\lambda}_s = \boldsymbol{\lambda}(\boldsymbol{x}_s), \quad D_T = D(\boldsymbol{x}_T), \tag{4.49}$$

where $\boldsymbol{\mu}_x(\cdot)$, $\underline{\underline{\sigma}}_x(\cdot)$, $r^f(\cdot)$, $\boldsymbol{\lambda}(\cdot)$, and $D(\cdot)$ denote well-behaved functions. As before, $\boldsymbol{z}$ is a standard Brownian motion of dimension d. Since $\boldsymbol{x}$ is a Markov process, the conditional expectation in the above valuation formula will depend only on time t and the current value $\boldsymbol{x}_t$ of the 'state variable' $\boldsymbol{x}$, that is we have $P_t = P(\boldsymbol{x}_t, t)$. The following theorem shows that the pricing function $P(\boldsymbol{x}_t, t)$ will satisfy a certain partial differential equation (PDE). Recall that, for any square matrix $\underline{\underline{A}}$, $\mathrm{tr}(\underline{\underline{A}})$ denotes the trace of the matrix, which is defined as the sum of the elements in the main diagonal.

Theorem 4.8 *Suppose Eqs.* (4.48) *and* (4.49) *are satisfied. Then, for any time $t \in [0, T)$, the price of the terminal dividend $D(\boldsymbol{x}_T)$ is given by $P_t = P(\boldsymbol{x}_t, t)$, where the function $P(\boldsymbol{x}, t)$ satisfies the PDE*

$$\begin{aligned}\frac{\partial P}{\partial t}(\boldsymbol{x}, t) &+ \left(\frac{\partial P}{\partial \boldsymbol{x}}(\boldsymbol{x}, t)\right)^{\top}\left(\boldsymbol{\mu}_x(\boldsymbol{x}) - \underline{\underline{\sigma}}_x(\boldsymbol{x})\boldsymbol{\lambda}(\boldsymbol{x})\right) + \frac{1}{2}\,\mathrm{tr}\left(\frac{\partial^2 P}{\partial \boldsymbol{x}^2}(\boldsymbol{x}, t)\underline{\underline{\sigma}}_x(\boldsymbol{x})\underline{\underline{\sigma}}_x(\boldsymbol{x})^{\top}\right) \\ &= r^f(\boldsymbol{x})P(\boldsymbol{x}, t), \qquad (\boldsymbol{x}, t) \in \mathcal{S} \times [0, T),\end{aligned} \tag{4.50}$$

with the terminal condition

$$P(\boldsymbol{x}, T-) = D(\boldsymbol{x}), \qquad \boldsymbol{x} \in \mathcal{S}, \tag{4.51}$$

where $\mathcal{S}$ is the value space of the diffusion process $\boldsymbol{x}$.

Here $P(\boldsymbol{x}, T-)$ denotes the price immediately before the terminal dividend is paid out. By our convention, the price at time T is exclusive of the dividend at time T and thus equal to zero.

Proof. Given the dynamics (4.48) of $\boldsymbol{x}$, it follows from the multidimensional version of Itô's Lemma, see Eq. (2.19), that the dynamics of the price $P_t = P(\boldsymbol{x}_t, t)$ is

$$dP_t = \left\{ \frac{\partial P}{\partial t}(\boldsymbol{x}_t, t) + \left(\frac{\partial P}{\partial \boldsymbol{x}}(\boldsymbol{x}_t, t)\right)^{\top} \boldsymbol{\mu}_x(\boldsymbol{x}_t) + \frac{1}{2}\operatorname{tr}\left(\frac{\partial^2 P}{\partial \boldsymbol{x}^2}(\boldsymbol{x}_t, t)\underline{\underline{\sigma}}_x(\boldsymbol{x}_t)\underline{\underline{\sigma}}_x(\boldsymbol{x}_t)^{\top}\right)\right\} dt$$
$$+ \left(\frac{\partial P}{\partial \boldsymbol{x}}(\boldsymbol{x}_t, t)\right)^{\top} \underline{\underline{\sigma}}_x(\boldsymbol{x}_t)\, d\boldsymbol{z}_t. \tag{4.52}$$

On the other hand, we know from Eq. (4.31) that the general price dynamics of an asset with no intermediate dividends is of the form

$$dP_t = P_t\left[\left(r_t^f + \boldsymbol{\sigma}_t^{\top}\boldsymbol{\lambda}_t\right) dt + \boldsymbol{\sigma}_t^{\top}\, d\boldsymbol{z}_t\right],$$

which under the above assumptions implies that

$$dP_t = \left(r^f(\boldsymbol{x}_t)P(\boldsymbol{x}_t, t) + P(\boldsymbol{x}_t, t)\boldsymbol{\sigma}_t^{\top}\boldsymbol{\lambda}(\boldsymbol{x}_t)\right) dt + P(\boldsymbol{x}_t, t)\boldsymbol{\sigma}_t^{\top}\, d\boldsymbol{z}_t. \tag{4.53}$$

By matching the sensitivity terms in Eqs. (4.52) and (4.53), we can conclude that

$$P(\boldsymbol{x}_t, t)\boldsymbol{\sigma}_t^{\top} = \left(\frac{\partial P}{\partial \boldsymbol{x}}(\boldsymbol{x}_t, t)\right)^{\top} \underline{\underline{\sigma}}_x(\boldsymbol{x}_t).$$

By substituting this into the drift term in Eq. (4.53) and matching that drift term with the drift term in Eq. (4.52), we conclude that

$$\frac{\partial P}{\partial t}(\boldsymbol{x}_t, t) + \left(\frac{\partial P}{\partial \boldsymbol{x}}(\boldsymbol{x}_t, t)\right)^{\top} \boldsymbol{\mu}_x(\boldsymbol{x}_t) + \frac{1}{2}\operatorname{tr}\left(\frac{\partial^2 P}{\partial \boldsymbol{x}^2}(\boldsymbol{x}_t, t)\underline{\underline{\sigma}}_x(\boldsymbol{x}_t)\underline{\underline{\sigma}}_x(\boldsymbol{x}_t)^{\top}\right)$$
$$= r^f(\boldsymbol{x}_t)P(\boldsymbol{x}_t, t) + \left(\frac{\partial P}{\partial \boldsymbol{x}}(\boldsymbol{x}_t, t)\right)^{\top} \underline{\underline{\sigma}}_x(\boldsymbol{x}_t)\boldsymbol{\lambda}(\boldsymbol{x}_t, t).$$

Rearranging, we find

$$\frac{\partial P}{\partial t}(\boldsymbol{x}_t, t) + \left(\frac{\partial P}{\partial \boldsymbol{x}}(\boldsymbol{x}_t, t)\right)^{\top} \left(\boldsymbol{\mu}_x(\boldsymbol{x}_t) - \underline{\underline{\sigma}}_x(\boldsymbol{x}_t)\boldsymbol{\lambda}(\boldsymbol{x}_t, t)\right)$$
$$+ \frac{1}{2}\operatorname{tr}\left(\frac{\partial^2 P}{\partial \boldsymbol{x}^2}(\boldsymbol{x}_t, t)\underline{\underline{\sigma}}_x(\boldsymbol{x}_t)\underline{\underline{\sigma}}_x(\boldsymbol{x}_t)^{\top}\right) = r^f(\boldsymbol{x}_t)P(\boldsymbol{x}_t, t).$$

Since this relation has to hold for any value of $\boldsymbol{x}_t$ and any t in the life of the asset, the pricing function must satisfy the PDE (4.50). □

Note that the PDE follows from the absence of arbitrage since that implies the existence of a state-price deflator and thus the existence of a market price of risk.[3]

In general, a PDE will have many solutions, but adding a terminal condition (and sometimes conditions on the value of P at the boundaries of $\mathcal{S}$) will lead to a unique solution. The PDE (4.50) is the same for all dividends that are functions of the same state variable x, but the terminal condition differs from asset to asset and therefore the pricing functions for the different assets will also differ.

Under certain assumptions of the functions r^f, $\boldsymbol{\lambda}$, D, $\boldsymbol{\mu}_x$, and $\underline{\underline{\sigma}}_x$, it is possible to derive a closed-form solution to the above PDE with the associated terminal condition. The most prominent example is when the model has an affine structure. In this case the risk-free rate is given by

$$r^f(\boldsymbol{x}) = \xi_0 + \boldsymbol{\xi}^\top \boldsymbol{x}$$

for a constant scalar ξ_0 and a constant vector $\boldsymbol{\xi}$ in $\mathbb{R}^m$. The volatility matrix of the state variable is of the form

$$\underline{\underline{\sigma}}_x(\boldsymbol{x}) = \underline{\underline{\Gamma}}\sqrt{\underline{\underline{V}}(\boldsymbol{x})},$$

where $\underline{\underline{\Gamma}}$ is a constant $m \times d$ matrix, $\underline{\underline{V}}(\boldsymbol{x})$ is the diagonal $d \times d$ matrix

$$\underline{\underline{V}}(\boldsymbol{x}) = \begin{pmatrix} \nu_1 + \boldsymbol{v}_1^\top \boldsymbol{x} & 0 & \dots & 0 \\ 0 & \nu_2 + \boldsymbol{v}_2^\top \boldsymbol{x} & \dots & 0 \\ \vdots & & \ddots & \vdots \\ 0 & 0 & \dots & \nu_d + \boldsymbol{v}_d^\top \boldsymbol{x} \end{pmatrix},$$

and $\sqrt{\underline{\underline{V}}(\boldsymbol{x}_t)}$ is the diagonal $d \times d$ matrix with entry (i, i) equal to $\sqrt{\nu_i + \boldsymbol{v}_i^\top \boldsymbol{x}_t}$. Furthermore, the 'risk-adjusted drift' is of the form

$$\boldsymbol{\mu}_x(\boldsymbol{x}) - \underline{\underline{\sigma}}_x(\boldsymbol{x})\boldsymbol{\lambda}(\boldsymbol{x}) = \boldsymbol{\varphi} - \underline{\underline{\kappa}}\boldsymbol{x},$$

where $\boldsymbol{\varphi} = (\varphi_1, \dots, \varphi_m)^\top$ is a constant vector and $\underline{\underline{\kappa}}$ is a constant $m \times m$ matrix. Obviously, we have to make sure that $\nu_j + \boldsymbol{v}_j^\top \boldsymbol{x}_t \geq 0$ for each $j = 1, \dots, d$ and for all possible values of $\boldsymbol{x}_t$. This is no problem if $\boldsymbol{v}_j = \boldsymbol{0}$ for all j, but in other cases some parameter restrictions will have to be imposed, compare Duffie and Kan (1996) and Dai and Singleton (2000). Finally, the dividend must have an exponential-affine form

[3] The PDE can also be derived by first rewriting the general pricing expression in the form $P_t = \mathrm{E}_t^{\mathbb{Q}}[\exp\{-\int_t^T r_s^f\, ds\} D_T]$ where $\mathbb{Q}$ is a risk-neutral probability measure (see Section 4.6.1 and Chapter 12) and then employing the so-called Feynman–Kač Theorem that links conditional expectations and partial differential equations, see for example Øksendal (2003). As will become clear in Chapter 12, $\boldsymbol{\mu}_x - \underline{\underline{\sigma}}_x\boldsymbol{\lambda}$ is the drift of the process $\boldsymbol{x}$ under the risk-neutral probability measure.

$$D(x) = e^{\psi^\top x}$$

for some constant vector $\psi \in \mathbb{R}^m$.

With this affine structure the solution to the PDE (4.50) with the terminal condition (4.51) is given by

$$\begin{aligned} P(x,t) &= \exp\left\{ - a(T-t) - b(T-t)^\top x\right\} \\ &= \exp\left\{ - a(T-t) - \sum_{j=1}^{m} b_j(T-t)x_j\right\} \end{aligned} \tag{4.54}$$

where the deterministic functions a and b satisfy the system of ordinary differential equations (ODEs)

$$b'(\tau) = -\underline{\underline{\kappa}}^\top b(\tau) - \frac{1}{2}\sum_{i=1}^{m} \left[\underline{\underline{\Gamma}}^\top b(\tau)\right]_i^2 \nu_i + \xi,$$

$$a'(\tau) = \varphi^\top b(\tau) - \frac{1}{2}\sum_{i=1}^{m} \left[\underline{\underline{\Gamma}}^\top b(\tau)\right]_i^2 \nu_i + \xi_0$$

with the initial conditions $a(0) = 0$, $b(0) = \psi$. Here $\left[\underline{\underline{\Gamma}}^\top b(\tau)\right]_i$ denotes element i of the vector $\underline{\underline{\Gamma}}^\top b(\tau)$. This can be seen directly by substitution of Eq. (4.54) into the PDE (4.50). We can write the ODEs without matrix and vector notation as

$$b_i'(\tau) = -\sum_{j=1}^{m} \kappa_{ji} b_j(\tau) - \frac{1}{2}\sum_{k=1}^{d} \nu_{ki}\left(\sum_{j=1}^{m} \Gamma_{jk} b_j(\tau)\right)^2 + \xi_i, \quad i = 1, \dots, m, \tag{4.55}$$

$$a'(\tau) = \sum_{j=1}^{m} \varphi_j b_j(\tau) - \frac{1}{2}\sum_{k=1}^{d} \nu_k\left(\sum_{j=1}^{m} \Gamma_{jk} b_j(\tau)\right)^2 + \xi_0 \tag{4.56}$$

with the initial conditions $a(0) = 0$, $b_i(0) = \psi_i$. Note that $a(\tau)$ can be found by integration once all $b_j(\tau)$ have been determined:

$$\begin{aligned} a(\tau) = a(\tau) - a(0) &= \int_0^\tau a'(u)\,du \\ &= \xi_0\tau + \sum_{j=1}^{m} \varphi_j \int_0^\tau b_j(u)\,du - \frac{1}{2}\sum_{k=1}^{d} \nu_k \int_0^\tau \left(\sum_{j=1}^{m} \Gamma_{jk} b_j(u)\right)^2 du. \end{aligned}$$

The main problem is thus to solve the ODEs for the b_j-functions. Under some additional assumptions about the constants of the model, these so-called Ricatti ODEs have closed-form solutions. In other cases, they can be solved by efficient numerical methods, see for example Press *et al.* (2007). Affine models are frequently applied in the pricing of bonds and derivatives on bonds. Simple examples are given in Section 11.5, whereas an in-depth coverage can be found in Munk (2011).

When the PDE cannot be solved in closed form and cannot be reduced to a system of ordinary differential equations, the PDE itself can be solved by numerical methods (computer-implemented algorithms) at least when the dimension of x does not exceed three. Such methods are quite common in the valuation of derivative assets such as options on stocks or bonds and are thus introduced in many derivatives textbooks, such as Hull (2009) and Munk (2011). For a more detailed coverage of the numerical solution of PDEs, see Tavella and Randall (2000).

The PDE approach can be extended to the situation with a continuous dividend stream in addition to the final lump-sum dividend. Following Eqs. (4.29) and (4.33), the time t price equals

$$\begin{aligned} P_t &= \mathrm{E}_t\left[e^{\int_t^T \delta_s\,ds} D_T \frac{\zeta_T}{\zeta_t}\right] \\ &= \mathrm{E}_t\left[D_T \exp\left\{ -\int_t^T \left(r_s^f - \delta_s\right) ds - \frac{1}{2}\int_t^T \|\boldsymbol{\lambda}_s\|^2\,ds - \int_t^T \boldsymbol{\lambda}_s^{\top}\,d\boldsymbol{z}_s \right\}\right]. \end{aligned}$$

If the continuous dividend yield is also a function of the state variable, $\delta_s = \delta(\boldsymbol{x}_s)$, the price will be $P_t = P(\boldsymbol{x}_t, t)$ where the function $P(\boldsymbol{x}, t)$ now satisfies the PDE

$$\begin{aligned} &\frac{\partial P}{\partial t}(\boldsymbol{x}, t) + \left(\frac{\partial P}{\partial \boldsymbol{x}}(\boldsymbol{x}, t)\right)^{\top} \left(\boldsymbol{\mu}_x(\boldsymbol{x}) - \underline{\underline{\sigma}}_x(\boldsymbol{x})\boldsymbol{\lambda}(\boldsymbol{x})\right) + \frac{1}{2}\operatorname{tr}\left(\frac{\partial^2 P}{\partial \boldsymbol{x}^2}(\boldsymbol{x}, t)\underline{\underline{\sigma}}_x(\boldsymbol{x})\underline{\underline{\sigma}}_x(\boldsymbol{x})^{\top}\right) \\ &\quad = \left(r^f(\boldsymbol{x}) - \delta(\boldsymbol{x})\right) P(\boldsymbol{x}, t), \qquad (\boldsymbol{x}, t) \in \mathcal{S} \times [0, T), \end{aligned}$$

still with the terminal condition (4.51). If all the above conditions for an affine structure are satisfied and furthermore $\delta(\boldsymbol{x}) = \hat{\delta}_0 + \sum_{i=1}^d \hat{\delta}_i x_i$, the PDE will again have a solution of the exponential-affine form (4.54), but in the ODEs each ξ_i will be replaced by $\xi_i - \hat{\delta}_i$.

4.5 NOMINAL AND REAL STATE-PRICE DEFLATORS

As explained in Section 1.3, it is important to distinguish between real and nominal dividends, prices, and returns. A nominal dividend is a dividend measured in units of a given currency, say US dollars. A real dividend is measured by the purchasing power that the dividend provides its recipient. We can pick a given consumption good as the *numeraire good* so that a real dividend means the number of units of the numeraire good that can be purchased using the dividend. More generally, we can think of a certain basket of different consumption goods as being the numeraire, for example the basket of goods used for computing the Consumer Price Index.[4]

A state-price deflator basically links future dividends to current prices. We can define a nominal state-price deflator so that the basic pricing condition holds for nominal prices and dividends and, similarly, define a real state-price deflator so that the basic pricing condition holds for real prices and dividends. If we indicate nominal quantities by a tilde and real quantities without a tilde, the definitions of state-price deflators given earlier in this chapter characterize real state-price deflators. Throughout, we let $\tilde{F}_t$ denote the monetary price of the consumption good (or the level of the Consumer Price Index) at time t. Then a nominal dividend of $\tilde{D}_t$ corresponds to a real dividend of $D_t = \tilde{D}_t/\tilde{F}_t$. Similarly for prices. In continuous time, a real dividend yield of δ_t over an instantaneous interval $[t, t + dt]$ means that the real, total dividend payment over the interval is $\delta_t P_t \, dt$. Similarly, a nominal dividend yield of $\tilde{\delta}_t$ means that the total nominal dividend payment over $[t, t + dt]$ is $\tilde{\delta}_t \tilde{P}_t \, dt$. The real value of that nominal payment is $\tilde{\delta}_t \tilde{P}_t \, dt/\tilde{F}_t = \tilde{\delta}_t P_t \, dt$. Hence, there is no difference between a nominal dividend yield and a real dividend yield.

For example, in a multiperiod discrete-time economy a nominal state-price deflator is a strictly positive stochastic process $\tilde{\zeta} = (\tilde{\zeta}_t)_{t \in \mathcal{T}}$ that has initial value $\tilde{\zeta}_0 = 1$, finite variance, and satisfies the condition

$$\tilde{P}_{it} = \mathrm{E}_t \left[\sum_{s=t+1}^{T} \tilde{D}_{is} \frac{\tilde{\zeta}_s}{\tilde{\zeta}_t} \right]$$

for all assets i. A similar definition can be stated for the one-period framework and the continuous-time framework. The link between real and nominal state-price deflators is simple:

Theorem 4.9 *If $\zeta = (\zeta_t)$ is a real state-price deflator, then $\tilde{\zeta} = (\tilde{\zeta}_t)$ defined by*

$$\tilde{\zeta}_t = \zeta_t \frac{\tilde{F}_0}{\tilde{F}_t},$$

is a nominal state-price deflator. Conversely, if $\tilde{\zeta} = (\tilde{\zeta}_t)$ is a nominal state-price deflator, then $\zeta = (\zeta_t)$ defined by

$$\zeta_t = \tilde{\zeta}_t \frac{\tilde{F}_t}{\tilde{F}_0}$$

is a real state-price deflator.

[4] Since different individuals will generally want to consume different baskets of goods, they may disagree about the 'real value' of a nominal dividend.

Proof. We consider the discrete-time case. If ζ is a real state-price deflator, then

$$P_{it} = \mathrm{E}_t\left[\sum_{s=t+1}^{T} D_{is}\frac{\zeta_s}{\zeta_t}\right].$$

Substituting $P_{it} = \tilde{P}_{it}/\tilde{F}_t$ and $D_{is} = \tilde{D}_{is}/\tilde{F}_s$ into the preceding equation and multiplying through by $\tilde{F}_t$, we obtain

$$\tilde{P}_{it} = \mathrm{E}_t\left[\sum_{s=t+1}^{T} \tilde{D}_{is}\frac{\zeta_s/\tilde{F}_s}{\zeta_t/\tilde{F}_t}\right].$$

Hence, $\tilde{\zeta}$ is a nominal state-price deflator (the initial value, strict positivity, and finite variance are also satisfied). The converse is similar. □

Next, let us try to derive some general links between real and nominal returns. We distinguish between the discrete-time and the continuous-time settings.

4.5.1 Real and Nominal Returns in Discrete Time

Recall from Section 1.3 that, in a discrete-time framework, the link between the gross real rate of return, the gross nominal rate of return, and the gross inflation rate $\Phi_{t+1} = \tilde{F}_{t+1}/\tilde{F}_t$ is

$$R_{i,t+1} = \frac{\tilde{R}_{i,t+1}}{\Phi_{t+1}},$$

whereas the link between net rate of return and the net inflation rate $\varphi_{t+1} = (F_{t+1} - F_t)/F_t = \Phi_{t+1} - 1$ is

$$r_{i,t+1} = \frac{\tilde{r}_{i,t+1} - \varphi_{t+1}}{1 + \varphi_{t+1}} \approx \tilde{r}_{i,t+1} - \varphi_{t+1}.$$

The realized gross inflation rate $\tilde{F}_{t+1}/\tilde{F}_t$ is generally not known in advance. Therefore the real return on a nominally risk-free asset is generally stochastic (and conversely). The link between the nominally risk-free gross rate of return $\tilde{R}^f_t$ and the real risk-free gross rate of return R^f_t is

$$\frac{1}{\tilde{R}^f_t} = \mathrm{E}_t\left[\frac{\tilde{\zeta}_{t+1}}{\tilde{\zeta}_t}\right] = \mathrm{E}_t\left[\frac{\zeta_{t+1}}{\zeta_t}\frac{\tilde{F}_t}{\tilde{F}_{t+1}}\right]$$

$$= \mathrm{E}_t\left[\frac{\zeta_{t+1}}{\zeta_t}\right]\mathrm{E}_t\left[\frac{\tilde{F}_t}{\tilde{F}_{t+1}}\right] + \mathrm{Cov}_t\left[\frac{\zeta_{t+1}}{\zeta_t}, \frac{\tilde{F}_t}{\tilde{F}_{t+1}}\right]$$

$$= \frac{1}{R^f_t}\mathrm{E}_t\left[\frac{\tilde{F}_t}{\tilde{F}_{t+1}}\right] + \mathrm{Cov}_t\left[\frac{\zeta_{t+1}}{\zeta_t}, \frac{\tilde{F}_t}{\tilde{F}_{t+1}}\right].$$

In order to obtain a simpler link between the nominal and the real risk-free returns, we specialize to a lognormal setting. Assume that the next-period state-price deflator ζ_{t+1}/ζ_t and the gross realized inflation $\tilde{F}_{t+1}/\tilde{F}_t$ are given by

$$\frac{\zeta_{t+1}}{\zeta_t} = e^{-a_t+b_t\varepsilon_{t+1}}, \qquad \frac{\tilde{F}_{t+1}}{\tilde{F}_t} = e^{h_t+k_t(\rho_t\varepsilon_{t+1}+\sqrt{1-\rho_t^2}\eta_{t+1})},$$

where $a = (a_t)$, $b = (b_t)$, $h = (h_t)$, $k = (k_t)$, and $\rho = (\rho_t)$ are adapted processes, and where the shocks ε_{t+1} and η_{t+1} are independent and identically $N(0, 1)$ distributed. Note that

$$\mathrm{E}_t\left[\ln\left(\frac{\zeta_{t+1}}{\zeta_t}\right)\right] = -a_t, \qquad \mathrm{Var}_t\left[\ln\left(\frac{\zeta_{t+1}}{\zeta_t}\right)\right] = b_t^2.$$

Using Theorem B.2 in Appendix B, the gross real risk-free rate of return becomes

$$R^f_t = \left(\mathrm{E}_t\left[\frac{\zeta_{t+1}}{\zeta_t}\right]\right)^{-1} = \left(e^{-a_t+\frac{1}{2}b_t^2}\right)^{-1} = e^{a_t-\frac{1}{2}b_t^2}$$

so that the continuously compounded real risk-free rate is

$$r^f_t = \ln R^f_t = a_t - \frac{1}{2}b_t^2. \tag{4.57}$$

Similarly, the expectation and the variance of the log-inflation rate are

$$\mathrm{E}_t\left[\ln\left(\frac{\tilde{F}_{t+1}}{\tilde{F}_t}\right)\right] = h_t, \qquad \mathrm{Var}_t\left[\ln\left(\frac{\tilde{F}_{t+1}}{\tilde{F}_t}\right)\right] = k_t^2,$$

implying an expected gross inflation of

$$\mathrm{E}_t\left[\frac{\tilde{F}_{t+1}}{\tilde{F}_t}\right] = e^{h_t+\frac{1}{2}k_t^2}. \tag{4.58}$$

Assuming that b_t and k_t are positive, ρ_t is the correlation between the log-real state-price deflator and the log-inflation rate.

Due to the lognormality assumption we can directly compute the expectation of the nominal state-price deflator over the next period:

$$\begin{aligned}
\mathrm{E}_t\left[\frac{\tilde{\zeta}_{t+1}}{\tilde{\zeta}_t}\right] &= \mathrm{E}_t\left[\frac{\zeta_{t+1}}{\zeta_t}\frac{\tilde{F}_t}{\tilde{F}_{t+1}}\right] = \mathrm{E}_t\left[e^{-a_t+b_t\varepsilon_{t+1}}e^{-h_t-k_t\rho_t\varepsilon_{t+1}-k_t\sqrt{1-\rho_t^2}\eta_{t+1}}\right] \\
&= e^{-a_t-h_t}\,\mathrm{E}_t\left[e^{(b_t-k_t\rho_t)\varepsilon_{t+1}}\right]\mathrm{E}_t\left[e^{-k_t\sqrt{1-\rho_t^2}\eta_{t+1}}\right] \\
&= e^{-a_t-h_t}e^{\frac{1}{2}(b_t-k_t\rho_t)^2}e^{\frac{1}{2}k_t^2(1-\rho_t^2)} = e^{-a_t-h_t+\frac{1}{2}b_t^2+\frac{1}{2}k_t^2-\rho_t b_t k_t}.
\end{aligned}$$

The gross nominal risk-free rate of return is thus

$$\tilde{R}_t^f = \left(\mathrm{E}_t\left[\frac{\tilde{\zeta}_{t+1}}{\tilde{\zeta}_t}\right]\right)^{-1} = e^{a_t+h_t-\frac{1}{2}b_t^2-\frac{1}{2}k_t^2+\rho_t b_t k_t},$$

and the continuously compounded nominal risk-free rate is

$$\tilde{r}_t^f = \ln \tilde{R}_t^f = a_t + h_t - \frac{1}{2}b_t^2 - \frac{1}{2}k_t^2 + \rho_t b_t k_t,$$

which we can rewrite using Eqs. (4.57) and (4.58) as

$$\begin{aligned}
\tilde{r}_t^f &= r_t^f + h_t - \frac{1}{2}k_t^2 + \rho_t b_t k_t \qquad (4.59)\\
&= r_t^f + \ln\left(\mathrm{E}_t\left[\frac{\tilde{F}_{t+1}}{\tilde{F}_t}\right]\right) - \mathrm{Var}_t\left[\ln\left(\frac{\tilde{F}_{t+1}}{\tilde{F}_t}\right)\right] \\
&\quad + \mathrm{Cov}_t\left[\ln\left(\frac{\zeta_{t+1}}{\zeta_t}\right), \ln\left(\frac{\tilde{F}_{t+1}}{\tilde{F}_t}\right)\right].
\end{aligned}$$

The nominal risk-free rate equals the real risk-free rate plus log-expected inflation minus inflation variance and adjusted by an inflation risk premium.

4.5.2 Real and Nominal Returns in Continuous Time

In a continuous-time framework, we can obtain an expression similar to Eq. (4.59) without imposing a distributional assumption. Let $\zeta = (\zeta_t)$ denote a real state-price deflator which evolves over time according to

$$d\zeta_t = -\zeta_t\left[r_t^f\,dt + \boldsymbol{\lambda}_t^{\top}\,d\boldsymbol{z}_t\right],$$

where $r^f = (r_t^f)$ is the short-term real interest rate and $\boldsymbol{\lambda} = (\boldsymbol{\lambda}_t)$ is the market price of risk. Assume that the dynamics of the price of the consumption good can be written as

$$d\tilde{F}_t = \tilde{F}_t \left[\mu_{Ft}\, dt + \boldsymbol{\sigma}_{Ft}^{\top}\, d\boldsymbol{z}_t \right].$$

We can interpret $\varphi_{t+dt} \equiv d\tilde{F}_t/\tilde{F}_t$ as the realized inflation rate over the next instant, $\mu_{Ft}\, dt = \mathrm{E}_t[\varphi_{t+dt}]$ as the expected inflation rate, and $\boldsymbol{\sigma}_{Ft}$ as the sensitivity vector of the inflation rate.

Consider now a nominal bank account which over the next instant promises a risk-free monetary return represented by the nominal short-term interest rate $\tilde{r}_t^f$. If we let $\tilde{N}_t$ denote the time t dollar value of such an account, we have that

$$d\tilde{N}_t = \tilde{r}_t^f \tilde{N}_t\, dt.$$

The real price of this account is $N_t = \tilde{N}_t/\tilde{F}_t$ since this is the number of units of the consumption good that has the same value as the account. An application of Itô's Lemma implies a real price dynamics of

$$dN_t = N_t \left[\left(\tilde{r}_t^f - \mu_{Ft} + \|\boldsymbol{\sigma}_{Ft}\|^2 \right) dt - \boldsymbol{\sigma}_{Ft}^{\top}\, d\boldsymbol{z}_t \right].$$

Note that the real return on this instantaneously nominally risk-free asset, dN_t/N_t, is risky. Since the percentage sensitivity vector is given by $-\boldsymbol{\sigma}_{Ft}$, the expected return is given by the real short rate plus $-\boldsymbol{\sigma}_{Ft}^{\top}\boldsymbol{\lambda}_t$. Comparing this with the drift term in the equation above, we have that

$$\tilde{r}_t^f - \mu_{Ft} + \|\boldsymbol{\sigma}_{Ft}\|^2 = r_t^f - \boldsymbol{\sigma}_{Ft}^{\top}\boldsymbol{\lambda}_t.$$

Consequently the nominal short-term interest rate is given by

$$\tilde{r}_t^f = r_t^f + \mu_{Ft} - \|\boldsymbol{\sigma}_{Ft}\|^2 - \boldsymbol{\sigma}_{Ft}^{\top}\boldsymbol{\lambda}_t, \tag{4.60}$$

that is the nominal short rate is equal to the real short rate plus the expected inflation rate minus the variance of the inflation rate minus a risk premium. The first three terms on the right-hand side are clearly analogous to those in the discrete-time relation (4.59). The continuous-time equivalent of the last term in Eq. (4.59) is

$$\mathrm{Cov}_t[d(\ln \zeta_t), d(\ln \tilde{F}_t)] = \mathrm{Cov}_t[-\boldsymbol{\lambda}_t^{\top}\, d\boldsymbol{z}_t, \boldsymbol{\sigma}_{Ft}^{\top}\, d\boldsymbol{z}_t] = -\boldsymbol{\sigma}_{Ft}^{\top}\boldsymbol{\lambda}_t\, dt,$$

which corresponds to the last term in Eq. (4.60). The discrete-time relation (4.59) and the continuous-time relation (4.60) are therefore completely analogous, but the discrete-time relation could only be derived in a lognormal setting.

The presence of the last two terms in Eq. (4.60) invalidates the so-called Fisher relation, according to which the nominal interest rate equals the sum of the real interest rate and the expected inflation rate. The Fisher relation holds if and only if the inflation rate is instantaneously risk-free. In Chapter 11 we will discuss the link between real and nominal interest rates and yields in more detail.

Individuals should primarily be concerned about real values since, in the end, they should care about the number of goods they can consume. Therefore, most theoretical asset pricing models make predictions about expected real returns.

4.6 A PREVIEW OF ALTERNATIVE FORMULATIONS

The previous sections have shown that a state-price deflator is a good way to represent the market-wide pricing mechanism in a financial market. Paired with characteristics of any individual asset, the state-price deflator leads to the price of the asset. This section shows that we can capture the same information in other ways. The alternative representations can be preferable for some specific purposes, and we will return to them in later chapters. Here we will only give a preview. For simplicity we keep the discussion in a one-period framework.

4.6.1 Risk-Neutral Probabilities

Suppose that a risk-free dividend can be constructed and that it provides a gross rate of return of R^f. A probability measure $\mathbb{Q}$ is called a risk-neutral probability measure if the following conditions are satisfied:

(i) $\mathbb{P}$ and $\mathbb{Q}$ are equivalent, that is they attach zero probability to the same events,

(ii) the random variable $d\mathbb{Q}/d\mathbb{P}$ (explained below) has finite variance,

(iii) the price of any asset $i = 1, \dots, I$ is given by

$$P_i = \mathrm{E}^{\mathbb{Q}}\left[(R^f)^{-1} D_i\right] = (R^f)^{-1}\,\mathrm{E}^{\mathbb{Q}}\left[D_i\right], \tag{4.61}$$

that is the price of any asset equals the expected discounted dividend using the risk-free interest rate as the discount rate and the risk-neutral probabilities when computing the expectation.

The risk-free return is not random and can therefore be moved in and out of expectations as in the above equation. Given the return (or, equivalently, the price) of the risk-free asset, all the market-wide pricing information is captured by a risk-neutral probability measure.

In the case of a finite state space $\Omega = \{1, 2, \dots, S\}$, a probability measure $\mathbb{Q}$ is fully characterized by the state probabilities $q_\omega = \mathbb{Q}(\omega)$, $\omega = 1, 2, \dots, S$. Since we have assumed that the real-world probability measure $\mathbb{P}$ is such that $p_\omega > 0$ for all ω, equivalence between $\mathbb{P}$ and $\mathbb{Q}$ demands that $q_\omega > 0$

for all ω. With finite Ω, the pricing equation in (iii) can be written as $P_i = (R^f)^{-1} \sum_{\omega=1}^{S} q_\omega D_{i\omega}$.

Why is $\mathbb{Q}$ called a risk-neutral probability measure? Since the gross rate of return on asset i is $R_i = D_i/P_i$, we can rewrite Eq. (4.61) as

$$\mathrm{E}^{\mathbb{Q}}[R_i] = R^f,$$

that is all assets have an expected return equal to the risk-free return under the risk-neutral probability measure. If all investors were risk-neutral, they would rank assets according to their expected returns only. Therefore the market could only be in equilibrium if all assets had the same expected returns. The definition of a risk-neutral probability measure $\mathbb{Q}$ thus implies that asset prices in the real world are just as they would have been in an economy in which all individuals are risk-neutral and the state probabilities are given by $\mathbb{Q}$. The price adjustments for risk are thus incorporated in the risk-neutral probabilities.

Next, let us explore the link between risk-neutral probability measures and state prices. First, assume a finite state space. Given a state-price vector $\boldsymbol{\psi}$ and the associated state-price deflator ζ, we can define

$$q_\omega = \frac{\psi_\omega}{\sum_{s=1}^{S} \psi_s} = R^f \psi_\omega = R^f p_\omega \zeta_\omega, \quad \omega = 1, \dots, S.$$

All the q_ω's are strictly positive and sum to one so they define an equivalent probability measure. Furthermore, (4.15) implies that

$$P_i = \boldsymbol{\psi} \cdot \boldsymbol{D}_i = \sum_{\omega=1}^{S} \psi_\omega D_{i\omega} = \sum_{\omega=1}^{S} (R^f)^{-1} q_\omega D_{i\omega} = \mathrm{E}^{\mathbb{Q}}\left[(R^f)^{-1} D_i\right],$$

so $\mathbb{Q}$ is indeed a risk-neutral probability measure. Note that $q_\omega > p_\omega$ if and only if $\zeta_\omega > (R^f)^{-1} = \mathrm{E}[\zeta]$, that is if the value of the state-price deflator for state ω is higher than average.

The change of measure from the real-world probability measure $\mathbb{P}$ to the risk-neutral probability measure $\mathbb{Q}$ is given by the ratios $\xi_\omega \equiv q_\omega/p_\omega = R^f \zeta_\omega$. The change of measure is fully captured by the random variable ξ that takes on the value ξ_ω if state ω is realized. This random variable is called the Radon–Nikodym derivative for the change of measure and is often denoted by $d\mathbb{Q}/d\mathbb{P}$. Note that the $\mathbb{P}$-expectation of any Radon–Nikodym derivative $\xi = d\mathbb{Q}/d\mathbb{P}$ must be 1 to ensure that the new measure is a probability measure. This is satisfied by our risk-neutral probability measure since

$$\mathrm{E}^{\mathbb{P}}\left[\frac{d\mathbb{Q}}{d\mathbb{P}}\right] = \sum_{\omega=1}^{S} p_\omega \xi_\omega = \sum_{\omega=1}^{S} p_\omega R^f \zeta_\omega = R^f \sum_{\omega=1}^{S} p_\omega \zeta_\omega = 1.$$

When the state space is infinite, state-price deflators still make sense. Given a state-price deflator ζ, we can define a risk-neutral probability measure $\mathbb{Q}$ by the random variable

$$\xi = \frac{d\mathbb{Q}}{d\mathbb{P}} = R^f \zeta.$$

Conversely, given a risk-neutral probability measure $\mathbb{Q}$ and the risk-free gross rate of return R^f, we can define a state-price deflator ζ by

$$\zeta = (R^f)^{-1} \frac{d\mathbb{Q}}{d\mathbb{P}}.$$

In the case of a finite state space, the risk-neutral probability measure is given by $\xi_\omega = q_\omega / p_\omega$, $\omega = 1, \dots, S$, and we can construct a state-price vector $\boldsymbol{\psi}$ and a state-price deflator $\boldsymbol{\zeta}$ as

$$\psi_\omega = (R^f)^{-1} q_\omega, \qquad \zeta_\omega = (R^f)^{-1} \xi_\omega = (R^f)^{-1} \frac{q_\omega}{p_\omega}, \quad \omega = 1, \dots, S.$$

We summarize the above observations in the following theorem:

Theorem 4.10 *Assume that a risk-free asset exists. Then there is a one-to-one correspondence between state-price deflators and risk-neutral probability measures.*

Combining this result with Theorems 4.5 and 4.6, we reach the next conclusion.

Theorem 4.11 *Assume that a risk-free asset exists. Prices admit no arbitrage if and only if a risk-neutral probability measure exists. The market is complete if and only if there is a unique risk-neutral probability measure. If the market is complete and arbitrage-free, the unique risk-neutral probability measure $\mathbb{Q}$ is characterized by $d\mathbb{Q}/d\mathbb{P} = R_f \zeta^*$, where ζ^* is given by Eq.* (4.39).

Risk-neutral probabilities are especially useful for the pricing of derivative assets. In Chapter 12 we will generalize the definition of risk-neutral probabilities to multiperiod settings and we will also define other probability measures that are useful in derivative pricing.

4.6.2 Pricing Factors

We will say that a (one-dimensional) random variable x is a pricing factor for the market if there exists some $\alpha, \eta \in \mathbb{R}$ so that

$$\mathrm{E}[R_i] = \alpha + \beta[R_i, x]\eta, \quad i = 1, \dots, I, \tag{4.62}$$

where the factor-beta of asset i is given by

$$\beta[R_i, x] = \frac{\mathrm{Cov}[R_i, x]}{\mathrm{Var}[x]}.$$

The constant η is called the factor risk premium and α the zero-beta return. Due to the linearity of expectations and covariance, Eq. (4.62) will also hold for all portfolios of the I assets. Note that if a risk-free asset is traded in the market, it will have a zero factor-beta and, consequently, $\alpha = R^f$.

The relation (4.62) does not directly involve prices. But since the expected gross rate of return is $\mathrm{E}[R_i] = \mathrm{E}[D_i]/P_i$, we have $P_i = \mathrm{E}[D_i]/\mathrm{E}[R_i]$ and hence the equivalent relation

$$P_i = \frac{\mathrm{E}[D_i]}{\alpha + \beta[R_i, x]\eta}.$$

The price is equal to the expected dividend discounted by a risk-adjusted rate. You may find this relation unsatisfactory since the price implicitly enters the right-hand side through the return-beta $\beta[R_i, x]$. However, we can define a dividend-beta by $\beta[D_i, x] = \mathrm{Cov}[D_i, x]/\mathrm{Var}[x]$ and inserting $D_i = R_i P_i$ we see that $\beta[D_i, x] = P_i \beta[R_i, x]$. Equation (4.62) now implies that

$$\frac{\mathrm{E}[D_i]}{P_i} = \alpha + \frac{1}{P_i}\beta[D_i, x]\eta$$

so that

$$P_i = \frac{\mathrm{E}[D_i] - \beta[D_i, x]\eta}{\alpha}.$$

Think of the numerator as a certainty equivalent to the risky dividend. The current price is the certainty equivalent discounted by the zero-beta return, which is the risk-free return if this exists.

What is the link between pricing factors and state-price deflators? It follows from Eq. (4.6) that any state-price deflator ζ itself is a pricing factor. That equation does not require positivity of the state-price deflator, only the pricing condition. Therefore any random variable x that satisfies $P_i = \mathrm{E}[x D_i]$ for all assets works as a pricing factor. More generally, if x is a random variable and a, b are constants so that $P_i = \mathrm{E}[(a + bx)D_i]$ for all assets i, then x is a pricing factor. In particular, whenever we have a state-price deflator of the form $\zeta = a + bx$, we can use x as a pricing factor.

Conversely, if we have a pricing factor x for which the associated zero-beta return α is non-zero, we can find constants a, b so that $\zeta = a + bx$ satisfies the pricing condition $P_i = \mathrm{E}[\zeta D_i]$ for $i = 1, \dots, I$. In order to see this let η denote the factor risk premium associated with the pricing factor x and define

$$b = -\frac{\eta}{\alpha \,\mathrm{Var}[x]}, \qquad a = \frac{1}{\alpha} - b\,\mathrm{E}[x].$$

Then $\zeta = a + bx$ works since

$$\begin{aligned}
\mathrm{E}[\zeta R_i] &= a\,\mathrm{E}[R_i] + b\,\mathrm{E}[R_i x] \\
&= a\,\mathrm{E}[R_i] + b\,(\mathrm{Cov}[R_i, x] + \mathrm{E}[R_i]\,\mathrm{E}[x])
\end{aligned}$$

$$
\begin{aligned}
&= (a + b\,\mathrm{E}[x])\,\mathrm{E}[R_i] + b\,\mathrm{Cov}[R_i, x] \\
&= \frac{1}{\alpha}\left(\mathrm{E}[R_i] - \frac{\mathrm{Cov}[R_i, x]}{\mathrm{Var}[x]}\eta\right) \\
&= \frac{1}{\alpha}\left(\mathrm{E}[R_i] - \beta[R_i, x]\eta\right) \\
&= 1
\end{aligned}
$$

for any $i = 1, \dots, I$. Inserting a and b, we get

$$\zeta = a + bx = \frac{1}{\alpha}\left(1 - \frac{\eta}{\mathrm{Var}[x]}\,(x - \mathrm{E}[x])\right).$$

Any pricing factor x gives us a candidate $a + bx$ for a state-price deflator but it will only be a true state-price deflator if it is strictly positive. The fact that we can find a pricing factor for a given market does not imply that the market is arbitrage-free.

Can the pricing factor be the return on some portfolio? No problem! Suppose x is a pricing factor. Look for a portfolio $\boldsymbol{\theta}$ which will generate the dividend as close as possible to x in the sense that it minimizes $\mathrm{Var}[D^{\boldsymbol{\theta}} - x]$. Since

$$
\begin{aligned}
\mathrm{Var}\left[D^{\boldsymbol{\theta}} - x\right] &= \mathrm{Var}\left[\boldsymbol{D}^{\top}\boldsymbol{\theta} - x\right] = \mathrm{Var}\left[\boldsymbol{D}^{\top}\boldsymbol{\theta}\right] + \mathrm{Var}[x] - 2\,\mathrm{Cov}\left[\boldsymbol{D}^{\top}\boldsymbol{\theta}, x\right] \\
&= \boldsymbol{\theta}^{\top}\,\mathrm{Var}[\boldsymbol{D}]\boldsymbol{\theta} + \mathrm{Var}[x] - 2\boldsymbol{\theta}^{\top}\,\mathrm{Cov}[\boldsymbol{D}, x],
\end{aligned}
$$

the minimum is obtained for

$$\boldsymbol{\theta} = (\mathrm{Var}[\boldsymbol{D}])^{-1}\,\mathrm{Cov}[\boldsymbol{D}, x].$$

This portfolio is called the factor-mimicking portfolio. Using Eqs. (3.9) and (3.10), the gross rate of return on this portfolio is

$$
\begin{aligned}
R^x &= \frac{\boldsymbol{\theta}^{\top}\,\mathrm{diag}(\boldsymbol{P})\boldsymbol{R}}{\boldsymbol{\theta}^{\top}\,\mathrm{diag}(\boldsymbol{P})\boldsymbol{1}} = \frac{\mathrm{Cov}[\boldsymbol{D}, x]^{\top}(\mathrm{Var}[\boldsymbol{D}])^{-1}\,\mathrm{diag}(\boldsymbol{P})\boldsymbol{R}}{\mathrm{Cov}[\boldsymbol{D}, x]^{\top}(\mathrm{Var}[\boldsymbol{D}])^{-1}\,\mathrm{diag}(\boldsymbol{P})\boldsymbol{1}} \\
&= \frac{\mathrm{Cov}[\boldsymbol{R}, x]^{\top}(\mathrm{Var}[\boldsymbol{R}])^{-1}\boldsymbol{R}}{\mathrm{Cov}[\boldsymbol{R}, x]^{\top}(\mathrm{Var}[\boldsymbol{R}])^{-1}\boldsymbol{1}}.
\end{aligned}
$$

The vector of covariances of the returns on the basic assets and the return on the factor-mimicking portfolio is

$$\mathrm{Cov}[\boldsymbol{R}, R^x] = \frac{\mathrm{Cov}[\boldsymbol{R}, x]}{\mathrm{Cov}[\boldsymbol{R}, x]^{\top}(\mathrm{Var}[\boldsymbol{R}])^{-1}\boldsymbol{1}},$$

and therefore the beta of asset i with respect to R^x is

$$\beta[R_i, R^x] = \frac{\mathrm{Cov}[R_i, R^x]}{\mathrm{Var}[R^x]} = \frac{\mathrm{Cov}[R_i, x]}{\mathrm{Var}[R^x]\,\mathrm{Cov}[\boldsymbol{R}, x]^\top (\mathrm{Var}[\boldsymbol{R}])^{-1}\mathbf{1}}$$
$$= \beta[R_i, x]\frac{\mathrm{Var}[x]}{\mathrm{Var}[R^x]\,\mathrm{Cov}[\boldsymbol{R}, x]^\top (\mathrm{Var}[\boldsymbol{R}])^{-1}\mathbf{1}}.$$

Consequently, if x is a pricing factor with zero-beta return α and factor risk premium η, then the corresponding factor-mimicking return R^x is a pricing factor with zero-beta return α and factor risk premium

$$\hat{\eta} = \frac{\eta\,\mathrm{Var}[R^x]\,\mathrm{Cov}[\boldsymbol{R}, x]^\top (\mathrm{Var}[\boldsymbol{R}])^{-1}\mathbf{1}}{\mathrm{Var}[x]}.$$

In that sense it is not restrictive to look for pricing factors only in the set of returns.

Note that when the factor x itself is a return, then it must satisfy

$$\mathrm{E}[x] = \alpha + \beta[x, x]\eta = \alpha + \eta \quad \Rightarrow \quad \eta = \mathrm{E}[x] - \alpha$$

so that

$$\mathrm{E}[R_i] = \alpha + \beta[R_i, x]\,(\mathrm{E}[x] - \alpha).$$

Now it is clear that the standard CAPM simply says that the return on the market portfolio is a pricing factor.

We will discuss factor models in detail in Chapter 10. We will also allow for multidimensional pricing factors there.

4.6.3 Mean-Variance Efficient Returns

A portfolio is said to be mean-variance efficient if there is no other portfolio with the same expected return and a lower return variance. The return on a mean-variance efficient portfolio is called a mean-variance efficient return. The mean-variance frontier is the curve in a $(\sigma[R], \mathrm{E}[R])$-plane traced out by all the mean-variance efficient returns.

The analysis of mean-variance efficient portfolios was introduced by Markowitz (1952, 1959) as a tool for investors in making portfolio decisions. Nevertheless, mean-variance efficient portfolios are also relevant for asset pricing purposes due to the following theorem:

Theorem 4.12 *A return is a pricing factor if and only if it is a mean-variance efficient return different from the minimum-variance return.*

Combining this with results from the previous subsection, we can conclude that (almost) any mean-variance return R^{mv} gives rise to a (candidate) state-price deflator of the form $\zeta = a + bR^{\text{mv}}$. And the standard CAPM can be reformulated as 'the return on the market portfolio is mean-variance efficient'.

We will not provide a proof of the theorem here but will return to the issue in Chapter 10.

4.7 CONCLUDING REMARKS

This chapter has introduced state-price deflators as a way to represent the general pricing mechanism of a financial market. Important properties of state-price deflators were discussed. Examples have illustrated the valuation of assets with a given state-price deflator. But what determines the state-price deflator? Intuitively, state prices reflect the value that market participants attach to an extra payment in a given state at a given point in time. This must be related to their marginal utility of consumption. To follow this idea, we must consider the optimal consumption choice of individuals. This is the topic of the next two chapters.

4.8 EXERCISES

Exercise 4.1 Imagine a one-period economy where the state-price deflator ζ is lognormally distributed with $\mathrm{E}[\ln \zeta] = \mu_\zeta$ and $\mathrm{Var}[\ln \zeta] = \sigma_\zeta^2$. What is the maximal Sharpe ratio of a risky asset? (Look at Eq. (4.8).) What determines the sign of an asset's Sharpe ratio?

Exercise 4.2 Consider a one-period, three-state economy with two assets traded. Asset 1 has a price of 0.9 and pays a dividend of 1 no matter what state is realized. Asset 2 has a price of 2 and pays 1, 2, and 4 in state 1, 2, and 3, respectively. The real-world probabilities of the states are 0.2, 0.6, and 0.2, respectively. Assume absence of arbitrage.

(a) Find the state-price vector ψ^* and the associated state-price deflator. What portfolio generates a dividend of ψ^*?

(b) Find the state-price deflator ζ^* and the associated state-price vector. What portfolio generates a dividend of ζ^*?

(c) Find a portfolio with dividends 4, 3, and 1 in states 1, 2, and 3, respectively. What is the price of the portfolio?

Exercise 4.3 Give a proof of Theorem 4.7 both for the one-period framework and the continuous-time framework.

Exercise 4.4 Show Lemma 4.1.

Exercise 4.5 Assume a one-period framework with no redundant assets. Show that ζ^* can be rewritten as in (4.47).

Exercise 4.6 Consider a one-period economy where the assets are correctly priced by a state-price deflator M. A nutty professor believes that the assets are priced according to a model in which Y is a state-price deflator, where Y is a random variable with $E[Y] = E[M]$. Refer to this model as the Y-model.

(a) Show that the Y-model prices a risk-free asset correctly.

(b) Argue that the expected return on an arbitrary asset i according to the Y-model is given by

$$\mathrm{E}_Y[R_i] \equiv \frac{1}{\mathrm{E}[M]} - \frac{1}{\mathrm{E}[M]}\mathrm{Cov}[Y, R_i].$$

(c) Show that

$$\frac{|\,\mathrm{E}[R_i] - \mathrm{E}_Y[R_i]\,|}{\sigma[R_i]} \leq \frac{\sigma[Y - M]}{\mathrm{E}[M]}$$

so that the mispricing of the Y-model (in terms of expected returns) is limited.

(d) What can you say about the returns for which the left-hand side in the above inequality will be largest?

(e) Under which condition on Y will the Y-model price all assets correctly?

Exercise 4.7 Consider a one-period economy where two basic financial assets are traded without portfolio constraints or transaction costs. There are three equally likely end-of-period states of the economy and the prices and state-contingent dividends of the two assets are given in the following table:

	State-contingent dividend			Price
	State 1	State 2	State 3	
Asset 1	1	1	0	0.5
Asset 2	2	2	2	1.8

The economy is known to be arbitrage-free.

(a) Characterize the set of state-contingent dividends that can be attained by combining the two assets.

(b) Characterize the set of state-price vectors $\psi = (\psi_1, \psi_2, \psi_3)$ consistent with the prices and dividends of the two basic assets.

(c) Find the state-price vector ψ^* that belongs to the set of attainable dividend vectors.

(d) Characterize the set of state-price deflators $\zeta = (\zeta_1, \zeta_2, \zeta_3)$ consistent with the prices and dividends of the two basic assets.

(e) What is the risk-free (gross) rate of return R^f over the period?

(f) What prices of the state-contingent dividend vector (1, 1, 5) are consistent with absence of arbitrage?

(g) What prices of the state-contingent dividend vector (1, 2, 5) are consistent with absence of arbitrage?

(h) Show that the state-price deflator ζ^* that belongs to the set of attainable dividend vectors is given by the vector $(0.75, 0.75, 1.2)$, that is it has the value 0.75 in states 1 and 2 and the value 1.2 in state 3.

Exercise 4.8 Consider a two-period economy where the resolution of uncertainty can be represented by the tree in Fig. 2.2 in Chapter 2. Assume that three assets are traded. Their dividend processes are illustrated in Fig. 4.1, where a triple (D_1, D_2, D_3) near a node means that asset $i = 1, 2, 3$ pays a dividend of D_i if/when that node is reached. For example, if the economy at time 2 is in the scenario F_{22}, assets 1 and 2 will pay a dividend of 1 and asset 3 will pay a dividend of 2. In Fig. 4.1, the numbers near the lines connecting nodes denote values of the next-period state-price deflator, that is $\zeta_1/\zeta_0 = \zeta_1$ over the first period and ζ_2/ζ_1 over the second period. For example, the value of ζ_2/ζ_1 given that the economy is in scenario F_{11} at time 1 is 1 if the economy moves to scenario F_{21} and 2/3 if the economy moves to scenario F_{22}. This characterizes completely the state-price deflator to be used in the computations below.

(a) Find the price processes of the three assets. (You should find that the time 0 price of asset 1 is 1.802.)

(b) Find the short-term (one-period) interest rate process. What are the one-period and the two-period zero-coupon yields at time 0?

(c) Is the market complete?

Exercise 4.9 Consider a discrete-time economy where a state-price deflator $\zeta = (\zeta_t)$ satisfies

$$\ln\left(\frac{\zeta_{t+1}}{\zeta_t}\right) \sim N(\mu_\zeta, \sigma_\zeta^2)$$

for each $t = 0, 1, \ldots, T - 1$. An asset pays a dividend process $D = (D_t)$ satisfying

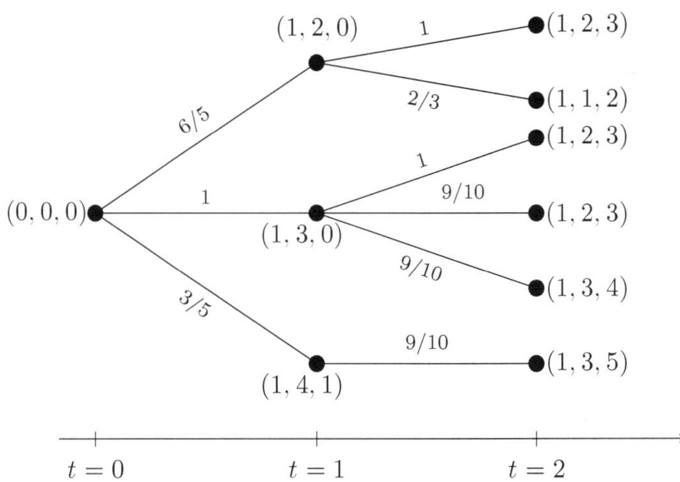

Fig. 4.1. Dividends and state prices.

$$\frac{D_{t+1}}{D_t} = a \left(\frac{\zeta_{t+1}}{\zeta_t} \right)^b + \varepsilon_{t+1}, \quad t = 0, 1, \dots, T-1,$$

where a and b are constants, and $\varepsilon_1, \dots, \varepsilon_T$ are independent with $\mathrm{E}_t[\varepsilon_{t+1}] = 0$ and $\mathrm{E}_t[\varepsilon_{t+1}\zeta_{t+1}] = 0$ for all t. What is the price of the asset at any time t (in terms of $D_t, a, b, \mu_\zeta, \sigma_\zeta^2$)?

Exercise 4.10 Assume a discrete-time model. As we shall see in later chapters, under some conditions a state-price deflator process $\zeta = (\zeta_t)_{t=0,1,2,\dots}$ is defined by $\zeta_0 = 1$ and

$$\frac{\zeta_{t+1}}{\zeta_t} = e^{-\delta} \left(\frac{c_{t+1}}{c_t} \right)^{-\gamma},$$

where c is the aggregate consumption in the economy, whereas δ is the time preference rate and γ the constant relative risk aversion of a so-called representative individual.

In this economy you want to value a stream of dividends $(D_t)_{t=0,1,2,\dots}$. Assume that $D_0 > 0$ is a fixed initial dividend and

$$\ln\left(\frac{D_{t+1}}{D_t} \right) = a + b \ln\left(\frac{c_{t+1}}{c_t} \right) + \varepsilon_{t+1}, \quad t = 0, 1, 2, \dots, T-1,$$

where $\ln(c_{t+1}/c_t)$ and ε_{t+1} are jointly normally distributed with

$$\ln\left(\frac{c_{t+1}}{c_t} \right) \sim N(\mu_c, \sigma_c^2), \; \varepsilon_{t+1} \sim N(-\frac{1}{2}\sigma_\varepsilon^2, \sigma_\varepsilon^2), \; \mathrm{Cov}_t\left[\ln\left(\frac{c_{t+1}}{c_t} \right), \varepsilon_{t+1} \right] = 0$$

for all $t = 0, 1, \dots, T-1$.

(a) Show that

$$\mathrm{E}_t\left[\frac{D_{t+1}}{D_t} \frac{\zeta_{t+1}}{\zeta_t} \right] = A,$$

where A is the constant

$$A = \exp\left\{ a - \delta + (b - \gamma)\mu_c + \frac{1}{2}(b-\gamma)^2\sigma_c^2 \right\}.$$

(b) Show that for each $t = 0, 1, \dots, T-1$ and each $s = 1, \dots, T-t$

$$\mathrm{E}_t\left[\frac{D_{t+s}}{D_t} \frac{\zeta_{t+s}}{\zeta_t} \right] = A^s.$$

(c) Show that the price at time t of the dividends received after time t is

$$P_t = D_t \frac{A}{1-A}\left(1 - A^{T-t} \right).$$

How does the price depend on the parameters a and b and is this dependence intuitively reasonable?

Exercise 4.11 Consider a continuous-time economy in which the state-price deflator follows a geometric Brownian motion:

$$d\zeta_t = -\zeta_t \left[r^f \, dt + \boldsymbol{\lambda}^\top \, dz_t \right],$$

where r^f and $\boldsymbol{\lambda}$ are constant.

(a) What is the price B_t^s of a zero-coupon bond maturing at time s with a face value of 1?

Define the continuously compounded yield y_t^s for maturity s via the equation $B_t^s = e^{-y_t^s(s-t)}$.

(b) Compute y_t^s. What can you say about the yield curve $s \mapsto y_t^s$?

Exercise 4.12 Show that $\zeta_t^* = V_0^*/V_t^*$, where V^* and ζ^* are given by Eqs. (4.42) and (4.41).

Exercise 4.13 In a one-period framework show that if x is a pricing factor and k_1, k_2 are constants with $k_2 \neq 0$, then $y = k_1 + k_2 x$ is also a pricing factor.

Exercise 4.14 Consider a two-period arbitrage-free economy where the resolution of uncertainty is illustrated in the following binomial tree.

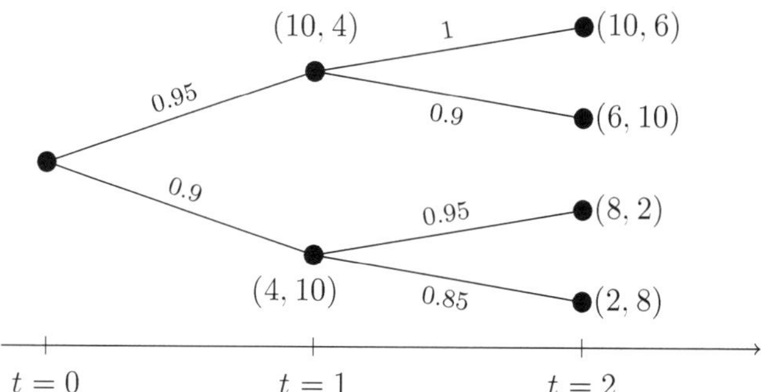

Each branch in the tree has a conditional probability of $\frac{1}{2}$. Assets in the economy are priced by a state-price deflator $\zeta = (\zeta_t)_{t \in \{0,1,2\}}$. The numbers along the branches show the possible values of the state-price deflator over that period, that is ζ_1/ζ_0 over the first period and ζ_2/ζ_1 over the second period. The pair of numbers written at each node shows the dividend payments of asset 1 and asset 2, respectively, if that node is reached. For example, if the up-branch is realized in both periods, then asset 1 will pay a dividend of 10 and asset 2 a dividend of 6 at time 2.

(a) For each of the two assets compute the following quantities in both the up-node and the down-node at time 1: (i) the conditional expectation of the dividend received at time 2, (ii) the ex-dividend price, and (iii) the expected net rate of return over the second period.

(b) For each of the two assets compute the following quantities at time 0: (i) the expectation of the dividend received at time 1, (ii) the price, and (iii) the expected net rate of return over the first period.

(c) Compare the prices of the two assets. Compare the expected returns of the two assets. Explain the differences.

(d) Is it always possible in this economy to construct a portfolio with a risk-free dividend over the next period? If so, find the one-period risk-free return at time 0 and in each of the two nodes at time 1.

(e) Is the market complete? Explain!

5

Preferences

5.1 INTRODUCTION

Before we can say anything concrete about the asset supply and demand of individuals we have to formalize the decision problem faced by them. We assume that individuals have preferences for consumption and have to choose between different consumption plans, which are plans for how much to consume at different points in time and in different states of the world. The financial market allows individuals to reallocate consumption over time and over states and hence to obtain a consumption plan different from their endowment.

Although an individual will typically obtain utility from consumption at many different dates (or in many different periods), we will first address the simpler case with consumption at only one future point in time. In such a setting a 'consumption plan' is simply a random variable representing the consumption at that date in the different states. Even in one-period models individuals should be allowed to consume both at the beginning of the period and at the end of the period, but we will first ignore the influence of current consumption on the well-being of the individual. We do this since current consumption is certain, and we want to focus on how preferences for uncertain consumption can be represented. Disregarding initial consumption will also simplify the notation and analysis somewhat. Since we have a one-period economy in mind, we basically have to model preferences for end-of-period consumption.

Sections 5.2–5.4 discuss how to represent individual preferences in a tractable way. We will demonstrate that under some fundamental assumptions ('axioms') on individual behaviour, the preferences can be modelled by a utility index which assigns a real number to each consumption plan with higher numbers to the more preferred plans. Under an additional axiom we can represent the preferences in terms of expected utility, which is even simpler to work with and used in most models of financial economics. Section 5.5 defines and discusses the important concept of risk aversion. Section 5.6 introduces the utility functions that are typically applied in models of financial economics and provides a short discussion on which utility functions and levels of risk aversions seem to be reasonable for representing the decisions of individuals. In Section 5.7 we discuss extensions to preferences for consumption at more than one point in time. This covers both the standard case of time-additive expected utility and extensions to habit formation, state-dependent preferences, and recursive utility.

There is a large literature on how to model the preferences of individuals for uncertain outcomes and the presentation here is by no means exhaustive. The literature dates back at least to the Swiss mathematician Daniel Bernoulli in 1738 (see English translation in Bernoulli (1954)), but was put on a firm formal setting by von Neumann and Morgenstern (1944).

5.2 CONSUMPTION PLANS AND PREFERENCE RELATIONS

It seems fair to assume that whenever an individual compares two different consumption plans, she will be able either to say that she prefers one of them to the other or to say that she is indifferent between the two consumption plans. Moreover, she should make such pairwise comparisons in a consistent way. For example, if she prefers plan 1 to plan 2 and plan 2 to plan 3, she should prefer plan 1 to plan 3. If these properties hold, we can formally represent the preferences of the individual by a so-called *preference relation*.

A preference relation itself is not very tractable. To find the best consumption plan among many feasible plans, we have to perform a large number of pairwise comparisons. Since the preference relation does not associate any number to each plan, we cannot use the standard mathematical optimization techniques. Therefore, we are looking for simpler ways of representing preferences.

First, we will find conditions under which it makes sense to represent preferences by a so-called *utility index* which attaches a real number to each consumption plan. If and only if plan 1 has a higher utility index than plan 2, the individual prefers plan 1 to plan 2. Attaching numbers to each possible consumption plan is not easy so we look for an even simpler representation. We show that under an additional condition we can represent preferences in an even simpler way in terms of the expected value of a *utility function*. A utility function is a function defined on the set of possible levels of consumption. Since consumption is random it then makes sense to talk about the expected utility of a consumption plan. The individual will prefer consumption plan 1 to plan 2 if and only if the expected utility from consumption plan 1 is higher than the expected utility from consumption plan 2. This representation of preferences turns out to be very tractable and is applied in the vast majority of asset pricing models.

We assume that there is uncertainty about how the variables affecting the well-being of an individual (such as asset returns) turn out. We model the uncertainty by a probability space $(\Omega, \mathcal{F}, \mathbb{P})$. In most of the chapter we will assume that the state space is finite, $\Omega = \{1, 2, \ldots, S\}$, so that there are S possible states of which exactly one will be realized. For simplicity, think of this as a model of a one-period economy with S possible states at the end of the period. The set $\mathcal{F}$ of events that can be assigned a probability is the collection of all subsets of Ω. The probability measure $\mathbb{P}$ is defined by the individual state probabilities $p_\omega = \mathbb{P}(\omega)$, $\omega = 1, 2, \ldots, S$. We assume that all $p_\omega > 0$ and, of course, that $p_1 + \cdots + p_S = 1$. We take the state probabilities as exogenously given and known to the individuals.

Individuals care about their consumption. It seems reasonable to assume that when an individual chooses between two different actions (for example two different portfolios), she only cares about the consumption plans generated by these choices. For example, she will be indifferent between two choices that generate exactly the same consumption plans, that is the same consumption levels in all states. In order to simplify the following analysis, we will assume a bit more, namely that the individual only cares about the probability distribution of consumption generated by each portfolio. This is effectively an assumption of *state-independent preferences.*

We can represent a consumption plan by a random variable c on $(\Omega, \mathcal{F}, \mathbb{P})$. We assume that there is only one consumption good and, since consumption should be non-negative, c is valued in $\mathbb{R}_+ = [0, \infty)$. As long as we are assuming a finite state space $\Omega = \{1, 2, \ldots, S\}$, we can equivalently represent the consumption plan by a vector $(c_1, \ldots, c_S)$, where $c_\omega \in [0, \infty)$ denotes the consumption level if state ω is realized, that is $c_\omega \equiv c(\omega)$. Let $\mathcal{C}$ denote the set of consumption plans that the individual can choose among. Let $Z \subseteq \mathbb{R}_+$ denote the set of all the possible levels of the consumption plans that are considered so that, no matter which of these consumption plans we take, its value will be in Z no matter which state is realized. Each consumption plan $c \in \mathcal{C}$ is associated with a probability distribution π_c, which is the function $\pi_c : Z \to [0, 1]$ given by

$$\pi_c(z) = \sum_{\omega \in \Omega:\, c_\omega = z} p_\omega, \tag{5.1}$$

that is the sum of the probabilities of those states in which the consumption level equals z.

As an example consider an economy with three possible states and four possible state-contingent consumption plans as illustrated in Table 5.1. These four consumption plans may be the product of four different portfolio choices. The set of possible end-of-period consumption levels is $Z = \{1, 2, 3, 4, 5\}$. Each consumption plan generates a probability distribution on the set Z. The

Table 5.1. The possible state-contingent consumption plans in the example.

State ω	1	2	3
State prob. p_ω	0.2	0.3	0.5
Cons. plan 1, $c^{(1)}$	3	2	4
Cons. plan 2, $c^{(2)}$	3	1	5
Cons. plan 3, $c^{(3)}$	4	4	1
Cons. plan 4, $c^{(4)}$	1	1	4

probability distributions corresponding to these consumption plans are as shown in Table 5.2. We see that although the consumption plans $c^{(3)}$ and $c^{(4)}$ are different, they generate identical probability distributions. By the assumption of state-independent preferences, individuals will be indifferent between these two consumption plans.

Given these assumptions, the individual will effectively choose between probability distributions on the set of possible consumption levels Z. We assume for simplicity that Z is a finite set, but the results can be generalized to the case of infinite Z at the cost of further mathematical complexity. We denote by $\mathcal{P}(Z)$ the set of all probability distributions on Z that are generated by consumption plans in $\mathcal{C}$. A probability distribution π on the finite set Z is simply a function $\pi : Z \rightarrow [0, 1]$ with the properties that $\sum_{z \in Z} \pi(z) = 1$ and $\pi(A \cup B) = \pi(A) + \pi(B)$ whenever $A \cap B = \emptyset$.

We assume that the preferences of the individual can be represented by a preference relation $\succeq$ on $\mathcal{P}(Z)$, which is a binary relation satisfying the following two conditions:

(i) if $\pi_1 \succeq \pi_2$ and $\pi_2 \succeq \pi_3$, then $\pi_1 \succeq \pi_3$ [transitivity]

(ii) $\forall \pi_1, \pi_2 \in \mathcal{P}(Z)$: either $\pi_1 \succeq \pi_2$ or $\pi_2 \succeq \pi_1$ [completeness]

Here, $\pi_1 \succeq \pi_2$ is to be read as 'π_1 is preferred to π_2'. We write $\pi_1 \not\succeq \pi_2$ if π_1 is not preferred to π_2. If both $\pi_1 \succeq \pi_2$ and $\pi_2 \succeq \pi_1$, we write $\pi_1 \sim \pi_2$ and say

Table 5.2. The probability distributions corresponding to the state-contingent consumption plans shown in Table 5.1.

Cons. level z	1	2	3	4	5
Cons. plan 1, $\pi_{c^{(1)}}$	0	0.3	0.2	0.5	0
Cons. plan 2, $\pi_{c^{(2)}}$	0.3	0	0.2	0	0.5
Cons. plan 3, $\pi_{c^{(3)}}$	0.5	0	0	0.5	0
Cons. plan 4, $\pi_{c^{(4)}}$	0.5	0	0	0.5	0

that the individual is indifferent between π_1 and π_2. If $\pi_1 \succeq \pi_2$, but $\pi_2 \not\succeq \pi_1$, we say that π_1 is strictly preferred to π_2 and write $\pi_1 \succ \pi_2$.

Note that if $\pi_1, \pi_2 \in \mathcal{P}(Z)$ and $\alpha \in [0,1]$, then $\alpha\pi_1 + (1-\alpha)\pi_2 \in \mathcal{P}(Z)$. The mixed distribution $\alpha\pi_1 + (1-\alpha)\pi_2$ assigns the probability $(\alpha\pi_1 + (1-\alpha)\pi_2)(z) = \alpha\pi_1(z) + (1-\alpha)\pi_2(z)$ to the consumption level z. We can think of the mixed distribution $\alpha\pi_1 + (1-\alpha)\pi_2$ as the outcome of a two-stage 'gamble'. The first stage is to flip a coin which with probability α shows heads and with probability $1-\alpha$ shows tails. If heads comes out, the second stage is the 'consumption gamble' corresponding to the probability distribution π_1. If tails is the outcome of the first stage, the second stage is the consumption gamble corresponding to π_2. When we assume that preferences are represented by a preference relation on the set $\mathcal{P}(Z)$ of probability distributions, we have implicitly assumed that the individual evaluates the two-stage gamble (or any multistage gamble) by the combined probability distribution, that is the ultimate consequences of the gamble.

Let z be some element of Z, that is some possible consumption level. By $\mathbf{1}_z$ we will denote the probability distribution that assigns a probability of one to z and a zero probability to all other elements in Z. Since we have assumed that the set Z of possible consumption levels only has a finite number of elements, it must have a maximum element, say z^u, and a minimum element, say z^l. Since the elements represent consumption levels, it is certainly natural that individuals prefer higher elements than lower. We will therefore assume that the probability distribution $\mathbf{1}_{z^u}$ is preferred to any other probability distribution. Conversely, any probability distribution is preferred to the probability distribution $\mathbf{1}_{z^l}$. We assume that $\mathbf{1}_{z^u}$ is strictly preferred to $\mathbf{1}_{z^l}$ so that the individual is not indifferent between all probability distributions. For any $\pi \in \mathcal{P}(Z)$ we thus have that,

$$\mathbf{1}_{z^u} \succ \pi \succ \mathbf{1}_{z^l} \quad \text{or} \quad \mathbf{1}_{z^u} \sim \pi \succ \mathbf{1}_{z^l} \quad \text{or} \quad \mathbf{1}_{z^u} \succ \pi \sim \mathbf{1}_{z^l}. \tag{5.2}$$

The 'extreme' consumption plans $\mathbf{1}_{z^u}$ and $\mathbf{1}_{z^l}$ will be used in the construction of utility indices which we turn to next.

5.3 UTILITY INDICES

A utility index for a given preference relation $\succeq$ is a function $\mathcal{U} : \mathcal{P}(Z) \to \mathbb{R}$ that to each probability distribution over consumption levels attaches a real-valued number such that

$$\pi_1 \succeq \pi_2 \quad \Leftrightarrow \quad \mathcal{U}(\pi_1) \geq \mathcal{U}(\pi_2).$$

Note that a utility index is only unique up to a strictly increasing transformation. If $\mathcal{U}$ is a utility index and $f : \mathbb{R} \to \mathbb{R}$ is any strictly increasing function, then the composite function $\mathcal{V} = f \circ \mathcal{U}$, defined by $\mathcal{V}(\pi) = f(\mathcal{U}(\pi))$, is also a utility index for the same preference relation.

We will show below that a utility index exists under the following two axiomatic assumptions on the preference relation $\succeq$:

Axiom 5.1 (Monotonicity). *Suppose that $\pi_1, \pi_2 \in \mathcal{P}(Z)$ with $\pi_1 \succ \pi_2$ and let $a, b \in [0, 1]$. The preference relation $\succeq$ has the property that*

$$a > b \quad \Leftrightarrow \quad a\pi_1 + (1 - a)\pi_2 \succ b\pi_1 + (1 - b)\pi_2.$$

This is certainly a very natural assumption on preferences. If you consider a weighted average of two probability distributions, you will prefer a high weight on the best of the two distributions.

Axiom 5.2 (Archimedean). *The preference relation $\succeq$ has the property that for any three probability distributions $\pi_1, \pi_2, \pi_3 \in \mathcal{P}(Z)$ with $\pi_1 \succ \pi_2 \succ \pi_3$, numbers $a, b \in (0, 1)$ exist such that*

$$a\pi_1 + (1 - a)\pi_3 \succ \pi_2 \succ b\pi_1 + (1 - b)\pi_3.$$

The axiom basically says that no matter how good a probability distribution π_1 is, then for any $\pi_2 \succ \pi_3$ we can find some mixture of π_1 and π_3 to which π_2 is preferred. We just have to put a sufficiently low weight on π_1 in the mixed distribution. Similarly, no matter how bad a probability distribution π_3 is, then for any $\pi_1 \succ \pi_2$ we can find some mixture of π_1 and π_3 that is preferred to π_2. We just have to put a sufficiently low weight on π_3 in the mixed distribution.

We shall say that a preference relation has the *continuity property* if for any three probability distributions $\pi_1, \pi_2, \pi_3 \in \mathcal{P}(Z)$ with $\pi_1 \succ \pi_2 \succ \pi_3$, a unique number $\alpha \in (0, 1)$ exists such that

$$\pi_2 \sim \alpha\pi_1 + (1 - \alpha)\pi_3.$$

We can easily extend this to the case where either $\pi_1 \sim \pi_2$ or $\pi_2 \sim \pi_3$. If $\pi_1 \sim \pi_2 \succ \pi_3$, then $\pi_2 \sim 1\pi_1 + (1 - 1)\pi_3$ corresponding to $\alpha = 1$. If $\pi_1 \succ \pi_2 \sim \pi_3$, then $\pi_2 \sim 0\pi_1 + (1 - 0)\pi_3$ corresponding to $\alpha = 0$. In words, the continuity property means that for any three probability distributions there is a unique combination of the best and the worst distribution so that the individual is indifferent between the third 'middle' distribution and this combination of the other two. This appears to be closely related to the Archimedean Axiom and, in fact, the next lemma shows that the Monotonicity Axiom and the Archimedean Axiom imply continuity of preferences.

Lemma 5.1 *Let $\succeq$ be a preference relation satisfying the Monotonicity Axiom and the Archimedean Axiom. Then it has the continuity property.*

Proof. Given $\pi_1 \succ \pi_2 \succ \pi_3$, define the number α by

$$\alpha = \sup\{k \in [0, 1] \mid \pi_2 \succ k\pi_1 + (1 - k)\pi_3\}.$$

By the Monotonicity Axiom we have that $\pi_2 \succ k\pi_1 + (1-k)\pi_3$ for all $k < \alpha$ and that $k\pi_1 + (1-k)\pi_3 \succeq \pi_2$ for all $k > \alpha$. We want to show that $\pi_2 \sim \alpha\pi_1 + (1-\alpha)\pi_3$. Note that by the Archimedean Axiom, there is some $k > 0$ such that $\pi_2 \succ k\pi_1 + (1-k)\pi_3$ and some $k < 1$ such that $k\pi_1 + (1-k)\pi_3 \succ \pi_2$. Consequently, α is in the open interval (0, 1).

Suppose that $\pi_2 \succ \alpha\pi_1 + (1-\alpha)\pi_3$. Then according to the Archimedean Axiom we can find a number $b \in (0,1)$ such that $\pi_2 \succ b\pi_1 + (1-b)\{\alpha\pi_1 + (1-\alpha)\pi_3\}$. The mixed distribution on the right-hand side has a total weight of $k = b + (1-b)\alpha = \alpha + (1-\alpha)b > \alpha$ on π_1. Hence we have found some $k > \alpha$ for which $\pi_2 \succ k\pi_1 + (1-k)\pi_3$. This contradicts the definition of α. Consequently, we must have that $\pi_2 \not\succ \alpha\pi_1 + (1-\alpha)\pi_3$.

Now suppose that $\alpha\pi_1 + (1-\alpha)\pi_3 \succ \pi_2$. Then we know from the Archimedean Axiom that a number $a \in (0,1)$ exists such that $a\{\alpha\pi_1 + (1-\alpha)\pi_3\} + (1-a)\pi_3 \succ \pi_2$. The mixed distribution on the left-hand side has a total weight of $a\alpha < \alpha$ on π_1. Hence we have found some $k < \alpha$ for which $k\pi_1 + (1-k)\pi_3 \succ \pi_2$. This contradicts the definition of α. We can therefore also conclude that $\alpha\pi_1 + (1-\alpha)\pi_3 \not\succ \pi_2$. In sum, we have $\pi_2 \sim \alpha\pi_1 + (1-\alpha)\pi_3$. □

The next result states that a preference relation which satisfies the Monotonicity Axiom and has the continuity property can always be represented by a utility index. In particular this is true when $\succeq$ satisfies the Monotonicity Axiom and the Archimedean Axiom.

Theorem 5.1 *Let $\succeq$ be a preference relation which satisfies the Monotonicity Axiom and has the continuity property. Then it can be represented by a utility index $\mathcal{U}$, that is a function $\mathcal{U} : \mathcal{P}(Z) \to \mathbb{R}$ with the property that*

$$\pi_1 \succeq \pi_2 \quad \Leftrightarrow \quad \mathcal{U}(\pi_1) \geq \mathcal{U}(\pi_2).$$

Proof. Recall that we have assumed a best probability distribution $\mathbf{1}_{z^u}$ and a worst probability distribution $\mathbf{1}_{z^l}$ so that Eq. (5.2) holds for any $\pi \in \mathcal{P}(Z)$. For any $\pi \in \mathcal{P}(Z)$ we know from the continuity property that a unique number $\alpha_\pi \in [0,1]$ exists such that

$$\pi \sim \alpha_\pi \mathbf{1}_{z^u} + (1-\alpha_\pi)\mathbf{1}_{z^l}.$$

If $\mathbf{1}_{z^u} \sim \pi \succ \mathbf{1}_{z^l}$, then $\alpha_\pi = 1$. If $\mathbf{1}_{z^u} \succ \pi \sim \mathbf{1}_{z^l}$, then $\alpha_\pi = 0$. If $\mathbf{1}_{z^u} \succ \pi \succ \mathbf{1}_{z^l}$, then $\alpha_\pi \in (0,1)$.

We define the function $\mathcal{U} : \mathcal{P}(Z) \to \mathbb{R}$ by $\mathcal{U}(\pi) = \alpha_\pi$. By the Monotonicity Axiom we know that $\mathcal{U}(\pi_1) \geq \mathcal{U}(\pi_2)$ if and only if

$$\mathcal{U}(\pi_1)\mathbf{1}_{z^u} + (1-\mathcal{U}(\pi_1))\,\mathbf{1}_{z^l} \succeq \mathcal{U}(\pi_2)\mathbf{1}_{z^u} + (1-\mathcal{U}(\pi_2))\,\mathbf{1}_{z^l},$$

and hence if and only if $\pi_1 \succeq \pi_2$. It follows that $\mathcal{U}$ is a utility index. □

In principle, we can find the optimal consumption plan by maximizing the utility index $\mathcal{U}(\pi)$ over all probability distributions $\pi \in \mathcal{P}(Z)$. However, with many states of the world and many assets to trade in, the set of such probability distributions will be very, very large. To simplify the analysis further, financial economists traditionally put more structure on the preferences so that they can be represented in terms of expected utility. This is explained in the following section.

5.4 EXPECTED UTILITY REPRESENTATION OF PREFERENCES

We say that a preference relation $\succeq$ on $\mathcal{P}(Z)$ has an expected utility representation if there exists a function $u : Z \to \mathbb{R}$ such that

$$\pi_1 \succeq \pi_2 \quad \Leftrightarrow \quad \sum_{z\in Z} \pi_1(z)u(z) \geq \sum_{z\in Z} \pi_2(z)u(z). \tag{5.3}$$

Note that, using Eq. (5.1), we have

$$\sum_{z\in Z} \pi_c(z)u(z) = \sum_{z\in Z} \sum_{\omega\in\Omega:\, c_\omega=z} p_\omega u(z) = \sum_{\omega\in\Omega} p_\omega u(c_\omega) = \mathrm{E}[u(c)]$$

so that $\sum_{z\in Z} \pi(z)u(z)$ is the expected utility of end-of-period consumption given the consumption plan associated with the probability distribution π. If we let c_i denote a consumption plan giving rise to the probability distribution π_i, the relation (5.3) says that c_1 is preferred to c_2 if and only if $\mathrm{E}[u(c_1)] \geq E[u(c_2)]$. The function u is called a von Neumann–Morgenstern utility function or simply a utility function. Note that u is defined on the set Z of consumption levels, which in general has a simpler structure than the set of probability distributions on Z. Given a utility function u, we can obviously define a utility index by $\mathcal{U}(\pi) = \sum_{z\in Z} \pi(z)u(z)$.

5.4.1 Conditions for Expected Utility

When can we use an expected utility representation of a preference relation? The next lemma is a first step in answering this question.

Lemma 5.2 *A preference relation $\succeq$ has an expected utility representation if and only if it can be represented by a linear utility index $\mathcal{U}$ in the sense that*

$$\mathcal{U}\left(a\pi_1 + (1-a)\pi_2\right) = a\mathcal{U}(\pi_1) + (1-a)\mathcal{U}(\pi_2)$$

for any $\pi_1, \pi_2 \in \mathcal{P}(Z)$ and any $a \in [0, 1]$.

Proof. Suppose that $\succeq$ has an expected utility representation with utility function u. Define $\mathcal{U}: \mathcal{P}(Z) \to \mathbb{R}$ by $\mathcal{U}(\pi) = \sum_{z \in Z} \pi(z)u(z)$. Then clearly $\mathcal{U}$ is a utility index representing $\succeq$, and $\mathcal{U}$ is linear since

$$\begin{aligned}\mathcal{U}(a\pi_1 + (1-a)\pi_2) &= \sum_{z\in Z} (a\pi_1(z) + (1-a)\pi_2(z))\, u(z) \\ &= a\sum_{z\in Z} \pi_1(z)u(z) + (1-a)\sum_{z\in Z} \pi_2(z)u(z) \\ &= a\mathcal{U}(\pi_1) + (1-a)\mathcal{U}(\pi_2).\end{aligned}$$

Conversely, suppose that $\mathcal{U}$ is a linear utility index representing $\succeq$. Define a function $u: Z \to \mathbb{R}$ by $u(z) = \mathcal{U}(\mathbf{1}_z)$. For any $\pi \in \mathcal{P}(Z)$ we have

$$\pi \sim \sum_{z\in Z} \pi(z)\mathbf{1}_z.$$

Therefore,

$$\mathcal{U}(\pi) = \mathcal{U}\left(\sum_{z\in Z} \pi(z)\mathbf{1}_z\right) = \sum_{z\in Z} \pi(z)\mathcal{U}(\mathbf{1}_z) = \sum_{z\in Z} \pi(z)u(z).$$

Since $\mathcal{U}$ is a utility index, we have $\pi_1 \succeq \pi_2 \Leftrightarrow \mathcal{U}(\pi_1) \geq \mathcal{U}(\pi_2)$, which the computation above shows is equivalent to $\sum_{z\in Z} \pi_1(z)u(z) \geq \sum_{z\in Z} \pi_2(z)u(z)$. Consequently, u gives an expected utility representation of $\succeq$. □

The question then is under what assumptions the preference relation $\succeq$ can be represented by a linear utility index. As shown by von Neumann and Morgenstern (1944) we need an additional axiom, the so-called Substitution Axiom.

Axiom 5.3 (Substitution). *For all $\pi_1, \pi_2, \pi_3 \in \mathcal{P}(Z)$ and all $a \in (0, 1]$, we have*

$$\pi_1 \succ \pi_2 \quad \Leftrightarrow \quad a\pi_1 + (1-a)\pi_3 \succ a\pi_2 + (1-a)\pi_3$$

and

$$\pi_1 \sim \pi_2 \quad \Leftrightarrow \quad a\pi_1 + (1-a)\pi_3 \sim a\pi_2 + (1-a)\pi_3.$$

The Substitution Axiom is sometimes called the Independence Axiom or the Axiom of the Irrelevance of the Common Alternative. Basically, it says that when the individual is to compare two probability distributions, she needs only to consider the parts of the two distributions which are different from each other. As an example, suppose the possible consumption levels are $Z = \{1, 2, 3, 4\}$ and consider the probability distributions on Z given in Table 5.3. Suppose you want to compare the distributions π_4 and π_5. They only differ in the probabilities they associate with consumption levels 2, 3, and 4 so it should only be necessary to focus on these parts. More formally observe that

Table 5.3. The probability distributions used in the illustration of the Substitution Axiom.

z	1	2	3	4
π_1	0	0.2	0.6	0.2
π_2	0	0.4	0.2	0.4
π_3	1	0	0	0
π_4	0.5	0.1	0.3	0.1
π_5	0.5	0.2	0.1	0.2

$$\pi_4 \sim 0.5\pi_1 + 0.5\pi_3 \quad \text{and} \quad \pi_5 \sim 0.5\pi_2 + 0.5\pi_3.$$

π_1 is the conditional distribution of π_4 given that the consumption level is different from 1, and π_2 is the conditional distribution of π_5 given that the consumption level is different from 1. The Substitution Axiom then says that

$$\pi_4 \succ \pi_5 \quad \Leftrightarrow \quad \pi_1 \succ \pi_2.$$

The next lemma shows that the Substitution Axiom is more restrictive than the Monotonicity Axiom.

Lemma 5.3 *If a preference relation $\succeq$ satisfies the Substitution Axiom, it will also satisfy the Monotonicity Axiom.*

Proof. Given $\pi_1, \pi_2 \in \mathcal{P}(Z)$ with $\pi_1 \succ \pi_2$ and numbers $a, b \in [0, 1]$, we have to show that

$$a > b \quad \Leftrightarrow \quad a\pi_1 + (1-a)\pi_2 \succ b\pi_1 + (1-b)\pi_2.$$

Note that if $a = 0$ we cannot have $a > b$, and if $a\pi_1 + (1-a)\pi_2 \succ b\pi_1 + (1-b)\pi_2$ we cannot have $a = 0$. We can therefore safely assume that $a > 0$.

First assume that $a > b$. Observe that it follows from the Substitution Axiom that

$$a\pi_1 + (1-a)\pi_2 \succ a\pi_2 + (1-a)\pi_2$$

and hence that $a\pi_1 + (1-a)\pi_2 \succ \pi_2$. The Substitution Axiom also implies that, for any $\pi_3 \succ \pi_2$,

$$\pi_3 \sim \left(1 - \frac{b}{a}\right)\pi_3 + \frac{b}{a}\pi_3 \succ \left(1 - \frac{b}{a}\right)\pi_2 + \frac{b}{a}\pi_3.$$

Due to our observation above, we can use this with $\pi_3 = a\pi_1 + (1-a)\pi_2$. Then we get

$$a\pi_1 + (1-a)\pi_2 \succ \frac{b}{a}\{a\pi_1 + (1-a)\pi_2\} + \left(1 - \frac{b}{a}\right)\pi_2$$
$$\sim b\pi_1 + (1-b)\pi_2,$$

as was to be shown.

Conversely, assuming that

$$a\pi_1 + (1-a)\pi_2 \succ b\pi_1 + (1-b)\pi_2,$$

we must argue that $a > b$. The above inequality cannot be true if $a = b$ since the two combined distributions are then identical. If b was greater than a, we could follow the steps above with a and b swapped and end up concluding that $b\pi_1 + (1-b)\pi_2 \succ a\pi_1 + (1-a)\pi_2$, which would contradict our assumption. Hence, we cannot have neither $a = b$ nor $a < b$ but must have $a > b$. □

Next we state the main result:

Theorem 5.2 *Assume that Z is finite and that $\succeq$ is a preference relation on $\mathcal{P}(Z)$. Then $\succeq$ can be represented by a linear utility index if and only if $\succeq$ satisfies the Archimedean Axiom and the Substitution Axiom.*

Proof. First suppose the preference relation $\succeq$ satisfies the Archimedean Axiom and the Substitution Axiom. Define a utility index $\mathcal{U} : \mathcal{P}(Z) \to \mathbb{R}$ exactly as in the proof of Theorem 5.1, that is $\mathcal{U}(\pi) = \alpha_\pi$, where $\alpha_\pi \in [0,1]$ is the unique number such that

$$\pi \sim \alpha_\pi \mathbf{1}_{z^u} + (1-\alpha_\pi)\mathbf{1}_{z^l}.$$

We intend to show that, as a consequence of the Substitution Axiom, $\mathcal{U}$ is indeed linear. For that purpose, pick any two probability distributions $\pi_1, \pi_2 \in \mathcal{P}(Z)$ and any number $a \in [0,1]$. We want to show that $\mathcal{U}(a\pi_1 + (1-a)\pi_2) = a\mathcal{U}(\pi_1) + (1-a)\mathcal{U}(\pi_2)$. We can do that by showing that

$$a\pi_1 + (1-a)\pi_2 \sim (a\mathcal{U}(\pi_1) + (1-a)\mathcal{U}(\pi_2))\,\mathbf{1}_{z^u}$$
$$+ (1 - \{a\mathcal{U}(\pi_1) + (1-a)\mathcal{U}(\pi_2)\})\,\mathbf{1}_{z^l}.$$

This follows from the Substitution Axiom:

$$a\pi_1 + (1-a)\pi_2 \sim a\{\mathcal{U}(\pi_1)\mathbf{1}_{z^u} + (1-\mathcal{U}(\pi_1))\,\mathbf{1}_{z^l}\}$$
$$+ (1-a)\{\mathcal{U}(\pi_2)\mathbf{1}_{z^u} + (1-\mathcal{U}(\pi_2))\,\mathbf{1}_{z^l}\}$$
$$\sim (a\mathcal{U}(\pi_1) + (1-a)\mathcal{U}(\pi_2))\,\mathbf{1}_{z^u}$$
$$+ (1 - \{a\mathcal{U}(\pi_1) + (1-a)\mathcal{U}(\pi_2)\})\,\mathbf{1}_{z^l}.$$

Now let us show the converse, that is if $\succeq$ can be represented by a linear utility index $\mathcal{U}$, then it must satisfy the Archimedean Axiom and the Substitution

Axiom. In order to show the Archimedean Axiom, we pick $\pi_1 \succ \pi_2 \succ \pi_3$, which means that $\mathcal{U}(\pi_1) > \mathcal{U}(\pi_2) > \mathcal{U}(\pi_3)$, and must find numbers $a, b \in (0,1)$ such that

$$a\pi_1 + (1-a)\pi_3 \succ \pi_2 \succ b\pi_1 + (1-b)\pi_3,$$

that is

$$\mathcal{U}\left(a\pi_1 + (1-a)\pi_3\right) > \mathcal{U}(\pi_2) > \mathcal{U}\left(b\pi_1 + (1-b)\pi_3\right).$$

Define the number a by

$$a = 1 - \frac{1}{2}\frac{\mathcal{U}(\pi_1) - \mathcal{U}(\pi_2)}{\mathcal{U}(\pi_1) - \mathcal{U}(\pi_3)}.$$

Then $a \in (0,1)$ and by linearity of $\mathcal{U}$ we get

$$\begin{aligned}
\mathcal{U}\left(a\pi_1 + (1-a)\pi_3\right) &= a\mathcal{U}(\pi_1) + (1-a)\mathcal{U}(\pi_3) \\
&= \mathcal{U}(\pi_1) + (1-a)\left(\mathcal{U}(\pi_3) - \mathcal{U}(\pi_1)\right) \\
&= \mathcal{U}(\pi_1) - \frac{1}{2}\left(\mathcal{U}(\pi_1) - \mathcal{U}(\pi_2)\right) \\
&= \frac{1}{2}\left(\mathcal{U}(\pi_1) + \mathcal{U}(\pi_2)\right) \\
&> \mathcal{U}(\pi_2).
\end{aligned}$$

Similarly for b. This proves that the Archimedean Axiom holds.

In order to show the Substitution Axiom, we take $\pi_1, \pi_2, \pi_3 \in \mathcal{P}(Z)$ and any number $a \in (0,1]$. We must show that $\pi_1 \succ \pi_2$ if and only if $a\pi_1 + (1-a)\pi_3 \succ a\pi_2 + (1-a)\pi_3$, that is

$$\mathcal{U}(\pi_1) > \mathcal{U}(\pi_2) \quad \Leftrightarrow \quad \mathcal{U}\left(a\pi_1 + (1-a)\pi_3\right) > \mathcal{U}\left(a\pi_2 + (1-a)\pi_3\right).$$

This follows immediately by linearity of $\mathcal{U}$:

$$\begin{aligned}
\mathcal{U}\left(a\pi_1 + (1-a)\pi_3\right) &= a\mathcal{U}(\pi_1) + \mathcal{U}\left((1-a)\pi_3\right) \\
&> a\mathcal{U}(\pi_2) + \mathcal{U}\left((1-a)\pi_3\right) \\
&= \mathcal{U}\left(a\pi_2 + (1-a)\pi_3\right)
\end{aligned}$$

with the inequality holding if and only if $\mathcal{U}(\pi_1) > \mathcal{U}(\pi_2)$. Similarly, we can show that $\pi_1 \sim \pi_2$ if and only if $a\pi_1 + (1-a)\pi_3 \sim a\pi_2 + (1-a)\pi_3$. □

The next theorem shows which utility functions represent the same preference relation. The proof is left for the reader as Exercise 5.1.

Theorem 5.3 *A utility function for a given preference relation is only determined up to a strictly increasing affine transformation: if u is a utility function for $\succeq$,* *then v will be so if and only if there exist constants $a > 0$ and b such that $v(z) = au(z) + b$ for all $z \in Z$.*

If one utility function is an affine function of another, we will say that they are equivalent. Note that an easy consequence of this theorem is that it does not really matter whether the utility is positive or negative. At first, you might find negative utility strange, but we can always add a sufficiently large positive constant without affecting the ranking of different consumption plans.

Suppose $\mathcal{U}$ is a utility index with an associated utility function u. If f is any strictly increasing transformation, then $\mathcal{V} = f \circ \mathcal{U}$ is also a utility index for the same preferences, but $f \circ u$ is only the utility function for $\mathcal{V}$ if f is affine.

The expected utility associated with the probability distribution π on Z equals $\sum_{z \in Z} \pi(z)u(z)$. Recall that the probability distributions we consider correspond to consumption plans. Given a consumption plan represented by the random variable c, the associated probability distribution is defined by the probabilities (5.1), and the expected utility associated with the consumption plan c is $\mathrm{E}[u(c)] = \sum_{z \in Z} \pi(z)u(z)$. Of course, if c is a risk-free consumption plan in the sense that a z exists such that $c(\omega) = z$ for all ω, then the expected utility is $\mathrm{E}[u(c)] = u(z)$. With a slight abuse of notation we will just write this as $u(c)$.

5.4.2 Some Technical Issues

5.4.2.1 Infinite Z

What if Z is infinite, for example $Z = \mathbb{R}_+ \equiv [0, \infty)$? It can be shown that in this case a preference relation has an expected utility representation if the Archimedean Axiom, the Substitution Axiom, an additional axiom ('the sure thing principle'), and 'some technical conditions' are satisfied. Fishburn (1970) gives the details. In this case, expected utility is $\mathrm{E}[u(c)] = \int_Z u(z)\pi(z)\,dz$, where π is a probability density function derived from the consumption plan c.

5.4.2.2 Boundedness of Expected Utility

Suppose the utility function u is unbounded from above and $\mathbb{R}_+ \subseteq Z$. Then there exists a sequence $(z_n)_{n=1}^{\infty} \subseteq Z$ with $z_n \to \infty$ and $u(z_n) \geq 2^n$. Consider a consumption plan corresponding to the probability distribution π_1 defined by $\pi_1(z_n) = 1/2^n$ (note that $\sum_{n=1}^{\infty} 1/2^n = 1$). The expected utility associated with that plan is then

$$\sum_{n=1}^{\infty} u(z_n)\pi_1(z_n) \geq \sum_{n=1}^{\infty} 2^n \frac{1}{2^n} = \infty.$$

If π_2, π_3 are such that $\pi_1 \succ \pi_2 \succ \pi_3$, then the expected utility of π_2 and π_3 must be finite. But for no $b \in (0, 1)$ do we have

$$\pi_2 \succ b\pi_1 + (1 - b)\pi_3$$

since the mixed distribution on the right-hand side leads to infinite expected utility. Therefore, the Archimedean Axiom will break down in this case.

This problem does not occur if Z is finite. Furthermore, it does not occur when $\mathbb{R}_+ \subseteq Z$ as long as u is concave and consumption plans have finite expectations. This is true because when u is concave, u will be differentiable in some point b and satisfy

$$u(z) \leq u(b) + u'(b)(z - b), \quad \forall z \in Z.$$

Therefore, if the consumption plan c has finite expectations, then

$$\mathrm{E}[u(c)] \leq \mathrm{E}[u(b) + u'(b)(c - b)] = u(b) + u'(b)\,(\mathrm{E}[c] - b) < \infty.$$

Typical applications do, in fact, assume a concave utility function and consider only consumption plans with finite expectations.

5.4.2.3 *Subjective Probability*

We have taken the probabilities of the states of nature as exogenously given, that is as *objective* probabilities. However, in real life individuals often have to form their own probabilities about many events, that is they form *subjective* probabilities. Although the analysis is a bit more complicated, Savage (1954) and Anscombe and Aumann (1963) show that the results developed above carry over to the case of subjective probabilities. For an introduction to this analysis, see Kreps (1990, Ch. 3).

5.4.3 Are the Axioms Reasonable?

The validity of the Substitution Axiom, which is necessary for obtaining the expected utility representation, has been intensively discussed in the literature. Some researchers have conducted experiments in which the decisions made by the participating individuals conflict with the Substitution Axiom.

The most famous challenge is the so-called *Allais Paradox* named after Allais (1953). Here is one example of the paradox. Suppose $Z = \{0, 1, 5\}$. Consider the consumption plans in Table 5.4. The Substitution Axiom implies that if an individual prefers π_1 to π_2, she should also prefer π_4 to π_3. In symbols: $\pi_1 \succ \pi_2 \Rightarrow \pi_4 \succ \pi_3$. This can be seen from the following:

Table 5.4. The probability distributions used in the illustration of the Allais Paradox.

z	0	1	5
π_1	0	1	0
π_2	0.01	0.89	0.1
π_3	0.9	0	0.1
π_4	0.89	0.11	0

$$0.11(\$1) + 0.89\boxed{(\$1)} \sim \pi_1 \succ \pi_2 \sim 0.11\left(\frac{1}{11}(\$0) + \frac{10}{11}(\$5)\right) + 0.89\boxed{(\$1)} \quad \Rightarrow$$

$$\underbrace{0.11(\$1) + 0.89\boxed{(\$0)}}_{\pi_4\sim} \succ 0.11\left(\frac{1}{11}(\$0) + \frac{10}{11}(\$5)\right) + 0.89\boxed{(\$0)} \sim \underbrace{0.9(\$0) + 0.1(\$5)}_{\pi_3\sim}$$

Nevertheless individuals preferring π_1 to π_2 often choose π_3 over π_4. Apparently people tend to over-weight small probability events, for example the event (\$0) in π_2.

Another problem with the standard mathematical models of preferences is that they assume individuals have unlimited rationality. They can identify all relevant states, assign appropriate probabilities to the states, and perform a potentially very complicated maximization to determine the optimal consumption plan. Many individuals may have a hard time doing that. For example, empirical experiments indicate that the *framing* of possible choices matters; the way in which the alternative choices are presented seems to affect the decision taken.

The standard models of preferences assume that the individual knows (or can easily assess) the probabilities of the different possible outcomes. However, for some decisions individuals do not know these probabilities. In order to make investment decisions, the individual will have to set up a model for the returns of different investment objects. In a one-period setting, this means identifying the correct type of probability distribution (such as the normal or lognormal distribution) and identifying the parameters of the distribution (such as mean, variance, and cross-asset correlations). Parameters can only be estimated with error, and it seems impossible to completely rule out alternative distribution types. Individuals thus face model and parameter uncertainty or, in other words, they are ambiguous about which probability distribution is correct. The experiments and accompanying discussions presented by Ellsberg (1961) illustrate that individuals might have different attitudes towards *ambiguity* than to the risks captured by a given model with given parameters. Ambiguity and ambiguity attitudes can be represented in different ways. The reader is referred to the original contributions by Gilboa and Schmeidler (1989), Anderson, Hansen, and Sargent (2003), and Klibanoff, Marinacci, and Mukerji (2005, 2009), as well as the survey by Gilboa and Marinacci (2011).

The completeness of preferences—the assumption that any two alternatives can be ranked—has been challenged and generalized by Aumann (1962), Bewley (2002), Kraus and Sagi (2006), and Gilboa *et al.* (2010), among others.

Over the last couple of decades a literature on *behavioural finance* has emerged, which investigates the impact of deviations from rational behaviour on individual decision-making and market equilibrium. Note that to obtain a significant effect on equilibrium prices, such behaviourial biases have to be systematic across individuals. We will not go into this literature here, but refer the reader to Hirshleifer (2001) and Barberis and Thaler (2003) for an introduction to behaviourial finance and to Constantinides (2002), Ross (2005), and Cochrane (2011) for a critique of that approach.

5.5 RISK AVERSION

In this section we focus on the attitudes towards risk reflected by the preferences of an individual. We assume that the preferences can be represented by a utility function u which is strictly increasing so that the individual is 'greedy' in the sense that she prefers high consumption to low consumption. We assume that the utility function is defined on some interval Z of $\mathbb{R}$. Since negative consumption does not make sense, the typical specification is that $Z = \mathbb{R}_+ \equiv [0, \infty)$, but sometimes a smaller set is appropriate as we shall see in Section 5.6.

5.5.1 Risk Attitudes

Fix a consumption level $c \in Z$. Consider a random variable ε with $\mathrm{E}[\varepsilon] = 0$. We can think of $c + \varepsilon$ as a random variable representing a consumption plan with consumption $c + \varepsilon(\omega)$ if state ω is realized. Note that $\mathrm{E}[c + \varepsilon] = c$. Such a random variable ε is called a fair gamble or a zero-mean risk.

An individual is said to be (strictly) *risk-averse* if she for all $c \in Z$ and all fair gambles ε (strictly) prefers the sure consumption level c to $c + \varepsilon$. In other words, a risk-averse individual rejects all fair gambles. Similarly, an individual is said to be (strictly) *risk-loving* if she for all $c \in Z$ (strictly) prefers $c + \varepsilon$ to c, and said to be *risk-neutral* if she for all $c \in Z$ is indifferent between accepting any fair gamble or not. Of course, individuals may be neither risk-averse, risk-neutral, nor risk-loving, for example if they reject fair gambles around some values of c and accept fair gambles around other values of c. Individuals may be locally risk-averse, locally risk-neutral, and locally risk-loving. Since it is generally believed that individuals are risk-averse, we focus on preferences exhibiting that feature.

We can think of any consumption plan c as the sum of its expected value $\mathrm{E}[c]$ and a fair gamble $\varepsilon = c - \mathrm{E}[c]$. It follows that an individual is risk-averse if she prefers the sure consumption $\mathrm{E}[c]$ to the random consumption c, that is if $u(\mathrm{E}[c]) \geq \mathrm{E}[u(c)]$. By Jensen's Inequality, this is true exactly when u is a concave function. The inequality is strict when u is strictly concave and c is a non-degenerate random variable so that it does not have the same value in all states. Recall that $u : Z \to \mathbb{R}$ being concave means that for all $z_1, z_2 \in Z$ and all $a \in (0, 1)$ we have

$$u\left(az_1 + (1-a)z_2\right) \geq au(z_1) + (1-a)u(z_2).$$

If the strict inequality holds in all cases, the function is said to be strictly concave. By the above argument, we have the following theorem:

Theorem 5.4 *An individual with a utility function u is (strictly) risk-averse if and only if u is (strictly) concave.*

Similarly, an individual is (strictly) risk-loving if and only if the utility function is (strictly) convex. An individual is risk-neutral if and only if the utility function is affine.

5.5.2 Quantitative Measures of Risk Aversion

We will focus on utility functions that are continuous and twice differentiable on the interior of Z. By our assumption of greedy individuals, we then have $u' > 0$, and the concavity of the utility function for risk-averse investors is then equivalent to $u'' \leq 0$.

The *certainty equivalent* of the random consumption plan c is defined as the $c^* \in Z$ such that

$$u(c^*) = \mathrm{E}[u(c)], \tag{5.4}$$

that is the individual is just as satisfied getting the consumption level c^* for sure as getting the random consumption c. With $Z \subseteq \mathbb{R}$, the certainty equivalent c^* exists and is unique due to our assumptions that u is continuous and strictly increasing. From the definition of the certainty equivalent, it is clear that an individual will rank consumption plans according to their certainty equivalents.

For a risk-averse individual the certainty equivalent c^* of a consumption plan is smaller than the expected consumption level $\mathrm{E}[c]$. The *consumption risk premium* associated with the consumption plan c is defined as $\lambda(c) = \mathrm{E}[c] - c^*$ so that

$$\mathrm{E}[u(c)] = u(c^*) = u(\mathrm{E}[c] - \lambda(c)).$$

The consumption risk premium is the consumption the individual is willing to give up in order to eliminate the uncertainty.

The degree of risk aversion is associated with u'', but a good measure of risk aversion should be invariant to strictly positive, affine transformations. This is satisfied by the Arrow–Pratt measures of risk aversion defined as follows. The *absolute risk aversion* is given by

$$\mathrm{ARA}(c) = -\frac{u''(c)}{u'(c)}.$$

The *relative risk aversion* is given by

$$\mathrm{RRA}(c) = -\frac{cu''(c)}{u'(c)} = c\,\mathrm{ARA}(c).$$

If $v(c) = au(c) + b$, then $v'(c) = au'(c)$ and $v''(c) = au''(c)$. Consequently, the absolute risk aversion computed from v equals the absolute risk aversion computed from u:

$$\mathrm{ARA}_v(c) = -\frac{v''(c)}{v'(c)} = -\frac{au''(c)}{au'(c)} = -\frac{u''(c)}{u'(c)} = \mathrm{ARA}_u(c).$$

Similarly for the relative risk aversion.

We can link the Arrow–Pratt measures to the consumption risk premium in the following way. Let $\bar{c} \in Z$ denote some fixed consumption level and let ε be a fair gamble. The resulting consumption plan is then $c = \bar{c} + \varepsilon$. Denote the corresponding consumption risk premium by $\lambda(\bar{c}, \varepsilon)$ so that

$$\mathrm{E}[u(\bar{c} + \varepsilon)] = u(c^*) = u\left(\bar{c} - \lambda(\bar{c}, \varepsilon)\right). \tag{5.5}$$

We can approximate the left-hand side of Eq. (5.5) by

$$\mathrm{E}[u(\bar{c} + \varepsilon)] \approx \mathrm{E}\left[u(\bar{c}) + \varepsilon u'(\bar{c}) + \frac{1}{2}\varepsilon^2 u''(\bar{c})\right] = u(\bar{c}) + \frac{1}{2}\,\mathrm{Var}[\varepsilon]u''(\bar{c}),$$

using $\mathrm{E}[\varepsilon] = 0$ and $\mathrm{Var}[\varepsilon] = \mathrm{E}[\varepsilon^2] - \mathrm{E}[\varepsilon]^2 = \mathrm{E}[\varepsilon^2]$, and we can approximate the right-hand side of Eq. (5.5) by

$$u\left(\bar{c} - \lambda(\bar{c}, \varepsilon)\right) \approx u(\bar{c}) - \lambda(\bar{c}, \varepsilon)u'(\bar{c}).$$

Hence we can write the consumption risk premium as

$$\lambda(\bar{c}, \varepsilon) \approx -\frac{1}{2}\,\mathrm{Var}[\varepsilon]\frac{u''(\bar{c})}{u'(\bar{c})} = \frac{1}{2}\,\mathrm{Var}[\varepsilon]\,\mathrm{ARA}(\bar{c}).$$

Of course, the approximation is more accurate for 'small' gambles. Thus the risk premium for a small fair gamble around $\bar{c}$ is roughly proportional to the absolute risk aversion at $\bar{c}$. We see that the absolute risk aversion $\text{ARA}(\bar{c})$ is constant if and only if $\lambda(\bar{c}, \varepsilon)$ is independent of $\bar{c}$.

Loosely speaking, the absolute risk aversion $\text{ARA}(c)$ measures the aversion to a fair gamble of a given dollar amount around c, such as a gamble where there is an equal probability of winning or losing 1000 dollars. Since we expect that a wealthy investor will be less averse to that gamble than a poor investor, the absolute risk aversion is expected to be a decreasing function of wealth. Note that

$$\text{ARA}'(c) = -\frac{u'''(c)u'(c) - u''(c)^2}{u'(c)^2} = \left(\frac{u''(c)}{u'(c)}\right)^2 - \frac{u'''(c)}{u'(c)},$$

so

$$\text{ARA}'(c) < 0 \quad \Rightarrow \quad u'''(c) > 0 \tag{5.6}$$

under our assumptions that $u'(c) > 0$ and $u''(c) < 0$. Hence, a positive third-order derivative of u is necessary for the utility function u to exhibit decreasing absolute risk aversion.

Now consider a 'multiplicative' fair gamble around $\bar{c}$ in the sense that the resulting consumption plan is $c = \bar{c}(1 + \varepsilon) = \bar{c} + \bar{c}\varepsilon$, where $\mathrm{E}[\varepsilon] = 0$. The consumption risk premium is then

$$\lambda(\bar{c}, \bar{c}\varepsilon) \approx \frac{1}{2}\,\text{Var}[\bar{c}\varepsilon]\,\text{ARA}(\bar{c}) = \frac{1}{2}\bar{c}^2\,\text{Var}[\varepsilon]\,\text{ARA}(\bar{c}) = \frac{1}{2}\bar{c}\,\text{Var}[\varepsilon]\,\text{RRA}(\bar{c})$$

implying that

$$\frac{\lambda(\bar{c}, \bar{c}\varepsilon)}{\bar{c}} \approx \frac{1}{2}\,\text{Var}[\varepsilon]\,\text{RRA}(\bar{c}). \tag{5.7}$$

The fraction of consumption you require to engage in the multiplicative fair gamble around $\bar{c}$ is thus (roughly) proportional to the relative risk aversion at $\bar{c}$. Note that utility functions with constant or decreasing (or even modestly increasing) relative risk aversion will display decreasing absolute risk aversion. For another perspective on the absolute and the relative risk aversion, see Exercise 5.5.

Some authors use terms like risk tolerance and risk cautiousness. The *absolute risk tolerance* at c is simply the reciprocal of the absolute risk aversion, that is

$$\text{ART}(c) = \frac{1}{\text{ARA}(c)} = -\frac{u'(c)}{u''(c)}.$$

Similarly, the *relative risk tolerance* is the reciprocal of the relative risk aversion. The *risk cautiousness* at c is defined as the rate of change in the absolute risk tolerance, that is $\text{ART}'(c)$.

5.5.3 Risk Aversion Towards Different Outcome Variables

Utility functions and risk aversions can be expressed in terms of various outcome variables such as consumption, wealth, income, and return. Moreover, these outcome variables can be measured in different ways. How can we relate the risk aversions computed using different measures of outcome? Following Meyer and Meyer (2005), suppose that X and Y are two such measures, related via a function $Y = Y(X)$, and suppose that X and Y are positive. Let $U(X)$ and $V(Y)$ denote the utility functions expressed in terms of X and Y, respectively, where

$$U(X) = V(Y(X))$$

for any value of X. We assume that both U and V are increasing and concave. Let $\mathrm{RRA}_U(X)$ and $\mathrm{RRA}_V(Y)$ denote the corresponding Arrow–Pratt relative risk aversions, that is

$$\mathrm{RRA}_U(X) = -\frac{XU''(X)}{U'(X)}, \qquad \mathrm{RRA}_V(Y) = -\frac{YV''(Y)}{V'(Y)}. \tag{5.8}$$

Then the following theorem holds (you are asked to provide a proof in Exercise 5.6):

Theorem 5.5 *The relative risk aversions* RRA_U *and* RRA_V *defined in Eq.* (5.8) *are related through*

$$\mathrm{RRA}_U(X) = \mathrm{RRA}_V(Y)\frac{XY'(X)}{Y} - \frac{XY''(X)}{Y'(X)}.$$

If $Y = a + bX$, *where* a *and* b *are positive constants, we have*

$$\mathrm{RRA}_U(X) \leq \mathrm{RRA}_V(Y),$$

and

$$\mathrm{RRA}'_V(Y) = 0 \Rightarrow \mathrm{RRA}'_U(X) > 0,$$
$$\mathrm{RRA}'_U(X) = 0 \Rightarrow \mathrm{RRA}'_V(Y) < 0.$$

The above results show that one has to be very careful when comparing two relative risk aversion measures that are computed with respect to different measures of outcome. Also, the magnitude of the relative risk aversion will generally depend on the underlying measure of outcome. Suppose, for example, that consumption is an affine function of wealth, $c = a + bW$, where a and b are positive constants. Then the relative risk aversion derived from consumption is greater than or equal to the relative risk aversion derived from wealth. Moreover, if the relative risk aversion based on consumption is constant (independent of the level of consumption), then the relative risk aversion based on wealth will be increasing (in the level of wealth).

Another example is when Y represents total wealth, which is the sum of human capital a (assumed constant) and financial wealth X. Since human capital is hard to measure, it is tempting just to use financial wealth as a proxy for total wealth. But the relative risk aversion based on financial wealth will be smaller than the relative risk aversion based on total wealth. And if the relative risk aversion based on total wealth is really constant, then the relative risk aversion derived from financial wealth will be increasing.

Meyer and Meyer (2005) show that some of the apparently very different estimates of relative risk aversion found in the literature are in fact much closer to each other once they have been adjusted for differences in the assumed outcome measures.

5.5.4 Comparison of Risk Aversion Between Individuals

An individual with utility function u is said to be *more risk-averse* than an individual with utility function v if for any consumption plan c and any fixed $\bar{c} \in Z$ with $\mathrm{E}[u(c)] \geq u(\bar{c})$, we have $\mathrm{E}[v(c)] \geq v(\bar{c})$. So the v-individual will accept all gambles that the u-individual will accept—and possibly some more. Pratt (1964) has shown the following theorem:

Theorem 5.6 *Suppose u and v are twice continuously differentiable and strictly increasing. Then the following conditions are equivalent:*

(a) u is more risk-averse than v,

(b) $\mathrm{ARA}_u(c) \geq \mathrm{ARA}_v(c)$ for all $c \in Z$,

(c) a strictly increasing and concave function f exists such that $u = f \circ v$.

Proof. First let us show (a) $\Rightarrow$ (b): suppose u is more risk-averse than v, but that $\mathrm{ARA}_u(\hat{c}) < \mathrm{ARA}_v(\hat{c})$ for some $\hat{c} \in Z$. Since ARA_u and ARA_v are continuous, we must then have that $\mathrm{ARA}_u(c) < \mathrm{ARA}_v(c)$ for all c in an interval around $\hat{c}$. Then we can surely find a small gamble around $\hat{c}$, which the u-individual will accept, but the v-individual will reject. This contradicts the assumption in (a).

Next, we show (b) $\Rightarrow$ (c): since v is strictly increasing, it has an inverse v^{-1} and we can define a function f by $f(x) = u\left(v^{-1}(x)\right)$. Then clearly $f(v(c)) = u(c)$ so that $u = f \circ v$. The first-order derivative of f is

$$f'(x) = \frac{u'\left(v^{-1}(x)\right)}{v'\left(v^{-1}(x)\right)},$$

which is positive since u and v are strictly increasing. Hence, f is strictly increasing. The second-order derivative is

$$f''(x) = \frac{u''\left(v^{-1}(x)\right) - \left\{v''\left(v^{-1}(x)\right) u'\left(v^{-1}(x)\right)\right\} / v'\left(v^{-1}(x)\right)}{v'\left(v^{-1}(x)\right)^2}$$

$$= \frac{u'\left(v^{-1}(x)\right)}{v'\left(v^{-1}(x)\right)^2} \left(\mathrm{ARA}_v\left(v^{-1}(x)\right) - \mathrm{ARA}_u\left(v^{-1}(x)\right)\right).$$

From (b), it follows that $f''(x) \leq 0$, hence f is concave.

Finally, we show that (c) $\Rightarrow$ (a): assume that for some consumption plan c and some $\bar{c} \in Z$, we have $\mathrm{E}[u(c)] \geq u(\bar{c})$ but $\mathrm{E}[v(c)] < v(\bar{c})$. We want to arrive at a contradiction. Under the stated assumptions, we see that

$$\begin{aligned} f\left(v(\bar{c})\right) = u(\bar{c}) \leq \mathrm{E}[u(c)] &= \mathrm{E}[f(v(c))] \\ &< f\left(\mathrm{E}[v(c)]\right) \\ &< f\left(v(\bar{c})\right), \end{aligned}$$

where we use the concavity of f and Jensen's Inequality to go from the first to the second line, and we use that f is strictly increasing to go from the second to the third line. Now the contradiction is clear. □

5.6 UTILITY FUNCTIONS IN MODELS AND IN REALITY

5.6.1 Frequently Applied Utility Functions

5.6.1.1 CRRA Utility

(Also known as power utility or isoelastic utility.) Utility functions in this class are defined for $c \geq 0$ and have the form

$$u(c) = \frac{c^{1-\gamma}}{1-\gamma}, \tag{5.9}$$

where $\gamma > 0$ and $\gamma \neq 1$. Since

$$u'(c) = c^{-\gamma} \quad \text{and} \quad u''(c) = -\gamma c^{-\gamma-1},$$

the absolute and relative risk aversions are given by

$$\mathrm{ARA}(c) = -\frac{u''(c)}{u'(c)} = \frac{\gamma}{c}, \qquad \mathrm{RRA}(c) = c\,\mathrm{ARA}(c) = \gamma.$$

The relative risk aversion is constant across consumption levels c, hence the label CRRA which is an acronym for Constant Relative Risk Aversion. Note that the absolute risk tolerance is linear in c:

$$\text{ART}(c) = \frac{1}{\text{ARA}(c)} = \frac{c}{\gamma}.$$

Since $u'(0+) \equiv \lim_{c \to 0} u'(c) = \infty$, marginal utility at zero is infinite. As a consequence, an optimal solution will have the property that consumption c will be strictly positive with probability one. We can then ignore the very appropriate non-negativity constraint on consumption since the constraint will never be binding. Furthermore, $u'(\infty) \equiv \lim_{c \to \infty} u'(c) = 0$ so that marginal utility goes to zero when consumption becomes infinitely large.

Some authors assume a utility function of the form $u(c) = c^{1-\gamma}$, but this only makes sense for $\gamma \in (0, 1)$ as $c^{1-\gamma}$ is decreasing for $\gamma > 1$. However, as will be discussed below, empirical studies indicate that most investors have a relative risk aversion above 1 which is also covered by the specification (5.9).

Except for a constant, the utility function

$$u(c) = \frac{c^{1-\gamma} - 1}{1 - \gamma}$$

is identical to the function specified in Eq. (5.9). The two utility functions are therefore equivalent in the sense that they generate the same ranking of consumption plans and, hence, the same optimal choices. The advantage in using the latter definition is that this function has a well-defined limit as $\gamma \to 1$. From l'Hôspital's rule we have that

$$\lim_{\gamma \to 1} \frac{c^{1-\gamma} - 1}{1 - \gamma} = \lim_{\gamma \to 1} \frac{-c^{1-\gamma} \ln c}{-1} = \ln c,$$

which is the important special case of *logarithmic utility*. When we consider CRRA utility, we will assume the simpler version of Eq. (5.9), but we will use the fact that we can obtain the optimal strategies of a log-utility investor as the limit of the optimal strategies of the general CRRA investor as $\gamma \to 1$.

Some CRRA utility functions are illustrated in Fig. 5.1. For relatively high values of the risk aversion parameter γ, the utility function is very steeply increasing just below 1 and almost flat just above 1. This can be seen from the curve corresponding to $\gamma = 5$ in the figure and is even more pronounced for higher values of γ.

5.6.1.2 HARA Utility

(Also known as extended power utility.) The absolute risk aversion for CRRA utility is hyperbolic in c. More generally a utility function is said to be a HARA (Hyperbolic Absolute Risk Aversion) utility function if

$$\text{ARA}(c) = -\frac{u''(c)}{u'(c)} = \frac{1}{\alpha c + \beta}$$

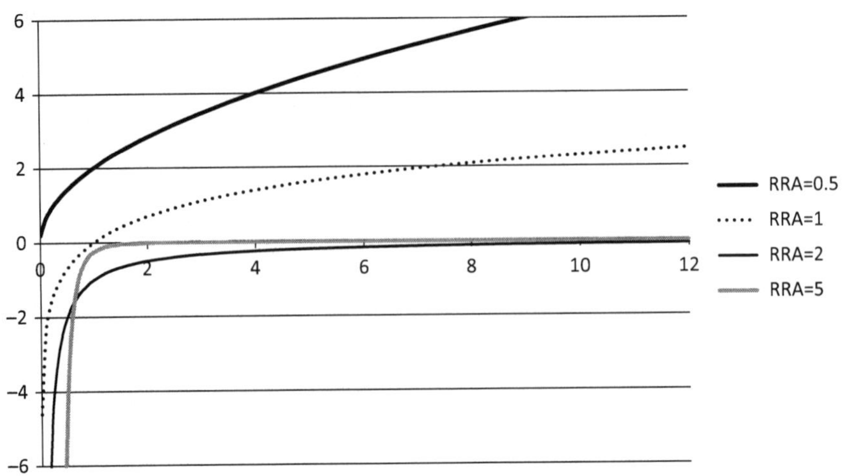

Fig. 5.1. Some CRRA utility functions.

for some constants α, β such that $\alpha c + \beta > 0$ for all relevant c. HARA utility functions are sometimes referred to as affine (or linear) risk tolerance utility functions since the absolute risk tolerance is

$$\mathrm{ART}(c) = \frac{1}{\mathrm{ARA}(c)} = \alpha c + \beta.$$

The risk cautiousness is $\mathrm{ART}'(c) = \alpha$.

What do the HARA utility functions look like? First, let us take the case $\alpha = 0$, which implies that the absolute risk aversion is constant (so-called CARA utility) and β must be positive. Since

$$\frac{d(\ln u'(c))}{dc} = \frac{u''(c)}{u'(c)} = -\frac{1}{\beta},$$

we must have

$$\ln u'(c) = -\frac{c}{\beta} + k_1 \quad \Rightarrow \quad u'(c) = e^{k_1} e^{-c/\beta}$$

for some constant k_1. Hence,

$$u(c) = -\beta e^{k_1} e^{-c/\beta} + k_2$$

for some other constant k_2. Applying the fact that increasing affine transformations do not change decisions, the basic representative of this class of utility functions is the *negative exponential utility* function

$$u(c) = -e^{-ac}, \quad c \in \mathbb{R},$$

where the parameter $a = 1/\beta$ is the absolute risk aversion. Constant absolute risk aversion is certainly not very reasonable. Nevertheless, the negative exponential utility function is sometimes used for computational purposes in connection with normally distributed returns, for example in one-period models.

Next, consider the case $\alpha \neq 0$. Applying the same procedure as above we find

$$\frac{d(\ln u'(c))}{dc} = \frac{u''(c)}{u'(c)} = -\frac{1}{\alpha c + \beta} \quad \Rightarrow \quad \ln u'(c) = -\frac{1}{\alpha} \ln(\alpha c + \beta) + k_1$$

so that

$$u'(c) = e^{k_1} \exp\left\{ -\frac{1}{\alpha} \ln(\alpha c + \beta) \right\} = e^{k_1} (\alpha c + \beta)^{-1/\alpha}. \tag{5.10}$$

For $\alpha = 1$, this implies that

$$u(c) = e^{k_1} \ln(c + \beta) + k_2.$$

The basic representative of such utility functions is the *extended log-utility* function

$$u(c) = \ln(c - \bar{c}), \quad c > \bar{c},$$

where we have replaced β by $-\bar{c}$. For $\alpha \neq 1$, Equation (5.10) implies that

$$u(c) = \frac{1}{\alpha} e^{k_1} \frac{1}{1 - \frac{1}{\alpha}} (\alpha c + \beta)^{1-1/\alpha} + k_2.$$

For $\alpha < 0$, we can write the basic representative as

$$u(c) = -(\bar{c} - c)^{1-\gamma}, \quad c < \bar{c},$$

where $\gamma = 1/\alpha < 0$. We can think of $\bar{c}$ as a satiation level, and we refer to utility functions of this type as *satiation HARA utility* functions. The absolute risk aversion is

$$\text{ARA}(c) = \frac{-\gamma}{\bar{c} - c},$$

which is increasing in c, conflicting with intuition and empirical studies. Some older financial models used the *quadratic utility* function which is the special case with $\gamma = -1$ so that $u(c) = -(\bar{c} - c)^2$. An equivalent utility function is $u(c) = c - ac^2$.

For $\alpha > 0$ (and $\alpha \neq 1$), the basic representative is

$$u(c) = \frac{(c - \bar{c})^{1-\gamma}}{1 - \gamma}, \quad c > \bar{c},$$

where $\gamma = 1/\alpha > 0$. The limit as $\gamma \to 1$ of the equivalent utility function $\frac{(c-\bar{c})^{1-\gamma}-1}{1-\gamma}$ is equal to the extended log-utility function $u(c) = \ln(c - \bar{c})$. We can think of $\bar{c}$ as a subsistence level of wealth or consumption (which makes sense only if $\bar{c} \geq 0$), and we refer to this subclass as *subsistence HARA utility* functions. The absolute and relative risk aversions are

$$\mathrm{ARA}(c) = \frac{\gamma}{c - \bar{c}}, \quad \mathrm{RRA}(c) = \frac{\gamma c}{c - \bar{c}} = \frac{\gamma}{1 - (\bar{c}/c)},$$

which are both decreasing in c. The relative risk aversion approaches ∞ for $c \to \bar{c}$ and decreases to the constant γ for $c \to \infty$. Clearly, for $\bar{c} = 0$, we are back to the CRRA utility functions so that these also belong to the HARA family.

5.6.1.3 Mean-Variance Preferences

For some problems it is convenient to assume that the expected utility associated with an uncertain consumption plan only depends on the expected value and the variance of the consumption plan. This is certainly true if the consumption plan is a normally distributed random variable since its probability distribution is fully characterized by the mean and variance. However, it is generally not appropriate to use a normal distribution for consumption (or wealth or asset returns).

For a quadratic utility function, $u(c) = c - ac^2$, the expected utility is

$$\mathrm{E}[u(c)] = \mathrm{E}\left[c - ac^2\right] = \mathrm{E}[c] - a\,\mathrm{E}\left[c^2\right] = \mathrm{E}[c] - a\left(\mathrm{Var}[c] + \mathrm{E}[c]^2\right),$$

which is indeed a function of the expected value and the variance of the consumption plan. Alas, the quadratic utility function is inappropriate for several reasons. Most importantly, it exhibits increasing absolute risk aversion.

For a general utility function the expected utility of a consumption plan will depend on all moments. This can be seen by the Taylor expansion of $u(c)$ around the expected consumption, $\mathrm{E}[c]$:

$$u(c) = u(\mathrm{E}[c]) + u'(\mathrm{E}[c])(c - \mathrm{E}[c]) + \frac{1}{2}u''(\mathrm{E}[c])(c - \mathrm{E}[c])^2 + \sum_{n=3}^{\infty} \frac{1}{n!} u^{(n)}(\mathrm{E}[c])(c - \mathrm{E}[c])^n,$$

where $u^{(n)}$ is the n'th order derivative of u. Taking expectations, we get

$$\mathrm{E}[u(c)] = u(\mathrm{E}[c]) + \frac{1}{2}u''(\mathrm{E}[c])\,\mathrm{Var}[c] + \sum_{n=3}^{\infty} \frac{1}{n!} u^{(n)}(\mathrm{E}[c])\,\mathrm{E}\left[(c - \mathrm{E}[c])^n\right].$$

Here $\mathrm{E}\left[(c - \mathrm{E}[c])^n\right]$ is the central moment of order n. The variance is the central moment of order 2. Obviously, a greedy investor (which just means that u is increasing) will prefer higher expected consumption to lower for fixed central moments of order 2 and higher. Moreover, a risk-averse investor (so that $u'' < 0$) will prefer lower variance of consumption to higher for fixed expected consumption and fixed central moments of order 3 and higher. But when the central moments of order 3 and higher are not the same for all alternatives, we cannot just evaluate them on the basis of their expectation and variance. With quadratic utility, the derivatives of u of order 3 and higher are zero so there it works. In general, mean-variance preferences can only serve as an approximation of the true utility function.

5.6.2 What Do We Know About Individuals' Risk Aversion?

From our discussion of risk aversion and various utility functions we expect that individuals are risk-averse and exhibit decreasing absolute risk aversion. But can this be supported by empirical evidence? Do individuals have constant relative risk aversion? And what is a reasonable level of risk aversion for individuals?

You can get an idea of the risk attitudes of individuals by observing how they choose between risky alternatives. Some researchers have studied this by setting up 'laboratory experiments' in which they present some risky alternatives to a group of individuals and simply see what they prefer. Some of these experiments suggest that expected utility theory is frequently violated, see for example Grether and Plott (1979). However, laboratory experiments are problematic for several reasons. You cannot be sure that individuals will make the same choice in what they know is an experiment as they would in real life. It is also hard to formulate alternatives that resemble the rather complex real-life decisions. It seems more fruitful to study actual data on how individuals have acted when confronted with real-life decision problems under uncertainty. A number of studies do just that.

Friend and Blume (1975) analyse data on household asset holdings. They conclude that the data are consistent with individuals having roughly constant relative risk aversion and that the coefficients of relative risk aversion are 'on average well in excess of one and probably in excess of two' (quote from page 900 in their paper). Pindyck (1988) finds support of a relative risk aversion between 3 and 4 in a structural model of the reaction of stock prices to fundamental variables.

Other studies are based on insurance data. Using US data on so-called property/liability insurance, Szpiro (1986) finds support of CRRA utility with a relative risk aversion coefficient between 1.2 and 1.8. Cicchetti and Dubin (1994) work with data from the US on whether individuals purchased an insurance against the risk of trouble with their home telephone line. They conclude that the data are consistent with expected utility theory and that a subsistence HARA utility function performs better than log utility or negative exponential utility.

Ogaki and Zhang (2001) study data on individual food consumption from Pakistan and India and conclude that relative risk aversion is decreasing for poor individuals, which is consistent with a subsistence HARA utility function.

When evaluating and comparing these findings, we have to recall the results of Section 5.5.3 which show that an estimate of the relative risk aversion will depend on the outcome variable (for example consumption or wealth). See also the discussion of various empirical estimates of risk aversion by Meyer and Meyer (2005).

It is an empirical fact that even though consumption and wealth have increased tremendously over the years, the magnitude of real rates of return has not changed dramatically. As indicated by Eq. (5.7) relative risk premia are approximately proportional to the relative risk aversion. As we shall see in later chapters, basic asset pricing theory implies that relative risk premia on financial assets (in terms of expected real return in excess of the real risk-free return) will be proportional to some sort of average relative risk aversion in the economy. If the average relative risk aversion was significantly decreasing (increasing) in the level of consumption or wealth, we should have seen decreasing (increasing) real returns on risky assets in the past. The data seem to be consistent with individuals having 'on average' close to CRRA utility.

To get a feeling of what a given risk aversion really means, suppose you are confronted with two consumption plans. One plan is a sure consumption of $\bar{c}$, the other plan gives you $(1-\alpha)\bar{c}$ with probability 0.5 and $(1+\alpha)\bar{c}$ with probability 0.5. If you have a CRRA utility function $u(c) = c^{1-\gamma}/(1-\gamma)$, the certainty equivalent c^* of the risky plan is determined by

$$\frac{1}{1-\gamma}\left(c^*\right)^{1-\gamma} = \frac{1}{2}\frac{1}{1-\gamma}\left((1-\alpha)\bar{c}\right)^{1-\gamma} + \frac{1}{2}\frac{1}{1-\gamma}\left((1+\alpha)\bar{c}\right)^{1-\gamma},$$

which implies that

$$c^* = \left(\frac{1}{2}\right)^{1/(1-\gamma)}\left[(1-\alpha)^{1-\gamma} + (1+\alpha)^{1-\gamma}\right]^{1/(1-\gamma)}\bar{c}.$$

The consumption risk premium $\lambda(\bar{c}, \alpha)$ is

$$\lambda(\bar{c}, \alpha) = \bar{c} - c^* = \left(1 - \left(\frac{1}{2}\right)^{1/(1-\gamma)}\left[(1-\alpha)^{1-\gamma} + (1+\alpha)^{1-\gamma}\right]^{1/(1-\gamma)}\right)\bar{c}.$$

Both the certainty equivalent and the consumption risk premium are thus proportional to the consumption level $\bar{c}$. The relative consumption risk premium $\lambda(\bar{c}, \alpha)/\bar{c}$ is simply one minus the relative certainty equivalent $c^*/\bar{c}$. These equations assume $\gamma \neq 1$. In Exercise 5.7 you are asked to find the certainty equivalent and the consumption risk premium for log-utility corresponding to $\gamma = 1$.

Table 5.5. Relative risk premia for a fair gamble of the fraction α of your consumption.

γ = RRA	$\alpha = 1\%$	$\alpha = 10\%$	$\alpha = 50\%$
0.5	0.00%	0.25%	6.70%
1	0.01%	0.50%	13.40%
2	0.01%	1.00%	25.00%
5	0.02%	2.43%	40.72%
10	0.05%	4.42%	46.00%
20	0.10%	6.76%	48.14%
50	0.24%	8.72%	49.29%
100	0.43%	9.37%	49.65%

Table 5.5 shows the relative risk premium for various values of the relative risk aversion coefficient γ and various values of α, the 'size' of the risk. For example, an individual with $\gamma = 5$ is willing to sacrifice 2.43% of the safe consumption in order to avoid a fair gamble of 10% of that consumption level. Of course, even extremely risk-averse individuals will not sacrifice more than they can lose but in some cases it is pretty close. Looking at these numbers, it is hard to believe in γ-values outside, say, the interval $[1, 10]$. In Exercise 5.8 you are asked to compare the exact relative risk premia shown in the table with the approximate risk premia given by Eq. (5.7).

5.6.3 Two-Good Utility Functions and the Elasticity of Substitution

Consider an atemporal utility function $f(c, q)$ of the consumption of two different goods at the same time. An indifference curve in the (c, q)-space is characterized by $f(c, q) = k$ for some constant k. Changes in c and q along an indifference curve are linked by

$$\frac{\partial f}{\partial c}\, dc + \frac{\partial f}{\partial q}\, dq = 0$$

so that the slope of the indifference curve (also known as the marginal rate of substitution) is

$$\frac{dq}{dc} = -\frac{\frac{\partial f}{\partial c}}{\frac{\partial f}{\partial q}}.$$

Unless the indifference curve is linear, its slope will change along the curve.

Indifference curves are generally assumed to be convex. The *elasticity of intratemporal substitution* tells you by which percentage you need to change q/c in order to obtain a 1% change in the slope of the indifference curve. It is a measure of the curvature or convexity of the indifference curve. If the indifference curve is very curved, you only have to move a little along the curve before its slope has changed by 1%. Hence, the elasticity of substitution is low. If the indifference curve is almost linear, you have to move far away to change the slope by 1%. In that case the elasticity of intratemporal substitution is very high. Formally, the elasticity of intratemporal substitution is defined as

$$\psi = -\frac{d\left(\frac{q}{c}\right)/\frac{q}{c}}{d\left(\frac{\frac{\partial f}{\partial q}}{\frac{\partial f}{\partial c}}\right)/\frac{\frac{\partial f}{\partial q}}{\frac{\partial f}{\partial c}}} = -\frac{\frac{\partial f}{\partial q}/\frac{\partial f}{\partial c}}{q/c}\frac{d\left(q/c\right)}{d\left(\frac{\partial f}{\partial q}/\frac{\partial f}{\partial c}\right)},$$

which is equivalent to

$$\psi = -\frac{d\ln\left(q/c\right)}{d\ln\left(\frac{\partial f}{\partial q}/\frac{\partial f}{\partial c}\right)}.$$

Assume now that

$$f(c,q) = \left(ac^{\alpha} + bq^{\alpha}\right)^{1/\alpha}, \tag{5.11}$$

where $\alpha < 1$ and $\alpha \neq 0$. Then

$$\frac{\partial f}{\partial c} = ac^{\alpha-1}\left(ac^{\alpha} + bq^{\alpha}\right)^{\frac{1}{\alpha}-1}, \qquad \frac{\partial f}{\partial q} = bq^{\alpha-1}\left(ac^{\alpha} + bq^{\alpha}\right)^{\frac{1}{\alpha}-1},$$

and thus

$$\frac{\frac{\partial f}{\partial q}}{\frac{\partial f}{\partial c}} = \frac{b}{a}\left(\frac{q}{c}\right)^{\alpha-1}.$$

Computing the derivative with respect to q/c, we get

$$\frac{d\left(\frac{\frac{\partial f}{\partial q}}{\frac{\partial f}{\partial c}}\right)}{d\left(\frac{q}{c}\right)} = \frac{b}{a}(\alpha-1)\left(\frac{q}{c}\right)^{\alpha-2}$$

and thus

$$\psi = -\frac{\frac{b}{a}\left(\frac{q}{c}\right)^{\alpha-1}}{\frac{q}{c}}\frac{1}{\frac{b}{a}(\alpha-1)\left(\frac{q}{c}\right)^{\alpha-2}} = -\frac{1}{\alpha-1} = \frac{1}{1-\alpha},$$

which is independent of (c, q). Therefore the utility function (5.11) is referred to as CES (Constant Elasticity of Substitution) utility. Since $\alpha = (\psi - 1)/\psi$, we can rewrite $f(c, q)$ directly in terms of the elasticity of intratemporal substitution as

$$f(c,q) = \left(ac^{\frac{\psi-1}{\psi}} + bq^{\frac{\psi-1}{\psi}}\right)^{\frac{\psi}{\psi-1}}. \tag{5.12}$$

Most applications embed $f(c,q)$ in a standard power one-good utility function so that the utility of consumption (c,q) is

$$u(c,q) = \frac{1}{1-\gamma} f(c,q)^{1-\gamma} = \frac{1}{1-\gamma}\left(ac^{\frac{\psi-1}{\psi}} + bq^{\frac{\psi-1}{\psi}}\right)^{\frac{\psi(1-\gamma)}{\psi-1}}.$$

For the Cobb–Douglas utility function

$$f(c,q) = c^a q^{1-a}, \quad 0 < a < 1, \tag{5.13}$$

the elasticity of substitution equals 1. In fact, the Cobb–Douglas utility function (5.13) can be seen as the limit of the utility function (5.11) assuming $b = 1-a$ as $\alpha \to 0$ (so that $\psi \to 1$). In order to see this, fix (c,q) and let $F(\alpha) = (ac^\alpha + (1-a)q^\alpha)^{1/\alpha}$. Then $\ln F(\alpha) = G(\alpha)/\alpha$, where $G(\alpha) = \ln(ac^\alpha + (1-a)q^\alpha)$. Note that $G(0) = 0$, so to figure out the limit of $\ln F(\alpha)$ as $\alpha \to 0$, we have to apply l'Hôspital's rule. Since

$$G'(\alpha) = \frac{ac^\alpha \ln c + (1-a)q^\alpha \ln q}{ac^\alpha + (1-a)q^\alpha},$$

we see that $G'(0) = a \ln c + (1-a)\ln q = \ln(c^a q^{1-a})$. Consequently, $\lim_{\alpha\to 0} \ln F(\alpha) = G'(0)/1 = \ln(c^a q^{1-a})$ and, therefore, $\lim_{\alpha \to 0} F(\alpha) = c^a q^{1-a}$ as claimed.

An interesting generalization of Eq. (5.11) is the so-called addilog function

$$f(c,q) = \left(ac^\alpha + b\frac{\alpha}{\beta}q^\beta\right)^{1/\alpha}.$$

The special case of $\beta = \alpha$ is exactly the CES function. With $\beta \neq \alpha$, the elasticity of intratemporal substitution is no longer constant. As we shall see in Example 6.2, the CES function has the property that the optimal expenditure share of each good will be independent of the total consumption expenditures (and wealth) of the individual. However, empirical studies indicate that this is not true. For example, the expenditure share of luxury goods is increasing in total consumption, whereas the expenditure share of food is decreasing in total consumption, see for example Wachter and Yogo (2010). The addilog function will allow the optimal expenditure shares of the goods to vary with the total consumption expenditures.

5.7 PREFERENCES FOR MULTIDATE CONSUMPTION PLANS

Above we implicitly considered preferences for consumption at one given future point in time. We need to generalize the ideas and results to settings with consumption at several dates. In one-period models individuals can consume both at time 0 (beginning-of-period) and at time 1 (end-of-period). In multi-period models individuals can consume either at each date in the discrete-time set $\mathcal{T} = \{0, 1, 2, \ldots, T\}$ or at each date in the continuous-time set $\mathcal{T} = [0, T]$. In both cases a consumption plan is a stochastic process $c = (c_t)_{t \in \mathcal{T}}$ where each c_t is a random variable representing the state-dependent level of consumption at time t.

Consider the discrete-time case and, for each t, let $Z_t \subseteq \mathbb{R}$ denote the set of all possible consumption levels at date t and define $Z = Z_0 \times Z_1 \times \cdots \times Z_T \subseteq \mathbb{R}^{T+1}$, then any consumption plan c can again be represented by a probability distribution π on the set Z. For finite Z, we can again apply Theorem 5.1 so that under the relevant axioms, we can represent preferences by a utility index $\mathcal{U}$, which to each consumption plan $(c_t)_{t \in \mathcal{T}} = (c_0, c_1, \ldots, c_T)$ assigns a real number $\mathcal{U}(c_0, c_1, \ldots, c_T)$ with higher numbers to the more preferred consumption plans. If we further impose the Substitution Axiom, Theorem 5.2 ensures an expected utility representation, that is the existence of a utility function $U : Z \to \mathbb{R}$ so that consumption plans are ranked according to their expected utility, that is

$$\mathcal{U}(c_0, c_1, \ldots, c_T) = \mathrm{E}\left[U(c_0, c_1, \ldots, c_T)\right] \equiv \sum_{\omega \in \Omega} p_\omega U\left(c_0, c_1(\omega), \ldots, c_T(\omega)\right).$$

We can call U a *multidate utility function* since it depends on the consumption levels at all dates. Again this result can be extended to the case of an infinite Z, for example $Z = \mathbb{R}_+^{T+1}$, but also to continuous-time settings where U will then be a function of the entire consumption process $c = (c_t)_{t \in [0,T]}$.

5.7.1 Additively Time-Separable Expected Utility

Often time-additivity is assumed so that the utility the individual gets from consumption in one period does not directly depend on what she consumed in earlier periods or what she plans to consume in later periods. For the discrete-time case, this means that

$$U(c_0, c_1, \ldots, c_T) = \sum_{t=0}^{T} u_t(c_t)$$

where each u_t is a valid 'single-date' utility function. Still, when the individual has to choose her current consumption rate, she will take her prospects for future consumption into account. The continuous-time analogue is

$$U((c_t)_{t \in [0,T]}) = \int_0^T u_t(c_t)\, dt.$$

In addition it is typically assumed that $u_t(c_t) = e^{-\delta t}u(c_t)$ for all t. This is to say that the direct utility the individual gets from a given consumption level is basically the same for all dates, but the individual prefers to consume any given number of goods sooner than later. This is modelled by the subjective time preference rate δ, which we assume to be constant over time and independent of the consumption level. More impatient individuals have higher δ's. In sum, the life-time utility is typically assumed to be given by

$$U(c_0, c_1, \ldots, c_T) = \sum_{t=0}^{T} e^{-\delta t} u(c_t)$$

in discrete-time models and

$$U((c_t)_{t\in[0,T]}) = \int_0^T e^{-\delta t} u(c_t)\, dt$$

in continuous-time models. In both cases, u is a 'single-date' utility function such as those discussed in Section 5.6.[1]

Time-additivity of preferences is mainly assumed for tractability. The time-additive specification does not follow from the basic axioms of choice under uncertainty, but is in fact a strong assumption which most economists agree is not very realistic. One problem is that time-additive preferences induce a close link between the willingness to substitute consumption across different states of the economy (which is measured by risk aversion) and the willingness to substitute consumption over time (which can be measured by the so-called elasticity of intertemporal substitution). The link is derived for specific preferences later in this chapter. Solving intertemporal utility maximization problems of individuals with time-additive CRRA utility, it turns out that an individual with a high relative risk aversion will also choose a very smooth consumption process, that is she will have a low elasticity of intertemporal substitution. There is nothing in the basic theory of choice that links the risk aversion and the elasticity of intertemporal substitution together. For one thing, risk aversion makes sense even in an atemporal (that is one-date) setting where intertemporal substitution is meaningless and, conversely, intertemporal substitution makes sense in a multiperiod setting without uncertainty in which risk aversion is meaningless. The close link between the two concepts in the multiperiod model with uncertainty is an unfortunate consequence of the assumption of time-additive expected utility.

[1] Some utility functions are negative, including the frequently used power utility $u(c) = c^{1-\gamma}/(1-\gamma)$ with a constant relative risk aversion $\gamma > 1$. When $\delta > 0$, we will then have that $e^{-\delta t}u(c)$ is in fact bigger (less negative) than $u(c)$, which may seem to destroy the interpretation of δ stated in the text. However, for the decisions made by the investor it is the marginal utilities that matter and, when $\delta > 0$ and u is increasing, $e^{-\delta t}u'(c)$ will be smaller than $u'(c)$ so that, other things being equal, the individual will choose higher current than future consumption. Therefore, it is fair to interpret δ as a time preference rate and expect it to be positive.

According to Browning (1991), non-additive preferences were already discussed in the 1890 book *Principles of Economics* by Alfred Marshall. See Browning's paper for further references to the critique on intertemporally separable preferences. Let us consider some alternatives that are more general and still tractable.

5.7.2 Habit Formation and State-Dependent Utility

The key idea of habit formation is to let the utility associated with the choice of consumption at a given date depend on past choices of consumption. In a discrete-time setting the utility index of a given consumption process c is now given as $\mathrm{E}[\sum_{t=0}^{T} e^{-\delta t} u(c_t, h_t)]$, where h_t is a measure of the standard of living or the habit level of consumption. For example, h_t can be a weighted average of past consumption rates such as

$$h_t = h_0 e^{-\beta t} + \alpha \sum_{s=1}^{t-1} e^{-\beta(t-s)} c_s,$$

where h_0, α, and β are non-negative constants. It is assumed that u is decreasing in h so that high past consumption generates a desire for high current consumption, that is preferences display intertemporal complementarity. For reasons of mathematical tractability, $u(c, h)$ is often assumed to be of the power-linear form

$$u(c, h) = \frac{1}{1-\gamma}(c-h)^{1-\gamma}, \quad \gamma > 0,\ c \geq h.$$

This is closely related to the subsistence HARA utility, but with habit formation the 'subsistence level' h is endogenously determined by past consumption. The corresponding absolute and relative risk aversions are

$$\mathrm{ARA}(c, h) \equiv -\frac{u_{cc}(c, h)}{u_c(c, h)} = \frac{\gamma}{c-h}, \quad \mathrm{RRA}(c, h) \equiv -c\frac{u_{cc}(c, h)}{u_c(c, h)} = \frac{\gamma c}{c-h}, \tag{5.14}$$

where u_c and u_{cc} are the first- and second-order derivatives of u with respect to c. In particular, the relative risk aversion is decreasing in c. Note that the habit formation preferences are still consistent with expected utility.

A related extension of the basic preferences is to allow for some external factors influencing the preferences of the individual, that is factors that are not fully determined by choices made by the individual. One example that has received some attention is where the utility that an individual associates with a given consumption plan also depends on the consumption plans of other individuals or maybe the aggregate consumption in the economy. This is often referred to as 'keeping up with the Joneses' preferences. If you see your neighbours consume at high rates, you want to consume at a high rate too. Utility is now state-dependent. Models of this type are sometimes said to have an *external* habit, whereas the genuine habit formation discussed above is then referred to as *internal* habit. If we denote the external factor by X_t, a time-additive life-time expected utility representation is $\mathrm{E}[\sum_{t=0}^{T} e^{-\delta t} u(c_t, X_t)]$, and a tractable version is $u(c, X) = \frac{1}{1-\gamma}(c - X)^{1-\gamma}$ very similar to the subsistence HARA or the specific habit formation utility given above. In this case, however, the 'subsistence' level is determined by external factors. Another tractable specification is $u(c, X) = \frac{1}{1-\gamma}(c/X)^{1-\gamma}$.

The empirical evidence of habit formation preferences is mixed. The time variation in risk aversion induced by habits as shown in (5.14) will generate variations in the Sharpe ratios of risky assets over the business cycle, which are not explained in simple models with CRRA preferences and appear to be present in the asset return data. Campbell and Cochrane (1999) construct a model with a representative individual having power-linear external habit preferences in which the equilibrium Sharpe ratio of the stock market varies counter-cyclically in line with empirical observations. However, a counter-cyclical variation in the relative risk aversion of a representative individual can also be obtained in a model in which each individual has a constant relative risk aversion, but the relative risk aversions are different across individuals, as explained for example by Chan and Kogan (2002). See Chapter 9 for more on asset pricing in the models of Campbell and Cochrane (1999) and Chan and Kogan (2002). Various studies have investigated whether a data set of individual decisions on consumption, purchases, or investments is consistent with habit formation in preferences. To mention a few studies, Ravina (2007) reports strong support for habit formation, whereas Dynan (2000), Gomes and Michaelides (2003), and Brunnermeier and Nagel (2008) find no evidence of habit formation at the individual level.

5.7.3 Recursive Utility in Discrete Time

Another preference specification gaining popularity is the so-called *recursive preferences* or Epstein–Zin preferences suggested and discussed by Koopmans (1960), Kreps and Porteus (1978), Epstein and Zin (1989, 1991), and Weil (1989), among others. The original motivation of this representation of preferences was to allow individuals to have preferences for the timing of resolution of uncertainty, which is inconsistent with the standard multidate time-additive expected utility theory. In this section we consider recursive preferences in a discrete-time setting. The subsequent section covers the continuous-time setting.

With recursive preferences the utility index $\mathcal{U}_t$ associated with a given consumption and investment strategy is defined recursively by

$$\mathcal{U}_t = f\left(c_t, q_t(\mathcal{U}_{t+1})\right), \quad q_t(\mathcal{U}_{t+1}) = \tilde{u}^{-1}\left(\mathrm{E}_t\left[\tilde{u}\left(\mathcal{U}_{t+1}\right)\right]\right) \tag{5.15}$$

for some increasing and concave functions f and $\tilde{u}$. Here, the so-called aggregator f captures how the current consumption and some 'present value' of future utility are combined into a current level of utility. Since

$$\tilde{u}\left(q_t(\mathcal{U}_{t+1})\right) = \mathrm{E}_t\left[\tilde{u}\left(\mathcal{U}_{t+1}\right)\right],$$

a comparison with Eq. (5.4) shows that we can interpret $q_t(\mathcal{U}_{t+1})$ as the time t certainty equivalent of the utility index $\mathcal{U}_{t+1}$ at time $t+1$, computed using $\tilde{u}$ as a utility function. At the terminal date T, assume that

$$\mathcal{U}_T = u(c_T),$$

where u could be a standard 'single-date' utility function.

Time-additive expected utility is the special case in which

$$f(c,q) = u(c) + e^{-\delta} q, \quad \tilde{u}(x) = x \tag{5.16}$$

so that $q_t(\mathcal{U}_{t+1}) = \mathrm{E}_t[\mathcal{U}_{t+1}]$ and

$$\mathcal{U}_t = u(c_t) + e^{-\delta}\, \mathrm{E}_t[\mathcal{U}_{t+1}].$$

Then, by unwinding the recursion, we get

$$\begin{aligned}
\mathcal{U}_t &= u(c_t) + e^{-\delta}\, \mathrm{E}_t\left[u(c_{t+1}) + e^{-\delta}\, \mathrm{E}_{t+1}[\mathcal{U}_{t+2}]\right] \\
&= u(c_t) + e^{-\delta} u(c_{t+1}) + e^{-2\delta}\, \mathrm{E}_t[\mathcal{U}_{t+2}] \\
&= \dots \\
&= \mathrm{E}_t\left[\sum_{s=t}^{T} e^{-\delta(s-t)} u(c_s)\right],
\end{aligned}$$

which shows the equivalence to time-additive expected utility.

Epstein and Zin (1989, 1991) assumed that f is identical to the two-good CES utility specification (5.11),

$$f(c,q) = \left(ac^{\alpha} + bq^{\alpha}\right)^{1/\alpha}.$$

Since q now refers to future consumption or utility, $\psi = 1/(1-\alpha)$ is called the *elasticity of intertemporal substitution*. Furthermore, assume that $q_t(\mathcal{U}_{t+1})$ is defined from the certainty equivalent of a power utility function, $\tilde{u}(x) = x^{1-\gamma}/(1-\gamma)$, where $\gamma > 0$ and $\gamma \neq 1$. This implies that

$$q_t(\mathcal{U}_{t+1}) = \left(\mathrm{E}_t[\mathcal{U}_{t+1}^{1-\gamma}]\right)^{\frac{1}{1-\gamma}}. \tag{5.17}$$

To sum up, *Epstein–Zin preferences* are defined recursively as

$$\mathcal{U}_t = \left(ac_t^{\alpha} + b \left(\mathrm{E}_t[\mathcal{U}_{t+1}^{1-\gamma}] \right)^{\frac{\alpha}{1-\gamma}} \right)^{1/\alpha}. \tag{5.18}$$

Introduce the new auxiliary constant $\theta = (1-\gamma)/(1-\frac{1}{\psi}) = (1-\gamma)/\alpha$. Then we can rewrite f as

$$f(c,q) = \left(ac^{\frac{1-\gamma}{\theta}} + bq^{\frac{1-\gamma}{\theta}} \right)^{\frac{\theta}{1-\gamma}}, \tag{5.19}$$

and the recursive definition of the utility index can be restated as

$$\mathcal{U}_t = \left(ac_t^{\frac{1-\gamma}{\theta}} + b \left(\mathrm{E}_t[\mathcal{U}_{t+1}^{1-\gamma}] \right)^{\frac{1}{\theta}} \right)^{\frac{\theta}{1-\gamma}}. \tag{5.20}$$

When the time horizon is finite, we need to specify the utility index $\mathcal{U}_T$ at the terminal date. If we allow for consumption at the terminal date and for a bequest motive, a specification like

$$\mathcal{U}_T = \left(ac_T^{\alpha} + \varepsilon a W_T^{\alpha} \right)^{1/\alpha} \tag{5.21}$$

assumes a CES-type weighting of consumption and bequest in the terminal utility with the same CES-parameter α as above. The parameter $\varepsilon \geq 0$ can be seen as a measure of the relative importance of bequest compared to consumption. Note that Eq. (5.21) involves no expectation as terminal wealth is known at time T. Alternatively, we can think of c_{T-1} as being the consumption over the final period and specify the terminal utility index as

$$\mathcal{U}_T = \left(\varepsilon a W_T^{\alpha} \right)^{1/\alpha} = (\varepsilon a)^{1/\alpha} W_T. \tag{5.22}$$

Bansal (2007) and other authors assume that $a = 1 - b$, but the value of a is in fact unimportant as it does not affect optimal decisions and therefore no interpretation can be given to a. At least this is true for an infinite time horizon and for a finite horizon when the terminal utility takes the form of Eqs. (5.21) or (5.22). In order to see this, first note that we can rewrite Eq. (5.18) as

$$\begin{aligned}\mathcal{U}_t &= a^{1/\alpha} \left(c_t^{\alpha} + ba^{-1} \left(\mathrm{E}_t \left[\mathcal{U}_{t+1}^{1-\gamma} \right] \right)^{\frac{\alpha}{1-\gamma}} \right)^{1/\alpha} \\ &= a^{1/\alpha} \left(c_t^{\alpha} + b \left(\mathrm{E}_t \left[\left\{ a^{-1/\alpha} \mathcal{U}_{t+1} \right\}^{1-\gamma} \right] \right)^{\frac{\alpha}{1-\gamma}} \right)^{1/\alpha},\end{aligned}$$

which implies that

$$a^{-1/\alpha} \mathcal{U}_t = \left(c_t^{\alpha} + b \left(\mathrm{E}_t \left[\left\{ a^{-1/\alpha} \mathcal{U}_{t+1} \right\}^{1-\gamma} \right] \right)^{\frac{\alpha}{1-\gamma}} \right)^{1/\alpha}.$$

Now define $\tilde{\mathcal{U}}_t = a^{-1/\alpha}\mathcal{U}_t$. Since $\tilde{\mathcal{U}}$ is just a scaling of $\mathcal{U}$, it is a utility index representing the same preferences as $\mathcal{U}$. Moreover, the above equation implies that

$$\tilde{\mathcal{U}}_t = \left(c_t^\alpha + b\left(\mathrm{E}_t\left[\tilde{\mathcal{U}}_{t+1}^{1-\gamma}\right]\right)^{\frac{\alpha}{1-\gamma}}\right)^{1/\alpha},$$

so the recursive relation for $\tilde{\mathcal{U}}$ does not involve a at all. With a finite time horizon and terminal utility given by Eq. (5.21), we see that

$$\tilde{\mathcal{U}}_T = a^{-1/\alpha}\mathcal{U}_T = \left(c_T^\alpha + \varepsilon W_T^\alpha\right)^{1/\alpha},$$

which also does not involve a. And similarly when terminal utility is specified as in Eq. (5.22). Without loss of generality we can therefore let $a = 1$.

Epstein–Zin utility is not of the form (5.16) for which we have shown that recursive utility specializes to time-additive expected utility. Nevertheless, time-additive power utility is the special case of Epstein–Zin utility in which $\gamma = 1/\psi$. In order to see this, first note that with $\gamma = 1/\psi$, we have $\alpha = 1-\gamma$ and $\theta = 1$ and thus

$$\mathcal{U}_t = \left(ac_t^{1-\gamma} + b\,\mathrm{E}_t[\mathcal{U}_{t+1}^{1-\gamma}]\right)^{\frac{1}{1-\gamma}}$$

or

$$\mathcal{U}_t^{1-\gamma} = ac_t^{1-\gamma} + b\,\mathrm{E}_t[\mathcal{U}_{t+1}^{1-\gamma}].$$

If we start unwinding the recursions, we get

$$\begin{aligned}\mathcal{U}_t^{1-\gamma} &= ac_t^{1-\gamma} + b\,\mathrm{E}_t\left[ac_{t+1}^{1-\gamma} + b\,\mathrm{E}_{t+1}[\mathcal{U}_{t+2}^{1-\gamma}]\right] \\ &= a\,\mathrm{E}_t\left[c_t^{1-\gamma} + bc_{t+1}^{1-\gamma}\right] + b^2\,\mathrm{E}_t\left[\mathcal{U}_{t+2}^{1-\gamma}\right].\end{aligned}$$

If we continue this way and the time horizon is infinite, we obtain

$$\mathcal{U}_t^{1-\gamma} = a\sum_{s=0}^{\infty}\mathrm{E}_t\left[b^s c_{t+s}^{1-\gamma}\right],$$

whereas with a finite time horizon and the terminal utility index (5.22), we obtain

$$\mathcal{U}_t^{1-\gamma} = a\left(\sum_{s=0}^{T-t} b^s\,\mathrm{E}_t\left[c_{t+s}^{1-\gamma}\right] + \varepsilon b^{T-t}\,\mathrm{E}_t\left[W_T^{1-\gamma}\right]\right).$$

In any case, observe that

$$\mathcal{V}_t = \frac{1}{a(1-\gamma)}\mathcal{U}_t^{1-\gamma}$$

is an increasing function of $\mathcal{U}_t$ and will therefore represent the same preferences as $\mathcal{U}_t$. Moreover, $\mathcal{V}_t$ is clearly equivalent to time-additive expected power utility.[2] Note that b plays the role of the subjective discount factor which we often represent by $e^{-\delta}$.

The Epstein–Zin preferences are characterized by three parameters:[3] the relative risk aversion γ, the elasticity of intertemporal substitution ψ, and the subjective discount factor $b = e^{-\delta}$. Relative to the standard time-additive power utility, the Epstein–Zin specification allows the relative risk aversion (attitudes towards atemporal risks) to be disentangled from the elasticity of intertemporal substitution (attitudes towards shifts in consumption over time). Moreover, Epstein and Zin (1989) show that when $\gamma > 1/\psi$, the individual will prefer early resolution of uncertainty. If $\gamma < 1/\psi$, late resolution of uncertainty is preferred. For the standard utility case $\gamma = 1/\psi$, the individual is indifferent about the timing of the resolution of uncertainty. Note that in the relevant case of $\gamma > 1$, the auxiliary parameter θ will be negative if and only if $\psi > 1$. Empirical studies disagree about reasonable values of ψ. Some studies find ψ smaller than one (for example Campbell 1999), other studies find ψ greater than one (for example Vissing-Jørgensen and Attanasio 2003).

5.7.4 Recursive Utility in Continuous Time: Stochastic Differential Utility

The continuous-time equivalent of recursive utility is called *stochastic differential utility* and has been studied by Duffie and Epstein (1992b) among others. The utility index $\mathcal{U}_t$ associated at time t with a given consumption process c over the remaining life-time $[t, T]$ is recursively given by

$$\mathcal{U}_t = \mathrm{E}_t\left[\int_t^T f(c_s, \mathcal{U}_s)\, ds\right]$$

where we assume a zero utility of terminal wealth, $\mathcal{U}_T = 0$. Here f is a so-called normalized aggregator.

Time-additive expected utility with utility function u and time preference rate δ is the special case where

$$f(c, \mathcal{U}) = \delta\,(u(c) - \mathcal{U}) \tag{5.23}$$

[2] Note that $\mathcal{V}_t = u(c_t) + b\,\mathrm{E}_t[\mathcal{V}_{t+1}]$ so that $\mathcal{V}_t$ *is* of the form (5.16), which confirms the equivalence of Epstein–Zin utility with $\gamma = 1/\psi$ to time-additive utility.

[3] With a finite time horizon and a bequest motive, there is really a fourth parameter, namely the relative weight of bequest and consumption, as represented by the constant ε in Eqs. (5.21) or (5.22).

so that

$$\mathcal{U}_t = \delta\,\mathrm{E}_t\left[\int_t^T u(c_s)\,ds\right] - \delta\,\mathrm{E}_t\left[\int_t^T \mathcal{U}_s\,ds\right]. \tag{5.24}$$

This recursive relation is solved by

$$\mathcal{U}_t = \delta\,\mathrm{E}_t\left[\int_t^T e^{-\delta(v-t)} u(c_v)\,dv\right], \tag{5.25}$$

because then

$$\begin{aligned}
\mathrm{E}_t\left[\int_t^T \mathcal{U}_s\,ds\right] &= \delta\,\mathrm{E}_t\left[\int_t^T \left(\int_s^T e^{-\delta(v-s)} u(c_v)\,dv\right) ds\right] \\
&= \delta\,\mathrm{E}_t\left[\int_t^T \left(\int_t^v e^{-\delta(v-s)}\,ds\right) u(c_v)\,dv\right] \\
&= \mathrm{E}_t\left[\int_t^T \left(1 - e^{-\delta(v-t)}\right) u(c_v)\,dv\right] \\
&= \mathrm{E}_t\left[\int_t^T u(c_v)\,dv\right] - \mathrm{E}_t\left[\int_t^T e^{-\delta(v-t)} u(c_v)\,dv\right]
\end{aligned}$$

from which (5.24) easily follows. The second equality in the preceding computation is due to a change of the order of integration. Obviously Eq. (5.25) is equivalent to time-additive expected utility.

A somewhat tractable version of f is[4]

$$f(c,\mathcal{U}) = \begin{cases} \frac{\delta}{1-1/\psi} c^{1-1/\psi}([1-\gamma]\mathcal{U})^{1-1/\theta} - \delta\theta\mathcal{U}, & \text{for } \gamma \neq 1, \psi \neq 1 \\ (1-\gamma)\delta\mathcal{U}\ln c - \delta\mathcal{U}\ln\left([1-\gamma]\mathcal{U}\right), & \text{for } \gamma \neq 1, \psi = 1 \\ \frac{\delta}{1-1/\psi} c^{1-1/\psi} e^{-(1-1/\psi)\mathcal{U}} - \frac{\delta}{1-1/\psi}, & \text{for } \gamma = 1, \psi \neq 1 \\ \delta \ln c - \delta\mathcal{U}, & \text{for } \gamma = \psi = 1 \end{cases} \tag{5.26}$$

where $\theta = (1-\gamma)/(1-\frac{1}{\psi})$. This can be seen as the continuous-time version of the discrete-time Epstein–Zin preferences in (5.20).[5] Again, δ is a subjective time preference rate, γ reflects the degree of risk aversion towards atemporal bets, and $\psi > 0$ reflects the intertemporal elasticity of substitution towards deterministic consumption plans. As in the discrete-time framework, the special case where $\psi = 1/\gamma$ (so that $\theta = 1$) corresponds to the classic time-additive power utility specification.

[4] It is also possible to define a normalized aggregator for $0 < \gamma < 1$ but such values are not supported empirically.

[5] The mathematical convergence of discrete-time recursive utility to continuous-time stochastic differential utility is non-trivial, but Kraft and Seifried (2011) are able to establish a convergence result.

Note that, in general, recursive preferences are not consistent with expected utility since $\mathcal{U}_t$ depends non-linearly on the probabilities of future consumption levels.

5.8 CONCLUDING REMARKS

This chapter has explained how the preferences for consumption of a rational individual can be represented in mathematically tractable ways. For decades, the most frequently used specification of preferences has been time-additive expected utility with constant relative risk aversion. However, recently a number of more advanced alternatives have been shown to lead to interesting conclusions about the optimal consumption and investment decisions of individuals and also the equilibrium prices of financial assets. The primary alternatives used involve habit formation, a 'keeping up with the Joneses' feature, and recursive utility. The following chapters will explore the decision-making of individuals and the equilibrium asset prices under the different preference specifications.

5.9 EXERCISES

Exercise 5.1 Give a proof of Theorem 5.3.

Exercise 5.2 (Adapted from Problem 3.3 in Kreps (1990).) Consider the following two probability distributions of consumption. π_1 gives 5, 15, and 30 (dollars) with probabilities 1/3, 5/9, and 1/9, respectively. π_2 gives 10 and 20 with probabilities 2/3 and 1/3, respectively.

(a) Show that we can think of π_1 as a two-step gamble, where the first gamble is identical to π_2. If the outcome of the first gamble is 10, then the second gamble gives you an additional 5 (total 15) with probability 1/2 and an additional -5 (total 5) also with probability 1/2. If the outcome of the first gamble is 20, then the second gamble gives you an additional 10 (total 30) with probability 1/3 and an additional -5 (total 15) with probability 2/3.

(b) Observe that the second gamble has mean zero and that π_1 is equal to π_2 plus mean-zero noise. Conclude that any risk-averse expected utility maximizer will prefer π_2 to π_1.

Exercise 5.3 (Adapted from Chapter 3 in Kreps (1990).) Imagine a greedy, risk-averse, expected utility maximizing consumer whose end-of-period income level is subject to some uncertainty. The income will be Y with probability $\bar{p}$ and $Y' < Y$ with probability $1 - \bar{p}$. Think of $\Delta = Y - Y'$ as some loss the consumer might incur due to an accident. An insurance company is willing to insure against this loss by paying Δ to the consumer if she sustains the loss. In return, the company wants an upfront premium of δ. The consumer may choose partial coverage in the sense that if she pays a premium of $a\delta$, she will receive

$a\Delta$ if she sustains the loss. Let u denote the von Neumann–Morgenstern utility function of the consumer. Assume for simplicity that the premium is paid at the end of the period.

(a) Show that the first-order condition for the choice of a is

$$\bar{p}\delta u'(Y - a\delta) = (1 - \bar{p})(\Delta - \delta)u'(Y - (1 - a)\Delta - a\delta).$$

(b) Show that if the insurance is actuarially fair in the sense that the expected payout $(1 - \bar{p})\Delta$ equals the premium δ, then the consumer will purchase full insurance, that is $a = 1$ is optimal.

(c) Show that if the insurance is actuarially unfair, meaning $(1 - \bar{p})\Delta < \delta$, then the consumer will purchase partial insurance, that is the optimal a is less than 1.

Exercise 5.4 Consider a one-period choice problem with four equally likely states of the world at the end of the period. The consumer maximizes expected utility of end-of-period wealth. The current wealth must be invested in a single financial asset today. The consumer has three assets to choose between. All three assets have a current price equal to the current wealth of the consumer. The assets have the following end-of-period values:

	State			
	1	2	3	4
Probability	0.25	0.25	0.25	0.25
asset 1	100	100	100	100
asset 2	81	100	100	144
asset 3	36	100	100	225

(a) What asset would a risk-neutral individual choose?

(b) What asset would a power utility investor, $u(W) = \frac{1}{1-\gamma}W^{1-\gamma}$ choose if $\gamma = 0.5$? If $\gamma = 2$? If $\gamma = 5$?

Now assume a power utility with $\gamma = 0.5$.

(c) Suppose the individual could obtain a perfect signal about the future state before she makes her asset choice. There are thus four possible signals, which we can represent by $s_1 = \{1\}$, $s_2 = \{2\}$, $s_3 = \{3\}$, and $s_4 = \{4\}$. What is the optimal asset choice for each signal? What is her expected utility before she receives the signal, assuming that the signals have equal probability?

(d) Now suppose that the individual can receive a less-than-perfect signal telling her whether the state is in $s_1 = \{1, 4\}$ or in $s_2 = \{2, 3\}$. The two possible signals are equally likely. What is the expected utility of the investor before she receives the signal?

Exercise 5.5 Consider an atemporal setting in which an individual has a utility function u of consumption. His current consumption is c. As always, the absolute risk aversion is $\text{ARA}(c) = -u''(c)/u'(c)$ and the relative risk aversion is $\text{RRA}(c) = -cu''(c)/u'(c)$.

Let $\varepsilon \in [0, c]$ and consider an additive gamble where the individual will end up with a consumption of either $c + \varepsilon$ or $c - \varepsilon$. Define the *additive indifference probability* $\pi(c, \varepsilon)$ for this gamble by

$$u(c) = \left(\frac{1}{2} + \pi(c,\varepsilon)\right) u(c+\varepsilon) + \left(\frac{1}{2} - \pi(c,\varepsilon)\right) u(c-\varepsilon). \qquad (*)$$

Assume that $\pi(c,\varepsilon)$ is twice differentiable in ε.

(a) Argue that $\pi(c,\varepsilon) \geq 0$ if the individual is risk-averse.

(b) Show that the absolute risk aversion is related to the additive indifference probability by the following relation

$$\text{ARA}(c) = 4 \lim_{\varepsilon \to 0} \frac{\partial \pi(c,\varepsilon)}{\partial \varepsilon}$$

and interpret this result. *Hint: differentiate twice with respect to* ε *in (*) and let* $\varepsilon \to 0$.

Now consider a multiplicative gamble where the individual will end up with a consumption of either $(1+\varepsilon)c$ or $(1-\varepsilon)c$, where $\varepsilon \in [0,1]$. Define the *multiplicative indifference probability* $\Pi(c,\varepsilon)$ for this gamble by

$$u(c) = \left(\frac{1}{2} + \Pi(c,\varepsilon)\right) u\left((1+\varepsilon)c\right) + \left(\frac{1}{2} - \Pi(c,\varepsilon)\right) u\left((1-\varepsilon)c\right).$$

Assume that $\Pi(c,\varepsilon)$ is twice differentiable in ε.

(c) Derive a relation between the relative risk aversion RRA(c) and $\lim_{\varepsilon \to 0} \frac{\partial \Pi(c,\varepsilon)}{\partial \varepsilon}$ and interpret the result.

Exercise 5.6 Provide a proof of Theorem 5.5.

Exercise 5.7 Consider an individual with log-utility, $u(c) = \ln c$. What is her certainty equivalent and consumption risk premium for the consumption plan which with probability 0.5 gives her $(1-\alpha)\bar{c}$ and with probability 0.5 gives her $(1+\alpha)\bar{c}$? Confirm that your results are consistent with the numbers for $\gamma = 1$ shown in Table 5.5.

Exercise 5.8 Use Eq. (5.7) to compute approximate relative risk premia for the consumption gamble underlying Table 5.5 and compare with the exact numbers given in the table.

6

Individual Optimality

6.1 INTRODUCTION

The general pricing mechanism of a financial market can be represented by a state-price deflator as explained in Chapter 4. Given a state-price deflator we can price all state-contingent dividends. Conversely, given the market prices of state-contingent dividends we can extract one or several state-price deflators. Market prices and hence the state-price deflator(s) are determined by the supply and demand of the individuals in the economy. Therefore, we have to study the portfolio decisions of individuals, which again cannot be disentangled from the consumption decisions. In this chapter we will therefore study the optimal consumption and investment decisions of utility-maximizing individuals.

The chapter is organized as follows: Section 6.2 studies the maximization problem of an individual under various preference specifications in the one-period setting. The mean-variance approach to optimal portfolios in a one-period economy is reviewed in Section 6.3. Sections 6.4 and 6.5 extend the utility maximization analysis to the discrete-time and the continuous-time framework, respectively. Sections 6.6 and 6.7 introduce the dynamic programming approach to the solution of multiperiod utility maximization problems. We consider both time-additive expected utility (with one or two consumption goods), habit formation, state-dependent preferences, and recursive utility.

A key result of the chapter is that the (marginal utility of) optimal consumption of any individual induces a valid state-price deflator, which gives us a link between individual optimality and asset prices. This is the cornerstone of the consumption-based asset pricing models studied in Chapters 8 and 9. Another important result is the so-called envelope condition that links marginal utility of consumption to marginal utility of optimal investments. In this way the state-price deflator is related to the optimally invested wealth of the individual plus some state variables capturing other information affecting the decisions of the individual. This will be useful for the theoretical underpinning of the factor pricing models studied in Chapter 10.

6.2 THE ONE-PERIOD FRAMEWORK

In the one-period framework the individual consumes at time 0 (the beginning of the period) and at time 1 (the end of the period). We denote time 0 consumption by c_0 and the state-dependent time 1 consumption by the random variable c. The individual has some initial wealth $e_0 \geq 0$ at time 0 and may receive a non-negative state-dependent endowment (income) at time 1 represented by the random variable e. The individual picks a portfolio $\boldsymbol{\theta}$ at time 0 with a time 0 price of $P^{\boldsymbol{\theta}} = \boldsymbol{\theta}^{\top}\boldsymbol{P} = \sum_{i=1}^{I} \theta_i P_i$, assuming the Law of One Price. The portfolio delivers a random dividend of $D^{\boldsymbol{\theta}} = \boldsymbol{\theta}^{\top}\boldsymbol{D} = \sum_{i=1}^{I} \theta_i D_i$ at time 1. The budget constraints are therefore

$$c_\omega \leq e_\omega + D^{\boldsymbol{\theta}}_\omega = e_\omega + \sum_{i=1}^{I} D_{i\omega}\theta_i, \qquad \text{for all } \omega \in \Omega, \tag{6.1}$$

$$c_0 \leq e_0 - P^{\boldsymbol{\theta}} = e_0 - \sum_{i=1}^{I} \theta_i P_i. \tag{6.2}$$

The individual can choose the consumption plan (c_0, c) and the portfolio $\boldsymbol{\theta}$. Since we will always assume that individuals prefer more consumption to less, it is clear that the budget constraints will hold as equalities. Therefore we can think of the individual choosing only the portfolio and then the consumption plan follows from the budget constraints above.

Consumption has to be non-negative both at time 0 and in all states at time 1 so we should add such constraints when looking for the optimal strategy. However, we assume throughout that the individual has infinite marginal utility at zero (or some positive level of) consumption which, in particular, is satisfied for the CRRA and subsistence HARA utility functions described in Section 5.6. Under this assumption the non-negativity constraints are automatically satisfied and can be ignored. We also assume that first-order conditions provide the optimal choice, which is definitely satisfied when preferences can be represented by a concave utility function since the second-order condition for a maximum is then automatically satisfied. Furthermore, when solving the problem we will also assume that the individual acts as a price taker so that prices are unaffected by the portfolio choice. Finally, we assume that prices admit no arbitrage. If there was an arbitrage, it would be possible to obtain infinite consumption. We do not impose any constraints on the portfolios the individual may choose among.

The following subsections characterize the optimal consumption plan for various preference specifications.

6.2.1 Time-Additive Expected Utility

With time-additive expected utility there is an increasing, concave, 'single-date' utility function $u : \mathbb{R}_+ \to \mathbb{R}$ such that the objective of the individual is

$$\max_{\boldsymbol{\theta}} u(c_0) + \mathrm{E}\left[e^{-\delta} u(c)\right],$$

where δ is a subjective time preference rate. Substituting in the budget constraints (6.1) and (6.2), we get

$$\max_{\boldsymbol{\theta}} u\left(e_0 - \sum_{i=1}^{I} \theta_i P_i\right) + \mathrm{E}\left[e^{-\delta} u\left(e + \sum_{i=1}^{I} \theta_i D_i\right)\right].$$

The first-order condition with respect to θ_i is

$$-P_i u'\left(e_0 - \sum_{i=1}^{I} \theta_i P_i\right) + \mathrm{E}\left[e^{-\delta} D_i u'\left(e + \sum_{i=1}^{I} \theta_i D_i\right)\right] = 0$$

which implies that

$$P_i u'(c_0) = \mathrm{E}\left[e^{-\delta} D_i u'(c)\right],$$

where c_0 and c denote the optimal consumption plan, that is the consumption plan generated by the optimal portfolio $\boldsymbol{\theta}$. We can rewrite the above equation as

$$P_i = \mathrm{E}\left[e^{-\delta} \frac{u'(c)}{u'(c_0)} D_i\right]. \tag{6.3}$$

This equation links prices to the optimal consumption plan of an individual investor. By comparing Eq. (6.3) and the pricing condition (4.1), we can draw the following conclusion:

Theorem 6.1 *In a one-period, arbitrage-free economy with a single consumption good, let δ be the time preference rate and u the utility function of an individual with time-additive expected utility. If (c_0, c) denotes the optimal consumption plan of the individual, then*

$$\zeta = e^{-\delta} \frac{u'(c)}{u'(c_0)} \tag{6.4}$$

defines a state-price deflator.

Since marginal utilities are positive, ζ defined by Eq. (6.4) is positive. By adding an appropriate condition on the variance of the consumption plan, we can also ensure that ζ has finite variance. Note that the state-price deflator is the marginal rate of substitution of the individual which is capturing the willingness of the individual to substitute a bit of time 0 consumption for some time 1 consumption.

The optimality condition (6.3) can also be justified by a variational argument which goes as follows. Assume that (c_0, c) denotes the optimal consumption plan for the individual. Then any deviation from this plan will give the individual a lower utility. One deviation is obtained by investing in $\varepsilon > 0$ additional units of asset i at the beginning of the period. This leaves an initial consumption of $c_0 - \varepsilon P_i$. On the other hand, the end-of-period consumption in any state ω becomes $c_\omega + \varepsilon D_{i\omega}$. By optimality of (c_0, c), we know that

$$u(c_0 - \varepsilon P_i) + e^{-\delta}\,\mathrm{E}\left[u(c + \varepsilon D_i)\right] \leq u(c_0) + e^{-\delta}\,\mathrm{E}\left[u(c)\right].$$

Subtracting the right-hand side from the left-hand side and dividing by ε yields

$$\frac{u(c_0 - \varepsilon P_i) - u(c_0)}{\varepsilon} + e^{-\delta}\,\mathrm{E}\left[\frac{u(c + \varepsilon D_i) - u(c)}{\varepsilon}\right] \leq 0.$$

Letting ε go to zero, the fractions on the left-hand side approach derivatives[1] and we obtain

$$-P_i u'(c_0) + e^{-\delta}\,\mathrm{E}\left[u'(c)D_i\right] \leq 0,$$

which implies that optimal consumption must be so that

$$P_i \geq \mathrm{E}\left[e^{-\delta}\frac{u'(c)}{u'(c_0)}D_i\right].$$

On the other hand, if we consider selling $\varepsilon > 0$ units of asset i at the beginning of the period, the same reasoning can be used to show that

$$P_i \leq \mathrm{E}\left[e^{-\delta}\frac{u'(c)}{u'(c_0)}D_i\right].$$

Hence, the relation must hold as an equality, just as in Eq. (6.3).

[1] By definition, the derivative of a function $f(x)$ is $f'(x) = \lim_{\varepsilon\to 0} \frac{f(x+\varepsilon)-f(x)}{\varepsilon}$, and hence

$$\lim_{\varepsilon\to 0}\frac{f(x+k\varepsilon)-f(x)}{\varepsilon} = k\lim_{\varepsilon\to 0}\frac{f(x+k\varepsilon)-f(x)}{k\varepsilon} = k\lim_{k\varepsilon\to 0}\frac{f(x+k\varepsilon)-f(x)}{k\varepsilon} = kf'(x).$$

Alternatively, you can apply l'Hôspital's rule to conclude that

$$\lim_{\varepsilon\to 0}\frac{u(c_0 - \varepsilon P_i) - u(c_0)}{\varepsilon} = \lim_{\varepsilon\to 0}\frac{-P_i u'(c_0 - \varepsilon P_i)}{1} = -P_i u'(c_0)$$

and analogously for the other utility quotient.

Example 6.1 For the case of CRRA utility, $u(c) = \frac{1}{1-\gamma}c^{1-\gamma}$, we have $u'(c) = c^{-\gamma}$. Therefore the optimal consumption plan satisfies

$$P_i = \mathrm{E}\left[e^{-\delta}\left(\frac{c}{c_0}\right)^{-\gamma} D_i\right],$$

and, hence,

$$\zeta = e^{-\delta}\left(\frac{c}{c_0}\right)^{-\gamma}$$

is the state-price deflator that can be derived from the individual's problem. □

Let us also consider the case with utility of two goods. Let good 1 be the numeraire so that the price of the other good as well as dividends and prices of all assets are measured in units of good 1. By P^q_0 we denote the price of good 2 at time 0, whereas P^q_ω is the price of good 2 at time 1 if state ω is realized. For simplicity, assume a finite state space $\Omega = \{1, 2, \dots, S\}$ so that the utility maximization problem is

$$\max u(c_0, q_0) + e^{-\delta}\sum_{\omega=1}^{S} p_\omega u(c_\omega, q_\omega),$$

$$\text{s.t. } c_0 + P^q_0 q_0 \leq e_0 - \sum_{i=1}^{I}\theta_i P_i,$$

$$c_\omega + P^q_\omega q_\omega \leq e_\omega + \sum_{i=1}^{I} D_{i\omega}\theta_i, \quad \omega = 1, \dots, S.$$

Here we assume that both goods are perishable so that the consumption of a good at a given date equals the purchases of the good at that date (we will consider the case in which one good is durable in the multiperiod setting in Section 6.4.2). With time-additive utility of non-durable goods, the utility of consumption at time 1 is independent of the purchases at time 0. In contrast, for a durable good the consumption at time 1 and thus the utility at time 1 will depend on the purchases at time 0 (possibly depreciated). The choice variables are the portfolio $\boldsymbol{\theta} = (\theta_1, \dots, \theta_I)^\top$, time 0 consumption (c_0, q_0), and state-dependent time 1 consumption $(c_1, q_1), \dots, (c_S, q_S)$. The Lagrangian associated with the above constrained optimization problem is

$$\mathcal{L} = u(c_0, q_0) + e^{-\delta}\sum_{\omega=1}^{S} p_\omega u(c_\omega, q_\omega) + \nu_0\left(e_0 - \sum_{i=1}^{I}\theta_i P_i - c_0 - P^q_0 q_0\right)$$
$$+ \sum_{\omega=1}^{S}\nu_\omega\left(e_\omega + \sum_{i=1}^{I} D_{i\omega}\theta_i - c_\omega - P^q_\omega q_\omega\right),$$

where $\nu_0, \nu_1, \ldots, \nu_S$ are the Lagrange multipliers.

The first-order conditions with respect to c_0 and q_0 imply that

$$u_c(c_0, q_0) = \nu_0, \quad u_q(c_0, q_0) = \nu_0 P_0^q, \tag{6.5}$$

where a subscript on u indicates the partial derivative of u with respect to that variable. In particular, the optimal time 0 consumption choice will satisfy

$$\frac{u_q(c_0, q_0)}{u_c(c_0, q_0)} = P_0^q. \tag{6.6}$$

This is intuitive: consuming one extra unit of good 2 increases utility by $u_q(c_0, q_0)$. Alternatively, the extra unit of good 2 can be swapped to P_0^q units of good 1 and, consuming those units, utility will increase by $P_0^q u_c(c_0, q_0)$. At the optimum, different alternatives will provide identical marginal utilities.

Similarly, the first-order conditions with respect to c_ω and q_ω imply that

$$e^{-\delta} p_\omega u_c(c_\omega, q_\omega) = \nu_\omega, \quad e^{-\delta} p_\omega u_q(c_\omega, q_\omega) = \nu_\omega P_\omega^q, \tag{6.7}$$

so, in particular,

$$\frac{u_q(c_\omega, q_\omega)}{u_c(c_\omega, q_\omega)} = P_\omega^q, \tag{6.8}$$

analogously to the result for time 0 decisions.

The first-order condition for θ_i leads to

$$\nu_0 P_i = \sum_{\omega=1}^{S} \nu_\omega D_{i\omega}.$$

Substituting in Eqs. (6.5) and (6.7), we see that

$$P_i = \sum_{\omega=1}^{S} p_\omega e^{-\delta} \frac{u_c(c_\omega, q_\omega)}{u_c(c_0, q_0)} D_{i\omega} = \mathrm{E}\left[e^{-\delta} \frac{u_c(c, q)}{u_c(c_0, q_0)} D_i \right].$$

Therefore, we have the next result:

Theorem 6.2 *In a one-period, arbitrage-free economy with two perishable consumption goods, let δ be the time preference rate and $u(c, q)$ the utility function of an individual with time-additive expected utility. If (c_0, c) and (q_0, q) denote the individual's optimal consumption plan for the numeraire good and the other good, respectively, then*

$$\zeta = e^{-\delta} \frac{u_c(c, q)}{u_c(c_0, q_0)}$$

defines a state-price deflator.

Because of the optimality conditions (6.6) and (6.8), we can equivalently express the state-price deflator as

$$\zeta = e^{-\delta} \frac{u_q(c,q)/P^q}{u_q(c_0,q_0)/P_0^q},$$

where P^q is the (state-dependent) end-of-period price of the second good.

In applications we will assume a CES-type utility function as studied in the following example.

Example 6.2 If we assume $u(c,q) = \frac{1}{1-\gamma} f(c,q)^{1-\gamma}$, we have

$$u_c(c,q) = f(c,q)^{-\gamma} f_c(c,q), \quad u_q(c,q) = f(c,q)^{-\gamma} f_q(c,q).$$

If we apply the CES function

$$f(c,q) = \left(ac^{\frac{\psi-1}{\psi}} + bq^{\frac{\psi-1}{\psi}}\right)^{\frac{\psi}{\psi-1}},$$

as in Eq. (5.12), we get

$$f_c(c,q) = ac^{-\frac{1}{\psi}} \left(ac^{\frac{\psi-1}{\psi}} + bq^{\frac{\psi-1}{\psi}}\right)^{\frac{1}{\psi-1}} = a\left(a + b\left(\frac{q}{c}\right)^{\frac{\psi-1}{\psi}}\right)^{\frac{1}{\psi-1}},$$

$$f_q(c,q) = bq^{-\frac{1}{\psi}} \left(ac^{\frac{\psi-1}{\psi}} + bq^{\frac{\psi-1}{\psi}}\right)^{\frac{1}{\psi-1}} = b\left(\frac{q}{c}\right)^{-\frac{1}{\psi}} \left(a + b\left(\frac{q}{c}\right)^{\frac{\psi-1}{\psi}}\right)^{\frac{1}{\psi-1}},$$

which also follows from the computations in Section 5.6.3. Hence, the optimal consumption combination of the two goods must satisfy

$$P^q = \frac{u_q(c,q)}{u_c(c,q)} = \frac{f_q(c,q)}{f_c(c,q)} = \frac{b}{a}\left(\frac{q}{c}\right)^{-\frac{1}{\psi}}, \tag{6.9}$$

both at time 0 and in any state possible at time 1. The state-price deflator becomes

$$\zeta = e^{-\delta} \frac{u_c(c,q)}{u_c(c_0,q_0)} = e^{-\delta} \left(\frac{f(c,q)}{f(c_0,q_0)}\right)^{-\gamma} \frac{f_c(c,q)}{f_c(c_0,q_0)}.$$

Rewriting $f(c,q)$ as

$$f(c,q) = c\left(a + b\left(\frac{q}{c}\right)^{\frac{\psi-1}{\psi}}\right)^{\frac{\psi}{\psi-1}},$$

we can express the state-price deflator as

$$\zeta = e^{-\delta}\left(\frac{c}{c_0}\right)^{-\gamma}\left(\frac{1+\frac{b}{a}\left(\frac{q}{c}\right)^{\frac{\psi-1}{\psi}}}{1+\frac{b}{a}\left(\frac{q_0}{c_0}\right)^{\frac{\psi-1}{\psi}}}\right)^{-\frac{\psi\gamma-1}{\psi-1}},$$

where the last fraction is new compared to the case of one-good power utility studied in Example 6.1.

If we define the expenditure share of good 1 as

$$\alpha = \frac{c}{c+P^q q},$$

we get

$$\alpha^{-1} = \frac{c+P^q q}{c} = 1 + P^q\frac{q}{c} = 1 + \frac{b}{a}\left(\frac{q}{c}\right)^{\frac{\psi-1}{\psi}}$$

by using Eq. (6.9). Therefore, the state-price deflator can alternatively be stated as

$$\zeta = e^{-\delta}\left(\frac{c}{c_0}\right)^{-\gamma}\left(\frac{\alpha}{\alpha_0}\right)^{\frac{\psi\gamma-1}{\psi-1}}.$$

Also note that Eq. (6.9) implies that

$$c = \left(\frac{a}{b}\right)^{\psi}\left(P^q\right)^{\psi} q$$

and, hence,

$$\alpha = \frac{1}{1+\left(\frac{a}{b}\right)^{-\psi}\left(P^q\right)^{1-\psi}}.$$

We see that the consumption share of each good does not depend on the level of consumption and, therefore, it does not depend on the wealth of the individual. □

6.2.2 Non-Additive Expected Utility

Next consider non-additive expected utility where the objective is to maximize $\mathrm{E}[U(c_0,c)]$ for some $U:\mathbb{R}_+\times\mathbb{R}_+\to\mathbb{R}$. Again, substituting in the budget constraints (6.1) and (6.2), the problem is

$$\max_{\theta} \mathrm{E}\left[U\left(e_0-\sum_{i=1}^{I}\theta_i P_i, e+\sum_{i=1}^{I}\theta_i D_i\right)\right].$$

The first-order condition with respect to θ_i is

$$-P_i \mathrm{E}\left[\frac{\partial U}{\partial c_0}\left(e_0 - \sum_{i=1}^{I}\theta_i P_i, e + \sum_{i=1}^{I}\theta_i D_i\right)\right]$$
$$+\mathrm{E}\left[D_i \frac{\partial U}{\partial c}\left(e_0 - \sum_{i=1}^{I}\theta_i P_i, e + \sum_{i=1}^{I}\theta_i D_i\right)\right] = 0$$

which implies that

$$P_i = \mathrm{E}\left[\frac{\frac{\partial U}{\partial c}(c_0, c)}{\mathrm{E}\left[\frac{\partial U}{\partial c_0}(c_0, c)\right]} D_i\right]$$

so that the corresponding state-price deflator is

$$\zeta = \frac{\frac{\partial U}{\partial c}(c_0, c)}{\mathrm{E}\left[\frac{\partial U}{\partial c_0}(c_0, c)\right]}. \tag{6.10}$$

This could be supported by a variational argument as in the case of time-additive expected utility. Again note that these equations hold only for the optimal consumption plan.

Example 6.3 Consider the very simple habit-style utility function

$$U(c_0, c) = \frac{1}{1-\gamma} c_0^{1-\gamma} + \frac{1}{1-\gamma} e^{-\delta} \left(c - \beta c_0\right)^{1-\gamma}.$$

The subsistence level for time 1 consumption is some fraction β of time 0 consumption. In this case the relevant marginal utilities are

$$\frac{\partial U}{\partial c_0}(c_0, c) = c_0^{-\gamma} - \beta e^{-\delta} \left(c - \beta c_0\right)^{-\gamma},$$
$$\frac{\partial U}{\partial c}(c_0, c) = e^{-\delta} \left(c - \beta c_0\right)^{-\gamma}.$$

The first-order condition therefore implies that

$$P_i = \mathrm{E}\left[\frac{e^{-\delta} \left(c - \beta c_0\right)^{-\gamma}}{\mathrm{E}\left[c_0^{-\gamma} - \beta e^{-\delta} \left(c - \beta c_0\right)^{-\gamma}\right]} D_i\right],$$

and the associated state-price deflator is

$$\zeta = \frac{e^{-\delta} \left(c - \beta c_0\right)^{-\gamma}}{\mathrm{E}\left[c_0^{-\gamma} - \beta e^{-\delta} \left(c - \beta c_0\right)^{-\gamma}\right]}.$$

This simple example indicates that (internal) habit formation leads to pricing expressions that are considerably more complicated than time-additive utility. □

6.2.3 A General Utility Index

A general utility index $\mathcal{U}$ is tractable for a finite state space where we can write the objective as

$$\max_{\theta} \mathcal{U}(c_0, c_1, \dots, c_S),$$

where c_ω is consumption in state ω, $\omega = 1, \dots, S$. In this case the first-order condition implies that

$$P_i = \sum_{\omega=1}^{S} \frac{\frac{\partial \mathcal{U}}{\partial c_\omega}(c_0, c_1, \dots, c_S)}{\frac{\partial \mathcal{U}}{\partial c_0}(c_0, c_1, \dots, c_S)} D_{i\omega}.$$

This defines a state-price vector $\boldsymbol{\psi}$ by

$$\psi_\omega = \frac{\frac{\partial \mathcal{U}}{\partial c_\omega}(c_0, c_1, \dots, c_S)}{\frac{\partial \mathcal{U}}{\partial c_0}(c_0, c_1, \dots, c_S)}. \tag{6.11}$$

By combining this expression with Eq. (4.16) we obtain the corresponding state-price deflator.

6.2.4 A Two-Step Procedure in a Complete Market

If the preferences of an individual in a one-period economy are given by a utility index $\mathcal{U}(c_0, c)$, then the individual wants to find the consumption and portfolio plan $(c_0, c, \boldsymbol{\theta})$ that maximizes this utility index over all feasible consumption and portfolio plans, that is the plans which satisfy the budget constraints (6.1) and (6.2). If the market is complete, we can separate the consumption and portfolio decision due to the following result. For simplicity, we assume a finite state space. We denote by $\boldsymbol{c}$ the vector of consumption rates in the different states at time 1, and $\boldsymbol{e}$ is the equivalent for income.

Lemma 6.1 *Assume the market is arbitrage-free and complete, and let $\boldsymbol{\psi}$ denote the unique state-price vector. If $(c_0, \boldsymbol{c}, \boldsymbol{\theta})$ is any feasible consumption and portfolio plan, then*

$$c_0 + \boldsymbol{\psi} \cdot \boldsymbol{c} \leq e_0 + \boldsymbol{\psi} \cdot \boldsymbol{e}. \tag{6.12}$$

Conversely, if a consumption plan (c_0, c) satisfies Eq. (6.12), then a portfolio $\boldsymbol{\theta}$ exists so that $(c_0, c, \boldsymbol{\theta})$ is feasible.

Proof. Given a feasible consumption and portfolio plan $(c_0, c, \boldsymbol{\theta})$, let $\boldsymbol{D} = \boldsymbol{D}^{\theta}$ denote the dividend vector of the portfolio $\boldsymbol{\theta}$. Then (c_0, c) and $\boldsymbol{D}$ satisfy

$$c \leq e + \boldsymbol{D}, \tag{6.13}$$

$$c_0 \leq e_0 - \boldsymbol{\psi} \cdot \boldsymbol{D}. \tag{6.14}$$

Multiplying Eq. (6.13) by $\boldsymbol{\psi}$, we get

$$\boldsymbol{\psi} \cdot c \leq \boldsymbol{\psi} \cdot e + \boldsymbol{\psi} \cdot \boldsymbol{D}.$$

Adding this to Eq. (6.14), we see that any feasible consumption plan $(c_0, \boldsymbol{c})$ must satisfy Eq. (6.12).

Conversely, suppose a consumption plan $(c_0, \boldsymbol{c})$ satisfies Eq. (6.12). Then it will also satisfy the conditions (6.13) and (6.14) with $\boldsymbol{D} = c - e$. Because the market is complete, a portfolio $\boldsymbol{\theta}$ exists so that $\boldsymbol{D}^{\theta} = \boldsymbol{D}$. By construction, the consumption and portfolio plan $(c_0, \boldsymbol{c}, \boldsymbol{\theta})$ is then feasible. □

The inequality (6.12) is natural since the left-hand side is the present value of the consumption plan and the right-hand side is the present value of the endowment, which is well-defined because market completeness ensures that some portfolio will provide a dividend identical to the endowment.

As a consequence of the lemma, we can find the utility-maximizing consumption and portfolio plan using a two-step procedure. *First*, solve

$$\max_{c_0, c} \mathcal{U}(c_0, \boldsymbol{c}) \tag{6.15}$$

$$\text{s.t. } c_0 + \boldsymbol{\psi} \cdot c \leq e_0 + \boldsymbol{\psi} \cdot e$$

$$c_0, \boldsymbol{c} \geq 0,$$

to find the optimal consumption plan. *Second*, find the portfolio financing that optimal consumption plan.

We still assume that the non-negativity constraint is automatically satisfied. The Lagrangian for the problem (6.15) is therefore

$$\mathcal{L} = \mathcal{U}(c_0, \boldsymbol{c}) + \nu \left(e_0 + \boldsymbol{\psi} \cdot e - c_0 - \boldsymbol{\psi} \cdot c\right),$$

where ν is the Lagrange multiplier. The first-order conditions are

$$\frac{\partial \mathcal{U}}{\partial c_0}(c_0, \boldsymbol{c}) = \nu, \quad \frac{\partial \mathcal{U}}{\partial \boldsymbol{c}}(c_0, \boldsymbol{c}) = \nu \boldsymbol{\psi}.$$

In particular, the optimal consumption plan satisfies

$$\frac{\frac{\partial \mathcal{U}}{\partial c}(c_0, \boldsymbol{c})}{\frac{\partial \mathcal{U}}{\partial c_0}(c_0, \boldsymbol{c})} = \boldsymbol{\psi},$$

which is consistent with Eq. (6.11).

With an infinite state space and an expected utility representation $\mathcal{U}(c_0, c) = \mathrm{E}[U(c_0, c)]$, we can formulate the complete markets problem as

$$\max_{c_0, c} \ \mathrm{E}[U(c_0, c)]$$
$$\text{s.t. } c_0 + \mathrm{E}[\zeta c] \leq e_0 + \mathrm{E}[\zeta e]$$
$$c_0, c \geq 0,$$

where ζ is the unique state-price deflator. The Lagrangian is

$$\begin{aligned}\mathcal{L} &= \mathrm{E}[U(c_0, c)] + \nu\,(e_0 - c_0 + \mathrm{E}[\zeta(e - c)]) \\ &= \nu\,(e_0 - c_0) + \mathrm{E}\left[U(c_0, c) + \nu\zeta(e - c)\right].\end{aligned}$$

We maximize the expectation $\mathrm{E}\left[U(c_0, c) + \nu\zeta(e - c)\right]$ by maximizing state-by-state, that is maximizing $U(c_0, c(\omega)) + \nu\zeta(\omega)\,(e(\omega) - c(\omega))$ for each state ω. The first-order condition with respect to $c(\omega)$ implies

$$\frac{\partial U}{\partial c}(c_0, c(\omega)) = \nu\zeta(\omega)$$

and the first-order condition with respect to c_0 implies that

$$\mathrm{E}\left[\frac{\partial U}{\partial c_0}(c_0, c)\right] = \nu$$

and, hence,

$$\frac{\frac{\partial U}{\partial c}(c_0, c)}{\mathrm{E}\left[\frac{\partial U}{\partial c_0}(c_0, c)\right]} = \zeta,$$

as found in Eq. (6.10). In particular, with time-additive expected utility $U(c_0, c) = u(c_0) + e^{-\delta}u(c)$, we get

$$e^{-\delta}\frac{u'(c)}{u'(c_0)} = \zeta$$

as found in Eq. (6.4).

If the market is incomplete, the individual cannot implement any consumption plan but only those that can be financed by portfolios of traded assets. Therefore, we cannot apply the above two-step technique.

6.3 OPTIMAL PORTFOLIOS AND MEAN-VARIANCE ANALYSIS

In the preceding section we did not explicitly solve for the optimal portfolio. A popular one-period model for portfolio choice is the mean-variance model introduced by Markowitz (1952, 1959). If the individual has mean-variance preferences, compare Section 5.6, her optimal portfolio will be a mean-variance efficient portfolio corresponding to a point on the upward-sloping branch of the mean-variance frontier. Mean-variance analysis does not by itself say anything about exactly which portfolio a given individual should choose, but if we assume a specific mean-variance utility function, the optimal portfolio can be derived.

We emphasize that the conditions justifying mean-variance portfolio choice are highly unrealistic: either returns must be normally distributed or individuals must have mean-variance preferences. Nevertheless, the mean-variance frontier remains an important concept in both portfolio choice and asset pricing (recall Theorem 4.12).

In this section we apply the traditional Lagrangian approach to characterize the mean-variance efficient portfolios. In Section 10.3 we will offer an alternative 'orthogonal' characterization and use that to show the link between mean-variance returns, pricing factors, and state-price deflators.

As before we assume that I assets are traded, and we let $\boldsymbol{R} = (R_1, \dots, R_I)^\top$ denote the vector of gross rates of return on these assets. Let $\boldsymbol{\mu} = \mathrm{E}[\boldsymbol{R}]$ denote the vector of expected gross rates of return, and let $\underline{\underline{\Sigma}} = \mathrm{Var}[\boldsymbol{R}]$ denote the $I \times I$ variance-covariance matrix of gross rates of return. In the characterization of mean-variance efficient portfolios, we are only interested in their returns so we can represent portfolios by portfolio weight vectors, that is vectors $\boldsymbol{\pi} = (\pi_1, \dots, \pi_I)^\top$ with $\boldsymbol{\pi}^\top \mathbf{1} = 1$, where π_i is the fraction of total portfolio value invested in asset i. The gross rate of return on a portfolio $\boldsymbol{\pi}$ is $R^{\boldsymbol{\pi}} = \boldsymbol{\pi}^\top \boldsymbol{R} = \sum_{i=1}^I \pi_i R_i$, compare Eq. (3.10). The expectation and the variance of the return on a portfolio $\boldsymbol{\pi}$ are

$$\mathrm{E}\left[R^{\boldsymbol{\pi}}\right] = \mathrm{E}\left[\sum_{i=1}^I \pi_i R_i\right] = \sum_{i=1}^I \pi_i \,\mathrm{E}[R_i] = \sum_{i=1}^I \pi_i \mu_i = \boldsymbol{\pi}^\top \boldsymbol{\mu},$$

$$\mathrm{Var}\left[R^{\boldsymbol{\pi}}\right] = \mathrm{Var}\left[\sum_{i=1}^I \pi_i R_i\right] = \sum_{i=1}^I \sum_{j=1}^I \pi_i \pi_j \,\mathrm{Cov}[R_i, R_j] = \boldsymbol{\pi}^\top \underline{\underline{\Sigma}} \boldsymbol{\pi}.$$

A portfolio $\boldsymbol{\pi}$ is said to be *mean-variance efficient* if an $m \in \mathbb{R}$ exists so that $\boldsymbol{\pi}$ solves

$$\min_{\boldsymbol{\pi}} \boldsymbol{\pi}^\top \underline{\underline{\Sigma}} \boldsymbol{\pi} \quad \text{s.t.} \quad \boldsymbol{\pi}^\top \boldsymbol{\mu} = m, \quad \boldsymbol{\pi}^\top \mathbf{1} = 1, \tag{6.16}$$

that is $\boldsymbol{\pi}$ has the lowest return variance among all portfolios with expected return m.

6.3.1 Risky Assets Only

Assume that $\underline{\underline{\Sigma}}$ is positive definite which means that $\pi^\top \underline{\underline{\Sigma}} \pi > 0$ for all π and, hence, the variance of the return on any portfolio is positive. Any portfolio of risky assets will be risky. There is no risk-free asset and no redundant assets. It follows that $\underline{\underline{\Sigma}}$ is non-singular and that the inverse $\underline{\underline{\Sigma}}^{-1}$ is also positive definite (see Appendix C). We will allow for a risk-free asset later.

The Lagrangian associated with the constrained minimization problem (6.16) is

$$\mathcal{L} = \pi^\top \underline{\underline{\Sigma}} \pi + \nu \left(m - \pi^\top \mu\right) + \xi \left(1 - \pi^\top \mathbf{1}\right),$$

where ν and ξ are Lagrange multipliers. The first-order condition with respect to π is

$$\frac{\partial \mathcal{L}}{\partial \pi} = 2\underline{\underline{\Sigma}} \pi - \nu \mu - \xi \mathbf{1} = 0,$$

which implies that

$$\pi = \frac{1}{2} \nu \underline{\underline{\Sigma}}^{-1} \mu + \frac{1}{2} \xi \underline{\underline{\Sigma}}^{-1} \mathbf{1}. \tag{6.17}$$

The first-order conditions with respect to the multipliers simply give the two constraints to the minimization problem. Substituting the expression (6.17) for π into the two constraints, we obtain the equations

$$\nu \mu^\top \underline{\underline{\Sigma}}^{-1} \mu + \xi \mathbf{1}^\top \underline{\underline{\Sigma}}^{-1} \mu = 2m,$$
$$\nu \mu^\top \underline{\underline{\Sigma}}^{-1} \mathbf{1} + \xi \mathbf{1}^\top \underline{\underline{\Sigma}}^{-1} \mathbf{1} = 2.$$

Defining the numbers A, B, C, D by

$$A = \mu^\top \underline{\underline{\Sigma}}^{-1} \mu, \;\; B = \mu^\top \underline{\underline{\Sigma}}^{-1} \mathbf{1} = \mathbf{1}^\top \underline{\underline{\Sigma}}^{-1} \mu, \;\; C = \mathbf{1}^\top \underline{\underline{\Sigma}}^{-1} \mathbf{1}, \;\; D = AC - B^2,$$

we can write the solution to the two equations in ν and ξ as

$$\nu = 2\frac{Cm - B}{D}, \qquad \xi = 2\frac{A - Bm}{D}.$$

Substituting this into (6.17) we arrive at the following result:

Theorem 6.3 *With risky assets only, the mean-variance efficient portfolio with expected gross rate of return m is given by the portfolio weight vector*

$$\pi = \pi(m) \equiv \frac{Cm - B}{D} \underline{\underline{\Sigma}}^{-1} \mu + \frac{A - Bm}{D} \underline{\underline{\Sigma}}^{-1} \mathbf{1}. \tag{6.18}$$

The variance of the return on this portfolio is given by

$$\sigma^2(m) \equiv \pi(m)^\top \underline{\underline{\Sigma}} \pi(m) = \frac{Cm^2 - 2Bm + A}{D}. \tag{6.19}$$

The expression (6.19) is to be verified in Exercise 6.4. This expression shows that the combinations of variance and mean form a parabola in a (mean, variance)-diagram.

Traditionally the portfolios are depicted in a (standard deviation, mean)-diagram. Equation (6.19) can be rewritten as

$$\frac{\sigma^2(m)}{1/C} - \frac{(m - B/C)^2}{D/C^2} = 1,$$

from which it follows that the optimal combinations of standard deviation and mean form a hyperbola in the (standard deviation, mean)-diagram. This hyperbola is called the *mean-variance frontier* of risky assets. The mean-variance efficient portfolios are sometimes called frontier portfolios.

Before we proceed, let us clarify a point in the derivation above. We need to divide by D so D has to be non-zero. In fact, $D > 0$. To see this, first note that since $\underline{\underline{\Sigma}}$ and therefore $\underline{\underline{\Sigma}}^{-1}$ are positive definite, we have $A > 0$ and $C > 0$. Moreover,

$$AD = A(AC - B^2) = (B\boldsymbol{\mu} - A\mathbf{1})^{\top}\underline{\underline{\Sigma}}^{-1}(B\boldsymbol{\mu} - A\mathbf{1}) > 0,$$

again using that $\underline{\underline{\Sigma}}^{-1}$ is positive definite. Since $A > 0$, we must have $D > 0$.

The (global) *minimum-variance portfolio* is the portfolio that has the minimum variance among all portfolios. We can find this directly by solving the constrained minimization problem

$$\min_{\boldsymbol{\pi}} \boldsymbol{\pi}^{\top}\underline{\underline{\Sigma}}\boldsymbol{\pi} \quad \text{s.t.} \quad \boldsymbol{\pi}^{\top}\mathbf{1} = 1$$

where there is no constraint on the expected portfolio return. Alternatively, we can minimize the variance $\sigma^2(m)$ in Eq. (6.19) over all m. Taking the latter route, we find that the minimum variance is obtained when the mean return is $m_{\min} = B/C$ and the minimum variance is given by $\sigma^2_{\min} = \sigma^2(m_{\min}) = 1/C$. From Eq. (6.18) we get that the minimum-variance portfolio is

$$\boldsymbol{\pi}_{\min} = \frac{1}{C}\underline{\underline{\Sigma}}^{-1}\mathbf{1} = \frac{1}{\mathbf{1}^{\top}\underline{\underline{\Sigma}}^{-1}\mathbf{1}}\underline{\underline{\Sigma}}^{-1}\mathbf{1}. \tag{6.20}$$

The following result turns out to be useful in the subsequent analysis:

Lemma 6.2 *For any constant α, the solution to the optimization problem*

$$\max_{\boldsymbol{\pi}} \frac{\boldsymbol{\pi}^{\top}\boldsymbol{\mu} - \alpha}{\left(\boldsymbol{\pi}^{\top}\underline{\underline{\Sigma}}\boldsymbol{\pi}\right)^{1/2}} \quad \textit{s.t.} \quad \boldsymbol{\pi}^{\top}\mathbf{1} = 1, \tag{6.21}$$

is obtained by the portfolio weight vector

$$\boldsymbol{\pi} = \frac{\underline{\underline{\Sigma}}^{-1}(\boldsymbol{\mu} - \alpha\mathbf{1})}{\mathbf{1}^{\top}\underline{\underline{\Sigma}}^{-1}(\boldsymbol{\mu} - \alpha\mathbf{1})}. \tag{6.22}$$

Note that the denominator in the objective of Eq. (6.21) is clearly the standard deviation of the return of the portfolio, whereas the numerator is the expected return in excess of α. This ratio is the slope of a straight line in the (standard deviation, mean)-diagram that goes through the point $\left((\boldsymbol{\pi}^\top \underline{\underline{\Sigma}} \boldsymbol{\pi})^{1/2}, \boldsymbol{\pi}^\top \boldsymbol{\mu}\right)$ corresponding to the portfolio $\boldsymbol{\pi}$ and intersects the mean-axis at α.

Proof. Applying the constraint, the objective function can be rewritten as

$$f(\boldsymbol{\pi}) = \frac{\boldsymbol{\pi}^\top(\boldsymbol{\mu} - \alpha \mathbf{1})}{\left(\boldsymbol{\pi}^\top \underline{\underline{\Sigma}} \boldsymbol{\pi}\right)^{1/2}} = \boldsymbol{\pi}^\top(\boldsymbol{\mu} - \alpha \mathbf{1}) \left(\boldsymbol{\pi}^\top \underline{\underline{\Sigma}} \boldsymbol{\pi}\right)^{-1/2}.$$

The derivative is

$$\frac{\partial f}{\partial \boldsymbol{\pi}} = (\boldsymbol{\mu} - \alpha \mathbf{1}) \left(\boldsymbol{\pi}^\top \underline{\underline{\Sigma}} \boldsymbol{\pi}\right)^{-1/2} - \left(\boldsymbol{\pi}^\top \underline{\underline{\Sigma}} \boldsymbol{\pi}\right)^{-3/2} \boldsymbol{\pi}^\top(\boldsymbol{\mu} - \alpha \mathbf{1}) \underline{\underline{\Sigma}} \boldsymbol{\pi},$$

and $\frac{\partial f}{\partial \boldsymbol{\pi}} = 0$ implies that

$$\frac{\boldsymbol{\pi}^\top(\boldsymbol{\mu} - \alpha \mathbf{1})}{\boldsymbol{\pi}^\top \underline{\underline{\Sigma}} \boldsymbol{\pi}} \boldsymbol{\pi} = \underline{\underline{\Sigma}}^{-1} (\boldsymbol{\mu} - \alpha \mathbf{1}), \tag{6.23}$$

which we want to solve for $\boldsymbol{\pi}$. Note that the equation has a vector on each side. If two vectors are identical, they will also be identical after a division by the sum of the elements of the vector. The sum of the elements of the vector on the left-hand side of Eq. (6.23) is

$$\mathbf{1}^\top \left(\frac{\boldsymbol{\pi}^\top(\boldsymbol{\mu} - \alpha \mathbf{1})}{\boldsymbol{\pi}^\top \underline{\underline{\Sigma}} \boldsymbol{\pi}} \boldsymbol{\pi} \right) = \frac{\boldsymbol{\pi}^\top(\boldsymbol{\mu} - \alpha \mathbf{1})}{\boldsymbol{\pi}^\top \underline{\underline{\Sigma}} \boldsymbol{\pi}} \mathbf{1}^\top \boldsymbol{\pi} = \frac{\boldsymbol{\pi}^\top(\boldsymbol{\mu} - \alpha \mathbf{1})}{\boldsymbol{\pi}^\top \underline{\underline{\Sigma}} \boldsymbol{\pi}},$$

where the last equality is due to the constraint in Eq. (6.21). The sum of the elements of the vector on the right-hand side of Eq. (6.23) is simply $\mathbf{1}^\top \underline{\underline{\Sigma}}^{-1} (\boldsymbol{\mu} - \alpha \mathbf{1})$. Dividing each side of Eq. (6.23) with the sum of the elements we obtain Eq. (6.22). □

In particular, by letting $\alpha = 0$, we can see that the portfolio

$$\boldsymbol{\pi}_{\text{slope}} = \frac{1}{\mathbf{1}^\top \underline{\underline{\Sigma}}^{-1} \boldsymbol{\mu}} \underline{\underline{\Sigma}}^{-1} \boldsymbol{\mu} = \frac{1}{B} \underline{\underline{\Sigma}}^{-1} \boldsymbol{\mu} \tag{6.24}$$

is the portfolio that maximizes the slope of a straight line between the origin and a point on the mean-variance frontier in the (standard deviation, mean)-diagram. Let us call $\boldsymbol{\pi}_{\text{slope}}$ the *maximum-slope portfolio*. This portfolio has mean A/B and variance A/B^2.

From Eqs. (6.18), (6.20), and (6.24), we see that any mean-variance efficient portfolio can be written as a linear combination of the maximum-slope portfolio and the minimum-variance portfolio:

$$\pi(m) = \frac{(Cm - B)B}{D}\pi_{\text{slope}} + \frac{(A - Bm)C}{D}\pi_{\min}.$$

Note that the two multipliers of the portfolios sum to one. This is a *two-fund separation* result. Any mean-variance efficient portfolio is a combination of two special portfolios or funds, namely the maximum slope portfolio and the minimum-variance portfolio. These two portfolios are said to generate the mean-variance frontier of risky assets. In fact, it can be shown that *any* two frontier portfolios generate the entire frontier.

The following result is both interesting and useful.

Theorem 6.4 *Let R^{π} denote the return on any mean-variance efficient portfolio different from the minimum-variance portfolio. Then there exists a unique mean-variance efficient portfolio with a return $R^{z(\pi)}$ such that* $\text{Cov}[R^{\pi}, R^{z(\pi)}] = 0$. *Furthermore,*

$$\text{E}[R^{z(\pi)}] = \frac{A - B\,\text{E}[R^{\pi}]}{B - C\,\text{E}[R^{\pi}]}$$

and the tangent to the mean-variance frontier at the point corresponding to R^{π} intersects the expected return axis exactly in $\text{E}[R^{z(\pi)}]$.

The return $R^{z(\pi)}$ is sometimes called the zero-beta return for R^{π}, which is consistent with the definition of betas in the context of pricing factors (see the preview on pricing factors in Section 4.6.2 and the detailed coverage in Chapter 10). Exercise 6.5 asks for a proof of the above theorem.

6.3.2 Allowing for a Risk-Free Asset

Now let us allow for a risk-free asset with a gross rate of return of R^f. The risk-free asset corresponds to the point $(0, R^f)$ in the (standard deviation, mean)-diagram. Either the risk-free asset is one of the I basic assets or it can be constructed as a portfolio of the basic assets. Without loss of generality we can assume that the risk-free asset is the I'th basic asset. The remaining $M \equiv I - 1$ basic assets are risky. Let $\tilde{R} = (R_1, \dots, R_M)^{\top}$ denote the gross rate of return vector of the risky assets with expectation $\tilde{\mu} = \text{E}[\tilde{R}]$ and variance $\underline{\underline{\tilde{\Sigma}}} = \text{Var}[\tilde{R}]$. Now assume that $\underline{\underline{\tilde{\Sigma}}}$ is positive definite. We assume that the risk-free return is smaller than the expected return on the minimum-variance portfolio of the risky assets.

A portfolio of all I assets can be represented by an M-dimensional vector $\tilde{\pi}$ of the portfolio weights invested in the risky assets, while the remaining fraction $\pi_f \equiv 1 - \tilde{\pi}^{\top}\mathbf{1}$ is the invested in the risk-free asset. A portfolio involving only the risky assets is an M-dimensional vector $\tilde{\pi}$ with $\tilde{\pi}^{\top}\mathbf{1} = 1$.

Fix for a moment a portfolio $\tilde{\pi}$ of risky assets only. The gross rate of return on this portfolio is $R^{\tilde{\pi}} = \tilde{\pi}^{\top}\tilde{R}$. Suppose you invest a fraction π_f of some amount in the risk-free asset and the remaining fraction $1 - \pi_f$ in this particular risky portfolio. The gross rate of return on this combination will be

$$R = \pi_f R^f + \left(1 - \pi_f\right) R^{\tilde{\pi}}$$

with mean and variance given by

$$\mathrm{E}[R] = \pi_f R^f + (1 - \pi_f)\,\mathrm{E}\left[R^{\tilde{\pi}}\right], \qquad \mathrm{Var}[R] = \left(1 - \pi_f\right)^2 \mathrm{Var}\left[R^{\tilde{\pi}}\right].$$

If $\pi_f \leq 1$, the standard deviation of the return is $\sigma[R] = (1 - \pi_f)\sigma\left[R^{\tilde{\pi}}\right]$ and we obtain

$$\mathrm{E}[R] = \pi_f R^f + \frac{\mathrm{E}\left[R^{\tilde{\pi}}\right]}{\sigma\left[R^{\tilde{\pi}}\right]}\sigma[R]$$

so, varying π_f, the set of points $\{(\sigma[R], \mathrm{E}[R]) \mid \pi_f \leq 1\}$ will form an upward-sloping straight line from $(0, R^f)$ through $(\sigma\left[R^{\tilde{\pi}}\right], \mathrm{E}\left[R^{\tilde{\pi}}\right])$. For $\pi_f > 1$, the standard deviation of the combined portfolio is $\sigma[R] = -(1 - \pi_f)\sigma\left[R^{\tilde{\pi}}\right]$, and we get

$$\mathrm{E}[R] = \pi_f R^f - \frac{\mathrm{E}\left[R^{\tilde{\pi}}\right]}{\sigma\left[R^{\tilde{\pi}}\right]}\sigma[R],$$

which defines a downward-sloping straight line from $(0, R^f)$ and to the right.

Minimizing variance for a given expected return we will move as far to the 'north-west' or to the 'south-west' as possible in the (standard deviation, mean)-diagram. Therefore the mean-variance efficient portfolios will correspond to points on a line which is tangent to the mean-variance frontier of risky assets and goes through the point $(0, R^f)$. There are two such lines, an upward-sloping and a downward-sloping line. The point where the upward-sloping line is tangent to the frontier of risky assets corresponds to a portfolio which we refer to as the *tangency portfolio*. This is a portfolio of risky assets only. It is the portfolio that maximizes the Sharpe ratio over all risky portfolios. The Sharpe ratio of a portfolio $\tilde{\pi}$ is the ratio $(\mathrm{E}[R^{\tilde{\pi}}] - R^f)/\sigma[R^{\tilde{\pi}}]$ between the excess expected return of a portfolio and the standard deviation of the return. To determine the tangency portfolio we must solve the problem

$$\max_{\tilde{\pi}} \frac{\tilde{\pi}^{\top}\tilde{\mu} - R^f}{\left(\tilde{\pi}^{\top}\underline{\underline{\tilde{\Sigma}}}\tilde{\pi}\right)^{1/2}} \quad \text{s.t.} \quad \tilde{\pi}^{\top}\mathbf{1} = 1.$$

Except for the tildes above the symbols, this problem is identical to the problem (6.21) with $\alpha = R^f$, which we have already solved in Lemma 6.2. We can therefore conclude that the tangency portfolio is given by

$$\tilde{\boldsymbol{\pi}}_{\tan} = \frac{\underline{\underline{\tilde{\Sigma}}}^{-1}\left(\tilde{\boldsymbol{\mu}} - R^f \mathbf{1}\right)}{\mathbf{1}^{\top}\underline{\underline{\tilde{\Sigma}}}^{-1}\left(\tilde{\boldsymbol{\mu}} - R^f \mathbf{1}\right)}. \tag{6.25}$$

The gross rate of return on the tangency portfolio is

$$R_{\tan} = \tilde{\boldsymbol{\pi}}_{\tan}^{\top} \tilde{\boldsymbol{R}}$$

with expectation and standard deviation given by

$$\mu_{\tan} = \tilde{\boldsymbol{\mu}}^{\top} \tilde{\boldsymbol{\pi}}_{\tan} = \frac{\tilde{\boldsymbol{\mu}}^{\top}\underline{\underline{\tilde{\Sigma}}}^{-1}\left(\tilde{\boldsymbol{\mu}} - R^f \mathbf{1}\right)}{\mathbf{1}^{\top}\underline{\underline{\tilde{\Sigma}}}^{-1}\left(\tilde{\boldsymbol{\mu}} - R^f \mathbf{1}\right)},$$

$$\sigma_{\tan} = \left(\tilde{\boldsymbol{\pi}}_{\tan}^{\top} \underline{\underline{\tilde{\Sigma}}} \tilde{\boldsymbol{\pi}}_{\tan}\right)^{1/2} = \frac{\left((\tilde{\boldsymbol{\mu}} - R^f \mathbf{1})^{\top}\underline{\underline{\tilde{\Sigma}}}^{-1}(\tilde{\boldsymbol{\mu}} - R^f \mathbf{1})\right)^{1/2}}{\mathbf{1}^{\top}\underline{\underline{\tilde{\Sigma}}}^{-1}\left(\tilde{\boldsymbol{\mu}} - R^f \mathbf{1}\right)}.$$

Now we can characterize the mean-variance frontier:

Theorem 6.5 *When investors have access to a risk-free asset and at least one risky asset, the mean-variance efficient portfolio with expected gross return equal to m consists of the fraction* $\alpha = (\mu_{tan} - m)/(\mu_{tan} - R^f)$ *of wealth in the risk-free asset and the fraction* $(1 - \alpha)$ *in the tangency portfolio of risky assets. The standard deviation of this portfolio is given by*

$$\sigma = \frac{\sigma_{tan}\,|m - R^f|}{\mu_{tan} - R^f}.$$

The straight line from the point $(0, R^f)$ and to and through $(\sigma_{\tan}, \mu_{\tan})$ constitutes the upward-sloping part of the mean-variance frontier of all assets. This line is sometimes referred to as the *capital market line*. There is a downward-sloping part of the frontier which starts out at $(0, R^f)$ and has a slope that equals the negative of the slope of the upward-sloping frontier. Again we have two-fund separation since all investors will combine just two funds, where one fund is simply the risk-free asset and the other is the tangency portfolio of only risky assets. If $\alpha \leq 1$, you will get a point on the upward-sloping part of the frontier. If $\alpha \geq 1$, you will get a point on the downward-sloping part. Of course, when a risk-free return is traded, it will be the minimum-variance return.

The maximum Sharpe ratio is the slope of the upward-sloping part of the mean-variance frontier and can be computed as follows:

$$\frac{\mu_{\tan} - R^f}{\sigma_{\tan}} = \frac{\frac{\tilde{\boldsymbol{\mu}}^\top \underline{\underline{\tilde{\Sigma}}}^{-1}(\tilde{\boldsymbol{\mu}} - R^f \mathbf{1})}{\mathbf{1}^\top \underline{\underline{\tilde{\Sigma}}}^{-1}(\tilde{\boldsymbol{\mu}} - R^f \mathbf{1})} - R^f}{\frac{\left((\tilde{\boldsymbol{\mu}} - R^f \mathbf{1})^\top \underline{\underline{\tilde{\Sigma}}}^{-1}(\tilde{\boldsymbol{\mu}} - R^f \mathbf{1})\right)^{1/2}}{\mathbf{1}^\top \underline{\underline{\tilde{\Sigma}}}^{-1}(\tilde{\boldsymbol{\mu}} - R^f \mathbf{1})}}$$

$$= \frac{\tilde{\boldsymbol{\mu}}^\top \underline{\underline{\tilde{\Sigma}}}^{-1}(\tilde{\boldsymbol{\mu}} - R^f \mathbf{1}) - R^f[\mathbf{1}^\top \underline{\underline{\tilde{\Sigma}}}^{-1}(\tilde{\boldsymbol{\mu}} - R^f \mathbf{1})]}{\left((\tilde{\boldsymbol{\mu}} - R^f \mathbf{1})^\top \underline{\underline{\tilde{\Sigma}}}^{-1}(\tilde{\boldsymbol{\mu}} - R^f \mathbf{1})\right)^{1/2}}$$

$$= \frac{(\tilde{\boldsymbol{\mu}} - R^f \mathbf{1})^\top \underline{\underline{\tilde{\Sigma}}}^{-1}(\tilde{\boldsymbol{\mu}} - R^f \mathbf{1})}{\left((\tilde{\boldsymbol{\mu}} - R^f \mathbf{1})^\top \underline{\underline{\tilde{\Sigma}}}^{-1}(\tilde{\boldsymbol{\mu}} - R^f \mathbf{1})\right)^{1/2}}$$

$$= \left((\tilde{\boldsymbol{\mu}} - R^f \mathbf{1})^\top \underline{\underline{\tilde{\Sigma}}}^{-1}(\tilde{\boldsymbol{\mu}} - R^f \mathbf{1})\right)^{1/2}.$$

6.4 THE DISCRETE-TIME FRAMEWORK

In the discrete-time framework each individual chooses a consumption process $c = (c_t)_{t \in \mathcal{T}}$ and a trading strategy $\boldsymbol{\theta} = (\boldsymbol{\theta}_t)_{t=0,1,\dots,T-1}$, where $\mathcal{T} = \{0, 1, \dots, T\}$. Here, c_t denotes the random, that is state-dependent, consumption at time t, and $\boldsymbol{\theta}_t$ represents the portfolio held from time t until time $t+1$. Again, c_t and $\boldsymbol{\theta}_t$ may depend on the information available to the individual at time t so c and $\boldsymbol{\theta}$ are adapted stochastic processes. The individual has an endowment or income process $e = (e_t)_{t \in \mathcal{T}}$, where e_0 is the initial endowment (wealth) and e_t is the possibly state-dependent income received at time t.

6.4.1 Time-Additive Expected Utility with One Good

Let us first focus on individuals with time-additive expected utility. Standing at time 0, the problem of an individual investor can then be written as

$$\max_{c,\boldsymbol{\theta}} u(c_0) + \sum_{t=1}^{T} e^{-\delta t} \, \mathrm{E}[u(c_t)]$$

$$\text{s.t. } c_0 \le e_0 - \boldsymbol{\theta}_0 \cdot \boldsymbol{P}_0,$$

$$c_t \le e_t + D_t^{\boldsymbol{\theta}}, \quad t = 1, \dots, T,$$

$$c_0, c_1, \dots, c_T \ge 0.$$

Applying Eq. (3.11), we can also write the constraint on time t consumption as

$$c_t \leq e_t + \boldsymbol{\theta}_{t-1} \cdot (\boldsymbol{P}_t + \boldsymbol{D}_t) - \boldsymbol{\theta}_t \cdot \boldsymbol{P}_t.$$

As in the one-period case, we will assume that the non-negativity constraint on consumption is automatically satisfied and that the budget constraints hold as equalities. Therefore the problem can be reformulated as

$$\max_{\boldsymbol{\theta}} u\left(e_0 - \boldsymbol{\theta}_0 \cdot \boldsymbol{P}_0\right) + \sum_{t=1}^{T} e^{-\delta t}\, \mathrm{E}\left[u\left(e_t + \boldsymbol{\theta}_{t-1} \cdot (\boldsymbol{P}_t + \boldsymbol{D}_t) - \boldsymbol{\theta}_t \cdot \boldsymbol{P}_t\right)\right].$$

The only terms involving the initially chosen portfolio $\boldsymbol{\theta}_0 = (\theta_{10}, \theta_{20}, \dots, \theta_{I0})^{\mathsf{T}}$ are

$$u\left(e_0 - \boldsymbol{\theta}_0 \cdot \boldsymbol{P}_0\right) + e^{-\delta}\, \mathrm{E}\left[u\left(e_1 + \boldsymbol{\theta}_0 \cdot (\boldsymbol{P}_1 + \boldsymbol{D}_1) - \boldsymbol{\theta}_1 \cdot \boldsymbol{P}_1\right)\right].$$

In the choice of the portfolio $\boldsymbol{\theta}_0$, the individual faces a tradeoff between consumption at time 0 and consumption at time 1. The first-order condition with respect to θ_{i0} implies that

$$u'(c_0)P_{i0} = \mathrm{E}\left[e^{-\delta}u'(c_1)(P_{i1} + D_{i1})\right],$$

and therefore

$$P_{i0} = \mathrm{E}\left[e^{-\delta}\frac{u'(c_1)}{u'(c_0)}(P_{i1} + D_{i1})\right].$$

When deciding on the portfolio $\boldsymbol{\theta}_t$, there is a similar tradeoff between consumption at time t and at time $t+1$. Since the individual can use all information available at time t before choosing $\boldsymbol{\theta}_t$, the optimal portfolio will align the marginal utility of consumption at time t (in each of the possible scenarios at that time) with the conditional expectation of the marginal utility of consumption at time $t+1$ (conditional on being in that particular scenario at time t). Therefore, the first-order condition with respect to θ_{it} implies that

$$P_{it}u'(c_t) = \mathrm{E}_t\left[e^{-\delta}u'(c_{t+1})(P_{i,t+1} + D_{i,t+1})\right].$$

Consequently,

$$P_{it} = \mathrm{E}_t\left[\frac{e^{-\delta}u'(c_{t+1})}{u'(c_t)}(P_{i,t+1} + D_{i,t+1})\right]. \tag{6.26}$$

Both the two preceding equations are sometimes called the consumption Euler Equation or just the *Euler Equation*. Note that c_t and c_{t+1} in these expressions are the optimal consumption rates of the individual. The above conclusions can alternatively be verified by a variational argument as in the one-period analysis. The Euler equation is also demonstrated using the dynamic programming approach in Section 6.6.

Not surprisingly, the relation (6.26) is consistent with the conclusion in the one-period framework. In particular, we can define a state-price deflator $\zeta = (\zeta_t)_{t\in\mathcal{T}}$ from the individual's optimal consumption process by $\zeta_0 = 1$ and

$$\frac{\zeta_{t+1}}{\zeta_t} = \frac{e^{-\delta}u'(c_{t+1})}{u'(c_t)},$$

which means that

$$\zeta_t = \frac{\zeta_t}{\zeta_{t-1}}\frac{\zeta_{t-1}}{\zeta_{t-2}}\cdots\frac{\zeta_1}{\zeta_0} = e^{-\delta}\frac{u'(c_t)}{u'(c_{t-1})}e^{-\delta}\frac{u'(c_{t-1})}{u'(c_{t-2})}\cdots e^{-\delta}\frac{u'(c_1)}{u'(c_0)} = e^{-\delta t}\frac{u'(c_t)}{u'(c_0)}.$$

We formulate this result in a theorem:

Theorem 6.6 *In a discrete-time, arbitrage-free economy with a single consumption good, let δ be the time preference rate and u the utility function of an individual with time-additive expected utility. If $c = (c_t)_{t\in\mathcal{T}}$ denotes the optimal consumption plan of the individual, then the process $\zeta = (\zeta_t)_{t\in\mathcal{T}}$ defined by*

$$\zeta_t = e^{-\delta t}\frac{u'(c_t)}{u'(c_0)}, \quad t = 0, 1, \dots, T, \tag{6.27}$$

is a state-price deflator.

The right-hand side of Eq. (6.27) is the individual's marginal rate of substitution between time 0 consumption and time t consumption. The value that the individual will attach at time 0 to getting a marginal extra payment at time t is measured by this marginal rate of substitution.

Note that with time-additive power utility $u(c) = \frac{1}{1-\gamma}c^{1-\gamma}$, the state-price deflator is obviously given by

$$\zeta_t = e^{-\delta t}\left(\frac{c_t}{c_0}\right)^{-\gamma}.$$

6.4.2 Time-Additive Expected Utility with Two Goods

If both goods are perishable goods, the analysis of the one-period framework of Section 6.2.1 is easily extended, which leads to the following result:

Theorem 6.7 *In a discrete-time, arbitrage-free economy with two perishable consumption goods, let δ be the time preference rate and $u(c, q)$ the utility function of an individual with time-additive expected utility. If $c = (c_t)_{t\in\mathcal{T}}$ and $q = (q_t)_{t\in\mathcal{T}}$ denote the individual's optimal consumption strategies for the numeraire good and the other good, respectively, then the process $\zeta = (\zeta_t)_{t\in\mathcal{T}}$ defined by*

$$\zeta_t = e^{-\delta t}\frac{u_c(c_t, q_t)}{u_c(c_0, q_0)}, \quad t = 0, 1, \dots, T,$$

is a state-price deflator.

In particular, if we embed the two-good CES utility function of Example 6.2 in a discrete-time framework, the state-price deflator can be written as

$$\zeta_t = e^{-\delta t}\left(\frac{c_t}{c_0}\right)^{-\gamma}\left(\frac{1+\frac{b}{a}\left(\frac{q_t}{c_t}\right)^{\frac{\psi-1}{\psi}}}{1+\frac{b}{a}\left(\frac{q_0}{c_0}\right)^{\frac{\psi-1}{\psi}}}\right)^{-\frac{\psi\gamma-1}{\psi-1}}, \tag{6.28}$$

and as

$$\zeta_t = e^{-\delta t}\left(\frac{c_t}{c_0}\right)^{-\gamma}\left(\frac{\alpha_t}{\alpha_0}\right)^{\frac{\psi\gamma-1}{\psi-1}}, \tag{6.29}$$

where c_t is the optimal consumption of good 1 at time t and α_t is the fraction of total consumption expenditures spent on good 1 at time t.

If good 2 is a durable good, we have to distinguish between the purchases of the good, the holdings of the good, and the consumption services derived from the good. This complicates the analysis somewhat. Let Q_t denote the number of units of the durable good purchased at time t, let $\bar{Q}_t$ denote the holdings of the durable good immediately after this purchase, and let q_t denote the consumption services derived from the durable good. If we assume that the durable good depreciates at a fixed rate of $\xi \in (0,1)$ per period, the holdings of the good evolve as

$$\bar{Q}_t = Q_t + (1-\xi)\bar{Q}_{t-1}.$$

Consequently, for any $s > t$,

$$\begin{aligned}\bar{Q}_s &= Q_s + (1-\xi)\bar{Q}_{s-1}\\ &= Q_s + (1-\xi)\left[Q_{s-1} + (1-\xi)\bar{Q}_{s-2}\right] = Q_s + (1-\xi)Q_{s-1} + (1-\xi)^2\bar{Q}_{s-2}\\ &= \ldots = (1-\xi)^{s-t+1}\bar{Q}_{t-1} + \sum_{j=0}^{s-t} Q_{t+j}(1-\xi)^{s-t-j}.\end{aligned}$$

In particular, purchasing an extra unit of the durable good at time t will increase the holdings at time s by $(1-\xi)^{s-t}$ units. The objective of the individual seen at time t is to maximize

$$\mathrm{E}_t\left[\sum_{s=t}^{T} e^{-\delta(s-t)}u(c_s, q_s)\right]$$

for some appropriate utility function $u(c,q)$ over all feasible strategies for perishable consumption, durable good purchases, and financial trading strategies. Let us assume that the consumption services derived from the durable good are proportional to the holdings of the good, that is $q_t = k\bar{Q}_t$ for all t.

Let us focus on the decisions c_t, Q_t, and $\boldsymbol{\theta}_t$ to be taken at time t. Since the budget constraints will hold as equalities for the optimal decisions, we have

$$c_t + P_t^q Q_t = W_t - \boldsymbol{\theta}_t^\top \boldsymbol{P}_t,$$

$$c_{t+1} + P_{t+1}^q Q_{t+1} = e_{t+1} + D_{t+1}^{\boldsymbol{\theta}} = e_{t+1} + \boldsymbol{\theta}_t^\top (\boldsymbol{P}_{t+1} + \boldsymbol{D}_{t+1}) - \boldsymbol{\theta}_{t+1}^\top \boldsymbol{P}_{t+1},$$

where W_t is the wealth of the individual at time t (after receiving dividends and income). The objective is thus to maximize

$$\begin{aligned} &u\left(W_t - \boldsymbol{\theta}_t^\top \boldsymbol{P}_t - P_t^q Q_t, k[Q_t + (1-\xi)\bar{Q}_{t-1}]\right) \\ &\quad + e^{-\delta}\, \mathrm{E}_t\Big[u\Big(e_{t+1} + \boldsymbol{\theta}_t^\top (\boldsymbol{P}_{t+1} + \boldsymbol{D}_{t+1}) - \boldsymbol{\theta}_{t+1}^\top \boldsymbol{P}_{t+1} - P_{t+1}^q Q_{t+1}, \\ &\qquad\qquad k[Q_{t+1} + (1-\xi)Q_t + (1-\xi)^2 \bar{Q}_{t-1}]\Big)\Big] \\ &\quad + \sum_{s=t+2}^{T} e^{-\delta(s-t)}\, \mathrm{E}_t\left[u\left(c_s, k[Q_s + \cdots + (1-\xi)^{s-t} Q_t + (1-\xi)^{s-t+1} \bar{Q}_{t-1}]\right)\right]. \end{aligned}$$

The first-order condition with respect to Q_t implies that

$$u_c(c_t, q_t) P_t^q = k\left(u_q(c_t, q_t) + \mathrm{E}_t\left[\sum_{s=t+1}^{T} u_q(c_s, q_s)(1-\xi)^{s-t}\right]\right), \tag{6.30}$$

which links the optimal consumption of the two goods. Note that if $\xi = 1$ and $k = 1$, good 2 is really a perishable good, and we are back to the condition

$$u_c(c_t, q_t) P_t^q = u_q(c_t, q_t)$$

as in Section 6.2.1. The first-order condition with respect to $\boldsymbol{\theta}_t$ implies that

$$u_c(c_t, q_t) \boldsymbol{P}_t = e^{-\delta}\, \mathrm{E}_t\left[u_c(c_{t+1}, q_{t+1}) \left(\boldsymbol{P}_{t+1} + \boldsymbol{D}_{t+1}\right)\right].$$

For any asset i, this leads to the pricing condition

$$P_{it} = \mathrm{E}_t\left[e^{-\delta} \frac{u_c(c_{t+1}, q_{t+1})}{u_c(c_t, q_t)} \left(P_{i,t+1} + D_{i,t+1}\right)\right].$$

This leads to the following theorem:

Theorem 6.8 *In a discrete-time, arbitrage-free economy with a perishable and a durable consumption good, let δ be the time preference rate and $u(c, q)$ the utility function of an individual with time-additive expected utility. Let the perishable good be the numeraire. Assume that consumption services derived from the durable good are proportional to the holdings of the good and that the holdings depreciate at a fixed rate. If $c = (c_t)_{t \in \mathcal{T}}$ denotes the individual's optimal consumption strategy for the perishable good and $q = (q_t)_{t \in \mathcal{T}}$ denotes* *the individual's consumption services optimally derived from the durable good, then c and q satisfy Eq. (6.30), and the process $\zeta = (\zeta_t)_{t\in\mathcal{T}}$ defined by*

$$\zeta_t = e^{-\delta t}\frac{u_c(c_t, q_t)}{u_c(c_0, q_0)}, \quad t = 0, 1, \ldots, T,$$

is a state-price deflator.

With the CES-type utility function

$$u(c, q) = \frac{1}{1-\gamma}\left(ac^{\frac{\psi-1}{\psi}} + bq^{\frac{\psi-1}{\psi}}\right)^{\frac{\psi}{\psi-1}(1-\gamma)},$$

the expressions (6.28) and (6.29) are still correct. Note, however, that the α_t in Eq. (6.29) can no longer be interpreted as an expenditure ratio since the consumption q_t differs from the purchases Q_t of the durable good.

6.4.3 Habit Formation and State-Dependent Preferences

Next let us consider a non-additive specification of preferences and for concreteness we study a single-good specification with habit formation. The objective of the individual is

$$\max_{\boldsymbol{\theta}=(\boldsymbol{\theta}_t)_{t=0,1,\ldots,T-1}} \mathrm{E}\left[\sum_{t=0}^{T} e^{-\delta t} u(c_t, h_t)\right],$$

where h_t is the habit level at time t. First assume that the habit level at time t is some fraction of the consumption level at time $t-1$,

$$h_t = \beta c_{t-1}, \quad t = 1, 2, \ldots, T,$$

and let $h_0 = 0$.

We apply the variational argument given earlier. Let $c = (c_t)_{t\in\mathcal{T}}$ denote the optimal consumption process, and let $h = (h_t)_{t\in\mathcal{T}}$ denote the resulting process for the habit level. What happens if the individual purchases $\varepsilon > 0$ units extra of asset i at time t and sells those ε units again at time $t+1$? Consumption at time t and $t+1$ will change to $c_t - \varepsilon P_{it}$ and $c_{t+1} + \varepsilon(D_{i,t+1} + P_{i,t+1})$, respectively. The perturbation will also affect the habit level. With the assumed habit formation, only the habit level at time $t+1$ and time $t+2$ will be changed. The new habit levels will be $h_{t+1} - \beta\varepsilon P_{it}$ at time $t+1$ and $h_{t+2} + \beta\varepsilon(D_{i,t+1} + P_{i,t+1})$ at time $t+2$. Therefore the change in total utility from time t and onwards will be

$$
\begin{aligned}
&u\left(c_t - \varepsilon P_{it}, h_t\right) - u(c_t, h_t) \\
&\quad + e^{-\delta}\,\mathrm{E}_t\left[u\big(c_{t+1} + \varepsilon(D_{i,t+1} + P_{i,t+1}), h_{t+1} - \beta\varepsilon P_{it}\big) - u\left(c_{t+1}, h_{t+1}\right)\right] \\
&\quad + e^{-2\delta}\,\mathrm{E}_t\left[u\big(c_{t+2}, h_{t+2} + \beta\varepsilon(D_{i,t+1} + P_{i,t+1})\big) - u(c_{t+2}, h_{t+2})\right] \leq 0.
\end{aligned}
$$

Dividing by ε and letting $\varepsilon \to 0$, we obtain

$$
\begin{aligned}
&- P_{it} u_c(c_t, h_t) + e^{-\delta}\,\mathrm{E}_t\left[u_c(c_{t+1}, h_{t+1})\left(D_{i,t+1} + P_{i,t+1}\right) - \beta P_{it} u_h(c_{t+1}, h_{t+1})\right] \\
&+ e^{-2\delta}\,\mathrm{E}_t\left[u_h(c_{t+2}, h_{t+2})\beta\left(D_{i,t+1} + P_{i,t+1}\right)\right] \leq 0.
\end{aligned}
$$

Again the opposite inequality can be reached by a similar argument. Replacing the inequality sign with an equality sign and rearranging, we arrive at

$$
\begin{aligned}
&P_{it}\left(u_c(c_t, h_t) + \beta e^{-\delta}\,\mathrm{E}_t\left[u_h(c_{t+1}, h_{t+1})\right]\right) \\
&= e^{-\delta}\,\mathrm{E}_t\left[\left(u_c(c_{t+1}, h_{t+1}) + \beta e^{-\delta} u_h(c_{t+2}, h_{t+2})\right)\left(D_{i,t+1} + P_{i,t+1}\right)\right] \\
&= e^{-\delta}\,\mathrm{E}_t\left[\left(u_c(c_{t+1}, h_{t+1}) + \beta e^{-\delta}\,\mathrm{E}_{t+1}[u_h(c_{t+2}, h_{t+2})]\right)\left(D_{i,t+1} + P_{i,t+1}\right)\right],
\end{aligned}
$$

where the last equality is due to the Law of Iterated Expectations. Consequently,

$$
P_{it} = \mathrm{E}_t\left[e^{-\delta}\frac{u_c(c_{t+1}, h_{t+1}) + \beta e^{-\delta}\,\mathrm{E}_{t+1}[u_h(c_{t+2}, h_{t+2})]}{u_c(c_t, h_t) + \beta e^{-\delta}\,\mathrm{E}_t\left[u_h(c_{t+1}, h_{t+1})\right]}\left(D_{i,t+1} + P_{i,t+1}\right)\right],
$$

and a state-price deflator can be defined by

$$
\zeta_t = e^{-\delta t}\frac{u_c(c_t, h_t) + \beta e^{-\delta}\,\mathrm{E}_t[u_h(c_{t+1}, h_{t+1})]}{u_c(c_0, h_0) + \beta e^{-\delta}\,\mathrm{E}\left[u_h(c_1, h_1)\right]}.
$$

Note that if $\beta = 0$ we are back to the case of time-additive utility.

It is probably more realistic that the habit level at time t depends on all the previous consumption rates but in such a way that the consumption in recent periods is more important for the habit level than consumption in the far past. This can be captured by a specification like

$$
h_t = \sum_{s=0}^{t-1} \beta^{t-s} c_s, \quad t = 1, 2, \ldots, T, \tag{6.31}
$$

where β is a constant between 0 and 1. A change in the consumption at time t will now affect the habit levels at all future dates $t+1, t+2, \ldots, T$. Following the same line of argumentation as above, we can show the following result:

Theorem 6.9 *In a discrete-time, arbitrage-free economy with a single consumption good, let δ be the time preference rate and $u(c,h)$ the utility function of an individual with habit formation, where the habit is given by Eq. (6.31). If $c = (c_t)_{t\in\mathcal{T}}$ denotes the optimal consumption plan of the individual and $h = (h_t)_{t\in\mathcal{T}}$ is the associated habit process, then the process $\zeta = (\zeta_t)_{t\in\mathcal{T}}$ defined by*

$$\zeta_t = e^{-\delta t} \frac{u_c(c_t, h_t) + \sum_{s=1}^{T-t} \beta^s e^{-\delta s} \mathrm{E}_t[u_h(c_{t+s}, h_{t+s})]}{u_c(c_0, h_0) + \sum_{s=1}^{T} \beta^s e^{-\delta s} \mathrm{E}\left[u_h(c_s, h_s)\right]}, \quad t = 0, 1, \dots, T, \tag{6.32}$$

is a state-price deflator.

Unfortunately, the complicated expression (6.32) for the state-price deflator makes it very difficult to work with. Consequently, only a few studies consider asset pricing models with habit formation. A much more tractable alternative is to keep a utility function of the form $u(c, h)$, but then assume that h is an exogenous variable not affected by the individual's decisions. For example, h could be a measure of the general standard of living in the economy in line with the idea of 'keeping up with the Joneses' mentioned in Section 5.7.2. Then we are back to the case of time-additive expected utility with the only exception that all marginal utilities now depend on the level of the exogenous variable:

Theorem 6.10 *In a discrete-time, arbitrage-free economy with a single consumption good, let δ be the time preference rate and $u(c, X)$ the utility function of an individual with time-additive preferences depending on some exogenous stochastic process $X = (X_t)_{t \in \mathcal{T}}$. If $c = (c_t)_{t \in \mathcal{T}}$ denotes the optimal consumption plan of the individual, then the process $\zeta = (\zeta_t)_{t \in \mathcal{T}}$ defined by*

$$\zeta_t = e^{-\delta t} \frac{u_c(c_t, X_t)}{u_c(c_0, X_0)}, \quad t = 0, 1, \dots, T,$$

is a state-price deflator.

Note that some authors also use the term 'habit formation' or 'external habit formation' for state-dependent preferences, although it is really something different.

6.4.4 Recursive Utility

Now assume that preferences are represented by a utility index $\mathcal{U}_t$ defined recursively by

$$\mathcal{U}_t = f\left(c_t, q_t(\mathcal{U}_{t+1})\right)$$

as introduced in Section 5.7.3. Extrapolating the intuition and results of the preceding sections, the state-price deflator ζ_{t+1}/ζ_t over the period between time t and time $t+1$ should be given by the marginal rate of substitution. This is generally the ratio between the marginal utility of consumption at time $t+1$ to the marginal utility of consumption at time t. With recursive preferences, this means

$$\frac{\zeta_{t+1}}{\zeta_t} = \frac{\partial \mathcal{U}_t / \partial c_{t+1}}{\partial \mathcal{U}_t / \partial c_t}.$$

Note that

$$\frac{\partial \mathcal{U}_t}{\partial c_t} = f_c\left(c_t, q_t(\mathcal{U}_{t+1})\right)$$

for any t. To simplify the expression for $\partial \mathcal{U}_t / \partial c_{t+1}$, we assume from now on that

$$q_t(\mathcal{U}_{t+1}) = \left(\mathrm{E}_t[\mathcal{U}_{t+1}^{1-\gamma}]\right)^{\frac{1}{1-\gamma}},$$

as in (5.17). Then

$$q_t'(\mathcal{U}_{t+1}) = \left(\mathrm{E}_t[\mathcal{U}_{t+1}^{1-\gamma}]\right)^{\frac{1}{1-\gamma}-1} \mathcal{U}_{t+1}^{-\gamma} = q_t(\mathcal{U}_{t+1})^{\gamma} \mathcal{U}_{t+1}^{-\gamma}$$

so the chain rule implies

$$\begin{aligned} \frac{\partial \mathcal{U}_t}{\partial c_{t+1}} &= f_q\left(c_t, q_t(\mathcal{U}_{t+1})\right) q_t'(\mathcal{U}_{t+1}) \frac{\partial \mathcal{U}_{t+1}}{\partial c_{t+1}} \\ &= f_q\left(c_t, q_t(\mathcal{U}_{t+1})\right) q_t(\mathcal{U}_{t+1})^{\gamma} \mathcal{U}_{t+1}^{-\gamma} f_c\left(c_{t+1}, q_{t+1}(\mathcal{U}_{t+2})\right). \end{aligned}$$

Hence, the state-price deflator with recursive utility is conjectured to be

$$\frac{\zeta_{t+1}}{\zeta_t} = f_q\left(c_t, q_t(\mathcal{U}_{t+1})\right) \left(\frac{\mathcal{U}_{t+1}}{q_t(\mathcal{U}_{t+1})}\right)^{-\gamma} \frac{f_c\left(c_{t+1}, q_{t+1}(\mathcal{U}_{t+2})\right)}{f_c\left(c_t, q_t(\mathcal{U}_{t+1})\right)}, \tag{6.33}$$

where the right-hand side is evaluated at the optimal consumption process. In Section 6.6.2 we confirm that Eq. (6.33) does indeed define a state-price deflator.

Recall from Section 5.7.3 that recursive utility with $f(c,q) = u(c) + e^{-\delta} q$ and $\gamma = 0$ collapses to time-additive expected utility. In this case $f_c(c,q) = u'(c)$ and $f_q(c,q) = e^{-\delta}$, so indeed the state-price deflator above reduces to $e^{-\delta} u'(c_{t+1})/u'(c_t)$.

From (5.19), Epstein–Zin preferences correspond to

$$f(c,q) = \left(ac^{\frac{1-\gamma}{\theta}} + bq^{\frac{1-\gamma}{\theta}}\right)^{\frac{\theta}{1-\gamma}}.$$

In this case, the derivatives are

$$f_c(c,q) = ac^{\frac{1-\gamma}{\theta}-1} \left(ac^{\frac{1-\gamma}{\theta}} + bq^{\frac{1-\gamma}{\theta}}\right)^{\frac{\theta}{1-\gamma}-1} = ac^{-1/\psi} f(c,q)^{1/\psi}, \tag{6.34}$$

$$f_q(c,q) = bq^{\frac{1-\gamma}{\theta}-1} \left(ac^{\frac{1-\gamma}{\theta}} + bq^{\frac{1-\gamma}{\theta}}\right)^{\frac{\theta}{1-\gamma}-1} = bq^{-1/\psi} f(c,q)^{1/\psi},$$

where we have used the relation $1 - (1-\gamma)/\theta = 1/\psi$. In particular,

$$f_c\left(c_{t+1}, q_{t+1}(\mathcal{U}_{t+2})\right) = ac_{t+1}^{-1/\psi} f\left(c_{t+1}, q_{t+1}(\mathcal{U}_{t+2})\right)^{1/\psi} \doteq ac_{t+1}^{-1/\psi} \mathcal{U}_{t+1}^{1/\psi}.$$

Substituting these derivatives in Eq. (6.33) for the state-price deflator can be reduced to

$$\frac{\zeta_{t+1}}{\zeta_t} = b\left(\frac{c_{t+1}}{c_t}\right)^{-1/\psi}\left(\frac{\mathcal{U}_{t+1}}{q_t(\mathcal{U}_{t+1})}\right)^{\frac{1}{\psi}-\gamma}. \tag{6.35}$$

In particular, for $\gamma = 1/\psi$ and $b = e^{-\delta}$ we are back to the previously found state-price deflator for time-additive CRRA utility.

While the expression (6.35) for the state-price deflator is nice, the dependence on the (unobservable) future utility index makes it hard to apply. As we shall demonstrate in Section 6.6.2, the state-price deflator can be restated in terms of the consumption growth and the return R^W_{t+1} on the optimally invested wealth as

$$\frac{\zeta_{t+1}}{\zeta_t} = b^{\theta}\left(\frac{c_{t+1}}{c_t}\right)^{-\theta/\psi}\left(R^W_{t+1}\right)^{\theta-1} = e^{-\delta\theta}\left(\frac{c_{t+1}}{c_t}\right)^{-\theta/\psi}\left(R^W_{t+1}\right)^{\theta-1},$$

where we have replaced b by $e^{-\delta}$.

6.5 THE CONTINUOUS-TIME FRAMEWORK

In a continuous-time setting an individual consumes according to a non-negative continuous-time process $c = (c_t)_{t\in\mathcal{T}}$, where $\mathcal{T} = [0, T]$. Suppose that the preferences of the individual are described by time-additive expected utility so that the objective is to maximize $\mathrm{E}[\int_0^T e^{-\delta t}u(c_t)\,dt]$.

We will again go through a variational argument giving a link between the optimal consumption process and asset prices. For simplicity assume that assets pay no intermediate dividends. Suppose $c = (c_t)$ is the optimal consumption process for some agent and consider the following deviation from this strategy: at time 0 increase the investment in asset i by ε units. The extra costs of εP_{i0} imply a reduced consumption now. Let us suppose that the individual finances this extra investment by cutting down the consumption rate in the time interval $[0, \Delta t]$ for some small positive Δt by $\varepsilon P_{i0}/\Delta t$. The extra ε units of asset i are resold at time $t < T$, yielding a revenue of εP_{it}. This finances an increase in the consumption rate over $[t, t+\Delta t]$ by $\varepsilon P_{it}/\Delta t$. The consumption rates outside the intervals $[0, \Delta t]$ and $[t, t+\Delta t]$ will be unaffected. Given the optimality of $c = (c_t)$, we must have that

$$\mathrm{E}\Bigg[\int_0^{\Delta t} e^{-\delta s}\left(u\left(c_s - \frac{\varepsilon P_{i0}}{\Delta t}\right) - u(c_s)\right) ds + \int_t^{t+\Delta t} e^{-\delta s}\left(u\left(c_s + \frac{\varepsilon P_{it}}{\Delta t}\right) - u(c_s)\right) ds\Bigg] \leq 0.$$

Dividing by ε and letting $\varepsilon \to 0$, we obtain

$$\mathrm{E}\left[-\frac{P_{i0}}{\Delta t}\int_0^{\Delta t} e^{-\delta s}u'(c_s)\,ds + \frac{P_{it}}{\Delta t}\int_t^{t+\Delta t} e^{-\delta s}u'(c_s)\,ds\right] \le 0.$$

Letting $\Delta t \to 0$, we arrive at

$$\mathrm{E}\left[-P_{i0}u'(c_0) + P_{it}e^{-\delta t}u'(c_t)\right] \le 0,$$

or, equivalently,

$$P_{i0}u'(c_0) \ge \mathrm{E}\left[e^{-\delta t}P_{it}u'(c_t)\right].$$

The reverse inequality can be shown similarly so, in total, we have that $P_{i0}u'(c_0) = \mathrm{E}[e^{-\delta t}P_{it}u'(c_t)]$ or, more generally, the continuous-time (consumption) Euler equation

$$P_{it} = \mathrm{E}_t\left[e^{-\delta(t'-t)}\frac{u'(c_{t'})}{u'(c_t)}P_{it'}\right], \quad t \le t' \le T.$$

With intermediate dividends this relation is slightly more complicated:

$$P_{it} = \mathrm{E}_t\left[\int_t^{t'} \delta_{is}P_{is}e^{-\delta(s-t)}\frac{u'(c_s)}{u'(c_t)}\,ds + e^{-\delta(t'-t)}\frac{u'(c_{t'})}{u'(c_t)}P_{it'}\right].$$

A comparison with (4.27) leads to the following conclusion:

Theorem 6.11 *In a continuous-time, arbitrage-free economy with a single consumption good, let δ be the time preference rate and u the utility function of an individual with time-additive expected utility. If $c = (c_t)_{t\in\mathcal{T}}$ denotes the optimal consumption plan of the individual, then the process $\zeta = (\zeta_t)_{t\in\mathcal{T}}$ defined by*

$$\zeta_t = e^{-\delta t}\frac{u'(c_t)}{u'(c_0)}, \quad t \in [0,T], \tag{6.36}$$

is a state-price deflator.

Note that the continuous-time state-price deflator in Eq. (6.36) is identical to the discrete-time state-price deflator in Eq. (6.27).

If the market is complete, we can easily reach Eq. (6.36) by solving step one of the two-step procedure suggested in Section 6.2.4. The problem is

$$\max_{c=(c_t)} \mathrm{E}\left[\int_0^T e^{-\delta t}u(c_t)\,dt\right] \quad \text{s.t. } \mathrm{E}\left[\int_0^T \zeta_t c_t\,dt\right] \le e_0 + \mathrm{E}\left[\int_0^T \zeta_t e_t\,dt\right],$$

where $\zeta = (\zeta_t)$ is the unique state-price deflator. The left-hand side of the constraint is the present value of the consumption process, the right-hand side is the sum of the initial wealth e_0 and the present value of the income process. The Lagrangian for this problem is

$$\begin{aligned}\mathcal{L} &= \mathrm{E}\left[\int_0^T e^{-\delta t} u(c_t)\,dt\right] + \alpha\left(e_0 + \mathrm{E}\left[\int_0^T \zeta_t e_t\,dt\right] - \mathrm{E}\left[\int_0^T \zeta_t c_t\,dt\right]\right) \\ &= \alpha\left(e_0 + \mathrm{E}\left[\int_0^T \zeta_t e_t\,dt\right]\right) + \mathrm{E}\left[\int_0^T \left(e^{-\delta t} u(c_t) - \alpha\zeta_t c_t\right)\,dt\right].\end{aligned}$$

By maximizing the integrand in the last integral above for each t and each state, we will surely maximize the Lagrangian. The first-order condition is $e^{-\delta t} u'(c_t) = \alpha\zeta_t$. Since $\zeta_0 = 1$, Eq. (6.36) follows.

We will confirm the above result in Section 6.7, where we shall also consider stochastic differential utility. Exercise 6.10 considers an individual with habit formation in a continuous-time setting.

6.6 DYNAMIC PROGRAMMING IN DISCRETE TIME

Above we have linked the optimal consumption plan of an individual to asset prices. In Chapter 8 we will see how this leads to consumption-based asset pricing models. While this link is quite intuitive and theoretically elegant, empirical tests and practical applications of the model suffer from the fact that available data on individual or aggregate consumption may be of poor quality. For that purpose it is tempting to link asset prices to other variables for which better data are available. One way to provide such a link is to explain optimal consumption in terms of other variables. If c_t is a function of some variable, say x_t, then the equations derived earlier in this chapter prove a link between asset prices and x.

In order to figure out what explains the consumption choice of an individual, we have to dig deeper into the utility maximization problem. The dynamic programming approach is one method for solving multiperiod dynamic decisions problems and will indeed lead to a useful expression for the optimal consumption strategy. Along the way we will also find interesting conclusions on the optimal trading strategy of the individual, and we will confirm the link between optimal consumption and state-price deflators derived earlier in this chapter.

In this section we focus on the discrete-time framework, whereas the next section covers continuous time. The basic references for the discrete-time models are Samuelson (1969), Hakansson (1970), Fama (1970, 1976), and (Ingersoll, 1987, Ch. 11). We begin with the case of time-additive expected utility and later extend the analysis to recursive utility.

6.6.1 Time-Additive Expected Utility

A central element of the analysis is the *indirect utility* of the individual, which is defined as the maximum expected utility of current and future consumption. In the discrete-time case with time-additive expected utility, the indirect utility at time t is defined as

$$J_t = \sup_{(c_s,\boldsymbol{\theta}_s)_{s=t}^T} \mathrm{E}_t\left[\sum_{s=t}^{T} e^{-\delta(s-t)} u(c_s)\right]. \tag{6.37}$$

There is no portfolio chosen at the final date so we can fix $\boldsymbol{\theta}_T = \mathbf{0}$. Consumption at the final date is equal to the time T value of the portfolio purchased at $T-1$.

For tractability it is necessary to assume that the indirect utility is a function of a limited number of variables. Surely the indirect utility of a finitely-lived individual will depend on the length of the remaining life and therefore on calendar time t. The indirect utility at a given time t will also depend on the wealth W_t of the individual at that point in time. Higher wealth allows for higher current consumption and larger investments that generate more consumption in the future. Other variables containing information about current and future investment opportunities or current and future income may have to be added. Suppose for notational simplicity that the extra information can be captured by a single variable x_t so that (W_t, x_t) together is a Markov process. In that case the indirect utility is of the form

$$J_t = J(W_t, x_t, t)$$

for some function J.

We show below that the optimal consumption strategy will satisfy the so-called *envelope condition*:

$$u'(c_t) = J_W(W_t, x_t, t), \tag{6.38}$$

where J_W is the partial derivative of J with respect to W. This is an intuitive optimality condition. The left-hand side is the marginal utility of an extra unit of consumption at time t. The right-hand side is the marginal utility from investing an extra unit at time t in the optimal way. In an optimum these marginal utilities have to be equal. If that was not the case, the allocation of wealth between consumption and investment should be reconsidered. For example, if $u'(c_t) > J_W(W_t, x_t, t)$, the consumption c_t should be increased and the amount invested should be decreased. Using the envelope condition, the state-price deflator derived from the individual's optimization problem can be rewritten as

$$\zeta_t = e^{-\delta t}\frac{u'(c_t)}{u'(c_0)} = e^{-\delta t}\frac{J_W(W_t, x_t, t)}{J_W(W_0, x_0, 0)},$$

which links state prices to the optimally invested wealth of the individual and the variable x_t. This will be useful in constructing factor models in Chapter 10.

Assume that a risk-free and d risky assets are traded. Let $\boldsymbol{\theta}_t$ denote the d-vector of units invested in the risky assets at time t, and let θ_{0t} denote the units of the risk-free asset. Assume for simplicity that the assets do not pay intermediate dividends. In accordance with Eq. (3.12), the change in the wealth of the individual between time t and time $t+1$ is

$$W_{t+1} - W_t = \sum_{i=0}^{d} \theta_{it} \left(P_{i,t+1} - P_{it} \right) + y_t - c_t,$$

where y_t denotes the income received at time t. After receiving income and consuming at time t, the funds invested will be $W_t + y_t - c_t$. Assuming this is positive, we can represent the portfolio in terms of the fractions of this total investment invested in the different assets, that is

$$\pi_{it} = \frac{\theta_{it} P_{it}}{W_t + y_t - c_t}, \qquad i = 0, 1, \dots, d.$$

Define the portfolio weight vector of the risky assets by $\boldsymbol{\pi}_t = (\pi_{1t}, \dots, \pi_{dt})^\top$. By construction the fraction $\pi_{0t} = 1 - \sum_{i=1}^{d} \pi_{it} = 1 - \boldsymbol{\pi}_t^\top \mathbf{1}$ of wealth is then invested in the risk-free asset. The wealth at the end of the period can then be restated as

$$\begin{aligned} W_{t+1} &= W_t + y_t - c_t + \sum_{i=0}^{d} \theta_{it} P_{it} r_{it} \\ &= \left(W_t + y_t - c_t \right) \left(1 + \sum_{i=0}^{d} \pi_{it} r_{it} \right) \\ &= \left(W_t + y_t - c_t \right) R^W_{t+1}, \end{aligned} \tag{6.39}$$

where

$$\begin{aligned} R^W_{t+1} &= 1 + \sum_{i=0}^{d} \pi_{it} r_{it} = 1 + r^f_t + \boldsymbol{\pi}_t^\top \left[\boldsymbol{r}_{t+1} - r^f_t \mathbf{1} \right] \\ &= R^f_t + \boldsymbol{\pi}_t^\top \left[\boldsymbol{R}_{t+1} - R^f_t \mathbf{1} \right] \end{aligned} \tag{6.40}$$

is the gross rate of return on the portfolio, r^f_t is the risk-free net rate of return, and $\boldsymbol{r}_{t+1}$ is the d-vector of the net rates of return of the risky assets over the period. Note that the only random variable (seen from time t) on the right-hand side of the above expressions is the vector of returns on the risky assets, that is either the net returns $\boldsymbol{r}_{t+1}$ or the gross returns $\boldsymbol{R}_{t+1}$.

In the definition of indirect utility in Eq. (6.37), the maximization is over both the current and all future consumption rates and portfolios. This is clearly a quite complicated maximization problem. Next, we show that we can alternatively perform a sequence of simpler maximization problems. This result is based on the following manipulations:

$$\begin{aligned}
J_t &= \sup_{(c_s,\pi_s)_{s=t}^T} \mathrm{E}_t\left[\sum_{s=t}^T e^{-\delta(s-t)} u(c_s)\right] \\
&= \sup_{(c_s,\pi_s)_{s=t}^T} \mathrm{E}_t\left[u(c_t) + \sum_{s=t+1}^T e^{-\delta(s-t)} u(c_s)\right] \\
&= \sup_{(c_s,\pi_s)_{s=t}^T} \mathrm{E}_t\left[u(c_t) + \mathrm{E}_{t+1}\left[\sum_{s=t+1}^T e^{-\delta(s-t)} u(c_s)\right]\right] \\
&= \sup_{(c_s,\pi_s)_{s=t}^T} \mathrm{E}_t\left[u(c_t) + e^{-\delta}\,\mathrm{E}_{t+1}\left[\sum_{s=t+1}^T e^{-\delta(s-(t+1))} u(c_s)\right]\right] \\
&= \sup_{c_t,\pi_t} \mathrm{E}_t\left[u(c_t) + e^{-\delta} \sup_{(c_s,\pi_s)_{s=t+1}^T} \mathrm{E}_{t+1}\left[\sum_{s=t+1}^T e^{-\delta(s-(t+1))} u(c_s)\right]\right].
\end{aligned}$$

Here, the first equality is simply due to the definition of indirect utility in Eq. (6.37), now representing the portfolio by $\boldsymbol{\pi}_s$ instead of $\boldsymbol{\theta}_s$. The second equality comes from separating out the first term of the sum. The third equality is valid according to the Law of Iterated Expectations, the fourth comes from separating out the discount term $e^{-\delta}$, and the final equality is due to the fact that only the inner expectation depends on future consumption rates and portfolios. Noting that the inner supremum is by definition the indirect utility at time $t+1$, we arrive at

$$J_t = \sup_{c_t,\pi_t} \mathrm{E}_t\left[u(c_t) + e^{-\delta} J_{t+1}\right] = \sup_{c_t,\pi_t} \left\{u(c_t) + e^{-\delta}\,\mathrm{E}_t\left[J_{t+1}\right]\right\}. \tag{6.41}$$

This equation is called the *Bellman Equation*, and the indirect utility J is said to have the *dynamic programming property*. The decision to be taken at time t is split up in two: (1) the consumption and portfolio decision for the current period and (2) the consumption and portfolio decisions for all future periods. We take the decision for the current period assuming that we will make optimal decisions in all future periods. Note that this does not imply that the decision for the current period is taken independently from future decisions. We take into account the effect that our current decision has on the maximum expected utility we can get from all future periods. The expectation $\mathrm{E}_t\left[J_{t+1}\right]$ will depend on our choice of c_t and $\boldsymbol{\pi}_t$.[2]

The dynamic programming property is the basis for a backward iterative solution procedure. First, we assume that all terminal wealth is used for consumption so that $J_T = u(c_T) = u(W_T)$, and c_{T-1} and $\boldsymbol{\pi}_{T-1}$ are chosen to maximize

$$u(c_{T-1}) + e^{-\delta}\,\mathrm{E}_{T-1}\left[u(W_T)\right],$$

where

$$W_T = \left(W_{T-1} + y_{T-1} - c_{T-1}\right) R_T^W, \quad R_T^W = 1 + r_{T-1}^f + \boldsymbol{\pi}_{T-1}^{\top}\left[\boldsymbol{r}_T - r_{T-1}^f \mathbf{1}\right].$$

This is done for each possible scenario at time $T-1$ and gives us J_{T-1}. Then c_{T-2} and $\boldsymbol{\pi}_{T-2}$ are chosen to maximize

$$u(c_{T-2}) + e^{-\delta}\,\mathrm{E}_{T-2}\left[J_{T-1}\right],$$

and so on until time zero is reached. Since we have to perform a maximization for each scenario of the world at every point in time, we have to make assumptions on the possible scenarios at each point in time before we can implement the recursive procedure. The optimal decisions at any time are expected to depend on the wealth level of the agent at that date, but also on the value of other time-varying state variables that affect future returns on investment (for example the interest rate level) and future income levels. To be practically implementable only a few state variables can be incorporated. Also, these state variables must follow Markov processes so only the current values of the variables are relevant for the maximization at a given point in time.

Suppose that the relevant information is captured by a one-dimensional Markov process $x = (x_t)$ so that the indirect utility at any time $t = 0, 1, \dots, T$ can be written as $J_t = J(W_t, x_t, t)$. Then the dynamic programming equation (6.41) becomes

$$J(W_t, x_t, t) = \sup_{c_t, \boldsymbol{\pi}_t}\left\{u(c_t) + e^{-\delta}\,\mathrm{E}_t\left[J(W_{t+1}, x_{t+1}, t+1)\right]\right\}$$

with terminal condition $J(W_T, x_T, T) = u(W_T)$. When maximizing, we have to remember that W_{t+1} will be affected by the choice of c_t and $\boldsymbol{\pi}_t$, compare Eq. (6.39). In particular, we see that

$$\frac{\partial W_{t+1}}{\partial c_t} = -R_{t+1}^W, \qquad \frac{\partial W_{t+1}}{\partial \boldsymbol{\pi}_t} = \left(W_t + y_t - c_t\right)\left(\boldsymbol{r}_{t+1} - r_t^f \mathbf{1}\right). \tag{6.42}$$

[2] Readers familiar with option pricing theory may note the similarity to the problem of determining the optimal exercise strategy of a Bermudan/American option. However, for that problem the decision to be taken is much simpler (exercise or not) than for the consumption/portfolio problem.

The first-order condition for the maximization with respect to c_t is

$$u'(c_t) + e^{-\delta} \operatorname{E}_t \left[J_W(W_{t+1}, x_{t+1}, t+1) \frac{\partial W_{t+1}}{\partial c_t} \right] = 0,$$

which implies that

$$u'(c_t) = e^{-\delta} \operatorname{E}_t \left[J_W(W_{t+1}, x_{t+1}, t+1) R^W_{t+1} \right]. \tag{6.43}$$

The first-order condition for the maximization with respect to $\boldsymbol{\pi}_t$ is

$$\operatorname{E}_t \left[J_W(W_{t+1}, x_{t+1}, t+1) \frac{\partial W_{t+1}}{\partial \boldsymbol{\pi}_t} \right] = 0,$$

which leads to

$$\operatorname{E}_t \left[J_W(W_{t+1}, x_{t+1}, t+1) \left(\boldsymbol{r}_{t+1} - r^f_t \boldsymbol{1} \right) \right] = 0. \tag{6.44}$$

While we cannot generally solve explicitly for the optimal decisions, we can show that the envelope condition (6.38) holds. First note that for the optimal choice $\hat{c}_t, \hat{\boldsymbol{\pi}}_t$ we have that

$$J(W_t, x_t, t) = u(\hat{c}_t) + e^{-\delta} \operatorname{E}_t \left[J(\hat{W}_{t+1}, x_{t+1}, t+1) \right], \tag{6.45}$$

where $\hat{W}_{t+1}$ is next period's wealth using $\hat{c}_t, \hat{\boldsymbol{\pi}}_t$. Taking derivatives with respect to W_t in this equation, and acknowledging that $\hat{c}_t$ and $\hat{\boldsymbol{\pi}}_t$ will in general depend on W_t, we get

$$J_W(W_t, x_t, t) = u'(\hat{c}_t) \frac{\partial \hat{c}_t}{\partial W_t} + e^{-\delta} \operatorname{E}_t \left[J_W(\hat{W}_{t+1}, x_{t+1}, t+1) \frac{\partial \hat{W}_{t+1}}{\partial W_t} \right],$$

where

$$\frac{\partial \hat{W}_{t+1}}{\partial W_t} = R^W_{t+1} \left(1 - \frac{\partial \hat{c}_t}{\partial W_t} \right) + (W_t + y_t - c_t) \left(\frac{\partial \hat{\boldsymbol{\pi}}_t}{\partial W_t} \right)^{\top} \left(\boldsymbol{r}_{t+1} - r^f_t \boldsymbol{1} \right). \tag{6.46}$$

Inserting this and rearranging terms, we get

$$\begin{aligned} J_W(W_t, x_t, t) &= e^{-\delta} \operatorname{E}_t \left[J_W(\hat{W}_{t+1}, x_{t+1}, t+1) R^W_{t+1} \right] \\ &+ \left(u'(\hat{c}_t) - e^{-\delta} \operatorname{E}_t \left[J_W(\hat{W}_{t+1}, x_{t+1}, t+1) R^W_{t+1} \right] \right) \frac{\partial \hat{c}_t}{\partial W_t} \\ &+ (W_t + y_t - c_t)\, e^{-\delta} \left(\frac{\partial \hat{\boldsymbol{\pi}}_t}{\partial W_t} \right)^{\top} \operatorname{E}_t \left[J_W(\hat{W}_{t+1}, x_{t+1}, t+1) \left(\boldsymbol{r}_{t+1} - r^f_t \boldsymbol{1} \right) \right]. \end{aligned}$$

On the right-hand side the last two terms are zero due to the first-order conditions and only the leading term remains, that is

$$J_W(W_t, x_t, t) = e^{-\delta} \mathrm{E}_t \left[J(\hat{W}_{t+1}, x_{t+1}, t+1) R^W_{t+1} \right].$$

Combining this with Eq. (6.43) we have the envelope condition (6.38).

Let us verify that the dynamic programming approach leads to the Euler Equation (6.26). By substituting Eq. (6.40) into Eq. (6.43), we obtain

$$\begin{aligned} u'(c_t) &= e^{-\delta} \mathrm{E}_t \left[J_W(W_{t+1}, x_{t+1}, t+1) \left(1 + r^f_t + \boldsymbol{\pi}_t^\top (\boldsymbol{r}_{t+1} - r^f_t \mathbf{1}) \right) \right] \\ &= e^{-\delta} \left(1 + r^f_t \right) \mathrm{E}_t \left[J_W(W_{t+1}, x_{t+1}, t+1) \right] \\ &\quad + e^{-\delta} \boldsymbol{\pi}_t^\top \mathrm{E}_t \left[J_W(W_{t+1}, x_{t+1}, t+1) (\boldsymbol{r}_{t+1} - r^f_t \mathbf{1}) \right] \\ &= e^{-\delta} R^f_t \mathrm{E}_t \left[J_W(W_{t+1}, x_{t+1}, t+1) \right], \end{aligned}$$

where we have exploited Eq. (6.44) and introduced the gross risk-free return $R^f_t = 1 + r^f_t$. Equation (6.44) also implies that, for any asset i,

$$\mathrm{E}_t \left[J_W(W_{t+1}, x_{t+1}, t+1) \left(r_{i,t+1} - r^f_t \right) \right] = 0,$$

and since the difference between two net returns is the same as the difference between the gross returns, we get

$$\mathrm{E}_t \left[J_W(W_{t+1}, x_{t+1}, t+1) R_{i,t+1} \right] = R^f_t \mathrm{E}_t \left[J_W(W_{t+1}, x_{t+1}, t+1) \right].$$

Hence, we obtain

$$u'(c_t) = e^{-\delta} \mathrm{E}_t \left[J_W(W_{t+1}, x_{t+1}, t+1) R_{i,t+1} \right].$$

If we use the envelope condition on the right-hand side of this expression and substitute in the definition of the gross return, $R_{i,t+1} = (P_{i,t+1} + D_{i,t+1})/P_{it}$, we arrive at

$$u'(c_t) = \mathrm{E}_t \left[e^{-\delta} u'(c_{t+1}) \frac{P_{i,t+1} + D_{i,t+1}}{P_{it}} \right],$$

which coincides with the Euler Equation (6.26) and confirms the link between marginal utilities and state-price deflators found earlier. We summarize our findings in the following theorem:

Theorem 6.12 *In a discrete-time setting, the optimal consumption strategy of an individual with time-additive expected utility satisfies the envelope condition (6.38). The optimal investment strategy is such that Eq. (6.44) holds. In these expressions, $J(W, x, t)$ is the indirect utility function which satisfies the recursive* *relation (6.45) with terminal condition $J(W,x,T) = u(W)$. Moreover, a state-price deflator is defined by*

$$\zeta_t = e^{-\delta t}\frac{u'(c_t)}{u'(c_0)} = e^{-\delta t}\frac{J_W(W_t,x_t,t)}{J_W(W_0,x_0,0)},$$

where c is optimal consumption and W is wealth under the optimal consumption and investment strategy.

Next, we extend these results to the case of recursive utility.

6.6.2 Recursive Utility

As in Eqs. (5.15) and (5.17), suppose the utility index $\mathcal{U}_t$ associated with a given consumption and investment strategy is defined recursively by

$$\mathcal{U}_t = f\left(c_t, q_t(\mathcal{U}_{t+1})\right), \quad q_t(\mathcal{U}_{t+1}) = \left(\mathrm{E}_t[\mathcal{U}_{t+1}^{1-\gamma}]\right)^{\frac{1}{1-\gamma}} \tag{6.47}$$

with a terminal condition of the form

$$\mathcal{U}_T = u(c_T).$$

The indirect utility is then $J_t = \sup \mathcal{U}_t$, where the maximization is over all feasible consumption and investment strategies from time t onwards. Assuming again that $J_t = J(W_t, x_t, t)$ at all dates t, the Bellman Equation now takes the following form:

$$J(W_t,x_t,t) = \sup_{c_t,\pi_t} f\left(c_t, \left(\mathrm{E}_t[J(W_{t+1},x_{t+1},t+1)^{1-\gamma}]\right)^{\frac{1}{1-\gamma}}\right). \tag{6.48}$$

The current consumption and portfolio choice still influences next period's wealth as in Eq. (6.39), which implies the derivatives in Eq. (6.42). At the terminal date, we assume all wealth is spent on consumption so that $J(W,x,T) = u(W)$. We proceed exactly as for time-additive expected utility.

Let f_c and f_q denote the derivatives of $f(c,q)$ with respect to the first and second variable, respectively. The first-order condition for c_t implies that

$$\begin{aligned} f_c\left(c_t, q_t(J_{t+1})\right) = f_q\left(c_t, q_t(J_{t+1})\right)&\left(\mathrm{E}_t[J_{t+1}^{1-\gamma}]\right)^{\gamma/(1-\gamma)} \\ &\times \mathrm{E}_t\left[J_{t+1}^{-\gamma} J_W(W_{t+1},x_{t+1},t+1) R_{t+1}^W\right]. \end{aligned} \tag{6.49}$$

The first-order condition for $\boldsymbol{\pi}_t$ leads to

$$\mathrm{E}_t\left[J_{t+1}^{-\gamma} J_W(W_{t+1},x_{t+1},t+1)\left(\boldsymbol{r}_{t+1} - r_t^f \mathbf{1}\right)\right] = 0. \tag{6.50}$$

These conditions implicitly characterize the optimal consumption and portfolio decision at time t, which we denote by $\hat{c}_t, \hat{\boldsymbol{\pi}}_t$. For the optimal decision, the Bellman Equation (6.48) holds without the supremum, that is

$$J(W_t, x_t, t) = f\left(\hat{c}_t, \left(\mathrm{E}_t[J(\hat{W}_{t+1}, x_{t+1}, t+1)^{1-\gamma}]\right)^{\frac{1}{1-\gamma}}\right), \tag{6.51}$$

where $\hat{W}_{t+1}$ is next period's wealth under the optimal consumption and portfolio decision at time t. Differentiation of the preceding equation with respect to W_t gives

$$\begin{aligned} J_W(W_t, x_t, t) &= f_c\left(\hat{c}_t, q_t(J_{t+1})\right) \frac{\partial \hat{c}_t}{\partial W_t} \\ &\quad + f_q\left(\hat{c}_t, q_t(J_{t+1})\right) q_t(J_{t+1})^{\gamma}\, \mathrm{E}_t\left[J_{t+1}^{-\gamma} J_W\left(\hat{W}_{t+1}, x_{t+1}, t+1\right) \frac{\partial \hat{W}_{t+1}}{\partial W_t}\right], \end{aligned}$$

where J_{t+1} is short for $J\left(\hat{W}_{t+1}, x_{t+1}, t+1\right)$. If we substitute Eq. (6.46) in and apply the first-order conditions (6.49) and (6.50), this expression simplifies to

$$\begin{aligned} J_W(W_t, x_t, t) &= f_q\left(\hat{c}_t, q_t(J_{t+1})\right) q_t(J_{t+1})^{\gamma} \\ &\quad \times \mathrm{E}_t\left[J_{t+1}^{-\gamma} J_W\left(\hat{W}_{t+1}, x_{t+1}, t+1\right) R^W_{t+1}\right]. \end{aligned} \tag{6.52}$$

Consequently, the first-order condition (6.49) for consumption can be rewritten as

$$f_c\left(c_t, q_t(J_{t+1})\right) = J_W(W_t, x_t, t). \tag{6.53}$$

This is the recursive utility version of the envelope condition.

Finally, we can deduce a state-price deflator from the individual's optimal decisions. Since we only consider the optimal strategies in what follows, we suppress the hat on consumption and wealth from now on. By substituting Eq. (6.40) into Eq. (6.52) and applying the optimality condition (6.50), we find that

$$J_W(W_t, x_t, t) = f_q\left(c_t, q_t(J_{t+1})\right) q_t(J_{t+1})^{\gamma}\, \mathrm{E}_t\left[J_{t+1}^{-\gamma} J_W\left(W_{t+1}, x_{t+1}, t+1\right) R_{i,t+1}\right]$$

for any risky asset i and similarly for the risk-free asset. Hence,

$$1 = \mathrm{E}_t\left[f_q\left(c_t, q_t(J_{t+1})\right) \left(\frac{J_{t+1}}{q_t(J_{t+1})}\right)^{-\gamma} \frac{J_W\left(W_{t+1}, x_{t+1}, t+1\right)}{J_W(W_t, x_t, t)} R_{i,t+1}\right].$$

Therefore,

$$\frac{\zeta_{t+1}}{\zeta_t} = f_q\left(c_t, q_t(J_{t+1})\right) \left(\frac{J_{t+1}}{q_t(J_{t+1})}\right)^{-\gamma} \frac{J_W\left(W_{t+1}, x_{t+1}, t+1\right)}{J_W(W_t, x_t, t)}$$

works as a state-price deflator over the period between t and $t+1$. Equivalently, a state-price deflator process is defined by

$$\zeta_t = \frac{J_W(W_t, x_t, t)}{J_W(W_0, x_0, 0)} \prod_{s=0}^{t-1} f_q\left(c_s, q_s(J_{s+1})\right) \left(\frac{J_{s+1}}{q_s(J_{s+1})}\right)^{-\gamma}, \tag{6.54}$$

where it is understood that optimal decisions are applied in the terms on the right-hand side. By help of the envelope condition (6.53), we can alternatively state these expressions as

$$\frac{\zeta_{t+1}}{\zeta_t} = f_q\left(c_t, q_t(J_{t+1})\right) \left(\frac{J_{t+1}}{q_t(J_{t+1})}\right)^{-\gamma} \frac{f_c\left(c_{t+1}, q_{t+1}(J_{t+2})\right)}{f_c\left(c_t, q_t(J_{t+1})\right)}$$

and

$$\zeta_t = \frac{f_c\left(c_t, q_t(J_{t+1})\right)}{f_c\left(c_0, q_0(J_1)\right)} \prod_{s=0}^{t-1} f_q\left(c_s, q_s(J_{s+1})\right) \left(\frac{J_{s+1}}{q_s(J_{s+1})}\right)^{-\gamma}, \tag{6.55}$$

again using optimal decisions on the right-hand side. This confirms the conjectured state-price deflator in Eq. (6.33).

We collect the above findings in the following theorem.

Theorem 6.13 *In a discrete-time setting, the optimal consumption strategy of an individual with recursive utility of the form* (6.47) *satisfies the envelope condition* (6.53). *The optimal investment strategy is such that Eq.* (6.50) *holds. In these expressions, $J(W, x, t)$ is the indirect utility function which satisfies the recursive relation* (6.51) *with terminal condition $J(W, x, T) = u(W)$. Moreover, a state-price deflator is defined by Eq.* (6.54) *or, equivalently, Eq.* (6.55).

In the case of Epstein–Zin preferences, the derivative $f_c(c, q)$ is given in (6.34) so that the envelope condition (6.53) leads to an optimal consumption rate of

$$c_t = a^{\psi} J(W_t, x_t, t) J_W(W_t, x_t, t)^{-\psi}.$$

The next-period state-price deflator simplifies to

$$\frac{\zeta_{t+1}}{\zeta_t} = b\left(\frac{c_{t+1}}{c_t}\right)^{-1/\psi} \left(\frac{J_{t+1}}{q_t(J_{t+1})}\right)^{\frac{1}{\psi}-\gamma} \tag{6.56}$$

as explained in Section 6.4.4.

Next, we want to rewrite the state-price deflator in terms of R^W_{t+1}, the gross return on optimally invested wealth over the period from time t to $t+1$, instead of the unobservable future utility index J_{t+1}. For this purpose, we need the following lemma:

Lemma 6.3 *With Epstein–Zin preferences and no labour income, the indirect utility satisfies*

$$J_t = f_c(c_t, q_t(J_{t+1}))W_t, \tag{6.57}$$

and the return on optimally invested wealth is

$$R^W_{t+1} = b^{-1}\left(\frac{c_{t+1}}{c_t}\right)^{1/\psi}\left(\frac{J_{t+1}}{q_t(J_{t+1})}\right)^{1-1/\psi}. \tag{6.58}$$

Proof. We have $W_{t+1} = (W_t - c_t)R^W_{t+1}$ in the absence of labour income. Since R^W_{t+1} is a return, we have

$$1 = \mathrm{E}_t\left[\frac{\zeta_{t+1}}{\zeta_t}R^W_{t+1}\right]$$

and hence

$$W_t = c_t + \mathrm{E}_t\left[\frac{\zeta_{t+1}}{\zeta_t}W_{t+1}\right]. \tag{6.59}$$

We will show that this recursive wealth relation is satisfied when $W_t = J_t/f_c(c_t, q_t(J_{t+1}))$ for all t. Because of Eq. (6.34), the conjecture is equivalent to

$$W_t = \frac{J_t}{f_c(c_t, q_t(J_{t+1}))} = \frac{1}{a}c_t^{1/\psi}J_t^{1-1/\psi}.$$

We substitute that and the state-price deflator (6.56) into the right-hand side of Eq. (6.59) and get

$$\begin{aligned}
\mathrm{E}_t\left[\frac{\zeta_{t+1}}{\zeta_t}W_{t+1}\right] &= \mathrm{E}_t\left[b\left(\frac{c_{t+1}}{c_t}\right)^{-1/\psi}\left(\frac{J_{t+1}}{q_t(J_{t+1})}\right)^{\frac{1}{\psi}-\gamma}\frac{1}{a}c_{t+1}^{1/\psi}J_{t+1}^{1-1/\psi}\right] \\
&= \frac{b}{a}c_t^{1/\psi}q_t(J_{t+1})^{\gamma-1/\psi}\,\mathrm{E}_t\left[J_{t+1}^{1-\gamma}\right] \\
&= \frac{b}{a}c_t^{1/\psi}q_t(J_{t+1})^{1-1/\psi}.
\end{aligned}$$

In order to verify Eq. (6.59), it remains to be shown that

$$\frac{1}{a}c_t^{1/\psi}J_t^{1-1/\psi} = c_t + \frac{b}{a}c_t^{1/\psi}q_t(J_{t+1})^{1-1/\psi}$$

or equivalently

$$J_t^{1-1/\psi} = ac_t^{1-1/\psi} + bq_t(J_{t+1})^{1-1/\psi}.$$

Since $1 - 1/\psi = (1-\gamma)/\theta$, this is satisfied because of the Epstein–Zin specification (5.20) of $J_t = f(c_t, q_t(J_{t+1}))$. This confirms Eq. (6.57).

The above computations imply that

$$W_t - c_t = \mathrm{E}_t\left[\frac{\zeta_{t+1}}{\zeta_t} W_{t+1}\right] = \frac{b}{a} c_t^{1/\psi} q_t(J_{t+1})^{1-1/\psi}.$$

Therefore, the return on wealth is

$$R^W_{t+1} = \frac{W_{t+1}}{W_t - c_t} = \frac{\frac{1}{a} c_{t+1}^{1/\psi} J_{t+1}^{1-1/\psi}}{\frac{b}{a} c_t^{1/\psi} q_t(J_{t+1})^{1-1/\psi}} = b^{-1}\left(\frac{c_{t+1}}{c_t}\right)^{1/\psi}\left(\frac{J_{t+1}}{q_t(J_{t+1})}\right)^{1-1/\psi}$$

as claimed. □

The return expression (6.58) implies that

$$\left(\frac{\mathcal{U}_{t+1}}{q_t(\mathcal{U}_{t+1})}\right)^{\frac{1}{\psi}-\gamma} = b^{\theta-1}\left(R^W_{t+1}\right)^{\theta-1}\left(\frac{c_{t+1}}{c_t}\right)^{(1-\theta)/\psi},$$

which allows us to restate the state-price deflator (6.56) in terms of consumption growth and return on wealth. If we replace b by $e^{-\delta}$, the result is as follows:

Theorem 6.14 *With Epstein–Zin preferences and no labour income,*

$$\frac{\zeta_{t+1}}{\zeta_t} = e^{-\delta\theta}\left(\frac{c_{t+1}}{c_t}\right)^{-\theta/\psi}\left(R^W_{t+1}\right)^{\theta-1},$$

defines a state-price deflator over the period from time t to time $t+1$, when the right-hand side is evaluated at the optimal consumption and investment decisions.

We shall apply this theorem in several model specifications in Chapter 9.

6.7 DYNAMIC PROGRAMMING IN CONTINUOUS TIME

In this section we develop the dynamic programming approach to dynamic consumption and investment decisions in continuous time. The basic references for the continuous-time models are Merton (1969, 1971, 1973b). More details and a lot of specific models are discussed in Munk (2012). First, we describe the general setting. Then we consider the case of time-additive expected utility, and finally we extend the analysis to the continuous-time version of recursive utility, namely stochastic differential utility.

6.7.1 The General Setting

As in the discrete-time setting above assume that an instantaneously risk-free asset with a continuously compounded risk-free rate of r^f_t and d risky assets are traded. We assume for simplicity that the assets pay no intermediate dividends and write their price dynamics as

$$dP_t = \operatorname{diag}(P_t)\left[\mu_t\,dt + \underline{\underline{\sigma}}_t\,dz_t\right],$$

where $z = (z_1, \ldots, z_d)^\top$ is a d-dimensional standard Brownian motion. We can write this componentwise as

$$dP_{it} = P_{it}\left[\mu_{it}\,dt + \sum_{j=1}^{d} \sigma_{ijt}\,dz_{jt}\right], \qquad i = 1, \ldots, d.$$

The instantaneous rate of return on asset i is given by dP_{it}/P_{it}. The d-vector $\mu_t = (\mu_{1t}, \ldots, \mu_{dt})^\top$ contains the expected rates of return and the $(d \times d)$-matrix $\underline{\underline{\sigma}}_t = (\sigma_{ijt})_{i,j=1}^{d}$ measures the sensitivities of the risky asset prices with respect to exogenous shocks so that the $(d \times d)$-matrix $\underline{\underline{\Sigma}}_t = \underline{\underline{\sigma}}_t \underline{\underline{\sigma}}_t^\top$ contains the variance and covariance rates of instantaneous rates of return. We assume that $\underline{\underline{\sigma}}_t$ is non-singular and, hence, we can define the market price of risk associated with z as

$$\lambda_t = \underline{\underline{\sigma}}_t^{-1}(\mu_t - r^f_t \mathbf{1})$$

so that

$$\mu_t = r^f_t \mathbf{1} + \underline{\underline{\sigma}}_t \lambda_t,$$

that is $\mu_{it} = r^f_t + \sum_{j=1}^{d} \sigma_{ijt}\lambda_{jt}$. We can now rewrite the price dynamics as

$$dP_t = \operatorname{diag}(P_t)\left[\left(r^f_t \mathbf{1} + \underline{\underline{\sigma}}_t \lambda_t\right)dt + \underline{\underline{\sigma}}_t\,dz_t\right].$$

We represent the trading strategy by the portfolio weight process $\pi = (\pi_t)$, where π_t is the d-vector of fractions of wealth invested in the d risky assets at time t. Again the weight of the risk-free asset is $\pi_{0t} = 1 - \pi_t^\top \mathbf{1} = 1 - \sum_{i=1}^{d} \pi_{it}$. Analogous to Eq. (3.14), the wealth dynamics can be written as

$$dW_t = W_t\left[r^f_t + \pi_t^\top \underline{\underline{\sigma}}_t \lambda_t\right]dt + \left[y_t - c_t\right]dt + W_t \pi_t^\top \underline{\underline{\sigma}}_t\,dz_t.$$

For simplicity we assume in the following that the agent receives no labour income, that is $y_t \equiv 0$. We also assume that a single variable x_t captures the time t information about investment opportunities so that, in particular,

$$r^f_t = r^f(x_t), \quad \mu_t = \mu(x_t, t), \quad \underline{\underline{\sigma}}_t = \underline{\underline{\sigma}}(x_t, t),$$

where r^f, $\boldsymbol{\mu}$, and $\underline{\underline{\sigma}}$ now (also) denote sufficiently well-behaved functions. The market price of risk is also given by the state variable:

$$\boldsymbol{\lambda}(x_t) = \underline{\underline{\sigma}}(x_t, t)^{-1} \left(\boldsymbol{\mu}(x_t, t) - r^f(x_t)\mathbf{1} \right).$$

Note that we have assumed that the short-term interest rate r_t^f and the market price of risk vector $\boldsymbol{\lambda}_t$ do not depend on calendar time directly. The fluctuations in r_t^f and $\boldsymbol{\lambda}_t$ over time are presumably not due to the mere passage of time, but rather due to variations in some more fundamental economic variables. In contrast, the expected rates of return and the price sensitivities of some assets will depend directly on time, for example the volatility and the expected rate of return on a bond will depend on its time to maturity and therefore on calendar time.

Now the wealth dynamics for a given portfolio and consumption strategy is

$$dW_t = W_t \left[r^f(x_t) + \boldsymbol{\pi}_t^\top \underline{\underline{\sigma}}(x_t, t) \boldsymbol{\lambda}(x_t) \right] dt - c_t\, dt + W_t \boldsymbol{\pi}_t^\top \underline{\underline{\sigma}}(x_t, t)\, d\boldsymbol{z}_t. \tag{6.60}$$

The state variable x is assumed to follow a one-dimensional diffusion process

$$dx_t = m(x_t)\, dt + \boldsymbol{v}(x_t)^\top\, d\boldsymbol{z}_t + \hat{v}(x_t)\, d\hat{z}_t, \tag{6.61}$$

where $\hat{z} = (\hat{z}_t)$ is a one-dimensional standard Brownian motion independent of $\boldsymbol{z} = (\boldsymbol{z}_t)$. Hence, if $\hat{v}(x_t) \neq 0$, there is an exogenous shock to the state variable that cannot be hedged by investments in the financial market. In other words, the financial market is incomplete. In contrast, if $\hat{v}(x_t)$ is identically equal to zero, the financial market is complete. The d-vector $\boldsymbol{v}(x_t)$ represents the sensitivity of the state variable with respect to the exogenous shocks to market prices. Note that the d-vector $\underline{\underline{\sigma}}(x, t)\boldsymbol{v}(x)$ is the vector of instantaneous covariance rates between the returns on the risky assets and the state variable.

6.7.2 Time-Additive Expected Utility

As in discrete time, the indirect utility function is a key object in the dynamic programming approach in continuous time. With time-additive expected utility, the indirect utility is defined as

$$J_t = \sup_{(c_s, \boldsymbol{\theta}_s)_{s \in [t,T]}} \mathrm{E}_t \left[\int_t^T e^{-\delta(s-t)} u(c_s)\, ds \right]. \tag{6.62}$$

Under the assumptions made above the indirect utility at time t is $J_t = J(W_t, x_t, t)$. Note that we will have $J_T = 0$, but we could allow for a separate utility of terminal wealth representing a bequest motive.

How do we implement the dynamic programming principle in continuous time? First consider a discrete-time approximation with time set $\{0, \Delta t, 2\Delta t, \dots, T = N\Delta t\}$. The Bellman Equation corresponding to this discrete-time utility maximization problem is

$$J(W,x,t) = \sup_{c_t \geq 0, \boldsymbol{\pi}_t \in \mathbb{R}^d} \left\{ u(c_t)\Delta t + e^{-\delta \Delta t} \mathrm{E}_t \left[J(W_{t+\Delta t}, x_{t+\Delta t}, t+\Delta t) \right] \right\},$$

compare Eq. (6.41). Here c_t and $\boldsymbol{\pi}_t$ are held fixed over the interval $[t, t+\Delta t)$. If we multiply by $e^{\delta \Delta t}$, subtract $J(W,x,t)$, and then divide by Δt, we get

$$\begin{aligned} &\frac{e^{\delta \Delta t} - 1}{\Delta t} J(W,x,t) \qquad (6.63) \\ &\quad = \sup_{c_t \geq 0, \boldsymbol{\pi}_t \in \mathbb{R}^d} \left\{ e^{\delta \Delta t} u(c_t) + \frac{1}{\Delta t} \mathrm{E}_t \left[J(W_{t+\Delta t}, x_{t+\Delta t}, t+\Delta t) - J(W,x,t) \right] \right\}. \end{aligned}$$

When we let $\Delta t \to 0$, we have that (by l'Hôspital's Rule)

$$\frac{e^{\delta \Delta t} - 1}{\Delta t} \to \delta,$$

and that (by definition of the drift of a process)

$$\frac{1}{\Delta t} \mathrm{E}_t \left[J(W_{t+\Delta t}, x_{t+\Delta t}, t+\Delta t) - J(W,x,t) \right]$$

will approach the drift of J at time t, which according to Itô's Lemma is given by

$$\begin{aligned} &\frac{\partial J}{\partial t}(W,x,t) + J_W(W,x,t) \left(W \left[r^f(x) + \boldsymbol{\pi}_t^\top \underline{\underline{\sigma}}(x,t) \boldsymbol{\lambda}(x) \right] - c_t \right) \\ &\quad + \frac{1}{2} J_{WW}(W,x,t) W^2 \boldsymbol{\pi}_t^\top \underline{\underline{\sigma}}(x,t) \underline{\underline{\sigma}}(x,t)^\top \boldsymbol{\pi}_t + J_x(W,x,t) m(x) \\ &\quad + \frac{1}{2} J_{xx}(W,x,t) (\boldsymbol{v}(x)^\top \boldsymbol{v}(x) + \hat{v}(x)^2) + J_{Wx}(W,x,t) W \boldsymbol{\pi}_t^\top \underline{\underline{\sigma}}(x,t) \boldsymbol{v}(x). \end{aligned}$$

The limit of Eq. (6.63) is therefore

$$\begin{aligned} \delta J(W,x,t) = \sup_{c \geq 0, \boldsymbol{\pi} \in \mathbb{R}^d} \Big\{ & u(c) + \frac{\partial J}{\partial t}(W,x,t) \\ & + J_W(W,x,t) \left(W \left[r^f(x) + \boldsymbol{\pi}^\top \underline{\underline{\sigma}}(x,t) \boldsymbol{\lambda}(x) \right] - c \right) \\ & + \frac{1}{2} J_{WW}(W,x,t) W^2 \boldsymbol{\pi}^\top \underline{\underline{\sigma}}(x,t) \underline{\underline{\sigma}}(x,t)^\top \boldsymbol{\pi} \\ & + J_x(W,x,t) m(x) + \frac{1}{2} J_{xx}(W,x,t) (\boldsymbol{v}(x)^\top \boldsymbol{v}(x) + \hat{v}(x)^2) \\ & + J_{Wx}(W,x,t) W \boldsymbol{\pi}^\top \underline{\underline{\sigma}}(x,t) \boldsymbol{v}(x) \Big\}. \end{aligned} \qquad (6.64)$$

This is called the *Hamilton–Jacobi–Bellman (HJB) Equation* corresponding to the dynamic optimization problem. Subscripts on J denote partial derivatives, however we write the partial derivative with respect to time as $\partial J/\partial t$ to distinguish it from the value J_t of the indirect utility process. The HJB Equation involves the supremum over the feasible time t consumption rates and portfolios (*not* the supremum over the entire processes) and is therefore a highly non-linear second-order partial differential equation.

From the analysis above we will expect that the indirect utility function $J(W, x, t)$ solves the HJB Equation for all possible values of W and x and all $t \in [0, T)$ and that it satisfies the terminal condition $J(W, x, T) = 0$.[3] This can be supported formally by the so-called verification theorem. The solution procedure is therefore as follows: (1) Solve the maximization problem embedded in the HJB Equation giving a candidate for the optimal strategies expressed in terms of the yet unknown indirect utility function and its derivatives. (2) Substitute the candidate for the optimal strategies into the HJB Equation, ignore the sup-operator, and solve the resulting partial differential equation for $J(W, x, t)$. Such a solution will then also give the candidate optimal strategies in terms of W, x, and t.[4]

Let us find the first-order conditions of the maximization in (6.64). The first-order condition with respect to c immediately gives us the important envelope condition (6.38). If we let I_u denote the inverse of the marginal utility function, we can thus write the optimal consumption as

$$c_t^* = I_u\left(J_W(W_t, x_t, t)\right). \tag{6.65}$$

Let us also look at the first-order condition with respect to $\boldsymbol{\pi}$, that is

$$\begin{aligned} J_W(W,x,t)W\underline{\underline{\sigma}}(x,t)\boldsymbol{\lambda}(x) + J_{WW}(W,x,t)W^2\underline{\underline{\sigma}}(x,t)\underline{\underline{\sigma}}(x,t)^{\top}\boldsymbol{\pi} \\ + J_{Wx}(W,x,t)W\underline{\underline{\sigma}}(x,t)\boldsymbol{\nu}(x) = 0 \end{aligned}$$

so that the optimal portfolio is

$$\begin{aligned} \boldsymbol{\pi}_t = &-\frac{J_W(W_t,x_t,t)}{W_tJ_{WW}(W_t,x_t,t)}\left(\underline{\underline{\sigma}}(x_t,t)^{\top}\right)^{-1}\boldsymbol{\lambda}(x_t) \\ &-\frac{J_{Wx}(W_t,x_t,t)}{W_tJ_{WW}(W_t,x_t,t)}\left(\underline{\underline{\sigma}}(x_t,t)^{\top}\right)^{-1}\boldsymbol{\nu}(x_t). \end{aligned} \tag{6.66}$$

[3] We could allow for some utility of terminal consumption or wealth, for example representing the utility of leaving money for your heirs. Then the terminal condition should be of the form $J(W, x, T) = \bar{u}(W)$.

[4] There is really also a third step, namely to check that the assumptions made along the way and the technical conditions needed for the verification theorem to apply are all satisfied. The standard version of the verification theorem is precisely stated and proved in Øksendal (2003, Ch. 11) and Fleming and Soner (1993, Thm III.8.1). The technical conditions of the standard version are not always satisfied in concrete consumption-portfolio problems, however. At least for some concrete problems a version with an appropriate set of conditions has been found, see for example Korn and Kraft (2001) and Kraft (2009).

Substituting the candidate optimal values of c and π back into the HJB Equation and gathering terms, we get the second-order PDE

$$\begin{aligned}\delta J(W,x,t) &= u\left(I_u(J_W(W,x,t))\right) - J_W(W,x,t)I_u(J_W(W,x,t)) + \frac{\partial J}{\partial t}(W,x,t) \\ &\quad + r^f(x)WJ_W(W,x,t) - \frac{1}{2}\frac{J_W(W,x,t)^2}{J_{WW}(W,x,t)}\|\boldsymbol{\lambda}(x)\|^2 \\ &\quad + J_x(W,x,t)m(x) + \frac{1}{2}J_{xx}(W,x,t)\left(\|\boldsymbol{v}(x)\|^2 + \hat{v}(x)^2\right) \\ &\quad - \frac{1}{2}\frac{J_{Wx}(W,x,t)^2}{J_{WW}(W,x,t)}\|\boldsymbol{v}(x)\|^2 - \frac{J_W(W,x,t)J_{Wx}(W,x,t)}{J_{WW}(W,x,t)}\boldsymbol{\lambda}(x)^{\top}\boldsymbol{v}(x).\end{aligned} \tag{6.67}$$

We can draw the following conclusion:

Theorem 6.15 *Under technical conditions, the optimal consumption and investment strategy with time-additive expected utility* (6.62) *is given by Eqs.* (6.65) *and* (6.66), *where the indirect utility function* $J(W,x,t)$ *solves the PDE* (6.67) *with terminal condition* $J(W,x,T)=0$.

Although the PDE (6.67) looks very complicated, closed-form solutions can be found for a number of interesting model specifications. See examples in Munk (2012).

Let us provide some intuition about the optimal portfolio in Eq. (6.66). As the horizon shrinks, the indirect utility function $J(W,x,t)$ approaches the terminal utility which is independent of the state x. Consequently, the derivative $J_{Wx}(W,x,t)$ and hence the last term of the portfolio will approach zero as $t \to T$. Short-sighted investors pick a portfolio given by the first term on the right-hand side. We can interpret the second term as an intertemporal hedge term since it shows how a long-term investor will deviate from the short-term investor. The last term will also disappear for 'non-instantaneous' investors in three special cases:

(1) There is no x: investment opportunities are constant; there is *nothing to hedge*.

(2) $J_{Wx}(W,x,t) \equiv 0$: the state variable does not affect the marginal utility of the investor. This turns out to be the case for investors with logarithmic utility. Such an investor is *not interested in hedging* changes in the state variable.

(3) $\boldsymbol{v}(x) \equiv 0$: the state variable is uncorrelated with instantaneous returns on the traded assets. In this case the investor is *not able to hedge* changes in the state variable.

In all other cases the state variable induces an additional term to the optimal portfolio relative to the case of constant investment opportunities.

In general, we have three-fund separation in the sense that all investors will combine the risk-free asset, the 'tangency portfolio' of risky assets given by the portfolio weights

$$\pi_t^{\tan} = \frac{1}{\mathbf{1}^\top \left(\underline{\underline{\sigma}}(x_t, t)^\top\right)^{-1} \boldsymbol{\lambda}(x_t)} \left(\underline{\underline{\sigma}}(x_t, t)^\top\right)^{-1} \boldsymbol{\lambda}(x_t),$$

and the 'hedge portfolio' given by the weights

$$\pi_t^{\text{hdg}} = \frac{1}{\mathbf{1}^\top \left(\underline{\underline{\sigma}}(x_t, t)^\top\right)^{-1} \nu(x_t)} \left(\underline{\underline{\sigma}}(x_t, t)^\top\right)^{-1} \nu(x_t).$$

Inserting the definition of $\boldsymbol{\lambda}$ we can rewrite the expression for the tangency portfolio as

$$\pi_t^{\tan} = \frac{1}{\mathbf{1}^\top \underline{\underline{\Sigma}}(x_t, t)^{-1} \left(\boldsymbol{\mu}(x_t, t) - r^f(x_t)\mathbf{1}\right)} \underline{\underline{\Sigma}}(x_t, t)^{-1} \left(\boldsymbol{\mu}(x_t, t) - r^f(x_t)\mathbf{1}\right),$$

which is analogous to the tangency portfolio in the one-period mean-variance analysis, compare Eq. (6.25).

If more than one, say k, variables are necessary to capture the information about investment opportunities, the optimal portfolio will involve k hedge portfolios beside the tangency portfolio and the risk-free asset so that $(k+2)$-fund separation holds.

Nielsen and Vassalou (2006) have shown that the only characteristic of investment opportunities that will induce intertemporal hedging is the short-term risk-free interest rate r_t^f and $\|\boldsymbol{\lambda}_t\|$, which is the maximum Sharpe ratio obtainable at the financial market. Since r_t^f is the intercept and $\|\boldsymbol{\lambda}_t\|$ the slope of the instantaneous mean-variance frontier, this result makes good sense. Long-term investors are concerned about the variations in the returns on investments that are good in the short run.

By substitution of the optimal portfolio into Eq. (6.60), the wealth dynamics under the optimal decision rules can be written as

$$\begin{aligned} dW_t = {} & \left(r^f(x_t) W_t - c_t^* - \frac{J_W}{J_{WW}} \|\boldsymbol{\lambda}(x_t)\|^2 - \frac{J_{Wx}}{J_{WW}} \nu(x_t)^\top \boldsymbol{\lambda}(x_t)\right) dt \\ & - \left(\frac{J_W}{J_{WW}} \boldsymbol{\lambda}(x_t) + \frac{J_{Wx}}{J_{WW}} \nu(x_t)\right)^\top dz_t, \end{aligned} \tag{6.68}$$

where all the derivatives of J are to be evaluated in (W_t, x_t, t). The optimal exposure to the shocks is determined by risk attitudes via the relevant derivatives of the indirect utility function.

Next we confirm that the optimal strategies give rise to a state-price deflator. Note that in the present set-up, the shocks to the economy are represented by the standard Brownian motions z and $\hat{z}$, but the prices of traded assets are only contemporaneously affected by z. In this setting, a state-price deflator is a stochastic process $\zeta = (\zeta_t)$ with initial value and finite variance and with dynamics of the form

$$d\zeta_t = -\zeta_t \left[r^f(x_t)\, dt + \boldsymbol{\lambda}(x_t)^\top\, dz_t + \hat{\lambda}_t\, d\hat{z}_t \right] \tag{6.69}$$

for any well-behaved process $\hat{\lambda} = (\hat{\lambda}_t)$, compare Theorem 4.4.

Theorem 6.16 *Let $W = (W_t)$ be the wealth process based on the optimal consumption and investment strategy. The process $\zeta = (\zeta_t)$ defined by*

$$\zeta_t = e^{-\delta t} \frac{J_W(W_t, x_t, t)}{J_W(W_0, x_0, 0)} \tag{6.70}$$

is a state-price deflator. Because of the envelope condition (6.38)*, this confirms that*

$$\zeta_t = e^{-\delta t} \frac{u'(c_t)}{u'(c_0)}$$

is a state-price deflator, where c denotes the optimal consumption strategy.

Proof. It is clear that with ζ_t defined as in Eq. (6.70), the initial value equals 1. The finite variance condition can be ensured by appropriate conditions on the preferences and shock terms of W and x. The central point of the proof is to show that the dynamics of ζ_t is of the form Eq. (6.69). We apply Itô's Lemma in Theorem 2.6 based on the relation (6.70) and the dynamics of W and x stated in Eqs. (6.68) and (6.61), respectively. After some simplification, this leads to the dynamics

$$\begin{aligned} d\zeta_t = -\zeta_t \Bigg\{ \Bigg[\delta - &\frac{J_{Wt}}{J_W} - \frac{J_{WW}}{J_W}\left(r^f W - c^*\right) + \|\boldsymbol{\lambda}\|^2 + \frac{J_{Wx}}{J_W}\boldsymbol{\nu}^\top \boldsymbol{\lambda} - \frac{1}{2}\frac{J_W J_{WWW}}{J_{WW}^2}\|\boldsymbol{\lambda}\|^2 \\ &- \frac{1}{2}\frac{J_{WWW} J_{Wx}^2}{J_w J_{WW}^2}\|\boldsymbol{\nu}\|^2 - \frac{J_{WWW} J_{Wx}}{J_{WW}^2}\boldsymbol{\nu}^\top\boldsymbol{\lambda} - \frac{J_{Wx}}{J_W} m \\ &- \frac{1}{2}\frac{J_{Wxx}}{J_W}\left(\|\boldsymbol{\nu}\|^2 + \hat{\nu}^2\right) + \frac{J_{WWx}}{J_{WW}}\boldsymbol{\nu}^\top\boldsymbol{\lambda} + \frac{J_{Wx} J_{WWx}}{J_W J_{WW}}\|\boldsymbol{\nu}\|^2 \Bigg] dt \\ + \boldsymbol{\lambda}^\top dz_t - &\frac{J_{Wx}}{J_W}\hat{\nu}\, d\hat{z}_t \Bigg\}, \end{aligned}$$

where again all the derivatives of J are to be evaluated in (W_t, x_t, t), and we have suppressed the dependence of r^f, $\boldsymbol{\nu}$, $\hat{\nu}$, and $\boldsymbol{\lambda}$ on x_t.

The shock terms in $d\zeta_t$ are already of the required form in Eq. (6.69), but the long expression in the square brackets in the drift must simplify to the risk-free rate. This is shown in the following manner. In the PDE (6.67), recall that

$I_u(J_W(W,x,t))$ equals the optimal consumption rate $c^*(W,x,t)$. Now differentiate with respect to W on both sides of the equation. This leads to

$$\begin{aligned}
\delta J_W &= u'(c^*)\frac{\partial c^*}{\partial W} - J_W\frac{\partial c^*}{\partial W} - J_{WW}c^* + J_{Wt} + r^f J_W + r^f WJ_{WW} \\
&- J_W\|\boldsymbol{\lambda}\|^2 + \frac{1}{2}\frac{J_W^2 J_{WWW}}{J_{WW}^2}\|\boldsymbol{\lambda}\|^2 + J_{Wx}m + \frac{1}{2}J_{Wxx}\left(\|\boldsymbol{v}\|^2 + \hat{v}^2\right) \\
&- \frac{J_{Wx}J_{WWx}}{J_{WW}}\|\boldsymbol{v}\|^2 + \frac{1}{2}\frac{J_{Wx}^2 J_{WWW}}{J_{WW}^2}\|\boldsymbol{v}\|^2 - J_{Wx}\boldsymbol{v}^\top\boldsymbol{\lambda} \\
&- \frac{J_W J_{WWx}}{J_{WW}}\boldsymbol{v}^\top\boldsymbol{\lambda} + \frac{J_W J_{Wx} J_{WWW}}{J_{WW}^2}\boldsymbol{v}^\top\boldsymbol{\lambda}.
\end{aligned}$$

Because of the envelope condition the first two terms on the right-hand side cancel. After dividing through by J_W, this equation implies that the drift term in the above expression for $d\zeta_t$ is, in fact, identical to r^f as it should be. □

6.7.3 Stochastic Differential Utility

The continuous-time version of recursive utility is often called stochastic differential utility and was introduced in Section 5.7.4. The objective of the individual is to maximize the utility index $\mathcal{U}_t$ recursively defined as

$$\mathcal{U}_t = \mathrm{E}_t\left[\int_t^T f(c_s, \mathcal{U}_s)\,ds\right], \quad \mathcal{U}_T = 0. \tag{6.71}$$

Here f is a normalized aggregator, and the prime example is the Epstein–Zin-type specification (5.26). The indirect utility is defined as $J_t = \sup \mathcal{U}_t$, where the supremum is over the consumption and investment strategies from time t onwards. We assume again that the indirect utility is a function of time, wealth, and some state variable x assumed one-dimensional for notational simplicity in what follows, that is $J_t = J(W_t, x_t, t)$. It follows from Duffie and Epstein (1992b) that the dynamic programming approach is also valid with stochastic differential utility so that J is expected to solve the following HJB Equation:

$$\begin{aligned}
0 = \sup_{c\geq 0, \boldsymbol{\pi}\in\mathbb{R}^d} &\Big\{ f\left(c, J(W,x,t)\right) + \frac{\partial J}{\partial t}(W,x,t) \\
&+ J_W(W,x,t)\left(W\left[r^f(x) + \boldsymbol{\pi}^\top \underline{\underline{\sigma}}(x,t)\boldsymbol{\lambda}(x)\right] - c\right) \\
&+ \frac{1}{2}J_{WW}(W,x,t)W^2\boldsymbol{\pi}^\top\underline{\underline{\sigma}}(x,t)\underline{\underline{\sigma}}(x,t)^\top\boldsymbol{\pi}
\end{aligned}$$

$$+ J_x(W,x,t)m(x) + \frac{1}{2}J_{xx}(W,x,t)(\nu(x)^\top \nu(x) + \hat{\nu}(x)^2)$$
$$+ J_{Wx}(W,x,t)W\boldsymbol{\pi}^\top \underline{\underline{\sigma}}(x,t)\nu(x)\Big\}. \tag{6.72}$$

In the special case where the aggregator is of the separable form (5.23) and thus consistent with time-additive expected utility, this HJB Equation is identical to Eq. (6.64). In particular, all the terms involving the portfolio $\boldsymbol{\pi}$ are exactly as in the case of time-additive utility. Therefore, the expression (6.66) for the optimal portfolio still holds.

In contrast, the expression for the optimal consumption is different. Let $f_c(c,J)$ denote the derivative of $f(c,J)$ with respect to c, and let $f_J(c,J)$ the derivative with respect to J. The first-order condition for consumption is then

$$f_c\big(c, J(W,x,t)\big) = J_W(W,x,t), \tag{6.73}$$

which is the recursive utility version of the envelope condition. If we let $a \mapsto I_f(a,J)$ denote the inverse of the function $c \mapsto f_c(c,J)$, we can formally write optimal consumption as

$$c^*(W,x,t) = I_f\big(J_W(W,x,t), J(W,x,t)\big). \tag{6.74}$$

When substituting the optimal values of c and π back into the HJB Equation (6.72) and gathering terms, we get the second-order PDE

$$\begin{aligned}
0 &= f\left(I_f\big(J_W(W,x,t), J(W,x,t)\big), J(W,x,t)\right) \\
&\quad - J_W(W,x,t) I_f\big(J_W(W,x,t), J(W,x,t)\big) + \frac{\partial J}{\partial t}(W,x,t) \\
&\quad + r^f(x) W J_W(W,x,t) - \frac{1}{2}\frac{J_W(W,x,t)^2}{J_{WW}(W,x,t)}\|\boldsymbol{\lambda}(x)\|^2 \\
&\quad + J_x(W,x,t)m(x) + \frac{1}{2}J_{xx}(W,x,t)\left(\|\nu(x)\|^2 + \hat{\nu}(x)^2\right) \\
&\quad - \frac{1}{2}\frac{J_{Wx}(W,x,t)^2}{J_{WW}(W,x,t)}\|\nu(x)\|^2 - \frac{J_W(W,x,t)J_{Wx}(W,x,t)}{J_{WW}(W,x,t)}\boldsymbol{\lambda}(x)^\top \nu(x),
\end{aligned} \tag{6.75}$$

which is very similar to the corresponding PDE (6.67) for time-additive utility. We summarize the results in the following theorem.

Theorem 6.17 *Under technical conditions, the optimal consumption and investment strategy with stochastic differential utility* (6.71) *is given by Eqs.* (6.74) *and* (6.66), *where the indirect utility function* $J(W,x,t)$ *solves the PDE* (6.75) *with terminal condition* $J(W,x,T) = 0$.

As for time-additive utility, we can link the optimal decisions to state-price deflators. Here is the precise result:

Theorem 6.18 *Let $J(W, x, t)$ be the indirect utility function for an individual with stochastic differential utility (6.71). Let $W = (W_t)$ be the wealth process based on the optimal consumption and investment strategy. The process $\zeta = (\zeta_t)$ defined by*

$$\zeta_t = e^{\int_0^t f_J\left(c(W_s,x_s,s),J(W_s,x_s,s)\right)\, ds} \frac{J_W(W_t, x_t, t)}{J_W(W_0, x_0, 0)} \tag{6.76}$$

is a state-price deflator. Because of the envelope condition (6.73), this implies that

$$\zeta_t = e^{\int_0^t f_J\left(c(W_s,x_s,s),J(W_s,x_s,s)\right)\, ds} \frac{f_c\big(c(W_t, x_t, t), J(W_t, x_t, t)\big)}{f_c\big(c(W_0, x_0, 0), J(W_0, x_0, 0)\big)}$$

is a state-price deflator, where c denotes the optimal consumption strategy.

Proof. The proof is similar to the proof for the time-additive case in Theorem 6.16. In the application of Itô's Lemma, the time derivative now equals $\zeta_t f_J(c_t, J_t)$ instead of $-\delta\zeta_t$. We leave the details for the reader. □

For the special case of Epstein–Zin utility with relative risk aversion $\gamma > 1$ and intertemporal elasticity of substitution $\psi \neq 1$, the aggregator is

$$f(c, J) = \frac{\delta}{1 - 1/\psi} c^{1-1/\psi} \left([1-\gamma]J\right)^{1-1/\theta} - \delta\theta J,$$

where $\theta = (1-\gamma)/(1-\frac{1}{\psi})$. In this case

$$f_c(c, J) = \delta c^{-1/\psi} \left([1-\gamma]J\right)^{1-1/\theta},$$

so the optimal consumption rate becomes

$$c^*(W, x, t) = \delta^{\psi} J_W(W, x, t)^{-\psi} \left([1-\gamma]J(W, x, t)\right)^{\frac{\gamma\psi-1}{\gamma-1}}.$$

Moreover,

$$f_J(c, J) = \delta(\theta - 1)c^{1-\frac{1}{\psi}} \left([1-\gamma]J\right)^{-\frac{1}{\theta}} - \delta\theta,$$

so the state-price deflator in (6.76) is

$$\zeta_t = e^{-\delta\theta t} \left(\frac{c_t}{c_0}\right)^{-\frac{1}{\psi}} e^{\delta(\theta-1)\int_0^t c_s^{1-1/\psi}([1-\gamma]J_s)^{-1/\theta}\, ds} \left(\frac{J_t}{J_0}\right)^{1-1/\theta}.$$

Note that for the special case of time-additive CRRA utility in which $\gamma = 1/\psi$ and $\theta = 1$, we are back to the well-known state-price deflator. The more general recursive utility complicates the expression for the state-price deflator considerably.

6.8 CONCLUDING REMARKS

This chapter has characterized the optimal consumption and portfolio choice of an individual by the first-order condition of her utility maximization problem. The characterization provides a link between asset prices and the optimal consumption plan of any individual. In the next chapter we will look at the market equilibrium.

6.9 EXERCISES

Exercise 6.1 Consider a one-period economy and an individual with a time-additive but state-dependent expected utility so that the objective is

$$\max_{\theta} u(c_0, X_0) + e^{-\delta} \, \mathrm{E}[u(c, X)].$$

The decisions of the individual do not affect X_0 or X. For example, X_0 and X could be the aggregate consumption in the economy at time 0 and time 1, respectively, which are not significantly affected by the consumption of a small individual. What is the link between prices and marginal utility in this case? What if $u(c,X) = \frac{1}{1-\gamma}(c-X)^{1-\gamma}$? What if $u(c,X) = \frac{1}{1-\gamma}(c/X)^{1-\gamma}$?

Exercise 6.2 Consider a one-period economy where four basic financial assets are traded without portfolio constraints or transaction costs. There are four possible end-of-period states of the economy. The objective state probabilities and the prices and state-contingent dividends of the assets are given in the following table:

State	1	2	3	4	
Probability	$\frac{1}{6}$	$\frac{1}{4}$	$\frac{1}{4}$	$\frac{1}{3}$	
		Dividends			Price
asset 1	1	2	2	2	$\frac{3}{2}$
asset 2	1	3	0	0	$\frac{7}{6}$
asset 3	0	0	1	1	$\frac{1}{3}$
asset 4	3	2	1	1	$\frac{3}{2}$

The economy is known to be arbitrage-free.

(a) Show that Asset 4 is redundant and verify that the price of Asset 4 is identical to the price of the portfolio of the other assets that replicates Asset 4.

(b) Is the market complete?

(c) Show that the vector $\psi^* = \left(\frac{1}{6}, \frac{1}{3}, \frac{1}{6}, \frac{1}{6}\right)^{\mathsf{T}}$ is a valid state-price vector and that it is in the set of dividends spanned by the basic assets. Characterize the set of all valid state-price vectors.

(d) Show that the vector $\zeta^* = \left(1, \frac{4}{3}, \frac{4}{7}, \frac{4}{7}\right)^{\mathsf{T}}$ is a valid state-price deflator and that it is in the set of dividends spanned by the basic assets. Show that any state-price deflator must be a vector of the form $\left(1, \frac{4}{3}, y, 1 - \frac{3}{4}y\right)^{\mathsf{T}}$, where $y \in \left(0, \frac{4}{3}\right)$.

(e) Show that it is possible to construct a risk-free asset from the four basic assets. What is the risk-free interest rate?

In the following consider an individual maximizing $u(c_0) + \beta \, \mathrm{E}[u(c)]$, where c_0 denotes consumption at the beginning of the period and c denotes the state-dependent consumption at the end of the period. Assume $u(c) = c^{1-\gamma}/(1-\gamma)$. For $\omega \in \{1, 2, 3, 4\}$, let c_ω denote the end-of-period consumption if state ω is realized.

(f) Show that the optimal consumption plan must satisfy

$$c_2 = c_1 \left(\frac{4}{3}\right)^{-1/\gamma}, \qquad c_4 = c_0 \left(\frac{1}{\beta} - \frac{3}{4}\left(\frac{c_3}{c_0}\right)^{-\gamma}\right)^{-1/\gamma}.$$

For the remainder of the problem it is assumed that the individual has identical income/endowment in States 3 and 4.

(g) Explain why c_3 and c_4 must be identical, and hence that the optimal consumption plan must have

$$c_3 = c_4 = c_0 \left(\frac{4}{7\beta}\right)^{-1/\gamma}.$$

(h) Assuming $\gamma = 2$, $\beta = \frac{6}{7}$, and $c_0 = 1$, find the optimal state-dependent end-of-period consumption, that is c_1, c_2, c_3, c_4.

(i) What is the present value of the optimal consumption plan?

(j) Assuming that the individual receives no end-of-period income in any state, find an optimal portfolio for this individual.

Exercise 6.3 Consider a one-period economy with four possible, equally likely, states at the end of the period. The agents in the economy consume at the beginning of the period (time 0) and at the end of the period (time 1). The agents can choose between three different consumption plans as shown in the following table:

	Consumption	Time 1 consumption			
	at time 0	State 1	State 2	State 3	State 4
consumption plan 1	8	9	16	9	4
consumption plan 2	8	9	9	9	9
consumption plan 3	8	4	16	25	4

Denote the time 0 consumption by c_0, the uncertain consumption at time 1 by c, and the consumption at time 1 in case state ω is realized by c_ω.

(a) Consider an agent with logarithmic utility,

$$U(c_0, c_1, c_2, c_3, c_4) = \ln c_0 + \mathrm{E}[\ln c] = \ln c_0 + \sum_{\omega=1}^{4} p_\omega \ln c_\omega,$$

where p_ω is the probability that state ω is realized. Compute the utility for each of the three possible consumption plans and determine the optimal consumption plan. Find the associated state-price vector. Using this state-price vector, what is the price at the beginning of the period of an asset that gives a payoff of 2 in States 1 and 4 and a payoff of 1 in States 2 and 3?

(b) Answer the same questions with the alternative time-additive square root utility,

$$U(c_0, c_1, c_2, c_3, c_4) = \sqrt{c_0} + \mathrm{E}[\sqrt{c}] = \sqrt{c_0} + \sum_{\omega=1}^{4} p_\omega \sqrt{c_\omega}.$$

(c) Answer the same questions with the alternative habit-style square root utility,

$$U(c_0, c_1, c_2, c_3, c_4) = \sqrt{c_0} + \mathrm{E}[\sqrt{c - 0.5c_0}] = \sqrt{c_0} + \sum_{\omega=1}^{4} p_\omega \sqrt{c_\omega - 0.5c_0}.$$

Exercise 6.4 Show Eq. (6.19).

Exercise 6.5 Give a proof of Theorem 6.4.

Exercise 6.6 Let $R_{\min}$ denote the return on the minimum-variance portfolio. Let R be any other return, efficient or not. Show that $\mathrm{Cov}[R, R_{\min}] = \mathrm{Var}[R_{\min}]$.

Exercise 6.7 Let R_1 denote the return on a mean-variance efficient portfolio and let R_2 denote the return on another not necessarily efficient portfolio with $\mathrm{E}[R_2] = \mathrm{E}[R_1]$. Show that $\mathrm{Cov}[R_1, R_2] = \mathrm{Var}[R_1]$ and conclude that R_1 and R_2 are positively correlated.

Exercise 6.8 Think of the mean-variance framework in a one-period economy. Show that if there is a risk-free asset, then any two mean-variance efficient returns (different from the risk-free return) are either perfectly positively correlated or perfectly negatively correlated. Is that also true if there is no risk-free asset?

Exercise 6.9 In a one-period model where the returns of all the risky assets are normally distributed, any greedy and risk-averse investor will place herself on the upward-sloping part of the mean-variance frontier. But where? Consider an agent that maximizes expected utility of end-of-period wealth with a negative exponential utility function $u(W) = -e^{-aW}$ for some constant a. Suppose that M risky assets (with normally distributed returns) and one risk-free asset are traded. What is the optimal portfolio of the agent? Where is the optimal portfolio located on the mean-variance frontier?

Exercise 6.10 Look at an individual with habit formation living in a continuous-time complete market economy. The individual wants to maximize his expected utility

$$\mathrm{E}\left[\int_0^T e^{-\delta t} u(c_t, h_t)\, dt\right],$$

where the habit level h_t is given by

$$h_t = h_0 e^{-\alpha t} + \beta \int_0^t e^{-\alpha(t-u)} c_u \, du.$$

We can write the budget constraint as

$$\mathrm{E}\left[\int_0^T \zeta_t c_t \, dt\right] \leq W_0,$$

where $\zeta = (\zeta_t)$ is the state-price deflator and W_0 is the initial wealth of the agent (including the present value of any future non-financial income).

(a) Show that $dh_t = (\beta c_t - \alpha h_t)\, dt$. What condition on α and β will ensure that the habit level declines, when current consumption equals the habit level?

(b) Show that the state-price deflator is linked to optimal consumption by the relation

$$\zeta_t = k e^{-\delta t} \left\{ u_c(c_t, h_t) + \beta \, \mathrm{E}_t \left[\int_t^T e^{-(\delta+\alpha)(s-t)} u_h(c_s, h_s) \, ds \right] \right\} \qquad (*)$$

for some appropriate constant k. *Hint: First consider what effect consumption at time t has on future habit levels.*

(c) How does (*) look when $u(c, h) = \frac{1}{1-\gamma}(c-h)^{1-\gamma}$?

Exercise 6.11 Consider an individual with a time-additive expected utility characterized by a utility function $u(c)$ and a time preference rate δ. The individual lives in a continuous-time economy. Let us write the dynamics of the optimal consumption process of the individual as

$$dc_t = c_t \left[\mu_{ct} \, dt + \boldsymbol{\sigma}_{ct}^{\top} \, d\boldsymbol{z}_t \right].$$

(a) What is the dynamics of the state-price deflator induced by this individual? Determine an expression for the continuously compounded short-term risk-free rate and a market price of risk for this economy in terms of the preferences and consumption process of this individual.

Bruce lives in a continuous-time complete market economy. Bruce has time-additive logarithmic utility, $u_B(c) = \ln c$, with a time preference rate of $\delta_B = 0.02$, and his optimal consumption process $c_B = (c_{Bt})$ has dynamics

$$dc_{Bt} = c_{Bt} \left[0.03 \, dt + 0.1 \, dz_t \right],$$

where $z = (z_t)$ is a standard Brownian motion.

(b) Identify the continuously compounded short-term risk-free interest rate and the market price of risk associated with z. Can there be any other 'priced risks' in the economy? What is the instantaneous Sharpe ratio of any risky asset?

Patti lives in the same economy as Bruce. She has time-additive expected utility with a HARA utility function $u_P(c) = \frac{1}{1-\gamma}(c - \bar{c})^{1-\gamma}$ and a time preference rate identical to Bruce's, that is $\delta_P = 0.02$.

(c) Explain why Patti's optimal consumption strategy $c_P = (c_{Pt})$ must satisfy

$$c_{Pt} = \bar{c} + \left(\frac{c_{Bt}}{c_{B0}} \right)^{1/\gamma} (c_{P0} - \bar{c}) \, .$$

Find the dynamics of Patti's optimal consumption process.

7

Market Equilibrium

7.1 INTRODUCTION

The key objective of asset pricing theories and models is to find asset prices for which the financial market is in equilibrium. Equilibrium prices are prices for which the optimal decisions of all individuals, given these asset prices, are such that the aggregate demand equals the aggregate supply of each asset.

Ideally, we would like to know under which conditions on the financial market and the investors an equilibrium exists and under which (stronger) conditions such an equilibrium is unique. We would like to study relevant properties of equilibria such as how the risks and resources of the economy are shared among the individuals and how this sharing depends on the market structure and investor preferences. We would like to know how the equilibrium is affected by a change in the market such as the introduction of a new asset. However, these questions are difficult to answer without imposing specific assumptions on the available assets and the preferences and endowments of the individuals.

We focus in this chapter on exchange economies which means that the endowments (initial wealth and state-dependent future incomes) and dividends are taken as given so that they are not affected by the decisions of any individuals in the economy. We assume that the economy offers a single consumption good, which is perishable. This good is the numeraire in the sense that all prices, dividends, and so on, are measured in units of the good. We assume that the individuals in the economy do not face any binding constraints on the portfolios they can form from the available financial assets. For example, they are allowed to take short positions and to borrow against future income, but of course they have to comply with the natural budget constraints. We assume that individuals agree on the set of possible future states of the economy and that they agree on the probabilities of these states. Finally, we assume that all investors are fully rational individuals with preferences that can be described by increasing and concave utility indices and for some results we even assume time-additive expected utility of consumption.

To further simplify the analysis, we will through most of the chapter assume a one-period model with a finite state space. In Section 7.2 we will formally define an equilibrium and introduce the relevant notation and assumptions. Section 7.3 reviews the concept of Pareto optimality and shows that Pareto-optimal consumption allocations can be seen as solutions to the decision problem of a hypothetical central planner in the economy. Pareto-optimal equilibria are shown to lead to efficient sharing of the risks in the economy. Furthermore, we will see that aggregate consumption is a central variable in Pareto-optimal equilibria, both in determining individual consumption and in pricing assets. Next, Section 7.4 shows that financial market equilibria will be Pareto optimal in all complete markets and in some 'slightly' incomplete markets. Section 7.5 introduces the idea of a representative individual and discusses how the preferences of a representative individual are linked to the preferences of all the individuals in the economy. Finally, Section 7.6 briefly explains how the findings can be generalized to a multiperiod setting.

The main references for this chapter are Arrow (1951, 1953, 1964), Debreu (1951, 1959), McKenzie (1954, 1959), Negishi (1960), Wilson (1968), Rubinstein (1974), Constantinides (1982), and Huang (1987). All of the assumptions mentioned above are questionable, but relaxing the assumptions complicates the analysis and results significantly. The interested reader is referred to Magill and Quinzii (1996) for a rigorous and comprehensive treatment of financial market equilibria in less restrictive settings that allow for incomplete markets, bounded rationality, production decisions, and other generalizations. The extension to recursive utility is studied by Duffie, Geoffard, and Skiadas (1994) and Dumas, Uppal, and Wang (2000), among others. Results for an infinite-dimensional state space are derived by Bewley (1972) and Mas-Colell (1986), among others. Christensen and Feltham (2003, 2005) focus on the role of public and private information in equilibria and investor welfare and the use of such information for performance evaluation, contracting, and the design of accounting systems.

7.2 DEFINITIONS AND ASSUMPTIONS

We will work throughout in a one-period model and assume that the state space is finite, $\Omega = \{1, 2, \dots, S\}$, and each state $\omega \in \Omega$ has a strictly positive probability of being realized. The one-period economy consists of I assets and L greedy and risk-averse individuals.

Each asset i is characterized by a random variable D_i representing the time 1 dividend, which we assume to be non-negative in all states and strictly positive in at least one state. All dividends are captured by the I-dimensional random variable $\boldsymbol{D} = (D_1, \dots, D_I)^\top$. Let $\mathcal{L}^I_+$ denote the set of such random variables.

Because of the finite state setting, we could equivalently represent a dividend vector $\boldsymbol{D}$ by an $I \times S$ matrix $\underline{\underline{D}}$.

Each individual is characterized by a utility index and an endowment. The utility index $\mathcal{U}_l$ depends on initial consumption c_0^l and the, possibly state-dependent, end-of-period consumption which we can represent by a random variable c^l. Let $\mathcal{C} \subseteq \mathbb{R}$ denote the set of possible consumption levels, and let $\mathcal{L}(\mathcal{C})$ denote the set of random variables with values in $\mathcal{C}$. Then the utility index is a function $\mathcal{U}_l : \mathcal{C} \times \mathcal{L}(\mathcal{C}) \to \mathbb{R}$. We assumed that $\mathcal{U}_l$ is strictly increasing and concave, and let $\mathbf{U}$ denote the set of such utility indices. Note that with our finite state space, we can equivalently think of $\mathcal{L}(\mathcal{C})$ as $\mathcal{C}^S$. The endowment is a pair (e_0^l, e^l), where $e_0^l \in \mathbb{R}_+ \equiv [0, \infty)$ is the initial endowment and e^l is a non-negative random variable representing the, possibly state-dependent, income at the end of the period. We allow for zero income so, using the notation introduced above, we require $e^l \in \mathcal{L}(\mathbb{R}_+)$. Again, because of the finite state space, we can equivalently represent the end-of-period income by a vector $\boldsymbol{e}^l = (e_1^l, \dots, e_S^l)^\top \in \mathbb{R}_+^S$.

With the above notation, we can formally collect the primitive ingredients of the finite-state, one-period economy in a set

$$\mathcal{E} = \{\boldsymbol{D} \in \mathcal{L}_+^I; \left(\mathcal{U}_l, e_0^l, e^l\right) \in \mathbf{U} \times \mathbb{R}_+ \times \mathcal{L}(\mathbb{R}_+), \, l = 1, \dots, L\}. \tag{7.1}$$

Each individual l faces the problem of maximizing $\mathcal{U}_l(c_0^l, c^l)$ subject to the budget constraints

$$\begin{aligned} c_0^l &\leq e_0^l - \boldsymbol{\theta}^l \cdot \boldsymbol{P}, \\ c_\omega^l &\leq e_\omega^l + \boldsymbol{\theta}^l \cdot \boldsymbol{D}_\omega, \quad \omega = 1, \dots, S, \end{aligned}$$

where $\boldsymbol{\theta}^l \in \mathbb{R}^I$ is the portfolio and where $\boldsymbol{P} = (P_1, \dots, P_I)^\top$ with P_i denoting the price of asset i. The individual can choose the consumption plan (c_0, c) and the portfolio $\boldsymbol{\theta}$. Since we will always assume that individuals prefer more consumption to less, it is clear that the budget constraints will hold as equalities. Therefore we can think of the individual choosing only the portfolio and then the consumption plan is given by

$$c_0^l = e_0^l - \boldsymbol{\theta}^l \cdot \boldsymbol{P}; \qquad c_\omega^l = e_\omega^l + \boldsymbol{\theta}^l \cdot \boldsymbol{D}_\omega, \quad \omega = 1, \dots, S. \tag{7.2}$$

Individual l thus maximizes $\mathcal{U}_l(c_0^l, c^l)$ over all feasible portfolios $\boldsymbol{\theta}^l$, which are the portfolios for which the corresponding consumption plan is well-defined so that $c_0^l, c_\omega^l \in \mathcal{C}$. Let Θ^l denote the set of feasible portfolios for individual l.

Now we can formally define an equilibrium in the economy described above.

Definition 7.1 *An equilibrium for the one-period economy $\mathcal{E}$ defined in* (7.1) *is a collection*

$$\left\{\boldsymbol{P} \in \mathbb{R}^I; (\boldsymbol{\theta}^1, \dots, \boldsymbol{\theta}^L) \in \Theta^1 \times \dots \times \Theta^L\right\}$$

of a price vector $\mathbf{P}$ *and feasible portfolios* $\boldsymbol{\theta}^l$ *satisfying the two conditions*

(i) *for each* $l = 1, \dots, L$*, the portfolio* $\boldsymbol{\theta}^l$ *is the optimal portfolio for individual* l *given asset prices* $\mathbf{P}$*,*

(ii) *markets clear so that* $\sum_{l=1}^{L} \theta_i^l = 0$ *for any asset* $i = 1, \dots, I$*.*

Associated with an equilibrium $\{\mathbf{P}; \boldsymbol{\theta}^1, \dots, \boldsymbol{\theta}^L\}$ is an *equilibrium consumption allocation* $\{(c_0^1, \mathbf{c}^1), \dots, (c_0^L, \mathbf{c}^L)\}$ defined by (7.2).

In the market clearing condition we have assumed that the traded assets are in a net supply of zero and, since the time 0 endowment is a certain number of units of the consumption good, no one owns any assets at time 0. This might seem restrictive but it does cover the case with initial asset holdings and positive net supply of assets. Just interpret $\boldsymbol{\theta}^l$ as individual l's net trade in the assets, that is the change in the portfolio relative to the initial portfolio, and interpret the time 1 endowment as the sum of some income from non-financial sources and the dividend from the initial portfolio.

The existence of an equilibrium is a delicate issue. Arrow and Debreu (1954) and McKenzie (1954, 1959) established the existence of an equilibrium in complete markets by use of a fixed-point argument. In various model settings with incomplete markets, the existence of an equilibrium has been studied by Radner (1972), Hart (1975), Duffie and Shafer (1985, 1986), Geanakoplos and Polemarchakis (1986), Repullo (1986), Polemarchakis and Siconolfi (1995), and Hellwig (1996), among others.

7.3 PROPERTIES OF PARETO-OPTIMAL EQUILIBRIA

Define the aggregate initial and future endowment in the economy as

$$\bar{e}_0 = \sum_{l=1}^{L} e_0^l, \quad \bar{e}_\omega = \sum_{l=1}^{L} e_\omega^l.$$

A consumption allocation $\{(c_0^1, \mathbf{c}^1), \dots, (c_0^L, \mathbf{c}^L)\}$ is said to be *feasible* with aggregate resources $(\bar{e}_0, \bar{\mathbf{e}})$ if

$$\sum_{l=1}^{L} c_0^l \leq \bar{e}_0; \quad \sum_{l=1}^{L} c_\omega^l \leq \bar{e}_\omega, \quad \omega \in \Omega$$

and $c_0^l, c_\omega^l \geq 0$ for all $l = 1, \dots, L$ and all $\omega = 1, \dots, S$. Let $\mathcal{A}(\bar{e}_0, \bar{\mathbf{e}})$ denote the set of feasible consumption allocations with aggregate resources $(\bar{e}_0, \bar{\mathbf{e}})$. Of course, for a given consumption allocation $\{(c_0^1, \mathbf{c}^1), \dots, (c_0^L, \mathbf{c}^L)\}$, the aggregate consumption is defined by

$$C_0 = \sum_{l=1}^{L} c_0^l, \quad C_\omega = \sum_{l=1}^{L} c_\omega^l.$$

Now we define the concept of a *Pareto-optimal* consumption allocation as follows:

Definition 7.2 *A consumption allocation* $\{(c_0^1, \boldsymbol{c}^1), \dots, (c_0^L, \boldsymbol{c}^L)\}$ *is Pareto-optimal for the economy* $\mathcal{E}$ *defined in Eq. (7.1) if*

(i) it is feasible, and

(ii) there is no other feasible consumption plan $\{(\hat{c}_0^1, \hat{\boldsymbol{c}}^1), \dots, (\hat{c}_0^L, \hat{\boldsymbol{c}}^L)\}$ *such that* $\mathcal{U}_l(\hat{c}_0^l, \hat{\boldsymbol{c}}^l) \geq \mathcal{U}_l(c_0^l, \boldsymbol{c}^l)$ *for all* $l = 1, \dots, L$ *with strict inequality for some* l.

To spell out, a consumption allocation is Pareto-optimal if it is impossible to reallocate the aggregate endowment in a way that makes one individual strictly better off without making at least one other individual strictly worse off. Pareto-optimality relates to how the aggregate consumption risk is shared among the individuals in the economy.

Pareto-optimality of consumption allocations is closely linked to the solution to the allocation problem of a hypothetical *central planner*. Let $\boldsymbol{\eta} = (\eta_1, \dots, \eta_L)^\top$ be a non-zero vector of non-negative numbers, one for each individual. Define the function $\mathcal{U}_{\boldsymbol{\eta}} : \mathbb{R}_+ \times \mathbb{R}_+^S \to \mathbb{R}$ by

$$\mathcal{U}_{\boldsymbol{\eta}}(\bar{e}_0, \bar{\boldsymbol{e}}) = \sup \left\{ \sum_{l=1}^{L} \eta_l \mathcal{U}_l(c_0^l, \boldsymbol{c}^l) \mid \{(c_0^1, \boldsymbol{c}^1), \dots, (c_0^L, \boldsymbol{c}^L)\} \in \mathcal{A}(\bar{e}_0, \bar{\boldsymbol{e}}) \right\}. \quad (7.3)$$

Here, $\sum_{l=1}^{L} \eta_l \mathcal{U}_l(c_0^l, \boldsymbol{c}^l)$ is a linear combination of the utilities of all individuals when each individual l follows the consumption plan $(c_0^l, \boldsymbol{c}^l)$. This linear combination is maximized over all feasible allocations of the total endowment $(\bar{e}_0, \bar{\boldsymbol{e}})$. Given the total endowment and the weights $\boldsymbol{\eta}$ on individuals, $\mathcal{U}_{\boldsymbol{\eta}}$ gives the best linear combination of utilities that can be obtained. As long as the individuals' utility indices are increasing and concave, $\mathcal{U}_{\boldsymbol{\eta}}$ will also be increasing and concave. We can thus think of $\mathcal{U}_{\boldsymbol{\eta}}$ as the utility index of a greedy and risk-averse individual, a central planner giving weights to the individual utility functions and having the right to redistribute consumption opportunities across individuals. Note that the multiplication of the weight vector $\boldsymbol{\eta}$ by a positive constant κ does not change the central planner's optimal consumption allocation.

The following theorem gives the link between the central planner and Pareto-optimality:

Theorem 7.1 *(i) Let* $\{(c_0^1, \boldsymbol{c}^1), \dots, (c_0^L, \boldsymbol{c}^L)\}$ *be a Pareto-optimal consumption allocation and let* $(C_0, \boldsymbol{C})$ *denote the corresponding aggregate consumption. Then a non-zero and non-negative vector* $\boldsymbol{\eta} = (\eta_1, \dots, \eta_L)^\top$ *of weights exists so that the same allocation maximizes* $\mathcal{U}_{\boldsymbol{\eta}}(C_0, \boldsymbol{C})$.

(ii) Given total endowment $(\bar{e}_0, \bar{\boldsymbol{e}})$. If a consumption allocation $\{(c_0^1, \boldsymbol{c}^1), \dots, (c_0^L, \boldsymbol{c}^L)\}$ solves the central planner's problem with non-zero and non-negative weights, then the allocation is Pareto-optimal.

Proof. (i) The proof applies the Separating Hyperplane Theorem.[1] Given aggregate resources $(C_0, \boldsymbol{C})$, the set of feasible consumption allocations is $\mathcal{A}(C_0, \boldsymbol{C})$. Define the set A as

$$A = \Big\{\boldsymbol{a} \in \mathbb{R}^L \;\big|\; a_l = \mathcal{U}_l(x_0^l, \boldsymbol{x}^l) - \mathcal{U}_l(c_0^l, \boldsymbol{c}^l), \quad l = 1, \dots, L,$$
$$\text{for some } \{(x_0^1, \boldsymbol{x}^1), \dots, (x_0^L, \boldsymbol{x}^L)\} \in \mathcal{A}(C_0, \boldsymbol{C})\Big\},$$

so that a_l is the increase in the individual l's utility when considering some alternative feasible consumption allocation. Note that $\mathbf{0} \in A$ since we can take $x_0^l = c_0^l$ and $\boldsymbol{x}^l = \boldsymbol{c}^l$ for all l. First, we show that A is convex. Assume $\boldsymbol{a}, \hat{\boldsymbol{a}} \in A$ and take $\alpha \in [0, 1]$. Then we have to show that $\bar{\boldsymbol{a}} \equiv \alpha \boldsymbol{a} + (1 - \alpha)\hat{\boldsymbol{a}} \in A$. Since $\boldsymbol{a}, \hat{\boldsymbol{a}} \in A$, we know that

$$a_l = \mathcal{U}_l(x_0^l, \boldsymbol{x}^l) - \mathcal{U}_l(c_0^l, \boldsymbol{c}^l), \quad \hat{a}_l = \mathcal{U}_l(\hat{x}_0^l, \hat{\boldsymbol{x}}^l) - \mathcal{U}_l(c_0^l, \boldsymbol{c}^l)$$

for some $\{(x_0^1, \boldsymbol{x}^1), \dots, (x_0^L, \boldsymbol{x}^L)\}$ and $\{(\hat{x}_0^1, \hat{\boldsymbol{x}}^1), \dots, (\hat{x}_0^L, \hat{\boldsymbol{x}}^L)\}$ in $\mathcal{A}(C_0, \boldsymbol{C})$. Now observe that

$$\begin{aligned}
\bar{a}_l &= \alpha a_l + (1 - \alpha)\hat{a}_l \\
&= \alpha \mathcal{U}_l(x_0^l, \boldsymbol{x}^l) + (1 - \alpha)\mathcal{U}_l(\hat{x}_0^l, \hat{\boldsymbol{x}}^l) - \mathcal{U}_l(c_0^l, \boldsymbol{c}^l) \\
&\leq \mathcal{U}_l\left(\alpha x_0^l + (1 - \alpha)\hat{x}_0^l, \alpha \boldsymbol{x}^l + (1 - \alpha)\hat{\boldsymbol{x}}^l\right) - \mathcal{U}_l(c_0^l, \boldsymbol{c}^l),
\end{aligned}$$

where the inequality is due to the assumed concavity of the utility index $\mathcal{U}_l$. Since $\mathcal{U}_l$ is increasing, we can certainly find $\{(\bar{x}_0^1, \bar{\boldsymbol{x}}^1), \dots, (\bar{x}_0^L, \bar{\boldsymbol{x}}^L)\}$ such that

$$\bar{a}_l = \mathcal{U}_l(\bar{x}_0^l, \bar{\boldsymbol{x}}^l) - \mathcal{U}_l(c_0^l, \boldsymbol{c}^l)$$

and

$$\bar{x}_0^l \leq \alpha x_0^l + (1 - \alpha)\hat{x}_0^l, \quad \bar{\boldsymbol{x}}^l \leq \alpha \boldsymbol{x}^l + (1 - \alpha)\hat{\boldsymbol{x}}^l$$

for all $l = 1, \dots, L$ so that $\{(\bar{x}_0^1, \bar{\boldsymbol{x}}^1), \dots, (\bar{x}_0^L, \bar{\boldsymbol{x}}^L)\}$ is feasible. Hence $\bar{\boldsymbol{a}} \in A$ so A is indeed convex.

Let $B = \mathbb{R}_+^L \setminus \{\mathbf{0}\}$ denote the set of non-negative vectors in $\mathbb{R}^L$ excluding the zero vector. Of course, B is also convex.

[1] The Separating Hyperplane Theorem comes in several different versions. The one applied here is as follows: suppose that A and B are non-empty, disjoint, convex subsets of $\mathbb{R}^n$ for some integer $n \geq 1$. Then there is a non-zero vector $\boldsymbol{\eta} \in \mathbb{R}^n$ and a scalar ξ so that $\boldsymbol{\eta}^\top \boldsymbol{a} \leq \xi \leq \boldsymbol{\eta}^\top \boldsymbol{b}$ for all $\boldsymbol{a} \in A$ and all $\boldsymbol{b} \in B$. Hence, A and B are separated by the hyperplane $H = \{\boldsymbol{x} \in \mathbb{R}^n | \boldsymbol{\eta}^\top \boldsymbol{x} = \xi\}$. See, for example, Sydsaeter *et al.* (2005, Thm. 13.6.3).

Observe that $A \cap B = \emptyset$: if you could find an $\boldsymbol{a} \in A$ with all $\boldsymbol{a} \geq \boldsymbol{0}$ and $a_l > 0$ for some l that would imply the existence of a feasible consumption allocation $\{(x_0^1, \boldsymbol{x}^1), \ldots, (x_0^L, \boldsymbol{x}^L)\}$ with

$$\mathcal{U}_k(x_0^k, \boldsymbol{x}^k) \geq \mathcal{U}_k(c_0^k, \boldsymbol{c}^k), \quad k = 1, \ldots, L,$$

and

$$\mathcal{U}_l(x_0^l, \boldsymbol{x}^l) > \mathcal{U}_l(c_0^l, \boldsymbol{c}^l),$$

which would contradict the Pareto optimality of the allocation $\{(c_0^1, \boldsymbol{c}^1), \ldots, (c_0^L, \boldsymbol{c}^L)\}$.

The Separating Hyperplane Theorem now implies the existence of a non-zero vector $\boldsymbol{\eta} = (\eta_1, \ldots, \eta_L)^\top \in \mathbb{R}^L$ so that

$$\boldsymbol{\eta} \cdot \boldsymbol{a} \leq \boldsymbol{\eta} \cdot \boldsymbol{b}, \quad \text{for all } \boldsymbol{a} \in A,\ \boldsymbol{b} \in B.$$

Because $\boldsymbol{0} \in A$, we have $\boldsymbol{\eta} \cdot \boldsymbol{a} \leq 0$ for all $\boldsymbol{a} \in A$, which means that

$$\sum_{l=1}^{L} \eta_l \mathcal{U}_l(x_0^l, \boldsymbol{x}^l) \leq \sum_{l=1}^{L} \eta_l \mathcal{U}_l(c_0^l, \boldsymbol{c}^l)$$

for all consumption allocations $\{(x_0^1, \boldsymbol{x}^1), \ldots, (x_0^L, \boldsymbol{x}^L)\} \in \mathcal{A}(C_0, \boldsymbol{C})$. This shows that $\{(c_0^1, \boldsymbol{c}^1), \ldots, (c_0^L, \boldsymbol{c}^L)\}$ maximizes $\mathcal{U}_{\boldsymbol{\eta}}(C_0, \boldsymbol{C})$ for that $\boldsymbol{\eta}$. Furthermore, we must have $\boldsymbol{\eta} \cdot \boldsymbol{b} \geq 0$ for all $\boldsymbol{b} \in B$, which requires $\boldsymbol{\eta} \geq 0$.

Proof of (ii): Since all the utility indices are increasing, the resource constraints are binding and it is impossible to allocate more consumption to anyone without reducing the consumption of at least one individual. □

Consequently, we can derive properties of Pareto-optimal allocations by studying the solution to the central planner's problem. The Lagrangian of the central planner's constrained maximization problem is

$$\mathcal{L} = \sum_{l=1}^{L} \eta_l \mathcal{U}_l(c_0^l, \boldsymbol{c}^l) + \alpha_0 \left(\bar{e}_0 - \sum_{l=1}^{L} c_0^l \right) + \sum_{\omega=1}^{S} \alpha_\omega \left(\bar{e}_\omega - \sum_{l=1}^{L} c_\omega^l \right),$$

where $\alpha_0, \alpha_1, \ldots, \alpha_S$ are Lagrange multipliers. The first-order conditions are

$$\frac{\partial \mathcal{L}}{\partial c_0^l} = 0 \quad \Leftrightarrow \quad \eta_l \frac{\partial \mathcal{U}_l}{\partial c_0^l} = \alpha_0, \quad l = 1, \ldots, L, \tag{7.4}$$

$$\frac{\partial \mathcal{L}}{\partial c_\omega^l} = 0 \quad \Leftrightarrow \quad \eta_l \frac{\partial \mathcal{U}_l}{\partial c_\omega^l} = \alpha_\omega, \quad \omega = 1, \ldots, S, \quad l = 1, \ldots, L, \tag{7.5}$$

$$\frac{\partial \mathcal{L}}{\partial \alpha_0} = 0 \quad \Leftrightarrow \quad \sum_{l=1}^{L} c_0^l = \bar{e}_0, \tag{7.6}$$

$$\frac{\partial \mathcal{L}}{\partial \alpha_\omega} = 0 \quad \Leftrightarrow \quad \sum_{l=1}^{L} c_\omega^l = \bar{e}_\omega, \quad \omega = 1, \dots, S. \tag{7.7}$$

Given strictly increasing and concave utility functions with infinite marginal utility at zero, the first-order conditions are both necessary and sufficient for optimality. We can thus conclude that a feasible consumption allocation is Pareto-optimal if and only if we can find a weighting vector $\boldsymbol{\eta} = (\eta_1, \dots, \eta_L)^\top$ so that (7.4) and (7.5) are satisfied. In particular, by dividing (7.5) by (7.4), it is clear that we need to have

$$\frac{\frac{\partial \mathcal{U}_l}{\partial c_\omega^l}}{\frac{\partial \mathcal{U}_l}{\partial c_0^l}} = \frac{\alpha_\omega}{\alpha_0}, \quad \omega = 1, \dots, S, \quad l = 1, \dots, L. \tag{7.8}$$

The left-hand side is the marginal rate of substitution of individual l.

Recall from (6.11) that the vector $\boldsymbol{\psi}^l = (\psi_1^l, \dots, \psi_S^l)^\top$ defined by

$$\psi_\omega^l = \frac{\frac{\partial \mathcal{U}_l}{\partial c_\omega^l}}{\frac{\partial \mathcal{U}_l}{\partial c_0^l}}, \quad \omega = 1, \dots, S,$$

is the state-price vector induced by individual l. According to Eq. (7.8), the central planner will optimally allocate consumption so that the marginal rates of substitution of all individuals—and therefore all the associated state-price vectors—are identical. A state-price vector $\boldsymbol{\psi}$ can be transformed into a state-price deflator ζ via $\zeta_\omega = \psi_\omega / p_\omega$, compare Eq. (4.16), so when individuals agree on the state probabilities, identical state-price vectors imply identical state-price deflators. For each ω, let $\psi_\omega = \alpha_\omega / \alpha_0$ denote the common value of $\psi_\omega^1, \dots, \psi_\omega^L$. Note that since we can scale all η_l's by a positive constant without affecting the maximizing consumption allocation, we might as well assume $\alpha_0 = 1$. Then $\alpha_\omega = \psi_\omega$, and we can rewrite the first-order conditions (7.4) and (7.5) as

$$\eta_l \frac{\partial \mathcal{U}_l}{\partial c_0^l} = 1, \quad l = 1, \dots, L, \tag{7.9}$$

$$\eta_l \frac{\partial \mathcal{U}_l}{\partial c_\omega^l} = \psi_\omega, \quad \omega = 1, \dots, S, \quad l = 1, \dots, L. \tag{7.10}$$

The alignment of the marginal rates of substitution of all individuals is referred to as *efficient risk-sharing*. The central planner will distribute aggregate consumption risk so that all individuals have the same marginal willingness to shift consumption across time and states.

Conversely, suppose a consumption allocation is feasible, that is it satisfies Eqs. (7.6) and (7.7), and the marginal rates of substitution of all individuals are identical so that

$$\frac{\frac{\partial \mathcal{U}_l}{\partial c^l_\omega}}{\frac{\partial \mathcal{U}_l}{\partial c^l_0}} = \psi_\omega, \quad \omega = 1, \dots, S, \quad l = 1, \dots, L.$$

for some $\psi_1, \dots, \psi_S$. If we define

$$\eta_l = \frac{1}{\frac{\partial \mathcal{U}_l}{\partial c^l_0}}, \quad l = 1, \dots, L,$$

then the first-order conditions (7.9) and (7.10) for the central planner will be satisfied with these weights. Consequently, the consumption allocation is Pareto-optimal. Hence, we have the following result:

Theorem 7.2 *A feasible consumption allocation is Pareto-optimal if and only if individuals share the aggregate risk efficiently, that is their marginal rates of substitution are identical.*

Let us specialize to the case where individuals have time-additive expected utility so that

$$\mathcal{U}_l(c_0, c) = u_l(c_0) + e^{-\delta_l}\,\mathrm{E}[u_l(c)] = u_l(c_0) + e^{-\delta_l}\sum_{\omega=1}^{S} p_\omega u_l(c_\omega).$$

Then we can replace Eqs. (7.9) and (7.10) by

$$\eta_l u_l'(c^l_0) = 1, \quad l = 1, \dots, L, \tag{7.11}$$

$$\eta_l e^{-\delta_l} p_\omega u_l'(c^l_\omega) = \psi_\omega, \quad \omega = 1, \dots, S, \quad l = 1, \dots, L. \tag{7.12}$$

Dividing the second equation by the first, we see that a Pareto-optimal consumption allocation has the property that

$$e^{-\delta_k}\frac{u_k'(c^k_\omega)}{u_k'(c^k_0)} = e^{-\delta_l}\frac{u_l'(c^l_\omega)}{u_l'(c^l_0)}, \quad \omega = 1, \dots, S, \tag{7.13}$$

for any two individuals k and l. Recall from Chapter 6 that the marginal rate of substitution of any individual works as a state-price deflator. Again we conclude that, with Pareto-optimal allocations, these state-price deflators are all identical so that individuals agree on the valuation of an extra bit of consumption in any given state.

The following theorem shows that all Pareto-optimal consumption allocations have the property that the consumption of each individual is an increasing function of the aggregate consumption. This is the so-called *mutuality property*. The consumption levels of different individuals move together.

Theorem 7.3 *Suppose that all individuals have time-additive expected utility. Let* $\{(c^1_0, \mathbf{c}^1), \dots, (c^L_0, \mathbf{c}^L)\}$ *be a Pareto-optimal consumption allocation and define* *the state-dependent aggregate consumption by* $C_\omega = \sum_{l=1}^{L} c_\omega^l$. *Then the consumption of any individual will be a strictly increasing function of aggregate consumption so that, for any* l, *we have* $c^l = f_l(C)$ *for some strictly increasing function* f_l.

Proof. Since we assume a Pareto-optimal allocation, we know from Theorem 7.1 that we can find a weighting vector $\eta = (\eta_1, \dots, \eta_L)^\top$ so that Eqs. (7.11) and (7.12) hold. In particular, we have

$$\eta_k u_k'(c_0^k) = \eta_l u_l'(c_0^l),$$
$$\eta_k e^{-\delta_k} u_k'(c_\omega^k) = \eta_l e^{-\delta_l} u_l'(c_\omega^l), \quad \omega = 1, \dots, S,$$

for any two individuals k and l. Moreover, it follows from the latter of these equations that

$$\frac{u_k'(c_\omega^k)}{u_k'(c_{\omega'}^k)} = \frac{u_l'(c_\omega^l)}{u_l'(c_{\omega'}^l)} \tag{7.14}$$

for any two states $\omega, \omega' \in \Omega$.

Suppose that aggregate consumption is higher in state ω than in state ω', that is $C_\omega > C_{\omega'}$. Then there must be at least one individual, say individual l, who consumes more in state ω than in state ω', $c_\omega^l > c_{\omega'}^l$. Consequently, $u_l'(c_\omega^l) < u_l'(c_{\omega'}^l)$. But then Eq. (7.14) implies that $u_k'(c_\omega^k) < u_k'(c_{\omega'}^k)$ and thus $c_\omega^k > c_{\omega'}^k$ for *all* individuals k. □

A consequence of the previous theorem is that, with Pareto-optimal allocations, individuals do not have to distinguish between states with identical aggregate consumption. Aggregate consumption C at time 1 is a random variable that induces a partition of the state space. Suppose that the possible values of aggregate consumption are $x_1, \dots, x_N$ where $N \leq S$. Let $\Omega_n = \{\omega \in \Omega | C_\omega = x_n\}$ denote the set of states in which aggregate consumption equals x_n. Then $\Omega = \Omega_1 \cup \dots \cup \Omega_N$. For any individual l, we can define a valid state-price vector by

$$\psi_\omega = e^{-\delta_l} \frac{p_\omega u_l'(c_\omega^l)}{u_l'(c_0^l)} = e^{-\delta_l} \frac{p_\omega u_l'(f_l(C_\omega))}{u_l'(c_0^l)}.$$

Recall that we can interpret ψ_ω as the time 0 price of an asset paying a dividend of 1 if state ω is realized and nothing in any other state. Hence,

$$\psi(n) \equiv \sum_{\omega \in \Omega_n} \psi_\omega$$

can be interpreted as the price of an asset paying a dividend of 1 if aggregate consumption turns out to be x_n and a 0 dividend in other cases. Combining the two preceding equations, we see that

$$\begin{aligned}\psi(n) &= \sum_{\omega\in\Omega_n} e^{-\delta_l}\frac{p_\omega u_l'(f_l(C_\omega))}{u_l'(c_0^l)}\\ &= e^{-\delta_l}\frac{u_l'(f_l(x_n))}{u_l'(c_0^l)}\sum_{\omega\in\Omega_n} p_\omega\\ &= e^{-\delta_l}\frac{u_l'(f_l(x_n))}{u_l'(c_0^l)}\mathbb{P}(C=x_n).\end{aligned}$$

The price of any marketed dividend D can now be written as

$$\begin{aligned}P &= \sum_{\omega=1}^{S}\psi_\omega D_\omega = \sum_{n=1}^{N}\sum_{\omega\in\Omega_n}\psi_\omega D_\omega\\ &= \sum_{n=1}^{N}\sum_{\omega\in\Omega_n} e^{-\delta_l}\frac{p_\omega u_l'(f_l(C_\omega))}{u_l'(c_0^l)}D_\omega = \sum_{n=1}^{N} e^{-\delta_l}\frac{u_l'(f_l(x_n))}{u_l'(c_0^l)}\sum_{\omega\in\Omega_n} p_\omega D_\omega\\ &= \sum_{n=1}^{N}\frac{\psi(n)}{\mathbb{P}(C=x_n)}\sum_{\omega\in\Omega_n} p_\omega D_\omega = \sum_{n=1}^{N}\psi(n)\sum_{\omega\in\Omega_n}\frac{p_\omega}{\mathbb{P}(C=x_n)}D_\omega\\ &= \sum_{n=1}^{N}\psi(n)\,\mathrm{E}[D|C=x_n],\end{aligned}$$

where $\mathrm{E}[D|C=x_n]$ is the expected dividend conditional on aggregate consumption being x_n. The last equality is due to the fact that $p_\omega/\mathbb{P}(C=x_n)$ is the conditional probability of the state ω given that aggregate consumption is x_n. To price any marketed dividend we thus need only prices of Arrow–Debreu-style assets on aggregate consumption and the expectation of the dividend conditional on the aggregate consumption. In Exercise 7.4, you are asked to show that if individuals can trade in a sufficiently large set of options on aggregate consumption with different strike prices, they can form such Arrow–Debreu-style assets. Hence, the values of the $\psi(n)$-terms in the pricing equation above could be derived from the prices of such options. This idea is due to Ross (1976b) and Breeden and Litzenberger (1978).

Note that the two preceding theorems do *not* imply that individuals have identical consumption growth rates in Pareto-optimal equilibria. Suppose, for example, individual k has constant relative risk aversion γ_k, individual l has constant relative risk aversion γ_l, and the two individuals have identical subjective time preference rates, $\delta_k=\delta_l$. Then it follows from Eq. (7.13) that the consumption growth rate of individual k is a power of the consumption growth rate of individual l:

$$\frac{c^k}{c_0^k} = \left(\frac{c^l}{c_0^l}\right)^{\gamma_l/\gamma_k}.$$

The consumption growth rates are identical only if $\gamma_l = \gamma_k$.

7.4 EXISTENCE OF PARETO-OPTIMAL EQUILIBRIA

The preceding section established a number of interesting properties of Pareto-optimal equilibria. But will equilibria in financial markets be Pareto-optimal? This section shows that when financial markets are complete or 'close to complete', then the equilibria will be Pareto-optimal.

7.4.1 Complete Markets

In the preceding section we concluded that in Pareto-optimal equilibria, the state-price deflators induced by all individuals are identical. From Theorem 4.6, we know that if the market is complete and arbitrage-free, the state-price deflator is unique. This suggests a close link between Pareto-optimal equilibria and market completeness. Indeed, we have the following result known as the *First Welfare Theorem*:

Theorem 7.4 *If the financial market is complete, then every equilibrium consumption allocation is Pareto-optimal.*

Proof. Recall from Eq. (6.15) that in a complete market the utility maximization problem of individual l can be written as

$$\begin{aligned}
&\max_{c_0, \boldsymbol{c}} \mathcal{U}_l(c_0, \boldsymbol{c}) \\
&\quad \text{s.t. } c_0 + \boldsymbol{\psi} \cdot \boldsymbol{c} \leq e_0^l + \boldsymbol{\psi} \cdot \boldsymbol{e}^l \\
&\quad\quad c_0, \boldsymbol{c} \geq 0,
\end{aligned}$$

where $\boldsymbol{\psi}$ is the unique state-price vector. Let $\{(c_0^l, \boldsymbol{c}^l), l = 1, \ldots, L\}$ be an equilibrium consumption allocation, but not Pareto-optimal. This would imply the existence of another consumption allocation $\{(\hat{c}_0^l, \hat{\boldsymbol{c}}^l), l = 1, \ldots, L\}$ that gives all individuals at least the same utility and some individuals a strictly higher utility than $\{(c_0^l, \boldsymbol{c}^l), l = 1, \ldots, L\}$. Since we assume strictly increasing utility and $(c_0^l, \boldsymbol{c}^l)$ maximizes individual l's utility subject to the constraint $c_0^l + \boldsymbol{\psi} \cdot \boldsymbol{c}^l \leq e_0^l + \boldsymbol{\psi} \cdot \boldsymbol{e}^l$, the inequality

$$\hat{c}_0^l + \boldsymbol{\psi} \cdot \hat{\boldsymbol{c}}^l \geq e_0^l + \boldsymbol{\psi} \cdot \boldsymbol{e}^l$$

must hold for all individuals with strict inequality for at least one individual. Summing up over all individuals we get

$$\sum_{l=1}^{L} \left(\hat{c}_0^l + \boldsymbol{\psi} \cdot \hat{\boldsymbol{c}}^l \right) > \sum_{l=1}^{L} \left(e_0^l + \boldsymbol{\psi} \cdot \boldsymbol{e}^l \right) = \bar{e}_0 + \boldsymbol{\psi} \cdot \bar{\boldsymbol{e}}.$$

Hence, the consumption allocation $\{(\hat{c}_0^l, \hat{\boldsymbol{c}}^l), l = 1, \dots, L\}$ is not feasible. Consequently, the consumption allocation $\{(c_0^l, \boldsymbol{c}^l), l = 1, \dots, L\}$ must be Pareto-optimal. □

A complete market equilibrium thus provides efficient risk-sharing. For the special case of time-additive expected utility—as already explained in the preceding section—this implies that

$$e^{-\delta_k} \frac{u_k'\left(c_\omega^k\right)}{u_k'\left(c_0^k\right)} = e^{-\delta_l} \frac{u_l'\left(c_\omega^l\right)}{u_l'\left(c_0^l\right)}$$

for any ω, and thus

$$\frac{u_k'\left(c_\omega^k\right)}{u_k'\left(c_{\omega'}^k\right)} = \frac{u_l'\left(c_\omega^l\right)}{u_l'\left(c_{\omega'}^l\right)} \tag{7.14}$$

for any two states ω and ω' and any two individuals k and l.

Suppose that Eq. (7.14) did not hold so that we could find two individuals k and l and two states ω and ω' such that

$$\frac{u_k'(c_\omega^k)}{u_k'(c_{\omega'}^k)} > \frac{u_l'(c_\omega^l)}{u_l'(c_{\omega'}^l)}. \tag{7.15}$$

Then the two agents could engage in a trade that makes both better off. What trade would facilitate this? Since the market is complete, Arrow–Debreu assets for all states are traded, in particular for states ω and ω'. Consider the following trade: individual k buys ε_ω Arrow–Debreu assets for state ω from individual l at a unit price of φ_ω. And individual l buys $\varepsilon_{\omega'}$ Arrow–Debreu assets for state ω' from individual k at a unit price of $\varphi_{\omega'}$. The deal is arranged so that the net price is zero, that is

$$\varepsilon_\omega \varphi_\omega - \varepsilon_{\omega'} \varphi_{\omega'} = 0 \quad \Leftrightarrow \quad \varepsilon_{\omega'} = \varepsilon_\omega \frac{\varphi_{\omega'}}{\varphi_\omega}.$$

The deal will change the consumption of the two individuals in states ω and ω' but not in other states, nor at time 0. The total change in the expected utility of individual k will be

$$p_\omega \left(u_k(c_\omega^k + \varepsilon_\omega) - u_k(c_\omega^k) \right) + p_{\omega'} \left(u_k \left(c_{\omega'}^k - \varepsilon_\omega \frac{\varphi_{\omega'}}{\varphi_\omega} \right) - u_k(c_{\omega'}^k) \right).$$

Dividing by ε_ω and letting $\varepsilon_\omega \to 0$, the additional expected utility approaches

$$p_\omega u_k'(c_\omega^k) - p_{\omega'} \frac{\varphi_{\omega'}}{\varphi_\omega} u_k'(c_{\omega'}^k),$$

which is strictly positive whenever

$$\frac{u_k'(c_\omega^k)}{u_k'(c_{\omega'}^k)} > \frac{p_{\omega'}\varphi_{\omega'}}{p_\omega \varphi_\omega}. \tag{7.16}$$

On the other hand, the total change in the expected utility of individual l will be

$$p_\omega \left(u_l(c_\omega^l - \varepsilon_\omega) - u_l(c_\omega^l)\right) + p_{\omega'} \left(u_l(c_{\omega'}^l + \varepsilon_\omega \frac{\varphi_{\omega'}}{\varphi_\omega}) - u_l(c_{\omega'}^l)\right).$$

Dividing by ε_ω and letting $\varepsilon_\omega \to 0$, we get

$$-p_\omega u_l'(c_\omega^l) + p_{\omega'} \frac{\varphi_{\omega'}}{\varphi_\omega} u_l'(c_{\omega'}^l),$$

which is strictly positive whenever

$$\frac{u_l'(c_\omega^l)}{u_l'(c_{\omega'}^l)} < \frac{p_{\omega'}\varphi_{\omega'}}{p_\omega \varphi_\omega}. \tag{7.17}$$

If the inequality (7.15) holds, the two individuals can surely find prices φ_ω and $\varphi_{\omega'}$ so that both Eqs. (7.16) and (7.17) are satisfied, which means that both individuals increase their expected utility.

If the market is incomplete, the individuals might not be able to implement this trade. In other words, we cannot be sure that the efficient risk-sharing condition (7.14) holds for states for which Arrow–Debreu assets are not traded, that is 'uninsurable' states. With incomplete markets, it is not always possible for individuals to align their marginal rates of substitution.

Complete markets have another interesting property: any (interior) Pareto-optimal consumption allocation is an equilibrium allocation after the aggregate endowment is reallocated appropriately. In other words, any particular Pareto-optimal allocation, which may be attractive from a social or political perspective, can be achieved by redistributing wealth (for example, via taxes and transfers) and then letting the individuals trade until the economy is in equilibrium. This is the so-called *Second Welfare Theorem*. See, for example, Kreps (1990, Sec. 6.3).

7.4.2 Pareto-Optimality in Some Incomplete Markets

As shown above, complete market equilibria are Pareto-optimal. However, as discussed earlier, real-life financial markets are probably not complete. Equilibrium consumption allocations in incomplete markets will generally not be

Pareto-optimal since the individuals cannot necessarily implement the trades needed to align their marginal rates of substitution. On the other hand, individuals do not have to be able to implement *any* possible consumption plan so we do not need markets to be complete in the strict sense. If every Pareto-optimal consumption allocation can be obtained by trading in the available assets, the market is said to be *effectively complete*. In this section we will discuss some examples of effectively complete markets.

For any Pareto-optimal consumption allocation we know from Theorem 7.3 that the consumption of any individual is an increasing function of aggregate consumption. Individual consumption is measurable with respect to aggregate consumption. As in the discussion below Theorem 7.3, suppose that the possible values of the aggregate consumption level are $x_1, \ldots, x_N$ and let $\Omega_n = \{\omega \in \Omega | C_\omega = x_n\}$ be the set of states in which aggregate consumption equals x_n. If it is possible for each n to form a portfolio that provides a payment of 1 if the state is in Ω_n and a 0 payment otherwise—an Arrow–Debreu-style asset for aggregate consumption—then the market is effectively complete (see also Exercise 7.4). The individuals are indifferent between states within a given subset Ω_n. Risk beyond aggregate consumption risk does not carry any premium. Assuming strictly increasing utility functions, aggregate time 1 consumption will equal aggregate time 1 endowment. If we think of the aggregate endowment as the total value of the market, aggregate consumption will equal the value of the market portfolio and we can partition the state space according to the value or return of the market portfolio. Risk beyond market risk is diversified away and does not carry any premium.

If a full set of Arrow–Debreu-style assets for aggregate consumption is traded, markets will be effectively complete for all strictly increasing and concave utility functions. The next theorem, which is due to Rubinstein (1974), shows that markets are effectively complete under weaker assumptions on the available assets if individuals have utility functions of the HARA class with identical risk cautiousness. Before stating the precise result, let us recall a few facts about the HARA utility functions which were defined in Section 5.6. A utility function u is of the HARA class, if the absolute risk tolerance is affine, that is

$$\mathrm{ART}(c) \equiv -\frac{u'(c)}{u''(c)} = \alpha c + \beta.$$

The risk cautiousness is $\mathrm{ART}'(c) = \alpha$. Ignoring insignificant constants, the marginal utility must be either

$$u'(c) = e^{-c/\beta},$$

for the case $\alpha = 0$ (corresponding to negative exponential utility, that is CARA utility), or

$$u'(c) = (\alpha c + \beta)^{-1/\alpha},$$

for the case $\alpha \neq 0$ (which encompasses extended log-utility, satiation HARA utility, and subsistence HARA utility).

Theorem 7.5 *Suppose that*

(i) all individuals have time-additive HARA utility functions with identical risk cautiousness,

(ii) a risk-free asset is traded,

(iii) the time 1 endowments of all individuals are spanned by traded assets, that is $e^l \in \mathcal{M}$, $l = 1, \dots, L$.

Then the equilibrium is Pareto-optimal and the optimal consumption for any individual is a strictly increasing affine function of aggregate consumption.

The property that individual optimal consumption is an affine function of aggregate consumption is referred to as a *linear sharing rule*.

Proof. Suppose first that the market is complete. Then we know that the equilibrium consumption allocation will be Pareto-optimal and we can find a weighting vector $\boldsymbol{\eta} = (\eta_1, \dots, \eta_L)^{\top}$ so that

$$\eta_k e^{-\delta_k} u_k'(c_\omega^k) = \eta_l e^{-\delta_l} u_l'(c_\omega^l)$$

for any two individuals k and l and any state ω. Assume that the common risk cautiousness α is different from zero so that

$$u_l'(c) = (\alpha c + \beta_l)^{-1/\alpha}, \quad l = 1, \dots, L.$$

(The proof for the CARA utility case $\alpha = 0$ is similar, see Exercise 7.8.) Substituting this into the previous equation, we obtain

$$\eta_k e^{-\delta_k} \left(\alpha c_\omega^k + \beta_k\right)^{-1/\alpha} = \eta_l e^{-\delta_l} \left(\alpha c_\omega^l + \beta_l\right)^{-1/\alpha},$$

which implies that

$$\left(\eta_k e^{-\delta_k}\right)^{-\alpha} \left(\alpha c_\omega^k + \beta_k\right) \left(\eta_l e^{-\delta_l}\right)^{\alpha} = \alpha c_\omega^l + \beta_l.$$

Summing up over $l = 1, \dots, L$, we get

$$\left(\eta_k e^{-\delta_k}\right)^{-\alpha} \left(\alpha c_\omega^k + \beta_k\right) \sum_{l=1}^{L} \left(\eta_l e^{-\delta_l}\right)^{\alpha} = \alpha \sum_{l=1}^{L} c_\omega^l + \sum_{l=1}^{L} \beta_l = \alpha C_\omega + \sum_{l=1}^{L} \beta_l,$$

where C_ω is aggregate consumption (or endowment) in state ω. Solving for c_ω^k, we find that

$$c_\omega^k = \frac{\alpha C_\omega + \sum_{l=1}^{L} \beta_l}{\alpha \left(\eta_k e^{-\delta_k}\right)^{-\alpha} \sum_{l=1}^{L} \left(\eta_l e^{-\delta_l}\right)^{\alpha}} - \frac{\beta_k}{\alpha} \equiv A_k C_\omega + B_k,$$

which is strictly increasing and affine in C_ω.

The same consumption allocation can be obtained in a market where a risk-free asset exists and the time 1 endowments of all individuals are spanned by traded assets. □

However, it is only under very special assumptions on preferences and endowments that incomplete markets lead to Pareto-optimal equilibrium consumption allocations. In fact, Geanakoplos and Polemarchakis (1986) show that with incomplete markets and under 'natural' assumptions on preferences, the equilibrium allocation will be Pareto-inefficient for almost any allocation of endowments.

7.5 THE REPRESENTATIVE INDIVIDUAL

Asset pricing models frequently refer to a *representative individual* or representative agent, as we shall see in subsequent chapters. The motivation is that it is much easier to analyse models with a single individual than a model with many heterogeneous individuals. Obviously, there will be no trade in a single-individual economy as the individual has no one to trade with. This implies that the consumption of the individual will equal the exogenously given endowment. Of course, to be of any interest for asset pricing purposes, such a single-individual economy should be constructed so that it will produce equilibrium asset prices identical to the equilibrium asset prices in a more realistic economy with many individuals. If that is the case, we refer to the single individual as a representative individual.

More formally, consider again the economy $\mathcal{E}$ defined in (7.1). If we want to construct a single-individual economy, we have to define the utility index and the endowment of that individual. It seems natural to define the endowment of the individual to be identical to the aggregate endowment in the multiagent economy $\mathcal{E}$,

$$\bar{e}_0 = \sum_{l=1}^{L} e_0^l, \quad \bar{e} = \sum_{l=1}^{L} e^l,$$

so the main challenge is to construct an appropriate utility index. Here, it is tempting to look for some combination $\mathcal{U}_\eta$ of the utility indices of the individuals in the original economy $\mathcal{E}$, as in the definition of the central planner's problem in Eq. (7.3).

Definition 7.3 *The economy $\mathcal{E}$ defined in* (7.1) *is said to have a representative individual if, for each equilibrium $\left\{\boldsymbol{P} \in \mathbb{R}^I; (\boldsymbol{\theta}^1, \dots, \boldsymbol{\theta}^L) \in \Theta^1 \times \cdots \times \Theta^L\right\}$, we can find a positive vector $\boldsymbol{\eta} = (\eta_1, \dots, \eta_L)^\top$ such that $\{\boldsymbol{P}; \boldsymbol{0}\}$ is an equilibrium in the hypothetical single-individual economy*

$$\mathcal{E}_{rep} = \left\{\boldsymbol{D} \in \mathcal{L}_+^I; \left(\mathcal{U}_\eta, \bar{e}_0, \bar{e}\right) \in \mathbf{U} \times \mathbb{R}_+ \times \mathcal{L}(\mathbb{R}_+)\right\},$$

where $\mathcal{U}_\eta$ is defined in (7.3).

Theorem 7.1 has the following immediate consequence:

Theorem 7.6 *The economy has a representative individual if and only if all possible equilibria are Pareto-optimal.*

It follows from the preceding section that if the market is complete or effectively complete, we can use the representative individual approach to asset pricing. Of course, if you want to model how financial assets are traded, a representative individual formulation is not fruitful, but if you just want to study equilibrium asset prices it can be very convenient.

Given that a representative individual exists, how can we find the preferences of the representative individual $\mathcal{U}_\eta(\bar{e}_0, \bar{e})$? What is the appropriate weighting vector $\boldsymbol{\eta}$? How is the utility index $\mathcal{U}_\eta$ of the representative individual related to the individual utility indices $\mathcal{U}_l$?

In some cases with time-additive expected utility we can easily determine the preferences of the representative individual. With time-additive expected utility the central planner's objective is to maximize

$$\sum_{l=1}^{L} \eta_l \mathcal{U}_l(c_0^l, c^l) = \sum_{l=1}^{L} \eta_l u_l(c_0^l) + \sum_{\omega=1}^{S} p_\omega \sum_{l=1}^{L} \eta_l e^{-\delta_l} u_l(c_\omega^l).$$

Since the central planner cannot transfer aggregate endowment over time or across states, the maximum is achieved by separately maximizing $\sum_{l=1}^{L} \eta_l u_l(c_0^l)$ over all $(c_0^1, \dots, c_0^L)$ satisfying $\sum_{l=1}^{L} c_0^l \leq \bar{e}_0$ and by maximizing, for each $\omega \in \{1, \dots, S\}$, the sum $\sum_{l=1}^{L} \eta_l e^{-\delta_l} u_l(c_\omega^l)$ over all $(c_\omega^1, \dots, c_\omega^L)$ satisfying $\sum_{l=1}^{L} c_\omega^l \leq \bar{e}_\omega$. The constraints will obviously be binding. If we simplify to two individuals, the consumption of individual 2 is thus equal to the aggregate endowment minus the consumption of individual 1, so we only have to maximize over the consumption of individual 1. For any state at time 1, the problem is then to maximize

$$\eta_1 e^{-\delta_1} u_1(c^1) + \eta_2 e^{-\delta_2} u_2(\bar{e} - c^1).$$

The first-order condition for c^1 leads to

$$\eta_1 e^{-\delta_1} u_1'(c^1) = \eta_2 e^{-\delta_2} u_2'(\bar{e} - c^1). \tag{7.18}$$

Of course, we have a similar optimality condition for time 0, just without the time preference terms. To proceed, we need to specify the utility functions.

Example 7.1 (CARA Utility). Suppose first that both individuals have negative exponential utility $u_l(c) = -e^{-a_l c}$, $l = 1, 2$, where a_l is the constant absolute risk aversion of individual l. Then the optimality condition (7.18) implies that

$$c^1 = \frac{a_2}{a_1+a_2}\bar{e} - \frac{1}{a_1+a_2}\ln\left(\frac{\eta_2 a_2 e^{-\delta_2}}{\eta_1 a_1 e^{-\delta_1}}\right),$$

$$c^2 \equiv \bar{e} - c^1 = \frac{a_1}{a_1+a_2}\bar{e} + \frac{1}{a_1+a_2}\ln\left(\frac{\eta_2 a_2 e^{-\delta_2}}{\eta_1 a_1 e^{-\delta_1}}\right).$$

After substituting these expressions into the objective function and simplifying, we can write the maximum value of the objective function as

$$\eta_1 e^{-\delta_1} u_1(c^1) + \eta_2 e^{-\delta_2} u_2(c^2) = -ke^{-\frac{\delta_1 a_2 + \delta_2 a_1}{a_1+a_2}} e^{-\frac{a_1 a_2}{a_1+a_2}\bar{e}} \equiv -ke^{-\delta} e^{-a\bar{e}},$$

where

$$k = \eta_1^{\frac{a_2}{a_1+a_2}} \eta_2^{\frac{a_1}{a_1+a_2}} \left(\frac{a_2}{a_1}\right)^{\frac{a_1}{a_1+a_2}} \left(1 + \frac{a_1}{a_2}\right)$$

is a positive constant and

$$\delta = \frac{\delta_1 a_2 + \delta_2 a_1}{a_1 + a_2}, \qquad a = \frac{a_1 a_2}{a_1 + a_2}.$$

Note that since k does not involve the time preference rates, the same constant works at time 0. Adding up over states and time, the maximized total objective of the central planner becomes

$$\mathcal{U}_\eta(\bar{e}_0, \bar{e}) = -ke^{-a\bar{e}_0} + \mathrm{E}\left[-ke^{-\delta}e^{-a\bar{e}}\right] = k\left(-e^{-a\bar{e}_0} + \mathrm{E}\left[-e^{-\delta}e^{-a\bar{e}}\right]\right).$$

This is utility-wise equivalent to $-e^{-a\bar{e}_0} + \mathrm{E}\left[-e^{-\delta}e^{-a\bar{e}}\right]$, which does not involve the weights η_1, η_2. We conclude that the representative individual also has time-additive expected utility with a time preference rate of δ and a constant absolute risk aversion a.

We can reformulate the result in terms of the absolute risk tolerance $\tau_l = 1/a_l$, the reciprocal of the absolute risk aversion. The absolute risk tolerance of the representative individual is

$$\tau = \frac{1}{a} = \frac{a_1 + a_2}{a_1 a_2} = \frac{1}{a_1} + \frac{1}{a_2} = \tau_1 + \tau_2,$$

that is the sum of the absolute risk tolerances of the individuals. The time preference rate of the representative individual can be rewritten as

$$\delta = \frac{\delta_1 a_2 + \delta_2 a_1}{a_1 + a_2} = \frac{\delta_1 \tau_2^{-1} + \delta_2 \tau_1^{-1}}{\tau_1^{-1} + \tau_2^{-1}} = \frac{\delta_1 \tau_1 + \delta_2 \tau_2}{\tau_1 + \tau_2} = \frac{\tau_1}{\tau_1 + \tau_2}\delta_1 + \frac{\tau_2}{\tau_1 + \tau_2}\delta_2,$$

that is a risk-tolerance-weighted average of the time preference rate of the individuals.

These conclusions generalize naturally to the case with many individuals as the reader is asked to confirm in Exercise 7.6.

Example 7.2 (CRRA Utility). Next, let us consider the case where both individuals have constant relative risk aversion so that individual l has a time preference rate δ_l and a utility function $u_l(c) = \frac{1}{1-\gamma_l} c^{1-\gamma_l}$, where γ_l is the relative risk aversion. The optimality condition (7.18) related to time 1 consumption then implies that

$$c^1 = \left(\frac{\eta_2 e^{-\delta_2}(1-\gamma_1)}{\eta_1 e^{-\delta_1}(1-\gamma_2)} \right)^{-\frac{1}{\gamma_1}} \left(\bar{e} - c^1\right)^{\frac{\gamma_2}{\gamma_1}}.$$

To proceed, we have to assume identical degrees of risk aversion, so let γ denote the common value of $\gamma_1 = \gamma_2$. Then the preceding equation can be solved for c^1 so that

$$c^1 = \frac{\left(\frac{\eta_2 e^{-\delta_2}}{\eta_1 e^{-\delta_1}}\right)^{-\frac{1}{\gamma}}}{1 + \left(\frac{\eta_2 e^{-\delta_2}}{\eta_1 e^{-\delta_1}}\right)^{-\frac{1}{\gamma}}} \bar{e},$$

$$c^2 \equiv \bar{e} - c^1 = \frac{1}{1 + \left(\frac{\eta_2 e^{-\delta_2}}{\eta_1 e^{-\delta_1}}\right)^{-\frac{1}{\gamma}}} \bar{e}.$$

The maximum value of the objective function at time 1 becomes

$$\eta_1 e^{-\delta_1} u_1(c^1) + \eta_2 e^{-\delta_2} u_2(c^2) = k e^{-\delta_2} \frac{1}{1-\gamma} \bar{e}^{1-\gamma},$$

where

$$k = \left(\eta_1^{1/\gamma} e^{(\delta_2 - \delta_1)/\gamma} + \eta_2^{1/\gamma} \right)^{\gamma}.$$

Note that if $\delta_1 \neq \delta_2$, the k that applies to time 1 will be different from the k that applies to time 0 (where the time preference terms are not included). Only if we assume $\delta_1 = \delta_2$, and let δ denote their common value, the maximized total objective of the central planner can be written as

$$\mathcal{U}_\eta(\bar{e}_0, \bar{e}) = k \left(\frac{1}{1-\gamma} \bar{e}_0^{1-\gamma} + \mathrm{E}\left[e^{-\delta} \frac{1}{1-\gamma} \bar{e}^{1-\gamma} \right] \right),$$

which is utility-wise equivalent to time-additive expected CRRA utility. Of course, this result is hardly surprising: if the economy is populated by individuals with identical time preference rates δ and identical constant relative risk aversions γ, then a representative individual has time preference rate δ and constant relative risk aversion γ. When individuals have constant relative risk aversion but different degrees of risk aversion, a representative agent will generally not have a constant relative risk aversion. Even if you believe that CRRA utility is appropriate for individual decision-makers, it is not necessarily appropriate for a representative individual. A simple example is given in Exercise 7.7.

In Section 9.2.4, we will consider a model suggested by Chan and Kogan (2002) in which all individuals have constant, but different, relative risk aversions. In that model, the representative individual turns out to have a relative risk aversion that varies counter-cyclically with the state of the economy so that it is high in bad times and low in good times. The intuition is simple. Individuals with low risk aversions invest more in the stock market (or risky assets in general), so if the stock market is booming their wealth will increase by more than the wealth of more risk-averse individuals. Hence, the highly risk-averse individuals will have a smaller share of the total wealth of the economy, whereas the little risk-averse individuals will have a higher share. A wealth-weighted average risk aversion is therefore quite low. Conversely, when the stock market is performing poorly, the wealth-weighted average risk aversion will be quite high. If we think of the representative individual's relative risk aversion as such a wealth-weighted average relative risk aversion (more on this below), we see that it will indeed vary counter-cyclically.

Example 7.3 (Subsistence HARA Utility). Suppose all individuals have time-additive subsistence HARA utility, that is $u_l(c) = \frac{1}{1-\gamma}(c - \bar{c}_l)^{1-\gamma}$, with the same time preference rate δ and the same curvature parameter γ, but possibly different subsistence consumption levels $\bar{c}_l$. Then it can be shown (see Exercise 7.5) that a representative individual will also have time-additive subsistence HARA utility with time preference rate δ, utility curvature parameter γ, and a subsistence consumption level which is given by the sum of the individual subsistence consumption levels, $\sum_{l=1}^{L} \bar{c}_l$.

The cases above in which we can compute the representative individual's preference all assume that individuals have time-additive HARA utility functions with identical risk cautiousness, compare the discussion before Theorem 7.5. With CARA utility, we can allow time preference rates to vary across individuals; in the other cases we need identical time preference rates. Under these assumptions the preferences of the representative individual only depend on the aggregate endowment and the preference parameters of the individuals, not on how the aggregate endowment is distributed across individuals. The state-price deflator derived from the representative individual and thus the price of all financial assets will therefore also be independent of the cross-sectional distribution of endowment. The economy is said to have the *aggregation property* if the equilibrium prices are independent of the endowment distribution. We can therefore state the following result:

Theorem 7.7 *Suppose the assumptions of Theorem 7.5 are satisfied (so that markets are effectively complete and allocations are Pareto-optimal). If the common risk cautiousness is different from zero, that is the absolute risk aversion is not constant, further assume that individuals have identical time preference rates. Then the economy has the aggregation property.*

Obviously, the preference assumptions made above are not that appealing. What can we say about the representative individual more generally? Suppose the market is complete so that a unique state-price vector $\boldsymbol{\psi}$ exists. The utility maximization problem of individual l can be formulated as in Eq. (6.15). The Lagrangian for this problem is

$$\mathcal{L}_l = \mathcal{U}_l(c_0^l, c^l) + \kappa_l \left(\sum_{\omega=1}^{S} \psi_\omega \left(e_\omega^l - c_\omega^l \right) + e_0^l - c_0^l \right),$$

where κ_l is the Lagrange multiplier, which is strictly positive since we assume strictly increasing utility. The first-order conditions are

$$\frac{\partial \mathcal{L}_l}{\partial c_0^l} = 0 \quad \Leftrightarrow \quad \frac{\partial \mathcal{U}_l}{\partial c_0^l} = \kappa_l,$$

$$\frac{\partial \mathcal{L}_l}{\partial c_\omega^l} = 0 \quad \Leftrightarrow \quad \frac{\partial \mathcal{U}_l}{\partial c_\omega^l} = \kappa_l \psi_\omega, \quad \omega = 1, \dots, S,$$

$$\frac{\partial \mathcal{L}_l}{\partial \kappa_l} = 0 \quad \Leftrightarrow \quad c_0^l + \sum_{\omega=1}^{S} \psi_\omega c_\omega^l = e_0^l + \sum_{\omega=1}^{S} \psi_\omega e_\omega^l.$$

If we set $\eta_l = 1/\kappa_l$ for each $l = 1, \dots, L$, we see from Eqs. (7.9) and (7.10) that the first-order conditions for the central planner equipped with these particular weights will also be satisfied with the same consumption allocation. So for each complete market equilibrium, the representative individual's preferences correspond to the maximized objective for the central planner with the weights $\eta_l = 1/\kappa_l, l = 1, \dots, L$.

The weight η_l associated with individual l is the reciprocal of the 'shadow price' of his budget constraint. Therefore, η_l will depend on the wealth of individual l, that is his initial endowment and the present value of his future endowment. The relative weights assigned to different individuals depend on the distribution of endowments across individuals. Redistributing the aggregate endowment will thus change the relative values of the weights η_l and, hence, the utility function of the representative individual and equilibrium asset prices. So, in general, the economy does not have the aggregation property. Other things being equal, increasing the wealth of individual l will lower his Lagrange multiplier κ_l and, therefore, increase his weight η_l in the representative individual's preferences.

Cuoco and He (2001) show that in incomplete markets a representative individual can still be constructed with a utility function being a linear combination of the individual utilities. However, the weights will in general be stochastic and correspond to the equilibrium marginal rates of substitution across individuals. See Dumas and Lyasoff (2012) for a recent approach to the computation of equilibria in incomplete markets.

7.6 MULTIPERIOD MODELS

Until now, this chapter has dealt with a one-period economy only. Next we discuss generalizations to a discrete-time, multiperiod model. In the discrete-time framework with time set $\mathcal{T} = \{0, 1, \dots, T\}$, the I assets are characterized by exogenously given, non-negative dividend processes $D_i = (D_{it})_{t\in\mathcal{T}}$. All assets are assumed to be long-lived in the sense that no matter what the state of the economy at time $T-1$ might be, there is a strictly positive probability that the terminal dividend D_{iT} is strictly positive for any $i = 1, \dots, I$. Each individual $l = 1, \dots, L$ is characterized by an exogenously given endowment process $e^l = (e^l_t)_{t\in\mathcal{T}}$ and an increasing and concave utility index $\mathcal{U}_l$ which now depends on consumption at all dates, $\mathcal{U}_l(c^l_0, c^l_1, \dots, c^l_T)$. Individuals choose trading strategies $\boldsymbol{\theta}^l = (\boldsymbol{\theta}^l_t)_{t\in\{0,1,\dots,T-1\}}$ which, together with their endowments and the dividend processes of the assets, determine the consumption processes $c^l = (c^l_t)_{t\in\mathcal{T}}$ through the relations

$$
\begin{aligned}
c^l_0 &= e^l_0 - \boldsymbol{\theta}^l_0 \cdot \boldsymbol{P}_0,\\
c^l_t &= e^l_t + \boldsymbol{\theta}^l_{t-1} \cdot (\boldsymbol{P}_t + \boldsymbol{D}_t) - \boldsymbol{\theta}^l_t \cdot \boldsymbol{P}_t, \quad t = 1, \dots, T-1,\\
c^l_T &= e^l_T + \boldsymbol{\theta}^l_{T-1} \cdot \boldsymbol{D}_T,
\end{aligned}
$$

where $\boldsymbol{P}_t$ is the vector of (ex-dividend) asset prices at time t. The equations for c^l_t and c^l_T have to hold for every state ω.

An equilibrium for the economy just described consists of a price process $\boldsymbol{P} = (\boldsymbol{P}_t)_{t\in\{0,1,\dots,T-1\}}$ and a trading strategy $\boldsymbol{\theta}^l$ for each individual $l = 1, \dots, L$ so that $\boldsymbol{\theta}^l$ is optimal given the price process $\boldsymbol{P}$ and markets clear at all points in time and for all assets. Assuming that each asset is in zero net supply, market clearing means that

$$\sum_{l=1}^{L} \theta_{it}^{l} = 0, \quad i = 1, \ldots, I, \quad t = 0, 1, \ldots, T-1.$$

This equilibrium definition is the natural generalization of Definition 7.1.

Also, the definition of Pareto-optimal consumption allocations in Definition 7.2 generalizes to the discrete-time setting in a straightforward way. The central planner's problem is now to maximize $\sum_{l=1}^{L} \eta_l \mathcal{U}_l(c_0^l, c_1^l, \ldots, c_T^l)$ for given weights $\eta_1, \ldots, \eta_L$ by allocating aggregate endowments to the individuals in the economy respecting the feasibility constraints

$$\sum_{l=1}^{L} c_t^l \leq \bar{e}_t \equiv \sum_{l=1}^{L} e_t^l, \quad t = 0, 1, \ldots, T.$$

The maximized value of the objective is denoted by $\mathcal{U}_\eta(\bar{e}_0, \bar{e}_1, \ldots, \bar{e}_T)$. The link given in Theorem 7.1 between Pareto-optimal allocations and solutions to the central planner's problem is also valid for the multiperiod economy.

In particular, when all individuals have time-additive expected utility so that

$$\mathcal{U}_l(c_0^l, c_1^l, \ldots, c_T^l) = \sum_{t=0}^{T} e^{-\delta_l t} \mathrm{E}\left[u(c_t^l)\right] = \sum_{t=0}^{T} e^{-\delta_l t} \sum_{\omega=1}^{S} p_\omega u(c_t^l(\omega)),$$

then the objective of the central planner becomes

$$\sum_{l=1}^{L} \eta_l \sum_{t=0}^{T} e^{-\delta_l t} \mathrm{E}\left[u(c_t^l)\right] = \sum_{t=0}^{T} \sum_{l=1}^{L} \eta_l e^{-\delta_l t} \mathrm{E}\left[u(c_t^l)\right].$$

Since aggregate endowments are not transferable across time, the problem can be decomposed into a number of optimization problems, one for each point in time. The maximized objective will then satisfy

$$\mathcal{U}_\eta(\bar{e}_0, \bar{e}_1, \ldots, \bar{e}_T) = \sum_{t=0}^{T} U_\eta(t, \bar{e}_t),$$

where

$$U_\eta(t, \bar{e}_t) = \sup \left\{ \sum_{l=1}^{L} \eta_l e^{-\delta_l t} \mathrm{E}\left[u(c_t^l)\right] \mid \sum_{l=1}^{L} c_t^l \leq \bar{e}_t \right\}.$$

The first-order conditions are similar to Eqs. (7.11) and (7.12) with appropriate time subscripts added. Efficient risk sharing follows again.

Just as in the one-period setting, equilibrium consumption allocations will be Pareto-optimal when markets are complete or effectively complete. Recall that a discrete-time, finite-state setting can be represented by a multinomial tree as illustrated by Fig. 2.2 for a simple two-period economy. As explained in

Section 3.6.2, the market is complete in such a model if, for any one-period subtree, there are as many sufficiently different assets as the number of branches leaving the node. Here the term 'sufficiently different' means that the matrix of the possible values of dividend plus price at the end of the period has full rank. Whether the market is complete or not is thus dependent on the price processes. More generally, the set of attainable dividend processes depends on the price processes which further complicates the search for conditions under which existence of an equilibrium is guaranteed.

If individuals have access to a sufficiently large set of claims on the aggregate consumption process, they can implement any Pareto-optimal allocation. Naturally, this includes trading in claims written on the aggregate consumption level at any date. Moreover, as time goes by, individuals will revise the probabilities they attach to future aggregate consumption levels, and the individuals must also be able to trade assets with payoffs depending on the variations in these probabilities, as emphasized by Christensen, Graversen, and Miltersen (2000) in a continuous-time setting.

The one-period results on the representative individual carry over to the multiperiod framework. The aggregation property (see Theorem 7.7) can be demonstrated for some specific time-additive preferences with limited heterogeneity in preference parameters. For more general preferences, the weights that the representative individual applies to different individuals will depend on the allocation of endowments across individuals.

All results can be generalized to the continuous-time setting under suitable regularity conditions. Key references include Duffie and Huang (1985), Duffie (1986), and Huang (1985, 1987).

7.7 CONCLUDING REMARKS

This chapter has defined an equilibrium in the financial market models considered in this book. We have seen that complete markets and effectively complete markets lead to Pareto-optimal equilibria which have the property that individuals share the risks efficiently. In such markets, equilibrium asset prices are the same as in a hypothetical representative-individual economy. The preferences of a representative individual are generally a complicated average of the preferences of all individuals with weights depending on the distribution of wealth across individuals. Only under strong assumptions on the preferences of the individuals will the weights be independent of the wealth distribution and then the representative individual's preferences will be simple. In the next chapter we will link state-price deflators to consumption growth. In particular, we will often assume the existence of a representative individual in which case we can link the state-price deflator to the growth rate of aggregate consumption.

7.8 EXERCISES

Exercise 7.1 Consider a discrete-time economy with L individuals with identical preferences so that agent $l = 1, \dots, L$ at time 0 wants to maximize

$$\mathrm{E}\left[\sum_{t=0}^{T} \beta^t \frac{1}{1-\gamma} c_{l,t}^{1-\gamma}\right]$$

where $c_{l,t}$ denotes the consumption rate of individual l at time t. Let $c_{l,t}^*$ be the optimal consumption rate of individual l at time t.

(a) Argue why

$$\frac{\zeta_{t+1}}{\zeta_t} = \frac{\beta}{L} \sum_{l=1}^{L} \left(\frac{c_{l,t+1}^*}{c_{l,t}^*}\right)^{-\gamma} \qquad (*)$$

is a state-price deflator between time t and time $t+1$.

(b) If the market is complete, explain why the next-period state-price deflator in (*) can be written as

$$\frac{\zeta_{t+1}}{\zeta_t} = \beta \left(\frac{\sum_{l=1}^{L} c_{l,t+1}^*}{\sum_{l=1}^{L} c_{l,t}^*}\right)^{-\gamma}.$$

Exercise 7.2 Assume a discrete-time economy with L agents. Each agent ℓ maximizes time-additive expected utility $\mathrm{E}\left[\sum_{t=0}^{T} \beta_\ell^t u_\ell(c_{\ell t})\right]$ where u_ℓ is strictly increasing and concave. Show that

$$\frac{\zeta_{t+1}}{\zeta_t} = \frac{\sum_{\ell=1}^{L} \beta_\ell u_\ell'(c_{\ell,t+1})}{\sum_{\ell=1}^{L} u_\ell'(c_{\ell t})}$$

is a valid one-period state-price deflator. How do you define the full state-price deflator process $\zeta = (\zeta_t)$?

Exercise 7.3 (Use a spreadsheet or similar computational tool.) Consider a one-period economy with 5 possible states and 5 assets traded. The state-contingent dividends and prices of the assets and the state probabilities are as follows:

	State 1	State 2	State 3	State 4	State 5	Price
asset 1	1	1	1	1	1	0.9
asset 2	0	2	4	6	8	1.7
asset 3	4	0	2	4	2	2.3
asset 4	10	0	0	2	2	4.3
asset 5	4	4	0	4	4	2.8
Probability	0.25	0.25	0.2	0.2	0.1	

(a) Verify that the market is complete and find the unique state-price deflator.

Consider an individual investor, Alex, with access to the above financial market with the given prices. Suppose Alex has time-additive expected utility with a time preference rate of $\delta = 0.03$ and a constant relative risk aversion of $\gamma = 2$. Suppose his optimal consumption at time 0 is 5 and that he will receive an income of 5 at time 1 no matter which state is realized.

(b) What is Alex's optimal time 1 consumption? What does it cost him to finance that consumption? What is the optimal portfolio for Alex?

Suppose now that there is only one other individual, Bob, in the economy. Bob also has time-additive expected utility with a time preference rate of 0.03 but a relative risk aversion of 5. Bob's optimal time 0 consumption is also 5.

(c) What is Bob's optimal time 1 consumption?

(d) What is the aggregate time 0 consumption and the state-dependent aggregate time 1 consumption?

(e) What is Bob's time 0 endowment and state-dependent time 1 endowment? What is Bob's optimal portfolio?

(f) Verify that the markets clear.

Exercise 7.4 Suppose that aggregate time 1 consumption can only take on the values $1, 2, \dots, K$ for some finite integer K. Assume that European call options on aggregate consumption are traded for any exercise price $0, 1, 2, \dots, K$. Consider a portfolio with one unit of the option with exercise price $k - 1$, one unit of the option with exercise price $k + 1$, and minus two units of the option with exercise price k. What is the payoff of this portfolio? Discuss the consequences of your findings for the (effective) completeness of the market. Could you do just as well with put options?

Exercise 7.5 Consider an economy with two individuals and Pareto-optimal equilibrium allocations. Both individuals have time-additive expected utility and their time preference rates are identical.

(a) Assume that $u_l(c) = \frac{1}{1-\gamma}(c - \bar{c}_l)^{1-\gamma}$ for $l = 1, 2$. Find the preferences of the representative individual.

(b) Assume that $u_l(c) = \ln(c - \bar{c}_l)$ for $l = 1, 2$. Find the preferences of the representative individual.

Exercise 7.6 Show how the results for CARA utility and CRRA utility stated in Section 7.5 generalize to economies with more than two individuals.

Exercise 7.7 George and John live in a continuous-time economy in which the relevant uncertainty is generated by a one-dimensional standard Brownian motion $z = (z_t)_{t \in [0,T]}$. Both have time-additive utility of their consumption process: George maximizes

$$U_G(c) = \mathrm{E}\left[\int_0^T e^{-0.02t} \ln c_t \, dt\right],$$

while John maximizes

$$U_J(c) = \mathrm{E}\left[\int_0^T e^{-0.02t} \left(-\frac{1}{c_t}\right) dt\right].$$

George's optimal consumption process $c_G = (c_{Gt})$ has a constant expected growth rate of 4% and a constant volatility of 5%, that is

$$dc_{Gt} = c_{Gt} \left[0.04 \, dt + 0.05 \, dz_t \right].$$

Two assets are traded in the economy. One asset is an instantaneously risk-free bank account with continuously compounded rate of return r_t^f. The other asset is a risky asset with price process $P = (P_t)$ satisfying

$$dP_t = P_t \left[\mu_{Pt} \, dt + 0.4 \, dz_t \right]$$

for some drift μ_{Pt}. The market is complete.

(a) What are the relative risk aversions of George and John, respectively?

(b) Using the fact that a state-price deflator can be derived from George's consumption process, determine the risk-free rate r_t^f and the market price of risk λ_t. What can you conclude about the price processes of the two assets?

(c) Find the drift and volatility of John's optimal consumption process, $c_J = (c_{Jt})$.

(d) Suppose George and John are the only two individuals in the economy. What can you say about the dynamics of aggregate consumption? Can the representative agent have constant relative risk aversion?

Exercise 7.8 Provide a proof of Theorem 7.5 in the case of CARA utility (corresponding to $\alpha = 0$ in the notation introduced just above the statement of the theorem).

8

Basic Consumption-Based Asset Pricing

8.1 INTRODUCTION

Consumption-based asset pricing models link asset prices to consumption. Chapter 6 showed that the marginal rate of substitution of any individual works as a state-price deflator. For an individual with time-additive expected utility, the marginal rate of substitution is fully specified by the optimal consumption process, the time preference rate, and the utility function of the individual. We can substitute this particular state-price deflator into the results derived in Chapter 4 that link state-price deflators to the risk-free rate and the risk premia (excess expected returns) on risky assets. This immediately produces a link between the growth in marginal utility of consumption and returns.

This chapter explores when this link leads to relations between the growth of consumption itself and returns so that, for example, the asset-specific part of the risk premium on a risky asset is given by the covariance between the return on the asset and the growth rate in consumption. We show that such relations can be established in continuous-time models without any additional assumptions. In discrete-time models, we obtain similar relations under the assumptions of constant relative risk aversion and a lognormally distributed consumption growth rate, the so-called CRRA-lognormal consumption-based model.

While these results hold for the consumption and preferences of any individual, they are often applied using aggregate consumption which is valid when a representative individual exists with the assumed utility function. We know from Chapter 7 that the representative-individual framework is appropriate in complete or effectively complete markets, but not necessarily in incomplete markets. The representative-individual version of the CRRA-lognormal consumption-based model thus predicts that the excess expected return on any risky asset equals the product of the representative individual's relative risk aversion and the covariance between the return on the asset and the growth rate of aggregate consumption. Furthermore, the model predicts that the risk-free rate is a specific function of the representative individual's time preference rate and relative risk aversion as well as the expected growth rate and volatility of aggregate consumption.

We explain how empirical studies come to the conclusion that the representative-individual CRRA-lognormal model cannot match the observed levels of the equity premium (the excess expected return on the stock market index) and the risk-free interest rate for reasonable values of the preference parameters. Other empirical return observations are also in conflict with this basic model. Therefore, the basic consumption-based CAPM leaves us with a number of asset pricing puzzles. We discuss some potential problems with the data and the approach used in such empirical tests which may exaggerate the magnitude of some of the problems. In the subsequent chapter we explore a number of recent, more advanced consumption-based asset pricing models that seem to be able to resolve some of these puzzles.

The consumption-based asset pricing models date back to Rubinstein (1976), Lucas (1978), and Breeden (1979). Note that the representative-individual models take the dynamics of aggregate consumption as exogenously given and are therefore models of an exchange economy in which aggregate resources cannot be moved across time periods or across states. Such an exchange economy model is also referred to as a 'Lucas fruit-tree model' since the exogenous aggregate resources can be thought of as fruits falling from a tree. This contrasts a production economy in which aggregate consumption is endogenously determined from productive investment decisions.

The outline of the chapter is as follows. Section 8.2 develops the consumption-CAPM in the one-period framework. Section 8.3 extends the analysis to the discrete-time and the continuous-time settings. Section 8.4 shows that the simple consumption-CAPM specification is unable to match important empirical features of aggregate consumption and returns, leaving a number of apparent asset pricing puzzles. Section 8.5 discusses some problems with such empirical studies.

8.2 THE ONE-PERIOD CONSUMPTION-CAPM

For simplicity let us first investigate the link between asset prices and consumption in the one-period framework. As explained in Chapter 6, the marginal rate of substitution of any individual defines a state-price deflator. If we assume time-additive expected utility with time preference rate δ and utility function u, this state-price deflator is

$$\zeta = e^{-\delta} \frac{u'(c)}{u'(c_0)},$$

where c_0 is optimal time 0 consumption and c is the state-dependent optimal time 1 consumption. If the economy can be modelled by a representative individual having such preferences, the equation holds for aggregate consumption.

If we assume that a risk-free asset is traded, it follows from Eq. (4.5) that the price of any asset i can be expressed as

$$\begin{aligned} P_i &= \left(R^f\right)^{-1}\left(\mathrm{E}[D_i] + \frac{\mathrm{Cov}[D_i, u'(c)/u'(c_0)]}{\mathrm{E}[u'(c)/u'(c_0)]}\right) \\ &= \left(R^f\right)^{-1}\left(\mathrm{E}[D_i] + \frac{\sigma\left[u'(c)/u'(c_0)\right]}{\mathrm{E}\left[u'(c)/u'(c_0)\right]}\sigma[D_i]\,\mathrm{Corr}\left[D_i, \frac{u'(c)}{u'(c_0)}\right]\right). \end{aligned} \tag{8.1}$$

As before, $\sigma[x]$ denotes the standard deviation of the random variable x, whereas $\mathrm{Corr}[x, y]$ is the correlation between the random variables x and y. The gross risk-free rate of return is

$$R^f = \frac{1}{\mathrm{E}[\zeta]} = e^{\delta}\frac{1}{\mathrm{E}[u'(c)/u'(c_0)]} \tag{8.2}$$

and the expected gross rate of return on any asset i is

$$\begin{aligned} \mathrm{E}[R_i] &= \frac{1}{\mathrm{E}[\zeta]} - \frac{\mathrm{Cov}[R_i, \zeta]}{\mathrm{E}[\zeta]} \\ &= R^f - \frac{\mathrm{Cov}[u'(c)/u'(c_0), R_i]}{\mathrm{E}[u'(c)/u'(c_0)]} \\ &= R^f - \frac{\sigma[u'(c)/u'(c_0)]}{\mathrm{E}[u'(c)/u'(c_0)]}\sigma[R_i]\,\mathrm{Corr}\left[R_i, u'(c)/u'(c_0)\right]. \end{aligned} \tag{8.3}$$

An asset with a return which is positively correlated with the marginal utility of consumption (and hence negatively correlated with the level of consumption) is attractive, has a high equilibrium price, and thus a low expected return.

In order to obtain a relation between expected returns and consumption itself (rather than marginal utility of consumption) we need to make further assumptions or approximations. Below we consider various cases.

8.2.1 Crude Approximations for a General Model

A first-order Taylor approximation of $u'(c)$ around c_0 gives that

$$\frac{u'(c)}{u'(c_0)} \approx \frac{u'(c_0) + u''(c_0)(c - c_0)}{u'(c_0)} = 1 - \gamma(c_0)g,$$

where $\gamma(c_0) = -c_0 u''(c_0)/u'(c_0)$ is the relative risk aversion of the individual evaluated at the time 0 consumption level, and $g = c/c_0 - 1$ is the (state-dependent) relative growth rate of consumption over the period. Note that

$$\mathrm{Corr}\left[x, \frac{u'(c)}{u'(c_0)}\right] \approx \mathrm{Corr}[x, 1 - \gamma(c_0)g] = -\,\mathrm{Corr}[x, g]$$

for any random variable x.

Applying the Taylor approximation in Eq. (8.1), we get that

$$P_i \approx (R^f)^{-1}\left(\mathrm{E}[D_i] - \frac{\gamma(c_0)\sigma[g]}{1-\gamma(c_0)\,\mathrm{E}[g]}\sigma[D_i]\,\mathrm{Corr}[D_i,g]\right)$$

from which it is clear that dividends that are positively correlated with consumption (growth) have a smaller present value. From Eq. (8.3), the expected excess return on a risky asset i becomes

$$\begin{aligned}\mathrm{E}[R_i] - R^f &\approx \frac{\gamma(c_0)}{1-\gamma(c_0)\,\mathrm{E}[g]}\,\mathrm{Cov}[g,R_i]\\ &= \frac{\gamma(c_0)}{1-\gamma(c_0)\,\mathrm{E}[g]}\,\mathrm{Corr}[g,R_i]\sigma[g]\sigma[R_i].\end{aligned}$$

If we further assume that $\mathrm{E}[g] \approx 0$, we get

$$\mathrm{E}[R_i] - R^f \approx \gamma(c_0)\,\mathrm{Cov}[g,R_i] = \gamma(c_0)\,\mathrm{Corr}[g,R_i]\sigma[g]\sigma[R_i], \tag{8.4}$$

where $\mathrm{Corr}[g,R_i]$ is the correlation between consumption growth and the return and $\sigma[g]$ and $\sigma[R_i]$ are the standard deviations of consumption growth and return, respectively. The above equation links expected excess returns to covariance with consumption growth. We can rewrite the equation as

$$\mathrm{E}[R_i] \approx R^f + \beta[R_i,g]\eta, \tag{8.5}$$

where $\beta[R_i,g] = \mathrm{Cov}[g,R_i]/\,\mathrm{Var}[g]$ and $\eta = \gamma(c_0)\,\mathrm{Var}[g]$. If we ignore the approximate nature of the equation, it shows that the growth rate of the individual's optimal consumption is a pricing factor, compare the introduction to pricing factors in Section 4.6.2.

Of course, we prefer exact asset pricing results to approximate. In a later section, we will show that in continuous-time models the analogues to the above relations will hold as exact equalities under certain assumptions.

8.2.2 The CRRA-Lognormal Model

If we are willing to assume that the individual has constant relative risk aversion and that the individual's consumption growth is lognormally distributed, we can show the following result:

Theorem 8.1 *In a one-period setting with a risk-free asset, consider an individual with time preference rate δ and constant relative risk aversion γ. If the consumption growth of the individual is lognormally distributed,*

$$\ln(1+g) \equiv \ln\left(\frac{c}{c_0}\right) \sim N(\bar{g},\sigma_g^2),$$

then the continuously compounded risk-free rate is

$$r^f \equiv \ln R^f = \delta + \gamma \bar{g} - \frac{1}{2}\gamma^2\sigma_g^2, \tag{8.6}$$

and the excess rate of return on any risky asset i is

$$\begin{aligned} \mathrm{E}[R_i] - R^f &= -\sigma[R_i]\sqrt{e^{\gamma^2\sigma_g^2} - 1}\ \mathrm{Corr}\left[R_i, (c/c_0)^{-\gamma}\right] \\ &\approx \gamma\sigma_g\sigma[R_i]\,\mathrm{Corr}[R_i, c/c_0]. \end{aligned} \tag{8.7}$$

Note that the approximate version of Eq. (8.7) is almost identical to the expression (8.4) derived for a general utility function using more dubious approximations. We can rewrite Eq. (8.7) in the beta-form (8.5).

Proof. The utility function is $u(c) = c^{1-\gamma}/(1-\gamma)$ so that

$$\frac{u'(c)}{u'(c_0)} = \left(\frac{c}{c_0}\right)^{-\gamma} = \exp\left\{-\gamma \ln\left(\frac{c}{c_0}\right)\right\},$$

which is lognormally distributed. It follows from Theorem B.2 in Appendix B that

$$\mathrm{E}\left[\frac{u'(c)}{u'(c_0)}\right] = \mathrm{E}\left[\exp\left\{-\gamma \ln\left(\frac{c}{c_0}\right)\right\}\right] = \exp\left\{-\gamma\bar{g} + \frac{1}{2}\gamma^2\sigma_g^2\right\} \tag{8.8}$$

and

$$\frac{\sigma\left[u'(c)/u'(c_0)\right]}{\mathrm{E}\left[u'(c)/u'(c_0)\right]} = \sqrt{e^{\gamma^2\sigma_g^2} - 1}. \tag{8.9}$$

Substituting Eq. (8.8) into Eq. (8.2), we obtain the gross risk-free return

$$R^f = e^{\delta}\left(\mathrm{E}\left[(c/c_0)^{-\gamma}\right]\right)^{-1} = \exp\left\{\delta + \gamma\bar{g} - \frac{1}{2}\gamma^2\sigma_g^2\right\},$$

which implies Eq. (8.6).

The exact expression in Eq. (8.7) follows immediately from Eqs. (8.3) and (8.9). The approximate expression is based on two approximations. First,

$$\sqrt{e^{\gamma^2\sigma_g^2} - 1} \approx \gamma\sigma_g,$$

which stems from the approximation $e^x \approx 1 + x$ for $x \approx 0$. Second, a first-order Taylor approximation of the function $f(x) = x^{-\gamma}$ around 1 gives $f(x) \approx f(1) + f'(1)(x-1) = 1 - \gamma(x-1)$. With $x = c/c_0$ we get

$$\left(\frac{c}{c_0}\right)^{-\gamma} \approx 1 - \gamma\left(\frac{c}{c_0} - 1\right)$$

and, consequently,

$$\operatorname{Corr}\left[R_i, \left(\frac{c}{c_0}\right)^{-\gamma}\right] \approx \operatorname{Corr}\left[R_i, 1-\gamma\left(\frac{c}{c_0}-1\right)\right]$$
$$= \frac{\operatorname{Cov}\left[R_i, 1-\gamma\left(\frac{c}{c_0}-1\right)\right]}{\sigma[R_i]\sigma\left[1-\gamma\left(\frac{c}{c_0}-1\right)\right]} = \frac{-\gamma \operatorname{Cov}[R_i, c/c_0]}{\sigma[R_i]\gamma\sigma[c/c_0]} = -\operatorname{Corr}[R_i, c/c_0].$$

Now, the approximate expression for the excess expected return in Eq. (8.7) follows. □

We can also derive an approximate pricing equation since Eq. (8.1) implies that

$$P_i \approx \left(R^f\right)^{-1}\left(\mathrm{E}[D_i] - \gamma\sigma_g\sigma[D_i]\operatorname{Corr}[D_i, g]\right)$$

under the stated assumptions.

If we make the stronger assumption that the gross rate of return R_i of the asset and the consumption growth c/c_0 are jointly lognormally distributed, we can derive an exact relation involving log returns. Note that the log of the state-price deflator is $\ln\zeta = -\delta - \gamma\ln(c/c_0)$. From Eq. (4.13), the expectation of the log return $r_i = \ln R_i$ of asset i satisfies

$$\begin{aligned}
\mathrm{E}[r_i] - r^f &= -\operatorname{Cov}[\ln\zeta, r_i] - \frac{1}{2}\operatorname{Var}[r_i] \\
&= \gamma\operatorname{Cov}\left[r_i, \ln\left(\frac{c}{c_0}\right)\right] - \frac{1}{2}\operatorname{Var}[r_i] \\
&= \gamma\sigma_g\operatorname{Corr}[r_i, \ln(c/c_0)]\sigma[r_i] - \frac{1}{2}\operatorname{Var}[r_i].
\end{aligned}$$

Likewise, the price can be expressed as

$$P_i = (R^f)^{-1}\,\mathrm{E}[D_i]\exp\{-\gamma\operatorname{Cov}[\ln(c/c_0), \ln D_i]\}.$$

These relations are exact but hold only under the more restrictive assumption of joint lognormality of returns (or, equivalently, dividends) and consumption.

8.2.3 Some Alternatives of Mainly Historical Interest

Much of the original work in financial economics was based on the assumptions of normally distributed returns and/or quadratic utility, although both are highly unrealistic. The mean-variance portfolio analysis in Section 6.3 is a prime example. It is also easy to derive an exact consumption-CAPM relation under such assumptions.

8.2.3.1 Normally distributed returns and consumption

Assume c and R_i are jointly *normally* distributed. We need the following result called Stein's Lemma:

Lemma 8.1 (Stein's Lemma). *If x and y are jointly normally distributed random variables and $g : \mathbb{R} \to \mathbb{R}$ is a differentiable function with* $\mathrm{E}[|g'(y)|] < \infty$, *then*

$$\operatorname{Cov}[x, g(y)] = \mathrm{E}[g'(y)] \operatorname{Cov}[x, y].$$

Proof. Define the random variable ε by $\varepsilon = x - \alpha - \beta y$, where $\beta = \operatorname{Cov}[x, y]/\operatorname{Var}[y]$, $\alpha = \mathrm{E}[x] - \beta\,\mathrm{E}[y]$, and $\operatorname{Cov}[\varepsilon, y] = 0$. Since ε and y are jointly normally distributed, the fact that they are uncorrelated implies that they will be independent. It follows that $\operatorname{Cov}[\varepsilon, g(y)] = 0$ for any function g. Therefore,

$$\operatorname{Cov}[x, g(y)] = \beta \operatorname{Cov}[y, g(y)] + \operatorname{Cov}[\varepsilon, g(y)] = \beta \operatorname{Cov}[y, g(y)].$$

Let us write the mean and variance of y as μ_y and σ_y^2, respectively. Then

$$\begin{aligned}\operatorname{Cov}[y, g(y)] &= \mathrm{E}[yg(y)] - \mathrm{E}[y]\,\mathrm{E}[g(y)] \\ &= \mathrm{E}[(y - \mu_y)g(y)] = \int_{-\infty}^{\infty} (y - \mu_y)g(y)f(y)\,dy,\end{aligned}$$

where

$$f(y) = \frac{1}{\sigma_y\sqrt{2\pi}} \exp\left\{-\frac{1}{2\sigma_y^2}(y - \mu_y)^2\right\}$$

is the probability density function of y. Noting that $f'(y) = -f(y)(y - \mu_y)/\sigma_y^2$, integration by parts gives

$$\begin{aligned}\int_{-\infty}^{\infty} (y - \mu_y)g(y)f(y)\,dy &= -\sigma_y^2 \int_{-\infty}^{\infty} g(y)f'(y)\,dy \\ &= \sigma_y^2 \int_{-\infty}^{\infty} g'(y)f(y)\,dy - \sigma_y^2 \Big[g(y)f(y)\Big]_{y=-\infty}^{\infty} \\ &= \sigma_y^2\,\mathrm{E}[g'(y)]\end{aligned}$$

provided that $g(y)$ does not approach plus or minus infinity faster than $f(y)$ approaches zero as $y \to \pm\infty$. Hence,

$$\operatorname{Cov}[x, g(y)] = \beta \operatorname{Cov}[y, g(y)] = \beta\sigma_y^2\,\mathrm{E}[g'(y)] = \operatorname{Cov}[x, y]\,\mathrm{E}[g'(y)]$$

as claimed. □

Applying Stein's Lemma, we get

$$\operatorname{Cov}[u'(c), D_i] = \mathrm{E}[u''(c)] \operatorname{Cov}[D_i, c]$$

and, substituting that into Eq. (8.1),

$$P_i = (R^f)^{-1}\left(\mathrm{E}[D_i] + \frac{\mathrm{E}[u''(c)]}{\mathrm{E}[u'(c)]}\operatorname{Cov}[D_i, c]\right)$$

Similarly, for returns, we obtain

$$\begin{aligned}
\mathrm{E}[R_i] &= R^f - \frac{\operatorname{Cov}[u'(c)/u'(c_0), R_i]}{\mathrm{E}[u'(c)/u'(c_0)]} \\
&= R^f - \frac{\operatorname{Cov}[u'(c), R_i]}{\mathrm{E}[u'(c)]} \\
&= R^f - \frac{\mathrm{E}[u''(c)]\operatorname{Cov}[R_i, c]}{\mathrm{E}[u'(c)]} \\
&= R^f + \beta[R_i, c]\left(\frac{-\mathrm{E}[u''(c)]\operatorname{Var}[c]}{\mathrm{E}[u'(c)]}\right),
\end{aligned} \tag{8.10}$$

which is of the desired form. Note that we need to have $\mathrm{E}[|u''(c)|] < \infty$ in order to apply Stein's Lemma and this is not a innocuous assumption. And, of course, the normality assumption is highly unrealistic.

8.2.3.2 *Quadratic utility*

If we assume quadratic utility

$$u(c) = -\frac{1}{2}(\bar{c} - c)^2 \quad \Rightarrow \quad u'(c) = \bar{c} - c,$$

we have

$$\mathrm{E}[u'(c)] = \bar{c} - \mathrm{E}[c], \quad \operatorname{Cov}[u'(c), D_i] = -\operatorname{Cov}[c, D_i].$$

Therefore the pricing expression (8.1) implies that

$$P_i = (R^f)^{-1}\left(\mathrm{E}[D_i] - \frac{1}{\bar{c} - \mathrm{E}[c]}\operatorname{Cov}[D_i, c]\right),$$

whereas the expected return on a risky asset in Eq. (8.3) can be rewritten as

$$\mathrm{E}[R_i] = R^f + \frac{\operatorname{Cov}[c, R_i]}{\bar{c} - \mathrm{E}[c]} = R^f + \beta[R_i, c]\left(\frac{\operatorname{Var}[c]}{\bar{c} - \mathrm{E}[c]}\right),$$

which has the form we were looking for.

8.2.4 The Consumption-Mimicking Portfolio

We have seen above that the expected excess returns are related to the beta of the asset with the growth rate of consumption via the equation

$$\mathrm{E}[R_i] \approx R^f + \beta[R_i, g]\eta, \tag{8.11}$$

compare Eq. (8.5). We will now show that we can replace the consumption growth rate by the return R^c on a portfolio $\boldsymbol{\pi}^c$ mimicking the consumption growth in the sense that π^c is the portfolio minimizing the variance of the difference between the portfolio return and the consumption growth. In fact, this consumption-mimicking portfolio has the property that its return has the highest absolute correlation with consumption growth. This is to be shown in Exercise 8.2.

Lemma 8.2 *The return R^c on the consumption-mimicking portfolio satisfies*

$$\mathrm{Cov}[R^c, g] = \mathrm{Var}[R^c]. \tag{8.12}$$

and, for any risky asset i,

$$\mathrm{Cov}[R_i, R^c] = \mathrm{Cov}[R_i, g]. \tag{8.13}$$

Proof. The portfolio characterized by the portfolio weight vector $\boldsymbol{\pi}$ has a return of $R^{\pi} = \boldsymbol{\pi}^{\top}\boldsymbol{R}$, where $\boldsymbol{R}$ is the vector of returns of the individual assets. The variance we seek to minimize is

$$\mathrm{Var}\left[R^{\pi} - g\right] = \boldsymbol{\pi}^{\top}\,\mathrm{Var}[\boldsymbol{R}]\boldsymbol{\pi} + \mathrm{Var}[g] - 2\boldsymbol{\pi}^{\top}\,\mathrm{Cov}[\boldsymbol{R}, g].$$

Here $\mathrm{Var}[\boldsymbol{R}]$ is the variance-covariance matrix of the returns and $\mathrm{Cov}[\boldsymbol{R}, g]$ is the vector of the covariances of each asset's return with consumption growth. The first-order condition determining the consumption growth mimicking portfolio $\boldsymbol{\pi} = \boldsymbol{\pi}^c$ is

$$2\,\mathrm{Var}[\boldsymbol{R}]\boldsymbol{\pi}^c - 2\,\mathrm{Cov}[\boldsymbol{R}, g] = 0 \quad \Leftrightarrow \quad \boldsymbol{\pi}^c = (\mathrm{Var}[\boldsymbol{R}])^{-1}\,\mathrm{Cov}[\boldsymbol{R}, g]$$

so that the return on that portfolio is

$$R^c = (\boldsymbol{\pi}^c)^{\top}\boldsymbol{R} = \left(\mathrm{Cov}[\boldsymbol{R}, g]\right)^{\top}(\mathrm{Var}[\boldsymbol{R}])^{-1}\,\boldsymbol{R}. \tag{8.14}$$

The variance of the return is

$$\mathrm{Var}[R^c] = \left(\mathrm{Cov}[\boldsymbol{R}, g]\right)^{\top}(\mathrm{Var}[\boldsymbol{R}])^{-1}\,\mathrm{Cov}[\boldsymbol{R}, g],$$

which implies that

$$\mathrm{Cov}[R^c, g] = \left(\mathrm{Cov}[\boldsymbol{R}, g]\right)^{\top}(\mathrm{Var}[\boldsymbol{R}])^{-1}\,\mathrm{Cov}[\boldsymbol{R}, g] = \mathrm{Var}[R^c],$$

confirming Eq. (8.12). Furthermore, it follows from Eqs. (8.14) and (A.2) that

$$\begin{aligned}\mathrm{Cov}[\boldsymbol{R}, R^c] &= \mathrm{Cov}\left[\boldsymbol{R}, \left(\mathrm{Cov}[\boldsymbol{R}, g]\right)^{\top} (\mathrm{Var}[\boldsymbol{R}])^{-1} \boldsymbol{R}\right] \\ &= \mathrm{Cov}\left[\boldsymbol{R}, \boldsymbol{R}\right] \left(\left(\mathrm{Cov}[\boldsymbol{R}, g]\right)^{\top} (\mathrm{Var}[\boldsymbol{R}])^{-1}\right)^{\top} \\ &= \mathrm{Var}[\boldsymbol{R}] \left(\mathrm{Var}[\boldsymbol{R}]\right)^{-1} \left(\mathrm{Cov}[\boldsymbol{R}, g]\right) = \mathrm{Cov}[\boldsymbol{R}, g],\end{aligned}$$

which shows Eq. (8.13). □

The equation (8.11) holds for all assets and portfolios. In particular, it must hold for the consumption-mimicking portfolio so that

$$\mathrm{E}[R^c] - R^f \approx \beta[R^c, g]\eta = \frac{\mathrm{Cov}[R^c, g]}{\mathrm{Var}[g]}\eta = \frac{\mathrm{Var}[R^c]}{\mathrm{Var}[g]}\eta,$$

where the last equality follows from Eq. (8.12). Solving for η in the above equation, we find

$$\eta \approx \frac{\mathrm{Var}[g]}{\mathrm{Var}[R^c]} \left(\mathrm{E}[R^c] - R^f\right).$$

Hence the expected excess return on any risky asset i can be rewritten as

$$\mathrm{E}[R_i] - R^f \approx \frac{\mathrm{Cov}[R_i, g]}{\mathrm{Var}[g]} \frac{\mathrm{Var}[g]}{\mathrm{Var}[R^c]} \left(\mathrm{E}[R^c] - R^f\right) = \frac{\mathrm{Cov}[R_i, g]}{\mathrm{Var}[R^c]} \left(\mathrm{E}[R^c] - R^f\right).$$

Applying Eq. (8.13), we conclude that

$$\mathrm{E}[R_i] - R^f \approx \beta[R_i, R^c] \left(\mathrm{E}[R^c] - R^f\right), \tag{8.15}$$

where $\beta[R_i, R^c] = \mathrm{Cov}[R_i, R^c]/\,\mathrm{Var}[R^c]$. Equation (8.15) is exactly as the classic CAPM but with the return on a consumption-mimicking portfolio instead of the return on the market portfolio.

8.2.5 Returns and Aggregate Consumption

If the economy has a representative individual we can use aggregate consumption instead of individual consumption in the relations derived in the preceding sections. Of course, it is then the relative risk aversion and the time preference rate of the representative individual that go into the equations. For example, if the representative individual has a constant relative risk aversion and aggregate consumption is lognormally distributed, then Theorem 8.1 provides a link between the expected excess rate of return on any risky asset and the covariance between this return and the growth in aggregate consumption.

What if the economy does not have a representative individual? Can we still relate returns to aggregate consumption? Equation (8.4) will still hold for any individual l, that is

$$\mathrm{E}[R_i] - R^f \approx \gamma_l(c_0^l)\,\mathrm{Cov}[c^l/c_0^l, R_i] = \mathrm{ARA}_l(c_0^l)\,\mathrm{Cov}[c^l, R_i],$$

where γ_l and ARA_l are the relative and absolute risk aversion of individual l (again, we have a similar relation in the CRRA-lognormal setting of Theorem 8.1). Consequently,

$$\left(\mathrm{E}[R_i] - R^f\right) \frac{1}{\mathrm{ARA}_l(c_0^l)} \approx \mathrm{Cov}[c^l, R_i], \quad l = 1, 2, \ldots, L.$$

Summing up over all individuals, we get

$$\begin{aligned}\left(\mathrm{E}[R_i] - R^f\right) \sum_{l=1}^{L} \frac{1}{\mathrm{ARA}_l(c_0^l)} &\approx \sum_{l=1}^{L} \mathrm{Cov}[c^l, R_i] \\ &= \mathrm{Cov}\left[\sum_{l=1}^{L} c^l, R_i\right] = \mathrm{Cov}[C, R_i],\end{aligned}$$

where C is aggregate time 1 consumption. If we let C_0 denote aggregate time 0 consumption, we obtain

$$\mathrm{E}[R_i] - R^f \approx \left(\sum_{l=1}^{L} \frac{1}{\mathrm{ARA}_l(c_0^l)}\right)^{-1} C_0\,\mathrm{Cov}[C/C_0, R_i].$$

Again ignoring the approximation, this equation shows that aggregate consumption growth is a pricing factor even if there is no representative individual. We just need to replace the relative risk aversion of the representative individual by some complex average of individual risk aversions. The absolute risk tolerance of individual l is exactly $1/\mathrm{ARA}_l(c_0^l)$ so the first term on the right-hand side of the above equation can be interpreted as the reciprocal of the aggregate absolute risk tolerance in the economy. The higher the aggregate absolute risk tolerance, the lower the equilibrium risk premium on risky assets. In Exercise 8.1 you are asked to find a similar approximate relation between the price of a risky asset and the covariance between its dividend and aggregate consumption.

8.3 THE MULTIPERIOD CONSUMPTION-CAPM

Now take the analysis to multiperiod settings. Assuming time-additive expected utility we can define a state-price deflator from the optimal consumption plan of any individual as

$$\zeta_t = e^{-\delta t} \frac{u'(c_t)}{u'(c_0)}. \tag{8.16}$$

This is true both in the discrete-time and in the continuous-time setting as shown in Chapter 6. If a representative individual exists, the equation holds for aggregate consumption.

8.3.1 Discrete Time

Not surprisingly, the multiperiod discrete-time setting leads to equations very similar to those derived in the one-period framework in the previous section. Since

$$\frac{\zeta_{t+1}}{\zeta_t} = e^{-\delta} \frac{u'(c_{t+1})}{u'(c_t)},$$

we get from Eqs. (4.21) and (4.22) that the risk-free gross rate of return is

$$R_t^f = e^{\delta} \left(\mathrm{E}_t \left[\frac{u'(c_{t+1})}{u'(c_t)} \right] \right)^{-1}$$

and that the conditionally expected excess gross rate of return on a risky asset is

$$\begin{aligned} \mathrm{E}_t[R_{i,t+1}] - R_t^f &= -\frac{\mathrm{Cov}_t[u'(c_{t+1})/u'(c_t), R_{i,t+1}]}{\mathrm{E}_t[u'(c_{t+1})/u'(c_t)]} \\ &= \mathrm{Corr}_t \left[R_{i,t+1}, \frac{u'(c_{t+1})}{u'(c_t)} \right] \sigma_t[R_{i,t+1}] \left(-\frac{\sigma_t[u'(c_{t+1})/u'(c_t)]}{\mathrm{E}_t[u'(c_{t+1})/u'(c_t)]} \right). \end{aligned}$$

These equations are the multiperiod equivalents of Eqs. (8.2) and (8.3) for the one-period model.

As in the one-period case, using crude approximations, we can obtain an approximate relation between expected returns and relative consumption growth, $g_{t+1} = c_{t+1}/c_t - 1$, over the next period:

$$\mathrm{E}_t[R_{i,t+1}] - R_t^f \approx \gamma(c_t) \, \mathrm{Cov}_t[g_{t+1}, R_{i,t+1}]. \tag{8.17}$$

With time-additive CRRA utility and lognormal periodic consumption growth, we have the following direct extension of Theorem 8.1.

Theorem 8.2 *In a discrete-time setting with a risk-free asset traded each period, consider an individual with time-additive expected utility with a time preference rate δ and a constant relative risk aversion γ. If the periodic consumption growth of the individual is lognormally distributed,*

$$\ln(1 + g_{t+1}) \equiv \ln\left(\frac{c_{t+1}}{c_t}\right) \sim N(\bar{g}_t, \sigma_{gt}^2), \quad t = 0, 1, \ldots, T-1,$$

then the continuously compounded risk-free rate between t and t + 1 is

$$r_t^f \equiv \ln R_t^f = \delta + \gamma \bar{g}_t - \frac{1}{2}\gamma^2 \sigma_{gt}^2, \tag{8.18}$$

and the excess rate of return on any risky asset i between t and t + 1 is

$$\begin{aligned} \mathrm{E}_t[R_{i,t+1}] - R_t^f &= -\sigma_t[R_{i,t+1}] \sqrt{e^{\gamma^2 \sigma_{gt}^2} - 1}\ \mathrm{Corr}_t\left[R_{i,t+1}, (c_{t+1}/c_t)^{-\gamma}\right] \\ &\approx \gamma \sigma_{gt} \sigma_t [R_{i,t+1}]\, \mathrm{Corr}_t[R_{i,t+1}, c_{t+1}/c_t]. \end{aligned} \tag{8.19}$$

If the periodic consumption growth has a constant mean $\bar{g}$ and a constant variance σ_g^2, then we have a 'constant-moments CRRA-lognormal' specification of the model. In this model, the one-period risk-free rate is constant over time and the conditional Sharpe ratio of asset i, that is $(\mathrm{E}_t[R_{i,t+1}] - R_t^f)/\sigma_t[R_{i,t+1}]$, can only vary if the correlation is time-varying.

If we further assume that the future asset price and the future consumption level are simultaneously lognormally distributed, we get

$$\begin{aligned} &\mathrm{E}_t[\ln R_{i,t+1}] - \ln R_t^f + \frac{1}{2} \mathrm{Var}_t[\ln R_{i,t+1}] \\ &\qquad = \gamma \sigma_{gt}\, \mathrm{Corr}_t \left[\ln R_{i,t+1}, \ln\left(\frac{C_{t+1}}{C_t}\right)\right] \sigma_t \left[\ln R_{i,t+1}\right] \end{aligned} \tag{8.20}$$

or, equivalently,

$$\ln\left(\mathrm{E}_t[R_{i,t+1}]\right) - \ln R_t^f = \gamma \sigma_{gt}\, \mathrm{Corr}_t \left[\ln R_{i,t+1}, \ln\left(\frac{C_{t+1}}{C_t}\right)\right] \sigma_t \left[\ln R_{i,t+1}\right].$$

As in the one-period framework, the expressions (8.17) and (8.19) for the conditionally expected excess return lead to a 'beta-version' of the consumption-based CAPM, where the beta is either with respect to consumption growth or with respect to the return on a consumption-mimicking portfolio. The latter can be expressed as

$$\mathrm{E}_t[R_{i,t+1}] - R_t^f \approx \beta_t[R_{i,t+1}, R_{t+1}^c] \left(\mathrm{E}_t[R_{t+1}^c] - R_t^f\right),$$

where $\beta_t[R_{i,t+1}, R_{t+1}^c] = \mathrm{Cov}_t[R_{i,t+1}, R_{t+1}^c]/\mathrm{Var}_t[R_{t+1}^c]$ and R_{t+1}^c is the gross rate of return on a portfolio mimicking consumption growth over this period.

8.3.2 Continuous Time

Now let us turn to the continuous-time setting. Suppose that the dynamics of consumption can be written as

$$dc_t = c_t\left[\mu_{ct}\, dt + \boldsymbol{\sigma}_{ct}^{\top}\, d\boldsymbol{z}_t\right] = c_t \mu_{ct}\, dt + c_t \boldsymbol{\sigma}_{ct}^{\top}\, d\boldsymbol{z}_t, \tag{8.21}$$

where μ_{ct} is the expected relative growth rate of consumption and $\boldsymbol{\sigma}_{ct}$ is the vector of sensitivities of consumption growth to the exogenous shocks to the economy. In particular, the variance of relative consumption growth is given by $\|\boldsymbol{\sigma}_{ct}\|^2$. Given the dynamics of consumption and the relation (8.16) we can obtain the dynamics of ζ_t by an application of Itô's Lemma on the function $g(t,c) = e^{-\delta t}u'(c)/u'(c_0)$. The relevant derivatives are

$$\frac{\partial g}{\partial t}(t,c) = -\delta e^{-\delta t}\frac{u'(c)}{u'(c_0)}, \quad \frac{\partial g}{\partial c}(t,c) = e^{-\delta t}\frac{u''(c)}{u'(c_0)}, \quad \frac{\partial^2 g}{\partial c^2}(t,c) = e^{-\delta t}\frac{u'''(c)}{u'(c_0)},$$

implying that

$$\begin{aligned}
\frac{\partial g}{\partial t}(t,c_t) &= -\delta e^{-\delta t}\frac{u'(c_t)}{u'(c_0)} = -\delta\zeta_t, \\
\frac{\partial g}{\partial c}(t,c_t) &= e^{-\delta t}\frac{u''(c_t)}{u'(c_0)} = \frac{u''(c_t)}{u'(c_t)}\zeta_t = -\gamma(c_t)c_t^{-1}\zeta_t, \\
\frac{\partial^2 g}{\partial c^2}(t,c_t) &= e^{-\delta t}\frac{u'''(c_t)}{u'(c_0)} = \frac{u'''(c_t)}{u'(c_t)}\zeta_t = \eta(c_t)c_t^{-2}\zeta_t,
\end{aligned}$$

where $\gamma(c_t) \equiv -c_t u''(c_t)/u'(c_t)$ is the relative risk aversion of the individual, and where $\eta(c_t) \equiv c_t^2 u'''(c_t)/u'(c_t)$ is positive under the very plausible assumption that the absolute risk aversion of the individual is decreasing in the level of consumption. Consequently, the dynamics of the state-price deflator can be expressed as

$$d\zeta_t = -\zeta_t\left[\left(\delta + \gamma(c_t)\mu_{ct} - \frac{1}{2}\eta(c_t)\|\boldsymbol{\sigma}_{ct}\|^2\right)dt + \gamma(c_t)\boldsymbol{\sigma}_{ct}^{\top}\,d\boldsymbol{z}_t\right].$$

Comparing this equation with Eq. (4.32), we can draw the conclusions summarized in the following theorem:

Theorem 8.3 *Assume a continuous-time economy in which the optimal consumption process of an individual with time-additive expected utility satisfies Eq. (8.21). Then the continuously compounded risk-free short-term interest rate is*

$$r_t^f = \delta + \gamma(c_t)\mu_{ct} - \frac{1}{2}\eta(c_t)\|\boldsymbol{\sigma}_{ct}\|^2, \tag{8.22}$$

where $\gamma(c_t) = -c_t u''(c_t)/u'(c_t)$ and $\eta(c_t) = c_t^2 u'''(c_t)/u'(c_t)$. The market price of risk process is

$$\boldsymbol{\lambda}_t = \gamma(c_t)\boldsymbol{\sigma}_{ct}, \tag{8.23}$$

which implies that the excess expected rate of return on asset i over the instant following time t can be written as

$$\mu_{it} + \delta_{it} - r_t^f = \gamma(c_t)\boldsymbol{\sigma}_{it}^{\top}\boldsymbol{\sigma}_{ct} = \gamma(c_t)\rho_{ict}\,\|\boldsymbol{\sigma}_{it}\|\,\|\boldsymbol{\sigma}_{ct}\|. \tag{8.24}$$

Here $\boldsymbol{\sigma}_{it}^{\top}\boldsymbol{\sigma}_{ct}$ and ρ_{ict} are the covariance rate and correlation between the rate of return on asset i and the consumption growth rate, respectively, whereas $\|\boldsymbol{\sigma}_{it}\|$ and $\|\boldsymbol{\sigma}_{ct}\|$ are volatilities of the rate of return on asset i and the consumption growth rate, respectively. The expression (8.24) follows from substituting Eq. (8.23) into Eq. (4.30). Note that the continuous-time relation (8.24) is exact in contrast to the discrete-time analogue in Eq. (8.17).

Equation (8.22) gives the interest rate at which the market for short-term borrowing and lending will clear. In the case of a representative individual, the equation relates the equilibrium short-term interest rate to the time preference rate and the expected growth rate μ_{ct} and the variance rate $\|\boldsymbol{\sigma}_{ct}\|^2$ of aggregate consumption growth over the next instant. We can observe the following relations:

- There is a positive relation between the time preference rate and the equilibrium interest rate. The intuition behind this is that when the individuals of the economy are impatient and have a high demand for current consumption, the equilibrium interest rate must be high in order to encourage the individuals to save now and postpone consumption.
- The multiplier of μ_{ct} in Eq. (8.22) is the relative risk aversion of the representative individual, which is positive. Hence, there is a positive relation between the expected growth in aggregate consumption and the equilibrium interest rate. This can be explained as follows: We expect higher future consumption and hence lower future marginal utility, so postponed payments due to saving have lower value. Consequently, a higher return on saving is needed to maintain market clearing.
- If u''' is positive, there will be a negative relation between the variance of aggregate consumption and the equilibrium interest rate. If the representative individual has decreasing absolute risk aversion, which is certainly a reasonable assumption, u''' has to be positive, compare Eq. (5.6). The intuition is that the greater the uncertainty about future consumption, the more the individuals will appreciate the sure payments from the risk-free asset and hence the lower a return necessary to clear the market for borrowing and lending.

Again, if we can find a trading strategy 'mimicking' the consumption process (maximal absolute correlation) we get the 'consumption-beta' relation

$$\mu_{it} + \delta_{it} - r_t^f = \beta_{it}^c \left(\mu_t^c + \delta_t^c - r_t^f \right),$$

where $\beta_{it}^c = \boldsymbol{\sigma}_{it}^{\top}\boldsymbol{\sigma}_{ct}/\|\boldsymbol{\sigma}_{ct}\|^2$, and where μ_t^c and δ_t^c refer to the expected capital gain and the dividend yield, respectively, of the consumption-mimicking trading strategy.

If the market is effectively complete, the above equations are valid for aggregate consumption if we apply the utility function and time preference rate of the representative individual. The representative individual version of Eq. (8.24) says that risky assets are priced so that the expected excess return on an asset is given by the product of the relative risk aversion of the representative individual and the covariance between the asset return and the growth rate of aggregate consumption.

As already indicated in the one-period framework, we can also obtain a relation between expected returns and aggregate consumption if the market is incomplete and no representative individual exists. Let us see how the argument goes in the continuous-time setting. Let $c_l = (c_{lt})$ denote the optimal consumption process of individual number l in the economy and assume that

$$dc_{lt} = c_{lt}\left[\mu_{clt}\,dt + \boldsymbol{\sigma}_{clt}^{\top}\,d\boldsymbol{z}_t\right].$$

If there are L individuals in the economy, aggregate consumption is $C_t = \sum_{l=1}^{L} c_{lt}$ and we have that

$$\begin{aligned} dC_t &= \sum_{l=1}^{L} dc_{lt} = \left(\sum_{l=1}^{L} c_{lt}\mu_{clt}\right) dt + \left(\sum_{l=1}^{L} c_{lt}\boldsymbol{\sigma}_{clt}\right)^{\top} d\boldsymbol{z}_t \\ &\equiv C_t\left[\mu_{Ct}\,dt + \boldsymbol{\sigma}_{Ct}^{\top}\,d\boldsymbol{z}_t\right], \end{aligned}$$

where $\mu_{Ct} \equiv \left(\sum_{l=1}^{L} c_{lt}\mu_{clt}\right)/C_t$ and $\boldsymbol{\sigma}_{Ct} = \left(\sum_{l=1}^{L} c_{lt}\boldsymbol{\sigma}_{clt}\right)/C_t$. We know from Eq. (8.24) that

$$\mu_{it} + \delta_{it} - r_t^f = A_l(c_{lt})c_{lt}\boldsymbol{\sigma}_{it}^{\top}\boldsymbol{\sigma}_{clt}, \quad l = 1, \ldots, L,$$

where $A_l(c_{lt}) \equiv -u_l''(c_{lt})/u_l'(c_{lt})$ is the *absolute* risk aversion of individual l. Consequently,

$$\left(\mu_{it} + \delta_{it} - r_t^f\right)\frac{1}{A_l(c_{lt})} = c_{lt}\boldsymbol{\sigma}_{it}^{\top}\boldsymbol{\sigma}_{clt}, \quad l = 1, \ldots, L,$$

and summing up over l, we get

$$\left(\mu_{it} + \delta_{it} - r_t^f\right)\sum_{l=1}^{L}\left(\frac{1}{A_l(c_{lt})}\right) = \boldsymbol{\sigma}_{it}^{\top}\left(\sum_{l=1}^{L} c_{lt}\boldsymbol{\sigma}_{clt}\right) = \boldsymbol{\sigma}_{it}^{\top}\left(C_t\boldsymbol{\sigma}_{Ct}\right).$$

Therefore, we have the following relation between excess expected returns and aggregate consumption:

$$\mu_{it} + \delta_{it} - r_t^f = \frac{C_t}{\sum_{l=1}^{L}\left(\frac{1}{A_l(c_{lt})}\right)}\boldsymbol{\sigma}_{it}^{\top}\boldsymbol{\sigma}_{Ct}.$$

Relative to the complete markets version Eq. (8.24), the only difference is that the relative risk aversion of the representative individual is replaced by some complicated average of the risk aversions of the individuals. Note that if all individuals have CRRA utility with identical relative risk aversions, then $A_l(c_{lt}) = \gamma/c_{lt}$ and the multiplier $C_t/\sum_{l=1}^{L}\left(\frac{1}{A_l(c_{lt})}\right)$ in the above equation reduces to γ.

While Theorem 8.3 provides the risk-free rate and the risk premia in a continuous-time model with a general utility function and a general consumption process, we can of course specialize to a constant-moments CRRA-lognormal setting. In continuous time, the assumption of a lognormal consumption growth means that μ_{ct} and $\boldsymbol{\sigma}_{ct}$ in the consumption process (8.21) are constant so that consumption is given by the geometric Brownian motion

$$dc_t = c_t\left[\mu_c\,dt + \boldsymbol{\sigma}_c^\top\,d\boldsymbol{z}_t\right].$$

It follows from Eqs. (8.22) and (8.24) that the model with these assumptions generates a constant continuously compounded short-term risk-free interest rate of

$$r^f = \delta + \gamma\mu_c - \frac{1}{2}\gamma(1+\gamma)\|\boldsymbol{\sigma}_c\|^2 \tag{8.25}$$

and a constant Sharpe ratio for asset i given by

$$\frac{\mu_{it} + \delta_{it} - r^f}{\|\boldsymbol{\sigma}_{it}\|} = \gamma\rho_{ic}\|\boldsymbol{\sigma}_c\|$$

if the asset has a constant correlation with consumption.

Note that when consumption follows the geometric Brownian motion $dc_t = c_t[\mu_c + \boldsymbol{\sigma}_c^\top\,d\boldsymbol{z}_t]$, we know from Section 2.6.7 that

$$\ln\left(\frac{c_{t+1}}{c_t}\right) \sim N\left(\mu_c - \frac{1}{2}\|\boldsymbol{\sigma}_c\|^2, \|\boldsymbol{\sigma}_c\|^2\right).$$

Rewriting the risk-free rate in Eq. (8.25) as

$$r^f = \delta + \gamma\left(\mu_c - \frac{1}{2}\|\boldsymbol{\sigma}_c\|^2\right) - \frac{1}{2}\gamma^2\|\boldsymbol{\sigma}_c\|^2,$$

we see that the continuous-time risk-free rate is consistent with the discrete-time risk-free rate we get with a constant $\bar{g}$ and σ_g^2 in Eq. (8.18).

8.4 THEORY MEETS DATA: ASSET PRICING PUZZLES

The implications of the consumption-based model have been exposed to numerous empirical tests and we will present the main conclusions from these tests below. But first, it is important to realize exactly what the tests are really testing.

The theoretical predictions of the risk-free rate and the risk premia on risky assets involve conditional expectations and variances of consumption growth, conditional expectations and variances of returns, and conditional correlations between returns and consumption growth. In standard empirical tests based on a time series of consumption growth rates and returns these conditional moments are replaced by sample means, variances, and correlations. This procedure presumes that all the observations of consumption growth rate are drawn from the same distribution with a constant conditional expectation and a constant conditional variance and similarly for returns. Likewise, when making inferences about the level of risk aversion, it is really assumed that the relative risk aversion is constant, although some formulations of the underlying theoretical model allow for time-varying risk aversion. In sum, the traditional empirical studies are testing the constant-moments CRRA-lognormal version of the consumption-CAPM.

As we shall see the tests conclude that the model cannot explain one or more stylized empirical facts. Hence, these facts are often referred to as asset pricing puzzles. We will introduce the puzzles one at a time, but note that some of the puzzles are closely related. We emphasize that while the existence of these puzzles disqualifies the basic constant-moments CRRA-lognormal consumption-based model, the general consumption-based framework is not questioned.

8.4.1 The Equity Premium Puzzle

In the constant-moments, representative-individual version of the discrete-time CRRA-lognormal model, we can rewrite the risk premium on any risky asset i from Eq. (8.19) as

$$\mu_i + \delta_i - r^f \approx \gamma \sigma_c \sigma_i \rho_{ic}, \tag{8.26}$$

where $\mu_i + \delta_i$ is the expected rate of return on asset i (the price appreciation plus the dividend), r^f is the one-period risk-free rate of return, σ_c is the standard deviation of the growth rate of aggregate consumption, σ_i is the standard deviation of the return, and ρ_{ic} the correlation between return and aggregate consumption growth. All returns and growth rates are measured over the same time interval, the length of a 'period' in the model. The continuous-time version of the model produces the same relation for every instant, but as an exact equality instead of an approximation. Some studies work with the discrete-time log-return version and use Eq. (8.20), again implicitly imposing constant moments.

Most tests focus on the question whether the risk premium relation (8.26) holds for a broad-based stock index for reasonable values of the relative risk aversion coefficient, that is whether the model can explain the observed equity premium. Let us use the following stylized figures that are roughly representative for the US economy over the second half of the twentieth century:

- the average annual real excess rate of return on the stock index (relative to the yield on a short-term government bond) is about 8%;
- the empirical standard deviation of the annual real rate of return on the stock index is about 20%;
- the empirical standard deviation of annual relative changes in aggregate consumption is about 2%;
- the empirical correlation between the real return on the stock index and changes in aggregate consumption is about 0.2.

If we insert these estimates into Eq. (8.26), it follows that the relative risk aversion coefficient γ must be 100. This is certainly an unrealistically high risk aversion for a typical individual, compare the discussion in Section 5.6.2.

In fact, this computation—which is standard in the literature—exaggerates the problem somewhat. If we drop the approximation of the square root in Eq. (8.19), the discrete-time simple model says that

$$\mu_i + \delta_i - r^f \approx \sqrt{e^{\gamma^2 \sigma_c^2} - 1}\, \sigma_i \rho_{ic}, \tag{8.27}$$

and plugging in the estimates, we need

$$\gamma \approx \frac{1}{\sigma_c} \sqrt{\ln\left[1 + \left(\frac{\mu_i + \delta_i - r^f}{\sigma_i \rho_{ic}}\right)^2\right]} = \frac{1}{0.02}\sqrt{\ln(5)} \approx 63.4.$$

But 63.4 is still an unreasonably high relative risk aversion.

For a reasonable level of risk aversion (probably in the range 2–5), the expected excess rate of return predicted by the theory is much smaller than the historical average. For example with $\gamma = 5$, the expected excess rate of return on the market portfolio should be $5 \cdot 0.2 \cdot 0.02 \cdot 0.2 = 0.004$ or 0.4% according to Eq. (8.26). The simple consumption-based asset pricing model cannot explain the high average stock returns observed in the data. This so-called *equity premium puzzle* was first pointed out by Mehra and Prescott (1985).

The equity premium puzzle is not specific to the US or to the post-World War II period. Similar results are obtained for other countries and other data periods. Table 8.1 is based on Campbell (2003) who considers the log-return

Table 8.1. The equity premium puzzle internationally.

Country	Period	$\tilde{\mu}_m$	$\tilde{\sigma}_m$	$\tilde{\sigma}_C$	$\tilde{\rho}_{mC}$	γ^*	γ^{**}
US	1947Q2–1998Q3	8.1	15.3	1.1	0.205	240.6	49.3
US	1970Q1–1998Q3	6.3	17.0	0.9	0.274	150.1	41.2
US	1891–1997	6.7	18.5	6.4	0.495	22.8	11.3
Australia	1970Q1–1998Q4	3.9	22.4	2.1	0.144	58.5	8.4
Canada	1970Q1–1999Q1	4.0	17.3	1.9	0.202	59.3	12.0
France	1973Q2–1998Q3	8.3	23.2	2.9	−0.093	negative	12.3
Germany	1978Q4–1997Q3	8.7	20.2	2.4	0.029	599.5	17.5
Italy	1971Q2–1998Q1	4.7	27.1	1.7	−0.006	negative	10.4
Japan	1970Q2–1998Q4	5.1	21.5	2.6	0.112	82.6	9.3
Netherlands	1977Q2–1998Q3	11.4	16.9	2.5	0.032	850.0	26.9
Sweden	1970Q1–1999Q2	11.5	23.5	1.9	0.015	1713.2	26.5
Sweden	1920–1997	6.5	18.8	5.6	0.0167	74.1	12.4
Switzerland	1982Q2–1998Q4	14.9	21.9	2.1	−0.112	negative	32.1
UK	1970Q1–1999Q1	9.2	21.2	2.5	0.093	186.0	17.2
UK	1919–1997	8.7	21.3	5.6	0.351	41.2	14.5

Notes: The information is taken from Table 4 in Campbell (2003). Data are quarterly when there are Qx suffices on the years in period column, otherwise annual data are used. The headings of the columns are explained in the text

equation (8.20). In the table, $\tilde{\mu}_m$ is the historical estimate of the left-hand side of Eq. (8.20), that is the average excess log return on the stock market adjusted by half the variance. $\tilde{\sigma}_m$ is the standard deviation of that excess return, and $\tilde{\sigma}_C$ is the standard deviation of the log growth rate of aggregate consumption. The means and standard deviations are annualized and in percentage terms. $\tilde{\rho}_{mC}$ is the historical correlation between the excess log return on the stock market and the log consumption growth. The values in the column γ^* are then computed as the value you need to apply for the relative risk aversion in order for Eq. (8.20) to hold given the estimates of the other parameters. The γ^{**} in the right-most column is the relative risk aversion needed if you fix the return-consumption correlation to 1.

It is clear from the table that the historical equity premium is quite high in all the countries and, given the other estimates, requires a very high level of risk aversion. In some of the countries, the estimated correlation between consumption growth and stock returns is negative so that the equity premium should be negative according to the model or you have to use a negative value for the risk aversion coefficient. The correlation may be difficult to estimate precisely but the right-most column shows that even if you pick the correlation values most favourable to the model (that is a correlation of 1), you still need a fairly high risk aversion coefficient. The value of the required risk aversion is very sensitive to the estimated consumption volatility. The table reveals that the post-World War II US consumption volatility is small compared to the other countries and also to a longer US data series. Consequently, fixing the correlation at 1, you need a particularly high risk aversion coefficient to match recent US data.

The simple consumption-based model seems unable to explain the observed equity premium, but what about more general consumption-based models? Equations like (8.17) and (8.24) provide a more general link between expected excess returns, risk aversion, and the asset-consumption covariance. If both the relative risk aversion and the asset-consumption covariance vary over time, and they are positively correlated so that risk aversion tends to be high when the asset-consumption covariance is high, then the average of the product of the risk aversion and the covariance will be higher than the product of the average risk aversion and the average covariance.[1] In other words, when risk and risk aversion are positively related, the equity premium is higher. This is a key aspect of the model of Campbell and Cochrane (1999) that we explore in Section 9.2.

Even the apparently general expressions (8.17) and (8.24) for the equity premium in consumption-based models are based on a number of questionable assumptions. By relaxing those assumptions we may be able to match the observed equity premium better. For example, we have assumed a single consumption good. In Section 9.5 we explore the consequences of distinguishing between different consumption goods, for example perishable goods and durable goods. The standard assumption of time-additive expected utility is also dubious. As we shall see in Section 9.3, the Bansal and Yaron (2004) model that combines Epstein–Zin preferences with certain long-run consumption risks can, in fact, produce an equity premium of the observed magnitude. Other authors have looked at the impact of so-called rare disasters on the equity premium and on various incomplete markets settings in which the standard representative individual approach does not apply. Details are given in various parts of Chapter 9. The overall conclusion is that there are several possible consumption-based explanations of the equity premium puzzle but, of course, you may disagree with some or all of these explanations.

8.4.2 The Risk-Free Rate Puzzle

The short-term risk-free rate in the constant-moments CRRA-lognormal model is given by Eq. (8.25) in the continuous-time setting and a similar expression in the discrete-time setting, see Eq. (8.18). As above, we assume a consumption volatility of $\sigma_c = 2\%$. The historical average annual growth rate of real consumption in the US has been around $\mu_c = 2\%$ with some variation between different time periods. Let us assume that the subjective time

[1] This is just an application of the standard covariance formula $\mathrm{E}[xy] = \mathrm{E}[x]\,\mathrm{E}[y] + \mathrm{Cov}[x, y]$.

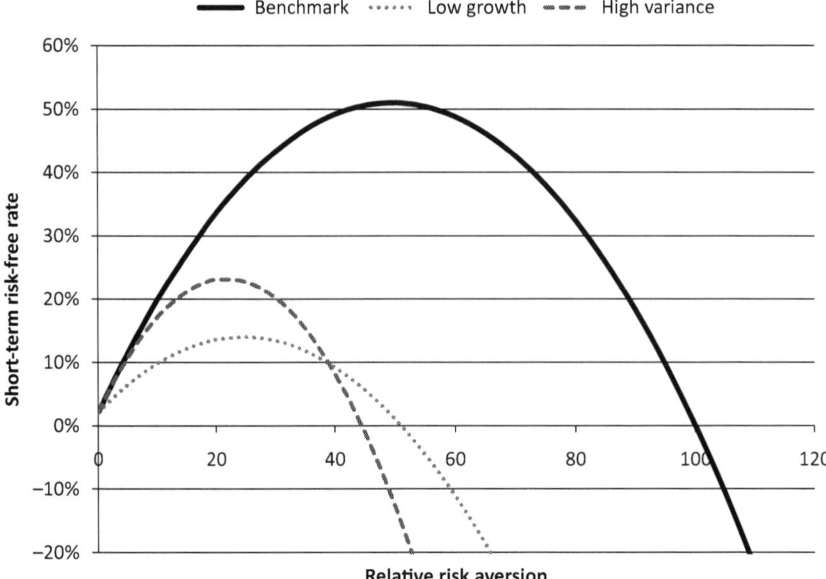

Fig. 8.1. The short-term risk-free rate as a function of the relative risk aversion in the simple consumption-based CAPM.

Notes: The time preference rate is fixed at $\delta = 2\%$. The benchmark values of the expected growth rate and the volatility of consumption are $\mu_c = 2\%$ and $\sigma_c = 2\%$, respectively. The dotted curve is for a lower expected growth rate of 1% and the dashed line for a higher volatility of 3%

preference rate δ is also 2% which seems to be a reasonable value. Given these numbers, Fig. 8.1 shows the risk-free rate of the model as a function of the relative risk aversion. If, for example, we assume that the relative risk aversion is 63.4 as implied by the observed equity premium (see above), then the risk-free rate should be 47%, which is obviously far above the observed level of interest rates. For apparently reasonable parameter values, the risk-free rate will be considerably higher than observed in the data. This is the so-called *risk-free rate puzzle* first identified by Weil (1989).

If you want the risk-free rate to be around the 2% assumed for the time preference, you need $\mu_c \approx (1 + \gamma)\sigma_c^2/2$, which requires a relatively low expected growth rate, high volatility, or a high risk aversion—or a combination thereof. Alternatively, you can lower the time preference rate, although it would have to be significantly negative to match the observed risk-free rate and consumption moments, and this is certainly unreasonable.

The level of the risk-free rate will be highly sensitive to the values of μ_c and σ_c, in particular for high or even moderate levels of risk aversion, as can be seen from the dotted line ($\mu_c = 1\%$) and the dashed line ($\sigma_c = 3\%$) in the graph. For example, with a risk aversion of 10, which seems moderate in light of the equity premium puzzle, the risk-free rate would be ten percentage points higher if the expected consumption growth was increased by one percentage point. In any case, parameter combinations that allow the model to match the observed interest rate level lie on a 'knife edge'.

Various of the advanced consumption-based models mentioned above can also match the low level and variability of short-term interest rates quite well. The use of Epstein–Zin preferences or the introduction of unhedgeable risks (for example risk stemming from labour income) seem particularly successful in dealing with the risk-free rate puzzle. Again, the reader is referred to Chapter 9 for details.

8.4.3 The Volatility Puzzle

An alternative perspective on the equity premium puzzle is that the consumption volatility is too low. Other things being equal, a higher consumption volatility on the right-hand side of Eq. (8.26) would boost the equity premium. Aggregate consumption is very smooth according to the data and, therefore, this must hold for the consumption of a representative individual. However, consumer surveys reveal that individual consumption is much more volatile than aggregate consumption. This could be due to problems in the aggregate consumption data which will be discussed in Section 8.5. But the difference between aggregate consumption volatility and individual consumption volatility can also be seen as an indication of incomplete markets and raises concerns about the representative individual interpretation of the consumption-based models. The average of consumption volatilities across individuals will exceed the volatility of aggregate consumption so using that average volatility would help in explaining the high observed equity premium.

Another volatility issue is that stock returns are very volatile relative to aggregate dividends. Is this possible in the simple CRRA-lognormal consumption-based model? In line with the assumptions listed in Section 8.3, write consumption dynamics as

$$\ln\left(\frac{C_{t+1}}{C_t}\right) = \mu_C + \sigma_C \varepsilon_{C,t+1},$$

where $\varepsilon_{C,t+1}$ follows a standard normal distribution (mean zero, variance one) and are independent over time, and assume the individual has time-additive power utility. The next-period state-price deflator is then

$$\frac{\zeta_{t+1}}{\zeta_t} = e^{-\delta}\left(\frac{C_{t+1}}{C_t}\right)^{-\gamma} = \exp\{-\delta - \gamma\left(\mu_C + \sigma_C \varepsilon_{C,t+1}\right)\}.$$

Assume a dividend stream (D_t) up to time T with a periodic growth given by

$$\ln\left(\frac{D_{t+1}}{D_t}\right) = \mu_D + \sigma_D\left(\rho_{CD}\varepsilon_{C,t+1} + \sqrt{1-\rho_{CD}^2}\varepsilon_{D,t+1}\right),$$

where $\varepsilon_{D,t+1}$ is also standard normally distributed and independent over time, and $\varepsilon_{C,t+1}$ and $\varepsilon_{D,t+1}$ are uncorrelated. Hence ρ_{CD} is the correlation between the log-growth rates of consumption and dividend. The time t value of the dividend at time $t+1$ is then

$$\begin{aligned}
\mathrm{E}_t\left[\frac{\zeta_{t+1}}{\zeta_t}D_{t+1}\right] &= D_t\,\mathrm{E}_t\left[\frac{\zeta_{t+1}}{\zeta_t}\frac{D_{t+1}}{D_t}\right] \\
&= D_t e^{-\delta-\gamma\mu_C+\mu_D}\,\mathrm{E}_t\left[e^{-(\gamma\sigma_C-\sigma_D\rho_{CD})\varepsilon_{C,t+1}+\sigma_D\sqrt{1-\rho_{CD}^2}\varepsilon_{D,t+1}}\right] \\
&= D_t\exp\left\{-\delta-\gamma\mu_C+\mu_D+\frac{1}{2}\left(\gamma\sigma_C-\sigma_D\rho_{CD}\right)^2+\frac{1}{2}\sigma_D^2(1-\rho_{CD}^2)\right\} \\
&= D_t\exp\left\{-\delta-\gamma\mu_C+\mu_D+\frac{1}{2}\gamma^2\sigma_C^2+\frac{1}{2}\sigma_D^2-\gamma\rho_{CD}\sigma_C\sigma_D\right\} \\
&\equiv AD_t,
\end{aligned}$$

where

$$A = \exp\left\{-\delta-\gamma\mu_C+\mu_D+\frac{1}{2}\gamma^2\sigma_C^2+\frac{1}{2}\sigma_D^2-\gamma\rho_{CD}\sigma_C\sigma_D\right\}$$

is obviously a positive constant. By proceeding as in Section 4.4.2, it can be shown that

$$\mathrm{E}_t\left[\frac{\zeta_{t+s}}{\zeta_t}D_{t+s}\right] = A^s D_t$$

and, summing up over s the present value of all future dividends is

$$P_t = D_t\frac{A}{1-A}\left(1-A^{T-t}\right). \tag{8.28}$$

The gross return is then

$$R_{t+1} = \frac{P_{t+1}+D_{t+1}}{P_t} = \frac{D_{t+1}}{D_t}\frac{1+\frac{A}{1-A}\left(1-A^{T-(t+1)}\right)}{\frac{A}{1-A}\left(1-A^{T-t}\right)} = \frac{1}{A}\frac{D_{t+1}}{D_t}$$

so that the log-return is $\ln R_{t+1} = -\ln A + \ln(D_{t+1}/D_t)$. Consequently, the volatility of the log-return must equal σ_D. The simple model cannot explain the observed difference between return volatility and dividend volatility. Apparently, this was first discussed by Grossman and Shiller (1981), LeRoy and Porter (1981), and Shiller (1981). Intuitively, we need more variation in the state-price deflator to boost the return volatility relative to the dividend volatility. This is satisfied in many of the extensions of the simple model covered by the next chapter.

8.4.4 The Price-Dividend Ratio Puzzle

Equation (8.28) above gives the price-dividend ratio in a simple CRRA-lognormal model. If we consider an infinite dividend stream and $A \leq 1$, the price-dividend ratio becomes a constant:

$$\frac{P_t}{D_t} = \frac{A}{1 - A}.$$

However, with the high relative risk aversion needed to match the level of the equity premium, the constant A will exceed 1 for some reasonable values of the other parameters. For example, if we assume that the dividend equals aggregate consumption so that $\mu_D = \mu_C$, $\sigma_D = \sigma_C$, and $\rho_{CD} = 1$, we have

$$A = e^{-\delta - (\gamma - 1)\mu_C + \frac{1}{2}(\gamma - 1)^2 \sigma_C^2}.$$

With $\delta = \mu_C = 0.02$ and $\sigma_C = 0.04$, we need $\gamma \approx 31.7$ to obtain an 8% equity premium (using the square root version in Eq. (8.27) and a correlation of 0.2). Then $A \approx 1.13$. In this case the price of the infinite dividend stream would be infinitely large, which is certainly not what we observe in reality. Parlour, Stanton, and Walden (2011) provide more details on this issue and suggest an alternative model that avoids the problem and may help in explaining some of the puzzles.

According to Fig. 1.2 in Chapter 1, the price-dividend ratio is typically around 25. Then we need $A = 25/26 \approx 0.96$. For given values of μ_C and σ_C^2, it will be impossible to find a δ and a γ so that the CRRA-lognormal can simultaneously match the equity premium, the risk-free rate, and the price-dividend ratio. Of course, opening up for a dividend process different from the aggregate consumption process adds flexibility, but still only carefully selected combinations of parameters will do the job.

8.4.5 The Predictability Puzzle

In the simple CRRA-lognormal model, the real short-term interest rate and the Sharpe ratios of risky assets are constant over time. The price-dividend ratio is deterministic and even constant if you consider an infinite time horizon. These properties are inconsistent with empirical observations. Interest rates vary over time, and recent studies indicate that Sharpe ratios, expected returns, and volatilities on stocks vary over the business cycle with high values in recessions and low values in periods of high economic growth rates, see for example Cochrane (2005) and Lettau and Ludvigson (2010). Returns of stocks and many other financial assets apparently have a predictable component so that it is possible to provide a better forecast of the future return than just the historical average return by conditioning on the current values of other variables, compare the brief overview of results in Section 1.5. Note, however, that the possibility of predicting stock returns by such variables is still debated in the academic literature, see for example Ang and Bekaert (2007). It is clear from the general version of the consumption-based CAPM developed in Section 8.3 that, within the time-additive utility, one-good model, expected returns will vary over time if the relative risk aversion or the asset-consumption covariance (or both) vary over time. Again, several of the extended models discussed in Chapter 9 have such features.

Even without going into specific models, we can obtain some insights about the causes of predictability. Start with the definition of the gross return over any time interval $[t, t+1]$:

$$R_{t+1} = \frac{P_{t+1} + D_{t+1}}{P_t}.$$

This definition implies that

$$P_t = R_{t+1}^{-1} \left(P_{t+1} + D_{t+1} \right)$$

and thus the price-dividend ratio at time t must satisfy

$$\begin{aligned} \frac{P_t}{D_t} &= R_{t+1}^{-1} \left(\frac{P_{t+1}}{D_t} + \frac{D_{t+1}}{D_t} \right) = R_{t+1}^{-1} \left(\frac{P_{t+1}}{D_{t+1}} \frac{D_{t+1}}{D_t} + \frac{D_{t+1}}{D_t} \right) \\ &= R_{t+1}^{-1} \frac{D_{t+1}}{D_t} \left(1 + \frac{P_{t+1}}{D_{t+1}} \right). \end{aligned}$$

Such an identity holds for any t, so we can iterate one step forward:

$$\begin{aligned} \frac{P_t}{D_t} &= R_{t+1}^{-1} \frac{D_{t+1}}{D_t} \left(1 + R_{t+2}^{-1} \frac{D_{t+2}}{D_{t+1}} \left(1 + \frac{P_{t+2}}{D_{t+2}} \right) \right) \\ &= R_{t+1}^{-1} \frac{D_{t+1}}{D_t} + R_{t+1}^{-1} R_{t+2}^{-1} \frac{D_{t+1}}{D_t} \frac{D_{t+2}}{D_{t+1}} \left(1 + \frac{P_{t+2}}{D_{t+2}} \right). \end{aligned}$$

If we proceed in the same way and assume that

$$\lim_{n \to \infty} \frac{P_{t+n}}{D_{t+n}} \prod_{j=1}^{n} R_{t+j}^{-1} \frac{D_{t+j}}{D_{t+j-1}} = 0,$$

we obtain

$$\frac{P_t}{D_t} = \sum_{j=1}^{\infty} \prod_{k=1}^{j} R_{t+k}^{-1} \frac{D_{t+k}}{D_{t+k-1}}. \tag{8.29}$$

Note that this is still an identity, there are no assumptions except for the zero limit assumption. Of course, the right-hand side of this equation involves values that are random variables as seen from time t. Taking expectations conditional on the information available at t in Eq. (8.29), we see that

$$\frac{P_t}{D_t} = \mathrm{E}_t\left[\sum_{j=1}^{\infty}\prod_{k=1}^{j} R_{t+k}^{-1}\frac{D_{t+k}}{D_{t+k-1}}\right]. \tag{8.30}$$

This relation confirms that a high current price-dividend ratio must reflect high (expected) future dividend growth or low (expected) future returns.

The non-linear nature of Eq. (8.30) prevents deeper insights. Campbell and Shiller (1988) introduce a linear, approximative relation between log-returns, log-dividends, and log-prices which is much more tractable. Write the gross rate of return on an asset as

$$\begin{aligned} R_{t+1} &= \frac{P_{t+1} + D_{t+1}}{P_t} = \frac{\frac{P_{t+1}}{D_t} + \frac{D_{t+1}}{D_t}}{\frac{P_t}{D_t}} = \frac{\frac{P_{t+1}}{D_{t+1}}\frac{D_{t+1}}{D_t} + \frac{D_{t+1}}{D_t}}{\frac{P_t}{D_t}} \\ &= \frac{e^{p_{t+1}-d_{t+1}+\Delta d_{t+1}} + e^{\Delta d_{t+1}}}{e^{p_t-d_t}} = \frac{e^{\Delta d_{t+1}}\left(e^{p_{t+1}-d_{t+1}} + 1\right)}{e^{p_t-d_t}}, \end{aligned}$$

where $d_t = \ln D_t$, $p_t = \ln P_t$, and $\Delta d_{t+1} = d_{t+1} - d_t = \ln \frac{D_{t+1}}{D_t}$. Then the log-return is

$$\begin{aligned} r_{t+1} \equiv \ln R_{t+1} &= \ln\left[e^{\Delta d_{t+1}}(1 + e^{p_{t+1}-d_{t+1}})\right] - (p_t - d_t) \\ &= -(p_t - d_t) + \Delta d_{t+1} + \ln(1 + e^{p_{t+1}-d_{t+1}}). \end{aligned}$$

A first-order Taylor approximation of $\ln(1 + e^z)$ around $\bar{z}$ gives

$$\ln(1 + e^z) \approx \ln(1 + e^{\bar{z}}) + \frac{e^{\bar{z}}}{1 + e^{\bar{z}}}(z - \bar{z}). \tag{8.31}$$

In our case it is natural to use the average value of the log-price-dividend ratio of the asset as the expansion point, $\bar{z} = \overline{p - d}$. Figure 8.2 illustrates the approximation when $\bar{z} = 3$ corresponding to a price-dividend ratio of $e^3 \approx 20.1$. In the typical range of price-dividend ratios, the approximation is relatively precise. For example, for a price-dividend ratio of 15, the approximation error is roughly -0.0021 so that the log-return is underestimated by -0.21%. For a price-dividend ratio of 30, the approximation error is roughly -0.0032 so that the log-return is underestimated by -0.32%.

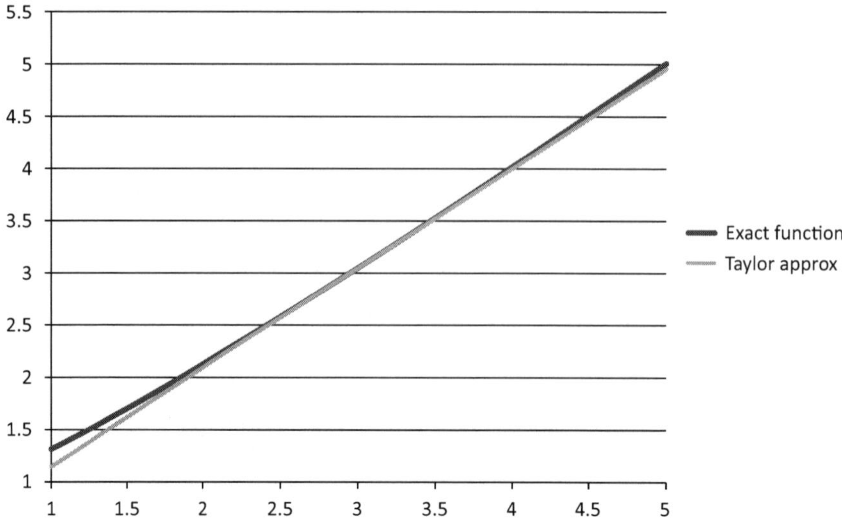

Fig. 8.2. The Taylor approximation.

Notes: (8.31) underlying the Campbell–Shiller return approximation. The Taylor approximation is a linear approximation of the function around $\bar{z} = 3$

With this approximation, the log-return can be approximated as

$$\begin{aligned} r_{t+1} &\approx -(p_t - d_t) + \Delta d_{t+1} + \ln(1 + e^{\overline{p-d}}) + \frac{e^{\overline{p-d}}}{1 + e^{\overline{p-d}}}(p_{t+1} - d_{t+1} - \overline{p-d}) \\ &= \kappa_0 + \kappa_1(p_{t+1} - d_{t+1}) - (p_t - d_t) + \Delta d_{t+1}, \end{aligned} \tag{8.32}$$

where

$$\kappa_1 = \frac{e^{\overline{p-d}}}{1 + e^{\overline{p-d}}} \in (0, 1), \qquad \kappa_0 = \ln(1 + e^{\overline{p-d}}) - \kappa_1 \overline{p-d}.$$

This return approximation is valuable in some models and will be used in Section 9.3. If we isolate the log-price-dividend ratio, we see that it must satisfy the recursive relation

$$p_t - d_t \approx \kappa_0 - r_{t+1} + \Delta d_{t+1} + \kappa_1(p_{t+1} - d_{t+1}),$$

and by iterating forward we obtain

$$p_t - d_t \approx \frac{\kappa_0}{1 - \kappa_1} + \sum_{j=1}^{\infty} \left(\Delta d_{t+j} - r_{t+j} \right), \tag{8.33}$$

under the assumption that

$$\lim_{n\to\infty} \kappa_1^n (p_{t+n} - d_{t+n}) = 0.$$

By taking conditional expectations in Eq. (8.33), it follows that

$$p_t - d_t \approx \frac{\kappa_0}{1-\kappa_1} + \sum_{j=1}^{\infty} \mathrm{E}_t\left[\Delta d_{t+j} - r_{t+j}\right],$$

which clearly shows that a high current price-dividend ratio reflects a high expected dividend growth and/or low expected future returns.

By taking an unconditional variance in (8.33), we see that

$$\begin{aligned} \mathrm{Var}[p_t - d_t] &= \mathrm{Cov}[p_t - d_t, p_t - d_t] \approx \mathrm{Cov}\left[p_t - d_t, \sum_{j=1}^{\infty} \left(\Delta d_{t+j} - r_{t+j}\right)\right] \\ &= \mathrm{Cov}\left[p_t - d_t, \sum_{j=1}^{\infty} \Delta d_{t+j}\right] - \mathrm{Cov}\left[p_t - d_t, \sum_{j=1}^{\infty} r_{t+j}\right]. \end{aligned}$$

Hence, variations in the price-dividend ratio must imply that price-dividend ratios either positively predict dividend growth or negatively predict returns (or both). Empirical studies conclude that there is a substantial variation over time in price-dividend ratios and that price-dividend ratios do not significantly predict dividend. Therefore, it seems that the price-dividend ratio has to predict returns, as has also been found in many studies (see below). However, this conclusion hinges on the linear approximation that has been criticized by Ang and Liu (2007) among others.

8.4.6 The Cross-Sectional Stock Return Puzzle

As described in Section 1.5, the standard CAPM cannot fully explain the observed systematic differences in average returns of different stocks. In particular, it fails to match the empirical fact that the expected return on a stock tends to increase with the book-to-market ratio and decrease with the market capitalization of the issuing company, the so-called value and size effects. Likewise, the simple consumption-based CAPM can only explain a small part of the differences in the average returns on different stocks and leaves a value and a size premium unaccounted for, see for example Mankiw and Shapiro (1986), Breeden, Gibbons, and Litzenberger (1989), and Lettau and Ludvigson (2001b). This is a *cross-sectional stock return puzzle.*

The value premium is very robust in the data and particularly intriguing from a theoretical perspective. Rational asset pricing demands that value stocks can only deliver higher expected returns than growth stocks if they are riskier. But intuitively you would expect growth stocks to be riskier than value stocks. Growth stocks are stocks in companies with low book equity value relative to the market equity value. An obvious reason for the higher market value is that the company has a number of valuable growth options, for example options to undertake new potentially profitable productive investments or options to scale existing production facilities up or down in response to market demand. As an option on an asset is generally considered riskier than already having the asset, growth stocks would seem riskier than value stocks.

A large number of recent papers have suggested various asset pricing models rationalizing the value premium by generalizing the assumptions of the simple model, for example, to the Bansal and Yaron (2004) setting with Epstein–Zin preferences and long-run consumption risks that will be explained in Chapter 9. Moreover, these papers explicitly include various features of the investment options such as the costs of exercising the options (possibly varying over the business cycle) and the possible irreversibility of the investments once the options are exercised. We will not dig deeper into the sources of the value premium here or in the subsequent chapter, but just refer the interested reader to Berk, Green, and Naik (1999), Gomes, Kogan, and Zhang (2003), Bansal, Dittmar, and Lundblad (2005), Zhang (2005), Cooper (2006), and Hansen, Heaton, and Li (2008).

The size effect refers to the observation that stocks in small firms on average offer higher returns than stocks in large firms having the same market-beta or consumption-beta. Berk (1995) argues that this is not really an anomaly, but exactly what you would expect to see. Small stocks are often less liquid, which can explain a higher average return, see for example Acharya and Pedersen (2005). Nevertheless, the size effect seems to have weakened considerably in the recent decades as reported by Schwert (2003) among others.

Empirical studies such as Liew and Vassalou (2000) indicate that both the value premium and the size premium are present because value stocks generally have different exposures to shifts in investment opportunities and business cycle risks than growth stocks do and similarly for small versus large stocks. Such time-varying risks can only be investigated in more general models than the simple CAPM or the simple CCAPM.

8.5 PROBLEMS WITH THE EMPIRICAL STUDIES

A number of issues should be taken into account when the conclusions of the empirical studies of the consumption-based model are evaluated. Below, we first discuss various issues related to the measurement of consumption and afterwards various other issues are listed.

8.5.1 Consumption Data

The application, estimation, and empirical evaluation of consumption-based asset pricing models require reliable data on consumption. Under the assumption of the existence of a representative individual, only aggregate consumption data or per capita consumption data are needed for asset pricing. For the US, a measure of the aggregate consumption at a quarterly frequency is published in the National Income and Product Accounts (NIPA) by the Bureau of Economic Analysis of the Department of Commerce. The consumption measure is split into the consumption of durable goods (items expected to last more than three years such as vehicles and durable household equipment), non-durable goods (such as food, clothing, and gasoline), and services (such as housing, utilities, heath care, transportation, communication, and insurance). The consumption estimates are primarily based on reported sales from retail stores.

Consumption data based on household surveys are also available. In the US, the Consumer Expenditure Survey (CEX) provides consumption expenditure data for a large cross-section of households sampled to be representative of the entire US population. The survey data are collected for the Bureau of Labor Statistics by the US Census Bureau. Since 1980, the CEX has been a continuing survey. Households are interviewed about their expenditures every three months over five consecutive quarters. After the last interview households are dropped and replaced by a new unit so that 20% of the sample exits the survey each quarter. Approximately 7000 households are interviewed each quarter. In addition, some households are asked to keep diaries of all their purchases during two one-week periods. About 7000 diaries are collected per year. Consumption is reported for a large number of different categories of goods and services. The average of the total consumption expenditures of the surveyed households represents an estimate of the US per capita consumption and constitutes an alternative to the NIPA consumption measure. However, the two consumption series exhibit significant differences, see for example Heathcote, Perri, and Violante (2010). The per capita CEX consumption falls below the per capita NIPA consumption, and the gap seems to be widening over time.[2]

Another US data set frequently used in finance research is the Panel Study of Income Dynamics (PSID) data. PSID is a longitudinal study of a sample of households starting from 1968 with 4800 families. When members of the surveyed families leave home and form a family of their own, they are also asked to participate in the surveys. Moreover, new families are sometimes added to the sample (and some eliminated) to retain a sample representative of the US population. The sample size has grown to more than 9000 families

[2] A similar comparison of micro-level consumption data and national accounts consumption data in several other countries can be found in the January 2010 issue of the journal *Review of Economic Dynamics*.

in the 2009 wave of the survey. Until 1996 individuals from these families were interviewed annually. Since then interviews have been biannual. PSID contains very useful, high-quality information on variables such as income, employment, and wealth. However, the data on consumption are limited. In the early years only food expenditures were reported. While expenditures on utilities and transportation have been added in the more recent surveys, data on total consumption expenditures are not directly available. However, as shown by Skinner (1987) and Guo (2010), total consumption expenditures extracted from CEX can be predicted quite well from the consumption items available in PSID, which opens up for application of PSID in consumption-based asset pricing studies.

Some obvious questions and problems arise when looking for consumption data to use in asset pricing studies.

Data source and data period. Since the consumption measures from the different data sources have different properties, they may lead to different conclusions when applied in asset pricing tests. Obviously, different time periods may also lead to different results. For example, for the period since the end of World War II aggregate consumption seems to be particularly smooth compared to longer time series, and the lower volatility makes it harder for the simple consumption-based model to match the observed equity premium. Even with a longer time series, the high equity premium remains a puzzle, though.

Consumption of which goods? The standard approach in the empirical literature is to use NIPA data on consumption of non-durables and services, but to exclude durable goods. However, a significant fraction of total consumption expenditures is spent on durable goods that offer consumption 'services' beyond the period of purchase. Moreover, some durable goods such as real estate and cars can be resold in later periods so that these goods play a dual role as a consumption good and an investment asset. The basic consumption-based asset pricing theory does not allow for durable goods, and it is not clear how to transform observed periodic expenditures on durable goods into the associated periodic consumption of durable goods. This explains why durable consumption is often excluded from the consumption measures used when testing consumption-based asset pricing models. More generally, individuals may have different preferences for different goods and these multi-good preferences are not well approximated by the standard power utility function applied to total consumption expenditures. In recent years, some multi-good consumption-based asset pricing models have been developed and show some potential in explaining various puzzles. We will describe some of these models in Section 9.5. Moreover, the consumption of some non-durable goods involves commitment (such as subscriptions and mobile phone services), whereas the consumption of other goods is costly to adjust (such as transportation or fuels), sometimes because the consumption of some non-durable goods is mainly determined by the holdings of major durable goods which are often very costly to adjust. See the discussions of such adjustment costs in Marshall and Parekh (1999) and Aït-Sahalia, Parker, and Yogo (2004).

The timing of consumption. The available consumption data reflect the aggregate consumption over a given period of time, which may disagree with the length of the time period of the model to be tested. In particular, this is a challenge for continuous-time models in which the relevant consumption measure is the instantaneous rate of consumption at a given point in time, as discussed by Grossman, Melino, and Shiller (1987). Such a time-aggregated consumption measure will imply a downward bias in the estimated covariance between consumption and asset returns, which again will lead to an upward bias in the required risk aversion coefficient. According to Breeden, Gibbons, and Litzenberger (1989), the covariance estimate may be biased downward by as much as 50% so that the risk aversion estimate may be biased upwards by a factor of 2.

Which households to include. Consumption-based asset pricing models with a representative individual find that the equity premium should be proportional to the covariance between equity returns and aggregate consumption. However, not all consumers invest in the stock market and, intuitively, the consumption of such individuals should really be excluded from the consumption measures applied in the asset pricing tests, as was first argued by Mankiw and Zeldes (1991). Based on consumer surveys, Ameriks and Zeldes (2004) estimate that roughly half of US households did not own stocks in 2001, although the stock market participation rate has increased over the years. Empirical studies have shown that the consumption of stockholders does indeed both (i) vary more than aggregate consumption and (ii) covary more with stock market returns than aggregate consumption. Therefore, the limited stock market participation can partially resolve the equity premium puzzle, but the implied relative risk aversion is still very high, see for example Brav, Constantinides, and Geczy (2002) and Vissing-Jørgensen (2002). Entering the stock market may be costly which can explain why low-wealth households do not invest in stocks, in particular if they also face credit constraints. However, even some of the more wealthy households do not participate in the stock market. Some households may also rationally stay out of the stock market because of exposure to other risks, such as labour income risks and risks associated with real estate. All these considerations fall outside the simple complete-market, representative-individual framework. We will return to some of these extensions in the following chapter, but it is generally very difficult to study asset prices in models with constraints, transaction costs, and non-traded risks. The intuitive 'fix' of just using the total consumption of stockholders instead of the aggregate consumption of all individuals seems hard to justify with a sound theoretical model.

Measurement errors. All the available consumption is potentially subject to measurement errors. Retail stores may unintentionally misreport their sales numbers that enter the aggregate consumption measures in the NIPA data. Consumers may misreport their consumption in surveys. Surveys may be non-representative. Errors can be made in the collection and handling of the data. Aggregate consumption numbers are undoubtedly subject to various sampling and measurement errors, see for example the discussion in Wilcox (1992). Koijen, Van Nieuwerburgh, and Vestman (2011) offer a recent investigation of the quality of survey household consumption data and also provide a number of references to papers on survey-based consumption measures.

According to Triplett (1997) and Savov (2011), the NIPA consumption data underestimate the true volatility of aggregate consumption. Likewise, survey consumption data show that the volatility of individual consumption is typically higher than the NIPA aggregate consumption volatility, and in particular for individuals who are actively investing in the stock market as mentioned above. The use of NIPA consumption data is therefore likely to exaggerate the magnitude of the equity premium puzzle.

More generally, all the apparent problems with consumption data motivate the development of asset pricing models that do not depend on consumption at all. This is for example the case of the so-called factor models discussed in Chapter 10.

8.5.2 Other Empirical Issues

Here are some other potential problems with the empirical tests of the simple consumption-based asset pricing model.

8.5.2.1 Statistical Significance

The 8% estimate of the average excess stock return is relatively imprecise. With 50 observations (one per year) and a standard deviation of 20%, the standard error equals $20\%/\sqrt{50} \approx 2.8\%$ so that a 95% confidence interval is roughly [2.5%, 13.5%]. With a mean return of 2.5% instead of 8.0%, the required value of the relative risk aversion drops to 31.25, which is certainly still very high but nevertheless considerably smaller than the original value of 100.

8.5.2.2 *Stock Return Data*

Data for stock returns have to be selected and applied with caution. Most tests of the asset pricing models are based on data from the US or other economies that have experienced relatively high growth at least throughout the last 50 years. Probably investors in these countries were not so sure 50 years ago that the economy would avoid major financial and political crises and outperform other countries. Brown, Goetzmann, and Ross (1995) point out that due to this *survivorship bias* the realized stock returns overstate the *ex-ante* expected rate of returns significantly by maybe as much as 2–4 percentage points. Note, however, that in many crises in which stocks do badly, bonds and deposits also tend to provide low returns so it is not clear how big the effect on the expected *excess* stock return is.

8.5.2.3 *Expectations vs. Realizations*

The pricing relations of the model involve the *ex-ante* expectations of individuals, while the tests of the model are based on a single realized sequence of market prices and consumption. Estimating and testing a model involving *ex-ante* expectations and other moments requires stationarity in data in the sense that it must be assumed that each of the annual observations is drawn from the same probability distribution. For example, the average of the observed annual stock market returns is only a reasonable estimate of the *ex-ante* expected annual stock market return if the stock market return in each of the 50 years is drawn from the same probability distribution. Some important changes in the investment environment over the past years invalidate the stationarity assumption. Mehra and Prescott (2003) note two significant changes in the US tax system in the period between 1960 and 2000, a period included in most tests of the consumption-based model:

- The marginal tax rate for stock dividends dropped from 43% to 17%.
- Stock returns in most pension savings accounts are now tax-exempt, which was not so in the 1960s. Bond returns in savings accounts have been tax-exempt throughout the period.

Both changes have led to increased demands for stocks with stock price increases as a result. These changes in the tax rules were hardly predicted by investors and, hence, they can partly explain why the model has problems explaining the high realized stock returns. Similarly, it can be argued that the reductions in direct and indirect transaction costs and the liberalizations of international financial markets experienced over the last decades have increased the demands for stocks and driven up stock returns above what could be expected *ex-ante*. The high transaction costs and restrictions on international investments particularly in the past may have made it impossible or at least very expensive for investors to obtain the optimal diversification of their investments so that even unsystematic risks may have been priced with higher required returns as a consequence.[3]

One can also argue theoretically that the returns of a given stock cannot be stationary. Here is the argument: in each period there is a probability that the issuing firm defaults and the stock stops existing. Then it no longer makes sense to talk about the return probability distribution of that stock. More generally, the probability distribution of the return in one period may very well depend on the returns in previous periods.

Moreover, as emphasized by Bossaerts (2002), standard tests assume that *ex-ante* expectations of individuals are correct in the sense that they are confirmed by realizations. The general asset pricing theory does allow individuals to have systematically over-optimistic or over-pessimistic expectations. The usual tests implicitly assume that market data can be seen as realizations of the *ex-ante* expectations of individuals. Bossaerts (2002) describes studies which indicate that this assumption is not necessarily valid.

8.6 CONCLUDING REMARKS

This chapter has developed consumption-based models of asset pricing. Under very weak assumptions, expected excess returns on risky assets will be closely related to the covariance of the asset return with aggregate consumption, giving a conditional consumption-based CAPM. The simple CRRA-lognormal consumption-based CAPM is unable to match some important empirical features of asset prices and leaves a number of asset pricing puzzles. The next chapter will explore a number of extensions of the simple model that perform better.

8.7 EXERCISES

Exercise 8.1 Consider a risky asset i in a one-period setting. Assume all individuals have time-additive expected utility.

(a) Explain why the price of asset i and the consumption of individual l are related as follows:

[3] It is technically complicated to include transaction costs and trading restrictions in asset pricing models, but a study of He and Modest (1995) indicates that such imperfections can at least in part explain the equity premium puzzle.

$$P_i = \frac{\mathrm{E}[D_i]}{R^f} + e^{-\delta_l} \operatorname{Cov}\left[D_i, \frac{u_l'(c^l)}{u_l'(c_0^l)}\right].$$

(b) Show the approximate relation

$$P_i \approx \frac{\mathrm{E}[D_i]}{R^f} - e^{-\delta_l} \operatorname{ARA}_l(c_0^l) \operatorname{Cov}\left[D_i, c^l\right].$$

(c) Show that the price of asset i and aggregate consumption $C = \sum_{l=1}^{L} c^l$ satisfy the approximation

$$P_i \approx \frac{\mathrm{E}[D_i]}{R^f} - \left(\sum_{l=1}^{L} \frac{1}{e^{-\delta_l} \operatorname{ARA}_l(c_0^l)}\right)^{-1} \operatorname{Cov}\left[D_i, C\right].$$

Exercise 8.2 Consider a one-period setting. Let g denote the growth rate of consumption over the period.

(a) For any portfolio π, show that

$$\left(\operatorname{Corr}[R^{\pi}, g]\right)^2 = \frac{\left(\pi^{\top} \operatorname{Cov}[R, g]\right)^2}{\pi^{\top} \operatorname{Var}[R]\pi \operatorname{Var}[g]}.$$

(b) Show that the first-order condition for the maximization of $\left(\operatorname{Corr}[R^{\pi}, g]\right)^2$ implies that

$$\operatorname{Cov}[R, g]\pi^{\top} \operatorname{Var}[R]\pi = \pi^{\top} \operatorname{Cov}[R, g] \operatorname{Var}[R]\pi.$$

(c) Explain why the consumption-mimicking portfolio of Lemma 8.2 is also the portfolio maximizing the absolute value of the correlation with consumption growth, that is $|\operatorname{Corr}[R^{\pi}, g]|$.

Exercise 8.3 Carl Smart is currently (at time $t = 0$) considering a couple of investment projects that will provide him with a dividend in one year from now (time $t = 1$) and a dividend in two years from now (time $t = 2$). He figures that the size of the dividends will depend on the growth rate of aggregate consumption over these two years. The first project Carl considers provides a dividend of

$$D_t = 60t + 5(C_t - \mathrm{E}[C_t])$$

at $t = 1$ and at $t = 2$. The second project provides a dividend of

$$D_t = 60t - 5(C_t - \mathrm{E}[C_t])$$

at $t = 1$ and at $t = 2$. Here E[ ] is the expectation computed at time 0 and C_t denotes aggregate consumption at time t. The current level of aggregate consumption is $C_0 = 1000$.

As a valuable input to his investment decision Carl wants to compute the present value of the future dividends of each of the two projects.

First, Carl computes the present values of the two projects using a 'risk-ignoring approach', that is by discounting the expected dividends using the riskless returns observed in the bond markets. Carl observes that a one-year zero-coupon bond with a face value of 1000 currently trades at a price of 960 and a two-year zero-coupon bond with a face value of 1000 trades at a price of 929.02.

(a) What are the expected dividends of project 1 and project 2?

(b) What are the present values of project 1 and project 2 using the risk-ignoring approach?

Suddenly, Carl remembers that he once took a great course on advanced asset pricing and that the present value of an uncertain dividend of D_1 at time 1 and an uncertain dividend of D_2 at time 2 should be computed as

$$P = \mathrm{E}\left[\frac{\zeta_1}{\zeta_0}D_1 + \frac{\zeta_2}{\zeta_0}D_2\right],$$

where the ζ_t's define a state-price deflator. After some reflection and analysis, Carl decides to value the projects using a conditional consumption-based CAPM so that the state-price deflator between time t and $t+1$ is of the form

$$\frac{\zeta_{t+1}}{\zeta_t} = a_t + b_t\frac{C_{t+1}}{C_t}, \quad t = 0, 1, \ldots.$$

Carl thinks it's fair to assume that aggregate consumption will grow by either 1% ('low') or 3% ('high') in each of the next two years. Over the first year he believes the two growth rates are equally likely. If the growth rate of aggregate consumption is high in the first year, he believes that there is a 30% chance that it will also be high in the second year and, thus, a 70% chance of low growth in the second year. On the other hand, if the growth rate of aggregate consumption is low in the first year, he estimates that there will be a 70% chance of high growth and a 30% chance of low growth in the second year.

In order to apply the consumption-based CAPM for valuing his investment projects, Carl has to identify the coefficients a_t and b_t for $t = 0, 1$. The values of a_0 and b_0 can be identified from the prices of two traded assets that only provide dividends at time 1. In addition to the one-year zero-coupon bond mentioned above, a one-year European call option on aggregate consumption is traded. The option has a strike price of $K = 1020$ so that the payoff of the option in one year is $\max(C_1 - 1020, 0)$, where C_1 is the aggregate consumption level at $t = 1$. The option trades at a price of 4.7.

(c) Using the information on the two traded assets, write up two equations that can be used for determining a_0 and b_0. Verify that the equations are solved for $a_0 = 3$ and $b_0 = -2$.

The values of a_1 and b_1 may depend on the consumption growth rate of the first year, that is Carl has to find a_1^h, b_1^h that defines the second-year state-price deflator if the first-year growth rate was high and a_1^l, b_1^l that defines the second-year state-price deflator if the first-year growth rate was low. Using the observed market prices of other assets, Carl concludes that

$$a_1^h = 2.5, \quad b_1^h = -1.5, \quad a_1^l = 3.5198, \quad b_1^l = -2.5.$$

(d) Verify that the economy is path-independent in the sense that the current price of an asset that will pay you 1 at $t = 2$ if the growth rate is high in the first year and low in the second year will be identical (at least to five decimal places) to the current price of an asset that will pay you 1 at $t = 2$ if the growth rate is low in the first year and high in the second year.

(e) Illustrate the possible dividends of the two projects in a two-period binomial tree.

(f) What are the correctly computed present values of the two projects?

(g) Carl notes that the expected dividends of the two projects are exactly the same but the present value of project 2 is higher than the present value of project 1. Although Carl is pretty smart, he cannot really figure out why this is so. Can you explain it to him?

Exercise 8.4 In the simple consumption-based asset pricing model, the growth rate of aggregate consumption is assumed to have a constant expectation and standard deviation (volatility). For example, in the continuous-time version aggregate consumption is assumed to follow a geometric Brownian motion. Consider the following alternative process for aggregate consumption:

$$dc_t = c_t[\mu\, dt + \sigma c_t^{\alpha-1}\, dz_t],$$

where μ, σ, and α are positive constants, and $z = (z_t)$ is a standard Brownian motion. As in the simple model, assume that a representative individual exists and that this individual has time-additive expected utility exhibiting constant relative risk aversion given by the parameter $\gamma > 0$ and a constant time preference rate $\delta > 0$.

(a) State an equation linking the expected excess return on an arbitrary risky asset to the level of aggregate consumption and the parameters of the aggregate consumption process. How does the expected excess return vary with the consumption level?

(b) State an equation linking the short-term continuously compounded risk-free interest rate r_t^f to the level of aggregate consumption and the parameters of the aggregate consumption process. How does the interest rate vary with the consumption level?

(c) Use Itô's Lemma to find the dynamics of the interest rate, dr_t^f. Can you write the drift and the volatility of the interest rate as functions of the interest rate level only?

Exercise 8.5 Consider a two-period binomial economy where the state-price deflator ζ is related to the growth rate of aggregate consumption C, that is,

$$\frac{\zeta_{t+1}}{\zeta_t} = a + b\frac{C_{t+1}}{C_t}, \quad t = 0, 1,$$

where a and b are constants with $b = -3$. Aggregate consumption may grow by either 1% or 5% over each period and the two outcomes are equally likely. The consumption growth rate in the second period is independent of the consumption growth rate in the first period.

(a) At time 0, a one-period zero-coupon bond with a face value of 100 is traded at a price of 96.00. Determine the value of a.

(b) What is the time 0 price of a two-period zero-coupon bond with a face value of 100?

Consider the following two assets with risky dividends. At time $t = 1$ and $t = 2$ asset 1 pays a dividend of 1000 if the aggregate consumption growth rate in the preceding period was 5% and a dividend of zero otherwise. Conversely, at $t = 1$ and $t = 2$ asset 2 pays a dividend of 1000 if the aggregate consumption growth rate in the preceding period was 1% and a dividend of zero otherwise. The dividends are illustrated in the tree below. At each node, the dividends of the two assets are written in the parenthesis with the first number being the dividend of asset 1.

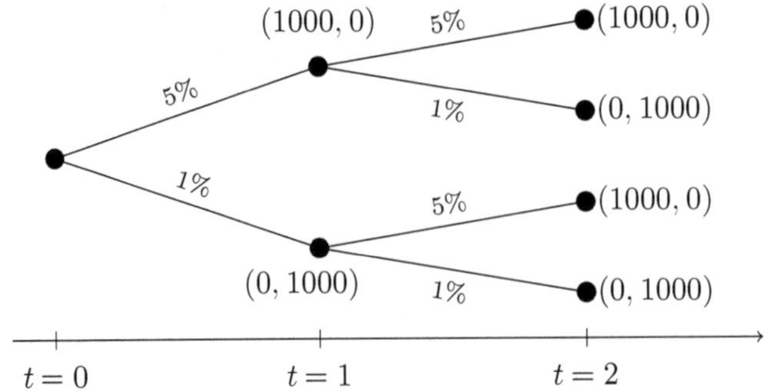

(c) What are the expected dividends of assets 1 and 2?

(d) Determine the prices of assets 1 and 2 at time 0. Can you provide an economic explanation for why one of the assets has a higher price than the other?

9

Advanced Consumption-Based Asset Pricing

9.1 INTRODUCTION

As explained in the previous chapter, the basic consumption-based asset pricing model is unable to match numerous stylized empirical facts. It is tempting to conclude that the consumption-based approach to asset pricing is not applicable, but this conclusion is unfair. First, due to the empirical issues also mentioned in the preceding chapter, the failure of the consumption-based CAPM may not be as severe as some studies seem to indicate. Second, it is only the very simple special case of the general consumption-based asset pricing model which is tested. The consumption-based approach in itself is based on only very few and relatively undisputed assumptions so the lack of empirical support must be blamed on the additional assumptions of the simple model.

Over the last two decades, a number of alternative specifications of the general consumption-based asset pricing model have been developed. These alternatives assume either a different representation of preferences than in the simple model, different aggregate consumption dynamics, or that the market is incomplete so that the representative individual approach is invalid. Section 9.2 focuses on alternative preferences including state-dependent utility, habit formation, and Epstein–Zin recursive utility. In particular, the important model of Campbell and Cochrane (1999) is described and discussed. Section 9.3 explores the idea of long-run risks in consumption which, in combination with Epstein–Zin utility, can reproduce a number of the salient features in the data, as shown by Bansal and Yaron (2004). Section 9.4 briefly discusses the idea that rare disasters may significantly impact risk premia. Standard models assume a single consumption good, but this is obviously a simplification of real life. Section 9.5 investigates some of the consequences of generalizing the theory to multiple consumption goods. As we shall see, such generalizations also have the potential of resolving some of the asset pricing puzzles. Finally, Section 9.6 looks at models with incomplete markets so that the standard representative individual approach fails.

9.2 CONSUMPTION-CAPM WITH ALTERNATIVE PREFERENCES

An interesting alternative to the simple consumption-based model is to allow the utility of a given consumption level at a given point in time t to depend on some benchmark X_t. Preferences are then modelled by $\mathrm{E}[\int_0^T e^{-\delta t} u(c_t, X_t)\, dt]$ in continuous time or $\mathrm{E}[\sum_{t=0}^T e^{-\delta t} u(c_t, X_t)]$ in discrete time. This incorporates the case of (internal) habit formation where X_t is determined as a weighted average of the previous consumption rates of the individual, and the case of state-dependent (or 'external habit') preferences where X_t is a variable not affected by the consumption decisions of the individual. To capture the intuition that a high value of the benchmark should make the individual more eager to increase consumption, we should have $u_{cX}(c, X) > 0$.

Typically models apply one of two tractable specifications of the utility function. The first specification is

$$u(c_t, X_t) = \frac{1}{1-\gamma} (c_t - X_t)^{1-\gamma}, \quad \gamma > 0, \tag{9.1}$$

which is defined for $c_t > X_t$. Marginal utility is

$$u_c(c_t, X_t) = (c_t - X_t)^{-\gamma},$$

and the relative risk aversion is

$$-\frac{c_t u_{cc}(c_t, X_t)}{u_c(c_t, X_t)} = \gamma \frac{c_t}{c_t - X_t} = \frac{\gamma}{1 - X_t/c_t}, \tag{9.2}$$

which is no longer constant and is greater than γ. This will allow us to match historical consumption and stock market data with a lower value of the parameter γ, but it is more reasonable to investigate whether we can match the data with a fairly low average value of the relative risk aversion given by Eq. (9.2). The second tractable specification is

$$u(c_t, X_t) = \frac{1}{1-\gamma} \left(\frac{c_t}{X_t}\right)^{1-\gamma}, \quad \gamma > 0, \tag{9.3}$$

which is defined for $c_t, X_t > 0$. Since

$$u_c(c, X) = c^{-\gamma} X^{\gamma-1}, \qquad u_{cX}(c, X) = (\gamma - 1) c^{-\gamma} X^{\gamma-2}$$

we need $\gamma > 1$ to ensure that marginal utility is increasing in X. Despite the generalization of the utility function relative to the standard model, the relative risk aversion is still constant:

$$-\frac{c u_{cc}(c, X)}{u_c(c, X; \gamma)} = \gamma.$$

9.2.1 Habit Formation

In the case with (internal) habit formation the individual will appreciate a given level of consumption at a given date more if she is used to low consumption than if she is used to high consumption. A rational individual with an internal habit will take into account the effects of her current decisions on the future habit levels. We saw in Chapter 6 that this will considerably complicate the formulas for optimal consumption and for the associated state-price deflator.

Individuals with habit formation in preferences will other things being equal invest more in the risk-free asset in order to ensure that future consumption will not come very close to (or even below) the future habit level. This extra demand for the risk-free asset will lower the equilibrium interest rate and, hence, help resolve the risk-free rate puzzle. Moreover, we see from Eq. (9.2) that the risk aversion is higher in 'bad states' where current consumption is close to the habit level than in 'good states' of high current consumption relative to the benchmark. This will be reflected by the risk premia of risky assets and has the potential to explain the observed cyclical behaviour of expected returns.

As we have seen in Chapter 6 the state-price deflators that can be derived from individuals with internal habit formation are considerably more complex than with time-additive preferences or external habit formation. See for example Theorem 6.9. A general and rather abstract continuous-time analysis for the case of an internal habit defined by a weighted average of earlier consumption rates is given by Detemple and Zapatero (1991).

Only very few concrete asset pricing models with internal habit have been developed with the continuous-time model of Constantinides (1990) as the most frequently cited. The model of Constantinides assumes a representative individual who can invest in a risk-free asset and a single risky asset. *A priori*, the risk-free rate and the expected rate of return and the volatility of the risky asset are assumed to be constant. The utility of the individual is given by Eq. (9.1), where the habit level is a weighted average of consumption at all previous dates. Constantinides solves for the optimal consumption and investment strategies of the individual and shows that the optimal consumption rate varies much less over time in the model with habit formation than with the usual time-additive specification of utility. A calibration of the model to historical data shows that the model is consistent with a large equity premium and a low risk aversion but, on the other hand, the consumption process of the model has an unrealistically high auto-correlation and the variance of long-term consumption growth is quite high. By construction, the model cannot explain variations in interest rates and expected returns on stocks.

Grischenko (2010) considers the case of a representative individual with power-habit utility of the form (9.1) and where the habit level is an exponentially weighted average of consumption over a long historic period. She finds that, given the observed US per capita consumption time series, the model is able to match the level of returns and the variations in short-term average returns over time. However, the average level of risk aversion is still high. The estimate of γ is around 6.3 and the long-run mean of the habit level is 89% of the long-run mean of aggregate consumption. From Eq. (9.2), a long-run estimate of the relative risk aversion is then $6.3/(1 - 0.89) \approx 57.3$. Therefore the equity premium puzzle is not resolved by habit formation. Also note that while power-habit utility might seem reasonable for each individual, it is unclear how that translates into the preferences of a representative individual, compare the discussion in Section 7.5.

9.2.2 State-Dependent Utility: General Results

With an external habit/benchmark, for example the aggregate consumption level, the state-price deflator is

$$\zeta_t = e^{-\delta t} \frac{u_c(c_t, X_t)}{u_c(c_0, X_0)},$$

where the only difference to the model without habit is that the marginal utilities depend on the habit level. An external habit formalizes the idea that the marginal utility of consumption of one individual is increasing in the consumption level of other individuals, the 'keeping up with the Joneses' effect. In this case, there is no effect of the consumption choice of the individual on the future benchmark levels, but of course the individual will include her knowledge of the dynamics of the benchmark when making consumption decisions.

In a discrete-time setting the one-period deflator is

$$\frac{\zeta_{t+1}}{\zeta_t} = e^{-\delta} \frac{u_c(c_{t+1}, X_{t+1})}{u_c(c_t, X_t)}.$$

Using the Taylor approximation

$$u_c(c_{t+1}, X_{t+1}) \approx u_c(c_t, X_t) + u_{cc}(c_t, X_t)\Delta c_{t+1} + u_{cX}(c_t, X_t)\Delta X_{t+1},$$

the approximate relation

$$\begin{aligned} \mathrm{E}_t[R_{i,t+1}] - R_t^f \approx & \left(-\frac{c_t u_{cc}(c_t, X_t)}{u_c(c_t, X_t)}\right) \mathrm{Cov}_t\left[R_{i,t+1}, \frac{\Delta c_{t+1}}{c_t}\right] \\ & - \frac{u_{cX}(c_t, X_t)}{u_c(c_t, X_t)} \mathrm{Cov}_t\left[R_{i,t+1}, \Delta X_{t+1}\right] \end{aligned}$$

can be derived. The covariance of return with the benchmark variable adds a term to the excess expected return of a risky asset. Moreover, the relative risk aversion in the first term will now generally vary with the benchmark variable.

In a continuous-time setting where the dynamics of consumption is again given by Eq. (8.21) and the dynamics of the benchmark process $X = (X_t)$ is of the form

$$dX_t = \mu_{Xt}\,dt + \boldsymbol{\sigma}_{Xt}^{\top}\,d\mathbf{z}_t, \tag{9.4}$$

an application of Itô's Lemma will give the dynamics of the state-price deflator. As before, the risk-free rate and the market price of risk can be identified from the drift and the sensitivity, respectively, of the state-price deflator. The following theorem states the conclusion. Exercise 9.1 asks for the proof.

Theorem 9.1 *In a continuous-time economy where the optimal consumption process of an individual with state-dependent expected utility satisfies Eq.* (8.21) *and the dynamics of the benchmark is given by Eq.* (9.4)*, the continuously compounded risk-free short-term interest rate satisfies*

$$\begin{aligned} r_t^f = \delta &+ \frac{-c_t u_{cc}(c_t, X_t)}{u_c(c_t, X_t)}\mu_{ct} - \frac{1}{2}\frac{c_t^2 u_{ccc}(c_t, X_t)}{u_c(c_t, X_t)}\|\boldsymbol{\sigma}_{ct}\|^2 \\ &- \frac{u_{cX}(c_t, X_t)}{u_c(c_t, X_t)}\mu_{Xt} - \frac{1}{2}\frac{u_{cXX}(c_t, X_t)}{u_c(c_t, X_t)}\|\boldsymbol{\sigma}_{Xt}\|^2 - \frac{c_t u_{ccX}(c_t, X_t)}{u_c(c_t, X_t)}\boldsymbol{\sigma}_{ct}^{\top}\boldsymbol{\sigma}_{Xt} \end{aligned}$$

and

$$\boldsymbol{\lambda}_t = \frac{-c_t u_{cc}(c_t, X_t)}{u_c(c_t, X_t)}\boldsymbol{\sigma}_{ct} - \frac{u_{cX}(c_t, X_t)}{u_c(c_t, X_t)}\boldsymbol{\sigma}_{Xt} \tag{9.5}$$

defines a market price of risk process. In particular, the excess expected rate of return on asset i is

$$\mu_{it} + \delta_{it} - r_t^f = \frac{-c_t u_{cc}(c_t, X_t)}{u_c(c_t, X_t)}\boldsymbol{\sigma}_{it}^{\top}\boldsymbol{\sigma}_{ct} - \frac{u_{cX}(c_t, X_t)}{u_c(c_t, X_t)}\boldsymbol{\sigma}_{it}^{\top}\boldsymbol{\sigma}_{Xt}.$$

Assuming $u_{cX}(c, X) > 0$, we see from Eq. (9.5) that, if $\boldsymbol{\sigma}_{Xt}$ goes in the same direction as $\boldsymbol{\sigma}_{ct}$, state-dependent utility will tend to lower the market price of risk, working against a resolution of the equity premium puzzle. On the other hand there is much more room for time variation in both the risk-free rate and the market price of risk, which can help explain the predictability puzzle.

Again, the above results hold for aggregate consumption if a representative individual with preferences of the given form exists. If $\boldsymbol{\sigma}_{Xt} = \mathbf{0}$, we can link asset prices to aggregate consumption without assuming the existence of a representative individual, as in the case of standard preferences. We obtain

$$\mu_{it} + \delta_{it} - r_t^f = \frac{C_t}{\sum_{l=1}^{L}\left(\frac{1}{A_l(c_{lt}, X_t)}\right)}\boldsymbol{\sigma}_{it}^{\top}\boldsymbol{\sigma}_{Ct}, \tag{9.6}$$

where C_t is aggregate consumption and $A_l(c_{lt}, X_t) = -u^l_{cc}(c_{lt}, X_t)/u^l_c(c_{lt}, X_t)$ is the (now state-dependent) absolute risk aversion of individual l.

9.2.3 The Campbell and Cochrane Model

Campbell and Cochrane (1999) suggest a discrete-time model of an economy with identical individuals with utility functions like Eq. (9.1), where X_t is the benchmark or external habit level.[1] The 'next-period deflator' is then

$$M_{t+1} \equiv \frac{\zeta_{t+1}}{\zeta_t} = e^{-\delta} \frac{(c_{t+1} - X_{t+1})^{-\gamma}}{(c_t - X_t)^{-\gamma}}.$$

The lognormal distributional assumption for aggregate consumption made in the simple model seems to be empirically reasonable so the Campbell and Cochrane model keeps that assumption. Since it is not obvious what distributional assumption on X_t will make the model computationally tractable, Campbell and Cochrane define the 'surplus consumption ratio' $S_t = (c_t - X_t)/c_t$ in terms of which the next-period deflator can be rewritten as

$$M_{t+1} = e^{-\delta} \left(\frac{c_{t+1}}{c_t}\right)^{-\gamma} \left(\frac{S_{t+1}}{S_t}\right)^{-\gamma} = \exp\left\{-\delta - \gamma \ln\left(\frac{c_{t+1}}{c_t}\right) - \gamma \ln\left(\frac{S_{t+1}}{S_t}\right)\right\}.$$

It is assumed that changes in both consumption growth and the surplus consumption ratio are conditionally lognormally distributed with

$$\ln\left(\frac{c_{t+1}}{c_t}\right) = \bar{g} + \varepsilon_{t+1},$$

$$\ln\left(\frac{S_{t+1}}{S_t}\right) = (1 - \varphi)\left(\ln \bar{S} - \ln S_t\right) + \Lambda(S_t)\varepsilon_{t+1}, \tag{9.7}$$

where $\varepsilon_{t+1} \sim N(0, \sigma^2)$ and the function Λ is specified below with the purpose of obtaining some desired properties. We assume $\varphi < 1$. With lognormality of c_{t+1} and S_{t+1}, then $c_{t+1} - X_{t+1} = c_{t+1}S_{t+1}$ and therefore the next-period deflator will also be lognormal. Note that $\ln S_t$ will fluctuate around $\ln \bar{S}$, and we can think of these fluctuations as representing business cycles with low values of $\ln S_t$ corresponding to bad times with relatively low consumption. Also note that the consumption and the surplus consumption ratios are perfectly correlated.

The distributional assumption on the surplus consumption ratio ensures that it stays positive so that $c_t > X_t$, as required by the utility specification. On the other hand, if you want the benchmark X_t to stay positive, the surplus

[1] The closely related model of Menzly, Santos, and Veronesi (2004) is studied in Exercise 9.6.

consumption ratio must be smaller than 1, which is not ensured by the lognormal distribution. However, with empirically reasonable parameters, it is highly unlikely that S_{t+1} will exceed 1. See also the remarks following the specification of $\Lambda(S_t)$ below.

According to Campbell, Lo, and MacKinlay (1997, p. 331), it can be shown that

$$\ln X_{t+1} \approx \ln(1-\bar{S}) + \frac{g}{1-\varphi} + (1-\varphi)\sum_{j=0}^{\infty} \varphi^j \ln c_{t-j}$$

so that the benchmark is related to a weighted average of past consumption levels.

With the above assumptions, the next-period deflator M_{t+1} is

$$M_{t+1} = \exp\left\{-\delta - \gamma\left[\bar{g} - (1-\varphi)\ln\frac{S_t}{\bar{S}}\right] - \gamma\left(1 + \Lambda(S_t)\right)\varepsilon_{t+1}\right\},$$

which is conditionally lognormally distributed with

$$\frac{\sigma_t[M_{t+1}]}{\mathrm{E}_t[M_{t+1}]} = \sqrt{\exp\left\{\gamma^2\sigma^2(1+\Lambda(S_t))^2\right\} - 1} \approx \gamma\sigma\left(1+\Lambda(S_t)\right).$$

As for the simple CCAPM in Chapter 8, the approximation is not that accurate for the parameter values necessary to match consumption and return data. It follows from Eq. (4.22) that the expected excess gross rate of return on a risky asset is

$$\mathrm{E}_t[R_{i,t+1}] - R_t^f \approx -\gamma\sigma\left(1+\Lambda(S_t)\right)\mathrm{Corr}_t\left[M_{t+1}, R_{i,t+1}\right]\sigma_t[R_{i,t+1}].$$

The variation in risk aversion through S_t increases the risk premium relative to the standard model as can be seen by comparing the preceding equation with Eq. (8.19). In order to obtain the counter-cyclical variation in risk premia observed in data, Λ has to be a decreasing function of S.

The continuously compounded short-term risk-free rate is

$$\begin{aligned}\ln R_t^f &= \ln\left(\frac{1}{\mathrm{E}_t[M_{t+1}]}\right)\\ &= \delta + \gamma\bar{g} - \frac{1}{2}\gamma^2\sigma^2 - \gamma(1-\varphi)\ln\frac{S_t}{\bar{S}} - \frac{1}{2}\gamma^2\sigma^2\Lambda(S_t)\left(\Lambda(S_t)+2\right).\end{aligned} \tag{9.8}$$

In comparison with the expression (8.18) for the risk-free rate in the simple model, the last two terms on the right-hand side are new. Note that S_t has opposite effects on the two new terms. A low value of S_t means that the marginal utility of consumption is high so that individuals will try to borrow money for current consumption. This added demand for short-term borrowing will drive up the equilibrium interest rate. On the other hand, a low S_t will also increase the risk aversion and, hence, precautionary savings with a lower equilibrium rate as a result. Campbell and Cochrane fix $\Lambda(\cdot)$ and $\bar{S}$ at

$$\Lambda(S_t) = \frac{1}{\bar{S}}\sqrt{1 - 2\ln(S_t/\bar{S})} - 1, \tag{9.9}$$

$$\bar{S} = \sigma\sqrt{\gamma/(1-\varphi)}. \tag{9.10}$$

Note that $\Lambda(\cdot)$ *is* decreasing. The specified function $\Lambda(S_t)$ is only well-defined for $\ln(S_t/\bar{S}) \leq \frac{1}{2}$, which is not guaranteed. We can rule out any problems with the square root by putting $\Lambda(S_t) = 0$ whenever $S_t \geq S_{\max} \equiv \bar{S}e^{\frac{1}{2}(1-\bar{S}^2)}$. While S_t may indeed exceed $S_{\max}$, this will only happen very rarely. Substituting Eq. (9.9) into Eq. (9.8), we find that the equilibrium interest rate is now given by the constant

$$\ln R^f = \delta + \gamma\bar{g} - \frac{1}{2}\sigma^2\left(\frac{\gamma}{\bar{S}}\right)^2.$$

Consequently, the yield curve will be flat and constant. In Section 11.3.2 we consider an extension of the model suggested by Wachter (2006) in which interest rates are stochastic and the yield curve non-flat, but we will focus on the original model here.

The authors calibrate the model to historical data for consumption growth, interest rates, and the average Sharpe ratio, which for example requires that $\gamma = 2$ and $\bar{S} = 0.057$. The calibrated model is consistent with the observed counter-cyclical variation in expected returns, standard deviations of returns, and the Sharpe ratio. With the given parameter values the model can therefore explain the predictability in those variables. The calibrated model yields empirically reasonable levels of the expected return and standard deviation of stock returns. Note, however, that although the calibrated value of the utility parameter γ is small, the relative risk aversion γ/S_t is still high. With $S_t = \bar{S} = 0.057$, the risk aversion is approximately 35, and the risk aversion is much higher in bad states where S_t is low. The model cannot therefore explain the equity premium puzzle. Also observe that the value of $\bar{S}$ implies that, on average, the minimum consumption level is only 5.7% lower than current consumption, which seems to be an extreme degree of 'habit formation'. Finally, note that the dynamics of the business cycle variable S_t is exogenously constructed to obtain the desired properties of the model. It would be interesting to understand how such a process could arise endogenously.

While the Campbell–Cochrane model is able to match some stylized facts, it is challenged empirically along several dimensions. First, the assumed preference structure implies that the individual's risk aversion, and thus their investment in risky assets, should vary with wealth but, according to Brunnermeier and Nagel (2008), this is hard to see in the data. Second, the model cannot generate the amount of cyclical variation in Sharpe ratios seen in the data, compare Lettau and Ludvigson (2010). Third, the model does not seem to be able to explain the observed value premium, compare Lettau and Wachter (2007), Møller (2009), and Santos and Veronesi (2010). See also van Binsbergen, Brandt, and Koijen (2011) for further empirical critique.

9.2.4 The Chan and Kogan Model

In many models for individual consumption and portfolio choice the individual is assumed to have constant relative risk aversion both because this seems quite reasonable and because this simplifies the analysis. If all individuals in an economy have constant relative risk aversion, you might think that a representative individual would also have constant relative risk aversion, but as we saw in Section 7.5 this is only true if they all have the same level of risk aversion. Chan and Kogan (2002) set up a model in which individuals have different, constant relative risk aversions. Individuals with a low (constant) relative risk aversion will other things being equal invest a larger fraction of their wealth in risky assets, for example stocks, than individuals with high (constant) relative risk aversion. Increasing stock prices will imply that the wealth of the relatively risk-tolerant individuals will grow more than the wealth of comparably more risk-averse individuals. Consequently, the aggregate risk aversion in the economy (corresponding to the risk aversion of a representative individual) will fall. Conversely, the aggregate risk aversion will increase when stock markets drop. This simple observation supports the assumption of Campbell and Cochrane (1999) discussed above that the risk aversion of the representative individual varies counter-cyclically, which helps in resolving asset pricing puzzles.

Let us take a closer look at the model of Chan and Kogan (2002). It is a continuous-time exchange economy in which the aggregate endowment/consumption $Y = (Y_t)$ follows the geometric Brownian motion

$$dY_t = Y_t[\mu\, dt + \sigma\, dz_t],$$

where $\mu > \sigma^2/2$, $\sigma > 0$, and $z = (z_t)$ is a one-dimensional standard Brownian motion. Two assets are traded: a risky asset which is a unit net supply and pays a continuous dividend equal to the aggregate endowment, and an instantaneously risk-free asset (a bank account) generating a continuously compounded short-term interest rate of r^f_t. The economy is populated with infinitely-lived individuals maximizing time-additive state-dependent utility given by Eq. (9.3), that is

$$\mathrm{E}\left[\int_0^\infty e^{-\delta t} u(c_t, X_t; \gamma)\, dt\right], \quad u(c, X; \gamma) = \frac{1}{1-\gamma}\left(\frac{c}{X}\right)^{1-\gamma}.$$

Here X is an external benchmark, for example an index of the standard of living in the economy. Let $x_t = \ln X_t$ and $y_t = \ln Y_t$. The dynamics of the benchmark is modelled through

$$x_t = e^{-\kappa t} x_0 + \kappa \int_0^t e^{-\kappa(t-s)} y_s\, ds$$

so that

$$dx_t = \kappa \left(y_t - x_t\right) dt.$$

The log-benchmark is a weighted average of past log-consumption. The relative log-consumption variable $\omega_t = y_t - x_t$ will be representative of the state of the economy. A high [low] value of ω_t represents a good [bad] state in terms of aggregate consumption relative to the benchmark. Note that

$$d\omega_t = dy_t - dx_t = \kappa\,(\bar{\omega} - \omega_t)\, dt + \sigma\, dz_t,$$

where $\bar{\omega} = (\mu - \sigma^2/2)/\kappa$.

Individuals are assumed to differ with respect to their relative risk aversion γ but to have identical subjective time preference parameters δ. Since the market is complete, an equilibrium in the economy will be Pareto-optimal and identical to the solution of the problem of a central planner or representative individual. Let $f(\gamma)$ denote the weight of the individuals with relative risk aversion γ in this problem, where f is normalized so that $\int_1^\infty f(\gamma) d\gamma = 1$. The problem of the central planner is to solve

$$\sup_{\{c_t(Y_t, X_t;\gamma);\gamma>1, t\geq 0\}} \mathrm{E}\left[\int_0^\infty e^{-\delta t}\left(\int_1^\infty f(\gamma)\frac{1}{1-\gamma}\left(\frac{c_t(Y_t, X_t;\gamma)}{X_t}\right)^{1-\gamma} d\gamma\right) dt\right]$$

$$\text{s.t.} \int_1^\infty c_t(Y_t, X_t; \gamma)\, d\gamma \leq Y_t, \quad t \geq 0.$$

In an exchange economy no intertemporal transfer of resources is possible at the aggregate level so the optimal value of the central planner's objective function will be $\mathrm{E}[\int_0^\infty e^{-\delta t} U(Y_t, X_t)\, dt]$, where

$$U(Y_t, X_t) = \sup_{\{c_t(Y_t, X_t;\gamma);\gamma>1\}} \left\{\int_1^\infty f(\gamma)\frac{1}{1-\gamma}\left(\frac{c_t(Y_t, X_t;\gamma)}{X_t}\right)^{1-\gamma} d\gamma,\right.$$
$$\left.\text{s.t.} \int_1^\infty c_t(Y_t, X_t; \gamma)\, d\gamma \leq Y_t\right\}. \tag{9.11}$$

The solution to this problem is characterized in the following theorem, which is the key to the asset pricing results in this model.

Theorem 9.2 *The optimal consumption allocation in the problem* (9.11) *is*

$$c_t(Y_t, X_t; \gamma) = \alpha_t(\omega_t; \gamma) Y_t, \quad \alpha_t(\omega_t; \gamma) = f(\gamma)^{1/\gamma} e^{-\frac{1}{\gamma} h(\omega_t) - \omega_t},$$

where the function h is implicitly defined by the identity

$$\int_1^\infty f(\gamma)^{1/\gamma} e^{-\frac{1}{\gamma} h(\omega_t) - \omega_t} \, d\gamma = 1. \tag{9.12}$$

The utility function of the representative individual is

$$U(Y_t, X_t) = \int_1^\infty \frac{1}{1-\gamma} f(\gamma)^{1/\gamma} e^{-\frac{1-\gamma}{\gamma} h(\omega_t)} \, d\gamma. \tag{9.13}$$

Proof. If we divide the constraint in Eq. (9.11) through by X_t and introduce the aggregate consumption share $\alpha_t(Y_t, X_t; \gamma) = c_t(Y_t, X_t; \gamma)/Y_t$, the Lagrangian for the optimization problem is

$$\begin{aligned}
\mathcal{L}_t &= \int_1^\infty f(\gamma) \frac{1}{1-\gamma} \left(\alpha_t(Y_t, X_t; \gamma) \frac{Y_t}{X_t} \right)^{1-\gamma} d\gamma \\
&\quad + H_t \left(\frac{Y_t}{X_t} - \int_1^\infty \alpha_t(Y_t, X_t; \gamma) \frac{Y_t}{X_t} \, d\gamma \right) \\
&= \frac{Y_t}{X_t} \int_1^\infty \left[f(\gamma) \frac{1}{1-\gamma} \alpha_t(Y_t, X_t; \gamma)^{1-\gamma} \left(\frac{Y_t}{X_t} \right)^{-\gamma} - H_t \alpha_t(Y_t, X_t; \gamma) \right] d\gamma \\
&\quad + H_t \frac{Y_t}{X_t},
\end{aligned}$$

where H_t is the Lagrange multiplier. The first-order condition for α_t implies that

$$\alpha_t(Y_t, X_t; \gamma) = H_t^{-1/\gamma} f(\gamma)^{1/\gamma} \left(\frac{Y_t}{X_t} \right)^{-1} = f(\gamma)^{1/\gamma} e^{-\frac{1}{\gamma} h_t - \omega_t},$$

where $h_t = \ln H_t$. The consumption allocated to all individuals must add up to the aggregate consumption, which implies the condition (9.12). From the condition, it is clear that h_t and therefore α_t depend on ω_t but not separately on Y_t and X_t.

The maximum of the objective function is

$$
\begin{aligned}
U(Y_t, X_t) &= \int_1^\infty f(\gamma)\frac{1}{1-\gamma}\left(\alpha_t(Y_t, X_t; \gamma)\frac{Y_t}{X_t}\right)^{1-\gamma} d\gamma \\
&= \int_1^\infty f(\gamma)\frac{1}{1-\gamma} f(\gamma)^{(1-\gamma)/\gamma} e^{-\frac{1-\gamma}{\gamma}h(\omega_t)-(1-\gamma)\omega_t} e^{(1-\gamma)\omega_t}\, d\gamma \\
&= \int_1^\infty \frac{1}{1-\gamma} f(\gamma)^{1/\gamma} e^{-\frac{1-\gamma}{\gamma}h(\omega_t)}\, d\gamma,
\end{aligned}
$$

which completes the proof. □

The optimal allocation of consumption to a given individual is a fraction of aggregate endowment, a fraction depending on the state of the economy and the relative risk aversion of the individual.

The next lemma summarizes some properties of the function h which will be useful in the following discussion.

Lemma 9.1 *The function h defined in Eq.* (9.12) *is decreasing and convex with*

$$
h'(\omega) = -\left(\int_1^\infty \frac{1}{\gamma} f(\gamma)^{1/\gamma} e^{-\frac{1}{\gamma}h(\omega)-\omega}\, d\gamma\right)^{-1} < -1. \tag{9.14}
$$

Proof. Differentiating with respect to ω_t in Eq. (9.12), we get

$$
\int_1^\infty f(\gamma)^{1/\gamma} e^{-\frac{1}{\gamma}h(\omega_t)-\omega_t}\left(-\frac{1}{\gamma}h'(\omega_t) - 1\right) d\gamma = 0,
$$

which implies that

$$
h'(\omega_t)\int_1^\infty \frac{1}{\gamma} f(\gamma)^{1/\gamma} e^{-\frac{1}{\gamma}h(\omega_t)-\omega_t}\, d\gamma = -\int_1^\infty f(\gamma)^{1/\gamma} e^{-\frac{1}{\gamma}h(\omega_t)-\omega_t}\, d\gamma = -1,
$$

from which the expression (9.14) for $h'(\omega_t)$ follows. Since we are integrating over $\gamma \geq 1$, we have

$$
\int_1^\infty \frac{1}{\gamma} f(\gamma)^{1/\gamma} e^{-\frac{1}{\gamma}h(\omega_t)-\omega_t}\, d\gamma < \int_1^\infty f(\gamma)^{1/\gamma} e^{-\frac{1}{\gamma}h(\omega_t)-\omega_t}\, d\gamma = 1,
$$

which gives the upper bound on $h'(\omega_t)$.

Convexity means $h''(\omega_t) \geq 0$ and by differentiating Eq. (9.14) we see that this is true if and only if

$$
-h'(\omega)\int_1^\infty \frac{1}{\gamma^2} f(\gamma)^{1/\gamma} e^{-\frac{1}{\gamma}h(\omega)-\omega}\, d\gamma \geq \int_1^\infty \frac{1}{\gamma} f(\gamma)^{1/\gamma} e^{-\frac{1}{\gamma}h(\omega)-\omega}\, d\gamma,
$$

that is if and only if

$$
\int_1^\infty \frac{1}{\gamma^2} f(\gamma)^{1/\gamma} e^{-\frac{1}{\gamma}h(\omega)-\omega}\, d\gamma \geq \left(\int_1^\infty \frac{1}{\gamma} f(\gamma)^{1/\gamma} e^{-\frac{1}{\gamma}h(\omega)-\omega}\, d\gamma\right)^2.
$$

In order to show this we apply the Cauchy–Schwartz inequality for integrals,

$$\left(\int_a^b F(x)G(x)\,dx\right)^2 \le \left(\int_a^b F(x)^2\,dx\right)\left(\int_a^b G(x)^2\,dx\right),$$

with $x = \gamma$, $a = 1$, $b = \infty$, and

$$F(x) = \frac{1}{\gamma}\left(f(\gamma)^{1/\gamma} e^{-\frac{1}{\gamma}h(\omega)-\omega}\right)^{1/2}, \quad G(x) = \left(f(\gamma)^{1/\gamma} e^{-\frac{1}{\gamma}h(\omega)-\omega}\right)^{1/2}.$$

By the Cauchy–Schwartz inequality and Eq. (9.12), we get exactly

$$\begin{aligned}
&\left(\int_1^\infty \frac{1}{\gamma} f(\gamma)^{1/\gamma} e^{-\frac{1}{\gamma}h(\omega)-\omega}\,d\gamma\right)^2 \\
&\le \left(\int_1^\infty \frac{1}{\gamma^2} f(\gamma)^{1/\gamma} e^{-\frac{1}{\gamma}h(\omega)-\omega}\,d\gamma\right)\left(\int_1^\infty f(\gamma)^{1/\gamma} e^{-\frac{1}{\gamma}h(\omega)-\omega}\,d\gamma\right) \\
&= \int_1^\infty \frac{1}{\gamma^2} f(\gamma)^{1/\gamma} e^{-\frac{1}{\gamma}h(\omega)-\omega}\,d\gamma
\end{aligned}$$

as was to be shown. □

Using Eqs. (9.12) and (9.14), straightforward differentiation of the utility function (9.13) gives that

$$U_Y(Y_t, X_t) = X_t^{-1} e^{h(\omega_t)}, \tag{9.15}$$

$$U_{YY}(Y_t, X_t) = h'(\omega_t) Y_t^{-1} U_Y(Y_t, X_t). \tag{9.16}$$

The relative risk aversion of the representative individual is therefore

$$-\frac{Y_t U_{YY}(Y_t, X_t)}{U_Y(Y_t, X_t)} = -h'(\omega_t).$$

It follows from Lemma 9.1 that this relative risk aversion is greater than 1 and decreasing in the state variable ω_t. The intuition is that the individuals with low relative risk aversion will other things being equal invest more in the risky asset—and their wealth will therefore fluctuate more—than individuals with high relative risk aversion. In good states a larger fraction of the aggregate resources will be held by individuals with low risk aversion than in bad states. The relative risk aversion of the representative individual, which is some sort of wealth-weighted average of the individual risk aversions, will therefore be lower in good states than in bad states. Aggregate relative risk aversion is counter-cyclical.

We can obtain the equilibrium risk-free rate and the market price of risk from Theorem 9.1. In the present model the dynamics of $X_t = e^{x_t}$ will be

$$dX_t = \kappa X_t \left(y_t - x_t\right)\,dt = \kappa X_t \omega_t\,dt, \tag{9.17}$$

which is locally insensitive to shocks corresponding to $\boldsymbol{\sigma}_{Xt} = \mathbf{0}$. This will simplify the formulas for the risk-free rate and the Sharpe ratio. Moreover,

$$U_{YX}(Y_t, X_t) = -X_t^{-1}(1 + h'(\omega_t))U_Y(Y_t, X_t), \tag{9.18}$$

$$Y_t^2 U_{YYY}(Y_t, X_t) = \left(h''(\omega_t) + h'(\omega_t)^2 - h'(\omega_t)\right) U_Y(Y_t, X_t). \tag{9.19}$$

We arrive at the following conclusion:

Theorem 9.3 *In the Chan and Kogan model the risk-free short-term interest rate is*

$$r_t^f = \delta - h'(\omega_t)\kappa(\bar{\omega} - \omega_t) + \kappa\omega_t - \frac{1}{2}\sigma^2 \left(h''(\omega_t) + h'(\omega_t)^2\right),$$

and the Sharpe ratio of a risky asset is

$$\frac{\mu_t + \delta_t - r_t^f}{\sigma_t} = -h'(\omega_t)\sigma, \tag{9.20}$$

which is decreasing in the state variable ω_t.

In Exercise 9.2 you are asked to provide the details. And in Exercise 9.3 you are asked to show how Eq. (9.20) follows from Eq. (9.6).

The Sharpe ratio in the model varies counter-cyclically. In good states of the economy the average relative risk aversion is relatively low and the risk premium necessary for markets clearing is therefore also low. And the converse in bad states where the average relative risk aversion is high.

9.2.5 Epstein–Zin Utility

Recall from Theorem 6.14 that in a discrete-time model with Epstein–Zin utility, the next-period state-price deflator is given by

$$M_{t+1} \equiv \frac{\zeta_{t+1}}{\zeta_t} = e^{-\delta\theta} \left(\frac{c_{t+1}}{c_t}\right)^{-\theta/\psi} \left(R_{t+1}^W\right)^{\theta-1}, \tag{9.21}$$

where δ is the subjective time preference rate, ψ is the elasticity of intertemporal substitution, and $\theta = (1-\gamma)/(1-\frac{1}{\psi})$, where γ is the relative risk aversion. Again note that if $\gamma = 1/\psi$ and thus $\theta = 1$, we are back to the traditional state-price deflator for time-additive power utility, $M_{t+1} = e^{-\delta}(c_{t+1}/c_t)^{-\gamma}$. Let $g_{t+1} = \ln\left(\frac{c_{t+1}}{c_t}\right)$ denote the log growth rate of consumption and let $r_{t+1}^w = \ln R_{t+1}^W$ denote the log-return on the wealth of the individual, which for a representative individual can be interpreted as the log-return on a claim to aggregate consumption (in equilibrium: aggregate dividends including labour income will equal aggregate consumption). We can then write the log of the state-price deflator, $m_{t+1} = \ln M_{t+1}$ as

$$m_{t+1} = -\delta\theta - \frac{\theta}{\psi} g_{t+1} + (\theta - 1)\, r^w_{t+1}. \tag{9.22}$$

Under the assumption that the consumption growth and return on wealth are jointly lognormally distributed, we have an Epstein–Zin-lognormal consumption-based asset pricing model in which we can establish the simple closed-form expressions for the risk-free rate and risk premia:

Theorem 9.4 *In a discrete-time setting, let g_{t+1} and r^w_{t+1} be the log-consumption growth and the log-return on investments, respectively, of an individual with Epstein–Zin preferences. Suppose that g_{t+1} and r^w_{t+1} are jointly normally distributed with $g_{t+1} \sim N(\mu_c, \sigma_c^2)$, $r^w_{t+1} \sim N(\mu_w, \sigma_w^2)$, and $\mathrm{Cov}_t[g_{t+1}, r^w_{t+1}] = \sigma_{cw}$. Then the one-period continuously compounded risk-free rate is*

$$r^f = \delta + \frac{\mu_c}{\psi} - \frac{1}{2}\frac{\theta}{\psi^2}\sigma_c^2 - \frac{1}{2}(1-\theta)\sigma_w^2, \tag{9.23}$$

and the excess expected log-return of any risky asset i satisfies

$$\begin{aligned}
\mathrm{E}_t[r^i_{t+1}] - r^f_t + \frac{1}{2}\mathrm{Var}_t[r^i_{t+1}] &= \frac{\theta}{\psi}\mathrm{Cov}_t[r^i_{t+1}, g_{t+1}] + (1-\theta)\,\mathrm{Cov}_t[r^i_{t+1}, r^w_{t+1}] \\
&= \sigma_t[r^i_{t+1}]\left(\frac{\theta}{\psi}\sigma_c\rho_{ic} + (1-\theta)\sigma_w\rho_{iw}\right) \\
&= \sigma_t[r^i_{t+1}]\left(\frac{\gamma-1}{1-\psi}\sigma_c\rho_{ic} + \frac{1-\psi\gamma}{1-\psi}\sigma_w\rho_{iw}\right).
\end{aligned} \tag{9.24}$$

Proof. Applying the state-price deflator to the 'wealth portfolio' implies

$$\mathrm{E}_t\left[\frac{\zeta_{t+1}}{\zeta_t}e^{r^w_{t+1}}\right] = \mathrm{E}_t\left[e^{m_{t+1}+r^w_{t+1}}\right] = 1 \quad \Rightarrow \quad \mathrm{E}_t\left[e^{-\delta\theta - \frac{\theta}{\psi}g_{t+1} + \theta r^w_{t+1}}\right] = 1. \tag{9.25}$$

By the use of Theorem B.2 in Appendix B we find that

$$\begin{aligned}
1 &= \mathrm{E}_t\left[e^{-\delta\theta - \frac{\theta}{\psi}g_{t+1} + \theta r^w_{t+1}}\right] \\
&= \exp\left\{-\delta\theta - \frac{\theta}{\psi}\mu_c + \theta\mu_w + \frac{1}{2}\frac{\theta^2}{\psi^2}\sigma_c^2 + \frac{1}{2}\theta^2\sigma_w^2 - \frac{\theta^2}{\psi}\sigma_{cw}\right\}.
\end{aligned}$$

This implies that

$$\mu_w = \delta + \frac{\mu_c}{\psi} - \frac{1}{2}\frac{\theta}{\psi^2}\sigma_c^2 - \frac{1}{2}\theta\sigma_w^2 + \frac{\theta}{\psi}\sigma_{cw}, \tag{9.26}$$

which we shall make use of below.

Applying the state-price deflator to the risk-free asset implies that the one-period risk-free log rate of return is

$$
\begin{aligned}
r_t^f &= -\ln \mathrm{E}_t\left[e^{m_{t+1}}\right] = -\ln \mathrm{E}_t\left[e^{-\delta\theta - \frac{\theta}{\psi}g_{t+1} + (\theta-1)r_{t+1}^w}\right] \\
&= \delta\theta + \frac{\theta}{\psi}\mu_c + (1-\theta)\mu_w - \frac{1}{2}\frac{\theta^2}{\psi^2}\sigma_c^2 - \frac{1}{2}(1-\theta)^2\sigma_w^2 - \frac{\theta}{\psi}(1-\theta)\sigma_{cw} \\
&= \delta + \frac{\mu_c}{\psi} - \frac{1}{2}\frac{\theta}{\psi^2}\sigma_c^2 - \frac{1}{2}(1-\theta)\sigma_w^2,
\end{aligned}
$$

where the last equality is due to Eq. (9.26). This shows Eq. (9.23).

The log-return r_{t+1}^i on an arbitrary risky claim must satisfy

$$
\mathrm{E}_t\left[e^{m_{t+1}+r_{t+1}^i}\right] = 1 \quad \Rightarrow \quad \mathrm{E}_t\left[e^{-\delta\theta - \frac{\theta}{\psi}g_{t+1} + (\theta-1)r_{t+1}^w + r_{t+1}^i}\right] = 1. \tag{9.27}
$$

Assuming that g_{t+1}, r_{t+1}^w, and r_{t+1}^i are jointly normally distributed, we get

$$
\begin{aligned}
\mathrm{E}_t[r_{t+1}^i] + \frac{1}{2}\operatorname{Var}_t[r_{t+1}^i] &= \delta\theta + \frac{\theta}{\psi}\mu_c + (1-\theta)\mu_w \\
&\quad - \frac{1}{2}\frac{\theta^2}{\psi^2}\sigma_c^2 - \frac{1}{2}(1-\theta)^2\sigma_w^2 - \frac{\theta}{\psi}(1-\theta)\sigma_{cw} \\
&\quad + \frac{\theta}{\psi}\operatorname{Cov}_t[r_{t+1}^i, g_{t+1}] + (1-\theta)\operatorname{Cov}_t[r_{t+1}^i, r_{t+1}^w] \\
&= \delta + \frac{\mu_c}{\psi} - \frac{1}{2}\frac{\theta}{\psi^2}\sigma_c^2 - \frac{1}{2}(1-\theta)\sigma_w^2 \\
&\quad + \frac{\theta}{\psi}\operatorname{Cov}_t[r_{t+1}^i, g_{t+1}] + (1-\theta)\operatorname{Cov}_t[r_{t+1}^i, r_{t+1}^w],
\end{aligned}
$$

again using Eq. (9.26). Applying Eq. (9.23) we can now verify Eq. (9.24). □

For the special case of power utility ($\gamma = 1/\psi, \theta = 1$), we are of course back to $r^f = \delta + \gamma\mu_c - \frac{1}{2}\gamma^2\sigma_c^2$ as in the constant-moments version of the CRRA-lognormal model, see Theorem 8.2. Likewise, the right-hand side of Eq. (9.24) reduces to $\gamma \operatorname{Cov}_t[r_{t+1}^i, g_{t+1}]$ in agreement with the basic CRRA-lognormal model.

Obviously, the extension from power utility to Epstein–Zin utility has some consequences for the risk-free rate. Not surprisingly, it is generally (the reciprocal of) the elasticity of intertemporal substitution that determines how expected consumption growth μ_c affects the equilibrium risk-free short rate. If investors expect a higher growth rate of consumption, they would want to borrow more in order to increase consumption now instead of in the next period, where the prospective high consumption would lead to low marginal utility. To ensure market clearing, the short rate would have to increase. If investors have a high elasticity of intertemporal substitution, a small increase in the short rate is sufficient. The last two terms in Eq. (9.23) can be seen as an adjustment for risk, which now includes both consumption risk and wealth risk. If we take the stock market volatility as a rough approximation to the volatility of the wealth portfolio, typical estimates suggest that σ_w^2 is considerably higher than σ_c^2. Clearly the precise values of the preferences parameters are therefore very important for the magnitude of the risk adjustment. In fact, if θ is (much) larger than 1, then $-\frac{1}{2}\frac{\theta}{\psi^2}\sigma_c^2 - \frac{1}{2}(1-\theta)\sigma_w^2$ can be positive.

In the power utility model with a high risk aversion, the average risk-free rate typically gets too high. With Epstein–Zin utility, we can have a high risk aversion without having a very low substitution parameter so Epstein–Zin utility can potentially help in explaining the risk-free rate puzzle.

For $\theta = 0$ (which requires a risk aversion of 1, that is log utility), the risk premium equals $\text{Cov}_t[r_{t+1}^i, r_{t+1}^w]$ as in the classic CAPM. In general, the risk premium is a combination of the asset's covariances with consumption and with wealth so the Epstein–Zin-lognormal consumption-CAPM can be seen as a combination of the CRRA-lognormal consumption-CAPM and the classic CAPM.

As mentioned above, σ_w may be considerably higher than σ_c. Let us assume that $\gamma > 1$. Then if $\psi > 1$, we have $\theta < 0$ and thus a high weight on σ_w. The right-hand side of Eq. (9.24) can therefore potentially be higher with Epstein–Zin utility than with power utility. As an example, suppose in line with the numbers used in the beginning of Section 8.4 that $\sigma_t[r_{t+1}^i] = 0.2$, $\sigma_c = 0.02$, $\rho_{ic} = 0.2$, and fix $\gamma = 5$, $\sigma_w = 0.2$, and $\rho_{iw} = 0.2$. Then the risk premium according to the power utility model is $5 \times 0.2 \times 0.02 \times 0.2 = 0.004 = 0.4\%$. With an elasticity of intertemporal substitution of $\psi = 1.5$ so that $\theta = -12$, the risk premium becomes

$$0.2 \times \left(\frac{-12}{1.5} \times 0.02 \times 0.2 + 13 \times 0.2 \times 0.2 \right) = 0.0976 = 9.76\%$$

which is not far from historical estimates (however, with these parameters and $\delta = \mu_c = 0.02$, the risk-free rate becomes -22.56% so not all problems are solved). The risk premium is highly sensitive to the value of ψ. If we instead use $\psi = 0.5$, we get $\theta = 4$ and a risk premium of -1.76%, which is not what we are looking for.

9.3 LONG-RUN RISKS AND EPSTEIN–ZIN UTILITY

Bansal and Yaron (2004) show that an exchange economy model with a representative individual having Epstein-Zin utility and with a 'long-run risk component' in aggregate consumption is able to explain some of the apparently puzzling features of consumption and return data. Both the assumptions on the preferences and the consumption dynamics are different from the simple consumption-based model, which is a special case. Bansal and Yaron emphasize that it is important to make both these extensions. Note that the log of the next-period state-price deflator is still given by Eq. (9.22). While Bansal and Yaron (2004) simply assume a long-run risk component in aggregate consumption, Kaltenbrunner and Lochstoer (2010) show that long-run consumption risk can arise endogenously in a relatively simple production economy model.

9.3.1 A Model with Long-Run Risks

We now take the following specific model for the dynamics of the log-consumption growth rate $g_{t+1} = \ln(c_{t+1}/c_t)$ as suggested by Bansal and Yaron (2004):

$$\begin{aligned} g_{t+1} &= \mu + x_t + \sigma_t \eta_{t+1}, \\ x_{t+1} &= \rho x_t + \varphi_e \sigma_t e_{t+1}, \\ \sigma^2_{t+1} &= \sigma^2 + \nu(\sigma^2_t - \sigma^2) + \sigma_v v_{t+1}. \end{aligned} \tag{9.28}$$

The shocks $\eta_{t+1}, e_{t+1}, v_{t+1}$ are assumed independent and $N(0,1)$-distributed for all t. The independence assumption simplifies notation and some of the computations in the following, but the shocks might very well be correlated and that may change the asset pricing conclusions of the model.

The process (x_t) drives variations in conditional expectations of consumption and dividend growth, while the process (σ^2_t) captures time-varying economic uncertainty. Note that the dynamics of these processes can be rewritten as

$$\begin{aligned} x_{t+1} - x_t &= (1-\rho)(0 - x_t) + \varphi_e \sigma_t e_{t+1}, \\ \sigma^2_{t+1} - \sigma^2_t &= (1-\nu)(\sigma^2 - \sigma^2_t) + \sigma_v v_{t+1}, \end{aligned}$$

from which it can be seen that the x_t variable is fluctuating around 0 and σ^2_t is fluctuating around σ^2 (unfortunately, with the proposed dynamics, σ^2_t is not guaranteed to stay positive). We will assume $0 < \rho < 1$ and $0 < \nu < 1$. In the simple constant-moments, CRRA-lognormal consumption-based model, the expected consumption growth rate is assumed constant so that the x_t variable is absent (or constant and equal to 0) and σ^2_t is constant and equal to σ^2.

Bansal and Yaron (2004) report an empirical estimate of ρ equal to 0.979, which means that the x_t variable is varying very slowly over time. Formulated differently, the speed of mean reversion, $1 - \rho$, is very close to zero. Variations in x matter for very long periods, hence the name 'long-run risk.' Empirical evidence for a long-run risk component in aggregate consumption is also provided by Hansen, Heaton, and Li (2008). Bansal and Yaron also present empirical support for variations in the volatility of consumption growth, which is captured by the σ_t of the above model. They find a high persistence in that process as well with an estimate of $\nu = 0.987$.

Turning to the market portfolio, assume that the log-growth rate of its dividends is given by

$$g_{d,t+1} = \mu_d + \varphi x_t + \varphi_d \sigma_t (\xi \eta_{t+1} + \sqrt{1-\xi^2}\, u_{t+1}), \tag{9.29}$$

where u_{t+1} is another $N(0,1)$ shock independent of the other shocks in Eq. (9.28), and where $\varphi, \varphi_d > 0$, and $\xi \in [-1,1]$ are additional constants. Then

$$\mathrm{Var}_t[g_{d,t+1}] = \varphi_d^2 \sigma_t^2, \qquad \mathrm{Corr}_t[g_{t+1}, g_{d,t+1}] = \xi.$$

In the discussion of the simple consumption-based model in the preceding chapter, we implicitly assumed in most of the analysis that the market portfolio was a claim to aggregate consumption so that $g_{d,t+1} = g_{t+1}$ in all periods. In the above model this requires that $\mu_d = \mu$, $\varphi = \varphi_d = 1$, and $\xi = 1$. In reality the dividends of the stock market portfolio fluctuate much more than aggregate consumption ($\varphi_d > 1$) and are not perfectly correlated with aggregate consumption ($\xi < 1$). Bansal and Yaron (2004) assume the above dividend growth model with $\xi = 0$, but we will allow for correlation. Following Abel (1999), Bansal and Yaron (2004) use $\varphi = 3$ so that expected dividend growth is considerably more sensitive to the persistent factor than expected consumption growth, which can be explained by the leverage of the companies issuing the stocks.

9.3.2 Return Approximations

The state prices and returns in the model will be driven by x_t and σ_t^2. As we have seen earlier, for example in Section 9.2.5, we can obtain closed-form expressions for the risk-free rate and expected excess returns when the log-state-price deflator and the log-returns are jointly normally distributed. The driving processes (x_t), (σ_t^2) are Gaussian processes so if the log-state-price deflator and the log-returns were linearly related to these variables, they would also be Gaussian. Such a linear relationship is not exact, however, but we can use the Campbell–Shiller linearization outlined in Section 8.4.5. This will allow us to obtain closed-form expressions for the risk-free return, the expected excess return on the market portfolio, and so on. Recall from Eq. (8.32) that the approximation of the log-return between time t and time $t+1$ is

$$r_{t+1} \approx \kappa_0 + \kappa_1 z_{t+1} - z_t + \Delta d_{t+1},$$

where

$$z_t = p_t - d_t = \ln P_t - \ln D_t = \ln \frac{P_t}{D_t}$$

is the log-price-dividend ratio and

$$\Delta d_{t+1} = d_{t+1} - d_t = \ln D_{t+1} - \ln D_t = \ln \frac{D_{t+1}}{D_t}$$

is the log-dividend growth rate. The constants κ_0 and κ_1 are defined by

$$\kappa_1 = \frac{e^{\bar{z}}}{1+e^{\bar{z}}} \in (0,1), \qquad \kappa_0 = \ln(1+e^{\bar{z}}) - \kappa_1 \bar{z},$$

where $\bar{z}$ is the average log-price-dividend ratio.

For an asset paying a dividend identical to the consumption stream, we can replace Δd_{t+1} by the log-growth rate of consumption, $g_{t+1} = \ln(C_{t+1}/C_t)$. In this case z_t is to be interpreted as the log-price-consumption ratio, and we have

$$r^w_{t+1} \approx \kappa_0 + \kappa_1 z_{t+1} - z_t + g_{t+1}. \tag{9.30}$$

Substituting this approximation into Eq. (9.25), we obtain

$$\mathrm{E}_t\left[e^{-\delta\theta+\theta\left(1-\frac{1}{\psi}\right)g_{t+1}+\theta\kappa_0+\theta\kappa_1 z_{t+1}-\theta z_t}\right] = 1. \tag{9.31}$$

For the market portfolio paying aggregate dividends, the analogous approximation of the log-return is

$$r^m_{t+1} \approx \kappa^m_0 + \kappa^m_1 z^m_{t+1} - z^m_t + g_{d,t+1}, \tag{9.32}$$

where z^m_t is the log-price-dividend ratio and $g_{d,t+1}$ is the log-growth rate of aggregate dividends. Substituting Eqs. (9.30) and (9.32) into Eq. (9.27), we obtain

$$\mathrm{E}_t\left[e^{-\delta\theta+\left[\theta\left(1-\frac{1}{\psi}\right)-1\right]g_{t+1}+(\theta-1)(\kappa_0+\kappa_1 z_{t+1}-z_t)+\kappa^m_0+\kappa^m_1 z^m_{t+1}-z^m_t+g_{d,t+1}}\right] = 1, \tag{9.33}$$

which we shall apply below.

We need the following lemmas:

Lemma 9.2 *Applying the Campbell–Shiller approximation in the long-run risk model, the log-price-consumption ratio $z_{t+1} \equiv \ln(P_{t+1}/C_{t+1})$ is given by*

$$z_{t+1} = A_0 + A_1 x_{t+1} + A_2 \sigma^2_{t+1}, \tag{9.34}$$

where A_0, A_1, and A_2 are constants defined through the equations

$$A_2 = \frac{\theta\left(1-\frac{1}{\psi}\right)^2}{2(1-\kappa_1\nu)}\left[1+\left(\frac{\kappa_1\varphi_e}{1-\rho\kappa_1}\right)^2\right], \qquad A_1 = \frac{1-\frac{1}{\psi}}{1-\rho\kappa_1},$$

$$(1-\kappa_1)A_0 = -\delta + \left(1-\frac{1}{\psi}\right)\mu + \kappa_0 + \kappa_1 A_2\sigma^2(1-\nu) + \frac{\theta}{2}\kappa_1^2 A_2^2\sigma_v^2.$$

Proof. Substituting the specific model equations into Eq. (9.31), we get

$$\mathrm{E}_t\left[e^{-\delta\theta+\theta\left(1-\frac{1}{\psi}\right)(\mu+x_t+\sigma_t\eta_{t+1})+\theta\kappa_0+\theta\kappa_1 z_{t+1}-\theta z_t}\right] = 1,$$

which has to be satisfied (approximately, at least) for all possible values of x_t and σ_t at any point in time t. Conjecture that z has the form (9.34) for all t. Substituting that and the equations for x_{t+1} and σ_{t+1}^2 from Eq. (9.28) into the previous equation and then collecting terms yields

$$\begin{aligned}
1 &= \exp\left\{\theta q + \theta\left(1-\frac{1}{\psi}-A_1\left[1-\rho\kappa_1\right]\right)x_t + \theta A_2\left(\kappa_1\nu-1\right)\sigma_t^2\right\} \\
&\quad\times \mathrm{E}_t\left[e^{\theta(1-\frac{1}{\psi})\sigma_t\eta_{t+1}+\theta\kappa_1\left[A_1\varphi_e\sigma_t e_{t+1}+A_2\sigma_v v_{t+1}\right]}\right] \\
&= \exp\left\{\theta q + \theta\left(1-\frac{1}{\psi}-A_1\left[1-\rho\kappa_1\right]\right)x_t - \theta A_2\left(1-\kappa_1\nu\right)\sigma_t^2\right\} \\
&\quad\times \exp\left\{\frac{1}{2}\theta^2\left(\left[(1-\frac{1}{\psi})^2+\kappa_1^2A_1^2\varphi_e^2\right]\sigma_t^2+\kappa_1^2A_2^2\sigma_v^2\right)\right\} \\
&= \exp\Bigg\{\theta q + \frac{1}{2}\theta^2\kappa_1^2A_2^2\sigma_v^2 + \theta\left(1-\frac{1}{\psi}-A_1\left[1-\rho\kappa_1\right]\right)x_t \\
&\qquad + \theta\left(\frac{1}{2}\theta\left[(1-\frac{1}{\psi})^2+\kappa_1^2A_1^2\varphi_e^2\right]-A_2\left(1-\kappa_1\nu\right)\right)\sigma_t^2\Bigg\},
\end{aligned}$$

where $q = -\delta + (1-\frac{1}{\psi})\mu + \kappa_0 + A_0(\kappa_1 - 1) + \kappa_1 A_2\sigma^2(1-\nu)$. Since this is to be satisfied for all values of x_t and σ_t^2, we need the coefficients of x_t and σ_t^2 to be zero, which leads to the expressions for A_1 and A_2. The constant A_0 which is included in q is then determined from the condition $\theta q + \frac{1}{2}\theta^2\kappa_1^2A_2^2\sigma_v^2 = 0$. This confirms the conjectured form of z. □

Lemma 9.3 *Applying the Campbell–Shiller approximation in the long-run risk model, the log-price-dividend ratio $z_{t+1}^m \equiv \ln(P_{t+1}/D_{t+1})$ is given by*

$$z_t^m = B_0 + B_1 x_t + B_2\sigma_t^2, \tag{9.35}$$

where B_0, B_1, and B_2 are constants defined through the equations

$$B_2 = \frac{(1-\theta)A_2(1-\kappa_1\nu) + \frac{1}{2}\gamma^2 - \gamma\varphi_d\xi + \frac{1}{2}\varphi_d^2 + \frac{1}{2}(\beta_e^m - \lambda_e)^2}{1-\nu\kappa_1^m},$$

$$B_1 = \frac{\varphi - \frac{1}{\psi}}{1-\rho\kappa_1^m},$$

$$(1-\kappa_1^m)B_0 = -\delta - \frac{\mu}{\psi} + \kappa_0^m + \mu_d + (\theta-1)\kappa_1\kappa_1^m A_2 B_2\sigma_v^2$$

$$+\frac{1-\theta}{2}\kappa_1^2 A_2^2\sigma_v^2 + \kappa_1^m B_2\sigma^2(1-\nu) + \frac{1}{2}(\kappa_1^m)^2 B_2^2\sigma_v^2.$$

Proof. If we substitute the modelling assumptions (9.28) and (9.29) together with (9.34) into Eq. (9.33), we find that

$$1 = \mathrm{E}_t\Big[\exp\Big\{\tilde{q} + (\varphi - \frac{1}{\psi})x_t + (\theta-1)A_2(\kappa_1\nu - 1)\sigma_t^2 + \kappa_1^m z_{t+1}^m - z_t^m$$

$$+ (\varphi_d\xi - \gamma)\sigma_t\eta_{t+1} + (\theta-1)\kappa_1 A_2\sigma_v v_{t+1} \tag{9.36}$$

$$+ \varphi_d\sqrt{1-\xi^2}\sigma_t u_{t+1} + (\theta-1)\kappa_1 A_1\varphi_e\sigma_t e_{t+1}\Big\}\Big],$$

where

$$\tilde{q} = -\delta + (\theta-1)q - \mu/\psi + \kappa_0^m + \mu_d$$

$$= -\delta - \frac{\mu}{\psi} + \kappa_0^m + \mu_d - \frac{1}{2}\theta(\theta-1)\kappa_1^2 A_2^2\sigma_v^2.$$

The conjectured form (9.35) implies that

$$\kappa_1^m z_{t+1}^m - z_t^m = (\kappa_1^m - 1)B_0 + \kappa_1^m B_2\sigma^2(1-\nu) + B_1(\rho\kappa_1^m - 1)x_t$$

$$+ B_2(\nu\kappa_1^m - 1)\sigma_t^2 + \kappa_1^m B_1\varphi_e\sigma_t e_{t+1} + \kappa_1^m B_2\sigma_v v_{t+1}.$$

If we substitute that into Eq. (9.36), we obtain

$$1 = \mathrm{E}_t\Big[\exp\Big\{q' + \left(\varphi - \frac{1}{\psi} + B_1(\rho\kappa_1^m - 1)\right)x_t$$

$$+\Big(A_2(\theta-1)(\kappa_1\nu - 1) + B_2(\nu\kappa_1^m - 1) + \frac{1}{2}\gamma^2 - \gamma\varphi_d\xi$$

$$+\frac{1}{2}\varphi_d^2 + \frac{1}{2}(\beta_e^m - \lambda_e)^2\Big)\sigma_t^2\Big\}\Big],$$

where

$$q' = \tilde{q} + (\kappa_1^m - 1)B_0 + \kappa_1^m B_2 \sigma^2 (1 - \nu) + \frac{1}{2}[(\theta - 1)\kappa_1 A_2 + \kappa_1^m B_2]^2 \sigma_v^2$$

and

$$\beta_e^m = \kappa_1^m B_1 \varphi_e, \qquad \lambda_e = (1 - \theta)\kappa_1 A_1 \varphi_e.$$

Since this must be satisfied for any values of x_t and σ_t^2, we need the coefficients of those terms to be zero and, consequently, the constant q' in the exponent to be zero as well, that is

$$B_1 = \frac{\varphi - \frac{1}{\psi}}{1 - \rho\kappa_{1,m}},$$

$$B_2 = \frac{(1 - \theta)A_2(1 - \kappa_1 \nu) + \frac{1}{2}\gamma^2 - \gamma\varphi_d \xi + \frac{1}{2}\varphi_d^2 + \frac{1}{2}(\beta_e^m - \lambda_e)^2}{1 - \nu\kappa_{1,m}},$$

and B_0 is such that $q' = 0$. This confirms the conjectured form of z^m. □

The two above lemmas are useful in deriving the asset pricing implications of the model, which we turn to now.

9.3.3 Asset Pricing Implications

In the general expression (9.22) for the log-state-price deflator, we substitute in Eq. (9.30), and apply Lemma 9.2. The log-state-price deflator can then be rewritten as

$$m_{t+1} = (\theta - 1)q - \delta - \frac{\mu}{\psi} - \frac{x_t}{\psi} + (\theta - 1)A_2(\kappa_1 \nu - 1)\sigma_t^2$$
$$+ \left(\theta - 1 - \frac{\theta}{\psi}\right)\sigma_t \eta_{t+1} + (\theta - 1)\kappa_1 A_1 \varphi_e \sigma_t e_{t+1} + (\theta - 1)\kappa_1 A_2 \sigma_v v_{t+1}.$$

Note that $\theta - 1 - \frac{\theta}{\psi} = \theta(1 - \frac{1}{\psi}) - 1 = 1 - \gamma - 1 = -\gamma$. Define

$$\lambda_\eta = \gamma, \quad \lambda_e = (1 - \theta)\kappa_1 A_1 \varphi_e, \quad \lambda_v = (1 - \theta)\kappa_1 A_2.$$

Then, from the distributional assumptions on the shocks, we conclude that we can rewrite m_{t+1} as

$$m_{t+1} = \mathrm{E}_t[m_{t+1}] - \lambda_\eta \sigma_t \eta_{t+1} - \lambda_e \sigma_t e_{t+1} - \lambda_v \sigma_v v_{t+1}, \qquad (9.37)$$

and that m_{t+1} is conditional lognormally distributed with

$$\mathrm{E}_t[m_{t+1}] = (\theta - 1)q - \delta - \frac{\mu + x_t}{\psi} + (\theta - 1)A_2(\kappa_1 \nu - 1)\sigma_t^2,$$

$$\mathrm{Var}_t[m_{t+1}] = \sigma_t^2\left(\lambda_\eta^2 + \lambda_e^2\right) + \lambda_v^2 \sigma_v^2.$$

The continuously compounded risk-free rate is now easily computed as

$$r_t^f = -\ln \mathrm{E}_t\left[e^{m_{t+1}}\right] = -\mathrm{E}_t[m_{t+1}] - \frac{1}{2}\mathrm{Var}_t[m_{t+1}] = \delta + (1-\theta)q$$
$$+ \frac{\mu + x_t}{\psi} - \frac{1}{2}\lambda_v^2\sigma_v^2 - \left((1-\theta)A_2(1-\kappa_1\nu) + \frac{1}{2}\gamma^2 + \frac{1}{2}\lambda_e^2\right)\sigma_t^2. \quad (9.38)$$

From Section 4.2.2, we have that for any normally distributed log-return $r_{i,t+1}$, the log-risk premium is

$$\mathrm{E}_t[r_{i,t+1}] - r_t^f = -\mathrm{Cov}_t\left[m_{t+1}, r_{i,t+1}\right] - \frac{1}{2}\mathrm{Var}_t[r_{i,t+1}].$$

After substitution of the expression (9.37) for the log-deflator, the risk premium can be rewritten as

$$\mathrm{E}_t[r_{i,t+1}] - r_t^f = \lambda_\eta \sigma_t \mathrm{Cov}_t[\eta_{t+1}, r_{i,t+1}] + \lambda_e \sigma_t \mathrm{Cov}_t[e_{t+1}, r_{i,t+1}]$$
$$+ \lambda_v \sigma_v \mathrm{Cov}_t[v_{t+1}, r_{i,t+1}] - \frac{1}{2}\mathrm{Var}_t[r_{i,t+1}]. \quad (9.39)$$

Now, let us focus on the market portfolio with log-return r_{t+1}^m. If we use Lemma 9.3 in the Campbell–Shiller approximation (9.32) and focus on the shock terms, we obtain

$$r_{t+1}^m = \mathrm{E}_t[r_{t+1}^m] + \beta_e^m \sigma_t e_{t+1} + \beta_v^m \sigma_v v_{t+1} + \beta_\eta^m \sigma_t \eta_{t+1} + \varphi_d \sqrt{1-\xi^2}\sigma_t u_{t+1},$$

where $\beta_v^m = \kappa_1^m B_2$ and $\beta_\eta^m = \varphi_d \xi$. Substituting this into Eq. (9.39) we find

$$\mathrm{E}_t[r_{t+1}^m] - r_t^f = \beta_\eta^m \lambda_\eta \sigma_t^2 + \beta_e^m \lambda_e \sigma_t^2 + \beta_v^m \lambda_v \sigma_v^2 - \frac{1}{2}\mathrm{Var}_t[r_{t+1}^m], \quad (9.40)$$

and

$$\mathrm{Var}_t[r_{t+1}^m] = \left((\beta_e^m)^2 + \varphi_d^2\right)\sigma_t^2 + (\beta_v^m)^2\sigma_v^2.$$

We summarize these findings in a theorem:

Theorem 9.5 *Using the Campbell–Shiller approximation in the discrete-time long-run risk model with Epstein–Zin preferences, the one-period continuously compounded risk-free rate is given by Eq.* (9.38) *and the excess expected log-return of any risky asset i satisfies Eq.* (9.40).

Let us first look at some special cases in which we either turn off the long-run risk element or Epstein–Zin preferences:

1. *Standard consumption dynamics.* In this case $x_t \equiv 0, \sigma_t^2 \equiv \sigma^2$ and $\sigma_v^2 = 0$ so that $q = 0$. Moreover, $\varphi_e = 0$ and thus $\lambda_e = 0$, and $A_2(1 - \kappa_1 \nu) = \theta(1 - \frac{1}{\psi})^2/2$. Hence, we get the constant risk-free rate

$$r_t^f = \delta + \frac{\mu}{\psi} - \frac{1}{2}\sigma^2\left(\theta(1 - \frac{1}{\psi})^2 + \gamma^2\right) = \delta + \frac{\mu}{\psi} - \frac{1}{2}\left(1 - \theta + \frac{\theta}{\psi^2}\right)\sigma^2.$$

   This is consistent with Eq. (9.23) because in this version of the model z_t in Eq. (9.34) is constant and, hence, r_{t+1}^w equals a constant plus log-consumption growth. Consequently, the variance of the wealth portfolio equals the variance of consumption growth, $\sigma_w^2 = \sigma^2$, and if you apply that in Eq. (9.23), you get the above expression for the risk-free rate.

   The risk premium becomes

$$\mathrm{E}_t[r_{t+1}^m] - r_t^f = \varphi_d \xi \gamma \sigma^2 - \frac{1}{2}\mathrm{Var}_t[r_{t+1}^m], \quad \mathrm{Var}_t[r_{t+1}^m] = \varphi_d^2 \sigma^2 \qquad (9.41)$$

   and $\varphi_d = \xi = 1$ if we assume the dividends are identical to aggregate consumption. This is consistent with Eq. (9.24) because in this special version of the model r_{t+1}^w equals a constant plus $g_{t+1} = \mu + \sigma \eta_{t+1}$ and $r_{t+1}^m = \mathrm{E}_t[r_{t+1}^m] + \varphi_d \xi \sigma \eta_{t+1} + \varphi_d \sqrt{1 - \xi^2} \sigma u_{t+1}$ so that

$$\mathrm{Cov}_t[r_{t+1}^m, g_{t+1}] = \mathrm{Cov}_t[r_{t+1}^m, r_{t+1}^w] = \varphi_d \xi \sigma^2.$$

   Since $\frac{\theta}{\psi} + 1 - \theta = \gamma$, it is now clear that Eqs. (9.24) and (9.41) agree.

2. *Power utility.* In this case the risk-free rate will be $r_t^f = \delta + \gamma(\mu + x_t) - \frac{1}{2}\gamma^2\sigma_t^2$. The level of the risk-free rate will be similar to the case with the simple model for consumption dynamics, but the fluctuations in expected consumption growth and consumption volatility generate fluctuations in the risk-free rate.

   In this case $\lambda_e = \lambda_v = 0$ and thus

$$\mathrm{E}_t[r_{t+1}^m] - r_t^f = \varphi_d \xi \gamma \sigma_t^2 - \frac{1}{2}\mathrm{Var}_t[r_{t+1}^m].$$

   Therefore, under a power utility assumption, introducing a long-run risk element in consumption dynamics does not change the level of excess expected returns on the market portfolio. We need the combination of Epstein–Zin utility and long-run risks in order to affect excess expected returns.

The general expression (9.38) allows for a time-varying risk-free rate and involves sufficiently many parameters that it may be possible to match the observed average level of the risk-free rate and the observed magnitude of variations. In the calibration of Bansal and Yaron (2004), the unconditional variance of the risk-free rate is

$$\operatorname{Var}[r_t^f] \approx \left(\frac{1}{\psi}\right)^2 \operatorname{Var}[x_t],$$

which is again decreasing in the elasticity of intertemporal substitution. In the long-run risk model with power utility briefly discussed above, we would similarly have $\operatorname{Var}[r_t^f] \approx \gamma^2 \operatorname{Var}[x_t]$. With power utility, a high risk aversion is needed to match the equity premium, but that may easily lead to an unrealistic high variance of the risk-free rate. With Epstein–Zin utility and a fairly high elasticity of intertemporal substitution, we can keep a relatively low and relatively stable risk-free rate.

In the general expression (9.40) for the market risk premium the first term—the standard term—is a premium for short-run risk, the second term is a premium for long-run risk, while the third term is a premium for consumption volatility risk. What can we say about the sign of the two latter premia? First consider $\lambda_e = (1-\theta)\kappa_1 A_1 \varphi_e$. We have $0 < \kappa_1 < 1$ and $\varphi_e > 0$. If we assume that $1 > 1/\psi$, we will have $A_1 > 0$. With $\gamma > 1/\psi$, we have $\theta < 1$, and thus all in all we get $\lambda_e > 0$. Next consider $\beta_e^m = \kappa_1^m B_1 \varphi_e$. Again κ_1^m and φ_e must be positive. If φ is greater than $1/\psi$, which holds for $\varphi > 1$ and $\psi > 1$, then B_1 will be positive and, hence, β_e^m is positive. Under such parameter values, the long-run risk premium $\beta_e^m \lambda_e \sigma_t^2$ is going to be positive. Also note that β_e^m and thus the long-run risk premium are increasing in ρ and φ, that is the risk premium increases with the persistence of the long-run growth component and the sensitivity of dividends to that long-run component.

What about the volatility risk premium? Assume $\gamma > 1 > 1/\psi$ so that $\theta < 0$. Then $A_2 < 0$ and $\lambda_v < 0$. When θ and A_2 are sufficiently negative, B_2 and thus β_v^m will be negative. Then the volatility risk premium $\beta_v^m \lambda_v \sigma_v^2$ will be positive.

From the preceding discussion it is clear that the long-run risk and volatility risk features of the model can add to the market risk premium when $\gamma > 1 > 1/\psi$. In particular, the elasticity of intertemporal substitution ψ has to exceed one. As discussed in Section 5.7.3, there is some debate about empirical realistic values of ψ, where some authors find ψ greater than one and others find ψ smaller than one.

The variations in consumption volatility induce variations in the excess expected return, the return volatility, and the Sharpe ratio of the market portfolio.

Above, we have not discussed the implications of the long-run risk model for the pricing of long-term bonds and thus for the shape of the yield curve. In Section 11.3.3 we will briefly explore these implications.

9.3.4 Evaluation of the Model

Bansal and Yaron (2004) calibrate their model to return and consumption data from the United States over the period 1929–1998. Table 9.1 contains statistics for the return data and for the calibrated model using an elasticity of intertemporal substitution equal to 1.5. With a modest level of risk aversion the model comes very close to matching the data.[2]

Including a long-run risk component in consumption also appears to be important for explaining the cross-section of returns. Bansal, Dittmar, and Lundblad (2005) show that the exposure of an asset's dividends to long-run consumption risks is an important explanatory variable in accounting for differences in mean returns across portfolios. For other applications of the long-run risk framework see Eraker and Shaliastovich (2008), Chen (2010), Chen, Collin-Dufresne, and Goldstein (2009), Malloy, Moskowitz, and Vissing-Jørgensen (2009), Bhamra, Kuehn, and Strebulaev (2010), Kaltenbrunner and Lochstoer (2010), and Colacito and Croce (2011). In related work, Lettau, Ludvigson, and Wachter (2008) built a regime switching model for the volatility and mean of consumption growth. They report evidence of a shift to lower consumption volatility at the beginning of the 1990s and explore the implications for the market risk premium.

As acknowledged by Bansal and Yaron, it is econometrically very difficult to detect a small but highly persistent component in a time series, but at least their study shows that if consumption growth has such a component, it may have significant effects on asset returns. Combined with the plausible Epstein–Zin preferences, long-run risks in consumption may explain (a substantial part of) the equity premium puzzle. Hansen, Heaton, and Li (2008) and Colacito and

Table 9.1. Asset pricing in the Bansal and Yaron model.

Variable	US data 1929–1998		Calibrated model	
	Estimate	Std. error	$\gamma = 7.5$	$\gamma = 10$
$\mathrm{E}[r^m - r^f]$	6.33	2.15	4.01	6.84
$\mathrm{E}[r^f]$	0.86	0.42	1.44	0.93
$\sigma[r^m]$	19.42	3.07	17.81	18.65
$\sigma[r^f]$	0.97	0.28	0.44	0.57

Notes: The information is taken from Table IV in Bansal and Yaron (2004). All returns are in percentage terms. The elasticity of intertemporal substitution is $\psi = 1.5$

[2] Obviously the analytical expressions for the risk-free rate and the risk premium derived above are only approximations. According to Bansal and Yaron (2004), the model-generated moments presented in Table 9.1 are based on a numerical solution method, but are 'quite close' to those based on the approximate analytical solutions.

Croce (2011) do report empirical evidence of long-horizon predictable variation in aggregate consumption growth. Bansal, Gallant, and Tauchen (2007) find empirical evidence of the long-run risk model and conclude that the model outperforms the Campbell–Cochrane model presented in Section 9.2.3 on several counts. Further empirical support is provided by Bansal, Kiku, and Yaron (2012). On the other hand, Constantinides and Ghosh (2011) reject the idea that the model can jointly match the cross-section of stock and bond returns and fit the time series moments of consumption and dividend growth, and Beeler and Campbell (2012) and van Binsbergen, Brandt, and Koijen (2011) provide further empirical critique.

9.4 RARE DISASTERS

The standard power utility aggregate consumption model assumes that log of consumption growth is normally distributed and typical empirical estimations suggest a low expected growth rate with a low standard deviation. Rietz (1988) proposed to add the risk of a large sudden decrease in consumption and provided numerical examples in which the associated disaster risk premium is large enough to account for the observed equity premium even with a relative risk aversion of around 10. According to this view, investors require a large equity premium because very bad shocks may hit the economy and stocks will then perform very poorly. The magnitude of this disaster risk premium depends crucially on the probability of disasters and how bad disasters really are. Mehra and Prescott (1988) argue that the examples of Rietz are based on sudden drops in consumption that are far bigger than those observed in the United States over the past century, even when the Great Depression is included and, therefore, Rietz grossly exaggerates the disaster risk premium.

The rare disaster explanation of the equity premium has been revived by Barro in a number of papers, including Barro (2006, 2009) and Barro and Ursua (2008). Based on long-term international GDP data, Barro (2006) defines an economic disaster as a drop of more than 15% GDP and concludes that such disasters are in fact relatively frequent (1.5–2% per year) and severe (between 15 and 64% with an average of 29%). With these disaster parameters he finds that the observed equity premium can be rationalized with a relative risk aversion as low as 3–4. Barro assumes that, when a consumption disaster occurs, the government will with some probability default on its debt and then only pay out a fraction of the face value to bond holders. With the parameter values he assumes, he can then also roughly match the observed level of interest rates and thus resolve the risk-free rate puzzle.

Barro's estimates of the frequency and size of economic disasters are controversial. When Barro measures the size of a disaster, he takes the decline in

GDP from the peak to trough of the disaster period, which is typically 3–5 years. But in the calibration of his model and the computation of the model's equity premium and risk-free rate, he assumes that such a decline in aggregate consumption happens over a single year. As pointed out by Constantinides (2008), this is inconsistent and leads to wrong conclusions. If, for example, a disaster lasts for four years, then Barro is really assuming that the equation

$$\mathrm{E}_t\left[e^{-\delta}\left(\frac{c_{t+4}}{c_t}\right)^{-\gamma} R_{t,t+1}\right] = 1$$

holds, but this does *not* follow from consumption-based asset pricing theory. As explained in earlier chapters, the power utility representative individual model implies that

$$\mathrm{E}_t\left[e^{-\delta}\left(\frac{c_{t+1}}{c_t}\right)^{-\gamma} R_{t,t+1}\right] = 1,$$

and also that

$$\mathrm{E}_t\left[e^{-4\delta}\left(\frac{c_{t+4}}{c_t}\right)^{-\gamma} R_{t,t+4}\right] = 1.$$

Either the annual decline in consumption should be compared with the annual stock market returns or the total decline in consumption over the disaster period should be compared with the stock market return over the same period. When applying the full consumption decline over the disaster period, it is really the four-year equity premium of around 20–30% that should be explained. Clearly, the disaster model is then much less successful. Julliard and Ghosh (2012) also conclude that the disaster risk premium is small since large consumption drops are rare. Backus, Chernov, and Martin (2011) calculate the disaster frequency and size implied by the prices of options on the S&P 500 stock index and conclude that large disasters are much less likely than assumed by Barro.

In Barro's papers the probability of a disaster is the same in all periods. Wachter (2012) extends the model by allowing a time-varying disaster probability as well as Epstein–Zin preferences. The time-varying disaster probability induces time-varying risk premia as observed in the data. The extension to Epstein–Zin preferences is important for the model to match the high stock market volatility, the low and stable risk-free rate, and the predictability of excess stock returns by the price-dividend ratio. Wachter's model is formulated in continuous time with a negative jump term added to the geometric Brownian motion usually assumed for aggregate consumption. The jump intensity follows a square-root process assumed independent of the shocks to consumption. She obtains closed-form expressions for the key quantities by focusing on the case of a unit elasticity of intertemporal substitution. Gabaix (2012) also allows the disaster risk to be time-varying, which can be caused either by a time-varying disaster probability or a time-varying magnitude of the disaster shock on consumption or dividends. Gabaix applies recently developed linearity-generating stochastic processes that lead to closed-form solutions for prices and expected returns. He claims that a calibrated version of his model can explain many different asset pricing puzzles.

Based on the observation that disasters tend to hit the economy in the form of a sequence of bad shocks of a moderate magnitude rather than an instantaneous very bad shock, Nowotny (2011) extends Wachter's model by letting the occurrence of a disaster increase the probability of further disasters in the near future. Whenever aggregate consumption jumps down, there is a simultaneous increase in the jump intensity. Disasters are bad not only because of the immediate effect on consumption but also because of the increased probability of further disasters. Therefore, although both the average size and probability of a disaster seem to be relatively small, the impact on the risk-free rate and risk premia will be substantial.

9.5 MULTIPLE CONSUMPTION GOODS

The asset pricing models studied above have all assumed a single, perishable consumption good. Of course, modern economies offer a large variety of different consumption goods. Some goods are durable so that purchasing and holding such goods will provide consumption benefits for a long period of time. Some durable goods can even be resold, although typically with significant transaction costs, which is why these goods have a dual role as consumption goods and investment objects. Furthermore, individuals may have different preferences for different goods so that concepts like marginal utility and relative risk aversion have to be defined and interpreted with care. Several recent papers have explored the consequences of incorporating multiple consumption goods into a representative individual framework. Below we will discuss some of these papers, but first we derive general expressions for the state-price deflator and risk premia in a discrete-time framework with two consumption goods.

9.5.1 General Derivations

Let c_t denote the time t consumption of good 1 and q_t the consumption of good 2. Good 1 is the numeraire so that all values and prices are expressed in terms of units of good 1. With time-additive expected utility, the individual maximizes

$$\mathrm{E}\left[\sum_{t=0}^{T} e^{-\delta t} u(c_t, q_t)\right],$$

which leads to the state-price deflator

$$\zeta_t = e^{-\delta t} \frac{u_c(c_t, q_t)}{u_c(c_0, q_0)},$$

compare Theorem 6.7. Most papers assume a utility function of the CES-power type

$$u(c,q) = \frac{1}{1-\gamma}\left([1-b]c^{\frac{\psi-1}{\psi}} + bq^{\frac{\psi-1}{\psi}}\right)^{\frac{\psi}{\psi-1}(1-\gamma)} = \frac{1}{1-\gamma} c^{1-\gamma} v(q/c)^{1-\gamma}, \tag{9.42}$$

where $\gamma > 1$, $\psi > 0$, $b \in (0,1)$, and v is the increasing function defined by

$$v(x) = \left(1 - b + bx^{\frac{\psi-1}{\psi}}\right)^{\frac{\psi}{\psi-1}}.$$

Note that

$$v'(x) = bx^{-1/\psi} v(x)^{1/\psi}.$$

As before γ is the constant relative risk aversion, b is a weighting parameter, and ψ is the constant elasticity of intratemporal substitution, as explained in Section 5.6.3 (the special case of Cobb–Douglas utility in which $\psi = 1$ is considered in Exercise 9.9). The marginal utility with respect to consumption of good 1 is then

$$\begin{aligned}
u_c(c,q) &= c^{-\gamma} v\left(\frac{q}{c}\right)^{1-\gamma} + c^{1-\gamma} v\left(\frac{q}{c}\right)^{-\gamma} v'\left(\frac{q}{c}\right)\left(\frac{-q}{c^2}\right) \\
&= c^{-\gamma} v\left(\frac{q}{c}\right)^{1-\gamma} - bc^{-\gamma}\left(\frac{q}{c}\right)^{\frac{\psi-1}{\psi}} v\left(\frac{q}{c}\right)^{-\gamma}\left(1 - b + b\left(\frac{q}{c}\right)^{\frac{\psi-1}{\psi}}\right)^{\frac{1}{\psi-1}} \\
&= c^{-\gamma} v\left(\frac{q}{c}\right)^{1-\gamma} - c^{-\gamma} v\left(\frac{q}{c}\right)^{-\gamma}\left(1 - b + b\left(\frac{q}{c}\right)^{\frac{\psi-1}{\psi}}\right)^{\frac{\psi}{\psi-1}} \\
&\quad + (1-b)c^{-\gamma} v\left(\frac{q}{c}\right)^{-\gamma}\left(1 - b + b\left(\frac{q}{c}\right)^{\frac{\psi-1}{\psi}}\right)^{\frac{1}{\psi-1}} \\
&= c^{-\gamma} v\left(\frac{q}{c}\right)^{1-\gamma} - c^{-\gamma} v\left(\frac{q}{c}\right)^{1-\gamma} + (1-b)c^{-\gamma} v\left(\frac{q}{c}\right)^{-\gamma} v\left(\frac{q}{c}\right)^{\frac{1}{\psi}} \\
&= (1-b)c^{-\gamma} v\left(\frac{q}{c}\right)^{\frac{1}{\psi}-\gamma}.
\end{aligned}$$

For a fixed c, the derivative of the marginal utility $u_c(c,q)$ with respect to the consumption ratio q/c is

$$\frac{\partial u_c}{\partial\left(\frac{q}{c}\right)}(c,q) = b(1-b)\left(\frac{1}{\psi}-\gamma\right)c^{-\gamma}\left(\frac{q}{c}\right)^{-\frac{1}{\psi}}v\left(\frac{q}{c}\right)^{\frac{2}{\psi}-\gamma-1}. \tag{9.43}$$

If $\gamma > 1/\psi$, the marginal utility $u_c(c,q)$ is decreasing in the consumption ratio q/c, hence the marginal utility of good 1 is particularly high when the consumption of good 2 is low compared to the consumption of good 1. We can loosely interpret a situation in which the consumption of good 1 is low as a 'recession'. If, in addition, the consumption of good 2 relative to the consumption of good 1 is low, the individual faces a 'severe recession' using the term of Piazzesi, Schneider, and Tuzel (2007), still assuming $\gamma > 1/\psi$. Rewriting this inequality as $\psi > 1/\gamma$, the condition means that the *intra*temporal elasticity of substitution exceeds the *inter*temporal elasticity of substitution (which is $1/\gamma$ with time-additive constant relative risk aversion). Hence, the individual would rather substitute consumption of good 1 by consumption of good 2 within a period than substitute overall consumption this period with overall consumption next period. When this relation between the preference parameters is satisfied, the individual will greatly appreciate an asset that pays out high dividends when the relative consumption of good 2 is low so that such assets will have low expected returns in equilibrium.

With the above expression for marginal utility the next-period state-price deflator is

$$\frac{\zeta_{t+1}}{\zeta_t} = e^{-\delta}\frac{u_c(c_{t+1},q_{t+1})}{u_c(c_t,q_t)} = e^{-\delta}\left(\frac{c_{t+1}}{c_t}\right)^{-\gamma}\left(\frac{v(q_{t+1}/c_{t+1})}{v(q_t/c_t)}\right)^{\frac{1}{\psi}-\gamma}. \tag{9.44}$$

Substituting this into the approximation (4.24), the conditional excess return on any risky asset i can be approximated by

$$\begin{aligned}\mathrm{E}_t\left[R_{i,t+1}\right] - R_t^f &\approx \gamma\,\mathrm{Cov}_t\left[R_{i,t+1}, \ln\frac{c_{t+1}}{c_t}\right] \\ &+ \left(\gamma-\frac{1}{\psi}\right)\mathrm{Cov}_t\left[R_{i,t+1}, \ln\frac{v(q_{t+1}/c_{t+1})}{v(q_t/c_t)}\right].\end{aligned}$$

To get rid of the v-function, note that

$$\ln v(x) = \frac{\psi}{\psi-1}\ln\left(1-b+bx^{\frac{\psi-1}{\psi}}\right).$$

Applying a first-order Taylor approximation of $\psi \ln\left(1 - b + bx^{\frac{\psi-1}{\psi}}\right)$ around $\psi = 1$, we can approximate $\ln v(x)$ by[3]

$$\ln v(x) \approx b \ln x.$$

Consequently, we obtain a risk premium of

$$\begin{aligned} \mathrm{E}_t\left[R_{i,t+1}\right] - R_t^f \approx & \left[\gamma - b\left(\gamma - \frac{1}{\psi}\right)\right] \mathrm{Cov}_t\left[R_{i,t+1}, \ln\frac{c_{t+1}}{c_t}\right] \\ & + b\left(\gamma - \frac{1}{\psi}\right) \mathrm{Cov}_t\left[R_{i,t+1}, \ln\frac{q_{t+1}}{q_t}\right]. \end{aligned}$$

If $\gamma > 1/\psi$ and

$$\mathrm{Cov}_t\left[R_{i,t+1}, \ln\frac{q_{t+1}}{q_t}\right] > \mathrm{Cov}_t\left[R_{i,t+1}, \ln\frac{c_{t+1}}{c_t}\right], \tag{9.45}$$

the above risk premium will exceed $\gamma \,\mathrm{Cov}_t[R_{i,t+1}, \ln \frac{c_{t+1}}{c_t}]$, which is the risk premium in the single-good model (corresponding to $b = 0$). The two-good model can thus imply a larger equity premium. If the conditional return covariance with respect to good 2, $\mathrm{Cov}_t[R_{i,t+1}, \ln \frac{q_{t+1}}{q_t}]$, varies counter-cyclically and more so than the conditional return covariance with respect to good 1, $\mathrm{Cov}_t[R_{i,t+1}, \ln \frac{c_{t+1}}{c_t}]$, the two-good model will also produce a larger counter-cyclical variation in expected excess returns than the one-good model provided that $\gamma > 1/\psi$. Moreover, cross-sectional differences in stock returns can now be due to differences in their betas with respect to both goods, so the addition of the second good may help in explaining the cross-section of stock returns.

Yogo (2006) generalizes these results by embedding the two-good CES utility in an Epstein–Zin recursive utility setting, that is he applies a utility index $\mathcal{U}_t$ satisfying

$$\mathcal{U}_t = \left\{(1 - e^{-\delta}) f(c_t, q_t)^{\frac{\nu-1}{\nu}} + e^{-\delta}\left(\mathrm{E}_t\left[\mathcal{U}_{t+1}^{1-\gamma}\right]\right)^{\theta}\right\}^{\frac{\nu}{\nu-1}},$$

where $\theta = (1-\gamma)/(1-1/\nu)$ and

$$f(c,q) = \left([1-b]c^{\frac{\psi-1}{\psi}} + bq^{\frac{\psi-1}{\psi}}\right)^{\frac{\psi}{\psi-1}}.$$

In this specification, γ is the relative risk aversion, ν is the elasticity of *inter*temporal substitution, ψ is the elasticity of *intra*temporal substitution, and

[3] With $f(\psi) = \psi \ln\left(1 - b + bx^{1-1/\psi}\right)$, we have $f(1) = 0$. Moreover, we obtain $f'(\psi) = \ln\left(1 - b + bx^{1-1/\psi}\right) + b\psi^{-1}x^{1-1/\psi}(1 - b + bx^{1-1/\psi})^{-1} \ln x$ and thus $f'(1) = b \ln x$. Therefore, $f(\psi) \approx f(1) + f'(1)(\psi - 1) = b(\psi - 1) \ln x$ and $f(\psi)/(\psi - 1) \approx b \ln x$.

$b \in (0, 1)$ is a weighting constant. According to Yogo, the next-period state-price deflator is then

$$\frac{\zeta_{t+1}}{\zeta_t} = e^{-\delta\theta} \left(\frac{c_{t+1}}{c_t}\right)^{-\frac{\theta}{\nu}} \left(\frac{v(q_{t+1}/c_{t+1})}{v(q_t/c_t)}\right)^{\theta\left(\frac{1}{\psi}-\frac{1}{\nu}\right)} (R^W_{t+1})^{\theta-1},$$

where R^W_{t+1} is the gross return over the period from t to $t+1$ on the portfolio optimally chosen at time t. This combines Eqs. (9.21) and (9.44). The approximation (4.24) now implies a conditional expected excess return of

$$\begin{aligned} \mathrm{E}_t\left[R_{i,t+1}\right] - R^f_t \approx \frac{\theta}{\nu} \operatorname{Cov}_t\left[R_{i,t+1}, \ln \frac{c_{t+1}}{c_t}\right] + (1-\theta) \operatorname{Cov}_t\left[R_{i,t+1}, \ln R^W_{t+1}\right] \\ + \theta\left(\frac{1}{\nu} - \frac{1}{\psi}\right) \operatorname{Cov}_t\left[R_{i,t+1}, \ln \frac{v(q_{t+1}/c_{t+1})}{v(q_t/c_t)}\right]. \end{aligned} \tag{9.46}$$

As above, another approximation can eliminate the v-function so that the conditional expected excess return is

$$\begin{aligned} \mathrm{E}_t\left[R_{i,t+1}\right] - R^f_t &\approx \theta\left[\frac{1}{\nu} - b\left(\frac{1}{\nu} - \frac{1}{\psi}\right)\right] \operatorname{Cov}_t\left[R_{i,t+1}, \ln \frac{c_{t+1}}{c_t}\right] \\ &\quad + \theta b\left(\frac{1}{\nu} - \frac{1}{\psi}\right) \operatorname{Cov}_t\left[R_{i,t+1}, \ln \frac{q_{t+1}}{q_t}\right] \\ &\quad + (1-\theta) \operatorname{Cov}_t\left[R_{i,t+1}, \ln R^W_{t+1}\right]. \end{aligned} \tag{9.47}$$

If $\theta b\left(\frac{1}{\nu} - \frac{1}{\psi}\right) > 0$, there is a positive contribution to the risk premium from the covariance with the growth in consumption of the second good. This is satisfied when $\psi > \nu$ and $\gamma > 1 > \nu$. However, if $\gamma > 1/\nu > 1$, then $\theta > 1$ and the last term in Eq. (9.47) will tend to lower the risk premium.

Note that the above conclusions hold whether good 2 is a perishable or a durable good, compare the discussions in Section 6.4.2. If good 2 is a durable good, q_t in the above expressions represents the consumption services derived from the holdings (that is the stock) of the good at time t, not the purchases of the good at time t. If these consumption services are proportional to the holdings of the good, the utility can be expressed in the same form as Eq. (9.42) in terms of perishable consumption and the holdings of the durable good, although with a different weighting constant b. Hence, we can think of q_t in the above results as the holdings of the good.[4] As always, the state-price deflator is the marginal rate of substitution evaluated at the optimal consumption rate of the goods, and the optimal mix of consumption of the two goods will depend

[4] In the recursive utility framework, there is a small twist: R^W_{t+1} is then (a normalization of) the gross return on the optimal investment of the individual, including capital gains on the holdings of the durable good, compare Yogo (2006).

on the relative price of good 2 as well as the nature of good 2 (perishable or durable). But a representative individual must consume the aggregate supply of the two goods and assuming some exogenous processes for that supply, we can just substitute them in to get the appropriate state-price deflator and the induced risk premium.

With time-additive CES-power utility (9.42) we know from Eq. (6.29) that the next-period state-price deflator can be expressed as

$$\frac{\zeta_{t+1}}{\zeta_t} = e^{-\delta} \left(\frac{c_{t+1}}{c_t} \right)^{-\gamma} \left(\frac{\alpha_{t+1}}{\alpha_t} \right)^{\frac{\psi\gamma-1}{\psi-1}}, \tag{9.48}$$

where $\alpha_t = \frac{c_t}{c_t + P_t^q q_t}$, P_t^q is the price of good 2 (relative to good 1), and c_t and q_t are the optimal consumption rates of the two goods. If both goods are perishable, we can interpret α_t as the expenditure share of the first good at time t. Substituting Eq. (9.48) into the approximation (4.24), the risk premium on asset i can be approximated by

$$\mathrm{E}_t\left[R_{i,t+1}\right] - R_t^f \approx \gamma \operatorname{Cov}_t\left[R_{i,t+1}, \ln \frac{c_{t+1}}{c_t}\right] - \frac{\psi\gamma - 1}{\psi - 1} \operatorname{Cov}_t\left[R_{i,t+1}, \ln \frac{\alpha_{t+1}}{\alpha_t}\right].$$

Alternatively, define $z_t = \frac{c_t}{P_t^q q_t}$ which, if both goods are perishable, is the expenditure ratio (of good 1 to good 2). Note that $\alpha_t = z_t/(1+z_t)$ and substituting that into Eq. (9.48), we can express the state-price deflator as

$$\frac{\zeta_{t+1}}{\zeta_t} = e^{-\delta} \left(\frac{c_{t+1}}{c_t} \right)^{-\gamma} \left(\frac{z_{t+1}/(1+z_{t+1})}{z_t/(1+z_t)} \right)^{\frac{\psi\gamma-1}{\psi-1}}.$$

Due to the first-order Taylor approximation

$$\begin{aligned}
\ln(1+z_{t+1}) = \ln\left(1+e^{\ln z_{t+1}}\right) &\approx \ln\left(1+e^{\ln z_t}\right) + \frac{e^{\ln z_t}}{1+e^{\ln z_t}}\left(\ln z_{t+1} - \ln z_t\right) \\
&= \ln(1+z_t) + \frac{z_t}{1+z_t} \ln\left(\frac{z_{t+1}}{z_t}\right),
\end{aligned}$$

the log-state-price deflator is

$$\begin{aligned}
\ln\left(\frac{\zeta_{t+1}}{\zeta_t}\right) &= -\delta - \gamma \ln\left(\frac{c_{t+1}}{c_t}\right) + \frac{\psi\gamma - 1}{\psi - 1}\left(\ln\left(\frac{z_{t+1}}{z_t}\right) - \ln\left(\frac{1+z_{t+1}}{1+z_t}\right)\right) \\
&\approx -\delta - \gamma \ln\left(\frac{c_{t+1}}{c_t}\right) + \frac{\psi\gamma - 1}{\psi - 1} \frac{1}{1+z_t} \ln\left(\frac{z_{t+1}}{z_t}\right).
\end{aligned} \tag{9.49}$$

By Eq. (4.24), the risk premium on asset i is thus approximately

$$\begin{aligned}\mathrm{E}_t\left[R_{i,t+1}\right] - R_t^f \approx \gamma \operatorname{Cov}_t\left[R_{i,t+1}, \ln \frac{c_{t+1}}{c_t}\right] \\ - \frac{\psi\gamma - 1}{\psi - 1} \frac{1}{1+z_t} \operatorname{Cov}_t\left[R_{i,t+1}, \ln \frac{z_{t+1}}{z_t}\right].\end{aligned} \tag{9.50}$$

Note that these expressions are not true if good 2 is a durable good, at least not with the interpretation given for α and z.

9.5.2 Perishable and Durable Goods

Yogo (2006) divides the consumption data in the US national accounts into perishable (non-durable) and durable consumption. Perishable consumption is measured as expenditures on, for example, food, clothing, transportation, and housing. Durable consumption consists of motor vehicles, furniture and appliances, and jewellery and watches. He shows that the relative price of durable goods to perishable goods has a clear downward trend and the ratio of durable to perishable consumption has a clear upward trend over the period 1951–2001. Moreover, the ratio of durable to perishable consumption is strongly procyclical: it rises during booms and falls during recessions. Perishable consumption is less procyclical. For most stocks, the inequality (9.45) will therefore be satisfied in the data.

Yogo estimates and tests the durable-consumption model with recursive utility on observed returns on a short-term government bond and various portfolios of stocks in the same period. In all cases the estimate of the relative risk aversion γ is above 170 (and thus way too high), the elasticity of intertemporal substitution ν is around 0.02 (very low, but significantly different from $1/\gamma$), the elasticity of intratemporal substitution ψ is between 0.52 and 0.87, the weighting parameter b is around 0.8, whereas the subjective time preference rate is around 10% per quarter (and thus very high). Several of the parameter estimates are thus unrealistic.

The model requires a very high risk aversion to match the observed level of average stock returns so it is therefore not able to explain the equity premium puzzle. The Epstein–Zin separation of γ and $1/\nu$ helps to avoid the risk-free rate puzzle, in combination with a high time preference rate, but cannot at the same time solve the equity premium puzzle, compare the discussions earlier in the chapter. Yogo's study shows that even when adding durable goods, the model cannot explain the observed equity premium.

However, the durable consumption model succeeds along two other dimensions. First, it can explain observed differences in average stock returns across the firm size and the book-to-market equity value. It is well known that small stocks and value stocks (high book-to-market) tend to provide higher returns. This could be explained by a one-good consumption-based model if small stocks and value stocks have sufficiently higher betas with respect to the growth rate of the consumption of that good, relative to large stocks and growth stocks (low book-to-market). Small stocks do generally have somewhat higher betas with respect to perishable consumption than large stocks, but the difference is not large enough to explain the differences in average returns. And there seems to be no systematic variation in perishable consumption betas across different book-to-market values. Yogo shows that betas with respect to durable consumption growth are generally higher for small stocks than large stocks and considerably higher for high book-to-market stocks than low book-to-market stocks. Small stocks and value stocks deliver especially low returns during recessions when durable consumption decreases. With a positive risk premium on durable consumption growth, this helps in explaining the size and value anomalies. In fact, the model clearly outperforms the Fama–French three-factor model, which is otherwise considered to be a very successful empirical model, compare the discussion in Section 10.6.

Second, the model provides an explanation for variations in risk premia over time or, more precisely, over the business cycle. In recessions, durable consumption falls sharply relative to perishable consumption. As long as $\psi > \nu$ and $\gamma > 1 > \nu$, which is satisfied by Yogo's estimates, this implies a higher risk premium, as can be seen from Eqs. (9.46) or (9.47). The risk premium will vary counter-cyclically over time as observed in the data, at least for the stock market index.

For other studies of durable goods and asset prices, see Siegel (2005) and Gomes, Kogan, and Yogo (2009). The optimal consumption and portfolio decisions in the presence of a durable good have been discussed in a partial equilibrium setting by Grossman and Laroque (1990), Hindy and Huang (1993), Detemple and Giannikos (1996), Cuoco and Liu (2000), and Damgaard, Fuglsbjerg, and Munk (2003).

9.5.3 Housing

Other authors consider housing as the second good, whereas the consumption of all other goods is lumped together in the first good. Let us focus on the study of Piazzesi, Schneider, and Tuzel (2007) who develop a 'housing consumption-based CAPM'. They assume the CES-power utility function (9.42) in which q is interpreted as the quantity of housing services consumed and c is the consumption of all other goods. The state-price deflator (9.44) depends on the ratio of the consumption of housing services to the consumption of other goods, and the authors refer to variations in this ratio as *composition risk*.

The authors recognize that it is difficult to measure the quantity q_t of housing consumption, so they formulate the state-price deflator and the induced risk premium in terms of the expenditure share α_t. For the expenditures on housing consumption each period, they apply data from the US national accounts, which are based on surveys. Renters are asked for the dollar amount spent on rent, whereas home owners are asked for an estimate of how much they would rent their house/appartment for. This is taken to be an estimate of the costs $P^q_t q_t$ of the housing consumption. Housing services is then treated as a second perishable good, which is paid for and consumed each period.

Based on these data, the expenditure share of non-housing consumption is shown to fluctuate relatively little from year to year over the period 1929–2001 with an average value of 82.6% with a standard deviation of 1.5%, but there are some large periodic trends (upwards in 1930s and early 1940s, downwards in the 1950s, and a smaller upward trend in the 1990s). The limited fluctuations indicate that the elasticity of intratemporal substitution is different from one (so Cobb–Douglas utility is invalid), but close to one. The non-housing expenditure share is highly persistent, so even small shocks will have long-term effects. The non-housing consumption rate itself is much less persistent and the apparent persistence may be due to time aggregation.

Piazzesi, Schneider, and Tuzel formulate and calibrate the following model of the dynamics of non-housing consumption c_t and the expenditure ratio $z_t = c_t/(P^q_t q_t)$:

$$\ln \frac{c_{t+1}}{c_t} = \mu_c + \varepsilon^c_{t+1}, \quad \ln \frac{z_{t+1}}{z_t} = (1-\rho)(\mu_z - \ln z_t) + \varepsilon^z_{t+1},$$

where $\Delta \ln c_{t+1} = \ln c_{t+1} - \ln c_t$ and similarly for $\Delta \ln z_{t+1}$. Here, ε^c_{t+1} and ε^z_{t+1} are uncorrelated and normally distributed mean-zero shocks so that ε^c_{t+1} has a constant variance σ^2_c whereas the variance σ^2_{zt} of ε^z_{t+1} is an increasing function of $\ln z_t$ to capture the significant heteroskedasticity in the data.

For the stock market index, they assume dividend growth of the form

$$\ln \frac{D_{t+1}}{D_t} = \ln \frac{c_{t+1}}{c_t} + \varepsilon^D_{t+1},$$

where $\varepsilon^D_{t+1} \sim N(0, \sigma^2_D)$ is independent of the other shocks. Hence, aggregate dividend growth follows aggregate non-housing consumption growth but with higher volatility. Unfortunately, it is not possible to compute the price of this dividend stream,

$$P_t = \sum_{s=1}^{\infty} \mathrm{E}_t \left[\frac{\zeta_{t+s}}{\zeta_t} D_{t+s} \right],$$

in closed form, not even by applying the conditionally lognormal approximation (9.49) of the state-price deflator. But the price-dividend ratio of the stock index satisfies the recursive relation

$$\frac{P_t}{D_t} = \mathrm{E}_t\left[\frac{\zeta_{t+1}}{\zeta_t}\frac{P_{t+1}+D_{t+1}}{D_t}\right] = \mathrm{E}_t\left[\frac{\zeta_{t+1}}{\zeta_t}\left(\frac{P_{t+1}}{D_{t+1}}+1\right)\frac{D_{t+1}}{D_t}\right],$$

and the authors solve numerically for a stationary solution. The price-dividend ratio will depend on z_t. The expected return is then computed from

$$\mathrm{E}_t[R_{t+1}] = \mathrm{E}_t\left[\frac{P_{t+1}+D_{t+1}}{P_t}\right] = \mathrm{E}_t\left[\frac{P_{t+1}/D_{t+1}+1}{P_t/D_t+1}\frac{D_{t+1}}{D_t}\right].$$

While the equity premium reported by the authors is based on this exact expression, intuition can be gained by the approximation (9.50), which shows that the risk premium on the asset consists of a premium due to the covariance of the return with non-housing consumption and a premium due to the covariance with the ratio of non-housing to housing expenditures. The first covariance is small and, since this is the only premium in the simple consumption-based CAPM, this is the source of the equity premium puzzle. The covariance of the return of the stock market with the expenditure ratio is negative in the data, so we need $(\psi\gamma - 1)/(\psi - 1)$ to be positive to help explain the high equity premium. This is the case when $\psi\gamma > 1$ and $\psi > 1$ (under the reasonable assumption that $\gamma > 1$, the condition $\psi > 1$ is redundant).

As explained by Eq. (9.43) and the subsequent discussion, an individual with $\psi\gamma > 1$ greatly appreciates an asset that pays out a lot when the relative consumption of good 2 is low. Empirically, the stock market is negatively covarying with the expenditure ratio and therefore positively correlated with the relative consumption of good 2. Stocks perform badly when overall consumption is low and exceptionally badly when the housing consumption relative to overall consumption is also low—exactly when the individual needs extra funds the most. To hold the stock market, the individual therefore requires an extra risk premium.

The continuously compounded one-period risk-free rate can be approximated using Eq. (9.49):

$$\begin{aligned} r_t^f &= -\ln \mathrm{E}_t\left[\frac{\zeta_{t+1}}{\zeta_t}\right] \\ &\approx -\ln \mathrm{E}_t\left[\exp\left\{-\delta - \gamma\ln\left(\frac{c_{t+1}}{c_t}\right) + \frac{\psi\gamma-1}{\psi-1}\frac{1}{1+z_t}\ln\left(\frac{z_{t+1}}{z_t}\right)\right\}\right] \\ &= \delta + \gamma\mu_c - \frac{1}{2}\gamma^2\sigma_c^2 \\ &\quad - \frac{1}{1+z_t}\left(\frac{\psi\gamma-1}{\psi-1}(1-\rho)(\mu_z - \ln z_t) + \frac{1}{2}\left(\frac{\psi\gamma-1}{\psi-1}\right)^2\frac{1}{1+z_t}\sigma_{zt}^2\right). \end{aligned} \tag{9.51}$$

The first three terms on the right-hand side constitute the risk-free rate in the basic consumption-based CAPM. On average, $\ln z_t$ is equal to μ_z, and the last term is then positive, that is the risk-free rate tends to be lower in the housing CCAPM than in the simple one-good CCAPM (assuming the same γ in the two models). When individuals are averse to uncertainty about the composition of their consumption mix, an uncertainty represented by σ_{zt}^2, their precautionary savings are higher, which leads to a lower equilibrium interest rate.

The authors try various combinations of the preference parameters δ, γ, and ψ. In particular, with the apparently reasonable values $e^{-\delta} = 0.99$, $\gamma = 5$, and $\psi = 1.05$, they report a sizeable annual equity premium of 3.5% (roughly half of the equity premium in their data) with a standard deviation of 11.4% (compared to roughly 16% in their data). Their model delivers an average one-year risk-free rate of 1.8% (around 1% in their data) with a standard deviation of 0.9% (around 3% in their data). Hence, the model provides at least a partial resolution of the equity premium and the risk-free rate puzzles. A disturbing feature of their model is the fact that these numbers are highly sensitive to ψ. For example, increasing ψ to just 1.10, the equity premium drops to 1.4%, and the risk-free rate increases to 9.0%. In fact, when the authors implement a certain procedure to estimate ψ, they find a ψ of approximately 1.25. The key return statistics can be matched even with that value of ψ, but that requires a relative risk aversion of $\gamma = 16$ as well as a highly negative subjective time preference rate so that $e^{-\delta} = 1.24$, which seems absurd.

It is also clear from Eqs. (9.50) and (9.51) that both the expected excess return on risky assets and the risk-free rate vary with z_t. In severe recessions, individuals want to borrow to increase current consumption that has a high marginal utility and then pay back the loan next period, where the economy is expected to do better and marginal utility is lower. Therefore, to maintain market clearing, the risk-free rate goes up. This effect is captured by the first of the new terms in the expression for the risk-free rate since $\ln z_t > \mu_z$ in severe recessions. On the other hand, the composition risk is also higher in severe recessions, as σ_{zt}^2 is increasing in z_t, so precautionary savings increase in severe recessions, which leads to a lower risk-free rate. The two effects are thus counteracting. According to the authors, the net effect is that the risk-free rate increases in severe recessions. Except for the extreme situations, the risk-free rate is very stable.

The expected excess return on risky assets will also vary with the expenditure ratio z_t or, equivalently, the expenditure share α_t. For typical stocks, the covariance $\mathrm{Cov}_t[R_{i,t+1}, \ln(z_{t+1}/z_t)]$ is negative. If the absolute value of the covariance increases sufficiently fast with z_t, then the expected excess return in Eq. (9.50) will also increase with z_t. Hence, the expected excess return is higher in severe recessions. The expenditure ratio z_t or the expenditure share α_t should then be able to predict excess stock returns. Indeed, the authors confirm that this is the case in their data set. As the expenditure share moves slowly over time, so will expected returns.

For other studies of the impact of housing on equilibrium asset prices, the reader is referred to Lustig and van Nieuwerburgh (2005) and Favilukis, Ludvigson, and van Nieuwerburgh (2011). Portfolio choice in the presence of housing has been analysed by Campbell and Cocco (2003), Cocco (2005), Sinai and Souleles (2005), Yao and Zhang (2005), and Kraft and Munk (2011), among others.

9.5.4 Other Candidates for the Second Good

Another obvious candidate for a second good is leisure. Classic theories of labour economics assume that the utility of an individual is increasing in leisure or, equivalently, decreasing in the number of working hours supplied by the individual. You can think of leisure as a consumption good with a price equal to the wage income you give up when not working. Leisure and labour income are thus closely connected.

The human wealth of an individual is generally defined as the present value of the future labour income stream of the individual. If the labour income is either deterministic or is risky but spanned by the traded financial assets, and the individual can use his future income as collateral for a loan, then the human wealth can be computed just like the present value of any dividend stream. However, labour income is risky and not spanned and it cannot be fully collateralized, so the computation of human wealth is not that simple. According to empirical studies the correlation between the labour income of an individual and the overall stock market index is typically close to zero (Heaton and Lucas 2000; Campbell and Viceira 2002). Although you might be able to construct a different portfolio of traded assets that has a return which is more correlated with your income, a perfect correlation seems unattainable. Nevertheless, it is clear that human wealth is a major asset for many, in particular young, individuals. Therefore, it is potentially very important to include labour income and leisure in asset pricing models.

It is straightforward to include labour income in a representative agent modelling framework. Santos and Veronesi (2006) consider a representative individual economy in which consumption is the sum of a given labour income stream and dividends from financial assets. The relative weights of income and dividend in consumption vary over time, which lead to time-varying covariances between the stock market's dividend process and the state prices. Consequently, the stock market risk premium is time-varying in line with the evidence from empirical studies. Recall from Chapter 7 that the representative individual approach presumes (effectively) complete markets. But, as explained above, labour income is not spanned by traded assets and therefore individuals cannot fully hedge their labour income risk, which means that the financial market is incomplete. We return to the discussion of labour income in Section 9.6.2 below.

Aït-Sahalia, Parker, and Yogo (2004) suggest distinguishing between basic goods and luxury goods. Luxury goods are mostly consumed by rich individuals, who also own a large part of the stocks. Therefore, it is potentially important to include luxury consumption in consumption-based asset pricing studies. However, the authors argue that the consumption of luxury goods is not well covered either by typical survey consumption data or by aggregate consumption data in the national accounts. They form time series of luxury good consumption from the sales of luxury good retailers and show that luxury consumption has a significantly higher covariance with returns on the stock market than basic consumption has. They model preferences over basic consumption B and luxury consumption L by the additively separable utility function

$$u(B, L) = \frac{1}{1-\varphi}(B - \underline{B})^{1-\varphi} + \frac{1}{1-\psi}(L + \underline{L})^{1-\psi},$$

where $\varphi, \psi, \underline{B}, \underline{L} > 0$ with $\varphi > \psi$. Here $\underline{B}$ denotes a positive subsistence level of basic consumption, whereas $-\underline{L}$ denotes a negative subsistence level of luxury consumption. The relative risk aversion is $\varphi B/(B - \underline{B})$ with respect to gambles over basic consumption and $\psi L/(L + \underline{L})$ with respect to gambles over luxury consumption. Basic consumption dominates for poor individuals. In fact, individuals will not consume luxury goods as long as basic consumption does not exceed a certain level (which is higher than $\underline{B}$). Luxury consumption dominates for rich individuals. As total consumption expenditures increase towards infinity, the expenditure share of luxury consumption will approach one. The relative risk aversion with respect to total consumption expenditures is a weighted sum of φ and ψ and will decrease towards ψ as total consumption expenditures increase towards infinity. Based on their data, they estimate the relative risk aversion with respect to gambles over luxury consumption to be around 10 and conclude that, for the very rich, the equity premium is much less of a puzzle. However, the relative risk aversion with respect to luxury good consumption should probably be significantly lower than the relative risk aversion with respect to basic consumption so even the estimate of 10 seems much too high.

Lochstoer (2009) assumes instead a utility function of the form

$$u(B, L; X) = \frac{1}{1-\gamma}\left(L^{\alpha}[B - X]^{1-\alpha}\right)^{1-\gamma},$$

where $\alpha \in (0, 1)$ and $\gamma > 1$. Also here B is the consumption of basic goods and L the consumption of luxury goods. Furthermore, X is an external benchmark for basic consumption and works as a time-varying subsistence level of basic consumption similar to the Campbell–Cochrane model of Section 9.2.3. If P^L denotes the price of the luxury good relative to the price of the basic good, it can be shown (see Exercise 9.7) that the optimal consumption mix must satisfy $B - X = \frac{1-\alpha}{\alpha} P^L L$ and substituting that into the utility function, we get

$$\tilde{u}(L;P^L) = \left(\frac{1-\alpha}{\alpha}\right)^{1-\alpha} \left(P^L\right)^{(1-\alpha)(1-\gamma)} \frac{1}{1-\gamma} L^{1-\gamma}.$$

Therefore, Lochstoer interprets γ as a relative risk aversion with respect to gambles over luxury consumption. Note, however, that by differentiating the original utility function, we get a relative risk aversion of $-Lu_{LL}/u_L = 1 + \alpha(\gamma - 1)$, which is smaller than γ. He sets $\gamma = 10$ and $\alpha = 0.05$, in which case the latter risk aversion is just 1.45, which seems reasonable for luxury consumption. The relative risk aversion with respect to gambles over basic consumption is $-Bu_{BB}/u_B = [\gamma - \alpha(\gamma - 1)]B/(B - X)$. With an average value of the 'surplus basic consumption ratio' $(B - X)/B$ of 0.057 as in the Campbell–Cochrane paper, this relative risk aversion becomes $9.55/0.057 \approx 168$, which is way too high. Lochstoer specifies the dynamics in aggregate luxury consumption and the price of luxury goods with GARCH-type processes exhibiting time-varying volatility, which will then induce fluctuations in the risk-free rate and the Sharpe ratio of the stock market, compare Exercise 9.7, in line with observed variations. For more on luxury goods, see Wachter and Yogo (2010).

9.6 INCOMPLETE MARKETS

9.6.1 Evidence that Market Incompleteness Matters

Some empirical asset pricing studies indicate that markets are incomplete so that the traditional representative-individual approach may break down. The marginal rate of substitution of each individual defines a state-price deflator. It follows from Theorem 4.7 that a weighted average of state-price deflators is also a state-price deflator. Brav, Constantinides, and Geczy (2002) assume that all individuals have time-additive CRRA utility with the same time preference rate δ and the same relative risk aversion γ so that the state-price deflator for individual l is $e^{-\delta t}\,(c_{lt}/c_{l0})^{-\gamma}$. An equally-weighted average over L individuals gives the state-price deflator

$$\zeta_t = e^{-\delta t} \frac{1}{L} \sum_{l=1}^{L} \left(\frac{c_{lt}}{c_{l0}}\right)^{-\gamma}.$$

Using data on the consumption of individual households, the authors find that this state-price deflator is consistent with the historical excess returns on the US stock market for a risk aversion parameter as low as 3. If the market were complete, consumption growth c_{lt}/c_{l0} would be the same for all individuals under these assumptions, and

$$\zeta_t = e^{-\delta t} \left(\frac{\sum_{l=1}^{L} c_{lt}}{\sum_{l=1}^{L} c_{l0}}\right)^{-\gamma} \tag{9.52}$$

would be a valid state-price deflator. Summing up over all individuals in this formula, we get the state-price deflator for a representative individual, who will also have relative risk aversion equal to γ, but this is inconsistent with data except for unreasonably high values of γ. This study therefore indicates that financial markets are incomplete and do not allow individuals to align their marginal rates of substitution.

As already mentioned in Section 8.5, a large, but declining, fraction of individuals do not invest in stock markets at all or only to a very limited extent. Brav, Constantinides, and Geczy (2002) show that if in Eq. (9.52) you only sum up over individuals holding financial assets with a value higher than some threshold, this state-price deflator is consistent with historical data for a relative risk aversion which is relatively high, but much lower than the required risk aversion using aggregate consumption. The higher the threshold, the lower the required risk aversion. This result reflects that only the individuals active in the financial markets contribute to the setting of prices. Other empirical studies report similar findings, and Başak and Cuoco (1998) set up a formal asset pricing model that explicitly distinguishes between individuals owning stocks and individuals not owning stocks.

9.6.2 Unspanned Labour Income Risk

In Section 9.5.4 we briefly discussed the impact of labour income and leisure in a representative individual framework. However, to be sure a representative individual exists, the financial markets have to be complete or effectively complete, which is not the case when investors have non-traded income streams. The labour income of individuals is not fully insurable, either through investments in financial assets or through existing insurance contracts. A number of papers investigate how non-hedgeable income shocks may affect the pricing of financial assets. If unexpected changes in labour income are temporary, individuals may self-insure by building up a buffer of savings in order to even out the consumption effects of the income shocks over the entire life. The effects on equilibrium asset prices will be insignificant, compare Telmer (1993). Similar computational results are reported by Aiyagari and Gertler (1991) and Heaton and Lucas (1996), whereas Levine and Zame (2002) arrive at the same conclusion in a theoretical study. If income shocks are to help resolve the equity premium puzzle, the shocks have to affect income beyond the current period. In addition, the magnitude of the income shocks has to be negatively related to the level of stock prices. Both the persistency of income shocks and the counter-cyclical variation in income seem reasonable in light of the risk of layoffs and find empirical support, compare Storesletten, Telmer, and Yaron (2004). Individuals facing such an income uncertainty will demand higher risk premia on stocks than in a model without labour income because stocks do badly exactly when individuals face the highest risk of an unexpected decline in income.

In a model where all individuals have time-additive CRRA utility, Constantinides and Duffie (1996) show by construction that if the income processes of different individuals are sufficiently different in a certain sense then their model with any given risk aversion can generate basically any pattern in aggregate consumption and financial prices, including the puzzling historical pattern. However, Cochrane (2005, Ch. 21) argues that with a realistic degree of cross-sectional variation in individual labour income, a relatively high value of the risk aversion parameter is still needed to match historical data. Nevertheless, it seems to be important to incorporate the labour income uncertainty of individuals and in particular the difference between the labour income processes of different individuals in the development of better asset pricing models.

Constantinides, Donaldson, and Mehra (2002) emphasize that individuals choose consumption and investment from a life-cycle perspective and face different opportunities and risks at different ages. They divide individuals into young, middle-aged, and old individuals. Old individuals only consume the savings they have built up earlier, do not receive further income, and do not invest in financial assets. Young individuals typically have a low financial wealth and a low current labour income but a high human capital (the present value of their future labour income). Many young individuals would prefer borrowing significant amounts both in order to smooth out consumption over life and to be able to invest in the stock market to generate additional consumption opportunities and obtain the optimal risk/return tradeoff. The empirically observed low correlation between labour income and stock returns makes stock investments even more attractive for young individuals. Unfortunately it is difficult to borrow significant amounts just because you expect to get a high future income and, therefore, the young individuals can only invest very little, if anything, in the stock market. Middle-aged individuals face a different situation. Their future labour income is limited and relatively certain. Their future consumption opportunities are primarily depending on the return on their investments. For middle-aged individuals the correlation between stock returns and future consumption is thus quite high so stocks are not as attractive for them. Nevertheless, due to the borrowing constraints on the young individuals, the stocks have to be owned by the middle-aged individuals and, hence, the equilibrium expected rate of return has to be quite high. The authors set up a relatively simple model formalizing these thoughts, and the model is able to explain an equity premium significantly higher than in the standard model, but still below the historically observed premium.

Christensen, Larsen, and Munk (2012) provide a closed-form solution for the equilibrium risk-free rate and the equilibrium stock price in a continuous-time economy with heterogeneous investor preferences and unspanned income risk. They show that lowering the fraction of income risk spanned by the market produces a lower equilibrium risk-free rate and a lower stock market Sharpe ratio, partly due to changes in the aggregate consumption dynamics. When they fix the aggregate consumption dynamics, the Sharpe ratio is the same as in an otherwise identical representative agent economy in which all risks are spanned, whereas the risk-free rate (and the expected stock return) is lower in the economy with unspanned income risk due to an increased demand for precautionary savings. The reduction in the risk-free rate is highest when the more risk-averse investors face the largest unspanned income risk. In numerical examples with reasonable parameters, they show that the risk-free rate is reduced by several percentage points. The closed-form solution hinges on negative exponential utility and normally distributed dividends and income but, nevertheless, the results show that unspanned income risk may in more general settings play an important role in explaining the so-called risk-free rate puzzle.

Other studies of the impact of labour income on financial asset prices include Eichenbaum, Hansen, and Singleton (1988), Weil (1992), Huggett (1993), Lucas (1994), Jagannathan and Wang (1996), Elul (1997), Krusell and Smith (1997), Storesletten, Telmer, and Yaron (2004, 2007), Krueger and Lustig (2010), Krusell, Mukoyama, and Smith (2011), Kuehn, Petrosky-Nadeau, and Zhang (2011), and Favilukis and Lin (2011). The effect of labour income on the optimal consumption and investment decisions of an individual has been investigated in various models by Bodie, Merton, and Samuelson (1992), Heaton and Lucas (1997), Munk (2000), Viceira (2001), Cocco, Gomes, and Maenhout (2005), Munk and Sørensen (2010), Lynch and Tan (2011), and Kraft and Munk (2011), among others.

9.7 CONCLUDING REMARKS

The previous chapter concluded that the simple consumption-based CAPM is unable to match a number of features of consumption and return data. This chapter has shown that a number of relatively recent theoretical and empirical studies identify extensions of the simple model that are able to eliminate (or at least reduce the magnitude of) several of the puzzles left by the simple model. These extensions include state-dependent preferences, heterogeneous risk aversion, long-run risks, disastrous consumption shocks, durable consumption, and labour income risk. The consumption-based asset pricing framework is alive and kicking.

In addition to the models and ideas described in this chapter, there are numerous other consumption-based models. For example, a number of papers have investigated the asset pricing implications of assuming that aggregate consumption is the sum of a number of simple exogenous stochastic processes, which can represent the consumption opportunities generated by different asset classes, industries, or countries. In the standard model the exogenous consumption is often referred to as the fruits falling from a tree—sometimes called a Lucas tree due to the important paper of Lucas (1978)—so the extensions are termed multiple-tree models. This idea was initiated by Cochrane, Longstaff, and Santa-Clara (2008) in a simple setting with two independent trees both generating dividends or consumption following a geometric Brownian motion as well as a representative individual with time-additive log utility. Subsequently, the work has been extended to general power and Epstein–Zin utility, dependent trees, and more general dividend processes, see for example Buraschi, Porchia, and Trojani (2010), Branger, Schlag, and Wu (2011), Martin (2011), and Branger, Kraft, and Meinerding (2012). The most fundamental insight of the multiple-tree models is that the market-clearing mechanism has an important impact on asset price dynamics at least in the short run where the size of each tree cannot be adjusted by reallocating investments across the different dividend-producing trees. When there is a positive shock to one tree, investors want to reduce their holdings of shares of that tree and increase their holdings of shares of the other trees in order to restore optimal diversification. In the short run, however, the aggregate supply of shares of each tree is fixed, so prices have to adjust to maintain market clearing. Even when the dividend processes of the individual trees are very simple, the market clearing effects generate interesting price dynamics.

A potential problem of all the tests and practical implementations of consumption-based models, however, is the need for good data on individual or aggregate consumption. As explained in Section 8.5.1, there are many concerns about the available consumption data. This motivates the next chapter which discusses asset pricing models not relying on consumption data.

9.8 EXERCISES

Exercise 9.1 Give a proof of Theorem 9.1.

Exercise 9.2 Consider the Chan and Kogan model. Show the expressions in Eqs. (9.15), (9.16), (9.17), (9.18), and (9.19). Show Theorem 9.3.

Exercise 9.3 In the Chan and Kogan model, show how Eq. (9.20) follows from Eq. (9.6). Note: with a continuum of individuals, the sum over individuals should be replaced by an integral, that is $\sum_{l=1}^{L}\left(\frac{1}{A_l(c_{lt},X_t)}\right)$ is replaced by $\int_1^{\infty}\left(\frac{1}{A(c_t,X_t;\gamma)}\right)\,d\gamma$, where $A(c_t,X_t;\gamma)$ is the absolute risk aversion of the individual with utility parameter γ.

Exercise 9.4 Consider a continuous-time economy with complete markets and a representative individual having an 'external habit formation' or 'keeping up with the

Joneses' utility function so that, at any time t, the individual wants to maximize $\mathrm{E}_t\left[\int_t^T e^{-\delta(s-t)} u(c_s, X_s)\, ds\right]$, where $u(c, X) = \frac{1}{1-\gamma}(c - X)^{1-\gamma}$ for $c > X \geq 0$.

Define $Y_t = -\ln\left(1 - \frac{X_t}{c_t}\right)$.

(a) Argue that Y_t is positive. Would you call a situation where Y_t is high a 'good state' or a 'bad state'? Explain!

(b) Argue that the unique state-price deflator is given by

$$\zeta_t = e^{-\delta t} \frac{c_t^{-\gamma} e^{\gamma Y_t}}{c_0^{-\gamma} e^{\gamma Y_0}}.$$

First, write the dynamics of consumption and the variable Y_t in the general way:

$$dc_t = c_t[\mu_{ct}\, dt + \boldsymbol{\sigma}_{ct}^{\mathsf{T}}\, d\boldsymbol{z}_t],$$
$$dY_t = \mu_{Yt}\, dt + \boldsymbol{\sigma}_{Yt}^{\mathsf{T}}\, d\boldsymbol{z}_t,$$

where $\boldsymbol{z} = (\boldsymbol{z}_t)$ is a multidimensional standard Brownian motion.

(c) Find the dynamics of the state-price deflator and identify the continuously compounded short-term risk-free interest rate r_t^f and the market price of risk $\boldsymbol{\lambda}_t$.

An asset i pays an uncertain terminal dividend but no intermediate dividends. The price dynamics is of the form

$$dP_{it} = P_{it}\left[\mu_{it}\, dt + \boldsymbol{\sigma}_{it}^{\mathsf{T}}\, d\boldsymbol{z}_t\right].$$

(d) Explain why

$$\mu_{it} - r_t^f = \beta_{ict}\eta_{ct} + \beta_{iYt}\eta_{Yt},$$

where $\beta_{ict} = (\boldsymbol{\sigma}_{it}^{\mathsf{T}}\boldsymbol{\sigma}_{ct})/\|\boldsymbol{\sigma}_{ct}\|^2$ and $\beta_{iYt} = (\boldsymbol{\sigma}_{it}^{\mathsf{T}}\boldsymbol{\sigma}_{Yt})/\|\boldsymbol{\sigma}_{Yt}\|^2$. Express η_{ct} and η_{Yt} in terms of previously introduced parameters and variables.

Next, consider the specific model:

$$dc_t = c_t[\mu_c\, dt + \sigma_c\, dz_{1t}],$$
$$dY_t = \kappa[\bar{Y} - Y_t]\, dt + \sigma_Y\sqrt{Y_t}\left(\rho\, dz_{1t} + \sqrt{1-\rho^2}\, dz_{2t}\right),$$

where $(z_1, z_2)^{\mathsf{T}}$ is a two-dimensional standard Brownian motion, μ_c, σ_c, κ, $\bar{Y}$, and σ_Y are positive constants, and $\rho \in (-1, 1)$.

(e) What is the short-term risk-free interest rate and the market price of risk in the specific model?

Assume that the price dynamics of asset i is

$$dP_{it} = P_{it}\left[\mu_{it}\, dt + \sigma_{it}\left(\psi\, dz_{1t} + \sqrt{1-\psi^2}\, dz_{2t}\right)\right],$$

where $\sigma_{it} > 0$ and $\psi \in (-1, 1)$.

(f) What is the Sharpe ratio of asset i in the specific model? Can the specific model generate counter-cyclical variation in Sharpe ratios (if necessary, provide parameter conditions ensuring this)?

Exercise 9.5 Consider the set-up of Exercise 6.10 with $u(c,h) = \frac{1}{1-\gamma}\,(c-h)^{1-\gamma}$.

(a) Can optimal consumption follow a geometric Brownian motion under these assumptions?

(b) Assume that the *excess* consumption rate $\hat{c}_t = c_t - h_t$ follows a geometric Brownian motion. Show that the state-price deflator will be of the form $\zeta_t = f(t)e^{-\delta t}\hat{c}_t^{-\gamma}$ for some deterministic function $f(t)$ (and find that function). Find an expression for the equilibrium interest rate and the market price of risk. Compare with the 'simple model' with no habit, CRRA utility, and consumption following a geometric Brownian motion.

Exercise 9.6 (This problem is based on Menzly, Santos, and Veronesi (2004).) Consider an economy with a representative agent with life-time utility given by

$$U(C) = \mathrm{E}\left[\int_0^\infty e^{-\varphi t}\ln(C_t - X_t)\,dt\right],$$

where X_t is an external habit level and φ is a subjective discount rate. As in Campbell and Cochrane (1999) define the surplus ratio as $S_t = (C_t - X_t)/C_t$. Define $Y_t = 1/S_t$. Aggregate consumption C_t is assumed to follow a geometric Brownian motion

$$dC_t = C_t\left[\mu_C\,dt + \sigma_C\,dz_t\right],$$

where μ_C and σ_C are constants and z is a one-dimensional standard Brownian motion. The dynamics of the habit level is modelled through

$$dY_t = k[\bar{Y} - Y_t]\,dt - \alpha(Y_t - \kappa)\sigma_C\,dz_t,$$

where $k, \bar{Y}, \alpha$, and κ are constants.

(a) Show that $\mathrm{E}_t[Y_\tau] = \bar{Y} + (Y_t - \bar{Y})e^{-k(\tau - t)}$.

(b) For any given dividend process $D = (D_t)$ in this economy, argue that the price is given by

$$P_t^D = (C_t - X_t)\,\mathrm{E}_t\left[\int_t^\infty e^{-\varphi(\tau - t)}\frac{D_\tau}{C_\tau - X_\tau}\,d\tau\right].$$

Let $s_\tau^D = D_\tau/C_\tau$ denote the dividend's share of aggregate consumption. Show that the price P_t^D satisfies

$$\frac{P_t^D}{C_t} = \frac{1}{Y_t}\,\mathrm{E}_t\left[\int_t^\infty e^{-\varphi(\tau - t)}s_\tau^D Y_\tau\,d\tau\right].$$

(c) Show that the price P_t^C of a claim to the aggregate consumption stream $D_\tau = C_\tau$ is given by

$$\frac{P_t^C}{C_t} = \frac{1}{\varphi + k}\left(1 + \frac{k\bar{Y}}{\varphi} S_t\right).$$

(d) Find the dynamics of the state-price deflator. Find and interpret expressions for the risk-free interest rate and the market price of risk in this economy.

Exercise 9.7 (This problem is based on Lochstoer (2009).) Suppose a representative individual has preferences of the form

$$\mathrm{E}\left[\sum_{t=0}^{T} e^{-\delta t} u(B_t, L_t; X_t)\right], \qquad u(B, L; X) = \frac{1}{1-\gamma}\left(L^{\alpha}[B-X]^{1-\alpha}\right)^{1-\gamma},$$

where $\alpha \in (0,1)$ and $\gamma > 1$. Here B_t denotes the time t consumption of basic goods and L_t the consumption of luxury goods. X is an external benchmark for basic consumption and works as a time-varying subsistence level of basic consumption similar to the Campbell–Cochrane model of Section 9.2.3. Let the basic good be the numeraire and let P_t^L denote the time t price of the luxury good (in units of the basic good).

(a) Argue why the optimal consumption of the two goods must be so that

$$B_t - X_t = \frac{1-\alpha}{\alpha} P_t^L L_t.$$

The state-price deflator process is in this case given by

$$\zeta_t = e^{-\delta t} \frac{u_B(B_t, L_t; X_t)}{u_B(B_0, L_0; X_0)}.$$

Let $M_{t+1} = \zeta_{t+1}/\zeta_t$ denote the next-period state-price deflator.

(b) Show that

$$M_{t+1} = e^{-\delta}\left(\frac{L_{t+1}}{L_t}\right)^{-\gamma}\left(\frac{P_{t+1}^L}{P_t^L}\right)^{-\gamma+\alpha(\gamma-1)}.$$

Let $\ell_t = \ln L_t$, $p_t^L = \ln P_t^L$, $\Delta\ell_{t+1} = \ell_{t+1} - \ell_t$, and $\Delta p_{t+1}^L = p_{t+1}^L - p_t^L$. Suppose that

$$\begin{aligned}
\Delta\ell_{t+1} &= a_\ell + b_\ell \sigma_{\ell,t}^2 + \sigma_{\ell,t}\varepsilon_{\ell,t+1}, \\
\ln \sigma_{\ell,t}^2 &= \omega_\ell + \beta_{1,\ell}\varepsilon_{\ell,t} + \beta_{2,\ell} \ln \sigma_{\ell,t-1}^2, \\
\Delta p_{t+1}^L &= a_p + b_p \sigma_{p,t}^2 + \sigma_{p,t}^2 \varepsilon_{p,t+1}, \\
\ln \sigma_{p,t}^2 &= \omega_p + \beta_{1,p}\varepsilon_{p,t} + \beta_{2,p} \ln \sigma_{p,t-1}^2,
\end{aligned}$$

where $\varepsilon_{\ell,t+1}, \varepsilon_{p,t+1} \sim N(0,1)$ with $\mathrm{Corr}[\varepsilon_{\ell,t+1}, \varepsilon_{p,t+1}] = \rho$.

(c) Compute the continuously compounded one-period risk-free interest rate, r_t^f.

(d) Compute the maximal conditional Sharpe ratio based on log-returns, that is the maximal possible value of

$$\frac{\mathrm{E}_t[r_{i,t+1}] - r_t^f + \frac{1}{2}\sigma_{i,t}^2}{\sigma_{i,t}}$$

over all risky assets i, compare Eq. (4.25). Here $\sigma_{i,t}^2 = \mathrm{Var}_t[r_{i,t+1}]$.

(e) Discuss the potential of this model in explaining asset pricing puzzles.

Exercise 9.8 (This problem is based on Longstaff and Piazzesi (2004).) Consider a continuous-time model of an economy with a representative agent and a single non-durable good. The objective of the agent at any time t is to maximize the expected time-additive CRRA utility,

$$\mathrm{E}_t\left[\int_t^\infty e^{-\delta(s-t)}\frac{C_s^{1-\gamma}}{1-\gamma}\,ds\right],$$

where $\gamma > 0$ and C_s denotes the consumption rate at time s. The agent can invest in a bank account, that is borrow and lend at a short-term interest rate of r_t. The bank account is in zero net supply. A single stock with a net supply of one share is available for trade. The agent is initially endowed with this share. The stock pays a continuous dividend at the rate D_t. The agent receives an exogenously given labour income at the rate I_t.

(a) Explain why the equilibrium consumption rate must equal the sum of the dividend rate and the labour income rate, that is $C_t = I_t + D_t$.

Let F_t denote the dividend-consumption ratio, that is $F_t = D_t/C_t$. Assume that $F_t = \exp\{-X_t\}$, where $X = (X_t)$ is the diffusion process

$$dX_t = (\mu - \kappa X_t)\,dt - \eta\sqrt{X_t}\,dz_{1t}.$$

Here μ, κ, and η are positive constants and $z_1 = (z_{1t})$ is a standard Brownian motion.

(b) Explain why F_t is always between zero and one.

Assume that the aggregate consumption process is given by the dynamics

$$dC_t = C_t\left[\alpha\,dt + \sigma\sqrt{X_t}\rho\,dz_{1t} + \sigma\sqrt{X_t}\sqrt{1-\rho^2}\,dz_{2t}\right],$$

where α, σ, and ρ are constants and $z_2 = (z_{2t})$ is another standard Brownian motion, independent of z_1.

(c) What is the equilibrium short-term interest rate in this economy?

(d) Use Itô's Lemma to derive the dynamics of F_t and of D_t.

(e) Show that the volatility of the dividend rate (the standard deviation of the relative changes in the dividend rate) is greater than the volatility of the consumption rate (the standard deviation of the relative changes in the consumption rate) if and only if $\sigma\rho > -\eta/2$.

Let P_t denote the price of the stock, that is the present value of all the future dividends.

(f) Show that the stock price can be written as

$$P_t = C_t^\gamma \, \mathrm{E}_t\left[\int_t^\infty e^{-\delta(s-t)} C_s^{1-\gamma} F_s \, ds\right].$$

It can be shown that P_t can be written as a function of t, C_t, and F_t:

$$P_t = C_t \int_t^\infty e^{-\delta(s-t)} A(t,s) F_t^{-B(t,s)} \, ds.$$

Here $A(t,s)$ and $B(t,s)$ are some deterministic functions of time that we will leave unspecified.

(g) Use Itô's Lemma to show that

$$dP_t = P_t\left[\dots dt + (\rho\sigma + \eta H_t)\sqrt{X_t}\, dz_{1t} + \sigma\sqrt{1-\rho^2}\sqrt{X_t}\, dz_{2t}\right],$$

where the drift term is left out (you do not have to compute the drift term!) and where

$$H_t = \frac{-\int_t^\infty e^{-\delta(s-t)} A(t,s) B(t,s) F_t^{-B(t,s)} \, ds}{\int_t^\infty e^{-\delta(s-t)} A(t,s) F_t^{-B(t,s)} \, ds}.$$

(h) Show that the expected excess rate of return on the stock at time t can be written as

$$\psi_t = \gamma X_t \left(\sigma^2 + \sigma\rho\eta H_t\right)$$

and as

$$\psi_t = \gamma \sigma_{Ct}^2 + \gamma \rho H_t \sigma_{Ct} \sigma_{Ft},$$

where σ_{Ct} and σ_{Ft} denote the percentage volatility of C_t and F_t, respectively.

(i) What would the expected excess rate of return on the stock be if the dividend-consumption ratio was deterministic? Explain why the model with stochastic dividend-consumption ratio has the potential to resolve (at least partially) the equity premium puzzle.

Exercise 9.9 Consider a discrete-time representative individual economy equipped with preferences $\mathrm{E}[\sum_{t=0}^\infty e^{-\delta t} u(c_t, q_t)]$, where c_t is the consumption of good 1 and q_t is the consumption of good 2. Assume a Cobb–Douglas type utility function,

$$u(c,q) = \frac{1}{1-\gamma}\left(c^\alpha q^{1-\alpha}\right)^{1-\gamma}$$

where $\gamma > 0$ and $\alpha \in [0,1]$.

(a) Determine the next-period state-price deflator ζ_{t+1}/ζ_t in terms of c_{t+1}/c_t, q_{t+1}/q_t, and the preference parameters.

Assume that

$$\ln\left(\frac{c_{t+1}}{c_t}\right) = \mu_c + \sigma_c \varepsilon^c_{t+1},$$

$$\ln\left(\frac{q_{t+1}}{q_t}\right) = \mu_{qt} + \sigma_{qt}\left(\rho\varepsilon^c_{t+1} + \sqrt{1-\rho^2}\varepsilon^q_{t+1}\right),$$

where $\sigma_c > 0$, $\rho \in (-1, 1)$, σ_{qt} is a positive stochastic process, and ε^c_{t+1} and ε^q_{t+1} are independent $N(0, 1)$-distributed random variables.

(b) Determine the equilibrium one-period risk-free interest rate (with continuous compounding).

(c) What can you say about expected excess returns and Sharpe ratios on risky assets without additional assumptions? What if you assume that the log-return satisfies

$$\ln R_{i,t+1} = \mu_{it} + \sigma_{it}\left(\xi_1\varepsilon^c_{t+1} + \xi_2\varepsilon^q_{t+1} + \xi_3\varepsilon^i_{t+1}\right),$$

where ε^i_{t+1} is also $N(0, 1)$-distributed and independent of ε^c_{t+1} and ε^q_{t+1} and $\xi_3 = \sqrt{1-\xi_1^2-\xi_2^2}$?

(d) Discuss the potential of such a model for explaining the equity premium puzzle, the risk-free rate puzzle, and the predictability puzzle.

Exercise 9.10 Consider a continuous-time economy with a representative agent with time-additive subsistence HARA utility, that is the objective of the agent is to maximize

$$\mathrm{E}\left[\int_0^T e^{-\delta t}\frac{1}{1-\gamma}\left(c_t - \bar{c}\right)^{1-\gamma}\, dt\right],$$

where $\bar{c} \geq 0$ is the subsistence consumption level. Assume that aggregate consumption $c = (c_t)$ evolves as

$$dc_t = \mu c_t\, dt + \sigma\sqrt{c_t(c_t - \bar{c})}\, dz_t,$$

where $z = (z_t)$ is a (one-dimensional) standard Brownian motion. Find the equilibrium short-term interest rate r^f_t and the market price of risk λ_t, expressed in terms of c_t and the parameters introduced above. How do r^f_t and λ_t depend on the consumption level? Are r^f_t and λ_t higher or lower or unchanged relative to the standard case in which $\bar{c} = 0$?

Exercise 9.11 Consider a one-period, finite-state economy where an individual has utility from the consumption of two goods. The consumption of the first good is denoted by c, and the consumption of the second good is denoted by q. The first good is the numeraire good, and P^q denotes the price of the second good. The individual is assumed to have time-additive expected utility and therefore faces the problem

$$\max u(c_0, q_0) + e^{-\delta} \sum_{\omega=1}^{S} p_\omega u(c_\omega, q_\omega),$$

$$\text{s.t. } c_0 + P_0^q q_0 \leq e_0 - \sum_{i=1}^{I} \theta_i P_i,$$

$$c_\omega + P_\omega^q q_\omega \leq e_\omega + \sum_{i=1}^{I} D_{i\omega}\theta_i, \quad \omega = 1, \dots, S,$$

where we assume the separable utility function

$$u(c, q) = \frac{1}{1-\gamma} c^{1-\gamma} + b \frac{1}{1-\gamma} q^{1-\gamma}$$

for some constants $b > 0$ and $\gamma > 1$. The choice variables are the portfolio $\boldsymbol{\theta} = (\theta_1, \dots, \theta_I)^\mathsf{T}$, time 0 consumption (c_0, q_0), and state-dependent time 1 consumption $(c_1, q_1), \dots, (c_S, q_S)$.

(a) Set up the Lagrangian associated with the problem and show that the first-order conditions with respect to c_0 and q_0 imply that

$$c_0 = b^{-1/\gamma} (P_0^q)^{1/\gamma} q_0.$$

Similarly, show that the first-order conditions with respect to c_ω and q_ω imply that

$$c_\omega = b^{-1/\gamma} (P_\omega^q)^{1/\gamma} q_\omega, \quad \omega = 1, \dots, S.$$

Explain why these relations make economic sense.

(b) Show that the first-order condition with respect to θ_i implies that

$$\zeta = e^{-\delta} \left(\frac{c}{c_0} \right)^{-\gamma}$$

is a valid state-price deflator.

(c) Discuss the potential of a model with the above preferences for explaining the standard asset pricing puzzles.

10

Factor Models

10.1 INTRODUCTION

The consumption-based asset pricing models studied in the preceding chapters are very elegant and provide an intuitive link between asset prices and consumption decisions. Unfortunately, the quality of the available consumption data is questionable, as discussed in Section 8.5, which complicates tests and applications of the models. Most tests find it problematic to match the (simple) consumption-based model and historical return and consumption data (of poor quality). This motivates a search for models linking asset prices and returns to other factors than consumption.

The classic CAPM is the 'mother of all factor models'. It links expected excess returns (on stocks) to the return on the market portfolio (of stocks). It was originally developed in a one-period framework but can be generalized to multiperiod settings. The model is based on rather unrealistic assumptions and the empirical success of the CAPM is modest.

Many, many papers have tried to identify factor models that perform better, mostly by adding factors supplementing the return on the stock market portfolio. However, this should only be done with extreme care. In a given data set of historical returns it is always possible to find a return that works as a pricing factor, as already indicated in Chapter 4. In fact, any ex-post mean-variance efficient return will work. On the other hand, there is generally no reason to believe that the same return will work as a pricing factor in the future. Factors should be justified by economic arguments or even backed by a formal asset pricing model.

It is worth emphasizing that the general theoretical results of the consumption-based asset pricing framework are not challenged by factor models. The problem with the consumption-based models is the implementation. Factor models do not invalidate the consumption-based asset pricing framework but are special cases that may be easier to apply and test. Therefore factors should generally help explain typical individuals' marginal utilities of consumption.

Section 10.2 defines and studies pricing factors in the one-period setting. In particular, pricing factors are linked to state-price deflators. The classic CAPM and the Arbitrage Pricing Theory are also reviewed. The relation between mean-variance efficient returns and pricing factors is the topic of Section 10.3. Pricing factors in discrete-time, multiperiod models are introduced in Section 10.4 with a discussion of the distinction between conditional and unconditional pricing factors. Section 10.5 considers the continuous-time case. Finally, Section 10.6 offers a brief overview of empirical studies of factor models.

10.2 PRICING FACTORS IN A ONE-PERIOD FRAMEWORK

We already defined a pricing factor in the one-period framework in Section 4.6.2, where we also briefly touched upon the relation between pricing factors and state-price deflators. But there we considered only the one-dimensional version of a pricing factor, and we did not give a complete presentation of the properties of pricing factors. Below we generalize the analysis to the case of multidimensional factors and give a more rigorous and complete treatment.

10.2.1 Definition and Basic Properties

Recall that for any K-dimensional random variable $\boldsymbol{x} = (x_1, \ldots, x_K)^\top$, the variance-covariance matrix $\mathrm{Var}[\boldsymbol{x}]$ is the $K \times K$ matrix with entry (i,j) given by $\mathrm{Cov}[x_i, x_j]$. If y is a one-dimensional random variable, then $\mathrm{Cov}[\boldsymbol{x}, y]$ is the K-dimensional vector with i'th entry given by $\mathrm{Cov}[x_i, y]$. We now formally define a pricing factor in a one-period setting:

Definition 10.1 *In a one-period framework, a pricing factor is a random variable $\boldsymbol{x} = (x_1, \ldots, x_K)^\top$ of some dimension K so that (i) the variance-covariance matrix* $\mathrm{Var}[\boldsymbol{x}]$ *is non-singular and (ii) constants $\alpha \in \mathbb{R}$ and $\boldsymbol{\eta} \in \mathbb{R}^K$ exist so that*

$$\mathrm{E}[R_i] = \alpha + \boldsymbol{\beta}[R_i, \boldsymbol{x}]^\top \boldsymbol{\eta}, \quad i = 1, \ldots, I, \tag{10.1}$$

where the factor-beta of asset i is the K-dimensional vector $\boldsymbol{\beta}[R_i, \boldsymbol{x}]$ given by

$$\boldsymbol{\beta}[R_i, \boldsymbol{x}] = (\mathrm{Var}[\boldsymbol{x}])^{-1} \mathrm{Cov}[\boldsymbol{x}, R_i].$$

The vector $\boldsymbol{\eta}$ is called the factor risk premium and α the zero-beta return associated with the pricing factor $\boldsymbol{x}$.

In general the k'th element of the factor-beta vector $\boldsymbol{\beta}[R_i, \boldsymbol{x}]$ is not equal to $\tilde{\beta}_{ik} \equiv \mathrm{Cov}[x_k, R_i]/\mathrm{Var}[x_k]$. However, we can rewrite the total risk premium $\boldsymbol{\beta}[R_i, \boldsymbol{x}]^\top \boldsymbol{\eta}$ in terms of $\tilde{\beta}_{i1}, \ldots, \tilde{\beta}_{iK}$. Let V_{jk} denote entry (j, k) in the inverse variance-covariance matrix $(\mathrm{Var}[\boldsymbol{x}])^{-1}$. Then

$$\begin{aligned}\boldsymbol{\beta}[R_i,\boldsymbol{x}]^\top\boldsymbol{\eta} &= \boldsymbol{\eta}^\top\boldsymbol{\beta}[R_i,\boldsymbol{x}] = \boldsymbol{\eta}^\top\left(\operatorname{Var}[\boldsymbol{x}]\right)^{-1}\operatorname{Cov}[\boldsymbol{x},R_i]\\ &= \sum_{j=1}^K \eta_j \sum_{k=1}^K V_{jk}\operatorname{Cov}[x_k,R_i]\\ &= \sum_{k=1}^K\left(\sum_{j=1}^K \eta_j V_{jk}\right)\operatorname{Cov}[x_k,R_i]\\ &= \sum_{k=1}^K \tilde{\eta}_k\tilde{\beta}_{ik},\end{aligned}$$

where $\tilde{\eta}_k = \operatorname{Var}[x_k]\sum_{j=1}^K \eta_j V_{jk}$. If the elements of the factor $\boldsymbol{x}$ are independent, the variance-covariance matrix and its inverse are diagonal so that $V_{jk} = 0$ for $j \neq k$ and $V_{kk} = 1/\operatorname{Var}[x_k]$. In this special case, $\tilde{\beta}_{ik}$ is indeed equal to the k'th element of $\boldsymbol{\beta}[R_i,\boldsymbol{x}]$ and $\tilde{\eta}_k = \eta_k$ for all $k = 1,\dots,K$.

We can write Eq. (10.1) more compactly as

$$\mathrm{E}[\boldsymbol{R}] = \alpha\mathbf{1} + \underline{\underline{\beta}}[\boldsymbol{R},\boldsymbol{x}]\boldsymbol{\eta},$$

where $\boldsymbol{R} = (R_1,\dots,R_I)^\top$ is the return vector, $\mathbf{1}$ is the K-dimensional vector $(1,\dots,1)^\top$, and $\underline{\underline{\beta}}[\boldsymbol{R},\boldsymbol{x}]$ is the $I \times K$ matrix with $\boldsymbol{\beta}[R_i,\boldsymbol{x}]$ as the i'th row. Due to the linearity of expectations and covariance, Eq. (10.1) will also hold for all portfolios of the I assets. Note that if a risk-free asset is traded in the market, it will have a zero factor-beta and, consequently, $\alpha = R^f$.

Equation (10.1) involves the gross rate of return R_i on asset i. What about the rate of return $r_i = R_i - 1$? Clearly, $\mathrm{E}[R_i] = 1 + \mathrm{E}[r_i]$, and the properties of covariance give

$$\operatorname{Cov}[\boldsymbol{x},R_i] = \operatorname{Cov}[\boldsymbol{x},1+r_i] = \operatorname{Cov}[\boldsymbol{x},r_i] \quad\Rightarrow\quad \boldsymbol{\beta}[R_i,\boldsymbol{x}] = \boldsymbol{\beta}[r_i,\boldsymbol{x}].$$

Consequently, Eq. (10.1) implies that

$$\mathrm{E}[r_i] = (\alpha - 1) + \boldsymbol{\beta}[r_i,\boldsymbol{x}]^\top\eta.$$

If a risk-free asset exists, we have $\alpha - 1 = R^f - 1 = r^f$, the risk-free net rate of return.

The relation (10.1) does not directly involve prices. But since the expected gross rate of return is $\mathrm{E}[R_i] = \mathrm{E}[D_i]/P_i$, we have $P_i = \mathrm{E}[D_i]/\mathrm{E}[R_i]$ and hence the equivalent relation

$$P_i = \frac{\mathrm{E}[D_i]}{\alpha + \boldsymbol{\beta}[R_i,\boldsymbol{x}]^\top\boldsymbol{\eta}}.$$

The price is equal to the expected dividend discounted by a risk-adjusted rate. You may find this relation unsatisfactory since the price implicitly enters the right-hand side through the return in the 'return-beta' $\boldsymbol{\beta}[R_i,\boldsymbol{x}]$. However, we can define a 'dividend-beta' by

$$\boldsymbol{\beta}[D_i, \boldsymbol{x}] = (\mathrm{Var}[\boldsymbol{x}])^{-1} \mathrm{Cov}[\boldsymbol{x}, D_i]$$

and inserting $D_i = R_i P_i$ we see that $\boldsymbol{\beta}[D_i, \boldsymbol{x}] = P_i \boldsymbol{\beta}[R_i, \boldsymbol{x}]$. Equation (10.1) now implies that

$$\frac{\mathrm{E}[D_i]}{P_i} = \alpha + \frac{1}{P_i} \boldsymbol{\beta}[D_i, \boldsymbol{x}]^\top \boldsymbol{\eta}$$

so that

$$P_i = \frac{\mathrm{E}[D_i] - \boldsymbol{\beta}[D_i, \boldsymbol{x}]^\top \boldsymbol{\eta}}{\alpha}.$$

Think of the numerator as a certainty equivalent of the risky dividend. The current price is the certainty equivalent discounted by the zero-beta return, which is the risk-free return if this exists.

The following result shows that pricing factors are not unique.

Theorem 10.1 *If the K-dimensional random variable $\boldsymbol{x}$ is a pricing factor, then any $\hat{\boldsymbol{x}}$ of the form $\hat{\boldsymbol{x}} = \boldsymbol{a} + \underline{\underline{A}}\boldsymbol{x}$ where $\boldsymbol{a} \in \mathbb{R}^K$ and $\underline{\underline{A}}$ is a non-singular $K \times K$ matrix is also a pricing factor.*

Proof. According to Eqs. (A.1), (A.2), and (C.1) in the Appendices, we have

$$\begin{aligned}
\mathrm{Cov}[\hat{\boldsymbol{x}}, R_i] &= \mathrm{Cov}[\boldsymbol{a} + \underline{\underline{A}}\boldsymbol{x}, R_i] = \underline{\underline{A}}\, \mathrm{Cov}[\boldsymbol{x}, R_i], \\
\left(\mathrm{Var}[\hat{\boldsymbol{x}}]\right)^{-1} &= \left(\mathrm{Var}[\boldsymbol{a} + \underline{\underline{A}}\boldsymbol{x}]\right)^{-1} = \left(\mathrm{Var}[\underline{\underline{A}}\boldsymbol{x}]\right)^{-1} \\
&= \left(\underline{\underline{A}}\, \mathrm{Var}[\boldsymbol{x}] \underline{\underline{A}}^\top\right)^{-1} = \left(\underline{\underline{A}}^\top\right)^{-1} (\mathrm{Var}[\boldsymbol{x}])^{-1} \underline{\underline{A}}^{-1},
\end{aligned}$$

and thus

$$\begin{aligned}
\boldsymbol{\beta}[R_i, \hat{\boldsymbol{x}}] &= \left(\mathrm{Var}[\hat{\boldsymbol{x}}]\right)^{-1} \mathrm{Cov}[\hat{\boldsymbol{x}}, R_i] \\
&= \left(\underline{\underline{A}}^\top\right)^{-1} (\mathrm{Var}[\boldsymbol{x}])^{-1} \underline{\underline{A}}^{-1} \underline{\underline{A}}\, \mathrm{Cov}[\boldsymbol{x}, R_i] = \left(\underline{\underline{A}}^\top\right)^{-1} \boldsymbol{\beta}[R_i, \boldsymbol{x}].
\end{aligned}$$

By defining $\hat{\boldsymbol{\eta}} = \underline{\underline{A}}\boldsymbol{\eta}$, we obtain

$$\boldsymbol{\beta}[R_i, \hat{\boldsymbol{x}}]^\top \hat{\boldsymbol{\eta}} = \left(\left(\underline{\underline{A}}^\top\right)^{-1} \boldsymbol{\beta}[R_i, \boldsymbol{x}]\right)^\top \underline{\underline{A}}\boldsymbol{\eta} = \boldsymbol{\beta}[R_i, \boldsymbol{x}]^\top \boldsymbol{\eta}$$

and, hence,

$$\mathrm{E}[R_i] = \alpha + \boldsymbol{\beta}[R_i, \hat{\boldsymbol{x}}]^\top \hat{\boldsymbol{\eta}}, \quad i = 1, \ldots, I,$$

which confirms that $\hat{\boldsymbol{x}}$ is a pricing factor. □

This theorem has the following important consequences.

First, we can orthogonalize any pricing factor $\boldsymbol{x}$, that is transform it into a pricing factor with uncorrelated components. The argument goes as follows: we can find a non-singular $K \times K$ matrix $\underline{\underline{V}}$ so that $\underline{\underline{V}}\,\underline{\underline{V}}^{\top} = \operatorname{Var}[\boldsymbol{x}]$. Then, defining $\hat{\boldsymbol{x}} = \underline{\underline{V}}^{-1}\boldsymbol{x}$, we know from above that $\hat{\boldsymbol{x}}$ is also a pricing factor and the variance-covariance matrix is

$$\operatorname{Var}[\hat{\boldsymbol{x}}] = \underline{\underline{V}}^{-1} \operatorname{Var}[\boldsymbol{x}] \left(\underline{\underline{V}}^{-1}\right)^{\top} = \underline{\underline{V}}^{-1}\underline{\underline{V}}\,\underline{\underline{V}}^{\top} \left(\underline{\underline{V}}^{\top}\right)^{-1} = \underline{\underline{I}},$$

where $\underline{\underline{I}}$ denotes the $K \times K$ identity matrix. It is therefore no restriction to look only for uncorrelated pricing factors.

Second, pricing factors can be chosen to have zero mean: if $\boldsymbol{x}$ is any pricing factor, just define $\hat{\boldsymbol{x}} = \boldsymbol{x} - \mathrm{E}[\boldsymbol{x}]$. Clearly, $\hat{\boldsymbol{x}}$ has mean zero and, due to the previous theorem, it is also a pricing factor. It is therefore no restriction to look only for zero-mean pricing factors.

Finally, note that we can replace the constant vector $\boldsymbol{a}$ in the above theorem with a K-dimensional random variable $\boldsymbol{\varepsilon}$ with the property that $\operatorname{Cov}[R_i, \boldsymbol{\varepsilon}] = \boldsymbol{0}$ for all i. In particular we have that if $\boldsymbol{x}$ is a pricing factor and $\boldsymbol{\varepsilon}$ is such a random variable, then $\boldsymbol{x} + \boldsymbol{\varepsilon}$ is also a pricing factor.

The consumption-based CAPM is a prime example of a factor model. The results of Section 8.2.3 show that the future consumption (of either a single individual or a representative individual) is a pricing factor if either (a) the individual has quadratic utility or (b) consumption and returns are jointly normally distributed. For example, in case (b), Eq. (8.10) is of the form (10.1) with future consumption c playing the role of a one-dimensional pricing factor with associated factor risk premium $\eta = -\mathrm{E}[u''(c)] \operatorname{Var}[c]/\mathrm{E}[u'(c)]$ and zero-beta return equal to the risk-free gross return. Since consumption growth $g = c/c_0$ is just a simple affine transformation of consumption, we can just as well use consumption growth as the pricing factor. Under the more attractive assumption of power utility and lognormally distributed consumption, Theorem 8.1 shows that an equation like (10.1) is approximately true, so in that sense consumption (or consumption growth) is an approximate pricing factor (see more below).

10.2.2 Returns as Pricing Factors

Suppose now that the pricing factor is a vector of returns on portfolios of the I assets. Then Eq. (10.1) holds with each x_k replacing R_i. We have $\operatorname{Cov}[\boldsymbol{x}, \boldsymbol{x}] = \operatorname{Var}[\boldsymbol{x}]$ and hence $\underline{\underline{\beta}}[\boldsymbol{x}, \boldsymbol{x}] = \underline{\underline{I}}$, the $K \times K$ identity matrix. Consequently,

$$\mathrm{E}[\boldsymbol{x}] = \alpha\mathbf{1} + \boldsymbol{\eta} \quad \Rightarrow \quad \boldsymbol{\eta} = \mathrm{E}[\boldsymbol{x}] - \alpha\mathbf{1},$$

where $\mathbf{1}$ is a K-dimensional vector of ones. In this case we can therefore rewrite Eq. (10.1) as

$$\mathrm{E}[R_i] = \alpha + \boldsymbol{\beta}[R_i, \boldsymbol{x}]^{\top} (\mathrm{E}[\boldsymbol{x}] - \alpha \mathbf{1}), \quad i = 1, \dots, I.$$

It is now clear that the classic CAPM has the return on the market portfolio as the single pricing factor. More generally, we will demonstrate in Section 10.3.3 that a return works as a single pricing factor if and only if it is the return on a mean-variance efficient portfolio (different from the minimum-variance portfolio).

For the case of a one-dimensional pricing factor x, Section 4.6.2 explained that the return R^x on the factor-mimicking portfolio also works as a pricing factor. We can generalize this to a multidimensional pricing factor in the following way. Given a pricing factor $\boldsymbol{x} = (x_1, \dots, x_K)^{\top}$, orthogonalize to obtain $\hat{\boldsymbol{x}} = (\hat{x}_1, \dots, \hat{x}_K)^{\top}$. For each $\hat{x}_k$ construct a factor-mimicking portfolio with corresponding return $R^{\hat{x}_k}$. Then the return vector $\boldsymbol{R}^{\hat{x}} = \left(R^{\hat{x}_1}, \dots, R^{\hat{x}_K}\right)^{\top}$ will work as a pricing factor and we have an equation like

$$\mathrm{E}[R_i] = \alpha + \boldsymbol{\beta}[R_i, \boldsymbol{R}^{\hat{x}}] \cdot \left(\mathrm{E}[\boldsymbol{R}^{\hat{x}}] - \alpha \mathbf{1}\right), \quad i = 1, \dots, I.$$

It is therefore no restriction to assume that pricing factors are returns.

10.2.3 The Classic One-Period CAPM

The classic CAPM developed by Sharpe (1964), Lintner (1965), Mossin (1966), and Black (1972) states that the return on the market portfolio is a pricing factor so that

$$\mathrm{E}[R_i] = \alpha + \beta[R_i, R_M] (\mathrm{E}[R_M] - \alpha), \quad i = 1, 2, \dots, I,$$

for some zero-beta return α, which is identical to the risk-free rate if such exists. Here the market-beta is defined as $\beta[R_i, R_M] = \mathrm{Cov}[R_i, R_M] / \mathrm{Var}[R_M]$.

The classic CAPM is usually derived from mean-variance analysis. If all individuals have quadratic utility or returns are normally distributed, any individual will optimally pick a mean-variance efficient portfolio. If R_l denotes the return on the portfolio chosen by individual l and w_l denotes individual l's share of total wealth, the return on the market portfolio will be $R_M = \sum_{l=1}^{L} w_l R_l$ and the market portfolio will be mean-variance efficient. As was already stated in Theorem 4.12 (demonstrated later in this chapter), the return R^{mv} on any mean-variance efficient portfolio is such that an $\alpha \in \mathbb{R}$ exists so that $\mathrm{E}[R_i] = \alpha + \beta[R_i, R^{\mathrm{mv}}](\mathrm{E}[R^{\mathrm{mv}}] - \alpha)$. In particular, this is true for the market portfolio when it is efficient.

To see how the classic CAPM fits into the consumption-based asset pricing framework, consider a model in which all individuals have time-additive expected utility and are endowed with some time 0 wealth but receive no time 1 income from non-financial sources. Let us consider an arbitrary individual with initial wealth endowment e_0. If the individual consumes c_0 at time 0, she will invest $e_0 - c_0$ in the financial assets. Representing the investment by the portfolio weight vector $\boldsymbol{\pi}$, the gross rate of return on the portfolio will be $R^{\pi} = \boldsymbol{\pi} \cdot \boldsymbol{R} = \sum_{i=1}^{I} \pi_i R_i$. The time 1 consumption will equal the total dividend of the portfolio, which is the gross rate of return multiplied by the initial investment, that is

$$c = R^{\pi}(e_0 - c_0).$$

We can substitute this into the marginal rate of substitution of the individual so that the associated state-price deflator becomes

$$\zeta = e^{-\delta}\frac{u'(c)}{u'(c_0)} = e^{-\delta}\frac{u'\left(R^{\pi}(e_0 - c_0)\right)}{u'(c_0)}. \tag{10.2}$$

If the economy has a representative individual, she has to own all the assets, that is she has to invest in the market portfolio. We can then replace R^{π} by R_M, the gross rate of return on the market portfolio. We can obtain the classic CAPM from this relation if we either assume that the utility function is quadratic or that the return on the market portfolio is normally distributed.

Quadratic utility. The quadratic utility function $u(c) = -(\bar{c} - c)^2$ is a special case of the satiation HARA utility functions. Marginal utility $u'(c) = 2(\bar{c} - c)$ is positive for $c < \bar{c}$ so that consumption in excess of $\bar{c}$ will decrease utility. Another problem is that the absolute risk aversion $\text{ARA}(c) = 1/(\bar{c} - c)$ is increasing in the level of consumption. For quadratic utility, Eq. (10.2) becomes

$$\zeta = e^{-\delta}\frac{\bar{c} - R^{\pi}(e_0 - c_0)}{\bar{c} - c_0} = e^{-\delta}\frac{\bar{c}}{\bar{c} - c_0} - e^{-\delta}\frac{e_0 - c_0}{\bar{c} - c_0}R^{\pi},$$

which is affine in the portfolio return. It now follows from the discussion in Section 4.6.2 (also see Section 10.2.4 below) that the portfolio return is a pricing factor so that

$$\mathrm{E}[R_i] = \alpha + \beta[R_i, R^{\pi}]\left(\mathrm{E}[R^{\pi}] - \alpha\right).$$

Again, if this applies to a representative individual, we can replace R^{π} by the market portfolio return R_M and we have the classic CAPM.

Normally distributed returns. We will show that for almost any utility function we can derive the classic CAPM relation if returns are jointly normally distributed. We assume that the state-price deflator is of the form $\zeta = g(x)$

where x and R_i are jointly normally distributed. According to Stein's Lemma, that is Lemma 8.1, we thus have that

$$\begin{aligned}
1 &= \mathrm{E}[g(x)R_i] = \mathrm{E}[g(x)]\,\mathrm{E}[R_i] + \mathrm{Cov}[g(x), R_i] \\
&= \mathrm{E}[g(x)]\,\mathrm{E}[R_i] + \mathrm{E}[g'(x)]\,\mathrm{Cov}[x, R_i] \\
&= \mathrm{E}[g(x)]\,\mathrm{E}[R_i] + \mathrm{E}[g'(x)]\,\mathrm{E}[(x - \mathrm{E}[x])R_i] \\
&= \mathrm{E}\left[\left\{\mathrm{E}[g(x)] - \mathrm{E}[x]E[g'(x)] + \mathrm{E}[g'(x)]x\right\} R_i\right] \\
&= \mathrm{E}[(a + bx)R_i],
\end{aligned}$$

for some constants a and b. Therefore, we can safely assume that $g(x)$ is affine in x.

In Eq. (10.2) we have

$$\zeta = e^{-\delta} \frac{u'\left(R^\pi (e_0 - c_0)\right)}{u'(c_0)} = g(R^\pi),$$

and if the individual asset returns are jointly normally distributed, the return on any portfolio and the return on any individual asset will also be jointly normally distributed. According to Stein's Lemma we can then safely assume that ζ is affine in R^π. Again, this implies that R^π is a pricing factor. Note, however, that to apply Stein's Lemma, we have to check that $\mathrm{E}[|g'(R^\pi)|]$ is finite. In our case,

$$g'(R^\pi) = e^{-\delta}(e_0 - c_0) \frac{u''\left(R^\pi (e_0 - c_0)\right)}{u'(c_0)}.$$

With log-utility, $u''(c) = -1/c^2$, and since $\mathrm{E}[1/(R^\pi)^2]$ is infinite (or undefined if you like) when R^π is normally distributed, we cannot apply Stein's Lemma. In fact, when R^π is normally distributed, we really need the utility function to be defined on the entire real line, which is not the case for the most reasonable utility functions. For negative exponential utility, there is no such problem.

The assumptions leading to the classic CAPM are clearly problematic. Preferences are poorly represented by quadratic utility functions or other mean-variance utility functions. Returns are not normally distributed. A more fundamental problem is the static nature of the one-period CAPM. Later in this chapter we will discuss how the CAPM can be extended to a dynamic setting. It turns out that we can derive an intertemporal CAPM under much more appropriate assumptions about utility functions and return distributions. We will need CRRA utility and lognormally distributed returns. In addition, we will need the return distribution to be stationary, that is the same for all future periods of the same length.

10.2.4 Pricing Factors and State-Price Deflators

From the definition of a covariance we have that $\operatorname{Cov}[R_i, \zeta] = \mathrm{E}[R_i\zeta] - \mathrm{E}[\zeta]\,\mathrm{E}[R_i]$. From Eq. (4.2), we now get that

$$\mathrm{E}[R_i] = \frac{1}{\mathrm{E}[\zeta]} - \frac{\operatorname{Cov}[R_i, \zeta]}{\mathrm{E}[\zeta]}. \tag{10.3}$$

With $\beta[R_i, \zeta] = \operatorname{Cov}[R_i, \zeta]/\operatorname{Var}[\zeta]$ and $\eta = -\operatorname{Var}[\zeta]/\mathrm{E}[\zeta]$, we can rewrite the above equation as

$$\mathrm{E}[R_i] = \frac{1}{\mathrm{E}[\zeta]} + \beta[R_i, \zeta]\eta,$$

which shows that the state-price deflator is a pricing factor. Although the proof is simple, the result is important enough to deserve its own theorem:

Theorem 10.2 *Any state-price deflator ζ is a pricing factor. The associated zero-beta return is $\alpha = 1/\mathrm{E}[\zeta]$, and the associated factor risk premium is $\eta = -\operatorname{Var}[\zeta]/\mathrm{E}[\zeta]$.*

In the above argument we did not use positivity of the state-price deflator, only the pricing equation (4.1) or, rather, the return version (4.2). Any random variable x that satisfies $P_i = \mathrm{E}[xD_i]$ for all assets works as a pricing factor. In particular, this is true for the random variable ζ^* defined in Eq. (4.39) whether it is positive or not. We therefore have that

$$\mathrm{E}[R_i] = \alpha^* + \beta[R_i, \zeta^*]\eta^*, \quad i = 1, \dots, I,$$

where $\alpha^* = 1/\mathrm{E}[\zeta^*]$ and $\eta^* = -\operatorname{Var}[\zeta^*]/\mathrm{E}[\zeta^*]$. Alternatively, we can scale by the price of ζ^* and use the return R^* defined in (4.45) as the factor so that

$$\mathrm{E}[R_i] = \alpha^* + \beta[R_i, R^*]\eta^*, \quad i = 1, \dots, I,$$

where $\alpha^* = 1/\mathrm{E}[\zeta^*]$ as before but now $\eta^* = -\operatorname{Var}[\zeta^*]/\left(\mathrm{E}[\zeta^*]\,\mathrm{E}[(\zeta^*)^2]\right)$.

More generally, we have the following result:

Theorem 10.3 *If the K-dimensional random variable $\boldsymbol{x}$ satisfies*

(i) $\operatorname{Var}[\boldsymbol{x}]$ *is non-singular;*

(ii) $a \in \mathbb{R}$ *and* $\boldsymbol{b} \in \mathbb{R}^K$ *exist so that* $\zeta = a + \boldsymbol{b}^\top \boldsymbol{x}$ *has the properties* $\mathrm{E}[\zeta] \neq 0$ *and* $\mathrm{E}[\zeta R_i] = 1$ *for* $i = 1, \dots, I$,

then $\boldsymbol{x}$ is a pricing factor.

Proof. Substituting $\zeta = a + \boldsymbol{b}^{\top}\boldsymbol{x}$ into Eq. (10.3), we get

$$\begin{aligned} \mathrm{E}[R_i] &= \frac{1}{a + \boldsymbol{b}^{\top} \mathrm{E}[\boldsymbol{x}]} - \frac{\boldsymbol{b}^{\top} \mathrm{Cov}[R_i, \boldsymbol{x}]}{a + \boldsymbol{b}^{\top} \mathrm{E}[\boldsymbol{x}]} \\ &= \frac{1}{a + \boldsymbol{b}^{\top} \mathrm{E}[\boldsymbol{x}]} - \frac{(\mathrm{Var}[\boldsymbol{x}]\boldsymbol{b})^{\top} (\mathrm{Var}[\boldsymbol{x}])^{-1} \mathrm{Cov}[R_i, \boldsymbol{x}]}{a + \boldsymbol{b}^{\top} \mathrm{E}[\boldsymbol{x}]} \\ &= \alpha + \beta[R_i, \boldsymbol{x}]^{\top} \boldsymbol{\eta}, \end{aligned}$$

where $\alpha = 1/\left(a + \boldsymbol{b}^{\top} \mathrm{E}[\boldsymbol{x}]\right)$ and $\boldsymbol{\eta} = -\alpha \,\mathrm{Var}[\boldsymbol{x}]\boldsymbol{b}$. □

Whenever we have a state-price deflator of the form $\zeta = a + \boldsymbol{b}^{\top}\boldsymbol{x}$, we can use $\boldsymbol{x}$ as a pricing factor.

Conversely, the following result holds:

Theorem 10.4 *Assume the K-dimensional random variable $\boldsymbol{x}$ is a pricing factor with an associated zero-beta return α different from zero. Then we can find $a \in \mathbb{R}$ and $\boldsymbol{b} \in \mathbb{R}^K$ so that $\zeta = a + \boldsymbol{b}^{\top}\boldsymbol{x}$ satisfies $\mathrm{E}[\zeta R_i] = 1$ for $i = 1, \dots, I$.*

Proof. Let $\boldsymbol{\eta}$ denote the factor risk premium associated with the pricing factor $\boldsymbol{x}$. Define

$$\boldsymbol{b} = -\frac{1}{\alpha} (\mathrm{Var}[\boldsymbol{x}])^{-1} \boldsymbol{\eta}, \quad a = \frac{1}{\alpha} - \boldsymbol{b}^{\top} \mathrm{E}[\boldsymbol{x}].$$

Then $\zeta = a + \boldsymbol{b}^{\top}\boldsymbol{x}$ works since

$$\begin{aligned} \mathrm{E}[\zeta R_i] &= a \,\mathrm{E}[R_i] + \boldsymbol{b}^{\top} \mathrm{E}[R_i \boldsymbol{x}] \\ &= a \,\mathrm{E}[R_i] + \boldsymbol{b}^{\top} \left(\mathrm{Cov}[R_i, \boldsymbol{x}] + \mathrm{E}[R_i] \,\mathrm{E}[\boldsymbol{x}]\right) \\ &= \left(a + \boldsymbol{b}^{\top} \mathrm{E}[\boldsymbol{x}]\right) \mathrm{E}[R_i] + \mathrm{Cov}[R_i, \boldsymbol{x}]^{\top}\boldsymbol{b} \\ &= \frac{1}{\alpha} \left(\mathrm{E}[R_i] - \mathrm{Cov}[R_i, \boldsymbol{x}]^{\top} (\mathrm{Var}[\boldsymbol{x}])^{-1} \boldsymbol{\eta}\right) \\ &= \frac{1}{\alpha} \left(\mathrm{E}[R_i] - \boldsymbol{\beta}[R_i, \boldsymbol{x}]^{\top} \boldsymbol{\eta}\right) \\ &= 1 \end{aligned}$$

for any $i = 1, \dots, I$. □

Inserting a and $\boldsymbol{b}$ from the proof, we get

$$\zeta = a + \boldsymbol{b}^{\top}\boldsymbol{x} = \frac{1}{\alpha} \left(1 - \boldsymbol{\eta}^{\top} (\mathrm{Var}[\boldsymbol{x}])^{-1} (\boldsymbol{x} - \mathrm{E}[\boldsymbol{x}])\right).$$

Any pricing factor $\boldsymbol{x}$ gives us a *candidate* $a + \boldsymbol{b}^{\top}\boldsymbol{x}$ for a state-price deflator but it will only be a true state-price deflator if it is strictly positive. The fact that we can find a pricing factor for a given market does not imply that the market is arbitrage-free.

Next suppose that a state-price deflator is given on the exponential form

$$\zeta = e^{a+b^\top x}, \tag{10.4}$$

where x is a random variable, a is a constant scalar, and b a constant vector of the same dimension as x. Assume the existence of a risk-free asset and substitute the above exponential form into Eq. (4.11). This implies the approximate relation

$$\mathrm{E}[R_i] - R^f \approx -b^\top \operatorname{Cov}[R_i, x] = \beta[R_i, x]^\top \eta,$$

where $\eta = -\operatorname{Var}[x]b$. In this sense x is an *approximate pricing factor.*

If a state-price deflator is given by Eq. (10.4) and x and all log-returns $r_i = \ln R_i$ are jointly normally distributed, then it follows by substituting Eq. (10.4) into Eq. (4.13) that

$$\mathrm{E}[r_i] - r^f = -b^\top \operatorname{Cov}[x, r_i] - \frac{1}{2}\operatorname{Var}[r_i] = \beta[r_t, x]^\top \eta - \frac{1}{2}\operatorname{Var}[r_i], \tag{10.5}$$

where $\eta = -\operatorname{Var}[x]b$. In this sense x can be called a *log-pricing factor.*

10.2.5 The Arbitrage Pricing Theory

Ross (1976a) introduced the Arbitrage Pricing Theory as an alternative to the classic CAPM. The basic assumption is that a K-dimensional random variable $x = (x_1, \dots, x_K)^\top$ exists so that the return on any asset $i = 1, \dots, I$ can be decomposed as

$$R_i = \mathrm{E}[R_i] + \beta[R_i, x]^\top x + \varepsilon_i = \mathrm{E}[R_i] + \sum_{k=1}^{K} \beta_{ik} x_k + \varepsilon_i, \tag{10.6}$$

where $\mathrm{E}[x_k] = 0$, $\mathrm{E}[\varepsilon_i] = 0$, $\operatorname{Cov}[\varepsilon_i, x_k] = 0$, and $\operatorname{Cov}[\varepsilon_i, \varepsilon_j] = 0$ for all $i, j \neq i$, and k. Due to the constraints on means and covariances, we have $\beta[R_i, x] = (\operatorname{Var}[x])^{-1} \operatorname{Cov}[R_i, x]$ as before. Note that one can always make a decomposition as in the equation above. Just think of regressing returns on the vector x. The real content of the assumption lies in the restriction that the residuals are uncorrelated, that is $\operatorname{Cov}[\varepsilon_i, \varepsilon_j] = 0$ whenever $i \neq j$. This implies that the vector x is the source of all the common variations in returns across assets.

Suppose you have invested some wealth in a portfolio. We can represent a zero net investment deviation from this portfolio by a vector $w = (w_1, \dots, w_I)^\top$ satisfying $w \cdot \mathbf{1} = 0$, where w_i is the fraction of wealth additionally invested in asset i. In other words, we increase the investment in some assets and decrease the investment in other assets. The additional portfolio return is

$$R^w = w^\top R = \sum_{i=1}^{I} w_i R_i$$

$$= \sum_{i=1}^{I} w_i \, \mathrm{E}[R_i] + \left(\sum_{i=1}^{I} w_i \beta_{i1} \right) x_1 + \cdots + \left(\sum_{i=1}^{I} w_i \beta_{iK} \right) x_K + \sum_{i=1}^{I} w_i \varepsilon_i,$$

where we have used Eq. (10.6). Suppose we can find $w_1, \ldots, w_I$ (not all zero) so that

(i) $\sum_{i=1}^{I} w_i \beta_{ik} = 0$ for $k = 1, \ldots, K$,
(ii) $\sum_{i=1}^{I} w_i \varepsilon_i = 0$.

Then we see that

$$R^w = \sum_{i=1}^{I} w_i \, \mathrm{E}[R_i]$$

so that the added return is risk-free. To rule out arbitrage, a risk-free zero net investment should give a zero return so we can conclude that

$$R^w = \sum_{i=1}^{I} w_i \, \mathrm{E}[R_i] = 0.$$

In linear algebra terms, we have thus seen that if a vector $\boldsymbol{w}$ is orthogonal to $\mathbf{1}$ and to each of the vectors $(\beta_{1k}, \ldots, \beta_{Ik})^\top$, $k = 1, \ldots, K$, then it must also be orthogonal to the vector of expected returns $\mathrm{E}[\boldsymbol{R}]$. It follows that $\mathrm{E}[\boldsymbol{R}]$ must be spanned by the vectors $\mathbf{1}$, $(\beta_{1k}, \ldots, \beta_{Ik})^\top$, $k = 1, \ldots, K$. This means that constants $\alpha, \eta_1, \ldots, \eta_K$ exist with the property that

$$\mathrm{E}[R_i] = \alpha + \beta_{i1}\eta_1 + \cdots + \beta_{iK}\eta_K = \alpha + \boldsymbol{\beta}[R_i, \boldsymbol{x}]^\top \boldsymbol{\eta}, \quad i = 1, 2, \ldots, I,$$

and hence $\boldsymbol{x}$ is a pricing factor.

With at least K sufficiently different assets, we can satisfy condition (i) above. We just need the $I \times K$ matrix $\underline{\underline{\beta}}[\boldsymbol{R}, \boldsymbol{x}]$ to have rank K. What about condition (ii)? The usual argument given is that if we pick w_i to be of the order $1/I$ and I is a very large number, then $\sum_{i=1} w_i \varepsilon_i$ will be close to zero and we can ignore it. But close to zero does not mean equal to zero and if the residual portfolio return is non-zero, the portfolio is not risk-free and the argument breaks down. Even a very small dividend or return in a particular state can have a large influence on the current price and, hence, the expected return. With finitely many assets, we can only safely ignore the residual portfolio return if the residual returns of all the individual assets are zero, that is $\varepsilon_i = 0$ for all $i = 1, \ldots, I$.

Theorem 10.5 *If individual asset returns are of the form*

$$R_i = \mathrm{E}[R_i] + \boldsymbol{\beta}[R_i, \boldsymbol{x}]^\top \boldsymbol{x}, \quad i = 1, 2, \dots, I,$$

and the $I \times K$ matrix $\underline{\underline{\beta}}[\boldsymbol{R}, \boldsymbol{x}]$ has rank K, then $\boldsymbol{x}$ is a pricing factor, that is $\alpha \in \mathbb{R}$ and $\boldsymbol{\eta} \in \mathbb{R}^K$ exist so that

$$\mathrm{E}[R_i] = \alpha + \boldsymbol{\beta}[R_i, \boldsymbol{x}]^\top \boldsymbol{\eta}, \quad i = 1, 2, \dots, I.$$

It is, however, fairly restrictive to assume that *all* the variation in the returns on a large number of assets can be captured by a low number of factors.

See Huberman (1982), Chen and Ingersoll (1983), Dybvig (1983), Grinblatt and Titman (1983, 1985, 1987), Connor (1984), and Ingersoll (1984) for more on the theoretical developments of the Arbitrage Pricing Theory.

10.3 MEAN-VARIANCE EFFICIENT RETURNS AND PRICING FACTORS

We have introduced the mean-variance frontier earlier in Sections 4.6.3 and 6.3. Here we provide an alternative characterization of the mean-variance efficient returns and study the link between mean-variance efficiency and asset pricing theory. The most important conclusion is Theorem 10.9 which shows that every mean-variance efficient return, except for the global minimum-variance return, works as a pricing factor. The alternative characterization of the mean-variance frontier is useful for the proof of that theorem.

As before let $\boldsymbol{R} = (R_1, \dots, R_I)^\top$ denote the vector of gross rates of return on the I traded assets and define $\boldsymbol{\mu} = \mathrm{E}[\boldsymbol{R}]$ and $\underline{\underline{\Sigma}} = \mathrm{Var}[\boldsymbol{R}]$. A portfolio $\boldsymbol{\pi}$ is mean-variance efficient if there is an $m \in \mathbb{R}$ so that $\boldsymbol{\pi}$ solves

$$\min_{\boldsymbol{\pi}} \boldsymbol{\pi}^\top \underline{\underline{\Sigma}} \boldsymbol{\pi} \quad \text{s.t.} \quad \boldsymbol{\pi}^\top \boldsymbol{\mu} = m, \quad \boldsymbol{\pi}^\top \mathbf{1} = 1, \tag{6.16}$$

that is $\boldsymbol{\pi}$ has the lowest return variance among all portfolios with expected return m.

10.3.1 Orthogonal Characterization

Following Hansen and Richard (1987) we will show that a return R is mean-variance efficient if and only if it can be written in the form $R = R^* + wR^{e*}$ for some number w. Here R^* is the return on the portfolio corresponding to the dividend ζ^* defined in Eq. (4.39). If $\boldsymbol{R}$ denotes the vector of gross rates of return, and we assume that no assets are redundant, this portfolio is characterized by the portfolio weight vector

$$\pi^* = \frac{\left(\mathrm{E}\left[RR^\top\right]\right)^{-1} \mathbf{1}}{\mathbf{1}^\top \left(\mathrm{E}\left[RR^\top\right]\right)^{-1} \mathbf{1}} \tag{4.44}$$

and its gross rate of return is

$$R^* = (\pi^*)^\top R = \frac{\mathbf{1}^\top \left(\mathrm{E}\left[RR^\top\right]\right)^{-1} R}{\mathbf{1}^\top \left(\mathrm{E}\left[RR^\top\right]\right)^{-1} \mathbf{1}}. \tag{4.45}$$

R^{e*} is a particular excess return to be defined shortly.

10.3.1.1 R^* and Mean-Variance Analysis

How does R^* fit into the mean-variance framework? The following lemma shows that it is a mean-variance efficient return on the downward-sloping part of the mean-variance frontier. Furthermore, it is the return with minimum second moment (recall that the second moment of a random variable x is $\mathrm{E}[x^2]$).

Lemma 10.1 *R^* has the following properties:*

(a) R^* is the return that has the minimum second moment,

(b) R^* is a mean-variance efficient return located on the downward-sloping part of the efficient frontier.

Proof. The return on a portfolio π is the random variable $R^\pi = \pi^\top R$. The second moment of this return is $\mathrm{E}[(R^\pi)^2] = \pi^\top \mathrm{E}[RR^\top]\pi$. Consider the minimization problem

$$\min_{\pi} \pi^\top \mathrm{E}[RR^\top]\pi \qquad \text{s.t.} \quad \pi^\top \mathbf{1} = 1.$$

The Lagrangian is $\mathcal{L} = \pi^\top \mathrm{E}[RR^\top]\pi + \lambda\,(1 - \pi^\top \mathbf{1})$, where λ is the Lagrange multiplier. The first-order condition for π is

$$2\,\mathrm{E}[RR^\top]\pi - \lambda \mathbf{1} = 0 \quad \Rightarrow \quad \pi = \frac{\lambda}{2}\left(\mathrm{E}[RR^\top]\right)^{-1} \mathbf{1}.$$

Imposing the constraint $\pi^\top \mathbf{1} = 1$, we get $\lambda/2 = 1/(\mathbf{1}^\top(\mathrm{E}[RR^\top])^{-1}\mathbf{1})$, and substituting this into the above expression for π, we see that π is indeed identical to π^* in Eq. (4.44).

Since π^* is the portfolio minimizing the second moment of gross rates of return among all portfolios, it is also the portfolio minimizing the second moment of gross rates of return among the portfolios with the same mean return as π^*, that is portfolios with $\mathrm{E}[R^\pi] = \mathrm{E}[R^*]$. For these portfolios the variance of return is

$$\mathrm{Var}\left[R^\pi\right] = \mathrm{E}[(R^\pi)^2] - \left(\mathrm{E}[R^\pi]\right)^2 = \mathrm{E}[(R^\pi)^2] - \left(\mathrm{E}[R^*]\right)^2.$$

It then follows that π^* is the portfolio minimizing the variance of return among all the portfolios having the same mean return as π^*. Hence, π^* is indeed a mean-variance efficient portfolio. In a (standard deviation, mean)-diagram returns with same second moment $K = \mathrm{E}[(R^\pi)^2]$ correspond to points on a circle with radius $\sqrt{K}$ centred in (0,0) since $(\sigma(R^\pi))^2 + (\mathrm{E}[R^\pi])^2 = \mathrm{E}[(R^\pi)^2]$. The return R^* therefore corresponds to a point on the downward-sloping part of the efficient frontier. □

10.3.1.2 The Constant-Mimicking Return

In a market without a risk-free asset you may wonder how close you can get to a risk-free dividend. Of course this will depend on what you mean by 'close'. If you apply a mean-square measure, the distance between the dividend $D^\theta = \boldsymbol{\theta}^\top \boldsymbol{D}$ of a portfolio $\boldsymbol{\theta}$ and a risk-free dividend of 1 is

$$
\begin{aligned}
\mathrm{E}\left[(D^\theta - 1)^2\right] &= \mathrm{E}\left[\left(\boldsymbol{\theta}^\top \boldsymbol{D} - 1\right)^2\right] \\
&= \mathrm{E}\left[\boldsymbol{\theta}^\top \boldsymbol{D}\boldsymbol{D}^\top \boldsymbol{\theta} + 1 - 2\boldsymbol{\theta}^\top \boldsymbol{D}\right] \\
&= \boldsymbol{\theta}^\top \mathrm{E}\left[\boldsymbol{D}\boldsymbol{D}^\top\right] \boldsymbol{\theta} + 1 - 2\boldsymbol{\theta}^\top \mathrm{E}\left[\boldsymbol{D}\right].
\end{aligned}
$$

Minimizing with respect to $\boldsymbol{\theta}$, we get $\boldsymbol{\theta}_{\mathrm{cm}} = (\mathrm{E}\left[\boldsymbol{D}\boldsymbol{D}^\top\right])^{-1}\,\mathrm{E}\left[\boldsymbol{D}\right]$ where the subscript 'cm' is short for 'constant-mimicking'. Let us transform this to a vector $\boldsymbol{\pi}_{\mathrm{cm}}$ of portfolio weights by using Eq. (3.9). Applying Eqs. (3.2) and (4.43), we get

$$
\begin{aligned}
\mathrm{diag}(\boldsymbol{P})\boldsymbol{\theta}_{\mathrm{cm}} &= \mathrm{diag}(\boldsymbol{P}) \left(\mathrm{E}\left[\boldsymbol{D}\boldsymbol{D}^\top\right]\right)^{-1} \mathrm{E}\left[\boldsymbol{D}\right] \\
&= \mathrm{diag}(\boldsymbol{P})[\mathrm{diag}(\boldsymbol{P})]^{-1} \left(\mathrm{E}\left[\boldsymbol{R}\boldsymbol{R}^\top\right]\right)^{-1} [\mathrm{diag}(\boldsymbol{P})]^{-1}\, \mathrm{E}\left[\boldsymbol{D}\right] \\
&= \left(\mathrm{E}\left[\boldsymbol{R}\boldsymbol{R}^\top\right]\right)^{-1} \mathrm{E}\left[\boldsymbol{R}\right]
\end{aligned}
$$

so that

$$
\boldsymbol{\pi}_{\mathrm{cm}} = \frac{1}{\boldsymbol{1}^\top \left(\mathrm{E}\left[\boldsymbol{R}\boldsymbol{R}^\top\right]\right)^{-1} \mathrm{E}\left[\boldsymbol{R}\right]} \left(\mathrm{E}\left[\boldsymbol{R}\boldsymbol{R}^\top\right]\right)^{-1} \mathrm{E}\left[\boldsymbol{R}\right] = \frac{\mathrm{E}[(R^*)^2]}{\mathrm{E}[R^*]} \left(\mathrm{E}\left[\boldsymbol{R}\boldsymbol{R}^\top\right]\right)^{-1} \mathrm{E}\left[\boldsymbol{R}\right],
$$

where the last equality comes from Eq. (4.46). The constant-mimicking return is thus

$$
R_{\mathrm{cm}} = (\boldsymbol{\pi}_{\mathrm{cm}})^\top \boldsymbol{R} = \frac{\mathrm{E}[(R^*)^2]}{\mathrm{E}[R^*]}\, \mathrm{E}\left[\boldsymbol{R}\right]^\top \left(\mathrm{E}\left[\boldsymbol{R}\boldsymbol{R}^\top\right]\right)^{-1} \boldsymbol{R}.
$$

10.3.1.3 Excess Returns and R^{e*}

An excess return is simply the difference between two returns. Since any return corresponds to a dividend for a unit initial payment, an excess return can be seen as a dividend for a zero initial payment. Of course, in the absence of arbitrage, a non-zero excess return will turn out positive in some states and negative in other states.

Typically, excess returns on different portfolios relative to the same 'reference' return are considered. For a reference return $\breve{R} = \breve{\pi}^{\top} R$, the set of all possible excess returns are given by

$$\mathcal{R}^e[\breve{R}] = \left\{ \pi^{\top} R - \breve{R} \mid \pi^{\top} \mathbf{1} = 1 \right\},$$

where, as before, R is the I-dimensional vector of returns on the basic assets, and π denotes a portfolio weight vector of these I assets.

It is useful to observe that the set of excess returns is the same for all reference returns. An excess return relative to a reference return $\breve{R}$ is given by $\pi^{\top} R - \breve{R} = (\pi - \breve{\pi})^{\top} R$ for some portfolio weight vector π. We can obtain the same excess return relative to another reference return $\dot{R} = \dot{\pi}^{\top} R$ using the portfolio $\pi + \dot{\pi} - \breve{\pi}$ (check for yourself!). Hence, we can simply talk about *the* set of excess returns, $\mathcal{R}^e$, without specifying any reference return, and we can write it as

$$\mathcal{R}^e = \{(\pi^e)^{\top} R \mid (\pi^e)^{\top} \mathbf{1} = 0\}.$$

The set of excess returns is a linear subspace of the set of all random variables (in the case with S possible outcomes this is equivalent to $\mathbb{R}^S$) in the sense that

1. if w is a number and R^e is an excess return, then wR^e is an excess return; *Check:* $R^e = (\pi^e)^{\top} R$ with $(\pi^e)^{\top} \mathbf{1} = 0$ implies that $wR^e = (w\pi^e)^{\top} R$ with $(w\pi^e)^{\top} \mathbf{1} = w(\pi^e)^{\top} \mathbf{1} = 0$;
2. if R^{e1} and R^{e2} are two excess returns, then $R^{e1} + R^{e2}$ is also an excess return. *Check:* $R^{ei} = (\pi^{ei})^{\top} R$ with $(\pi^{ei})^{\top} \mathbf{1} = 0$ implies that $R^{e1} + R^{e2} = (\pi^{e1} + \pi^{e2})^{\top} R$, where $(\pi^{e1} + \pi^{e2})^{\top} \mathbf{1} = 0$.

Define

$$R^{e*} = \frac{\mathrm{E}[R^*]}{\mathrm{E}[(R^*)^2]} \left(R_{\mathrm{cm}} - R^* \right) = \mathrm{E}[R]^{\top} \left(\mathrm{E}[RR^{\top}] \right)^{-1} R - \frac{\mathrm{E}[R^*]}{\mathrm{E}[(R^*)^2]} R^*. \tag{10.7}$$

Of course, $R_{\mathrm{cm}} - R^*$ is an excess return, and since R^{e*} is a multiplum of that, we can conclude that R^{e*} is an excess return. Here are some important properties of R^{e*}:

Lemma 10.2 *(a) For any excess return R^e, we have*

$$\mathrm{E}[R^e R^*] = 0. \tag{10.8}$$

In particular,

$$\mathrm{E}[R^{e*} R^*] = 0.$$

(b) For any excess return R^e we have

$$\mathrm{E}[R^e] = \mathrm{E}[R^{e*}R^e]. \tag{10.9}$$

(c) $\mathrm{E}[R^{e*}] = \mathrm{E}[(R^{e*})^2]$ *and* $\mathrm{Var}[R^{e*}] = \mathrm{E}[R^{e*}](1 - \mathrm{E}[R^{e*}])$.

Proof. (a) For any return R^i, we have $\mathrm{E}[R^*R^i] = \mathrm{E}[(R^*)^2]$, compare Lemma 4.1. Consequently, for any excess return $R^e = R^i - R^j$, we have

$$\mathrm{E}[R^*R^e] = \mathrm{E}[R^*(R^i - R^j)] = \mathrm{E}[R^*R^i] - \mathrm{E}[R^*R^j] = \mathrm{E}[(R^*)^2] - \mathrm{E}[(R^*)^2] = 0.$$

In particular, this is true for the excess return R^{e*}.

(b) Write the excess return R^e as the difference between the return on some portfolio $\boldsymbol{\pi}$ and R^*, that is $R^e = \boldsymbol{\pi}^\top \boldsymbol{R} - R^*$. Then

$$\mathrm{E}[R^{e*}R^e] = \mathrm{E}[R^{e*}\left(\boldsymbol{\pi}^\top \boldsymbol{R} - R^*\right)] = \boldsymbol{\pi}^\top \mathrm{E}[R^{e*}\boldsymbol{R}] - \mathrm{E}[R^{e*}R^*] = \boldsymbol{\pi}^\top \mathrm{E}[R^{e*}\boldsymbol{R}]. \tag{10.10}$$

Using (10.7), we get

$$\mathrm{E}[R^{e*}\boldsymbol{R}] = \mathrm{E}\left[\left(\mathrm{E}[\boldsymbol{R}]^\top \left(\mathrm{E}[\boldsymbol{R}\boldsymbol{R}^\top]\right)^{-1} \boldsymbol{R}\right)\boldsymbol{R}\right] - \frac{\mathrm{E}[R^*]}{\mathrm{E}[(R^*)^2]}\,\mathrm{E}[R^*\boldsymbol{R}]. \tag{10.11}$$

Let us first consider the last term on the right-hand side of Eq. (10.11). From Lemma 4.1, we have $\mathrm{E}[R^*R_i] = \mathrm{E}[(R^*)^2]$ for each i so that $\mathrm{E}[R^*\boldsymbol{R}] = \mathrm{E}[(R^*)^2]\mathbf{1}$. Now look at the first term on the right-hand side of (10.11). It can be shown in general that any vector $\boldsymbol{x}$ satisfies $\mathrm{E}[\boldsymbol{x}^\top \boldsymbol{R}\boldsymbol{R}] = \mathrm{E}[\boldsymbol{R}\boldsymbol{R}^\top]\boldsymbol{x}$. Applying this with $\boldsymbol{x} = (\mathrm{E}[\boldsymbol{R}\boldsymbol{R}^\top])^{-1}\,\mathrm{E}[\boldsymbol{R}]$ we obtain

$$\mathrm{E}\left[\left(\mathrm{E}[\boldsymbol{R}]^\top \left(\mathrm{E}[\boldsymbol{R}\boldsymbol{R}^\top]\right)^{-1} \boldsymbol{R}\right)\boldsymbol{R}\right] = \mathrm{E}[\boldsymbol{R}\boldsymbol{R}^\top]\left(\mathrm{E}[\boldsymbol{R}\boldsymbol{R}^\top]\right)^{-1}\mathrm{E}[\boldsymbol{R}] = \mathrm{E}[\boldsymbol{R}].$$

We can now rewrite Eq. (10.11):

$$\mathrm{E}[R^{e*}\boldsymbol{R}] = \mathrm{E}[\boldsymbol{R}] - \mathrm{E}[R^*]\mathbf{1}.$$

Going back to Eq. (10.10), we have

$$\mathrm{E}[R^{e*}R^e] = \boldsymbol{\pi}^\top \mathrm{E}[R^{e*}\boldsymbol{R}] = \boldsymbol{\pi}^\top\left(\mathrm{E}[\boldsymbol{R}] - \mathrm{E}[R^*]\mathbf{1}\right) = \boldsymbol{\pi}^\top \mathrm{E}[\boldsymbol{R}] - \mathrm{E}[R^*] = \mathrm{E}[R^e],$$

as was to be shown.

(c) The first part follows immediately from (b). The second part comes from

$$\mathrm{Var}[R^{e*}] = \mathrm{E}[(R^{e*})^2] - (\mathrm{E}[R^{e*}])^2 = \mathrm{E}[R^{e*}] - (\mathrm{E}[R^{e*}])^2 = \mathrm{E}[R^{e*}]\left(1 - \mathrm{E}[R^{e*}]\right)$$

where we have used the first part. □

10.3.1.4 A Characterization of the Mean-Variance Frontier in Terms of R^* and R^{e*}

First we show that any return can be decomposed using R^*, R^{e*}, and some 'residual' excess return.

Theorem 10.6 *For any return R_i, we can find a number w_i and an excess return $\eta_i \in \mathcal{R}^e$ so that*

$$R_i = R^* + w_i R^{e*} + \eta_i \tag{10.12}$$

and

$$\mathrm{E}[\eta_i] = \mathrm{E}[R^* \eta_i] = \mathrm{E}[R^{e*} \eta_i] = 0.$$

Proof. Define $w_i = (\mathrm{E}[R_i] - \mathrm{E}[R^*]) \,/\, \mathrm{E}[R^{e*}]$ and $\eta_i = R_i - R^* - w_i R^{e*}$. Then (10.12) and $\mathrm{E}[\eta_i] = 0$ hold by construction. η_i is the difference between the two excess returns $R_i - R^*$ and $w_i R^{e*}$ and therefore itself an excess return. Now $\mathrm{E}[R^* \eta_i] = 0$ follows from Eq. (10.8), whereas from Eq. (10.9) we have $\mathrm{E}[\eta_i R^{e*}] = \mathrm{E}[\eta_i]$ which we know is zero. □

Due to the relations $\mathrm{E}[R^* R^{e*}] = \mathrm{E}[R^* \eta_i] = \mathrm{E}[R^{e*} \eta_i] = 0$, the decomposition is said to be orthogonal.

Note that the same w_i applies for all returns with the same expected value. The return variance is

$$\begin{aligned}
\mathrm{Var}[R_i] &= \mathrm{Var}\left[R^* + w_i R^{e*}\right] + \mathrm{Var}[\eta_i] + 2\,\mathrm{Cov}\left[R^* + w_i R^{e*}, \eta_i\right] \\
&= \mathrm{Var}\left[R^* + w_i R^{e*}\right] + \mathrm{Var}[\eta_i] \\
&\qquad + 2\left\{\mathrm{E}\left[\left(R^* + w_i R^{e*}\right)\eta_i\right] - \mathrm{E}[R^* + w_i R^{e*}]\,\mathrm{E}[\eta_i]\right\} \\
&= \mathrm{Var}\left[R^* + w_i R^{e*}\right] + \mathrm{Var}[\eta_i].
\end{aligned}$$

Clearly the minimum variance for a given mean, that is a given w_i, is obtained for $\eta_i = 0$. We therefore have the following result:

Theorem 10.7 *A return R_i is mean-variance efficient if and only if it can be written as*

$$R_i = R^* + w_i R^{e*}$$

for some number w_i.

Varying w_i from $-\infty$ to $+\infty$, $R_i = R^* + w_i R^{e*}$ runs through the entire mean-variance frontier in the direction of higher and higher expected returns (since $\mathrm{E}[R^{e*}] = \mathrm{E}[(R^{e*})^2] > 0$).

Note that from Eq. (10.7) the constant-mimicking return can be written as

$$R_{\mathrm{cm}} = R^* + \frac{\mathrm{E}\left[(R^*)^2\right]}{\mathrm{E}[R^*]} R^{e*} \tag{10.13}$$

so the constant-mimicking return is mean-variance efficient.

10.3.1.5 Allowing for a Risk-Free Asset

Now let us assume that a risk-free asset with return R^f exists (or can be constructed as a portfolio of the basic assets). Then from Lemma 4.1 we have that $R^f\,\mathrm{E}[R^*] = \mathrm{E}[R^* R^f] = \mathrm{E}[(R^*)^2]$, and hence

$$R^f = \frac{\mathrm{E}[(R^*)^2]}{\mathrm{E}[R^*]} = \frac{1}{\mathbf{1}^\top\left(\mathrm{E}[\boldsymbol{R}\boldsymbol{R}^\top]\right)^{-1}\mathrm{E}[\boldsymbol{R}]}. \tag{10.14}$$

In addition we have

$$\mathrm{E}[\boldsymbol{R}]^\top\left(\mathrm{E}[\boldsymbol{R}\boldsymbol{R}^\top]\right)^{-1}\boldsymbol{R} = 1. \tag{10.15}$$

Let us just show this for the case with two assets, a risk-free and a risky so that $\boldsymbol{R} = (\tilde{R}, R^f)^\top$, where $\tilde{R}$ is the return on the risky asset. Then

$$\begin{aligned}
&\mathrm{E}[\boldsymbol{R}]^\top\left(\mathrm{E}[\boldsymbol{R}\boldsymbol{R}^\top]\right)^{-1}\boldsymbol{R}\\
&= \left(\mathrm{E}[\tilde{R}], R^f\right)\begin{pmatrix}\mathrm{E}[\tilde{R}^2] & R^f\,\mathrm{E}[\tilde{R}]\\ R^f\,\mathrm{E}[\tilde{R}] & (R^f)^2\end{pmatrix}^{-1}\begin{pmatrix}\tilde{R}\\ R^f\end{pmatrix}\\
&= \frac{1}{(R^f)^2\left(\mathrm{E}[\tilde{R}^2] - (\mathrm{E}[\tilde{R}])^2\right)}\left(\mathrm{E}[\tilde{R}], R^f\right)\begin{pmatrix}(R^f)^2 & -R^f\,\mathrm{E}[\tilde{R}]\\ -R^f\,\mathrm{E}[\tilde{R}] & \mathrm{E}[\tilde{R}^2]\end{pmatrix}\begin{pmatrix}\tilde{R}\\ R^f\end{pmatrix}\\
&= \frac{1}{(R^f)^2\left(\mathrm{E}[\tilde{R}^2] - (\mathrm{E}[\tilde{R}])^2\right)}\left(\mathrm{E}[\tilde{R}], R^f\right)\begin{pmatrix}(R^f)^2\left(\tilde{R} - \mathrm{E}[\tilde{R}]\right)\\ R^f\left(\mathrm{E}[\tilde{R}^2] - \mathrm{E}[\tilde{R}]\tilde{R}\right)\end{pmatrix}\\
&= 1.
\end{aligned}$$

Substituting Eqs. (10.14) and (10.15) into the general definition of R^{e*} in Eq. (10.7), we get

$$R^{e*} = 1 - \frac{1}{R^f}R^*. \tag{10.16}$$

Consequently,

$$R^f = R^* + R^f R^{e*} \tag{10.17}$$

so the w_i corresponding to the risk-free return is R^f itself. With $R^f > 1$, we see that $R^* + R^{e*}$ corresponds to a point on the frontier below the risk-free rate (again we use the fact that $\mathrm{E}[R^{e*}] > 0$).

10.3.1.6 The Minimum-Variance Return

With the decomposition in Theorem 10.7, it is easy to find the minimum-variance return. The variance of any mean-variance efficient return is

$$\begin{aligned}\operatorname{Var}\left[R^* + wR^{e*}\right] &= \mathrm{E}\left[(R^* + wR^{e*})^2\right] - \left(\mathrm{E}\left[R^* + wR^{e*}\right]\right)^2 \\ &= \mathrm{E}\left[(R^*)^2\right] + w^2\,\mathrm{E}\left[(R^{e*})^2\right] + 2w\,\mathrm{E}\left[R^* R^{e*}\right] \\ &\quad - \left(\mathrm{E}[R^*]\right)^2 - w^2\left(\mathrm{E}[R^{e*}]\right)^2 - 2w\,\mathrm{E}[R^*]\,\mathrm{E}[R^{e*}] \\ &= \mathrm{E}\left[(R^*)^2\right] + w^2\,\mathrm{E}\left[R^{e*}\right]\left(1 - \mathrm{E}\left[R^{e*}\right]\right) - \left(\mathrm{E}[R^*]\right)^2 \\ &\quad - 2w\,\mathrm{E}[R^*]\,\mathrm{E}[R^{e*}],\end{aligned}$$

where the simplifications leading to the last expression are due to Lemma 10.2. The first-order condition with respect to w implies that

$$w = \frac{\mathrm{E}[R^*]}{1 - \mathrm{E}[R^{e*}]}.$$

The minimum-variance return is thus

$$R_{\min} = R^* + \frac{\mathrm{E}[R^*]}{1 - \mathrm{E}[R^{e*}]} R^{e*} = R^* + \frac{\mathrm{E}[R^*]\,\mathrm{E}[R^{e*}]}{\operatorname{Var}[R^{e*}]} R^{e*}.$$

When a risk-free asset exists, this simplifies to $R_{\min} = R^f$ because $\mathrm{E}[R^*]/(1 - \mathrm{E}[R^{e*}]) = R^f$ using (10.16).

10.3.2 Mean-Variance Efficient Returns and State-Price Deflators

We can apply the above characterization of the mean-variance efficient returns to show the following result:

Theorem 10.8 *Let R denote a gross rate of return. Then there exists $a, b \in \mathbb{R}$ so that $\zeta = a + bR$ satisfies $P_i = \mathrm{E}[\zeta D_i]$ for $i = 1, \dots, I$ if and only if R is a mean-variance efficient return different from the constant-mimicking return.*

Proof. According to Theorem 10.6 we can decompose the return R as

$$R = R^* + wR^{e*} + \eta$$

for some $w \in \mathbb{R}$ and some excess return η with $\mathrm{E}[\eta] = \mathrm{E}[R^*\eta] = \mathrm{E}[R^{e*}\eta] = 0$. Obviously, R is mean-variance efficient if and only if $\eta = 0$. We need to show that, for suitable $a, b \in \mathbb{R}$,

$$\zeta = a + bR = a + b\left(R^* + wR^{e*} + \eta\right)$$

will satisfy $P_i = \mathrm{E}[\zeta D_i]$ for all i if and only if $\eta = 0$ and $w \neq \mathrm{E}[(R^*)^2]/\mathrm{E}[R^*]$.

Recall that $P_i = \mathrm{E}[\zeta D_i]$ for all i implies that $\mathrm{E}[\zeta R_i] = 1$ for all returns R_i and $\mathrm{E}[\zeta R^e] = 0$ for all excess returns R^e. In particular,

$$1 = \mathrm{E}[\zeta R^*] = \mathrm{E}\left[\left(a + b\left(R^* + wR^{e*} + \eta\right)\right) R^*\right] = a\,\mathrm{E}[R^*] + b\,\mathrm{E}\left[(R^*)^2\right]$$

$$0 = \mathrm{E}[\zeta R^{e*}] = \mathrm{E}\left[\left(a + b\left(R^* + wR^{e*} + \eta\right)\right) R^{e*}\right]$$
$$= a\,\mathrm{E}[R^{e*}] + bw\,\mathrm{E}\left[(R^{e*})^2\right] = (a + bw)\,\mathrm{E}[R^{e*}].$$

Solving for a and b, we get

$$a = \frac{w}{w\,\mathrm{E}[R^*] - \mathrm{E}\left[(R^*)^2\right]}, \qquad b = -\frac{1}{w\,\mathrm{E}[R^*] - \mathrm{E}\left[(R^*)^2\right]}$$

so that

$$\zeta = \frac{w - (R^* + wR^{e*} + \eta)}{w\,\mathrm{E}[R^*] - \mathrm{E}\left[(R^*)^2\right]}.$$

To avoid division by zero we have to assume that $w\,\mathrm{E}[R^*] \neq \mathrm{E}\left[(R^*)^2\right]$, which rules out the constant-mimicking return, compare Eq. (10.13).

Now consider any other return R_i and decompose to $R_i = R^* + w_i R^{e*} + \eta_i$. Then

$$\mathrm{E}[\zeta R_i] = \frac{1}{w\,\mathrm{E}[R^*] - \mathrm{E}\left[(R^*)^2\right]}\,\mathrm{E}\left[\left(w - \left(R^* + wR^{e*} + \eta\right)\right)\left(R^* + w_i R^{e*} + \eta_i\right)\right]$$
$$= \frac{1}{w\,\mathrm{E}[R^*] - \mathrm{E}\left[(R^*)^2\right]}\left(w\,\mathrm{E}[R^*] - \mathrm{E}\left[(R^*)^2\right] - \mathrm{E}[\eta\eta_i]\right),$$

where we have applied various results from earlier. We can now see that we will have $\mathrm{E}[\zeta R_i] = 1$ for all returns R_i if and only if $\mathrm{E}[\eta\eta_i] = 0$ for all excess returns η_i. In particular $\mathrm{E}[\eta^2] = 0$, which together with $\mathrm{E}[\eta] = 0]$ imply that $\eta = 0$. □

This result is remarkable: any mean-variance efficient return (except one) defines a state-price deflator or, more precisely, a candidate for a state-price deflator since positivity is not guaranteed. Note that we have not made any assumptions about preferences nor the distribution of returns. As explained in Section 6.3, the use of mean-variance analysis for portfolio choice requires an assumption of normally distributed returns. Even in that case mean-variance portfolio choice is problematic in the sense that it does not work for many frequently used utility functions and it does not directly identify the optimal portfolio for a given individual. In that light, it is surprising that mean-variance returns play such a powerful role in asset pricing theory as reflected by Theorem 10.8.

10.3.3 Mean-Variance Efficient Returns and Pricing Factors

Together with earlier results of this chapter, Theorem 10.8 indicates that mean-variance efficient returns can act as pricing factors. Here is the precise result:

Theorem 10.9 *A return R^{mv} is a pricing factor, that is an $\alpha \in \mathbb{R}$ exists so that*

$$\mathrm{E}[R_i] = \alpha + \beta[R_i, R^{mv}]\left(\mathrm{E}[R^{mv}] - \alpha\right), \quad i = 1, \dots, I, \tag{10.18}$$

if and only if R^{mv} is a mean-variance efficient return different from the minimum-variance return.

The constant α must then be equal to the zero-beta return corresponding to R^{mv}, which is equal to the risk-free return if a risk-free asset exists.

Proof. ('If' part.) First, let us show that if R^{mv} is mean-variance efficient and different from the minimum-variance return, it will work as a pricing factor. This result is originally due to Roll (1977). For some w, we have $R^{\mathrm{mv}} = R^* + wR^{e*}$. Consider a general return R_i and decompose as

$$R_i = R^* + w_i R^{e*} + \eta_i$$

as in Theorem 10.6. Then

$$\mathrm{E}[R_i] = \mathrm{E}[R^*] + w_i\,\mathrm{E}[R^{e*}]$$

and

$$\begin{aligned}\mathrm{Cov}[R_i, R^{\mathrm{mv}}] &= \mathrm{Var}[R^*] + ww_i\,\mathrm{Var}[R^{e*}] + (w + w_i)\,\mathrm{Cov}[R^*, R^{e*}] \\ &= \mathrm{Var}[R^*] + ww_i\,\mathrm{Var}[R^{e*}] - (w + w_i)\,\mathrm{E}[R^*]\,\mathrm{E}[R^{e*}]\end{aligned}$$

which implies that

$$\mathrm{Cov}[R_i, R^{\mathrm{mv}}] - \mathrm{Var}[R^*] + w\,\mathrm{E}[R^*]\,\mathrm{E}[R^{e*}] = w_i\left(w\,\mathrm{Var}[R^{e*}] - \mathrm{E}[R^*]\,\mathrm{E}[R^{e*}]\right).$$

If $w \neq \mathrm{E}[R^*]\,\mathrm{E}[R^{e*}]/\,\mathrm{Var}[R^{e*}]$, which according to Eq. (10.17) means that R^{mv} is different from the minimum-variance return, then we can solve the above equation for w_i with the solution

$$w_i = \frac{\mathrm{Cov}[R_i, R^{\mathrm{mv}}] - \mathrm{Var}[R^*] + w\,\mathrm{E}[R^*]\,\mathrm{E}[R^{e*}]}{w\,\mathrm{Var}[R^{e*}] - \mathrm{E}[R^*]\,\mathrm{E}[R^{e*}]}.$$

Hence

$$\begin{aligned}\mathrm{E}[R_i] &= \mathrm{E}[R^*] + w_i\,\mathrm{E}[R^{e*}] \\ &= \mathrm{E}[R^*] + \frac{\mathrm{Cov}[R_i, R^{\mathrm{mv}}] - \mathrm{Var}[R^*] + w\,\mathrm{E}[R^*]\,\mathrm{E}[R^{e*}]}{w\,\mathrm{Var}[R^{e*}] - \mathrm{E}[R^*]\,\mathrm{E}[R^{e*}]}\,\mathrm{E}[R^{e*}] \\ &= \alpha + \frac{\mathrm{Cov}[R_i, R^{\mathrm{mv}}]}{w\,\mathrm{Var}[R^{e*}] - \mathrm{E}[R^*]\,\mathrm{E}[R^{e*}]}\,\mathrm{E}[R^{e*}]\end{aligned}$$

where we have defined the constant α as

$$\alpha = \mathrm{E}[R^*] + \frac{w\,\mathrm{E}[R^*]\,\mathrm{E}[R^{e*}] - \mathrm{Var}[R^*]}{w\,\mathrm{Var}[R^{e*}] - \mathrm{E}[R^*]\,\mathrm{E}[R^{e*}]}\,\mathrm{E}[R^{e*}].$$

This applies to any return R_i and in particular to R^{mv} itself, which implies that

$$\mathrm{E}[R^{\mathrm{mv}}] = \alpha + \frac{\mathrm{Var}[R^{\mathrm{mv}}]}{w\,\mathrm{Var}[R^{e*}] - \mathrm{E}[R^*]\,\mathrm{E}[R^{e*}]}\,\mathrm{E}[R^{e*}]$$

and hence

$$\frac{\mathrm{E}[R^{e*}]}{w\,\mathrm{Var}[R^{e*}] - \mathrm{E}[R^*]\,\mathrm{E}[R^{e*}]} = \frac{\mathrm{E}[R^{\mathrm{mv}}] - \alpha}{\mathrm{Var}[R^{\mathrm{mv}}]}.$$

Substituting this back in, we get

$$\mathrm{E}[R_i] = \alpha + \frac{\mathrm{Cov}[R_i, R^{\mathrm{mv}}]}{\mathrm{Var}[R^{\mathrm{mv}}]}\left(\mathrm{E}[R^{\mathrm{mv}}] - \alpha\right) = \alpha + \beta[R_i, R^{\mathrm{mv}}]\left(\mathrm{E}[R^{\mathrm{mv}}] - \alpha\right),$$

which verifies that R^{mv} is a valid pricing factor.

('Only if' part.) Next, let us show that if a return works as a pricing factor, it must be mean-variance efficient and different from the minimum-variance return. This proof is due to Hansen and Richard (1987). Assume that R^{mv} is a pricing factor. Decomposing as in Theorem 10.6

$$R^{\mathrm{mv}} = R^* + wR^{e*} + \eta,$$

we need to show that $\eta = 0$ (so that R^{mv} is mean-variance efficient) and that $w \neq \mathrm{E}[R^*]\,\mathrm{E}[R^{e*}]/\,\mathrm{Var}[R^{e*}]$ (so that R^{mv} is different from the minimum-variance return).

Define a new return R as the 'efficient part' of R^{mv}, that is

$$R = R^* + wR^{e*}.$$

Since

$$\mathrm{Cov}[\eta, R^{\mathrm{mv}}] = \mathrm{E}[\eta R^{\mathrm{mv}}] - \mathrm{E}[\eta]\,\mathrm{E}[R^{\mathrm{mv}}] = \mathrm{E}[\eta R^{\mathrm{mv}}] = \mathrm{E}[\eta^2],$$

we get

$$\begin{aligned}\mathrm{Cov}[R, R^{\mathrm{mv}}] &= \mathrm{Cov}[R^{\mathrm{mv}} - \eta, R^{\mathrm{mv}}] = \mathrm{Cov}[R^{\mathrm{mv}}, R^{\mathrm{mv}}] - \mathrm{Cov}[\eta, R^{\mathrm{mv}}]\\ &= \mathrm{Var}[R^{\mathrm{mv}}] - \mathrm{E}[\eta^2].\end{aligned}$$

On the other hand, $\mathrm{E}[R] = \mathrm{E}[R^{\mathrm{mv}}]$ so applying (10.18) for $R_i = R$, we obtain

$$\mathrm{E}[R^{\mathrm{mv}}] - \alpha = \mathrm{E}[R] - \alpha = \frac{\mathrm{Cov}[R, R^{\mathrm{mv}}]}{\mathrm{Var}[R^{\mathrm{mv}}]}\left(\mathrm{E}[R^{\mathrm{mv}}] - \alpha\right)$$

and hence $\mathrm{Cov}[R, R^{\mathrm{mv}}] = \mathrm{Var}[R^{\mathrm{mv}}]$. We conclude that $\mathrm{E}[\eta^2] = 0$, which together with $\mathrm{E}[\eta] = 0$ imply $\eta = 0$.

Suppose that $w = \mathrm{E}[R^*]\,\mathrm{E}[R^{e*}]/\,\mathrm{Var}[R^{e*}]$ and define a new gross rate of return

$$R = R^{\mathrm{mv}} + \frac{1}{\mathrm{E}[R^{e*}]}R^{e*}.$$

Clearly, $\mathrm{E}[R] = \mathrm{E}[R^{\mathrm{mv}}] + 1$, and furthermore

$$\mathrm{Cov}[R, R^{\mathrm{mv}}] = \mathrm{Var}[R^{\mathrm{mv}}] + \frac{1}{\mathrm{E}[R^{e*}]} \mathrm{Cov}[R^{e*}, R^{\mathrm{mv}}] = \mathrm{Var}[R^{\mathrm{mv}}]$$

since

$$\begin{aligned}\mathrm{Cov}[R^{e*}, R^{\mathrm{mv}}] &= \mathrm{Cov}[R^{e*}, R^* + wR^{e*}] = \mathrm{Cov}[R^{e*}, R^*] + w\,\mathrm{Var}[R^{e*}] \\ &= \mathrm{Cov}[R^{e*}, R^*] + \mathrm{E}[R^*]\,\mathrm{E}[R^{e*}] = \mathrm{E}[R^{e*}R^*] = 0.\end{aligned}$$

Applying (10.18) to the return R, we get

$$\mathrm{E}[R] = \alpha + \frac{\mathrm{Cov}[R, R^{\mathrm{mv}}]}{\mathrm{Var}[R^{\mathrm{mv}}]} \left(\mathrm{E}[R^{\mathrm{mv}}] - \alpha\right) = \alpha + \left(\mathrm{E}[R^{\mathrm{mv}}] - \alpha\right) = \mathrm{E}[R^{\mathrm{mv}}],$$

which contradicts our early conclusion that $\mathrm{E}[R] = \mathrm{E}[R^{\mathrm{mv}}] + 1$. Hence our assumption about w cannot hold. □

One implication of this theorem is that we can always find some returns that work as a pricing factor, namely the mean-variance efficient returns. Another implication is that the conclusion of the classic CAPM can be restated as 'the market portfolio is mean-variance efficient'.

10.4 PRICING FACTORS IN A DISCRETE-TIME FRAMEWORK

In the one-period framework we defined a pricing factor to be a K-dimensional random variable $\boldsymbol{x}$ such that there exists some $\alpha \in \mathbb{R}$ and some $\boldsymbol{\eta} \in \mathbb{R}^K$ so that

$$\mathrm{E}[R_i] = \alpha + \boldsymbol{\beta}[R_i, \boldsymbol{x}]^{\top}\boldsymbol{\eta}, \quad i = 1, \dots, I,$$

where $\boldsymbol{\beta}[R_i, \boldsymbol{x}] = (\mathrm{Var}[\boldsymbol{x}])^{-1}\,\mathrm{Cov}[\boldsymbol{x}, R_i]$. We saw that any state-price deflator works as a pricing factor and, more generally, if $\zeta = a + \boldsymbol{b}^{\top}\boldsymbol{x}$ is a state-price deflator for constants $a, \boldsymbol{b}$ then $\boldsymbol{x}$ is a pricing factor. On the other hand, given any pricing factor $\boldsymbol{x}$, we can find constants $a, \boldsymbol{b}$ such that $\zeta = a + \boldsymbol{b}^{\top}\boldsymbol{x}$ is a candidate state-price deflator (not necessarily strictly positive, alas).

Now think of a multiperiod, discrete-time framework with the set of time points where trading and consumption take place is given by $\mathcal{T} = \{0, 1, 2, \dots, T\}$. Here a pricing factor should be so that a relation like the above holds for every period, that is between any two adjacent time points. But the expectation, covariance, and variance in such an expression can either be conditional or unconditional. We will therefore distinguish between a *conditional pricing factor* and an *unconditional pricing factor*.

10.4.1 Conditional Pricing Factors

We define a conditional pricing factor as follows:

Definition 10.2 *In a multiperiod, discrete-time framework, a conditional pricing factor is a stochastic process $\boldsymbol{x} = (\boldsymbol{x}_t)_{t\in\mathcal{T}}$ of some dimension K so that*

(i) *the conditional variance-covariance matrix* $\mathrm{Var}_t[\boldsymbol{x}_{t+1}]$ *is non-singular for all $t = 0, 1, \dots, T-1$ and in all states, and*

(ii) *adapted stochastic processes $\alpha = (\alpha_t)_{t\in\mathcal{T}}$ and $\boldsymbol{\eta} = (\boldsymbol{\eta}_t)_{t\in\mathcal{T}}$ exist so that*

$$\mathrm{E}_t[R_{i,t+1}] = \alpha_t + \boldsymbol{\beta}_t[R_{i,t+1}, \boldsymbol{x}_{t+1}]^\top \boldsymbol{\eta}_t, \quad i = 1, \dots, I,$$

for any $t = 0, 1, 2, \dots, T-1$. Here, the conditional factor-beta is defined as

$$\boldsymbol{\beta}_t[R_{i,t+1}, \boldsymbol{x}_{t+1}] = (\mathrm{Var}_t[\boldsymbol{x}_{t+1}])^{-1} \,\mathrm{Cov}_t[\boldsymbol{x}_{t+1}, R_{i,t+1}].$$

Note that if a conditionally risk-free asset—an asset which is risk-free over the next period—exists then $\alpha_t = R^f_t$ implying that

$$\mathrm{E}_t[R_{i,t+1}] = R^f_t + \boldsymbol{\beta}_t[R_{i,t+1}, \boldsymbol{x}_{t+1}]^\top \boldsymbol{\eta}_t, \quad i = 1, \dots, I.$$

As in the one-period framework, conditional pricing factors are not unique. Suppose $\boldsymbol{x}$ is a conditional pricing factor, and let $a = (a_t)_{t\in\mathcal{T}}$ be an adapted one-dimensional process and $\underline{\underline{A}} = (\underline{\underline{A}}_t)_{t\in\mathcal{T}}$ be an adapted process whose values $\underline{\underline{A}}_t$ are non-singular $K \times K$ matrices. Then $\hat{\boldsymbol{x}}$ defined by

$$\hat{\boldsymbol{x}}_{t+1} = a_t + \underline{\underline{A}}_t \boldsymbol{x}_{t+1} \tag{10.19}$$

will also be a conditional pricing factor.

If $\zeta = (\zeta_t)_{t\in\mathcal{T}}$ is a state-price deflator process, the one-period analysis implies that the ratios ζ_{t+1}/ζ_t define a conditional pricing factor (see Theorem 10.2). Since $\zeta_{t+1} = 0 + \zeta_t(\zeta_{t+1}/\zeta_t)$ is a transformation of the form (10.19), we see that any state-price deflator is a conditional pricing factor.

As in the one-period case (Theorems 10.3 and 10.4), we have a close relation between conditional pricing factors and state-price deflators. If a state-price deflator $\zeta = (\zeta_t)_{t\in\mathcal{T}}$ satisfies

$$\frac{\zeta_{t+1}}{\zeta_t} = a_t + \boldsymbol{b}_t^\top \boldsymbol{x}_{t+1}, \quad t = 0, 1, \dots, T-1, \tag{10.20}$$

for some adapted processes $\boldsymbol{x}$, a, and $\boldsymbol{b}$, then $\boldsymbol{x}$ is a conditional pricing factor. This result follows by substituting the affine expression for the state-price deflator into Eq. (4.23), which implies that

$$\begin{aligned}\mathrm{E}_t[R_{i,t+1}] &= \frac{1}{a_t + \boldsymbol{b}_t^\top E_t\left[\boldsymbol{x}_{t+1}\right]} - \frac{\boldsymbol{b}_t^\top \mathrm{Cov}_t\left[R_{i,t+1}, \boldsymbol{x}_{t+1}\right]}{a_t + \boldsymbol{b}_t^\top E_t\left[\boldsymbol{x}_{t+1}\right]} \\ &= \alpha_t + \boldsymbol{\beta}_t[R_{i,t+1}, \boldsymbol{x}_{t+1}]^\top \boldsymbol{\eta}_t,\end{aligned} \tag{10.21}$$

where

$$\alpha_t = \frac{1}{a_t + \boldsymbol{b}_t^\top \mathrm{E}_t\left[\boldsymbol{x}_{t+1}\right]}, \qquad \boldsymbol{\eta}_t = -\alpha_t \operatorname{Var}_t[\boldsymbol{x}_{t+1}]\boldsymbol{b}_t. \tag{10.22}$$

Conversely, for any conditional pricing factor $\boldsymbol{x}$, we can find adapted process $a = (a_t)_{t\in\mathcal{T}}$ and $\boldsymbol{b} = (\boldsymbol{b}_t)_{t\in\mathcal{T}}$ so that Eq. (10.20) defines a candidate for a next-period state-price deflator which is not necessarily positive, however.

If we apply the relation between the next-period state-price deflator and the pricing factor in the recursive pricing relation (4.19), we obtain

$$\begin{aligned} P_{it} &= \mathrm{E}_t\left[\left(a_t + \boldsymbol{b}_t^\top \boldsymbol{x}_{t+1}\right)\left(P_{i,t+1} + D_{i,t+1}\right)\right] \\ &= \mathrm{E}_t\left[a_t + \boldsymbol{b}_t^\top \boldsymbol{x}_{t+1}\right]\mathrm{E}_t\left[P_{i,t+1} + D_{i,t+1}\right] + \boldsymbol{b}_t^\top \operatorname{Cov}_t\left[\boldsymbol{x}_{t+1}, P_{i,t+1} + D_{i,t+1}\right] \\ &= \frac{\mathrm{E}_t\left[P_{i,t+1} + D_{i,t+1}\right] - \boldsymbol{\beta}[P_{i,t+1} + D_{i,t+1}, \boldsymbol{x}_{t+1}]^\top \boldsymbol{\eta}_t}{\alpha_t}, \end{aligned}$$

which illustrates the use of pricing factors for valuation purposes. See also Exercise 10.3.

Likewise the notion of an approximate pricing factor can be extended to the multiperiod setting. Recall from Theorem 8.2 the simple discrete-time consumption-based CAPM in which an individual with time-additive power utility enjoys lognormally distributed consumption. By rewriting Eq. (8.19), the excess expected return on a risky asset in that model will satisfy

$$\mathrm{E}_t[R_{i,t+1}] - R_t^f \approx \beta_t[R_{i,t+1}, g_{t+1}]\eta_t, \tag{10.23}$$

where $g_{t+1} = c_{t+1}/c_t$ is the gross consumption growth between time t and $t+1$ and $\eta_t = \gamma\sigma_{gt}^2$, the product of the relative risk aversion and the variance of consumption growth. Hence, under the stated assumptions, consumption growth is an approximate pricing factor.

Approximate pricing factors can also be identified as follows. Assume the existence of a risk-free asset and suppose a next-period state-price deflator is given in the exponential-affine form

$$\frac{\zeta_{t+1}}{\zeta_t} = e^{a_t + \boldsymbol{b}_t^\top \boldsymbol{x}_{t+1}}.$$

Substituting that into Eq. (4.24), we obtain

$$\mathrm{E}_t[R_{i,t+1}] - R_t^f \approx -\boldsymbol{b}_t^\top \operatorname{Cov}_t\left[R_{i,t+1}, \boldsymbol{x}_{t+1}\right] = \boldsymbol{\beta}_t[R_{i,t+1}, \boldsymbol{x}_{t+1}]^\top \boldsymbol{\eta}_t,$$

where $\boldsymbol{\eta}_t = -\operatorname{Var}_t[\boldsymbol{x}_{t+1}]\boldsymbol{b}_t$. We could also generalize the log pricing factor and the associated relation (10.5) to a multiperiod setting.

10.4.2 Unconditional Pricing Factors

Next we turn to the definition of an unconditional pricing factor:

Definition 10.3 *In a multiperiod, discrete-time framework, an unconditional pricing factor is a stochastic process* $\boldsymbol{x} = (\boldsymbol{x}_t)_{t\in\mathcal{T}}$ *of some dimension K so that*

(i) the unconditional variance-covariance matrix $\mathrm{Var}[\boldsymbol{x}_{t+1}]$ *is non-singular for all* $t = 0, 1, \dots, T-1$, *and*

(ii) constants $\alpha \in \mathbb{R}$ *and* $\boldsymbol{\eta} \in \mathbb{R}^K$ *exist so that*

$$\mathrm{E}[R_{i,t+1}] = \alpha + \boldsymbol{\beta}[R_{i,t+1}, \boldsymbol{x}_{t+1}]^\top \boldsymbol{\eta}, \quad i = 1, \dots, I, \tag{10.24}$$

for any $t = 0, 1, 2, \dots, T-1$. *Here, the unconditional factor-beta is defined as*

$$\boldsymbol{\beta}[R_{i,t+1}, \boldsymbol{x}_{t+1}] = (\mathrm{Var}[\boldsymbol{x}_{t+1}])^{-1} \mathrm{Cov}[\boldsymbol{x}_{t+1}, R_{i,t+1}]. \tag{10.25}$$

Testing factor models on actual data really requires an unconditional model since we need to replace expected returns by average returns, and so on. Similarly, if we want to estimate factor-betas from a time series of observations of returns and the factor.

How are unconditional pricing factors related to state-price deflators? First note that $\mathrm{E}_t[R_{i,t+1}\frac{\zeta_{t+1}}{\zeta_t}] = 1$ implies that $\mathrm{E}[R_{i,t+1}\frac{\zeta_{t+1}}{\zeta_t}] = 1$ and thus

$$\mathrm{E}\left[R_{i,t+1}\right] = \frac{1}{\mathrm{E}\left[\frac{\zeta_{t+1}}{\zeta_t}\right]} - \frac{\mathrm{Cov}\left[R_{i,t+1}, \frac{\zeta_{t+1}}{\zeta_t}\right]}{\mathrm{E}\left[\frac{\zeta_{t+1}}{\zeta_t}\right]}.$$

Suppose the next-period state-price deflator can be expressed as

$$\frac{\zeta_{t+1}}{\zeta_t} = a + \boldsymbol{b}^\top \boldsymbol{x}_{t+1}$$

for some K-dimensional stochastic process $\boldsymbol{x} = (\boldsymbol{x}_t)_{t\in\mathcal{T}}$ and some constants $a \in \mathbb{R}$, $\boldsymbol{b} \in \mathbb{R}^K$, and furthermore the unconditional moments $\mathrm{E}[\boldsymbol{x}_{t+1}]$, $\mathrm{Var}[\boldsymbol{x}_{t+1}]$, and $\mathrm{Cov}[\boldsymbol{x}_{t+1}, R_{i,t+1}]$ are independent of t (stationarity assumption). Then we get an unconditional factor model because

$$\begin{aligned}
\mathrm{E}[R_{i,t+1}] &= \frac{1}{a + \boldsymbol{b}^\top \mathrm{E}[\boldsymbol{x}_{t+1}]} - \frac{\boldsymbol{b}^\top \mathrm{Cov}\left[R_{i,t+1}, \boldsymbol{x}_{t+1}\right]}{a + \boldsymbol{b}^\top \mathrm{E}[\boldsymbol{x}_{t+1}]} \\
&= \alpha + \left((\mathrm{Var}[\boldsymbol{x}_{t+1}])^{-1} \mathrm{Cov}\left[R_{i,t+1}, \boldsymbol{x}_{t+1}\right]\right)^\top \left(-\frac{1}{\alpha} \mathrm{Var}[\boldsymbol{x}_{t+1}]\boldsymbol{b}\right) \\
&= \alpha + \boldsymbol{\beta}[R_{i,t+1}, \boldsymbol{x}_{t+1}]^\top \boldsymbol{\eta}
\end{aligned}$$

with the obvious definition of α and $\boldsymbol{\eta}$.

Can we deduce a (candidate) state-price deflator from an unconditional pricing factor? If $\boldsymbol{x}$ is an unconditional pricing factor, we can go backwards in the above derivation to show that

$$\mathrm{E}\left[R_{i,t+1}\left(a+\boldsymbol{b}^{\top}\boldsymbol{x}_{t+1}\right)\right]=1 \tag{10.26}$$

with

$$\boldsymbol{b}=-\frac{1}{\alpha}\left(\mathrm{Var}[\boldsymbol{x}_{t+1}]\right)^{-1}\boldsymbol{\eta}, \quad a=\frac{1}{\alpha}-\boldsymbol{b}^{\top}\,\mathrm{E}[\boldsymbol{x}_{t+1}],$$

which are constants if the unconditional moments $\mathrm{E}[\boldsymbol{x}_{t+1}]$, $\mathrm{Var}[\boldsymbol{x}_{t+1}]$ are independent of t. However, Eq. (10.26) does *not* imply that

$$\mathrm{E}_t\left[R_{i,t+1}\left(a+\boldsymbol{b}^{\top}\boldsymbol{x}_{t+1}\right)\right]=1, \quad t=0,1,\ldots,T-1,$$

nor that

$$\mathrm{E}_t\left[R_{i,t+1}\frac{a+\boldsymbol{b}^{\top}\boldsymbol{x}_{t+1}}{a+\boldsymbol{b}^{\top}\boldsymbol{x}_t}\right]=1, \quad t=0,1,\ldots,T-1,$$

which is a necessary condition for $a+\boldsymbol{b}^{\top}\boldsymbol{x}_{t+1}$ to define a state-price deflator. Therefore, we cannot generally deduce a state-price deflator from an unconditional pricing factor.

10.4.3 From Conditional to Unconditional Pricing Factors

As a first attempt to identify an unconditional pricing factor, suppose that x is a one-dimensional conditional pricing factor so that

$$\mathrm{E}_t[R_{i,t+1}]=\alpha_t+\beta_t[R_{i,t+1},x_{t+1}]\eta_t$$

holds for any t and any i. Taking unconditional expectations implies that

$$\begin{aligned}
\mathrm{E}[R_{i,t+1}] &= \mathrm{E}[\alpha_t]+\mathrm{E}\left[\beta_t[R_{i,t+1},x_{t+1}]\eta_t\right] \\
&= \mathrm{E}[\alpha_t]+\mathrm{E}\left[\beta_t[R_{i,t+1},x_{t+1}]\right]\mathrm{E}[\eta_t]+\mathrm{Cov}\left[\beta_t[R_{i,t+1},\boldsymbol{x}_{t+1}],\eta_t\right] \\
&= \alpha+\bar{\beta}[R_{i,t+1},x_{t+1}]\eta+\mathrm{Cov}\left[\beta_t[R_{i,t+1},\boldsymbol{x}_{t+1}],\eta_t\right]
\end{aligned} \tag{10.27}$$

with $\alpha=\mathrm{E}[\alpha_t]$, $\eta=\mathrm{E}[\eta_t]$, and $\bar{\beta}[R_{i,t+1},x_{t+1}]=\mathrm{E}\left[\beta_t[R_{i,t+1},x_{t+1}]\right]$. If the covariance is zero, this simplifies to

$$\mathrm{E}[R_{i,t+1}]=\alpha+\bar{\beta}[R_{i,t+1},x_{t+1}]\eta,$$

which is of the form (10.24) although the expected conditional beta $\bar{\beta}[R_{i,t+1},x_{t+1}]$ is not necessarily equal to the unconditional beta defined in Eq. (10.25). Note that the covariance $\mathrm{Cov}\left[\beta_t[R_{i,t+1},\boldsymbol{x}_{t+1}]\eta_t\right]$ above is, of course, zero if either the conditional beta or the conditional factor risk premium are constant. It seems likely that both conditional betas and conditional factor risk premia vary with the state of the economy in which case the covariance would generally be non-zero.

The above considerations show that a conditional pricing factor does typically not work as an unconditional pricing factor by itself. However, in some cases we can obtain an unconditional pricing factor from a conditional pricing factor by adding appropriate factors. Suppose that the next-period state-price deflator is of the form (10.20) so that $\boldsymbol{x}$ is a conditional pricing factor. Furthermore suppose that the variations in the coefficients a_t and $\boldsymbol{b}_t$ can be captured by affine functions of some other stochastic process $\boldsymbol{y} = (\boldsymbol{y}_t)_{t\in\mathcal{T}}$:

$$a_t = A_0 + \boldsymbol{A}_1^\top \boldsymbol{y}_t, \quad \boldsymbol{b}_t = \boldsymbol{B}_0 + \underline{\underline{B}}_1 \boldsymbol{y}_t,$$

where $A_0, \boldsymbol{A}_1, \boldsymbol{B}_0, \underline{\underline{B}}_1$ are constants of suitable dimensions. If, in addition, the unconditional moments of $\boldsymbol{x}_{t+1}$ and $\boldsymbol{y}_t$ are independent of t, then we have an unconditional factor model with factors $x_i, y_j, x_i y_j$. For example, if both x and y are one-dimensional, then

$$\frac{\zeta_{t+1}}{\zeta_t} = (A_0 + A_1 y_t) + (B_0 + B_1 y_t) x_{t+1} = A_0 + A_1 y_t + B_0 x_{t+1} + B_1 y_t x_{t+1},$$

which defines a three-dimensional *unconditional* pricing factor $(y_t, x_{t+1}, y_t x_{t+1})^\top$. Hence, the one-factor conditional model corresponds to a three-factor unconditional model.

To understand the role of the 'instrument vector' $\boldsymbol{y}_t$, recall from Theorem 4.3 that if a risk-free asset is traded, then the gross risk-free rate R^f_t satisfies

$$\left(R^f_t\right)^{-1} = \mathrm{E}_t\left[\frac{\zeta_{t+1}}{\zeta_t}\right] = a_t + \boldsymbol{b}_t^\top \mathrm{E}_t[\boldsymbol{x}_{t+1}]$$

and the maximum Sharpe ratio is given by

$$\sigma_t\left[\frac{\zeta_{t+1}}{\zeta_t}\right] / \mathrm{E}_t\left[\frac{\zeta_{t+1}}{\zeta_t}\right] = \frac{\sqrt{\boldsymbol{b}_t^\top \mathrm{Var}_t[\boldsymbol{x}_{t+1}]\boldsymbol{b}_t}}{a_t + \boldsymbol{b}_t^\top \mathrm{E}_t[\boldsymbol{x}_{t+1}]}.$$

Therefore the instruments in $\boldsymbol{y}_t$ must capture the variations over time in the risk-free rate and the maximum Sharpe ratio as well as variations in the conditional moments of the conditional pricing factor.

10.4.4 A Discrete-Time CAPM

The one-period CAPM reviewed in Section 10.2.3 states that the return on a market portfolio is a pricing factor. This is theoretically correct under the dubious assumption of either quadratic utility or normally distributed returns. Moreover, the market portfolio should, strictly speaking, include all assets, although applications often use a stock market index as a proxy. A discrete-time version of the CAPM could either be in form of a conditional CAPM with

$$\mathrm{E}_t[R_{i,t+1}] = \alpha_t + \beta_{iW,t}\left(\mathrm{E}_t[R_{W,t+1}] - \alpha_t\right)$$

or an unconditional CAPM with

$$\mathrm{E}[R_{i,t+1}] = \alpha + \beta_{iW}\left(\mathrm{E}[R_{W,t+1}] - \alpha\right).$$

The conditional CAPM is roughly equivalent to having a next-period state-price deflator of the form $\zeta_{t+1}/\zeta_t = a_t + b_t R_{W,t+1}$, whereas the unconditional CAPM corresponds to $\zeta_{t+1}/\zeta_t = a + bR_{W,t+1}$ with constant a and b.

Is there any theoretical support for either of these discrete-time versions of the CAPM? First, let us derive a more general CAPM-type model. We consider an individual with time-additive expected utility and recall the envelope condition $u'(c_t) = J_W(W_t, x_t, t)$ from Eq. (6.38). Here, $J(W, x, t)$ denotes the indirect utility of an individual, which is the maximum obtainable expected utility over the remaining lifetime from time t and onward when the individual has wealth W at time t. The state variable x captures all other variables that may affect the well-being of the individual and, consequently, the indirect utility. This could be variables containing relevant information about future investment opportunities (the risk-free rate, volatilities, Sharpe ratios, etc.) or about future labour income. We assume for notational simplicity that x is one-dimensional.

The next-period state-price deflator can be stated in terms of marginal utilities of consumption, see Theorem 6.6, and due to the envelope condition we can rewrite the deflator in terms of the derivative of indirect utility with respect to wealth:

$$\frac{\zeta_{t+1}}{\zeta_t} = e^{-\delta}\frac{u'(c_{t+1})}{u'(c_t)} = e^{-\delta}\frac{J_W(W_{t+1}, x_{t+1}, t+1)}{J_W(W_t, x_t, t)}.$$

Seen at time t, the random variables on the right-hand side are W_{t+1} and x_{t+1}. In order to identify pricing factors, we have to linearize using the first-order Taylor approximation

$$\begin{aligned} J_W(W_{t+1}, x_{t+1}, t+1) \approx\ & J_W(W_t, x_t, t) + J_{WW}(W_t, x_t, t)\Delta W_{t+1} \\ & + J_{Wx}(W_t, x_t, t)\Delta x_{t+1} + J_{Wt}(W_t, x_t, t), \end{aligned}$$

where $\Delta W_{t+1} = W_{t+1} - W_t$ and $\Delta x_{t+1} = x_{t+1} - x_t$. This implies that

$$\begin{aligned} \frac{\zeta_{t+1}}{\zeta_t} \approx\ & e^{-\delta}\left(1 + \frac{J_{Wt}(W_t, x_t, t)}{J_W(W_t, x_t, t)}\right) - e^{-\delta}\left(\frac{-W_t J_{WW}(W_t, x_t, t)}{J_W(W_t, x_t, t)}\right)\frac{\Delta W_{t+1}}{W_t} \\ & + e^{-\delta}\left(\frac{x_t J_{Wx}(W_t, x_t, t)}{J_W(W_t, x_t, t)}\right)\frac{\Delta x_{t+1}}{x_t}, \end{aligned}$$

which is affine in ΔW_{t+1} and Δx_{t+1} (and thus affine in W_{t+1} and x_{t+1}). Therefore, from Eqs. (10.20)–(10.22), we obtain the approximate, conditional two-factor model

$$\mathrm{E}_t[R_{i,t+1}] \approx \alpha_t + \boldsymbol{\beta}_{it}^{\top}\boldsymbol{\eta}_t,$$

where

$$\alpha_t^{-1} = e^{-\delta}\left(1 + \frac{J_{Wt}(W_t,x_t,t)}{J_W(W_t,x_t,t)} - \frac{-W_tJ_{WW}(W_t,x_t,t)}{J_W(W_t,x_t,t)}\mathrm{E}_t\left[\frac{\Delta W_{t+1}}{W_t}\right] + \frac{x_tJ_{Wx}(W_t,x_t,t)}{J_W(W_t,x_t,t)}\mathrm{E}_t\left[\frac{\Delta x_{t+1}}{x_t}\right]\right)$$

and

$$\begin{aligned}
\boldsymbol{\beta}_{it}^{\top}\boldsymbol{\eta}_t &= \boldsymbol{\eta}_t^{\top}\boldsymbol{\beta}_{it} \\
&= \alpha_t e^{-\delta}\left(\frac{-W_tJ_{WW}(W_t,x_t,t)}{J_W(W_t,x_t,t)}, \frac{-x_tJ_{Wx}(W_t,x_t,t)}{J_W(W_t,x_t,t)}\right)\begin{pmatrix}\mathrm{Cov}_t\left[R_{i,t+1}, \Delta W_{t+1}/W_t\right] \\ \mathrm{Cov}_t\left[R_{i,t+1}, \Delta x_{t+1}/x_t\right]\end{pmatrix} \\
&= \tilde{\beta}_{iW,t}\tilde{\eta}_{Wt} + \tilde{\beta}_{ix,t}\tilde{\eta}_{xt},
\end{aligned}$$

where we have defined

$$\begin{aligned}
\tilde{\beta}_{iW,t} &= \frac{\mathrm{Cov}_t\left[R_{i,t+1}, \Delta W_{t+1}/W_t\right]}{\mathrm{Var}_t\left[\Delta W_{t+1}/W_t\right]}, \\
\tilde{\beta}_{ix,t} &= \frac{\mathrm{Cov}_t\left[R_{i,t+1}, \Delta x_{t+1}/x_t\right]}{\mathrm{Var}_t\left[\Delta x_{t+1}/x_t\right]}, \\
\tilde{\eta}_{Wt} &= \alpha_t e^{-\delta}\frac{-W_tJ_{WW}(W_t,x_t,t)}{J_W(W_t,x_t,t)}\mathrm{Var}_t\left[\frac{\Delta W_{t+1}}{W_t}\right], \\
\tilde{\eta}_{xt} &= \alpha_t e^{-\delta}\frac{-x_tJ_{Wx}(W_t,x_t,t)}{J_W(W_t,x_t,t)}\mathrm{Var}_t\left[\frac{\Delta x_{t+1}}{x_t}\right].
\end{aligned}$$

Hence, the expected return on any asset i can be written as

$$\mathrm{E}_t[R_{i,t+1}] \approx \alpha_t + \tilde{\beta}_{iW,t}\tilde{\eta}_{Wt} + \tilde{\beta}_{ix,t}\tilde{\eta}_{xt}. \tag{10.28}$$

For a representative individual, the growth in wealth can be interpreted on the return on a market portfolio of all assets. Therefore, we have an approximate, two-factor conditional version of the CAPM. Because the preceding equation holds for any asset i, it will also hold for the wealth portfolio itself. Since $\tilde{\beta}_{WW,t} = 1$, we see that

$$\tilde{\eta}_{Wt} \approx \mathrm{E}_t[R_{W,t+1}] - \alpha_t - \tilde{\beta}_{Wx,t}\tilde{\eta}_{xt}$$

so that

$$\mathrm{E}_t[R_{i,t+1}] \approx \alpha_t + \tilde{\beta}_{iW,t}\left(\mathrm{E}_t[R_{W,t+1}] - \alpha_t\right) + \left(\tilde{\beta}_{ix,t} - \tilde{\beta}_{iW,t}\tilde{\beta}_{Wx,t}\right)\tilde{\eta}_{xt},$$

which looks more like the standard CAPM.

In the more general case where the state variable x affecting indirect utility has dimension m, the same derivations as above would lead to an approximate, $(m+1)$-factor conditional CAPM. The additional factors relate to variables capturing variations in investment opportunities and labour income rates. We can only obtain a single-factor discrete-time CAPM if the indirect utility depends solely on time and wealth. This would be true if there were no variations in investment opportunities and labour income or if the individual would not care about such variations. Obviously, investment opportunities and labour income rates do vary stochastically over time, and individuals care about these variations unless they have log-utility of consumption. Log-utility corresponds to a constant relative risk aversion equal to one, which is not supported by empirical evidence or theoretical considerations, see Section 5.6.

The derived CAPM is a discrete-time version of the intertemporal CAPM that was introduced by Merton (1973b) in a continuous-time setting. We will develop the continuous-time equivalent in Section 10.5.2.

Note that the discrete-time CAPM above is approximate and conditional. The approximation is due to the linearization of $J_W(W_{t+1}, x_{t+1}, t+1)$. If J_W is quadratic in W_{t+1} and x_{t+1}, we could avoid the approximation, but for this to hold the utility function $u(c)$ would have to be quadratic, which is implausible. It is also clear that very particular assumptions on preferences and the distributions of changes in wealth and the state variable are required for obtaining constant α_t, η_{Wt}, and η_{xt} and thus an unconditional CAPM. In sum, there is no convincing theoretical support for a discrete-time version of the unconditional CAPM. We discuss some empirical findings on the CAPM in Section 10.6.2.

10.5 PRICING FACTORS IN A CONTINUOUS-TIME FRAMEWORK

Now let us turn to the continuous-time setting with time set $\mathcal{T} = [0, T]$. Recall that our general notation for the price dynamics of an asset i is

$$dP_{it} = P_{it}\left[\mu_{it}\, dt + \boldsymbol{\sigma}_{it}^{\top}\, d\boldsymbol{z}_t\right],$$

where $\boldsymbol{z} = (\boldsymbol{z}_t)$ is a standard Brownian motion of dimension d. Furthermore, $\delta_i = (\delta_{it})_{t\in\mathcal{T}}$ denotes the dividend yield process of asset i. The total expected rate of return on asset i over an infinitesimally short interval $[t, t+dt]$ is then $(\mu_{it} + \delta_{it})\, dt$.

10.5.1 General Definition and Results

The natural analogue to the discrete-time definition of a conditional pricing factor is therefore the following:

Definition 10.4 *In a continuous-time framework, a conditional pricing factor is a stochastic process $\boldsymbol{x} = (\boldsymbol{x}_t)_{t\in\mathcal{T}}$ of some dimension K with dynamics of the form*

$$d\boldsymbol{x}_t = \boldsymbol{\mu}_{xt}\, dt + \underline{\underline{\sigma}}_{xt}\, d\boldsymbol{z}_t, \tag{10.29}$$

which satisfies

(i) the conditional variance-covariance matrix $\underline{\underline{\sigma}}_{xt}\underline{\underline{\sigma}}_{xt}^{\top}$ is non-singular for all t and in all states, and

(ii) adapted stochastic processes $\alpha = (\alpha_t)_{t\in\mathcal{T}}$ and $\boldsymbol{\eta} = (\boldsymbol{\eta}_t)_{t\in\mathcal{T}}$ exist so that for any asset i

$$\mu_{it} + \delta_{it} = \alpha_t + (\boldsymbol{\beta}_t^{ix})^{\top}\boldsymbol{\eta}_t, \quad t \in [0, T),$$

where the conditional factor-beta is defined as

$$\boldsymbol{\beta}_t^{ix} = \left(\underline{\underline{\sigma}}_{xt}\underline{\underline{\sigma}}_{xt}^{\top}\right)^{-1} \underline{\underline{\sigma}}_{xt}\boldsymbol{\sigma}_{it}. \tag{10.30}$$

If a 'bank account' exists that continuously is paying interest equal to the short-term risk-free rate r_t^f, it follows immediately that $\alpha_t = r_t^f$. In the following we will assume that this is the case.

Again, factors are closely linked to market prices of risk and hence to state-price deflators. Let us assume that a risk-free bank account is traded. If $\boldsymbol{x} = (\boldsymbol{x}_t)$ is a factor in an expected return-beta relation, we can define a market price of risk as (note that it is d-dimensional)

$$\boldsymbol{\lambda}_t = \underline{\underline{\sigma}}_{xt}^{\top}\left(\underline{\underline{\sigma}}_{xt}\underline{\underline{\sigma}}_{xt}^{\top}\right)^{-1}\boldsymbol{\eta}_t$$

since we then have

$$\boldsymbol{\sigma}_{it}^{\top}\boldsymbol{\lambda}_t = \boldsymbol{\sigma}_{it}^{\top}\underline{\underline{\sigma}}_{xt}^{\top}\left(\underline{\underline{\sigma}}_{xt}\underline{\underline{\sigma}}_{xt}^{\top}\right)^{-1}\boldsymbol{\eta}_t = \left(\boldsymbol{\beta}_t^{ix}\right)^{\top}\boldsymbol{\eta}_t = \mu_{it} + \delta_{it} - r_t^f.$$

The market price of risk $\boldsymbol{\lambda}_t$ and the risk-free rate r_t^f define a state-price deflator through

$$d\zeta_t = -\zeta_t\left(r_t^f\, dt + \boldsymbol{\lambda}_t^{\top}\, d\boldsymbol{z}_t\right),$$

see Theorem 4.4.

Conversely, let $\boldsymbol{\lambda} = (\boldsymbol{\lambda}_t)$ be any market price of risk and let $\zeta = (\zeta_t)$ be the associated state-price deflator. Then we can use ζ as a one-dimensional factor in an expected return-beta relation. Since this corresponds to a factor 'sensitivity' vector $-\zeta_t \boldsymbol{\lambda}_t$ replacing the matrix $\underline{\underline{\sigma}}_{xt}$, the relevant 'beta' is

$$\beta_t^{i\zeta} = \frac{-\zeta_t \boldsymbol{\sigma}_{it}^{\top} \boldsymbol{\lambda}_t}{\zeta_t^2 \boldsymbol{\lambda}_t^{\top} \boldsymbol{\lambda}_t} = -\frac{1}{\zeta_t} \frac{\boldsymbol{\sigma}_{it}^{\top} \boldsymbol{\lambda}_t}{\boldsymbol{\lambda}_t^{\top} \boldsymbol{\lambda}_t}.$$

We can use $\eta_t = -\zeta_t \boldsymbol{\lambda}_t^{\top} \boldsymbol{\lambda}_t$ since then

$$\beta_t^{i\zeta} \eta_t = -\frac{1}{\zeta_t} \frac{\boldsymbol{\sigma}_{it}^{\top} \boldsymbol{\lambda}_t}{\boldsymbol{\lambda}_t^{\top} \boldsymbol{\lambda}_t} \left(-\zeta_t \boldsymbol{\lambda}_t^{\top} \boldsymbol{\lambda}_t\right) = \boldsymbol{\sigma}_{it}^{\top} \boldsymbol{\lambda}_t = \mu_{it} + \delta_{it} - r_t^f$$

for any asset i. We can even use $a_t + b_t \zeta_t$ as a factor for any sufficiently well-behaved adapted processes $a = (a_t)$ and $b = (b_t)$.

More generally, suppose that a state-price deflator is given as $\zeta_t = g(\boldsymbol{x}_t, t)$ for some function g and some K-dimensional process $\boldsymbol{x}$ with dynamics of the form (10.29). Assuming that g is sufficiently differentiable, we can compute the dynamics of ζ by applying Itô's Lemma in Theorem 2.8. Focusing on the shock term, we obtain

$$\begin{aligned} d\zeta_t &= \dots\, dt + \left(\frac{\partial g}{\partial \boldsymbol{x}}(\boldsymbol{x}_t, t)\right)^{\top} \underline{\underline{\sigma}}_{xt}\, d\boldsymbol{z}_t \\ &= -\zeta_t \left[\dots\, dt + \left(-\frac{\frac{\partial g}{\partial x}(\boldsymbol{x}_t, t)}{g(\boldsymbol{x}_t, t)}\right)^{\top} \underline{\underline{\sigma}}_{xt}\, d\boldsymbol{z}_t\right], \end{aligned}$$

so that $\boldsymbol{\lambda}_t = -\underline{\underline{\sigma}}_{xt}^{\top} \frac{\partial g}{\partial x}(\boldsymbol{x}_t, t)/g(\boldsymbol{x}_t, t)$ defines a market price of risk. Consequently, assuming that a risk-free asset exists, the excess expected rate of return on any asset i is

$$\begin{aligned} \mu_{it} + \delta_{it} - r_t^f &= \boldsymbol{\sigma}_{it}^{\top} \underline{\underline{\sigma}}_{xt}^{\top} \left(-\frac{\frac{\partial g}{\partial x}(\boldsymbol{x}_t, t)}{g(\boldsymbol{x}_t, t)}\right) \\ &= \boldsymbol{\sigma}_{it}^{\top} \underline{\underline{\sigma}}_{xt}^{\top} \left(\underline{\underline{\sigma}}_{xt} \underline{\underline{\sigma}}_{xt}^{\top}\right)^{-1} \left(\underline{\underline{\sigma}}_{xt} \underline{\underline{\sigma}}_{xt}^{\top}\right) \left(-\frac{\frac{\partial g}{\partial x}(\boldsymbol{x}_t, t)}{g(\boldsymbol{x}_t, t)}\right) \\ &= \left(\left(\underline{\underline{\sigma}}_{xt} \underline{\underline{\sigma}}_{xt}^{\top}\right)^{-1} \underline{\underline{\sigma}}_{xt} \boldsymbol{\sigma}_{it}\right)^{\top} \left(\underline{\underline{\sigma}}_{xt} \underline{\underline{\sigma}}_{xt}^{\top}\right) \left(-\frac{\frac{\partial g}{\partial x}(\boldsymbol{x}_t, t)}{g(\boldsymbol{x}_t, t)}\right) \\ &= \boldsymbol{\beta}_{ix,t}^{\top} \boldsymbol{\eta}_t, \end{aligned}$$

where $\boldsymbol{\beta}_{ix,t}$ is defined in Eq. (10.30) and

$$\boldsymbol{\eta}_t = \left(\underline{\underline{\sigma}}_{xt} \underline{\underline{\sigma}}_{xt}^{\top}\right) \left(-\frac{\frac{\partial g}{\partial x}(\boldsymbol{x}_t, t)}{g(\boldsymbol{x}_t, t)}\right).$$

Hence, x works as a pricing factor. In the discrete-time setting the analogous conclusion is only valid if the state-price deflator is an affine function of x, but in the continuous-time setting any functional relationship is allowed.

If we use the 'spanned' state-price deflator ζ^* defined in Eqs. (4.40) and (4.41) as the factor, the relevant η is

$$\eta_t = -\zeta_t^* \left(\boldsymbol{\lambda}_t^*\right)^\top \boldsymbol{\lambda}_t^* = -\zeta_t^* \|\boldsymbol{\lambda}_t^*\|^2.$$

From Eq. (4.42), we see that $\|\boldsymbol{\lambda}_t^*\|^2$ is exactly the excess expected rate of return of the growth-optimal strategy, which we can also write as $\mu_t^* - r_t^f$. Hence, we can write the excess expected rate of return on any asset (or trading strategy) as

$$\mu_{it} + \delta_{it} - r_t^f = \beta_t^{i\zeta^*}\left(-\zeta_t^*[\mu_t^* - r_t^f]\right) = \frac{\boldsymbol{\sigma}_{it}^\top \boldsymbol{\lambda}_t^*}{\left(\boldsymbol{\lambda}_t^*\right)^\top \boldsymbol{\lambda}_t^*}\left(\mu_t^* - r_t^f\right) \equiv \beta_t^{i\lambda^*}\left(\mu_t^* - r_t^f\right).$$

The consumption-based CAPM can be seen as a factor pricing model also in a continuous-time setting. Assuming only time-additive utility and some Itô-process for consumption, expected excess returns are given by Eq. (8.24), which is easily rewritten as

$$\mu_{it} + \delta_{it} - r_t^f = \beta_t^{ic}\eta_t,$$

where $\eta_t = \gamma(c_t)\|\boldsymbol{\sigma}_{ct}\|^2$, the product of the relative risk aversion and the variance rate of consumption. Note that, in contrast to the analogous discrete-time result, we do not have to assume constant relative risk aversion or a specific distribution for future consumption rates.

As in the discrete-time case, we could also introduce unconditional pricing factors in the continuous-time setting, but we will not pursue this further. Note that general continuous-time consumption-based CAPM says that consumption growth is a *conditional* pricing factor since, for example, the factor risk premium η_t is generally time-varying.

Whether we want to use a discrete-time or a continuous-time model, the key question is what factors to include in order to get prices or returns that are consistent with the data. Due to the link between state-price deflators and (marginal utility of) consumption, we should look for factors among variables that may affect (marginal utility of) consumption.

10.5.2 The Continuous-Time CAPM

As for the discrete-time case in Section 10.4.4, we assume time-additive expected utility and exploit the envelope condition $u'(c_t) = J_W(W_t, x_t, t)$, which we derived in the continuous-time setting in Section 6.7. Again, J is the indirect utility function of the individual, that is the maximum obtainable expected utility of future consumption, and W_t is the financial wealth of the investor at time t. Furthermore, x_t is the time t value of a variable that explains the variations in investment opportunities (captured by the risk-free interest rate, expected returns and volatilities on risky assets, and correlations between risky assets) and investor-specific variables (for example labour income). For notational simplicity, x is assumed to be one-dimensional, but this could be generalized.

Write the dynamics of wealth compactly as

$$dW_t = W_t \left[\mu_{Wt}\, dt + \boldsymbol{\sigma}_{Wt}^{\top}\, d\boldsymbol{z}_t \right]$$

and assume that the state variable x follows a diffusion process

$$dx_t = \mu_{xt}\, dt + \boldsymbol{\sigma}_{xt}^{\top}\, d\boldsymbol{z}_t,$$
$$\mu_{xt} = \mu_x(x_t, t), \quad \boldsymbol{\sigma}_{xt} = \boldsymbol{\sigma}_x(x_t, t).$$

The envelope condition implies that the state-price deflator derived from this individual can be written as

$$\zeta_t = e^{-\delta t} \frac{J_W(W_t, x_t, t)}{J_W(W_0, x_0, 0)}.$$

An application of Itô's Lemma yields a new expression for the dynamics of ζ. Focusing on the shock terms, the relevant derivatives are

$$\frac{\partial \zeta_t}{\partial W_t} = e^{-\delta t} \frac{J_{WW}(W_t, x_t, t)}{J_W(W_0, x_0, 0)} = \frac{J_{WW}(W_t, x_t, t)}{J_W(W_t, x_t, t)} \zeta_t,$$
$$\frac{\partial \zeta_t}{\partial x_t} = e^{-\delta t} \frac{J_{Wx}(W_t, x_t, t)}{J_W(W_0, x_0, 0)} = \frac{J_{Wx}(W_t, x_t, t)}{J_W(W_t, x_t, t)} \zeta_t,$$

so that

$$d\zeta_t = -\zeta_t \left[\dots\, dt - \left(\frac{W_t J_{WW}(W_t, x_t, t)}{J_W(W_t, x_t, t)} \boldsymbol{\sigma}_{Wt} + \frac{J_{Wx}(W_t, x_t, t)}{J_W(W_t, x_t, t)} \boldsymbol{\sigma}_{xt} \right)^{\top} d\boldsymbol{z}_t \right].$$

By comparing with the general expression for the state-price deflator dynamics in Eq. (4.32), we conclude that

$$\boldsymbol{\lambda}_t = \left(\frac{-W_t J_{WW}(W_t, x_t, t)}{J_W(W_t, x_t, t)} \right) \boldsymbol{\sigma}_{Wt} + \left(\frac{-J_{Wx}(W_t, x_t, t)}{J_W(W_t, x_t, t)} \right) \boldsymbol{\sigma}_{xt}$$

is a market price of risk. Consequently, the expected excess rate of return on asset i can be written as

$$\mu_{it} + \delta_{it} - r^f_t = \left(\frac{-W_t J_{WW}(W_t, x_t, t)}{J_W(W_t, x_t, t)} \right) \boldsymbol{\sigma}^\top_{it} \boldsymbol{\sigma}_{Wt} + \left(\frac{-J_{Wx}(W_t, x_t, t)}{J_W(W_t, x_t, t)} \right) \boldsymbol{\sigma}^\top_{it} \boldsymbol{\sigma}_{xt}, \tag{10.31}$$

which can be rewritten as

$$\mu_{it} + \delta_{it} - r^f_t = \tilde{\beta}_{iWt} \tilde{\eta}_{Wt} + \tilde{\beta}_{ixt} \tilde{\eta}_{xt},$$

where

$$\tilde{\beta}_{iWt} = \frac{\boldsymbol{\sigma}^\top_{it} \boldsymbol{\sigma}_{Wt}}{\|\boldsymbol{\sigma}_{Wt}\|^2}, \quad \tilde{\beta}_{ixt} = \frac{\boldsymbol{\sigma}^\top_{it} \boldsymbol{\sigma}_{xt}}{\|\boldsymbol{\sigma}_{xt}\|^2},$$

$$\tilde{\eta}_{Wt} = \|\boldsymbol{\sigma}_{Wt}\|^2 \left(\frac{-W_t J_{WW}(W_t, x_t, t)}{J_W(W_t, x_t, t)} \right), \quad \tilde{\eta}_{xt} = \|\boldsymbol{\sigma}_{xt}\|^2 \left(\frac{-J_{Wx}(W_t, x_t, t)}{J_W(W_t, x_t, t)} \right).$$

We now have a two-factor model with the wealth of the individual and the state variable as the factors. It is the continuous-time analogue of the discrete-time relation (10.28), but the continuous-time version does not rely on any approximations. If it takes m state variables to describe the variations in investment opportunities, labour income, and so on, we get an $(m + 1)$-factor model. Note that factor risk premia, betas, and so on, will generally vary over time as indicated by their t-subscripts so that (W, x) is a *conditional* pricing factor.

If the individual is taken to be a representative individual, her wealth will be identical to the aggregate value of all assets in the economy, including all traded financial assets and non-traded assets such as human capital. This is like the market portfolio in the traditional static CAPM. The first term on the right-hand side of Eq. (10.31) is then the product of the relative risk aversion of the representative individual (derived from her indirect utility) and the covariance between the rate of return on asset i and the rate of return on the market portfolio. In the special case where the indirect utility is a function of wealth and time only, the last term on the right-hand side will be zero, and we get the well-known relation

$$\mu_{it} + \delta_{it} - r^f_t = \beta_{iWt} \left(\mu_{Wt} + \delta_{Wt} - r^f_t \right),$$

where β_{iWt} is the 'market-beta' of asset i. This is a continuous-time version of the traditional static CAPM. This single-factor model is only true under the strong assumption that individuals do not care about variations in investment opportunities, income, and so on, which is satisfied for log-utility but not for more realistic preferences. In general we have to add factors describing the future investment opportunities, future labour income, and so on. This extension of the CAPM is called the intertemporal CAPM and was first derived by Merton (1973b).

10.6 EMPIRICAL FACTOR MODELS

This section gives a short overview of the empirical literature on factor models. As the literature is abundant, such a short overview will necessarily omit many interesting aspects and relevant papers. The reader is referred to the more comprehensive surveys by Campbell (2000), Fama and French (2004), Levy (2010), Subrahmanyam (2010), Cochrane (2011), Goyal (2012), and Ludvigson (2012), as well as the textbook treatments by Campbell, Lo, and MacKinlay (1997), Cochrane (2005), and Singleton (2006). We first discuss empirical studies related to the consumption-based CAPM and subsequently studies addressing the market-based CAPM.

10.6.1 The Consumption-Based CAPM

Most theoretical models leading to a consumption-based CAPM imply that consumption growth is a conditional pricing factor. For example, in Eq. (10.23) the factor risk premium η_t is generally time-varying. The simple version with constant relative risk aversion and lognormal consumption growth with a constant mean and variance over all periods leads to an unconditional factor model if the assets have constant consumption-betas. Breeden, Gibbons, and Litzenberger (1989) show that empirically this unconditional single-factor CCAPM can only explain a small part of the differences in the average returns on different stocks. Various authors show that an extended two-factor unconditional CCAPM is much better at capturing return differences.

Lettau and Ludvigson (2001b) add the so-called *cay* or log-consumption-wealth ratio $\text{cay}_t = \ln(c_t/W_t)$ as the second factor. This is supported by the conditional one-factor CCAPM if the log-consumption-wealth ratio works as an instrument capturing variations in the risk-free rate and the factor risk premium, which theoretically should be the product of the relative risk aversion and the variance of consumption growth. As Lettau and Ludvigson argue, a high consumption-wealth ratio is likely to indicate that individuals expect good times are ahead, which can make them lower the risk premium they require on stock investments. Also, the consumption-wealth ratio may be able to explain variations in the conditional consumption-betas over time. Some stocks are more highly correlated with consumption growth in bad times than in good times. For further discussion of the role of *cay*, see Brennan and Xia (2005), Lettau and Ludvigson (2005), and Gao and Huang (2008).

As another example of a multifactor unconditional consumption-based model, Jacobs and Wang (2004) include the dispersion in consumption growth across individuals as a second factor in addition to the growth in aggregate consumption. Consumption dispersion tends to be higher in recessions than in booms due to the larger unemployment rate in recessions. Hence, stocks that are negatively correlated with consumption dispersion will typically provide high returns when dispersion is low, which is in good times where extra payments are not so highly appreciated. Consequently, such stocks have low prices and high expected returns, other things being equal. Jacobs and Wang confirm this intuition empirically and show that the extended unconditional model explains cross-sectional differences in average returns much better than the single-factor unconditional model. That consumption dispersion is a priced unconditional factor is consistent with the representative-individual consumption-based CAPM if consumption dispersion acts as an instrument explaining variations in the short-term risk-free rate and the conditional risk premium on aggregate consumption risk. Alternatively, the significance of consumption dispersion for the cross-section of returns may indicate that the representative-individual version of the CCAPM is invalid so that the consumption growth rates of individuals do not follow each other in lockstep.

Santos and Veronesi (2006) illustrate that the ratio of aggregate labour income to aggregate consumption is a useful instrument in the conditional CCAPM, which makes sense since this ratio fluctuates with the business cycle. Lustig and van Nieuwerburgh (2005) investigate the role of the ratio of housing wealth to human wealth as a conditioning variable in a consumption-based CAPM.

Many of the extensions of the consumption-based CAPM described in Chapter 9 have also been documented to improve the fit of the model to the cross-sectional returns. For example, Bansal, Dittmar, and Lundblad (2005), Bansal, Dittmar, and Kiku (2009), and Malloy, Moskowitz, and Vissing-Jørgensen (2009) report that the long-run risk model discussed in Section 9.3, in which the short-run consumption risk factor is supplemented by a long-run consumption risk factor and a volatility factor, can explain the cross-section of average stock returns relatively well. In contrast, Lettau and Ludvigson (2009), Constantinides and Ghosh (2011), and Beeler and Campbell (2012) raise doubts about the empirical success of the long-run risk model.

Any direct test of a consumption-CAPM has to rely on consumption data. As explained in Section 8.5.1, there are several concerns about the quality of the available data on aggregate consumption. Jagannathan and Wang (2007) show that the unconditional CCAPM performs much better using the year-to-year growth rate in the fourth-quarter aggregate consumption instead of the usual quarterly growth rate. Savov (2011) argues that the growth in garbage may constitute a better estimate of the actual consumption growth than the official aggregate consumption statistics, and he documents that the consumption-CAPM performs better when using garbage growth as a proxy for consumption growth.

10.6.2 The CAPM and Extensions

Based on a time series of returns of various (portfolios of) stocks, numerous empirical studies have tested whether the unconditional CAPM with the market return as the only factor can explain observed cross-sectional differences in average stock returns. After some initial apparently supporting results (Black, Jensen, and Scholes 1972; Fama and MacBeth 1973), most of the later studies conclude that the unconditional CAPM is insufficient. As the unconditional CAPM also has very weak theoretical support, this conclusion is not surprising.

10.6.2.1 Conditioning Information

Several authors report significant improvements from taking conditioning information into account. Jagannathan and Wang (1996) decompose the conditional market-beta of asset i as

$$\beta_{it} = \bar{\beta}_i + \theta_i (\eta_t - \bar{\eta}) + \varepsilon_{it},$$

where ε_{it} and η_t are uncorrelated, $\mathrm{E}[\varepsilon_{it}] = 0$, and $\bar{\eta} = \mathrm{E}[\eta_{t+1}]$. The constant θ_i measures the sensitivity of the market-beta of asset i towards variations in the conditional risk premium. Consequently,

$$\mathrm{E}[\beta_{it}] = \bar{\beta}_i, \qquad \mathrm{Cov}\,[\beta_{it}, \eta_t] = \theta_i \,\mathrm{Var}[\eta_t].$$

If we substitute this into Eq. (10.27), we obtain

$$\mathrm{E}[R_{i,t+1}] = \alpha + \bar{\beta}_i \bar{\eta} + \theta_i \,\mathrm{Var}[\eta_{t+1}].$$

In this case, the conditional one-factor CAPM implies an unconditional two-factor version of the CAPM.

Jagannathan and Wang show that adding the second factor leads to a dramatic improvement of the cross-sectional fit by increasing the R^2 from a meagre 1.35% to a respectable 29.32%. They also add the growth rate of per capita income as a third factor, which further improves the R^2 to 55.21%. From a theoretical perspective the addition of an income factor is natural since human wealth (the present value of future income) is a major asset for most individuals and should be included in the market portfolio used in tests of the CAPM. However, most such tests take a broad portfolio of stocks as a proxy for the market portfolio, and the study of Jagannathan and Wang does not deviate from this practice. Campbell (1996) and Eiling (2012) confirm that human capital is important in explaining cross-sectional returns. Stambaugh (1982) finds that the inclusion of bonds, real estate, or consumer durables in the proxy for the market portfolio does not significantly change the empirical results, but he does not consider including human capital.

As mentioned above, Lettau and Ludvigson (2001b) find it useful to apply their *cay*-factor, the log-consumption-wealth ratio, as an instrument in the consumption-based CAPM. They also demonstrate that using *cay* as an instrument leads to a significant improvement in the fit of the standard CAPM, which provides some support for the conditional version of the one-factor CAPM.

10.6.2.2 The Fama–French Three-Factor Model

A large part of the empirical literature on factor models identifies a number of priced factors in a given cross-section of stocks without much concern about which underlying mechanisms could explain such factors. The best known studies of this kind were carried out by Fama and French, who find support for a model with three factors:

1. *market*: the return on a broad stock market index;
2. *small-minus-big* or *SMB*: the return on a portfolio of stocks in small companies (according to the market value of all stocks issued by the firm) minus the return on a portfolio of stocks in large companies;
3. *high-minus-low* or *HML*: the return on a portfolio of stocks issued by firms with a high book-to-market value (value stocks) minus the return on a portfolio of stocks in firms with a low book-to-market value (growth stocks).

Probably starting with Banz (1981), numerous studies report that stocks in small companies provide a higher average return than stocks in large companies also after correcting for any differences in market-betas. This motivates the use of the small-minus-big factor. Similarly, the high-minus-low factor is motivated by the observation of Rosenberg, Reid, and Lanstein (1985), Fama and French (1992), and others that value stocks provide a higher average return than growth stocks, even after controlling for differences in market-betas. Note that the Fama–French model is a partial pricing model since the factors themselves are derived from prices of financial assets.

The market values and book values of companies vary over time, and the small-minus-big and high-minus-low portfolios are rebalanced regularly. According to Fama and French (1996) such a model gives a good fit of US stock market data over the period 1963–1993, and Fama and French (2011) show that the same is true in many other countries.

As recognized by Fama and French, their empirical analysis does not explain *why* this three-factor model performs well and what the underlying pricing mechanisms might be. Maybe the small-minus-big and the high-minus-low portfolios are mimicking some underlying state variables capturing relevant information about future consumption and investment opportunities in line with the intertemporal CAPM, but the link is not clear. Fama and French suggest that the success of their three-factor model comes from a premium on financial distress. Small value stocks tend to be the stocks of firms that have performed rather poorly in the recent past and are thus more likely to experience financial distress, see Chan and Chen (1991). There are also various explanations of the value premium and the associated high-minus-low factor. See, for example, Carlson, Fisher, and Giammarino (2004), Zhang (2005), Cooper (2006), Gomes, Yaron, and Zhang (2006), and Garlappi and Yan (2011). Liew and Vassalou (2000) show that the SMB and HML factors are highly correlated with future growth in GDP and thus future consumption and investment opportunities.

10.6.2.3 Momentum

In recent years the three Fama–French factors are often augmented by a *momentum factor*. As mentioned in Section 1.5, returns on many stocks and stock portfolios exhibit short-term momentum in the sense that a positive [negative] return over the previous days, weeks, or months tends to be followed by another positive [negative] return over the subsequent days, weeks, or months. The momentum strategy consisting of buying past winners and selling past losers provides a high average return even after controlling for the risks represented by the Fama–French three-factor model. The momentum factor is the return on a portfolio of stocks with high past returns minus the return on a portfolio of stock with low past returns. The factor was introduced by Carhart (1997) and is often referred to as the up-minus-down factor or just UMD factor. The momentum effect is also present in international stock markets as documented by Rouwenhorst (1998) among others. Since the momentum strategy requires knowledge of past prices only, its profitability is seen by some researchers (and many practitioners) as an indication of market inefficiency. See for example the discussion in Fama and French (2008). However, some explanations of the momentum effect have been suggested. Empirical results presented by Hvidkjær (2006) indicate that the momentum effect is linked to liquidity issues. Avramov *et al.* (2007) report that most of the momentum profits come from trades in stocks of firms with low credit quality. Hence, the momentum factor may be capturing some liquidity risk or credit risk, and that such risks are priced is economically intuitive. Furthermore, Liu and Zhang (2008) show that the momentum factor is closely related to the growth rate of industrial production, a key business cycle indicator.

10.6.2.4 Idiosyncratic risk

Studies by Ang *et al.* (2006, 2007) and others conclude that idiosyncratic risk is priced, which is inconsistent with typical asset pricing models in which only exposure to systematic risks affects the prices and expected returns of individual assets. The conclusion by Ang *et al.* is questioned by other studies, for example Bali and Cakici (2008) and Fu (2009). A premium on idiosyncratic risk could arise if investors hold undiversified portfolios. Levy (1978) and Merton (1987) develop extensions of the CAPM in which investors hold undiversified portfolios in equilibrium.

10.6.2.5 Liquidity

Liquidity has received much attention in recent years. In the asset pricing models studied in this book, individuals are assumed to have the opportunity to trade all financial assets at any point in time and without paying any transaction costs. This assumption is obviously not satisfied in real-life financial markets. For some financial assets transaction costs are so small that they can safely be neglected, but for other assets transaction costs are economically significant. Moreover, transaction costs can vary significantly over time so that some assets may be very liquid (trade with low costs) in some periods and very illiquid (trade with high costs) in other periods, a fact that often becomes very clear during major financial crises. Investors care about returns net of transaction costs, and cross-sectional differences in liquidity will therefore induce cross-sectional differences in expected returns.

The asset pricing implications of liquidity risk is explained in the relatively simple liquidity-adjusted CAPM of Acharya and Pedersen (2005). They set up a model with overlapping generations of investors who live for one period. Each investor is born with a given endowment, purchases a portfolio of assets immediately, then liquidates the portfolio one period later, consumes the dividends and the proceeds from the sale, and leaves the economy. Investors are assumed to have CARA utilities (see Section 5.6). The financial market offers a perfectly liquid risk-free asset with gross return $R^f > 1$. The sale of a risky asset implies a transaction cost. Dividends and transaction costs are assumed to follow AR(1) processes (see Section 2.5). Short-selling of the risky assets is prohibited. Under these assumptions, the authors show that the expected excess gross return on any risky asset i (computed without adjusting for transaction costs) is

$$
\begin{aligned}
\mathrm{E}_t[R^i_{t+1}] - R^f &= \mathrm{E}_t[c^i_{t+1}] + \lambda_t \frac{\mathrm{Cov}_t[R^i_{t+1}, R^M_{t+1}]}{\mathrm{Var}_t[R^M_{t+1} - c^M_{t+1}]} + \lambda_t \frac{\mathrm{Cov}_t[c^i_{t+1}, c^M_{t+1}]}{\mathrm{Var}_t[R^M_{t+1} - c^M_{t+1}]} \\
&\quad - \lambda_t \frac{\mathrm{Cov}_t[R^i_{t+1}, c^M_{t+1}]}{\mathrm{Var}_t[R^M_{t+1} - c^M_{t+1}]} - \lambda_t \frac{\mathrm{Cov}_t[c^i_{t+1}, R^M_{t+1}]}{\mathrm{Var}_t[R^M_{t+1} - c^M_{t+1}]},
\end{aligned}
$$

where $\lambda_t = \mathrm{E}_t[R^M_{t+1} - c^M_{t+1} - R^f] > 0$. Here, R^M_{t+1} is the market return (without transaction costs), c^i_{t+1} is the transaction cost on asset i as a fraction of the price, and c^M_{t+1} is a weighted average of the relative transaction costs of the individual assets and thus a measure of the market illiquidity. The excess expected return consists of the expected transaction cost and four terms compensating for risk, where each term is the product of a specific 'beta' and the common market risk premium λ_t. The first beta corresponds to the usual CAPM market-beta. The three new liquidity-related beta-terms have intuitive signs. An asset that tends to be very liquid (low c^i_{t+1}) when the general market is illiquid (high c^M_{t+1}) is very attractive, and therefore will have a high price and a low expected return. An asset that tends to provide high returns when the market is very illiquid will likewise have low expected returns. Finally, an asset that tends to be illiquid only when the market return is high is also relatively attractive and will thus offer low expected returns.

In an empirical study based on US stocks, Acharya and Pedersen estimate that the expected or average transaction cost can explain around 3.5% of the expected return, whereas the three liquidity risk terms add up to around 1.1%. These estimates indicate that liquidity and liquidity risk are important elements in explaining the cross-sectional differences in expected returns.

Amihud, Mendelson, and Pedersen (2005) survey both the theoretical and the empirical literature on the impact of illiquidity on asset prices. More recent studies include Brunnermeier and Pedersen (2009), Hasbrouck (2009), and Brennan *et al.* (2012).

10.6.3 Discussion

It is important to realize that while a given factor model does well in a given market over a given period, it may perform very badly in other markets or other periods, and the relevant risk premia may be different for other data sets. For example, some recent studies indicate that the small-minus-big factor (and the associated 'size effect') seems to have disappeared (Schwert 2003; Goyal 2012). Another critique is that over the last 30 years empirical researchers have tried so many factors that it is hardly surprising that they have found some statistically significant factors. Explanations of the success of Fama–French type models that are related to data snooping and biases are emphasized by Lo and MacKinlay (1990) and Kothari, Shanken, and Sloan (1995). In fact, we know that in any given sample of historical returns it is possible to find a portfolio so that a factor model with the return on this portfolio as the only factor will perfectly explain all returns in the sample!

There are also a number of statistical issues in the empirical factor modelling literature. Problems in the measurement of beta have been documented by Berk, Green, and Naik (1999) and Gomes, Kogan, and Zhang (2003), among others. See also Berk (1995), Liew and Vassalou (2000), Lettau and Ludvigson (2001a), Vassalou (2003), and Petkova (2006), as well as the general discussion about standard tests of asset pricing models in Lewellen, Nagel, and Shanken (2010).

For these reasons the purely empirically based 'factor models' do not contribute much to the understanding of the pricing mechanisms of financial markets. Ideally, there should be an intuitive or theory-backed explanation for why the factors are priced in the cross-section of assets either because they should work as an instrument representing relevant conditioning information or because they somehow provide information about future consumption and investment opportunities.

Some empirical studies of factor models refer to Merton's intertemporal CAPM when motivating the choice of factors. Brennan, Wang, and Xia (2004) set up a simple model with the short-term real interest rate and the slope of the capital market line as the factors since these variables capture the investment opportunities. In an empirical test, this model performs as well as the Fama–French model, which is encouraging for the development of theoretically well-founded and empirically viable factor models. Campbell and Vuolteenaho (2004) find supportive empirical evidence for a two-factor CAPM, where the market return factor is supplemented by the market discount rate. The latter is related to future investment opportunities so the model is in the spirit of the intertemporal CAPM.

10.7 CONCLUDING REMARKS

Factor models aim at relating the expected returns on a broad set of assets to a relatively low number of common factors. Much of the literature on factor models is empirically oriented and attempts to identify such common factors in a given data set of stock returns, although most studies also try to provide some intuition for why these factors should be priced. This chapter has formally defined and analysed the properties of pricing factors. A close link between pricing factors and state-price deflators has been demonstrated. This link highlights that pricing factors should be variables affecting the marginal utilities of investors.

10.8 EXERCISES

Exercise 10.1 Consider a discrete-time economy with a one-dimensional conditional pricing factor $x = (x_t)$ so that, for some adapted processes $\alpha = (\alpha_t)$ and some $\eta = (\eta_t)$,

$$\mathrm{E}_t[R_{i,t+1}] = \alpha_t + \beta_t[R_{i,t+1}, x_{t+1}]\,\eta_t,$$

for all assets i and all $t = 0, 1, \ldots, T-1$.

(a) Show that

$$\frac{\zeta_{t+1}}{\zeta_t} = \frac{1}{\alpha_t}\left(1 - \frac{x_{t+1} - \mathrm{E}_t[x_{t+1}]}{\mathrm{Var}_t[x_{t+1}]}\eta_t\right)$$

satisfies the pricing condition for a state-price deflator, that is

$$\mathrm{E}_t\left[\frac{\zeta_{t+1}}{\zeta_t}R_{i,t+1}\right] = 1$$

for all assets i.

(b) Show that ζ_{t+1}/ζ_t will only be a true one-period state-price deflator for the period between time t and time $t+1$ if you impose some condition on parameters and/or distributions and provide that condition. If such a condition is not satisfied, what can you conclude about the asset prices in this economy?

(c) Now suppose that the factor is the return on some particular portfolio, that is $x_{t+1} = \tilde{R}_{t+1}$. Answer question (b) again.

(d) Consider the good (?) old (!) CAPM where $x_{t+1} = R_{M,t+1}$, the return on the market portfolio. Suppose that $\mathrm{E}_t[R_{M,t+1}] = 1.05$, $\sigma_t[R_{M,t+1}] = 0.2$, and $R_t^f = 1.02$. What do you need to assume about the distribution of the market return to ensure that the model is free of arbitrage? Is an assumption like this satisfied in typical derivations of the CAPM?

Exercise 10.2 Using the orthogonal characterization of the mean-variance frontier, show that for any mean-variance efficient return R^π different from the minimum-variance portfolio there is a unique mean-variance efficient return $R^{z(\pi)}$ satisfying $\mathrm{Cov}[R^\pi, R^{z(\pi)}] = 0$. Show that

$$\mathrm{E}[R^{z(\pi)}] = \mathrm{E}[R^*] - \mathrm{E}[R^{e*}]\frac{\mathrm{E}[(R^*)^2] - \mathrm{E}[R^\pi]\,\mathrm{E}[R^*]}{\mathrm{E}[R^\pi] - \mathrm{E}[R^*] - \mathrm{E}[R^\pi]\,\mathrm{E}[R^{e*}]}.$$

Exercise 10.3 Consider a discrete-time economy in which asset prices are described by an unconditional linear factor model

$$\frac{\zeta_{t+1}}{\zeta_t} = a + \boldsymbol{b}\cdot\boldsymbol{x}_{t+1}, \quad t = 0, 1, \ldots, T-1,$$

where the conditional mean and second moments of the factor are constant, that is $\mathrm{E}_t[\boldsymbol{x}_{t+1}] = \boldsymbol{\mu}$ and $\mathrm{E}_t[\boldsymbol{x}_{t+1}\boldsymbol{x}_{t+1}^\top] = \underline{\underline{\Sigma}}$ for all t.

You want to value an uncertain stream of dividends $D = (D_t)$. You are told that dividends evolve as

$$\frac{D_{t+1}}{D_t} = m + \boldsymbol{\psi}\cdot\boldsymbol{x}_{t+1} + \varepsilon_{t+1}, \quad t = 0, 1, \ldots, T-1,$$

where $\mathrm{E}_t[\varepsilon_{t+1}] = 0$ and $\mathrm{E}_t[\varepsilon_{t+1}\boldsymbol{x}_{t+1}] = \boldsymbol{0}$ for all t.

The first three questions will lead you through the valuation based directly on the pricing condition of the state-price deflator.

(a) Show that, for any $t = 0, 1, \ldots, T-1$,

$$\mathrm{E}_t\left[\frac{D_{t+1}}{D_t}\frac{\zeta_{t+1}}{\zeta_t}\right] = ma + (m\boldsymbol{b} + a\boldsymbol{\psi})\cdot\boldsymbol{\mu} + \boldsymbol{\psi}^\top\underline{\underline{\Sigma}}\boldsymbol{b} \equiv A.$$

(b) Show that

$$\mathrm{E}_t\left[\frac{D_{t+s}}{D_t}\frac{\zeta_{t+s}}{\zeta_t}\right] = A^s.$$

(c) Show that the value at time t of the future dividends is

$$P_t = D_t \frac{A}{1-A}\left(1 - A^{T-t}\right).$$

Next, consider an alternative valuation technique. From Eq. (4.26) we know that the dividends can be valued by the formula

$$P_t = \sum_{s=1}^{T-t} \frac{\mathrm{E}_t[D_{t+s}] - \beta_t\left[D_{t+s}, \frac{\zeta_{t+s}}{\zeta_t}\right]\eta_{t,t+s}}{(1+\hat{y}_t^{t+s})^s}, \qquad (*)$$

where

$$\beta_t\left[D_{t+s}, \frac{\zeta_{t+s}}{\zeta_t}\right] = \mathrm{Cov}_t\left[D_{t+s}, \frac{\zeta_{t+s}}{\zeta_t}\right] / \mathrm{Var}_t\left[\frac{\zeta_{t+s}}{\zeta_t}\right],$$

$$\eta_{t,t+s} = -\mathrm{Var}_t\left[\frac{\zeta_{t+s}}{\zeta_t}\right] / \mathrm{E}_t\left[\frac{\zeta_{t+s}}{\zeta_t}\right].$$

In the next questions you have to compute the ingredients to this valuation formula.

(d) What is the one-period risk-free rate of return r_t^f? What is the time t annualized yield $\hat{y}_t^{t+s}$ on a zero-coupon bond maturing at time $t+s$? (If B_t^{t+s} denotes the price of the bond, the annualized gross yield is defined by the equation $B_t^{t+s} = (1+\hat{y}_t^{t+s})^{-s}$.)

(e) Show that $\mathrm{E}_t[D_{t+s}] = D_t\,(m + \boldsymbol{\psi}\cdot\boldsymbol{\mu})^s$.

(f) Compute $\mathrm{Cov}_t\left[D_{t+s}, \frac{\zeta_{t+s}}{\zeta_t}\right]$.

(g) Compute $\beta_t\left[D_{t+s}, \frac{\zeta_{t+s}}{\zeta_t}\right]$.

(h) Compute $\eta_{t,t+s}$.

(i) Verify that the time t value of the future dividends satisfies (*).

Exercise 10.4 In a continuous-time framework an individual with time-additive expected power utility induces the state-price deflator

$$\zeta_t = e^{-\delta t}\left(\frac{c_t}{c_0}\right)^{-\gamma},$$

where γ is the constant relative risk aversion, δ is the subjective time preference rate, and $c = (c_t)_{t\in[0,T]}$ is the optimal consumption process of the individual. If the dynamics of the optimal consumption process is of the form

$$dc_t = c_t\left[\mu_{ct}\,dt + \boldsymbol{\sigma}_{ct}^{\mathsf{T}}\,d\boldsymbol{z}_t\right]$$

then the dynamics of the state-price deflator is

$$d\zeta_t = -\zeta_t\left[\left(\delta + \gamma\mu_{ct} - \frac{1}{2}\gamma(1+\gamma)\|\boldsymbol{\sigma}_{ct}\|^2\right)dt + \gamma\boldsymbol{\sigma}_{ct}^{\mathsf{T}}\,d\boldsymbol{z}_t\right].$$

(a) State the market price of risk $\boldsymbol{\lambda}_t$ in terms of the preference parameters and the expected growth rate and sensitivity of the consumption process.

In many concrete models of the individual consumption and portfolio decisions, the optimal consumption process will be of the form

$$c_t = W_t e^{f(X_t,t)},$$

where W_t is the wealth of the individual at time t, X_t is the time t value of some state variable, and f is some smooth function. Here X can potentially be multidimensional.

(b) Give some examples of variables other than wealth that may affect the optimal consumption of an individual and which may therefore play the role of X_t.

Suppose the state variable X is one-dimensional and write the dynamics of the wealth of the individual and the state variable as

$$dW_t = W_t \left[\left(\mu_{Wt} - e^{f(X_t,t)} \right) dt + \boldsymbol{\sigma}_{Wt}^{\top} d\boldsymbol{z}_t \right],$$

$$dX_t = \mu_{Xt}\, dt + \boldsymbol{\sigma}_{Xt}^{\top} d\boldsymbol{z}_t.$$

(c) Characterize the market price of risk in terms of the preference parameters and the drift and sensitivity terms of W_t and X_t.
Hint: Apply Itô's Lemma to $c_t = W_t e^{f(X_t,t)}$ to express the required parts of the consumption process in terms of W and X.

(d) Show that the instantaneous excess expected rate of return on risky asset i can be written as

$$\mu_{it} + \delta_{it} - r_t^f = \beta_{iW,t}\eta_{Wt} + \beta_{iX,t}\eta_{Xt},$$

where $\beta_{iW,t}$ and $\beta_{iX,t}$ are the instantaneous betas of the asset with respect to wealth and the state variable, respectively. Relate η_{Wt} and η_{Xt} to preference parameters and the drift and sensitivity terms of W and X.

11

The Economics of the Term Structure of Interest Rates

11.1 INTRODUCTION

The primary focus of the previous chapters were the implications of asset pricing models for the level of stock market excess returns and the cross-section of stock returns. This chapter focuses on the consequences of asset pricing theory for the pricing of bonds and for the term structure of interest rates implied by bond prices.

A bond is a standardized and transferable loan agreement. The issuer of the bond is borrowing money from the holder of the bond and promises to pay back the loan according to a predefined payment scheme. The presence of the bond market allows individuals to trade consumption opportunities at different points in time among each other. An individual having a clear preference for current capital to finance investments or current consumption can borrow by issuing a bond to an individual having a clear preference for future consumption opportunities. The price of a bond of a given maturity is, of course, set to align the demand and supply of that bond. Consequently, the price will depend on the attractiveness of the real investment opportunities and on the individual's preferences for consumption over the maturity of the bond. The term structure of interest rates will reflect these dependencies.

After a short introduction to the notation and the bond market terminology in Section 11.2, we derive in Sections 11.3 and 11.4 relations between equilibrium interest rates and aggregate consumption and production in settings with a representative individual. In Section 11.5 we give some examples of equilibrium term structure models that are derived from the basic relations between interest rates, consumption, and production. The famous Vasicek model and Cox–Ingersoll–Ross model are presented.

Since individuals are concerned with the number of units of goods they consume and not the dollar value of these goods, the relations found in the above-mentioned sections apply to real interest rates. However, most traded bonds are nominal, that is they promise the delivery of certain dollar amounts, not the delivery of a certain number of consumption goods. The real value of a nominal bond depends on the evolution of the price of the consumption good. In Section 11.6 we explore the relations between real rates, nominal rates, and inflation. We consider both the case where money has no real effects on the economy and the case where money does impact the real economy.

The development of arbitrage-free dynamic models of the term structure was initiated in the 1970s. Until then, the discussions among economists about the shape of the term structure were based on some relatively loose hypotheses. The most well-known of these is the expectation hypothesis which postulates a close relation between current interest rates or bond yields and expected future interest rates or bond returns. Many economists still seem to rely on the validity of this hypothesis, and a lot of manpower has been spent on testing the hypothesis empirically. In Section 11.7, we review several versions of the expectation hypothesis and discuss the consistency of these versions. We argue that neither of these versions will hold for any reasonable dynamic term structure model. Some alternative traditional hypotheses are briefly reviewed in Section 11.8.

Throughout the chapter we assume that the bonds in question will pay the promised future payments for sure. Hence, we ignore any credit risk or default risk, and the analysis is therefore applicable to government bonds issued by countries having a limited public debt relative to the tax incomes or the GDP of the country. If a government has issued bonds and subsequently faces financial troubles, it has the opportunity of raising taxes, cutting public spending, or—if the bonds are denominated in the domestic currency—printing enough money so that it will be able to honour its nominal debts. Nevertheless, there are plenty of historical examples of countries defaulting on part or all of their debt. Credit risk plays a major role in the valuation of corporate bonds. For more about the valuation of defaultable bonds, see Chapter 13 in Munk (2011) for an overview or the specialized textbooks by Bielecki and Rutkowski (2002), Duffie and Singleton (2003), and Lando (2004) for detailed coverage. Some papers study interrelations between variations in credit risk premia and variations in equity premia, risk-free rates, and aggregate consumption. See, for example, Almeida and Philippon (2007), Bhamra, Kuehn, and Strebulaev (2010), Chen, Collin-Dufresne, and Goldstein (2009), and Chen (2010).

11.2 BASIC INTEREST RATE CONCEPTS AND RELATIONS

As in earlier chapters we will denote by B_t^T the price at time t of a zero-coupon bond paying a dividend of one (unit of the consumption good) at time T and no other dividends. If many zero-coupon bonds with different maturities are traded, we can form the function $T \mapsto B_t^T$, which we refer to as the *discount function* prevailing at time t. Of course, we must have $B_t^t = 1$, and we expect the discount function to be decreasing since all individuals will presumably prefer getting the dividend sooner than later.

Next, consider a coupon bond with payment dates $t_1, t_2, \dots, t_n$, where we assume without loss of generality that $t_1 < t_2 < \dots < t_n$. The payment at date t_i is denoted by Y_i. Such a coupon bond can be seen as a portfolio of zero-coupon bonds, namely a portfolio of Y_1 zero-coupon bonds maturing at t_1, Y_2 zero-coupon bonds maturing at t_2, and so on. If all these zero-coupon bonds are traded in the market, the coupon bond is a redundant asset with a unique no-arbitrage time t price of

$$B_t = \sum_{t_i > t} Y_i B_t^{t_i}, \tag{11.1}$$

where the sum is over all future payment dates of the coupon bond. If not all the relevant zero-coupon bonds are traded, we cannot justify the relation (11.1) as a result of the no-arbitrage principle. Still, it is a valuable relation. Suppose that an investor has determined (from private and/or macro economic information) a discount function showing the value *she* attributes to payments at different future points in time. Then she can value all non-risky cash flows in a consistent way by substituting that discount function into Eq. (11.1).

The information incorporated in prices of the many different bonds is usually better understood when transforming the bond prices into interest rates. Interest rates are always quoted on an annual basis, that is as some percentage per year. However, to apply and assess the magnitude of an interest rate, we also need to know the compounding frequency of that rate. More frequent compounding of a given interest rate per year results in higher 'effective' interest rates. Furthermore, we need to know at which time the interest rate is set or observed and for which period of time the interest rate applies. Spot rates apply to a period beginning at the time the rate is set, whereas forward rates apply to a future period of time. The precise definitions follow below.

Annual compounding Given the price B_t^T at time t on a zero-coupon bond maturing at time T, the relevant discount rate between time t and time T is the yield on the zero-coupon bond, the so-called *zero-coupon rate* or *spot rate* for date T. That $\hat{y}_t^T$ is the annually compounded zero-coupon rate means that

$$B_t^T = (1 + \hat{y}_t^T)^{-(T-t)} \quad \Leftrightarrow \quad \hat{y}_t^T = \left(B_t^T\right)^{-1/(T-t)} - 1.$$

The zero-coupon rates as a function of maturity constitute the so-called *zero-coupon yield curve* or simply the *yield curve*. It is one way to express the term structure of interest rates.

While a zero-coupon or spot rate reflects the price on a loan between today and a given future date, a *forward rate* reflects the price on a loan between two future dates. The annually compounded relevant forward rate at time t for the period between time T and time S is denoted by $\hat{f}_t^{T,S}$. Here, we have $t \leq T < S$. This is the rate which is appropriate at time t for discounting between time T and S. We can think of discounting from time S back to time t by first discounting from time S to time T and then discounting from time T to time t. We must therefore have that

$$\left(1 + \hat{y}_t^S\right)^{-(S-t)} = \left(1 + \hat{y}_t^T\right)^{-(T-t)} \left(1 + \hat{f}_t^{T,S}\right)^{-(S-T)},$$

from which we find that

$$\hat{f}_t^{T,S} = \frac{(1 + \hat{y}_t^T)^{-(T-t)/(S-T)}}{(1 + \hat{y}_t^S)^{-(S-t)/(S-T)}} - 1.$$

We can also link forward rates to bond prices:

$$B_t^S = B_t^T \left(1 + \hat{f}_t^{T,S}\right)^{-(S-T)} \quad \Leftrightarrow \quad \hat{f}_t^{T,S} = \left(\frac{B_t^T}{B_t^S}\right)^{1/(S-T)} - 1. \quad (11.2)$$

Note that since $B_t^t = 1$, we have

$$\hat{f}_t^{t,S} = \left(\frac{B_t^t}{B_t^S}\right)^{1/(S-t)} - 1 = \left(B_t^S\right)^{-1/(S-t)} - 1 = \hat{y}_t^S,$$

that is the forward rate for a period starting today equals the zero-coupon rate or spot rate for the same period.

Compounding over other discrete periods—LIBOR rates. In practice, many interest rates are quoted using semi-annually, quarterly, or monthly compounding. An interest rate of R per year compounded m times a year corresponds to a discount factor of $(1 + R/m)^{-m}$ over a year. The annually compounded interest rate that corresponds to an interest rate of R compounded m times a year is $(1 + R/m)^m - 1$. This is sometimes called the 'effective' interest rate corresponding to a nominal interest rate R and a compounding frequency m. Interest rates are set for loans with various maturities and currencies at the international money markets, the most commonly used being the LIBOR rates that are fixed in London. Traditionally these rates are quoted using a compounding period equal to the maturity of the interest rate. For example, if the three-month interest rate is $l_t^{t+0.25}$ per year, it means that

$$B_t^{t+0.25} = \frac{1}{1 + 0.25\, l_t^{t+0.25}} \quad \Leftrightarrow \quad l_t^{t+0.25} = \frac{1}{0.25}\left(\frac{1}{B_t^{t+0.25}} - 1\right).$$

More generally, the relations are

$$B_t^T = \frac{1}{1 + l_t^T (T-t)} \quad \Leftrightarrow \quad l_t^T = \frac{1}{T-t}\left(\frac{1}{B_t^T} - 1\right). \tag{11.3}$$

Similarly, discretely compounded forward rates can be computed as

$$L_t^{T,S} = \frac{1}{S-T}\left(\frac{B_t^T}{B_t^S} - 1\right). \tag{11.4}$$

Continuous compounding. By increasing the compounding frequency m, the effective annual return on one dollar invested at the interest rate R per year increases to e^R, due to the mathematical result saying that

$$\lim_{m\to\infty}\left(1 + \frac{R}{m}\right)^m = e^R.$$

A continuously compounded interest rate R is equivalent to an annually compounded interest rate of $e^R - 1$ (which is bigger than R). Similarly, the zero-coupon bond price B_t^T is related to the continuously compounded zero-coupon rate y_t^T by

$$B_t^T = e^{-y_t^T (T-t)} \quad \Leftrightarrow \quad y_t^T = -\frac{1}{T-t} \ln B_t^T. \tag{11.5}$$

The function $T \mapsto y_t^T$ is also a zero-coupon yield curve that contains exactly the same information as the discount function $T \mapsto B_t^T$ and also the same information as the annually compounded yield curve $T \mapsto \hat{y}_t^T$. The relation is $y_t^T = \ln(1 + \hat{y}_t^T)$.

If $f_t^{T,S}$ denotes the continuously compounded forward rate prevailing at time t for the period between T and S, we must have that $B_t^S = B_t^T e^{-f_t^{T,S}(S-T)}$, in analogy with Eq. (11.2). Consequently,

$$f_t^{T,S} = -\frac{\ln B_t^S - \ln B_t^T}{S-T} \tag{11.6}$$

and hence

$$f_t^{T,S} = \frac{y_t^S (S-t) - y_t^T (T-t)}{S-T}. \tag{11.7}$$

Analytical studies of the term structure of interest rates often focus on forward rates for future periods of infinitesimal length. The forward rate for an infinitesimal period starting at time T is simply referred to as the forward rate for time T and is defined as $f_t^T = \lim_{S\to T} f_t^{T,S}$. The function $T \mapsto f_t^T$ is called the *term structure of forward rates*. Assuming differentiability of the discount function, Eq. (11.6) implies that

$$f_t^T = -\frac{\partial \ln B_t^T}{\partial T} = -\frac{\partial B_t^T/\partial T}{B_t^T} \qquad \Leftrightarrow \qquad B_t^T = e^{-\int_t^T f_t^u\, du}.$$

Applying Eq. (11.7), the relation between the infinitesimal forward rate and the spot rates can be written as

$$f_t^T = \frac{\partial\left[y_t^T(T-t)\right]}{\partial T} = y_t^T + \frac{\partial y_t^T}{\partial T}(T-t)$$

under the assumption of a differentiable term structure of spot rates $T \mapsto y_t^T$. The forward rate reflects the slope of the zero-coupon yield curve. In particular, the forward rate f_t^T and the zero-coupon rate y_t^T will coincide if and only if the zero-coupon yield curve has a horizontal tangent at T. Conversely,

$$y_t^T = \frac{1}{T-t}\int_t^T f_t^u\, du,$$

that is the zero-coupon rate is an average of the forward rates.

It is important to realize that discount factors, spot rates, and forward rates (with any compounding frequency) are perfectly equivalent ways of expressing the same information. If a complete yield curve of, say, quarterly compounded spot rates is given, we can compute the discount function as well as spot rates and forward rates for any given period and with any given compounding frequency. If a complete term structure of forward rates is known, we can compute discount functions and spot rates, and so on. Academics frequently apply continuous compounding since the mathematics involved in many relevant computations is more elegant when exponentials are used.

There are even more ways of representing the term structure of interest rates. Since most bonds are bullet bonds, many traders and analysts are used to thinking in terms of yields of bullet bonds rather than in terms of discount factors or zero-coupon rates. The *par yield* for a given maturity is the coupon rate that causes a bullet bond of the given maturity to have a price equal to its face value. Again we have to fix the coupon period of the bond. US Treasury bonds typically have semi-annual coupons which are therefore often used when computing par yields. Given a discount function $T \mapsto B_t^T$, the n-year par yield is the value of c satisfying

$$\sum_{i=1}^{2n}\left(\frac{c}{2}\right)B_t^{t+0.5i} + B_t^{t+n} = 1 \Rightarrow \qquad c = \frac{2\left(1 - B_t^{t+n}\right)}{\sum_{i=1}^{2n} B_t^{t+0.5i}}.$$

It reflects the current market interest rate for an n-year bullet bond. The par yield is closely related to the so-called swap rate, which is a key concept in the swap markets, see Section 13.4.

11.3 REAL INTEREST RATES AND AGGREGATE CONSUMPTION

This section explores the link between aggregate consumption and current real interest rates. We assume the existence of a representative individual, which holds at least when financial markets are complete or effectively complete as discussed in Chapter 7. We consider time-additive expected utility, state-dependent utility, and Epstein–Zin recursive utility in separate subsections.

11.3.1 Time-Additive Expected Utility

Assume a continuous-time setting in which the representative individual maximizes the expected time-additive utility $\mathrm{E}[\int_0^T e^{-\delta t} u(c_t)\, dt]$. Recall that the parameter δ is the subjective time preference rate with higher δ representing a more impatient individual. Furthermore, c_t is the consumption rate of the individual, which is then also the aggregate consumption level in the economy. In terms of the utility and time preference of the representative individual the state-price deflator is therefore characterized by

$$\zeta_t = e^{-\delta t} \frac{u'(c_t)}{u'(c_0)}$$

as shown in Eq. (6.36).

Assume that aggregate consumption follows a stochastic process $c = (c_t)$ characterized by the dynamics

$$dc_t = c_t \left[\mu_{ct}\, dt + \boldsymbol{\sigma}_{ct}^{\top}\, d\boldsymbol{z}_t \right], \tag{11.8}$$

where $\boldsymbol{z} = (\boldsymbol{z}_t)$ is a (possibly multidimensional) standard Brownian motion. Then Theorem 8.3 states that the equilibrium continuously compounded short-term interest rate is given by

$$r_t = \delta + \gamma(c_t)\mu_{ct} - \frac{1}{2}\eta(c_t)\|\boldsymbol{\sigma}_{ct}\|^2, \tag{11.9}$$

and that

$$\boldsymbol{\lambda}_t = \gamma(c_t)\boldsymbol{\sigma}_{ct}$$

defines a market price of risk process. Here $\gamma(c_t) \equiv -c_t u''(c_t)/u'(c_t)$ is the relative risk aversion and $\eta(c_t) \equiv c_t^2 u'''(c_t)/u'(c_t)$, which is positive under the very plausible assumption of decreasing absolute risk aversion. For notational simplicity we leave out the f superscript on the short-term interest rate in this chapter. The short rate in Eq. (11.9) was already interpreted in Section 8.3.

In the special case of constant relative risk aversion, $u(c) = c^{1-\gamma}/(1-\gamma)$, Eq. (11.9) simplifies to

$$r_t = \delta + \gamma \mu_{ct} - \frac{1}{2}\gamma(1+\gamma)\|\boldsymbol{\sigma}_{ct}\|^2. \tag{11.10}$$

In particular, we see that if the drift and variance rates of aggregate consumption are constant, that is aggregate consumption follows a geometric Brownian motion, then the short-term interest rate will be constant over time. In that case the time t price of the zero-coupon bond maturing at time s is

$$B_t^s = \mathrm{E}_t\left[\frac{\zeta_s}{\zeta_t}\right] = \mathrm{E}_t\left[\exp\left\{-r(s-t) - \frac{1}{2}\|\boldsymbol{\lambda}\|^2(s-t) - \boldsymbol{\lambda}^{\top}(\boldsymbol{z}_s - \boldsymbol{z}_t)\right\}\right] = e^{-r(s-t)}$$

and the corresponding continuous compounded yield is $y_t^s = r$. Consequently, the yield curve will be flat and constant over time. This is clearly an unrealistic case. To obtain interesting models we must either allow for variations in the expectation and the variance of aggregate consumption growth or allow for non-constant relative risk aversion—or both.

What can we say about the relation between the equilibrium yield curve and the expectations and uncertainty about future aggregate consumption? Given the consumption dynamics in Eq. (11.8), we have

$$\frac{c_T}{c_t} = \exp\left\{\int_t^T \left(\mu_{cs} - \frac{1}{2}\|\boldsymbol{\sigma}_{cs}\|^2\right) ds + \int_t^T \boldsymbol{\sigma}_{cs}^{\top} d\boldsymbol{z}_s\right\}.$$

Assuming that the consumption sensitivity $\boldsymbol{\sigma}_{cs}$ is constant and that the drift rate is so that $\int_t^T \mu_{cs}\, ds$ is normally distributed, we see that c_T/c_t is lognormally distributed. Assuming time-additive power utility, the state-price deflator $\zeta_T/\zeta_t = e^{-\delta(T-t)}(c_T/c_t)^{-\gamma}$ will then also be lognormally distributed. Consequently, the price of the zero-coupon bond maturing at time T is given by

$$\begin{aligned} B_t^T &= \mathrm{E}_t\left[\frac{\zeta_T}{\zeta_t}\right] = e^{-\delta(T-t)}\,\mathrm{E}_t\left[e^{-\gamma \ln(c_T/c_t)}\right] \\ &= \exp\left\{-\delta(T-t) - \gamma\,\mathrm{E}_t\left[\ln\left(\frac{c_T}{c_t}\right)\right] + \frac{1}{2}\gamma^2\,\mathrm{Var}_t\left[\ln\left(\frac{c_T}{c_t}\right)\right]\right\}, \end{aligned}$$

where we have applied Theorem B.2 in Appendix B.

Combining the above expression with Eq. (11.5), the continuously compounded zero-coupon rate or yield y_t^T for maturity T is

$$y_t^T = \delta + \gamma \frac{\mathrm{E}_t[\ln(c_T/c_t)]}{T-t} - \frac{1}{2}\gamma^2 \frac{\mathrm{Var}_t[\ln(c_T/c_t)]}{T-t}.$$

Since

$$\ln \mathrm{E}_t\left[\frac{c_T}{c_t}\right] = \mathrm{E}_t\left[\ln\left(\frac{c_T}{c_t}\right)\right] + \frac{1}{2}\mathrm{Var}_t\left[\ln\left(\frac{c_T}{c_t}\right)\right],$$

the zero-coupon rate can be rewritten as

$$y_t^T = \delta + \gamma \frac{\ln \mathrm{E}_t[c_T/c_t]}{T-t} - \frac{1}{2}\gamma(1+\gamma)\frac{\mathrm{Var}_t[\ln(c_T/c_t)]}{T-t}, \tag{11.11}$$

which is very similar to the short-rate equation (11.10). The yield is increasing in the subjective rate of time preference. The equilibrium yield for the period $[t, T]$ is positively related to the expected growth rate of aggregate consumption over the period and negatively related to the uncertainty about the growth rate of consumption over the period. The intuition for these results is the same as for short-term interest rate. We see that the shape of the equilibrium time t yield curve $T \mapsto y_t^T$ is determined by how expectations and variances of consumption growth rates depend on the length of the forecast period. For example, if the economy is expected to enter a short period of high growth rates, real short-term interest rates tend to be high and the yield curve downward-sloping.

Equation (11.11) is based on a lognormal future consumption and power utility. We will discuss such a setting in more detail in Section 11.5.1. It appears impossible to obtain an exact relation of the same structure as Eq. (11.11) for a more general model, where future consumption is not necessarily lognormal and preferences are different from power utility. However, following Breeden (1986), we can derive an approximate relation of a similar form. The equilibrium time t price of a zero-coupon bond paying one consumption unit at time $T \geq t$ is given by

$$B_t^T = \mathrm{E}_t\left[\frac{\zeta_T}{\zeta_t}\right] = e^{-\delta(T-t)}\frac{\mathrm{E}_t\left[u'(c_T)\right]}{u'(c_t)}, \tag{11.12}$$

where c_T is the uncertain future aggregate consumption level. We can write the left-hand side of the equation above in terms of the yield y_t^T of the bond as

$$B_t^T = e^{-y_t^T(T-t)} \approx 1 - y_t^T(T-t),$$

using a first-order Taylor expansion. Turning to the right-hand side of the equation, we will use a second-order Taylor expansion of $u'(c_T)$ around c_t:

$$u'(c_T) \approx u'(c_t) + u''(c_t)(c_T - c_t) + \frac{1}{2}u'''(c_t)(c_T - c_t)^2.$$

This approximation is reasonable when c_T stays relatively close to c_t, which is the case for fairly low and smooth consumption growth and fairly short time horizons. Applying the approximation, the right-hand side of Eq. (11.12) becomes

$$
\begin{aligned}
e^{-\delta(T-t)} \frac{\mathrm{E}_t\left[u'(c_T)\right]}{u'(c_t)} &\approx e^{-\delta(T-t)} \left(1 + \frac{u''(c_t)}{u'(c_t)} \mathrm{E}_t[c_T - c_t] + \frac{1}{2}\frac{u'''(c_t)}{u'(c_t)} \mathrm{E}_t\left[(c_T - c_t)^2\right]\right) \\
&\approx 1 - \delta(T-t) + e^{-\delta(T-t)} \frac{c_t u''(c_t)}{u'(c_t)} \mathrm{E}_t\left[\frac{c_T}{c_t} - 1\right] \\
&\quad + \frac{1}{2} e^{-\delta(T-t)} c_t^2 \frac{u'''(c_t)}{u'(c_t)} \mathrm{E}_t\left[\left(\frac{c_T}{c_t} - 1\right)^2\right],
\end{aligned}
$$

where we have used the approximation $e^{-\delta(T-t)} \approx 1 - \delta(T-t)$. Substituting the approximations of both sides into Eq. (11.12) and rearranging, we find the following approximate expression for the zero-coupon yield:

$$
\begin{aligned}
y_t^T &\approx \delta + e^{-\delta(T-t)} \left(\frac{-c_t u''(c_t)}{u'(c_t)}\right) \frac{\mathrm{E}_t\left[\frac{c_T}{c_t} - 1\right]}{T-t} \\
&\quad - \frac{1}{2} e^{-\delta(T-t)} c_t^2 \frac{u'''(c_t)}{u'(c_t)} \frac{\mathrm{E}_t\left[\left(\frac{c_T}{c_t} - 1\right)^2\right]}{T-t}.
\end{aligned}
$$

We can replace $\mathrm{E}_t\left[((c_T/c_t) - 1)^2\right]$ by $\mathrm{Var}_t\left[c_T/c_t\right] + (\mathrm{E}_t\left[(c_T/c_t) - 1\right])^2$ and consider the effect of a shift in variance for a fixed expected consumption growth. Again assuming $u' > 0$, $u'' < 0$, and $u''' > 0$, we see that the yield of a given maturity is positively related to the expected growth rate of consumption up to the maturity date and negatively related to the variance of the consumption growth rate up to maturity.

11.3.2 State-Dependent Utility

The Campbell–Cochrane model outlined in Section 9.2.3 is constructed to have a constant real, short-term risk-free rate and, consequently, the term structure of real interest rates is flat. Wachter (2006) extends the model to stochastic interest rates and a non-flat term structure. The extension is simply to replace the expression (9.10) for the constant $\bar{S}$ by

$$
\bar{S} = \sigma \sqrt{\frac{\gamma}{1 - \varphi - (b/\gamma)}},
$$

where b is a new constant. The original specification corresponds to $b = 0$. The key function $\Lambda(S_t)$ is still given by Eq. (9.9), but with the new value of $\bar{S}$. Substituting into the general expression (9.8), the continuously compounded, short-term, real risk-free rate becomes

$$r_t = \delta + \gamma\bar{g} - \frac{\gamma^2\sigma^2}{2\bar{S}^2} - b\ln\frac{S_t}{\bar{S}}.$$

The real risk-free rate now varies with the surplus consumption ratio S_t and thus the state of the economy. If $b > 0$, the real risk-free rate will be low in good times where surplus consumption is high and vice versa. If $b < 0$, the real risk-free rate is low in bad times and high in good times.

Let B_t^{t+n} denote the time t real price of a real zero-coupon bond paying out one (unit of the consumption good) at time $t + n$ for sure. With the state-price deflator in the Campbell–Cochrane framework, we have

$$B_t^{t+n} = \mathrm{E}_t\left[\frac{\zeta_{t+n}}{\zeta_t}\right] = e^{-\delta n}\,\mathrm{E}_t\left[\left(\frac{C_{t+n}}{C_t}\right)^{-\gamma}\left(\frac{S_{t+n}}{S_t}\right)^{-\gamma}\right].$$

Unfortunately, there is no explicit solution for this expectation. Bond prices can be computed numerically based on the relation

$$\begin{aligned} B_t^{t+n} &= \mathrm{E}_t\left[\frac{\zeta_{t+1}}{\zeta_t}B_{t+1}^{t+n}\right] \\ &= e^{-\delta}\,\mathrm{E}_t\left[\left(\frac{C_{t+1}}{C_t}\right)^{-\gamma}\left(\frac{S_{t+1}}{S_t}\right)^{-\gamma}B_{t+1}^{t+n}\right] \\ &= e^{-\delta-\gamma\bar{g}-\gamma(1-\varphi)\ln\bar{S}}\,\mathrm{E}_t\left[e^{-\gamma[1+\Lambda(S_t)]\nu_{t+1}}B_{t+1}^{t+n}\right], \end{aligned} \tag{11.13}$$

which is simply an application of the general recursive pricing rule (4.19). All information about the state of the economy at time t is captured by the current surplus consumption ratio S_t or, equivalently, the log of the surplus consumption ratio $s_t = \ln S_t$, so we can write $B_t^{t+n} = F_n(s_t)$ for some series of functions $F_0, F_1, \dots$. Since $B_t^t = 1$ for all t, we need $F_0(s) = 1$ for any s. From Eqs. (9.7) and (11.13), it follows that

$$F_n(s) = e^{-\delta-\gamma\bar{g}-\gamma(1-\varphi)\ln\bar{S}}\,\mathrm{E}\left[e^{-\gamma[1+\Lambda(e^s)]\tilde{\nu}}F_{n-1}\left(\varphi s + (1-\varphi)\ln\bar{S} + \Lambda(e^s)\tilde{\nu}\right)\right],$$

where $\tilde{\nu}$ is a standardized normal random variable. Wachter suggests to set up a grid approximating the possible values of s. Given $F_0(s) = 1$ for all s, we can compute $F_1(s)$ for any s on the grid from the above equation using numerical integration techniques to approximate the expectation.[1] Subsequently, $F_2(s)$ can be computed for all s based on the computed values of F_1. This procedure is continued until bond prices of all desired maturities have been calculated.

Because bond prices are determined numerically it seems impossible to say anything general about the possible shape and dynamics of the real discount

[1] According to Wachter, numerical integration is superior to Monte Carlo in this case 'because the sensitivity of asset prices to rare events makes simulation unreliable.'

function $n \mapsto B_t^{t+n}$ and the corresponding real yield curve $n \mapsto y_t^{t+n}$. However, Wachter provides some valuable intuition regarding the slope of the real yield curve. Suppose $b > 0$. Then the short-term rate r_t covaries negatively with the state s_t. Bond returns generally move in the opposite direction from the short-term rate, so bond prices covary positively with s_t, which means that bonds have high returns in good times and low returns in bad times. Therefore investors demand a risk premium to hold bonds so that long-term bonds offer higher expected returns than the one-period risk-free rate. The high expected return leads to a low price and a high yield. More precisely, a long-term bond will have a yield which is above the short-term risk-free rate, that is the real yield curve will be upward-sloping, and conversely, if $b < 0$.

Wachter adds a stochastic inflation component to the model and calibrates the model to US data on nominal bonds of different maturities over the period 1952–2004. The key parameter b is set so to obtain reasonable levels of the means and standard deviations of nominal yields and to generate a nominal yield curve that is upward-sloping in normal times. This requires a positive value of b. As discussed above, the real yield curve is then also typically upward-sloping and real bonds have positive risk premia. Piazzesi and Schneider (2006) report that the real yield curve derived from prices of the inflation-protected US government bonds (the so-called TIPS) indeed seems to be upward-sloping, but data are scarce since the bonds were not introduced until 1997 and there have been relatively few issues of TIPS. Moreover, at least in the early years, the TIPS market was highly illiquid which may have depressed prices. In fact, for the longer sample of indexed government bonds in the UK, Piazzesi and Schneider (2006) find that the real yield curve is typically downward-sloping.

11.3.3 Epstein–Zin Recursive Utility and Long-Run Risks

The long-run risk model of Bansal and Yaron (2004) was outlined and discussed in Section 9.3. It deviates from the simple consumption-based model by assuming (i) that the representative individual has Epstein–Zin recursive utility and (ii) that the expectation and variance of consumption growth have time-varying, persistent components x_t and σ_t^2, respectively. According to Eq. (9.38), the continuously compounded equilibrium real short-term risk-free rate is

$$\begin{aligned} r_t = \delta + (1-\theta)q + \frac{\mu + x_t}{\psi} - \frac{1}{2}\lambda_v^2\sigma_v^2 \\ - \left(\frac{1}{2}\gamma^2 + (1-\theta)A_2(1-\kappa_1 \nu) + \frac{1}{2}\lambda_e^2\right)\sigma_t^2, \end{aligned}$$

where we notice some new terms relative to the standard case of power utility and lognormal consumption. The risk-free rate is increasing in the expected consumption growth, which is $\mu + x_t$ in the long-run risk model, but the slope is $1/\psi$ which is generally different than the slope γ for power utility. In fact, if $\psi > 1/\gamma$ as supported by most estimates, the slope is smaller with recursive utility. Assuming a relatively high value of γ in order to match the equity premium, the risk-free rate would be extremely sensitive to swings in the expected consumption growth, but the sensitivity is lower and more realistic with recursive utility featuring an elasticity of intertemporal substitution near 1. As explained in Section 9.3, we have $\kappa_1 \nu < 1$ and, assuming $\gamma > 1$ and $\psi > 1$, we have $\theta < 0$ and $A_2 < 0$ so that the term $(1-\theta)A_2(\kappa_1\nu - 1)$ is positive. Therefore, the risk-free rate is unambiguously decreasing in the consumption variance σ_t^2, which is consistent with the precautionary savings motive for risk-free investments. Variations in the expectation and/or the variance of consumption growth are necessary to obtain a non-constant real short rate and a non-flat real term structure of interest rates. Recall from Section 9.3 that a calibrated version of the model with potentially reasonable preference parameters provides a good match of the level of the real short-term risk-free rate and its volatility.

In an early version of their 2004 paper, Bansal and Yaron (2000) derive some implications of their model for real bonds and the term structure of real interest rates. They show (using a different notation than here) that the price B_t^{t+n} at time t of a real zero-coupon bond paying one (unit of the consumption good) n periods into the future can be approximated by

$$B_t^{t+n} = e^{-\Gamma_{0,n} - \Gamma_{1,n} x_t - \Gamma_{2,n}\sigma_t^2}. \tag{11.14}$$

Here the Γ_1-coefficients satisfy $\Gamma_{1,0} = 0$ and the recursive relation

$$\Gamma_{1,n} = \rho \Gamma_{1,n-1} + \frac{1}{\psi},$$

which has the solution

$$\Gamma_{1,n} = \frac{1}{\psi(1-\rho)} \left(1 - \rho^n\right).$$

With $\psi > 0$ and $\rho \in (0,1)$, we see that $\Gamma_{1,n}$ is positive and increasing in n. A positive shock to the long-run consumption growth variable x leads to decreasing prices of real bonds with the biggest effect on long-term bonds. In line with intuition, higher values of the elasticity of intertemporal substitution ψ dampen the influence of expected consumption growth on real bond prices. The Γ_2-coefficients satisfy $\Gamma_{2,0} = 0$ and the recursive relation

$$\Gamma_{2,n} = \nu \Gamma_{2,n-1} + (1-\theta)A_2(\kappa_1\nu - 1) - \frac{1}{2}\lambda_\eta^2 - \frac{1}{2}\left(\lambda_e + \varphi_e \Gamma_{1,n-1}\right)^2,$$

whereas $\Gamma_{0,n}$ is not reported. Again, the term $(1-\theta)A_2(\kappa_1\nu - 1)$ is positive under the assumption that $\gamma > 1$ and $\psi > 1$. Therefore, the sign of $\Gamma_{2,n}$ is not obvious. According to Hasseltoft (2011), $\Gamma_{2,n}$ is negative for reasonable values of the preference parameters. Therefore real bond prices are increasing in consumption variance, which is consistent with the precautionary savings motive for bond investments.

The continuously compounded periodic yield corresponding to the real bond price in (11.14) is

$$y_t^{t+n} = \frac{\Gamma_{0,n}}{n} + \frac{\Gamma_{1,n}}{n} x_t + \frac{\Gamma_{2,n}}{n} \sigma_t^2.$$

It seems impossible to deduce general properties of the real yield curve $n \mapsto y_t^{t+n}$ by analytical arguments. Based on an estimated version of the model, Hasseltoft (2011) reports that the real yield curve is typically downward-sloping, which is consistent with data on inflation-indexed bonds in the UK as mentioned above. In a differently specified long-run risk model with a unit elasticity of intertemporal substitution, Piazzesi and Schneider (2006) also obtain a downward-sloping real yield curve. Real long-term bonds perform well in bad times, that is times of low expected consumption growth and high consumption uncertainty, and are therefore attractive for risk-averse investors. Hence, long-term bonds have a high price and a corresponding low yield and low expected return. For further discussion of bond prices in long-run risk models, the reader is referred to Bansal, Kiku, and Yaron (2012) and Beeler and Campbell (2012).

11.4 REAL INTEREST RATES AND AGGREGATE PRODUCTION

In order to study the relation between interest rates and production, we will look at a slightly simplified version of the general equilibrium model of Cox, Ingersoll, and Ross (1985a).

Consider an economy with a single physical good that can be used either for consumption or investment. All values are expressed in units of this good. The instantaneous rate of return on an investment in the production of the good is

$$\frac{d\eta_t}{\eta_t} = g(x_t)\,dt + \xi(x_t)\,dz_{1t},$$

where z_1 is a standard one-dimensional Brownian motion and g and ξ are well-behaved real-valued functions (given by Mother Nature) of some state variable x_t. We assume that $\xi(x)$ is non-negative for all values of x. The above dynamics means that η_0 goods invested in the production process at time 0 will grow to η_t goods at time t if the output of the production process is continuously reinvested in this period. We can interpret g as the expected real growth rate of production in the economy and the volatility ξ (assumed positive for all x) as a measure of the uncertainty about the growth rate of production in the economy. The production process has constant returns to scale in the sense that the distribution of the rate of return is independent of the scale of the investment. There is free entry to the production process. We can think of individuals investing in production directly by forming their own firm or indirectly by investing in stocks of production firms. For simplicity we take the first interpretation. All producers act competitively so that firms have zero profits and just pass production returns on to their owners. All individuals and firms act as price takers.

We assume that the state variable is a one-dimensional diffusion with dynamics

$$dx_t = m(x_t)\,dt + \nu_1(x_t)\,dz_{1t} + \nu_2(x_t)\,dz_{2t},$$

where z_2 is another standard one-dimensional Brownian motion independent of z_1, and m, ν_1, and ν_2 are well-behaved real-valued functions. The instantaneous variance rate of the state variable is $\nu_1(x)^2 + \nu_2(x)^2$, the covariance rate of the state variable and the real growth rate is $\xi(x)\nu_1(x)$ so that the correlation between the state and the growth rate is $\nu_1(x)/\sqrt{\nu_1(x)^2 + \nu_2(x)^2}$. Unless $\nu_2 \equiv 0$, the state variable is imperfectly correlated with the real production returns. If ν_1 is positive [negative], then the state variable is positively [negatively] correlated with the growth rate of production in the economy. Since the state determines the expected returns and the variance of returns on real investments, we may think of x_t as a productivity or technology variable.

In addition to the investment in the production process, we assume that the individuals have access to a financial asset with a price P_t with dynamics of the form

$$\frac{dP_t}{P_t} = \mu_t\,dt + \sigma_{1t}\,dz_{1t} + \sigma_{2t}\,dz_{2t}.$$

As a part of the equilibrium we will determine the relation between the expected return μ_t and the sensitivity coefficients σ_{1t} and σ_{2t}. Finally, the individuals can borrow and lend funds at an instantaneously risk-free interest rate r_t, which is also determined in equilibrium. With the two Brownian motion shocks and the three assets, the market is complete. Other financial assets affected by z_1 and z_2 may be traded, but they will be redundant. We will get the same equilibrium relation between expected returns and sensitivity coefficients for these other assets as for the one modelled explicitly. For simplicity we stick to the case with a single financial asset.

If an individual at each time t consumes at a rate of $c_t \geq 0$, invests a fraction α_t of his wealth in the production process, invests a fraction π_t of wealth in the financial asset, and invests the remaining fraction $1 - \alpha_t - \pi_t$ of wealth in the risk-free asset, his wealth W_t will evolve as

$$dW_t = \left\{ r_t W_t + W_t \alpha_t \left(g(x_t) - r_t \right) + W_t \pi_t \left(\mu_t - r_t \right) - c_t \right\} dt + W_t \alpha_t \xi(x_t)\, dz_{1t} + W_t \pi_t \sigma_{1t}\, dz_{1t} + W_t \pi_t \sigma_{2t}\, dz_{2t}.$$

Since a negative real investment is physically impossible, we should restrict α_t to the non-negative numbers. However, we will assume that this constraint is not binding.

Let us look at an individual maximizing expected utility of future consumption. The indirect utility function is defined as

$$J(W, x, t) = \sup_{(\alpha_s, \pi_s, c_s)_{s \in [t,T]}} \mathrm{E}_t \left[\int_t^T e^{-\delta(s-t)} u(c_s)\, ds \right],$$

that is the maximal expected utility the individual can obtain given his current wealth and the current value of the state variable. The dynamic programming technique of Section 6.7 leads to the Hamilton–Jacobi–Bellman Equation

$$\delta J = \sup_{\alpha, \pi, c} \Big\{ u(c) + \frac{\partial J}{\partial t} + J_W \left(rW + \alpha W(g - r) + \pi W(\mu - r) - c \right) + \frac{1}{2} J_{WW} W^2 \left([\alpha \xi + \pi \sigma_1]^2 + \pi^2 \sigma_2^2 \right) + J_x m + \frac{1}{2} J_{xx} (v_1^2 + v_2^2) + J_{Wx} W v_1 (\alpha \xi + \pi \sigma_1) \Big\}.$$

The first-order conditions for α and π imply that

$$\alpha^* = \frac{-J_W}{W J_{WW}} \left[(g - r) \frac{\sigma_1^2 + \sigma_2^2}{\xi^2 \sigma_2^2} - (\mu - r) \frac{\sigma_1}{\xi \sigma_2^2} \right] + \frac{-J_{Wx}}{W J_{WW}} \frac{\sigma_2 v_1 - \sigma_1 v_2}{\xi \sigma_2}, \tag{11.15}$$

$$\pi^* = \frac{-J_W}{W J_{WW}} \left[-\frac{\sigma_1}{\xi \sigma_2^2} (g - r) + \frac{1}{\sigma_2^2} (\mu - r) \right] + \frac{-J_{Wx}}{W J_{WW}} \frac{v_2}{\sigma_2}. \tag{11.16}$$

In equilibrium, prices and interest rates are such that (a) all individuals act optimally and (b) all markets clear. In particular, summing up the positions of all individuals in the financial asset we should get zero, and the total amount borrowed by individuals on a short-term basis should equal the total amount lent by individuals. Since the available production apparatus is to be held by some investors, summing the optimal α's over investors we should get 1. Since we have assumed a complete market, we can construct a representative individual, that is an individual with a given utility function so that the equilibrium interest rates and price processes are the same in the single individual economy as in the larger multi-individual economy. (Alternatively, we may think of the case where all individuals in the economy are identical so that they will have the same indirect utility function and always make the same consumption and investment choice.)

In an equilibrium, we have $\pi^* = 0$ for a representative individual, and hence Eq. (11.16) implies that

$$\mu - r = \frac{\sigma_1}{\xi}(g - r) - \frac{\left(\frac{-J_{Wx}}{WJ_{WW}}\right)}{\left(\frac{-J_W}{WJ_{WW}}\right)}\sigma_2 \nu_2. \tag{11.17}$$

Substituting this into the expression for α^* and using the fact that $\alpha^* = 1$ in equilibrium, we get that

$$\begin{aligned}1 &= \left(\frac{-J_W}{WJ_{WW}}\right)\left[(g-r)\frac{\sigma_1^2+\sigma_2^2}{\xi^2\sigma_2^2} - \frac{\sigma_1}{\xi}\frac{\sigma_1}{\xi\sigma_2^2}(g-r) + \frac{\left(\frac{-J_{Wx}}{WJ_{WW}}\right)}{\left(\frac{-J_W}{WJ_{WW}}\right)}\sigma_2\nu_2\frac{\sigma_1}{\xi\sigma_2^2}\right] \\ &\quad + \left(\frac{-J_{Wx}}{WJ_{WW}}\right)\frac{\sigma_2\nu_1 - \sigma_1\nu_2}{\xi\sigma_2} \\ &= \left(\frac{-J_W}{WJ_{WW}}\right)\frac{g-r}{\xi^2} + \left(\frac{-J_{Wx}}{WJ_{WW}}\right)\frac{\nu_1}{\xi}.\end{aligned}$$

Consequently, the equilibrium short-term interest rate can be written as

$$r = g - \left(\frac{-WJ_{WW}}{J_W}\right)\xi^2 + \frac{J_{Wx}}{J_W}\xi\nu_1. \tag{11.18}$$

This equation ties the equilibrium real short-term interest rate to the production side of the economy. Let us address each of the three right-hand side terms:

- The equilibrium real interest rate r is positively related to the expected real growth rate g of the economy. The intuition is that for higher expected growth rates, the productive investments are more attractive relative to the risk-free investment, so to maintain market clearing the interest rate has to be higher as well.
- The term $-WJ_{WW}/J_W$ is the relative risk aversion of the representative individual's indirect utility. This is assumed to be positive. Hence, we see that the equilibrium real interest rate r is negatively related to the uncertainty about the growth rate of the economy, represented by the instantaneous variance ξ^2. For a higher uncertainty, the safe returns of a risk-free investment are relatively more attractive, so to establish market clearing the interest rate has to decrease.
- The last term in Eq. (11.18) is due to the presence of the state variable. The covariance rate of the state variable and the real growth rate of the economy is equal to $\xi\nu_1$. Suppose that high values of the state variable

represent good states of the economy, where the wealth of the individual is high. Then the marginal utility J_W will be decreasing in x, that is $J_{Wx} < 0$. If instantaneous changes in the state variable and the growth rate of the economy are positively correlated, we see from Eq. (11.15) that the hedge demand of the productive investment is decreasing, and hence the demand for depositing money at the short rate is increasing, in the magnitude of the correlation (both J_{Wx} and J_{WW} are negative). To maintain market clearing, the interest rate must be decreasing in the magnitude of the correlation as reflected by Eq. (11.18).

We see from Eq. (11.17) that the market prices of risk are given by

$$\lambda_1 = \frac{g - r}{\xi}, \qquad \lambda_2 = -\frac{\left(\frac{-J_{Wx}}{WJ_{WW}}\right)}{\left(\frac{-J_W}{WJ_{WW}}\right)} \nu_2 = -\frac{J_{Wx}}{J_W} \nu_2. \tag{11.19}$$

Applying the relation

$$g - r = \left(\frac{-WJ_{WW}}{J_W}\right) \xi^2 - \frac{J_{Wx}}{J_W} \xi \nu_1,$$

we can rewrite λ_1 as

$$\lambda_1 = \left(\frac{-WJ_{WW}}{J_W}\right) \xi - \frac{J_{Wx}}{J_W} \nu_1. \tag{11.20}$$

We discuss a special case of this model in Section 11.5.2 below.

11.5 EQUILIBRIUM INTEREST RATE MODELS

11.5.1 The Vasicek Model

A classic but still widely used model of interest rate dynamics and the pricing of bonds and interest rate derivatives is the model proposed by Vasicek (1977). The basic assumption of the model is that the continuously compounded short-term interest rate r_t has dynamics

$$dr_t = \kappa \left(\bar{r} - r_t\right) dt + \sigma_r \, dz_t, \tag{11.21}$$

where κ, $\bar{r}$, and σ_r are positive constants, and that the market price of risk associated with the shock z is a constant λ.

Before we study the consequences of these assumptions, let us see how they can be supported by a consumption-based equilibrium model. Following Goldstein and Zapatero (1996) assume that aggregate consumption evolves as

$$dc_t = c_t \left[\mu_{ct}\, dt + \sigma_c\, dz_t\right],$$

where z is a one-dimensional standard Brownian motion, σ_C is a constant, and the expected consumption growth rate μ_{ct} follows the process

$$d\mu_{ct} = \kappa\left(\bar{\mu}_c - \mu_{ct}\right) dt + \theta\, dz_t.$$

The representative individual is assumed to have a constant relative risk aversion of γ. It follows from Eq. (11.10) that the equilibrium real short-term interest rate is

$$r_t = \delta + \gamma\mu_{ct} - \frac{1}{2}\gamma(1+\gamma)\sigma_C^2$$

with dynamics $dr_t = \gamma\, d\mu_{ct}$, which gives Eq. (11.21) with $\sigma_r = \gamma\theta$ and $\bar{r} = \gamma\bar{\mu}_c + \delta - \frac{1}{2}\gamma(1+\gamma)\sigma_c^2$. The market price of risk is $\lambda = \gamma\sigma_c$, a constant.

The process (11.21) is a so-called Ornstein-Uhlenbeck process. The process exhibits *mean reversion* in the sense that the drift is positive when $r_t < \bar{r}$ and negative when $x_t > \bar{r}$. The process is therefore always pulled towards a long-term level of $\bar{r}$. However, the random shock to the process through the term $\sigma_r\, dz_t$ may cause the process to move further away from $\bar{r}$. The parameter κ controls the size of the expected adjustment towards the long-term level and is often referred to as the mean reversion parameter or the speed of adjustment.

The distribution of the future value of the short-term interest rate is given in the following theorem:

Theorem 11.1 *Suppose that $r = (r_t)$ is given by the Ornstein–Uhlenbeck process (11.21). Then for any $t, t' \in [0, T]$ with $t \leq t'$,*

$$r_{t'} = e^{-\kappa(t'-t)} r_t + \bar{r}\left(1 - e^{-\kappa(t'-t)}\right) + \int_t^{t'} \sigma_r e^{-\kappa(t'-u)}\, dz_u, \tag{11.22}$$

and $r_{t'}$ (given r_t) is normally distributed with mean and variance given by

$$\mathrm{E}_t[r_{t'}] = e^{-\kappa(t'-t)} r_t + \bar{r}\left(1 - e^{-\kappa(t'-t)}\right), \tag{11.23}$$

$$\mathrm{Var}_t[r_{t'}] = \frac{\sigma_r^2}{2\kappa}\left(1 - e^{-2\kappa(t'-t)}\right). \tag{11.24}$$

Proof. The idea is to define a new process y_t as some function of r_t such that $y = (y_t)_{t\geq 0}$ is a generalized Brownian motion. It turns out that this is satisfied for $y_t = g(r_t, t)$, where $g(r, t) = e^{\kappa t} r$. From Itô's Lemma we get

$$\begin{aligned}
dy_t &= \left[\frac{\partial g}{\partial t}(r_t, t) + \frac{\partial g}{\partial r}(r_t, t)\kappa\left(\bar{r} - r_t\right) + \frac{1}{2}\frac{\partial^2 g}{\partial r^2}(r_t, t)\sigma_r^2\right] dt + \frac{\partial g}{\partial r}(r_t, t)\sigma_r\, dz_t \\
&= \left[\kappa e^{\kappa t} r_t + \kappa e^{\kappa t}\left(\bar{r} - r_t\right)\right] dt + e^{\kappa t}\sigma_r\, dz_t \\
&= \kappa\bar{r}e^{\kappa t}\, dt + \sigma_r e^{\kappa t}\, dz_t.
\end{aligned}$$

This implies that

$$y_{t'} = y_t + \kappa\bar{r}\int_t^{t'} e^{\kappa u}\,du + \int_t^{t'} \sigma_r e^{\kappa u}\,dz_u.$$

After substitution of the definition of y_t and $y_{t'}$ and a multiplication by $e^{-\kappa t'}$, we arrive at the expression

$$\begin{aligned} r_{t'} &= e^{-\kappa(t'-t)}r_t + \kappa\bar{r}\int_t^{t'} e^{-\kappa(t'-u)}\,du + \int_t^{t'} \sigma_r e^{-\kappa(t'-u)}\,dz_u \\ &= e^{-\kappa(t'-t)}r_t + \bar{r}\left(1 - e^{-\kappa(t'-t)}\right) + \int_t^{t'} \sigma_r e^{-\kappa(t'-u)}\,dz_u \end{aligned}$$

as claimed. According to Theorem 2.3, the integral $\int_t^{t'} \sigma_r e^{-\kappa(t'-u)}\,dz_u$ is normally distributed with mean zero and variance $\int_t^{t'} \sigma_r^2 e^{-2\kappa(t'-u)}\,du = \frac{\sigma_r^2}{2\kappa}\left(1 - e^{-2\kappa(t'-t)}\right)$. This implies that $r_{t'}$ is normally distributed with the mean and variance stated in Eqs. (11.23) and (11.24), respectively. □

Note that the value space of an Ornstein–Uhlenbeck process is $\mathbb{R}$. For $t' \to \infty$, the mean approaches $\bar{r}$, and the variance approaches $\sigma_r^2/(2\kappa)$. For $\kappa \to \infty$, the mean approaches $\bar{r}$, and the variance approaches 0. For $\kappa \to 0$, the mean approaches the current value r_t, and the variance approaches $\sigma_r^2(t'-t)$. Observe that $\mathrm{E}_t[r_{t'}] - \bar{r} = \frac{1}{2}(r_t - \bar{r})$ implies that $e^{-\kappa(t'-t)} = \frac{1}{2}$ and, hence, $t' - t = (\ln 2)/\kappa$ is the time it takes for the distance between the level of the process and the long-term level to be halved, in expectations.

The effect of the different parameters can also be evaluated by looking at the paths of the process, which can be simulated by

$$r_{t_i} = r_{t_{i-1}} + \kappa[\bar{r} - r_{t_{i-1}}](t_i - t_{i-1}) + \sigma_r \varepsilon_i \sqrt{t_i - t_{i-1}},$$

where $\varepsilon_i \sim N(0,1)$. Figure 11.1 shows a single path for different combinations of r_0, κ, $\bar{r}$, and σ_r. In each sub-figure one of the parameters is varied and the others fixed. The base values of the parameters are $r_0 = 0.04$, $\bar{r} = 0.04$, $\kappa = \ln 2 \approx 0.69$, and $\sigma_r = 0.02$. All paths are computed using the same sequence of random numbers $\varepsilon_1, \dots, \varepsilon_n$ and are therefore directly comparable. None of the paths shown involve negative values of the process, but other paths will as shown, for example, in Fig. 11.2 in the next subsection. As a matter of fact, it can be shown that an Ornstein–Uhlenbeck process with probability one will become negative sooner or later.

Given Vasicek's assumptions, the prices of zero-coupon bonds can be computed in closed form as shown in the following theorem. First, we introduce some notation. For any positive constant α, define the function

$$\mathcal{B}_\alpha(\tau) = \frac{1}{\alpha}\left(1 - e^{-\alpha\tau}\right), \quad \tau \geq 0. \tag{11.25}$$

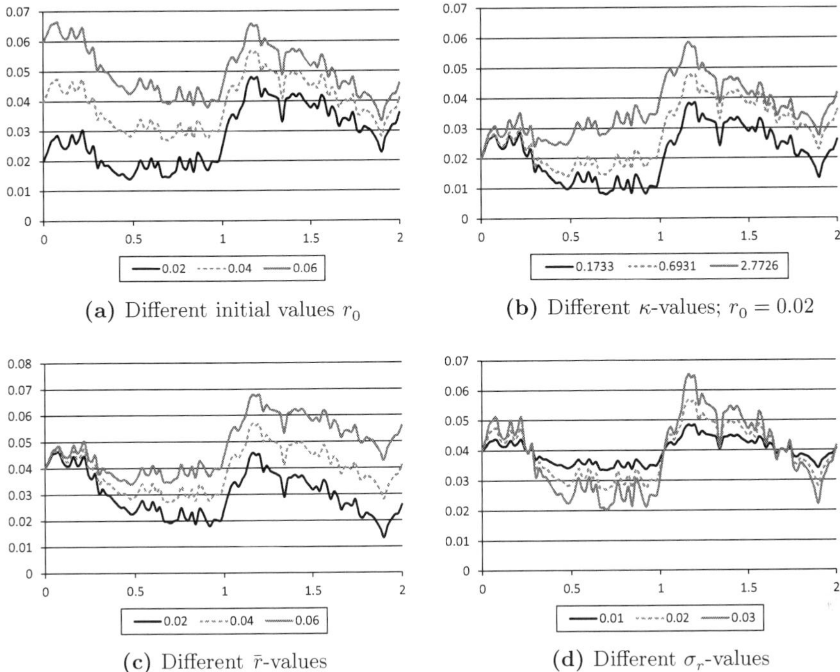

(a) Different initial values r_0

(b) Different κ-values; $r_0 = 0.02$

(c) Different $\bar{r}$-values

(d) Different σ_r-values

Fig. 11.1. Simulated paths for an Ornstein–Uhlenbeck process. The basic parameter values are $r_0 = \bar{r} = 0.04$, $\kappa = \ln 2 \approx 0.69$, and $\sigma_r = 0.02$.

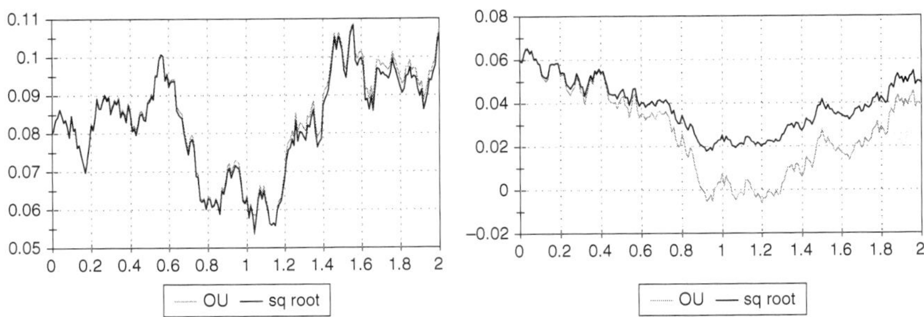

Fig. 11.2. A comparison of simulated paths for an Ornstein–Uhlenbeck process (grey) and a square root process (black).

Notes: For both processes, the parameters $\bar{r} = 0.08$ and $\kappa = \ln 2 \approx 0.69$ are used, while σ_r is set to 0.03 for the Ornstein–Uhlenbeck process and to $0.03/\sqrt{0.08} \approx 0.1061$ for the square root process

Straightforward integration leads to

$$\int_t^s \mathcal{B}_\alpha(s-u)\,du = \frac{1}{\alpha}(s-t-\mathcal{B}_\alpha(s-t)), \tag{11.26}$$

$$\int_t^s \mathcal{B}_\alpha(s-u)^2\,du = \frac{1}{\alpha^2}(s-t-\mathcal{B}_\alpha(s-t)) - \frac{1}{2\alpha}\mathcal{B}_\alpha(s-t)^2, \tag{11.27}$$

which will be useful below.

Theorem 11.2 *Assume that the short-term risk-free interest rate follows the Ornstein–Uhlenbeck process* (11.21) *and that the market price of risk associated with the standard Brownian motion z is a constant λ. Then the time t price of a zero-coupon bond maturing at time s is given by*

$$B_t^s = \exp\left\{-\mathcal{A}(s-t) - \mathcal{B}_\kappa(s-t)r_t\right\}, \tag{11.28}$$

where $\mathcal{B}_\kappa$ is given by Eq. (11.25) *and*

$$\mathcal{A}(\tau) = y_\infty(\tau - \mathcal{B}_\kappa(\tau)) + \frac{\sigma_r^2}{4\kappa}\mathcal{B}_\kappa(\tau)^2 \tag{11.29}$$

with

$$y_\infty = \bar{r} - \frac{\lambda\sigma_r}{\kappa} - \frac{\sigma_r^2}{2\kappa^2}.$$

Proof. Let ζ denote the state-price deflator. Then the time t price of a zero-coupon bond maturing at time s is given by

$$B_t^s = \mathrm{E}_t\left[\frac{\zeta_s}{\zeta_t}\right] = \mathrm{E}_t\left[\exp\left\{-\int_t^s r_u\,du - \frac{1}{2}\int_t^s \lambda^2\,du - \int_t^s \lambda\,dz_u\right\}\right],$$

where we have applied Eq. (4.33) and the assumption of a constant market price of risk. In order to compute this expectation, first use Eq. (11.22) to find that

$$\int_t^s r_u\,du = \int_t^s e^{-\kappa(u-t)}r_t\,du + \int_t^s \bar{r}\left(1-e^{-\kappa(u-t)}\right)\,du + \int_t^s\int_t^u \sigma_r e^{-\kappa(u-v)}\,dz_v\,du.$$

Interchange the order of integration in the double integral (this follows from the so-called Fubini Theorem of stochastic calculus):

$$\int_t^s\left[\int_t^u \sigma_r e^{-\kappa(u-v)}\,dz_v\right]du = \int_t^s\left[\int_v^s \sigma_r e^{-\kappa(u-v)}\,du\right]dz_v.$$

Further note that $\int_t^s e^{-\kappa(u-t)}\,du = \mathcal{B}_\kappa(s-t)$.

It now follows that

$$\int_t^s r_u\,du = r_t\mathcal{B}_\kappa(s-t) + \bar{r}\,(s-t-\mathcal{B}_\kappa(s-t)) + \int_t^s \sigma_r\mathcal{B}_\kappa(s-u)\,dz_u. \tag{11.30}$$

By using Theorem 2.3 and results in Appendix B we obtain

$$\begin{aligned}
B_t^s &= \exp\left\{-r_t\mathcal{B}_\kappa(s-t) - \bar{r}(s-t-\mathcal{B}_\kappa(s-t)) - \frac{1}{2}\lambda^2(s-t)\right\} \\
&\quad \times \mathrm{E}_t\left[\exp\left\{-\int_t^s (\lambda + \sigma_r\mathcal{B}_\kappa(s-u))\, dz_u\right\}\right] \\
&= \exp\left\{-r_t\mathcal{B}_\kappa(s-t) - \bar{r}(s-t-\mathcal{B}_\kappa(s-t)) - \frac{1}{2}\lambda^2(s-t)\right\} \\
&\quad \times \exp\left\{\frac{1}{2}\int_t^s (\lambda + \sigma_r\mathcal{B}_\kappa(s-u))^2\, du\right\} \\
&= \exp\Bigg\{-r_t\mathcal{B}_\kappa(s-t) - \bar{r}(s-t-\mathcal{B}_\kappa(s-t)) + \lambda\sigma_r\int_t^s \mathcal{B}_\kappa(s-u)\, du \\
&\qquad + \frac{1}{2}\sigma_r^2\int_t^s \mathcal{B}_\kappa(s-u)^2\, du\Bigg\} \\
&= \exp\{-\mathcal{A}(s-t) - \mathcal{B}_\kappa(s-t)r_t\},
\end{aligned}$$

where $\mathcal{A}$ is defined by Eq. (11.29).

Alternatively, we can derive the bond price formula (11.28) using the PDE approach described in Section 4.4.3. In the Vasicek model, the short rate r_t itself is the only state variable, so it is clear that the bond price is of the form $B_t^s = B^s(r,t)$ for some function B^s. The general valuation PDE (4.50) specializes to

$$\begin{aligned}
&\frac{\partial B^s}{\partial t}(r,t) + \frac{\partial B^s}{\partial r}(r,t)\,(\kappa[\bar{r} - r] - \sigma_r\lambda) \\
&\qquad + \frac{1}{2}\frac{\partial^2 B^s}{\partial r^2}(r,t)\sigma_r^2 = rB^s(r,t), \qquad (r,t) \in \mathbb{R} \times [0,s),
\end{aligned}$$

with the terminal condition $B^s(r,s) = 1$ for all $r \in \mathbb{R}$. The Vasicek model has an affine structure as outlined in Section 4.4.3. Therefore we conjecture a solution of the form $B^s(r,t) = \exp\{-\mathcal{A}(s-t) - \mathcal{B}_\kappa(s-t)r\}$ for some functions $\mathcal{A}$ and $\mathcal{B}_\kappa$, substitute that into the above PDE, divide through by B^s, and collect terms. We obtain

$$\begin{aligned}
&\left\{\mathcal{A}'(s-t) - (\kappa\bar{r} - \sigma_r\lambda)\,\mathcal{B}_\kappa(s-t) + \frac{1}{2}\sigma_r^2\mathcal{B}_\kappa(s-t)^2\right\} \\
&\qquad + \left\{\mathcal{B}_\kappa'(s-t) + \kappa\mathcal{B}_\kappa(s-t) - 1\right\} r = 0, \quad (r,t) \in \mathbb{R} \times [0,s).
\end{aligned}$$

This can only hold for all (r,t) and for all maturities s if a and $\mathcal{B}_\kappa$ solve the ordinary differential equations (ODEs)

$$\mathcal{B}'_\kappa(\tau) + \kappa \mathcal{B}_\kappa(\tau) - 1 = 0, \; \mathcal{A}'(\tau) = (\kappa \bar{r} - \sigma_r \lambda)\, \mathcal{B}_\kappa(T-t) - \frac{1}{2}\sigma_r^2 \mathcal{B}_\kappa(T-t)^2$$

for $\tau > 0$. These ODEs are special cases of the general ODEs in Eqs. (4.55)–(4.56). The terminal condition on the bond price implies that $\mathcal{A}(0) = \mathcal{B}_\kappa(0) = 0$. It is easy to verify that the functions $\mathcal{B}_\kappa$ and $\mathcal{A}$ defined in the theorem indeed satisfy the ODEs and the terminal condition. □

The continuously compounded yield of the zero-coupon bond maturing at time s is

$$y_t^s = -\frac{\ln B_t^s}{s-t} = \frac{\mathcal{A}(s-t)}{s-t} + \frac{\mathcal{B}_\kappa(s-t)}{s-t} r_t, \tag{11.31}$$

which is affine in the current short rate r_t. It can be shown that $y_t^s \to y_\infty$ for $s \to \infty$, which explains the notation. The asymptotic long yield is a constant in the Vasicek model. Concerning the shape of the yield curve $s \to y_t^s$ it can be shown that

(i) if $r_t < y_\infty - \frac{\sigma_r^2}{4\kappa^2}$, the yield curve is increasing;

(ii) if $r_t > y_\infty + \frac{\sigma_r^2}{2\kappa^2}$, the yield curve is decreasing;

(iii) for intermediate values of r_t, the yield curve is humped, that is increasing in s up to some maturity s^* and then decreasing for longer maturities.

A proof can be found in Munk (2011, Sec. 7.4.3). Within the Vasicek model it is possible to find closed-form expressions for the prices of many other interesting assets, such as forwards and futures on bonds, Eurodollar futures, and European options on bonds, see Chapter 13.

The Vasicek model is an example of an affine term structure model. There are many other affine term structure models and they can basically all be supported by a consumption-based asset pricing model in the same way as the Vasicek model. Assume that the expected growth rate and the variance rate of aggregate consumption are affine in some state variables, that is

$$\mu_{ct} = a_0 + \sum_{i=1}^n a_i x_{it}, \qquad \|\boldsymbol{\sigma}_{ct}\|^2 = b_0 + \sum_{i=1}^n b_i x_{it},$$

then the equilibrium short rate will be

$$r_t = \left(\delta + \gamma a_0 - \frac{1}{2}\gamma(1+\gamma) b_0\right) + \gamma \sum_{i=1}^n \left(a_i - \frac{1}{2}(1+\gamma) b_i\right) x_{it}.$$

Of course, we should have $b_0 + \sum_{i=1}^n b_i x_{it} \geq 0$ for all values of the state variables. The market price of risk is $\lambda_t = \gamma \sigma_{ct}$. If the state variables x_i follow processes of the affine type, we have an affine term structure model.

For other term structure models developed with the consumption-based approach, see, for example, Bakshi and Chen (1997).

11.5.2 The Cox–Ingersoll–Ross Model

Another widely used model of interest rate dynamics was suggested by Cox, Ingersoll, and Ross (1985b). They assume that the short-term interest rate r_t follows a so-called square root process

$$dr_t = \kappa\,(\bar{r} - r_t)\,dt + \sigma_r \sqrt{r_t}\,d\bar{z}_t, \tag{11.32}$$

where κ, $\bar{r}$, and σ_r are positive constants. Furthermore, the associated market price of risk is assumed to be

$$\lambda_t = \lambda \sqrt{r_t}/\sigma_r, \tag{11.33}$$

where the λ on the right-hand side is a constant.

Cox, Ingersoll, and Ross (1985b) derive their model as a special case of their general equilibrium model with production which we reviewed in Section 11.4. The representative individual is assumed to have a logarithmic utility so that the relative risk aversion of the direct utility function equals one. In addition, the individual is assumed to have an infinite time horizon, which implies that the indirect utility function will be independent of time. It can be shown that under these assumptions the indirect utility function of the individual is of the form $J(W,x) = A \ln W + B(x)$. In particular, $J_{Wx} = 0$ and the relative risk aversion of the indirect utility function is also one. It follows from Eq. (11.18) that the equilibrium real short-term interest rate is equal to

$$r(x_t) = g(x_t) - \xi(x_t)^2.$$

The authors further assume that the expected rate of return and the variance rate of the return on the productive investment are both proportional to the state, that is

$$g(x) = k_1 x, \qquad \xi(x)^2 = k_2 x,$$

where $k_1 > k_2$. Then the equilibrium short rate becomes $r(x) = (k_1 - k_2)x \equiv kx$. Assume now that the state variable follows a square root process

$$\begin{aligned} dx_t &= \kappa\,(\bar{x} - x_t)\,dt + \rho\sigma_x\sqrt{x_t}\,dz_{1t} + \sqrt{1-\rho^2}\sigma_x\sqrt{x_t}\,dz_{2t} \\ &= \kappa\,(\bar{x} - x_t)\,dt + \sigma_x\sqrt{x_t}\,d\bar{z}_t, \end{aligned}$$

where $\bar{z}$ is a standard Brownian motion with correlation ρ with the standard Brownian motion z_1 and correlation $\sqrt{1-\rho^2}$ with z_2. Then the dynamics of the real short rate is $dr_t = k\,dx_t$, which yields

$$dr_t = \kappa\,(\bar{r} - r_t)\,dt + \sigma_r \sqrt{r_t}\,d\bar{z}_t,$$

where $\bar{r} = k\bar{x}$ and $\sigma_r = \sqrt{k}\sigma_x$. The market prices of risk given in Eqs. (11.19) and (11.20) simplify to

$$\lambda_1 = \xi(x) = \sqrt{k_2 x} = \sqrt{k_2/k}\,\sqrt{r}, \qquad \lambda_2 = 0.$$

The market price of risk associated with the combined shock $\bar{z}$ is $\rho\lambda_1 + \sqrt{1-\rho^2}\lambda_2$, which is proportional to $\sqrt{r}$. These conclusions support the assumptions (11.32) and (11.33).

Before we discuss the implications for bond prices and the yield curve, let us look at the properties of the square root process. The only difference to the Ornstein–Uhlenbeck process is the square root term in the volatility. The variance rate is now $\sigma_r^2 r_t$ which is proportional to the level of the process. A square root process also exhibits mean reversion. A square root process can only take on non-negative values. To see this, note that if the value should become zero, then the drift is positive and the volatility zero, and therefore the value of the process will with certainty become positive immediately after (zero is a so-called reflecting barrier). It can be shown that if $2\kappa\bar{r} \geq \sigma_r^2$, the positive drift at low values of the process is so big relative to the volatility that the process cannot even reach zero, but stays strictly positive.[2] Hence, the value space for a square root process is either $\mathcal{S} = [0, \infty)$ or $\mathcal{S} = (0, \infty)$.

Paths for the square root process can be simulated by successively calculating

$$r_{t_i} = r_{t_{i-1}} + \kappa[\bar{r} - r_{t_{i-1}}](t_i - t_{i-1}) + \sigma_r \sqrt{r_{t_{i-1}}}\varepsilon_i \sqrt{t_i - t_{i-1}}.$$

Variations in the different parameters will have similar effects as for the Ornstein–Uhlenbeck process, which is illustrated in Fig. 11.1. Instead, let us compare the paths for a square root process and an Ornstein-Uhlenbeck process using the same drift parameters κ and $\bar{r}$, but where the σ_r-parameter for the Ornstein–Uhlenbeck process is set equal to the σ_r-parameter for the square root process multiplied by the square root of $\bar{r}$, which ensures that the processes will have the same variance rate at the long-term level. Figure 11.2 compares two pairs of paths of the processes. In part (a), the initial value is set equal to the long-term level, and the two paths continue to be very close to each other. In part (b), the initial value is lower than the long-term level so that the variance rates of the two processes differ from the beginning. For the given sequence of random numbers, the Ornstein-Uhlenbeck process becomes negative, whereas the square root process of course stays positive. In this case there is a clear difference between the paths of the two processes.

Since a square root process cannot become negative, the future values of the process cannot be normally distributed. The following theorem provides the relevant distribution.

[2] To show this, the results of Karlin and Taylor (1981, pp. 226ff.) can be applied.

Theorem 11.3 *Given the short rate r_t at time t, the value of the short rate $r_{t'}$ at time $t' > t$ is non-centrally χ^2-distributed. More precisely, the probability density function for $r_{t'}$ is*

$$f_{r_{t'}|r_t}(x) = f_{\chi^2_{a,b}}(2cx),$$

where

$$c = \frac{2\kappa}{\sigma_r^2\left(1 - e^{-\kappa(t'-t)}\right)}, \qquad b = cr_t e^{-\kappa(t'-t)}, \qquad a = \frac{4\kappa\bar{r}}{\sigma_r^2},$$

and where $f_{\chi^2_{a,b}}(\cdot)$ denotes the probability density function for a non-centrally χ^2-distributed random variable with a degrees of freedom and non-centrality parameter 2b. The mean and the variance are given by

$$\mathrm{E}_t[r_{t'}] = e^{-\kappa(t'-t)}r_t + \bar{r}\left(1 - e^{-\kappa(t'-t)}\right) = \bar{r} + (r_t - \bar{r})\,e^{-\kappa(t'-t)},$$

$$\mathrm{Var}_t[r_{t'}] = \frac{\sigma_r^2 r_t}{\kappa}\left(e^{-\kappa(t'-t)} - e^{-2\kappa(t'-t)}\right) + \frac{\sigma_r^2\bar{r}}{2\kappa}\left(1 - e^{-\kappa(t'-t)}\right)^2,$$

respectively.

Proof. Let us try the same trick as for the Ornstein–Uhlenbeck process, that is we look at $y_t = e^{\kappa t}r_t$. By Itô's Lemma,

$$\begin{aligned} dy_t &= \kappa e^{\kappa t} r_t\,dt + \kappa e^{\kappa t}(\bar{r} - r_t)\,dt + e^{\kappa t}\sigma_r\sqrt{r_t}\,dz_t \\ &= \kappa\bar{r}e^{\kappa t}\,dt + \sigma_r e^{\kappa t}\sqrt{r_t}\,dz_t \end{aligned}$$

so that

$$y_{t'} = y_t + \kappa\bar{r}\int_t^{t'} e^{\kappa u}\,du + \int_t^{t'} \sigma_r e^{\kappa u}\sqrt{r_u}\,dz_u.$$

Computing the ordinary integral and substituting the definition of y, we get

$$r_{t'} = r_t e^{-\kappa(t'-t)} + \bar{r}\left(1 - e^{-\kappa(t'-t)}\right) + \sigma_r\int_t^{t'} e^{-\kappa(t'-u)}\sqrt{r_u}\,dz_u.$$

Since r enters the stochastic integral we cannot immediately determine the distribution of $r_{t'}$ given r_t from this equation. We can, however, use it to obtain the mean and variance of $r_{t'}$. Due to the fact that the stochastic integral has mean zero, compare Theorem 2.2, we easily confirm the mean stated in the theorem. To compute the variance the second equation of Theorem 2.2 can be applied, which will eventually lead to the expression stated in the theorem.

The proof of the claim that future short rates are non-centrally χ^2-distributed with the postulated parameters is complicated and will be omitted here. It follows from the analysis by Feller (1951). □

Note that the mean is identical to the mean for an Ornstein–Uhlenbeck process, whereas the variance is more complicated for the square root process.

Although the assumed short rate process and the resulting distribution is more complex than for the Vasicek model, the Cox–Ingersoll–Ross model is still in the affine class introduced in Section 4.4.3. Consequently, the prices of zero-coupon bonds will have the same exponential-affine structure as in the Vasicek model.

Theorem 11.4 *Assume that the short-term risk-free interest rate follows the square root process* (11.32) *and that the market price of risk associated with the standard Brownian motion z is given by Eq.* (11.33). *Then the time t price of a zero-coupon bond maturing at time s is given by*

$$B_t^s = \exp\left\{-\mathcal{A}(s-t) - \mathcal{B}(s-t)r_t\right\},$$

where

$$\mathcal{B}(\tau) = \frac{2(e^{\nu\tau}-1)}{(\nu+\hat{\kappa})(e^{\nu\tau}-1)+2\nu},$$

$$\mathcal{A}(\tau) = -\frac{2\kappa\bar{r}}{\sigma_r^2}\left(\ln(2\nu) + \frac{1}{2}(\hat{\kappa}+\nu)\tau - \ln\left[(\nu+\hat{\kappa})(e^{\nu\tau}-1)+2\nu\right]\right),$$

with $\hat{\kappa} = \kappa + \lambda$ *and* $\nu = \sqrt{\hat{\kappa}^2 + 2\sigma_r^2}$.

Proof. The complexity of the non-central χ^2 distribution makes the computation of the bond price B_t^T via the expectation $E_t[\zeta_T/\zeta_t]$ more difficult than in the Vasicek model. Instead, we can exploit the fact that also the Cox–Ingersoll–Ross model has an affine structure, so it is clear from Section 4.4.3 that the price of a zero-coupon bond maturing at time s is of the form

$$B_t^s = e^{-\mathcal{A}(s-t)-\mathcal{B}(s-t)r_t}.$$

The bond price is a function $B^s(r,t)$ of the short rate and time, and this function will satisfy a certain PDE as explained in Section 4.4.3. Substituting the conjectured form of B^s into the PDE will lead to ODEs that $\mathcal{A}$ and $\mathcal{B}$ have to solve. The solution is as stated in the theorem. Exercise 11.10 asks for the details of this proof. □

As in the Vasicek model, the yields are affine in the current short rate,

$$y_t^s = \frac{\mathcal{A}(s-t)}{s-t} + \frac{\mathcal{B}(s-t)}{s-t}r_t.$$

It can be shown that the asymptotic long yield is

$$y_\infty \equiv \lim_{s\to\infty} y_t^s = \frac{2\kappa\bar{r}}{\hat{\kappa}+\nu},$$

and that the yield curve can have the following shapes (Kan 1992):

(i) if $\kappa + \lambda > 0$, the yield curve is decreasing for $r_t \geq \kappa\bar{r}/(\kappa + \lambda)$ and increasing for $0 \leq r_t \leq \kappa\bar{r}/\nu$. For $\kappa\bar{r}/\nu < r_t < \kappa\bar{r}/(\kappa + \lambda)$, the yield curve is humped, that is first increasing, then decreasing;

(ii) if $\kappa + \lambda \leq 0$, the yield curve is increasing for $0 \leq r_t \leq \kappa\bar{r}/\nu$ and humped for $r_t > \kappa\bar{r}/\nu$.

Also in this model closed-form expressions can be derived for many popular interest rate related assets, see Chapter 13.

Longstaff and Schwartz (1992) study a two-factor version of the model. They assume that the production returns are given by

$$\frac{d\eta_t}{\eta_t} = g(x_{1t}, x_{2t})\, dt + \xi(x_{2t})\, dz_{1t},$$

where

$$g(x_1, x_2) = k_1 x_1 + k_2 x_2, \qquad \xi(x_2)^2 = k_3 x_2$$

so that the state variable x_2 affects both expected returns and uncertainty of production, while the state variable x_1 only affects the expected return. With log-utility the short rate is again equal to the expected return minus the variance,

$$r(x_1, x_2) = g(x_1, x_2) - \xi(x_2)^2 = k_1 x_1 + (k_2 - k_3) x_2.$$

The state variables are assumed to follow independent square root processes,

$$dx_{1t} = (\varphi_1 - \kappa_1 x_{1t})\, dt + \beta_1 \sqrt{x_{1t}}\, dz_{2t},$$
$$dx_{2t} = (\varphi_2 - \kappa_2 x_{2t})\, dt + \beta_2 \sqrt{x_{2t}}\, dz_{3t},$$

where z_2 are independent of z_1 and z_3, but z_1 and z_3 may be correlated. The market prices of risk associated with the Brownian motions are

$$\lambda_1(x_2) = \xi(x_2) = \sqrt{k_2}\sqrt{x_2}, \quad \lambda_2 = \lambda_3 = 0.$$

11.6 REAL AND NOMINAL INTEREST RATES AND TERM STRUCTURES

In the following we shall first derive some generally valid relations between real rates, nominal rates, and inflation and investigate the differences between real and nominal bonds. Then we will discuss two different types of models in which we can say more about real and nominal rates. The first setting follows the neoclassic tradition in assuming that monetary holdings do not affect the preferences of the individuals so that the presence of money has no effects on real rates and real asset returns. Hence, the relations derived earlier in this chapter still apply. However, several empirical findings indicate that the existence of money does have real effects. For example, real stock returns are negatively correlated with inflation and positively correlated with money growth. Also, assets that are positively correlated with inflation have a lower expected return. Such results are reported by Fama (1981), Fama and Gibbons (1982), Chen, Roll, and Ross (1986), and Marshall (1992). In the second setting we consider below, money is allowed to have real effects. Economies with this property are called *monetary economies*.

11.6.1 Real and Nominal Asset Pricing

Earlier in this chapter we derived relations between interest rates or yields on one side and aggregate consumption or production on the other side. These relations apply to real interest rates or yields. The real short-term interest rate is the rate of return over the next instant of an asset which is risk-free in real terms so that it provides a certain purchasing power. A real yield of maturity T is derived from the real price of a real zero-coupon bond maturing at time T, that is a bond paying one unit of the consumption good (or a well-defined basket of different goods) at time T. In reality most deposit arrangements and traded bonds are nominal in the sense that the dividends they promise are pre-specified units of some currency, not some units of consumption goods. In this section we search for the link between real and nominal interest rates and yields.

Recall the results we derived on real and nominal pricing in Section 4.5. Let us stick to the continuous-time framework. Let $\tilde{F}_t$ denote the price of the good in currency units at time t (or think of $\tilde{F}_t$ as the value of the Consumer Price Index at time t). A nominal dividend of $\tilde{D}_t$ corresponds to a real dividend of $D_t = \tilde{D}_t/\tilde{F}_t$ and a nominal price of $\tilde{P}_t$ corresponds to a real price of $P_t = \tilde{P}_t/\tilde{F}_t$. We have seen that a nominal state-price deflator $\tilde{\zeta} = (\tilde{\zeta}_t)$ is related to a real state-price deflator $\zeta = (\zeta_t)$ via the equation

$$\tilde{\zeta}_t = \zeta_t \frac{\tilde{F}_0}{\tilde{F}_t}, \qquad \text{all } t \in [0, T].$$

The nominal state-price deflator links nominal dividends to nominal prices in the same way that a real state-price deflator links real dividends to real prices.

The real return on a nominally risk-free asset is generally stochastic (and conversely). The dynamics of the real state-price deflator is

$$d\zeta_t = -\zeta_t \left[r_t \, dt + \boldsymbol{\lambda}_t^{\top} \, d\boldsymbol{z}_t \right],$$

where $r = (r_t)$ is the short-term real interest rate and $\boldsymbol{\lambda} = (\boldsymbol{\lambda}_t)$ is the market price of risk. The dynamics of the price of the consumption good is written as

$$d\tilde{F}_t = \tilde{F}_t \left[\mu_{Ft}\, dt + \boldsymbol{\sigma}_{Ft}^{\top}\, d\boldsymbol{z}_t \right].$$

We interpret $d\tilde{F}_t/\tilde{F}_t$ as the realized inflation rate over the next instant $[t, t + dt]$, that is $\mu_{Ft} = \mathrm{E}_t[d\tilde{F}_t/\tilde{F}_t]/dt$ is the expected inflation rate, and $\boldsymbol{\sigma}_{Ft}$ is the sensitivity vector of the inflation rate. Then we have shown that the nominal and the real short-term interest rates are related as follows

$$\tilde{r}_t = r_t + \mu_{Ft} - \|\boldsymbol{\sigma}_{Ft}\|^2 - \boldsymbol{\sigma}_{Ft}^{\top}\boldsymbol{\lambda}_t, \tag{11.34}$$

that is the nominal short rate equals the real short rate plus the expected inflation rate minus the variance of the inflation rate minus a risk premium. The presence of the last two terms invalidates the Fisher relation, which says that the nominal interest rate is equal to the sum of the real interest rate and the expected inflation rate.

An application of Itô's Lemma (Exercise 11.2) shows that the dynamics of the nominal state-price deflator is

$$d\tilde{\zeta}_t = -\tilde{\zeta}_t \left[\tilde{r}_t\, dt + \tilde{\boldsymbol{\lambda}}_t^{\top}\, d\boldsymbol{z}_t \right], \tag{11.35}$$

where $\tilde{\boldsymbol{\lambda}}_t = \boldsymbol{\lambda}_t + \boldsymbol{\sigma}_{Ft}$ is the nominal market price of risk.

The time t real price of a real zero-coupon bond maturing at time s is

$$B_t^s = \mathrm{E}_t\left[\frac{\zeta_s}{\zeta_t}\right] = \mathrm{E}_t\left[\exp\left\{-\int_t^s r_u\, du - \frac{1}{2}\int_t^s \|\boldsymbol{\lambda}_u\|^2\, du - \int_t^s \boldsymbol{\lambda}_u^{\top}\, d\boldsymbol{z}_u\right\}\right].$$

The time t nominal price of a nominal zero-coupon bond maturing at s is

$$\tilde{B}_t^s = \mathrm{E}_t\left[\frac{\tilde{\zeta}_s}{\tilde{\zeta}_t}\right] = \mathrm{E}_t\left[\exp\left\{-\int_t^s \tilde{r}_u\, du - \frac{1}{2}\int_t^s \|\tilde{\boldsymbol{\lambda}}_u\|^2\, du - \int_t^s \tilde{\boldsymbol{\lambda}}_u^{\top}\, d\boldsymbol{z}_u\right\}\right].$$

Clearly the prices of nominal bonds are related to the nominal short rate and the nominal market price of risk in exactly the same way as the prices of real bonds are related to the real short rate and the real market price of risk. Models that are based on specific exogenous assumptions about the short rate dynamics and the market price of risk can be applied both to real term structures and to nominal term structures—but not simultaneously for both real and nominal term structures. This is indeed the case for most popular term structure models. However, the equilibrium arguments that some authors offer in support of a particular term structure model, compare Section 11.5, typically apply to real interest rates and real market prices of risk. The same arguments cannot generally support similar assumptions on nominal rates and market price of risk. Nevertheless, these models are often applied on nominal bonds and term structures.

Above we derived an equilibrium relation between real and nominal short-term interest rates. What can we say about the relation between longer-term real and nominal interest rates? Applying the well-known relation $\mathrm{Cov}[x,y] = \mathrm{E}[xy] - \mathrm{E}[x]\,\mathrm{E}[y]$, we can write

$$\begin{aligned}
\tilde{B}_t^T &= \mathrm{E}_t\left[\frac{\zeta_T}{\zeta_t}\frac{\tilde{F}_t}{\tilde{F}_T}\right] \\
&= \mathrm{E}_t\left[\frac{\zeta_T}{\zeta_t}\right]\mathrm{E}_t\left[\frac{\tilde{F}_t}{\tilde{F}_T}\right] + \mathrm{Cov}_t\left[\frac{\zeta_T}{\zeta_t}, \frac{\tilde{F}_t}{\tilde{F}_T}\right] \\
&= B_t^T\,\mathrm{E}_t\left[\frac{\tilde{F}_t}{\tilde{F}_T}\right] + \mathrm{Cov}_t\left[\frac{\zeta_T}{\zeta_t}, \frac{\tilde{F}_t}{\tilde{F}_T}\right].
\end{aligned}$$

From the dynamics of the state-price deflator and the price index, we get

$$\frac{\zeta_T}{\zeta_t} = \exp\left\{-\int_t^T \left(r_s + \frac{1}{2}\|\boldsymbol{\lambda}_s\|^2\right) ds - \int_t^T \boldsymbol{\lambda}_s^{\top}\, d\boldsymbol{z}_s\right\}, \tag{11.36}$$

$$\frac{\tilde{F}_t}{\tilde{F}_T} = \exp\left\{-\int_t^T \left(\mu_{Fs} - \frac{1}{2}\|\boldsymbol{\sigma}_{Fs}\|^2\right) ds - \int_t^T \boldsymbol{\sigma}_{Fs}^{\top}\, d\boldsymbol{z}_s\right\}, \tag{11.37}$$

which can be substituted into the above relation between prices on real and nominal bonds. However, the covariance-term on the right-hand side can only be explicitly computed under very special assumptions about the variations over time in r, $\boldsymbol{\lambda}$, μ_F, and $\boldsymbol{\sigma}_F$.

Let us consider a specific model in which a more explicit relation between real and nominal yields can be derived. Assume that shocks are represented by a multidimensional standard Brownian motion $\boldsymbol{z}$, that the real market price of risk is a constant $\boldsymbol{\lambda}$, and that the real short rate follows the Ornstein–Uhlenbeck process

$$dr_t = \kappa\,[\bar{r} - r_t]\,dt + \boldsymbol{\sigma}_r^{\top}\, d\boldsymbol{z}_t. \tag{11.38}$$

Furthermore, assume that the Consumer Price Index $\tilde{F}_t$ has a constant sensitivity towards the shocks, whereas the expected inflation rate μ_{Ft} also follows an Ornstein–Uhlenbeck process, that is

$$d\tilde{F}_t = \tilde{F}_t\left[\mu_{Ft}\,dt + \boldsymbol{\sigma}_F^{\top}\, d\boldsymbol{z}_t\right], \tag{11.39}$$

$$d\mu_{Ft} = \beta\,[\bar{\mu}_F - \mu_{Ft}]\,dt + \boldsymbol{\sigma}_{\mu_F}^{\top}\, d\boldsymbol{z}_t. \tag{11.40}$$

Let us define the *inflation yield* between time t and time T as the value of ι_t^T satisfying the relation

$$\mathrm{E}_t\left[\frac{\tilde{F}_T}{\tilde{F}_t}\right] = e^{\iota_t^T(T-t)}.$$

The inflation yield between t and T is a measure of the annualized, expected inflation rate of that time period. The inflation yield and the prices of real and nominal bonds are connected as shown in the following theorem:

Theorem 11.5 *Suppose that the dynamics of the real short rate, the Consumer Price Index, and the expected inflation rate are given by Eqs.* (11.38)–(11.40) *and that the market price of risk associated with* $\boldsymbol{z}$ *is a constant vector* $\boldsymbol{\lambda}$. *Then the nominal price* $\tilde{B}_t^T$ *of a nominal zero-coupon bond and the real price* B_t^T *of a real zero-coupon bond satisfy*

$$\tilde{B}_t^T = B_t^T\left(\mathrm{E}_t\left[\frac{\tilde{F}_T}{\tilde{F}_t}\right]\right)^{-1} e^{\mathcal{H}(T-t)},$$

for a certain deterministic function $\mathcal{H}$. *The relation between the nominal yield* $\tilde{y}_t^T$, *the real yield* y_t^T, *and the inflation yield* ι_t^T *is given by*

$$\tilde{y}_t^T = y_t^T + \iota_t^T - \frac{\mathcal{H}(T-t)}{T-t}. \tag{11.41}$$

Proof. Analogously to the computation (11.30) of the integral of the short rate, it can be shown that

$$\int_t^T \mu_{Fu}\, du = \mu_{Ft}\mathcal{B}_\beta(T-t) + \bar{\mu}_F\left[T-t-\mathcal{B}_\beta(T-t)\right] + \int_t^T \mathcal{B}_\beta(T-u)\boldsymbol{\sigma}_{\mu_F}^{\top}\, d\boldsymbol{z}_u.$$

It then follows (see for example Eq. (11.37)) that

$$\tilde{F}_T = \tilde{F}_t \exp\Big\{\mu_{Ft}\mathcal{B}_\beta(T-t) + \bar{\mu}_F\left[T-t-\mathcal{B}_\beta(T-t)\right] - \frac{1}{2}\|\boldsymbol{\sigma}_F\|^2(T-t) + \int_t^T \left(\boldsymbol{\sigma}_F + \mathcal{B}_\beta(T-u)\boldsymbol{\sigma}_{\mu_F}\right)^{\top} d\boldsymbol{z}_u\Big\}. \tag{11.42}$$

By applying the properties of stochastic integrals stated in Theorem 2.3, the results on expectations of lognormal random variables in Appendix B, as well as Eqs. (11.26) and (11.27), we find that

$$\mathrm{E}_t\left[\frac{\tilde{F}_T}{\tilde{F}_t}\right] = e^{\mathcal{A}_F(T-t)+\mu_{Ft}\mathcal{B}_\beta(T-t)},$$

where

$$\mathcal{A}_F(\tau) = \left(\bar{\mu}_F + \frac{\|\boldsymbol{\sigma}_{\mu_F}\|^2}{2\beta^2} + \frac{\boldsymbol{\sigma}_F^\top \boldsymbol{\sigma}_{\mu_F}}{\beta}\right)\left(T - t - \mathcal{B}_\beta(T-t)\right) - \frac{\|\sigma_{\mu_F}\|^2}{4\beta}\mathcal{B}_\beta(T-t)^2.$$

The inflation yield over the period $[t, T]$ is thus

$$\iota_t^T = \frac{\mathcal{A}_F(T-t)}{T-t} + \mu_{Ft}\frac{\mathcal{B}_\beta(T-t)}{T-t}.$$

From Eqs. (11.30) and (11.36), it follows that

$$\begin{aligned}\zeta_T &= \zeta_t \exp\left\{-\int_t^T r_s\,ds - \frac{1}{2}\|\boldsymbol{\lambda}\|^2(T-t) - \int_t^T \boldsymbol{\lambda}^\top d\boldsymbol{z}_s\right\} \\ &= \zeta_t \exp\Big\{-r_t\mathcal{B}_\kappa(T-t) - \bar{r}\left[T-t-\mathcal{B}_\kappa(T-t)\right] - \frac{1}{2}\|\boldsymbol{\lambda}\|^2(T-t) \\ &\qquad - \int_t^T \left(\boldsymbol{\lambda} + \mathcal{B}_\kappa(T-s)\boldsymbol{\sigma}_r\right)^\top d\boldsymbol{z}_s\Big\}.\end{aligned}$$

By combining this with Eq. (11.42), we can compute the nominal price of a nominal zero-coupon bond as

$$\begin{aligned}\tilde{B}_t^T &= \mathrm{E}_t\left[\frac{\zeta_T}{\zeta_t}\frac{\tilde{F}_t}{\tilde{F}_T}\right] \\ &= \exp\Big\{-r_t\mathcal{B}_\kappa(T-t) - \mu_{Ft}\mathcal{B}_\beta(T-t) - \bar{r}\left[T-t-\mathcal{B}_\kappa(T-t)\right] \\ &\qquad - \frac{1}{2}\|\boldsymbol{\lambda}\|^2(T-t) - \bar{\mu}_F\left[T-t-\mathcal{B}_\beta(T-t)\right] + \frac{1}{2}\|\boldsymbol{\sigma}_F\|^2(T-t)\Big\} \\ &\quad \times \mathrm{E}_t\left[\exp\left\{-\int_t^T \left(\boldsymbol{\lambda} + \mathcal{B}_\kappa(T-s)\boldsymbol{\sigma}_r + \boldsymbol{\sigma}_F + \mathcal{B}_\beta(T-s)\boldsymbol{\sigma}_{\mu_F}\right)^\top d\boldsymbol{z}_s\right\}\right].\end{aligned}$$

Since the integrand of the stochastic integral is deterministic, the integral is normally distributed, so that we again have to compute the expectation of a lognormally distributed random variable. In this case, we get

$$\begin{aligned}&\mathrm{E}_t\left[\exp\left\{-\int_t^T \left(\boldsymbol{\lambda} + \mathcal{B}_\kappa(T-s)\boldsymbol{\sigma}_r + \boldsymbol{\sigma}_F + \mathcal{B}_\beta(T-s)\boldsymbol{\sigma}_{\mu_F}\right)^\top d\boldsymbol{z}_s\right\}\right] \\ &= \exp\Big\{\frac{1}{2}(\|\boldsymbol{\lambda}\|^2 + \|\boldsymbol{\sigma}_F\|^2 + 2\boldsymbol{\lambda}^\top\boldsymbol{\sigma}_F)(T-t) + \frac{1}{2}\|\boldsymbol{\sigma}_r\|^2\int_t^T \mathcal{B}_\kappa(T-s)^2\,ds\end{aligned}$$

$$+\frac{1}{2}\|\boldsymbol{\sigma}_{\mu_F}\|^2\int_t^T \mathcal{B}_\beta(T-s)^2\,ds+\boldsymbol{\sigma}_r^\top(\boldsymbol{\lambda}+\boldsymbol{\sigma}_F)\int_t^T \mathcal{B}_\kappa(T-s)\,ds$$
$$+\boldsymbol{\sigma}_{\mu_F}^\top(\boldsymbol{\lambda}+\boldsymbol{\sigma}_F)\int_t^T \mathcal{B}_\beta(T-s)\,ds+\boldsymbol{\sigma}_r^\top\boldsymbol{\sigma}_{\mu_F}\int_t^T \mathcal{B}_\kappa(T-s)\mathcal{B}_\beta(T-s)\,ds\Bigg\}.$$

We compute the integrals using Eqs. (11.26), (11.27), and

$$\int_t^T \mathcal{B}_\beta(T-s)\mathcal{B}_\kappa(T-s)\,ds$$
$$=\frac{1}{\beta\kappa}\left(T-t-\mathcal{B}_\beta(T-t)-\mathcal{B}_\kappa(T-t)+\mathcal{B}_{\beta+\kappa}(T-t)\right).$$

Substituting back into the above expression for the nominal bond price, we can rewrite it in the form

$$\tilde{B}_t^T=\exp\left\{-\mathcal{A}(T-t)-r_t\mathcal{B}_\kappa(T-t)-\mathcal{A}_F(T-t)-\mu_{Ft}\mathcal{B}_\beta(T-t)+\mathcal{H}(T-t)\right\}$$
$$=B_t^T\left(\mathrm{E}_t\left[\frac{\tilde{F}_T}{\tilde{F}_t}\right]\right)^{-1}e^{\mathcal{H}(T-t)},$$

where

$$\mathcal{H}(\tau)=\left(\|\boldsymbol{\sigma}_F\|^2+\boldsymbol{\lambda}^\top\sigma_F\right)\tau-\frac{\|\boldsymbol{\sigma}_{\mu_F}\|^2}{2\beta}\mathcal{B}_\beta(\tau)^2$$
$$+\left(\frac{\|\boldsymbol{\sigma}_{\mu_F}\|^2}{\beta^2}+\frac{\boldsymbol{\lambda}^\top\boldsymbol{\sigma}_{\mu_F}}{\beta}+\frac{\boldsymbol{\sigma}_F^\top\boldsymbol{\sigma}_{\mu_F}}{\beta}+\frac{\boldsymbol{\sigma}_r^\top\boldsymbol{\sigma}_{\mu_F}}{\beta\kappa}\right)\left(\tau-\mathcal{B}_\beta(\tau)\right)$$
$$-\frac{\boldsymbol{\sigma}_r^\top(\beta\boldsymbol{\sigma}_F+\boldsymbol{\sigma}_{\mu_F})}{\beta\kappa}\left(\tau-\mathcal{B}_\kappa(\tau)\right)-\frac{\boldsymbol{\sigma}_r^\top\boldsymbol{\sigma}_{\mu_F}}{\beta\kappa}\left(\tau-\mathcal{B}_{\kappa+\beta}(\tau)\right).$$

In terms of yields, this gives

$$e^{-\tilde{y}_t^T(T-t)}=e^{-y_t^T(T-t)}e^{-\iota_t^T(T-t)}e^{\mathcal{H}(T-t)},$$

which immediately leads to Eq. (11.41). □

Under the stated assumptions, the nominal yield for a given maturity equals the real yield plus the expected, annualized inflation rate over the life of the bond, adjusted by a maturity-dependent, deterministic term that depends on risk premia as well as variances and covariances of interest rates, realized inflation, and expected inflation. While such a relation among yields has intuitive appeal, it seems to be true only in a Gaussian model like the above model.

11.6.2 No Real Effects of Inflation

In this subsection we will take as given some process for the Consumer Price Index and assume that monetary holdings do not affect the utility of the individuals directly. As before the aggregate consumption level is assumed to follow the process

$$dc_t = c_t \left[\mu_{ct}\, dt + \boldsymbol{\sigma}_{ct}^{\top}\, dz_t \right]$$

so that the dynamics of the real state-price density is

$$d\zeta_t = -\zeta_t \left[r_t\, dt + \boldsymbol{\lambda}_t^{\top}\, dz_t \right].$$

The short-term real rate is given by

$$r_t = \delta + \frac{-c_t u''(c_t)}{u'(c_t)} \mu_{ct} - \frac{1}{2} c_t^2 \frac{u'''(c_t)}{u'(c_t)} \|\boldsymbol{\sigma}_{ct}\|^2$$

and the market price of risk vector is given by

$$\boldsymbol{\lambda}_t = \left(-\frac{c_t u''(c_t)}{u'(c_t)} \right) \boldsymbol{\sigma}_{ct}. \tag{11.43}$$

By substituting the expression (11.43) for λ_t into Eq. (4.60), we can write the short-term nominal rate as

$$\tilde{r}_t = r_t + \mu_{Ft} - \|\boldsymbol{\sigma}_{Ft}\|^2 - \left(-\frac{c_t u''(c_t)}{u'(c_t)} \right) \boldsymbol{\sigma}_{Ft}^{\top} \boldsymbol{\sigma}_{ct}.$$

In the special case where the representative individual has constant relative risk aversion, that is $u(c) = c^{1-\gamma}/(1-\gamma)$, and both the aggregate consumption and the price index follow geometric Brownian motions, we get constant rates

$$r = \delta + \gamma \mu_c - \frac{1}{2} \gamma (1 + \gamma) \|\boldsymbol{\sigma}_c\|^2, \tag{11.44}$$

$$\tilde{r} = r + \mu_F - \|\boldsymbol{\sigma}_F\|^2 - \gamma \boldsymbol{\sigma}_F^{\top} \boldsymbol{\sigma}_c.$$

Breeden (1986) considers the relations between interest rates, inflation, and aggregate consumption and production in an economy with multiple consumption goods. In general the presence of several consumption goods complicates the analysis considerably. Breeden shows that the equilibrium nominal short rate will depend on both an inflation rate computed using the average weights of the different consumption goods and an inflation rate computed using the marginal weights of the different goods, which are determined by the optimal allocation to the different goods of an extra dollar of total consumption expenditure. The average and the marginal consumption generally differ since the representative individual may shift to other consumption goods as his wealth increases. However, in the special (probably unrealistic) case of Cobb–Douglas type utility function, the relative expenditure weights of the different consumption goods are constant. For that case Breeden obtains results similar to our one-good conclusions.

11.6.3 A Model with Real Effects of Money

In the next model we consider, cash holdings enter the direct utility function of the individual(s). This may be rationalized by the fact that cash holdings facilitate frequent consumption transactions.[3] In such a model the price of the consumption good is determined as a part of the equilibrium of the economy, in contrast to the models studied above where we took an exogenous process for the Consumer Price Index. We follow the set-up of Bakshi and Chen (1996) closely.

We assume the existence of a representative individual who chooses a consumption process $c = (c_t)$ and a cash process $\tilde{M} = (\tilde{M}_t)$, where $\tilde{M}_t$ is the dollar amount held at time t. As before, let $\tilde{F}_t$ be the unit dollar price of the consumption good. Assume that the representative individual has an infinite time horizon, no endowment stream, and an additively time-separable utility of consumption and the real value of the monetary holdings, that is $M_t = \tilde{M}_t/\tilde{F}_t$. At time t the individual has the opportunity to invest in a nominally risk-free bank account with a nominal rate of return of $\tilde{r}_t$. When the individual chooses to hold $\tilde{M}_t$ dollars in cash over the period $[t, t + dt]$, she therefore gives up a dollar return of $\tilde{M}_t\tilde{r}_t\, dt$, which is equivalent to a consumption of $\tilde{M}_t\tilde{r}_t\, dt/\tilde{F}_t$ units of the good. Given a (real) state-price deflator $\zeta = (\zeta_t)$, the total cost of choosing c and M is thus $\mathrm{E}\left[\int_0^\infty \zeta_t(c_t + \tilde{M}_t\tilde{r}_t/\tilde{F}_t)\, dt\right]$. In sum, the optimization problem of the individual can be written as follows:

$$\sup_{(c_t,\tilde{M}_t)} \mathrm{E}\left[\int_0^\infty e^{-\delta t} u\left(c_t, \tilde{M}_t/\tilde{F}_t\right)\, dt\right] \tag{11.45}$$

$$\text{s.t. } \mathrm{E}\left[\int_0^\infty \zeta_t \left(c_t + \frac{\tilde{M}_t}{\tilde{F}_t}\tilde{r}_t\right)\, dt\right] \leq W_0,$$

where W_0 is the initial (real) wealth of the individual.

[3] Apparently, the first research paper studying a model with money in the utility function was Sidrauski (1967). Economists have debated whether money should enter directly as an argument of the utility function or rather in the budget constraints, see for example Samuelson (1968, p. 8). As shown by Feenstra (1986), the two approaches can be seen as equivalent, at least in the framework he considers.

The Lagrangian associated with the optimization problem is

$$\mathcal{L} = \mathrm{E}\left[\int_0^\infty e^{-\delta t} u\left(c_t, \tilde{M}_t/\tilde{F}_t\right) dt\right] + \psi\left(W_0 - \mathrm{E}\left[\int_0^\infty \zeta_t\left(c_t + \frac{\tilde{M}_t}{\tilde{F}_t}\tilde{r}_t\right) dt\right]\right)$$

$$= \psi W_0 + \mathrm{E}\left[\int_0^\infty \left(e^{-\delta t} u\left(c_t, \tilde{M}_t/\tilde{F}_t\right) - \psi\zeta_t\left(c_t + \frac{\tilde{M}_t}{\tilde{F}_t}\tilde{r}_t\right)\right) dt\right].$$

If we maximize the integrand 'state-by-state', we will also maximize the expectation. The first-order conditions are

$$e^{-\delta t} u_c(c_t, \tilde{M}_t/\tilde{F}_t) = \psi\zeta_t, \tag{11.46}$$

$$e^{-\delta t} u_M(c_t, \tilde{M}_t/\tilde{F}_t) = \psi\zeta_t\tilde{r}_t, \tag{11.47}$$

where u_c and u_M are the first-order derivatives of u with respect to the first and second argument, respectively. The Lagrange multiplier ψ is set so that the budget condition holds as an equality. Again, we see that the state-price deflator is given in terms of the marginal utility with respect to consumption. Imposing the initial value $\zeta_0 = 1$ and recalling the definition of M_t, we have

$$\zeta_t = e^{-\delta t}\frac{u_c(c_t, M_t)}{u_c(c_0, M_0)}. \tag{11.48}$$

We can apply the state-price deflator to value all payment streams. For example, an investment of one dollar at time t in the nominal bank account generates a continuous payment stream at the rate of $\tilde{r}_s$ dollars to the end of all time. The corresponding real investment at time t is $1/\tilde{F}_t$ and the real dividend at time s is $\tilde{r}_s/\tilde{F}_s$. Hence, we have the relation

$$\frac{1}{\tilde{F}_t} = \mathrm{E}_t\left[\int_t^\infty \frac{\zeta_s}{\zeta_t}\frac{\tilde{r}_s}{\tilde{F}_s}\, ds\right],$$

or, equivalently,

$$\frac{1}{\tilde{F}_t} = \mathrm{E}_t\left[\int_t^\infty e^{-\delta(s-t)}\frac{u_c(c_s, M_s)}{u_c(c_t, M_t)}\frac{\tilde{r}_s}{\tilde{F}_s}\, ds\right]. \tag{11.49}$$

Substituting the first optimality condition (11.46) into the second (11.47), we see that the nominal short rate is given by

$$\tilde{r}_t = \frac{u_M(c_t, \tilde{M}_t/\tilde{F}_t)}{u_c(c_t, \tilde{M}_t/\tilde{F}_t)}. \tag{11.50}$$

The intuition behind this relation can be explained in the following way. If you have an extra dollar now you can either keep it in cash or invest it in the nominally risk-free bank account. If you keep it in cash your utility grows by $u_M(c_t, \tilde{M}_t/\tilde{F}_t)/\tilde{F}_t$. If you invest it in the bank account you will earn a dollar interest of $\tilde{r}_t$ that can be used for consuming $\tilde{r}_t/\tilde{F}_t$ extra units of consumption, which will increase your utility by $u_c(c_t, \tilde{M}_t/\tilde{F}_t)\tilde{r}_t/\tilde{F}_t$. At the optimum, these utility increments must be identical. Combining (11.49) and (11.50), we get that the price index must satisfy the recursive relation

$$\frac{1}{\tilde{F}_t} = \mathrm{E}_t\left[\int_t^\infty e^{-\delta(s-t)}\frac{u_M(c_s, M_s)}{u_c(c_t, M_t)}\frac{1}{\tilde{F}_s}\,ds\right]. \tag{11.51}$$

Let us find expressions for the equilibrium real short rate and the market price of risk in this setting. As always, the real short rate equals minus the percentage drift of the state-price deflator, whereas the market price of risk equals minus the percentage sensitivity vector of the state-price deflator. In an equilibrium, the representative individual must consume the aggregate consumption and hold the total money supply in the economy. Suppose that the aggregate consumption and the money supply follow exogenous processes of the form

$$dc_t = c_t\left[\mu_{ct}\,dt + \boldsymbol{\sigma}_{ct}^\top\,d\boldsymbol{z}_t\right], \tag{11.52}$$

$$d\tilde{M}_t = \tilde{M}_t\left[\tilde{\mu}_{Mt}\,dt + \tilde{\boldsymbol{\sigma}}_{Mt}^\top\,d\boldsymbol{z}_t\right]. \tag{11.53}$$

Assuming that the endogenously determined price index will follow a similar process,

$$d\tilde{F}_t = \tilde{F}_t\left[\mu_{Ft}\,dt + \boldsymbol{\sigma}_{Ft}^\top\,d\boldsymbol{z}_t\right], \tag{11.54}$$

the dynamics of $M_t = \tilde{M}_t/\tilde{F}_t$ will be

$$dM_t = M_t\left[\mu_{Mt}\,dt + \boldsymbol{\sigma}_{Mt}^\top\,d\boldsymbol{z}_t\right],$$

where

$$\mu_{Mt} = \tilde{\mu}_{Mt} - \mu_{Ft} + \|\boldsymbol{\sigma}_{Ft}\|^2 - \tilde{\boldsymbol{\sigma}}_{Mt}^\top\boldsymbol{\sigma}_{\varphi t}, \qquad \boldsymbol{\sigma}_{Mt} = \tilde{\boldsymbol{\sigma}}_{Mt} - \boldsymbol{\sigma}_{Ft}.$$

Given these equations and the relation (11.48), we can find the drift and the sensitivity vector of the state-price deflator by an application of Itô's Lemma. A comparison with the general state-price deflator dynamics established in Theorem 4.4 then leads to the following theorem (Exercise 11.5 asks for the details of this derivation).

Theorem 11.6 *Assume a continuous-time economy with a representative individual maximizing time-additive expected utility of consumption and cash holdings as in Eq. (11.45). Suppose that the dynamics of aggregate consumption, money supply, and consumer prices are given by Eqs. (11.52)–(11.54). Then the equilibrium real short-term interest rate is*

$$r_t = \delta + \left(\frac{-c_t u_{cc}(c_t, M_t)}{u_c(c_t, M_t)} \right) \mu_{ct} + \left(\frac{-M_t u_{cM}(c_t, M_t)}{u_c(c_t, M_t)} \right) \mu_{Mt}$$
$$- \frac{1}{2} \frac{c_t^2 u_{ccc}(c_t, M_t)}{u_c(c_t, M_t)} \|\boldsymbol{\sigma}_{ct}\|^2 - \frac{1}{2} \frac{M_t^2 u_{cMM}(c_t, M_t)}{u_c(c_t, M_t)} \|\boldsymbol{\sigma}_{Mt}\|^2 \tag{11.55}$$
$$- \frac{c_t M_t u_{ccM}(c_t, M_t)}{u_c(c_t, M_t)} \boldsymbol{\sigma}_{ct}^{\top} \boldsymbol{\sigma}_{Mt},$$

and the market price of risk vector is

$$\begin{aligned} \boldsymbol{\lambda}_t &= \left(-\frac{c_t u_{cc}(c_t, M_t)}{u_c(c_t, M_t)} \right) \boldsymbol{\sigma}_{ct} + \left(\frac{-M_t u_{cM}(c_t, M_t)}{u_c(c_t, M_t)} \right) \boldsymbol{\sigma}_{Mt} \\ &= \left(-\frac{c_t u_{cc}(c_t, M_t)}{u_c(c_t, M_t)} \right) \boldsymbol{\sigma}_{ct} + \left(\frac{-M_t u_{cM}(c_t, M_t)}{u_c(c_t, M_t)} \right) (\tilde{\boldsymbol{\sigma}}_{Mt} - \boldsymbol{\sigma}_{Ft}) . \end{aligned} \tag{11.56}$$

With $u_{cM} < 0$, we see that assets that are positively correlated with the inflation rate will have a lower expected real return, other things being equal. Intuitively such assets are useful for hedging inflation risk so that they do not have to offer as high an expected return.

The relation (11.34) is also valid in the present setting. Substituting in the expression (11.56) for the market price of risk, we obtain

$$\tilde{r}_t - r_t - \mu_{Ft} + \|\boldsymbol{\sigma}_{Ft}\|^2 = - \left(-\frac{c_t u''(c_t)}{u'(c_t)} \right) \boldsymbol{\sigma}_{Ft}^{\top} \boldsymbol{\sigma}_{ct} - \left(\frac{-M_t u_{cM}(c_t, M_t)}{u_c(c_t, M_t)} \right) \boldsymbol{\sigma}_{Ft}^{\top} \boldsymbol{\sigma}_{Mt}.$$

To obtain more concrete results, we must specify the utility function and the exogenous processes c and $\tilde{M}$. We will present two examples from Bakshi and Chen (1996).

Example 11.1 Assume a utility function of the Cobb–Douglas type,

$$u(c, M) = \frac{\left(c^{\varphi} M^{1-\varphi}\right)^{1-\gamma}}{1-\gamma},$$

where φ is a constant between zero and one, and γ is a positive constant. The limiting case for $\gamma = 1$ is log-utility,

$$u(c, M) = \varphi \ln c + (1 - \varphi) \ln M.$$

By inserting the relevant derivatives into (11.55), we see that the real short rate becomes

$$r_t = \delta + [1 - \varphi(1-\gamma)]\mu_{ct} - \frac{1}{2}[1 - \varphi(1-\gamma)][2 - \varphi(1-\gamma)]\|\boldsymbol{\sigma}_{ct}\|^2$$
$$- (1-\varphi)(1-\gamma)\mu_{Mt} + \frac{1}{2}(1-\varphi)(1-\gamma)[1 - (1-\varphi)(1-\gamma)]\|\boldsymbol{\sigma}_{Mt}\|^2$$
$$+ (1-\varphi)(1-\gamma)[1 - \varphi(1-\gamma)]\boldsymbol{\sigma}_{ct}^{\top}\boldsymbol{\sigma}_{Mt}, \tag{11.57}$$

which for $\gamma = 1$ simplifies to

$$r_t = \delta + \mu_{ct} - \|\boldsymbol{\sigma}_{ct}\|^2.$$

We see that with log-utility, the real short rate will be constant if aggregate consumption $c = (c_t)$ follows a geometric Brownian motion. From Eq. (11.50), the nominal short rate is

$$\tilde{r}_t = \frac{1-\varphi}{\varphi}\frac{c_t}{M_t}.$$

The ratio c_t/M_t is called the *velocity of money*. If the velocity of money is constant, the nominal short rate will be constant. Since $M_t = \tilde{M}_t/\tilde{F}_t$ and $\tilde{F}_t$ is endogenously determined, the velocity of money will also be endogenously determined.

We have to determine the price level in the economy, which is given only recursively in Eq. (11.51). This is possible under the assumption that both C and $\tilde{M}$ follow geometric Brownian motions. We conjecture that $\tilde{F}_t = k\tilde{M}_t/c_t$ for some constant k. From Eq. (11.51), we get

$$\frac{1}{k} = \frac{1-\varphi}{\varphi}\int_t^\infty e^{-\delta(s-t)}\,\mathrm{E}_t\left[\left(\frac{c_s}{c_t}\right)^{1-\gamma}\left(\frac{\tilde{M}_s}{\tilde{M}_t}\right)^{-1}\right] ds.$$

Inserting the relations

$$\frac{c_s}{c_t} = \exp\left\{\left(\mu_c - \frac{1}{2}\|\boldsymbol{\sigma}_c\|^2\right)(s-t) + \boldsymbol{\sigma}_c^{\top}(\boldsymbol{z}_s - \boldsymbol{z}_t)\right\},$$
$$\frac{\tilde{M}_s}{\tilde{M}_t} = \exp\left\{\left(\tilde{\mu}_M - \frac{1}{2}\|\tilde{\boldsymbol{\sigma}}_M\|^2\right)(s-t) + \tilde{\boldsymbol{\sigma}}_M^{\top}(\boldsymbol{z}_s - \boldsymbol{z}_t)\right\},$$

and applying a standard rule for expectations of lognormal variables, we get

$$\frac{1}{k} = \frac{1-\varphi}{\varphi}\int_t^\infty \exp\Big\{\Big(-\delta + (1-\gamma)(\mu_c - \frac{1}{2}\|\boldsymbol{\sigma}_c\|^2) - \tilde{\mu}_M + \|\tilde{\boldsymbol{\sigma}}_M\|^2$$
$$+ \frac{1}{2}(1-\gamma)^2\|\tilde{\boldsymbol{\sigma}}_c\|^2 - (1-\gamma)\boldsymbol{\sigma}_c^{\top}\tilde{\boldsymbol{\sigma}}_M\Big)(s-t)\Big\}\, ds,$$

which implies that the conjecture is true with

$$k = \frac{\varphi}{1-\varphi}\Big(\delta - (1-\gamma)(\mu_c - \frac{1}{2}\|\boldsymbol{\sigma}_c\|^2) + \tilde{\mu}_M - \|\tilde{\boldsymbol{\sigma}}_M\|^2 - \frac{1}{2}(1-\gamma)^2\|\boldsymbol{\sigma}_c\|^2 + (1-\gamma)\boldsymbol{\sigma}_c^\top\tilde{\boldsymbol{\sigma}}_M\Big).$$

Of course, conditions ensuring $k > 0$ must be imposed. From an application of Itô's Lemma, it follows that the price index also follows a geometric Brownian motion

$$d\tilde{F}_t = \tilde{F}_t\left[\mu_F\, dt + \boldsymbol{\sigma}_F^\top\, d\boldsymbol{z}_t\right],$$

where

$$\mu_F = \tilde{\mu}_M - \mu_c + \|\boldsymbol{\sigma}_c\|^2 - \tilde{\boldsymbol{\sigma}}_M^\top\boldsymbol{\sigma}_c, \qquad \boldsymbol{\sigma}_F = \tilde{\boldsymbol{\sigma}}_M - \boldsymbol{\sigma}_c.$$

With $\tilde{F}_t = k\tilde{M}_t/c_t$, we have $M_t = c_t/k$ so that the velocity of money $c_t/M_t = k$ is constant, and the nominal short rate becomes

$$\tilde{r}_t = \frac{1-\varphi}{\varphi}k = \delta - (1-\gamma)(\mu_c - \frac{1}{2}\|\boldsymbol{\sigma}_c\|^2) + \tilde{\mu}_M - \|\tilde{\boldsymbol{\sigma}}_M\|^2 - \frac{1}{2}(1-\gamma)^2\|\boldsymbol{\sigma}_c\|^2 + (1-\gamma)\boldsymbol{\sigma}_c^\top\tilde{\boldsymbol{\sigma}}_M,$$

which is again a constant. With log-utility, the nominal rate simplifies to $\delta + \tilde{\mu}_M - \|\tilde{\boldsymbol{\sigma}}_M\|^2$. In order to obtain the real short rate in the non-log case, we have to determine μ_{Mt} and $\boldsymbol{\sigma}_{Mt}$ and plug into Eq. (11.57). We get $\mu_{Mt} = \mu_c + \frac{1}{2}\|\boldsymbol{\sigma}_c\|^2 + \tilde{\boldsymbol{\sigma}}_M^\top\boldsymbol{\sigma}_c$ and $\boldsymbol{\sigma}_{Mt} = \boldsymbol{\sigma}_c$ and hence

$$r_t = \delta + \gamma\mu_c - \gamma\|\boldsymbol{\sigma}_c\|^2\left[\frac{1}{2}(1+\gamma) + \varphi(1-\gamma)\right],$$

which is also a constant. In comparison to Eq. (11.44) for the case where money has no real effects, the last term in the equation above is new. □

Example 11.2 In this example, both nominal and real short rates are time-varying, but evolve independently of each other. To obtain stochastic interest rates we have to specify more general processes for aggregate consumption and money supply than the geometric Brownian motions used above. Assume log-utility ($\gamma = 1$) in which case we have already seen that

$$r_t = \delta + \mu_{ct} - \|\boldsymbol{\sigma}_{ct}\|^2, \qquad \tilde{r}_t = \frac{1-\varphi}{\varphi}\frac{c_t}{M_t} = \frac{1-\varphi}{\varphi}\frac{c_t\tilde{F}_t}{\tilde{M}_t}.$$

The dynamics of aggregate consumption is assumed to be

$$dc_t = c_t\left[(\alpha_c + \kappa_c X_t)\, dt + \sigma_c\sqrt{X_t}\, dz_{1t}\right],$$

where X can be interpreted as a technology variable and is assumed to follow the process

$$dX_t = \kappa_x(\theta_x - X_t)\,dt + \sigma_x\sqrt{X_t}\,dz_{1t}.$$

The money supply is assumed to be $\tilde{M}_t = \tilde{M}_0 e^{\mu_M^* t} g_t/g_0$, where

$$dg_t = g_t\left[\kappa_g(\theta_g - g_t)\,dt + \sigma_g\sqrt{g_t}\left(\rho_{CM}\,dz_{1t} + \sqrt{1-\rho_{CM}^2}\,dz_{2t}\right)\right],$$

and where z_1 and z_2 are independent one-dimensional Brownian motions. Following the same basic procedure as in the previous model specification, Bakshi and Chen show that the real short rate is

$$r_t = \delta + \alpha_c + (\kappa_c - \sigma_c^2)X_t,$$

while the nominal short rate is

$$\tilde{r}_t = \frac{(\delta + \mu_M^*)(\delta + \mu_M^* + \kappa_g\theta_g)}{\delta + \mu_M^* + (\kappa_g + \sigma_g^2)g_t}.$$

Both rates are time-varying. The real rate is driven by the technology variable X, while the nominal rate is driven by the monetary shock process g. In this set-up, shocks to the real economy have opposite effects of the same magnitude on real rates and inflation so that nominal rates are unaffected.

The real price of a real zero-coupon bond maturing at time T is of the form

$$B_t^T = e^{-a(T-t)-b(T-t)X_t},$$

whereas the nominal price of a nominal zero-coupon bond maturing at T is

$$\tilde{B}_t^T = \frac{\tilde{a}(T-t) + \tilde{b}(T-t)g_t}{\delta + \mu_M^* + (\kappa_g + \sigma_g^2)g_t}.$$

Here a, b, $\tilde{a}$, and $\tilde{b}$ are deterministic functions of time for which Bakshi and Chen provide closed-form expressions.

In the very special case where these processes are uncorrelated, that is $\rho_{CM} = 0$, the real and nominal term structures of interest rates are independent of each other! Although this is an extreme result, it does point out that real and nominal term structures in general may have quite different properties. □

11.7 THE EXPECTATION HYPOTHESIS

The *expectation hypothesis* relates the current interest rates and yields to expected future interest rates or returns. This basic issue was discussed already by Fisher (1896) and further developed and concretized by Hicks (1939) and

Lutz (1940). The original motivation of the hypothesis is that when lenders (bond investors) and borrowers (bond issuers) decide between long-term or short-term bonds, they will compare the price or yield of a long-term bond to the expected price or return on a roll-over strategy in short-term bonds. Hence, long-term rates and expected future short-term rates will be linked. Of course, a cornerstone of modern finance theory is that, when comparing different strategies, investors will also take the risks into account. So even before going into the specifics of the hypothesis you should really be quite sceptical, at least when it comes to very strict interpretations of the expectation hypothesis.

The vague idea that current yields and interest rates are linked to expected future rates and returns can be concretized in a number of ways. Below we will present and evaluate a number of versions. This analysis follows Cox, Ingersoll, and Ross (1981a) quite closely. We find that some versions are equivalent, some versions inconsistent. We end up concluding that none of the variants of the expectation hypothesis are consistent with any realistic behaviour of interest rates. Hence, the analysis of the shape of the yield curve and models of term structure dynamics should not be based on this hypothesis. Hence, it is surprising, maybe even disappointing, that empirical tests of the expectation hypothesis have generated such a huge literature in the past and that the hypothesis still seems to be widely accepted among economists.

11.7.1 Versions of the Pure Expectation Hypothesis

The first version of the pure expectation hypothesis that we will discuss says that prices in the bond markets are set so that the expected gross rates of return on all self-financing trading strategies over a given period are identical. In particular, the expected gross rate of return from buying at time t a zero-coupon bond maturing at time T and reselling it at time $t' \leq T$, which is given by $\mathrm{E}_t[B_{t'}^T/B_t^T]$, will be independent of the maturity date T of the bond (but generally not independent of t'). Let us refer to this as the *gross return* pure expectation hypothesis.

This version of the hypothesis is consistent with pricing in a world of risk-neutral investors. If we have a representative individual with time-additive expected utility, we know that zero-coupon bond prices satisfy

$$B_t^T = \mathrm{E}_t\left[e^{-\delta(t'-t)}\frac{u'(c_{t'})}{u'(c_t)}B_{t'}^T\right],$$

where u is the instantaneous utility function, δ is the time preference rate, and c denotes aggregate consumption. If the representative individual is risk-neutral, his marginal utility is constant, which implies that

$$\mathrm{E}_t\left[\frac{B_{t'}^T}{B_t^T}\right] = e^{\delta(t'-t)},$$

which is clearly independent of T. Obviously, the assumption of risk-neutrality is not very attractive. There is also another serious problem with this hypothesis. As is to be shown in Exercise 11.4, it cannot hold when interest rates are uncertain.

A slight variation of the above is to align all expected continuously compounded returns, that is $\frac{1}{t'-t}\,\mathrm{E}_t[\ln\left(B_{t'}^T/B_t^T\right)]$ for all T. In particular with $T = t'$, the expected continuously compounded rate of return is known to be equal to the zero-coupon yield for maturity t', which we denote by $y_t^{t'} = -\frac{1}{t'-t}\ln B_t^{t'}$. We can therefore formulate the hypothesis as

$$\frac{1}{t'-t}\,\mathrm{E}_t\left[\ln\left(\frac{B_{t'}^T}{B_t^T}\right)\right] = y_t^{t'}, \text{ all } T \geq t'.$$

Let us refer to this as the *rate of return* pure expectation hypothesis. For $t' \to t$, the right-hand side approaches the current short rate r_t, while the left-hand side approaches the absolute drift rate of $\ln B_t^T$.

An alternative specification of the pure expectation hypothesis postulates that the expected return over the next time period is the same for all investments in bonds and deposits. In other words there is no difference between expected returns on long-maturity and short-maturity bonds. In the continuous-time limit we consider returns over the next instant. The risk-free return over $[t, t+dt]$ is $r_t\,dt$, so for any zero-coupon bond, the hypothesis claims that

$$\mathrm{E}_t\left[\frac{dB_t^T}{B_t^T}\right] = r_t\,dt, \qquad \text{for all } T > t, \tag{11.58}$$

or, using Theorem 2.7, that

$$B_t^T = \mathrm{E}_t\left[e^{-\int_t^T r_s\,ds}\right], \qquad \text{for all } T > t.$$

This is the *local* pure expectation hypothesis.

Yet another interpretation says that the return from holding a zero-coupon bond to maturity should equal the expected return from rolling over short-term bonds over the same time period. If 'short-term' is interpreted as instantaneous, the rolling over in short-term bonds corresponds to a money market account earning the short-term interest rates. Hence, this interpretation of the expectation hypothesis means that

$$\frac{1}{B_t^T} = \mathrm{E}_t\left[e^{\int_t^T r_s\,ds}\right], \qquad \text{for all } T > t \tag{11.59}$$

or, equivalently,

$$B_t^T = \left(\mathrm{E}_t\left[e^{\int_t^T r_s\,ds}\right]\right)^{-1}, \qquad \text{for all } T > t.$$

This is the *return-to-maturity* pure expectation hypothesis.

A related claim is that the yield on any zero-coupon bond should equal the 'expected yield' on a roll-over strategy in short bonds. Since an investment of one at time t in the bank account generates $e^{\int_t^T r_s\,ds}$ at time T, the ex-post realized yield is $\frac{1}{T-t}\int_t^T r_s\,ds$. Hence, this *yield-to-maturity* pure expectation hypothesis says that

$$y_t^T = -\frac{1}{T-t}\ln B_t^T = \mathrm{E}_t\left[\frac{1}{T-t}\int_t^T r_s\,ds\right], \tag{11.60}$$

or, equivalently,

$$B_t^T = e^{-\mathrm{E}_t\left[\int_t^T r_s\,ds\right]}, \qquad \text{for all } T > t.$$

Finally, the *unbiased* pure expectation hypothesis states that the forward rate for time T prevailing at time $t < T$ is equal to the time t expectation of the short rate at time T, that is that forward rates are unbiased estimates of future spot rates. In symbols,

$$f_t^T = \mathrm{E}_t[r_T], \qquad \text{for all } T > t.$$

This implies that

$$-\ln B_t^T = \int_t^T f_t^s\,ds = \int_t^T \mathrm{E}_t[r_s]\,ds = \mathrm{E}_t\left[\int_t^T r_s\,ds\right],$$

from which we see that the unbiased version of the pure expectation hypothesis is indistinguishable from the yield-to-maturity version.

We will first show that *the different versions are inconsistent* when future rates are uncertain. This follows from an application of Jensen's inequality which states that if X is a random variable and f is a convex function, that is $f'' > 0$, then $\mathrm{E}[f(X)] > f(\mathrm{E}[X])$. Since $f(x) = e^x$ is a convex function, we have $\mathrm{E}[e^X] > e^{\mathrm{E}[X]}$ for any random variable X. In particular for $X = \int_t^T r_s\,ds$, we get

$$\mathrm{E}_t\left[e^{\int_t^T r_s\,ds}\right] > e^{\mathrm{E}_t\left[\int_t^T r_s\,ds\right]} \quad \Rightarrow \quad e^{-\mathrm{E}_t\left[\int_t^T r_s\,ds\right]} > \left(\mathrm{E}_t\left[e^{\int_t^T r_s\,ds}\right]\right)^{-1}.$$

This shows that the bond price according to the yield-to-maturity version is strictly greater than the bond price according to the return-to-maturity version. For $X = -\int_t^T r_s\,ds$, we get

$$\mathrm{E}_t\left[e^{-\int_t^T r_s\,ds}\right] > e^{\mathrm{E}_t\left[-\int_t^T r_s\,ds\right]} = e^{-\mathrm{E}_t\left[\int_t^T r_s\,ds\right]},$$

hence the bond price according to the local version of the hypothesis is strictly greater than the bond price according to the yield-to-maturity version. We can conclude that at most one of the versions of the local, return-to-maturity, and yield-to-maturity pure expectation hypothesis can hold.

11.7.2 The Pure Expectation Hypothesis and Equilibrium

Next, let us see whether the different versions can be consistent with any equilibrium. Assume that interest rates and bond prices are generated by a d-dimensional standard Brownian motion z. Assuming absence of arbitrage there exists a market price of risk process $\boldsymbol{\lambda}$ so that for any maturity T, the zero-coupon bond price dynamics is of the form

$$dB_t^T = B_t^T \left[\left(r_t + \left(\boldsymbol{\sigma}_t^T\right)^{\top} \boldsymbol{\lambda}_t \right) dt + \left(\boldsymbol{\sigma}_t^T\right)^{\top} dz_t \right], \tag{11.61}$$

where $\boldsymbol{\sigma}_t^T$ denotes the d-dimensional sensitivity vector of the bond price. Recall that the same $\boldsymbol{\lambda}_t$ applies to all zero-coupon bonds so that $\boldsymbol{\lambda}_t$ is independent of the maturity of the bond. Comparing to Eq. (11.58), we see that the local expectation hypothesis will hold if and only if $\left(\boldsymbol{\sigma}_t^T\right)^{\top} \boldsymbol{\lambda}_t = 0$ for all T. This is true if either investors are risk-neutral or interest rate risk is uncorrelated with aggregate consumption. Neither of these conditions hold in real life.

To evaluate the return-to-maturity version, first note that an application of Itô's Lemma on Eq. (11.61) shows that

$$d\left(\frac{1}{B_t^T}\right) = \frac{1}{B_t^T} \left[\left(-r_t - \left(\boldsymbol{\sigma}_t^T\right)^{\top} \boldsymbol{\lambda}_t + \|\boldsymbol{\sigma}_t^T\|^2 \right) dt - \left(\boldsymbol{\sigma}_t^T\right)^{\top} dz_t \right].$$

On the other hand, according to the hypothesis (11.59) and Theorem 2.7, the relative drift of $1/B_t^T$ equals $-r_t$. To match the two expressions for the drift, we must have

$$\left(\boldsymbol{\sigma}_t^T\right)^{\top} \boldsymbol{\lambda}_t = \|\boldsymbol{\sigma}_t^T\|^2, \qquad \text{for all } T. \tag{11.62}$$

Is this possible? Cox, Ingersoll, and Ross (1981a) conclude that it is impossible. They are definitely right if the exogenous shock z and therefore $\boldsymbol{\sigma}_t^T$ and $\boldsymbol{\lambda}_t$ are one-dimensional since $\boldsymbol{\lambda}_t$ must then equal $\boldsymbol{\sigma}_t^T$, and this must hold for all T. Since $\boldsymbol{\lambda}_t$ is independent of T and the volatility $\boldsymbol{\sigma}_t^T$ approaches zero for $T \to t$, this can only hold if $\boldsymbol{\lambda}_t \equiv 0$ (risk-neutral investors) or $\boldsymbol{\sigma}_t^T \equiv 0$ (deterministic interest rates). However, as pointed out by McCulloch (1993) and Fisher and Gilles (1998), in multidimensional cases the key condition (11.62) may indeed hold, although only in very special cases. Let $\boldsymbol{\varphi}$ be a d-dimensional function with the property that $\|\boldsymbol{\varphi}(\tau)\|^2$ is independent of τ. Define $\boldsymbol{\lambda}_t = 2\boldsymbol{\varphi}(0)$ and $\boldsymbol{\sigma}_t^T = \boldsymbol{\varphi}(0) - \boldsymbol{\varphi}(T-t)$. Then Eq. (11.62) is indeed satisfied. However, all such functions $v\varphi$ seem to generate very strange bond price dynamics. The examples given in the two papers mentioned above are

$$\varphi(\tau) = k \begin{pmatrix} \sqrt{2e^{-\tau} - e^{-2\tau}} \\ 1 - e^{-\tau} \end{pmatrix}, \qquad \varphi(\tau) = k_1 \begin{pmatrix} \cos(k_2\tau) \\ \sin(k_2\tau) \end{pmatrix},$$

where k, k_1, and k_2 are constants.

As discussed above, the rate of return version implies that the absolute drift rate of the log-bond price equals the short rate. We can see from Eq. (11.60) that the same is true for the yield-to-maturity version and hence the unbiased version.[4] On the other hand Itô's Lemma and Eq. (11.61) imply that

$$d\left(\ln B_t^T\right) = \left(r_t + (\boldsymbol{\sigma}_t^T)^{\top}\boldsymbol{\lambda}_t - \frac{1}{2}\|\boldsymbol{\sigma}_t^T\|^2\right) dt + \left(\boldsymbol{\sigma}_t^T\right)^{\top} dz_t. \tag{11.63}$$

Hence, these versions of the hypothesis will hold if and only if

$$(\boldsymbol{\sigma}_t^T)^{\top}\boldsymbol{\lambda}_t = \frac{1}{2}\|\boldsymbol{\sigma}_t^T\|^2, \qquad \text{for all } T.$$

Again, it is possible that the condition holds. Just let φ and $\boldsymbol{\sigma}_t^T$ be as for the return-to-maturity hypothesis and let $\boldsymbol{\lambda}_t = \varphi(0)$. But such specifications are not representing real-life term structures.

The conclusion to be drawn from this analysis is that neither of the different versions of the pure expectation hypothesis seem to be consistent with any reasonable description of the term structure of interest rates.

11.7.3 The Weak Expectation Hypothesis

Above we looked at versions of the *pure* expectation hypothesis that all align an expected return or yield with a current interest rate or yield. However, as emphasized by Campbell (1986), there is also a *weak* expectation hypothesis that allows for a difference between the relevant expected return/yield and the current rate/yield, but restricts this difference to be constant over time.

The local weak expectation hypothesis says that

$$\mathrm{E}_t\left[\frac{dB_t^T}{B_t^T}\right] = \left(r_t + g(T-t)\right)\, dt$$

[4] According to the yield-to-maturity hypothesis

$$\begin{aligned} \frac{1}{\Delta t}\mathrm{E}_t\left[\ln B_{t+\Delta t}^T - \ln B_t^T\right] &= \frac{1}{\Delta t}\mathrm{E}_t\left[-\mathrm{E}_{t+\Delta t}\left[\int_{t+\Delta t}^T r_s\, ds\right] + \mathrm{E}_t\left[\int_t^T r_s\, ds\right]\right] \\ &= \frac{1}{\Delta t}\mathrm{E}_t\left[\int_t^{t+\Delta t} r_s\, ds\right], \end{aligned}$$

which approaches r_t as $\Delta t \to 0$. This means that the absolute drift of $\ln B_t$ equals r_t.

for some deterministic function g. In the pure version g is identically zero. For a given time-to-maturity there is a constant 'instantaneous holding term premium'. Comparing to Eq. (11.61), we see that this hypothesis will hold when the market price of risk $\boldsymbol{\lambda}_t$ is constant and the bond price sensitivity vector $\boldsymbol{\sigma}_t^T$ is a deterministic function of time-to-maturity. These conditions are satisfied in the Vasicek (1977) model and in other models of the Gaussian class.

Similarly, the weak yield-to-maturity expectation hypothesis says that

$$f_t^T = \mathrm{E}_t[r_T] + h(T-t)$$

for some deterministic function h with $h(0) = 0$ so that there is a constant 'instantaneous forward term premium'. The pure version requires h to be identically equal to zero. It can be shown that this condition implies that the drift of $\ln B_t^T$ equals $r_t + h(T-t)$.[5] Comparing to Eq. (11.63), we see that also this hypothesis will hold when λ_t is constant and σ_t^T is a deterministic function of $T-t$ as is the case in the Gaussian models.

The class of Gaussian models has several unrealistic properties. For example, such models allow (unbounded) negative interest rates and require bond and interest rate volatilities to be independent of the level of interest rates. So far, the validity of even weak versions of the expectation hypothesis has not been shown in more realistic term structure models.

11.8 OTHER HYPOTHESES ABOUT THE YIELD CURVE

Another traditional explanation of the shape of the yield curve is given by the *liquidity preference hypothesis* introduced by Hicks (1939). He realized that the expectation hypothesis basically ignores investors' aversion towards risk and argued that expected returns on long-term bonds should exceed the expected

[5] From the weak yield-to-maturity hypothesis, it follows that $-\ln B_t^T = \int_t^T (\mathrm{E}_t[r_s] + h(s-t))\,ds$. Hence,

$$\begin{aligned}
&\frac{1}{\Delta t}\,\mathrm{E}_t\left[\ln B_{t+\Delta t}^T - \ln B_t^T\right] \\
&\quad= \frac{1}{\Delta t}\,\mathrm{E}_t\left[-\int_{t+\Delta t}^T (\mathrm{E}_{t+\Delta t}[r_s] + h(s-(t+\Delta t)))\,ds + \int_t^T (\mathrm{E}_t[r_s] + h(s-t))\,ds\right] \\
&\quad= \frac{1}{\Delta t}\,\mathrm{E}_t\left[\int_t^{t+\Delta t} r_s\,ds\right] - \frac{1}{\Delta t}\left(\int_{t+\Delta t}^T h(s-(t+\Delta t))\,ds - \int_t^T h(s-t)\,ds\right).
\end{aligned}$$

The limit of $\frac{1}{\Delta t}\left(\int_{t+\Delta t}^T h(s-(t+\Delta t))\,ds - \int_t^T h(s-t)\,ds\right)$ as $\Delta t \to 0$ is exactly the derivative of $\int_t^T h(s-t)\,ds$ with respect to t. Applying Leibnitz' rule and $h(0) = 0$, this derivative equals $-\int_t^T h'(s-t)\,ds = -h(T-t)$. In sum, the drift rate of $\ln B_t^T$ becomes $r_t + h(T-t)$ according to the hypothesis.

returns on short-term bonds to compensate for the higher price fluctuations of long-term bonds. According to this view the yield curve should tend to be increasing. Note that the word 'liquidity' in the name of the hypothesis is not used in the usual sense of the word. Short-term bonds are not necessarily more liquid than long-term bonds. A better name would be 'the maturity preference hypothesis'.

In contrast the *market segmentation hypothesis* introduced by Culbertson (1957) claims that investors will typically prefer to invest in bonds with time-to-maturity in a certain interval, a maturity segment, perhaps in an attempt to match liabilities with similar maturities. For example, a pension fund with liabilities due in 20–30 years can reduce risk by investing in bonds of similar maturity. On the other hand, central banks typically operate in the short end of the market. Hence, separated market segments can exist without any relation between the bond prices and the interest rates in different maturity segments. If this is really the case, we cannot expect to see continuous or smooth yield curves and discount functions across the different segments.

A more realistic version of this hypothesis is the *preferred habitats hypothesis* put forward by Modigliani and Sutch (1966). An investor may prefer bonds with a certain maturity, but should be willing to move away from that maturity if she is sufficiently compensated in terms of a higher yield.[6] The different segments are therefore not completely independent of each other, and yields and discount factors should depend on maturity in a smooth way.

It is really not possible to quantify the market segmentation or the preferred habitats hypothesis without setting up an economy with individuals having different favourite maturities. The resulting equilibrium yield curve will depend heavily on the degree of risk aversion of the various individuals as illustrated by an analysis of Cox, Ingersoll, and Ross (1981a).

11.9 CONCLUDING REMARKS

This chapter has derived a number of general insights about interest rates and bond prices and has studied various specific models. Numerous dynamic term structure models have been suggested for the purpose of pricing various interest rate derivatives. Some of these are briefly mentioned in Chapter 13, but a more comprehensive overview is given in specialized textbooks such as Brigo and Mercurio (2006) and Munk (2011). For models of the equilibrium term structure of interest rates with investor heterogeneity or more general utility functions than studied in this chapter, see Duffie and Epstein (1992a),

[6] In a sense the liquidity preference hypothesis simply says that all investors prefer short-term bonds.

Wang (1996), Riedel (2000, 2004), and Wachter (2006). The effects of central banks on the term structure are discussed and modelled by Babbs and Webber (1994), Balduzzi, Bertola, and Foresi (1997), and Piazzesi (2005).

11.10 EXERCISES

Exercise 11.1 Show that if there is no arbitrage and the short rate can never go negative, then the discount function is non-increasing and all forward rates are non-negative.

Exercise 11.2 Show Eq. (11.35).

Exercise 11.3 The term premium at time t for the future period $[t', T]$ is the current forward rate for that period minus the expected spot rate, that is $f_t^{t',T} - \mathrm{E}_t[y_{t'}^T]$. This exercise will give a link between the term premium and a state-price deflator $\zeta = (\zeta_t)$.

(a) Show that

$$B_t^T = B_t^{t'}\,\mathrm{E}_t\left[B_{t'}^T\right] + \mathrm{Cov}_t\left[\frac{\zeta_{t'}}{\zeta_t}, \frac{\zeta_T}{\zeta_{t'}}\right]$$

for any $t \le t' \le T$.

(b) Using the above result, show that

$$\mathrm{E}_t\left[e^{-y_{t'}^T(T-t')}\right] - e^{-f_t^{t',T}(T-t')} = -\frac{1}{B_t^{t'}}\,\mathrm{Cov}_t\left[\frac{\zeta_{t'}}{\zeta_t}, \frac{\zeta_T}{\zeta_{t'}}\right].$$

Using the previous result and the approximation $e^x \approx 1 + x$, show that

$$f_t^{t',T} - \mathrm{E}_t[y_{t'}^T] \approx -\frac{1}{(T-t')B_t^{t'}}\,\mathrm{Cov}_t\left[\frac{\zeta_{t'}}{\zeta_t}, \frac{\zeta_T}{\zeta_{t'}}\right].$$

Exercise 11.4 The purpose of this exercise is to show that the claim of the gross return pure expectation hypothesis is inconsistent with interest rate uncertainty. In the following we consider time points $t_0 < t_1 < t_2$.

(a) Show that if the hypothesis holds, then

$$\frac{1}{B_{t_0}^{t_1}} = \frac{1}{B_{t_0}^{t_2}}\,\mathrm{E}_{t_0}\left[B_{t_1}^{t_2}\right].$$

Hint: Compare two investment strategies over the period $[t_0, t_1]$. The first strategy is to buy at time t_0 zero-coupon bonds maturing at time t_1. The second strategy is to buy at time t_0 zero-coupon bonds maturing at time t_2 and to sell them again at time t_1.

(b) Show that if the hypothesis holds, then

$$\frac{1}{B_{t_0}^{t_2}} = \frac{1}{B_{t_0}^{t_1}}\,\mathrm{E}_{t_0}\left[\frac{1}{B_{t_1}^{t_2}}\right].$$

(c) Show from the two previous questions that the hypothesis implies that

$$\mathrm{E}_{t_0}\left[\frac{1}{B_{t_1}^{t_2}}\right] = \frac{1}{\mathrm{E}_{t_0}\left[B_{t_1}^{t_2}\right]}. \qquad (*)$$

(d) Show that (*) can only hold under full certainty. *Hint: Use Jensen's inequality.*

Exercise 11.5 Show Eqs. (11.55) and (11.56).

Exercise 11.6 Go through the derivations in Example 11.1.

Exercise 11.7 Constantinides (1992) develops the so-called SAINTS model of the nominal term structure of interest rates by specifying exogenously the nominal state-price deflator $\tilde{\zeta}$. In a slightly simplified version, his assumption is that

$$\tilde{\zeta}_t = ke^{-gt+(X_t-\alpha)^2},$$

where k, g, and α are constants, and $X = (X_t)$ follows the Ornstein–Uhlenbeck process

$$dX_t = -\kappa X_t\, dt + \sigma\, dz_t,$$

where κ and σ are positive constants with $\sigma^2 < \kappa$ and $z = (z_t)$ is a standard one-dimensional Brownian motion.

(a) Derive the dynamics of the nominal state-price deflator. Express the nominal short-term interest rate, $\tilde{r}_t$, and the nominal market price of risk, $\tilde{\lambda}_t$, in terms of the variable X_t.

(b) Find the dynamics of the nominal short rate.

(c) Find parameter constraints that ensure that the short rate stays positive. *Hint: The short rate is a quadratic function of X. Find the minimum value of this function.*

(d) What is the distribution of X_T given X_t?

(e) Let Y be a normally distributed random variable with mean μ and variance ν^2. Show that

$$\mathrm{E}\left[e^{-\gamma Y^2}\right] = (1 + 2\gamma\nu^2)^{-1/2} \exp\left\{-\frac{\gamma\mu^2}{1 + 2\gamma\nu^2}\right\}.$$

(f) Use the results of the two previous questions to derive the time t price of a nominal zero-coupon bond with maturity T, that is $\tilde{B}_t^T$. It will be an exponential-quadratic function of X_t. What is the yield on this bond?

(g) Find the percentage volatility σ_t^T of the price of the zero-coupon bond maturing at T.

(h) The instantaneous expected excess rate of return on the zero-coupon bond maturing at T is often called the term premium for maturity T. Explain why the term premium is given by $\sigma_t^T \tilde{\lambda}_t$ and show that the term premium can be written as

$$4\sigma^2\alpha^2 (1 - F(T-t)) \left(\frac{X_t}{\alpha} - 1\right) \left(\frac{X_t}{\alpha} - \frac{1 - F(T-t)e^{\kappa(T-t)}}{1 - F(T-t)}\right),$$

where

$$F(\tau) = \frac{1}{\frac{\sigma^2}{\kappa} + \left(1 - \frac{\sigma^2}{\kappa}\right) e^{2\kappa\tau}}.$$

For which values of X_t will the term premium for maturity T be positive/negative? For a given state X_t, is it possible that the term premium is positive for some maturities and negative for others?

Exercise 11.8 Assume a continuous-time economy where the state-price deflator $\zeta = (\zeta_t)$ has dynamics

$$d\zeta_t = -\zeta_t \left[r_t\, dt + \lambda\, dz_{1t} \right],$$

where $z_1 = (z_{1t})$ is a (one-dimensional) standard Brownian motion, λ is a constant, and $r = (r_t)$ follows the Ornstein–Uhlenbeck process

$$dr_t = \kappa [\bar{r} - r_t]\, dt + \sigma_r\, dz_{1t}.$$

This is the Vasicek model so we know that the prices of zero-coupon bonds are given by Eq. (11.28) and the corresponding yields are given by (11.31).

Suppose you want to value a real uncertain cash flow of F_T coming at time T. Let $x_t = \mathrm{E}_t[F_T]$ and assume that

$$dx_t = x_t \left[\mu_x\, dt + \sigma_x \rho\, dz_{1t} + \sigma_x \sqrt{1 - \rho^2}\, dz_{2t} \right],$$

where μ_x, σ_x, and ρ are constants, and where $z_2 = (z_{2t})$ is another (one-dimensional) standard Brownian motion independent of z_1.

(a) Argue that $x = (x_t)$ must be a martingale and hence that $\mu_x = 0$.

(b) Show that the time t value of the claim to the cash flow F_T is given by

$$V_t \equiv V(t, r_t, x_t) = x_t e^{-A(T-t) - B(T-t) r_t}, \qquad (*)$$

where $B(\tau) = \mathcal{B}_\kappa(\tau)$ and

$$A(\tau) = \mathcal{A}(\tau) + \rho\lambda\sigma_x\tau + \frac{\rho\sigma_x\sigma_r}{\kappa}\left(\tau - \mathcal{B}_\kappa(\tau)\right).$$

(c) Write the dynamics of $V = (V_t)$ as $dV_t = V_t[\mu_t^V\, dt + \sigma_{1t}^V\, dz_{1t} + \sigma_{2t}^V\, dz_{2t}]$. Use (*) to identify μ_t^V, σ_{1t}^V, and σ_{2t}^V. Verify that $\mu_t^V = r_t + \left(\boldsymbol{\sigma}_t^V\right)^\top \boldsymbol{\lambda}_t$, where $\boldsymbol{\sigma}^V = (\sigma_1^V, \sigma_2^V)^\top$ and $\boldsymbol{\lambda}$ is the market price of risk vector (the market price of risk associated with z_2 is zero! Why?).

(d) Define the risk-adjusted discount rate R_t for the cash flow by the relation $V_t = \mathrm{E}_t[F_T]e^{-R_t[T-t]}$. What is the difference between R_t and y_t^T? How does this difference depend on the cash flow payment date T?

Exercise 11.9 Consider an economy with complete financial markets and a representative agent with CRRA utility, $u(C) = \frac{C^{1-\gamma}}{1-\gamma}$, where $\gamma > 0$, and a time preference rate of δ. The aggregate consumption level C is assumed to follow the stochastic process

$$dc_t = c_t \left[\left(a_1 X_t^2 + a_2 X_t + a_3 \right) dt + \sigma_c \, dz_t \right],$$

where $z = (z_t)$ is a standard one-dimensional Brownian motion under the real-life probability measure $\mathbb{P}$ and where a_1, a_2, a_3, σ_c are constants with $\sigma_c > 0$. Furthermore, $X = (X_t)$ is a stochastic process with dynamics

$$dX_t = -\kappa X_t \, dt + dz_t,$$

where κ is a positive constant.

(a) Show that the short-term interest rate is of the form $r_t = d_1 X_t^2 + d_2 X_t + d_3$ and determine the constants d_1, d_2, d_3.

(b) Find a parameter condition under which the short-term interest rate is always non-negative.

(c) Write up the dynamics of r_t.

(d) What is the market price of risk in this economy?

Suppose that the above applies to the real economy and that money has no effect on the real economy. The Consumer Price Index $\tilde{F}_t$ is supposed to have dynamics

$$d\tilde{F}_t = \tilde{F}_t \left[\mu_{Ft} \, dt + \rho_{CF} \sigma_{Ft} \, dz_t + \sqrt{1 - \rho_{CF}^2} \sigma_{Ft} \, d\hat{z}_t \right],$$

where ρ_{CF} is a constant correlation coefficient and $\hat{z} = (\hat{z}_t)$ is another standard Brownian motion independent of z. Assume that μ_{Ft} and σ_{Ft} are of the form

$$\mu_{Ft} = b_1 X_t^2 + b_2 X_t + b_3, \qquad \sigma_{Ft} = k X_t.$$

(e) Write up an expression for the nominal short-term interest rate, $\tilde{r}_t$.

Assume in the rest of the problem that $\gamma a_1 + b_1 = k^2$.

(f) Show that the nominal short rate $\tilde{r}_t$ is affine in X_t and express X_t as an affine function of $\tilde{r}_t$.

(g) Compute the nominal market price of risk $\tilde{\lambda}_t$.

(h) Determine the dynamics of the nominal short rate. The drift and volatility should be expressed in terms of $\tilde{r}_t$, not X_t.

Exercise 11.10 Provide a detailed proof of the bond price expression in the Cox–Ingersoll–Ross model as stated in Theorem 11.4.

12

Risk-Adjusted Probabilities

12.1 INTRODUCTION

A standard method in option pricing is to compute the price of an option as the risk-neutral expectation of the discounted payoff of the option. Here, the 'risk-neutral expectation' refers to an expectation under a hypothetical probability measure which is a transformation of the true, real-world probability measure. Finance students are often introduced to the risk-neutral valuation technique in simple option pricing models. If the underlying asset price under the risk-neutral probability measure follows a discrete-time binomial process (Cox, Ross, and Rubinstein 1979) or a continuous-time geometric Brownian motion (Black and Scholes 1973; Merton 1973c), a closed-form expression for the price of a European option can be derived by computing the risk-neutral expected discounted payoff.

The risk-neutral valuation approach applies to all financial assets, not just derivatives. As indicated in a one-period framework in Section 4.6.1, the general pricing mechanism in a financial market can be represented by a risk-neutral probability measure and a risk-free return. In this sense, the risk-neutral probability measure together with the risk-free return carry the same information as a state-price deflator. Intuitively, the adjustment for risk is built into the state probabilities, and then risky dividends can be valued as the expected dividend discounted by the risk-free rate, but where the expectation is calculated using the risk-adjusted probabilities. In contrast, when using the state-price deflator the present value is computed as the expected dividend adjusted by a term involving the covariance of the dividend and the state-price deflator, and then this adjusted expected dividend is discounted by the risk-free rate, see Eq. (4.5). Alternatively, the present value is the expected dividend discounted by an appropriately risk-adjusted discount rate as in Eq. (4.9). In both these cases, expectations are calculated using the true probabilities. Apparently, the idea of risk-neutral valuation dates back to Arrow (1971) and Drèze (1971) and was further explored by Cox and Ross (1976a, 1976b) and Harrison and Kreps (1979).

The risk-neutral probability measure of the simple option pricing models is just one out of many probability measures that are useful for pricing purposes. In this chapter we will introduce a number of specific probability measures and derive some general pricing expressions involving these probability measures. The next chapter will illustrate the use of the various risk-adjusted probability measures for the pricing of a number of important derivative securities.

The rest of this chapter is organized in the following way. Section 12.2 outlines how a general change of the probability measure is formalized. The risk-neutral probability measure is defined and studied in Section 12.3, whereas the so-called forward risk-adjusted probability measures are introduced in Section 12.4. Section 12.5 shows that an appropriate risk-adjusted probability measure can be defined for any given asset or trading strategy with a positive value. Section 12.6 demonstrates that the risk-adjusted probability measure associated with the so-called growth-optimal trading strategy is identical to the real-world probability measure.

12.2 CHANGE OF PROBABILITY MEASURE

Any financial model with uncertainty formally builds on a probability space $(\Omega, \mathcal{F}, \mathbb{P})$. Here Ω is the state space (the set of possible realizations of all relevant uncertain objects), $\mathcal{F}$ is the set of events that can be assigned a probability, and $\mathbb{P}$ is a probability measure assigning probabilities to events. It is implicitly understood that $\mathbb{P}$ gives the true or real-world probabilities of events. The consumption and investment decisions of individuals will depend on the probabilities they associate with different events and, hence, the equilibrium asset prices will reflect those probabilities. However for some purposes, as we will see in the following sections, it is relevant to consider other probability measures on the same set of events. We will use the term real-world probability measure for $\mathbb{P}$, but in the literature $\mathbb{P}$ is also referred to as the true, the physical, or the empirical probability measure.

A word on notation. Whenever the expectation operator is written without a superscript, it means the expectation using the probability measure $\mathbb{P}$. The expectation under a different probability measure $\mathbb{Q}$ will be denoted by $\mathrm{E}^{\mathbb{Q}}$. Similarly for variances and covariances and for conditional moments.

The alternative probability measures we will consider will be equivalent to $\mathbb{P}$. Two probability measures $\mathbb{P}$ and $\mathbb{Q}$ on the same set of events $\mathcal{F}$ are said to be *equivalent probability measures* if they assign probability zero to exactly the same events, that is

$$\mathbb{P}(F) = 0 \quad \Leftrightarrow \quad \mathbb{Q}(F) = 0.$$

The link between two equivalent probability measures $\mathbb{P}$ and $\mathbb{Q}$ can be represented by a random variable, which is typically denoted by $\frac{d\mathbb{Q}}{d\mathbb{P}}$ and referred to as the *Radon–Nikodym derivative* of $\mathbb{Q}$ with respect to $\mathbb{P}$. For any state $\omega \in \Omega$, the value of $\frac{d\mathbb{Q}}{d\mathbb{P}}$ shows what the $\mathbb{P}$-probability of ω should be multiplied by in order to get the $\mathbb{Q}$-probability of ω. In the special case of a finite state space $\Omega = \{1, 2, \dots, S\}$, the probability measures $\mathbb{P}$ and $\mathbb{Q}$ are defined by the probabilities p_ω and q_ω, respectively, of the individual states $\omega = 1, 2, \dots, S$. The Radon–Nikodym derivative of $\mathbb{Q}$ with respect to $\mathbb{P}$ is then captured by the S possible realizations

$$\frac{d\mathbb{Q}}{d\mathbb{P}}(\omega) = \frac{q_\omega}{p_\omega}, \qquad \omega = 1, \dots, S.$$

The Radon–Nikodym derivative $\frac{d\mathbb{Q}}{d\mathbb{P}}$ must be strictly positive on all events having a non-zero $\mathbb{P}$-probability. Furthermore, to ensure that the $\mathbb{Q}$-probabilities sum up to one, we must have $\mathrm{E}\left[\frac{d\mathbb{Q}}{d\mathbb{P}}\right] = 1$. For example, with a finite state space

$$\mathrm{E}\left[\frac{d\mathbb{Q}}{d\mathbb{P}}\right] = \sum_{\omega=1}^{S} p_\omega \frac{d\mathbb{Q}}{d\mathbb{P}}(\omega) = \sum_{\omega=1}^{S} p_\omega \frac{q_\omega}{p_\omega} = \sum_{\omega=1}^{S} q_\omega = 1.$$

The expected value under the measure $\mathbb{Q}$ of a random variable X is given by

$$\mathrm{E}^{\mathbb{Q}}[X] = \mathrm{E}\left[\frac{d\mathbb{Q}}{d\mathbb{P}} X\right]. \tag{12.1}$$

Again, this is easily demonstrated with a finite state space:

$$\mathrm{E}^{\mathbb{Q}}[X] = \sum_{\omega=1}^{S} q_\omega X(\omega) = \sum_{\omega=1}^{S} p_\omega \frac{q_\omega}{p_\omega} X(\omega) = \sum_{\omega=1}^{S} p_\omega \frac{d\mathbb{Q}}{d\mathbb{P}}(\omega) X(\omega) = \mathrm{E}\left[\frac{d\mathbb{Q}}{d\mathbb{P}} X\right].$$

In a multiperiod model where all the uncertainty is resolved at time T, the Radon–Nikodym derivative $\frac{d\mathbb{Q}}{d\mathbb{P}}$ will be known at time T, but usually not known before. Define the stochastic process $\xi = (\xi_t)_{t \in \mathcal{T}}$ by

$$\xi_t = \mathrm{E}_t\left[\frac{d\mathbb{Q}}{d\mathbb{P}}\right]. \tag{12.2}$$

In particular, $\xi_T = \frac{d\mathbb{Q}}{d\mathbb{P}}$. The process ξ is called the change-of-measure process or the likelihood ratio process. Note that the process ξ is a $\mathbb{P}$-martingale since, for any $t < t' \leq T$, we have

$$\mathrm{E}_t\left[\xi_{t'}\right] = \mathrm{E}_t\left[\mathrm{E}_{t'}\left[\xi_T\right]\right] = \mathrm{E}_t\left[\xi_T\right] = \xi_t.$$

Here the first and the third equalities follow from the definition of ξ. The second equality follows from the Law of Iterated Expectations, Theorem 2.1.

In multiperiod models we often work with conditional probabilities and the following result, the so-called Bayes' Formula, turns out to be very useful.

Theorem 12.1 (Bayes). *Let $\mathbb{Q}$ and $\mathbb{P}$ be equivalent probability measures, and let $\xi = (\xi_t)$ denote the likelihood ratio process as defined in Eq. (12.2). Let $X = (X_t)_{t \in \mathcal{T}}$ be any stochastic process. Then we have*

$$\mathrm{E}_t^{\mathbb{Q}}\left[X_{t'}\right] = \frac{\mathrm{E}_t\left[\xi_{t'} X_{t'}\right]}{\mathrm{E}_t[\xi_{t'}]} = \mathrm{E}_t\left[\frac{\xi_{t'}}{\xi_t} X_{t'}\right]. \tag{12.3}$$

For a proof, see Björk (2009, Prop. B.41).

A change of the probability measure can be handled very elegantly in continuous-time models in which the underlying uncertainty is represented by a standard Brownian motion $z = (z_t)_{t \in [0,T]}$ (under the real-world probability measure $\mathbb{P}$), and this is the case in all the continuous-time models considered in this book. Let $\lambda = (\lambda_t)_{t \in [0,T]}$ be any adapted and sufficiently well-behaved stochastic process.[1] Here, z and λ must have the same dimension. For notational simplicity, we assume in the following that they are one-dimensional, but the results generalize naturally to the multidimensional case. We can generate an equivalent probability measure $\mathbb{Q}^\lambda$ in the following way. Define the process $\xi^\lambda = (\xi_t^\lambda)_{t \in [0,T]}$ by

$$\xi_t^\lambda = \exp\left\{-\int_0^t \lambda_s \, dz_s - \frac{1}{2}\int_0^t \lambda_s^2 \, ds\right\}.$$

Then $\xi_0^\lambda = 1$, ξ^λ is strictly positive, and an application of Itô's Lemma shows that $d\xi_t^\lambda = -\xi_t^\lambda \lambda_t \, dz_t$ so that ξ^λ is a $\mathbb{P}$-martingale (see Exercise 2.4) and $\mathrm{E}[\xi_T^\lambda] = \xi_0^\lambda = 1$. Consequently, an equivalent probability measure $\mathbb{Q}^\lambda$ can be defined by the Radon–Nikodym derivative

$$\frac{d\mathbb{Q}^\lambda}{d\mathbb{P}} = \xi_T^\lambda = \exp\left\{-\int_0^T \lambda_s \, dz_s - \frac{1}{2}\int_0^T \lambda_s^2 \, ds\right\}.$$

From Eq. (12.3), we get that

$$\mathrm{E}_t^{\mathbb{Q}^\lambda}\left[X_{t'}\right] = \mathrm{E}_t\left[\frac{\xi_{t'}^\lambda}{\xi_t^\lambda} X_{t'}\right] = \mathrm{E}_t\left[X_{t'} \exp\left\{-\int_t^{t'} \lambda_s \, dz_s - \frac{1}{2}\int_t^{t'} \lambda_s^2 \, ds\right\}\right]$$

for any stochastic process $X = (X_t)_{t \in [0,T]}$. A central result is Girsanov's Theorem (see, for example, Øksendal 2003):

[1] Basically, λ must be square-integrable in the sense that $\int_0^T \lambda_t^2 \, dt$ is finite with probability 1, and λ must satisfy Novikov's condition, that is the expectation $\mathrm{E}\left[\exp\left\{\frac{1}{2}\int_0^T \lambda_t^2 \, dt\right\}\right]$ is finite.

Theorem 12.2 (Girsanov). *The process $z^\lambda = (z^\lambda_t)_{t\in[0,T]}$ defined by*

$$z^\lambda_t = z_t + \int_0^t \lambda_s \, ds, \quad 0 \le t \le T,$$

is a standard Brownian motion under the probability measure $\mathbb{Q}^\lambda$. In differential notation,

$$dz^\lambda_t = dz_t + \lambda_t \, dt.$$

This theorem has the attractive consequence that the effects on a stochastic process of changing the probability measure from $\mathbb{P}$ to some $\mathbb{Q}^\lambda$ are captured by a simple adjustment of the drift. If $X = (X_t)$ is an Itô-process with dynamics

$$dX_t = \mu_t \, dt + \sigma_t \, dz_t,$$

then

$$dX_t = \mu_t \, dt + \sigma_t \left(dz^\lambda_t - \lambda_t \, dt \right) = (\mu_t - \sigma_t \lambda_t) \, dt + \sigma_t \, dz^\lambda_t. \tag{12.4}$$

Since z^λ is a standard Brownian motion under $\mathbb{Q}^\lambda$, we have $\mathrm{E}^{\mathbb{Q}^\lambda}_t [dz^\lambda_t] = 0$ and thus

$$\mathrm{E}^{\mathbb{Q}^\lambda}_t [dX_t] = (\mu_t - \sigma_t \lambda_t) \, dt.$$

Hence, $\mu - \sigma\lambda$ is the drift under the probability measure $\mathbb{Q}^\lambda$, and this is different from the drift under the original measure $\mathbb{P}$ unless σ or λ are identically equal to zero. In contrast, the volatility remains the same as under the original measure. We will say that Eq. (12.4) shows the $\mathbb{Q}^\lambda$-dynamics of the process X.

In many financial models, the relevant change of measure is such that the distribution under $\mathbb{Q}^\lambda$ of the future value of the central processes is of the same class as under the original $\mathbb{P}$ measure, but with different moments. However, in general, a shift of probability measure may change not only some or all moments of future values, but also the distributional class.

12.3 RISK-NEUTRAL PROBABILITIES

12.3.1 Definition

A risk-neutral probability measure for a given financial market can only be defined if the investors at any point in time considered in the model and for any state can trade in an asset which provides a risk-free return until the next point in time where the investors can rebalance their portfolios. In a one-period economy, this is simply a one-period risk-free asset. As before, R^f denotes the gross rate of return on that asset. In a discrete-time economy with trading at $t = 0, 1, 2, \ldots, T-1$, the assumption is that investors can roll over in one-period risk-free investments. Investing one unit in a one-period risk-free investment at time t will give you R^f_t at time $t+1$. Reinvesting that in a risk-free manner over the next period will give you $R^f_{t,t+2} = R^f_t R^f_{t+1}$ at time $t+2$. Continuing that procedure, you end up with

$$R^f_{t,t+n} = R^f_t R^f_{t+1} R^f_{t+2} \ldots R^f_{t+n-1} = \prod_{m=0}^{n-1} R^f_{t+m}$$

at time $t+n$. Note that, in general, this return is not known before time $t+n-1$ and in particular not at time t where the investment strategy is initiated. An investment with a truly risk-free return between time t and $t+n$ is a zero-coupon bond maturing at time $t+n$. If B^{t+n}_t denotes the price of this bond at time t and the face value of the bond is normalized at 1, the gross risk-free rate of return between t and $t+n$ is $1/B^{t+n}_t$.

In a continuous-time economy we can think of the limit of the above roll-over strategy. If r^f_t denotes the continuously compounded risk-free net rate of return at time t (the interest rate over the instant following time t), an investment of 1 in this roll-over strategy at time t will give you

$$R^f_{t,t'} = \exp\left\{\int_t^{t'} r^f_u \, du\right\}$$

at time t'.

Whether the model is formulated in discrete or continuous time, we refer to the roll-over strategy in short risk-free investments as the *bank account* and refer to $R^f_{t,s}$ as the gross rate of return on the bank account between time t and time $s > t$. In the one-period model, the bank account is simply a one-period risk-free asset.

We can now give a unified definition of a risk-neutral probability measure:

Definition 12.1 *A probability measure $\mathbb{Q}$ is called a* risk-neutral probability measure *for a given financial market in which a bank account is traded if the following conditions are satisfied:*

(i) $\mathbb{P}$ and $\mathbb{Q}$ are equivalent;

(ii) the Radon–Nikodym derivative $\frac{d\mathbb{Q}}{d\mathbb{P}}$ has finite variance;

(iii) the price of a future dividend equals the $\mathbb{Q}$-expectation of the ratio of the dividend to the gross rate of return on the bank account between the pricing date and the dividend payment date.

When $\mathbb{Q}$ is a risk-neutral probability measure, we will refer to the $\mathbb{Q}$-expectation as the risk-neutral expectation.

The pricing condition (iii) is a bit vague at this point. In a one-period framework, it means that

$$P_i = \mathrm{E}^{\mathbb{Q}}\left[\frac{D_i}{R^f}\right] = (R^f)^{-1}\,\mathrm{E}^{\mathbb{Q}}\left[D_i\right], \tag{12.5}$$

and, consequently, $\mathrm{E}^{\mathbb{Q}}[R_i] = R^f$. In a discrete-time model, the pricing condition (iii) means

$$P_{it} = \mathrm{E}_t^{\mathbb{Q}}\left[\sum_{s=t+1}^{T} \frac{D_{is}}{R^f_{t,s}}\right], \tag{12.6}$$

which is equivalent to

$$P_{it} = \mathrm{E}_t^{\mathbb{Q}}\left[\frac{P_{it'}}{R^f_{t,t'}} + \sum_{s=t+1}^{t'} \frac{D_{is}}{R^f_{t,s}}\right], \quad t < t' \le T, \tag{12.7}$$

compare Exercise 12.1. In particular, for $t' = t+1$ this reduces to

$$P_{it} = \frac{1}{R^f_t}\,\mathrm{E}_t^{\mathbb{Q}}\left[P_{i,t+1} + D_{i,t+1}\right]$$

so that $\mathrm{E}_t^{\mathbb{Q}}[R_{i,t+1}] = R^f_t$. In the continuous-time framework, the pricing condition (iii) is interpreted as

$$\begin{aligned} P_{it} &= \mathrm{E}_t^{\mathbb{Q}}\left[\int_t^T (R^f_{t,s})^{-1}\delta_{is}P_{is}\,ds + (R^f_{t,T})^{-1}D_{iT}\right] \\ &= \mathrm{E}_t^{\mathbb{Q}}\left[(R^f_{t,T})^{-1}e^{\int_t^T \delta_{is}\,ds}D_{iT}\right] = \mathrm{E}_t^{\mathbb{Q}}\left[e^{-\int_t^T (r^f_s - \delta_{is})\,ds}D_{iT}\right], \end{aligned}$$

where $\delta_i = (\delta_{it})$ is the dividend yield process of asset i. The relation

$$P_{it} = \mathrm{E}_t^{\mathbb{Q}}\left[\int_t^{t'} (R^f_{t,s})^{-1}\delta_{is}P_{is}\,ds + (R^f_{t,t'})^{-1}P_{it'}\right] = \mathrm{E}_t^{\mathbb{Q}}\left[e^{-\int_t^{t'} (r^f_s - \delta_{is})\,ds}P_{it'}\right] \tag{12.8}$$

then follows. Applying Theorem 2.7, we get

$$dP_{it} = P_{it}\left[(r^f_t - \delta_{it})\,dt + \boldsymbol{\sigma}_{it}^{\top}\,d\boldsymbol{z}_t^{\mathbb{Q}}\right]$$

so that the total instantaneous rate of return has a risk-neutral expectation equal to the risk-free rate. Therefore, in all of the modelling frameworks, the risk-neutral expected return on any asset over the next period equals the risk-free return over that period. The above considerations also hold for all trading strategies (as always, in the continuous-time framework some 'wild' trading strategies must be ruled out).

We can see from the above equations that given the stochastic process for the risk-free return and a risk-neutral probability measure, we can price any dividend process. Therefore, the risk-free return process and a risk-neutral probability measure jointly capture the market-wide pricing mechanism of the financial market.

A risk-neutral probability measure is sometimes called an *equivalent martingale measure*. Of course, the word *equivalent* refers to the equivalence of the risk-neutral probability measure and the real-world probability measure. The word *martingale* is used here since the risk-free discounted gains process of any asset will be a $\mathbb{Q}$-martingale. The risk-free discounted gains process of asset i is denoted by $\bar{G}_i = (\bar{G}_{it})_{t\in\mathcal{T}}$. In the discrete-time setting, it is defined as

$$\bar{G}_{it} = \frac{P_{it}}{R^f_{0,t}} + \sum_{s=1}^{t} \frac{D_{is}}{R^f_{0,s}}.$$

Since $R^f_{0,s} = R^f_{0,t} R^f_{t,s}$ for all $t < s$, the pricing condition (12.7) can be rewritten as

$$\frac{P_{it}}{R^f_{0,t}} = \mathrm{E}^{\mathbb{Q}}_t\left[\frac{P_{it'}}{R^f_{0,t'}} + \sum_{s=t+1}^{t'} \frac{D_{is}}{R^f_{0,s}}\right], \quad t < t' \leq T,$$

which is equivalent to

$$\frac{P_{it}}{R^f_{0,t}} + \sum_{s=1}^{t} \frac{D_{is}}{R^f_{0,s}} = \mathrm{E}^{\mathbb{Q}}_t\left[\frac{P_{it'}}{R^f_{0,t'}} + \sum_{s=1}^{t'} \frac{D_{is}}{R^f_{0,s}}\right], \quad t < t' \leq T.$$

This means that $\bar{G}_{it} = \mathrm{E}^{\mathbb{Q}}_t[\bar{G}_{it'}]$ so that $\bar{G}_i$ indeed is a $\mathbb{Q}$-martingale. In the continuous-time setting, the discounted gains process of asset i is defined as

$$\bar{G}_{it} = \frac{P_{it}}{R^f_{0,t}} + \int_0^t \frac{\delta_{is} P_{is}}{R^f_{0,s}}\, ds,$$

and again it can be shown that the pricing condition (12.8) is equivalent to $\bar{G}_i$ being a $\mathbb{Q}$-martingale.

12.3.2 Relation to State-Price Deflators

Since we can represent the general pricing mechanism of a financial market either by a state-price deflator or by a risk-neutral probability measure and the risk-free return process, it should come as no surprise that there is a close relation between these quantities.

First, consider a one-period economy with a risk-free asset. Here, the following theorem states the precise relation between state-price deflators and risk-neutral probability measures.

Theorem 12.3 *Consider a one-period economy in which a risk-free asset is traded with gross risk-free return $R^f > 0$. Let $\mathbb{P}$ denote the real-world probability measure.*

(i) If ζ is a state-price deflator, then the Radon–Nikodym derivative

$$\frac{d\mathbb{Q}}{d\mathbb{P}} = R^f \zeta = \frac{\zeta}{\mathrm{E}[\zeta]} \tag{12.9}$$

defines a risk-neutral probability measure $\mathbb{Q}$.

(ii) If $\mathbb{Q}$ is a risk-neutral probability measure, then

$$\zeta = (R^f)^{-1} \frac{d\mathbb{Q}}{d\mathbb{P}}$$

defines a state-price deflator.

Proof. (i) Since ζ is a state-price deflator, it is strictly positive and, consequently, has a positive expectation. Hence, $d\mathbb{Q}/d\mathbb{P}$ is a strictly positive random variable with

$$\mathrm{E}\left[\frac{d\mathbb{Q}}{d\mathbb{P}}\right] = \mathrm{E}\left[\frac{\zeta}{\mathrm{E}[\zeta]}\right] = 1.$$

Therefore, $\frac{d\mathbb{Q}}{d\mathbb{P}}$ defines a probability measure $\mathbb{Q}$ which is equivalent to $\mathbb{P}$. Since a state-price deflator has finite variance and R^f is a constant, $\frac{d\mathbb{Q}}{d\mathbb{P}}$ has finite variance. Furthermore, from Eq. (12.1) we get

$$\mathrm{E}^{\mathbb{Q}}\left[\frac{D_i}{R^f}\right] = \mathrm{E}\left[\frac{d\mathbb{Q}}{d\mathbb{P}} \frac{D_i}{R^f}\right] = \mathrm{E}[\zeta D_i] = P_i.$$

Hence, $\mathbb{Q}$ is indeed a risk-neutral probability measure.

(ii) Since $\mathbb{Q}$ is a risk-neutral probability measure, $d\mathbb{Q}/d\mathbb{P}$ is strictly positive and has finite variance. Therefore, ζ will be strictly positive and have finite variance. Moreover, by applying Eqs. (12.1) and (12.5) we see that

$$P_i = \mathrm{E}^{\mathbb{Q}}\left[\left(R^f\right)^{-1} D_i\right] = \mathrm{E}\left[\frac{d\mathbb{Q}}{d\mathbb{P}} \left(R^f\right)^{-1} D_i\right] = \mathrm{E}\left[\zeta D_i\right].$$

This confirms that ζ is a state-price deflator. □

A change of the probability measure is a reallocation of probability mass over the states. We can see that the risk-neutral measure allocates a higher probability to states ω for which $\zeta_\omega > \mathrm{E}[\zeta]$, that is if the value of the state-price deflator for state ω is higher than average.

Example 12.1 Consider the same one-period economy as in Examples 3.1 and 4.2. The real-world probabilities of the three states are $p_1 = 0.5, p_2 = p_3 = 0.25$, respectively. The state-price deflator is given by $\zeta_1 = 0.6$, $\zeta_2 = 0.8$, and $\zeta_3 = 1.2$. Since

$$\mathrm{E}[\zeta] = 0.5 \cdot 0.6 + 0.25 \cdot 0.8 + 0.25 \cdot 1.2 = 0.8,$$

the gross risk-free rate of return is $R^f = 1/\mathrm{E}[\zeta] = 1.25$ corresponding to a 25% risk-free net rate of return. It follows that the risk-neutral probabilities are

$$q_1 = R^f \zeta_1 p_1 = 0.375, \quad q_2 = R^f \zeta_2 p_2 = 0.25, \quad q_3 = R^f \zeta_3 p_3 = 0.375.$$

The risk-neutral measure allocates a larger probability to state 3, the same probability to state 2, and a lower probability to state 1 than the real-world measure. □

Example 12.2 Suppose a representative individual with time-additive power utility exists so that the state-price deflator is given by the marginal rate of substitution, $\zeta = e^{-\delta}(c/c_0)^{-\gamma}$. Assume that $\delta = 0.02$ and normalize current aggregate consumption to $c_0 = 1$. Suppose that there are five possible levels of aggregate consumption at the end of the period and that these are equally likely according to the real-world probability measure $\mathbb{P}$. The five consumption levels can be seen in Table 12.1. Note that the distribution is somewhat extreme in the sense that there is a 20% chance for a consumption growth of 50% and also a 20% chance for a drop of 50% in consumption.

If the relative risk aversion of the representative individual is $\gamma = 2$, the state-price deflator for the five states will be as shown in the fourth column of the table with an expected value of 1.4389. The associated risk-neutral probabilities for the five states then follow from Eq. (12.9) and are displayed in the fifth column. Note that the risk-neutral probability for the very bad state 5 is much higher than the true probability. This simply reflects the fact that

Table 12.1. Change of measure in Example 12.2.

			$\gamma = 2$		$\gamma = 10$	
State	$\mathbb{P}$-prob	c	ζ	$\mathbb{Q}$-prob	ζ	$\mathbb{Q}$-prob
1	0.2	1.5	0.4356	0.0606	0.0170	0.000017
2	0.2	1.1	0.8101	0.1126	0.3779	0.00038
3	0.2	1.02	0.9421	0.1309	0.8041	0.00080
4	0.2	0.95	1.0861	0.1510	1.6371	0.0016
5	0.2	0.5	3.9208	0.5450	1003.7	0.9972
sum	1			1		1
$\mathbb{P}$-expectation		1.014	1.4389		201.31	

the risk-averse representative individual will value an extra payment highly in that state where the overall consumption is extremely low. This is even more pronounced for higher levels of risk aversion as can be seen from the two rightmost columns in the table. With a relative risk aversion of $\gamma = 10$, the risk-neutral probability for the very bad state is very close to one, whereas the other states are assigned very low probabilities. □

The following theorem states the link between state-price deflators and risk-neutral probability measures in a multiperiod setting. Note that if $\zeta = (\zeta_t)_{t\in\mathcal{T}}$ is a state-price deflator, then the gross return on the bank account between any two dates $t, t' \in \mathcal{T}$ with $t \le t'$ satisfies

$$R^f_{t,t'} = \left(\mathrm{E}_t\left[\frac{\zeta_{t+1}}{\zeta_t}\right] \mathrm{E}_{t+1}\left[\frac{\zeta_{t+2}}{\zeta_{t+1}}\right] \dots \mathrm{E}_{t'-1}\left[\frac{\zeta_{t'}}{\zeta_{t'-1}}\right]\right)^{-1}$$

in a discrete-time setting where $\mathcal{T} = \{0, 1, 2, \dots, T\}$, and

$$R^f_{t,t'} = \exp\left\{\int_t^{t'} r^f_u \, du\right\}$$

with $r^f_u \, du = -\mathrm{E}_u[d\zeta_u/\zeta_u]$ in a continuous-time setting where $\mathcal{T} = [0, T]$.

Theorem 12.4 *Consider a multiperiod economy in which investors have access to a bank account. Let $R^f_{t,t'} > 0$ denote the gross return on the bank account between any two dates $t, t' \in \mathcal{T}$ with $t \le t'$, and let $\mathbb{P}$ denote the real-world probability measure.*

(i) If $\zeta = (\zeta_t)_{t\in\mathcal{T}}$ is a state-price deflator, then the Radon–Nikodym derivative

$$\frac{d\mathbb{Q}}{d\mathbb{P}} = R^f_{0,T}\zeta_T$$

defines a risk-neutral probability measure $\mathbb{Q}$.

(ii) If $\mathbb{Q}$ is a risk-neutral probability measure, then $\zeta = (\zeta_t)_{t\in\mathcal{T}}$ with

$$\zeta_t = \frac{1}{R^f_{0,t}} \mathrm{E}_t\left[\frac{d\mathbb{Q}}{d\mathbb{P}}\right]$$

defines a state-price deflator.

In terms of the likelihood ratio process ξ defined by $\xi_t = \mathrm{E}_t[\frac{d\mathbb{Q}}{d\mathbb{P}}]$ as before, the link between state-price deflators and risk-neutral measures can be written compactly as

$$\zeta_t = \frac{1}{R^f_{0,t}} \mathrm{E}_t\left[\frac{d\mathbb{Q}}{d\mathbb{P}}\right] = \frac{\xi_t}{R^f_{0,t}}, \quad t \in \mathcal{T}. \tag{12.10}$$

Proof. For concreteness, take a discrete-time framework. An analogous procedure works in the continuous-time setting.

(i) First note that when ζ is a state-price deflator, then

$$1 = \mathrm{E}_t\left[\frac{\zeta_T}{\zeta_t} R^f_{t,T}\right]$$

and hence

$$\xi_t = \mathrm{E}_t\left[\frac{d\mathbb{Q}}{d\mathbb{P}}\right] = \mathrm{E}_t\left[\zeta_T R^f_{0,T}\right] = \zeta_t R^f_{0,t}\,\mathrm{E}_t\left[\frac{\zeta_T}{\zeta_t} R^f_{t,T}\right] = \zeta_t R^f_{0,t}$$

so that

$$\xi_t = \zeta_t R^f_{0,t}, \quad t = 0, 1, \dots, T,$$

and thus

$$\frac{\xi_s}{\xi_t} = \frac{\zeta_s}{\zeta_t} R^f_{t,s}, \quad t < s \leq T. \tag{12.11}$$

We now have that

$$\begin{aligned}
\mathrm{E}^{\mathbb{Q}}_t\left[\frac{P_{it'}}{R^f_{t,t'}} + \sum_{s=t+1}^{t'} \frac{D_{is}}{R^f_{t,s}}\right] &= \mathrm{E}^{\mathbb{Q}}_t\left[\frac{P_{it'}}{R^f_{t,t'}}\right] + \sum_{s=t+1}^{t'} \mathrm{E}^{\mathbb{Q}}_t\left[\frac{D_{is}}{R^f_{t,s}}\right] \\
&= \mathrm{E}_t\left[\frac{\xi_{t'}}{\xi_t}\frac{P_{it'}}{R^f_{t,t'}}\right] + \sum_{s=t+1}^{t'} \mathrm{E}_t\left[\frac{\xi_s}{\xi_t}\frac{D_{is}}{R^f_{t,s}}\right] \\
&= \mathrm{E}_t\left[\frac{\xi_{t'}}{\xi_t}\frac{P_{it'}}{R^f_{t,t'}} + \sum_{s=t+1}^{t'} \frac{\xi_s}{\xi_t}\frac{D_{is}}{R^f_{t,s}}\right] \\
&= \mathrm{E}_t\left[\frac{\zeta_{t'}}{\zeta_t} P_{it'} + \sum_{s=t+1}^{t'} \frac{\zeta_s}{\zeta_t} D_{is}\right] \\
&= P_{it},
\end{aligned}$$

as was to be shown. Here the second equality is due to the relation (12.3), the fourth equality comes from inserting Eq. (12.11), and the final equality holds since ζ is a state-price deflator.

(ii) To show that ζ defined in Eq. (12.10) satisfies the appropriate pricing condition, follow the steps in part (i) of the proof in the reverse order. □

Combining the relation between risk-neutral measures and state-price deflators with the results on the existence and uniqueness of state-price deflators derived in Section 4.3, we can draw the following conclusions:

Theorem 12.5 *Assume that a bank account is traded. Prices admit no arbitrage if and only if a risk-neutral probability measure exists. An arbitrage-free market is complete if and only if there is a unique risk-neutral probability measure.*

In the continuous-time framework some technical conditions have to be added or the definition of arbitrage must be slightly adjusted, see for example Björk (2009). In that framework, we know from Chapter 4 that a state-price deflator is of the form

$$\zeta_t = \exp\left\{-\int_0^t r_s^f\, ds - \frac{1}{2}\int_0^t \|\boldsymbol{\lambda}_s\|^2\, ds - \int_0^t \boldsymbol{\lambda}_s^\top\, d\boldsymbol{z}_s\right\}, \tag{12.12}$$

where $\boldsymbol{\lambda} = (\boldsymbol{\lambda}_t)$ is a market price of risk process so that

$$\boldsymbol{\mu}_t + \boldsymbol{\delta}_t - r_t^f \mathbf{1} = \underline{\underline{\sigma}}_t \boldsymbol{\lambda}_t.$$

The corresponding risk-neutral probability measure is defined by

$$\frac{d\mathbb{Q}}{d\mathbb{P}} = R_{0,T}^f \zeta_T = e^{\int_0^T r_s^f\, ds}\zeta_T = \exp\left\{-\frac{1}{2}\int_0^T \|\boldsymbol{\lambda}_s\|^2\, ds - \int_0^T (\boldsymbol{\lambda}_s)^\top\, d\boldsymbol{z}_s\right\}$$

and

$$\xi_t = \mathrm{E}_t\left[\frac{d\mathbb{Q}}{d\mathbb{P}}\right] = \exp\left\{-\frac{1}{2}\int_0^t \|\boldsymbol{\lambda}_s\|^2\, ds - \int_0^t (\boldsymbol{\lambda}_s)^\top\, d\boldsymbol{z}_s\right\}.$$

It follows by the Girsanov Theorem 12.2 that the process $\boldsymbol{z}^{\mathbb{Q}} = (\boldsymbol{z}^{\mathbb{Q}})_{t\in[0,T]}$ defined by $\boldsymbol{z}_0^{\mathbb{Q}} = \mathbf{0}$ and

$$d\boldsymbol{z}_t^{\mathbb{Q}} = d\boldsymbol{z}_t + \boldsymbol{\lambda}_t\, dt$$

is a standard Brownian motion under the risk-neutral probability measure. We can then transform the dynamics of any process $X = (X_t)_{t\in[0,T]}$ as follows:

$$\begin{aligned}
dX_t &= \mu_{Xt}\, dt + \boldsymbol{\sigma}_{Xt}^\top\, d\boldsymbol{z}_t \\
&= \mu_{Xt}\, dt + \boldsymbol{\sigma}_{Xt}^\top\left(d\boldsymbol{z}_t^{\mathbb{Q}} - \boldsymbol{\lambda}_t\, dt\right) \\
&= \left(\mu_{Xt} - \boldsymbol{\sigma}_{Xt}^\top \boldsymbol{\lambda}_t\right)\, dt + \boldsymbol{\sigma}_{Xt}^\top d\boldsymbol{z}_t^{\mathbb{Q}}.
\end{aligned}$$

The instantaneous sensitivity is unchanged, but the product of the sensitivity vector and the market price of risk is subtracted from the drift. In particular, for a price process we get

$$\begin{aligned}
dP_{it} &= P_{it}\left[\mu_{it}\, dt + \boldsymbol{\sigma}_{it}^\top\, d\boldsymbol{z}_t\right] \\
&= P_{it}\left[\left(\mu_{it} - \boldsymbol{\sigma}_{it}^\top \boldsymbol{\lambda}_t\right)\, dt + \boldsymbol{\sigma}_{it}^\top\, d\boldsymbol{z}_t^{\mathbb{Q}}\right] \\
&= P_{it}\left[\left(r_t^f - \delta_{it}\right)\, dt + \boldsymbol{\sigma}_{it}^\top\, d\boldsymbol{z}_t^{\mathbb{Q}}\right],
\end{aligned}$$

where the last equality follows from the definition of a market price of risk. Again we see that the risk-neutral expectation of the total instantaneous rate of return is identical to the risk-free interest rate.

12.3.3 Valuation with Risk-Neutral Probabilities

From the pricing condition in the definition of a risk-neutral probability measure, it is clear that the valuation of an asset requires knowledge of the joint risk-neutral probability distribution of the risk-free discount factor $(R^f_{t,s})^{-1}$ and the asset dividend D_{is}. More precisely, we have to know the covariance under the risk-neutral probability measure of the two variables. For example, in the discrete-time setting, Eq. (12.6) implies that

$$P_{it} = \sum_{s=t+1}^{T} \left(\mathrm{E}_t^{\mathbb{Q}} \left[\left(R^f_{t,s} \right)^{-1} \right] \mathrm{E}_t^{\mathbb{Q}} \left[D_{is} \right] + \mathrm{Cov}_t^{\mathbb{Q}} \left[\left(R^f_{t,s} \right)^{-1}, D_{is} \right] \right).$$

Note that $\mathrm{E}_t^{\mathbb{Q}} \left[\left(R^f_{t,s} \right)^{-1} \right] = B_t^s$, the time t price of a zero-coupon bond maturing with a unit payment at time s. Therefore, we can rewrite the above equation as

$$P_{it} = \sum_{s=t+1}^{T} B_t^s \left(\mathrm{E}_t^{\mathbb{Q}} \left[D_{is} \right] + \frac{\mathrm{Cov}_t^{\mathbb{Q}} \left[\left(R^f_{t,s} \right)^{-1}, D_{is} \right]}{B_t^s} \right).$$

Example 12.3 Consider the two-period economy illustrated in Figs. 2.1 and 2.2 and also studied in Exercise 4.8. There are six states. The real-world state probabilities and the assumed values of the state-price deflator at time 1 and time 2 are listed in left-most columns of Table 12.2. Figure 12.1 illustrates the economy as a two-period tree. Each state corresponds to a path through the tree. Two numbers are written along each branch. The left-most number is the

Table 12.2. $\mathbb{P}$, $\mathbb{Q}$, R^f, and ζ in Example 12.3.

ω	p	ζ_1	ζ_2/ζ_1	ζ_2	R^f_1	$R^f_{0,2}$	$\frac{d\mathbb{Q}}{d\mathbb{P}}$	q
1	0.24	1.2	1	1.2	1.0714	1.1398	1.3678	0.3283
2	0.06	1.2	0.6667	0.8	1.0714	1.1398	0.9119	0.0547
3	0.04	1	1	1	1.0989	1.1690	1.1690	0.0468
4	0.16	1	0.9	0.9	1.0989	1.1690	1.0521	0.1683
5	0.2	1	0.9	0.9	1.0989	1.1690	1.0521	0.2104
6	0.3	0.6	0.9	0.54	1.1111	1.1820	0.6383	0.1915

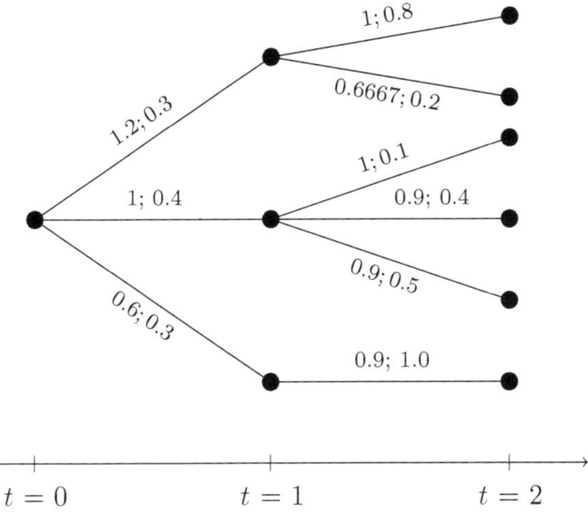

Fig. 12.1. The state-price deflator and real-world probabilities in Example 12.3.

value of the next-period deflator along that branch (ζ_1 over the first period and ζ_2/ζ_1 over the second period). The right-most number is the conditional real-world probability of that branch. The conditional probabilities can be computed from the state probabilities, for example the conditional probability for the upward branch leaving the upper node at time 1 is the probability that state 1 is realized given that it is known that the true state is either 1 or 2, that is $0.24/(0.24 + 0.06) = 0.8$.

Before the risk-neutral probabilities can be computed, we have to find the gross rate of return $R^f_{0,2} = R^f_0 R^f_1$ on the bank account. We can identify this from the state-price deflator and the real-world probabilities. Over the first period the risk-free gross rate of return is

$$R^f_0 = \frac{1}{\mathrm{E}[\zeta_1]} = \frac{1}{0.3 \times 1.2 + 0.4 \times 1 + 0.3 \times 0.6} = \frac{1}{0.94} \approx 1.0638.$$

Over the second period the risk-free gross rate of return depends on the information at time 1. In the upper node at time 1 the one-period risk-free gross rate of return is

$$R^f_1 = \frac{1}{\mathrm{E}_1[\zeta_2/\zeta_1]} = \frac{1}{0.8 \times 1 + 0.2 \times 0.6667} = \frac{1}{0.9333} \approx 1.0714.$$

Similarly, $R^f_1 \approx 1.0989$ in the middle node and $R^f_1 \approx 1.1111$ in the lower node at time 1. Now the risk-neutral probabilities can be computed as shown in the right-most part of Table 12.2.

Given the risk-neutral probabilities of each state, we can compute the conditional risk-neutral probabilities of transitions from one point in time to the next, exactly as for the real-world probabilities. Together with the one-period risk-free returns, the conditional risk-neutral probabilities contain all the necessary information to price a given dividend process by backwards recursions through the tree. This information is illustrated in Fig. 12.2. The conditional risk-neutral probabilities can also be computed directly from the conditional real-world probabilities and the risk-free return and the state-price deflator for that transition. For example, the conditional risk-neutral probability of the upper branch leaving the upper node at time 1 equals $1.0714 \times 1 \times 0.8 \approx 0.8571$.

Let us compute the price process of an asset with the dividends written below or to the right of the nodes in Fig. 12.3 (this is asset 2 from Exercise 4.8). The ex-dividend price in the upper node at time 1 is

$$P_1^u = \frac{1}{1.0714}\,(0.8571 \times 2 + 0.1429 \times 1) \approx 1.7333.$$

Similarly, the time 1 prices in the middle and lower node are $P_1^m = 2.27$ and $P_1^l = 2.7$, respectively. The time 0 price is then computed as

$$\begin{aligned} P_0 &= \frac{1}{1.0638}\,(0.3830 \times [1.7333 + 2] + 0.4255 \times [2.27 + 3] + 0.1915 \times [2.7 + 4]) \\ &= 4.658. \end{aligned}$$

□

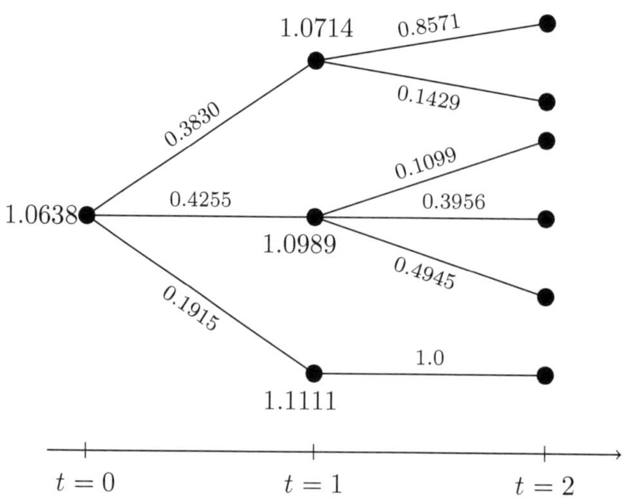

Fig. 12.2. Risk-neutral probabilities and one-period risk-free returns in Example 12.3.

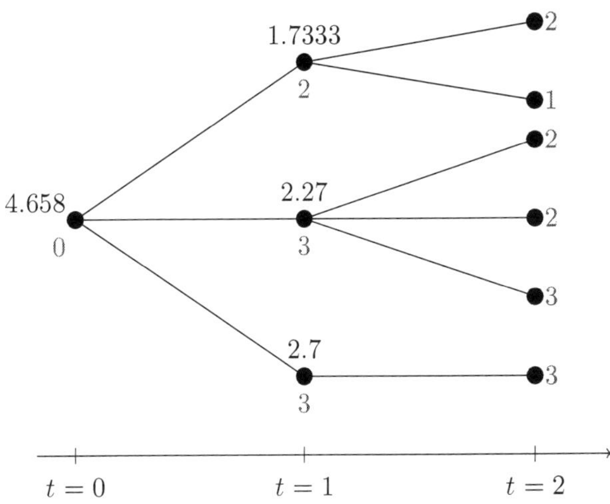

Fig. 12.3. Risk-neutral valuation of a dividend process in Example 12.3.

12.4 FORWARD RISK-ADJUSTED PROBABILITY MEASURES

When valuing an asset with the risk-neutral valuation approach, we have to know the risk-neutral covariance between the risk-free discount factor $(R^f_{t,s})^{-1}$ and the asset dividend D_{is}. Except for simple cases, such covariances are hard to compute analytically. In this section we introduce an alternative probability measure where we do not need to deal with such covariances. The downside is that we have to use a separate probability measure for each payment date.

12.4.1 Definition

We define the so-called forward risk-adjusted probability measures as follows:

Definition 12.2 *Consider a financial market in which a zero-coupon bond maturing at time $s \in \mathcal{T}$ with a face value of one is traded. A probability measure $\mathbb{Q}^s$ is called a* forward risk-adjusted probability measure *for maturity s if the following conditions are satisfied:*

(i) $\mathbb{P}$ and $\mathbb{Q}^s$ are equivalent;

(ii) the Radon–Nikodym derivative $\frac{d\mathbb{Q}^s}{d\mathbb{P}}$ has finite variance;

(iii) the time t price of a dividend paid at time $s \geq t$ equals the product of the zero-coupon bond price B^s_t and the $\mathbb{Q}^s$-expectation of the dividend.

Sometimes the measure $\mathbb{Q}^s$ is just called a forward measure for maturity s. Some authors also use the names forward neutral measure and forward martingale measure. Apparently, forward measures were introduced by Jamshidian (1987) and Geman (1989).

It follows from the definition that the time t price of a discrete-time dividend process $D_i = (D_{is})$ can be computed as

$$P_{it} = \sum_{s=t+1}^{T} B_t^s \, \mathrm{E}_t^{\mathbb{Q}^s}[D_{is}].$$

No covariance or joint distribution is necessary, but a separate probability measure must be used for each payment date. If you trust the market valuation of bonds, you can observe B_t^s in the bond market and you only have to find the expected dividend under the appropriate forward measure. If zero-coupon bonds are not traded, implicit zero-coupon bond prices can be derived or estimated from market prices of traded coupon bonds, see for example Munk (2011, Ch. 2).

The word *forward* can be explained as follows. A forward (contract) on a given asset, say asset i, is a binding agreement between two parties stipulating that one party has to sell a unit of the asset to the other party at a given future point in time, say time s, for a price already set today. The (unique) delivery price that ensures that the present value of this contract equals zero is called the forward price of asset i with delivery at time s. We will show in Theorem 13.1 that if asset i pays no dividends before time s, the forward price for delivery at time s equals P_{it}/B_t^s, that is the current price of the asset 'discounted forward in time' using the zero-coupon bond price maturing at the delivery date. The $\mathbb{Q}^s$-measure is defined such that the $\mathbb{Q}^s$-expectation of the dividend equals the forward price of the asset with delivery at time s (in case of no intermediary dividends).

12.4.2 Relation to State-Price Deflators and Risk-Neutral Measures

The time 0 price of a dividend payment of D_s at time s is given by both $\mathrm{E}[\zeta_s D_s]$ and

$$B_0^s \, \mathrm{E}^{\mathbb{Q}^s}[D_s] = B_0^s \, \mathrm{E}\left[\frac{d\mathbb{Q}^s}{d\mathbb{P}} D_s\right].$$

Therefore, a forward measure for maturity s is related to a state-price deflator through

$$B_0^s \frac{d\mathbb{Q}^s}{d\mathbb{P}} = \zeta_s \quad \Leftrightarrow \quad \frac{d\mathbb{Q}^s}{d\mathbb{P}} = \frac{\zeta_s}{B_0^s} = \frac{\zeta_s}{\mathrm{E}[\zeta_s]}.$$

The zero-coupon bond price and therefore the Radon–Nikodym derivative $\frac{d\mathbb{Q}^s}{d\mathbb{P}}$ only 'make sense' up to time s. Results on the existence and uniqueness of $\mathbb{Q}^s$ follow from the corresponding conclusions about state-price deflators.

In terms of a risk-neutral probability measure $\mathbb{Q}$, the time 0 value of the dividend D_s is $\mathrm{E}^{\mathbb{Q}}[(R^f_{0,s})^{-1}D_s]$ and therefore a forward measure for maturity s is related to a risk-neutral probability measure through the equation

$$B_0^s \frac{d\mathbb{Q}^s}{d\mathbb{Q}} = \left(R^f_{0,s}\right)^{-1} \quad \Leftrightarrow \quad \frac{d\mathbb{Q}^s}{d\mathbb{Q}} = \left(B_0^s\right)^{-1}\left(R^f_{0,s}\right)^{-1} = \frac{\left(R^f_{0,s}\right)^{-1}}{\mathrm{E}^{\mathbb{Q}}\left[\left(R^f_{0,s}\right)^{-1}\right]}.$$

In a continuous-time framework, the last equality can be rewritten as

$$\frac{d\mathbb{Q}^s}{d\mathbb{Q}} = \frac{e^{-\int_0^s r^f_u\,du}}{\mathrm{E}^{\mathbb{Q}}\left[e^{-\int_0^s r^f_u\,du}\right]}.$$

If the future short-term interest rates are non-random, we see that the forward measure for maturity s and the risk-neutral probability measure will assign identical probabilities to all events that are decidable at time s, that is $\mathbb{Q}^s = \mathbb{Q}$ on $\mathcal{F}_s$. In a one-period economy, $\mathbb{Q}$ and $\mathbb{Q}^1$ are always identical.

Assume a continuous-time setting and write the dynamics of the zero-coupon bond price maturing at time s as

$$dB_t^s = B_t^s\left[\left(r^f_t + \left(\boldsymbol{\sigma}_t^s\right)^{\top}\boldsymbol{\lambda}_t\right)dt + \left(\boldsymbol{\sigma}_t^s\right)^{\top} d\boldsymbol{z}_t\right].$$

This implies that

$$1 = B_s^s = B_0^s \exp\left\{\int_0^s \left(r^f_t + \left(\boldsymbol{\sigma}_t^s\right)^{\top}\boldsymbol{\lambda}_t - \frac{1}{2}\|\boldsymbol{\sigma}_t^s\|^2\right)dt + \int_0^s \left(\boldsymbol{\sigma}_t^s\right)^{\top} d\boldsymbol{z}_t\right\},$$

which immediately gives an expression for $1/B_0^s$. Combining this with Eq. (12.12), we conclude that the Radon–Nikodym derivative of the forward measure with respect to the real-world probability measure is

$$\frac{d\mathbb{Q}^s}{d\mathbb{P}} = \frac{\zeta_s}{B_0^s} = \exp\left\{-\frac{1}{2}\int_0^s \|\boldsymbol{\lambda}_t - \boldsymbol{\sigma}_t^s\|^2\,dt - \int_0^s \left(\boldsymbol{\lambda}_t - \boldsymbol{\sigma}_t^s\right)^{\top} d\boldsymbol{z}_t\right\}.$$

According to the Girsanov Theorem 12.2 the process $\boldsymbol{z}^s = (\boldsymbol{z}^s)_{t\in[0,T]}$ defined by $\boldsymbol{z}_0^s = \boldsymbol{0}$ and

$$d\boldsymbol{z}_t^s = d\boldsymbol{z}_t + \left(\boldsymbol{\lambda}_t - \boldsymbol{\sigma}_t^s\right)dt$$

is a standard Brownian motion under the forward measure for maturity s. The dynamics of any process $X = (X_t)_{t\in[0,T]}$ is transformed via

Table 12.3. The $\mathbb{Q}^2$-probabilities in Example 12.4.

ω	p	ζ_2	$\frac{d\mathbb{Q}^2}{d\mathbb{P}}$	$q^{(2)}$
1	0.24	1.2	1.3921	0.3341
2	0.06	0.8	0.9281	0.0557
3	0.04	1	1.1601	0.0464
4	0.16	0.9	1.0441	0.1671
5	0.2	0.9	1.0441	0.2088
6	0.3	0.54	0.6265	0.1879

$$dX_t = \mu_{Xt}\,dt + \boldsymbol{\sigma}_{Xt}^{\top}\,d\boldsymbol{z}_t = \left(\mu_{Xt} - \boldsymbol{\sigma}_{Xt}^{\top}\left(\boldsymbol{\lambda}_t - \boldsymbol{\sigma}_t^{s}\right)\right)\,dt + \boldsymbol{\sigma}_{Xt}^{\top} d\boldsymbol{z}_t^{s} \tag{12.13}$$

and for a price process the analogue is

$$dP_{it} = P_{it}\left[\mu_{it}\,dt + \boldsymbol{\sigma}_{it}^{\top}\,d\boldsymbol{z}_t\right] = P_{it}\left[\left(r_t^f - \delta_{it} + \boldsymbol{\sigma}_{it}^{\top}\boldsymbol{\sigma}_t^{s}\right)\,dt + \boldsymbol{\sigma}_{it}^{\top}\,d\boldsymbol{z}_t^{s}\right].$$

12.4.3 Valuation with Forward Measures

The following example illustrates how a forward measure can be used in the valuation of a risky dividend.

Example 12.4 Consider the same two-period economy as in Example 12.3. Let us find the forward measure for maturity at time 2, that is $\mathbb{Q}^2$. First, we must find the price of the zero-coupon bond maturing at time 2:

$$B_0^2 = \mathrm{E}[\zeta_2] = 0.862.$$

Now the forward probabilities of the states can be computed as $q_\omega^{(2)} = \zeta_2(\omega)p_\omega/B_0^2$ yielding the numbers in Table 12.3. Note that the forward probabilities are different from the risk-neutral probabilities computed in Table 12.2.

Given the forward probabilities for maturity 2, it is easy to value a dividend received at time 2. The time 0 value of the time 2 dividend illustrated in Fig. 12.3 is

$$\begin{aligned} B_0^2\,\mathrm{E}^{\mathbb{Q}^2}[D_2] &= 0.862 \times \left(1 \times q_2^{(2)} + 2 \times [q_1^{(2)} + q_3^{(2)} + q_4^{(2)}] + 3 \times [q_5^{(2)} + q_6^{(2)}]\right) \\ &= 2.018. \end{aligned}$$

The dividend received at time 1 is not valued using the forward measure for maturity 2 but with the forward measure for time 1, that is $\mathbb{Q}^1$. The forward measure at time 1 only assigns probabilities to the decidable events at time 1, that is the events $\{1,2\}$, $\{3,4,5\}$, $\{6\}$, and unions of these events. Since the one-period bond is the risk-free asset over the first period, the $\mathbb{Q}^1$-probabilities are identical to the risk-neutral probabilities of these events, which are depicted in

Fig. 12.2. Note that these are different from the $\mathbb{Q}^2$-probabilities of the same events, for example $q_1^{(2)} + q_2^{(2)} = 0.3898$ while $q_1 + q_2 = 0.3830$. The time 0 value of the time 1 dividend illustrated in Fig. 12.3 is

$$B_0^1 \,\mathrm{E}^{\mathbb{Q}^1}[D_1] = (R_0^f)^{-1}\,\mathrm{E}^{\mathbb{Q}}[D_1] = 2.64$$

so that the total time 0 value of the asset is $2.64 + 2.018 = 4.658$ as found in Example 12.3. Exercise 12.3 has more on the forward measures in this example. □

12.5 GENERAL RISK-ADJUSTED PROBABILITY MEASURES

Consider an asset with a single dividend payment of D_s at time s. Using the risk-neutral probability measure $\mathbb{Q}$ the price at time $t < s$ of this asset is

$$P_t = \mathrm{E}_t^{\mathbb{Q}}\left[\left(R_{t,s}^f\right)^{-1} D_s\right].$$

If we invest 1 in the bank account at time 0 and roll-over at the short-term interest rate, the value at time t will be $P_t^f = R_{0,t}^f$. We can think of $P^f = (P_t^f)$ as the price process of the bank account. Since $R_{t,s}^f = R_{0,s}^f / R_{0,t}^f = P_s^f / P_t^f$, we can rewrite the above equation as

$$\frac{P_t}{P_t^f} = \mathrm{E}_t^{\mathbb{Q}}\left[\frac{D_s}{P_s^f}\right].$$

Both the current price and the future dividend of the asset are measured relative to the price of the bank account, that is the bank account is used as the numeraire. By the Law of Iterated Expectations (Theorem 2.1),

$$\frac{P_t}{P_t^f} = \mathrm{E}_t^{\mathbb{Q}}\left[\mathrm{E}_{t'}^{\mathbb{Q}}\left[\frac{D_s}{P_s^f}\right]\right] = \mathrm{E}_t^{\mathbb{Q}}\left[\frac{P_{t'}}{P_{t'}^f}\right], \quad t < t' \le s,$$

so the relative price process (P_t / P_t^f) is a $\mathbb{Q}$-martingale.

Valuation with the forward measure for maturity s involves using the zero-coupon bond maturing at s as the numeraire. The price of the bond B_t^s converges to its face value of 1 as $t \to s$. If we let $B_s^s = 1$ denote the cum-dividend price of the bond at maturity, the price P_t of the asset paying D_s at time $s > t$ will satisfy

$$\frac{P_t}{B_t^s} = \mathrm{E}_t^{\mathbb{Q}^s}\left[\frac{D_s}{B_s^s}\right]$$

from which it is clear that the zero-coupon bond is used as a numeraire. The relative price process (P_t/B_t^s) is a $\mathbb{Q}^s$-martingale.

In fact we can use any asset or self-financing trading strategy having a strictly positive price process as the numeraire and find an equivalent probability measure under which the relative price processes are martingales. Recall from Chapter 3 the definition of the value process $V^{\boldsymbol{\theta}} = (V_t^{\boldsymbol{\theta}})_{t\in\mathcal{T}}$ associated with a self-financing trading strategy $\boldsymbol{\theta}$. We say that $\boldsymbol{\theta}$ has a strictly positive value process if $V_t^{\boldsymbol{\theta}} > 0$ with probability 1 for all $t \in \mathcal{T}$.

Definition 12.3 *Let $\boldsymbol{\theta}$ be a self-financing trading strategy with a strictly positive value process $V^{\boldsymbol{\theta}}$. A probability measure $\mathbb{Q}^{\boldsymbol{\theta}}$ is said to be a risk-adjusted measure for $\boldsymbol{\theta}$ if the following conditions are satisfied:*

(i) $\mathbb{P}$ and $\mathbb{Q}^{\boldsymbol{\theta}}$ are equivalent;

(ii) the Radon–Nikodym derivative $\frac{d\mathbb{Q}^{\boldsymbol{\theta}}}{d\mathbb{P}}$ has finite variance;

(iii) the time t price of an asset paying a dividend of D_s at time $s > t$ is

$$P_t = V_t^{\boldsymbol{\theta}}\, \mathrm{E}_t^{\mathbb{Q}^{\boldsymbol{\theta}}}\left[\frac{D_s}{V_s^{\boldsymbol{\theta}}}\right]. \tag{12.14}$$

Clearly, the pricing condition (12.14) can be rewritten as

$$\frac{P_t}{V_t^{\boldsymbol{\theta}}} = \mathrm{E}_t^{\mathbb{Q}^{\boldsymbol{\theta}}}\left[\frac{D_s}{V_s^{\boldsymbol{\theta}}}\right],$$

and the relative price process $(P_t/V_t^{\boldsymbol{\theta}})$ is a $\mathbb{Q}^{\boldsymbol{\theta}}$-martingale. Since the trading strategy $\boldsymbol{\theta}$ is self-financing, its gross rate of return between t and s will be $R_{t,s}^{\boldsymbol{\theta}} = V_s^{\boldsymbol{\theta}}/V_t^{\boldsymbol{\theta}}$ so that the pricing condition can also be written as

$$P_t = \mathrm{E}_t^{\mathbb{Q}^{\boldsymbol{\theta}}}\left[\left(R_{t,s}^{\boldsymbol{\theta}}\right)^{-1} D_s\right]. \tag{12.15}$$

For a full discrete dividend process $D_i = (D_{it})_{t=1,2,\dots,T}$, the price will be

$$P_{it} = V_t^{\boldsymbol{\theta}}\, \mathrm{E}_t^{\mathbb{Q}^{\boldsymbol{\theta}}}\left[\sum_{s=t+1}^{T} \frac{D_{is}}{V_s^{\boldsymbol{\theta}}}\right].$$

Comparing the pricing expressions involving expectations under $\mathbb{P}$ and $\mathbb{Q}^{\boldsymbol{\theta}}$, we see that the Radon–Nikodym derivative $\frac{d\mathbb{Q}^{\boldsymbol{\theta}}}{d\mathbb{P}}$ is linked to a state-price deflator through the relations

$$\zeta_t = \frac{V_0^{\boldsymbol{\theta}}}{V_t^{\boldsymbol{\theta}}}\, \mathrm{E}_t\left[\frac{d\mathbb{Q}^{\boldsymbol{\theta}}}{d\mathbb{P}}\right], \quad \frac{d\mathbb{Q}^{\boldsymbol{\theta}}}{d\mathbb{P}} = \zeta_T \frac{V_T^{\boldsymbol{\theta}}}{V_0^{\boldsymbol{\theta}}}.$$

Now take a continuous-time framework and write the real-world dynamics of the value of the numeraire as

$$dV_t^{\theta} = V_t^{\theta}\left[\left(r_t^f + \left(\sigma_t^{\theta}\right)^{\top}\lambda_t\right)dt + \left(\sigma_t^{\theta}\right)^{\top}dz_t\right],$$

which implies that

$$\frac{V_T^{\theta}}{V_0^{\theta}} = \exp\left\{\int_0^T \left(r_t^f + \left(\sigma_t^{\theta}\right)^{\top}\lambda_t - \frac{1}{2}\|\sigma_t^{\theta}\|^2\right)dt + \int_0^T \left(\sigma_t^{\theta}\right)^{\top}dz_t\right\}.$$

Hence,

$$\frac{d\mathbb{Q}^{\theta}}{d\mathbb{P}} = \zeta_T\frac{V_T^{\theta}}{V_0^{\theta}} = \exp\left\{-\frac{1}{2}\int_0^T \|\lambda_t - \sigma_t^{\theta}\|^2\,dt - \int_0^T \left(\lambda_t - \sigma_t^{\theta}\right)^{\top}dz_t\right\},$$

and it follows from the Girsanov Theorem 12.2 that the process z^{θ} defined by

$$dz_t^{\theta} = dz_t + \left(\lambda_t - \sigma_t^{\theta}\right)dt$$

is a standard Brownian motion under the measure $\mathbb{Q}^{\theta}$. The dynamics of any process $X = (X_t)_{t\in[0,T]}$ is transformed via

$$dX_t = \mu_{Xt}\,dt + \sigma_{Xt}^{\top}\,dz_t = \left(\mu_{Xt} - \sigma_{Xt}^{\top}\left(\lambda_t - \sigma_t^{\theta}\right)\right)dt + \sigma_{Xt}^{\top}dz_t^{\theta}$$

and for a price process the analogue is

$$dP_{it} = P_{it}\left[\mu_{it}\,dt + \sigma_{it}^{\top}\,dz_t\right] = P_{it}\left[\left(r_t^f - \delta_{it} + \sigma_{it}^{\top}\sigma_t^{\theta}\right)dt + \sigma_{it}^{\top}\,dz_t^{\theta}\right].$$

In particular for the numeraire itself,

$$dV_t^{\theta} = V_t^{\theta}\left[\left(r_t^f + \|\sigma_t^{\theta}\|^2\right)dt + \left(\sigma_t^{\theta}\right)^{\top}dz_t^{\theta}\right]. \qquad (12.16)$$

Suppose we want to use asset j as a numeraire. If asset j does not pay any dividends in the relevant time period, a position in asset j is just a very special self-financing portfolio and the above analysis is directly applicable. If asset j pays dividends, we have to be more careful. Let δ_j be the dividend yield process and P_j the price process of asset j. Then, beginning at time t, a self-financing portfolio is defined by holding $A_{ju} = \exp\{\int_t^u \delta_{jv}\,dv\}$ units of the asset at time $u \geq t$. The continuously received dividends are reinvested in the asset itself as explained in Section 3.2.3. The time u value of the position is thus $V_{ju} = A_{ju}P_{ju}$, $u \geq t$. Since this is the (positive) value process of a self-financing trading strategy, we can use it as a numeraire. Let $\mathbb{Q}^j$ denote the associated risk-adjusted measure. Then Eq. (12.14) implies that the time t price of an asset paying a dividend of D_s at time $s > t$ is

$$P_t = V_{jt}\,\mathrm{E}_t^{\mathbb{Q}^j}\left[\frac{D_s}{V_{js}}\right] = P_{jt}\,\mathrm{E}_t^{\mathbb{Q}^j}\left[\exp\left\{-\int_t^s \delta_{jv}\,dv\right\}\frac{D_s}{P_{js}}\right].$$

The gross return on asset j between time t and time s is $R^j_{t,s} = \exp\{\int_t^s \delta_{jv}\,dv\}P_{js}/P_{jt}$, so we can rewrite the above as

$$P_t = \mathrm{E}_t^{\mathbb{Q}^j}\left[\left(R^j_{t,s}\right)^{-1} D_s\right]$$

in accordance with Eq. (12.15).

Risk-adjusted probability measures are often used in the pricing of derivatives. If the payoff of the derivative is fully determined by some underlying asset, it is sometimes helpful to express the price of the derivative using the risk-adjusted probability measure with the underlying asset as the numeraire. Some examples will be given in Chapter 13.

12.6 CHANGING THE NUMERAIRE WITHOUT CHANGING THE MEASURE

Now consider the following question: is there a trading strategy $\boldsymbol{\theta}$ for which the associated risk-adjusted probability measure is identical to the real-world probability measure, that is $\mathbb{Q}^{\boldsymbol{\theta}} = \mathbb{P}$? The answer is affirmative. The so-called growth-optimal portfolio (or just GOP) strategy does the job.

Let us first consider a one-period setting. Here, the growth-optimal portfolio is defined as the portfolio maximizing the expected log-return (or expected log-growth rate of the invested amount) among all portfolios, that is it solves

$$\max_{\boldsymbol{\pi}} \mathrm{E}[\ln(\boldsymbol{\pi}^\top \boldsymbol{R})] \quad \text{s.t. } \boldsymbol{\pi}^\top \mathbf{1} = 1.$$

The Lagrangian for this problem is $\mathcal{L} = \mathrm{E}[\ln(\boldsymbol{\pi}^\top \boldsymbol{R})] + \nu(1 - \boldsymbol{\pi}^\top \mathbf{1})$, where ν is the Lagrange multiplier, with first-order condition

$$\mathrm{E}\left[\frac{1}{\boldsymbol{\pi}^\top \boldsymbol{R}}\boldsymbol{R}\right] = \nu \mathbf{1}.$$

We cannot solve explicitly for the portfolio $\boldsymbol{\pi}_{\mathrm{GOP}}$ satisfying this equation, but we can see that its gross rate of return $R_{\mathrm{GOP}} = (\boldsymbol{\pi}_{\mathrm{GOP}})^\top \boldsymbol{R}$ satisfies

$$\mathrm{E}\left[\frac{1}{R_{\mathrm{GOP}}}\boldsymbol{R}\right] = \nu \mathbf{1}.$$

Pre-multiplying by any portfolio $\boldsymbol{\pi}$ we get

$$\mathrm{E}\left[\frac{R^{\boldsymbol{\pi}}}{R_{\mathrm{GOP}}}\right] = \nu \boldsymbol{\pi}^\top \mathbf{1} = \nu.$$

In particular, with $\boldsymbol{\pi} = \boldsymbol{\pi}_{\text{GOP}}$, we see that

$$\nu = \mathrm{E}\left[\frac{R_{\text{GOP}}}{R_{\text{GOP}}}\right] = \mathrm{E}[1] = 1.$$

We can thus conclude that for any asset i, we have

$$\mathrm{E}\left[\frac{R_i}{R_{\text{GOP}}}\right] = 1 \quad \Leftrightarrow \quad P_i = \mathrm{E}\left[(R_{\text{GOP}})^{-1} D_i\right]. \tag{12.17}$$

Note that the expectations are under the real-world probability measure.

If the state space is finite, $\Omega = \{1, 2, \dots, S\}$, and the market is complete, it is possible to construct an Arrow–Debreu asset for any state $\omega \in \Omega$, that is an asset with a dividend of 1 if state ω is realized and a zero dividend otherwise. In this case, any portfolio $\boldsymbol{\pi}$ of the basic assets can be seen as a portfolio $\hat{\boldsymbol{\pi}}$ of the S Arrow–Debreu assets. If ψ_ω denotes the state price of state ω, the gross rate of return on the Arrow–Debreu asset for state ω will be a random variable $R^{\text{AD}(\omega)}$, which if state s is realized takes on the value

$$R_s^{\text{AD}(\omega)} = \begin{cases} \frac{1}{\psi_s} & \text{if } s = \omega, \\ 0 & \text{otherwise.} \end{cases}$$

Let $\boldsymbol{R}^{\text{AD}} = \left(R^{\text{AD}(1)}, \dots, R^{\text{AD}(S)}\right)^{\top}$ denote the random return vector of the S Arrow–Debreu assets. The gross rate of return on a portfolio $\hat{\boldsymbol{\pi}}$ of Arrow–Debreu assets will be

$$R_s^{\hat{\pi}} = \hat{\boldsymbol{\pi}}^{\top} \boldsymbol{R}_s^{\text{AD}} = \frac{\hat{\pi}_s}{\psi_s}, \quad s = 1, 2, \dots, S.$$

If we use the first-order condition (12.17) for the Arrow–Debreu asset for state ω, we therefore get

$$1 = \mathrm{E}\left[\frac{R^{\text{AD}(\omega)}}{R_{\text{GOP}}^{\hat{\pi}}}\right] = p_\omega \frac{1/\psi_\omega}{\hat{\pi}_\omega/\psi_\omega} = \frac{p_\omega}{\hat{\pi}_\omega},$$

where p_ω is the real-world probability of state ω. Therefore, in terms of the Arrow–Debreu assets, the GOP consists of p_ω units of the Arrow–Debreu asset for state ω for each $\omega = 1, 2, \dots, S$.

In a multiperiod setting the growth-optimal trading strategy is the trading strategy maximizing $\mathrm{E}[\ln V_T^{\boldsymbol{\pi}}]$ among all self-financing trading strategies. Hence, it also maximizes $\mathrm{E}[\ln(V_T^{\boldsymbol{\pi}}/V_0^{\boldsymbol{\pi}})]$, the expected log-growth rate between time 0 and time T. For now, focus on the discrete-time framework. Note that

$$\ln\left(\frac{V_T^\pi}{V_0^\pi}\right) = \ln\left(\frac{V_1^\pi}{V_0^\pi}\frac{V_2^\pi}{V_1^\pi}\cdots\frac{V_T^\pi}{V_{T-1}^\pi}\right)$$
$$= \ln\left(\frac{V_1^\pi}{V_0^\pi}\right) + \ln\left(\frac{V_2^\pi}{V_1^\pi}\right) + \cdots + \ln\left(\frac{V_T^\pi}{V_{T-1}^\pi}\right)$$
$$= \ln R_1^\pi + \ln R_2^\pi + \cdots + \ln R_T^\pi,$$

where $R_{t+1}^\pi = V_{t+1}^\pi / V_t^\pi$ is the gross rate of return on the trading strategy between time t and time $t+1$, that is the gross rate of return on the portfolio $\boldsymbol{\pi}_t$ chosen at time t. Therefore the growth-optimal trading strategy $\boldsymbol{\pi} = (\boldsymbol{\pi}_t)_{t\in\mathcal{T}}$ is such that each $\boldsymbol{\pi}_t$ maximizes $\mathrm{E}_t[\ln R_{t+1}^{\pi_t}] = \mathrm{E}_t[\ln(\boldsymbol{\pi}_t^\top \boldsymbol{R}_{t+1})]$, where $\boldsymbol{R}_{t+1}$ is the vector of gross rates of return on all the basic assets between time t and time $t+1$. As in the one-period setting, the first-order condition implies that

$$\mathrm{E}_t\left[\frac{R_{i,t+1}}{R_{t+1}^\pi}\right] = 1$$

for all assets i (and portfolios). Again, it is generally not possible to solve explicitly for the portfolio $\boldsymbol{\pi}_t$.

In the continuous-time framework assume that a bank account is traded with instantaneous risk-free rate of return r_t^f and let $\boldsymbol{\pi}_t$ denote the portfolio weights of the instantaneously risky assets. Then the dynamics of the value V_t^π of a self-financing trading strategy $\boldsymbol{\pi} = (\boldsymbol{\pi}_t)_{t\in[0,T]}$ is given by

$$dV_t^\pi = V_t^\pi\left[\left(r_t^f + \boldsymbol{\pi}_t^\top[\boldsymbol{\mu}_t + \boldsymbol{\delta}_t - r_t^f\mathbf{1}]\right)dt + \boldsymbol{\pi}_t^\top \underline{\underline{\sigma}}_t\, d\boldsymbol{z}_t\right],$$

compare Sections 3.3.3 and 6.7. This implies that

$$V_T^\pi = V_0^\pi \exp\left\{\int_0^T \left(r_t^f + \boldsymbol{\pi}_t^\top[\boldsymbol{\mu}_t + \boldsymbol{\delta}_t - r_t^f\mathbf{1}] - \frac{1}{2}\boldsymbol{\pi}_t^\top \underline{\underline{\sigma}}_t \underline{\underline{\sigma}}_t^\top \boldsymbol{\pi}_t\right)dt + \int_0^T \boldsymbol{\pi}_t^\top \underline{\underline{\sigma}}_t\, d\boldsymbol{z}_t\right\},$$

and thus

$$\ln\left(\frac{V_T^\pi}{V_0^\pi}\right) = \int_0^T \left(r_t^f + \boldsymbol{\pi}_t^\top[\boldsymbol{\mu}_t + \boldsymbol{\delta}_t - r_t^f\mathbf{1}] - \frac{1}{2}\boldsymbol{\pi}_t^\top \underline{\underline{\sigma}}_t \underline{\underline{\sigma}}_t^\top \boldsymbol{\pi}_t\right)dt + \int_0^T \boldsymbol{\pi}_t^\top \underline{\underline{\sigma}}_t\, d\boldsymbol{z}_t.$$

If the process $\boldsymbol{\pi}_t^\top \underline{\underline{\sigma}}_t$ is sufficiently nice, the stochastic integral in the above equation will have mean zero so that the growth-optimal trading strategy is maximizing the expectation of the first integral, which can be found by maximizing $\boldsymbol{\pi}_t^\top[\boldsymbol{\mu}_t + \boldsymbol{\delta}_t - r_t^f\mathbf{1}] - \frac{1}{2}\boldsymbol{\pi}_t^\top \underline{\underline{\sigma}}_t \underline{\underline{\sigma}}_t^\top \boldsymbol{\pi}_t$ for each t and each state. The first-order condition implies that

$$\underline{\underline{\sigma}}_t \underline{\underline{\sigma}}_t^\top \boldsymbol{\pi}_t = \boldsymbol{\mu}_t + \boldsymbol{\delta}_t - r_t^f \mathbf{1},$$

which means that

$$\underline{\underline{\sigma}}_t^\top \boldsymbol{\pi}_t = \boldsymbol{\lambda}_t$$

for some market price of risk process $\boldsymbol{\lambda} = (\boldsymbol{\lambda}_t)$. If $\underline{\underline{\sigma}}_t$ is a square, non-singular matrix, the unique GOP strategy is given by the fractions

$$\boldsymbol{\pi}_t = \left(\underline{\underline{\sigma}}_t^{\top}\right)^{-1} \boldsymbol{\lambda}_t = \left(\underline{\underline{\sigma}}_t \underline{\underline{\sigma}}_t^{\top}\right)^{-1} \left(\boldsymbol{\mu}_t + \boldsymbol{\delta}_t - r_t^f \mathbf{1}\right)$$

of wealth invested in the risky assets and the fraction $1 - \boldsymbol{\pi}_t^{\top}\mathbf{1}$ of wealth invested in the risk-free asset. This shows that the GOP strategy is a combination of the instantaneously risk-free asset and the tangency portfolio of risky assets, introduced in Section 6.7. The GOP strategy is the optimal trading strategy for an individual with time-additive logarithmic utility. Substituting the expression for $\boldsymbol{\pi}_t$ back into the value dynamics, we see that the value of the GOP strategy evolves as

$$dV_t^{\pi} = V_t^{\pi} \left[\left(r_t^f + \|\boldsymbol{\lambda}_t\|^2 \right) dt + \boldsymbol{\lambda}_t^{\top} d\boldsymbol{z}_t \right].$$

The value process of the GOP strategy contains sufficient information to price any specific dividend process. Since knowing the value process of the GOP strategy boils down to knowing the risk-free rate process and the market price of risk process, this is not a surprise. Also note that $\zeta_t = V_0^{\pi} / V_t^{\pi}$ defines a state-price deflator.

12.7 CONCLUDING REMARKS

This chapter has introduced several risk-adjusted probability measures and discussed the application of these measures in the pricing of assets. Each risk-adjusted probability measure (in conjunction with the price process for the associated numeraire) is in a one-to-one relation with a state-price deflator. The models for state-price deflators developed in the previous chapters are therefore also models concretizing the risk-adjusted probability measures. For example, the consumption-based CAPM will define a risk-neutral probability measure in terms of the (aggregate) consumption of a given (representative) individual. Any full factor pricing model will also nail down the risk-neutral probability measure.

As discussed in Chapter 4, there is a distinction between *real* state-price deflators and *nominal* state-price deflators. Similarly, we can distinguish between a real risk-neutral probability measure and a nominal risk-neutral probability measure. The real (nominal, respectively) risk-neutral probability measure is defined with a bank account yielding the real (nominal, respectively) short-term risk-free interest rate as the numeraire. In the same manner real and nominal forward measures are defined with a real and nominal, respectively, zero-coupon bond as the numeraire.

12.8 EXERCISES

Exercise 12.1 Show that Eqs. (12.6) and (12.7) are equivalent.

Exercise 12.2 Take a continuous-time framework and assume that $\zeta = (\zeta_t)_{t\in[0,T]}$ is a state-price deflator. What is the $\mathbb{Q}$-dynamics of ζ?

Exercise 12.3 Consider Example 12.4. Compute the conditional $\mathbb{Q}^2$-probabilities of the transitions over the second period of the tree. Compare with conditional $\mathbb{Q}$-probabilities illustrated in Fig. 12.2 and explain why they are (not?) different.

Exercise 12.4 In the same two-period economy considered in Examples 12.3 and 12.4, compute the price of an asset giving a time 1 dividend of 0 in the upper or middle node and 1 in the lower node and a time 2 dividend of 3, 2, 3, 3, 4, or 5 from the top node and down (this is asset 3 in Exercise 4.8).

13

Derivatives

13.1 INTRODUCTION

A derivative is an asset whose dividend(s) and price are derived from the price of another asset, the underlying asset, or the value of some other variable such as an interest rate. The main types of derivatives are forwards, futures, options, and swaps. While a large number of different derivatives are traded in today's financial markets, most of them are variations of these four main types.

A *forward* is the simplest derivative. A forward contract is an agreement between two parties on a given transaction at a given future point in time and at a price that is already fixed when the agreement is made. For example, a forward on a bond is a contract where the parties agree to trade the bond at a future point in time for a price which is already fixed today. This fixed price is usually set so that the value of the contract at the time of inception is equal to zero so that no money changes hands before the delivery date. Forward contracts are not traded or listed at financial exchanges but are traded in over-the-counter (OTC) markets dominated by large financial institutions. For example, forwards on foreign exchange are quite common.

As a forward contract, a *futures* contract is an agreement upon a specified future transaction, for example a trade of a given security. The special feature of a future is that changes in its value are settled continuously throughout the life of the contract (usually once every trading day). This so-called *marking-to-market* ensures that the value of the contract (that is the value of the payments still to come) is zero immediately following a settlement. This procedure makes it practically possible to trade futures at organized exchanges, since there is no need to keep track of when the futures position was originally taken. Futures on many different assets or variables are traded at different exchanges around the world, including futures on stocks, bonds, interest rates, foreign exchange, oil, metals, frozen concentrate orange juice, live cattle, and the temperature in Las Vegas!

An *option* gives the holder the right to make some specified future transaction at terms that are already fixed. A *call* option gives the holder the right to buy a given security at a given price at or before a given date. Conversely, a *put* option gives the holder the right to sell a given security. If the option gives the right to make the transaction at only one given date, the option is said to be *European*-style. If the right can be exercised at any point in time up to some given date, the option is said to be *American*-style. Both European- and American-style options are traded. Options on stocks, bonds, foreign exchange, and many other assets, commodities, and variables are traded at many exchanges around the world and also on the OTC markets. Also options on futures on some asset or variable are traded, that is a derivative on a derivative! In addition, many financial assets or contracts have 'embedded' options. For example, many mortgage-backed bonds and corporate bonds are callable in the sense that the issuer has the right to buy back the bond at a pre-specified price.

A *swap* is an exchange of two dividend streams between two parties. In a 'plain vanilla' interest rate swap, two parties exchange a stream of fixed interest rate payments and a stream of floating interest rate payments. In a currency swap, streams of payments in different currencies are exchanged. Many exotic swaps with special features are widely used.

The markets for derivatives are of an enormous size. Based on BIS statistics published in Bank for International Settlements (2010), henceforth referred to as BIS (2010), Table 13.1 provides some interesting statistics on the size of derivatives markets at organized exchanges. The markets for interest rate derivatives are much larger than the markets for currency- or equity-linked derivatives. The option markets generally dominate futures markets measured by the amounts outstanding, but ranked according to turnover futures markets are larger than options markets.

The BIS statistics also contain information about the size of OTC markets for derivatives. BIS estimates that in June 2009 the total amount outstand-

Table 13.1. Derivatives traded on organized exchanges.

Instruments/ Location	Futures		Options	
	Outstanding	Turnover	Outstanding	Turnover
All markets	21,749	307,315	51,388	137,182
Interest rate	20,623	276,215	46,435	106,523
Currency	164	7677	147	582
Equity index	962	23,423	4807	30,077
North America	10,716	156,160	23,875	55,216
Europe	8054	129,016	26,331	62,937
Asia-Pacific	2446	18,567	310	17,235
Other markets	532	3573	873	1793

Notes: All amounts are in billions of US dollars. The amount outstanding is of December 2009, whereas the turnover figures are for the fourth quarter of 2009

Source: Table 23A in BIS (2010)

Table 13.2. Amounts outstanding (billions of US dollars) on OTC single-currency interest rate derivatives as of June 2009.

Contracts	total	Maturity in years		
		≤ 1	1–5	≥ 5
All interest rate	437,198	159,143	128,301	149,754
Forward rate agreements	46,798	150,630	111,431	126,623
Swaps	341,886			
Options	48,513	8,513	16,870	23,130

Source: Tables 21A and 21C in BIS (2010)

ing on OTC derivative markets was 604,622 billions of US dollars, of which single-currency interest rate derivatives account for 72.3%, currency derivatives account for 8.1%, credit default swaps for 6.0%, equity-linked derivatives for 1.1%, commodity contracts for 0.6%, while the remainder cannot be split into any of these categories, compare Table 19 in BIS (2010). Table 13.2 shows how the interest rate derivatives market can be disaggregated according to instrument and maturity. Approximately 36.7% of these OTC-traded interest rate derivatives are denominated in Euros, 35.3% in US dollars, 13.1% in yen, 7.5% in pounds sterling, and the remaining 7.4% in other currencies, compare Table 21B in BIS (2010).

This chapter gives an introduction to frequently traded derivatives and their valuation. We will specify the payments of these derivatives, discuss the links between different derivatives, and we will also indicate what we can conclude about their prices from general asset pricing theory. Throughout the chapter we assume that prices are arbitrage-free and that a bank account and zero-coupon bonds of relevant maturities are traded so that we can define and work with the risk-neutral probability measures and forward measures introduced in Chapter 12. We will denote the continuously compounded risk-free short-term interest rate by r_t instead of r_t^f.

Section 13.2 deals with forwards and futures, Section 13.3 with options, and Section 13.4 with swaps and swaptions. Some features of American-style derivatives are discussed in Section 13.5.

13.2 FORWARDS AND FUTURES

13.2.1 General Results on Forward Prices and Futures Prices

A forward with maturity date T and delivery price K provides a dividend of $P_T - K$ at time T, where P is the underlying variable, typically the price of an asset or a specific interest rate. If you plan to buy a unit of an asset at time T, you can lock in the effective purchase price with a forward on that asset. Conversely, if you plan to sell a unit of an asset, you can lock in the effective selling price by taking a short position in a forward on the asset, which will give a terminal dividend of $K - P_T$. Of course, forwards can also be used for speculation. If you believe in high values of P_T, you can take a long position in a forward. If you believe in low values of P_T, you can take a short position in a forward.

In terms of a risk-neutral probability measure $\mathbb{Q}$, the time t value of such a future payoff can be written as

$$\begin{aligned} V_t &= \mathrm{E}_t^{\mathbb{Q}}\left[\left(R^f_{t,T}\right)^{-1}(P_T - K)\right] \\ &= \mathrm{E}_t^{\mathbb{Q}}\left[\left(R^f_{t,T}\right)^{-1} P_T\right] - K\,\mathrm{E}_t^{\mathbb{Q}}\left[\left(R^f_{t,T}\right)^{-1}\right] \\ &= \mathrm{E}_t^{\mathbb{Q}}\left[\left(R^f_{t,T}\right)^{-1} P_T\right] - KB_t^T, \end{aligned}$$

where $B_t^T = \mathrm{E}_t^{\mathbb{Q}}[(R^f_{t,T})^{-1}]$ is the price of the zero-coupon bond maturing at time T with a unit payment. Here $R^f_{t,T}$ is the gross rate of return between time t and T on the bank account, that is a roll-over in short risk-free investments, compare the discussion in Section 12.3.

For forwards contracted upon at time t, the delivery price K is typically set so that the value of the forward at time t is zero. This value of K is called the forward price at time t (for the delivery date T) and is denoted by F_t^T. We define the terminal forward price to be $F_T^T = P_T$, the only reasonable price for immediate delivery. Solving the equation $V_t = 0$ for K, we get that the forward price is given by

$$F_t^T = \frac{\mathrm{E}_t^{\mathbb{Q}}\left[\left(R^f_{t,T}\right)^{-1} P_T\right]}{B_t^T}.$$

If the underlying variable is the price of a traded asset with no payments in the period $[t, T]$, we have

$$\mathrm{E}_t^{\mathbb{Q}}\left[\left(R^f_{t,T}\right)^{-1} P_T\right] = P_t$$

so that the forward price can be written as $F_t^T = P_t/B_t^T$. Applying a well-known property of covariances, we have that

$$\mathrm{E}_t^{\mathbb{Q}}\left[\left(R_{t,T}^f\right)^{-1} P_T\right] = \mathrm{Cov}_t^{\mathbb{Q}}\left[\left(R_{t,T}^f\right)^{-1}, P_T\right] + \mathrm{E}_t^{\mathbb{Q}}\left[\left(R_{t,T}^f\right)^{-1}\right] \mathrm{E}_t^{\mathbb{Q}}[P_T]$$
$$= \mathrm{Cov}_t^{\mathbb{Q}}\left[\left(R_{t,T}^f\right)^{-1}, P_T\right] + B_t^T \, \mathrm{E}_t^{\mathbb{Q}}[P_T]$$

and therefore

$$F_t^T = \mathrm{E}_t^{\mathbb{Q}}[P_T] + \frac{\mathrm{Cov}_t^{\mathbb{Q}}\left[\left(R_{t,T}^f\right)^{-1}, P_T\right]}{B_t^T}. \tag{13.1}$$

We can also characterize the forward price in terms of the forward measure for maturity T. The forward price process for contracts with delivery date T is a $\mathbb{Q}^T$-martingale. This is clear from the following considerations. With B_t^T as the numeraire, we have that the forward price F_t^T is set so that

$$\frac{0}{B_t^T} = \mathrm{E}_t^{\mathbb{Q}^T}\left[\frac{P_T - F_t^T}{B_T^T}\right]$$

and hence

$$F_t^T = \mathrm{E}_t^{\mathbb{Q}^T}[P_T] = \mathrm{E}_t^{\mathbb{Q}^T}[F_T^T],$$

which implies that the forward price F_t^T is a $\mathbb{Q}^T$-martingale.

We summarize our findings in the following theorem.

Theorem 13.1 *The forward price for delivery at time T is given by*

$$F_t^T = \frac{\mathrm{E}_t^{\mathbb{Q}}\left[\left(R_{t,T}^f\right)^{-1} P_T\right]}{B_t^T} = \mathrm{E}_t^{\mathbb{Q}^T}[P_T].$$

If the underlying variable is the price of a traded asset with no payments in the period $[t, T]$, the forward price can be written as

$$F_t^T = \frac{P_t}{B_t^T}. \tag{13.2}$$

Note that when Eq. (13.2) holds, the forward price of an asset follows immediately from the spot price of the asset and the price of the zero-coupon bond maturing at the delivery date. No model for the price dynamics of the underlying asset is needed. This is because the forward is perfectly replicated by a portfolio of one unit of the underlying asset and a short position in K zero-coupon bonds maturing at the delivery date of the forward.

Consider now a futures contract with final settlement at time T. The marking-to-market at a given date involves the payment of the change in the so-called futures price of the contract relative to the previous settlement date.

Let Φ_t^T be the futures price at time t. The futures price at the settlement time is by definition equal to the price of the underlying security, $\Phi_T^T = P_T$. At maturity of the contract the futures thus gives a payoff equal to the difference between the price of the underlying asset at that date and the futures price at the previous settlement date. After the last settlement before maturity, the futures is therefore indistinguishable from the corresponding forward contract, so the values of the futures and the forward at that settlement date must be identical. At the next-to-last settlement date before maturity, the futures price is set to that value that ensures that the net present value of the upcoming settlement at the last settlement date before maturity (which depends on this futures price) *and* the final payoff is equal to zero. Similarly at earlier settlement dates. We assume that the futures is marked-to-market at every trading date considered in the model. In the discrete-time framework, the dividend from the futures at time $t+1$ is therefore $\Phi_{t+1}^T - \Phi_t^T$. In a continuous-time setting, the dividend over any infinitesimal interval $[t, t+dt]$ is $d\Phi_t^T$. The following theorem characterizes the futures price:

Theorem 13.2 *The futures price Φ_t^T is a martingale under the risk-neutral probability measure $\mathbb{Q}$. In particular,*

$$\Phi_t^T = \mathrm{E}_t^{\mathbb{Q}}\left[P_T\right]. \tag{13.3}$$

Proof. We give a proof in the discrete-time framework, a proof originally due to Cox, Ingersoll, and Ross (1981b). Then the continuous-time version of the result follows by taking a limit. For a proof based on the same idea but formulated directly in continuous time, see Duffie and Stanton (1992).

Consider a discrete-time setting in which positions can be changed and the futures contracts marked-to-market at times $t, t+\Delta t, t+2\Delta t, \dots, t+N\Delta t \equiv T$. Let R_t^f denote the risk-free gross rate of return between t and $t+\Delta t$ and let $R_{t,t+n\Delta t}^f = R_t^f R_{t+\Delta t}^f \cdots R_{t+(n-1)\Delta t}^f$. The idea is to set up a self-financing strategy that requires an initial investment at time t equal to the futures price Φ_t^T. Hence, at time t, Φ_t^T is invested in the bank account. In addition, R_t^f futures contracts are acquired (at a price of zero).

At time $t+\Delta t$, the deposit at the bank account has grown to $R_t^f \Phi_t^T$. The marking-to-market of the futures position yields a payoff of $R_t^f \left(\Phi_{t+\Delta t}^T - \Phi_t^T\right)$, which is deposited at the bank account. Thus, the balance of the account becomes $R_t^f \Phi_{t+\Delta t}^T$. The position in futures is increased (at no extra costs) to a total of $R_t^f R_{t+\Delta t}^f = R_{t,t+2\Delta t}^f$ contracts.

At time $t+2\Delta t$, the deposit has grown to $R_{t,t+2\Delta t}^f \Phi_{t+\Delta t}^T$. After addition of the marking-to-market payment of $R_{t,t+2\Delta t}^f \left(\Phi_{t+2\Delta t}^T - \Phi_{t+\Delta t}^T\right)$, the new balance of the account is $R_{t,t+2\Delta t}^f \Phi_{t+2\Delta t}^T$.

Continuing this way, the balance of the bank account at time $T = t + N\Delta t$ will be

$$R^f_{t,t+N\Delta t}\Phi^T_{t+N\Delta t} = R^f_{t,T}\Phi^T_T = R^f_{t,T}P_T.$$

This is true for any value of Δt and $\Delta t = 1$ covers our standard discrete-time framework, whereas $\Delta t \to 0$ gives the continuous-time limit.

So a self-financing trading strategy with an initial time t investment of Φ^T_t will give a dividend of $R^f_{t,T}P_T$ at time T. On the other hand, we can value the time T dividend by multiplying by $(R^f_{t,T})^{-1}$ and taking the risk-neutral expectation. Hence,

$$\Phi^T_t = \mathrm{E}^{\mathbb{Q}}_t\left[\left(R^f_{t,T}\right)^{-1} R^f_{t,T}P_T\right] = \mathrm{E}^{\mathbb{Q}}_t[P_T],$$

as was to be shown. □

Note that in order to compute the futures price of an asset we generally have to model the dynamics of the underlying spot price.

Comparing Eq. (13.3) to Eq. (12.8), we see that we can think of the futures price as the price of a traded asset with a continuous dividend given by the product of the current price and the short-term interest rate, that is an asset with a dividend yield equal to the short-term interest rate.

From Eqs. (13.1) and (13.3) we get that the difference between the forward price F^T_t and the futures price Φ^T_t is given by

$$F^T_t - \Phi^T_t = \frac{\mathrm{Cov}^{\mathbb{Q}}_t\left[\left(R^f_{t,T}\right)^{-1}, P_T\right]}{B^T_t}.$$

The forward price and the futures price will only be identical if the two random variables P_T and $(R^f_{t,T})^{-1}$ are uncorrelated under the risk-neutral probability measure. In particular, this is true if the short-term risk-free rate is constant or deterministic.

The forward price is larger [smaller] than the futures price if the variables $(R^f_{t,T})^{-1}$ and P_T are positively [negatively] correlated under the risk-neutral probability measure. An intuitive, heuristic argument for this goes as follows. If the forward price and the futures price are identical, the total undiscounted payments from the futures contract will be equal to the terminal payment of the forward. Suppose the interest rate and the spot price of the underlying asset are positively correlated, which ought to be the case whenever $(R^f_{t,T})^{-1}$ and P_T are negatively correlated. Then the marking-to-market payments of the futures tend to be positive when the interest rate is high and negative when the interest rate is low. So positive payments can be reinvested at a high interest rate, whereas negative payments can be financed at a low interest rate. With such a correlation, the futures contract is clearly more attractive than a forward contract when the futures price and the forward price are identical. To maintain a zero initial value of both contracts, the futures price has to be larger than the forward price. Conversely, if the sign of the correlation is reversed.

If the underlying asset has a constant or deterministic volatility and pays no dividends before time T, we can write the risk-neutral price dynamics as

$$dP_t = P_t \left[r_t\, dt + \sigma(t)\, dz_t^{\mathbb{Q}} \right],$$

where $z^{\mathbb{Q}} = (z_t^{\mathbb{Q}})$ is a standard Brownian motion under the risk-neutral measure $\mathbb{Q}$. If, furthermore, the short-term risk-free rate is constant or follows a Gaussian process as for example in the Vasicek model introduced in Section 11.5.1, the future values of P_T will be lognormally distributed under the risk-neutral measure. In that case, the futures price can be stated in closed form. In Exercise 13.6 you are asked to compute and compare the forward price and the futures price on a zero-coupon bond under the assumptions of the Vasicek model of interest rate dynamics introduced in Section 11.5.1.

13.2.2 Interest Rates Forwards and Futures

Forward interest rates are rates for a future period relative to the time where the rate is set. Many participants in the financial markets may on occasion be interested in 'locking in' an interest rate for a future period, either in order to hedge risk involved with varying interest rates or to speculate in specific changes in interest rates. In the money markets the agents can lock in an interest rate by entering a forward rate agreement (FRA). Suppose the relevant future period is the time interval between T and S, where $S > T$. In principle, a forward rate agreement with a face value H and a contract rate of K involves two payments: a payment of $-H$ at time T and a payment of $H[1 + (S - T)K]$ at time S. (Of course, the payments to the other part of the agreement are H at time T and $-H[1 + (S - T)K]$ at time S.) In practice, the contract is typically settled at time T so that the two payments are replaced by a single payment of $B_T^S H[1 + (S - T)K] - H$ at time T.

Usually the contract rate K is set so that the present value of the future payment(s) is zero at the time the contract is made. Suppose the contract is made at time $t < T$. Then the time t value of the two future payments of the contract is equal to $-HB_t^T + H[1 + (S - T)K]B_t^S$. This is zero if and only if

$$K = \frac{1}{S - T} \left(\frac{B_t^T}{B_t^S} - 1 \right) = L_t^{T,S},$$

compare Eq. (11.4), that is when the contract rate equals the forward rate prevailing at time t for the period between T and S. For this contract rate, we can think of the forward rate agreement having a single payment at time T, which is given by

$$B_T^S H[1 + (S - T)K] - H = H\left(\frac{1 + (S - T)L_t^{T,S}}{1 + (S - T)l_T^S} - 1\right)$$
$$= \frac{(S - T)(L_t^{T,S} - l_T^S)H}{1 + (S - T)l_T^S}. \tag{13.4}$$

The numerator is exactly the interest lost by lending out H from time T to time S at the forward rate given by the FRA rather than the realized spot rate. Of course, this amount may be negative so that a gain is realized. The division by $1 + (S - T)l_T^S$ corresponds to discounting the gain/loss from time S back to time T.

Interest rate futures trade with a very high volume at several international exchanges, for example CME (Chicago Mercantile Exchange), LIFFE (London International Financial Futures & Options Exchange), and MATIF (Marché à Terme International de France). The CME interest rate futures involve the three-month Eurodollar deposit rate and are called Eurodollar futures. The interest rate involved in the futures contracts traded at LIFFE and MATIF is the three-month LIBOR rate on the Euro currency. We shall simply refer to all these contracts as Eurodollar futures and refer to the underlying interest rate as the three-month LIBOR rate, whose value at time t we denote by $l_t^{t+0.25}$.

The price quotation of Eurodollar futures is a bit complicated since the amounts paid in the marking-to-market settlements are not exactly the changes in the quoted futures price. We must therefore distinguish between the *quoted* futures price, $\tilde{\mathcal{E}}_t^T$, and the *actual* futures price, $\mathcal{E}_t^T$, with the settlements being equal to changes in the actual futures price. At the maturity date of the contract, T, the quoted Eurodollar futures price is defined in terms of the prevailing three-month LIBOR rate according to the relation

$$\tilde{\mathcal{E}}_T^T = 100\left(1 - l_T^{T+0.25}\right), \tag{13.5}$$

which using Eq. (11.3) can be rewritten as

$$\tilde{\mathcal{E}}_T^T = 100\left(1 - 4\left(\frac{1}{B_T^{T+0.25}} - 1\right)\right) = 500 - 400\frac{1}{B_T^{T+0.25}}.$$

Traders and analysts typically transform the Eurodollar futures price to an interest rate, the so-called *LIBOR futures rate*, which we denote by φ_t^T and define by

$$\varphi_t^T = 1 - \frac{\tilde{\mathcal{E}}_t^T}{100} \quad \Leftrightarrow \quad \tilde{\mathcal{E}}_t^T = 100\left(1 - \varphi_t^T\right).$$

It follows from Eq. (13.5) that the LIBOR futures rate converges to the three-month LIBOR spot rate, as the maturity of the futures contract approaches.

The actual Eurodollar futures price is given by

$$\mathcal{E}_t^T = 100 - 0.25(100 - \tilde{\mathcal{E}}_t^T) = \frac{1}{4}\left(300 + \tilde{\mathcal{E}}_t^T\right) = 100 - 25\varphi_t^T$$

per 100 dollars of nominal value. It is the change in the actual futures price which is exchanged in the marking-to-market settlements. At the CME the nominal value of the Eurodollar futures is 1 million dollars. A quoted futures price of $\tilde{\mathcal{E}}_t^T = 94.47$ corresponds to a LIBOR futures rate of 5.53% and an actual futures price of

$$\frac{1\,000\,000}{100} \times [100 - 25 \times 0.0553] = 986\,175.$$

If the quoted futures price increases to 94.48 the next day, corresponding to a drop in the LIBOR futures rate of one basis point (0.01 percentage points), the actual futures price becomes

$$\frac{1\,000\,000}{100} \times [100 - 25 \times 0.0552] = 986\,200.$$

An investor with a long position will therefore receive 986 200 − 986 175 = 25 dollars at the settlement at the end of that day.

If we simply sum up the individual settlements without discounting them to the terminal date, the total gain on a long position in a Eurodollar futures contract from t to expiration at T is given by

$$\mathcal{E}_T^T - \mathcal{E}_t^T = \left(100 - 25\varphi_T^T\right) - \left(100 - 25\varphi_t^T\right) = -25\left(\varphi_T^T - \varphi_t^T\right)$$

per 100 dollars of nominal value. Hence, the total gain on a contract with nominal value H is equal to $-0.25\left(\varphi_T^T - \varphi_t^T\right)H$. The gain will be positive if the three-month spot rate at expiration turns out to be below the futures rate when the position was taken. Conversely for a short position. The gain/loss on a Eurodollar futures contract is closely related to the gain/loss on a forward rate agreement, as can be seen from substituting $S = T + 0.25$ into Eq. (13.4). Recall that the rates φ_T^T and $l_T^{T+0.25}$ are identical. However, it should be emphasized that in general the futures rate φ_t^T and the forward rate $L_t^{T,T+0.25}$ will be different due to the marking-to-market of the futures contract.

The final settlement is based on the terminal actual futures price

$$\begin{aligned}
\mathcal{E}_T^T &\equiv 100 - 0.25\left(100 - \tilde{\mathcal{E}}_T^T\right) \\
&= 100 - 0.25\left(400\left[(B_T^{T+0.25})^{-1} - 1\right]\right) \\
&= 100\left[2 - (B_T^{T+0.25})^{-1}\right].
\end{aligned}$$

It follows from Theorem 13.2 that the actual futures price at any earlier point in time t can be computed as

$$\mathcal{E}_t^T = \mathrm{E}_t^{\mathbb{Q}}\left[\mathcal{E}_T^T\right] = 100\left(2 - \mathrm{E}_t^{\mathbb{Q}}\left[(B_T^{T+0.25})^{-1}\right]\right).$$

The quoted futures price is therefore

$$\tilde{\mathcal{E}}_t^T = 4\mathcal{E}_t^T - 300 = 500 - 400\,\mathrm{E}_t^{\mathbb{Q}}\left[(B_T^{T+0.25})^{-1}\right]. \tag{13.6}$$

In several models of interest rate dynamics and bond prices, including the Vasicek and Cox–Ingersoll–Ross models introduced in Chapter 11, the expectation in Eq. (13.6) can be computed in closed form, see for example Munk (2011).

13.3 OPTIONS

In this section, we focus on European options. Some aspects of American options are discussed in Section 13.5.

13.3.1 General Pricing Results for European Options

A European call option with an exercise price of K and expiration at time T gives a dividend at T of

$$C_T = \max(P_T - K, 0),$$

where P_T is the value at time T of the underlying variable of the option. For an option on a traded asset, P_T is the price of the underlying asset at the expiry date. For an option on a given interest rate, P_T denotes the value of this interest rate at the expiry date. With a call option you can speculate in high values of P_T. A call option on an asset offers protection to an investor who wants to purchase the underlying asset at time T. The call option ensures that the investor effectively pays at most K for the underlying asset. The call option price is the price of that protection.

Similarly, a European put option with an exercise price of K and expiration at time T gives a dividend at T of

$$\pi_T = \max(K - P_T, 0).$$

With a put option you can speculate in low values of P_T. A put option offers protection to an investor who wants to sell the underlying asset at time T. The put option ensures that the effective selling price is at least K.

Prices of European call and put options on the same underlying variable are closely related. Since $C_T + K = \pi_T + P_T$, it is clear that

$$C_t + KB_t^T = \pi_t + B_t^T \operatorname{E}_t^{\mathbb{Q}^T}[P_T],$$

where $\mathbb{Q}^T$ is the T-forward martingale measure. In particular, if the underlying variable is the price of a non-dividend paying asset, we have $P_t = B_t^T \operatorname{E}_t^{\mathbb{Q}^T}[P_T]$ and thus the following result:

Theorem 13.3 (Put-call parity). *The prices of a European call option and a European put option on a non-dividend paying asset are related through the equation*

$$C_t + KB_t^T = \pi_t + P_t. \tag{13.7}$$

A portfolio of a call option and K zero-coupon bonds maturing at time T gives exactly the same dividend as a portfolio of a put option and the underlying asset. The put-call parity (13.7) follows by absence of arbitrage. A consequence of the put-call parity is that we can focus on the pricing of European call options. The prices of European put options will then follow immediately.

Now let us focus on the call option. In terms of the forward measure $\mathbb{Q}^T$ for maturity T, the time t price of the option is

$$C_t = B_t^T \operatorname{E}_t^{\mathbb{Q}^T}[\max(P_T - K, 0)]. \tag{13.8}$$

We can rewrite the payoff as

$$C_T = (P_T - K)\,\mathbf{1}_{\{P_T > K\}},$$

where $\mathbf{1}_{\{P_T>K\}}$ is the indicator for the event $P_T > K$. This indicator is a random variable whose value will be 1 if the realized value of P_T turns out to be larger than K and the value is 0 otherwise. Hence, the option price can be rewritten as[1]

$$\begin{aligned} C_t &= B_t^T \operatorname{E}_t^{\mathbb{Q}^T}\left[(P_T - K)\mathbf{1}_{\{P_T>K\}}\right] \\ &= B_t^T \left(\operatorname{E}_t^{\mathbb{Q}^T}\left[P_T\mathbf{1}_{\{P_T>K\}}\right] - K \operatorname{E}_t^{\mathbb{Q}^T}\left[\mathbf{1}_{\{P_T>K\}}\right]\right) \\ &= B_t^T \left(\operatorname{E}_t^{\mathbb{Q}^T}\left[P_T\mathbf{1}_{\{P_T>K\}}\right] - K\mathbb{Q}_t^T(P_T > K)\right) \\ &= B_t^T \operatorname{E}_t^{\mathbb{Q}^T}\left[P_T\mathbf{1}_{\{P_T>K\}}\right] - KB_t^T\mathbb{Q}_t^T(P_T > K). \end{aligned} \tag{13.9}$$

[1] Since the indicator $\mathbf{1}_{\{P_T>K\}}$ takes on the value 1 or 0, its expected value equals 1 times the probability that it will have the value 1 plus 0 times the probability that it will have the value 0, that is the expected value equals the probability that the indicator will have the value 1, which again equals the probability that $P_T > K$.

Here $\mathbb{Q}_t^T(P_T > K)$ denotes the probability (using the probability measure $\mathbb{Q}^T$) of $P_T > K$ given the information known at time t, that is the forward risk-adjusted probability of the option finishing in-the-money.

The term $B_t^T \mathrm{E}_t^{\mathbb{Q}^T}[P_T \mathbf{1}_{\{P_T > K\}}]$ is the value at time t of a dividend of $P_T \mathbf{1}_{\{P_T > K\}}$ at time T. For an option on a traded asset with a strictly positive price we can value the same payment using that underlying asset as the numeraire. Assume for simplicity that the underlying asset pays no dividends in the life of the option. In terms of the associated risk-adjusted measure $\mathbb{Q}^P$, the time t value of getting a dividend of D_T at time T is $P_t \mathrm{E}_t^{\mathbb{Q}^P}[D_T/P_T]$. Using this with $D_T = P_T \mathbf{1}_{\{P_T > K\}}$, we conclude that

$$B_t^T \mathrm{E}_t^{\mathbb{Q}^T}\left[P_T \mathbf{1}_{\{P_T > K\}}\right] = P_t \mathrm{E}_t^{\mathbb{Q}^P}\left[\mathbf{1}_{\{P_T > K\}}\right] = P_t \mathbb{Q}_t^P(P_T > K).$$

Now the call price formula in the following theorem is clear. The put price can be derived analogously or from the put-call parity.

Theorem 13.4 *The price of a European call option on a non-dividend paying asset is given by*

$$C_t = P_t \mathbb{Q}_t^P(P_T > K) - K B_t^T \mathbb{Q}_t^T(P_T > K). \tag{13.10}$$

The price π_t of a put option is given as

$$\pi_t = K B_t^T \mathbb{Q}_t^T(P_T \leq K) - P_t \mathbb{Q}_t^P(P_T \leq K).$$

Both probabilities in Eq. (13.10) show the probability of the option finishing in-the-money, but under two different probability measures. To compute the price of the European call option in a concrete model we 'just' have to compute these probabilities. In some cases, however, it is easier to work directly on Eq. (13.8) or (13.9).

In Exercise 13.3 you are asked to demonstrate that the price of a European call option has to stay between certain bounds to avoid arbitrage opportunities. More results of the same kind can be found in Merton (1973c) and Munk (2002).

13.3.2 European Option Prices when the Underlying Variable is Lognormal

If we assume that the value of the underlying variable at the maturity of the option is lognormally distributed under the forward measure for maturity T, a more explicit option pricing formula can be derived without too much work. For this reason many specific option pricing models build on assumptions leading to P_T being lognormal under the measure $\mathbb{Q}^T$.

If $\ln P_T \sim N(m, v^2)$ under the $\mathbb{Q}^T$-measure conditional on the information at time $t < T$, it follows that

$$\mathbb{Q}_t^T(P_T > K) = \mathbb{Q}_t^T(\ln P_T > \ln K) = \mathbb{Q}_t^T\left(\frac{\ln P_T - m}{v} > \frac{\ln K - m}{v}\right)$$
$$= \mathbb{Q}_t^T\left(\frac{\ln P_T - m}{v} < -\frac{\ln K - m}{v}\right) = N\left(\frac{m - \ln K}{v}\right),$$

where $N(\cdot)$ is the cumulative probability distribution function of a normally distributed random variable with mean zero and variance one. The last equality follows since $(\ln P_T - m)/v \sim N(0, 1)$. Moreover, it follows from Theorem B.3 in Appendix B that

$$\mathrm{E}_t^{\mathbb{Q}^T}\left[P_T \mathbf{1}_{\{P_T > K\}}\right] = \mathrm{E}_t^{\mathbb{Q}^T}[P_T] N\left(\frac{m - \ln K}{v} + v\right)$$
$$= \mathrm{E}_t^{\mathbb{Q}^T}[P_T] N\left(\frac{\ln\left(\mathrm{E}_t^{\mathbb{Q}^T}[P_T]/K\right) + \frac{1}{2}v^2}{v}\right).$$

Substituting these results into Eq. (13.9), we get

$$C_t = B_t^T \mathrm{E}_t^{\mathbb{Q}^T}[P_T] N(d) - K B_t^T N(d - v),$$

where

$$d = \frac{\ln\left(\mathrm{E}_t^{\mathbb{Q}^T}[P_T]/K\right) + \frac{1}{2}v^2}{v}.$$

In the typical case where P is the price of a non-dividend paying asset, we know that $P_t = B_t^T \mathrm{E}_t^{\mathbb{Q}^T}[P_T]$. Let us identify the relevant v^2. By convention the forward price of the underlying variable at time T for immediate delivery is $F_T^T = P_T$ so we can focus on the dynamics of the forward price $F_t^T = P_t/B_t^T$. This is easier since we know that the forward price is a martingale under the measure $\mathbb{Q}^T$ so that the drift is zero. By Itô's Lemma the sensitivity of the forward price is given by the sensitivity of the underlying variable and the sensitivity of the zero-coupon bond price so for this purpose we can ignore the drift terms in P_t and B_t^T. If we write their $\mathbb{Q}^T$-dynamics as

$$dP_t = P_t\left[\ldots\, dt + \sigma(t)\, dz_{1t}^T\right],$$
$$dB_t^T = B_t^T\left[\ldots\, dt + \sigma_B(T-t)\rho\, dz_{1t}^T + \sigma_B(T-t)\sqrt{1-\rho^2}\, dz_{2t}^T\right],$$

where (z_1^T, z_2^T) is a two-dimensional standard Brownian motion under $\mathbb{Q}^T$, then $\sigma(t)$ is the volatility of the underlying asset, $\sigma_B(T-t)$ is the volatility of the zero-coupon bond price, and ρ is the correlation between shocks to those two prices. We have assumed that ρ is a constant, that the volatility of the underlying asset $\sigma(t)$ is a deterministic function of time, and that $\sigma_B(\cdot)$ is a deterministic function of the time-to-maturity of the bond since these are the only reasonable assumptions that will lead to P_T being lognormal under $\mathbb{Q}^T$. Now the forward price dynamics will be

$$\begin{aligned} dF_t^T &= \frac{1}{B_t^T}\sigma(t)S_t\, dz_{1t}^T - \frac{S_t}{(B_t^T)^2}B_t^T\left(\sigma_B(T-t)\rho\, dz_{1t}^T + \sigma_B(T-t)\sqrt{1-\rho^2}\, dz_{2t}^T\right) \\ &= F_t^T\left[(\sigma(t) - \rho\sigma_B(T-t))\, dz_{1t}^T - \sqrt{1-\rho^2}\sigma_B(T-t)\, dz_{2t}^T\right], \end{aligned}$$

which implies that

$$\begin{aligned} \ln P_T = \ln F_T^T = \ln F_t^T - \frac{1}{2}v_F(t,T)^2 + \int_t^T (\sigma(u) - \rho\sigma_B(T-u))\, dz_{1u}^T \\ - \int_t^T \sqrt{1-\rho^2}\sigma_B(T-u)\, dz_{2u}^T, \end{aligned}$$

where

$$v_F(t,T) = \left(\int_t^T \left(\sigma(u)^2 + \sigma_B(T-u)^2 - 2\rho\sigma(u)\sigma_B(T-u)\right) du\right)^{1/2} \tag{13.11}$$

is the volatility of the forward price. Now we see that, under the measure $\mathbb{Q}^T$, we have $\ln P_T \sim N(\ln F_t^T - \frac{1}{2}v_F(t,T)^2, v_F(t,T)^2)$.

We summarize the above results in the following theorem:

Theorem 13.5 *If $\ln P_T$ conditional on time t information is normally distributed with variance v^2 under the forward measure $\mathbb{Q}^T$, the price of a European option maturing at time T is given by*

$$C_t = B_t^T\, \mathrm{E}_t^{\mathbb{Q}^T}[P_T]N(d) - KB_t^T N(d - v),$$

where

$$d = \frac{\ln\left(\mathrm{E}_t^{\mathbb{Q}^T}[P_T]/K\right) + \frac{1}{2}v^2}{v}.$$

In particular, if P is the price of a non-dividend paying asset and $\ln P_T$ is normally distributed under $\mathbb{Q}^T$, the call price is

$$C_t = P_t N\left(d(F_t^T, t)\right) - KB_t^T N\left(d(F_t^T, t) - v_F(t,T)\right),$$

where $F_t^T = P_t/B_t^T$,

$$d(F_t^T, t) = \frac{\ln\left(F_t^T/K\right) + \frac{1}{2}v_F(t,T)^2}{v_F(t,T)}$$

and $v_F(t,T)$ is given by Eq. (13.11).

13.3.3 The Black–Scholes–Merton model for stock option pricing

While option pricing models date back at least to Bachelier (1900), the most famous model is the Black–Scholes–Merton model developed by Black and Scholes (1973) and Merton (1973c) for the pricing of a European option on a stock. The model is formulated in continuous time and assumes that the risk-free interest rate r (continuously compounded) is constant over time and that the price S_t of the underlying stock follows a continuous stochastic process with a constant relative volatility, that is

$$dS_t = \mu_t S_t \, dt + \sigma S_t \, dz_t, \tag{13.12}$$

where σ is a constant and μ is a 'nice' process. Furthermore, we assume that the underlying stock pays no dividends in the life of the option. Exercise 13.4 explores extensions to the case with intermediate dividends.

With constant interest rates, $B_t^T = e^{-r(T-t)}$ and the risk-neutral measure is identical to the forward measure, $\mathbb{Q} = \mathbb{Q}^T$. Since the risk-neutral expected rate of return of any asset is equal to the risk-free rate of return, the risk-neutral dynamics of the stock price is

$$dS_t = S_t \left[r \, dt + \sigma \, dz_t^{\mathbb{Q}} \right], \tag{13.13}$$

where $z^{\mathbb{Q}} = (z_t^{\mathbb{Q}})$ is a standard Brownian motion under $\mathbb{Q}$. It follows that the stock price is a geometric Brownian motion under $\mathbb{Q} = \mathbb{Q}^T$ and, in particular, we know from Section 2.6.7 that

$$\ln S_T = \ln S_t + \left(r - \frac{1}{2}\sigma^2 \right)(T-t) + \sigma (z_T^{\mathbb{Q}} - z_t^{\mathbb{Q}}).$$

Hence S_T is lognormal and $\mathrm{Var}_t^{\mathbb{Q}}[\ln S_T] = \sigma^2 (T-t)$. We can apply Theorem 13.5, and since $\sigma_B(T-t) = 0$ with constant interest rates we have $v_F = \sigma\sqrt{T-t}$. The forward price of the stock is $F_t^T = S_t e^{r(T-t)}$. We summarize this in the following theorem:

Theorem 13.6 (Black–Scholes–Merton). *Assume that the stock pays no dividend, the stock price dynamics is of the form* (13.12), *and the short-term risk-free rate is constant. Then the price of a European call option on the stock is given by*

$$C_t = S_t N\left(d(S_t, t)\right) - K e^{-r(T-t)} N\left(d(S_t, t) - \sigma\sqrt{T-t} \right), \tag{13.14}$$

where

$$d(S_t, t) = \frac{\ln(S_t/K) + \left(r + \frac{1}{2}\sigma^2\right)(T-t)}{\sigma\sqrt{T-t}}.$$

Equation (13.14) is the famous Black–Scholes–Merton formula.

Alternatively, we can derive the above result using Eq. (13.10) which implies that the price of a European call option on a stock is given by

$$C_t = S_t \mathbb{Q}_t^S(S_T > K) - KB_t^T \mathbb{Q}_t(S_T > K),$$

where $\mathbb{Q}^S$ is the risk-adjusted measure associated with the underlying stock. With the risk-neutral dynamics (13.13), we have

$$\begin{aligned}
\mathbb{Q}_t(S_T > K) &= \mathbb{Q}_t(\ln S_T > \ln K) \\
&= \mathbb{Q}_t\left(\ln S_t + \left(r - \frac{1}{2}\sigma^2\right)(T-t) + \sigma\left(z_T^{\mathbb{Q}} - z_t^{\mathbb{Q}}\right) > \ln K\right) \\
&= \mathbb{Q}_t\left(\frac{z_T^{\mathbb{Q}} - z_t^{\mathbb{Q}}}{\sqrt{T-t}} > -\frac{\ln(S_t/K) + \left(r - \frac{1}{2}\sigma^2\right)(T-t)}{\sigma\sqrt{T-t}}\right) \\
&= \mathbb{Q}_t\left(\frac{z_T^{\mathbb{Q}} - z_t^{\mathbb{Q}}}{\sqrt{T-t}} < \frac{\ln(S_t/K) + \left(r - \frac{1}{2}\sigma^2\right)(T-t)}{\sigma\sqrt{T-t}}\right) \\
&= N\left(\frac{\ln(S_t/K) + \left(r - \frac{1}{2}\sigma^2\right)(T-t)}{\sigma\sqrt{T-t}}\right).
\end{aligned}$$

According to Eq. (12.16), the dynamics of the stock price under the measure $\mathbb{Q}^S$ is

$$dS_t = S_t\left[\left(r + \sigma^2\right) dt + \sigma\, dz_t^S\right]$$

so that S is also a geometric Brownian motion under the measure $\mathbb{Q}^S$. Analogously to the above equations it can be shown that

$$\mathbb{Q}_t^S(S_T > K) = N\left(\frac{\ln(S_t/K) + \left(r + \frac{1}{2}\sigma^2\right)(T-t)}{\sigma\sqrt{T-t}}\right).$$

Now the option price in Eq. (13.14) follows.

The Black–Scholes–Merton equation states the call option price in terms of five quantities:

(1) the price of the underlying stock,
(2) the price of the zero-coupon bond maturing at expiry of the option (or, equivalently, the risk-free interest rate),
(3) the time-to-expiration of the option,
(4) the exercise price (or, equivalently, the *moneyness* S_t/K of the option),
(5) the volatility of the underlying stock.

It can be shown (you are asked to do this in Exercise 13.2) by straightforward differentiation that

$$\frac{\partial C_t}{\partial S_t} = N\left(d(S_t, t)\right), \quad \frac{\partial^2 C_t}{\partial S_t^2} = \frac{n\left(d(S_t, t)\right)}{S_t \sigma \sqrt{T-t}}, \tag{13.15}$$

where $n(\cdot) = N'(\cdot)$ is the probability density function of an $N(0, 1)$ random variable, and

$$\frac{\partial C_t}{\partial t} = -\frac{-S_t \sigma n\left(d(S_t, t)\right)}{2\sqrt{T-t}} - rKB_t^T N\left(d(S_t, t) - \sigma\sqrt{T-t}\right), \tag{13.16}$$

using that $B_t^T = \exp\{-r(T-t)\}$. In particular, the call option price is an increasing, convex function of the price of the underlying stock. The call price is increasing in the volatility σ, (obviously) decreasing in the exercise price K, and increasing in the zero-coupon bond price (and, hence, decreasing in the risk-free rate r).

Note that the Black–Scholes–Merton price of the call option does not involve any preference parameters or a market price of risk associated with the shock z to the underlying stock price. On the other hand, it involves the price of the underlying stock. In the Black–Scholes–Merton model the option is a redundant asset. There is only one source of risk, and with the stock and the risk-free asset the market is already complete. Any additional asset affected only by the same shock will be redundant.

The option can be perfectly replicated by a trading strategy in the stock and the risk-free asset. At any time $t < T$, the portfolio consists of $\theta_t^S = N\left(d(S_t, t)\right) \in (0, 1)$ units of the stock and $\theta_t^B = -KN\left(d(S_t, t) - \sigma\sqrt{T-t}\right) \in (-K, 0)$ units of the zero-coupon bond maturing at time T. Clearly, the value of this portfolio is identical to the value of the call option, $\theta_t^S S_t + \theta_t^B B_t^T = C_t$. Since $C_t = C(S_t, t)$, it follows from Itô's Lemma and the derivatives of C computed above that the dynamics of the call price is

$$\begin{aligned} dC_t &= \frac{\partial C_t}{\partial t}\, dt + \frac{\partial C_t}{\partial S_t}\, dS_t + \frac{1}{2}\frac{\partial^2 C_t}{\partial S_t^2}(dS_t)^2 \\ &= \left(N\left(d(S_t, t)\right)\mu(S_t, t) - rKB_t^T N\left(d(S_t, t) - \sigma\sqrt{T-t}\right)\right) dt \\ &\quad + N\left(d(S_t, t)\right)\sigma S_t\, dz_t. \end{aligned}$$

The dynamics of the value of the trading strategy is

$$\begin{aligned} \theta_t^S\, dS_t + \theta_t^B\, dB_t^T &= N\left(d(S_t, t)\right)\, dS_t - KN\left(d(S_t, t) - \sigma\sqrt{T-t}\right)\, dB_t^T \\ &= \left(N\left(d(S_t, t)\right)\mu(S_t, t) - rKB_t^T N\left(d(S_t, t) - \sigma\sqrt{T-t}\right)\right) dt \\ &\quad + N\left(d(S_t, t)\right)\sigma S_t\, dz_t, \end{aligned}$$

which is identical to dC_t. The trading strategy is therefore replicating the option.

Applying the put-call parity (13.7), we obtain a European put option price of

$$\pi(S_t, t) = KB_t^T N\left(-[d(S_t, t) - \sigma\sqrt{T-t}]\right) - S_t N\left(-d(S_t, t)\right).$$

In the above model, interest rates and hence bond prices were assumed to be non-stochastic. However, we can easily generalize to the case where bond prices vary stochastically with a deterministic volatility and a constant correlation with the stock price. Assuming that the dynamics of the stock price and the price of the zero-coupon bond maturing at time T are given by

$$dS_t = S_t\left[\dots\, dt + \sigma\, dz_{1t}\right],$$

$$dB_t^T = B_t^T\left[\dots\, dt + \sigma_B(T-t)\rho\, dz_{1t} + \sigma_B(T-t)\sqrt{1-\rho^2}\, dz_{2t}\right],$$

we are still in the setting of Section 13.3.2 and can apply Theorem 13.5.

Theorem 13.7 *Suppose the stock pays no dividend, has a constant volatility σ, and a constant correlation ρ with the price of the zero-coupon bond maturing at time T, and suppose that this bond has a deterministic volatility $\sigma_B(T-t)$. Then the price of a European call option on the stock is given by*

$$C_t = S_t N\left(d(F_t^T, t)\right) - KB_t^T N\left(d(F_t^T, t) - v_F(t, T)\right), \tag{13.17}$$

where $F_t^T = S_t/B_t^T$,

$$d(F_t^T, t) = \frac{\ln(F_t^T/K) + \frac{1}{2}v_F(t, T)^2}{v_F(t, T)},$$

$$v_F(t, T) = \left(\int_t^T \left(\sigma^2 + \sigma_B(T-u)^2 - 2\rho\sigma\sigma_B(T-u)\right) du\right)^{1/2}.$$

In practice $\sigma_B(T-t)$ is typically much smaller than σ, and the approximation

$$v_F(t, T) \approx \sqrt{\int_t^T \sigma^2\, du} = \sigma\sqrt{T-t}$$

is not too bad. With that approximation you will get the same call price using Eq. (13.17) as by using the Black–Scholes–Merton formula (13.14) with the zero-coupon yield $y_t^T = -(\ln B_t^T)/(T-t)$ replacing r. In this sense the above theorem supports the use of the Black–Scholes–Merton equation even when interest rates are stochastic. Note, however, that the above theorem requires the bond price volatility to be a deterministic function of the time-to-maturity of the bond. This will only be satisfied if the short-term risk-free interest rate r_t follows a Gaussian process, such as an Ornstein–Uhlenbeck process as assumed in the Vasicek model introduced in Section 11.5.1. While such models are very nice to work with, they are not terribly realistic. On the other hand, for short maturities and relatively stable interest rates, it is probably reasonable to approximate the bond price volatility with a deterministic function or even approximate it with zero as the Black–Scholes–Merton model implicitly does.

The assumption of a constant stock price volatility is important for the derivations of the Black–Scholes–Merton option pricing formula. Alas, it is not realistic. The volatility of a stock can be estimated from historical variations in the stock price and the estimate varies with the time period used in the estimation—both over short periods and long periods. Another measure of the volatility of a stock is its *implied volatility*. Given the current stock price S_t and interest rate r, we can define an implied volatility of the stock for any option traded upon that stock (that is for any exercise price K and any maturity T) as the value of σ you need to plug into the Black–Scholes–Merton formula to get a match with the observed market price of the option. Since the Black–Scholes–Merton option price is an increasing function of the volatility, there will be a unique value of σ that does the job. Looking at simultaneous prices of different options on the same stock, the implied volatility is found to vary with the exercise price and the maturity of the option. If the Black–Scholes–Merton assumptions were correct, you would find the same implied volatility for all options on the same underlying.

Various alternatives to the constant volatility assumption have been proposed. Black and Cox (1976) replace the constant σ by σS_t^{α} for some power α. Here the volatility is a function of the stock price and therefore perfectly correlated with the stock price. This extension does not seem sufficient. The stochastic volatility models of Hull and White (1987) and Heston (1993) allow the volatility to be affected by another exogenous shock than the shock to the stock price itself. With these extensions it is possible to match the option prices in the model relatively well to observed option prices. In the stochastic volatility models, the market is no longer complete, and the option prices will depend on the market price of volatility risk, which then has to be specified and estimated.

Occasionally stock prices change a lot over a very short period of time, for example in the so-called stock market crashes. Such dramatic variations are probably better modelled by jump processes than by pure diffusion models like those discussed in this book. Several papers study the pricing of options on stocks when the stock price can jump. Some prominent examples are Merton (1976) and Madan, Carr, and Chang (1998). There is even empirical support of and theoretical work on jumps in the volatilities, see Eraker, Johannes, and Polson (2003) and Eraker (2004).

Obviously, the addition of stochastic volatility and jump components complicates the computation of the option price. The general results from Section 13.3.1 still hold, of course, and the challenge is to compute the relevant exercise probabilities. As long as the model belongs to the class of affine jump-diffusion models, these probabilities can be efficiently computed by the so-called Fourier transform technique as explained by Duffie, Pan, and Singleton (2000).

13.3.4 Options on Bonds

Consider a European call option on a zero-coupon bond. Let T be the maturity of the option and $T^* > T$ the maturity of the bond. As before K is the exercise price. Let C_t^{K,T,T^*} denote the price at time t of a European call option on this zero-coupon bond. The dividend of the option at time T is

$$C_T^{K,T,T^*} = \max\left(B_T^{T^*} - K, 0\right).$$

According to Theorem 13.4 the option price is generally characterized by

$$C_t^{K,T,T^*} = B_t^{T^*} \mathbb{Q}_t^{T^*}\left(B_T^{T^*} > K\right) - KB_t^T \mathbb{Q}_t^T\left(B_T^{T^*} > K\right),$$

where $\mathbb{Q}^{T^*}$ and $\mathbb{Q}^T$ are the forward measures for maturities T^* and T, respectively.

If $B_T^{T^*}$ is lognormally distributed under the forward measure for maturity T, we know from Theorem 13.5 that we can find a nice closed-form solution. This is for example the case in the Vasicek model introduced in Section 11.5.1. Given the Ornstein–Uhlenbeck process for the short-term risk-free rate,

$$dr_t = \kappa\left(\bar{r} - r_t\right) dt + \sigma_r\, dz_t,$$

and a constant market price of interest rate risk λ, the price of a zero-coupon bond price maturing at time s is

$$B_t^s = e^{-\mathcal{A}(s-t) - \mathcal{B}_\kappa(s-t) r_t},$$

compare (11.28), where $\mathcal{A}(\cdot)$ and $\mathcal{B}_\kappa(\cdot)$ are defined in Eqs. (11.29) and (11.25), respectively. The change to the forward measure requires identification of the bond price sensitivity. An application of Itô's Lemma gives the bond price dynamics

$$dB_t^s = B_t^s\left[\dots\, dt - \sigma_r \mathcal{B}_\kappa(s-t)\, dz_t\right]$$

so that the bond price sensitivity is $\sigma_B(s-t) = -\sigma_r \mathcal{B}_\kappa(s-t)$. Since this is negative, the bond price volatility is really $-\sigma_B(s-t) = \sigma_r \mathcal{B}_\kappa(s-t)$. It now follows from Eq. (12.13) that the $\mathbb{Q}^T$-dynamics of the short-term interest rate is

$$\begin{aligned} dr_t &= \left(\kappa\left[\bar{r} - r_t\right] - \sigma_r\left[\lambda - \sigma_B(T-t)\right]\right) dt + \sigma_r\, dz_t^T \\ &= \kappa\left(\tilde{r}(T-t) - r_t\right) dt + \sigma_r\, dz_t^T, \end{aligned}$$

where $\tilde{r}(\tau) = \bar{r} - \sigma_r\lambda/\kappa - \sigma_r^2 \mathcal{B}_\kappa(\tau)/\kappa$ and $z^T = (z_t^T)$ is a standard Brownian motion under $\mathbb{Q}^T$. Under the $\mathbb{Q}^T$-measure, the short rate behaves as an

Ornstein–Uhlenbeck process, but with a deterministically changing mean-reversion level $\tilde{r}(T-t)$. Hence, r_T will be normally distributed under $\mathbb{Q}^T$ and, consequently, the price of the underlying zero-coupon bond at the maturity of the option, $B_T^{T^*} = \exp\{-\mathcal{A}(T^*-T) - \mathcal{B}_\kappa(T^*-T)r_T\}$, will be lognormally distributed under $\mathbb{Q}^T$. We can therefore apply Theorem 13.5 and conclude that the price of the option is

$$C_t^{K,T,T^*} = B_t^{T^*} N(d) - KB_t^T N\left(d - v_F(t,T,T^*)\right), \tag{13.18}$$

where

$$d = \frac{\ln\left(\frac{B_t^{T^*}}{KB_t^T}\right) + \frac{1}{2}v_F(t,T,T^*)^2}{v_F(t,T,T^*)}.$$

Furthermore, by using the fact that the underlying zero-coupon bond price is perfectly correlated with the price of the zero-coupon bond maturing at T, we obtain

$$\begin{aligned}
v_F(t,T,T^*)^2 &= \int_t^T \left(\sigma_B(T^*-u) - \sigma_B(T-u)\right)^2 du \\
&= \sigma_r^2 \int_t^T \left(\mathcal{B}_\kappa(T^*-u) - \mathcal{B}_\kappa(T-u)\right)^2 du \\
&= \frac{\sigma_r^2}{\kappa^2} \int_t^T \left(e^{-\kappa(T-u)} - e^{-\kappa(T^*-u)}\right)^2 du \\
&= \frac{\sigma_r^2}{\kappa^3}\left(1 - e^{-\kappa(T^*-T)}\right)^2\left(1 - e^{-2\kappa(T-t)}\right).
\end{aligned}$$

In many other models of interest rates and bond prices, an option pricing formula very similar to Eq. (13.18) can be derived. For example, in the Cox–Ingersoll–Ross model introduced in Section 11.5.2, the price of a European call option on a zero-coupon bond is of the form

$$C_t^{K,T,T^*} = B_t^{T^*}\chi^2(h_1;f,g_1) - KB_t^T\chi^2(h_2;f,g_2),$$

where $\chi^2(\cdot;f,g)$ is the cumulative probability distribution function of a non-centrally χ^2-distributed random variable with f degrees of freedom and non-centrality parameter g. For details see Munk (2011, Ch. 7).

The options considered above are options on zero-coupon bonds. Traded bond options usually have a coupon bond as the underlying. Fortunately, the pricing formulas for options on zero-coupon bonds can, under some assumptions, be used in the pricing of options on coupon bonds. First some notation. The underlying coupon bond is assumed to pay Y_i at time T_i ($i = 1, 2, \dots, n$), where $T_1 < T_2 < \cdots < T_n$, so that the price of the bond is

$$B_t = \sum_{T_i > t} Y_i B_t^{T_i},$$

where we sum over all the future payment dates. Let $C_t^{K,T,\mathrm{cpn}}$ denote the price at time t of a European call option on the coupon bond, where K is the exercise price and T is the expiration date of the option. In reasonable one-factor models, the price of a given zero-coupon bond will be a decreasing function of the short-term interest rate. In both the Vasicek model and the Cox–Ingersoll–Ross model the zero-coupon bond price is of the form $B_t^T = \exp\{-\mathcal{A}(T-t) - \mathcal{B}(T-t)r_t\}$ and since the $\mathcal{B}$-function is positive in both models, the bond price is indeed decreasing in maturity. Then the following result, first derived by Jamshidian (1989), applies:

Theorem 13.8 *Suppose that the zero-coupon bond prices are of the form $B_t^T = B^T(r_t, t)$ and $B^T(\cdot, t)$ is decreasing in r_t. Then the price of a European call on a coupon bond is*

$$C_t^{K,T,cpn} = \sum_{T_i > T} Y_i C_t^{K_i,T,T_i},$$

where $K_i = B^{T_i}(r^*, T)$, and r^* is defined as the solution to the equation

$$B(r^*, T) \equiv \sum_{T_i > T} Y_i B^{T_i}(r^*, T) = K. \tag{13.19}$$

Proof. The payoff of the option on the coupon bond is

$$\max(B(r_T, T) - K, 0) = \max\left(\sum_{T_i > T} Y_i B^{T_i}(r_T, T) - K, 0\right).$$

Since every zero-coupon bond price $B^{T_i}(r_T, T)$ is a monotonically decreasing function of the interest rate r_T, the whole sum $\sum_{T_i > T} Y_i B^{T_i}(r_T, T)$ is monotonically decreasing in r_T. Therefore, exactly one value r^* of r_T will make the option finish *at the money* so that Eq. (13.19) holds. Letting $K_i = B^{T_i}(r^*, T)$, we have that $\sum_{T_i > T} Y_i K_i = K$.

For $r_T < r^*$,

$$\sum_{T_i > T} Y_i B^{T_i}(r_T, T) > \sum_{T_i > T} Y_i B^{T_i}(r^*, T) = K, \quad B^{T_i}(r_T, T) > B^{T_i}(r^*, T) = K_i$$

so that

$$\begin{aligned} \max\left(\sum_{T_i > T} Y_i B^{T_i}(r_T, T) - K, 0\right) &= \sum_{T_i > T} Y_i B^{T_i}(r_T, T) - K \\ &= \sum_{T_i > T} Y_i \left(B^{T_i}(r_T, T) - K_i\right) \\ &= \sum_{T_i > T} Y_i \max\left(B^{T_i}(r_T, T) - K_i, 0\right). \end{aligned}$$

For $r_T \geq r^*$,

$$\sum_{T_i > T} Y_i B^{T_i}(r_T, T) \leq \sum_{T_i > T} Y_i B^{T_i}(r^*, T) = K, \quad B^{T_i}(r_T, T) \leq B^{T_i}(r^*, T) = K_i$$

so that

$$\max\left(\sum_{T_i > T} Y_i B^{T_i}(r_T, T) - K, 0\right) = 0 = \sum_{T_i > T} Y_i \max\left(B^{T_i}(r_T, T) - K_i, 0\right).$$

Hence, for *all* possible values of r_T we may conclude that

$$\max\left(\sum_{T_i > T} Y_i B^{T_i}(r_T, T) - K, 0\right) = \sum_{T_i > T} Y_i \max\left(B^{T_i}(r_T, T) - K_i, 0\right).$$

The payoff of the option on the coupon bond is thus identical to the payoff of a portfolio of options on zero-coupon bonds, namely a portfolio consisting (for each i with $T_i > T$) of Y_i options on a zero-coupon bond maturing at time T_i and an exercise price of K_i. Consequently, the value of the option on the coupon bond at time $t \leq T$ equals the value of that portfolio of options on zero-coupon bonds. A formal derivation goes as follows:

$$\begin{aligned}
C_t^{K,T,\text{cpn}} &= \mathrm{E}_{r,t}^{\mathbb{Q}}\left[e^{-\int_t^T r_u\,du} \max\left(B(r_T, T) - K, 0\right)\right] \\
&= \mathrm{E}_{r,t}^{\mathbb{Q}}\left[e^{-\int_t^T r_u\,du} \sum_{T_i > T} Y_i \max\left(B^{T_i}(r_T, T) - K_i, 0\right)\right] \\
&= \sum_{T_i > T} Y_i \, \mathrm{E}_{r,t}^{\mathbb{Q}}\left[e^{-\int_t^T r_u\,du} \max\left(B^{T_i}(r_T, T) - K_i, 0\right)\right] \\
&= \sum_{T_i > T} Y_i C_t^{K_i,T,T_i},
\end{aligned}$$

which completes the proof. □

To compute the price of a European call option on a coupon bond we must numerically solve one equation in one unknown (to find r^*) and calculate n' prices of European call options on zero-coupon bonds, where n' is the number of payment dates of the coupon bond after expiration of the option. For example, in the Vasicek model we can use Eq. (13.18).

Practitioners often use Black–Scholes–Merton type formulas for pretty much all types of options, including options on bonds. The formulas are based on the Black (1976a) variant of the Black–Scholes–Merton model developed for stock option pricing, originally developed for options on futures on an asset with a lognormally distributed value. Black's formula for a European call option on a bond is

$$C_t^{K,T,\text{cpn}} = B_t^T \left[F_t^{T,\text{cpn}} N\left(d(F_t^{T,\text{cpn}}, t) \right) - KN\left(d(F_t^{T,\text{cpn}}, t) - \sigma_B \sqrt{T-t} \right) \right],$$
$$= \tilde{B}_t N\left(d(F_t^{T,\text{cpn}}, t) \right) - KB_t^T N\left(d(F_t^{T,\text{cpn}}, t) - \sigma_B \sqrt{T-t} \right),$$

where σ_B is the volatility of the bond, $F_t^{T,\text{cpn}} = \tilde{B}_t / B_t^T$ is the forward price of the bond, $\tilde{B}_t = B_t - \sum_{t<T_i<T} Y_i B_t^{T_i}$ is the present value of the bond payments after maturity of the option, and

$$d(F_t^{T,\text{cpn}}, t) = \frac{\ln(F_t^{T,\text{cpn}}/K)}{\sigma\sqrt{T-t}} + \frac{1}{2}\sigma_B\sqrt{T-t}.$$

The use of Black's formula for bond options is not theoretically supported and may lead to prices allowing arbitrage. At best, it is a reasonable approximation to the correct price.

13.3.5 Interest Rate Options: Caps and Floors

An *(interest rate) cap* is designed to protect an investor who has borrowed funds on a floating interest rate basis against the risk of paying very high interest rates. Suppose the loan has a face value of H and payment dates $T_1 < T_2 < \cdots < T_n$, where $T_{i+1} - T_i = \delta$ for all i.[2] The interest rate to be paid at time T_i is determined by the δ-period money market interest rate prevailing at time $T_{i-1} = T_i - \delta$, that is the payment at time T_i is equal to $H\delta l_{T_i-\delta}^{T_i}$, compare the notation for interest rates introduced in Section 11.2. Note that the interest rate is set at the beginning of the period, but paid at the end. Define $T_0 = T_1 - \delta$. The dates $T_0, T_1, \ldots, T_{n-1}$ where the rate for the coming period is determined are called the *reset dates* of the loan.

A cap with a face value of H, payment dates T_i $(i = 1, \ldots, n)$ as above, and a so-called cap rate K yields a time T_i payoff of $H\delta \max(l_{T_i-\delta}^{T_i} - K, 0)$, for $i = 1, 2, \ldots, n$. If a borrower buys such a cap, the net payment at time T_i cannot exceed $H\delta K$. The period length δ is often referred to as the *frequency* or the *tenor* of the cap.[3] In practice, the frequency is typically either 3, 6, or 12 months. Note that the time distance between payment dates coincides with the 'maturity' of the floating interest rate. Also note that while a cap is tailored for interest rate hedging, it can also be used for interest rate speculation.

[2] In practice, there will not be exactly the same number of days between successive reset dates, and the calculations below must be slightly adjusted by using the relevant *day count convention*.

[3] The word tenor is sometimes used for the set of payment dates $T_1, \ldots, T_n$.

A cap can be seen as a portfolio of n *caplets*, namely one for each payment date of the cap. The i'th caplet yields a payoff at time T_i of

$$C^i_{T_i} = H\delta \max\left(l^{T_i}_{T_i-\delta} - K, 0\right)$$

and no other payments. A caplet is a call option on the zero-coupon yield prevailing at time $T_i - \delta$ for a period of length δ, but where the payment takes place at time T_i although it is already fixed at time $T_i - \delta$.

In the following we will find the value of the i'th caplet before time T_i. Since the payoff becomes known at time $T_i - \delta$, we can obtain its value in the interval between $T_i - \delta$ and T_i by a simple discounting of the payoff, that is

$$C^i_t = B^{T_i}_t H\delta \max\left(l^{T_i}_{T_i-\delta} - K, 0\right), \quad T_i - \delta \le t \le T_i.$$

In particular,

$$C^i_{T_i-\delta} = B^{T_i}_{T_i-\delta} H\delta \max\left(l^{T_i}_{T_i-\delta} - K, 0\right). \tag{13.20}$$

To find the value before the fixing of the payoff, that is for $t < T_i - \delta$, we shall use two strategies. The first is simply to take relevant expectations of the payoff. Since the payoff comes at T_i, we know from Section 12.4 that the value of the payoff can be found as the product of the expected payoff computed under the T_i-forward martingale measure and the current discount factor for time T_i payments, that is

$$C^i_t = H\delta B^{T_i}_t \, \mathrm{E}^{\mathbb{Q}^{T_i}}_t \left[\max\left(l^{T_i}_{T_i-\delta} - K, 0\right)\right], \quad t < T_i - \delta.$$

The price of a cap can therefore be determined as

$$C_t = H\delta \sum_{i=1}^{n} B^{T_i}_t \, \mathrm{E}^{\mathbb{Q}^{T_i}}_t \left[\max\left(l^{T_i}_{T_i-\delta} - K, 0\right)\right], \quad t < T_0.$$

If each LIBOR rate $l^{T-i}_{T_i-\delta}$ is lognormally distributed under the $\mathbb{Q}^{T_i}$-forward measure, we can obtain a nice closed-form pricing formula. This is satisfied in the so-called LIBOR market model introduced by Miltersen, Sandmann, and Sondermann (1997) and Brace, Gatarek, and Musiela (1997). See Munk (2011, Ch. 11) for a review. In fact, the resulting pricing formula is the Black formula often applied in practice:

$$C^i_t = H\delta B^{T_i}_t \Big[L^{T_i-\delta,T_i}_t N\left(d^i(L^{T_i-\delta,T_i}_t, t)\right) - KN\left(d^i(L^{T_i-\delta,T_i}_t, t) - \sigma_i\sqrt{T_i - \delta - t}\right)\Big],$$

for $t < T_i - \delta$. Here σ_i is the (relative) volatility of the forward LIBOR rate $L_t^{T_i-\delta,T_i}$, and d^i is given by

$$d^i(L_t^{T_i-\delta,T_i}, t) = \frac{\ln(L_t^{T_i-\delta,T_i}/K)}{\sigma_i\sqrt{T_i-\delta-t}} + \frac{1}{2}\sigma_i\sqrt{T_i-\delta-t}.$$

The second pricing strategy links caps to bond options. Applying Eq. (11.3), we can rewrite Eq. (13.20) as

$$\begin{aligned} C^i_{T_i-\delta} &= B^{T_i}_{T_i-\delta} H \max\left(1+\delta l^{T_i}_{T_i-\delta} - [1+\delta K], 0\right) \\ &= B^{T_i}_{T_i-\delta} H \max\left(\frac{1}{B^{T_i}_{T_i-\delta}} - [1+\delta K], 0\right) \\ &= H(1+\delta K)\max\left(\frac{1}{1+\delta K} - B^{T_i}_{T_i-\delta}, 0\right). \end{aligned}$$

We can now see that the value at time $T_i - \delta$ is identical to the payoff of a European put option expiring at time $T_i - \delta$ that has an exercise price of $1/(1+\delta K)$ and is written on a zero-coupon bond maturing at time T_i. Accordingly, the value of the i'th caplet at an earlier point in time $t \le T_i - \delta$ must equal the value of that put option, that is

$$C^i_t = H(1+\delta K)\pi_t^{(1+\delta K)^{-1}, T_i-\delta, T_i}.$$

To find the value of the entire cap contract we simply have to add up the values of all the caplets corresponding to the remaining payment dates of the cap. Before the first reset date, T_0, none of the cap payments are known, so the value of the cap is given by

$$C_t = \sum_{i=1}^{n} C^i_t = H(1+\delta K)\sum_{i=1}^{n} \pi_t^{(1+\delta K)^{-1}, T_i-\delta, T_i}, \quad t < T_0.$$

At all dates after the first reset date, the next payment of the cap will already be known. If we use the notation $T_{i(t)}$ for the nearest following payment date after time t, the value of the cap at any time t in $[T_0, T_n]$ (exclusive of any payment received exactly at time t) can be written as

$$\begin{aligned} C_t &= HB_t^{T_{i(t)}}\delta \max\left(l^{T_{i(t)}}_{T_{i(t)}-\delta} - K, 0\right) \\ &\quad + (1+\delta K)H \sum_{i=i(t)+1}^{n} \pi_t^{(1+\delta K)^{-1}, T_i-\delta, T_i}, \quad T_0 \le t \le T_n. \end{aligned}$$

If $T_{n-1} < t < T_n$, we have $i(t) = n$, and there will be no terms in the sum, which is then considered to be equal to zero. In various models of interest rate dynamics, nice pricing formulas for European options on zero-coupon bonds can be derived. This is for example the case in the Vasicek model studied above. Cap prices will then follow from prices of European puts on zero-coupon bonds.

Note that the interest rates and the discount factors appearing in the expressions above are taken from the money market, not from the government bond market. Also note that since caps and most other contracts related to money market rates trade OTC, one should take the default risk of the two parties into account when valuing the cap. Here, default simply means that the party cannot pay the amounts promised in the contract. Official money market rates and the associated discount function apply to loan and deposit arrangements between large financial institutions, and thus they reflect the default risk of these corporations. If the parties in an OTC transaction have a default risk significantly different from that, the discount rates in the formulas should be adjusted accordingly. However, it is quite complicated to do that in a theoretically correct manner, so we will not discuss this issue any further here.

An *(interest rate) floor* is designed to protect an investor who has lent funds on a floating rate basis against receiving very low interest rates. The contract is constructed just as a cap except that the payoff at time T_i ($i = 1, \dots, n$) is given by

$$\mathcal{F}^i_{T_i} = H\delta \max\left(K - l^{T_i}_{T_i-\delta}, 0\right), \tag{13.21}$$

where K is called the floor rate. Buying an appropriate floor, an investor who has provided another investor with a floating rate loan will in total at least receive the floor rate. Of course, an investor can also speculate in low future interest rates by buying a floor. The (hypothetical) contracts that only yield one of the payments in Eq. (13.21) are called *floorlets*. Obviously, we can think of a floorlet as a European put on the floating interest rate with delayed payment of the payoff.

Analogously to the analysis for caps, we can price the floor directly as

$$\mathcal{F}_t = H\delta \sum_{i=1}^{n} B^{T_i}_t \,\mathrm{E}^{\mathbb{Q}^{T_i}}_t \left[\max\left(K - L^{T_i-\delta, T_i}_{T_i-\delta}, 0\right)\right], \quad t < T_0.$$

Again a pricing formula consistent with the Black formula is obtained assuming lognormally distributed forward LIBOR rates. Alternatively, we can express the floorlet as a European call on a zero-coupon bond, and hence a floor is equivalent to a portfolio of European calls on zero-coupon bonds. More precisely, the value of the i'th floorlet at time $T_i - \delta$ is

$$\mathcal{F}^i_{T_i-\delta} = H(1+\delta K) \max\left(B^{T_i}_{T_i-\delta} - \frac{1}{1+\delta K}, 0\right).$$

The total value of the floor contract at any time $t < T_0$ is therefore given by

$$\mathcal{F}_t = H(1+\delta K)\sum_{i=1}^{n} C_t^{(1+\delta K)^{-1},T_i-\delta,T_i}, \quad t < T_0,$$

and later the value is

$$\mathcal{F}_t = HB_t^{T_{i(t)}}\delta \max\left(K - l_{T_{i(t)}-\delta}^{T_{i(t)}}, 0\right) + (1+\delta K)H\sum_{i=i(t)+1}^{n} C_t^{(1+\delta K)^{-1},T_i-\delta,T_i}, \quad T_0 \le t \le T_n.$$

13.4 INTEREST RATE SWAPS AND SWAPTIONS

13.4.1 Interest Rate Swaps

Many different types of swaps are traded on the OTC markets, for example currency swaps, credit swaps, asset swaps, but we focus here on interest rate swaps. An *(interest rate) swap* is an exchange of two cash flow streams that are determined by certain interest rates. In the simplest and most common interest rate swap, a *plain vanilla* swap, two parties exchange a stream of fixed interest rate payments and a stream of floating interest rate payments. The payments are in the same currency and are computed from the same (hypothetical) face value or notional principal. The floating rate is usually a money market rate, for example a LIBOR rate, possibly augmented or reduced by a fixed margin. The fixed interest rate is usually set so that the swap has zero net present value when the parties agree on the contract. While the two parties can agree upon any maturity, most interest rate swaps have a maturity between 2 and 10 years.

Let us briefly look at the uses of interest rate swaps. An investor can transform a floating rate loan into a fixed rate loan by entering into an appropriate swap, where the investor receives floating rate payments (netting out the payments on the original loan) and pays fixed rate payments. This is called a *liability transformation*. Conversely, an investor who has lent money at a floating rate, that is owns a floating rate bond, can transform this to a fixed rate bond by entering into a swap, where he pays floating rate payments and receives fixed rate payments. This is an *asset transformation*. Hence, interest rate swaps can be used for hedging interest rate risk on both (certain) assets and liabilities. On the other hand, interest rate swaps can also be used for taking advantage of specific expectations of future interest rates, that is for speculation.

Swaps are often said to allow the two parties to exploit their *comparative advantages* in different markets. Concerning interest rate swaps, this argument presumes that one party has a comparative advantage (relative to the other party) in the market for fixed rate loans, while the other party has a comparative advantage (relative to the first party) in the market for floating rate loans. However, these markets are integrated, and the existence of comparative advantages conflicts with modern financial theory and the efficiency of the money markets. Apparent comparative advantages can be due to differences in default risk premia. For details we refer the reader to the discussion in Hull (2009, Ch. 7).

Next, we will discuss the valuation of swaps. As for caps and floors, we assume that both parties in the swap have a default risk corresponding to the 'average default risk' of major financial institutions reflected by the money market interest rates. For a description of the impact on the payments and the valuation of swaps between parties with different default risk, see Duffie and Huang (1996) and Huge and Lando (1999). Furthermore, we assume that the fixed rate payments and the floating rate payments occur at exactly the same dates throughout the life of the swap. This is true for most, but not all, traded swaps. For some swaps, the fixed rate payments only occur once a year, whereas the floating rate payments are quarterly or semi-annual. The analysis below can easily be adapted to such swaps.

In a plain vanilla interest rate swap, one party pays a stream of fixed rate payments and receives a stream of floating rate payments. This party is said to have a pay fixed, receive floating swap or a fixed-for-floating swap or simply a *payer swap*. The counterpart receives a stream of fixed rate payments and pays a stream of floating rate payments. This party is said to have a pay floating, receive fixed swap or a floating-for-fixed swap or simply a *receiver swap*. Note that the names payer swap and receiver swap refer to the fixed rate payments.

We consider a swap with payment dates $T_1, \dots, T_n$, where $T_{i+1} - T_i = \delta$. The floating interest rate determining the payment at time T_i is the money market (LIBOR) rate $l_{T_i-\delta}^{T_i}$. In the following we assume that there is no fixed extra margin on this floating rate. If there were such an extra charge, the value of the part of the flexible payments that is due to the extra margin could be computed in the same manner as the value of the fixed rate payments of the swap, see below. We refer to $T_0 = T_1 - \delta$ as the starting date of the swap. As for caps and floors, we call $T_0, T_1, \dots, T_{n-1}$ the reset dates, and δ the frequency or the tenor. Typical swaps have δ equal to 0.25, 0.5, or 1 corresponding to quarterly, semi-annual, or annual payments and interest rates.

We will find the value of an interest rate swap by separately computing the value of the fixed rate payments (V^{fix}) and the value of the floating rate payments (V^{fl}). The fixed rate is denoted by K. This is a nominal, annual interest rate so that the fixed rate payments equal $HK\delta$, where H is the notional principal or face value (which is not swapped). The value of the remaining fixed payments is simply

$$V_t^{\text{fix}} = \sum_{i=i(t)}^{n} HK\delta B_t^{T_i} = HK\delta \sum_{i=i(t)}^{n} B_t^{T_i}. \tag{13.22}$$

The floating rate payments are exactly the same as the coupon payments on a floating rate bond with annualized coupon rate $l^{T_i}_{T_i-\delta}$. Immediately after each reset date, the value of such a bond will equal its face value. To see this, first note that immediately after the last reset date $T_{n-1} = T_n - \delta$, the bond is equivalent to a single-payment bond with a coupon rate equal to the market interest rate for the last coupon period. By definition of that market interest rate, the time T_{n-1} value of the bond will be exactly equal to the face value H. In mathematical terms, the market discount factor to apply for the discounting of time T_n payments back to time T_{n-1} is $(1 + \delta l^{T_n}_{T_{n-1}})^{-1}$, so the time T_{n-1} value of a payment of $H(1 + \delta l^{T_n}_{T_{n-1}})$ at time T_n is precisely H. Immediately after the next-to-last reset date T_{n-2}, we know that we will receive a payment of $H\delta l^{T_{n-1}}_{T_{n-2}}$ at time T_{n-1} and that the time T_{n-1} value of the following payment (received at T_n) equals H. We therefore have to discount the sum $H\delta l^{T_{n-1}}_{T_{n-2}} + H = H(1 + \delta l^{T_{n-1}}_{T_{n-2}})$ from T_{n-1} back to T_{n-2}. The discounted value is exactly H. Continuing this procedure, we get that immediately after a reset of the coupon rate, the floating rate bond is valued at par. Note that it is crucial for this result that the coupon rate is adjusted to the interest rate considered by the market to be 'fair'. Suppose we are interested in the value at some time t between T_0 and T_n. Let $T_{i(t)}$ be the nearest following payment date after time t. We know that the following payment at time $T_{i(t)}$ equals $H\delta l^{T_{i(t)}}_{T_{i(t)-1}}$ and that the value at time $T_{i(t)}$ of all the remaining payments will equal H. The value of the bond at time t will then be

$$B^{\mathrm{fl}}_t = H(1 + \delta l^{T_{i(t)}}_{T_{i(t)}-\delta})B^{T_{i(t)}}_t, \quad T_0 \le t < T_n.$$

This expression also holds at payment dates $t = T_i$, where it results in H, which is the value excluding the payment at that date.

The value of the floating rate bond is the value of both the coupon payments and the final repayment of face value so the value of the coupon payments only must be

$$\begin{aligned} V^{\mathrm{fl}}_t &= H(1 + \delta l^{T_{i(t)}}_{T_{i(t)}-\delta})B^{T_{i(t)}}_t - HB^{T_n}_t \\ &= H\delta l^{T_{i(t)}}_{T_{i(t)}-\delta}B^{T_{i(t)}}_t + H\left[B^{T_{i(t)}}_t - B^{T_n}_t\right], \quad T_0 \le t < T_n. \end{aligned}$$

At and before time T_0, the first term is not present, so the value of the floating rate payments is simply

$$V^{\mathrm{fl}}_t = H\left[B^{T_0}_t - B^{T_n}_t\right], \quad t \le T_0. \tag{13.23}$$

We will also develop an alternative expression for the value of the floating rate payments of the swap. The time $T_i - \delta$ value of the coupon payment at time T_i is

$$H\delta l^{T_i}_{T_i-\delta} B^{T_i}_{T_i-\delta} = H\delta \frac{l^{T_i}_{T_i-\delta}}{1+\delta l^{T_i}_{T_i-\delta}},$$

where we have applied Eq. (11.3). Consider a strategy of buying a zero-coupon bond with face value H maturing at $T_i - \delta$ and selling a zero-coupon bond with the same face value H but maturing at T_i. The time $T_i - \delta$ value of this position is

$$HB^{T_i-\delta}_{T_i-\delta} - HB^{T_i}_{T_i-\delta} = H - \frac{H}{1+\delta l^{T_i}_{T_i-\delta}} = H\delta \frac{l^{T_i}_{T_i-\delta}}{1+\delta l^{T_i}_{T_i-\delta}},$$

which is identical to the value of the floating rate payment of the swap. Therefore, the value of this floating rate payment at any time $t \leq T_i - \delta$ must be

$$H\left(B^{T_i-\delta}_t - B^{T_i}_t\right) = H\delta B^{T_i}_t \frac{\frac{B^{T_i-\delta}_t}{B^{T_i}_t} - 1}{\delta} = H\delta B^{T_i}_t L^{T_i-\delta,T_i}_t,$$

where we have applied Eq. (11.4). Thus, the value at time $t \leq T_i - \delta$ of getting $H\delta l^{T_i}_{T_i-\delta}$ at time T_i is equal to $H\delta B^{T_i}_t L^{T_i-\delta,T_i}_t$, that is the unknown future spot rate $l^{T_i}_{T_i-\delta}$ in the payoff is replaced by the current forward rate for $L^{T_i-\delta,T_i}_t$ and then discounted by the current risk-free discount factor $B^{T_i}_t$. The value at time $t > T_0$ of all the remaining floating coupon payments can therefore be written as

$$V^{\text{fl}}_t = H\delta B^{T_{i(t)}}_t l^{T_{i(t)}}_{T_{i(t)}-\delta} + H\delta \sum_{i=i(t)+1}^{n} B^{T_i}_t L^{T_i-\delta,T_i}_t, \quad T_0 \leq t < T_n.$$

At or before time T_0, the first term is not present, so we get

$$V^{\text{fl}}_t = H\delta \sum_{i=1}^{n} B^{T_i}_t L^{T_i-\delta,T_i}_t, \quad t \leq T_0. \tag{13.24}$$

The value of a payer swap is

$$\mathbf{P}_t = V^{\text{fl}}_t - V^{\text{fix}}_t,$$

while the value of a receiver swap is

$$\mathbf{R}_t = V^{\text{fix}}_t - V^{\text{fl}}_t.$$

In particular, the value of a payer swap at or before its starting date T_0 can be written as

$$\mathbf{P}_t = H\delta \sum_{i=1}^{n} B^{T_i}_t \left(L^{T_i-\delta,T_i}_t - K\right), \quad t \leq T_0, \tag{13.25}$$

using Eqs. (13.22) and (13.24), or as

$$\mathbf{P}_t = H\left(\left[B_t^{T_0} - B_t^{T_n}\right] - \sum_{i=1}^{n} K\delta B_t^{T_i}\right), \quad t \le T_0, \tag{13.26}$$

using Eqs. (13.22) and (13.23). If we let $Y_i = K\delta$ for $i = 1, \dots, n-1$ and $Y_n = 1 + K\delta$, we can rewrite Eq. (13.26) as

$$\mathbf{P}_t = H\left(B_t^{T_0} - \sum_{i=1}^{n} Y_i B_t^{T_i}\right), \quad t \le T_0. \tag{13.27}$$

Also note the following relation between a cap, a floor, and a payer swap having the same payment dates and where the cap rate, the floor rate, and the fixed rate in the swap are all identical:

$$\mathcal{C}_t = \mathcal{F}_t + \mathbf{P}_t.$$

This follows from the fact that the payments from a portfolio of a floor and a payer swap exactly match the payments of a cap.

The *swap rate* $\tilde{l}^{\delta}_{T_0}$ prevailing at time T_0 for a swap with frequency δ and payment dates $T_i = T_0 + i\delta$, $i = 1, 2, \dots, n$, is defined as the unique value of the fixed rate that makes the present value of a swap starting at T_0 equal to zero, that is $\mathbf{P}_{T_0} = \mathbf{R}_{T_0} = 0$. The swap rate is sometimes called the equilibrium swap rate or the par swap rate. Applying Eq. (13.25), we can write the swap rate as

$$\tilde{l}^{\delta}_{T_0} = \frac{\sum_{i=1}^{n} L_{T_0}^{T_i-\delta, T_i} B_{T_0}^{T_i}}{\sum_{i=1}^{n} B_{T_0}^{T_i}},$$

which can also be written as a weighted average of the relevant forward rates:

$$\tilde{l}^{\delta}_{T_0} = \sum_{i=1}^{n} w_i L_{T_0}^{T_i-\delta, T_i},$$

where $w_i = B_{T_0}^{T_i} / \sum_{i=1}^{n} B_{T_0}^{T_i}$. Alternatively, we can let $t = T_0$ in Eq. (13.26) yielding

$$\mathbf{P}_{T_0} = H\left(1 - B_{T_0}^{T_n} - K\delta \sum_{i=1}^{n} B_{T_0}^{T_i}\right)$$

so that the swap rate can be expressed as

$$\tilde{l}^{\delta}_{T_0} = \frac{1 - B_{T_0}^{T_n}}{\delta \sum_{i=1}^{n} B_{T_0}^{T_i}}. \tag{13.28}$$

Substituting Eq. (13.28) into the expression just above it, the time T_0 value of an agreement to pay a fixed rate K and receive the prevailing market rate at each of the dates $T_1, \dots, T_n$, can be written in terms of the current swap rate as

$$\mathbf{P}_{T_0} = H\left(\tilde{l}^{\delta}_{T_0}\delta\left(\sum_{i=1}^{n} B^{T_i}_{T_0}\right) - K\delta\left(\sum_{i=1}^{n} B^{T_i}_{T_0}\right)\right)$$
$$= \left(\sum_{i=1}^{n} B^{T_i}_{T_0}\right) H\delta\left(\tilde{l}^{\delta}_{T_0} - K\right). \tag{13.29}$$

A *forward swap* (or deferred swap) is an agreement to enter into a swap with a future starting date T_0 and a fixed rate which is already set. Of course, the contract also fixes the frequency, the maturity, and the notional principal of the swap. The value at time $t \leq T_0$ of a forward payer swap with fixed rate K is given by the equivalent expressions Eqs. (13.25)–(13.27). The *forward swap rate* $\tilde{L}^{\delta,T_0}_t$ is defined as the value of the fixed rate that makes the forward swap have zero value at time t. The forward swap rate can be written as

$$\tilde{L}^{\delta,T_0}_t = \frac{B^{T_0}_t - B^{T_n}_t}{\delta\sum_{i=1}^{n} B^{T_i}_t} = \frac{\sum_{i=1}^{n} L^{T_i-\delta,T_i}_t B^{T_i}_t}{\sum_{i=1}^{n} B^{T_i}_t}.$$

Note that both the swap rate and the forward swap rate depend on the frequency and the maturity of the underlying swap. To indicate this dependence, let $\tilde{l}^{\delta}_t(n)$ denote the time t swap rate for a swap with payment dates $T_i = t + i\delta$, $i = 1, 2, \dots, n$. If we depict the swap rate as a function of the maturity, that is the function $n \mapsto \tilde{l}^{\delta}_t(n)$ (only defined for $n = 1, 2, \dots$), we get a *term structure of swap rates* for the given frequency. Many financial institutions participating in the swap market will offer swaps of varying maturities under conditions reflected by their posted term structure of swap rates. In Exercise 13.7, you are asked to show how the discount factors $B^{T_i}_{T_0}$ can be derived from a term structure of swap rates.

13.4.2 Swaptions

A swaption is an option on a swap. A European *swaption* gives its holder the right, but not the obligation, at the expiry date T_0 to enter into a specific interest rate swap that starts at T_0 and has a given fixed rate K. No exercise price is to be paid if the right is utilized. The rate K is sometimes referred to as the exercise rate of the swaption. We distinguish between a *payer swaption*, which gives the right to enter into a payer swap, and a *receiver swaption*, which gives the right to enter into a receiver swap. As for caps and floors, two different pricing strategies can be taken. One strategy is to link the swaption payoff to the payoff of another well-known derivative. The other strategy is to directly take relevant expectations of the swaption payoff.

Let us first see how we can link swaptions to options on bonds. Let us focus on a European receiver swaption. At time T_0, the value of a receiver swap with payment dates $T_i = T_0 + i\delta$, $i = 1, 2, \ldots, n$, and a fixed rate K is given by

$$\mathbf{R}_{T_0} = H\left(\sum_{i=1}^{n} Y_i B_{T_0}^{T_i} - 1\right),$$

where $Y_i = K\delta$ for $i = 1, \ldots, n-1$ and $Y_n = 1 + K\delta$, compare Eq. (13.27). Hence, the time T_0 payoff of a receiver swaption is

$$\mathcal{R}_{T_0} = \max\left(\mathbf{R}_{T_0} - 0, 0\right) = H \max\left(\sum_{i=1}^{n} Y_i B_{T_0}^{T_i} - 1, 0\right),$$

which is equivalent to the payoff of H European call options on a bullet bond with face value 1, n payment dates, a period of δ between successive payments, and an annualized coupon rate K. The exercise price of each option equals the face value 1. The price of a European receiver swaption must therefore be equal to the price of these call options. In many models of interest rate dynamics, we can compute such prices quite easily. For the Vasicek model, the swaption prices follow from Eq. (13.18) and Theorem 13.8.

Similarly, a European payer swaption yields a payoff of

$$\mathcal{P}_{T_0} = \max\left(\mathbf{P}_{T_0} - 0, 0\right) = \max\left(-\mathbf{R}_{T_0}, 0\right) = H \max\left(1 - \sum_{i=1}^{n} Y_i B_{T_0}^{T_i}, 0\right).$$

This is identical to the payoff from H European put options expiring at T_0 and having an exercise price of 1 with a bond paying Y_i at time T_i, $i = 1, 2, \ldots, n$, as its underlying asset.

Alternatively, we can apply Eq. (13.29) to express the payoff of a European payer swaption as

$$\mathcal{P}_{T_0} = \left(\sum_{i=1}^{n} B_{T_0}^{T_i}\right) H\delta \max\left(\tilde{l}_{T_0}^{\delta} - K, 0\right),$$

where $\tilde{l}_{T_0}^{\delta}$ is the (equilibrium) swap rate prevailing at time T_0. What is an appropriate numeraire for pricing this swaption? If we were to use the zero-coupon bond maturing at T_0 as the numeraire, we would have to find the expectation of the payoff $\mathcal{P}_{T_0}$ under the T_0-forward martingale measure $\mathbb{Q}^{T_0}$. But since the payoff depends on several different bond prices, the distribution of $\mathcal{P}_{T_0}$ under $\mathbb{Q}^{T_0}$ is rather complicated. It is more convenient to use another numeraire, namely the annuity bond, which at each of the dates $T_1, \ldots, T_n$ provides a payment of 1 dollar. The value of this annuity at time $t \leq T_0$ equals $G_t = \sum_{i=1}^{n} B_t^{T_i}$. In particular, the payoff of the swaption can be restated as

$$\mathcal{P}_{T_0} = G_{T_0} H\delta \max\left(\tilde{l}^{\delta}_{T_0} - K, 0\right),$$

and the payoff expressed in units of the annuity bond is simply $H\delta \max\left(\tilde{l}^{\delta}_{T_0} - K, 0\right)$. The risk-adjusted probability measure corresponding to the annuity being the numeraire is sometimes called the *swap martingale measure* and will be denoted by $\mathbb{Q}^G$ in the following. The price of the European payer swaption can now be written as

$$\mathcal{P}_t = G_t \, \mathrm{E}_t^{\mathbb{Q}^G}\left[\frac{\mathcal{P}_{T_0}}{G_{T_0}}\right] = G_t H\delta \, \mathrm{E}_t^{\mathbb{Q}^G}\left[\max\left(\tilde{l}^{\delta}_{T_0} - K, 0\right)\right],$$

so we only need to know the distribution of the swap rate $\tilde{l}^{\delta}_{T_0}$ under the swap martingale measure. In the so-called lognormal swap rate model introduced by Jamshidian (1997), the swap rate $\tilde{l}^{\delta}_{T_0}$ is assumed to be lognormally distributed under the $\mathbb{Q}^G$-measure and the resulting swaption pricing formula is identical to the Black formula for swaptions often applied by practitioners:

$$\mathcal{P}_t = H\delta\left(\sum_{i=1}^{n} B_t^{T_i}\right)\left[\tilde{L}_t^{\delta,T_0} N\left(d(\tilde{L}_t^{\delta,T_0}, t)\right) - KN\left(d(\tilde{L}_t^{\delta,T_0}, t) - \tilde{\sigma}\right)\right], \quad t < T_0,$$

where $\tilde{\sigma}$ is the (relative) volatility of the foward swap rate $\tilde{L}_t^{\delta,T_0}$ and

$$d(\tilde{L}_t^{\delta,T_0}, t) = \frac{\ln(\tilde{L}_t^{\delta,T_0}/K)}{\tilde{\sigma}\sqrt{T_0 - t}} + \frac{1}{2}\tilde{\sigma}\sqrt{T_0 - t}.$$

See Munk (2011, Ch. 11) for a presentation and discussion of the lognormal swap rate model.

Similar to the put-call parity for options we have the following *payer-receiver parity* for European swaptions having the same underlying swap and the same exercise rate:

$$\mathcal{P}_t - \mathcal{R}_t = \mathbf{P}_t, \quad t \leq T_0, \tag{13.30}$$

compare Exercise 13.8. In words, a payer swaption minus a receiver swaption is indistinguishable from a forward payer swap.

13.5 AMERICAN-STYLE DERIVATIVES

Consider an American-style derivative where the holder has the right to choose when to exercise the derivative, at least within some limits. Typically exercise can take place at the expiration date T or at any time before T. Let P_τ denote the payoff if the derivative is exercised at time $\tau \leq T$. In general, P_τ may depend on the evolution of the economy up to and including time τ, but it is usually a simple function of the time τ price of an underlying security or the time τ value of a particular interest rate. At each point in time the holder of the derivative must decide whether or not he will exercise. Of course, this decision must be based on the available information, so we are seeking an entire exercise strategy that tells us exactly in what states of the world we should exercise the derivative. We can represent an exercise strategy by an indicator function $I(\omega, t)$, which for any given state of the economy ω at time t either has the value 1 or 0, where the value 1 indicates exercise and 0 indicates non-exercise. For a given exercise strategy I, the derivative will be exercised the first time $I(\omega, t)$ takes on the value 1. We can write this point in time as

$$\tau(I) = \min\{s \in [t, T] \mid I(\omega, s) = 1\}.$$

This is called a stopping time in the literature on stochastic processes. By our earlier analysis, the value of getting $V_{\tau(I)}$ at time $\tau(I)$ equals $\mathrm{E}_t^{\mathbb{Q}}\left[e^{-\int_t^{\tau(I)} r_u\,du} P_{\tau(I)}\right]$. If we let $\mathcal{I}[t, T]$ denote the set of all possible exercise strategies over the time period $[t, T]$, the time t value of the American-style derivative must therefore be

$$V_t = \sup_{I \in \mathcal{I}[t,T]} \mathrm{E}_t^{\mathbb{Q}}\left[e^{-\int_t^{\tau(I)} r_u\,du} P_{\tau(I)}\right].$$

An optimal exercise strategy I^* is such that

$$V_t = \mathrm{E}_t^{\mathbb{Q}}\left[e^{-\int_t^{\tau(I^*)} r_u\,du} P_{\tau(I^*)}\right].$$

Note that the optimal exercise strategy and the price of the derivative must be solved for simultaneously. This complicates the pricing of American-style derivatives considerably. In fact, in all situations where early exercise may be relevant, we will not be able to compute closed-form pricing formulas for American-style derivatives. We have to resort to numerical techniques. See Hull (2009) or Munk (2011) for an introduction to the standard techniques of binomial or trinomial trees, finite difference approximation of the partial differential equation that the pricing function must satisfy, and Monte Carlo simulation.

It is well-known that it is never strictly advantageous to exercise an American call option on a non-dividend paying asset before the final maturity date T, compare Merton (1973c) and Hull (2009, Ch. 9). In contrast, premature exercise of an American put option on a non-dividend paying asset will be advantageous for sufficiently low prices of the underlying asset. If the underlying asset pays dividends at discrete points in time, it can be optimal to exercise an American call option prematurely, but only immediately before each dividend payment date. Regarding early exercise of put options, it can never be optimal to exercise an American put on a dividend-paying asset just before a dividend payment, but at all other points in time early exercise will be optimal for sufficiently low prices of the underlying asset.

13.6 CONCLUDING REMARKS

This chapter has given an introduction to standard derivatives and the pricing of such derivatives. Numerous continuous-time models have been proposed in the literature for the pricing of derivatives on stocks, interest rates, bonds, commodities, foreign exchange, and other variables. Also many 'exotic' variations of the basic derivatives are traded and studied in the literature. In many cases the prices of some relevant derivatives cannot be computed explicitly given the modelling assumptions found to be reasonable so the prices have to be computed by approximations or numerical solution techniques. The design of efficient computational techniques for derivatives pricing is also an active research area.

The interested reader can find much more information on derivatives in specialized textbooks such as Musiela and Rutkowski (1997), James and Webber (2000), Brigo and Mercurio (2006), Björk (2009), Hull (2009), and Munk (2011). The market for derivatives with payoffs depending on credit events, such as the default of a given corporation, has been rapidly growing recently. Such derivatives and their pricing are studied in textbooks such as Bielecki and Rutkowski (2002), Duffie and Singleton (2003), Lando (2004), and Schönbucher (2003).

13.7 EXERCISES

Exercise 13.1 Consider a coupon bond with payment dates $T_1 < T_2 < \cdots < T_n$. For each $i = 1, 2, \ldots, n$, let Y_i be the sure payment at time T_i. For some $t < T < T_i$, let Φ_t^{T,T_i} denote the futures price at time t for delivery at time T of the zero-coupon bond maturing at time T_i with a unit payment. Show that futures price at time t for delivery at time T of the coupon bond satisfies

$$\Phi_t^{T,\text{cpn}} = \sum_{T_i > T} Y_i \Phi_t^{T,T_i}.$$

Exercise 13.2 Show by differentiation that the Black–Scholes–Merton call option price satisfies Eqs. (13.15) and (13.16). *Hint: First show that* $S_t n(d) = Ke^{-r[T-t]} n(d - \sigma\sqrt{T-t})$.

Exercise 13.3 Show that the no-arbitrage price of a European call option on a non-dividend paying stock must satisfy

$$\max\left(0, S_t - KB_t^T\right) \leq C_t \leq S_t.$$

Show that the no-arbitrage price of a European call on a zero-coupon bond will satisfy

$$\max\left(0, B_t^S - KB_t^T\right) \leq C_t^{K,T,S} \leq B_t^S(1-K)$$

provided that all interest rates are non-negative.

Exercise 13.4 We will adapt the Black–Scholes–Merton model and option pricing formula to three cases in which the underlying asset provides dividend payments before the expiration of the option at time T.

I. Discrete dividends known in absolute terms.
Suppose that the underlying asset pays dividends at n points in time before time T, namely $t_1 < t_2 < \cdots < t_n$. All the dividends are known already. Let D_j denote the dividend at time t_j. The time t value of all the remaining dividends is then

$$D_t^* = \sum_{t_j > t} D_j e^{-r(t_j - t)},$$

where r is the constant interest rate. Define $S_t^* = S_t - D_t^*$. Note that $S_T^* = S_T$.

(a) Show that S_t^* is the necessary investment at time t to end up with one unit of the underlying asset at time T.

(b) Assuming that S_t^* has constant volatility σ so that

$$dS_t^* = S_t^* \left(\mu(\cdot)\, dt + \sigma\, dz_t\right)$$

for some drift term $\mu(\cdot)$, derive a Black–Scholes–Merton-type equation for a European call option on this asset. State the option price in terms of S_t (and the remaining dividends). Compare with the standard Black–Scholes–Merton formula—in particular, check whether σ is equal to the volatility of S_t under the assumptions on S^*.

II. Discrete dividends known as a percentage of the price of the underlying asset.
Again assume that dividends are paid at $t_1 < t_2 < \cdots < t_n$, but now assume that the dividend at time t_j is known to be $D_j = \delta_j S_{t_j-}$, where δ_j is a known constant and S_{t_j-} is the price just before the dividend is paid out. The ex-dividend price is then $S_{t_j} = (1-\delta_j)S_{t_j-}$. Define the process S^* by

$$S_t^* = S_t \prod_{t_j > t} (1 - \delta_j), \quad t < t_n,$$

and $S_t^* = S_t$ for $t \geq t_n$. Answer the questions (a) and (b) above using this definition of S^*.

III. Continuous dividend payments at a known rate.
Now suppose that the underlying asset pays dividends continuously at a constant and known relative rate δ. This means that over any very short time interval $[t, t+\Delta t]$, the total dollar dividends is $\int_t^{t+\Delta t} \delta S_u\, du$ or approximately $\delta S_{t+\Delta t} \Delta t$. Define

$$S_t^* = S_t e^{-\delta(T-t)}.$$

Again, answer the questions (a) and (b) using this new definition of S^*. *Hint: For part (a), you may want to divide the interval $[t, T]$ into N equally long subintervals and assume that* *dividends are paid only at the end of each subinterval. Use the result* $\lim_{N\to\infty}(1+\delta\frac{T-t}{N})^N = e^{\delta(T-t)}$ *to go to the continuous-time limit.*

Exercise 13.5 Let $S_1 = (S_{1t})$ and $S_2 = (S_{2t})$ be the price processes of two assets. Consider the option to exchange (at zero cost) one unit of asset 2 for one unit of asset 1 at some prespecified date T. The payoff is thus $\max(S_{1T} - S_{2T}, 0)$. The assets have no dividends before time T.

(a) Argue that the time t value of this option can be written as

$$V_t = S_{2t}\,\mathrm{E}_t^{\mathbb{Q}_2}\left[\max\left(\frac{S_{1T}}{S_{2T}} - 1, 0\right)\right],$$

where $\mathbb{Q}_2$ is the risk-adjusted probability measure associated with asset 2.

Suppose that S_1 and S_2 are both geometric Brownian motions so that we may write their joint dynamics as

$$dS_{1t} = S_{1t}\left[\mu_1\,dt + \sigma_1\,dz_{1t}\right],$$
$$dS_{2t} = S_{2t}\left[\mu_2\,dt + \rho\sigma_2\,dz_{1t} + \sqrt{1-\rho^2}\sigma_2\,dz_{2t}\right].$$

(b) Find the dynamics of S_{1t}/S_{2t} under the probability measure $\mathbb{Q}_2$.

(c) Use the two previous questions and your knowledge of lognormal random variables to show that

$$V_t = S_{1t}N(d_1) - S_{2t}N(d_2), \tag{13.31}$$

where

$$d_1 = \frac{\ln(S_{1t}/S_{2t})}{v} + \frac{1}{2}v,\ d_2 = d_1 - v,\ v = \sqrt{(\sigma_1^2 + \sigma_2^2 - 2\rho\sigma_1\sigma_2)(T-t)}.$$

This formula was first given by Margrabe (1978).

(d) Give pricing formulas (in terms of S_{1t} and S_{2t}) for an option with payoff $\max(S_{1T}, S_{2T})$ and an option with payoff $\min(S_{1T}, S_{2T})$.

(e) What happens to the pricing formula (13.31) if asset 2 is a zero-coupon bond maturing at time T with a payment of K? And if, furthermore, interest rates are constant, what then?

Exercise 13.6 Let $F_t^{T,S}$ and $\Phi_t^{T,S}$ denote the forward price and futures price at time t, respectively, for delivery at time $T > t$ of a zero-coupon bond maturing at time $S > T$. Under the assumptions of the Vasicek model introduced in Section 11.5.1, show that

$$F_t^{T,S} = \exp\{-[\mathcal{A}(S-t) - \mathcal{A}(T-t)] - [\mathcal{B}_\kappa(S-t) - \mathcal{B}_\kappa(T-t)]r_t\},$$
$$\Phi_t^{T,S} = \exp\{-\tilde{\mathcal{A}}(T-t, S-T) - [\mathcal{B}_\kappa(S-t) - \mathcal{B}_\kappa(T-t)]r_t\},$$

where $\mathcal{A}(\cdot)$ and $\mathcal{B}_\kappa(\cdot)$ are given by Eqs. (11.29) and (11.25),

$$\tilde{\mathcal{A}}(T-t, S-T) = \mathcal{A}(S-T) + \kappa\hat{r}\mathcal{B}_\kappa(S-T)\mathcal{B}_\kappa(T-t) \\ - \frac{\sigma_r^2}{2}\mathcal{B}_\kappa(S-T)^2\left(\mathcal{B}_\kappa(T-t) - \frac{\kappa}{2}\mathcal{B}_\kappa(T-t)^2\right)$$

and $\hat{r} = \bar{r} - \sigma_r\lambda/\kappa$. Compare the forward price and the futures price.

Exercise 13.7 Let $\tilde{l}^\delta_{T_0}(k)$ be the equilibrium swap rate for a swap with payment dates $T_1, T_2, \ldots, T_k$, where $T_i = T_0 + i\delta$ as usual. Suppose that $\tilde{l}^\delta_{T_0}(1), \ldots, \tilde{l}^\delta_{T_0}(n)$ are known. Find a recursive procedure for deriving the associated discount factors $B^{T_1}_{T_0}, B^{T_2}_{T_0}, \ldots, B^{T_n}_{T_0}$.

Exercise 13.8 Show the parity (13.30). Show that a payer swaption and a receiver swaption (with identical terms) will have identical prices, if the exercise rate of the contracts is equal to the forward swap rate $\tilde{L}^{\delta,T_0}_t$.

Exercise 13.9 Consider a swap with starting date T_0 and a fixed rate K. For $t \leq T_0$, show that $V^{\mathrm{fl}}_t / V^{\mathrm{fix}}_t = \tilde{L}^{\delta,T_0}_t / K$, where $\tilde{L}^{\delta,T_0}_t$ is the forward swap rate.

APPENDIX A

A Review of Basic Probability Concepts

Risk is a key concept in asset pricing so we need to apply some concepts and results from probability theory. This appendix gives a short introduction, which is a bit more formal than many textbooks on statistics for business and economics. Some further issues are introduced and discussed in the main text when needed.

The basic mathematical object for studies of uncertain events is a *probability space*, which is a triple $(\Omega, \mathcal{F}, \mathbb{P})$ consisting of a state space Ω, a sigma-algebra $\mathcal{F}$, and a probability measure $\mathbb{P}$. Any study of uncertain events must explicitly or implicitly specify the probability space. Let us discuss each of the three elements of a probability space in turn.

The *state space* Ω is the set of possible states or outcomes of the uncertain object. Only one of these states will be realized. For example, if one studies the outcome of a throw of a die (the number of 'eyes' on the upside), the state space is $\Omega = \{1, 2, 3, 4, 5, 6\}$. An event is a set of possible outcomes, that is a subset of the state space. In the example with the die, some events are $\{1, 2, 3\}$, $\{4, 5\}$, $\{1, 3, 5\}$, $\{6\}$, and $\{1, 2, 3, 4, 5, 6\}$. This is an example where a finite state space is natural. For other uncertain objects it is natural to take an infinite state space. If we only want to study the dividend of a given stock at a given point in time, an appropriate state space is $\mathbb{R}_+ \equiv [0, \infty)$ since the dividend may in principle be any non-negative real number. In our asset pricing models we want to study the entire economy over a certain time span so the state space has to list all the possible realizations of dividends of all assets and incomes of all individuals. Of course, this requires a large state space. Note that some authors use the term sample space instead of state space.

The second component of a probability space, $\mathcal{F}$, is the set of events to which a probability can be assigned, that is the *set of 'probabilizable' or 'measurable' events.* Hence, $\mathcal{F}$ is a set of subsets of the state space! It is required that

(i) the entire state space can be assigned a probability, that is $\Omega \in \mathcal{F}$;

(ii) if some event $F \subseteq \Omega$ can be assigned a probability, so can its complement $F^c \equiv \Omega \setminus F$, that is $F \in \mathcal{F} \Rightarrow F^c \in \mathcal{F}$; and

(iii) given a sequence of probabilizable events, the union is also probabilizable, that is $F_1, F_2, \dots \in \mathcal{F} \Rightarrow \cup_{i=1}^{\infty} F_i \in \mathcal{F}$.

A set $\mathcal{F}$ with these properties is called a *sigma-algebra*, a sigma-field, or a tribe. We will stick to the term sigma-algebra.

Alternatively, we can use a partition of the state space to represent the probabilizable events. By a partition $\mathbb{F}$ of Ω we mean a collection $A_1, \dots, A_k$ of disjoint subsets of Ω, that is $A_i \cap A_j = \emptyset$ for $i \neq j$, so that the union of these subsets equals the entire set Ω, that is $\Omega = A_1 \cup \dots \cup A_k$. With a finite state space $\Omega = \{\omega_1, \omega_2, \dots, \omega_S\}$ the natural partition is

$$\mathbb{F} = \Big\{\{\omega_1\}, \{\omega_2\}, \dots, \{\omega_S\}\Big\},$$

which intuitively means that we will learn exactly which state is realized. Given a partition F we can define an associated sigma-algebra $\mathcal{F}$ as the set of all unions of (countably many) sets in F including the 'empty union', that is the empty set $\emptyset$. Again, if $\Omega = \{\omega_1, \omega_2, \dots, \omega_S\}$ and $\mathrm{F} = \left\{\{\omega_1\}, \{\omega_2\}, \dots, \{\omega_S\}\right\}$, the corresponding sigma-algebra is the set of all subsets of Ω. On the other hand we can also go from a sigma-algebra $\mathcal{F}$ to a partition F. Just remove all sets in $\mathcal{F}$ that are unions of the sets in $\mathcal{F}$. Again this includes the empty set $\emptyset$ since that is an 'empty union' of the other sets in $\mathcal{F}$. If the state space is infinite, the equivalence between a partition and a sigma-algebra may break down, and the sigma-algebra formulation is the preferred one; see for example the discussion in Björk (2009, App. B).

We can think of the sigma-algebra $\mathcal{F}$ or the associated partition F as representing full information about the realization of the state. In some cases it can be relevant also to model some limited information about the realized state. Many models in financial economics are designed to capture uncertainty about many different variables or objects, for example the dividends on a large number of stocks. It may be relevant to formalize what can be learned about the true state by just observing the dividends of one particular stock. In other models some individuals are assumed to know more about some uncertain objects than other individuals. Less-than-full information can be represented formally by a sigma-algebra $\mathcal{G}$ on Ω, which is coarser than $\mathcal{F}$ in the sense that any set in $\mathcal{G}$ is also in $\mathcal{F}$. In terms of partitions, a partition G of Ω represents less information than F if any set in G is the union of sets in F. In the example with the throw of a die, full information is represented by the partition

$$\mathrm{F} = \left\{\{1\}, \{2\}, \{3\}, \{4\}, \{5\}, \{6\}\right\}$$

or the associated sigma-algebra. An example of less-than-perfect information is represented by the partition

$$\mathrm{G} = \left\{\{1, 3, 5\}, \{2, 4, 6\}\right\}$$

or the associated sigma-algebra

$$\mathcal{G} = \left\{\emptyset, \{1, 3, 5\}, \{2, 4, 6\}, \Omega\right\}.$$

With G, you will only know whether the die will show an odd or an even number of eyes on the upside. As mentioned above the link between partitions and sigma-algebras is more delicate in infinite state spaces and so is the notion of information. Dubra and Echenique (2004) give an example in an economic setting where one partition represents more information than another partition but the sigma-algebra associated with the second partition seems to represent more information than the sigma-algebra associated with the first!

The final component of a probability space is a *probability measure* $\mathbb{P}$, which formally is a function from the sigma-algebra $\mathcal{F}$ into the interval $[0, 1]$. To each event $F \in \mathcal{F}$, the probability measure assigns a number $\mathbb{P}(F)$ in the interval $[0, 1]$. This number is called the $\mathbb{P}$-probability (or simply the probability) of F. A probability measure must satisfy the following conditions:

(i) $\mathbb{P}(\Omega) = 1$ and $\mathbb{P}(\emptyset) = 0$;

(ii) the probability of the state being in the union of disjoint sets is equal to the sum of the probabilities for each of the sets, that is given $F_1, F_2, \dots \in \mathcal{F}$ with $F_i \cap F_j = \emptyset$ for all $i \neq j$, we have $\mathbb{P}(\cup_{i=1}^{\infty} F_i) = \sum_{i=1}^{\infty} \mathbb{P}(F_i)$.

If the state space Ω is finite, say $\Omega = \{\omega_1, \omega_2, \dots, \omega_S\}$, and each $\{\omega_i\}$ is probabilizable, a probability measure $\mathbb{P}$ is fully specified by the individual state probabilities $\mathbb{P}(\omega_i)$, $i = 1, 2, \dots, S$.

Many different probability measures can be defined on the same sigma-algebra, $\mathcal{F}$, of events. In the example of the die, a probability measure $\mathbb{P}$ corresponding to the idea that the die is 'fair' is defined by

$$\mathbb{P}(\{1\}) = \mathbb{P}(\{2\}) = \dots = \mathbb{P}(\{6\}) = 1/6.$$

Another probability measure, $\mathbb{Q}$, can be defined by

$$\mathbb{Q}(\{1\}) = 1/12, \quad \mathbb{Q}(\{2\}) = \dots = \mathbb{Q}(\{5\}) = 1/6, \quad \mathbb{Q}(\{6\}) = 3/12,$$

which may be appropriate if the die is believed to be 'unfair'.

Two probability measures $\mathbb{P}$ and $\mathbb{Q}$ defined on the same state space and sigma-algebra $(\Omega, \mathcal{F})$ are called *equivalent probability measures* if the two measures assign probability zero to exactly the same events, that is if $\mathbb{P}(A) = 0 \Leftrightarrow \mathbb{Q}(A) = 0$. The two probability measures in the die example are equivalent. In the stochastic models of financial markets switching between equivalent probability measures turns out to be useful.

A *random variable* is a function X from the state space Ω into the real numbers $\mathbb{R}$. To each possible outcome $\omega \in \Omega$ the function assigns a real number $X(\omega)$. A random variable is thus the formal way to represent a state-dependent quantity. To be meaningful, the function X must be $\mathcal{F}$-measurable. This means that for any interval $I \in \mathbb{R}$, the set $\{\omega \in \Omega | X(\omega) \in I\}$ belongs to $\mathcal{F}$, that is we can assign a probability to the event that the random variable takes on a value in the interval I. A random variable is thus defined relative to a probability space $(\Omega, \mathcal{F}, \mathbb{P})$.

Any random variable is associated with a probability distribution. We can represent the distribution of the random variable X by the *cumulative distribution function* $F_X : \mathbb{R} \to \mathbb{R}$ defined for any $x \in \mathbb{R}$ by

$$F_X(x) = \mathbb{P}(X \leq x) \equiv \mathbb{P}(\{\omega \in \Omega | X(\omega) \leq x\}).$$

A random variable X is said to be a discrete-valued or simply a *discrete random variable* if it can only take on finitely many different values $x_1, x_2, \dots, x_m \in \mathbb{R}$. In that case we can represent the probability distribution by the numbers $f_X(x_i) \equiv \mathbb{P}(X = x_i) \equiv \mathbb{P}(\{\omega \in \Omega | X(\omega) = x_i\})$. Note that this is surely the case if the state space Ω itself is finite. A random variable X is said to be a continuous-valued or simply a *continuous random variable* if it can take on a continuum of possible values and a function $f_X : \mathbb{R} \to \mathbb{R}$ exists such that

$$F_X(x) = \int_{-\infty}^{x} f_X(y)\, dy.$$

The function f_X is then called the *probability density function* of X. It is also possible to construct random variables that are neither discrete nor continuous but they will not be important for our purposes. In any case we can represent the probability distribution more abstractly by a *distribution measure* μ_X, which is a probability measure on the real numbers $\mathbb{R}$ equipped with the so-called Borel-algebra $\mathcal{B}$. The Borel-algebra can be defined as the smallest sigma-algebra that includes all intervals. The Borel-algebra includes all subsets of $\mathbb{R}$ 'you can think of' but there are in fact some very obscure subsets of $\mathbb{R}$ which are not in the Borel-algebra. Fortunately, this will be unimportant for our purposes. The distribution measure is defined for any $B \in \mathcal{B}$ by

$$\mu_X(B) = \mathbb{P}(X \in B) \equiv \mathbb{P}(\{\omega \in \Omega | X(\omega) \in B\}).$$

It is often useful to summarize the probability distribution of a random variable in a few informative numbers. The most frequently used are the expected value (or mean) and the variance. For a discrete random variable X that can take on the values $x_1, \dots, x_m \in \mathbb{R}$, the *expected value* $\mathrm{E}[X]$ is defined by

$$\mathrm{E}[X] = \sum_{i=1}^{m} x_i \mathbb{P}(X = x_i).$$

For a continuous random variable X with probability density function f_X, the expected value is defined as

$$\mathrm{E}[X] = \int_{-\infty}^{\infty} x f_X(x)\, dx$$

if this integral is finite; otherwise the random variable does not have an expected value. Similarly we can define the expected value of a function $g(X)$ as $\mathrm{E}[g(X)] = \sum_{i=1}^{m} g(x_i)\mathbb{P}(X = x_i)$ or $\mathrm{E}[g(X)] = \int_{-\infty}^{\infty} g(x) f_X(x)\, dx$, respectively.

For a general random variable X we can define the expected value of $g(X)$ as

$$\mathrm{E}[g(X)] = \int_{\Omega} g(X(\omega))\, d\mathbb{P}(\omega)$$

which is an integral with respect to the probability measure $\mathbb{P}$. For functions that are just modestly nice (so-called Borel functions) one can rewrite the expected value as

$$\mathrm{E}[g(X)] = \int_{-\infty}^{\infty} g(x)\, d\mu_X(x)$$

which is an integral with respect to the distribution measure μ_X of the random variable. We do not want to go into the theory of integration with respect to various measures so let us just note that for discrete and continuous random variables the general definition simplifies to the definitions given in the paragraph above.

The *variance* of a random variable X is generally defined as

$$\mathrm{Var}[X] = \mathrm{E}\left[(X - \mathrm{E}[X])^2\right] = \mathrm{E}\left[X^2\right] - (\mathrm{E}[X])^2.$$

The *standard deviation* of X is $\sigma[X] = \sqrt{\mathrm{Var}[X]}$. The n'th moment of the random variable X is $\mathrm{E}[X^n]$, while the n'th central moment is $\mathrm{E}\left[(X - \mathrm{E}[X])^n\right]$. In particular, the variance is the second central moment.

It can be shown that, for any constants a and b,

$$\mathrm{E}[aX + b] = a\,\mathrm{E}[X] + b, \quad \mathrm{Var}[aX + b] = a^2\,\mathrm{Var}[X], \quad \sigma[aX + b] = |a|\,\sigma[X],$$

where $|a|$ denotes the absolute value of a.

In the example with the throw of a die, the random variable X defined by $X(\omega) = \omega$ for all $\omega \in \Omega$ simply represents the uncertain number of eyes on the upside of the die after the throw. Other random variables may be relevant also. Suppose that you bet 10 dollars with a friend that the number of eyes on the upside will be even or odd. If even, you will win 10 dollars, if odd, you will lose 10 dollars. A random variable Y capturing your uncertain gain on the bet can be defined as follows:

$$Y(\omega) = \begin{cases} 10, & \text{if } \omega \in \{2,4,6\}, \\ -10, & \text{if } \omega \in \{1,3,5\}. \end{cases}$$

If the die is believed to be fair, corresponding to the probability measure $\mathbb{P}$, the distribution associated with the random variable Y is given by

$$\mathbb{P}(Y = -10) = \mathbb{P}(\omega \in \{1,3,5\}) = \frac{1}{2},$$

$$\mathbb{P}(Y = 10) = \mathbb{P}(\omega \in \{2,4,6\}) = \frac{1}{2},$$

or by the cumulative distribution function

$$F_Y(x) \equiv \mathbb{P}(Y(\omega) \leq x) = \begin{cases} 0, & \text{for } x < -10, \\ \frac{1}{2}, & \text{for } -10 \leq x < 10, \\ 1, & \text{for } x \geq 10. \end{cases}$$

Observing the realization of a random variable can give you some information about which state ω was realized. If the random variable X takes on different values in all states, that is you cannot find $\omega_1, \omega_2 \in \Omega$ with $\omega_1 \neq \omega_2$ and $X(\omega_1) \neq X(\omega_2)$, observing the realized value $X(\omega)$ will tell you exactly which state was realized. On the other extreme, if X takes on the same value in all states, you cannot infer anything from observing $X(\omega)$. Other random variables will tell you something, but not everything. In the example above, observing the realization of the random variable Y will tell you either that the realized state is in $\{1,3,5\}$ or in $\{2,4,6\}$. We can represent this by the partition

$$\mathbb{F}_Y = \Big\{\{1,3,5\}, \{2,4,6\}\Big\}$$

or the associated sigma-algebra

$$\mathcal{F}_Y = \Big\{\emptyset, \{1,3,5\}, \{2,4,6\}, \Omega\Big\}.$$

More generally, we can define the sigma-algebra associated with a random variable $X : \Omega \to \mathbb{R}$ to be the smallest sigma-algebra on Ω with respect to which X is a measurable function. This sigma-algebra will be denoted $\mathcal{F}_X$. Just think of this as the information generated by X.

We have defined a random variable to be a function from Ω to $\mathbb{R}$. Given two random variables X_1 and X_2 on the same probability space, we can form the vector $(X_1, X_2)^\top$, which is then a (measurable) function from Ω to $\mathbb{R}^2$ said to be a two-dimensional random variable. For example, X_1 could represent the uncertain dividend of one asset and X_2 the uncertain dividend of another asset. Similarly we can define random variables of any other (integer) dimension. This will often be notationally convenient.

For a two-dimensional random variable $(X_1, X_2)^\top$, the *joint or simultaneous cumulative distribution function* is the function $F_{(X_1,X_2)} : \mathbb{R}^2 \to \mathbb{R}$ defined by

$$\begin{aligned}F_{(X_1,X_2)}(x_1, x_2) &= \mathbb{P}(X_1 \leq x_1, X_2 \leq x_2)\\ &\equiv \mathbb{P}(\{\omega \in \Omega | X_1(\omega) \leq x_1 \text{ and } X_2(\omega) \leq x_2\}).\end{aligned}$$

If both X_1 and X_2 are discrete random variables, the vector random variable $(X_1, X_2)^\top$ is also discrete, and the joint probability distribution is characterized by probabilities $\mathbb{P}(X_1 = x_1, X_2 = x_2)$. The two-dimensional random variable $(X_1, X_2)^\top$ is said to be continuous if a function $f_{(X_1,X_2)} : \mathbb{R}^2 \to \mathbb{R}$ exists such that

$$F_{(X_1,X_2)}(x_1, x_2) = \int_{-\infty}^{x_1} \int_{-\infty}^{x_2} f_{(X_1,X_2)}(y_1, y_2)\, dy_1\, dy_2$$

and $f_{(X_1,X_2)}$ is then called the joint or simultaneous probability density function of $(X_1, X_2)^\top$.

Given the joint distribution of $(X_1, X_2)^\top$, we can find the distributions of X_1 and X_2, the so-called *marginal distributions*. For example, if $(X_1, X_2)^\top$ is continuous with joint probability density function $f_{(X_1,X_2)}$, we can find the marginal probability density function of X_1 by integrating over all possible values of X_2, that is

$$f_{X_1}(x_1) = \int_{-\infty}^{+\infty} f_{(X_1,X_2)}(x_1, x_2)\, dx_2.$$

Two random variables X_1 and X_2 are said to be *independent* if

$$\mathbb{P}(X_1 \in B_1, X_2 \in B_2) = \mathbb{P}(X_1 \in B_1)\, \mathbb{P}(X_2 \in B_2)$$

for all Borel sets $B_1, B_2 \subseteq \mathbb{R}$ or, equivalently, if

$$F_{(X_1,X_2)}(x_1, x_2) = F_{X_1}(x_1)\, F_{X_2}(x_2)$$

for all $(x_1, x_2) \in \mathbb{R}^2$.

We can easily extend the definition of the expected value to functions of multidimensional random variables. If $(X_1, X_2)^\top$ is a two-dimensional continuous random variable and $g : \mathbb{R}^2 \to \mathbb{R}$, the expected value of $g(X_1, X_2)$ is defined as

$$\mathrm{E}[g(X_1, X_2)] = \int_{-\infty}^{+\infty} \int_{-\infty}^{+\infty} g(x_1, x_2) f_{(X_1,X_2)}(x_1, x_2)\, dx_1\, dx_2.$$

We define the *covariance* between X_1 and X_2 by

$$\mathrm{Cov}[X_1, X_2] = \mathrm{E}\left[(X_1 - \mathrm{E}[X_1])(X_2 - \mathrm{E}[X_2])\right] = \mathrm{E}[X_1 X_2] - \mathrm{E}[X_1]\, \mathrm{E}[X_2].$$

In particular, $\mathrm{Cov}[X_1, X_1] = \mathrm{Var}[X_1]$. The *correlation* between X_1 and X_2 is

$$\mathrm{Corr}[X_1, X_2] = \frac{\mathrm{Cov}[X_1, X_2]}{\sigma[X_1]\sigma[X_2]},$$

which is a number in the interval $[-1, 1]$. Some useful properties of covariances are

$$\begin{aligned}\mathrm{Cov}[X_1, X_2] &= \mathrm{Cov}[X_2, X_1],\\ \mathrm{Cov}[aX_1 + bX_2, X_3] &= a\,\mathrm{Cov}[X_1, X_3] + b\,\mathrm{Cov}[X_2, X_3],\end{aligned}$$

where X_1, X_2, X_3 are three random variables and $a, b \in \mathbb{R}$. An often used result is

$$\operatorname{Var}[X_1 + X_2] = \operatorname{Var}[X_1] + \operatorname{Var}[X_2] + 2\operatorname{Cov}[X_1, X_2].$$

If X_1 and X_2 are independent, one can show that $\operatorname{Cov}[X_1, X_2] = 0$ and, consequently, $\operatorname{Corr}[X_1, X_2] = 0$.

If $\boldsymbol{X} = (X_1, \dots, X_K)^\top$ is a K-dimensional random variable, its variance-covariance matrix is the $K \times K$ matrix $\operatorname{Var}[\boldsymbol{X}]$ with (i,j)'th entry given by $\operatorname{Cov}[X_i, X_j]$. If $\boldsymbol{X}$ is a K-dimensional random variable and $\underline{\underline{A}}$ is an $M \times K$ matrix, then

$$\operatorname{Var}[\underline{\underline{A}}\boldsymbol{X}] = \underline{\underline{A}}\operatorname{Var}[\boldsymbol{X}]\underline{\underline{A}}^\top. \tag{A.1}$$

If $\boldsymbol{X} = (X_1, \dots, X_K)^\top$ is a K-dimensional random variable and $\boldsymbol{Y} = (Y_1, \dots, Y_L)^\top$ is an L-dimensional random variable, their covariance matrix $\operatorname{Cov}[\boldsymbol{X}, \boldsymbol{Y}]$ is the $K \times L$ matrix whose (k, l)'th entry is $\operatorname{Cov}[X_k, Y_l]$. If, furthermore, $\underline{\underline{A}}$ is an $M \times K$ matrix and $\underline{\underline{B}}$ is an $N \times L$ matrix, then

$$\operatorname{Cov}[\underline{\underline{A}}\boldsymbol{X}, \underline{\underline{B}}\boldsymbol{Y}] = \underline{\underline{A}}\operatorname{Cov}[\boldsymbol{X}, \boldsymbol{Y}]\underline{\underline{B}}^\top. \tag{A.2}$$

If, in addition, $\boldsymbol{a}$ is a non-random M-dimensional vector and $\boldsymbol{b}$ is a non-random N-dimensional vector, then

$$\operatorname{Cov}[\underline{\underline{A}}\boldsymbol{X} + \boldsymbol{a}, \underline{\underline{B}}\boldsymbol{Y} + \boldsymbol{b}] = \underline{\underline{A}}\operatorname{Cov}[\boldsymbol{X}, \boldsymbol{Y}]\underline{\underline{B}}^\top.$$

APPENDIX B

Results on the Lognormal Distribution

A random variable Y is said to be lognormally distributed if the random variable $X = \ln Y$ is normally distributed. In the following we let m be the mean of X and s^2 be the variance of X so that

$$X = \ln Y \sim N(m, s^2).$$

The probability density function for X is given by

$$f_X(x) = \frac{1}{\sqrt{2\pi s^2}} \exp\left\{-\frac{(x-m)^2}{2s^2}\right\}, \qquad x \in \mathbb{R}.$$

Theorem B.1 *The probability density function for Y is given by*

$$f_Y(y) = \frac{1}{\sqrt{2\pi s^2}\,y} \exp\left\{-\frac{(\ln y - m)^2}{2s^2}\right\}, \qquad y > 0,$$

and $f_Y(y) = 0$ for $y \leq 0$.

This result follows from the general result on the distribution of a random variable which is given as a function of another random variable; see any introductory textbook on probability theory and distributions.

Theorem B.2 *For $X \sim N(m, s^2)$ and $\gamma \in \mathbb{R}$ we have*

$$\mathrm{E}\left[e^{-\gamma X}\right] = \exp\left\{-\gamma m + \frac{1}{2}\gamma^2 s^2\right\},$$

$$\mathrm{Var}\left[e^{-\gamma X}\right] = \left(\mathrm{E}[e^{-\gamma X}]\right)^2 \left[e^{\gamma^2 s^2} - 1\right].$$

Proof. Per definition we have

$$\mathrm{E}\left[e^{-\gamma X}\right] = \int_{-\infty}^{+\infty} e^{-\gamma x} \frac{1}{\sqrt{2\pi s^2}} e^{-\frac{(x-m)^2}{2s^2}}\, dx.$$

Manipulating the exponent we get

$$\begin{aligned}
\mathrm{E}\left[e^{-\gamma X}\right] &= e^{-\gamma m + \frac{1}{2}\gamma^2 s^2} \int_{-\infty}^{+\infty} \frac{1}{\sqrt{2\pi s^2}} e^{-\frac{1}{2s^2}\left[(x-m)^2 + 2\gamma(x-m)s^2 + \gamma^2 s^4\right]}\, dx \\
&= e^{-\gamma m + \frac{1}{2}\gamma^2 s^2} \int_{-\infty}^{+\infty} \frac{1}{\sqrt{2\pi s^2}} e^{-\frac{(x-[m-\gamma s^2])^2}{2s^2}}\, dx \\
&= e^{-\gamma m + \frac{1}{2}\gamma^2 s^2},
\end{aligned}$$

where the last equality is due to the fact that the function

$$x \mapsto \frac{1}{\sqrt{2\pi s^2}} e^{-\frac{(x-[m-\gamma s^2])^2}{2s^2}}$$

is a probability density function, namely the density function for an $N(m-\gamma s^2, s^2)$ distributed random variable.

The variance is now computed as

$$\begin{aligned}
\mathrm{Var}[e^{-\gamma x}] &= \mathrm{E}[(e^{-\gamma x})^2] - \left(\mathrm{E}[e^{-\gamma x}]\right)^2 = \mathrm{E}[e^{-2\gamma x}] - \left(e^{-\gamma m+\frac{1}{2}\gamma^2 s^2}\right)^2 \\
&= e^{-2\gamma m+2\gamma^2 s^2} - \left(e^{-\gamma m+\frac{1}{2}\gamma^2 s^2}\right)^2 = \left(e^{-\gamma m+\frac{1}{2}\gamma^2 s^2}\right)^2 \left[e^{\gamma^2 s^2} - 1\right] \\
&= \left(\mathrm{E}[e^{-\gamma x}]\right)^2 \left[e^{\gamma^2 s^2} - 1\right],
\end{aligned}$$

where we have applied the result for the expectation with 2γ replacing γ. □

Using this theorem, we can easily compute the mean and the variance of the lognormally distributed random variable $Y = e^X$. The mean is (let $\gamma = -1$)

$$\mathrm{E}[Y] = \mathrm{E}\left[e^X\right] = \exp\left\{m + \frac{1}{2}s^2\right\}$$

and the variance is

$$\mathrm{Var}[Y] = e^{2m+s^2}\left(e^{s^2} - 1\right).$$

The next theorem provides an expression of the truncated mean of a lognormally distributed random variable, that is the mean of the part of the distribution that lies above some level. We define the indicator variable $\mathbf{1}_{\{Y>K\}}$ to be equal to 1 if the outcome of the random variable Y is greater than the constant K and equal to 0 otherwise.

Theorem B.3 *If $X = \ln Y \sim N(m, s^2)$ and $K > 0$, then we have*

$$\begin{aligned}
\mathrm{E}\left[Y\mathbf{1}_{\{Y>K\}}\right] &= e^{m+\frac{1}{2}s^2} N\left(\frac{m - \ln K}{s} + s\right) \\
&= \mathrm{E}\left[Y\right] N\left(\frac{m - \ln K}{s} + s\right).
\end{aligned}$$

Proof. Because $Y > K \Leftrightarrow X > \ln K$, it follows from the definition of the expectation of a random variable that

$$\begin{aligned}
\mathrm{E}\left[Y\mathbf{1}_{\{Y>K\}}\right] &= \mathrm{E}\left[e^X \mathbf{1}_{\{X>\ln K\}}\right] \\
&= \int_{\ln K}^{+\infty} e^x \frac{1}{\sqrt{2\pi s^2}} e^{-\frac{(x-m)^2}{2s^2}}\, dx \\
&= \int_{\ln K}^{+\infty} \frac{1}{\sqrt{2\pi s^2}} e^{-\frac{(x-[m+s^2])^2}{2s^2}} e^{\frac{2ms^2+s^4}{2s^2}}\, dx \\
&= e^{m+\frac{1}{2}s^2} \int_{\ln K}^{+\infty} f_{\bar{X}}(x)\, dx,
\end{aligned}$$

where

$$f_{\bar{X}}(x) = \frac{1}{\sqrt{2\pi s^2}} e^{-\frac{(x-[m+s^2])^2}{2s^2}}$$

is the probability density function for an $N(m + s^2, s^2)$ distributed random variable. The calculations

$$\begin{aligned}
\int_{\ln K}^{+\infty} f_{\bar{X}}(x)\,dx &= \text{Prob}(\bar{X} > \ln K) \\
&= \text{Prob}\left(\frac{\bar{X} - [m + s^2]}{s} > \frac{\ln K - [m + s^2]}{s}\right) \\
&= \text{Prob}\left(\frac{\bar{X} - [m + s^2]}{s} < -\frac{\ln K - [m + s^2]}{s}\right) \\
&= N\left(-\frac{\ln K - [m + s^2]}{s}\right) \\
&= N\left(\frac{m - \ln K}{s} + s\right)
\end{aligned}$$

complete the proof. □

Theorem B.4 *If $X = \ln Y \sim N(m, s^2)$ and $K > 0$, we have*

$$\begin{aligned}
\text{E}\left[\max(0, Y - K)\right] &= e^{m+\frac{1}{2}s^2} N\left(\frac{m - \ln K}{s} + s\right) - KN\left(\frac{m - \ln K}{s}\right) \\
&= \text{E}\left[Y\right] N\left(\frac{m - \ln K}{s} + s\right) - KN\left(\frac{m - \ln K}{s}\right).
\end{aligned}$$

Proof. Note that

$$\begin{aligned}
\text{E}\left[\max(0, Y - K)\right] &= \text{E}\left[(Y - K)\mathbf{1}_{\{Y>K\}}\right] \\
&= \text{E}\left[Y\mathbf{1}_{\{Y>K\}}\right] - K\text{Prob}\,(Y > K).
\end{aligned}$$

The first term is known from Theorem B.3. The second term can be rewritten as

$$\begin{aligned}
\text{Prob}\,(Y > K) &= \text{Prob}\,(X > \ln K) \\
&= \text{Prob}\left(\frac{X - m}{s} > \frac{\ln K - m}{s}\right) \\
&= \text{Prob}\left(\frac{X - m}{s} < -\frac{\ln K - m}{s}\right) \\
&= N\left(-\frac{\ln K - m}{s}\right) \\
&= N\left(\frac{m - \ln K}{s}\right).
\end{aligned}$$

The claim now follows immediately. □

APPENDIX C

Results from Linear Algebra

This appendix is a collection of definitions and results from linear algebra that are applied in the main text. Proofs and additional results can be found, for example, in Sydsaeter and Hammond (2005) and Sydsaeter *et al.* (2005).

Vector.

A vector of dimension $n \in \{1, 2, \dots\}$ – or just an n-vector – is an ordered collection of n elements or so-called components, coordinates, or entries. An n-vector $\boldsymbol{x}$ with elements $x_1, \dots, x_n$ is typically written as

$$\boldsymbol{x} = \begin{pmatrix} x_1 \\ x_2 \\ \vdots \\ x_n \end{pmatrix}.$$

A vector with all entries equal to zero is denoted by $\mathbf{0}$, and a vector with all entries equal to the number one is denoted by $\mathbf{1}$.

Matrix.

A matrix of dimension (m, n) – or just an $m \times n$ matrix – is a collection of mn elements or entries ordered in a rectangular array with $m \in \{1, 2, \dots\}$ rows and $n \in \{1, 2, \dots\}$ columns. For example, an $m \times n$ matrix $\underline{\underline{A}}$ is typically written as

$$\underline{\underline{A}} = \begin{pmatrix} A_{11} & A_{12} & \dots & A_{1n} \\ A_{21} & A_{22} & \dots & A_{2n} \\ \vdots & \vdots & \ddots & \vdots \\ A_{m1} & A_{m2} & \dots & A_{mn} \end{pmatrix}$$

or more shortly as $\underline{\underline{A}} = [A_{ij}]$, where it is then understood that A_{ij} is the element in the position where row i crosses column j, where $i = 1, \dots, m$ and $j = 1, \dots, n$. Sometimes A_{ij} is called entry (i, j) of $\underline{\underline{A}}$.

Unless otherwise mentioned, an n-vector is seen as an $n \times 1$ matrix, that is as a column vector.

A matrix with equally many rows and columns is called a square matrix. The identity matrix of dimension n is the $n \times n$ matrix $\underline{\underline{I}} = [I_{ij}]$ with one along the diagonal and zeros elsewhere, that is $I_{ii} = 1$, $i = 1, \dots, n$, and $I_{ij} = 0$ for $i, j = 1, \dots, n$ with $i \neq j$.

Adding and scaling vectors and matrices.

Given two vectors $\boldsymbol{x} = (x_1, \dots, x_n)^\top$ and $\boldsymbol{y} = (y_1, \dots, y_n)^\top$ of the same dimension and a scalar $\alpha \in \mathbb{R}$, the vectors $\boldsymbol{x} + \boldsymbol{y}$ and $\alpha\boldsymbol{x}$ are defined as

$$x+y=\begin{pmatrix}x_1+y_1\\x_2+y_2\\\vdots\\x_n+y_n\end{pmatrix},\qquad \alpha x=\begin{pmatrix}\alpha x_1\\\alpha x_2\\\vdots\\\alpha x_n\end{pmatrix}.$$

Given two matrices $\underline{\underline{A}} = [A_{ij}]$ and $\underline{\underline{B}} = [B_{ij}]$ of the same dimension (m, n) and a scalar $\alpha \in \mathbb{R}$, the matrices $\underline{\underline{A}} + \underline{\underline{B}}$ and $\alpha\underline{\underline{A}}$ are defined as

$$\underline{\underline{A}}+\underline{\underline{B}}=\begin{pmatrix}A_{11}+B_{11} & A_{12}+B_{12} & \dots & A_{1n}+B_{1n}\\A_{21}+B_{21} & A_{22}+B_{22} & \dots & A_{2n}+B_{2n}\\\vdots & \vdots & \ddots & \vdots\\A_{m1}+B_{m1} & A_{m2}+B_{m2} & \dots & A_{mn}+B_{mn}\end{pmatrix},$$

$$\alpha\underline{\underline{A}}=\begin{pmatrix}\alpha A_{11} & \alpha A_{12} & \dots & \alpha A_{1n}\\\alpha A_{21} & \alpha A_{22} & \dots & \alpha A_{2n}\\\vdots & \vdots & \ddots & \vdots\\\alpha A_{m1} & \alpha A_{m2} & \dots & \alpha A_{mn}\end{pmatrix}.$$

Transpose.

The transpose of an $m \times n$ matrix $\underline{\underline{A}} = [A_{ij}]$ is the $n \times m$ matrix $\underline{\underline{A}}^\top = [A_{ji}]$ with columns and rows interchanged. An n-dimensional column vector $\boldsymbol{x}$ with elements $x_1, \dots, x_n$ can then be written as $\boldsymbol{x} = (x_1, \dots, x_n)^\top$.

A matrix $\underline{\underline{A}}$ is called symmetric if $\underline{\underline{A}}^\top = \underline{\underline{A}}$, which is only possible if $\underline{\underline{A}}$ is a square matrix.

Dot product.

Given two vectors $\boldsymbol{x} = (x_1, \dots, x_n)^\top$ and $\boldsymbol{y} = (y_1, \dots, y_n)^\top$ of the same dimension, the dot product (or vector product or inner product) of $\boldsymbol{x}$ and $\boldsymbol{y}$ is defined as $\boldsymbol{x} \cdot \boldsymbol{y} = x_1y_1 + \dots + x_ny_n = \sum_{i=1}^n x_iy_i$.

The vectors $\boldsymbol{x}$ and $\boldsymbol{y}$ are said to be orthogonal if $\boldsymbol{x} \cdot \boldsymbol{y} = 0$.

Length of vector.

The length of a vector $\boldsymbol{x} = (x_1, \dots, x_n)^\top$ is defined by

$$\|\boldsymbol{x}\| = \sqrt{\boldsymbol{x}\cdot\boldsymbol{x}} = \sqrt{\sum_{i=1}^n x_i^2}.$$

The Cauchy–Schwartz Inequality says that $|\boldsymbol{x} \cdot \boldsymbol{y}| \leq \|\boldsymbol{x}\| \cdot \|\boldsymbol{y}\|$.

Matrix product.

Given an $m \times n$ matrix $\underline{\underline{A}} = [A_{ij}]$ and an $n \times p$ matrix $\underline{\underline{B}} = [B_{kl}]$, the product $\underline{\underline{A}}\,\underline{\underline{B}}$ is the $m \times p$ matrix with (i, j)'th entry given by $(\underline{\underline{A}}\,\underline{\underline{B}})_{ij} = \sum_{k=1}^n A_{ik}B_{kj}$, which can be seen as the dot product of the i'th row of $\underline{\underline{A}}$ and the j'th column of $\underline{\underline{B}}$. In particular with $m = p = 1$, we see that for two vectors $\boldsymbol{x} = (x_1, \dots, x_n)^\top$ and $\boldsymbol{y} = (y_1, \dots, y_n)^\top$, we have $\boldsymbol{x}^\top\boldsymbol{y} = \boldsymbol{x} \cdot \boldsymbol{y}$, so the matrix product generalizes the dot product for vectors. Generally, $\underline{\underline{A}}\,\underline{\underline{B}} \neq \underline{\underline{B}}\,\underline{\underline{A}}$.

Inverse.

An $n \times n$ matrix $\underline{\underline{A}}$ is said to be non-singular if there exists a matrix $\underline{\underline{A}}^{-1}$ so that $\underline{\underline{A}}\underline{\underline{A}}^{-1} = \underline{\underline{I}}$, where $\underline{\underline{I}}$ is the $n \times n$ identity matrix, and then $\underline{\underline{A}}^{-1}$ is called the inverse of $\underline{\underline{A}}$.

A 2×2 matrix $\begin{pmatrix} a & b \\ c & d \end{pmatrix}$ is non-singular if $ad - bc \neq 0$ and the inverse is then given by

$$\begin{pmatrix} a & b \\ c & d \end{pmatrix}^{-1} = \frac{1}{ad - bc} \begin{pmatrix} d & -b \\ -c & a \end{pmatrix}.$$

If $\underline{\underline{A}}$ and $\underline{\underline{B}}$ are non-singular matrices of appropriate dimensions,

$$\left(\underline{\underline{A}}\,\underline{\underline{B}}\right)^{-1} = \underline{\underline{B}}^{-1}\underline{\underline{A}}^{-1}. \tag{C.1}$$

Furthermore, $(\underline{\underline{A}}^{-1})^{-1} = \underline{\underline{A}}$.

Rules for transposition.

If $\underline{\underline{A}}$ is non-singular, then the transposed matrix $\underline{\underline{A}}^{\top}$ is also non-singular and $(\underline{\underline{A}}^{\top})^{-1} = (\underline{\underline{A}}^{-1})^{\top}$.

Given an $m \times n$ matrix $\underline{\underline{A}}$ and an $n \times p$ matrix $\underline{\underline{B}}$, then $\left(\underline{\underline{A}}\,\underline{\underline{B}}\right)^{\top} = \underline{\underline{B}}^{\top}\underline{\underline{A}}^{\top}$.

Linear dependence and rank.

The m vectors $\boldsymbol{x}_1, \dots, \boldsymbol{x}_m$ of dimension n are said to be linearly dependent if

$$\alpha_1 \boldsymbol{x}_1 + \cdots + \alpha_m \boldsymbol{x}_m = \boldsymbol{0}$$

for some scalars $\alpha_1, \dots, \alpha_m \in \mathbb{R}$ that are not all zero. If the equation only holds when $\alpha_1 = \cdots = \alpha_m = 0$, the vectors $\boldsymbol{x}_1, \dots, \boldsymbol{x}_m$ are called linearly independent.

The rank$(\underline{\underline{A}})$ of a matrix $\underline{\underline{A}} = [A_{ij}]$ is the maximum number of linearly independent column vectors in $\underline{\underline{A}}$. This is also equal to the maximum number of linearly independent row vectors in $\underline{\underline{A}}$ so that rank$(\underline{\underline{A}}^{\top}) =$ rank$(\underline{\underline{A}})$. If $\underline{\underline{A}}$ is an $m \times n$ matrix, the rank$(\underline{\underline{A}})$ is smaller than or equal to the minimum of m and n, and if rank$(\underline{\underline{A}})$ is equal to that minimum $\underline{\underline{A}}$ is said to have full rank.

A square matrix $\underline{\underline{A}}$ is non-singular if and only $\underline{\underline{A}}$ has full rank.

For any matrix $\underline{\underline{A}}$, rank$(\underline{\underline{A}}\,\underline{\underline{A}}^{\top}) =$ rank$(\underline{\underline{A}}^{\top}\underline{\underline{A}}) =$ rank$(\underline{\underline{A}}) =$ rank$(\underline{\underline{A}}^{\top})$.

Equation system.

A system of m linear equations

$$\begin{aligned} A_{11}x_1 + A_{12}x_2 + \ldots + A_{1n}x_n &= b_1, \\ A_{21}x_1 + A_{22}x_2 + \ldots + A_{2n}x_n &= b_2, \\ \vdots \qquad\qquad & \quad \vdots \\ A_{m1}x_1 + A_{m2}x_2 + \ldots + A_{mn}x_n &= b_m \end{aligned}$$

in n unknowns $x_1, \dots, x_n$ can be written in matrix-vector form as $\underline{\underline{A}}\boldsymbol{x} = \boldsymbol{b}$, where $\underline{\underline{A}} = [A_{ij}]$ is an $m \times n$ matrix, $\boldsymbol{x} = (x_1, \dots, x_n)^{\top} \in \mathbb{R}^n$, and $\boldsymbol{b} = (b_1, \dots, b_m)^{\top} \in \mathbb{R}^m$.

If $m = n$ and $\underline{\underline{A}}$ is non-singular, then the system has the unique solution $\boldsymbol{x} = \underline{\underline{A}}^{-1}\boldsymbol{b}$.

Define the augmented coefficient matrix

$$\underline{\underline{A}}_b = \begin{pmatrix} A_{11} & A_{12} & \dots & A_{1n} & b_1 \\ A_{21} & A_{22} & \dots & A_{2n} & b_2 \\ \vdots & \vdots & \ddots & \vdots & \vdots \\ A_{m1} & A_{m2} & \dots & A_{mn} & b_m \end{pmatrix}.$$

The system has a solution if and only if $\text{rank}(\underline{\underline{A}}) = \text{rank}(\underline{\underline{A}}_b)$.

If $\text{rank}(\underline{\underline{A}}) = \text{rank}(\underline{\underline{A}}_b) = k$ and $k < m$, then the system has $m - k$ superfluous equations that can be removed without affecting the solutions to the system.

If $\text{rank}(\underline{\underline{A}}) = \text{rank}(\underline{\underline{A}}_b) = k$ and $k < n$, then the system has infinitely many solutions. If $\text{rank}(\underline{\underline{A}}) = \text{rank}(\underline{\underline{A}}_b) = m < n$ so that no equations are superfluous, then one solution is $\boldsymbol{x} = \underline{\underline{A}}^\top \left(\underline{\underline{A}}\,\underline{\underline{A}}^\top\right)^{-1} \boldsymbol{b}$, where $\left(\underline{\underline{A}}\,\underline{\underline{A}}^\top\right)^{-1}$ exists since $\text{rank}(\underline{\underline{A}}\,\underline{\underline{A}}^\top) = \text{rank}(\underline{\underline{A}}) = m$ so that $\underline{\underline{A}}\,\underline{\underline{A}}^\top$ is a square matrix of full rank.

A system of equations of the form $\underline{\underline{A}}\boldsymbol{x} = \boldsymbol{0}$ is called homogeneous. If $\underline{\underline{A}}$ is an $m \times n$ matrix, the homogeneous system has a solution $\boldsymbol{x}$ different from $\boldsymbol{0}$ if and only if $\text{rank}(\underline{\underline{A}}) < n$.

Trace.

tr denotes the trace of a quadratic matrix, that is the sum of the diagonal elements. For example, if $\underline{\underline{A}} = [A_{ij}]$ is a $K \times K$ matrix, then $\text{tr}(\underline{\underline{A}}) = \sum_{i=1}^{K} A_{ii}$.

Positive definite or semi-definite matrix.

A square matrix $\underline{\underline{A}}$, say an $n \times n$ matrix, is said to be positive semi-definite if $\boldsymbol{x}^\top \underline{\underline{A}}\boldsymbol{x} \geq 0$ for all $\boldsymbol{x} \in \mathbb{R}^n$. Likewise, $\underline{\underline{A}}$ is called positive definite if $\boldsymbol{x}^\top \underline{\underline{A}}\boldsymbol{x} > 0$ for all $\boldsymbol{x} \in \mathbb{R}^n$ with $\boldsymbol{x} \neq \boldsymbol{0}$. Any positive definite matrix is non-singular and the inverse matrix is also positive definite.

Cholesky decomposition of matrix.

If $\underline{\underline{A}}$ is a symmetric and positive semi-definite matrix of real numbers, then $\underline{\underline{A}}$ can be decomposed as $\underline{\underline{A}} = \underline{\underline{C}}\,\underline{\underline{C}}^\top$, where $\underline{\underline{C}}$ is a lower triangular matrix with diagonal entries that are non-negative. That $\underline{\underline{C}} = [C_{ij}]$ is lower triangular means that $C_{ij} = 0$ for $j > i$.

Differentiation.

If $\boldsymbol{a}$ and $\boldsymbol{x}$ are vectors of the same dimension, then $\frac{\partial \boldsymbol{a}^\top \boldsymbol{x}}{\partial \boldsymbol{x}} = \frac{\partial \boldsymbol{x}^\top \boldsymbol{a}}{\partial \boldsymbol{x}} = \boldsymbol{a}$.

If $\boldsymbol{x}$ is a vector of dimension n and $\underline{\underline{A}}$ is an $n \times n$ matrix, then $\frac{\partial \boldsymbol{x}^\top \underline{\underline{A}}\boldsymbol{x}}{\partial \boldsymbol{x}} = \left(\underline{\underline{A}} + \underline{\underline{A}}^\top\right)\boldsymbol{x}$. In particular, if $\underline{\underline{A}}$ is symmetric, that is $\underline{\underline{A}}^\top = \underline{\underline{A}}$, we have $\frac{\partial \boldsymbol{x}^\top \underline{\underline{A}}\boldsymbol{x}}{\partial \boldsymbol{x}} = 2\underline{\underline{A}}\boldsymbol{x}$.

Bibliography

Abel, A. B. (1999). Risk Premia and Term Premia in General Equilibrium. *Journal of Monetary Economics* 43(1), 3–33.

Acharya, V. V. and L. H. Pedersen (2005). Asset Pricing with Liquidity Risk. *Journal of Financial Economics* 77(2), 375–410.

Aït-Sahalia, Y., J. A. Parker, and M. Yogo (2004). Luxury Goods and the Equity Premium. *Journal of Finance* 59(6), 2959–3004.

Aiyagari, S. R. and M. Gertler (1991). Asset Returns with Transactions Costs and Uninsured Individual Risk. *Journal of Monetary Economics* 27(3), 311–331.

Albuquerque, R. (2012). Skewness in Stock Returns: Reconciling the Evidence on Firm versus Aggregate Returns. *Review of Financial Studies* 25(5), 1630–1673.

Allais, M. (1953). Le Comportement de l'Homme Rationnel devant le Risque—Critique des Postulats et Axiomes de l'École Américaine. *Econometrica* 21(4), 503–546.

Almeida, H. and T. Philippon (2007). The Risk-Adjusted Cost of Financial Distress. *Journal of Finance* 62(6), 2557–2586.

Altug, S. and P. Labadie (2008). *Asset Pricing for Dynamic Economies.* Cambridge University Press.

Ameriks, J. and S. P. Zeldes (2004, September). How Do Household Portfolio Shares Vary With Age? Working paper, The Vanguard Group and Columbia University.

Amihud, Y., H. Mendelson, and L. H. Pedersen (2005). Liquidity and Asset Prices. *Foundations and Trends in Finance* 1(4), 269–364.

Anderson, E. W., L. P. Hansen, and T. J. Sargent (2003). A Quartet of Semi-Groups for Model Specification, Robustness, Prices of Risk, and Model Detection. *Journal of the European Economic Association* 1(1), 68–123.

Anderson, R. M. and R. C. Raimondo (2008). Equilibrium in Continuous-Time Financial Markets: Endogenously Dynamically Complete Markets. *Econometrica* 76(4), 841–907.

Andersson, M., E. Krylova, and S. Vähämaa (2008). Why Does the Correlation between Stock and Bond Returns Vary over Time? *Applied Financial Economics* 18(2), 139–151.

Ang, A. and G. Bekaert (2007). Stock Return Predictability: Is It There? *Review of Financial Studies* 20(3), 651–707.

Ang, A. and J. Liu (2007). Risk, Return and Dividends. *Journal of Financial Economics* 85(1), 1–38.

Ang, A., R. J. Hodrick, Y. Xing, and X. Zhang (2006). The Cross-Section of Volatility and Expected Returns. *Journal of Finance* 61(1), 259–299.

Ang, A., R. J. Hodrick, Y. Xing, and X. Zhang (2007). High Idiosyncratic Volatility and Low Returns: International and Further US Evidence. *Journal of Financial Economics* 91(1), 1–23.

Anscombe, F. and R. Aumann (1963). A Definition of Subjective Probability. *Annals of Mathematical Statistics* 34(1), 199–205.

Arrow, K. J. (1951). An Extension of the Basic Theorems of Classical Welfare Economics. In J. Neyman (ed.), *Proceedings of the Second Berkeley Symposium on Mathematical Statistics and Probability*, pp. 507–532. University of California Press.

Arrow, K. J. (1953). Le Rôle des Valeurs Boursières pour la Repartition la Meillure des Risques. *Econometrie* 40, 41–47. English translation: Arrow (1964).

Arrow, K. J. (1964). The Role of Securities in the Optimal Allocation of Risk-Bearing. *Review of Economic Studies* 31(2), 91–96.

Arrow, K. J. (1971). *Essays in the Theory of Risk Bearing*. North-Holland.

Arrow, K. J. and G. Debreu (1954). Existence of an Equilibrium for a Comptetitive Economy. *Econometrica* 22(3), 265–290.

Asness, C. S., T. J. Moskowitz, and L. H. Pedersen (2012). Value and Momentum Everywhere. *Journal of Finance*, forthcoming.

Aumann, R. J. (1962). Utility Theory without the Completeness Axiom. *Econometrica* 30(3), 445–462.

Avramov, D., T. Chordia, G. Jostova, and A. Philipov (2007). Momentum and Credit Rating. *Journal of Finance* 62(5), 2503–2520.

Babbs, S. H. and N. J. Webber (1994). A Theory of the Term Structure with an Official Short Rate. Working paper, Warwick Business School, University of Warwick.

Bachelier, L. (1900). *Théorie de la Spéculation*, Volume 3 of *Annales de l'Ecole Normale Supérieure*. Gauthier-Villars. English translation in Cootner (1964).

Backus, D., M. Chernov, and I. Martin (2011). Disasters Implied by Equity Index Options. *Journal of Finance* 66(6), 1969–2012.

Bakshi, G. S. and Z. Chen (1996). Inflation, Asset Prices and the Term Structure of Interest Rates in Monetary Economies. *Review of Financial Studies* 9(1), 241–275.

Bakshi, G. S. and Z. Chen (1997). An Alternative Valuation Model for Contingent Claims. *Journal of Financial Economics* 44(1), 123–165.

Balduzzi, P., G. Bertola, and S. Foresi (1997). A Model of Target Changes and the Term Structure of Interest Rates. *Journal of Monetary Economics* 39(2), 223–249.

Bali, T. G. and N. Cakici (2008). Idiosyncratic Volatility and the Cross Section of Expected Returns. *Journal of Financial and Quantitative Analysis* 43(1), 29–58.

Bank for International Settlements (2010, March). *BIS Quarterly Review: International Banking and Financial Market Developments. Statistical Annex*. Bank for International Settlements. Available at <http://www.bis.org/publ> [Accessed October 2012].

Bansal, R. (2007). Long-Run Risks and Financial Markets. *Federal Reserve Bank of St. Louis Review* 89(4), 283–300.

Bansal, R. and A. Yaron (2000). Risks for the Long Run: A Potential Resolution of Asset Pricing Puzzles. Working paper 8059, NBER.

Bansal, R. and A. Yaron (2004). Risks for the Long Run: A Potential Resolution of Asset Pricing Puzzles. *Journal of Finance* 59(4), 1481–1509.

Bansal, R., R. F. Dittmar, and D. Kiku (2009). Cointegration and Consumption Risks in Equity Returns. *Review of Financial Studies* 22(3), 1343–1375.

Bansal, R., R. F. Dittmar, and C. T. Lundblad (2005). Consumption, Dividends, and the Cross-Section of Equity Returns. *Journal of Finance* 60(4), 1639–1672.

Bansal, R., R. Gallant, and G. Tauchen (2007). Rational Pessimism, Rational Exuberance, and Asset Pricing Models. *Review of Economic Studies* 74(4), 1005–1033.

Bansal, R., D. Kiku, and A. Yaron (2012). An Empirical Evaluation of the Long-Run Risks Model for Asset Prices. *Critical Finance Review* 1(1), 183–221.

Banz, R. W. (1981). The Relationship between Return and Market Value of Common Stocks. *Journal of Financial Economics* 9(1), 3–18.

Barberis, N. and R. Thaler (2003). A Survey of Behavioral Finance. In G. M. Constantinides, M. Harris, and R. M. Stulz (eds.), *Handbook of the Economics of Finance*, Volume 1B, Chapter 18. Elsevier.

Barro, R. J. (2006). Rare Disasters and Asset Markets in the Twentieth Century. *The Quarterly Journal of Economics* 121(3), 823–866.

Barro, R. J. (2009). Rare Disasters, Asset Prices, and Welfare Costs. *American Economic Review* 99(1), 243–264.

Barro, R. J. and J. F. Ursua (2008). Macroeconomic Crises since 1870. *Brookings Papers on Economic Activity* (1), 255–335.

Başak, S. and D. Cuoco (1998). An Equilibrium Model with Restricted Stock Market Participation. *Review of Financial Studies* 11(2), 309–341.

Beeler, J. and J. Y. Campbell (2012). The Long-Run Risks Model and Aggregate Asset Prices: An Empirical Assessment. *Critical Finance Review* 1(1), 141–182.

Berk, J. B. (1995). A Critique of Size-Related Anomalies. *Review of Financial Studies* 8(2), 275–286.

Berk, J., R. Green, and V. Naik (1999). Optimal Investment, Growth Options, and Security Returns. *Journal of Finance* 54(5), 1553–1608.

Bernoulli, D. (1954). Exposition of a New Theory on the Measurement of Risk. *Econometrica* 22(1), 23–36. Translation of the 1738 version.

Bewley, T. F. (1972). Existence of Equilibria in Economies with Infinitely Many Commodities. *Journal of Economic Theory* 4(3), 514–540.

Bewley, T. F. (2002). Knightian Decision Theory. Part I. *Decisions in Economics and Finance* 25(2), 79–110.

Bhamra, H. S., L.-A. Kuehn, and I. A. Strebulaev (2010). The Aggregate Dynamics of Capital Structure and Macroeconomic Risk. *Review of Financial Studies* 23(12), 4187–4241.

Bielecki, T. R. and M. Rutkowski (2002). *Credit Risk: Modeling, Valuation and Hedging*. Springer.

Björk, T. (2009). *Arbitrage Theory in Continuous Time* (third edn.). Oxford University Press.

Black, F. (1972). Capital Market Equilibrium with Restricted Borrowing. *Journal of Business* 45, 444–454.

Black, F. (1976a). The Pricing of Commodity Contracts. *Journal of Financial Economics* 3(1–2), 167–179.

Black, F. (1976b). Studies of Stock Price Volatility Changes. In *Proceedings of the 1976 Meetings of the Business and Economics Statistics Section*, pp. 177–181. American Statistical Association.

Black, F. and J. Cox (1976). Valuing Corporate Securities: Some Effects of Bond Indenture Provisions. *Journal of Finance* 31(2), 351–367.

Black, F. and M. Scholes (1973). The Pricing of Options and Corporate Liabilities. *Journal of Political Economy* 81(3), 637–654.

Black, F., M. C. Jensen, and M. Scholes (1972). The Capital Asset Pricing Model: Some Empirical Tests. In M. C. Jensen (ed.), *Studies in the Theory of Capital Markets*, pp. 79–121. Praeger.

Bloom, N. (2009). The Impact of Uncertainty Shocks. *Econometrica* 77(3), 623–685.

Bodie, Z., R. C. Merton, and W. F. Samuelson (1992). Labor Supply Flexibility and Portfolio Choice in a Life Cycle Model. *Journal of Economic Dynamics and Control* 16(3–4), 427–449.

Bollerslev, T. (1986). Generalized Autoregressive Conditional Heteroskedasticity. *Journal of Econometrics* 31(3), 307–327.

Bossaerts, P. (2002). *The Paradox of Asset Pricing*. Princeton University Press.

Boudoukh, J., R. Michaely, M. Richardson, and M. R. Roberts (2007). On the Importance of Measuring Payout Yield: Implications for Empirical Asset Pricing. *Journal of Finance* 62(2), 877–916.

Boudoukh, J., M. Richardson, and R. F. Whitelaw (2008). The Myth of Long-Horizon Predictability. *Review of Financial Studies* 21(4), 1577–1605.

Brace, A., D. Gatarek, and M. Musiela (1997). The Market Model of Interest Rate Dynamics. *Mathematical Finance* 7(2), 127–155.

Branger, N., H. Kraft, and C. Meinerding (2012, March). Pricing Two Trees When Mildew Infests the Orchard: How Does Contagion Affect General Equilibrium Asset Prices? Available at SSRN: <http://ssrn.com/abstract=1633480> [Accessed 1 October 2012].

Branger, N., C. Schlag, and L. Wu (2011). Pricing Two Heterogeneous Trees. *Journal of Financial and Quantitative Analysis* 46(5), 1437–1462.

Brav, A., G. M. Constantinides, and G. C. Geczy (2002). Asset Pricing with Heterogenous Consumers and Limited Participation: Empirical Evidence. *Journal of Political Economy* 110(4), 793–824.

Breeden, D. T. (1979). An Intertemporal Asset Pricing Model with Stochastic Consumption and Investment Opportunities. *Journal of Financial Economics* 7(3), 265–296.

Breeden, D. T. (1986). Consumption, Production, Inflation and Interest Rates. *Journal of Financial Economics* 16(1), 3–39.

Breeden, D. T. and R. H. Litzenberger (1978). Prices of State-Contingent Claims Implicit in Option Prices. *Journal of Business* 51(4), 621–651.

Breeden, D. T., M. R. Gibbons, and R. H. Litzenberger (1989). Empirical Tests of the Consumption-Oriented CAPM. *Journal of Finance* 44(2), 231–262.

Brennan, M. J. and Y. Xia (2005). *tay*'s as good as *cay*. *Finance Research Letters* 2(1), 1–14.

Brennan, M. J., T. Chordia, A. Subrahmanyam, and Q. Tong (2012). Sell-Order Liquidity and the Cross-Section of Expected Stock Returns. *Journal of Financial Economics*, forthcoming.

Brennan, M. J., A. W. Wang, and Y. Xia (2004). Estimation and Test of a Simple Model of Intertemporal Capital Asset Pricing. *Journal of Finance* 59(4), 1743–1775.

Brigo, D. and F. Mercurio (2006). *Interest Rate Models – Theory and Practice* (second edn.). Springer-Verlag.

Brown, S., W. Goetzmann, and S. A. Ross (1995). Survival. *Journal of Finance* 50(3), 853–873.

Browning, M. (1991). A Simple Nonadditive Preference Structure for Models of Household Behavior over Time. *Journal of Political Economy* 99(3), 607–637.

Brunnermeier, M. K. and S. Nagel (2008). Do Wealth Fluctuations Generate Time-Varying Risk Aversion? Micro-Evidence on Individuals' Asset Allocation. *American Economic Review* 98(3), 713–736.

Brunnermeier, M. K. and L. H. Pedersen (2009). Market Liquidity and Funding Liquidity. *Review of Financial Studies* 22(6), 2201–2238.

Buraschi, A., P. Porchia, and F. Trojani (2010). The Cross-Section of Expected Stock Returns: Learning about Distress and Predictability in Heterogeneous Orchards. Available at SSRN: <http://ssrn.com/abstract=1573015> [Accessed 1 October 2012].

Campbell, J. Y. (1986). A Defense of Traditional Hypotheses About the Term Structure of Interest Rates. *Journal of Finance* 41(1), 183–193.

Campbell, J. Y. (1996). Understanding Risk and Return. *Journal of Political Economy* 104(2), 298–345.

Campbell, J. Y. (1999). Asset Prices, Consumption, and the Business Cycle. In J. B. Taylor and M. Woodford (eds.), *Handbook of Macroeconomics*, Volume 1. Elsevier.

Campbell, J. Y. (2000). Asset Pricing at the Millennium. *Journal of Finance* 55(4), 1515–1567.

Campbell, J. Y. (2003). Consumption-Based Asset Pricing. In G. M. Constantinides, M. Harris, and R. Stulz (eds.), *Handbook of the Economics of Finance*, Volume 1B, Chapter 13, pp. 803–887. Elsevier.

Campbell, J. Y. and J. Ammer (1993). What Moves the Stock and Bond Markets? A Variance Decomposition for Long-Term Asset Returns. *Journal of Finance* 48(1), 3–37.

Campbell, J. Y. and J. F. Cocco (2003). Household Risk Management and Optimal Mortgage Choice. *The Quarterly Journal of Economics* 118(4), 1449–1494.

Campbell, J. Y. and J. H. Cochrane (1999). By Force of Habit: A Consumption-Based Explanation of Aggregate Stock Market Behavior. *Journal of Political Economy* 107(2), 205–251.

Campbell, J. Y. and R. J. Shiller (1988). The Dividend-Price Ratio and Expectations of Future Dividends and Discount Factors. *Review of Financial Studies* 1(3), 195–227.

Campbell, J. Y. and R. J. Shiller (1991). Yield Spreads and Interest Rate Movements: A Bird's Eye View. *Review of Economic Studies* 58(3), 495–514.

Campbell, J. Y. and S. B. Thompson (2008). Predicting Excess Stock Returns Out of Sample: Can Anything Beat the Historical Average? *Review of Financial Studies* 21(4), 1509–1531.

Campbell, J. Y. and L. M. Viceira (2002). *Strategic Asset Allocation*. Oxford University Press.

Campbell, J. Y. and T. Vuolteenaho (2004). Bad Beta, Good Beta. *American Economic Review* 94(5), 1249–1275.

Campbell, J. Y., A. W. Lo, and A. C. MacKinlay (1997). *The Econometrics of Financial Markets*. Princeton University Press.

Cappiello, L., R. F. Engle, and K. Sheppard (2006). Asymmetric Dynamics in the Correlations of Global Equity and Bond Returns. *Journal of Financial Econometrics* 4(4), 537–572.

Carhart, M. (1997). On Persistence in Mutual Fund Performance. *Journal of Finance* 52(1), 57–82.

Carlson, M., A. Fisher, and R. Giammarino (2004). Corporate Investment and Asset Price Dynamics: Implications for the Cross-Section of Returns. *Journal of Finance* 59(6), 2577–2603.

Chan, K. C. and N.-F. Chen (1991). Structural and Return Characteristics of Small and Large Firms. *Journal of Finance* 46(4), 1467–1484.

Chan, K. C., G. A. Karolyi, F. A. Longstaff, and A. Sanders (1992). An Empirical Comparison of Alternative Models of the Short-Term Interest Rate. *Journal of Finance* 47(3), 1209–1227.

Chan, Y. L. and L. Kogan (2002). Catching Up with the Joneses: Heterogeneous Preferences and the Dynamics of Asset Prices. *Journal of Political Economy* 110(6), 1255–1285.

Chen, H. (2010). Macroeconomic Conditions and the Puzzles of Credit Spreads and Capital Structure. *Journal of Finance* 65(6), 2171–2212.

Chen, L. (2009). On the Reversal of Return and Dividend Growth Predictability: A Tale of Two Periods. *Journal of Financial Economics* 92(1), 128–151.

Chen, L., P. Collin-Dufresne, and R. S. Goldstein (2009). On the Relation Between the Credit Spread Puzzle and the Equity Premium Puzzle. *Review of Financial Studies* 22(9), 3367–3409.

Chen, N.-F. (1991). Financial Investment Opportunities and the Macroeconomy. *Journal of Finance* 46(2), 529–554.

Chen, N.-F. and J. E. Ingersoll, Jr. (1983). Exact Pricing in Linear Factor Models with Finitely Many Assets: A Note. *Journal of Finance* 38(3), 985–988.

Chen, N.-F., R. Roll, and S. A. Ross (1986). Economic Forces and the Stock Market. *Journal of Business* 59(3), 383–403.

Christensen, P. O. and G. A. Feltham (2003). *Economics of Accounting*, Volume I: *Information in Markets*. Kluwer Academic Publishers.

Christensen, P. O. and G. A. Feltham (2005). *Economics of Accounting*, Volume II: *Performance Evaluation*. Springer.

Christensen, P. O., S. E. Graversen, and K. R. Miltersen (2000). Dynamic Spanning in the Consumption-Based Capital Asset Pricing Model. *European Finance Review* 4(2), 129–156.

Christensen, P. O., K. Larsen, and C. Munk (2012). Equilibrium in Securities Markets with Heterogeneous Investors and Unspanned Income Risk. *Journal of Economic Theory* 147(3), 1035–1063.

Cicchetti, C. J. and J. A. Dubin (1994). A Microeconomic Analysis of Risk Aversion and the Decision to Self-Insure. *Journal of Political Economy* 102(1), 169–186.

Cocco, J. F. (2005). Portfolio Choice in the Presence of Housing. *Review of Financial Studies* 18(2), 535–567.

Cocco, J. F., F. J. Gomes, and P. J. Maenhout (2005). Consumption and Portfolio Choice over the Life Cycle. *Review of Financial Studies* 18(2), 491–533.

Cochrane, J. H. (2005). *Asset Pricing* (revised edn.). Princeton University Press.

Cochrane, J. H. (2008). The Dog That Did Not Bark: A Defense of Return Predictability. *Review of Financial Studies* 21(4), 1533–1575.

Cochrane, J. H. (2011). Discount Rates. *Journal of Finance* 66(4), 1047–1108.

Cochrane, J. H. and M. Piazzesi (2005). Bond Risk Premia. *American Economic Review* 95(1), 138–160.

Cochrane, J. H., F. A. Longstaff, and P. Santa-Clara (2008). Two Trees. *Review of Financial Studies* 21(1), 347–385.

Colacito, R. and M. M. Croce (2011). Risks for the Long Run and the Real Exchange Rate. *Journal of Political Economy* 119(1), 153–181.

Collin-Dufresne, P. and R. S. Goldstein (2002). Do Bonds Span the Fixed Income Markets? Theory and Evidence for Unspanned Stochastic Volatility. *Journal of Finance* 57(4), 1685–1730.

Connor, G. (1984). A Unified Beta Pricing Theory. *Journal of Economic Theory* 34(1), 13–31.

Constantinides, G. M. (1982). Intertemporal Asset Pricing with Heterogeneous Consumers and without Demand Aggregation. *Journal of Business* 55(2), 253–267.

Constantinides, G. M. (1990). Habit Formation: A Resolution of the Equity Premium Puzzle. *Journal of Political Economy* 98(3), 519–543.

Constantinides, G. M. (1992). A Theory of the Nominal Term Structure of Interest Rates. *Review of Financial Studies* 5(4), 531–552.

Constantinides, G. M. (2002). Rational Asset Prices. *Journal of Finance* 57(4), 1567–1591.

Constantinides, G. M. (2008). Comments on "Macroeconomic Crises since 1870". *Brookings Papers on Economic Activity* (1), 341–349.

Constantinides, G. M. and D. Duffie (1996). Asset Pricing with Heterogeneous Consumers. *Journal of Political Economy* 104(2), 219–240.

Constantinides, G. M. and A. Ghosh (2011). Asset Pricing Tests with Long Run Risks in Consumption Growth. *Review of Asset Pricing Studies* 1(1), 96–136.

Constantinides, G. M., J. B. Donaldson, and R. Mehra (2002). Junior Can't Borrow: A New Perspective on the Equity Premium Puzzle. *Quarterly Journal of Economics* 117(1), 269–296.

Cont, R. and P. Tankov (2004). *Financial Modeling with Jump Processes*. Chapman & Hall.

Cooper, I. (2006). Asset Pricing Implications of Nonconvex Adjustment Costs and Irreversibility of Investment. *Journal of Finance* 61(1), 139–170.

Cooper, I. and R. Priestley (2009). Time-Varying Risk Premiums and the Output Gap. *Review of Financial Studies* 22(7), 2801–2833.

Cootner, P. H. (1964). *The Random Character of Stock Market Prices*. MIT Press.

Cox, J. C. and S. A. Ross (1976a). A Survey of Some New Results in Financial Option Pricing Theory. *Journal of Finance* 31(2), 383–402.

Cox, J. C. and S. A. Ross (1976b). The Valuation of Options for Alternative Stochastic Processes. *Journal of Financial Economics* 3(1–2), 145–166.

Cox, J. C., J. E. Ingersoll, Jr., and S. A. Ross (1981a). A Re-examination of Traditional Hypotheses about the Term Structure of Interest Rates. *Journal of Finance* 36(4), 769–799.

Cox, J. C., J. E. Ingersoll, Jr., and S. A. Ross (1981b). The Relation between Forward Prices and Futures Prices. *Journal of Financial Economics* 9(4), 321–346.

Cox, J. C., J. E. Ingersoll, Jr., and S. A. Ross (1985a). An Intertemporal General Equilibrium Model of Asset Prices. *Econometrica* 53(2), 363–384.

Cox, J. C., J. E. Ingersoll, Jr., and S. A. Ross (1985b). A Theory of the Term Structure of Interest Rates. *Econometrica* 53(2), 385–407.

Cox, J. C., S. A. Ross, and M. Rubinstein (1979). Option Pricing: A Simplified Approach. *Journal of Financial Economics* 7(3), 229–263.

Culbertson, J. M. (1957). The Term Structure of Interest Rates. *Quarterly Journal of Economics* 71(4), 489–504.

Cuoco, D. and H. He (2001). Dynamic Aggregation and Computation of Equilibria in Finite-Dimensional Economies with Incomplete Financial Markets. *Annals of Economics and Finance* 2(2), 265–296.

Cuoco, D. and H. Liu (2000). Optimal Consumption of a Divisible Durable Good. *Journal of Economic Dynamics and Control* 24(4), 561–613.

Cuthbertson, K. and D. Nitzsche (2004). *Quantitative Financial Economics* (second edn.). Wiley.

Dai, Q. and K. J. Singleton (2000). Specification Analysis of Affine Term Structure Models. *Journal of Finance* 55(5), 1943–1978.

Damgaard, A., B. Fuglsbjerg, and C. Munk (2003). Optimal Consumption and Investment Strategies with a Perishable and an Indivisible Durable Consumption Good. *Journal of Economic Dynamics and Control* 28(2), 209–253.

Debreu, G. (1951). The Coefficient of Resource Utilization. *Econometrica* 19(3), 257–273.

Debreu, G. (1954). Valuation Equilibrium and Pareto Optimum. *Proceedings of the National Academy of Sciences* 40(7), 588–592.

Debreu, G. (1959). *Theory of Value*. Yale University Press.

Detemple, J. B. and C. I. Giannikos (1996). Asset and Commodity Prices with Multi-Attribute Durable Goods. *Journal of Economic Dynamics and Control* 20(8), 1451–1504.

Detemple, J. B. and F. Zapatero (1991). Asset Prices in an Exchange Economy with Habit Formation. *Econometrica* 59(6), 1633–1658.

Dimson, E., P. Marsh, and M. Staunton (2002). *Triumph of the Optimists: 101 Years of Global Investment Returns*. Princeton University Press.

Drèze, J. (1971). Market Allocation under Uncertainty. *European Economic Review* 2(2), 133–165.

Dubra, J. and F. Echenique (2004). Information is not about Measurability. *Mathematical Social Sciences* 47(2), 177–185.

Duffie, D. (1986). Stochastic Equilibria: Existence, Spanning Number, and the "No Expected Financial Gain from Trade" Hypothesis. *Econometrica* 54(5), 1161–1183.

Duffie, D. (2001). *Dynamic Asset Pricing Theory* (third edn.). Princeton University Press.

Duffie, D. and L. G. Epstein (1992a). Asset Pricing with Stochastic Differential Utility. *Review of Financial Studies* 5(3), 411–436.

Duffie, D. and L. G. Epstein (1992b). Stochastic Differential Utility. *Econometrica* 60(2), 353–394.

Duffie, D. and C.-F. Huang (1985). Implementing Arrow–Debreu Equilibria by Continuous Trading of Few Long-Lived Securities. *Econometrica* 53(6), 1337–1356.

Duffie, D. and M. Huang (1996). Swap Rates and Credit Quality. *Journal of Finance* 51(3), 921–949.

Duffie, D. and R. Kan (1996). A Yield-Factor Model of Interest Rates. *Mathematical Finance* 6(4), 379–406.

Duffie, D. and W. Shafer (1985). Equilibrium in Incomplete Markets: I. A Basic Model of Generic Existence. *Journal of Mathematical Economics* 14(3), 285–300.

Duffie, D. and W. Shafer (1986). Equilibrium in Incomplete Markets: II. Generic Existence in Stochastic Economies. *Journal of Mathematical Economics* 15(3), 199–216.

Duffie, D. and K. Singleton (2003). *Credit Risk: Pricing, Measurement, and Management.* Princeton University Press.

Duffie, D. and R. Stanton (1992). Pricing Continuously Resettled Contingent Claims. *Journal of Economic Dynamics and Control* 16(3–4), 561–574.

Duffie, D., P.-Y. Geoffard, and C. Skiadas (1994). Efficient and Equilibrium Allocations with Stochastic Differential Utility. *Journal of Mathematical Economics* 23(2), 133–146.

Duffie, D., J. Pan, and K. Singleton (2000). Transform Analysis and Asset Pricing for Affine Jump-Diffusions. *Econometrica* 68(6), 1343–1376.

Dumas, B. and A. Lyasoff (2012). Incomplete-Market Equilibria Solved Recursively on an Event Tree. *Journal of Finance*, forthcoming.

Dumas, B., R. Uppal, and T. Wang (2000). Efficient Intertemporal Allocations with Recursive Utility. *Journal of Economic Theory* 93, 240–259.

Dybvig, P. H. (1983). An Explicit Bound on Individual Assets' Deviations from APT Pricing in a Finite Economy. *Journal of Financial Economics* 12(4), 483–496.

Dybvig, P. H. and C.-F. Huang (1988). Nonnegative Wealth, Absence of Arbitrage, and Feasible Consumption Plans. *Review of Financial Studies* 1(4), 377–401.

Dynan, K. E. (2000). Habit Formation in Consumer Preferences: Evidence from Panel Data. *American Economic Review* 90(3), 391–406.

Eichenbaum, M., L. P. Hansen, and K. Singleton (1988). A Time Series Analysis of Representative Agent Models of Consumption and Leisure Choice under Uncertainty. *The Quarterly Journal of Economics* 103(1), 51–78.

Eiling, E. (2012). Industry-Specific Human Capital, Idiosyncratic Risk and the Cross-Section of Expected Stock Returns. *Journal of Finance*, forthcoming.

Ellsberg, D. (1961). Risk, Ambiguity, and the Savage Axioms. *The Quarterly Journal of Economics* 75(4), 643–669.

Elul, R. (1997). Financial Innovation, Precautionary Saving and the Risk-Free Rate. *Journal of Mathematical Economics* 27(1), 113–131.

Engle, R. F. (1982). Autoregressive Conditional Heteroscedasticity with Estimates of the Variance of United Kingdom Inflation. *Econometrica* 50(4), 987–1007.

Engsted, T. and T. Q. Pedersen (2010). The Dividend-Price Ratio Does Predict Dividend Growth: International Evidence. *Journal of Empirical Finance* 17(4), 585–605.

Epstein, L. G. and S. E. Zin (1989). Substitution, Risk Aversion, and the Temporal Behavior of Consumption and Asset Returns: A Theoretical Framework. *Econometrica* 57(4), 937–969.

Epstein, L. G. and S. E. Zin (1991). Substitution, Risk Aversion, and the Temporal Behavior of Consumption and Asset Returns: An Empirical Analysis. *Journal of Political Economy* 99(2), 263–286.

Eraker, B. (2004). Do Stock Prices and Volatility Jump? Reconciling Evidence from Spot and Option Prices. *Journal of Finance* 59(3), 1367–1403.

Eraker, B. and I. Shaliastovich (2008). An Equilibrium Guide to Designing Affine Pricing Models. *Mathematical Finance* 18(4), 519–543.

Eraker, B., M. S. Johannes, and N. G. Polson (2003). The Impact of Jumps in Returns and Volatility. *Journal of Finance* 53(3), 1269–1300.

Estrella, A. and G. A. Hardouvelis (1991). The Term Structure as a Predictor of Real Economic Activity. *Journal of Finance* 46(2), 555–576.

Fama, E. F. (1970). Multiperiod Consumption-Investment Decisions. *American Economic Review* 60(1), 163–174. Correction: Fama (1976).

Fama, E. F. (1976). Multiperiod Consumption-Investment Decisions: A Correction. *American Economic Review* 66(4), 723–724.

Fama, E. F. (1981). Stock Returns, Real Activity, Inflation, and Money. *American Economic Review* 71(4), 545–565.

Fama, E. F. and R. R. Bliss (1987). The Information in Long-Maturity Forward Rates. *American Economic Review* 77(4), 680–692.

Fama, E. F. and K. R. French (1988). Permanent and Temporary Components of Stock Prices. *Journal of Political Economy* 96(2), 246–273.

Fama, E. F. and K. R. French (1989). Business Conditions and Expected Returns on Stocks and Bonds. *Journal of Financial Economics* 25(1), 23–49.

Fama, E. F. and K. R. French (1992). The Cross-Section of Expected Stock Returns. *Journal of Finance* 47(2), 427–465.

Fama, E. F. and K. R. French (1996). The CAPM is Wanted, Dead or Alive. *Journal of Finance* 51(5), 1947–1958.

Fama, E. F. and K. R. French (2004). The Capital Asset Pricing Model: Theory and Evidence. *Journal of Economic Perspectives* 18(3), 25–46.

Fama, E. F. and K. R. French (2008). Dissecting Anomalies. *Journal of Finance* 63(4), 1653–1678.

Fama, E. F. and K. R. French (2011). Size, Value, and Momentum in International Stock Returns. Available at SSRN: <http://ssrn.com/abstract=1720139> [Accessed 1 October 2012].

Fama, E. F. and M. Gibbons (1982). Inflation, Real Returns and Capital Investment. *Journal of Monetary Economics* 9(3), 297–323.

Fama, E. F. and J. D. MacBeth (1973). Risk, Return, and Equilibrium: Some Empirical Tests. *Journal of Political Economy* 81(3), 607–636.

Favilukis, J. and X. Lin (2011, March). Wage Rigidity: A Solution to Several Asset Pricing Puzzles. Available at SSRN: <http://ssrn.com/abstract=1786838> [Accessed 1 October 2012].

Favilukis, J., S. C. Ludvigson, and S. van Nieuwerburgh (2011, January). The Macroeconomic Effects of Housing Wealth, Housing Finance, and Limited Risk-Sharing in General Equilibrium. Available at SSRN: <http://ssrn.com/abstract=1602163> [Accessed 1 October 2012].

Feenstra, R. C. (1986). Functional Equivalence between Liquidity Costs and the Utility of Money. *Journal of Monetary Economics* 17(2), 271–291.

Feller, W. (1951). Two Singular Diffusion Problems. *The Annals of Mathematics* 54(1), 173–182.

Fishburn, P. (1970). *Utility Theory for Decision Making*. John Wiley and Sons.

Fisher, I. (1896). Appreciation and Interest. *Publications of the American Economic Association*, 23–29 and 88–92.

Fisher, M. and C. Gilles (1998). Around and Around: The Expectations Hypothesis. *Journal of Finance* 52(1), 365–383.

Fleming, W. H. and H. M. Soner (1993). *Controlled Markov Processes and Viscosity Solutions*, Volume 25 of *Applications of Mathematics*. Springer-Verlag.

Friend, I. and M. E. Blume (1975). The Demand for Risky Assets. *American Economic Review* 65(5), 900–922.

Fu, F. (2009). Idiosyncratic Risk and the Cross Section of Expected Stock Returns. *Journal of Financial Economics* 91(1), 24–37.

Gabaix, X. (2012). Variable Rare Disasters: An Exactly Solved Framework for Ten Puzzles in Macro-Finance. *The Quarterly Journal of Economics* 127(2), 645–700.

Gao, P. P. J. and K. X. D. Huang (2008). Aggregate Consumption-Wealth Ratio and the Cross-Section of Stock Returns: Some International Evidence. *Annals of Economics and Finance* 9(1), 1–37.

Garlappi, L. and H. Yan (2011). Financial Distress and the Cross-Section of Equity Returns. *Journal of Finance* 66(3), 789–822.

Geanakoplos, J. and H. Polemarchakis (1986). Existence, Regularity, and Constrained Suboptimality of Competitive Allocations when the Asset Market is Incomplete. In W. Heller and D. Starrett (eds.), *Essays in Honor of Kenneth J. Arrow*, Volume III, pp. 65–96. Cambridge University Press.

Geman, H. (1989). The Importance of the Forward Neutral Probability in a Stochastic Approach of Interest Rates. Working paper, ESSEC.

Gilboa, I. and M. Marinacci (2011). *Ambiguity and the Bayesian Paradigm. Advances in Economics and Econometrics: Theory and Applications, Tenth World Congress of the Econometric Society*. Cambridge University Press.

Gilboa, I. and D. Schmeidler (1989). Maximin Expected Utility with Non-Unique Prior. *Journal of Mathematical Economics* 18(2), 141–153.

Gilboa, I., F. Maccheroni, M. Marinacci, and D. Schmeidler (2010). Objective and Subjective Rationality in a Multiple Prior Model. *Econometrica* 78(2), 755–770.

Goldstein, R. and F. Zapatero (1996). General Equilibrium with Constant Relative Risk Aversion and Vasicek Interest Rates. *Mathematical Finance* 6(3), 331–340.

Gomes, F. and A. Michaelides (2003). Portfolio Choice with Internal Habit Formation: A Life-Cycle Model with Uninsurable Labor Income Risk. *Review of Economic Dynamics* 6(4), 729–766.

Gomes, J., L. Kogan, and M. Yogo (2009). Durability of Output and Expected Stock Returns. *Journal of Political Economy* 117(5), 941–986.

Gomes, J., L. Kogan, and L. Zhang (2003). Equilibrium Cross-Section of Returns. *Journal of Political Economy* 111(4), 693–732.

Gomes, J. F., A. Yaron, and L. Zhang (2006). Asset Pricing Implications of Firms' Financing Constraints. *Review of Financial Studies* 19(4), 1321–1356.

Gordon, M. (1962). *The Investment Financing and Valuation of the Corporation*. Richard D. Irwin.

Goyal, A. (2012). Empirical Cross-Sectional Asset Pricing: A Survey. *Financial Markets and Portfolio Management* 26(1), 3–38.

Goyal, A. and P. Santa-Clara (2003). Idiosyncratic Risk Matters! *Journal of Finance* 58(3), 975–1007.

Goyal, A. and I. Welch (2008). A Comprehensive Look at the Empirical Performance of Equity Premium Prediction. *Review of Financial Studies* 21(4), 1455–1508.

Grether, D. M. and C. R. Plott (1979). Economic Theory of Choice and the Preference Reversal Phenomenon. *American Economic Review* 69(4), 623–638.

Grinblatt, M. and S. Titman (1983). Factor Pricing in a Finite Economy. *Journal of Financial Economics* 12(4), 497–507.

Grinblatt, M. and S. Titman (1985). Approximate Factor Structures: Interpretations and Implications for Empirical Tests. *Journal of Finance* 40(5), 1367–1373.

Grinblatt, M. and S. Titman (1987). The Relation Between Mean-Variance Efficiency and Arbitrage Pricing. *Journal of Business* 60(1), 97–112.

Grischenko, O. V. (2010). Internal vs. External Habit Formation: The Relative Importance for Asset Pricing. *Journal of Economics and Business* 62(3), 176–194.

Grossman, S. J. and G. Laroque (1990). Asset Pricing and Optimal Portfolio Choice in the Presence of Illiquid Durable Consumption Goods. *Econometrica* 58(1), 25–51.

Grossman, S. J. and R. J. Shiller (1981). The Determinants of the Variability of Stock Market Prices. *American Economic Review* 71(2), 222–227.

Grossman, S. J., A. Melino, and R. J. Shiller (1987). Estimating the Continuous-Time Consumption-Based Asset-Pricing Model. *Journal of Business & Economic Statistics* 5(3), 315–327.

Guo, S. (2010). The Superior Measure of PSID Consumption: An Update. *Economics Letters* 108(3), 253–256.

Hakansson, N. H. (1970). Optimal Investment and Consumption Strategies Under Risk for a Class of Utility Functions. *Econometrica* 38(5), 587–607.

Hansen, L. P. and R. Jagannathan (1991). Implications of Security Market Data for Models of Dynamic Economies. *Journal of Political Economy* 99(2), 225–262.

Hansen, L. P. and S. F. Richard (1987). The Role of Conditioning Information in Deducing Testable Restrictions Implied by Dynamic Asset Pricing Models. *Econometrica* 55(3), 587–614.

Hansen, L. P., J. C. Heaton, and N. Li (2008). Consumption Strikes Back? Measuring Long-Run Risk. *Journal of Political Economy* 116(2), 260–302.

Harrison, J. M. and D. M. Kreps (1979). Martingales and Arbitrage in Multiperiod Securities Markets. *Journal of Economic Theory* 20(3), 381–408.

Harrison, J. M. and S. R. Pliska (1981). Martingales and Stochastic Integrals in the Theory of Continuous Trading. *Stochastic Processes and their Applications* 11(3), 215–260.

Harrison, J. M. and S. R. Pliska (1983). A Stochastic Calculus Model of Continuous Trading: Complete Markets. *Stochastic Processes and their Applications* 15(3), 313–316.

Hart, O. D. (1975). On the Optimality of Equilibrium when the Market Structure is Incomplete. *Journal of Economic Theory* 11(3), 418–443.

Hasbrouck, J. (2009). Trading Costs and Returns for U.S. Equities: Estimating Effective Costs from Daily Data. *Journal of Finance* 64(3), 1445–1477.

Hasseltoft, H. (2011). Stocks, Bonds, and Long-Run Consumption Risks. *Journal of Financial and Quantitative Analysis* 47(2), 309–332.

He, H. and D. M. Modest (1995). Market Frictions and Consumption-Based Asset Pricing. *Journal of Political Economy* 103(11), 94–117.

Heathcote, J., F. Perri, and G. L. Violante (2010). Unequal We Stand: An Empirical Analysis of Economic Inequality in the United States, 1967–2006. *Review of Economic Dynamics* 13(1), 15–51.

Heaton, J. and D. Lucas (1996). Evaluating the Effects of Incomplete Markets on Risk Sharing and Asset Pricing. *Journal of Political Economy* 104(3), 443–487.

Heaton, J. and D. Lucas (1997). Market Frictions, Savings Behavior, and Portfolio Choice. *Macroeconomic Dynamics* 1(1), 76–101.

Heaton, J. and D. Lucas (2000). Portfolio Choice and Asset Prices: The Importance of Entrepreneurial Risk. *Journal of Finance* 55(3), 1163–1198.

Hellwig, M. (1996). Rational Expectations Equilibria in Sequence Economies with Symmetric Information: The Two-Period Case. *Journal of Mathematical Economics* 26(1), 9–49.

Heston, S. L. (1993). A Closed-Form Solution for Options with Stochastic Volatility with Applications to Bond and Currency Options. *Review of Financial Studies* 6(2), 327–343.

Hicks, J. R. (1939). *Value and Capital*. Clarendon Press.

Hindy, A. and C.-F. Huang (1993). Optimal Consumption and Portfolio Rules with Durability and Local Substitution. *Econometrica* 61(1), 85–121.

Hirshleifer, D. (2001). Investor Psychology and Asset Pricing. *Journal of Finance* 56(4), 1533–1597.

Huang, C.-F. (1985). Information Structure and Equilibrium Asset Prices. *Journal of Economic Theory* 35(1), 33–71.

Huang, C.-F. (1987). An Intertemporal General Equilibrium Asset Pricing Model: The Case of Diffusion Information. *Econometrica* 55(1), 117–142.

Huang, C.-F. and R. H. Litzenberger (1988). *Foundations for Financial Economics*. Prentice-Hall.

Huberman, G. (1982). A Simple Approach to Arbitrage Pricing Theory. *Journal of Economic Theory* 28(1), 183–191.

Huge, B. and D. Lando (1999). Swap Pricing with Two-Sided Default Risk in a Rating-Based Model. *European Finance Review* 3(3), 239–268.

Huggett, M. (1993). The Risk-Free Rate in Heterogeneous-Agent Incomplete-Insurance Economies. *Journal of Economic Dynamics and Control* 17(5–6), 953–969.

Hull, J. and A. White (1987). The Pricing of Options on Assets with Stochastic Volatility. *Journal of Finance* 42(2), 281–300.

Hull, J. C. (2009). *Options, Futures, and Other Derivatives* (seventh edn). Prentice-Hall.

Hvidkjær, S. (2006). A Trade-Based Analysis of Momentum. *Review of Financial Studies* 19(2), 457–491.

Ibbotson Associates (2000). *Stocks, Bonds, Bills, and Inflation. 2000 Year Book*. Ibbotson Associates.

Ilmanen, A. (2003). Stock-Bond Correlations. *Journal of Fixed Income* 13(2), 55–66.

Ingersoll, Jr., J. E. (1984). Some Results in the Theory of Arbitrage Pricing. *Journal of Finance* 39(4), 1021–1039.

Ingersoll, Jr., J. E. (1987). *Theory of Financial Decision Making*. Rowman & Littlefield.

Jacobs, K. and K. Q. Wang (2004). Idiosyncratic Consumption Risk and the Cross Section of Asset Returns. *Journal of Finance* 59(5), 2211–2252.

Jagannathan, R. and Y. Wang (2007). Lazy Investors, Discretionary Consumption, and the Cross-Section of Stock Returns. *Journal of Finance* 62(4), 1623–1661.

Jagannathan, R. and Z. Wang (1996). The Conditional CAPM and the Cross-Section of Expected Returns. *Journal of Finance* 51(1), 3–53.

James, J. and N. Webber (2000). *Interest Rate Modelling*. Wiley.

Jamshidian, F. (1987). Pricing of Contingent Claims in the One Factor Term Structure Model. Working paper, Merrill Lynch Capital Markets.

Jamshidian, F. (1989). An Exact Bond Option Formula. *Journal of Finance* 44(1), 205–209.

Jamshidian, F. (1997). LIBOR and Swap Market Models and Measures. *Finance and Stochastics* 1(4), 293–330.

Jegadeesh, N. and S. Titman (1993). Returns to Buying Winners and Selling Losers: Implications for Stock Market Efficiency. *Journal of Finance* 48(1), 65–91.

Julliard, C. and A. Ghosh (2012). Can Rare Events Explain the Equity Premium Puzzle? *Review of Financial Studies*, forthcoming.

Kaltenbrunner, G. and L. A. Lochstoer (2010). Long-Run Risk through Consumption Smoothing. *Review of Financial Studies* 23(8), 3190–3224.

Kan, R. (1992). Shape of the Yield Curve under CIR Single Factor Model: A Note. Working paper, University of Chicago.

Karlin, S. and H. M. Taylor (1981). *A Second Course in Stochastic Processes*. Academic Press.

Klibanoff, P., M. Marinacci, and S. Mukerji (2005). A Smooth Model of Decision Making under Ambiguity. *Econometrica* 73(6), 1849–1892.

Klibanoff, P., M. Marinacci, and S. Mukerji (2009). Recursive Smooth Ambiguity Preferences. *Journal of Economic Theory* 144(3), 930–976.

Koijen, R. S. J. and S. Van Nieuwerburgh (2011). Predictability of Returns and Cash Flows. *Annual Review of Financial Economics* 3, 467–491.

Koijen, R. S. J., S. Van Nieuwerburgh, and R. Vestman (2011). Judging the Quality of Survey Data by Comparison with "Truth" as Measured by Administrative Records: Evidence from Sweden. Working paper.

Koopmans, T. C. (1960). Stationary Ordinal Utility and Impatience. *Econometrica* 28(2), 287–309.

Korn, R. and H. Kraft (2001). A Stochastic Control Approach to Portfolio Problems with Stochastic Interest Rates. *SIAM Journal on Control and Optimization* 40(4), 1250–1269.

Kothari, S. P. and J. Shanken (1997). Book-to-Market, Dividend Yield, and Expected Market Returns: A Time-Series Analysis. *Journal of Financial Economics* 44(2), 169–203.

Kothari, S. P., J. Shanken, and R. G. Sloan (1995). Another Look at the Cross-Section of Expected Stock Returns. *Journal of Finance* 50(1), 185–224.

Kraft, H. (2009). Optimal Portfolios with Stochastic Short Rate: Pitfalls when the Short Rate is Non-Gaussian or the Market Price of Risk is Unbounded. *International Journal of Theoretical and Applied Finance* 12(6), 767–796.

Kraft, H. and C. Munk (2011). Optimal Housing, Consumption, and Investment Decisions over the Life-Cycle. *Management Science* 57(6), 1025–1041.

Kraft, H. and F. T. Seifried (2011, June). Stochastic Differential Utility as the Continuous-time Limit of Recursive Utility. Available at SSRN: <http://ssrn.com/abstract=1873572> [Accessed 1 October 2012].

Kraus, A. and J. S. Sagi (2006). Intertemporal Preference for Flexibility and Risky Choice. *Journal of Mathematical Economics* 42(6), 698–709.

Kreps, D. M. (1990). *A Course in Microeconomic Theory*. Harvester Wheatsheaf.

Kreps, D. M. and E. Porteus (1978). Temporal Resolution of Uncertainty and Dynamic Choice Theory. *Econometrica* 46(1), 185–200.

Krueger, D. and H. Lustig (2010). When is Market Incompleteness Irrelevant for the Price of Aggregate Risk (and when is it not)? *Journal of Economic Theory* 145(1), 1–41.

Krusell, P. and A. A. Smith, Jr. (1997). Income and Wealth Heterogeneity, Portfolio Choice and Equilibrium Asset Returns. *Macroeconomic Dynamics* 1(2), 387–422.

Krusell, P., T. Mukoyama, and A. A. Smith, Jr. (2011). Asset Prices in a Huggett Economy. *Journal of Economic Theory* 146(3), 812–844.

Kuehn, L.-A., N. Petrosky-Nadeau, and L. Zhang (2011, December). An Equilibrium Asset Pricing Model with Labor Market Search. Available at SSRN: <http://ssrn.com/abstract=1979625> [Accessed 1 October 2012].

Lando, D. (2004). *Credit Risk Modeling*. Princeton University Press.

Lengwiler, Y. (2004). *Microfoundations of Financial Economics*. Princeton University Press.

LeRoy, S. F. and R. D. Porter (1981). The Present-Value Relation: Tests Based on Implied Variance Bounds. *Econometrica* 49(3), 555–574.

LeRoy, S. F. and J. Werner (2001). *Principles of Financial Economics*. Cambridge University Press.

Lettau, M. and S. C. Ludvigson (2001a). Consumption, Aggregate Wealth and Expected Stock Returns. *Journal of Finance* 56(3), 815–849.

Lettau, M. and S. C. Ludvigson (2001b). Resurrecting the (C)CAPM: A Cross-Sectional Test when Risk Premia are Time-Varying. *Journal of Political Economy* 109(6), 1238–1287.

Lettau, M. and S. C. Ludvigson (2005). *tay*'s as good as *cay*: Reply. *Finance Research Letters* 2(1), 15–22.

Lettau, M. and S. C. Ludvigson (2009). Euler Equation Errors. *Review of Economic Dynamics* 12(2), 255–283.

Lettau, M. and S. C. Ludvigson (2010). Measuring and Modeling Variation in the Risk-Return Tradeoff. In Y. Ait-Sahalia and L. P. Hansen (eds.), *Handbook of Financial Econometrics*, Volume 1, pp. 618–682. North Holland.

Lettau, M. and S. Van Nieuwerburgh (2008). Reconciling the Return Predictability Evidence. *Review of Financial Studies* 21(4), 1607–1652.

Lettau, M. and J. A. Wachter (2007). Why is Long-Horizon Equity Less Risky? A Duration-Based Explanation of the Value Premium. *Journal of Finance* 62(1), 55–92.

Lettau, M., S. C. Ludvigson, and J. A. Wachter (2008). The Declining Equity Premium: What Role Does Macroeconomic Risk Play? *Review of Financial Studies* 21(4), 1653–1687.

Levine, D. K. and W. R. Zame (2002). Does Market Incompleteness Matter? *Econometrica* 70(5), 1805–1839.

Levy, H. (1978). Equilibrium in an Imperfect Market: A Constraint on the Number of Securities in the Portfolio. *American Economic Review* 68(4), 643–658.

Levy, H. (2010). The CAPM is Alive and Well: A Review and Synthesis. *European Financial Management* 16(1), 43–71.

Lewellen, J., S. Nagel, and J. Shanken (2010). A Skeptical Appraisal of Asset Pricing Tests. *Journal of Financial Economics* 96(2), 175–194.

Liew, J. and M. Vassalou (2000). Can Book-to-Market, Size, and Momentum Be Risk Factors that Predict Economic Growth? *Journal of Financial Economics* 57(2), 221–245.

Lintner, J. (1965). The Valuation of Risky Assets and the Selection of Risky Investment in Stock Portfolios and Capital Budgets. *Review of Economics and Statistics* 47(1), 13–37.

Liu, L. X. and L. Zhang (2008). Momentum Profits, Factor Pricing, and Macroeconomic Risk. *Review of Financial Studies* 21(6), 2417–2448.

Lo, A. W. and A. C. MacKinlay (1990). Data-Snooping Biases in Tests of Financial Asset Pricing Models. *Review of Financial Studies* 3(3), 431–467.

Lochstoer, L. A. (2009). Expected Returns and the Business Cycle: Heterogeneous Goods and Time-Varying Risk Aversion. *Review of Financial Studies* 22(12), 5251–5294.

Longstaff, F. A. and M. Piazzesi (2004). Corporate Earnings and the Equity Premium. *Journal of Financial Economics* 74(3), 401–421.

Longstaff, F. A. and E. S. Schwartz (1992). Interest Rate Volatility and the Term Structure: A Two-Factor General Equilibrium Model. *Journal of Finance* 47(4), 1259–1282.

Lucas, D. J. (1994). Asset Pricing with Undiversifiable Income Risk and Short Sales Constraints: Deepening the Equity Premium Puzzle. *Journal of Monetary Economics* 34(3), 325–341.

Lucas, R. E. (1978). Asset Prices in an Exchange Economy. *Econometrica* 46(6), 1429–1445.

Ludvigson, S. C. (2012). Advances in Consumption-Based Asset Pricing: Empirical Tests. Forthcoming in G. Constantinides, M. Harris, and R. Stulz (eds.), Volume 2 of the *Handbook of the Economics of Finance*.

Lustig, H. N. and S. G. van Nieuwerburgh (2005). Housing Collateral, Consumption Insurance, and Risk Premia: An Empirical Perspective. *Journal of Finance* 60(3), 1167–1219.

Lutz, F. (1940). The Structure of Interest Rates. *Quarterly Journal of Economics* 55(1), 36–63.

Lynch, A. W. and S. Tan (2011). Labor Income Dynamics at Business-Cycle Frequencies: Implications for Portfolio Choice. *Journal of Financial Economics* 101(2), 333–359.

McCulloch, J. H. (1993). A Reexamination of Traditional Hypotheses about the Term Structure of Interest Rates: A Comment. *Journal of Finance* 48(2), 779–789.

McKenzie, L. (1954). On Equilibrium in Graham's Model of World Trade and Other Competitive Systems. *Econometrica* 22(2), 147–161.

McKenzie, L. (1959). On the Existence of General Equilibrium for a Competitive Market. *Econometrica* 27(1), 54–71.

Madan, D. B., P. P. Carr, and E. C. Chang (1998). The Variance-Gamma Process and Option Pricing. *European Finance Review* 2(1), 79–105.

Magill, M. and M. Quinzii (1996). *Theory of Incomplete Markets*. MIT Press.

Malloy, C., T. Moskowitz, and A. Vissing-Jørgensen (2009). Long-Run Stockholder Consumption Risk and Asset Returns. *Journal of Finance* 64(6), 2427–2479.

Mandelbrot, B. (1963). The Variation of Certain Speculative Prices. *Journal of Business* 36(4), 394–419.

Mankiw, N. G. and M. D. Shapiro (1986). Risk and Return: Consumption Beta Versus Market Beta. *Review of Economics and Statistics* 68(3), 452–459.

Mankiw, N. G. and S. P. Zeldes (1991). The Consumption of Stockholders and Non-stockholders. *Journal of Financial Economics* 29(1), 97–112.

Margrabe, W. (1978). The Value of an Option to Exchange One Asset for Another. *Journal of Finance* 33(1), 177–198.

Markowitz, H. (1952). Portfolio Selection. *Journal of Finance* 7(1), 77–91.

Markowitz, H. (1959). *Portfolio Selection: Efficient Diversification of Investment*. Wiley.

Marshall, D. (1992). Inflation and Asset Returns in a Monetary Economy. *Journal of Finance* 47(4), 1315–1342.

Marshall, D. A. and N. G. Parekh (1999). Can Costs of Consumption Adjustment Explain Asset Pricing Puzzles? *Journal of Finance* 54(2), 623–654.

Martin, I. (2011). The Lucas Orchard. Working paper, Stanford University. Available at <http://www.stanford.edu/ iwrm/> [Accessed 1 October 2012].

Mas-Colell, A. (1986). Valuation Equilibrium and Pareto Optimum Revisited. In W. Hildebrand and A. Mas-Colell (eds.), *Contributions to Mathematical Economics*, pp. 317–332. North-Holland.

Mehra, R. and E. C. Prescott (1985). The Equity Premium: A Puzzle. *Journal of Monetary Economics* 15(2), 145–162.

Mehra, R. and E. C. Prescott (1988). The Equity Risk Premium: A Solution? *Journal of Monetary Economics* 22(1), 133–136.

Mehra, R. and E. C. Prescott (2003). The Equity Premium in Retrospect. In G. M. Constantinides, M. Harris, and R. Stulz (eds.), *Handbook of the Economics of Finance*, Volume 1B, Chapter 14, pp. 889–938. Elsevier.

Menzly, L., T. Santos, and P. Veronesi (2004). Understanding Predictability. *Journal of Political Economy* 112(1), 1–46.

Merton, R. C. (1969). Lifetime Portfolio Selection Under Uncertainty: The Continuous-Time Case. *Review of Economics and Statistics* 51(3), 247–257. Reprinted as Chapter 4 in Merton (1992).

Merton, R. C. (1971). Optimum Consumption and Portfolio Rules in a Continuous-Time Model. *Journal of Economic Theory* 3(4), 373–413. Erratum: Merton (1973a). Reprinted as Chapter 5 in Merton (1992).

Merton, R. C. (1973a). Erratum. *Journal of Economic Theory* 6(2), 213–214.

Merton, R. C. (1973b). An Intertemporal Capital Asset Pricing Model. *Econometrica* 41(5), 867–887. Reprinted in an extended form as Chapter 15 in Merton (1992).

Merton, R. C. (1973c). Theory of Rational Option Pricing. *Bell Journal of Economics and Management Science* 4(1), 141–183. Reprinted as Chapter 8 in Merton (1992).

Merton, R. C. (1976). Option Pricing When Underlying Stock Returns are Discontinuous. *Journal of Financial Economics* 3(1–2), 125–144. Reprinted as Chapter 9 in Merton (1992).

Merton, R. C. (1987). A Simple Model of Capital Market Equilibrium with Incomplete Information. *Journal of Finance* 42(3), 483–510.

Merton, R. C. (1992). *Continuous-Time Finance*. Basil Blackwell.

Meyer, D. J. and J. Meyer (2005). Relative Risk Aversion: What Do We Know? *Journal of Risk and Uncertainty* 31(3), 243–262.

Miltersen, K. R., K. Sandmann, and D. Sondermann (1997). Closed Form Solutions for Term Structure Derivatives with Log-Normal Interest Rates. *Journal of Finance* 52(1), 409–430.

Modigliani, F. and R. Sutch (1966). Innovations in Interest Rate Policy. *American Economic Review* 56(1–2), 178–197.

Møller, S. V. (2009). Habit Persistence: Explaining Cross-Sectional Variation in Returns and Time-Varying Expected Returns. *Journal of Empirical Finance* 16(4), 525–536.

Moskowitz, T., Y. H. Ooi, and L. H. Pedersen (2012). Time Series Momentum. *Journal of Financial Economics* 104(2), 228–250.

Mossin, J. (1966). Equilibrium in a Capital Asset Market. *Econometrica* 34(4), 768–783.

Munk, C. (2000). Optimal Consumption-Investment Policies with Undiversifiable Income Risk and Liquidity Constraints. *Journal of Economic Dynamics and Control* 24(9), 1315–1343.

Munk, C. (2002). Price Bounds on Bond Options, Swaptions, Caps, and Floors Assuming Only Nonnegative Interest Rates. *International Review of Economics and Finance* 11(4), 335–347.

Munk, C. (2011). *Fixed Income Modelling*. Oxford University Press.

Munk, C. (2012). Dynamic Asset Allocation. Lecture notes, Copenhagen Business School.

Munk, C. and C. Sørensen (2010). Dynamic Asset Allocation with Stochastic Income and Interest Rates. *Journal of Financial Economics* 96(3), 433–462.

Musiela, M. and M. Rutkowski (1997). *Martingale Methods in Financial Modelling*, Volume 36 of *Applications of Mathematics*. Springer-Verlag.

Negishi, T. (1960). Welfare Economics and Existence of an Equilibrium for a Competitive Economy. *Metroeconometrica* 12(2–3), 92–97.

Nielsen, L. T. and M. Vassalou (2006). The Instantaneous Capital Market Line. *Economic Theory* 28(3), 651–664.

Nowotny, M. (2011, March). Disaster Begets Crisis: The Role of Contagion in Financial Markets. Available at <http://sites.google.com/site/nowotnym/> [Accessed 1 October 2012].

Ogaki, M. and Q. Zhang (2001). Decreasing Relative Risk Aversion and Tests of Risk Sharing. *Econometrica* 69(2), 515–526.

Øksendal, B. (2003). *Stochastic Differential Equations* (sixth edn). Springer-Verlag.

Omberg, E. (1989). The Expected Utility of the Doubling Strategy. *Journal of Finance* 44(2), 515–524.

Parlour, C. A., R. Stanton, and J. Walden (2011). Revisiting Asset Pricing Puzzles in an Exchange Economy. *Review of Financial Studies* 24(3), 629–674.

Petkova, R. (2006). Do the Fama–French Factors Proxy for Innovations in Predictive Variables? *Journal of Finance* 61(2), 581–612.

Piazzesi, M. (2005). Bond Yields and the Federal Reserve. *Journal of Political Economy* 113(2), 311–344.

Piazzesi, M. and M. Schneider (2006). Equilibrium Yield Curves. *NBER Macroeconomics Annual* 21, 389–457.

Piazzesi, M., M. Schneider, and S. Tuzel (2007). Housing, Consumption, and Asset Pricing. *Journal of Financial Economics* 83(3), 531–569.

Pindyck, R. S. (1988). Risk Aversion and the Determinants of Stock Market Behavior. *Review of Economic Studies* 70(2), 183–190.

Polemarchakis, H. M. and P. Siconolfi (1995). Generic Existence of Competitive Equilibria when the Asset Market is Incomplete: A Symmetric Argument. *Economic Theory* 6(3), 495–510.

Pratt, J. (1964). Risk Aversion in the Small and the Large. *Econometrica* 32(1–2), 122–136.

Press, W. H., S. A. Teukolsky, W. T. Vetterling, and B. P. Flannery (2007). *Numerical Recipes: The Art of Scientific Computing* (third edn). Cambridge University Press.

Radner, R. (1972). Existence of Equilibrium of Plans, Prices, and Price Expectations in a Sequence of Markets. *Econometrica* 40(2), 289–303.

Rangvid, J. (2006). Output and Expected Returns. *Journal of Financial Economics* 81(3), 595–624.

Rangvid, J., M. Schmeling, and A. Schrimpf (2011, August). Dividend Predictability Around the World. Available at SSRN: <http://ssrn.com/abstract=1542592> [Accessed 1 October 2012].

Ravina, E. (2007, November). Habit Persistence and Keeping Up with the Joneses: Evidence from Micro Data. Available at SSRN: <http://ssrn.com/abstract=928248> [Accessed 1 October 2012].

Repullo, R. (1986). On the Generic Existence of Radner Equilibria When There Are as Many Securities as States of Nature. *Economics Letters* 21(2), 101–105.

Riedel, F. (2000). Decreasing Yield Curves in a Model with an Unknown Constant Growth Rate. *European Finance Review* 4(1), 51–67.

Riedel, F. (2004). Heterogeneous Time Preferences and Humps in the Yield Curve: The Preferred Habitat Theory Revisited. *European Journal of Finance* 10(1), 3–22.

Rietz, T. A. (1988). The Equity Risk Premium: A Solution. *Journal of Monetary Economics* 22(1), 117–131.

Roll, R. (1977). A Critique of the Asset Pricing Theory's Tests. *Journal of Financial Economics* 4(2), 129–176.

Rosenberg, B., K. Reid, and R. Lanstein (1985). Persuasive Evidence of Market Inefficiency. *Journal of Portfolio Management* 11, 9–16.

Ross, S. A. (1976a). The Arbitrage Theory of Capital Asset Pricing. *Journal of Economic Theory* 13(3), 341–360.

Ross, S. A. (1976b). Options and Efficiency. *The Quarterly Journal of Economics* 90(1), 75–89.

Ross, S. A. (1978). A Simple Approach to the Valuation of Risky Streams. *Journal of Business* 51(3), 453–475.

Ross, S. A. (2005). *Neoclassical Finance*. Princeton University Press.

Rouwenhorst, K. G. (1998). International Momentum Strategies. *Journal of Finance* 53(1), 267–284.

Rubinstein, M. (1974). An Aggregation Theorem for Securities Markets. *Journal of Financial Economics* 1(3), 225–244.

Rubinstein, M. (1976). The Strong Case for the Generalized Logarithmic Utility Model as the Premier Model of Financial Markets. *Journal of Finance* 31(2), 551–571.

Samuelson, P. A. (1965). Proof that Properly Anticipated Prices Fluctuate Randomly. *Industrial Management Review* 6(2), 41–49.

Samuelson, P. A. (1968). What Classical and Neoclassical Monetary Theory Really Was. *The Canadian Journal of Economics* 1(1), 1–15.

Samuelson, P. A. (1969). Lifetime Portfolio Selection by Dynamic Stochastic Programming. *Review of Economics and Statistics* 51(3), 239–246.

Santos, T. and P. Veronesi (2006). Labor Income and Predictable Stock Returns. *Review of Financial Studies* 19(1), 1–44.

Santos, T. and P. Veronesi (2010). Habit Formation, the Cross Section of Stock Returns and the Cash-Flow Risk Puzzle. *Journal of Financial Economics* 98(2), 385–413.

Savage, L. J. (1954). *The Foundations of Statistics.* Wiley.

Savov, A. (2011). Asset Pricing with Garbage. *Journal of Finance* 66(1), 177–201.

Schönbucher, P. (2003). *Credit Derivatives Pricing Models: Models, Pricing, and Implementation.* Wiley.

Schwert, G. W. (2003). Anomalies and Market Efficiency. In G. M. Constantinides, M. Harris, and R. M. Stulz (eds.), *Handbook of the Economics of Finance*, Volume 1B, Chapter 15, pp. 937–972. Elsevier.

Sharpe, W. (1964). Capital Asset Prices: A Theory of Market Equilibrium under Conditions of Risk. *Journal of Finance* 19(3), 425–442.

Shiller, R. J. (1981). Do Stock Prices Move Too Much to be Justified by Subsequent Changes in Dividends? *American Economic Review* 71(3), 421–436.

Shiller, R. J. and A. E. Beltratti (1992). Stock Prices and Bond Yields: Can Their Comovements be Explained in Terms of Present Value Models? *Journal of Monetary Economics* 30(1), 25–46.

Sidrauski, M. (1967). Rational Choice and Patterns of Growth in a Monetary Economy. *American Economic Review* 57(2), 534–544.

Siegel, S. (2005, November). Consumption-Based Asset Pricing: Durable Goods, Adjustment Costs, and Aggregation. Available at SSRN: <http://ssrn.com/abstract=545882> [Accessed 1 October 2012].

Sinai, T. and N. S. Souleles (2005). Owner-Occupied Housing as a Hedge Against Rent Risk. *The Quarterly Journal of Economics* 120(2), 763–789.

Singleton, K. J. (2006). *Empirical Dynamic Asset Pricing.* Princeton University Press.

Skinner, J. (1987). A Superior Measure of Consumption from the Panel Study of Income Dynamics. *Economics Letters* 23(2), 213–216.

Stambaugh, R. F. (1982). On the Exclusion of Assets from Tests of the Two Parameter Model. *Journal of Financial Economics* 10(3), 235–268.

Stambaugh, R. F. (1988). The Information in Forward Rates: Implications for Models of the Term Structure. *Journal of Financial Economics* 21(1), 41–70.

Storesletten, K., C. I. Telmer, and A. Yaron (2004). Cyclical Dynamics in Idiosyncratic Labor Market Risk. *Journal of Political Economy* 112(3), 695–717.

Storesletten, K., C. I. Telmer, and A. Yaron (2007). Asset Pricing with Idiosyncratic Risk and Overlapping Generations. *Review of Economic Dynamics* 10(4), 519–548.

Subrahmanyam, A. (2010). The Cross-Section of Expected Stock Returns: What Have We Learnt from the Past Twenty-Five Years of Research? *European Financial Management* 16(1), 27–42.

Sydsaeter, K. and P. J. Hammond (2005). *Essential Mathematics for Economic Analysis* (second edn). Prentice-Hall, Pearson Education.

Sydsaeter, K., P. J. Hammond, A. Seierstad, and A. Strom (2005). *Further Mathematics for Economic Analysis* (first edn). Prentice-Hall, Pearson Education.

Sydsaeter, K., A. Strom, and P. Berck (2000). *Economists' Mathematical Manual* (third edn). Springer-Verlag.

Szpiro, G. G. (1986). Measuring Risk Aversion: An Alternative Approach. *Review of Economic Studies* 68(1), 156–159.

Tavella, D. and C. Randall (2000). *Pricing Financial Instruments: The Finite Difference Method*. Wiley.

Telmer, C. I. (1993). Asset-Pricing Puzzles and Incomplete Markets. *Journal of Finance* 48(5), 1803–1832.

Triplett, J. E. (1997). Measuring Consumption: The Post-1973 Slowdown and the Research Issues. *Federal Reserve Bank of St. Louis Review* 79(May/June), 9–42.

van Binsbergen, J. H. and R. S. J. Koijen (2010). Predictive Regressions: A Present-Value Approach. *Journal of Finance* 65(4), 1439–1471.

van Binsbergen, J. H., M. W. Brandt, and R. S. J. Koijen (2011). On the Timing and Pricing of Dividends. Available at SSRN: <http://ssrn.com/abstract=1551654> [Accessed 1 October 2012].

Vasicek, O. (1977). An Equilibrium Characterization of the Term Structure. *Journal of Financial Economics* 5(2), 177–188.

Vassalou, M. (2003). News Related to Future GDP Growth as a Risk Factor in Equity Returns. *Journal of Financial Economics* 68(1), 47–73.

Viceira, L. M. (2001). Optimal Portfolio Choice for Long-Horizon Investors with Nontradable Labor Income. *Journal of Finance* 56(2), 433–470.

Vissing-Jørgensen, A. (2002). Limited Asset Market Participation and the Elasticity of Intertemporal Substitution. *Journal of Political Economy* 110(4), 825–853.

Vissing-Jørgensen, A. and O. P. Attanasio (2003). Stock Market Participation, Intertemporal Substitution, and Risk-Aversion. *American Economic Review* 93(2), 383–391.

von Neumann, J. and O. Morgenstern (1944). *Theory of Games and Economic Behavior*. Princeton University Press.

Wachter, J. A. (2006). A Consumption-Based Model of the Term Structure of Interest Rates. *Journal of Financial Economics* 79(2), 365–399.

Wachter, J. A. (2012, March). Can Time-Varying Risk of Rare Disasters Explain Aggregate Stock Market Volatility. Working paper, Wharton. Available at <http://finance.wharton.upenn.edu/ jwachter/> [Accessed 1 October 2012].

Wachter, J. A. and M. Yogo (2010). Why Do Household Portfolio Shares Rise in Wealth? *Review of Financial Studies* 23(11), 3929–3965.

Wang, J. (1996). The Term Structure of Interest Rates in a Pure Exchange Economy with Heterogeneous Investors. *Journal of Financial Economics* 41(1), 75–110.

Weil, P. (1989). The Equity Premium Puzzle and the Risk-free Rate Puzzle. *Journal of Monetary Economics* 24(3), 401–421.

Weil, P. (1992). Equilibrium Asset Prices with Undiversifiable Labor Income Risk. *Journal of Economic Dynamics and Control* 16(3–4), 769–790.

Wilcox, D. W. (1992). The Construction of U.S. Consumption Data: Some Facts and Their Implications for Empirical Work. *American Economic Review* 82(4), 922–941.

Wilson, R. (1968). The Theory of Syndicates. *Econometrica* 36(1), 119–132.

Yao, R. and H. H. Zhang (2005). Optimal Consumption and Portfolio Choices with Risky Housing and Borrowing Constraints. *Review of Financial Studies* 18(1), 197–239.

Yogo, M. (2006). A Consumption-Based Explanation of Expected Stock Returns. *Journal of Finance* 61(2), 539–580.

Zhang, L. (2005). The Value Premium. *Journal of Finance* 60(1), 67–103.

Index

Printed and bound by CPI Group (UK) Ltd, Croydon, CR0 4YY